THE SOCIOLOG
www.pearsoned.co.uk/plummer

Select from the links in the drop-down menu to access the student study materials.

1. **Internet sociologist** – improve your internet research skills using this tutorial.

2. **Web resources for critical thinking** – links to Part Six of the book. A range of materials that link to films, art and novels of sociological interest. It also includes links to the websites.

3. **Website links** – a major listing of websites of interest to sociologists.

4. **Chapter resources** – a collection of resources including PowerPoint slides for use in classes, interactive questions, an online glossary and revision flashcards.

5. **Reading supplements** – a selection of short pieces to read which will add to each chapter.

6. **Tutor's section** – some comments chapter by chapter which may be of particular interest to tutors.

7. **Podcasts** – introducing each part of the textbook and global voices on sociology.

8. **The Big Vote** – allowing you to give your view on key debates and see what other students think.

9. **The Sociology Blog** – check this regularly for current and 'hot' topics to update your knowledge.

10. **Pearson** – learn more about the textbook, including how to order this title or obtain an inspection copy.

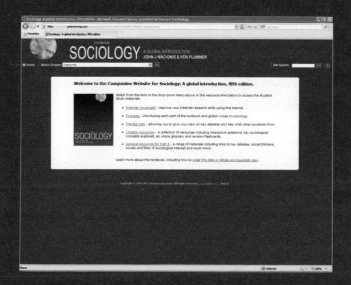

Dedicated to all those involved in the saving of lives through transplant surgery: especially the skills of doctors, the kindness of carers and the greatest gift of life from the donors and their loved ones.

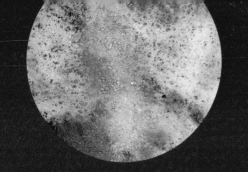

SOCIOLOGY

A GLOBAL INTRODUCTION

FIFTH EDITION

JOHN J. MACIONIS & KEN PLUMMER

Prentice Hall
is an imprint of

PEARSON

Harlow, England • London • New York • Boston • San Francisco • Toronto • Sydney • Singapore • Hong Kong
Tokyo • Seoul • Taipei • New Delhi • Cape Town • Madrid • Mexico City • Amsterdam • Munich • Paris • Milan

Pearson Education Limited
Edinburgh Gate
Harlow
Essex CM20 2JE
England

and Associated Companies throughout the world

Visit us on the World Wide Web at:
www.pearson.com/uk

Authorised adaptation from the United States edition, entitled SOCIOLOGY, 13th Edition,
ISBN: 9780205735747 by MACIONIS, JOHN J., published by Pearson Education, Inc., publishing
as Prentice Hall, Copyright © 2010.
All rights reserved. No part of this book may be reproduced or transmitted in any form or by any means,
electronic or mechanical, including photocopying, recording or by any information storage retrieval system,
without permission from Pearson Education, Inc.
European adaptation edition published by PEARSON EDUCATION LTD, Copyright © 2012

First published 1997
Second edition 2002
Third edition 2005
Fourth edition 2008
Fifth edition published 2012

ISBN: 978-0-273-72791-0

British Library Cataloguing-in-Publication Data
A catalogue record for this book is available from the British Library

Library of Congress Cataloging-in-Publication Data
Macionis, John J.
    Sociology : a global introduction / John J. Macionis, Ken Plummer. -- 5th ed.
        p. cm.
    ISBN 978-0-273-72791-0 (pbk.)
1. Sociology.   I. Plummer, Kenneth.   II. Title.
    HM586.M34 2011
    301--dc23

                                                2011020369

10 9 8
18

Typeset in 10/12pt Minion by 35
Printed and bound by L.E.G.O. S.p.A., Italy

BRIEF CONTENTS

CONTENTS

PREFACE: HOW TO USE THIS BOOK

Welcome to the fifth edition

The book *Sociology : A Global Introduction* has fast become one of the more prominent sociology texts in many countries. This *fifth edition* consolidates some of its past achievements, but also makes clearer its humanistic perspective on global concerns in a rapidly changing high-tech twenty-first century. Its key goals are:

- to introduce all the main areas of study, the key concepts, the historical debates and basic approaches to the discipline of sociology. It assumes you know nothing about sociology; and thus **it is not an advanced text**. It is only an introduction, but a challenging one we hope. It sets its goals as **opening up the field** of enquiry for the very first time; and to stimulate you to want to take it all further. And if you do want to go further, there are suggestions at the end of each chapter for doing this (Mytasklist), guidance at the end of the book (Part Six) as well as a website which has been designed to give you further links, readings, questions and food for thought. Indeed you could see this book as a key resource to link you up to many topics on your own personal website studies.
- to tell a story about the parallel rise of sociology and the modern world and how it is persistently shaped by both technologies and inequalities. This is not meant to be a text which just summarises vast streams of sociological studies. It does not aim to tell you everything that has ever been written on sociology (an impossible task). It aims, rather, to tell a story about how the contemporary world developed from more traditional ones, and how now in the twenty-first century it may well be moving into yet another new – possibly post-modern – phase. The term to be used to discuss this change is one that sociologists constantly discuss. The book provides some suggestions on evaluating whether the modern world is progressing or not.
- to recognise that sociology these days must be global. Many textbooks focus upon one country. Whilst this textbook does often focus on UK and Europe – its main readership – it also takes its orbit to be the world. It is impossible to understand one country in isolation from others. Indeed, a recurrent theme through this book is that the (post) modern world is becoming progressively globalised. One society cannot be understood in isolation.
- to be wide-ranging and hence to introduce analyses of a number of newer topics that are not always included in introductory sociology textbooks. We have selected some issues that are becoming increasingly critical in the twenty-first century. These include the role of globalisation (Chapter 2); the new areas of body, emotions and identity (Chapter 7); the importance of age, children and the growing number of the elderly (Chapter 13); the significance of disability in the modern world (Chapter 14); the emergence of a humanitarian society (Chapter 14); the importance of human rights regimes (Chapter 16); the rising (global) power of the mass media (Chapter 22); the significance of many countries outside the West that are facing poverty (Chapter 9); the importance of science, cyberspace and the new reproductive technologies (Chapter 23); the global significance of environmental hazards (Chapter 25); the sociological significance of AIDS (Chapter 21); and debates around post-modernity and the new kind of society that may be appearing in the twenty-first century (Chapters 2 and 26 in particular).
- to suggest that all the social sciences should work together and that they are inevitably bound up with political and ethical thought. Social science – despite its pretensions – cannot be value free. The position of this book is quite clear: it is a firm belief in the equal value of all human lives, to reduce human suffering across each generation, and to provide tools to help make the world a better place to live in. You do not have to agree with this, but you must debate the ethical and political foundations of sociology.
- to present all of this in a distinctly fresh and 'user friendly' way. We hope the book looks good with its crisp style, clean design and full colour. Although

we have tried to present it in a highly readable way, there is still a lot of material to digest, even in a book as introductory as this. It is worth spending a little bit of time looking at the book *as a whole* – its chapter organisation, why the Interludes have been written, what Part Six may be used for. There is a definite point to the structure of the book, a logic that should become apparent if you take time to grasp it. But in addition there are a number of tools that have been provided to help study. We hope the book is written in a lively style. Some sections will be easier to read than others. Skip around and enjoy what you find. We have tried to illustrate arguments with visuals, maps, debating boxes and charts which should stimulate discussions. Films and DVD – and sometimes novels – are suggested to take you further in your thinking. We encourage you to use Wikipedia, the YouTube and to blog away! But always – as we suggest throughout the book – work to develop your critical skills in all this: some material on the Internet is garbage and you need to spot it.

The set of *podcasts* – Studying Sociology – are designed to help you do this. These are 10 minute recordings which guide you through the book overall and through each Part. They aim to show you how to use the book as a whole. It is worth spending a little time listening to these. An hour of your time to break up some iPod listening! (Go to www.pearsoned.co.uk /plummer).

Above all, sociology is about lively and critical thinking about society. It is not in our view the learning of facts, theories or names of sociologists. It is driven by a passion to understand just what is going on in the modern world and to make it a better place for all.

Some features of the text and how to use it

Sociology: A Global Introduction not only aims to provide a highly readable text, it also provides a number of special features that will help you to study. We hope that this is a 'user friendly' book pitched at **an introductory level for those who have never studied sociology before**. Amongst the tools in the book that you should note and work with are the following:

1 **The boxes**. These are aimed at focusing you on specific issues. We believe, and hope you do too, that they provide handy tools for thinking and analysing. They come in six forms each identified by an icon.

Public Sociology boxes engage with key sociological issues and people in the real world.

Theory and Thinkers boxes which highlight both Classical and Contemporary Social Thinkers who have shaped or are shaping the discipline of sociology, and provide a capsule guide to some of their ideas.

Worldwatch boxes focus on issues over a range of different countries and provide **Fact Files** detailing these countries.

Research In Action boxes which show sociological research actually being conducted.

Methods and Research boxes examine different methods of sociological research.

Some miscellaneous boxes focus on a range of other issues that are of importance within sociology.

2 **The Interludes**. Each section of the book ends with a short interlude. This is designed to provide a topical issue through which you can now review the issues raised in each section. We hope it will be a good way to review the features of each section and think about what the section has tried to achieve. The topics raised in the Interludes are sport (Part One), food (Part Two), music and inequalities (Part Three), autobiography and lives (Part Four).

3 **Global and national maps**. These are aimed at helping you locate many of the issues discussed in the text through graphic illustration. They come in three forms:

   - **The Social Shapes of the World** global maps are sociological maps offering a comparative look at a range of sociological issues such as favoured languages and religions, permitted marriage forms, the degree of political freedom, the extent of the world's rain forests, and a host of other issues.
   - **National maps** focus on social diversity within a country or a group of countries.
   - **The World at a Glance** at the back of the book suggests very quickly some of the major regional divides in the world and can be used as a handy reference as you are studying the book.

4 **The Time Line**. This three-part time line found at the back of the book (page 1030) locates every era and important development mentioned in the text, and tracks the emergence of crucial trends.

5 **Glossary and Key Concepts**. A listing of key concepts with their definitions appears on the book's website, and a complete **Glossary** is to be found at the end of the book.

6 A numbered **Summary** of each chapter is given at the end of chapters and on the book's website.

7 Each chapter ends with MYTASKLIST. This is a short list of resources for going further. This aims to provide:

- a few key websites
- some probing questions
- a short introductory reading list
- a few videos or films of relevance
- links to other chapters
- and a novel or two that may be of interest

Again, you can take these further on the book's website.

8 **The Big Debate** section at the end of each chapter presents different points of view on an issue of contemporary importance.

9 **Part Six aims to be a handy standby resource centre for you to use in your own researches. Here you will find:**

- A list of suggestions for using the YouTube.
- A guide to the key 'sociological' artwork found in the book with questions to think about.
- Lists of novels and films that may connect to sociology and be of interest.
- A list of best websites (also see 'Search the Web' at the end of Chapter 1, pages 21–23).
- A glossary of key words used throughout the book.
- A consolidated/select end of book bibliography.
- Basic data lists: time lines, maps, statistics and key theorists.

10 In addition the book provides:

- **Images** A key opening image to each chapter as well as numerous photographs throughout.
- **Vignettes** that begin each chapter. These openings, we hope, will spark the interest of the reader as they introduce important themes.
- **Recognition of differences** Readers will encounter the diversity of societies. Although there is an emphasis on Europe and the USA in the book – the dominant Western cultures – there is also a concern with global issues and people from other cultures. There is also an inclusive focus on women and men. Beyond devoting a full chapter to the important concepts of sex and gender, the book mainstreams gender into most chapters, showing how the topic at hand affects women and men differently, and explaining how gender operates as a basic dimension of social organisation.

- **Theoretically clear and balanced presentation** The discipline's major theoretical approaches are introduced in Chapter 2. They are then systematically treated on the book's website and often reappear in later chapters. The text highlights not only the conflict, functional and action paradigms, but incorporates social-exchange analysis, ethnomethodology, cultural theory, sociobiology and developments in the newer postmodern theories where different voices can be heard.
- **A debate on value issues** which leads you into the value base line of this book which can be loosely defined as a critical humanism.
- **Key Theorists** Students are also provided with easy-to-understand brief introductions to important social theorists. The foundational ideas of Max Weber, Karl Marx and Emile Durkheim appear in distinct sections.
- **Emphasis on critical thinking** Critical-thinking skills include the ability to challenge common assumptions by formulating questions, identifying and weighing appropriate evidence, and reaching reasoned conclusions. This text not only teaches but encourages students to discover on their own recent sociological research. Part Six provides a major resource for doing this.

Sociology in a fast and hi-tech world

Computers and the new information technology are now playing a major role in sociology. The most common ways in which you use these in your daily studies are:

- Word processing (when you prepare your essays and projects).
- Linking to websites. The World Wide Web is a system that helps you gain systematic access to all the information housed in the vast worldwide computer network known as the Internet. It connects you to libraries, businesses, research centres, voluntary organisations, etc., all over the world.
- Research (when you need statistical techniques such as those discussed in Chapter 2).
- Searching various databases (the most common of which is probably your university library, when you retrieve information on books).

- Using e-mail and blogs to talk to both lecturers and fellow students. Often this can link students and others with similar interests (such as wanting to find out more about postmodern culture, feminism or Marx), who can then communicate readily with each other.
- Simulated gaming. A number of games help you create alternative realities and other societies.

A word of warning

There is a huge amount of sociological data on the Web, and although it can be very easy to access, it can also bring problems. Throughout this book, we will suggest useful websites, but we do so with some anxiety for the following reasons:

- Websites keep changing. There is no guarantee that a site will not be closed or its name changed. Even while preparing this book, we found a number had 'vanished' and others that had opened for just a few weeks.
- The quality of websites is very variable: we have checked most of the sites listed in this book and they were 'good' at that time. But they change, and sometimes they can be the home page of one 'crank' who is really only listing his or her own private interests. So use websites carefully and critically.
- The usage of websites at key times can be very intensive. So a cardinal rule is to be patient!
- And, finally, note that accuracy matters. Do not change addresses from lower-case to capitals, or miss out slashes and points. The website address must be precise.
- Look out for discussions throughout this book of the pitfalls and problems in using these technologies.

Organisation of this text

Part One introduces the foundations of sociology. Underlying the discipline is the sociological perspective, the focus of Chapter 1, which explains how this invigorating point of view brings the world to life in a new and instructive way. Chapter 2 spotlights some of the key sociological perspectives and suggests the importance of globalisation as an idea. Chapter 3 looks at some of the issues involved in the practice of sociology, and explains how to use the logic of science to study human society. It also provides a guide to planning research.

Part Two targets the foundations of social life. It may be useful to see this section as layered: society, culture, groups, interactions and biographies constitute the matrix of the social worlds we live in. Chapter 4 looks at the concept of society, presenting three time-honoured models of social organisation developed by Emile Durkheim, Karl Marx and Max Weber. It also looks at societies of the past and societies of the present. Chapter 5 focuses on the central concept of culture, emphasising the cultural diversity that makes up our society and our world. Chapter 6 offers coverage of groups and organisations, two additional and vital elements of social structure. Chapter 7 provides a micro-level look at the patterns of social interaction and biographical work that make up our everyday lives.

Part Three looks at the Unequal World we live in. It offers a wide discussion of social inequality, beginning with three chapters devoted to social stratification. Chapter 8 introduces major concepts and presents theoretical explanations of social inequality. This chapter is rich with illustrations of how stratification has changed historically, and how it varies around the world today. Chapter 9 extends the analysis with a look at global stratification, revealing the extent of differences in wealth and power between rich and poor societies. Chapter 10 surveys social inequality in a number of Western countries, but mainly the UK, exploring our perceptions of inequality and assessing how well they square with research findings. Race and ethnicity, additional important dimensions of social inequality in both Europe and the rest of the world, are detailed in Chapter 11. The focus of Chapter 12, gender and sexuality, explains how societies transform the distinction of biological sex into systems of gender stratification, and looks at the ways sexuality is produced. Childhood and the ageing process are addressed in Chapter 13. And in Chapter 14, we introduce a major new topic: disabilities and the ways in which equalities evolve around them. We also use it as an opportunity to discuss issues around care and the evolution of a more civilized humanitarian society.

Part Four includes a full chapter on major social institutions and the practices that accompany them. Chapter 15 leads off investigating the economy, consumption and work, because most sociologists recognise the economy as having the greatest impact on all other institutions. This chapter highlights the processes of industrialisation and postindustrialisation, explains the emergence of a global economy, and suggests what such transformations mean. Chapter 16 investigates the roots of social power and looks at the modern development of social movements. In addition, this chapter includes discussion of the threat of war, and the search for peace. Chapter 17 looks at the control process, as well as some of the theories that explain why crime and deviance appear in societies. Chapter 18, on families, examines the many changes taking place around our personal ways of living together in the modern world, looking at some of the diversity of family life. Chapter 19, on religion, addresses the human search for ultimate meaning, surveys world religions, and explains how religious beliefs are linked to other dimensions of social life. Chapter 20, on education, traces the expansion of schooling in industrial societies. Here again, educational patterns in the United Kingdom are brought to life through contrasts with those of many other societies. Chapter 21, on health and medicine, shows how health is a social issue just as much as it is a matter of biological processes, and compares UK patterns to those found in other countries. It also considers a major subject: HIV/AIDS. Chapter 22, on mass media, looks at forms of communications in societies, focusing especially on the rise of the modern global media. Lastly, in Chapter 23, we look at the institution of 'science' and consider some of its most recent manifestations, including the Human Genome Project, the New Reproductive Technologies and the importance of computing and the World Wide Web.

Part Five examines important dimensions of global social change. Chapter 24 focuses on the powerful impact of population growth and urbanisation in Europe and throughout the world. Chapter 25 presents issues of contemporary concern by highlighting the interplay of society and the natural environment. Chapter 26 concludes the text with an overview of social change that highlights traditional, modern and postmodern societies. This chapter rounds out the text by explaining how and why world societies change, and by critically analysing the benefits and liabilities of traditional, modern and postmodern ways of life.

Part Six provides a new, major resource for the critical student. Closely linked to the book's website, it provides 11 key resources which enable students to actively pursue ideas about society on their own. Not only does it provide the usual list of key words (Glossary) and reading lists (References), it also provides a major website listing. For the first time, a new key resource is suggested in the YouTube and a list of suggested searches are provided. In addition, the significance of the humanities for studying social life is indicated through guides for reading novels, watching films, and looking at art.

A note on authorship

This book is a radical re-writing of the highly successful North American textbook *Sociology* by John J. Macionis, which is now in its 13th edition (Macionis, 2010). In 1996, the UK sociologist, Ken Plummer, was commissioned to write an adaptation of this original text in order to make it more suitable for a European audience. Since that time it has grown and changed into a distinctively different book under the revisions progressively carried out by the adapting author working alone. Apart from nine completely new chapters, five 'Interludes', a new Part (Part Six) and substantial changes throughout the text, it also marks a major shift towards both a global and humanistic perspective as its foundation. John J. Macionis has not been involved with how this book has subsequently evolved, but a debt should be acknowledged to the original organisation of the American text, along with the original content, some of which endures in this latest European edition. This European edition of *Sociology: A global introduction*, 5th edition, is available worldwide, but not in the USA. Since sociology is a changing and conflictual discipline, neither author necessarily agrees with everything the other has written. But there is strong agreement that sociology is a lively and challenging discipline that should be presented in a lively and challenging way. We hope that this book succeeds in this aim.

GUIDED TOUR

Living in the C21st boxes highlight contemporary aspects of the topic.

Theory & Thinkers focus on key thinkers and their ideas in context.

Public Sociology and World Watch engage with key sociological issues from around the world.

Methods & Research examine different methods of social research, while Research In Action boxes show real sociological research being conducted.

PART 6

WEB RESOURCES FOR CRITICAL THINKING

CREATING SOCIOLOGICAL IMAGINATIONS

The Mytasklist for each chapter collects together key related sources – websites, key reading, novels, films and big debates – for you to follow up and consider.

Part Six: Web Resources for Critical Thinking brings together key words, film lists, a major webliography, YouTube themes, topical art works and key organisations.

On the web

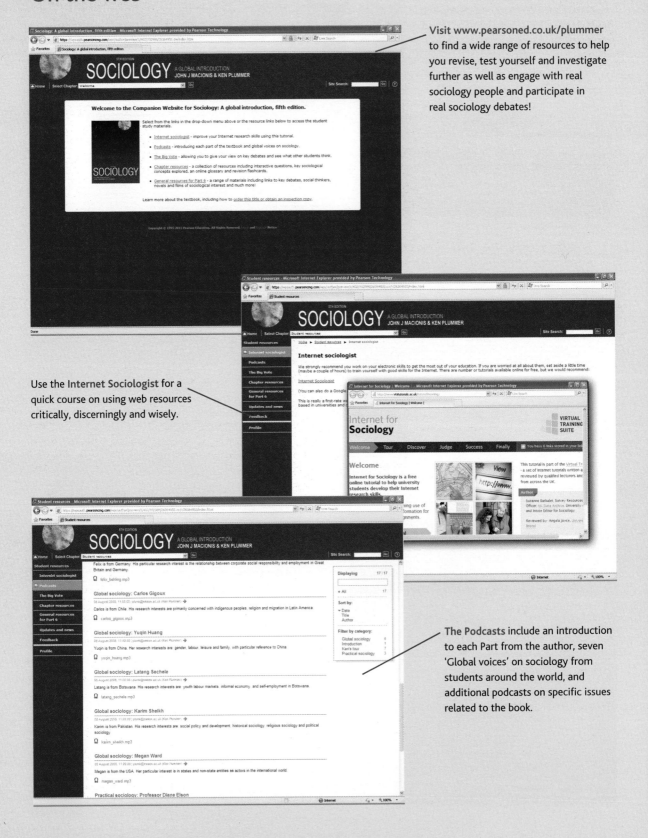

Visit www.pearsoned.co.uk/plummer to find a wide range of resources to help you revise, test yourself and investigate further as well as engage with real sociology people and participate in real sociology debates!

Use the Internet Sociologist for a quick course on using web resources critically, discerningly and wisely.

The Podcasts include an introduction to each Part from the author, seven 'Global voices' on sociology from students around the world, and additional podcasts on specific issues related to the book.

After you read a chapter, explore the related resources online: test your understanding of the text with **true/false questions**, use the interactive flashcards and key concepts explored to test your understanding of key terms, and explore the **links to websites and videography** for more information on films that deal with sociological issues.

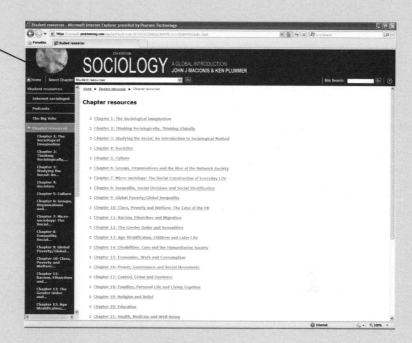

In the **General Web Resources for Part 6** you will find a wealth of information to help you go way beyond the textbook. Follow the links to films, key websites, YouTube clips, novels, art and much more to enrich your study of sociology.

PART 1

INTRODUCING
SOCIOLOGY

CHAPTER 1

THE SOCIOLOGICAL IMAGINATION

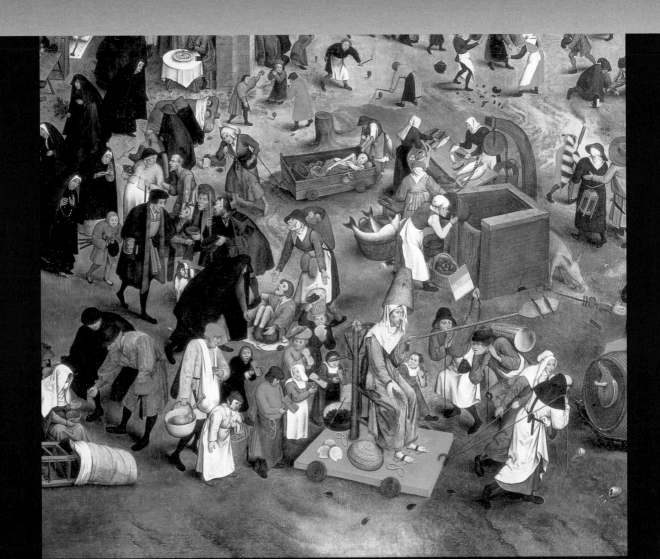

IMAGINE YOU WERE BORN SOME 300 YEARS AGO, IN THE YEAR 1700. Although this is very recent in terms of the billions of years of the existence of planet earth, you would still be living in a remarkably different world. You would probably be living in a very small community and you would not have travelled anywhere except perhaps to a nearby town.

You would never have been to a shop, let alone a shopping centre. You would not have encountered the world of railways, cars, telephones, cameras, PCs, faxes, mobile phones, planes, videos, McDonald's, holiday tours, laptops or DVDs. And more than this, the idea of voting for your government, going to a university, choosing your religion, or even choosing your identity would all have been bizarrely rare. And a map of the world would have been very different. Welcome, then, to our twenty-first century world!

Now imagine again: this time that you were born and living in Afghanistan, one of the poorest and most conflict-torn places in the world today. Your life expectancy at birth would be no more than 44.5 years. By contrast, if you were born in Japan, your expectations would be nearly double this. Indeed, in Afghanistan, 150 children out of every thousand born die shortly after birth; in Japan (and Sweden), it is less than 3 per thousand. Your chances of extended education will be low: boys will have on average 8 years of education whereas it is double that in Japan (or the United Kingdom). The situation is worse for girls: they are likely to have only four years of schooling and less than 15 per cent will be literate. Some 53 per cent of people live below the poverty line and 40 per cent are unemployed. In Norway, by contrast, some 2.5 per cent are unemployed and poverty seems too low to be recorded! Media

communications are also different. In Afghanistan, there are 500,000 internet users; in Japan there are 90 million.

But now have another leap of imagination: this time to a world that is yet to come – the world perhaps of your own grandchildren or great grandchildren. We cannot, of course, predict the future, but we can often see trends. For instance, 'babies in test tubes' and the new genetic engineering are now commonplace. The miniaturisation of electronics as new computers, cameras and I-phones become pocket size is ubiquitous in the rich world. Already these new technologies are being implanted into our bodies and secreted in public spaces. The home of the future will be driven by these. Medicine is prolonging many lives: and with many more people living longer and longer, some even predict that we may become immortal! Our music and media, shops and work situations, families and government structures are all changing beyond today's recognition. What once looked like science fiction a hundred years ago is the reality we now live in. Think up your own projections for the futuristic landscape of your old age!

The power of sociology is to demonstrate just how strong are the social forces that organise society in very, very different ways – and to demonstrate it in time (past societies, present societies and future societies) and space (across the 200 countries or so throughout the world). In this book, over and over again, you will see the variety of societies and the different opportunities that people have within them. Just where you were born – and when – has radically shaped much of what you know and what you can do. Having encountered sociology, you may never see the world with the same eyes again.

tip For more information and data on all this, and indeed for every country in the world, search online *The World Fact Book* compiled by the Central Intelligence Agency (CIA). For full details: type www.cia.gov/library/publications/the-world-factbook/index.html.

Note this is produced and kept up to date by the government of the United States of America.

The first wisdom of sociology is this: things are not what they seem.

Peter Berger

In this chapter, we ask:

- **What is sociology?**
- **How can sociological perspectives help us understand everyday life?**
- **What do sociologists do?**
- **How did sociology develop?**

(Left) Pieter Brueghel the Younger, *The Battle between Carnival and Lent*, 1559

Source: *The Battle between Carnival and Lent* (oil on canvas). Brueghel, Pieter the Younger, (c. 1564–1638)/Private Collection, Johnny Van Haeften Ltd, London/The Bridgeman Art Library.

Note: For more information, see: www.artcyclopedia.com/artists/bruegel_the_younger_pieter.html; http://wwar.com/masters/b/brueghel-pieter.html.

Q Brueghel's painting is a world classic. Examine it closely. What issues of social life does it depict? Can you imagine what a contemporary version of this would look like?

What is sociology?

Welcome to sociology – the *systematic, sceptical and critical study of the social.* It studies the way people do things together. At the heart of sociology is a distinctive point of view. It should be more than you find in a good documentary on a social issue. It is certainly more than listings of facts and figures about society. Instead it becomes *a form of consciousness, a way of thinking, a critical way of seeing the social.* It takes a while, sometimes years, for this 'consciousness' to become clear. And it brings the potential to change your life forever.

So a health warning is needed. Sociology could change your life – maybe even damage it! Contrary to the popular view that sociology is just common sense, it often strains against the common sense. Once it becomes ingrained in your thinking, it will always be asking for you to 'think the social', and it will entail *challenging the obvious, questioning the world as it is taken for granted,* and *de-familiarising the familiar.* This is personally enlightening, even empowering, but it can also make you a very critical person. It helps develop critical thinking and can help make critical citizens.

In this section, and subsequently in the whole book, we ask: what is distinctive about this way of seeing, this new consciousness? To get you going, the box below gives a few standard definitions to consider.

Seeing the general in the particular

Peter Berger's short book *Invitation to Sociology* (1963) has tempted several generations of students into seeing this perspective. In it he characterised the

PUBLIC SOCIOLOGY

So they ask me: what is sociology?

When you start to study sociology, people – friends, families, even strangers – will probably ask you what it is. You may well mumble something about 'the study of society', but that is very vague. Prepare a practical answer to give people. The following definitions might help you a little in this (but they all raise more questions than they resolve):

> The sociologist . . . is someone concerned with understanding society in a disciplined way. The nature of this discipline is scientific.
>
> (Peter Berger, *Invitation to Sociology*, 1963: 27)

> Sociology is . . . first and foremost a *way of thinking* about the human world . . . [It asks how] does it matter that humans live always (and cannot but live) in the company of, in communication with, in an exchange with,

in competition with, in cooperation with other human beings? . . . Its questions 'defamiliarise the familiar'.

(Zygmunt Bauman, *Thinking Sociologically*, 1990: 8, 15)

> The 'human world', or the 'world of humans', is the distinctive realm of human experience and existence . . . and the subject matter with which sociology is concerned.

(Richard Jenkins, *Foundations of Sociology*, 2002: 3)

> The term has two stems – the Latin *socius* (companionship) and the Greek *logos* (study of) – and literally means the study of the processes of companionship. In these terms, sociology may be defined as the study of the bases of social membership. More technically, sociology is the analysis of the structure of social relationships as constituted by social interaction, but no definition is entirely satisfactory because of the diversity of perspectives.

(Nicholas Abercrombie, *Sociology*, 2004: 232)

> The science or study of the origin, history and constitution of human society.

(*Shorter Oxford English Dictionary*)

> Defined in dictionaries as the science or study of society. The term was coined by Comte (1830), linking the Latin *socius* (originally a people, tribe or city allied to Rome, but later a society) to the Greek *logos* (reason or knowledge). The term spread rapidly and is now used in virtually all languages to denote any relatively rigorous, reasoned study of society.

(Michael Mann, *Encyclopedia of Sociology*, 1983: 370)

> A social science having as its main focus the study of the social institutions brought into being by the industrial transformations of the past two or three centuries . . . [It involves] an historical, an anthropological and a critical sensitivity.

(Anthony Giddens, *Sociology: A Brief but Critical Introduction*, 2nd edn, 1986: 9, 13)

sociological perspective as a way of *seeing the general in the particular*. He meant that sociologists can identify general patterns of social life by looking at concrete specific examples of social life. While acknowledging that each individual is unique, in other words, sociologists recognise that society acts differently on various *categories* of people (say, children compared to adults, women versus men, the rich as opposed to the poor). We begin to think sociologically once we start to realise how the general categories into which we happen to fall shape our particular life experiences.

Each chapter of this book illustrates the general impact of society on the actions, thoughts and feelings of particular people. For example, seeing the world sociologically also makes us aware of the importance of gender – as we will see in Chapter 12. Every society attaches meanings (though often different meanings) to gender, giving women and men different kinds of work, family responsibilities, dress codes and even differing expectations across the life cycle. At the same time, the lives of men and women in modern Iraq, North America and China have very significant differences. And as societies change, so do these meanings: the expectations around men and women now, at the start of the twenty-first century, are very different from what they were at the start of the twentieth and they are often loaded with political conflict across many countries around the world. In this book, for instance, we will address the low pay of women (Chapter 15), their lack of power (Chapter 16), the violence against them (Chapter 12), the issues debated around Muslim women and the veil (Chapter 11), and the emergence of controversies around transgender and gay/homosexual/queer life (Chapter 12). Individuals experience the workings of society as they encounter advantages and opportunities characteristic of each sex.

The images on pages 6–7 suggest that there are many factors that shape our lives; Table 1.1 suggests some of the different 'levels' of reality we need to consider.

Seeing the strange in the familiar

Especially at the beginning, using the sociological perspective amounts to *seeing the strange in the familiar*. As Peter Berger (1963: 34) says in his *Invitation to Sociology*, 'the first wisdom of sociology is this: things are not what they seem'. Or as Zygmunt Bauman (1990: 15) says in his *Sociological Thinking*, we need to 'defamiliarise the familiar'. For instance, observing

Table 1.1	The architecture of social life: the layers of reality

- *Cosmic* – the widest presence in the universe/cosmos. This is a vast level of reality and we do not often look at it – but it is important to be aware of it as the infinitely complex presence behind the way we think about our humanly constructed social world.
- *World and globe* – the interconnectedness of the social and cultural across the world: the global flows and movements of economies, political systems, people, media messages, the internet, etc.
- *Social and cultural* – communities, societies, institutions and nation-states that have an existence independently of us, and that have definite structures and symbolic meanings over and above us.
- *Interactional* – the experience of the world in the immediate face-to-face presence and awareness of others: self, inter-subjectivity, and encounters with family, friends, groups and strangers in specific places.
- *Individual* – the inner world: the psychic world of human subjectivity and the inner biological workings of genetics, hormones, brain structure and the like.

sociologically requires giving up the familiar idea that human behaviour is simply a matter of what people *decide* to do and accepting instead the initially strange notion that society guides our thoughts and deeds.

Learning to 'see' how society affects us may take a bit of practice. Asked why you 'chose' your particular college or university, you might offer any of the following personal reasons:

I wanted to stay close to home.

This college has the best women's rugby team.

A law degree from this university ensures a good job.

My girlfriend goes to university here.

I wasn't accepted by the university I really wanted to attend.

What else could I do? I just drifted here.

Such responses are certainly grounded in reality for the people expressing them. But do they tell the whole story? The sociological perspective provides deeper insights that may not be readily apparent.

Thinking sociologically about going on to further or higher education, we might first realise that, for most people throughout most of the world and for most of history, university is all but out of reach. Moreover, had we lived a century or two ago, the 'choice' to go to university was only an option for the smallest elite.

But even in the here and now, a look around the classroom suggests that social forces still have much to do with whether or not one pursues higher education. Typically, college students are relatively young – generally between 18 and 24 years of age. Why? Because in our society going to university is associated with this period of life. But it needn't be – there are many 'mature students' and there is a 'University of the Fourth Age'. Likewise, higher education is costly, so college students tend to come from families with above-average incomes – young people lucky enough to belong to families from the service (middle) classes are some ten times more likely to go to university than are those from manual working-class families. And in many low-income societies such as Afghanistan, the length of time spend in education is drastically reduced. There are also significant variations by ethnicity and gender.

So, at the broadest level, sociology sets out to show the patterns and processes by which society shapes what we do.

Individuality in social context: the strange case of suicide

The sociological perspective often challenges common sense by revealing that human behaviour is not as individualistic as we may think. For most of us, daily living seems very individual. We think we make our own choices, and have our own personal responsibilities – and we congratulate ourselves when we enjoy success and kick ourselves when things go wrong. Proud of our individuality, even in painful times, we resist the idea that we act in socially patterned ways. Yet much of social life is

Society as a prison
A key to sociological thinking is the basic idea that society guides our actions and life choices. In this painting, human beings are located at the centre of numerous social forces. Think about the forces that have shaped your own life – and consider how your life would be very different if you had been born into other languages, institutions or societies.

Maybe think of the 'walls of our imprisonment' – the constraints on our lives – as being linked to issues of:
- cultures (see Chapter 5)
- social divisions (see Part Three)
- economies (see Chapter 15)
- power structures (see Chapter 16)
- families (see Chapter 18)
- religion (see Chapter 19)
- education (see Chapter 20)
- media (see Chapter 22)
- science and technologies (see Chapter 23).

Source: Withdrawn Man.
© Paul Schulenburg/Stock Illustration Source.

Multiple lives
Differences are a key feature of social life. The power of society over the individual can easily be grasped by looking at the world through different cultures. (a) Teenage girl, Mali; (b) Teenage boy, England; (c) man, Egypt; (d) woman, Ivory coast; (e) Muslim woman

Sources: (a), (c), (d), (e) Getty Photodisk; (b) Pearson Education Ltd/BananaStock.

indeed shaped, even determined, by factors outside of our control.

Perhaps the most intriguing demonstration of how social forces affect human behaviour can be found in the study of suicide. It is a topic that has fascinated sociologists precisely because no act seems more individualistic – more driven by personal 'choice' – than the decision to take one's own life. This is why Emile Durkheim (1858–1917), a pioneer of sociology

writing a century ago who will reappear many times in this book, chose suicide as a topic of research. If he could show that an intensely individual act like suicide was socially shaped, then he would have made a strong case for sociological analysis. And many think he did! He showed that social forces help shape even the apparently most isolated act of self-destruction.

Durkheim began by examining suicide records in and around his native France. The statistics of his time (and 'statistics' was also a newly emerging field of study at this time) clearly showed that some *categories of people* were more likely than others to take their own lives. Specifically, Durkheim found that men, Protestants, wealthy people and the unmarried each had significantly higher suicide rates when compared with women, Roman Catholics and Jews, the poor and married people, respectively. Durkheim deduced that these differences corresponded to people's degree of *social integration: how they bonded, connected and tied into society*. Durkheim claimed that low suicide rates characterised categories of people with strong social ties; high suicide rates were found among those who were more socially isolated and individualistic. Working from this he developed a social classification (or typology) of different kinds of suicide. Too little integration – common at times of massive social change and social breakdown – could lead to *anomic suicide*; whilst too much integration could lead to *altruistic suicide*. A good example of this latter group would be suicide bombers, whose allegiance to a religion or a political group is so strong that they are literally willing to lay their lives down for it. (Durkheim also saw levels of regulation as another key to understanding suicide. He saw too little regulation leading to *egoistic suicide*, and too much to what he called *fatalistic suicide*; but we will not consider these here.)

Durkheim's analysis was poignant for the time he was writing, at the end of the nineteenth century. It was the time of the Great Transformation when the old order was breaking down (see pp. 17–19) and when industrialisation and market capitalism had led to a breakdown of the old integration. Suicide seemed to be on the rise everywhere. Durkheim started to make connections. And more: in the male-dominated societies studied by Durkheim, men certainly had more autonomy than women. Whatever freedom's advantages for men, concluded Durkheim, autonomy meant lower social integration, which contributed to a higher male suicide rate. Likewise, individualistic Protestants were more prone to suicide than Catholics and Jews, whose rituals fostered stronger social ties. The wealthy clearly have much more freedom of action than the poor but, once again, at the cost of a higher suicide rate. Finally, single people, with weaker social ties than married people, are also at greater risk of suicide.

Durkheim's study was very influential in helping people think about social influences and many of his correlations still hold. We discuss his work further in Chapters 2 and 4. But contemporary sociologists now claim that, as we have moved into the twenty-first century, and societies have continued to change, many of the factors that Durkheim raised are no longer so significant. Two recent French sociologists – Christian Baudelot and Roger Establet (2008) – have examined world changes and concluded that, although suicide is shaped by social factors, these have changed somewhat since the time that Durkheim was studying. Suicide, for example, has declined amongst the wealthy and grown amongst the poor.

The Chinese exception

Each year worldwide, approximately 1 million individuals die of suicide, 10–20 million attempt suicide and many more are affected by it. In some parts of the world, such as Iraq, suicide rates are very low; but Asia accounts for 60 per cent of the world's suicides. Table 1.2 shows a range of suicide rates across the world. Thus, for example, in almost every country of the world, men are more likely to commit suicide than women. Yet in China, this is not so. The statistics emerging from China on suicide – and they are quite hard to get, and we cannot be sure of their validity – suggest a very different pattern from the mainly Western one described by Durkheim. China, with 22 per cent of the world's people, accounts for some 40 per cent of suicides worldwide: a staggering higher rate. Indeed, suicide is the fifth largest cause of death in China, and each year more than a quarter of a million people take their own lives (and 2 million more attempt to do so). And whereas male suicides in the industrial West outnumber female suicides by roughly three or four to one, in China women's suicides outnumber men's. Likewise, whereas in the West suicide is linked to city life, in China it is three times higher in the countryside. Thus, suicide now accounts for a third of all deaths among women in the countryside. Sociologists, then, look at these statistics to detect broad social patterns that then need explaining.

Methods and research: what sociologists do

Throughout this book you will find a selection of boxes which highlight key issues in sociology. One set of boxes are organised under the theme of *Methods and research* (look out for them). In these boxes, we will give you some idea of the kind of practical work that sociologists do – along with a sense of the methods they use. Often these boxes

SUICIDE RATES AROUND THE WORLD: STUDY THE TABLE

Study this table and look at other countries on the original and fuller table which is accessible online.

Table 1.2	Selected suicide rates around the world per 100,000 population by country and gender (as of 2009)		
Country	Year of latest data	Males	Females
Argentina	2005	12.7	3.4 i
Australia	2004	16.7	4.4 d
Brazil	2005	7.3	1.9
Canada	2004	17.3	5.4 d
Chile	2005	17.4	3.4 i
China (selected rural and urban areas)	1999	13.0	14.8
China (Hong Kong SAR)	2006	19.3	11.5 i
Columbia	2005	7.8	2.1 i
Croatia	2006	26.9	9.7 d
Cuba	2006	19.6	4.9 d
Cyprus	2006	3.2	1.8
Czech Republic	2007	22.7	4.3 d
Denmark	2006	17.5	6.4 d
Estonia	2005	35.5	7.3 d
Finland	2007	28.9	9.0 d
France	2006	25.5	9.0 d
Germany	2006	17.9	6.0 d
Greece	1999	5.7	1.6
Iceland	2007	18.9	4.6 d
India	1998	12.2	9.1
Iran	1991	0.3	0.1 [?]
Ireland	2007	17.4	3.8
Israel	2005	8.7	3.3
Italy	2006	9.9	2.8 d
Japan	2007	35.8	13.7 d
Kazakhstan	2007	46.2	9.0
Latvia	2007	34.1	7.7 d
Lithuania	2007	53.9	9.8 d
Norway	2006	16.8	6.0 d
Portugal	2004	17.9	5.5 i
Russian Federation	2006	53.9	9.5 i
Spain	2005	12.0 d	16.8 i
Sweden	2006	18.1	8.3
United Kingdom	2007	10.1	2.8
United States of America	2005	17.7	4.5
Zimbabwe	1990	10.6	5.2

i = increasing; d = decreasing

Source: This has been adapted from World Health Organization (2009) www.who.int/mental_health/prevention/suicide_rates/en/index.html.

Note in general that:

- The eastern Mediterranean region and the central Asian republics have the lowest suicide rates.
- World suicide *rates* are highest amongst men in Russia, Estonia, Hungary, Slovenia, Khazakistan and the Ukraine. They are also high in Japan and Sri Lanka.
- The largest *numbers* of all suicides worldwide occur in India and China (some 30%).
- 55% of suicides are aged between 15 and 44 years and 45% are aged 45 years and over.
- Youth suicide is increasing at the greatest rate.

1　Consider what patterns are revealed.
2　Why do you think there are these variations?
3　Can you really trust such statistics? Start making a list of problems with statistics. You will encounter a lot of statistics during this book but they should always be read critically (see pp. 94–5 and 289).

will sample key studies. In them we will explore what sociology is for and what sociologists do. Here we look briefly at some of the key roles that a sociologist performs in a modern society.

First, sociologists are *researchers*: they document the nature of the social times we live in. We need data about the human world – otherwise we would be living in the dark. You will find a lot of 'data' in this book, and ways of finding more, and sociology maps information on such things as population size, economic functioning, shifts in religious belief, the move to the cities, the functioning state of whole countries and regions – along with concerns over crime, migration patterns, family life and the nature of social class.

A second task of the sociologist is that of the *theorists*: they aim to foster deeper understanding of what is going on, and provide a way for sociological knowledge to become cumulative – wisdom can be passed on and developed from generation to generation. Data from research never just speaks for itself. We need more than information and data: we need wider understanding and the capacity to make connections, sense links with the rich heritage of thinkers from the past, and shun seeing facts in isolation and out of context. Sociologists develop wider ideas and help facilitate theoretical and analytical thinking about society. Random facts and information are of little value.

A third role is the sociologist as *critic* (and, often, change agent). As we have already seen, sociology fosters a critical attitude to social life, seeing that things are never quite what they seem, and common sense never quite that common. Sociologists question and interrogate the taken-for-granted society, and connect it to other possible worlds. They subvert the thinking as usual. Behind this, quite often sociologists seek progress and a 'better' world. Sociology developed as tool to build an emancipatory knowledge: to help us understand the world in order to advance it.

Next comes the sociologist as *educator and teacher* (and these days the media disseminator and the web coordinator of social knowledge). Amongst the many things that sociologists can do in this applied role is writing and teaching. But they also can provide governments (and world organisations and non-governmental organisations) with information that helps in planning future

pathways for society, and nowadays they also work in media of all kinds (from journalism to websites), helping society to find its way around social knowledge.

There are many other roles for sociologists. Sociologists can be *artists*, generating ideas that can inform and enhance human creativity. Sociological ideas feed into worlds of art, literature, music, poetry and film. Sociologists can be *policy shapers*, advising governments and groups on the nature of the social world. They can also be *commentators* and *public intellectuals*, providing a social diagnosis of the ills of our time. Sociologists can help make a contribution to the human world by clarifying options, sensing alternatives and signposting directions for the future.

They are also *dialogists*, creating organised dialogues across the multiple different voices to be heard in a society. At every level of social life we confront conflicts, and sociologists can facilitate listening to different voices and maybe evolving common ground as a basis for discussions. They look at global conflicts (e.g. wars between nation-states, and conflicts between men and women), at national conflicts (e.g. ethnic, religious), at local conflicts (e.g. community politics, splits between social movements), and even at personal conflicts (e.g. domestic violence, breakdown of trust between friends). In all this, they can help lay out different arguments and sources of tension, and seek greater understanding on both sides.

Finally, then, sociology has a wide and generic role in society: the sociologist becomes the *critical citizen in society*. This is the most general and possibly the most valuable role of the sociologist. Here we *can all help create a widespread social awareness and what might be called social thinking*, which is often in contradistinction to common sense, which usually sees the world in more individualising and 'natural' terms. Sociology helps people to challenge what is taken for granted, to look at their social world creatively, and to make the link between the private problems of individuals and the public problems of cultures. Sociologists can help people to make social connections and can foster aware citizens who know what is going on around them. Sociology *can help create critical, socially aware citizens*, who can make informed and knowledgeable decisions.

What is public sociology?

Sociology involves multiple audiences and groups, as Figure 1.1 shows. It is an academic discipline to be studied (sometimes rather remotely) by students and lecturers in colleges and universities. But its subject matter also means that it is a matter of great general concern to the wider public. As you will see throughout this book, sociology's subjects are 'hot topics': the environment, pollution, family breakdown, religious conflicts, extreme differences of wealth and poverty, violence, terrorism, war, cyberspace, 'youth', women and men – and so on. Most people have views on such matters, and often like a good argument with friends and family about them. So sociology potentially has a very wide 'popular audience'. But can sociology help with all these issues?

Well, yes. Sociology's history can certainly show a strand of work that is indeed aloof. But many sociologists have wanted to make their work more accessible and less 'ivory tower'. They have also shown a passion for social change. Marx, for example, was a revolutionary, wanting to see the overthrow of the entire social order to bring about greater equality and social justice. He wrote very academic books, but also produced very readable tracts – see his *Manifesto of the Communist Party* (Marx and Engels, 1894). Others have not been so extreme but, as you will see throughout this book, over and over again, many sociologists study the world in order to provide a better understanding and achieve an improved social world. They want to make a difference. They work with social movements, speak through the media, write books, engage with public policy formation. Sociology is not all moribund theory abstraction and neither is it senseless fact grabbing: it often shows a deep concern and engagement with the social world and how sociology's findings and ideas can be made more accessible. It lives at the interface between everyday life, public life and academic/intellectual work. Throughout this book there will be 'boxes' where you can consider some of the issues involved.

We will look at the ways in which public sociology can:

- Understand the audiences it is trying to reach – help us to see how the understanding of students, a television audience, a website reader, a social activist, a policy-maker, a social worker or a politician will start from different positions; and the sociologist may well have to approach these different audiences in different ways.
- Clarify language and definitions – help us to know which words to use, to understand 'new words' which keep appearing, and to appreciate the pitfalls of jargon and the advantages of clear speaking.
- Recognise positions – help us to see the moral and political positions which surround all arguments.
- Provide basic knowledge backgrounds – such as legal frameworks and information databases (now made so much easier through access to the internet).
- Assist in understanding research findings – so we know enough about the methods of researchers to make sense of their data.
- Present public debates – help us to understand the issues involved on various sides.
- Appreciate the different kinds of media that can present these issues – from television and film to debate and website blogging.
- Identify key spokespeople and organisations that work on these public issues.

You can find out a great deal about public sociology on Michael Burawoy's website, including the original article. *See*: http://burawoy.berkeley.edu. You can also hear him lecturing on public sociology on YouTube.

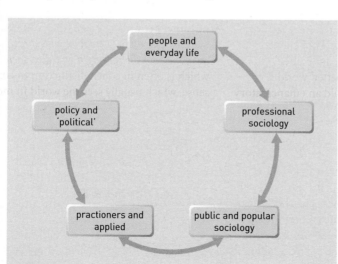

Figure 1.1 The 5 Ps: the circle of sociological life
Source: Plummer (2010: 192).

The sociologist as critical citizen: sociology in everyday life

Sociology and social marginality

Sociological thinking is especially common among social 'outsiders'. Social marginality is something we all experience from time to time. For some categories of people, however, being an outsider is part of daily living. Great literature often speaks from an outsider's point of view: Shakespeare's Shylock in *The Merchant of Venice* or Albert Camus's *The Outsider*, for example. The more acute people's social marginality, the more likely they are to be keenly aware of their surroundings and to see the world from a different perspective. To an extent, sociology is an outsider discipline.

No Turkish guest worker in Germany or Pakistani in England lives for long without learning how much 'race' affects personal experience. But white people, because they are the dominant majority in these countries, think about 'race' only occasionally and often take the attitude that race affects only people of colour rather than themselves as well.

Much the same is true of women, gays and lesbians, people with disabilities, the homeless and the very old. All those who can be relegated to the outskirts of social life typically become more aware of social patterns that others take for granted. Turning the argument around, for any of us to develop a sociological perspective we must step back a bit from our familiar routines to look on our lives with a new awareness and curiosity. Sociology leads to a questioning of all that is taken for granted. Seeing the world through the eyes of others 'on the margins' can help us to see the way the world works more clearly. And it raises challenging questions about how margins and boundaries come about.

Sociology and social crisis

Periods of massive social change or social crisis throw everyone a little off balance, and this, too, stimulates sociological vision. C. Wright Mills (1959), a noted US sociologist, illustrated this principle by recalling the Great Depression of the 1930s. As the unemployment rate in the United States soared to 25 per cent (as it did elsewhere – the depression was 'global'), people out of work could not help but see general social forces at work in their particular lives. Rather than personalising their plight by claiming 'Something is wrong with me. I can't find a job', they took a more sociological approach, observing: 'The economy has collapsed. There are no jobs to be found!'

Conversely, sociological thinking often fosters social change. The more we learn about the operation of 'the system', the more we may wish to change it in some way. As women and men have confronted the power of gender, for example, many have actively tried to reduce the traditional differences that distinguish men and women.

In short, an introduction to sociology is an invitation to learn a new way of looking at familiar patterns of social life. At this point, we might well consider whether this invitation is worth accepting. In other words, what are the benefits of learning to use the sociological perspective?

Benefits of the sociological perspective

As we learn to use the sociological perspective, we can readily apply it to our daily lives. Doing so provides four general benefits.

1 *It becomes a way of thinking, a 'form of consciousness' that challenges familiar understandings of ourselves and of others*, so that we can critically assess the truth of commonly held assumptions. Thinking sociologically, in other words, we may realise that ideas we have taken for granted are not always true. As we have already seen, a good example of a widespread but misleading 'truth' is that Europe is populated with 'autonomous individuals' who are personally responsible for their lives. Thinking this way, we are sometimes too quick to praise particularly successful people as superior to others whose more modest achievements mark them as personally deficient. A sociological approach becomes a way of thinking with an ingrained habit of asking awkward questions. It prompts us to ask whether these beliefs are actually true and, to the extent that they are not, why they are so widely held. Sociology challenges the 'taken for granted'.

2 *It enables us to assess both the opportunities and the constraints that characterise our lives*. Sociological thinking leads us to see that, for better or worse, our society operates in a particular way. It helps

PUBLIC SOCIOLOGY

Looking across divides: sociology and other disciplines

Sociology is a branch of the academic field of social science and the humanities, and hence has many friends it can work alongside. Of course, sociology does have its own distinctive take on matters, as we show in the text, but it overlaps with many other fields. At points in this book you will sense sociologists' close affinity to historians, philosophers, anthropologists, students of literature and many others. This should not be seen as a problem. Connecting with these, not breaking from other ways of thinking, is a feature of twenty-first-century thought.

To start with, you may like to consider how sociology connects to:

- *History*. All social phenomena – from politics, economies, religions and wars to shopping, celebrities, cooking, lovemaking and space travel – have histories. All social actions must be located in time. Sociologists must ask: 'Just when did this happen, and what were the circumstances that led to it?'

- *Philosophy*. Behind all theories and research findings are ideas and assumptions which shape them – about 'human nature', 'freedom', the 'reality of the world' and even what 'knowledge really is'. Philosophy is the under-labourer of all knowledge: it digs around in these assumptions and can help us to clarify them. (But if we are not careful, it can lose us in language that does not help.) Sociologists must ask: 'Just what are the assumptions – of human nature, of choice, of social order – that lie behind sociological study?'

- *Anthropology*. This is the study of people's ways of life and is the cornerstone of understanding 'ethnocentrism' – *the practice of judging another culture by the standard of one's own culture*. Sociology must always recognise that people inhabit very different social worlds, and anthropology – especially the variant that is called 'cultural anthropology' – is a great helper in this. Sociologists must ask: 'How are social things organised in different ways across different cultures?'

- *Literature*. Novels – and drama, poetry, film, art, music – are all visions of human life. They create little worlds we can enter to appreciate the nature of the social and the human. Sociologists have a similar task – though they do not create imaginary worlds so much as study existing ones. But common themes and understandings are everywhere. Sociologists must ask: 'What are the different social worlds that humans inhabit and create. Can we imagine other worlds in other times and places?'

We could ask similar questions through economics, politics, art and biology. In addition, there are also newer disciplines – found mainly towards the end of the twentieth century – which can play prominent roles within sociology. Thus, look for help from *women's/feminist studies, media/film studies, cultural studies, cyber studies, ethnic and race studies, human rights, postcolonial studies, citizenship studies, queer studies* and the like. Most of these newer disciplines focus on a particular issue – women, gender, media and human rights – and tend to be more interdisciplinary. But they all assist in our thinking about the social.

Sociology has much to offer, but it does not stand on its own. A sample of introductions to other disciplines includes the following:

John Tosh, *The Pursuit of History*, 2009

Nigel Warburton, *Philosophy*, 4th edn, 2004

Peter Metcalf, *Anthropology*, 2005

Hans Bertens, *Literary Theory*, 2007

us to see the pattern and order that is found in all societies. Moreover, in the game of life, we may decide how to play our cards, but it is society that deals us the hand. The more we understand the game, the more effective players we will be. Sociology helps us to understand what we are likely and unlikely to accomplish for ourselves and how we can pursue our goals most effectively.

3 *It helps us to be active participants in our society.* Without an awareness of how society operates, we are likely to accept the status quo. We might just think that this is how all societies are, or how all people behave 'naturally'. But the greater our understanding of the operation of society, the more we can take an active part in shaping social life. For some, this may mean embracing society as it is;

others, however, may attempt nothing less than changing the entire world in some way. The discipline of sociology advocates no one particular political orientation, and sociologists themselves weigh in at many points across the political spectrum. But it does have a built-in 'critical' tendency. And evaluating any aspect of social life – whatever one's eventual goal – depends on the ability to identify social forces and to assess their consequences. Some 50 years ago, C. Wright Mills claimed that developing what he called the 'sociological imagination' would help people to become more active citizens. This major sociological thinker is highlighted in the box on p. 21. Other notable sociologists are featured throughout this book.

4 *It enables us to recognise human differences and human suffering and to confront the challenges of living in a diverse world.* Sociological thinking highlights both the world's remarkable social variety and its sufferings, real and potential. 'The British', for example, represent only a small proportion of the world's population, and, as the remaining chapters of this book explain, many human beings live in dramatically different societies. People everywhere tend to define their own way of life as proper and 'natural', and to dismiss the lifestyles of those who differ. But the sociological perspective encourages us to think critically about the relative strengths and weaknesses of all ways of life – including our own. It also encourages us to see the many forms of suffering that occur – poverty,

THINKERS & THEORY

The Enlightenment and the Age of Reason

Key idea: the world can be made better through the application of human reason.
'Modern Sociology was born of Enlightenment Thinking. Its approximate boundaries are represented by – at its emergence – the work of Rene Descartes (1596–1650) born in France but spending much of his adult life in Holland, and, at its conclusion, the work of Immanuel Kant (1724–1804) living and working in Germany in the second half of the eighteenth century' (Evans, 2007: 23). Descartes wanted to know 'How do I know? And can I be certain?' He concluded with the famous aphorism: I think therefore I am. *Cogito ergo sum*. Kant characterised his difficult work as a bridge into eighteenth-century rationalism and empiricism.

The Enlightenment began in England (with Locke) and Scotland (with Adam Smith (1723–90) and David Hume

(1711–76)) and was developed in France in the eighteenth century (with Diderot, Voltaire and the Encyclopaediasts). In its broadest sense it takes in artists such as Hogarth, authors such as Jonathan Swift and maybe Jane Austen, and composers such as Mozart. Just as today we sense a new spirit of the times with the growth of the new information technology, this was also a time when new intellectul currents swept Europe. Rationality, science, progress and a certain questioning of religious dogma were among the hallmarks.

Jean-Jacques Rousseau (1712–78) said: 'Man is born free; and everywhere he is in chains.' This famous quote from Chapter 1 of *The Social Contract* opens up debates as to what human nature is and ultimately suggests that living under the 'general will' provides a remedy for the corruption by greed and meanness of the perfect state of nature into which man is born 'the noble savage'.

Voltaire (1694–1778) said: 'In this best of all possible worlds . . . all is for the best.' In his widely read work *Candide*, Voltaire suggests this is not true – indeed quite the opposite is

shown as 'our hero' Candide travels the world to face one horror after another. Life is not easy! It is better to cultivate one's own small garden and to ignore the rest, said Voltaire, ('Il faut cultiver son jardin'; Chapter 30).

Thomas Hobbes (1588–1679) said: 'No arts; no letters; no society; and which is worst of all, continual fear and danger of violent death; the life of man, solitary, poor, nasty, brutish and short.' Living through Britain's civil wars, Hobbes suggests in *Leviathan* that people should hand over power to a sovereign state and agree to live by its laws. The ruler's authority must be absolute, or there would be chaos.

John Locke (1632–1704) stated that knowledge depends upon our senses – we need to look at the material and empirical world. We need to recognise the supreme authority of the law; but it is conditional on an implied contract between subject and ruler. The ruler's authority is not absolute.

A good guide to the Enlightenment is: Paul Hyland, *The Enlightenment: A Sourcebook and Reader* (2003).

marital breakdown, illness, war and so on – and to see how such problems often arise because of the ways in which societies are organised.

Some opening problems with the sociological perspective

While approaching the world sociologically brings many benefits, it also harbours some distinctive problems. Three can be mentioned at the outset.

1 *Sociology is part of a changing world.* One of the difficult things about studying sociology is that we are studying a moving object: society can change just as quickly as we study it! A 'finding' from one day may soon be proved wrong when situations and circumstances change. And, since it is a feature of the modern world that societies are changing extraordinarily rapidly, we can expect our knowledge about them to change rapidly too. For instance, many of the statistics you find in this book will be out of date by the time you read them.

2 *Sociologists are part of what they study.* 'I have seen society, and it is me.' As we are all part of society, we are all part of what we study. This cannot be otherwise, but it makes the tasks of a sociologist very difficult. Many other 'sciences' study objects that are separate from the human species, but sociologists do not. Since we are part of the very world we study, we may find it hard to distance ourselves from this world. A sociologist born in Europe may have all kinds of European assumptions which do not hold in Thailand or Brazil. With the best intentions in the world, much sociology remains *ethnocentric* – bound to a particular cultural view. Sociologists have to be *reflexive* and see themselves as part of the very things they study.

3 *Sociological knowledge becomes part of society.* The research and study that sociologists do – the books they write, the arguments they make – eventually become part of a society's knowledge about itself. Sociologists create ideas that can shape the ways in which societies work. Their work is *recursive* – it feeds back on to itself. Findings on crime – for example, that crime rates are soaring – can be reported in the media, and people then become more conscious of crime. As a result, even more crime is reported and sociologists may even study it more! There is an odd circle or cycle of knowledge at work in society and sociology, being part of this, has an impact on society.

Social change and the Great Transformation 1

The origins of Western sociology

Major historical events rarely just happen. They are typically products of powerful social forces that are always complex and only partly predictable. So it was with the emergence of sociology itself. Having described the discipline's distinctive perspective and surveyed some of its benefits, we can now consider how and why sociology emerged in the first place.

Although human beings have mused about society since the beginning of our history, sociology is of relatively recent origin. In many ways it was the product of the **Enlightenment**. The *French philosophes* were the cornerstone of such thinking, a 'solid, respectable clan of revolutionaries' (Gay, 1970: 9) that included Montesquieu, Rousseau and Voltaire. Such thinking signposted the arrival of the 'modern world'. The world-view of the Enlightenment highlighted, amongst other things, the following ideas:

1 Rationality and reason became a key way of organising knowledge.
2 Empiricism – we need facts and observations apprehended through the senses.
3 Science – linked especially to experimental scientific revolution.
4 Universalism – the search was on for general laws of the universe (and society).
5 Progress – the 'human condition' can be improved.
6 Individualism – the starting point for all knowledge.
7 Toleration – in the world of religious conflicts, beliefs of other nations and groups are not inherently inferior to European Christianity and different religions should be tolerated.
8 Freedom – the human condition was that of a choosing self.
9 Human nature was uniform: rational, individual and free.
10 Secularism – despite toleration, or because of it, the Enlightenment was often opposed to the Church (Hamilton, 1996).

Later – as we shall see – thinkers became very critical of this kind of thinking, but it is still pervasive in much of the modern Western world. (Watch out for the ideas of Foucault (Chapter 17) and Adorno (Chapter 22).)

Auguste Comte: the French Revolution and positivism

Key idea: the study of sociology is a science.

What sort of person would invent sociology? Certainly someone living in times of momentous change. Auguste Comte (1798–1857) grew up in the wake of the French Revolution, which brought a sweeping transformation to his country. And if that wasn't sufficient, another revolution was under way: factories were sprouting up across continental Europe, recasting the lives of the entire population. Everyone living in this era became keenly aware of the state of society.

Auguste Comte (1798–1857) is usually seen as both the founder of sociology and of positivism in the social sciences. He sees them as the 'religion of humanity'. For an analysis of his work, see Mike Gane: *Auguste Comte* (2006)

Source: akg-images.

Drawn from his small home town by the bustle of Paris, Comte was soon deeply involved in the exciting events of his time. More than anything else, he wanted to understand the human drama that was unfolding all around him. Once equipped with knowledge about how society operates, Comte believed, people would be able to build for themselves a better future. He divided his new discipline into two parts: how society is held together (which he called social statics), and how society changes (social dynamics). From the Greek and Latin words meaning 'the study of society', Comte came to describe his work as sociology. He evolved an influential account of the stages of society – theological, metaphysical and positivist – and claimed that sociology should be part of this positivist, or scientific, phase (see pp. 63–5).

However, only in 1839 did the French social thinker Auguste Comte (introduced in the above box) coin the term *sociology* to describe a new way of looking at the world.

Science and Western sociology

The nature of society was a major topic of enquiry for virtually all the brilliant thinkers of the ancient world, including the Chinese philosopher K'ung Futzu, also known as Confucius (551–479 BCE), and the Greek philosophers Plato (*c.* 427–347 BCE) and Aristotle (384–322 BCE).[1] Similarly, the medieval thinker St Thomas Aquinas (*c.* 1225–74), the fourteenth-century Muslim Ibn Khaldun and the French philosopher Montesquieu (1689–1755) all examined the state of human society.

[1] Throughout this text, the abbreviation BCE designates 'before the common era'. We use this terminology in place of the traditional BC ('before Christ') in recognition of religious plurality. Similarly, in place of the traditional AD (*anno Domini*, or 'in the year of our Lord'), we employ the abbreviation CE ('common era'). See also the timelines at the front of the book. This reaming is controversial, and does not seem to be widely used yet in Europe. It shows the relativity of categories. But to use a Christian-based chronology is seen by many as offensive in a world where billions are not Christian.

There have been many such social thinkers. Yet, as Emile Durkheim noted almost a century ago, none of these approached society from a truly sociological point of view.

> Looking back in history . . . we find that no philosophers ever viewed matters [with a sociological perspective] until quite recently . . . It seemed to them sufficient to ascertain what the human will should strive for and what it should avoid in established societies . . . Their aim was not to offer us as valid a description of nature as possible, but to present us with the idea of a perfect society, a model to be imitated.

(Durkheim, 1972: 57; orig. 1918)

What sets sociology apart from earlier social thought? Prior to the birth of sociology, philosophers and theologians mostly focused on imagining the ideal society. None attempted to analyse society as it really was. Pioneers of the discipline such as Auguste Comte, Emile Durkheim and Ferdinand Toennies (see below) reversed these priorities. Although they were certainly concerned with how human society could be improved, their major goal was to understand how society actually operates.

The key to achieving this objective, according to Comte, was developing a scientific approach to society. Looking back in time, Comte sorted human efforts to comprehend the world into three distinct stages: theological, metaphysical and scientific (1975; orig. 1851–54). The earliest era, extending through to the medieval period in Europe, was the *theological stage*. At this point, thoughts about the world were guided by religion, so people regarded society as an expression of God's will – at least in so far as humans were capable of fulfilling a divine plan.

With the Renaissance, the theological approach to society gradually gave way to what Comte called the *metaphysical stage*. During this period, people came to understand society as a natural, rather than a supernatural, phenomenon. Human nature figured heavily in metaphysical visions of society: Thomas Hobbes (1588–1679), for example, posited that society reflected not the perfection of God as much as the failings of a rather selfish human nature.

What Comte heralded as the final, *scientific stage* in the long quest to understand society was propelled by scientists such as Copernicus (1473–1543), Galileo[2] (1564–1642) and Isaac Newton (1642–1727). Comte's contribution came in applying this scientific approach – first used to study the physical world – to the study of society.

Comte was thus a proponent of **positivism**, defined as *a means to understand the world based on science*. As a positivist, Comte believed that society conforms to invariable laws, much as the physical world operates according to gravity and other laws of nature. Even today, most sociologists agree that science plays a crucial role in sociology. But, as Chapter 3 explains, we now realise both that human behaviour is often far more complex than natural phenomena and that science is itself more sophisticated than we thought before. Thus human beings are creatures with considerable imagination and spontaneity, so that our behaviour can never be fully explained by any rigid 'laws of society'. Likewise, the universe may be much more 'chaotic' and 'emergent' than we previously thought, making observations and laws much more difficult.

Change, transformation and sociology

Sociology was born out of the 'massive social transformation' of the past two centuries. Two great revolutions – the French Revolution of 1789 and the more general 'Industrial Revolution' traced to England in the eighteenth century – 'have all but totally dissolved the forms of social organisation in which humankind has lived for thousands of years of its previous history' (Giddens, 1986: 4). Striking transformations in eighteenth- and nineteenth-century Europe, then, drove the development of sociology. As the social ground trembled under their feet, people understandably focused their attention on society. Traditions were crumbling.

First came scientific discoveries and technological advances that produced a factory-based industrial economy. Second, factories drew millions of people from the countryside, causing an explosive growth of cities. Third, people in these burgeoning industrial cities soon entertained new ideas about democracy and political rights. Finally, the stable communities in which most people had lived for centuries started to decline. We shall briefly describe each of these four changes – though they all reappear for more detailed analysis during this book.

1 A new industrial economy: the growth of modern capitalism

During the European Middle Ages, most people tilled fields near their homes or engaged in small-scale *manufacturing* (a word derived from Latin words meaning 'to make by hand'). But by the end of the eighteenth century, inventors had applied new sources of energy – first water power and then steam power – to the operation of large machines, which gave birth to factories. England, the home of the Industrial Revolution, was transformed. The landscape changed radically as new cities were built. And now, instead of labouring at home, workers became part of a large and anonymous industrial workforce, toiling for strangers who owned the factories. This drastic change in the system of production generated huge poverty and mass suffering; it weakened families and 'demoralised societies'; it eroded traditions that had guided members of small communities for centuries. For many, the progress of the new machines was also the breakdown of any kind of society or social order as we previously knew it. The development of modern capitalism is considered in Chapter 4.

[2] Illustrating Comte's stages, the ancient Greeks and Romans viewed the planets as gods; Renaissance metaphysical thinkers saw them as astral influences (giving rise to astrology); by the time of Galileo, scientists understood planets as natural objects behaving in orderly ways.

2 The growth of cities

Factories sprouting across much of Europe became magnets, attracting people in need of work. This 'pull' of work in the new industrialised labour force was accentuated by an additional 'push' as landowners fenced off more and more ground, turning farms into grazing land for sheep – the source of wool for the thriving textile mills. This 'enclosure movement' forced countless tenant farmers from the countryside towards cities in search of work in the new factories.

Many villages were soon abandoned; at the same time, however, factory towns swelled rapidly into large cities. Such urban growth dramatically changed people's lives. Cities churned with strangers, in numbers that overwhelmed available housing. Widespread social problems – including poverty, disease, pollution, crime and homelessness – were the order of the day. This was the world that Charles Dickens so vividly described in some of his nineteenth-century novels. Such social crises further stimulated development of the sociological perspective. We consider the rise of modern cities in Chapter 24.

3 Political change: control and democracy

During the Middle Ages, as Comte noted, most people thought of society as the expression of God's will. Royalty claimed to rule by 'divine right', and each person up and down the social hierarchy had some other part in the holy plan. Indeed, throughout history people have rarely seen themselves as being in control of their own lives. With economic development and the rapid growth of cities, changes in political thought were inevitable. Starting in the seventeenth century, every kind of tradition came under spirited attack. In the writings of Thomas Hobbes, John Locke (1632–1704) and Adam Smith (1723–90), we see a distinct shift in focus from people's moral obligations to remain loyal to their rulers, to the idea that society is the product of individual self-interest. The key phrases in the new political climate, therefore, were *individual liberty* and *individual rights*. Echoing the thoughts of Locke, the American Declaration of Independence asserts that each individual has 'certain unalienable rights', including 'life, liberty, and the pursuit of happiness'.

Table 1.3	Some early sociologists and how they viewed the social change of their time		
Sociologist	**Earlier societies**	**Newer societies arriving**	**Explanatory dynamic?**
Smith and Montesquieu	Hunting, herding, agricultural	Commercial	Rise of free markets
Comte	Theological, metaphysical	Scientific, positivist	Science
Maine	Status	Contract	Changes in law
Spencer	Homogeneous – simple, militant	Heterogeneous – complex, industrial	Changes in population
Toennies	*Gemeinschaft* – community based	*Gesellschaft* – association based	Community shifts
Marx	Primitive communism, slavery, feudalism	Capitalism (but leading to socialism)	Economic exploitation
Durkheim	Mechanical solidarity	Organic solidarity	Population density and division of labour
Weber	Traditional	Rational-bureaucratic, secular	Changes in religion and economy (capitalism and its affinity with the Protestant ethic)
Simmel	Primitive production	Money and modernity	Circulation of money; Group size grows

Source: Plummer (2010: 77).

The political revolution in France that began soon afterwards, in 1789, constituted an even more dramatic break with political and social traditions. As the French social analyst Alexis de Tocqueville (1805–59) surveyed his society after the French Revolution, he exaggerated only slightly when he asserted that the changes we have described amounted to 'nothing short of the regeneration of the whole human race' (1955: 13; orig. 1856). In this context, it is easy to see why Auguste Comte and other pioneers of sociology soon developed their new discipline. Sociology flowered in precisely those societies – France, Germany and England – where change was greatest.

4 The loss of Gemeinschaft: the eclipse of community

The German sociologist Ferdinand Toennies produced the theory of **Gemeinschaft** and **Gesellschaft** (see also Chapter 24). Toennies (1963; orig. 1887) saw the modern world as the progressive loss of *Gemeinschaft*, or human community. He argued that the Industrial Revolution had undermined the strong social fabric of family and tradition by fostering individualism and a business-like emphasis on facts and efficiency. European and North American societies gradually became rootless and impersonal as people came to associate mostly on the basis of self-interest – the condition Toennies dubbed *Gesellschaft*. Toennies' thesis was that traditional societies, built on kinship and neighbourhood, nourished collective sentiments, virtue and honour. Modernisation washes across traditional society like an acid, eroding human community and unleashing rampant individualism.

Through much of the twentieth century, at least some areas of the Western world approximated Toennies' concept of *Gemeinschaft*. Families that had lived for generations in rural towns and villages were tightly integrated into a hard-working, slow-moving way of life. Before telephones (invented in 1876) and television (introduced in 1939, widespread after 1950), families and communities entertained themselves, communicating with distant members by letter.

Before private cars became commonplace after the Second World War, many people viewed their home town as their entire world. Inevitable tensions and conflicts – sometimes based on race, ethnicity and religion – characterised past communities. According to Toennies, however, the traditional ties of *Gemeinschaft* bound people of a community together, 'essentially united in spite of all separating factors' (1963: 65; orig. 1887).

The modern world turned societies inside-out so that, as Toennies put it, people are 'essentially separated in spite of uniting factors' (1963: 65; orig. 1887). This is the world of *Gesellschaft* where, especially in large cities, most people live among strangers and ignore those they pass on the street. Trust is hard to come by in a mobile and anonymous society in which, according to researchers, people tend to put their personal needs ahead of group loyalty and a majority of adults claim that 'you can't be too careful' in dealing with people (Russell, 1993).

Toennies' work displays a deep distrust of the notion of 'progress', which he feared amounted to the steady loss of traditional morality. Toennies stopped short of claiming that modern society was 'worse' than societies of the past and he made a point of praising the spread of rational, scientific thinking. Nevertheless, the growing individualism and selfishness characteristic of modern societies troubled him. Knowing that there could be no return to the past, he looked to the future, hoping that new forms of social organisation would develop that would combine modern rationality with traditional collective responsibility.

 To develop timelines, see the inside cover of this book and examine:

Wikipedia Timeline of Sociology
http://en.wikipedia.org/wiki/Timeline_of_sociology

Hyper soc Timeline
www.timelineindex.com/content/view/160

Timeline of the American Sociological Association
www.asanet.org/cs/root/leftnav/asa_history/
a_history_of_asa_2005_appendix_1

Timeline Western sociology: some early landmarks in thinking about society

Before Western sociology

551–479 BCE   Confucius, *Analects of Confucius*
469–399 BCE   Socrates and Western philosophy
384–322 BCE   Aristotle, *Poetics*; *The Nicomachean Ethics*
360 BCE   Plato, *The Republic*
973–1048   Al-Biruni, Abu Rayhan Muhammad ibn Ahmad, Qanun-i-Masoodi
1332–1406   Ibn-Khaldun, *Muqaddimah*

Renaissance and Enlightenment

1651   Thomas Hobbes, *Leviathan*
1739   John Locke, *An Essay Concerning Human Understanding*
1751   William Hogarth, *Gin Lane*
1755   Jean-Jacques Rousseau, *Discourse on Inequality*
1759   Voltaire, *Candide*
1776   Adam Smith, *Wealth of Nations*
1784   Immanuel Kant, *What is Enlightenment?*

Origins and classics

1839   Comte defines sociology as a discipline – the term is invented.
       (published 1824 August Comte's *System of Positive Politics*: introduced the term 'sociology')
1846   Marx and Engels, *The German Ideology*: the theory of materialist history is outlined.
1987   Emile Durkheim, *Suicide* – suicide statistics show just how it varies socially.
1889   William E. Du Bois, *The Philadelphia Negro* – first major study of the American Negro.
1904   Max Weber, *The Protestant Ethic and the Spirit of Capitalism* – ideas shape history, and here religion shapes capitalism.
1900   Georg Simmel, *The Philosophy of Money* – changes in organisation of money shift human relations.

The rise of US sociology

1912   Charles Horton Cooley, *Human Nature and Social Order*.
1905   American Sociological Society formed (becoming American Sociological Association in 1959).
1915–30 The tradition of the 'Chicago School' associated with Robert Park and the examination of urban life.
1918–20 W. I. Thomas and Florian Znaniecki, *The Polish Peasant in Europe and America* – highly regarded five volumes
         of innovative method, theory and data on migrants and city life.
1921   Park and Burgess, *Introduction to the Science of Sociology* – first major textbook from a major new sociology
         department at Chicago University with a stress on city conflict.
1929   Robert and Helen Lynd, *Middletown* – small-town community life (Muncie) in the USA observed closely and
         especially through its class system.
1934   George Herbert Mead, *Mind, Self and Society*.

Mid-twentieth-century sociology

1944   Theodore Adorno and Max Horkheimer, *Dialectics of Enlightenment* – asks 'why mankind, instead of entering
         into a truly human condition, is sinking into a new kind of barbarism'.
1950   David Riesman et al.'s *The Lonely Crowd* – society has moved from tradition directed to outer directed.
1951   British Sociological Association founded.
1951   Indian Sociological Association founded.
1951   Talcott Parsons, *The Social System* – theoretical treatise about the integrated social order.
1956/59 Erving Goffman, *The Presentation of Everyday Life* – micro sociological argument about social life as drama.
1957   Peter Wilmott and Michael Young, *Family and Kinship in East London* – charts changes in community and family
         life in post-Second World War England.
1959   C. Wright Mills, *The Sociological Imagination* – left critique of grand theory and overworked methodology in sociology.

THINKERS & THEORY

C. Wright Mills: the sociological imagination

C. Wright Mills (1916–1962) was an outspoken, radical, and left wing sociologist of the mid twentieth century. His book *The Sociological Imagination* (1959) has been extremely influential on several generations of sociologists

Source: Archive Photos/Stringer/ Getty Images.

Charles Wright Mills (1916–62) managed to cause a stir with almost everything he did. Even arriving for a class at New York's Columbia University – clad in a sweatshirt, jeans and boots, astride his motorcycle – he usually turned some heads. During the conservative 1950s, Mills not only dressed a bit out of the mainstream, but he also produced a number of books that challenged most of the beliefs the majority of us take for granted. He was an American Marxist and he acquired both adherents and adversaries.

As Mills saw it, sociology is not some dry enterprise detached from life. Rather, he held up sociology as an escape from the 'traps' of our lives because it can show us that society – not our own foibles or failings – is responsible for many of our problems. In this way, Mills maintained, sociology transforms personal problems into public and political issues. For Mills, 'The sociological imagination enables us to grasp history and biography and the relations between the two within society. That is its task and its promise . . .' (Mills, 1967: 4; orig. 1957).

In the following excerpt, Mills describes both the power of society to shape our individual lives, and the importance of connecting our lives (biographies) to history and society:

> When a society becomes industrialised, a peasant becomes a worker; a feudal lord is liquidated or becomes a businessman. When classes rise or fall, a man is employed or unemployed; when the rate of investment goes up or down, a man takes new heart or goes broke. When wars happen, an insurance salesman becomes a rocket launcher; a store clerk, a radar man; a wife lives alone; a child grows up without a father. Neither the life of an individual nor the history of a society can be understood without understanding both.
>
> Yet men do not usually define the troubles they endure in terms of historical change . . . The well-being they enjoy, they do not usually impute to the big ups and downs of the society in which they live. Seldom aware of the intricate connection between the patterns of their own lives and the course of world history, ordinary men do not usually know what this connection means for the kind of men they are becoming and for the kinds of history-making in which they might take part. They do not possess the quality of mind essential to grasp the interplay of men and society, of biography and history, of self and world . . .
>
> What they need . . . is a quality of mind that will help them to [see] . . . what is going on in the world and . . . what may be happening within themselves. It is this quality . . . that . . . may be called the sociological imagination. Always keep your eyes open to the image of man – the generic notion of his human nature – which by your work you are assuming and implying; and also to the image of history – your notion of how history is being made. In a word, continually work out and revise your views of the problems of history, the problems of biography, and the problems of a social structure in which biography and history intersect. Keep your eyes open to the varieties of individuality, and to the modes of epochal change. Use what you see and what you imagine as the clues to your study of the human variety . . . know that many personal troubles cannot be solved merely as troubles, but must be understood in terms of public issues – and in terms of the problems of history making. Know that the human meaning of public issues must be revealed by relating them to personal troubles and to the problems of individual life. Know that the problems of social science, when adequately formulated, must include both troubles and issues, both biography and history, and the range of their intricate relations. Within that range the life of the individual and the making of societies occur; and within that range the sociological imagination has its chance to make a difference in the quality of human life in our time.

(Mills, 1967: 3–5, 225–6; orig. 1957)

This triple focus, on *biography, history and structure*, is sociology's heritage (see Bipul Kumar Bhadra, 1998).

(Notice that in this excerpt Mills uses male pronouns to apply to all people. It is interesting – even ironic – that an outspoken critic of society like Mills reflected the conventional writing practices of his time as far as gender was concerned. But he was writing in the 1950s, before gender became a key issue for sociology.)

Sociology and the significance of change

Living through the momentous changes brought about by the French Revolution and the Industrial Revolution must have been both exciting and dangerous. It is hard for the twenty-first-century person to grasp what it must have been like. But this was precisely the period that the earliest sociologists lived through and why they were driven to understand such changes and to consider where it may all have been heading. Sociology was born out of this firmament of change.

Yet sociologists reacted differently to the new social order then, just as they respond differently to society today. Some, including Auguste Comte and later Ferdinand Toennies, feared that people would be uprooted from long-established local communities and overpowered by change. So, in a conservative approach, Comte sought to shore up the family and traditional morality.

In contrast, Karl Marx (1818–83) worried little about the loss of tradition. But he could not condone the way industrial technology concentrated its great wealth in the hands of a small elite, while so many others faced hunger and misery. We examine his ideas at length in Chapter 4.

Clearly, Comte and Marx advanced radically different prescriptions for the problems of modernity. Yet they had in common the conviction that society rests on much more than individual choice. The sociological perspective animates the work of each, revealing that people's individual lives are framed by the broader society in which they live. This lesson, of course, remains as true today as it was a century ago.

Social change and the Great Transformation 2

The digital-information-network-cyborg society

Sociology may have been born of the Industrial Revolution but it has fast moved into the Cyber Revolution. In the twenty-first century, living in society – and studying it – is very different from the days of sociology's founders. The development of digital technologies, the spread of information technologies and the creation of new ways of communicating across the world since the later twentieth century has been an extraordinarily rapid development. In many countries across the world, it has become part of mainstream life in less than 20 years. Bearing in mind that the World Wide Web was not launched until 1991, already over 180 countries are connected and there are now over 100 million users in the United States alone. A new generation, the Net Generation, for whom the use of personal computers, information technology and the internet is taken for granted, is growing up. Brought up on Nintendo games and computers, they create a huge generation gap, often reversing adult–child roles as children come to know so much more about these things than either their teachers or their parents. Many 'users' are young, male and relatively wealthy: these are what Douglas Rushkoff (1999) calls the 'Digital Kids'. That said, more and more women are becoming involved; information technology is spreading through the classes and ethnicities; and it is moving through more groups across the world. One report in 2010 suggested that young people spent on average seven hours a day using the new technologies of various kinds; another recorded that there were at least 250 million Facebook sites in use by mid-2010. Growth in mobile phone use has been dramatic, as has growth in internet usage. Table 1.4 shows the numbers using the internet worldwide in 2009.

It is not quite clear yet what is the best term to use to describe this rapid change. Various suggestions have been made and we will use and discuss them variously though this book – as they highlight different aspects of the broad social change we are flagging here. They are:

- *The Digital Age.* This highlights the computerisation of life, the shift from analogue to digital, and the miniaturisation of these technologies which can now be found in all the smallest gadgets and gizmos of everyday life – from washing machines to watches to iPads and iPhones. Digitalisation is the key process here.

- *The Cyborg Age.* This highlights the ways in which human beings are more and more becoming adapted to and compelled to live with all manner of technologies, from transplants to space travel (see Chapter 20).

- *The Information Age.* This highlights the rapid growth of production and availability of all kinds of data and information. No society in history has been flooded with so much data that is available to so many. Wikipedia alone has in excess of 14 million articles – bigger than any encyclopedia ever imagined in the past.

Table 1.4	World internet usage and population statistics: 2010				
World regions	Population (2010 est.)	Internet users 31 Dec. 2000	Internet users Latest data	Penetration (% population)	Growth 2000–10
Africa	1,013,779,050	4,514,400	110,931,700	10.9%	2,357.3%
Asia	3,834,792,852	114,304,000	825,094,396	21.5%	621.8%
Europe	813,319,511	105,096,093	475,069,448	58.4%	352.0%
Middle East	212,336,924	9,284,800	63,240,946	29.8%	1,825.3%
North America	344,124,450	108,096,800	266,224,500	77.4%	146.3%
Latin America/Caribbean	592,556,972	18,068,919	204,689,836	34.5%	1,032.8%
Oceania/Australia	34,700,204	7,620,480	21,263,990	61.3%	179.0%
WORLD TOTAL	6,845,609,960	360,985,492	1,966,514,816	28.7%	444.8%

Notes: (1) Internet usage and world population statistics are for 30 June 2010. (2) Demographic (population) numbers are based on data from the US Census Bureau. (3) Internet usage information comes from data published by Nielsen Online, the International Telecommunications Union, GfK, local regulators and other reliable sources.

Source: www.internetworldstats.com. Copyright © 2000–10, Miniwatts Marketing Group. All rights reserved worldwide.

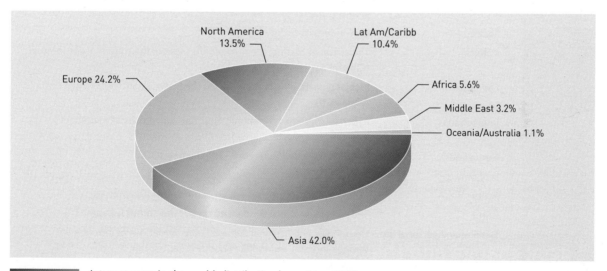

Figure 1.2	Internet users in the world: distribution by regions, 2010

Source: Internet World Stats, www.internetworldstats.com/stats.htm © 2010, Miniwatts Marketing Group.

- *The Network Society*. This highlights the ways in which new ways of communicating and relating have developed. Mobile phones have put us in 'perpetual contact' and Facebook (with some 500 million global users in mid-2010) has given us new ways of building friendship networks.

  (Both of these latter terms are used by the sociologist Manuel Castells in his major three volume book, *The Information Society* (see p. 200).)

- *The Virtual Age*. This highlights the mediated nature of reality. The twenty-first-century world is increasingly a world where reality is less direct and instead mediated through some technology – a mobile phone, a screen, a bar code.

Sociology and the new information order

In the face of this, sociology is changing its nature. It is doing this in two ways:

- *New topics*. Sociologists now have a vast array of new fields to examine – from digital dating to digital democracies. The list in the *Living in the twenty-first century* box shows some of the new topics that are emerging in sociology and which will be featured in this book.

- *New methods*. Sociologists now have a vast array of new tools with which to study society – along with new problems in doing research. How do Google, YouTube, Wikipedia, Twitter and Facebook help sociology? This is a challenge for contemporary sociology. What is the role of the new technologies (digital television, web, mobile, MP3, digital imagery, cybercam, etc.), their formats (Wikipedia,

Living the digital life

The Information Age is no longer new. It is well settled into twenty-first-century life across the world and many now move seamlessly across 'real' and 'virtual' worlds, making them interconnected on a daily basis. The recognition of this has had profound effects on sociological thinking. Here, together, is a guide to some of the issues raised about digital life in this book.

Studying sociology	Web search and Wikipedia (Chapter 1)
Globalisation	Network theory and global networks (Chapter 2)
Doing research	Transformation of research methods on line: Google, YouTube, network groups (Chapter 3)
Society	Post-industrial society (Chapter 4)
Culture	The arrival of texting; the flow of information; the culture of the internet (Chapter 5)
Organisations	Mobile phones, blogging, Facebook: the Network Society, Manuel Castells (Chapter 6)
Interactions	Cyber-self; internet communication; network groups like Facebook; 'Hi-Tech Harry Potters' (Chapter 7)
Inequalities	The digital divide (Chapters 8–14); the new ICT4
Economy	The global economy; outsourcing; teleworking, 'Disneyisation' (Chapter 15)
Polity	Online social movements; digital democracies (Chapter 16)
Crime	The surveillance society; identity theft; cybercrimes (Chapter 17)
Families and personal life	Households and personal cultures: transformations of intimate life through internet and mobile phones (Chapter 18)
Religion	Cyber-churches; growth of e-religions (Chapter 19)
Education	The 'e-revolution'; digital ways of thinking; Wikiworld (Chapter 20)
Health	Cyber-health (Chapter 21)
Media	Digitalisation; iPods; YouTube; Baudrillard (Chapter 22)
Science	Donna Haraway; biotechnology; space travel; cyberworlds (Chapter 23)
Cities	The digital city (Chapter 24)
The environment	High costs of all this to the environment (Chapter 25)
Part 6: Resources	This whole section is designed to connect you up with the large number of electronic resources available to the student (e.g. websites, YouTube, electronic maps) and also give a few more tips on things like 'developing a critical cyber attitude' and 'thinking visually'.

blogs, video-sharing websites, Google searches, etc.) and new social processes (e.g. e-education, i-labs, etc.) in social research? How can the new IT, which is clearly here to stay but is also likely to change in unexpected ways, be fruitfully and carefully used in doing sociology? We look at this more throughout the book but especially in Chapter 3 (and see the 'Big debate' on Wikipedia at the end of this chapter).

We now live in social worlds saturated with information about society and a startling array of ways of accessing it. We can access large amounts of social life at the press of a button – something our ancestors could not do. And we can find – on television, through photography, in film and documentary, in the everyday press and interviews, in the work and research of a myriad of pressure groups and non-governmental organisations – a staggering amount of stuff about society. In a way, everybody can now be their own sociologist: the material is there to be thought about. But thinking is just what is required. No data or information is just the automatic truth about society. The new technologies change patterns of communication and create new virtual worlds for many. They are profoundly shaping our relationship to information and knowledge. How does information technology shift the ways in which we do both our everyday life and our intellectual work? How does living in the Information Age shape the ways we now do sociology? These will be ongoing concerns in this book.

Futures: a world brimming with change

Just as the changes brought by the nineteenth and twentieth centuries were momentous, so too are the changes that are happening now in the twenty-first century. This is an era which is being revolutionised by digital technologies, new media, new sciences such as the new reproductive technologies, and new transnational movements and global interconnections. It is an era when traditional families, religions, patterns of work and government are often being rethought. More and more, people are not given a clear blueprint on how to live their lives, as they often were in the past. Instead they have to ask: what kind of life do I want to lead? They become more individualised, less committed to common standards, more prone to self-reflection. It is an era when divisions and inequalities of class, ethnicity, age and gender have become more and more noticeable and often increased, and it is a world where significant new conflicts over religion and culture seem rife. All of these ideas will need defining, describing, analysing and explaining, and this is the continuing task for sociologists in the new century – as well as the task for this introductory book. Just as sociology was born of the Industrial Revolution, now it finds renewed excitement at the challenge of what we shall call the postmodern or information society.

In subsequent chapters of this book, then, we delve into some of these changes. We will look at the steady move to modernity and modern societies, and how these days this may be transforming into other kinds of (global, digital, postmodern) society. We will discuss the major issues that concern contemporary sociologists. These pivotal social forces include culture, inequality, social class, race, ethnicity, gender, the economy and the family. They all involve ways in which individuals are guided, united and divided in the larger arena of society. Sociology is a challenging discipline, highly relevant to a world brimming with change. This book sets out to explore a little of this. Welcome to the challenge.

SUMMARY

1 Sociology is the systematic and critical study of society. It questions what people take for granted. It looks at social worlds as humanly produced.

2 The sociological perspective reveals 'the general in the particular' or the power of society to shape our lives. Because people in Western countries tend to think in terms of individual choice, recognising the impact of society on our lives initially seems like 'seeing the strange in the familiar' – 'defamiliarising the familiar'.

3 Public sociology tries to engage sociology with the wider world and the wider public. The circle of sociological life suggests groups involved in sociological knowledge. Sociologists have many roles and tasks to perform: as researchers, theorists, critics, educators, practitioners and critical citizens.

4 Socially marginal people are more likely than others to perceive the effects of society. For everyone, periods of social crisis foster sociological thinking.

5 There are at least four general benefits to using the sociological perspective. First, it challenges our familiar understandings of the world, helping us separate fact from fiction; second, it helps us appreciate the opportunities and constraints that frame our lives; third, it encourages more active participation in society; and fourth, it increases our awareness of social diversity locally and in the world as a whole.

6 There are three problems in studying sociology. First, societies change very rapidly; second, we are part of the societies we study; and third, sociology itself becomes a part of society.

7 Auguste Comte gave sociology its name in 1838. Whereas previous social thought had focused on what society ought to be, Comte's new discipline of sociology used scientific methods to understand society as it is. Sociology emerged as a reaction to the rapid transformation of Europe during the eighteenth and nineteenth centuries.

8 A first major transformation shows that four key dimensions of change – the rise of an industrial economy, the explosive growth of cities, the emergence of new political ideas and the decline of community – helped focus people's attention on the operation of society.

9 A second major transformation might be appearing, variously called the Digital, Cyborg, Information, Network or Virtual Age. Quite what it is to be called and what its features are will be raised throughout the book.

CONNECT UP: Turn to Part 6 of this book for key resources and link up with the book's website, which links to these resources
SEE: www.pearsoned.co.uk/plummer

MYTASKLIST

Ten suggestions for going further

1 Connect up with Part Six and the Sociology Web Resources

As you work through ideas and think about the issues raised in this chapter, look at the accompanying website and the resource centre at the end of this book which connects to it. There is a lot here to help you move on. To link up, see: www.pearson.co.uk/plummer.

- For a start, just spend some time surfing around and glancing over the final section of this book.

2 Review the chapter

Briefly summarise (in a paragraph) just what this chapter has been about. Consider: (a) What have you learned? (b) What do you disagree with? Be critical. And (c) How would you develop all this? How could you get more detail on matters that interest you?

3 Pose questions

(a) Consider how sociology differs from economics, politics, psychology, history, literature and journalism. Using the box on p. 4, try to define sociology and see what is distinctive about it.
(b) How does using the sociological perspective make us seem less in control of our lives? In what ways does it give us greater power over our surroundings?
(c) Give a sociological explanation of why sociology developed where and when it did. Examine whether it had 'biases' and, if so, what they were.
(d) Read or watch some science fiction, then write a futuristic account of the society in which your grandchildren will live, based upon your current knowledge of any new social trends.

(e) Discuss the nature of public sociology. What does the term mean? Scan the book to see what sorts of things are going to be discussed in these boxes.

4 Explore key words

Many concepts have been introduced in this chapter. There is a glossary of key concepts at the end of this book, but sometimes you will wish to explore the meanings of concepts more fully. For this, you will need a dictionary of sociology. There are many available. Among them are:

> *The Penguin Dictionary of Sociology* (5th rev. edn, 2006)
> *The Concise Oxford Dictionary of Sociology* (4th edn, 2009)
> *The Cambridge Dictionary of Sociology* (1st edn, 2006)
> Tony Lawson and Joan Garrod, *The Complete A–Z Sociology Handbook* (4th edn, 2009)
> *The Concise Encyclopedia of Sociology* (1st edn, 2010)

5 Search the Web

Be critical when you look at websites – see the box on p. 940 in the Resources section.

There are now a large number of websites devoted to social science and to sociology. There is a major list in Part 6 of this book – usually with links on the book's website.

For a general start look at:

The Internet Sociologist
www.vts.intute.ac.uk/he/tutorial/sociologist

This is one of a national series of tutorials written by qualified tutors, lecturers and librarians from across the UK. It is part of the Intute: Virtual Training Suite, funded by JISC.

The following sites may also be helpful:

Sociology Central
www.sociology.org.uk

The Sociolog
www.sociolog.com

SocioSite
www.pscw.uva.nl/sociosite

The SocioWeb
www.socioweb.com/~markbl/socioweb

6 Watch a DVD

Each chapter will suggest a few films that may be worth a look. As an opener, you might like to look at three 'classic' films that hold very different views of what society is like:

- Fritz Lang's *Metropolis* (1926): a futuristic account.
- Frank Capra's *It's a Wonderful Life* (1946): a tale of small-town America.
- David Lynch's *Blue Velvet* (1986): another tale of small-town America but one that is very different and not for the weak-hearted or squeamish (be warned: this last film is strong stuff and not recommended for all).

A comparison of the three kinds of society depicted would make for an interesting discussion! Look also at:

- Harold Ramis's *Groundhog Day* (1993): in which everybody pretty much does the same thing every day. It is a good way of thinking about the ways in which everyday life is often routine and taken for granted.

A good book that will help you to 'see' films sociologically is Jean-Anne Sutherand and Kathryn Fettey *Cinematic Sociology* (2010).

7 Read and think

Two classic introductions to the field, now read by millions of students and still worth a look at are:

Peter Berger, *Invitation to Sociology* (1963)

C. Wright Mills, *The Sociological Imagination* (1959)

There are many other recent ones: see for example:

Pamela Abbott, Claire Wallace and Melissa Tyler, *An Introduction to Sociology: Feminist Perspectives* (3rd edn, 2005) – an introductory text which provides a strong feminist perspective.

Zygmunt Bauman and Tim May, *Thinking Sociologically* (rev. edn, 2001) – a leading sociologist updates his views on what it means to be a sociologist.

Charles Lemert, *Social Things* (4th edn, 2008) – a very lively, often personal but also comprehensive coverage. Strongly recommended.

Ken Plummer, *Sociology: The Basics* (2010) – from one of the authors of this book, eight pathways into sociology are introduced for fostering a sociological imagination.

A useful guide to the Enlightenment is:

Paul Hyland, *The Enlightenment: A Sourcebook and Reader* (2003)

A good overview of Western society is:

Mary Evans, *A Short History of Society* (2006).

Newspapers, magazines and journals

Much useful reading is contained in magazines or journals which come out at regular intervals, and all sociologists must read the news (but maybe on websites) regularly. In fact, sociologists can become very dependent on these for the latest findings. Key world newspapers (such as the *Guardian*, the *Washington Post* and *Le Monde*) all have their own websites.

> **tip** Make sure you read a good newspaper – one with world news and serious discussion. Search for its home page by its title, then make it an online favourite so you can look at it regularly.

Two very readable popular magazines for sociology students – even worth subscribing to – are:

- *Sociology Review*: Search Philip Allan Publishers. Published four times a year. Full of short, up-to-date articles on key issues in sociology and well illustrated. With a strong focus on the UK, this is useful for the emerging sociologist. See: www.philipallan.co.uk/sociologyreview/index.htm

- *New Internationalist*. Search New Internationalist. Published monthly. This takes a clear political stance and is packed full of valuable information on the 'global state' of the world. The magazine is a must for world activists for change. See: www.newint.org

8 Connect and integrate

Many of the ideas in this chapter can also be developed by looking at other chapters. For example:

- For more on the positivist method, see Chapter 3.
- For more on explanations of social change, see Chapter 4.
- For more on anomie and suicide, see Chapter 17.
- Get clear the ideas of *Public sociology* (p. 11) and *Living the digital life* (p. 24) – and follow these features as they appear throughout the book.
- But, of course, this is just the introductory chapter. Read the book!

9 Relax with a novel

A good start for thinking about Enlightenment thought is to read some classics of Enlightenment literature like Voltaire's *Candide* (1759) and Jonathan Swift's *Gulliver's Travels* (1726).

10 Engage in THE BIG DEBATE

Debate Wikipedia and other digital tools for a digital generation

Sociology was born of the Industrial Revolution and used the growing tools of 'science' to develop. Now, in the twenty-first century, we live in the world of information science and high tech. Studying society now is very different from in the past. We are now fortunate enough to be able to access large amounts of social life at the press of a mouse, something our ancestors could never do. There are now a very large number of websites devoted to social science and to sociology – but a much vaster number which are simply devoted to social life in all its forms around the world. Quickly, and across the world, students now have access to sociology writings and world statistics online. You have access to almost any social 'scene', subculture or group you wish to know about (from alcoholics anonymous to asexuals; from xenophobia to extreme sports). You can enter the worlds of film, television and music too – saving them, filing them, editing them later. You can make digital images of anything instantly. You can chat with many specialist groups on Facebook. Indeed, you can blog and tweet your life away. It seems that the new young generation may spend as many as seven hours of each day living life through the new electronic gadgets.

All this means that the ways of doing sociology have changed. Even the way you read this book will be different – it has a website that accompanies it, and this will link you up immediately with thousands of online sites of interest. These are massive resources that were simply unavailable for students or sociologists before. As we have seen, sociology is becoming a very different enterprise. In every chapter of this book you will confront it head on. Old methods and old theories are changing: in many ways, you are the first true digital generation – the new pioneers with new challenges. These are exciting times for you. In this book you will find:

- key resources listed at the end of each chapter
- a major listing of websites and video-sharing resources in Part 6 of the book. This connects to our online website, which is very full and includes podcasts.

We no longer always use full addresses, as this is a fast-moving world and many will have changed.

But a few seconds on a search engine will usually take you there. You might want to create some home pages and 'favourites'.

So here you are, living in the digital world. And now, at the start of your course, is the time to debate some of the problems it raises. To start with, why not just look at the pros and cons of a number of the tools you are likely to use? As an exercise, spend some time surfing the net and looking for sociological entries on:

- *Google*: sensitises the first approximation of a field of inquiry and provides access to seemingly unlimited data resources.
- *Wikipedia*: raises issues about the democratisation of knowledge.
- *Amazon*: can suggest the books we want to read before we even know it ourselves.
- *YouTube*: shows the significance of a new visual (and blip) screen culture.
- *Blogs*: suggest that ongoing diaries, life stories and interviews are being made before our very eyes.
- *Facebook*: brings together new group styles that are shifting identities and patterns of communication.

 Remember, four matters are usually seen as important in evaluating material found on a website (Wilson and Carson, 2007). These concern:

- *The source.* Where does the information come from?
- *The objectivity of the author.* Might they have a particular point to push? Could it be 'propaganda'?
- *The logic of the argument.* Does it actually make sense?
- *Independent sources for the arguments or claims made.* Can you check them out elsewhere?

1 **Discuss Wikipedia.** This is the web's ever-expanding online encyclopedia. Many students rush to it these days. It seems to have all the answers, and can easily be cribbed for your essays! But this whole site also raises the question: *Just what is an encyclopedia and what is it for?* Conventionally, an encyclopedia provides stable answers to problems provided by experts in their fields. It does not change, so an encyclopedia often gets out of date quite quickly. But with Wikipedia, anyone can provide information and it will be as up to date as anyone wants to make it. It is also wide open to abuse: anyone could put anything on it! A lot of errors could be posted. And this raises the issue about what knowledge is. Is it to be fixed by experts – as in the past – or is it to be more

open, fluid and even democratic? But if this is to be the case, do you really want to risk filling up your minds with false, misleading information? This is a hot and contentious issue and now is the time for you to discuss it and ponder its implications.

Wikipedia raises major issues for the sociology of knowledge. Comparing it with any standard book encyclopedia will lead to a discussion of at least four critical issues. First, *how is this knowledge actually assembled – is it just there as a given, or is it selected by human agency?* And if it is the latter (which it is), then how does this social process take place. 'What are the social conditions for organising knowledge?' can become a topic for discussion.

Secondly, *what is the authority of the author for doing this?* Why should you trust an ageing professor who writes the entry to a standard published encyclopedia more than your friends who know nothing about it really but who can – if they want – submit entries? I know who I would trust more. A discussion of how knowledge, truth and authority are being questioned can follow.

Thirdly, *how can encyclopedias deal with the ways in which knowledge changes rapidly?* In their book forms, they often remain static for decades. Wikipedia opens up the possibility of an encyclopedia being dynamic and constantly responding to changes.

Fourthly, some of the above discussions could lead to a consideration of the democratisation of knowledge: *can ideas and knowledge be more usefully assembled through collective work than through individual expertise?* It would help here if you did a case study of the way in which Wikipedia entries are constructed – maybe constructing one, or modifying an entry. Guidelines for doing this can be found on Wikipedia itself, as well as in the useful handbook by John Broughton, *Wikipedia: The Missing Manual* (Cambridge: O'Reilly, 2008) – which perhaps your library should purchase.

To have an informed discussion on all these issues, look through some of the myriad back-up pages to Wikipedia, which show how entries are made, how changes can be made, and how records are kept for

all to see of who writes the entries and of all record modifications. Thousands of dedicated people all over the world are working to improve a fallible system, and it is good to understand this wider social process at work.

 For a really positive assessment of how Wikipeda mighty radically change the world for the better, see Juha Suoranta and Tere Vaden, *Wikiworld* (2010).

2 **Discuss Google searches** for something that interests you. Discuss the process of surfing with your friends, and share what you have come up with. Consider some of the problems that such data raise. Is all the information equally reliable, valid and truthful? Does it even make sense? Is it hurtful or even hateful in some way? What is its bias? What sources do you think you can rely on most?

3 **Discuss YouTube.** Now look at the lists of DVDs at the end of each chapter and see if you can track any of them down. Take this further: how central to social life now is the textual image? Is it becoming more important than books?

4 **Finally, read a book!** Consider whether reading books and articles is a better way to deal with issues than surfing. Does anyone in the class use an e-reader? Will books survive? Should they survive?

Later in the book we will suggest key issues to consider in using the digital world (see especially p. 939). Remember that the net is a public space – information on your site travels to you in complicated ways and leaves traces in many places. Watch out for sensitive and personal information and make sure it is restricted or encrypted. As we will see later in the book, many forms of 'deviance' have emerged around the net. And there are problems of surveillance, we will discuss in Chapter 17.

 Remember, since access to websites is open to anybody, anything could be said with no regard to truth, logic, rationality or even human kindness! So watch out and always scrutinise your data. *Develop a cyber critical attitude*: see p. 940.

CHAPTER 2

THINKING SOCIOLOGICALLY, THINKING GLOBALLY

IN THE MILLENNIUM YEAR OF 2000, the earth was home to some 6 billion people who lived in the cities and countryside of nearly 200 nations (by 2010 it had already grown another million). To grasp the social 'shape' of this world, imagine for a moment the planet's population reduced to a single settlement of 100 people. A visit to this 'global village' would reveal that more than half (61) of the inhabitants are from Asia, including 21 from the People's Republic of China and 17 from India. Next, in terms of numbers, we would find 13 from Africa, 12 from Europe, 8 from South America, 5 from North America and 1 from Oceania.

A study of this settlement would reveal some startling conclusions. People believe in very different 'gods': of the 100 people, 32 are Christian, 19 Muslim, 13 Hindus, 12 practise folk religions (like shamanism), 6 are Buddhists, 2 belong to other religions like Confucianism and the Bahai'i faith, 1 is Jewish and 15 are non-religious. There are some 6,000 languages but over half of the 100 speak Chinese, 9 English, 8 Hindi, 7 Spanish, 4 Arabic, 4 Bengali, 3 Portugese and 3 Russian.

The village is a rich place, with a vast array of goods and services for sale. Yet most people can do no more than dream of such treasures, because 80 per cent of the village's total income is earned by just 20 individuals.

Food is the greatest worry for the majority of the population. Every year, workers produce more than enough food to feed everyone; even so, half the village's people – including most of the children – go hungry. The worst-off 20 residents (who together have less money than the richest person in the village!) lack food, safe drinking water and secure shelter. They are weak and unable to work. Every day some of

them fall ill with life-threatening diseases. Another 50 do not have a reliable source of food and are hungry much of the time.

Villagers talk of their community's many schools, including colleges and universities. Of 38 school-aged villagers, 31 attend school but few (7.5) reach university. Half of the village's people can neither read nor write.

The sociological perspective reminds us of these many differences in the world. Our life chances and our very experiences of social life will differ dramatically according to what kind of society we are born into. Human lives do not unfold according to sheer chance; nor do people live isolated lives, relying solely on what philosophers call 'free will' in choosing every thought and action. On the contrary, while individuals make many important decisions every day, we do so within a larger arena called 'society' – a friendship, a family, a university, a nation, an entire world. The essential wisdom of sociology is that the social world guides and constrains our actions and life choices just as the seasons influence our choices of activities and clothing. It sets the framework in which we make decisions about our lives. And, because sociologists know a great deal about how society works, they can analyse and predict with insight and a fair degree of accuracy how we all behave. Many of the achievements we attribute to our personal abilities are products of the privileged position we occupy in the worldwide social system.[1]

[1] Global village scenario adapted from United Nations data. This is now widely taught in primary schools, and has been developed in posters and on T-shirts. In my view, it is still worth citing. See Smith and Armstrong (2003).

Queremos un mundo donde quepan muchos mundos. We want one world, one that can accommodate many worlds.

The Zapatistas, Chiapas, Mexico

From now on, nothing that happens on our planet is only a limited local event.

Ulrich Beck, *What is Globalization?* (2000)

Globalization debates transform many existing sociological controversies. . . .

John Urry, *Global Complexity* (2003)

In this chapter, we ask:

- What are the 'classical' ways of thinking about society and how are they being challenged and modified by a range of new perspectives?

- Why do we need a global perspective in sociology?

- What is meant by globalisation and how will it be developed as an idea in this book?

(Left) Michael Simpson, *World in Sky*
Source: Getty Images/Taxi/Michael Simpson.

Q Where are you in this image? What does the image say about you and your position in the world? What does it say about the 7 billions of planet earth's population?

How to think about society: a short tour of sociological theory

The task of weaving isolated observations into understanding brings us to another dimension of sociology: theory. Students are often put off by theory, believing it to be obscure and difficult. In fact, theory is what makes sociology different from, say, journalism or popular documentary television of social issues. For a **theory** is a *statement of how and why specific facts are related*. In a sense, we all theorise or generalise all the time. But sociology aims to do this more systematically (see Lee and Newby, 1983; Craib, 1992). Recall that Emile Durkheim observed that certain categories of people (men, Protestants, the wealthy and the unmarried) have higher suicide rates than others (women, Catholics and Jews, the poor and the married). He explained these observations by creating a theory: a high risk of suicide stems from a low level of social integration.

Of course, as Durkheim pondered the issue of suicide, he considered any number of possible theories. But merely linking facts together is no guarantee that a theory is correct. To evaluate a theory, as the next chapter explains, sociologists use critical and logical thinking along with an array of research tools to gather evidence. 'Facts', as we shall see, are always a bit of a problem – consider, for example, how the very idea of a suicide rate used by Durkheim brings problems. Just what does such a rate measure? Does it really record all the suicides? How can we really tell that a death has been a suicide? Nevertheless, sociologists do strive for 'facts', which often allow them to confirm some theories while rejecting or modifying others. As a sociologist, Durkheim was not content merely to identify a plausible cause of suicide; he set about collecting data to see precisely which categories of people committed suicide with the highest frequency.

Poring over his data, Durkheim settled on a theory that best squared with all the available evidence.

In attempting to develop theories about human society, sociologists face a wide range of choices. What issues should we study? How should we link facts together to form theories? What assumptions might underpin our theories? In making sense of society, sociologists are guided by one or more theoretical 'road maps' or perspectives. A **theoretical perspective** can be seen as *a basic image that guides thinking and research.*

We noted earlier that two of sociology's founders – Auguste Comte and Karl Marx – made sense of the emerging modern society in strikingly different ways. Such differences persist today as some sociologists highlight how societies stay the same, while others focus on patterns of change. Similarly, some sociological theorists focus on what joins people together, while others investigate how society divides people according to gender, race, ethnicity or social class. Some sociologists seek to understand the operation of society as it is, while others actively promote what they view as desirable social change.

In short, sociologists often disagree about what the most interesting questions are; even when they agree on the questions, they may still differ over the answers. Nonetheless, the discipline of sociology is far from chaotic. Like many disciplines, it has built-in controversies and has multiple perspectives, containing *an array of basic images that guide thinking and research.* See Figure 2.1 for a summary of various positions. Over the past hundred years, sociologists have developed three major theoretical ways of thinking about society. We will introduce these next – and they will reappear at various points in the book. They may be called the *classical perspectives* that have shaped sociology in the past. But, like any growing discipline, these are constantly being refined and developed, while at the same time newer ones are appearing alongside them. After outlining these mainstream, or classical, stances, we will turn to some *emerging perspectives*.

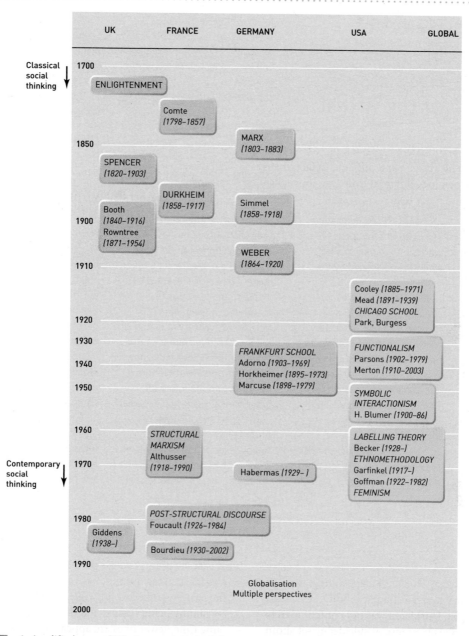

Figure 2.1

A simplified map of Western sociological theory, 1700–2000

The sociological map shows some key Western sociologists – when they were born and where. When presented like this, it is easy to detect a very strong male bias.

Source: Plummer, with suggestions from Tabitha Freeman.

THINKERS & THEORY

Herbert Spencer: the survival of the fittest

The most memorable idea of the English philosopher Herbert Spencer (1820–1903) was his assertion that the passing of time witnesses 'the survival of the fittest'. Many people associate this immortal phrase with the theory of species evolution developed by the natural scientist Charles Darwin (1809–82). The expression was actually Spencer's, however, and he used it to refer to society, not to living creatures. In it, we find not only an example of early structural–functional analysis, but also a controversial theory that reflects the popular view in Spencer's day that society mirrored biology.

Spencer's ideas, which came to be known as social Darwinism, rested on the assertion that, if left to compete among themselves, the most intelligent, ambitious and productive people will inevitably win out. Spencer endorsed a world of fierce competition, thinking that as the 'fittest' survived, society would undergo steady improvements.

Society rewards its best members, Spencer continued, by allowing a free-market economy to function without government interference. Welfare, or other programmes aimed at redistributing money to benefit the poor, Spencer maintained, do just the opposite: they drag society down by elevating its weakest and least worthy members. For such opinions, nineteenth-century industrialists loudly applauded Spencer, and the rich saw in Spencer's analysis a scientific justification for big business to remain free of government regulation or social conscience. Indeed, John D. Rockefeller, who built a vast financial empire that included most of the US oil industry, often recited Spencer's 'social gospel' to young children in Sunday school, casting the growth of giant corporations as merely the naturally ordained 'survival of the fittest'.

But others objected to the idea that society amounted to little more than a jungle where self-interest reigned supreme. Gradually, social Darwinism fell out of favour among social scientists, though it still surfaces today as an influential element of conservative political thought. From a sociological point of view, Spencer's thinking is flawed because we now realise that ability only partly accounts for personal success, and favouring the rich and powerful does not necessarily benefit society as a whole. In addition, the heartlessness of Spencer's ideas strikes many people as cruel, with little room for human compassion.

For a positive appraisal of Spencer's life and work, see Mark Francis, *Herbert Spencer and the Invention of Modern Life* (2007).

SOCIOLOGICAL THEORY:

A MULTI-PARADIGMATIC DISCIPLINE WITH MANY THEORIES AND WAYS OF THINKING

A key challenge for sociology is to search for general ways of understanding social life. Sociologists are always developing sociological theories to help us make sense of this social world, and in this book you will be briefly introduced to a wide range of them. What you will find is that they tend to provide partial accounts – they take an angle, adopt a perspective and give you one way of seeing the world. Sociology is best seen as multi-paradigmatic and suggests a range of perspectives on social life. At its best it draws together a wide range of these perspectives to help provide the fullest picture.

We suggest you start your sociological theorising by trying to grasp the broadest 'image' of each theory. Table 2.1 provides some details of where you can find them discussed more in this book. Finally, if you want to take any theory further, look at some of the suggestions for further reading at the end of the chapter and book.

Table 2.1

Look at the social as:	Key theories and ideas to develop	Follow up in this book by looking at:
A series of unfolding stages.	Evolutionary theories of society.	Early versions are Comte (Ch. 1); Spencer (Ch. 1). Modern variants such as 'multiple modernities' are discussed in Ch. 4.
An integrated whole where the parts and institutions work to hold it all together. Sometimes it falls apart and things do not function well.	Functionalism and neofunctionalism; ecological theory; modern social systems theory and cybernetics.	Classic version is Durkheim (Ch. 2 and 4); and Park (Ch. 24). Parsons' systems theory (Ch. 2); Mary Douglas and the natural order (Ch. 14); and Jeffrey Alexander (neofunctionalism and civic society, Ch. 26).
Composed of different groups with different interests which are in conflict. Dominant groups over exploited and dominated groups. These are commonly identified as class, race, gender, nation, sexual, disability and age interests.	Conflict theories of many and all kinds: which can include Marxism, feminism, anti-racist theories, queer theory, and postcolonial theories. They are also widely found in cultural studies, in the idea of hegemony and in notions of symbolic violence.	Can be found in Marx (Ch. 2 and 4); C. Wright Mills (Ch. 1); Du Bois (Ch. 11); Patricia Hill Collins (Ch. 11); Feminism (Ch. 2 and 12); queer theory (Ch. 12); Paulo Freiere (Ch. 20); Intersections (Ch. 8).
Ways in which we orientate ourselves to meaning and interact with each other and develop culture and symbols – society is meaningful interaction.	Action theory, symbolic interactionism, phenomenological sociology, constructionism.	Most explicitly found in the works of Max Weber (Ch. 2 and 4); G. H. Mead (Ch. 7) and Goffman (Ch. 7).
The habits we create, change and live with in different arenas of life.	The psychology of William James on 'habits'; institutionalisation theory; the idea of habitus.	See especially Pierre Bourdieu (Ch. 8 and 10).
Drama, the roles we play and the selves we present.	Role theory, dramaturgy, theories of identity; ideas of performativity. Symbolic interactions.	See especially discussions of self and Goffman (Ch. 7) and Judith Butler (Ch. 12); Norman Denzin (Ch. 3).
Languages and discourses we live our lives through. Communication.	Social linguistics, conversational analysis, ethnomethodology, discourse analysis and hermeneutics. Symbolic interaction	Key recent influence is the work of Foucault (Ch. 17). Present in linguistics (Ch. 5), narrative and ethnomethodology (Ch. 7); Habermas.
A civilizing process	Configurational theory	Key proponent is Norbert Elias (see Ch. 7).
Creating a bridge between action and structure	See action–structure debate	See the big debate at the end of Ch. 2 and Giddens (Ch. 16).
Underlying forms of sociability and sociation	Formal sociology	See Simmel (Ch. 6).
Networks and flows	Network theory, mobilities theory. The term 'network' is used in a number of different ways: simple mapping of friends and contacts to a new cybernetic reality of high tech.	See discussions in Ch. 6. Note in particular the work of Manuel Castells. The work of Zygmunt Bauman on fluid society (Ch. 4) and of John Urry on mobilities (Ch. 26) see society as a flow.
Logo and brand	Many recent theories have been developed by a focus on a specific brand.	Most famous is George Ritzer's McDonaldisation of society (Ch. 6); see also Disneyisation etc.
Flourishing capabilities	Human capabilities theory, being developed by human development theorists like Nussbaum and Sen.	Discussed mainly in Ch. 9 and 14.
Global	Globalisation, world systems, cosmopolitanism.	See chart on p. 53.

The 'classical', traditional perspectives of sociology

Broadly, three perspectives dominated sociological thinking for a long while, and it is important to know about them. We will return to them in many chapters of this book. The three traditions are called by many different names but we will identify them very simply as *functionalism*, *conflict* and *action theory*. These terms are now old fashioned, but the ideas they capture are still very much alive today. Here, we briefly describe each.

1 The functionalist perspective: a world of balance

Functionalism is *a framework for building theory that sees society as a complex system whose parts work together and interconnect – often to promote solidarity and stability*. This perspective begins by recognising that our lives are guided by **social structure**, meaning relatively stable patterns of social behaviour. Social structure is what gives shape to the family, directs people to exchange greetings on the street, or steers events in a university classroom. Second, this perspective leads us to understand social structure in terms of its **social functions**, or consequences for the operation of society. All social structure – from family life to a simple handshake – contributes to the operation of society, at least in its present form.

Functionalism owes much to the ideas of Auguste Comte who, as we have already explained, sought to promote social integration during a time of tumultuous change. A second architect of this theoretical approach, the influential English sociologist Herbert Spencer (1820–1903), is introduced in the box on p. 36. Spencer was a student of both the human body and society, and he came to see that the two have much in common. The structural parts of the human body include the skeleton, muscles and various internal organs. These elements are interdependent, each contributing to the survival of the entire organism. In the same way, reasoned Spencer, various social structures are interdependent, working in concert to preserve society. The structural–functional perspective, then, organises sociological observations by identifying various structures of society and investigating the function of each one.

In France, several decades after Comte's death, Emile Durkheim continued the development of sociology. Durkheim did not share the social Darwinist thinking of his English colleague Spencer; rather, his work is primarily concerned with the issue of *social solidarity*, or how societies 'hang together'. Because of the extent of Durkheim's influence on sociology, his work is detailed in Chapter 4.

As sociology developed in the United States, many of the ideas of Herbert Spencer and Emile Durkheim were carried forward by Talcott Parsons (1902–79). The major US proponent of the functional perspective, Parsons treated society as a system, identifying the basic tasks that all societies must perform to survive and the ways they accomplish these tasks. All societies, he argued, need to be able to adapt, achieve their goals, maintain themselves and have members who are well socialised into their order. Without this, societies may begin to break down.

A contemporary of Parsons was the major US sociologist Robert K. Merton (1910–2003) , who expanded our understanding of the concept of social function in novel ways. Merton (1968) explains, first, that the consequences of any social pattern are likely to differ for various members of a society. For example, conventional families may provide crucial support for the development of children, but they also confer privileges on men while limiting the opportunities of women.

Second, Merton notes, people rarely perceive all the functions of a particular social structure. He described as **manifest functions** the *recognised and intended consequences of any social pattern*. By contrast, **latent functions** are *consequences that are largely unrecognised and unintended*. To illustrate, the obvious functions of higher education include providing people with the information and skills they need to perform jobs effectively. But perhaps just as important, although rarely acknowledged, is a university's function as a chance to meet potential partners. Another function may be to keep millions of young people out of a labour market where, presumably, many of them would not find jobs. And a third, less obvious function may well be to reinforce a system of prestige and inequality – by excluding those who do not go to universities from all sorts of work.

Merton makes a third point: not *all* the effects of any social structure turn out to be useful. Thus we designate as **social dysfunctions** *any social pattern's undesirable consequences for the operation of society*. And, to make matters still more complex, people may well disagree about what is useful or harmful. So some might argue that higher education promotes left-wing thinking that threatens traditional values. Others might dismiss such charges as trivial or simply wrong; higher education is dysfunctional for conferring further privileges on the wealthy (who disproportionately attend university), while poorer families find a university course beyond their financial reach.

Critical comment

The most salient characteristic of the functional perspective is its vision of society as a whole being comprehensible, orderly and stable. Sociologists typically couple this approach with scientific methods of research aimed at learning 'what makes society tick'.

Until the 1960s, the functional perspective dominated sociology. In recent decades, however, its influence has waned. How can we assume that society has a 'natural' order, critics ask, when social patterns vary from place to place and change over time? Further, by emphasising social integration, functionalism tends to gloss over inequality based on social class, race, ethnicity and gender – divisions that may generate considerable tension and conflict. This focus on stability at the expense of conflict and change can give the functional perspective a conservative character. In the main, functionalism is a theory that is much less discussed and used these days.

2 The conflict perspective: a world of difference

The **conflict perspective** is *a framework for building theory that sees society as an arena of differences and inequalities that generate conflict and change.* This approach complements the functional perspective by highlighting not solidarity but division based on different interests and potential inequality. Guided by this perspective, sociologists investigate how factors such as social class, race, ethnicity, sex, disability and age are linked to unequal distribution of money, power, education and social prestige. We look at these in detail in Part Three of this book. A conflict analysis points out that, rather than promoting the operation of society as a whole, social structure typically benefits some people while depriving others.

Working within the conflict perspective, sociologists spotlight ongoing differences and conflict between dominant and disadvantaged categories of people – the rich in relation to the poor, white people as opposed to black, men versus women. Typically, those on top strive to protect their privileges; the disadvantaged counter by attempting to gain more resources for themselves.

To illustrate, a conflict analysis of our educational system might highlight how schooling perpetuates

inequality by helping to reproduce the class structure in every new generation. The process may start in primary schools and continue as secondary schools stream students. From a functional point of view, this may benefit all of society because, ideally, students receive the training appropriate to their academic abilities. But conflict analysis counters that streaming often has less to do with talent than with a student's social background, as well-to-do students are placed in higher streams and poor students end up in the lower ones.

In this way, privileged families gain favoured treatment for their children from schools. And, with the best schooling behind them, these young people leave university to pursue occupations that confer both prestige and high income. By contrast, the children of poor families are less prepared for college. So, like their parents before them, these young people typically move straight from secondary school into low-paying jobs. In both cases, the social standing of one generation is passed on to another, with schools justifying the practice in terms not of privilege but of individual merit (Bowles and Gintis, 1976; and see Chapter 20).

Social conflict extends well beyond schools. Later chapters of this book highlight efforts by working people, women, racial, ethnic, gay and lesbian minorities to improve their lives. In each of these cases, the conflict perspective helps us to see how inequality and the conflict it generates are rooted in the organisation of society itself.

Finally, many sociologists who embrace the conflict perspective attempt not just to understand society but to reduce social inequality. This was the goal of Karl Marx, the social thinker whose ideas underlie the conflict perspective. Marx did not seek merely to understand how society works. In a well-known declaration (inscribed on his monument in London's Highgate Cemetery), Marx asserted: 'The philosophers have only interpreted the world, in various ways; the point, however, is to change it.'

Critical comment

The conflict perspective developed rapidly during the 1960s and the 1970s. Yet, like other approaches, it has come in for its share of criticism. Because this perspective highlights inequality and division, it glosses over how shared values or interdependence generate unity among members of a society. In addition, say critics, to the extent that the conflict approach explicitly pursues political goals, it can relinquish any claim to scientific objectivity. As the next chapter explains in detail, conflict theorists are uneasy with the notion that science can be 'objective'. They contend, on the contrary, that the conflict perspective as well as *all* theoretical approaches have political consequences, albeit different ones. Like functionalism, the language of conflict theory has gone more and more out of fashion in recent years.

One additional criticism, which applies equally to both the functional and conflict perspectives, is that they envisage society in very broad terms. 'Society' becomes a thing in itself, describing our lives as a composite of 'family', 'social class', and so on. A third theoretical perspective depicts society less in terms of abstract generalisations and more in terms of people's everyday, situational experiences.

THINKERS & THEORY

The foundational three: a very brief introduction

Since the 1950s, when sociology really entered the university curriculum, the 'holy trinity' of Marx, Durkheim and Weber have been taught as the central founders of sociology. There is a good reason for this. Each provides a core understanding of the arrival of modern capitalist societies, the rapid changes that were going on with the Industrial Revolution and the key political transformation of the late eighteenth and nineteenth centuries. As the landscape of the world changed dramatically, so Marx, Durkheim and Weber provided key accounts to guide contemporary understanding. Their ideas still shape sociological analysis in the twenty-first century, so below we give a very brief introduction to them. Their ideas – and those of their

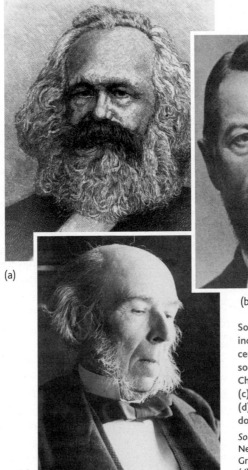

(a)

(b)

(c)

(d)

Some shapers of a modern sociology. With the rise of industrial capitalism, the nineteenth and twentieth centuries saw an explosion of significant thinkers about society. Above are just four of them: (a) Karl Marx (see Chapters 2 and 4); (b) Max Weber (see Chapters 2 and 4); (c) Emile Durkheim (see Chapters 1, 2 and 4); and (d) Herbert Spencer (see Chapter 2). What characteristics do they have in common?

Source: (a) © Pearson Education Ltd/The Illustrated London News Picture Library/Ingram Publishing/Alamy; (b) © The Granger Collection, New York; (c) © Bettmann/Corbis; (d) © Hulton-Deutsch Collection/Corbis.

THINKERS & THEORY

contemporary followers – are discussed more fully throughout the book.

Marx (1803–83)

Marx claimed that 'the history of all hitherto existing societies is the history of class struggle' (opening statement in *The Communist Manifesto*) and saw a flow of conflict between groups as the hallmark of histories everywhere. People are born into a history that is not of their making; but people also make history. People can change the world they are born into. In the nineteenth century, Marx saw that industrial capitalism (see Chapter 4) was developing into a system which would bring exploitation and a suffering lower class. As people became aware of their situation, so change – revolution – would come about; and create a new order of equality.

Marx's work has had a huge impact upon intellectual life, political activity and society. Few people have heard of Weber and Durkheim, but Marx became a household name in much of the twentieth century. He argued that 'the philosophers have only interpreted the world, the point is to change it' and claimed that 'The ideas of the ruling class are in every epoch the ruling ideas'. His work had a profound impact on the development of communist societies such as the Soviet Union and Mao's China. In the middle part of the twentieth century, more than a fifth of the world lived in communist societies inspired by him. Whilst these societies are now considered short-term failures which harboured deeply authoritarian structures and major genocidal tendencies,

many of his ideas have remained influential. In sociology, his work continues to flag the centrality of oppression and conflict in social life and the ubiquitous nature of inequality and exploitation.

Born in Germany, he eventually had to leave it because his relentless social criticism got him into trouble with the authorities. He lived much of his later life in relative poverty in Victorian London and was buried at Highgate Cemetery in 1883.

Durkheim (1858–1917)

Durkheim saw societies as changing too. They were moving from societies based on great similarities to ones characterised by a rapid growth of division of labour. This increased differentiation (which he called a shift from mechanical society to organic society), which could become associated with a breakdown of integration and ultimate anomie – a state of normlessness. He suggested that new groups (guilds) could create a new sense of community and belonging. He was one of the main architects of the structural–functional tradition we locate throughout this book. His influence can be found today in the many theories of community and social bonding, as well as in studies of the power of symbols and rituals in everyday life.

Durkheim was the only one of our 'holy three' to work in a sociology department and identify as a sociologist. He outlined how sociology should study the social world – to '*treat social facts as things*', as matters that arise outside human consciousness and which shape the way we live in the world.

Weber (1864–1920)

Weber saw societies as becoming increasingly dominated by rational thought. He highlighted the growth of bureaucracies (which we discuss in Chapter 6). While this brought benefits, it also brought an increasing 'disenchantment' with the world – men became trapped in an 'iron cage' in which they had little hope of change. Religions were likely to decline. Capitalism came about mainly because of shifts in the organisation of religion – the rise of an individualistic Protestant ethic (see Chapter 4).

Weber was very concerned with the ways in which human actions and meanings played their role in social life. His work ranged over many areas: music, religion, love, law, the economy, politics. He looked at a wide range of civilisations. He also engaged with politics (and his wife, Marianne, was a leading feminist of her time). He struggled with the balance between his personal political commitments and his view of sociology as being scientifically neutral – or value-free. He was the most pessimistic of our three thinkers. And, indeed, in his personal life he waged war with perpetual depression.

 Brush up on your Marx, Durkheim and Weber. If you want to understand how sociological ideas have developed, you could read:

John Hughes, Wes Sharrock and Peter Martin, *Understanding Classical Social Theory: Marx, Weber, Durkheim* (2nd edn, 2003)

Kenneth Morrison, *Marx, Durkheim, Weber: Formations of Modern Social Thought* (2006)

Most of the originals of these authors can be found online (see end of chapter).

3 The social action perspective: a world of meaning

Both the functional and conflict perspectives share a **macro-level orientation**, meaning *a focus on broad social structures that characterise society as a whole*. Macro-level sociology takes in the big picture, rather like observing a city from high above in a helicopter, noting how highways carry traffic from place to place and the striking contrasts between rich and poor neighbourhoods. Action theory, by contrast, starts with the ways in which people (or actors) orientate themselves to each other, and how they do so on the basis of meanings. This provides a *micro-level orientation*, meaning *a focus on the emerging meanings of social interaction in specific situations*. The distinction between macro and micro is an important one in sociology and it appears in a number of guises. The *Big debate* at the end of the chapter introduces some of these ideas.

One founder of the action perspective – a micro-theory that focuses on how actors assemble social meanings – is the highly influential Max Weber (1864–1920), a German sociologist who emphasised the need to understand a setting from the point of view of the people in it. Weber's approach is presented at length in Chapter 4, but here a few ideas can be introduced.

His approach emphasises how human meanings and action shape society. Weber understood the power of technology, and he shared many of Marx's ideas about social conflict. But he departed from Marx's materialist analysis, arguing that societies differ primarily in terms of the ways in which their members think about the world. For Weber, ideas – especially beliefs and values – have transforming power. Thus he saw modern society as the product not just of new technology and capitalism, but of a new way of thinking. This emphasis on ideas contrasts with Marx's focus on material production, leading scholars to describe Weber's work as 'a debate with the ghost of Karl Marx' (Cuff and Payne, 1979: 73–4).

In all his work, Weber contrasted social patterns in different times and places. To sharpen comparisons, he relied on the ideal type, an abstract statement of the essential, though often exaggerated, characteristics of any social phenomenon. He explored religion by contrasting the ideal 'Protestant' with the ideal 'Jew', 'Hindu' and 'Buddhist', knowing that these models precisely described no actual individuals. These 'ideal types' can then be contrasted with actual, empirical forms found in reality. Note that Weber's use of the word 'ideal' does not mean that something is 'good' or 'the best'; we could analyse 'criminals' as well as 'priests' as ideal types.

Closely allied to Weber is the American tradition of symbolic interactionism. The perspective emerges in the work of the philosopher George Herbert Mead (1863–1931), who looked at how we assemble our sense of self over time based on social experience. His ideas are explored in Chapter 7. The theory is also connected to the Chicago School of Sociology (explored more in Chapter 24), which examined city life in this way. The theory leads to careful observation of how people interact. **Symbolic interactionism**, then, is *a theoretical framework that envisages society as the product of the everyday interactions of people doing things together*. In order to understand such interactions, great emphasis is placed on studying everyday social life through tools such as life stories and observation. Sociology must proceed in this view through an intimate familiarity with everyday real-life events and not through abstract social theory.

How does 'society' result from the ongoing experiences of tens of millions of people? One answer, detailed in Chapter 7, is that society arises as a shared reality that its members construct as they interact with one another. Through the human process of finding meaning in our surroundings, we define our identities, bodies and feelings, and come to 'socially construct' the world around us.

Of course, this process of definition varies a great deal from person to person. On a city street, for example, one person may define a homeless woman as 'a no-hoper looking for a handout' and ignore her. Another, however, might define her as a 'fellow human being in need' and offer assistance. In the same way, one pedestrian may feel a sense of security passing by a police officer walking the beat, while another may be seized by nervous anxiety. Sociologists guided by the symbolic interaction approach, therefore, view society as a mosaic of subjective meanings and variable responses.

On this foundation, others have devised their own micro-level approaches to understanding social life. Chapter 7 presents the work of Erving Goffman (1922–82), whose *dramaturgical analysis* emphasises how we resemble actors on a stage as we play out our various roles before others. Other sociologists, including George Homans and Peter Blau, have developed *social exchange analysis*. In their view, social interaction amounts to a negotiation in which individuals are guided by what they stand to gain and lose from others. In the ritual of courtship, for example, people typically seek mates who offer at least as much – in terms of physical attractiveness, intelligence and social background – as they provide in return.

Critical comment

The action perspective helps to correct a bias inherent in all macro-level approaches to understanding society. Without denying the usefulness of abstract social structures such as 'the family' and 'social class', we must bear in mind that society basically amounts to *people interacting*. Put another way, this micro-level approach helps convey more of how individuals actually experience society and how they do things together (Becker, 1986).

The trouble is that by focusing on day-to-day interactions, these theorists can obscure larger social structures. Highlighting what is unique in each social scene risks overlooking the widespread effects of our culture, as well as factors such as class, gender and race.

Table 2.2 summarises the important characteristics of the functional, conflict and action perspectives. As we have explained, each perspective is partially helpful in answering particular kinds of question. By and large, however, the fullest understanding of society comes from linking the sociological perspective to all three. Sociologists examine the social world by looking at *functions and dysfunctions, conflicts and consensus, actions and meanings*. The three theoretical perspectives certainly offer different insights, but none is more correct than the others, and all three have become increasingly modified in the light of newer theories.

Table 2.2	Three traditional perspectives: a summary		
Theoretical perspective	**Orientation**	**Image of society**	**Core questions**
Functional	Macro-level	A system of interrelated parts that is relatively stable based on widespread consensus as to what is morally desirable; each part has functional consequences for the operation of society as a whole	• How is society integrated? • What are the major parts of society? • How are these parts interrelated? • What are the consequences of each one for the operation of society?
Conflict	Macro-level	A system characterised by social inequality; each part of society benefits some categories of people more than others; conflict-based social inequality promotes social change	• How is society divided? • What are the major patterns of social inequality? • How do some categories of people attempt to protect their privileges? • How do other categories of people challenge the status quo?
Symbolic interaction	Micro-level	An ongoing process of social interaction in specific settings based on symbolic communications; individual perceptions of reality are variable and changing	• How is society experienced? • How do human beings interact to create, sustain and change social patterns? • How do individuals attempt to shape the reality perceived by others? • How does individual behaviour change from one situation to another?

LIVING IN THE C 21ST

The capitalist world: the neoliberal model

One of the key challenges for social theory is to grasp the changing nature of capitalism – which, in the twenty-first century, has become the dominant system organising principle of most societies. **Capitalism** is *the economic system in which resources and the means of producing goods and services are privately owned.* There are many kinds of capitalist economy, but commonly there will be three distinctive features:

1 *Private ownership of property.* A capitalist economy supports the right of individuals to own almost anything. The more capitalist an economy is, the more private ownership there is of wealth-producing property such as factories and land. The downside of this can be a mass accumulation of profits by relatively few people, which can generate polarisation and cleavages between groups – the 'haves' and the 'have nots'. A potential for conflict is generated.

2 *Pursuit of personal profit.* A capitalist society encourages the accumulation of private property and defines a profit-minded orientation as natural and simply a matter of 'doing business'. The classical Scottish Enlightenment economist Adam Smith (1723–90) claimed that the individual pursuit of self-interest helps an entire society prosper (1937: 508; orig. 1776). Others argue that it leads to the exploitation of the mass by the few, and consolidates a class system.

3 *Free competition, consumer sovereignty and markets.* A purely capitalist economy would operate with no government interference, sometimes called a *laissez-faire* approach. Adam Smith contended that a freely competitive economy regulates itself by the 'invisible hand' of the laws of supply and demand.

Capitalism takes many different forms across the world and we look at these in more detail in Chapter 15. But it is important to grasp how central the free market, the pursuit of profit and freed competition are in structuring much of world social life. The most prevalent system which was developed under the government of President Reagan in the USA and Prime Minister Margaret Thatcher is often called Reaganism, Thatcherism or more formally neoliberalism (the term used by the economist Friedrich Hayek who championed it). *Neoliberal market capitalism* involves highly competitive, decentralised, open markets. It is anti-trust and unions, and seeks the freest flows of capital markets. There should be minimum state involvement and planning and the maximising of returns to owners of capital. It champions the free individual – but is uncritical of the way it fosters poverty and injustice for large numbers of people.

For more on capitalism, see p. 503 *et seq*; and pp. 533–5. Read: Geoffrey Ingham, *Capitalism* (2008); and on neoliberalism, see David Harvey, *A Brief History of Neo-Liberalism* (2005).

Contemporary perspectives in sociology: multiple perspectives, other voices and the postmodern

Although functionalism, conflict theory and action sociology are still common positions within sociology, many others have emerged over the past three decades. As we have seen, sociology is often seen as containing multiple perspectives, which means that it takes on many perspectives for looking at social life rather than just one. It is the sign of a lively subject that, as society changes, so too do some of the approaches being adopted within it.

Some of them are really just further developments of the above theories. Thus, they may, for example, focus on different aspects of 'action', such as language and conversation (**conversational analysis** is an approach which does this: see Chapter 7). Or they may develop the idea that societies are structures through a focus either on the system of signs and languages that often organise them (as **semiotics** does: see Chapter 5) or on the way the state works (as in Althusserian Marxism: see Chapter 22). We will say a little more about these theories when we discuss the mass media later in the book (Chapter 22).

Other developments, however, are seen by some to go deeper than this. A number of critics of sociology suggest that the discipline has now entered a stage of 'crisis' in which many of its older ideas and perspectives are seen as being too narrowly conceived. Broadly, the newer approaches highlight **different** *perspectives*, *standpoints*, *cultures* or *voices*: they are much more self-conscious that all of sociology has to come from a perspective, a position or a point of view. We can never grasp the 'full truth' of a society, a completely full picture of it, even though we should try. Hence we should be more open about the partial perspectives we adopt and understand where we stand in relation to these partial perspectives. Sociology will always be selective. Max Weber himself recognised this long ago when he said:

> There is no absolutely 'objective' scientific analysis of culture or . . . of 'social phenomena' independent of special and 'one-sided' viewpoints according to which . . . they are selected, analysed and organised.

(Weber, 1949: 72)

This recognition of *perspectives*, *points of view*, *different cultures* or *standpoints* from which analysis proceeds has become more and more important for modern sociology. And this means that it helps to be explicit and open about the perspective we take. At its most critical, many of the new perspectives suggest that the major perspective of the past has been that of white, Western, Anglo-American, heterosexual men. This may sound a cliché, but as you read this book you should look for authors and sociologists who lie outside this tradition. They will, sadly, be somewhat hard to find. Whether using a functionalist, conflict or (inter)action perspective, they all shared common assumptions derived from their male and Western position.

In contrast, the newer perspectives generally see a range of other voices that were missed out of sociology in the past. Taken together, they provide a lot more 'angles' from which to approach society as a whole. They help to enrich the openness of the discipline to the range of ways of seeing society. This does *not* mean that everything is relative and anything goes. Quite the opposite: it means that, by carefully and systematically unpacking different perspectives, we can come to see societies more deeply and in a more rounded way. The aim of sociology is still to be 'objective' even if, as we shall see in Chapter 3, this is much harder than sociologists used to think and even if we can only ever approximate truth.

Many of these newer approaches are very critical of the dominant, earlier approaches – what we have called the classical perspectives. At present, however, it may be most helpful to see them as complementing and challenging these earlier perspectives, but not as entirely replacing them. They do, however, disagree with these early theories whenever they suggest they are telling the whole story of society: only partial stories are now possible in this newer view. Some of these newer sociologies thus speak of the 'death of the metanarrative' – a term coined by the French philosopher Lyotard – as a way of rejecting any idea that there is one, and only one, 'Big Story of Sociology'.

What, then, are these new voices? They include women, racial and ethnic minorities, colonised peoples throughout the world, gays and lesbians, the elderly, disabled people and various other marginalised or overlooked groups. You may well belong to one or more of these many groups, and should read this book with this in mind.

Taken together, a number of criticisms of classical sociology can be briefly summarised as follows:

1 That sociology has mainly been by men for men and about men – and for 'men', read white and heterosexual and usually privileged and relatively affluent. As such, it has had a persistently limited, even biased approach.
2 That areas of significance to other groups – 'racism' for ethnic groups, 'patriarchy' for women, 'homophobia' for gays, 'colonisation' for many non-Western groups, 'disablement' for disabled people – have often been overlooked. You may like to think about what each of these terms means; they will be introduced later in this book.
3 That these areas of significance, when they have been included, have often been presented in a distorted fashion: often sociology has been sexist, racist, homophobic, etc.

Many voices have been missing in sociology, and they have led to a number of newer sociological stances that will be introduced throughout the book.

An example: the case of a feminist sociology and the missing voice of women

To illustrate: the most apparent absence until the 1970s was that of women's voices. Until then, sociology had mainly been by men, about men and for men. All this started to change with the development of a second wave of feminism (see Chapter 12), which helped to

(a)

(b)

(c)

A multicultural world. Sociology used to be the study of white Western men by white Western men. This is no longer always so. It has become far more multicultural and listens more attentively to the voices of a whole array of different groups: (a) Pataxou Indians in Brazil; (b) a lesbian couple in New York; (c) a Navaho matriarch in Arizona

Source: (a) © Mike Goldwater/Alamy; (b) © Homer Sykes; Archive/Alamy; (c) © Eve Arnold; Magnum Photos.

foster both a *feminist sociology* and a *feminist methodology*. Broadly, these place either women or gender at the centre of their specific analysis. They do this because they see the need for a more political role for sociologists in trying to reduce or eliminate women's subordination and oppression in societies across the world. Although you will find a chapter in this book that looks at gender specifically (Chapter 12), you will also find that gender as an issue will be considered in nearly every chapter. Bringing a feminist gender perspective to any analysis helps to widen and deepen understanding (see Abbott and Wallace, 1992).

Once we enter a feminist sociology, however, we will find that there is no one or unified voice here either! To put it bluntly, not all women are the same across the globe! When we start suggesting that women are all the same, we start to engage in what has been called essentialist thinking – **essentialism** is the belief in essences that are similar. It is to suggest here that there is an 'essence' or pure core to what it is to be a woman. Yet we will find a plurality of women's stances too – ranging, as we shall see, from those who adopt

conflict perspectives to those who focus more on action perspectives; from those who highlight postcolonialist perspectives to those who focus on 'black' perspectives. For example, the experiences of a black woman living in poverty in Sierra Leone are very different from those of most white women studying in European universities.

Some do try to bring all these different voices together. But to do this, there has to be a major recognition that voices are not unified but fragmentary and multi-situated. As you will start to sense, this is no easy task!

And other voices: postmodernism and a multi-paradigmatic sociology

Following on from all this, then, there are many new developments in sociology and you will encounter these throughout this book. For instance, Chapter 5 introduces ideas around multiculturalism; Chapter 7 introduces ideas around social constructionism; Chapter 11 debates postcolonial theory; Chapter 12 will extend feminist theory and introduce queer theory; Chapter 17 introduces ideas around Foucault's 'discourse theory'; Chapter 21 will introduce disablement theory; while Chapter 26 will further present some ideas around postmodern social theory. As in any introduction, we cannot take these newer ideas very far. But at least you will sense that sociology is a continuously growing and changing discipline of study that is always bringing new challenges to its students.

Some sociologists have started to suggest that in the twenty-first century a new generation of sociology is in the making, and that it is bringing what has sometimes been called a postmodern stance. Although sociology was born of the modern world – industrialisation, capitalism, the growth of big cities, the rise of democracies, the decline of traditional communities, etc. – it is now finding itself in a world where the features of modernity are accelerating: modernity is speeding up and going faster. It is what Giddens has called 'a runaway world' (Giddens, 1999). Over the past 30 years or so, there have been many rapid changes both within society and in our understanding of ways of approaching society. Sociology itself, therefore, has had to rethink some of its key ideas to at least accommodate these changes – which have been increasingly identified as 'postmodern' or a 'late modern turn' (see Giddens, 1992).

For some thinkers these changes have been so extreme as to question the very foundations of sociology. Two French thinkers, for example, have more or less proclaimed the death of sociology and suggested that we have moved into a postmodern world. Thus Baudrillard writes that:

> **It has all been done. The extreme limit of . . . possibilities has been reached. It has destroyed itself. It has deconstructed its entire universe. So all that are left are pieces. All that remains to be done is play with the pieces. Playing with the pieces – that is post-modern.**

(Baudrillard, 1984: 24)

This is an extreme position which will not be adopted in this book. Rather, this textbook will tell the story of the shift from a traditional form of society, one which was usually authoritarian with strong religious commitments to an overarching belief system, towards what we might see as *a more provisional world – one that is altogether less sure of itself*. Modernity has

In the early days of sociology, men dominated its concerns. Today, there has been the growth of a much more feminist-based sociology. Jane Addams (above) is often seen as a pioneer of sociology through her concern with city life in Chicago. Some have argued that she is the true founder of the Chicago School (see Chapter 24)
Source: © Bettmann/Corbis.

brought many changes; and in the twenty-first century this modern world is an accelerating one where there is an increased sensitivity to diversities and differences. In this view the world becomes less dominated by generalities and 'master narratives', and there is a turn towards 'local cultures' and their 'multiplicity of stories'. We could see postmodernism as:

> . . . the liberation of differences, of local elements, of what could generally be called dialect. With the demise of the idea of a central rationality of history, the world of generalised communication explodes like a multiplicity of 'local' rationalities

Table 2.3	Summary: six recent political influences on sociological thinking		
Theory	**Search for**	**Challenge**
Feminism	Equality of sexes	Analyse gender differences
Anti-racism	Equality of ethnicities	Analyse nation and ethnicities
Queer theory	Equality of sexualities	Analyse sexualities
Post-colonialism and multiculturalism	Equality of cultures	Analyse different cultural positions and understandings
Postmodernism	Recognition of differences	Analyse differences, multiplicities and complexities
Globalisation	Interconnections across cultures	Globalisation and glocalisation as key social processes

– ethnic, sexual, religious, cultural or aesthetic minorities – that finally speak up for themselves. They are no longer repressed and cowed into silence by the idea of a single pure form of humanity that must be realised irrespective of particularity and individual finitude, transience and contingency . . .

(Vattimo, 1992: 8–9)

All this leads to a new approach to sociology, but not one that has to reject its past. Rob Stones suggests that a postmodern sociology has three concerns:

Postmodernists argue . . . for respecting the existence of a plurality of perspectives, as against a notion that there is one single truth from a privileged perspective; local, contextual studies in place of grand narratives; an emphasis on disorder, flux and openness, as opposed to order, continuity and restraint.

(Stones, 1996: 22)

Thinking globally: a global perspective in sociology

Part of this shift in voice and concern within sociology over recent years has involved recognising the position of different, local voices around the world. In recent years, as even the furthest reaches of the earth have become more easily accessible through advances in technology, many academic disciplines have been forced to incorporate a **global perspective**, *the study of the larger world and each society's place in it*. Instead of the overwhelming dominance in sociology of Western

voices, we can now pay attention to voices heard in all parts of the world – from various African states to those found in Latin American countries. They often see the world in radically different ways and it is important, if sociology is to develop, to take these voices seriously.

Many sociology textbooks in the recent past have tended to focus on one country only. While this certainly deepens understanding of *one* society, it is insular and limited. This book therefore tries to look outwards to a range of societies, while at the same time maintaining some kind of focus on Europe and the UK, the societies which most of its readers are likely to come from, and maybe therefore the societies that will probably interest the readers of this book most. But we have tried to avoid too much of a bias towards 'the West'.

How does a global perspective enhance sociology?

Very often sociology looks too narrowly at specific cultures – usually of the West. Yet global awareness is a logical extension of the sociological perspective and greatly enhances it. Sociology's basic insight is that where we are placed in a society profoundly affects individual experiences – and the position of a society in the larger world system affects everyone. The opening story provided a brief sketch of our global village, indicating that people the world over are far from equal in their quality of life. Every chapter of this text will highlight life in the world beyond the borders of our own society. Here are three reasons to consider why global thinking should figure prominently in the sociological perspective.

Raewyn Connell: from men's studies to globalisation and southern theory

Raewyn Connell is one of Australia's leading sociologists, professor at the University of Sydney and globally influential. Her earliest work was on class and education, and she was extremely influential in the1980s and 1990s in the development of 'men and masculinity' as a sociological problem of study. She suggested the importance of **'hegemonic masculinity'** – *the dominant way of being a man in society* – and the variety of global masculinities (ways of being men) that could be discovered (see Chapter 12).

Her work broadened out in the 1990s to study the development of sociology itself and she was not very happy with what she found. She discovered that sociology was not only a product of men, but of a certain kind of men. They were part of the Western, male Enlightenment; and as such they provided a rather specialised and limited view of the world. Her subsequent work turned to ideas about society that had been developed in different countries around the world. She examined the poetry and oral traditions in Africa and the development of an 'indigenous sociology'. The work of Al-Afghani and the Nigerian sociologist Akinsola Akiwowoo were considered. And then she reviewed developments and sociologists around the world: Raul Prebisch in Latin America, Ali Shariati in revolutionary Iran, Paulin Hountondji in Benin, Vienna Das and Ashes Nandi in India – and many others. Her aim was to introduce 'Western sociology' to a wider range of theorists and thinkers beyond the West, which should start to shape sociology in the future. Her book *Southern Theory* (2007) is a major challenge to the tradition of Western sociology and is likely to have a major impact on twenty-first-century sociology.

Raewyn Connell is a transsexual woman and was formally known as R. W. Connell or Robert Connell.

National flags provide unique symbolic identities in a global world. Here are the flags for Pakistan, Japan, South Africa, Nigeria, and Iran. Can you identify which is which?

Source: Corel Flags of the World.

1 *Societies the world over are increasingly interconnected.* A feature of the world over the past 300 years or so has been the ways in which countries have become more and more internationally connected, initially through 'the great explorers', then through colonialism, slavery and mass migrations, and nowadays through high finance, tourism and the electronic world. In recent times, the world has become linked as never before. Jet aircraft whisk people across continents in hours, while new electronic devices transmit pictures, sounds and written documents around the globe in seconds.

One consequence of this new technology, as later chapters explain, is that people all over the world now share many tastes in music, clothing and food. With their economic strength, high-income nations cast a global shadow, influencing members of other societies who eagerly gobble up American hamburgers, dance to British 'pop music' and, more and more, speak the English language.

Commerce across national borders has also propelled a global economy. Large corporations manufacture and market goods worldwide, just as global financial markets linked by satellite communications now operate around the clock. Today, no stock trader in London dares to ignore what happens in the financial markets in Tokyo and Hong Kong, just as no fisherman in Scotland can afford to ignore the European common fishing policy! But as the West projects its way of life on to much of the world, the larger world also reacts back. All of this is linked to the process of **globalisation**, *the increasing interconnectedness of societies*. This process will be discussed further in the next section and in many parts of this book.

2 *A global perspective enables us to see that many human problems we face in Europe are far more serious elsewhere.* Poverty is certainly a serious problem in Europe, and especially eastern Europe. But, as Chapter 9 explains, poverty is both more widespread and more severe throughout Latin America, Africa and Asia. Similarly, the social standing of women, children and the disabled is especially low in poor countries of the world. And, although racism may be pronounced in the UK,

it has even harsher forms throughout many parts of the world. Ethnic cleansings in Bosnia, 'Islamophobia', and hostility to German 'guest workers' are three examples that will be considered later (Chapter 11). Then, too, many of the toughest problems we grapple with at home are global in scope. Environmental pollution is one example: as Chapter 25 demonstrates, the world is a single ecosystem in which the action (or inaction) of one nation has implications for all others.

3 *Thinking globally is also an excellent way to learn more about ourselves.* We cannot walk the streets of a distant city without becoming keenly aware of what it means to live in western Europe at the beginning of the twenty-first century. Making global comparisons also leads to unexpected lessons. For instance, Chapter 9 transports us to a squatter settlement in Madras, India. There we are surprised to find people thriving in the love and support of family members, despite a desperate lack of basic material comforts. Such discoveries prompt us to think about why poverty in Europe so often involves isolation and anger, and whether material things – so crucial to our definition of a 'rich' life – are the best way to gauge human well-being.

In sum, in an increasingly interconnected world, we can understand ourselves only to the extent that we comprehend others.

Goma Zaire Rwandan refugee camp near Goma. Cholera victims July 1994. Baby sitting next to her sick mother
Source: © Jenny Mattthews/Alamy.

Table 2.4	Making the modern global world: Roland Robertson's six stages of globalisation
1 1400–1750s (germinal)	Start of modern geography, Gregorian calendar, a bringing together of ideas about humanity
2 1750s–1870s (incipient)	Emergence of nation states; transnational regulation and communication; nationalism versus internationalism
3 1875–mid-1920s (take-off)	Growth of global communications; First World War; League of Nations; Olympics
4 1920s–mid-1960s (struggle for hegemony)	United Nations formed in 1942; worldwide conflicts and growth of concern over common humanity; expansion of capital and capitalism
5 1969–early 1990s (uncertainty)	Number of global 'problems', organisations and movement sharply increases – facing nuclear destruction and environment crisis
6 Late 1990s (antagonism)	World Trade Organization; Kyoto Agreements, terrorism, the internet, global media, global capitalism

Source: Based on Giulianto and Robertson (2009).

Globalisation and sociology

Since the 1990s, sociologists have increasingly used the term 'globalisation' to capture the movements across world cultures. It has become one of the most influential of sociological ideas in the past two decades and it is still (in 2011) at the centre of many of its debates. The term itself is used across the globe: for the Germans it is *Globalisierung*; in Spain and Latin America it is *globalización*; and in France it is *mondialisation*! Yet even though it translates into many languages, its meaning is far from clear. It has now almost become a cliché and the term is often trotted out with little meaning. Most simply, we can start by defining **globalisation** as capturing *the increasing interconnectedness of societies*.

But hereafter we will find a lot of disagreement about the term. It brings different 'ideological baggage'. Some people embrace the term, seeing globalisation as everywhere and usually doing a lot of good. Thus it creates greater awareness of diversity and **hybridisation**; it stimulates international markets and wealth; it helps towards a more universal humankind – through awareness of common environmental problems, and international organisations like the United Nations. This is the dawning of the global age and it is to be celebrated. (David Held and others call those holding this view 'transformationalists' or 'hyperglobalisers'; Held et al., 1999: 10).

Critics, by contrast, suggest that there is nothing new about globalisation. History, they argue, shows that nations have a constant tendency to exploit, colonise and raid other cultures, and matters are getting worse. 'Global' in contemporary times usually means that dominant (capitalist) societies are taking over the finances and cultures of other societies (indeed, for some it means Americanisation, not globalisation!). Thus certain trading blocks and nation-states (largely in Europe, North America and the Pacific Rim) have become stronger, so there is no great tendency towards a greater universality at all. (These critics of globalisation are sometimes called 'sceptics'; see Hirst and Thompson, 2009).

The *Public sociology* box suggests a number of other definitions you may like to consider.

At the most basic, the term 'globalisation' can be grasped through the imagery of worldwide multicultural companies such as *Coca-Cola*, *McDonald's* and *Nike*. These companies exist across the globe – and in a number of ways. They *produce* goods across many countries; they *market* goods across many countries; and they *present* their logos and images which travel the globe ahead of them. Think of how McDonald's can be found across the world – even though it had its origins in the United States (see Chapter 5). Likewise, a Nike shoe – with its characteristic logo of the swoosh – is produced in many parts of the poorer world and yet sold everywhere. As we shall see, they are simultaneously loved by millions and hated by millions – as signs of convenience and the modern world, and as signs of corporate takeover of mass culture. We will have a lot more to say on all this in later chapters. They capture the economic, social and cultural impact of this process and simultaneously symbolise what may be good and bad about it. Globalisation is thus a controversial term.

Some meanings of globalisation

Ideas of the 'global' and 'globalisation' are widespread in public debate and discussion. The term itself has been given many different meanings. Listen to discussions of globalisation and consider which position it might be coming from, and to get you going here are some recent discussions of its meaning:

- Globalization has something to do with the thesis that we all now live in one world . . . (Anthony Giddens, *A Runaway World*, 1999: 7)
- Globalization is the widening, deepening and speeding up of worldwide interconnectedness in all aspects of contemporary life, from the cultural to the criminal, the financial to the spiritual. (David Held et al., *Global Transformations*, 1999: 14–16)
- Globalization . . . denotes the processes through which sovereign national states are criss-crossed and undermined by transnational actors with varying prospects of power, orientations, identities and networks. (Ulrich Beck, *What is Globalization?*, 2000b: 11)
- The Global Age involves the supplanting of modernity with globality . . . [This includes] the global environmental consequences of aggregate human activities; the loss of security where weaponry has global destructiveness; the globality of communication systems; the rise of a global economy; and the reflexivity of globalism, where people and groups of all kinds refer to the globe as the frame for their beliefs. (Martin Albrow, *The Global Age*, 1996: 4)
- Globalization is a transplanetary process . . . involving increasing liquidity and growing multidirectional flows of people, objects, places, and information as well as the structures they encounter and create that are barriers to, or expedite, those flows. (George Ritzer, *Globalization: A Basic Text*, 2010: 519)

As we shall see (Chapter 16), major social movements have developed in the past few years to protest against it: in Seattle, in Prague, in London, in Genoa. For the time being we will just suggest a few of the key features of globalisation. We suggest that globalisation:

1 *Shifts the borders of economic transactions* – bringing a marked change in the pace of economic development in the world. Business companies, banking and investment now cross more national borders than ever before. In many instances these huge companies (TNCs or *transnational corporations*) have incomes and expenditures which are bigger than those of whole countries! Many argue that this has led to growing inequalities across the world, both within countries and between them. We will consider this in Chapters 9 and 16.

2 *Expands communications into global networks.* Television satellites, digital media, personal computers, mobile phones and all the information technologies help to 'shrink the world'. This has led to a major rethinking of ideas of *space and time*. We now no longer think mainly in terms of very local places. Instead we have entered a world where telephones, jet planes and now the internet make communications with others all over the globe instantaneous and hence very different from the past. Think especially of the phenomenal growth in the use of the mobile phone – handies, cellphones, etc. – and how this makes communications so much less restricted to face-to-face relations. Of course, telephones are not new, but the idea of being able to keep a phone on one's body wherever you are does make for a different pattern of communication. For growing numbers of people the whole world can be accessed instantly. Whereas a few hundred years ago it would take years for people to know what was happening in other parts of the world, now ideas can be moved instantly. We will consider this further in Chapters 22 and 23.

3 *Fosters a new, widespread 'global culture'.* Many urban areas come to look like each other, and many television programmes, much music, film and so on travels easily around the world. MTV has become a global youth form. And if you go to your local record store, the chances are you will now find quite a large section on global music! Not only do we have Hollywood but we have Bollywood. We will consider all this in Chapters 5 and 22.

4 *Develops new forms of international governance.* Some suggest that globalisation means the weakening of the nation-state. Though this is controversial, what is not in doubt is the growth of international agencies such as the United Nations, the European Court of Human Rights and the World Health Organization. These enact programmes that are publicly committed to what has been called 'the

democratisation of the world' – a growing belief that democracy as a political system will become dominant in the world. We consider this in Chapter 16.

5 *Creates a growing awareness of shared common world problems.* It is harder and harder to think of the world's problems as just the problems belonging to any one country. For instance, crime – as we shall see in Chapter 17 – has become increasingly global: drugs markets spread across continents, cyber-crimes push against the laws of any one country, international courts proclaim international justice. Likewise, the major impact of industrialisation on the environment becomes a compelling common problem in all countries (which is discussed in Chapters 24 and 25). Meanwhile, world poverty studies highlight growing inequalities both between and within nations; while debates on migration, refugees, wars and terrorism bring an international focus.

6 *Fosters a growing sense of risk* – what the German sociologist Ulrich Beck (1992) has called the *World Risk Society.* New technologies are generating risks which are of a quite different order from those found throughout earlier human history. Of course, past societies were risky and dangerous places too – whole populations could be wiped out by major earthquakes, floods or plagues, for example. Life for most people throughout history has been nasty, brutish and short. Nature brought with it its own dangers and risks. But Beck argues that new kinds of risk appear with the industrial world which are not 'in nature' but 'manufactured'.

These risks are associated with the many new technologies which generate new dangers to lives and the planet itself. These are humanly produced, may have massively unforeseen consequences, and may take many, many thousands of years to reverse. These 'manufactured risks' are taking us to the edge of catastrophe: to 'threats to all forms of life on this planet', to 'the exponential growth of risks and the impossibility of escaping them'. Risk, then, is associated with a globalising world that tries to break away from tradition and the past, and where change and the future become more valued. All these changes – from the railway to the computer, from genetic engineering to nuclear weapons – have unforeseen consequences that we cannot easily predict. The list of examples of new risks could be quite long: the changes in work and family patterns, fallout from the atomic bomb, the spread of networks of cars and planes throughout the planet,

the arrival of AIDS as a major world pandemic, the development of genetically modified crops, the cloning of animals (and people), the deforestation of the planet, 'designer children and surrogate mothering', the intensity of computer games and the new ways of relating (or not relating!) this might bring, and the arrival of new forms of terrorism where suicide bombers are willing to fly into major buildings (such as happened at the World Trade Center on 11 September 2001), and on and on. All have consequences which may be far reaching and are at present unpredictable. In some of the chapters that follow, we look at some of these main 'risks' and how they affect all countries and people. We consider this in many places, but especially in Chapters 23, 24 and 25.

7 *Leads to the emergence of 'transnational global actors' who 'network'.* From Greenpeace to Disneyworld, from the United Nations to tourism, from the Moonies to the women's movement, there are more and more people who move in networks that are not just bound to a fixed spatial community. Instead, they connect across the globe, making the global their local. They are global citizens.

The globalisation guide

You can find more detail on globalisation throughout the book:

1 *Global economy*: Chapters 9 and 16.
2 *Global politics, war and terrorism*: Chapter 16.
3 *Global media, networks and communications*: Chapters 6, 22 and 23.
4 *Global inequalities*: Chapters 8–14
5 *Global people – migration, trafficking, refugees, the rich*: especially Chapter 11.
6 *Global education*: Chapter 20.
7 *Global technologies*: outer space, computer revolution: Chapter 23.
8 *Global culture/culture industries*: Chapters 5 and 22.
9 *Global conflicts, governance and social movements*: Chapter 16.
10 *Globalisation of crime*: Chapter 17.
11 *Global world problems*: Chapters 9, 24 and 25.
12 *Global environment and the risk society*: Chapters 23, 24 and 25.
13 *Global religions*: Chapter 19.
14 *Global cities*: Chapter 24.

See also Martell (2010) and Ritzer (2010).

In recent years, as ideas around globalisation have grown, many different stances have been taken on the relevance and usefulness of the idea. Two can be singled out here. *Globalisers* argue that there is a growing global economy which is transcending nations and providing the motor force of change. They tend to be the 'modernisers' and see the dynamic of international capitalism as a force for generating more and more wealth, from which more and more countries will be able to gain. By contrast, there are the *sceptics* who are critical of the globalisation thesis. They argue that there is much more economic independence among individual states than globalisers allow for. They also claim that there has been little real convergence of state policies across the globe. For them, real inequalities across countries can be shown to have actually grown. Sceptics often mirror a newer version of dependency theory (for example, Hirst and Thompson, 2009; Held et al., 1999).

WORLD WATCH

The globalisation of music: Hip Hop in Japan

In the past, except for the very rich and the world travellers, music has been limited to the local community and handed on by tradition. But today, music increasingly flows through worldwide cultures. Music has become part of the globalisation process. We can now find 'world music', cultures of international music celebrities, worldwide fan cultures, and the creation of music media companies worldwide that dominate music markets across the world. We can see examples of world music cultures everywhere: from global music festivals (often to raise money for charities) to 'global musicals' like *Les Misérables* – seen by 55 million people worldwide in some 40 countries and recorded in 21 languages. When the the Three Tenors (Domingo, Carreras and Pavarotti) performed at the 1990 FIFA World Cup in Italy in 1990, it led to a mass global phenomenon continuing well into 2005 and a new interest in classical music 'for the millions' (though the term has two different meanings!). Music is now part of the world economy and world media.

Central to all this, and indeed to much of globalisation, is the idea of **commodification** (*aspects of life are turned into things – commodities for sale*). Music has been turned into a

You can see how widespread globalisation has been by looking at different musical forms and youth culture styles and dress. The rap of late 1970s black US ghettos turns into 1980s hip-hop and then travels the world, being modified in the process by different cultures. Depicted here is Japanese hip-hop

Source: © PYMCA/Alamy.

sellable object. This has meant not just the selling of concerts, CDs, DVDs and music generally – but also an aggressive merchandising of adjuncts like posters, books, concert programmes and the like. Tickets for a world tour concert of the singer Barbara Streisand in 2007 were sold out at £500 a ticket! Globalisation leads to developed markets around the world for music. Up to 90 per cent of the global music market is accounted for by just five corporations: EMI Records, Sony, AOI Time Warner, BMG and Vivendi Universal. The latter is the largest with 29 per cent of the market share, and owning operations in some 63 countries. But it is interesting to note that certain areas of the world are not well marketed by the 'Big Five'. India resists their domination because it has its own very large industry (for example, in what has been called Bollywood). Africa's weak economic situation also means that, outside South Africa, the market does not seem attractive.

Global music appears to be increasingly Westernised. To some extent local cultures all over the world have been invaded by Western music – from 'classical concerts and opera'

(often seen as a sign of status), to modern rock, pop, MTV and all the spin-offs that largely reproduce the Western status quo. Some have claimed that this is a new form of colonialism, where local cultures lose their musical traditions at the expense of Western dominance. Nowhere is this more clearly seen than in the convergence of youth cultures and the convergence in their musical styles.

But global music is also shaped and adapted to local trends and cultures. Sociologists might call this 'the **glocalisation** of world music'. (Glocalisation *means the process by which local communities respond differently to global changes* – see Chapter 5.) Musical traditions are rarely 'pure': they get spliced into hybrid forms. Classical music goes 'light' with Classic FM; rap, itself a hybrid of African-American black music becomes Japanese hip hop. Japan has a vibrant hip hop scene which has borrowed heavily from Afro-American music and been remade in Tokyo clubs and recording studios. In a major study of this process, Ian Condry went to more than 120 hip hop performances in clubs in and around Tokyo, sat in on dozens of studio recording sessions, and

interviewed rappers, music company executives, music store owners and journalists. He shows how young Japanese combine the figure of the samurai with American rapping techniques and gangsta imagery, and how self-described 'yellow B-Boys' express their devotion to 'black culture'. Here there is mix (a blend, a hybridity) of black and yellow, classical Japanese and black America. Condry shows how rappers manipulate the Japanese language to achieve rhyme and rhythmic flow. This is a fascinating study (which could probably be redone in many other cultures). It shows how cultural musical globalisation often depends on grassroots connections and individual performers rather than just the control of big media corporation markets (though they may have initially started the popular concern). Hip hop is constantly made and remade in specific locations through local activities and for particular audiences (Condry, 2006). Local cultures embrace musical forms from other cultures while modifying them.

Look at YouTube for examples of 'Japan hip hop'. And see the website by Ian Condry at http://web.mit.edu/condry/www/jhh.

Futures: a multi-paradigm discipline in a global world

This chapter has aimed to introduce you to some of the perspectives needed to think about society. We have suggested some classical ways (looking at society as functions, as structures, as actions, as conflicts, as consensus) and some emerging ways (looking at societies as an array of competing perspectives: from feminism to the postcolonial). We have suggested that some of the classical ways are now being questioned by

what might be seen as a postmodern perspective. These diverse positions suggest that sociology is not one position but many: sociologists call this **multi-paradigmatic**. This is a view we take throughout this book, and you will hence find a range of views – some of which many even conflict. Do not expect sociology to give you neat answers and tidy solutions!

Perhaps the most significant development in all this has been to push for sociology to focus on not just one country, but many. Here we have suggested that sociologists should take a global perspective and a helpful idea in doing this is globalisation. We will regularly return to all this throughout the book.

SUMMARY

1 Building theory involves linking insights to gain understanding. Various theoretical perspectives guide sociologists as they construct theories.

2 The functional perspective is a framework for exploring how social structures promote the stability and integration of society. This approach minimises the importance of social inequality, conflict and change, whereas the conflict perspective highlights these aspects. At the same time, the conflict approach downplays the extent of society's integration and stability. In contrast to these broad, macro-level approaches, the action perspective is a micro-level theoretical framework that focuses on face-to-face interaction in specific settings. Because each perspective spotlights different dimensions of any social issue, the richest sociological understanding is derived from applying all three. Sociological thinking involves the action–structure debate.

3 Newer developments in sociological theory have highlighted how all sociology must work from perspectives or different voices. It is multi-paradigmatic. Classically, sociology has heard only the voices of white, Western, heterosexual men: other voices are now being heard. Feminist sociology is a prime example. Postmodernism suggests that a new social order is in the making that is accelerating social change and creating a more 'provisional' world. Postmodern sociology stresses the need to look at multiple perspectives, takes seriously the local elements, and tries to keep a provisional 'openness' in its ideas.

4 A key feature of the modern word is that it is organised through capitalism. It highlights private ownership of property, pursuit of personal profit and free competition.

5 A global perspective enhances the sociological perspective because, first, societies of the world are becoming more and more interconnected; secondly, many social problems are most serious beyond the borders of European countries; and, thirdly, recognising how others live helps us better understand ourselves. Globalisation is an emerging widespread process by which social relations acquire relatively distanceless and borderless qualities. Globalisation highlights the interconnectedness of business and TNCs, the development of global media, and the emergence of global cultures, international governance and world citizens.

CONNECT UP: Turn to Part 6 of this book for key resources and link up
with the book's website, which links to these resources
SEE: www.pearsoned.co.uk/plummer

MYTASKLIST

Ten suggestions for going further

1 Connect up with Part Six and the Sociology Web Resources

As you work through ideas and think about the issues raised in this chapter, look at the accompanying website and the resource centre at the end of this book which connects to it. There is a lot here to help you move on. To link up, see: www.pearson.co.uk/plummer.

2 Review the chapter

Briefly summarise (in a paragraph) just what this chapter has been about. Consider: (a) What have you learned? (b) What do you disagree with? Be critical. And (c) How would you develop all this? How could you get more detail on matters that interest you?

3 Pose questions

(a) Start keeping a list of sociologists you encounter throughout this book. Locate them historically, the name of the theory they are identified with, some examples of what they looked at and examined, and the key features and problems of their theories.

(b) What are the key theories discussed in this chapter? Be guided by some of these theoretical perspectives and ask yourself what kinds of question might a sociologist ask about (i) television, (ii) war, (iii) sport, (iv) colleges and universities, and (v) men and women?

(c) Start keeping a 'sociological glossary' of key new words you find in sociology. Try to make sure you can say (i) what the word means, (ii) what debates and research it is applied in, and (iii) whether you find it helpful or not: does it enable you to see society more sharply or does it confuse and hinder?

(d) Is globalisation a new phenomenon and is it really such a different world from that of the past? Consider what the term means and draw out some illustrations of it. How has your own life been touched by globalisation?

4 Explore key words

Many concepts have been introduced in this chapter. You can review them from the website or from the listing at the back of this book. You might like to give special attention to just five words and think them through – how would you define them, what are they dealing with, and do they help you see the social world more clearly or not? A useful additional dictionary for this chapter might be:

Andrew Jones *Dictionary of Globalization*, Polity (2006)

You may find it useful to have by you three books by John Scott:

Sociology: The Key Concepts (2006)

Fifty Key Sociologists: The Formative Theorists (2006)

Fifty Key Sociologists: The Contemporary Theorists (2006)

5 Search the Web

Be critical when you look at websites – see the box on p. 940 in the Resources section. For this chapter look at:

Sociological theory

SocioSite www.sociosite.net/topics/theory.php – provides a general introduction.

Durkheim

www.emile-durkheim.com
www.faculty.rsu.edu/~felwell/Theorists/Durkheim/index.htm
http://durkheim.itgo.com

Marx

www.marxists.org
www.spartacus.schoolnet.co.uk/TUmarx.htm
http://plato.stanford.edu/entries/marx
www.bbc.co.uk/history/historic_figures/marx_karl.shtml

www.historyguide.org/intellect/marx.html
www.faculty.rsu.edu/~felwell/Theorists/Marx

Weber

Verstehen: Max Weber's home page
www.faculty.rsu.edu/~felwell/Theorists/Weber/Whome.htm
Weberian sociology of religion
www.ne.jp/asahi/moriyuki/abukuma

Feminism

Feminist theory website
www.cddc.vt.edu/feminism/enin.html

Globalisation

Two introductory sites are:

The globalization website
www.sociology.emory.edu/globalization

Globalization 101: a student's guide
www.globalization101.org

See also:
Forces of globalisation
www.humanities.uci.edu/critical/html/Projects%20
+%20Events/Forces.html

International Forum on Globalization (IFG)
www.ifg.org

World Bank: globalisation
www.worldbank.org/globalization

World Commission on the Social Dimensions of Globalization
www.ilo.org/public/english/wcsdg

6 Watch a DVD

Look at the films of other cultures across the world
and see how they are interconnecting with your own.
One way into issues of globalisation is through international
film and video. A good source for such films is
http://worldfilm.about.com – a major site for world films.

On globalisation, see: Tom Zaniello, *The Cinema of
Globalization: A Guide to Films about the New Economic
Order* (2007).

For some opening examples, try:

- Ang Lee's *The Wedding Banquet* (1993): a romantic
  comedy about a gay Asian man in the USA who marries
  a Chinese girl to please his parents.
- Carlos Saura's *Blood Wedding* (1981): a powerful dance
  movie based on a Garcia Lorca story, starring Antonio
  Gades and Christina Hoyos.
- Bahman Ghobadi's *A Time for Drunken Horses* (2000): a
  film about the suffering and hard lot of Kurdish children.
- Marziyeh Meshkini's *The Day I Became a Woman* (2001):
  a disturbing portrayal of the role of women in Iran.

7 Think and read

Introduction to social theory

Michele Dillon, *Introduction to Sociological Theory* (2009)
is a clear and illustrated introductory tour. Shaun Best,
A Beginner's Guide to Social Theory (2003) and E. C. Cuff,
Wes Sharrock and D. Francis, *Perspectives in Sociology*
(5th rev edn, 2006) outline most of the major positions.

Rob Stones (ed.), *Key Sociological Thinkers* (2nd edn, 2008)
provides 21 short and readable essays on many of the
key sociologists, past and present.

Charles Lemert (ed.), *Social Theory: The Multicultural and
Classic Readings* (3rd edn, 2004) is a major compendium
of articles that debates the full range of sociological
theories – classical and newer. It is a very large volume!
But for anyone very interested in the full range of
sociological theory from the original authors it is an
invaluable starting point.

Introductions to globalisation

Zygmunt Bauman, *Globalization: The Human Consequences*
(1998) and Anthony Giddens, *Runaway World: How
Globalization is Reshaping Our Lives* (1999) provide two
short, readable guides to the idea of globalisation.

Jan Nederveen Pieterse, *Globalization and Culture* (2004)
and Malcolm Waters, *Globalization* (2000) are also short
but more detailed and systematic treatments – a little
more advanced.

George Ritzer, *Globalization: A Basic Text* (2010) and Luke
Martell, *The Sociology of Globalization* (2010) are both
major readable textbooks which introduce key ideas
around globalisation.

David Held et al., *Global Transformations* (2nd edn, 2007).
This is an altogether more advanced, very detailed and
long account of globalisation. A shorter version is
Globalization/Anti Globalization: Beyond the Great Divide
(with Andrew McGrew) (2nd edn, 2007).

Understanding Global Issues: The Facts behind the News is a
very useful series of booklets which are issued regularly and
cover current global issues. Details can be accessed on its
website at: www.global-issues.co.uk/index.php

8 Relax with a novel

You will get the idea of a postmodern novel from reading:
John Fowles's *The French Lieutenant's Woman*, Umberto Eco's
The Name of the Rose, and Brett Easton's *American Pyscho*
(all are also films). Pico Iyer's *The Global Soul: Jet Lag,
Shopping Malls and the Search for Home* (2000) could be fun!

9 Connect to other chapters

- For more on Marx, Durkheim and Weber, see Chapter 4.
- For more on action and interaction, see Chapter 7.
- For more on feminism and queer theory, see Chapter 12.
- For more on globalisation, see all chapters but especially Chapters 9 and 22–25.

10 Engage in THE BIG DEBATE

The sociological puzzle: do we make social life or does social life make us?

Which comes first: the chicken or the egg? This classic conundrum has a parallel question for sociology which has persisted throughout the discipline's history. It can be put like this: which comes first – society or the individual? And like the chicken and egg problem, there is no simple solution. Indeed, what has to be recognised is that one does not come first – eggs cannot simply come before chickens, any more than chickens can simply come before eggs. Both are needed. And it is the interaction of the two that has to be seen. You cannot, in short, have one without the other. And the same is true for individuals and societies. What sociologists do is look at both individuals and societies, and at their best they look at them together through dialectical thinking which requires looking at two seeming opposites (like individual and society) and how a new form emerges through them.

Making it happen: individuals and action

One phase of sociological analysis is indeed to look at human beings. Not as a psychologist would – in terms of individual attributes like drives or personalities. Rather, the task is to look at the ways in which human beings are orientated towards action, to being world makers, creators of history and social life. Human beings make history, and sociology should look at the ways this happens.

For instance, if you want to understand how our current education system works, one task is to look at the ways in which people make it what it is. This means examining the ways in which legislators passed laws that provided the framework for schools, teaching, curriculum and exams. These did not just happen: they were made, and sociologists need to look at how they were made. Likewise, a pupil arrives in a class and, along with other students and teachers, sets about making the class happen. Sociologists like to get into the classrooms and observe this 'action' – to see just how human beings make the social world work.

Pattern and prison: social structures as maps

Yet people are also born into worlds that are not of their own making. Indeed, as the sociologist Peter Berger says, 'society is the walls of our imprisonment' (Berger, 1963: 109). We are born into families, communities and nations over which we have little immediate control; our lives are heavily shaped by the class, gender and ethnicity we are born into; indeed, even the very language we think with and talk with helps set a pattern to our life. And we had no initial choice over which language we speak: it is given to us from early childhood. (It would be very odd, if you were born in England, if you were made to speak Swahili.) Thus, one moment of sociological analysis is to look at these broadest patterns of social organisation that shape our lives. Recurrent and habitual patterns of social life may be seen as structures. Think for a moment of the ways in which your own life is 'imprisoned'.

Putting 'action' and 'structure' together

So, a structural approach tends to map out society as a whole, while an action approach tends to examine the ways in which individuals and small groups come to make their social worlds. Of course, ideally both will be done. This is a task for more advanced social theory.

British sociologist Anthony Giddens, for example, has introduced the idea of structuration to focus on both simultaneously, to suggest a process whereby action and structure are always two sides of the same coin (Giddens, 1984). For him, people engage in social actions that create social structures, and it is through these social actions that the structures themselves are produced, maintained and eventually changed over time. Language is a good example of this. Language is a structure of rules, but people speak, write and act it in different ways, changing it as they go along. Without the rules, they would be incomprehensible, so the structures are needed. But just slavishly adhering to the structure would allow for no change, no creativity, no humanity. Looking at both individuals and structures at the same time is what is required. This is no easy task.

As you read this book, keep this puzzle in mind. And take the discussion further.

Continue the debate

1 Do you see yourself as 'determined' by social structure? Look at the image on p. 6 again (Society as a prison).
2 How much control do you have over your life? How far do you think you can change the world? Are you a world maker?
3 Look at attempts that have been made to resolve the problem between individual and society.

CHAPTER 3

STUDYING THE SOCIAL: AN INTRODUCTION TO SOCIOLOGICAL METHOD

SUDHIR VENKATESH STYLES HIMSELF AS A 'ROGUE SOCIOLOGIST'. He was a student and a budding sociologist at the University of Chicago in the late 1980s, but is now a major professor at New York's Columbia University. When at university he started long walks around the city and found himself intrigued by the neighbourhood that bordered his elite university. Right next to the elite Chicago University stands a major Chicago ghetto. Sudhir Venkatesh decided to study it.

There is a very long tradition of researching the life of this city (often called Chicago Sociology) and much of it has focused on delinquents, gangs and the race issue. For a decade in the 1990s, Sudir hung around with some of the most violent gangs of Chicago for his sociological studies. The Black Kings operated a hugely profitable drug ring – selling crack in the corridors of old buildings and extorting protection money from residents. They were not averse to violence. Sudhir got to know some of the dealers, the prostitutes, the pimps, the organisers, the cops and the officials – a good few of whom were corrupt and willing to take money from the gang for looking the other way. He watched them all 'misbehave' in many criminal situations and he became so accepted that for one day he was delegated with key decisions – acting as a 'Gang Leader for a Day'. He saw how they laundered money; he had to organise the selling and distribution of drugs; he lived the criminal life to see how it was done. His supervisors back at the university were not too keen on his approach – he seemed to be taking a lot of personal risks. After all the gang was quite a heavy one, even capable of killing! To start with Sudhir was indeed very uneasy, but bit by bit he started

to build up a strong bond with J.T., a gang leader, and he spent the better part of a decade inside the projects under JT's protection. Whilst he started the project thinking he would do a multiple-choice survey on urban poverty, he soon learnt that this was not a good way to get his data.

Sudhir was not the first to do this. William Whyte half a century before him had produced his famous study *Street Corner Society*, and many a young sociologist has spent their formative days studying 'youth cultures'. But Sudhir's work was written up in a way that made it very accessible – it reads like a good novel, with no academic jargon or references at all. Yet it bristles with sociological insights. It rapidly became a kind of sociological pop best seller – you will probably find it a local good bookshop in a Penguin paperback. This does not happen a lot in sociology.

You can find more about Sudhir Vankatesh and his projects on his website at: www.sudhirvenkatesh.org. Here you can:

- find reviews and press coverage for *Gang Leader for a Day*
- watch online video interviews with Sudhir Venkatesh
- listen to audio interviews with Sudhir Venkatesh

He is also on YouTube – reading extracts from his work.

I have striven not to laugh at human actions, not to weep at them, not to hate them, but to understand them.

Benedict Spinoza

There is no best way to tell a story about society. Many genres, many methods, many

formats – they can all do the trick. Instead of ideal ways to do it, the world gives us possibilities among which we choose. Every way of telling the story of a society does some of the job superbly but other parts not so well . . .

Howard S. Becker

In this chapter, we ask:

- How can we do sociological research?

- What is the nature of sociological knowledge, evidence and 'truth'?

- What are the key tools of sociological research?

- What are the major political and ethical issues in research?

- What are the new developments in research methods?

(Left) Leonardo da Vinci, *Vitruvian Man*, c. 1492

Source: Bridgeman Art Library Ltd/Galleria dell'Accademia, Venice, Italy/BAL.

Note: For more information go to: www.artcyclopedia.com/artists/leonardo_da_vinci.html; www.willamette.edu/cla/exsci/info/history/vitruvian.htm; http://leonardodavinci.stanford.edu/submissions/clabaugh/history/leonardo.html; and elsewhere in this chapter too.

Leonardo da Vinci (1452–1519) was one of the leading figures in Renaissance art. Why is this particular drawing so significant? Consider how you have seen it represented over and over again in the modern world. What does this suggest to you about studying social life?

Just how do social scientists get their data? The sociologist Sudhir Venkatesh went into the field and observed the daily life of a Chicago gang. Others interview, survey, give out questionnaires, draw upon documents of all kinds, set up focus groups. Some even monitor their own conduct. Such research may then get written up as stories and narratives; other researchers turn them into statistical reports. The ways of doing social science are many and varied. In this chapter we provide a brief review of some of the issues involved in 'doing social science'.

As we have seen, sociology involves a way of thinking; but it also involves a way of doing. It is a practice that looks at problems and then digs out the best 'data', 'evidence' or 'facts' that it can. This chapter will look at some of the ways sociologists actually go about studying the social world. It will ask about the very nature of 'knowledge'. It will highlight the methods that sociologists use to conduct research, and suggest appropriate questions to raise in assessing the value of any particular sociological study or 'finding'. Along the way, we shall see that sociological research involves not just procedures for gathering information but also controversies about whether that research should strive to be objective or to offer a bolder prescription for social change. Can it be neutral or is it bound up with politics and values? Sociologists are divided on all these issues.

The issues this chapter raises should help you think about the adequacy of the methods used in the sociological studies you read about. It should also enable you to start thinking about how you could conduct your own research – the chapter ends with some basic guidelines for you to plan your own project.

The basics of sociological investigation

Sociological investigation begins with two simple requirements. The first was the focus of Chapters 1 and 2: *look at the world using the sociological perspective.* Suddenly, from this point of view, all around us we see curious patterns of social life that call out for further theoretical study. This brings us to the second requirement for sociological investigation: *be curious and critical by asking sociological questions.*

These two requirements – seeing the world sociologically and asking critical sociological questions – are fundamental to sociological investigation. Yet they are only the beginning. They draw us into the

social world, stimulating our imagination. But then we face the challenging task of finding answers to our questions. To understand the kinds of insight sociology offers, it helps to divide the research process into the following three types of issue:

- *Theoretical/epistemological questions.* Here we ask about the *kind* of truth we are trying to produce. Do we, for example, want to produce a strong 'factual' scientific kind of truth with lots of evidence? Or do we wish to provide a wider theoretical understanding of what is going on? As we shall see, there are different versions of sociology and it helps to be clear which kind of sociology is being done.

- *Technical questions.* Here we ask questions about how to use tools and procedures which enable our 'findings' to be as good as they can be. There is the matter of the kinds of research tool to use – interviewing, observing, questionnaires, statistical calculations, for example; and then making sure they perform their tasks well and do not mislead us. We must always remember, though, that methods like this are a means to an end and should never be an end in themselves (sadly, a lot of social science forgets this and elevates the idea of methods to a fetish).

- *Ethical, political and policy questions.* Here we ask questions about the *point* of doing the research and consider what consequences it might have: for us, for our research subjects, and even for the wider world. All sociology is embroiled with politics and ethics: if it looks like it is being neutral, you may well want to be suspicious.

The discussion in this chapter will be framed by these questions. You can use them as a guide for thinking about your own research projects. But they are only a guide, and suggestions for taking them further will – as usual – be found at the end of the chapter.

What is a sociological 'truth'? Matters of epistemology

A key question to ask of social investigation is a very hard one: 'What kind of truth am I trying to produce?' This raises questions of **epistemology**, *that branch of philosophy that investigates the nature of knowledge and truth.* Our opening concern is to realise that there are different kinds of 'truth'.

People's 'truths' differ the world over, and we often encounter 'facts' at odds with our own. Imagine being a volunteer with Voluntary Service Overseas (VSO) and arriving in a small, traditional village in Africa. With the job of helping the local people to grow more food, you take to the fields, observing a curious practice: farmers carefully planting seeds and then placing a dead fish directly on top of each one. In response to your question, they reply that the fish is a gift to the god of the harvest. A local elder adds sternly that the harvest was poor one year when no fish were offered as gifts.

From that society's point of view, using fish as gifts to the harvest god makes sense. The people believe in it, their experts endorse it, and everyone seems to agree that the system works. But, with scientific training in agriculture, you have to shake your head and wonder. The scientific 'truth' in this situation is something entirely different: the decomposing fish fertilise the ground, producing a better crop.

Our VSO worker example does not mean, of course, that people in traditional villages ignore what their senses tell them, or that members of technologically advanced societies reject non-scientific ways of knowing. A medical researcher using science to seek an effective treatment for cancer, for example, may still practise her religion as a matter of faith; she may turn to experts when making financial decisions; and she may derive political opinions from family and friends. In short, we all embrace various kinds of truth at the same time.

But science represents a very distinctive way of knowing, and one that has come to dominate in the modern Western world.

Common sense versus scientific evidence

Scientific evidence sometimes challenges our common sense. Here are four statements that many people might assume to be 'true', even though each is at least partly contradicted by scientific research.

1 *Poor people are far more likely than rich people to break the law.* Watching a crime show on TV, one might well conclude that police arrest only people from 'bad' neighbourhoods. And, as Chapter 17 explains, poor people are arrested in disproportionate numbers. But research also reveals that police and prosecutors are likely to treat apparent wrongdoing by well-to-do people more leniently. Further, some researchers argue that our society drafts laws in such a way as to reduce the risk that affluent people will be criminalised.

2 *We now live in a middle-class society in which most people are more or less equal.* Data presented in Chapter 9 show that a very small group of people throughout the world control wealth. If people are equal, then some are much 'more equal' than others.

3 *Differences in the behaviour of females and males reflect 'human nature'.* Much of what we call 'human nature' is created by the society in which we are raised, as Chapter 5 details. Further, as Chapter 12 argues, some societies define 'feminine' and 'masculine' very differently from the way we do.

4 *Most people marry because they are in love.* To members of our society, few statements are so self-evident. But, surprising as it may seem, research shows that, in most societies, marriage has little to do with love. Chapter 18 explains why.

These examples confirm the old saying that 'It's not what we don't know that gets us into trouble as much as the things we *do* know that just aren't so.' We have all been brought up believing conventional truths, bombarded by expert advice, and pressured to accept the opinions of people around us. Sociology teaches us to evaluate critically what we see, read and hear. Like any way of knowing, sociology has limitations, as we shall see. But sociology gives us the tools to assess many kinds of information.

A starting point: the positivist and humanistic traditions

The trouble is that precisely what is meant even by 'science' is not agreed upon by philosophers of knowledge. Traditionally, they take one of two views: positivist or humanist (often called interpretivist).

Positivism is *a logical system that bases knowledge on direct, systematic observation.* It usually seeks out law-like statements of social life that can be tested. The work of Durkheim on suicide introduced in Chapter 1 would be an instance of this. Scientific knowledge rests on **empirical evidence** (for Durkheim, recall, these were suicide rates), meaning *information we can verify with our senses.* But even here there is controversy among philosophers over the true nature of science, as we shall soon see.

The second position is interpretivism or humanism. **Humanist epistemology** sees that studying the human world is very different from studying the physical, biological or material world. There is a focus on the human and the symbolic. As such, social science must produce a different kind of knowledge, one that seeks to understand meanings. Research in this tradition will look at the empirical world (as in positivism) but will highlight the importance of understanding and interpretation.

Below, we will look at these two basic positions in a little more detail.

The positivist baseline

Positivist sociologists apply science to the study of society in much the same way that natural scientists investigate the physical world. Whether they end up confirming a widely held opinion or revealing that it is completely groundless, sociologists use scientific techniques to gather empirical evidence. The following sections of this chapter introduce the major elements of positivist investigation.

The ideal of objectivity

Assume that ten writers who work for a magazine in Amsterdam are collaborating on a story about that city's best restaurants. With their editor paying, they head out on the town for a week of fine dining. Later, they get together to compare notes. Do you think one restaurant would be everyone's clear favourite? That hardly seems likely.

In scientific terms, each of the ten reporters probably operationalises the concept 'best restaurant' differently. For one, it might be a place that serves Indonesian food at reasonable prices; for another, the choice might turn on a superb view of the canals; for yet another, stunning decor and attentive service might be the deciding factors. Like so many other things in life, the best restaurant turns out to be mostly a matter of individual taste.

Personal values are fine when it comes to restaurants, but they pose a challenge to scientific research. On the one hand, every scientist has personal opinions about the world. On the other, science endorses the goal of **objectivity**, *a state of personal neutrality in conducting research*. Objectivity in research depends on carefully adhering to scientific procedures in order not to bias the results. Scientific objectivity is an ideal rather than a reality, of course, since complete impartiality is virtually impossible for any researcher to achieve. Even the subject a researcher selects to study and the framing of the questions are likely to grow out of personal interest. But scientists cultivate detachment and follow specific methods to lessen the chance that conscious or unconscious biases will distort their work.

As an additional safeguard, researchers should try to identify and report their personal leanings to help readers evaluate their conclusions in the proper context.

The influential German sociologist Max Weber expected personal beliefs to play a part in a sociologist's selection of research topic. Why, after all, would one person study world hunger, another investigate the effects of racism, and still another examine one-parent families? But Weber (1958; orig. 1905) warned that, even though sociologists select topics that are *value-relevant*, they should conduct research that is *value-free* in their pursuit of conclusions. Only by being dispassionate in their work (as we expect any professional to be) can researchers study the world *as it is* rather than telling others how they think *it should be*. In Weber's view, this detachment was a crucial element of science that sets it apart from politics. Politicians, in other words, are committed to a particular outcome; scientists try to maintain an open-minded readiness to accept the results of their investigations, whatever they may be.

By and large, sociologists accept Weber's argument, though most concede that we can never be completely value-free or even aware of all our biases. Moreover, sociologists are not 'average' people: most are white people who are highly educated and more politically liberal than the population as a whole. Sociologists need to remember that they, too, are affected by their own social backgrounds.

One strategy for limiting distortion caused by personal values is **replication**, *repetition of research by other investigators*. If other researchers repeat a study using the same procedures and obtain the same results, they gain confidence that the original research (as well as their own) was conducted objectively. The need for replication in scientific investigation is probably the reason why the search for knowledge is called *research* in the first place.

In any case, keep in mind that the logic and methodology of science hold out no guarantee that we will grasp objective, absolute truth. What science offers is an approach to knowledge that is *self-correcting* so that, in the long run, researchers stand the best chance of overcoming their own biases and achieving greater understanding. Objectivity and truth, then, lie not in any particular research method, but in the scientific process itself.

Some limitations of scientific sociology

The first scientists probed the operation of the natural world. Many sociologists use science to study the social world; however, the scientific study of people has several important limitations.

1 *Human behaviour is too complex to allow sociologists to predict precisely any individual's actions.* Astronomers calculate the movement of planets with remarkable precision, announcing years in advance when a comet will next pass near the earth. But planets and comets are unthinking objects; humans, by contrast, have minds of their own. Because no two people react to any event in exactly the same way, the best that sociologists can do is to show that categories of people typically act in one way or another. This is no failing of sociology; it is simply consistent with the nature of our task: studying creative, spontaneous people.

2 *Because humans respond to their surroundings, the mere presence of a researcher may affect the behaviour being studied.* An astronomer gazing at the moon has no effect whatever on that celestial body. But people usually react to being observed. Some may become anxious, angry or defensive; others may try to 'help' by providing the answers or actions they think researchers expect of them.

3 *Social patterns change constantly; what is true in one time or place may not hold true in another.* The laws of physics apply tomorrow as well as today; they hold true all around the world. But human behaviour is too variable for us to set down immutable sociological laws. In fact, some of the most interesting sociological research focuses on social diversity and social change.

4 *Because sociologists are part of the social world they study, being value-free when conducting social research can be difficult.* Barring a laboratory mishap, chemists are rarely personally affected by what goes on in test tubes. But sociologists live in their 'test tube' – the society they study. Therefore, social scientists face a greater challenge in controlling – or even recognising – personal values that may distort their work.

5 *Human behaviour differs from all other phenomena precisely because human beings are symbolic, subjective creatures.* Human beings – unlike planets or molecules – are always constructing meaning. And what marks us off from other animals is the elaborate symbolic systems we weave for ourselves. Therefore, sociologists cannot simply study societies from outside; they have to take on board ways of 'entering' these worlds of meaning.

The humanistic stance: the importance of subjective interpretation

As we have explained, scientists tend to think of 'subjectivity' as 'bias' – a source of error to be avoided as much as possible. But there is also a good side to subjectivity, since creative thinking is vital to sociological investigation in three key ways.

First, science is basically a series of rules that guide research, rather like a recipe for cooking. But just as more than a recipe is required to make a great chef, so scientific procedure does not, by itself, produce a great sociologist. Also needed is an inspired human imagination. After all, insight comes not from science itself but from the lively thinking of creative human beings (Nisbet, 1970). The genius of physicist Albert Einstein or sociologist Max Weber lay not only in their use of the scientific method, but also in their curiosity and ingenuity.

Second, science cannot account for the vast and complex range of human motivations and feelings, including greed, love, pride and despair. Science certainly helps us gather facts about how people act, but it can never fully explain the complex meanings people attach to their behaviour (Berger and Kellner, 1981).

Third, we also do well to remember that scientific data never speak for themselves. After sociologists and other scientists 'collect the numbers', they face the ultimate task of *interpretation* – creating meaning from their observations. For this reason, good sociological investigation is as much art as science.

Sociology and the humanities

The recognition of all these limitations leads many sociologists to adopt a somewhat different stance towards their study. They do not claim to be scientists as above, but instead try to make sociology a more humanistic discipline concerned with understanding. In his study of *Sociology as an Art Form*, Nisbet reflects 'How different things would be . . . if the social sciences at the time of their systematic formation in the nineteenth century had taken the arts in the same degree they took the physical science as models' (Nisbet, 1976: 16).

This corrective sociology may be called 'humanistic' and has at least four central criteria. It must pay tribute to *human subjectivity and creativity*, showing how individuals respond to social constraints and actively assemble social worlds. It must deal with concrete

Being observed. A basic lesson of social research is that being observed affects how people behave. Researchers can never be certain precisely how this will occur; while some people resent public attention, others become highly animated when they think they have an audience

Source: © Jenny Matthews/Alamy.

Q Does the camera ever tell the truth? How do people behave in front of cameras? What does this suggest to you as a major problem for all research?

human experiences – talk, feelings, actions – through their *social, and especially economic, organisation* (and not just their inner, psychic or biological structuring). It must show a naturalistic *intimate familiarity* with such experiences – abstractions untempered by close involvement are ruled out. And there must be a self-awareness by the sociologist of the ultimate *moral and political role* in moving towards a social structure

in which there is less exploitation, oppression and injustice and more creativity, diversity and equality. A list like this is open to detailed extension and revision, but it is hard to imagine a humanistic sociology which is not so minimally committed to these criteria.

Table 3.1 summarises some of the wide-ranging contrasts between the positivistic and humanistic approaches to sociological investigation.

Table 3.1	A bridgeable divide? Humanistic and positivist research contrasted	
	Towards the humanities	**Towards the sciences**
Foci	Unique and idiographic Human-centred The inner: subjective, meaning, feeling, experience	General and nomothetic Structure-centred The outer: objective, 'things', events, facts
Epistemology	Phenomenalist Relational/relativist Perspectivist/pragmatist	Realist Absolutist/essentialist Logical positivist
Task	Interpret, understand Describe, observe Appreciate	Causal explanation Measure Theorise
Style	'Soft', 'warm' Imaginative Valid, 'real', 'rich' Personal research	'Hard', 'cold' Systematic Reliable, 'replicable' Large-scale funding
Theory	Inductive and grounded 'Storytelling'	Deductive and abstract 'Operationalism'
Values	Ethically and politically committed Egalitarianism	Ethically and politically neutral 'Expertise and elites'

Source: Adapted from Plummer, 2001a: 9.

Emergent epistemologies

The traditional debates in sociology over epistemology have been between the positivist stance and the humanist stance. Unfortunately, matters are not quite as simple as this, as there are a number of other positions that are important. We will look further at science in Chapter 23. But here we briefly raise five others: realism, critical stances, standpoints, queer theory and postmodernism.

1 The realist stance: theorising science

Realism is *a theoretical system of concepts that are evolved to handle a particular problem* (like how the economy, our minds or even the solar system works). While it may also gather empirical evidence, this is not central to its research – since it argues that 'empirical evidence' is never straightforward. We can never be sure of 'facts'. What we need, therefore, are strong explanations – built up from theoretical tools that will help us do this. The work of Marx is usually seen as a realist theory. For him, the problem was how capitalism works. To explain this, he did not simply go out and talk with people or simply look at documents (although he did do both these things). Instead he developed the idea of the **mode of production**, *the way a society is organised to produce goods and services*. From this concept, he could start to evolve an understanding of how societies work and change.

2 Critical sociology

Critical sociology developed in reaction to positivist science, and is often inspired by Marx. It rejects the idea that society exists as a 'natural' system open to discovery. Critical sociologists suggest that not only should the social world be understood, it should ultimately be changed. They see the task of sociology as avowedly political, tying knowledge to action. They look at *all knowledge as harbouring political interests and the task of sociology as being critically to unmask what is actually going on*. Thus, for example, much sociology may suggest that we are free-thinking rational agents with choices: critical sociology would take this as a problem and try to show how all of this is shaped by social institutions. It subverts societies' dominant ideologies and beliefs. (For more on this, see Chapter 5, p. 163.)

3 Standpoint theory/standpoint epistemologies

Linked to the 'voices' raised in Chapter 1, **standpoint epistemologies** suggest that knowledge always comes out of specific kinds of social experience. *All knowledge is grounded in standpoints and standpoint theory enables groups to analyse their situation (problems and oppressions) from within the context of their own experiences.* The standpoint for most of social science has routinely been that of white, heterosexual, middle-class and middle-aged men – conventionally the dominant group in studying society. They have made their own standpoint appear to be 'the truth'.

But there is a range of other standpoints in the world: just as we saw in Chapter 2, there may be a feminist standpoint, which arises from the experiences and situations of women; a black standpoint, which arises from the situation of black people; or a gay standpoint, which arises from the experiences of lesbians and gays. The starting point, then, of this kind of epistemology is with the experience of these varied groups. The point is that starting from the (many different) daily activities of, for instance, lesbians enables us to see things in the social world that might otherwise have been invisible to us, not just about those lives but about heterosexual women's lives and men's lives, straight as well as gay (Harding, 1991: 252).

But problems can soon arise. For in taking, say, a feminist standpoint, it soon becomes clear that there is not just one position or stand to take – there is no universal (or essential) women's view. Women in low-income societies will almost certainly have different standpoints from those of middle-class white feminists in high-income societies. As we have already seen (Chapter 2), to work from a position which suggests there is only one standpoint of women would be to engage in **essentialism** – *the belief that qualities are inherent (essential to) specific objects*. A non-essentialising stance has to be taken which recognises how standpoints interweave (Collins, 1990; Harding, 1991).

4 Queer theory

Queer theory argues that *most sociological theory still has a bias towards 'heterosexuality' and that non-heterosexual voices need to be heard*. Such theorists would argue that all the topics discussed in this book – from stratification and ethnicity, to religion and economy – would be greatly enhanced if the position of 'non-heterosexual voices' were placed at the centre.

For example, it suggests that many religions have been organised around 'homophobic' persecutions; that a new form of economy is emerging that is based upon the spending power of young middle-class gay men – the pink economy; and that the experience of being lesbian or gay can differ significantly across different ethnic minority communities (Seidman, 1996). New insights can be provided for all the traditional concerns of sociology once we give a focus to a different group such as 'queers'. This is a position that is a little like standpoint theory. It is discussed further in Chapter 12.

5 Postmodern methodology

We could go on with other standpoints. As we have seen in Chapter 2, a number of different approaches have emerged within sociology over the past two decades which stress differing voices and an anti-essentialism. Most prominently, and most generally, there has been the arrival of what may be called postmodern methodology.

This suggests that any strong search for *the* truth (like the positivism discussed above) is part of the (now doomed) Enlightenment project of science. Postmodernists hold that this view of an absolute, scientific truth has now been discredited: truths are much more multiple, fluid, changing and fragmentary. Postmodern epistemology would highlight the following:

- The death of the meta-narrative, i.e. the end of any one big claim to truth.
- The need for local knowledges produced out of particular contexts, i.e. our truths must be located in specific situations.
- The need to be aware of the contexts which shape this knowledge. Part of this means a much greater self-awareness on the part of the researchers – knowing how they come to do this research and their involvement in it.
- The need to understand the ways in which this knowledge is then told – how it is represented through 'writing strategies'. This means an awareness of how knowledge is represented. Metaphors such as stories, discourses and narratives become part of this. Part may also be the visual turn – the importance given to film, video, cam-recording and the like as new tools for gathering data and new tools for presenting it.
- The need to know why this knowledge is being produced and how it will be used. Here sociological knowledge is rarely just 'knowledge for knowledge's

sake': it is bound up with moral, political and ethical judgements. Sociology becomes a moral and political tale.

A caution

We have to be careful. Ever since its birth, sociology has been locked into controversy as to its true character. A lot of recent debates are not in the end that recent – they have often been voiced, slightly differently, at earlier moments. The work of C. Wright Mills, for example, introduced in Chapter 1, was an earlier version of some of these ideas. What is important for you to sense at this stage is that the character of sociological knowledge itself has always been discussed and has led to many battles. These still continue today.

Making sense of sociological data

Whichever epistemology is to be claimed, sociological research also always involves learning some 'tricks of the trade'. These are very practical matters – tools that are needed to make sure that you are doing the research as best you can.

1 Concepts, variables and measurement

A crucial element of all 'science' is the **concept**, *a mental construct that represents some part of the world, inevitably in a simplified form*. 'Society' is itself a concept, as are the structural parts of societies, including 'the family' and 'the economy'. Sociologists also use concepts to describe individuals, by noting, for example, their 'sex', 'race' or 'social class'.

A **variable** is *a concept whose value changes from case to case*. The familiar variable 'price', for example, changes from item to item in a supermarket. Similarly, people use the concept 'social class' to evaluate people as 'upper class', 'middle class', 'working class' or 'lower class'.

The use of variables depends on **measurement**, *the process of determining the value of a variable in a specific case*. Some variables are easy to measure, such as adding up income at tax time. But measuring many sociological variables can be far more difficult.

For example, how would you measure a person's 'social class'? You might be tempted to look at clothing, listen to patterns of speech, or note a home address. Or, trying to be more precise, you might ask about someone's income, occupation and education.

Researchers know that almost any variable can be measured in more than one way. Having a very high income might qualify a person as 'upper class'. But what if the income is derived from selling cars, an occupation most people think of as middle or even working class? And would leaving school at 16 make a person 'lower class'? To resolve such a dilemma, sociologists sensibly (if somewhat arbitrarily) combine these three measures – income, occupation and education – into a single composite assessment of social class, called socioeconomic status, which is described in Chapters 8 and 10.

Sociologists also face the challenge of describing thousands or even millions of people according to some variable of interest such as income. Reporting an interminable stream of numbers would carry little meaning and tell us nothing about the people as a whole. Hence sociologists use *statistical measures* to describe people efficiently and collectively. The box below explains how.

Measurement is always a bit arbitrary because the value of any variable depends, in part, on how one defines it. **Operationalising a variable** means *specifying exactly what one is to measure in assigning a value to a variable*. If we were measuring people's social class, for example, we would have to decide whether we were going to measure income, occupational prestige, education or something else and, if we measure more than one of these, how we will combine the scores. When reporting their results, researchers should specify how they operationalised each variable, so that readers can evaluate the research and fully understand the conclusions.

2 Reliability and validity of measurement

Useful measurement involves two further considerations. **Reliability** is *the quality of consistent measurement*. For a measure to be reliable, in other words, repeating the process should yield the same result. But consistency is no guarantee of **validity**, which is *the quality of measuring precisely what one intends to measure*. Valid measurement, in other words,

PUBLIC SOCIOLOGY

Knowing your 'averages': three useful (and simple) statistical measures

We all talk about 'averages': the average price of a litre of petrol or the average salary for graduates. Sociologists, too, are interested in averages, and they use three different statistical measures to describe what is typical. They often say 'means, medians or modes'. What does this mean?

Assume that we wish to describe the salaries paid to seven members of a company: £23,000, £28,500, £27,800, £28,000, £23,000, £52,000 and £23,000.

The simplest statistical measure is **the mode**, defined as *the value that occurs most often in a series of numbers*. In this example, the mode is £23,000 because that value occurs three times, while each of the others occurs only once. If all the values were to occur only once, there would be no mode; if two values occurred three times (or twice), there would be two modes. Although the mode is easy to identify, sociologists rarely make use of it because this statistic provides at best only a crude measure of the 'average'.

A more common statistical measure, **the mean**, refers to *the arithmetic average of a series of numbers*, and is calculated by adding all the values together and dividing by the number of cases. The sum of the seven incomes is £205,300; dividing by 7 yields a mean income of £29,329. But notice that the

mean is actually higher than the income of six of the seven members. Because the mean is 'pulled' up or down by an especially high or low value (in this case, the £52,000 paid to one member who also serves as a director), it has the drawback of giving a distorted picture of any distribution with extreme scores.

The median is *the value that occurs midway in a series of numbers arranged in order of magnitude* or, simply, the middle case. Here the median income for the seven people is £27,800, because three incomes are higher and three are lower. (With an even number of cases, the median is halfway between the two middle cases.) Since a median is unaffected by an extreme score, it usually gives a more accurate picture of what is 'average' than the mean does.

means more than getting the same result time and again – it means obtaining a *correct* measurement.

To illustrate the difficulty of valid measurement, say you want to investigate how religious people are. A reasonable strategy would be to ask how often they attend religious services. But, in trying to gauge *religiosity* in this way, what you are actually measuring is *attendance at services*, which may or may not amount to the same thing. Generally, religious people do attend services more frequently, but people also participate in religious rituals out of habit or because of a sense of duty to someone else. Moreover, some devout believers shun organised religion altogether. Thus, even when a measurement yields consistent results (making it reliable), it can still miss the real, intended target (and lack validity). In sum, sociological research is no better than the quality of its measurement.

3 Relationships among variables

Once they achieve valid measurement, investigators can pursue the real pay-off, which is determining how variables are related. The scientific ideal is **cause and effect**, *a relationship in which we know that change in one variable causes change in another*. A familiar cause-and-effect relationship occurs when a girl teases her brother until he becomes angry. *The variable that causes the change* (in this case, the teasing) is called the **independent variable**. *The variable that changes* (the behaviour of the brother) is known as the **dependent variable**. The value of one variable, in other words, is dependent on the value of another. Why is linking variables in terms of cause and effect important? Because doing so is the basis of **prediction**: that is, *researchers using what they do know to predict what they don't know.*

Because science puts a premium on prediction, people may be tempted to think that a cause-and-effect relationship is present whenever variables change together. Consider, for instance, that the marriage rate in the United Kingdom falls to its lowest point in January, exactly the same month our national death rate peaks. This hardly means that people die because they fail to marry (or that they don't marry because they die). In fact, it is the dreary weather during January (and perhaps also the post-holiday blues) that causes both a low marriage rate and a high death rate. The converse holds as well: the warmer and sunnier summer months have the highest marriage rate as well as the lowest death rate. Thus, researchers often have to untangle cause-and-effect relationships that are not readily apparent.

To take a second case, sociologists have long recognised that juvenile delinquency is more common among young people who live in crowded housing. Say we operationalise the variable 'juvenile delinquency' as the number of times (if any) a person under the age of 18 has been arrested, and assess 'crowded housing' by looking at the total square footage of living space per person in a home. We would find the variables related: that is, delinquency rates are, indeed, high in densely populated neighbourhoods. But should we conclude that crowding in the home (the independent variable) is what causes delinquency (the dependent variable)?

Not necessarily. **Correlation** is *a relationship by which two (or more) variables change together*. We know that density and delinquency are correlated because they change together, as shown in Figure 3.1(a). This relationship *may* mean that crowding causes misconduct, but often some third factor is at work, causing change in both the variables under observation. To see how, think what kind of people live in crowded housing: people with less money, power and choice – the poor. Poor children are also more likely to end up with police records. Thus, crowded housing and juvenile delinquency are found together because *both* are caused by a third factor – poverty – as shown in Figure 3.1(b). In other words, the apparent connection between crowding and delinquency is 'explained away' by a third variable – low income – that causes them both to change. So our original connection turns out to be a **spurious correlation**, *an apparent, though false, association between two (or more) variables caused by some other variable*.

Unmasking a correlation as spurious requires a bit of detective work, assisted by a technique called **control**, *holding constant all relevant variables except one in order to see its effect clearly*. In the example above, we suspect that income level may be behind a spurious connection between housing density and delinquency. To check, we control for income (that is, we hold it constant) by using as research subjects only young people of the same income level and looking again for a correlation between density and delinquency. If, by doing this, a correlation between density and delinquency remains (that is, if young people living in more crowded housing show higher rates of delinquency than young people with the same family income in less crowded housing), we gain confidence that crowding does, in fact, cause delinquency. But if the relationship disappears when we control for income, as shown in Figure 3.1(c), we confirm that we have been dealing with a spurious correlation. Research has, in fact, shown that virtually all correlation between crowding and delinquency disappears if income is controlled. So we have now sorted out the relationship among the three variables, as illustrated in Figure 3.1(d). Housing density and juvenile delinquency have a spurious correlation; evidence shows that both variables rise or fall according to people's income.

(a)

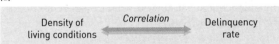

If two variables vary together, they are said to be correlated. In this example, density of living conditions and juvenile delinquency increase and decrease together.

(b)

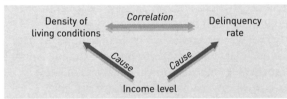

Here we consider the effect of a third variable: income level. Low income level may cause both high-density living conditions and a high delinquency rate. In other words, as income level decreases, both density of living conditions and the delinquency rate increase.

(c)

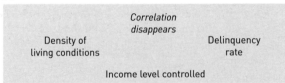

If we control income level – that is, examine only cases with the same income level – do those with higher-density living conditions still have a higher delinquency rate? The answer is no. There is no longer a correlation between these two variables.

(d)

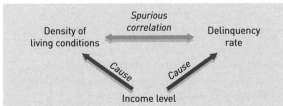

This finding leads us to conclude that income level is a cause of both density of living conditions and the delinquency rate. The original two variables (density of living conditions and delinquency rate) are thus correlated, but neither one causes the other. Their correlation is therefore spurious.

Figure 3.1   Correlation and cause: an example

To sum up, correlation means only that two (or more) variables change together. Cause and effect rests on three conditions: (1) a demonstrated correlation, but also (2) that the independent (or causal) variable precedes the dependent variable in time, and (3) that no evidence suggests a third variable is responsible for a spurious correlation between the two.

Natural scientists identify cause-and-effect relationships more easily than social scientists because the laboratories used for study of the physical world allow control of many variables at one time. The sociologist, carrying out research in a workplace or on the streets, faces a considerably more difficult task. Often, sociologists must be satisfied with demonstrating only correlation. In every case, moreover, human behaviour is highly complex, involving dozens of causal variables at any one time.

4 Issues of sampling

One of the key issues of research is to know just how representative of a wider group are the people you study. For example, if you want to speak about the population of Australia as a whole, it would be sheer folly just to interview Australian students on campus. They would not be representative. You would need a much wider sampling frame – maybe a list of everybody who lives in Australia. But clearly, obtaining such a list would be very costly, and contacting everybody on it would be prohibitively expensive and time consuming. Hence full-scale population surveys – the census found in many countries – usually take place only every ten years or so. The United States census for 2000 (which can be found on the website www.census.gov) and the UK census for 2001 are the most recent of such censuses and are discussed in the *Methods and research* box, below (see www.census.ac.uk).

Much more commonly, social scientists engage in *sampling*. Usually, a researcher begins a survey by designating a **population**, *the people who are the focus of research*. For example, if you wanted a random sample of your college or university, you would initially need a sampling frame of everybody attending it. Researchers then collect data from a **sample**, *a part of a population that represents the whole*. The now familiar national political surveys utilise a sample of some 1,500 people to gauge the political mood of the entire country. You use the logic of sampling all the time. If you look around a lecture room and notice five or six students nodding off, you might conclude that the class finds the day's lecture dull. Such a conclusion

Argentine family answers questions during the nationwide Census

Source: Reuters/Corbis.

involves making an inference about *all* the people (the 'population') from observing *some* of the people (the 'sample'). But how do we know whether a sample actually represents the entire population? There are a number of different sampling strategies.

The main distinction made in sampling theory is usually between probability sampling and non-probability (convenience) sampling. The former is more sophisticated, for each of the elements of the sample has the same probability of being included. This is the only approach for a truly representative sample. It usually comes in two forms – simple random samples (something like every tenth person), or stratified random samples (where the population is divided into known strata or groups in advance, such as gender or age). In *random sampling*, researchers draw a sample from the population in such a way that every element in the population has the same chance of ending up in the sample. If this is the case, the mathematical laws of probability dictate that the sample they select will, in the vast majority of cases, represent the population with a minimal amount of error. Experienced researchers use special computer programs to generate random samples. Novice researchers, however, sometimes make the mistake of assuming that 'randomly' walking up to people on the street produces a sample representative of an entire city. This is a serious error, for such a strategy does not give every person an equal chance to be included in the sample. For one thing, any street – whether in a rich or a poor neighbourhood or in a 'university city' – contains more of some kinds of people than others. For another, any researcher is apt to find some people more approachable than others, again introducing a bias.

Examples of non-probability samples include *quota samples* and *snowball samples*. A quota sample represents the group of people it wants to make statements about. Thus interviewers may be told how many respondents with particular kinds of characteristic are needed for the study: if we know that the population has equal numbers of men and women, then interviewers are asked to interview equal numbers of each. If we know that it is likely to be an older group, then we make sure the sample contains an appropriate mix of ages. This is not a random sample, but one that is purposely constructed with people in their correct proportions or ratios.

Snowball sampling also does not aim at real representativeness and is usually associated with case studies and qualitative research, often in areas of research where respondents are hard to find. The basic method relies upon searching out more respondents from the respondents you interview, and building up a network of contacts through each interview. In a research project on drug users or alcoholics, for example, it is impossible to find a full sampling frame that lists 'all drug users', from which you can draw a random sample. Instead, a more common method is to make contact with some drug users and then ask about their friends and acquaintances and subsequently interview them. Such a method, of course, can never provide a truly representative sample, but it is convenient.

Although good sampling is no simple task, it offers a considerable saving in time and expense. We are spared the tedious work of contacting everyone in a population, while obtaining useful results.

5 Sociological thinking: the interplay of theory and method

Sociological investigators move back and forth between facts and theory. **Inductive logical thought** is *reasoning that transforms specific observations into general theory*. In this mode, a researcher's thinking runs from the specific to the general, something like this: 'I have some interesting data here; what are the data saying about human behaviour?'

A second type of logical thought works 'downwards' in the opposite direction. **Deductive logical thought** is *reasoning that transforms general theory into specific*

METHODS & RESEARCH

The population census

A **census** is *a count of everyone who lives in the country*. It is seen as crucial for broad planning and the shaping of policies. Most countries try to have one, but the problems it can pose are formidable. India has a population in 2011 of around 1,210,000,000 (1.21 billion – the second largest population in the world) and its census started in 1872 – a history of 140 years. It conducted the most recent in 2011 – and every time it is a major challenge.

In the UK, the census has been held every ten years since 1801 (with the exception of 1841) when the population was 9 million. In 2001, it cost £255 million – but the 2011 census is well over half a million pounds. Run by the Office for National Statistics (ONS), it tries to count every person in the UK at the same moment. Although a lot of attention is given to the design of the questionnaire, it is getting longer and longer. By 2011 it had become a 32 page booklet. And for the first time it was also accessible online. (There was also a follow-up survey – some 4,000 professional interviewers conducting some 32,000 ten-minute interviews.)

It was becoming clear that the scale of the census is heading towards trouble and the census of 2011 is predicted by many to be the last in the UK. It now is too unwieldy, too costly and too unreliable. Some statisticians often choose to ignore its data because its return rate was only 96 per cent, and indeed was much lower in some inner-city regions. Nowadays, the figures do not seem to tally: in 2001, there were some 900,000 people fewer than predicted – this was eventually put down to an increased emigration (possibly of young men). But there were other discrepancies. In Westminster, the population was revised downwards by a quarter, and in Manchester by a tenth. All this mattered because lower populations meant lower government grants.

Among the most commonly cited problems with the census are:

- *Undercounting*: some councils have complained that their populations are undercounted, and are suggesting a recount.
- *Cost*: as populations grow, the costs of a census can become prohibitive.
- *Distribution*: it is becoming harder both to get the forms to the right people and to get them to complete and return the forms.
- *Immigration*: there were more immigrants and some cannot read English.
- *Civil liberties*: there are suspicions about the nature of the questions in the census and how they impinge on civil liberties.
- *Ethics*: the questions asked are becoming more and more numerous – and more personally intrusive.

The census may be discontinued from 2011. Follow up the debates: on the UK census, see www.ons.gov.uk/census/2011-census/index.html; on the India census, see http://censusindia.gov.in; on wordwide census, see www.census.gov/ipc/www/cendates.

---

hypotheses suitable for scientific testing. This time, the researcher's thinking goes from the general to the specific: 'I have this hunch about human behaviour; let's put it in a form we can test, collect some data, and see if it is correct.' Working deductively, the researcher first states the theory in the form of a hypothesis and then selects a method by which to test it. To the extent that the data support the hypothesis, we conclude that the theory is correct; data that refute the hypothesis alert the researcher that the theory should be revised or perhaps rejected entirely.

Just as researchers commonly employ several methods over the course of one study, they typically make use of *both* types of logical thought. Figure 3.2 illustrates the two phases of scientific thinking: inductively building theory from observations and deductively making observations to test our theory.

Finally, it is worth noting that statistics, too, play a key part in the process of turning facts into meaning. Commonly, sociological researchers provide quantitative data as part of their research results. And precisely how they present their numbers affects the conclusions their readers draw. In other words, data presentation always provides the opportunity to 'spin' reality in one way or another.

Often, we conclude that an argument must be true simply because there are statistics to back it up. However, readers must use a cautious eye when encountering statistical data. After all, researchers choose what data to present, they offer interpretations of the statistics, and they may use tables or graphs to encourage others to reach particular conclusions. *The big debate* at the end of this chapter takes a closer look at these important issues.

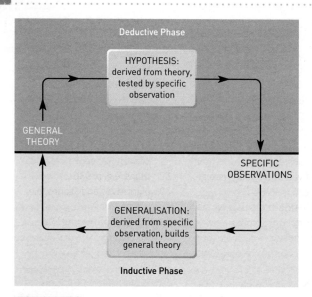

| Figure 3.2 | Deductive and inductive logical thought |

The tools of sociological research

A **research tool** is *a systematic technique for conducting research*. The *Methods and research* box suggests a wide range of research tools that can be used by sociologists, and this section then briefly discusses a few of them. None is inherently better or worse than any other. Rather, in the same way that a carpenter selects a particular tool for a specific task, researchers choose a tool according to what they wish to learn. Each one of these requires their own skill – and there are numerous books published that provide such advice on all the above (see the guide at the end of the chapter).

   To give some order to all of this, such data are often divided into *quantitative* materials involving statistics and requiring numeracy skills; and *qualitative* materials involving less measurable matter and requiring interpretive skills. Surveys and formal questionnaires are good examples of the former; and historical documents and fieldwork are good examples of the latter (but their paths often cross: there is statistical history and qualitative surveys). And although sociologists often make much of this divide (they split into 'the hard', with statistical tables, and the 'soft', without any tables), sociologists usually need both kind of data. The former help them make generalisations and often map trends – even when blind to inner meanings and idiosyncrasy; the latter help provide a deeper sense of meaning and

understanding – even if they fail to help map out broader trends. They are correctives to each other.

Core tools

1 The experiment

The logic of positivist science is most clearly expressed in the **experiment**, *a research method for investigating cause and effect under highly controlled conditions*. This is used rarely by sociologists, but more commonly by psychologists and social psychologists. However, it is a pure form of research: it is *explanatory*, and asks not just what happens but why. Typically, researchers turn to an experiment to test a specific **hypothesis**, *an unverified statement of a relationship between variables*.

   Ideally, we evaluate a hypothesis in three steps. First, the experimenter measures the dependent variable (the 'effect'); second, the investigator exposes the dependent variable to the independent variable (the 'cause' or 'treatment'); and third, the researcher again measures the dependent variable to see if the predicted change took place. If the expected change did occur, the experiment lends support to the hypothesis; if not, the hypothesis is discounted.

2 The survey

A **survey** is *a research method in which subjects respond to a series of items in a questionnaire or an interview*. Surveys are particularly well suited to studying attitudes that investigators cannot observe directly, including political and religious beliefs or the subjective effects of racism. Although surveys can shed light on cause and effect, most often they yield *descriptive* findings, as researchers seek to paint a picture of subjects' views on some issue.

3 Questionnaires

A **questionnaire** is *a series of written questions that a researcher supplies to subjects requesting their responses*. One type of questionnaire provides not only the questions but a series of fixed responses (similar to a multiple-choice examination). This *closed-ended format* makes the task of analysing the results relatively easy, yet narrows the range of responses in a way that might distort the findings. By contrast, a second type of questionnaire, using an open-ended format, allows subjects to respond freely, expressing various shades of opinion. The drawback of this approach is that the researcher later has to make sense out of what can be a bewildering array of answers.

METHODS & RESEARCH

The research tool kit

Sociological data are the various bit of information that sociologists collect. In the past, the sociologist has been characterised as a person who uses interviews, surveys and statistics – but this is now a very limited view and only partially true. Research tools are used across a wide range of fields, and sociologists' work is much broader than this. Where possible, we signpost where you can find examples of research tools in this book.

30 research tools for sociologists

1. Artefacts and things (personal possessions, archaeological 'finds', consumer objects), e.g. p. 87

2. Art, e.g. pp. 930–5
3. Attitudes, e.g. pp. 152; 356
4. Autobiographies/life stories, e.g. pp. 77; 509; 613; 714
5. Auto/ethnographies/ personal experience, e.g. p. 86
6. Biography, e.g. pp. 823–5
7. Census, e.g. p. 73
8. Conversation analysis, e.g. p. 226
9. Cybermethods/netnography, e.g. pp. 24; 84–5
10. Diaries, e.g p. 78
11. Discourse analysis, e.g. p. 594
12. Documentary, e.g. p. 75
13. Ethnography, see Participant observation
14. Field research, see Participant observation
15. Experiments, e.g. pp. 178–80

16. Fiction, e.g. *mytasklist* (each chapter); Part 6
17. Film and video, e.g. p. 87; youth; Part 6
18. Historical research, e.g. pp. 186; 363
19. Interviews, e.g. p. 255
20. Letters, p.79
21. Longitudinal, panel and cohort, e.g. pp. 218–9; 825
22. Maps, e.g. p. 936
23. Narratives and stories, e.g. p. 824
24. Oral history, e.g. p. 506
25. Participant observation, e.g. pp. 61; 155; 225; 507; 699
26. Performance, e.g. pp. 86–7; 222
27. Photographs, e.g. pp. 79–82
28. Postcodes, e.g. p. 325
29. Statistics and surveys, e.g. pp. 8–9; 282–3; 288; 585–7
30. Video, see film

Drama and documentary in sociology

Nick Broomfield is a leading UK documentary film-maker. In a style he calls 'Direct Cinema', he uses non-actors to play themselves. In 2006, he completed a drama called *Ghosts* for Channel 4 which was inspired by the 2004 Morecambe Bay Cockling Disaster (You can read about this in the opening of Chapter 15). In this incident, 23 immigrants were drowned after being cut off by the tides. *Ghosts* won numerous awards and helped raise nearly half a million pounds to help the victims' families. In many ways it is a more striking document than a lot of mainstream sociology and really worth a look. You can find most of it on YouTube. Think about and discuss the value of documentary film, drama and performance as sociological methods

See also: http://www.nickbroomfield.com/home.html and especially: http://www.nickbroomfield.com/ghosts.html.

Source: Nick Broomfield, from the film *Ghosts*.

4 Interviews

An **interview** is *a series of questions a researcher addresses personally to respondents*. Interviews come in several forms. In a *closed-ended* interview, researchers would read a question or statement and then ask the subject to select a response from several alternatives. Generally, however, interviews are *open-ended* so that subjects can respond in whatever way they choose and researchers can probe with follow-up questions.

Closed-ended and open-ended interviews are both relatively formal. But there is another kind of informal conversational interview, which is more commonly used in the qualitative field research described in the next section. With this mode of interviewing, the goal is to encourage the respondent to participate fully and equally in discussion with the interviewer. Certain key themes provide the shape for the discussion, but there is no questionnaire as such, and the relationship between interviewer and respondent is much more casual, friendly and egalitarian. This mode of research is more suitable to gaining 'in-depth' understanding and for researching more sensitive topics. The 'conversations' are usually taped. This can lead to problems of a mass of data that are much less organised and accessible to analysis than the data found with more formal interviewing. See Table 3.2 for some key differences in interview forms.

Table 3.2	A continuum of interview forms
Positivist	**Interpretative**
Interviews 'collect' data	Interviews 'construct' data
Standardised	Flexible
Mass	Formative
Focused	Open
Structured	Unstructured
Survey	Ethnographic
'Objective'	Phenomenological/'subjective'
Passive	Active
Short	Long

Source: Plummer (2001a).

5 Fieldwork, ethnography and participant observation

The most widely used strategy for humanistic field study is **participant observation**, *a method by which researchers systematically observe people while joining in their routine activities*. Researchers choose participant observation in order to gain an inside look at social life in settings ranging from nightclubs to religious seminaries. Cultural anthropologists commonly employ participant observation (which they call *fieldwork*) to study communities in other societies. They term their descriptions of unfamiliar cultures *ethnographies*; sociologists prefer to describe their accounts of people in particular settings as *case studies*.

At the outset of a field study, social scientists typically have just a vague idea of what they will encounter. Thus, most field research is *exploratory* and *descriptive*. Researchers might have hypotheses in mind, but it is just as likely that they may not yet realise what the important questions will turn out to be.

As its name suggests, participant observation has two facets. Gaining an 'insider's look' depends on becoming a participant in the setting – 'hanging out' with others, attempting to act, think and even feel the way they do. Compared to experiments and survey research, then, participant observation has fewer hard-and-fast rules. But it is precisely this flexibility that allows investigators to explore the unfamiliar and to adapt to the unexpected.

Unlike other research methods, participant observation requires a researcher to become immersed in the setting, not for a week or two, but for months or even years. For the duration of the study, however, the researcher must maintain some distance as an 'observer', mentally stepping back to record field notes and, eventually, to make sense of the action. The tension inherent in this method comes through in the name: 'playing the *participant*' gains for the researcher acceptance and access to people's lives; yet 'playing the *observer*' affords the distance and perspective needed for thoughtful analysis. The twin roles of 'insider' participant and 'outsider' observer, then, often come down to a series of careful compromises.

Most sociologists carry out participant observation alone, so they must remain mindful that results depend on the interpretations of a single individual.

An aside: qualitative and quantitative research

Participant observation is typically **qualitative research**, meaning *investigation by which a researcher gathers subjective, not numerical, data*. (The informal conversational interviews we encountered earlier are also part of this approach.) Unlike experiments or surveys, participant observation and informal interviews usually involve little **quantitative research**, *investigation by which a researcher collects numerical data*. Some scientists disparage a 'soft' method such as participant observation as lacking in scientific rigour. Yet, much qualitative research has become very rigorous in recent years, even to the point of having computer programs such as *NVivo, Atlas, The Ethnograph* and *NUDIST* to enable a rigorous analysis of 'soft' data. Furthermore, its personal approach – relying so heavily on personal impressions – is also a strength: while a highly visible team of sociologists attempting to administer formal surveys would disrupt many social settings, a sensitive participant-observer can often gain considerable insight into people's natural day-to-day behaviour.

 For Advice on using qualitative software in research, see:

Computer assisted qualitative data analysis
http://caqdas.soc.surrey.ac.uk/index.html

6 Secondary and historical analysis

Not all research requires investigators to collect their own data personally. In many cases, sociologists engage in **secondary analysis**, *a research method in which a researcher utilises data collected by others*.

The most widely used statistics in social science are gathered by government agencies. The Office for National Statistics in the UK continuously updates information about the UK population, and offers much of interest to sociologists. Comparable data on Europe are available via *Eurostat*, from the Office for Official Publications of the European Communities in Luxembourg. Global investigations benefit from various publications of the United Nations and the World Bank. And much of the data of previous research is housed in archives such as the Social Science Research Data Archive at the University of Essex, UK. In short, a wide range of data about the whole world is as close as the university library. And most of these data sets, these days, are available on CD-Rom or on the World Wide Web.

Clearly, using available data – whether government statistics or the findings of individuals – saves researchers time and money. Therefore, this approach holds special appeal to sociologists with low budgets. Just as important, the quality of government data is generally better than what even well-funded researchers could hope to obtain on their own.

Still, secondary analysis has inherent problems. For one thing, available data may not exist in precisely the form one might wish; furthermore, there are always questions about the meaning and accuracy of work done by others. For example, in his classic study of suicide, Emile Durkheim realised that he could not be sure that a death classified as an 'accident' was not, in reality, a 'suicide' and vice versa. And he also knew that various agencies use different procedures and categories in collecting data, making comparisons difficult. In the end, then, using second-hand data is a little like shopping for a used car: bargains are plentiful, but you have to shop carefully to avoid being stuck with a 'lemon'.

Emerging research tools: from life stories to visual sociology

So far, we have described the four most common tools used by sociologists to dig out data and understand the world. They are compared in Table 3.3. But there are others that are becoming increasingly common: we call them *documents of life* (see Plummer, 2001a). These are accounts of people's lives told by themselves – usually in words, but sometimes through other media such as video. The world is crammed full of these personal documents. People keep diaries, send letters, take photos, make their own video diaries, write memos, tell biographies, scrawl graffiti, publish their memoirs, write letters to the papers, leave suicide notes, inscribe memorials on tombstones, shoot films, paint pictures, make music and try to record their personal dreams. All of these expressions of personal life are hurled out into the world by the millions and can be of interest to anyone who cares to seek them out. They are all in the broadest sense 'documents of life', and are there to be gathered and analysed by sociologists. They come in a number of forms, which include the following.

1 Life stories

The life history method was established with the 300-page story of a Polish émigré to Chicago, Wladek Wisniewski, written in three months before the outbreak of the First World War. It was one volume of the massive study by W. I. Thomas and F. Znaniecki, *The Polish Peasant in Europe and America*, first published between 1918 and 1920. Wladek describes the early phases of his life in the Polish village of Lubotynborn as the son of a rural blacksmith, his early schooling, his entry to the baker's trade, his migration to Germany to seek work, and his ultimate arrival in Chicago and his plight there. Following the classic work, life histories became an important tool in the work of Chicago and

Table 3.3	**Four classic research methods: a summary**		
Method	**Application**	**Advantages**	**Limitations**
Experiment	For explanatory research that specifies relationships among variables; generates quantitative data	Provides greatest ability to specify cause-and-effect relationships; replication of research is relatively easy	Laboratory settings have artificial quality; unless research environment is carefully controlled, results may be biased
Survey	For gathering information about issues that cannot be directly observed, such as attitudes and values; useful for descriptive and explanatory research; generates quantitative or qualitative data	Sampling allows surveys of large populations using questionnaires; interviews provide in-depth responses	Questionnaires must be carefully prepared and may produce a low return rate; interviews are expensive and time consuming
Participant observation	For exploratory and descriptive study of people in a 'natural' setting; generates qualitative data	Allows study of 'natural' behaviour; usually inexpensive	Time consuming; replication of research is difficult; researcher must balance roles of participant and observer
Secondary analysis	For exploratory, descriptive or explanatory research whenever suitable data are available	Saves time and expense of data collection; makes historical research possible	Researcher has no control over possible bias in data; data may not be suitable for current research needs

Polish sociologists. The authors have claimed this to be the best form of sociological method.

> We are safe in saying that personal life records, as complete as possible, constitute the perfect type of sociological material, and that if social science has to use other materials at all it is only because of the practical difficulty of obtaining at the moment a sufficient number of such records to cover the totality of sociological problems, and of the enormous amount of work demanded for an adequate analysis of all the personal material necessary to characterise the life of a social group.

(Thomas and Znaniecki, 1958: 1832–3)

2 Diaries

For Allport (1942: 95), the diary is the document of life *par excellence*, chronicling as it does the immediately contemporaneous flow of public and private events that are significant to the diarist. The word 'contemporary' is crucial here, for each diary entry – unlike life histories – is sedimented into a particular moment in time. In some recent research on sexual behaviour and AIDS, researchers have asked subjects to keep diaries of their sexual activities and they have then analysed them (Coxon, 1997).

3 'Logs' and 'time budgets'

Sorokin pioneered this method when he asked informants to keep detailed 'time-budget schedules' showing just how they allocated their time during a day (Sorokin and Berger, 1938). The anthropologist Oscar Lewis's particular method focused on a few specific families in Mexico, and the analysis of a 'day' in each of their lives. Of course, his actual familiarity with each family was in no way limited to a day. He 'spent hundreds of hours with them in their homes, ate with them, joined in their fiestas and dances, listened to their troubles, and discussed with them the history of their lives' (Lewis, 1959: 5). But in the end he decided that it would be analytically more valuable, for both humanistic and scientific purposes, to focus upon 'the day' as a unit of study. Thus each family – Martinez, Gomez, Gutierez, Sanchez and Castro – is first presented as a 'cast of characters' and then followed through one arbitrarily chosen but not untypical day of their life. Lewis believed that a study of a day had at least a threefold value: practically, it was small enough

Asking questions of photographs

In a general study of photography, Akeret (1973) coins the term 'photoanalysis' and suggests the following useful scheme of questions to be asked. We suggest you keep this question list to hand – and add some of your own – when you look at some of the photos in this book.

What is your immediate impression (of the photograph)? Who and what do you see? What is happening in the photo? Is the background against which the photo was taken of any significance, either real or symbolic? What feelings does it evoke in you? What do you notice about physical intimacy or distance? Are people touching physically? How are they touching? How do the people in the photo feel about their bodies? Are they using their bodies to show them off, to hide behind, to be seductive, are they proud of their bodies, ashamed? What do you notice about the emotional state of each person? Is (s)he shy, compliant, aloof, proud, fearful, mad, suspicious, introspective, superior, confused, happy, anxious, angry, weak, pained, suffering, bright, curious, sexy, distant, etc.? Can you visualise how those emotions are expressed in facial dynamics and body movement? If there is more than one person in the photo, what do you notice about the group mood? Is there harmony or chaos? How do people relate? Are they tense or relaxed? What are their messages towards each other? Who has the power, the grace? Do you see love present? What do you notice about the various parts of each person? Look carefully at the general body posture and then the hands, the legs, the arms, the face, the eyes, the mouth. What does each part tell you? Are the parts harmonious or are there inconsistencies? Pay particular attention to the face, always the most expressive part of the person. Learn to read any photo as you would read a book from left to right then downwards. Go over it again and again, each time trying to pick out something you have missed. Ask yourself more general questions, as many as you can think of. What is obvious and what is subtle? What is the sense of movement or is there any? What memories and experiences does the photo stir in you? How do you identify with the people in the photo? How are you alike, how different? What moves you most about the photo? What do you find distasteful about it? Is there anything that disturbs you? Try to define the social and economic class of the people photographed. What is their cultural background? If it is a family, would you want to be a member of it? Would you want your children to play with theirs? If the photos are personal – of you, your family, friends or associates – try to remember the exact circumstances of the photo session. How have you changed since then? How have you remained the same? (Akeret, 1973: 35–6).

---

to allow for intensive observation; quantitatively, it permitted controlled comparisons across family units; and qualitatively, it encouraged a sensitivity to the subtlety, immediacy and wholeness of life.

4 Letters

Letters remain a relatively rare document of life in the social sciences. The most thoroughgoing use of letters is still to be found in Thomas and Znaniecki's *Polish Peasant* (see p. 77), where on discovering that there was extensive correspondence between Poles and Polish émigrés to America, an advertisement was placed in a Chicago journal offering to pay between 10 and 20 cents for each letter received. Through this method they were able to gain many hundreds of letters, 764 of which are printed in the first volume of their study, totalling some 800 pages and arranged in 50 family sequences. Each sequence is prefaced with a commentary that introduces the family members and the main concerns.

5 Visual sociology: photography

Invented at approximately the same time as sociology, photography has only occasionally figured in sociological research. It is true that in the earliest days of the *American Journal of Sociology*, photographs were a regular feature of its muck-raking, reformist articles: between 1896 and 1916, 31 articles used 244 photographs. Likewise many early fieldwork studies were illustrated with photographs. Thrasher's *The Gang*, for example, contains nearly 40 photos of boys and boy gangs. The lead has primarily come from anthropologists, and in particular the pioneering work of Gregory Bateson and Margaret Mead (1942), who provided a volume devoted entirely to photographic images from the culture of the Balinese. The photo

ALIVE WITH ALZHEIMER'S

Cathy Stein Greenblat

Cathy Greenblat combines sociology with photography. Working to dispel myths and cut into common assumptions, her work focuses on care for the dependent elderly and for the end of life. She looks especially at those with Alzheimer's and dementia and shows how people with these illnesses are far from being 'empty shells' but come alive in diverse ways. Her work combines photographs with text – the images do not stand on their own; and she finds still photography a better medium to work in than film because, as she says, 'People need time to stop and reflect on the images, to deal with their emotions and thoughts at their own pace'. Her book *Alive with Alzheimer's* (2002) can be found online at her website: http://www.cathygreenblat.com/category.cfm?nL=0&nS=9

We also use some of her images in Chapters 13 and 21.

Source: Cathy Greenblat.

below is drawn from this book. Oddly, one of the most frequent places to find visuals is in sociology textbooks like this one. Indeed, throughout this book you will find many images: you may like to consider their value and use in sociology as you look at them (see the *Research in action* box above).

In the main, sociologists have not taken much interest in what should now be viewed as a major tool for investigation. Yet recently there has been growing interest in what has been called *visual sociology*.

Thus Cathy Greenblat takes photos of residents in an Alzheimer's home – her book shows their daily

round of ordinary activities (Greenblat, 2004); Mitch Dunier worked with Hakim Hassan to study the street vendors in New York City (Duneier, 2000) whilst Kevin Bales worked with documentary photographers to show the nature of contemporary slavery (2009). Douglas Harper is one of the leading developers of visual sociology. His work can be found in a range of studies looking at migrant labour in Hong Kong, agricultural change and human values, the sociology of the small shop, and *The Italian Way*, a study of food in family life in contemporary Italy. These books include innovative uses of photography as well as other qualitative methods, and highlight the ways in which

Balinese cockfighting

Source: Bateson and Mead (1942: 140). Reprinted by permission of the New York Academy of Sciences.

 This image comes from one of the earliest attempts to use photography in field research. The authors – Gregory Bateson and Margaret Mead – were leaders in this field for much of the twentieth century. What does this picture depict? Why might it be significant? Consider the role of images in sociology.

See: The Institute for Intercultural Studies: www.interculturalstudies.org/resources.

sociologists are starting at last to take the visual much more seriously in their research.

6 Visual sociology: film and video

The twentieth century has been called by Norman Denzin 'the cinematic century' (1995). Film, and later television, video and DVD, became prime modes for looking at social life. Yet few sociologists have seriously engaged with it as a tool for research.

It is the documentary film-makers and anthropologists who have been most adept at exploiting this medium to date. At the start of the century, ethnographers started to film various tribal peoples engaged in social rituals. In 1901 Spencer filmed Australian aborigines in kangaroo dances and rain ceremonies, while in 1914 Curtis filmed the Kwakiutl Indians. But the birth of the documentary film is commonly agreed to be Robert Flaherty's *Nanook of the North* (1922) about 'Eskimo' life.

Flaherty, a compassionate romantic appalled by the dehumanisation of modern technology, lived in 'Eskimo' country for 11 years, and shot his film under the most adverse conditions on the life of one specific individual – Nanook. In this film he reveals the constant struggle for life in a hostile environment. Sensitively, the power of the image is left behind.

One of Flaherty's most successful visual techniques was to follow an exotic act visually, showing it step by step as it developed, not explaining it in words. In one sequence we see Nanook tugging on a line leading into a hole in the ice. We are engaged in that act, and think about it. Eventually, the suspense is broken: our questions are answered when Nanook pulls out a seal. Flaherty creates the same visual involvement when Nanook makes the igloo, especially at the end of the sequence, when Nanook cuts a slab of ice for a window, sets it in place, and fixes a snow slab reflector along one side. For a time we are puzzled and, therefore, involved.

But when Nanook steps back, finished, we understand (Heider, 1976: 24).

In the main sociologists have either ignored the medium or used the documentaries created by film-makers like Frederick Wiseman. His films perhaps come closest to embodying sociological concerns: most deal directly with the ways in which individuals, in their social hierarchies, cope (or fail to cope) with the day-to-day pressures of social institutions. As he puts it:

> **What I'm aiming at is a series on American institutions, using the word 'institutions' to cover a series of activities that take place in a limited geographical area with a more or less consistent group of people being involved. I want to use film technology to have a look at places like high schools, hospitals, prisons, and police, which seems to be very fresh material for film; I want to get away from the typical documentary where you follow one charming person or one Hollywood star around. I want to make films where the institutions will be the star but will also reflect larger issues in general society.**

(In Rosenthal, 1971: 69)

Hence Wiseman's 'documents' treat not 'lives' but 'institutions' – the police in *Law and Order* (1969), hospitals for the criminally insane in *The Titicut Follies* (1969), army life in *Basic Training* (1971) as well as films on *Welfare* (1975), *High School* (1968) and *Hospital* (1970).

Feminist methodology: gender and research

One major development in sociology over the past 30 years has been the development of feminist methodology. Sociologists have (gradually) come to realise that gender often plays a significant part in their work. Margrit Eichler (1988) identifies the following five threats to sound research that relate to gender.

1 *Androcentricity*. Androcentricity (*andro* is the Greek word for 'male'; *centricity* means 'being centred on') refers to approaching an issue from a male perspective. Sometimes researchers enter a setting as if only the activities of men are important while ignoring what women do. For years, for example, researchers studying occupations focused on the paid work of men while overlooking the housework and childcare traditionally performed by women.

Clearly, research that seeks to understand human behaviour cannot ignore half of humanity.

Eichler notes that the parallel situation of *gynocentricity* – seeing the world from a female perspective – is equally limiting to sociological investigation. However, in our male-dominated society, this narrowness of vision arises less frequently.

2 *Overgeneralising*. This problem occurs when researchers use data drawn from only people of one sex to support conclusions about both sexes. Historically, sociologists have studied men and then made sweeping claims about 'humanity' or 'society'. Gathering information about a community from a handful of public officials (typically, men) and then drawing conclusions about the entire community illustrates the problem of overgeneralising. Here, again, the bias can occur in reverse. For example, in an investigation of child-rearing practices, collecting data only from women would allow researchers to draw conclusions about 'motherhood' but not about the more general issue of 'parenthood'.

3 *Gender blindness*. This refers to the failure of a researcher to consider the variable of gender at all. As we note throughout this book, the lives of men and women typically differ in virtually every setting. A study of growing old in Europe that overlooked the fact that most elderly men live with spouses while elderly women generally live alone would be weakened by its gender blindness.

4 *Double standards*. Researchers must be careful not to distort what they study by applying different standards to men and women. For example, a family researcher who labels a couple as 'man and wife' may define the man as the 'head of household' and treat him accordingly, while assuming that the woman simply engages in family 'support work'.

5 *Interference*. In this case, gender distorts a study because a subject reacts to the sex of the researcher in ways that interfere with the research operation. While studying a small community in Sicily, for instance, Maureen Giovannini found that many men responded to her as a woman rather than as a researcher, compromising her research efforts. Gender dynamics precluded her from certain activities, such as private conversations with men, that were deemed inappropriate for single women. In addition, local residents denied Giovannini access to places considered off-limits to members of her sex.

Of course, there is nothing wrong with focusing research on one sex or the other. But all sociologists, as well as people who read their work, should stay mindful about how gender can affect the process of sociological investigation.

Feminist research

Sociology's pervasive attention to men in the past has prompted some contemporary researchers to make special efforts to investigate the lives of women. Advocates of feminist research embrace two key tenets: (1) that their research should focus on the condition of women in society, and (2) that the research must be grounded in the assumption that women generally experience subordination. Some proponents of feminist research advocate the use of conventional scientific techniques, including all those described in this chapter. Others maintain that feminist research must transform the essence of science, which they see as a masculine form of knowledge. Whereas scientific investigation has traditionally demanded detachment, feminists deliberately foster a sympathetic understanding between investigator and subject. Moreover, conventional scientists take charge of the research agenda by deciding in advance what issues to raise and how to study them. Feminist researchers, by contrast, favour a less structured approach to gathering information so that participants in research can offer their own ideas on their own terms (Stanley and Wise, 1983; Nielsen, 1990; Stanley, 1990; Reinharz, 1992).

Such alterations in research premises and methods have led more conventional sociologists to charge that feminist research is less science than simple political activism. Feminists respond that research and politics should not – indeed cannot – ever be distinct. Therefore, traditional notions that placed politics and science in separate spheres have now given way to some new thinking that merges these two dimensions.

Twenty-first-century methods: new directions ahead

Although we can find traces of twenty-first-century developments in research methods and methodologies tracing back over generations and decades, there is a certain 'turning point' – even 'tipping point' – at the start of the twenty-first-century which has rendered some trends more and more significant for certain clusters of researchers. Eight major trends can be detected and in your studies it will be worth looking out for them.

1 'New' technologies and research

Most conspicuous is the development of the new technologies which are profoundly shaping the ways we do sociology. What once might have taken months to unearth can now be found at the click of a mouse. Major data sets can be created, stored, found and analysed through a large range of statistical and qualitative research packages. Large data sets such as those provided by the United Nations, the European Union and most governments can now be accessed instantly. Any research can usually start with a Google search or an Amazon book search and you will be on your way. Wikipedia can sometimes be a valuable resource and is usually a good first point of call. The ability to create images and videos – and store and present them easily – via web cam, digital camera, YouTube, PowerPoint and the rest has brought the visual world to sociology in a much more accessible way. Facebook can be homed into friends researching the same area. Blogs can provide access to research groups. Postcode searches can open up routes into lifestyle analysis. And so on. Table 3.4 suggests some of the ways in which the new technologies – not available a quarter of a century ago – are now to be found everywhere and shaping sociological research. Many of the older tools – interviews or surveys – are also being reshaped through these new technologies.

2 Global research

These new tools also aid in research that is going global. The internet is not bound to one country and so more and more research becomes accessible not just to one local community but to global ones. If you want to find people with a common experience – sickness, migration, work, families, sex or sport – you can find people to interview, blog, web cam or tweet online across many countries and even as they travel. It has made the possibilities of global research more and more possible – even for students. No longer is there the practical need for research to simply stay local – it can go global. But there is more than just a practical

Table 3.4	Digital culture and the transformation of twenty-first-century research	
Research tasks	**New digital research methods**	**A few examples (this is not meant to be comprehensive)**
Preliminary overview of the field	Do key word online searches, which will help you sketch out an area of research and see what already exists.	Search engines like Lycos (formed in 1994), Google (formed in 1998, and the world leader) and Bing (formed in 2009). The now ubiquitous Wikipedia which, despite its limitations, is 'good enough' for a starting point.
Accessing data	Get data. A core feature of the twenty-first-century world is its developing and managing of information which has never been possible before. You can now access both primary and secondary data online, with ease and little cost, as never before.	For secondary data, major statistical resources are provided by organisations, such as *Eurostats* (on the EU), *World Factbook* (CIA) and *United Nations Statistics*. But there are also databases for films (IMDb), literature (Project Gutenberg), and online archives for newspapers, sociology books, etc. (see Part Six of this book for much more on this).
Using internet tools for accessing original data	Do original research. Web 2 is highly interactive and enables you to gather data from your informants in many different ways.	Online and phone interviewing. Online ethnographies of networking groups from many spheres of social life (netnography). Analysing life stories and data found on blogs, Twitter and other sources.
Storing and managing the data you collect	Put in folders and files, and use table management. This is a core function of the information technologies.	Save your own data in well-organised and easily accessible files and folders on well-labelled and coded discs and memory sticks. Use programmes which analyse content of data.
Organising your research project	Plan frames and lists. Set up your research website, possibly including a blog where you can communicate with an emerging online research community working in similar areas.	Apart from setting up a website, this is where skills with Facebook, blogging and other network sites become important.
Constructing and managing bibliographies and reading	Nearly all sociologically relevant books and articles are electronically catalogued – often with abstracts, sometimes in e-book format.	Become familiar with the systems of your local library; use INTUTE; use search engines for recent books – and sites like Amazon. Keep all this catalogued in a database programme like EndNote.
Taking seriously the visual side of social life	Much sociology of the past has ignored the visual world but new technologies have created key ways of capturing and storing the world we live in through photographs and video.	The use of digital cameras makes on the spot image possible. Digital camera for ease of documentary work. Ubiqitous web cams. Visual websites like Flickr (for photo sharing). The value and use of YouTube.

Table 3.4	*continued*	
Research tasks	**New digital research methods**	**A few examples (this is not meant to be comprehensive)**
Using programmes for the analysis of your data	Tools for inspecting your data range from simple table making (like Access and Excel) to the more elaborate but widespread softwares for data analysis.	NVivo 8 is the most common qualitative programme and it lets you combine detailed analysis with linking, searching, modelling and charting. The most common quantitative package is SPSS for Windows, which has become increasingly user-friendly over the last few years.
The presentation of your data	No longer do you have to stick with the straight essay and paper – there are many tools to help you enhance your presentation.	PowerPoint needs to be used creatively and imaginatively – never use it for plain text that you could put in a book or an essay. There are many programmes to help you design maps, charts and visuals of all kinds. Think of photos and how these lead you on to think.

reason for this turn to global research: there is an intellectual and political one.

As we have seen, globalisation is a key feature of the contemporary world. But it is also the case that much sociology has been seriously limited to European and North American ideas: the history of sociology is largely Western (see Chapter 2, p. 49). With the rise of postcolonial theory it has become more and more apparent that many more voices around the world need to be heard to challenge the rather limited one of current sociology. People in North America and Europe constitute a very small part of the world's population (Europe and North America together make up scarcely one-seventh of the world's population but almost all mainstream sociology has been by them, about them and for them). What we are starting to see are many developments – global ethnography, postcolonial research, standpoint theory – that give priority to the full range of cultures and society across the world, and adopting stances that take seriously as the baseline for research the world view and understandings of the people who inhabit these worlds.

3 Narrative research

More and more social researchers are beginning to understand that most of social life is actually conducted through narratives and stories. They take their lead from Roland Barthes (1915–80),

an important and influential French literary theorist, philosopher, critic and semiotician) when he says:

> **Narratives and stories are among the most powerful instruments for ordering human experience. Narrative can be expressed in oral or written language, still or moving pictures, or a mixture of these media. It is present in myths, legends, fables, tales, short stories, epics, history, tragedy, drama, comedy, pantomime, paintings, stained glass windows, movies, local news, and conversation. In its almost infinite variety of forms, it is present at all times, in all places, and in all societies. Indeed, narrative starts with the very history of mankind ...**

(Barthes, 1975)

Human beings are *homo narrans* – narrating animals. We are story-telling animals and as we go through our lives we are ceaselessly narrating them. Even sociology itself can be seen as one form of story telling and narrative.

As more and more sociologists have come to understand this, they have started to speak of 'narrative reality' as one key focus for sociologists to study (see Gubrium and Holstein, 2009). This means that they are developing tools for understanding three things:

1 How do people come to tell stories of their lives?
2 How do these stories then take definite shapes, patterns and forms?
3 What are the social consequences of telling some stories – rather than others?

To do such work, narrative analysts draw from many disciplines – history, communications, semiology, literature and philosophy – to aid in the understanding of narrative construction.

4 Sensory research

Until recently, research methods have tended to neglect the senses. Most sociology has been spoken and written about lives without detailing how people feel, see, hear, smell and touch. As we will see in Chapter 7, some sociologists have recently started to take a major interest in the body and its emotions. Sarah Pink, for example, talks about *Doing Sensory Ethnography* (2009). As a result, sociologists have had to start to develop strategies for studying these things – to *get close to people's feelings*, *listen* to what they have to say, *attend* to how we and others perceive and see the world around us. Neglecting the senses in sociology has led to a very restricted, myopic account of the world – and sociologists are only just starting to rectify this. There is now a sociology developing which focuses on how we listen and hear (e.g. Back, 2007) and how we study a full range of senses – a sensory methodology (Pink, 2009).

Consider just one neglected sense: the eye and the visual. Clearly human beings organise social life in ways that are very dependent on what we see. Yet most sociology for its first 150 years never even bothered to look at photographs; few even today use videos; film is relegated to a side interest of a few. As we have suggested, the growth of many new visual technologies – as well as the massive increase of media in our lives – have made our lives more and more mediated lives: lives which are organised through mass media. How we see these media and how this in turn plays a role in social life has become more and more a key to understanding it. We will have more to say about media analysis in Chapter 22.

5 The reflexivity turn

Sociologists have long recognised that their presence in the social world partially shapes the nature of the social knowledge they 'find'. Think of the simplest interview – and how the interviewer plays some human role in shaping the outcome. People interact with each other and this shapes how knowledge gets produced. As sociologists come to understand their own position in shaping sociological findings, many find it more and more necessary to reflect upon their own role in the research. They ask questions about themselves – why are they interested in this research, what do they think

and feel about the people they are studying and the 'findings' they get, how does the research process have an impact on their own life and the life of the people they study? They try to include a sense of themselves in the very knowledge they produce – and write themselves into the findings.

Critics say that this is self-indulgent and distracts from the findings. But the argument that these researchers make is simply that no human knowledge can be devoid of its human creation and that it enhances our understanding of the knowledge to see how it was made by people.

6 Auto-ethnography in research

It is but a short step from this to the idea of auto-ethnography. This is the sociological version of autobiography, where there is a linking of the sociologist's own life to their research area. Here sociologists are willing to write in the first person and place their own self on the line: his or her voice has to come out, and be discussed and situated at the forefront of the analysis. Often this is claimed to be self-indulgent and it can lead to awkwardness and embarrassment. In doing this, however, the auto-ethnographer will explicitly connect to the wider aspects of studying the culture of which they are a part. Such tellings raise all kinds of methodological questions linked to the truth of the story and the life that tells it. They show how ideas are shaped in the very context which produces them.

7 Material culture and research on 'things'

Another range of new research focuses on what we could call 'the social life of things'. Here almost any material object in the world – a house, a photo, a concert, a house – can be examined through the relations in which it is enmeshed. Typically this kind of research examines the biography or history of the thing and traces its life through a series of events and people who have helped shape it. Table 3.5 outlines a few of the topics that have been studied.

8 Performance theory

One strand of new methods and approaches to research has been very critical of the over-reliance of sociology (and other branches of social science) on written texts and the pursuit of objective science.

Table 3.5	The sociology of consumer objects: a quick review	
Material object of consumption	**The study**	**The book**
T-shirt	Traces the production of a T-shirt from start to end across the world economy	Pietra Rivoli, *The Travels of a T-shirt in the Global Economy* (2nd edn, 2009)
Tomatoes	Traces evolution of the tomato within the development of the capitalist market	Mark Harvey, Steve Quilley and Huw Benyon, *Exploring the Tomato* (2002)
Coca-Cola	Traces the globalisation of consumption through the famous soft drink: the role of the transnational company as it spreads the drink to Papua New Guinea	Robert J. Foster, *Coca-Globalization* (2008)
Nike	Traces the cycle of production, distribution and consumption of the famous shoe and its logo	Robert Goldman and Stephen Papson, *Nike Culture* (1998)
Sony Walkman	Now of historical interest as a major commodity that had mass sales but was morphed into other newer technologies	Paul du Gay et al., *Doing Cultural Studies: The Story of the Sony Walkman* (1996)
The McDonald's hamburger	The classic study which takes McDonald's as a paradigm for the shifts in bureaucratic social organisation	George Ritzer, *The McDonaldization of Society* (6th edn, in 2010)

THINKERS & THEORY

Norman Denzin: from life stories and film to performance radicalism

Norman Denzin has been very prominent in shaping new directions in qualitative research, primarily through his editorship of *The Handbook of Qualitative Research* (4th edn, 2011), which has provided a forum for all kinds of new developments – from poetry and drama to film and photography: all of which are now being encouraged as tools for sociology.

Denzin rose to prominence with his book *The Research Act* in the 1970s, where he demonstrated how social research should be analysed as a social process. Interviews and questionnaires are not simply neutral tools of research, but are deeply shaped by social encounters. In a sense he was writing a sociology of research methods.

In his later work he focused on children, emotion and alcohol, and found increasingly that life stories and film were key media for sociologists to work with. He claimed that film and cinema had become the media of the twentieth century and sociology neglected them at its peril. At the time he argued this, few sociologists were taking film seriously as a method.

More recently, Denzin has spearheaded the use of performance in sociology – suggesting that sociologists should write and perform dramas that come out of their ethnographic studies and which capture the rich emotional and political complexities of life. Social life always involves performance, and sociologists need both to enter the performing worlds of others and then to present them back to the world through their own performances which capture the stumbling difficulties of social life.

His latest book, *The Qualitative Manifesto: A Call to Arms* (2010), outlines a challenging new view of methods and champions what he calls 'social justice inquiry'. The social sciences should be value committed and should aim to improve the quality of life. A key factor here is the need to conduct research that will reduce inequalities and enhance social justice.

See: Norman Denzin, *The Research Act* (1970/1999); *Performance Ethnography* (2003); *The Qualitative Manifesto: A Call to Arms* (2010).

This critique wants to find better ways to capture and display the embodied lived experience – and to this end advocates using methods engaging with drama and performance. The claim is made that we live in a dramaturgical performance culture and we should be increasingly concerned with 'how to construct, perform and critically analyze performance texts' (Denzin, 2003: xi).

Ethical, political and policy questions

As Max Weber observed long ago, a fine line separates politics from science. Most sociologists endorse Weber's goal of value-free research, but a growing number of researchers are challenging the notion that politics and science can – or should – be distinct. Many sociologists now argue that the ideal of 'value-free' research paints a 'storybook picture' of sociology. Every element of social life is political, they claim, in that it benefits some people more than others. In this view, sociology is saturated with values and politics from top to bottom. There is a long history, then, of discussing the role of politics, values and ideologies in sociology – and they are usually discussed using Max Weber's distinctions between value-free and value-relevant. Without detailing his work here, we can find three key issues:

1 *Value relevance.* In the early stages of research (choosing areas of research, etc.), values become crucial in making selections and phrasing problems. The tip here is to think about the value of your research and choose your area carefully – often on political and moral grounds.

2 *Value neutrality but ethical responsibility.* Whilst doing research, adequate objectivity has to be attained. The tip here is to follow a number of the guidelines of science whilst being aware, *at the same time*, that sociology always deals with human life and people, and there will be a need to think about your responsibilities towards the people you are studying.

3 *Value implications.* Most sociology can have an impact on the world and the sociologist has to think

about this impact. The tip here is to think carefully about the implications of what you are going to say. Who will this impact and how? In particular, is there political fallout out here?

There are some who will suggest that values should be kept strictly out of sociology. Simply look at the great sociologists of the past – and indeed the key names of the present – and what you will almost invariably find is a passion drenched in languages of values. Much contemporary sociology is often quite explicit about its moral and political imagination: feminist sociology declares the need to remove women's inequalities; anti-racism sociology critiques racism; queer sociology destabilises gender and sexual categories; and postcolonial sociologies critique the supremacy of the European/American model that dominates thinking. Sociology asks: whose side are you on? Sociologists have to juggle their science with their politics, their ethics and their passions.

Debating ethics and politics in sociology

Throughout this book you will encounter many political issues. Be sure to look at the boxes on *Public sociology* which often raise thorny issues and also turn to the Epilogue (p. 921) where some possible key ethical and political stances to help shape sociology are outlined. Many of the contemporary thinkers we encounter in this book are very politically engaged. Look at the boxes on Stuart Hall, Judith Butler, Donna Haraway, Martha Nussbaum, Raewyn Connell, Michel Foucault, Anthony Giddens, Norman Denzin, Patricia Hill Collins, Jürgen Habermas and Stanley Cohen, who are deeply partisan and explicitly political. They want, at the least, a world of greater justice.

 Look at the ethical codes of sociological professions. See, for example, the Code of the British Sociological Association at:

www.britsoc.co.uk/equality/ Statement+Ethical+Practice.htm.

Issues in ethics and politics

As a village schoolmaster said to anthropologist Nancy Scheper-Hughes:

> It's not your science I am questioning, but this: don't we have the right to lead unexamined lives, the right not to be analysed? Don't we have a right to hold on to an image of ourselves as different to be sure, but as innocent and unblemished all the same?

All researchers should be aware that research can be harmful as well as helpful to subjects or communities. The major professional associations of sociologists in the UK establish formal guidelines for the conduct of research. The prime directive here is that sociologists should strive to be both technically able and humanly ethical in conducting their research. Sociologists, for example, must disclose all their findings, without omitting significant data. Furthermore, they must point out various interpretations of data, and they are ethically bound to make their results available to other sociologists, some of whom may wish to replicate the study. Yet what if this harms their subjects?

There are many ethical issues that face sociologists. Below are a few to consider:

- *Confidentiality*. In most sociology, research subjects need to be guaranteed confidentiality. Thus names of people are changed; schools studied get 'pseudonyms'.

- *Informed consent*. Respondents in research should know that they are involved in a research undertaking and roughly what this research is about.

- *Honesty*. As in life, so in research, 'honesty' would seem to be a fairly basic requirement! So a minimal canon of 'science' might well be seen as suggesting that the researcher should be as accurate, painstaking and honest as possible.

- *Deception*. A related form of dishonesty arises with deception. In sociology, the dilemma appears where the researcher conceals his or her identity and 'cons' his way into a new group – an issue that is often dubbed the overt/covert debate.

- *Exploitation*. A subject is asked by a sociologist to give up hours – often hundreds of hours – of his or her life to tell their story. It might be very painful and involve a great deal of effort. And at the end of it all – for reasons of confidentiality – the subject must remain anonymous while the sociologist publishes. And certainly there have been prosecutions over such alleged abuses: the mother of one 'case study' – that of Genie, a 'wild child' found at the age of 13 to be living in complete isolation and subsequently studied in detail by psychologists – filed a suit against the researchers on the grounds that private and confidential information had been disclosed for 'prestige and profit' and that Genie had been subjected to 'unreasonable and outrageous' testing.

- *Hurt and harm*. A final worry is the hurt and harm that may befall the subject through the researcher's activities. Social science has produced many instances where communities have been upset by community studies on them – feeling they have been misrepresented; or where individual people feel they have told a story in good faith only for it to result in a kind of damaging or sensational exposure.

Putting it all together: steps in planning a sociological project

Drawing together the elements of sociological investigation presented in this chapter, a typical project in sociology will include each of the following 14 steps. The emphasis here is upon planning the project well.

1 *Get yourself a research problem and define the topic of investigation.* Nothing is more important than getting yourself a good question. Being curious and looking at the world sociologically can generate ideas for social research anywhere. The issue you choose to study is likely to have some personal significance. But a social problem is not a sociological problem and you need to be clear how you can pose a sociological question.

2 *Start keeping a log and record files.* Keep a log of how you develop your research, how you change your views and problems, and how you make key decisions. This will be useful in helping you reflect, but it may also provide good source material for writing up the methodology chapter in your study – if you are to have one. Keep all your notes well organised, and plan this early.

3 *Find out what others have learned about the topic.* You are probably not the first person to develop an interest in a particular issue. Spend time in the library to see what theories and methods researchers have applied to your topic in the past. In reviewing existing research, note problems that may have come up before. Check on the findings.

4 *Assess the requirements for carrying out the research.* How much time and money will the research require? What special equipment or skills are necessary? Can you do the work yourself? What sources of funding are available to support the research? You should answer all these questions before beginning to design the research project.

5 *Specify the research questions.* Are you seeking to explore an unfamiliar social setting? To describe some category of people? Or to investigate cause and effect among variables? If your study is exploratory, identify general questions that will guide the work. If it is descriptive, specify the population and the variables of interest. If it is explanatory, state the hypothesis to be tested and carefully operationalise each variable. Make a long list of what puzzles you; and then work to narrow it to a firmer focus.

6 *Specify your theoretical orientation, and perhaps your disciplinary links.* You should try to locate your own research within certain traditions. For example, some research might be historical, some anthropological, and some more theoretical. And if it is to be theoretical, what kinds of theory will you use: to return to Chapter 1, would you find a functionalist, conflict or action approach most suitable?

7 *Consider ethical issues.* Not all research raises serious ethical issues, but you should be sensitive to this matter throughout your investigation. Could the research harm anyone? How might you design the study to minimise the chances of injury? Do you plan to promise anonymity to the subjects? If so, how will you ensure that anonymity will be maintained?

8 *Devise a research strategy or design.* Consider all major research strategies – as well as innovative combinations of approaches. Keep in mind that the appropriate method depends on the kinds of question you are asking as well as the resources available to support your research.

9 *Draw up a written research proposal in which you outline the above stages and say what you will be doing.* This is very valuable in providing a guide and checklist for doing the research.

10 *Do the research – gather and record your data.* The way you collect data depends on the research method you choose. Be sure to record all the information accurately in a way that will make sense later (it may be some time before you actually write up the results of your work). Remain vigilant for any bias that may creep into the research. Bias may be inevitable, but you should be aware of it.

11 *Interpret the data.* Scrutinise the data in terms of the initial questions and decide what answers they suggest. If your study involves a specific hypothesis, you should be able to confirm, reject or modify the hypothesis based on the data. In writing up your research report, keep in mind that there may be several ways to interpret the results of your study, consistent with different theoretical paradigms, and you should consider them all.

12 *Report your findings and conclusions.* As you write your final report, specify conclusions supported by the data. Consider the significance of your work both to sociological theory and to improving research methods. Of what value is your research to people outside sociology? Finally, evaluate your own work, noting problems that arose and questions that were left unanswered. Note ways in which your own biases may have coloured your conclusions.

13 *Share your results.* Consider submitting your research paper to a campus newspaper or magazine, or making a presentation to a seminar, a meeting of any people you have been involved in studying, or perhaps a meeting of professional sociologists. The important point is to share what you have learned with others and to let others respond to your work.

14 *Where possible, store your data in an archive.* You never know, at some point some other researchers may want to see your data, or even reuse it. So it is always wise to think about ways of storing it or keeping it available for others to see and use.

 See the project 'Writing Across Boundaries'. This is a project which gets various social scientists who have published quite a bit to reflect on the nature of their writing. It includes pieces by Howard Becker, Harvey Molotch, Marilyn Strathborn and Liz Stanley, myself and many others: see www.dur.ac.uk/writingacrossboundaries.

On this website you will also find resources relating to a variety of themes that engage writers in the social sciences. These include drafting and plotting; the data–theory relationship; narrative, rhetoric and representation; and hints and tips on writing.

SUMMARY

1 Two basic requirements for sociological investigation are (1) viewing the world from a sociological perspective, and (2) being curious and asking questions about society.

2 Sociological research involves asking questions about three issues: (1) epistemology, (2) technical tools, and (3) ethics and politics.

3 Two major approaches to epistemology are positivism and humanism. Others include realism, critical sociology, standpoint theory, queer theory and postmodernism.

4 Measurement is the process of determining the value of a variable in any specific case. Sound measurement is both reliable and valid. A goal of science is discovering how variables are related. Correlation means that two or more variables change value together. Knowledge about cause-and-effect relationships is more powerful, however, because a researcher can use an independent variable to predict change in a dependent variable.

5 There are four major research tools. Experiments, which are performed under controlled conditions, attempt to specify causal relationships between two (or more) variables. Surveys, which gather people's responses to statements or questions, may employ questionnaires or interviews. Through participant observation, a form of field research, sociologists directly observe a social setting while participating in it for an extended period of time. Secondary analysis, or making use of available data, is often preferable to collecting one's own data; it is also essential in the study of historical questions. Other tools include 'documents of life', which are records of personal lives recorded by the subjects themselves. They help to gain an understanding of subjective experience, and include life histories, diaries and letters.

6 Visual sociology is a growing area of interest – as is the use of the personal computer in doing research.

7 Although investigators select topics according to their personal interests, the scientific ideal of objectivity demands that they try to suspend personal values and biases as they conduct research. Rejecting conventional ideas about scientific objectivity, some sociologists argue that research inevitably involves political values and that, with this in mind, research should be directed towards promoting desirable social change. Feminist methodologies take gender bias very seriously and aim to correct it.

8 Because sociological research has the potential to cause discomfort and harm to subjects, sociological investigators are bound by ethical guidelines.

CONNECT UP: Turn to Part 6 of this book for key resources and link up
with the book's website, which links to these resources
SEE: www.pearsoned.co.uk/plummer

MYTASKLIST

Ten suggestions for going further

1 Connect up with Part Six and the Sociology Web Resources

As you work through ideas and think about the issues raised in this chapter, look at the accompanying website and the resource centre at the end of this book which connects to it. There is a lot here to help you move on. To link up, see: www.pearson.co.uk/plummer.

2 Review the chapter

Briefly summarise (in a paragraph) just what this chapter has been about. Consider: (a) What have you learned? (b) What do you disagree with? Be critical. And (c) How would you develop all this? How could you get more detail on matters that interest you?

3 Pose questions

(a) What does it mean to state that there are various kinds of truth? What is the basic rationale for relying on science as a way of knowing? Is sociology a science? Should it be? And if so, what kind? Identify several ways in which sociological research is similar to – and different from – research in the natural sciences.

(b) What sorts of measure do scientists adopt as they strive for objectivity? Why do some sociologists consider objectivity an undesirable goal?

(c) Dissect any one sociological study in order to evaluate its methodology.

(d) If there can be a feminist methodology, can there also be an anti-racist methodology, or a gay/queer methodology?

(e) Examine the ways in which the internet and new technologies are changing the nature of social research.

4 Explore key words

Many concepts have been introduced in this chapter. You can review them from the website or from the listing at the back of this book. You might like to give special attention to just five words and think them through – how would you define them, what are they dealing with, and do they help you see the social world more clearly or not?

See: Victor Jupp, *The Sage Dictionary of Social Research Methods* (2006).

5 Search the Web

Be critical when you look at websites – see the box on p. 940 in the Resources section. Some useful sources for this chapter are:

The Qualitative Report
www.nova.edu/ssss/QR – an online journal that provides a major listing of qualitative research websites.

Data on the Net
http://3stages.org/idata – based at the University of California at San Diego, this is a useful site for quantitative data. It houses some 850 sources for gathering data.

National Statistics
www.statistics.gov.uk – the British government's website for all official statistics.

UK Data Archive
www.data-archive.ac.uk – this site, based at Essex University, is home for most of the major surveys and researches conducted in the UK.

6 Watch a DVD

- Akira Kurosawa's *Rashomon* (1951): a much celebrated introduction to the idea of different perspectives capturing a common reality.

It will be valuable now to watch *some classic documentary films* and consider whether they can offer more to understanding than conventional sociological research. For example, see:

- Robert Flaherty's *Nanook of the North* (1922): a classic early documentary about the Innu.
- Leni Riefenstahl's *Triumph of the Will* (1935): a controversial documentary made at the start of Hitler's rule.
- Tod Browning's *Freaks* (1932): a very disturbing introduction to deviance, not really a documentary. See also Chapter 14.

These give you a little sense of how new film-makers in the earliest days attempted to capture social life – and, indeed, how they often got this very wrong.

7 Think and read

C. Wright Mills, *The Sociological Imagination* (1959). This has already been introduced in Chapter 1. It has a very useful appendix on how to do sociology and is strongly recommended.

Alan Bryman, *Social Research Methods* (3rd edn, 2008). This is one of a large number of wide-ranging textbooks that cover the whole field.

Ann Gray, *Research Practice for Cultural Studies* (2003). A helpful guide to methods for cultural studies.

Robert Kozinets, *Netnography* (2010). A guide to researching online communities.

Karen O'Reilly, *Ethnographic Methods* (2nd edn, 2011). A useful guide to fieldwork in sociology.

Gillian Rose, *Visual Methodologies* (2nd edn, 2007). A good general introductory textbook on visual research.

Gerard Delanty, *Social Science: Philosophical and Methodological Foundations* (2005). A good background guide to the philosophical issues of social science.

8 Connect to other chapters

- Inspect some of the many tables and statistics throughout this book. Ask how they were produced and how valid and reliable they are. View them critically.
- See the life stories in the *speaking lives* boxes throughout this book. What are the problems with such stories?
- For more on the growth of multiple voices and feminism, see Chapter 2.

9 Relax with a novel

Several novels have tried to capture the life of a social researcher. See Alison Lurie's *Imaginary Friends* (1967), which looks at the researchers of a strange religious cult.

10 Engage in THE BIG DEBATE

Damned lies and statistics: so do statistics tell the truth?

'Fact, fact, fact!' said the gentleman . . . 'You are to be in all things regulated and governed' . . . by fact. We hope to have, before long, a board of fact, composed of commissioners of fact. Who will force the people to be a people of fact, and of nothing but fact. You must discard the word Fancy altogether.

(Charles Dickens, Hard Times, Chapter 2)

You will soon notice that this book is littered with statistics. That is the sociologist's weakness, and you cannot trust him or her! As the English politicia Benjamin Disraeli once noted wryly: 'There are three kinds of lies: lies, damned lies, and statistics!' Every method of data collection is prone to error, and data do not speak for themselves. Throughout this book – as well as in much of the press – you will find a generous sprinkling of 'statistics' as well as 'statistical tables' that aim to summarise much data. Indeed, we live in a world that bombards us with 'scientific facts' and 'official figures' and it is well worth pausing to consider what such 'statistical evidence' means. People are so fond of saying: 'As the evidence shows . . . ' But what does it show?

As you find statistics in this book, ask yourself some of the questions below. You will soon learn that statistics should never be taken at simple face value and you will start to see that some seem more reasonable than others. Some of the questions you should ask of data include:

1 Are the statistics valid? Do they measure what they say they are trying to measure – like the 'suicide' rate, the 'crime' rate or 'human development'? If you simply think of the problems of just how 'suicide' (see Chapter 1), 'crime' (Chapter 17), 'class' (Chapter 10) or 'human development' (Chapter 4) can be defined (and indeed what they mean), you should soon see some of the problems.

2 Are the statistics possible to disaggregate or break down into different parts? Thus statistics can conceal differences between groups – such as men and women, or young and old, or region to region. Is it possible to break the statistics down to see these differences at work?

3 Are the statistics consistently measured over time? Statistics may be produced at different times using different measuring devices. Again, you need to check how the statistics were made in order to see if they were measuring the same things.

4 Who created this statistic? There is always someone who made the statistic – from a big world agency like the United Nations to the smallest undergraduate survey. Knowing a bit about them may help you see possible sources of error and bias.

5 Why was this statistic created? What were the author(s) trying to achieve by making these statistics? For example, if it is a poverty statistic produced by campaigners against poverty, it is good to know this. And if it is a measure of church memberships produced by devout Christians, it is good to know this too!

6 How was this statistic actually created? Was it, for example, part of a multi-million-pound bureaucratic enterprise involving the filling in of many forms by many different people across the world? If it was bureaucratically produced, how did the various contributors play their role – what rules guided them?

7 How is the statistic being used? Was the statistic produced as part of a political campaign and is it being used perhaps to get more resources? How statistics are used may give clues to hidden biases. There are usually plenty of statistics available for people on all sides of a political debate to use as ammunition to bolster their arguments. Watch out for over-use, under-use, misuse, political abuse and oversimplification.

8 Why was this statistic selected to be presented? Often the data we confront are not wrong; they just do not tell the whole story.

9 How is the statistic being presented? Very often graphs and charts can be used to 'spin' the truth. The picture tells only part of the story. A graph of the crime rate over only the last several years, for example, would reveal a downward trend; shifting the time frame to include the last few decades, however, would show a sharp increase.

Above all, initially be suspicious of all statistics. Put them through some of the above tests, and then make your mind up about them.

Continue the debate

1 Look at some of the statistics in this book. Consider where they have come from, why they are being used and just what it is they purport to measure.

2 When would you trust a statistic?

3 Why do you think people are so quick to accept 'statistics' as true?

4 Consider the opening quote from the hugely insightful Victorian novelist Charles Dickens. Do we now have this 'Board of Fact' and 'People of Fact' and is it a sign of our progress as a civilisation?

5 More questions are asked about statistics in Chapter 9. See the *Public sociology* box on p. 288.

6 See Joel Best, *Damned Lies and Statistics* (2001).

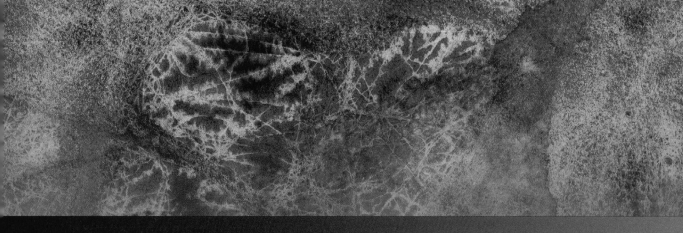

Researching sport

Sport seems to be found in all societies and throughout history. In its many varieties, it is often among the most popular of social activities. The '10' box below suggests the ten most popular sports in the UK in 2008. Having read the first three chapters of this book, we can now ask just what sociology brings to our understanding of sport.

Chapter 1 asked questions about **the sociological imagination**; here, our concern lies with just how we can apply this imagination to 'sport' – indeed, just what is a sociology of sport? What is 'taken for granted' about sport? And how might it have been shaped or constructed by the great transformations of the nineteenth and twentieth centuries? Chapter 2 asked questions about different 'theoretical approaches', a nd here we consider their relevance to sport. And how has sport become globalised? Finally, Chapter 3 would help us pose questions about research and sport. In what follows, there are some hints on how you can develop all this.

TOP 10

Active sports:[1] by sex, 2007/08

England

Men	%	Women	%
Indoor swimming and diving	28	Indoor swimming or diving	35
Snooker, pool, billiards[2]	23	Health, fitness, gym or conditioning activities	22
Cycling[3]	21	Keepfit, aerobics and dance exercise[6]	16
Health, fitness, gym or conditioning activities	21	Outdoor swimming or diving	14
Outdoor football[4]	20	Tenpin bowling	13
Golf, pitch and putt, putting	18	Cycling[3]	13
Outdoor swimming or diving	16	Jogging[5]	8
Tenpin bowling	15	Snooker, pool, billiards[2]	7
Darts	12	Badminton	7
Jogging[5]	12	Yoga	6

1 Adults aged 16 and over.
2 Excludes bar billiards.
3 Includes for health, recreation, training or competition.
4 Includes 5-a-side and 6-a-side.
5 Includes cross-country and road running.
6 Includes exercise bike.

Source: *Social Trends 40* (2010) Table 13.12, p. 193.

Sport is not what it seems: questioning the taken for granted

At the surface level, sport is just that – sport: good fun for healthy bodies perhaps. But sociology always invites you to look a little deeper and challenge what is taken for granted. You need to **defamiliarise yourself with the familiar**.

In this sense it may help to assume the guise of a Martian visitor to planet earth, who comes to see what is going on with no prior 'human' assumptions. The visitor would observe millions of people running, jumping, swimming, hitting each other, and chasing balls in various ways. For instance, just one thing our visitor could not help noticing pretty soon would be that little boys, adolescents, middle-aged men and older men too all seem preoccupied with 'balls'. They kick them around at the earliest of ages, organise into groups around them, build stadiums to them across the world, and dress in special clothing when they do this. Indeed, it all seems to generate a huge industry of 'goods to be sold'. They fight over the balls locally and internationally, they talk and write endlessly about them, and they create mass global gatherings screened across global television – from the favelas of Rio and São Paulo and the slums of Lagos to the Congo jungle and school playgrounds in India, everyone is talking about and kicking balls. And the visitor would also note a special gathering called 'The football World Cup Final' on 11 July 2010, which attracted a television audience of over 700 million people. Despite all the many seeming differences between people, they were all watching the same images, wherever they could.

Beijing Olympics and the globalisation of sport
The modern Olympic Games have been held every four years since 1896 (except during World Wars I and II). In 2008, there were some 11,028 competitors in the games held in Beijing, China with 204 nations participating. This is global sport at its most extreme. It is estimated that some 4.7 billion people watched the opening on television and some 7 million tickets were sold. You can watch the spectacular opening on YouTube. The London Olympics are scheduled for July–August 2012 and are bound to raise a lot of sociological debate. See: http://www.culturalolympics.org.uk/2010/06/sociology-and-the-2012-olympic-games/
Source: © Aflo Foto Agency/Alamy.

The visitor sees all this as very curious, and baffling: what is to be made of it all? One thing is clear, football is very important on planet earth in human societies: billions embrace it; indeed, they often seem to be obsessed with it; there is an intoxication by it; the media devote a huge amount of space to it; they fight over it. Football becomes a major symbol of many societies. So what then does a 'football' signify?

Although football is a major sport, it is not even our most popular sport. So what in the end is going on here? The visitor's first task must be to describe it. The second is to try to explain just what is going on. This is, in effect, the sociologist's task too.

1 Describing sport, researching sport

As we saw in Chapter 3, there are various ways of gathering materials and describing social worlds: we could collect statistics around sport to sense its social shape; we could interview people involved in sports – players, managers, funders, spectators – and find out what they do and why; we could observe the sports, see how people do things together and find out what it all seems to mean to them – and others; we could study documents that surround sports – press cuttings, books, films, fan magazines, photos, videos and websites; we could dig around in the historical archives and see how it developed; we could look at individual life stories and see the role sport has played in them. There is an enormous amount of descriptive work to do. In all of this, what we will be doing is social research.

Let's take just one example. French sociologist Loïc Wacquant's research on boxing on Chicago's South Side is a prime example of observational participation of a sport which connects to wider theory (his ideas have been shaped by the work of Bourdieu – see Chapter 8, p. 263). It is a case study with rich sociological implications. The book *Body and Soul: Notebooks of an Apprentice Boxer* (2004) is full of black boxers busily talking about boxing, many vivid descriptions of the actual boxing experience in the ring, and many photographs in the ring and around it. It is a 'hard-hitting' and very readable piece of sociology; and it will certainly give you a rich description of boxing as it is done.

Unusually, Wacquant is himself right there in the book (some sociologists would not approve of this). He signed himself up at a boxing gym in a black neighbourhood and spent three years immersed among local fighters, amateur and professional. Thus, a brainy white academic sociologist entered the world of black macho boxers! A scholar becomes a boxer. Here Wacquant hangs around at the Woodland boxing gym; learns 'bruising', 'shadow-boxing drills', 'sparring'; and ends up fighting in the Golden Gloves tournament. Never previously contemplating getting close to a ring, let alone climbing into it, he studied, lived and described boxing for three years.

Wacquant started with many popular assumptions about this sport as scary: very violent, utterly 'macho' and not a little dehumanising. Equally, it is sometimes seen as a sort of heroic style for black men – the world of Muhammad Ali and the like. It is a pretty rough and macho sport, but one which gives daily meaning to a lot of men. This is a study of sport. But it is much more: it looks at the way the body works in sport as a means of transcending the mundane; it is a study of personal transformation in the black American ghetto.

Sport in the media

We live in a media world. Chapter 22 examines this in more detail. For the time being, you may like to consider the ways in which sport is ubiquitous in the media. Not only do sports have their own media forms (think of sports magazines, TV sports stations and sports programmes), but sport is also to be found in film, literature and on the internet.

Some interesting films on sport would include *Chariots of Fire* (competition and the male gazes), Scorseses's *Raging Bull* and Stallone's *Rocky* (is masculinity in crisis?) and *Field of Dreams* (with its famous line: 'If you build it, he will come'). *Rollerball* (1975) captures a (then) futuristic aggressive scenario. *Million Dollar Baby* (2004) confronts women's boxing and was very controversial in its death scene. *Hoop Dreams* (1994) is the classic documentary on two African-American college basketball players struggling to go professional.

Media also produce sports stars and celebrities. Consider the social significance of 'Beckham'. In the USA, consider 'the black bodies' of Michael Jordan and Mike Tyson.

Sport is also now to be found everywhere in cyberspace. On the web, you can look up any sport. Try extreme sports/alternative sports: for example, the world of boarders (of surf, on skate, on snow, in the sky), as well as bungy jumping, barefoot snow skiing, parachute skiing and much more.

In all of this, think of the ways in which sport permeates our everyday social worlds and consider the ways in which it shapes our social lives.

How does all this differ from what you read in the newspaper: why is it sociology? First, the data you gather need to be analysed as objectively as you can. Chapter 3 discusses some of the tools for appraising validity, reliability and representatives – as well as contrasting accounts of what social science is: positivistic, realist and interpretive. You might now like to consider the above examples and their links to all this.

2 Explaining sport: theory and sport

But all these 'little' or specific descriptions we have suggested above will probably be just that: little descriptions. These are very valuable, but we need a way to relate these to wider social understanding. Just how do they work in society and, more ambitiously, why do they take the forms that they do?

In Chapter 1 we saw the importance of structure and action; in Chapter 2 various positions – functionalist, conflict, interactionist, postmodern – were outlined. Can such theories be used to make sense of sport?

Functionalism. Put simply, we can see a traditional approach through the functionalist who explains sport as meeting certain 'needs', be they manifest or latent (see p. 38 for this distinction), as performing certain functions in making the society work and hold together. Among the key functions that sport could perform to make societies function or work well are:

* As an outlet for biologically active and healthy bodies.
* As a symbolic marker of certain groups. Thus sports mark out men from women, and various social classes: polo for the posh and wrestling for the lumpen.
* As a programmed channel for conflicts, competitions and social tensions. Sport manages to regulate conflicts which otherwise might erupt more violently in society.
* As a social ritual, or 'spectacle'. It gathers large numbers of people to celebrate and sometimes to attempt to reach a kind of transcendence of the banality of the daily round of work, sleep and everyday life.

We know that major sporting events capture enormous audiences and become global events (see below). It could be that they often condense major symbolic matters – of nationalism, gender, race.

Action/Interaction. Put simply, we look here at how people do things together and the meanings this generates. Here the emphasis becomes that of looking at specific situations and contexts. We look at the social worlds of sports – players, teams, managers, businesses, organisations, media professionals, spectators, families, communities – and inspect the ways in which 'action' builds these worlds and meaning is constructed. The work of Loïc Wacquant on boxers would be a very good example of such research. Our interest would mainly be with 'sport scenes' or subcultures (and we discuss them more in Chapter 5).

Sociologists have looked at the social worlds (ethnographies) of athletes, wrestlers, horse racing, pool hustlers, hockey players, baseball players, rugby players, racing cyclists, rock climbers, surfers, soccer hooligans, body builders, tennis clubs and 'little league baseball' teams – among many others. Here the explanation of sport is much less general than the functionalist. By looking closely at how people do their body movements and play out their sense of self and being in sports, we come to see the interaction of people as generating various meanings. Contexts can be used to explain sports. Thus sport can come to be seen as a celebration, as a means of self-control, as work, as play, as a mechanism of maintaining masculinity – or femininity – as sexuality, as a way of ordering time, as a means of generating thrills, as violence, as a transcendence of the everyday, as a means of escapism from the everyday, as a meaning for life! Consider for example:

* What are the social meanings of 'Formula 1' racing? It seems to be thrill-seeking, death-defying (or not: and that is the risk), very speedy, and the global rich flock to it at romantic places such as the Italian and Monaco Grand Prix. To top it all, they spray champagne over each other. It can bring 'glittering prizes' and the 'glamorous life'.
* In contrast, what meanings do 'runners' bring to their runs? Greg Smith (2003) shows how runners have to build up a different sense of time. When they train, when they plan their careers, and when they actually do their 'body work' of running, they build very different senses of time and what it means to them.
* For some, sport can mean narcissism and hyper-masculinity. Alan M. Klein looks at bodybuilding among men and a distinctive culture of masculinity. See his *Little Big Men: Bodybuilding subculture and gender construction* (1993).

Conflict. Other sociologists see sport as much more obviously linked to social conflicts. One approach here would be to see sport as a market involving consumerism, exploitation and the 'opium of the masses' (terms discussed in Chapters 15 and 19). Watching sport may well be a spectator sport, but it is also a consumer sport – a commodity sold for large sums of money. Commodification, as we have seen in the box on music in Chapter 2 (p. 54), involves turning things into objects for sale. There is the commodification of players and teams – sold for huge sums of money. There is the commodification of merchandise – shirts, balls, games, etc. And there is the commodification by media – the selling of sports in advertising and communication. For example, the sporting goods business is now huge and growing. In 2003, the US retail sales of sporting goods reached $45.8 billion.

Social divisions in sport

In Part Three, we outline the main areas of social division and sport could be examined for its role in social inequalities. Here, we can see that sport is organised through class, gender, age, race, sexuality, disability and nation. There is much that could be said on all this and much research has been conducted in the growing field of the 'sociology of sport'. For the time being, just consider the ways in which sports can establish hierarchy and authority structures within themselves and the ways they reproduce the wider patterns of social divisions.

Thus, sports have been heavily organised by class and gender. Football belongs (at least initially) to working-class men, and it has a long history of being linked to 'macho' violence and 'hooliganism' (well studied by sociologists). More recently, it has become increasingly middle class, and there are now many women's teams. This reflects some of the wider shifts in class and gender that we will discuss in Chapters 10–13. Boxing and wrestling seem to have a concentration in the lower class. We can also see a strong ethnicity issue: many sports stars – especially in the USA – are 'black'. Some have argued that this concentration of black Americans has provided a success route for young people who might not otherwise have opportunities for success. Other groups too have new voices to be heard in sporting arenas: gays now have their own 'Gay Olympics', as do disabled people.

The 'Premiership' makes big money: some €2 billion during the 2008–9 season. It has regulated football hooligans, attracted funding at home, and expanded overseas. It lags behind major US leagues like the National Basketball Association (NBA) and the National Football League (NFL) (which made more than $6 billion in the same period). Television is crucial: events like the World Cup in South Africa in 2010 fetch deals in their billions for domestic TV rights. In 2007, the then new superstar Lewis Hamilton earned around £50 million a year (*Telegraph*: 17/06/07: 21). Young gifted and black, he was an advertiser's dream. The box provides details of the top-earning 20 football players in 2009.

The transformation of sport

People make 'sports' throughout history, and 'sport', in turn, then makes them. Without going back too far in time, some see Renaissance Italy and France as the founding eras of what we could call 'modern sport' (as opposed to more traditional forms?); others see it as appearing with the growth of the modern world in eighteenth-century England. In any event, sport came to be seen as both a potentially civilising and a rationalising form of social life. It takes the

Highest-paid footballers in the world, 2009

1   Cristiano Ronaldo (Real Madrid, £11.3 million)
2   Zlatan Ibrahimovic (Barcelona, £10.4 million)
3   Lionel Messi (Barcelona, £9.1 million)
4   Samuel Eto'o (Internazionale, £9.1 million)
5   Kaka (Real Madrid, £8.7 million)
6   Emmanuel Adebayor (Manchester City, £7.4 million)
7   Karim Benzema (Real Madrid, £7.4 million)
8   Carlos Tevez (Manchester City, £7 million)
9   John Terry (Chelsea, £6.5 million)
10 Frank Lampard (Chelsea, £6.5 million)
11 Thierry Henry (Barcelona, £6.5 million)
12 Xavi (Barcelona, £6.5 million)
13 Ronaldinho (AC Milan, £6.5 million)
14 Steven Gerrard (Liverpool, £6.5 million)
15 Daniel Alves (Barcelona, £6.1 million)
16 Michael Ballack (Chelsea, £5.6 million)
17 Raul (Real Madrid, £5.6 million)
18 Rio Ferdinand (Manchester United, £5.6 million)
19 Kolo Toure (Manchester City, £5.6 million)
20 Wayne Rooney (Manchester United, £5.2 million)

Source: www.caughtoffside.com/2010/02/17/50-highest-paid-footballers-in-the-world-be-prepared-to-be-slightly-surprised.

more chaotic, violent and competitive worlds of the past (?) and 'civilises it' (see the box on Elias in Chapter 7, p. 233). With the rise of capitalism we see the growth of 'sports markets' (Guttmann and Allen, 'The development of modern sports', in Jay Oakley and Eric Dunning, *Handbook of Sports Studies*, London: Sage, 2000, 248–59). To take the history of football, David Goldblatt has shown how it moves from a chaotic folk ritual to a sector of the global entertainment industry.

The transformations of modern sport can be seen through six key terms (some of which we have already encountered and some of which will be discussed later):

• *Commercialisation* – more and more, sports are subject to market forces and develop large industries around them.

• *Globalisation* – sport is no longer bounded by one country (see below).

• *Professionalisation* – sports are not just played. Now they have 'elite groups' – the professional organisations which mark both standards (and boundaries) of skill. Sports are socially controlled and regulated.

• *Consumption* – more and more people, often across the world, spend large sums of money on sports and all its merchandise. Sport is objectified; sports people become consumers.

• *Spectacularisation* – more and more watch the sports across the globe. Sport becomes increasingly audience centred, and sport becomes a 'mediated simulacrum' (see p. 780 for the meaning of this term).

- *Postmodernisation* – sports worlds split into more and more different groups. There is now, for example, a large world of queer sport (including the Gay Olympics) and of disability sport (including the Paralympics and the Special Olympics). Sports themselves also become more 'X-treme' (the X Games: some 'respectable' – deep sea diving, ocean yacht racing, hot balloons; others less so – mud wrestling, etc.). Sport also becomes increasingly a media event.

The globalisation of sport

Almost anywhere on earth, one of the quickest ways to enter a particular society or culture is to look at its world of sports. Initially we can think of sport as a very local thing: your local college football team, your local gym. Yet whereas, in the past, most sports were local – a few friends kicking a ball about, the rivalry between schools – they have increasingly become embedded in worldwide dimensions. Sport has become part of the globalisation process. We can now see sports as matters of global finance, international superstars, teams and supporters who travel the world, the development of international mass media coverage, the creation of an array of new logos known worldwide, advertising and commercial products. Think of the Olympics, the World Cup, Wimbledon, European football: sport is now part of the world economy, world media, world travel. The globalisation of sport has meant that sport is becoming truly international – and a big business. It has meant:

- *The commodification of sport.* Sport now means an aggressive merchandising of products, where multinationals sell replica team shirts, training shoes, wall posters, etc. In the USA alone, the retail sales of sporting goods reached $45.8 billion in 2003. Globalisation also leads to branding: company logos go on sports shirts, their adverts dominate sports fields, their sponsorship hooks them into the media, their shops and outlets are closely connected to the various games. Companies with a major impact on global sport include Murdoch's empire (Fox, Sky, Star), Nike, Time Warner, Kirch Group, Disney, Coca-Cola, ISL and NBC.

- *The creation of sports cities.* Cities bid for various world events not just because of the sporting activity but because of the ways in which this can rejuvenate their cities (in the 1984 Olympic Games based at Los Angeles,

a profit of $215 million was made for the city; in 2006, the UK won a bid for the 2012 Olympic Games, which it is hoped will regenerate much of East London).

- *Global superstars and global identities.* Sporting events are now part of the global media world – sporting celebrities play a world role. From Tiger Woods and Michael Jordan (the sale of Nike shoes bearing his name totalled some $1.4 billion) to David Beckham, sports stars become worldwide superheroes and can command enormous salaries – teams and regions foster an international rivalry. David Beckham, for example, is much more than a football player: he is a brand. In 2003, David Beckham was bought by Real Madrid, for a transfer payment of £25 million to his original club (Manchester United, the richest soccer club in the world) in addition to the £4.2 million it paid Beckham. Real Madrid now starts to rival Man U as a brand! In 2006, he was bought as a 'coach' in Los Angeles to promote football – an alleged $250 million for a five-year contract. Vodafone and Pepsi used to pay him at least £2 million a year, and his wider impact is to increase the sale of some commodities to over £1 billion (see Cashmore, 2002).

And in addition, consider the ways in which:

- Global supporters become international travellers and sports stars become sporting migrants.

- International scandals from bribery to drug taking become commonplace.

- Sports violence becomes a feature of some sports – as teams become 'national icons' and their winning or losing becomes a kind of neo-nationalism. Other groups – women, the disabled, gays – come to hold their own international games.

Sport: going further

Richard Giulianotti and Roland Robertson, *Globalization and Football* (2009)

Tim Delaney and Tim Madigon, *The Sociology of Sports* (2009)

D. Goldblatt, *The Ball is Round: A Global History of Football* (2006)

Jay Coakley and Eric Dunning, *Handbook of Sport Studies* (2002)

Loïc Wacquant, *Body and Soul: Notes of an Apprentice Boxer* (2007)

Ellis Cashmore, *Beckham* (2002)

PART 2

THE FOUNDATIONS OF SOCIETY

FROM MACRO TO MICRO

CHAPTER 4
SOCIETIES

同 歡 共 樂

IN JUNE 2008, THERE WAS MUCH EXCITEMENT IN THE PRESS ABOUT THE SIGHTING OF AN 'UNKNOWN AND UNEXPLORED' AMAZON BASIN TRIBE. A plane flying over the Brazilian state of Acre (on the borders of Peru), saw dozens of people dotted around a clearing with two communal huts. When they returned later the same day, the impact of the earlier flight was clear. Most of the women and children had fled into the forest. Only three near-naked figures were now visible in the forest clearing – and they were aiming their bows at the sky. A third figure appeared to be a woman. This remarkable photograph has been seen as evidence of the existence of one of the world's last uncontacted tribes.

'We did the overflight to show their houses, to show they are there, to show they exist,' said José Carlos dos Reis Meirelles Junior, an expert on the remote tribal people who live beyond the boundaries of the modern world. 'This is very important because there are some who doubt their existence.'

Look at the photograph on page 106 (over). With planes flying over, it clearly looks as if the tribe sensed that the outside world brought danger.

And there is a long history of earlier societies and tribes being destroyed by 'newcomers' who plunder resources, bring aggression, and spread disease. There was every reason to fear these strangers. Across the borders of Peru, and across the world, similar tribes are under threat.

The Akuntsu tribe in neighbouring Rondônia is an example and tells a very sad story. Here a tiny tribe is now reduced to just five individuals who live in two small community houses made of straw. They hunt, cultivate small gardens and paint their bodies for ceremonies. They have their own language and culture. But soon they will be extinct.

And we will have lost another unique and distinct society.

 You can read and see more about all this, and watch a view of the Akuntsu through the website for Survival International: www.survivalinternational.org/tribes/akuntsu. This website is a useful guide to the smaller and neglected societies of the world.

There is no such thing as society.

Margaret Thatcher, UK Conservative prime minister (1979–90)

We are taking to help make the Big Society a reality.

David Cameron, UK Conservative prime minister (2010–)

(Left) *Happy Together As One*, Chinese School (1963)

In this chapter, we ask:
- What are the main different types of society throughout history?
- How can we explain the rise of modern industrial societies?
- What are the broad shapes of contemporary world societies?

Mao Zedong (1893–1976) (Mao Tse Tung) is one of the most important but controversial political figures of the twentieth century. In 1949, he established the People's Republic of China and became its first leader, spearheading the Cultural Revolution to rid China of old ways of thinking and unseat any 'ruling class', putting art and literature into the hands of the ordinary people: a 'perpetual revolution' that served the interests of the majority, not a tiny elite. Chinese art of this period advanced the principle that art must serve the workers and peasants, portraying the heroism of the Communists. The masses needed educating with true descriptions of valiant deeds and model conduct.

Source: Happy Together as One, August 1963 (colour litho), Chinese School (20th Century)/ Private Collection/© The Chambers Gallery/ London/The Bridgeman Art Library.

See: Chinese Art Portal: http://www. artzinechina.com/display.php?a=746

Chiu, M *Art and China's Revolution* 2008 Princeton University Press

 Look at this painting. What does it suggest to you about the nature of art under Chinese communist rule?

In 2010, there were around 200 major societies in the world (192 of them in the United Nations). But once you start to count small groups, numbers grow – for example, there are probably around 7,000 different languages in the world, which usually indicate different social groupings. Parts of the world – such as the Amazonian basin and the New Guinea highlands – have still not been fully explored. And, as we saw in the opening story, some new languages and societies are still being discovered.

Chapter 1 explained that sociology was born out of a concern with the decline of these traditional societies and the rapidly changing character of the newly arriving modern, industrial world: with where we have come from and where we are heading. New technologies, the advance of capitalism, the growth of cities and the rise of democratic politics all ushered in this new world. This chapter both reaches back into the different kinds of society that existed before the arrival of the modern world and looks forward into the changing shape of the contemporary world. Along the way, it offers some major reasons for the changes that have happened and that are even now accelerating. The central concept of **society** refers to *people who interact in a defined space and share culture*. In this sense, both Europe as a whole and specific countries such as Norway and England may be seen as societies.

A society under threat

Look at the opening story to this chapter. This is the photo taken from a plane of the trip described in the story. It is a photo that has captured the public's imagination. Several near-naked tribesmen can be seen firing arrows at the plane – thinking they are under threat. This remarkable photograph has been seen as evidence of the existence of one of the world's last uncontacted tribes. In Brazil today there are around 650,000 Indians in Brazil in over 200 tribes, who live scattered across the country speaking a huge number of languages, many of which are fast becoming extinct. Some of these tribes number thousands – the Guarani and Yanomami. But hidden deep in the Amazon rainforest, there may be an estimated 40 groups of truly isolated indigenous people. Centuries of exposure to disease, violence and dispossession has wiped out the vast majority.

The discovery of new tribes is a tricky business: the skill is to locate such tribes but without disturbing their ways of life and ensuring their survival

See: Survival International http://www.survivalinternational.org/.

Source: Reuters/Funai-Frente de Proteção Etno-Ambiental Envira/Handout (Brazil).

We shall start by describing the changing character of human society over the last 10,000–12,000 years. This is a very difficult task. The remainder of the chapter then analyses some of the main patterns of different kinds of society, and presents classic visions of society developed by three of sociology's founders, already introduced in earlier chapters. Karl Marx understood human history as a long and complex process of economic conflict. His concern was with the ways in which the economy generates *conflicts and inequalities* around the production of material goods in order to live (to eat and have shelter, for instance), and how these conflicts provided the motor force for change. Max Weber recognised the importance of productive forces as well, but he sought to demonstrate the power of *human ideas* (especially those found in religions) to animate society. Weber believed that rational thinking underlies modern society and promotes change. Finally, Emile Durkheim investigated patterns of *social solidarity*, noting that the bonds uniting traditional societies are strikingly different from those uniting their modern counterparts. All of them were concerned with the momentous changes taking place in European societies in their times, and with how the future would develop. At the end of the chapter we will turn to just what the 200 or so societies in the world today look like, and how they may be characterised. But we will be returning to much of this later in the book.

Changing patterns of society

Sociologists who study the past (working with archaeologists and anthropologists) have learned quite a bit about our human heritage. Gerhard Lenski and Jean Lenski have chronicled the great differences among societies that have flourished and declined throughout human history. Just as important, the work of these researchers helps us better understand how we live today. The Lenskis call the focus of their research **sociocultural evolution**, *the process of change that results from a society's gaining new information, particularly technology* (Nolan and Lenski, 2010). Rather like a biologist examining how a living species evolves over millennia, a sociologist employing this approach observes how societies change over centuries as they gain a greater ability to manipulate their physical environments. It suggests that societies with rudimentary technology can support only a small

number of people, who enjoy few choices about how to live. Technologically complex societies – while not necessarily 'better' in any absolute sense – develop larger populations which are more likely to be characterised by diverse, highly specialised lives.

The greater the amount of technological information a society has in its grasp, the faster the rate at which it changes. Technologically less complex societies, then, change very slowly. By contrast, industrial, high-technology societies can start to change so quickly that people witness dramatic transformations in the span of their lifetimes. Again, consider some familiar elements of contemporary culture that would probably puzzle, delight, but most likely alarm people who lived just a few generations ago: fast food, faxes, mobile phones, computer 'cybersex', artificial hearts, laser surgery, test-tube babies, genetic engineering, computer-based virtual reality, fibre optics, smart bombs, the threat of nuclear holocaust, space shuttles, transsexual surgery, and 'tell-all' talk shows transmitted across the world to all countries! It is indeed a strange modern world we have arrived in – even when compared with the world of the recent past.

As a society extends its technological reach, the effects ripple through the cultural system, generating countless repercussions. When our ancestors first harnessed the power of the wind by using a sail, they set the stage for discovering kites, sailing ships, windmills and, eventually, aircraft. Consider, as more recent examples, the many ways modern life has been changed by atomic energy or the computer. Drawing on the Lenskis' work, we will describe five general types of society distinguished by their technology: hunting and gathering societies; horticultural and pastoral societies; agrarian societies; industrial societies; and post-industrial societies. We could equally well describe societies as distinguished by their political systems, or their kinds of community.

1 Hunting and gathering societies

Hunting and gathering refers to *simple technology for hunting animals and gathering vegetation*. From the emergence of our species until about 12,000 years ago, all humans were hunters and gatherers. Hunting and gathering societies remained common several centuries ago, but today they are in sharp decline as they are more and more ravaged by the advance of industrial societies. Still, estimates suggest there may still be – across some 70 countries – at least 370 million

indigenous peoples worldwide: *peoples with ties to the land, water and wildlife of their ancestral domain.* Many of these have been or still are hunter-gatherers. Today these include the Aka and Pygmies of central Africa, the Bushmen of south-western Africa, the Aborigines and Torres Strait Islanders of Australia, the Maori of New Zealand, the Kaska Indians of north-west Canada, and the Batek and Semai of Malaysia.

Most members of these societies looked continually for game and edible plants. Only in lush areas where food was plentiful would hunters and gatherers have much leisure time. Moreover, foraging for food demands a large amount of land, so hunting and gathering societies comprise small bands of a few dozen people living at some distance from one another. These groups were also nomadic, moving on as they depleted vegetation in one area or in pursuit of migratory animals. Although they periodically returned to favoured sites, they rarely formed permanent settlements.

Hunting and gathering societies are based on kinship. The family obtains and distributes food, protects its members, and teaches necessary skills to children. Most activities are common to everyone and centre on seeking the next meal; some specialisation, however, corresponds to age and sex. The very young and the very old contribute only what they can, while healthy adults secure most of the food. The gathering of vegetation – the most reliable food source – is typically the work of women, while men take on the less certain job of hunting. Although the two sexes have somewhat different responsibilities, then, most hunters and gatherers probably accorded men and women comparable social importance (Leacock, 1978).

Hunting and gathering societies have few formal leaders. Most recognise a shaman, or spiritual leader, who enjoys high prestige but receives no greater material rewards than other members of the society and must help procure food like everyone else. Other individuals who are especially skilful at obtaining food may also have high prestige; overall, however, the social organisation of hunters and gatherers is relatively simple and egalitarian.

Hunting and gathering societies rarely use their weapons – the spear, the bow and arrow, and stone knife – to wage war. Nonetheless, they are often ravaged by the forces of nature. Storms and droughts can easily destroy their food supply, and they stand vulnerable to accident and disease. Such risks encourage cooperation and sharing, a strategy that increases everyone's odds of survival. Even so, many die in childhood, and perhaps half perish before the age of 20 (Brody, 2000; Lenski and Nolan, 2010).

During the twentieth century, technologically complex societies slowly closed in on the remaining hunters and gatherers, reducing their landholdings and depleting game and vegetation. Many of these 'indigenous' peoples, such as the Inuit in Canada and Alaska, are finding their cultures increasingly destroyed by the industrial West. In the first half of the twentieth century, Brazil alone lost some 87 tribes. They live under conditions where their human rights are abused and where they are under constant threat of extinction. Yet at the same time, there are signs that such cultures are also fighting back to protect their own ways of life. There is also now a Charter of Rights of Indigenous Peoples which was drawn up by the United Nations.

 There is a lot of information on the web about indigenous people. You could check out:

Native Web: www.nativeweb.com/resources

Survival International: www.survivalinternational.org

Indigenous People: www.indigenouspeople.net/sidemenu.html

The UN Permananent Forum on Indigenous Issues: www.un.org/esa/socdev/unpfii

Indigenous Peoples: Issues and resources: http://indigenouspeoplesissues.com

2 Horticultural and pastoral societies

Ten to twelve thousand years ago, a new technology began to change many hunting and gathering societies. **Horticulture** is *technology based on using hand tools to cultivate plants.* The most important tools of horticulturists are the hoe to work the soil and the digging stick to punch holes in the ground for seeds. Humans first used these tools in fertile regions of the Middle East and, later, in Latin America and Asia. Cultural diffusion spread knowledge of horticulture throughout most of the world by about 6,000 years ago.

Not all societies were quick to abandon hunting and gathering in favour of horticulture. Hunters and gatherers living amid plentiful vegetation and game probably saw little reason to embrace the new technology. The Yanomami of the Brazilian rainforest illustrate the common practice of combining horticulture with more traditional hunting and gathering. They are one of the last large isolated groups of indigenous peoples in the Americas.

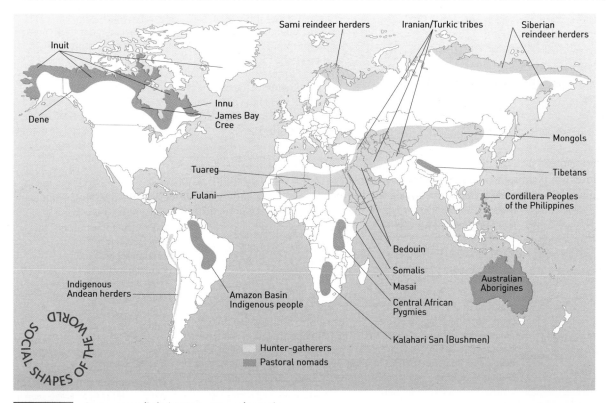

Inuit

Innu
James Bay
Cree

Dene

Sami reindeer herders

Iranian/Turkic tribes

Siberian
reindeer herders

Mongols

Tibetans

Cordillera Peoples
of the Philippines

Tuareg

Fulani

Bedouin

Somalis

Masai

Central African
Pygmies

Australian
Aborigines

Indigenous
Andean herders

Amazon Basin
Indigenous people

Kalahari San (Bushmen)

Hunter-gatherers

Pastoral nomads

SOCIAL SHAPES OF THE WORLD

Map 4.1

Some nomadic/migratory groups by region

See also: genographic.nationalgeographic.com.

Source: Adapted from A. M. Khazanov, *Nomads and the Outside World*. Cambridge: Cambridge University Press, 1984: 185.

Then, too, people in particularly arid regions (such as the Middle East) or mountainous areas (such as in the Alps, where the Iceman lived) found horticulture to be of little value. Such people turned to a different strategy for survival, **pastoralism**, which is *technology based on the domestication of animals*. Still others combined horticulture and pastoralism to produce a variety of foods. Today, many horticultural–pastoral societies thrive in South America, Africa and Asia.

The domestication of plants and animals greatly increased food production, enabling societies to support not dozens but hundreds of people. Pastoralists remained nomadic, leading their herds to fresh grazing lands. Horticulturalists, by contrast, formed settlements, moving on only when they depleted the soil. These settlements, joined by trade, comprised multi-centred societies with overall populations often in the thousands.

Domesticating plants and animals generates a *material surplus* – more resources than are necessary to sustain day-to-day living. A surplus frees some people from the job of securing food, allowing them to create crafts, engage in trade, cut hair, apply tattoos or serve as

priests. In comparison to hunting and gathering societies, then, horticultural and pastoral societies display more specialised and complex social arrangements.

Hunters and gatherers recognise numerous spirits inhabiting the world. Horticulturalists, however, practise ancestor worship and conceive of God as creator. Pastoral societies carry this belief further, viewing God as directly involved in the well-being of the entire world. This view of God ('The Lord is my shepherd', Psalm 23) is widespread among members of contemporary societies because Christianity, Islam and Judaism originated as Middle Eastern, pastoral religions.

Expanding productive technology also intensifies social inequality. As some families produce more food than others, they assume positions of relative power and privilege. Forging alliances with other elite families ensures that social advantages endure over generations, and a formal system of social inequality emerges. Along with social hierarchy, rudimentary government – backed by military force – is formed to shore up the power of elites. However, without the ability to communicate or to travel quickly, a ruler can control

What is 'Chinese society'?

The twenty-first century is tipped to become the Chinese Century. In 2010, China also became the world's second leading economic state (after the USA). Chinese society is one of the oldest and biggest societies in the world. In area, China is as large as the USA. In population it is about 1.3 billion – the largest population in the world (and increasing by about 14 million a year despite its policy of controlling family size). In land area, it is the fourth largest country. The first dynasty – the Xia dynasty – is conventionally thought to have begun in the twenty-first century BCE, and for a long while before the 'West' developed, it seems to have been one of a very few ancient civilisations. Strongly influenced by Confucianism, Taoism and Buddhism, Chinese society was not (and still is not) a religious society as we use the term 'religion' today (see Chapter 19). Confucianism is more of a moral code than a religion. Most people are influenced by these traditions, embedding belief rituals like ancestor worshipping in local communities and economies.

In the twentieth century, communism was the country's creed under Mao Tse Tung (1893–1976). More recently it has opened up markets internally and throughout the world, becoming semi-capitalist and partially 'democratised'. Major economic transformations towards a free market are under way (see Chapters 15 and 26). China, then, is a curious mixture of Confucian, socialist, capitalist and patriarchal societies (all terms that should become increasingly clear as you read this book!). It was once imperial, then republican, communist in the latter part of the twentieth century and now in the twenty-first century a hybrid of many shapes.

Indeed, today it is one of the most prominent societies in the world, predicted by many to become the most important country of the twenty-first century – as the USA was for the twentieth, and the UK was in the nineteenth (see Chapter 26, p. 902 for a discussion of this).

So what is Chinese society? This box shows some of its elements for you to consider and discuss.

China as diverse

If it is defined by geography, we can soon see it as a society of vast diversity. We could at least speak of the 'five Chinas' (see Map 4.2).

The margins: mountainous; least populated and developed. The vast north of China is relatively lightly populated, partly because of inhospitable terrain and a climate that makes only around 10% of the area possible to cultivate.

Xinjiang: enclosed by mountain ranges to the north, south and west. Much of the province is barren.

Tibet: China's invasion of Tibet in 1950 and its bloody crackdown of an anti-government uprising in 1959 make Tibet one of China's most controversial regions.

The hinterland: dense population.

Coastal strip: flood plains and low land with the densest populations and the most economic activity. From China's largest city of Shanghai down to its tropical tourist island of Hainan, the coastal strip has been transformed by the pursuit of wealth.

The rust belt: was the industrial centre but there is now much unemployment.

The 'state' of China

How can such a huge space be governed? In general, for much of its 12,000-year history, China has had a centralised imperial monarchy with between 17 and 22 'dynasties' between 1766 BCE and 1911 CE – from the Shang dynasty in 1766 BCE to the Qing dynasty (which ended in 1911). The monarchy goes back through 4,000 years of history with 22 dynasties united by the 'First Emperor' of the Qin (Ch'in) in Shi Huangdi (Shih Huang-ti) (221–206 BCE) and consolidated by the Han dynasty (206 BCE to CE 220). The Chinese Empire may be seen to have lasted from 221 BCE to 1911–12 CE, although this was punctuated by long periods when a central government was lacking (Braudel, 1963). But with such a large land mass, it was also a very decentralised state. China has had a strongly agrarian society and has been administered for the last 2,000 years by a complex legal framework and large-scale bureaucracies. Warring and conflict were common.

Most of the twentieth century witnessed the rise of 'Marxist' ideas and the growth of communism. Although this seems like a radical change, it does need to be seen in the context of a very long history. In a sense, it is a simple blip in the twentieth century that certainly worked to modernise the country – albeit at high human cost.

Chinese culture: 'Chineseness'

The belief system of China today is a curious mixture of three 'high traditions': Confucianism, Taoism and Buddhism. Ancestor worship is often part of this. But beliefs are ritualised in local forms.

Confucianism was closely linked with the teaching of the educated classes and aimed to explain the world, respecting its past and rejecting popular primitive beliefs and superstitions. It was constructed as a set of cosmological and ethical doctrines intended to serve the interests of the state, and for almost 2,000 years it functioned as the moral orthodoxy of the Imperial Order. As we will see in Chapter 19, it was originated by Confucius (Kong Fuzi) around 550 BCE. The *Yijing* (Book of Changes, fourth century BCE)

WORLD WATCH

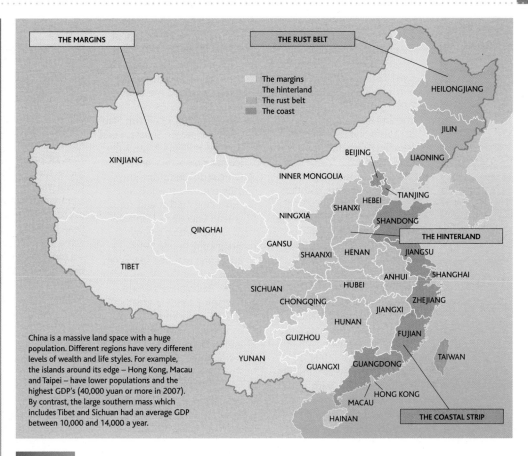

THE MARGINS

THE RUST BELT

The margins
The hinterland
The rust belt
The coast

HEILONGJIANG

JILIN

XINJIANG

BEIJING

LIAONING

INNER MONGOLIA

TIANJING

HEBEI

SHANXI

NINGXIA

SHANDONG

QINGHAI

THE HINTERLAND

GANSU

SHAANXI

HENAN

JIANGSU

TIBET

ANHUI

SHANGHAI

SICHUAN

HUBEI

ZHEJIANG

CHONGQING

JIANGXI

HUNAN

FUJIAN

GUIZHOU

YUNAN

GUANGXI

GUANGDONG

TAIWAN

HONG KONG

MACAU

HAINAN

THE COASTAL STRIP

China is a massive land space with a huge population. Different regions have very different levels of wealth and life styles. For example, the islands around its edge – Hong Kong, Macau and Taipei – have lower populations and the highest GDP's (40,000 yuan or more in 2007). By contrast, the large southern mass which includes Tibet and Sichuan had an average GDP between 10,000 and 14,000 a year.

Map 4.2   The Five Chinas

highlights the complementary aspects of the universe, which are in perpetual mutual opposition (day and night, cold and heat, love and hatred, anger and joy): 'One yin and one yang make the whole, Tao'. It integrates opposites via yin (the dark side, earth) and yang (the light side, heaven). It suggests an ethic in which the powerful gain moral serenity and inculcate respect and humility in the masses, and it functioned well to maintain hierarchy.

Taoism (Laozi, from Lao-Tse, 'the Master') was more mystical and recommended the many ways for a long life (through breathing, dieting and alchemy). Confucianism stressed tradition and harmony, whereas Taoism stressed individual freedom and rebellion.

Buddhism arose in India in the sixth and fifth centuries BCE and entered China around the second century BCE, causing conflicts and schisms with the more established Confucianism and Taoism.

Timeline of China

Early days

- 18–12th centuries BCE: transition from a tribal to a feudal way of life
- 1766–1122 BCE: the first major dynasty: the Shang dynasty
- 1279–1368: Genghis Khan establishes the Mongol Yuan dynasty
- 4th century BCE: Kung Fu-Tzu Confucius (551–479 BCE). The I Ching Book. The Tao Te Ching: well-being, harmony and virtue
- 136 BCE: these ideas become central to the Chinese state

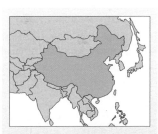

COUNTRY FACT FILE

CHINA

Population	1,338.6 million
Per capita GDP	$2,430
Life expectancy	Male: 71.3
	Female: 74.8
Adult literacy	93.3%
Key languages	Standard Chinese or Mandarin
Key religions	Daoist (Taoist), Buddhist
	Note: officially atheist
Key city	Beijing
Human development index	0.663 (89th, 2010)

WORLD WATCH

Before the twentieth century
- 221: Unification: Qin adopted title of First Emperor
- Great Wall constructed to repel 'barbarians' from the north (4,000 miles long and 2,000 years old)
- 2nd and 3rd centuries: spread of Taoism and neo-Taoism (conflicts with Buddhism and Confucianism)
- 1127–1279: 'second golden age' (printing press, compass invented)
- 1644–1911: The Qing (Ch'ing) Manchu dynasty
- 1839–60: Opium Wars with French and English

The twentieth century
- Chinese Revolution (1911): overthrow of Qing Manchu dynasty by nationalists and creation of republic
- The Long March (1934–5): conflict between nationalists and communists, with communists moving to north-west China under Mao Zedong (Mao Tse-tung)

- 1949: the People's Republic of China proclaimed; capital at Beijing (Peking)
- 1950s–1960s: the Great Leap Forward (established rural communes) and the Cultural Revolution
- 1976: Death of 'Chairman Mao'
- 1989: Tiananmen Square; world outrage at killing of student-led pro-democracy protesters. Official deaths: 200.
- 1990s: moves towards an expanding market and greater liberalism. Handover of former British colony Hong Kong in July 1997
- 2003: first manned spacecraft launched
- 2008: Beijing hosts World Olympic Games in great style
- 2010: Google ends its compliance with China's internet regulations and restrictions.

For a more detailed timeline and updates: search BBC China timeline at news.bbc.co.uk/1/hi/world/asia-pacific/1288392.stm

Going further

See Norman Stockman, *Understanding Chinese Society* (2000) and Robert E. Gamer, *Understanding Contemporary China* (3rd edn, 2008).

Watch the Oscar-winning film by Bernardo Bertolucci, *The Last Emperor* (1987), which shows the transformation of China from imperialism to communism through the life of the last absolute monarch. Read Jung Chang's *Wild Swans: Three Daughters of China* (1993) – a modern classic which tells the story of life in China through three generations of women. Philip Short's *Mao: A Life* (1999) is a human account of one of the twentieth century's major tyrants.

For more details see:
http://news.bbc.co.uk/1/hi/world/asia-pacific/2188605.stm
http://www.scotland.gov.uk/Topics/Government/International-Relations/china/Regional-Links (an interactive map of regions produced in Scotland!).

---

only a limited number of people, so empire building proceeds on a small scale.

The domestication of plants and animals surely made simpler societies more productive. But advancing technology is never entirely beneficial. Compared to hunters and gatherers, horticulturists and pastoralists display more social inequality and, in many cases, engage in slavery, protracted warfare and even cannibalism.

3 Agrarian societies

About 5,000 years ago – at about the time the Iceman roamed the earth – another technological revolution was under way in the Middle East that would eventually transform most of the world. This was the discovery of **agriculture**, *the technology of large-scale farming using ploughs harnessed to animals or more powerful sources of energy*. The social significance of the animal-drawn plough, along with other technological innovations of the period – including irrigation, the wheel, writing, numbers and the expanding use of metals – clearly suggests the arrival of a new kind of society.

Farmers with animal-drawn ploughs cultivated fields vastly larger than the garden-sized plots worked by horticulturists. Ploughs have the additional advantage of turning, and thereby aerating, the soil to increase fertility. Such technology encouraged agrarian societies to farm the same land for decades, which in turn led to humanity's first permanent settlements. Large food surpluses, transported on animal-powered wagons, allowed agrarian societies to expand to an unprecedented land area and population. As an extreme case, the Roman Empire at its height (about 100 CE) boasted a population of 70 million spread over some 2 million square miles (Lenski and Nolan, 2010).

As always, increasing production meant greater specialisation. Tasks once performed by everyone, such as clearing land and securing food, became distinct occupations. Specialisation made the early barter system obsolete and prompted the invention of money as a common standard of exchange. The appearance of money facilitated trade, sparking the growth of cities as economic centres with populations soaring into the millions.

Agrarian societies exhibit dramatic social inequality. In many cases, peasants or slaves constitute a significant

Of Egypt's 130 pyramids, the Great Pyramids at Giza are the largest. Each of the three major structures stands more than 40 storeys high and is composed of about 3 million massive stone blocks. Some 4,500 years ago, tens of thousands of people laboured to construct these pyramids so that one man, the pharaoh, might have a god-like monument for his tomb. Clearly social inequality in this agrarian society was extreme

Source: Getty Photodisk.

share of the population and labour for elites. Freed from manual work, elites can then devote their time to the study of philosophy, art and literature.

Among hunters and gatherers, and also among horticulturists, women are the primary providers of food. The development of agriculture, however, appears to have propelled men into a position of social dominance.

Religion reinforces the power of agricultural elites. Religious doctrine typically propounds the idea that people are morally obligated to perform whatever tasks correspond to their place in the social order. Many of the 'wonders of the ancient world', such as the Great Wall of China and the Great Pyramids of Egypt, were possible because emperors and pharaohs wielded virtually absolute power to mobilise their people to endure a lifetime of labour without pay.

In agrarian societies, then, elites gain unparalleled power. To maintain control of large empires, leaders require the services of a wide range of administrators. Consequently, along with the growing economy, the political system becomes established as a distinct sphere of life.

Agrarian societies have greater specialisation and more social inequality. And, compared to horticultural and pastoral societies, agrarian societies differ more from one another because advancing technology can increase human control over the natural world.

4 Industrial societies

Industrialism is *technology that powers sophisticated machinery with advanced sources of energy*. Until the industrial era, the major source of energy was the muscle power of humans and other animals. At the dawning of the *Industrial Revolution*, about 1750, mills and factories relied on flowing water and later steam to power ever-larger and more efficient machinery.

Once this technology was at hand, societies began to change faster, as shown in Figure 4.1. Industrial

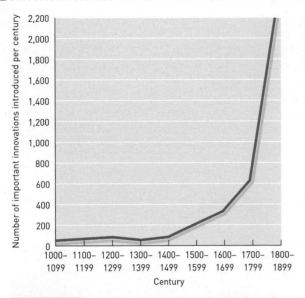

Figure 4.1 The increasing number of technological innovations

This figure illustrates the number of technological innovations in western Europe after the beginning of the Industrial Revolution in the mid-eighteenth century. Technological innovation occurs at an accelerating rate because each innovation spins off existing cultural elements to produce many further innovations.

Source: Adapted from Lenski and Nolan (2006) p. 62, Fig. 3.1.

societies transformed themselves more in a century than they had in thousands of years before. As explained in Chapter 1, this stunning change stimulated the birth of sociology itself. During the nineteenth century, railways and steamships revolutionised transportation, and steel-framed skyscrapers recast the urban landscape, dwarfing the cathedrals that symbolised an earlier age.

As the twentieth century opened, the internal combustion engine further reshaped Western societies, and electricity was fast becoming the basis for countless 'modern conveniences'. Electronic communication, including the telephone, radio and television, was mass-producing cultural patterns and gradually making a large world seem smaller and smaller. More recently, transportation technology has given humanity the capacity to fly faster than sound and even to break the bonds of earth. Nuclear power has also changed the world for ever. And, during the last generation, computers have ushered in the *Information Revolution*, dramatically increasing humanity's capacity to process words and numbers.

Work, too, has changed. In agrarian societies, most men and women work in the home and on the land.

Industrialisation, however, creates factories near centralised machinery and energy sources. Lost in the process are close working relationships and strong kinship ties, as well as many of the traditional values, beliefs and customs that guide agrarian life.

Industrialism engenders societies of unparalleled prosperity. Although health in the industrial cities of Europe and North America was initially poor, a rising standard of living and advancing health-related technology gradually brought infectious diseases under control. Consequently, life expectancy increased, fuelling rapid population growth. Industrialisation also draws people from the countryside to the cities where the factories are built. So, while roughly one in ten members of agrarian societies lives in cities, three out of four people in industrial societies are urbanites.

Occupational specialisation, which expanded over the long course of sociocultural evolution, has become more pronounced than ever. Industrial people often size up one another in terms of their jobs, rather than according to their kinship ties as agrarian people do. Rapid change and movement from place to place also generate anonymity and cultural diversity, sparking the formation of numerous subcultures and countercultures, as described in Chapter 5.

Industrial technology recasts the family, too, diminishing its traditional significance as the centre of social life. No longer does the family serve as the primary setting for economic production, learning and religious worship. And, as Chapter 18 explains in detail, technological change also underlies the trend away from so-called traditional families to greater numbers of single people, divorced people, single-parent families, lesbian and gay couples and stepfamilies.

Early industrialisation concentrated the benefits of advancing technology on a small segment of the population, with the majority living in poverty. In time, however, the material benefits of industrial productivity spread more widely. Poverty remains a serious problem in industrial societies, but compared to the situation a century ago, the standard of living has risen fivefold, and economic, social and political inequality has declined. Some social levelling, detailed in Chapter 8, occurs because industrial societies demand a literate and skilled labour force. While most people in agrarian societies are illiterate, industrial societies provide state-funded schooling and confer numerous political rights on virtually everyone. Industrialisation, in fact, intensifies demands for political participation, as seen recently in South Korea, Taiwan, the People's Republic of China, the former Soviet Union, and the societies of eastern Europe.

5 Post-industrial societies

Many industrial societies now appear to be entering yet another phase of technological development. In the early 1970s, Daniel Bell (1976) coined the term **post-industrialism** to refer to *computer-linked technology that supports an information-based economy*. While production in industrial societies focuses on factories and machinery that generate material goods, post-industrial production focuses on computers and other electronic devices that create, process, store and apply information. It is the *information society, the network society, the cyber-society, the postmodern society* (all terms now in common sociological usage). At the individual level, members of industrial societies concentrate on learning mechanical skills; people in post-industrial societies, however, work on honing information-based skills for work involving computers, facsimile machines, satellites and other forms of communication technology.

As this shift in key skills indicates, the emergence of post-industrialism dramatically changes a society's occupational structure. Chapter 15 examines this process in detail, explaining that a post-industrial society utilises less and less of its labour force for industrial production. At the same time, the ranks of clerical workers, managers and other people who process information (in fields ranging from academia and advertising to marketing and public relations) swell rapidly. New skills – often less physical and more mental – are needed to handle fragmented work, multi-tasking and non-linear patterns of work.

The Information Revolution is, of course, most pronounced in industrial, high-income societies, yet the reach of this new technology is so great that it is affecting the entire world. As will be explained further in Chapters 6 and 23, the unprecedented worldwide flow of information originating in rich nations has the predictable effect of tying far-flung societies together and fostering common patterns of global culture. This extends the process of globalisation. And as we saw in Chapter 2, this also brings a society that some speak of as being postmodern (**postmodernism** is *the ways of thinking which stress a plurality of perspectives as opposed to a unified, single core*). It is a world where change is greatly speeding up, where classical boundaries across societies are breaking down, and a new sense of society is in the making.

At the same time, it is important to remember that all five of the different kinds of society we have outlined here still coexist (and there are others not discussed). There are still societies which focus on agriculture, and the industrial world still tends to dominate. But as this book will show over and over again, there is a sense that as the twenty-first century continues to unfold, many changes will accelerate – making the world of 3001 (if it comes to exist!), or even maybe the world of 2050, a quite different order from that we live in now.

Table 4.1 summarises how technology helps shape societies at different stages of sociocultural evolution.

Technological determinism: a cautious word

While different kinds of technology may well create preconditions for different kinds of society, there are four cautions that need to be given.

First, the technology does not *determine* societies. There is no automatic connection between the kinds of technology a society has available and the form of that society. It takes people to decide how to use technologies – and they may use them in very different ways, developing different skills and meanings. In Nazi Germany, for example, the weight of modern technology was used to exterminate millions of people. The technologies of the Incas or the Egyptians were very sophisticated, but also involved systems of domination and slavery. As we will see later, modern information or computer societies need actions from people to use them – and they may be used for good or bad. Technology is neutral: it is people who shape technology.

Second, we must be very wary of saying that these five societies *evolve* from one to the next, as if there is some kind of automatic progress. In fact, in the twenty-first century all of these societies may be said to coexist. Many indigenous peoples may have hunting, pastoral or agrarian societies with highly evolved technologies of their own. It is often a 'Eurocentric' view that wants to see them as prior to or simpler than European culture. We will return to some of these problems when we discuss multiculturalism in the next chapter.

Third, we must recognise *the limits of technology*. While technology remedies many human problems by raising productivity, by eliminating disease and sometimes simply by relieving boredom, it provides no 'quick fix' for deeply rooted social problems. *Poverty* remains the plight of billions of people worldwide (see Chapter 9). Moreover, with the capacity to reshape the world, technology has created new problems that our ancestors could hardly have imagined. Industrial societies provide more personal freedom, often at the

Table 4.1   Kinds of society: a summary

Type of society	Historical period	Productive technology	Population size	Settlement pattern	Social organisation	Examples
Hunting and gathering societies	Only type of society until about 12,000 years ago; still common several centuries ago; the few examples remaining today are threatened with extinction	Primitive weapons	25–40 people	Often nomadic, but can be settled (Brody, 2000)	Family centred; specialisation limited to age and sex; little social inequality	Pygmies of central Africa Bushmen of south-western Africa Aborigines of Australia Semai of Malaysia Kaska Indians of Canada
Horticultural and pastoral societies	From about 12,000 years ago, with decreasing numbers after about 3000 BCE	Horticultural societies use hand tools for cultivating plants; pastoral societies are based on the domestication of animals	Settlements of several hundred people, interconnected through trading ties to form societies of several thousand people	Horticulturalists form relatively small permanent settlements; pastoralists are nomadic	Family centred; religious system begins to develop; moderate specialisation; increased social inequality	Middle Eastern societies about 5000 BCE Various societies today in New Guinea and other Pacific islands Yanomami today in South America
Agrarian societies	From about 5,000 years ago with large but decreasing numbers today	Animal-drawn plough	Millions of people	Cities become common, though they generally contain only a small proportion of the population today	Family loses significance as distinctive religious, political and economic systems emerge; extensive specialisation; increased social inequality	Egypt during construction of the Great Pyramids Medieval Europe Numerous non-industrial societies of the world
Industrial societies	From about 1750 to the present	Advanced sources of energy; mechanised production	Millions of people	Cities contain most of the population	Distinct religious, political, economic, educational and family systems; highly specialised; marked social inequality persists, diminishing somewhat over time	Most societies today in Europe and North America, Australia and Japan generate most of the world's industrial production
Post-industrial societies: Information Network Cyber Postmodern	Emerging in recent decades	Computers that support an information-based economy	Millions of people	Population remains concentrated in cities but now globalisation is the dominant experience	Industrial work downgraded to poorer societies. Information processing and other service work replace industrial production in rich societies. Consumption is key	Industrial societies noted above are now entering post-industrial stage

cost of the sense of community that characterised agrarian life. Further, although the most powerful societies of today's world infrequently engage in all-out warfare, *international conflict* now poses unimaginable horrors. Should nations ever unleash even a fraction of their present stockpiles of nuclear weapons, human society would almost certainly regress to a technologically primitive state if, indeed, we survived at all.

Finally, another stubborn social problem linked to technology involves humanity's relation to the *physical environment*. Each stage in sociocultural evolution has introduced more powerful sources of energy and accelerated our appetite for the earth's resources at a rate even faster than the population is growing. We now face an issue of vital concern – one that is the focus of Chapter 24: can humanity continue to pursue material prosperity without subjecting the planet to damage and strains from which it will never recover?

In some respects, then, technological advances have improved life and brought the world's people closer together within a 'global village'. Yet in technology's wake are daunting problems of establishing peace, ensuring justice, and sustaining a safe environment – problems that technology alone can never solve.

Explaining modern industrial society: the classical sociological accounts

There have been many attempts to explain how the modern industrial world was created. Sociology has its classic interpretations; and we saw at the start of this chapter three key visions of modern industrial society in the work of three of the key 'founders' of modern sociology: Karl Marx, Max Weber and Emile Durkheim. All three of their visions of society try to answer key questions:

- How do societies of the past and present differ from one another?
- How and why does a society change? What forces divide a society? What forces hold it together?
- Are societies getting better or worse?

The theorists profiled in this chapter all probed these questions, but they disagree on the answers. We shall highlight the similarities and differences in their views as we go along.

Karl Marx: capitalism and conflict

The first of our classic visions of society comes from Karl Marx (1818–83). Few observed the industrial transformation of Europe as keenly as he did. Marx spent most of his adult life in London, then the capital of the vast British Empire. He was awed by the productive power of the new factories; not only were European societies producing more goods than ever before, but a global system of commerce was funnelling resources from around the world through British factories at a dizzying rate.

Marx saw that industry's riches were increasingly concentrated in the hands of a few. A walk almost anywhere in London revealed dramatic extremes of splendid affluence and wretched squalor. A handful of aristocrats and industrialists lived in fabulous mansions, well staffed by servants, where they enjoyed luxury and privileges barely imaginable by the majority of their fellow Londoners. Most people laboured long hours for low wages, living in slums or even sleeping in the streets, where many eventually succumbed to poor nutrition and infectious disease.

Throughout his life, Marx wrestled with a basic contradiction: in a society so rich, how could so many be so poor? Just as important, Marx asked, how can this situation be changed? He was motivated by compassion for humanity, and sought to help a society already badly divided forge what he hoped would be a new and just social order.

The key to Marx's thinking is the idea of **social conflict**, *struggle between segments of society over valued resources*. Social conflict can, of course, take many forms: individuals may quarrel, some towns have long-standing rivalries, and nations sometimes go to war. For Marx, however, the most significant form of social conflict involved clashes between social classes that arise from the way a society produces material goods.

Society and production

Living in the nineteenth century, Marx observed the early stage of industrial capitalism in Europe. This economic system, Marx noted, transformed a small part of the population into *capitalists*, people who own factories and other productive enterprises. A capitalist's goal is profit, which results from selling a product for more than it costs to produce. Capitalism transforms most of the population into industrial workers, whom Marx called the **proletariat**, *people who provide labour necessary to operate factories and other productive enterprises.* Workers sell their labour for the wages they need to live. To Marx, an inevitable conflict between capitalists and workers has its roots in the productive process itself. To maximise profits, capitalists must minimise wages, generally their single greatest expense. Workers, however, want wages to be as high as possible. Since profits and wages come from the same pool of funds, ongoing conflict occurs. Marx argued that this conflict would end only when people abandoned the capitalist system.

All societies are composed of **social institutions**, defined as *the major spheres of social life, or society's subsystems, organised to meet basic human needs.* In his analysis of society, Marx contended that one specific institution – the economy – dominates all others when it comes to steering the direction of a society. Drawing on the philosophical doctrine of historical *materialism*, which asserts that how humans produce material goods shapes the rest of society, Marx claimed that all the other major social institutions – the political system, family, religion and education – operated under the influence of a society's economy. Marx argued that the economy is 'the real foundation. . . . The mode of production in material life determines the general character of the social, political, and spiritual processes of life' (1959: 43; orig. 1859).

Marx therefore viewed the economic system as the base or social *infrastructure* (*infra* is Latin for 'below'). Other social institutions, including the family, the political system and religion, which are built on this foundation, form society's *superstructure* (*supra* meaning 'above' in Latin). These institutions extend economic principles into other areas of life, as illustrated in Figure 4.2. In practical terms, social institutions reinforce the domination of the capitalists, by legally protecting their wealth, for example, and by transferring property from one generation to the next through the family.

Generally speaking, members of industrial–capitalist societies do not view their legal or family systems as hotbeds of social conflict. On the contrary, individuals come to see their rights to private property as 'natural'. Many people find it easy to think that affluent people have earned their wealth, while those who are poor or out of work lack skills or motivation. Marx rejected this kind of reasoning as rooted in a capitalist preoccupation with the 'bottom line' that treats human well-being as a market commodity. Poverty and unemployment are not inevitable; as Marx saw it, grand wealth clashing with grinding poverty represents

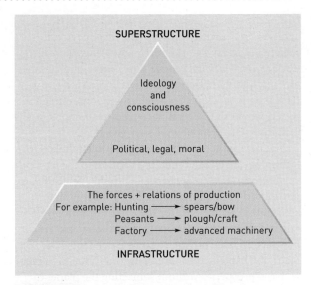

	Karl Marx's model of society
Figure 4.2	This diagram illustrates Marx's materialist view that the process of economic

production underlies and shapes the entire society. Economic production involves both technology (industry, in the case of capitalism) and social relationships (for capitalism, the relationship between the capitalists, who control the process of economic production, and the workers, who are simply a source of labour). Upon this infrastructure, or foundation, are built the major social institutions as well as core cultural values and ideas. Taken together, these additional social elements represent the society's superstructure. Marx maintained that every part of a society operates in concert with the economic system.

merely one set of human possibilities generated by capitalism (Cuff and Payne, 1979).

Marx rejected capitalist common sense, therefore, as **false consciousness**, *explanations of social problems grounded in the shortcomings of individuals rather than the flaws of society.* Marx was saying, in effect, that industrial capitalism itself is responsible for many of the social problems he saw all around him. False consciousness, he maintained, victimises people by obscuring the real cause of their problems.

Conflict in history

Marx studied how societies have changed throughout history, noting that they often evolve gradually, though they sometimes change in rapid, revolutionary fashion. Marx observed that change is partly prompted by technological advance. But he steadfastly held that conflict between economic groups is the major engine of change.

Early hunters and gatherers formed primitive communist societies. The word 'communism' refers to a social system in which the production of food and other material goods is a common effort shared more or less equally by all members of society. Because the resources of nature were available to all hunters and gatherers (rather than privately owned), and because everyone performed similar work (rather than dividing work into highly specialised tasks), there was little possibility for social conflict.

Horticulture, Marx noted, introduced significant social inequality. Among horticultural, pastoral and early agrarian societies – which Marx lumped together as the 'ancient world' – the victors in frequent warfare forced their captives into servitude. A small elite (the 'masters') and their slaves were thus locked in an irreconcilable pattern of social conflict (Zeitlin, 1981).

Agriculture brought still more wealth to members of the elite, fuelling further social conflict. Agrarian serfs, occupying the lowest reaches of European feudalism from about the twelfth to the eighteenth centuries, were only slightly better off than slaves. In Marx's view, the power of both the church and the state defended feudal inequality by defining the existing social order as God's will. Thus, to Marx, feudalism amounted to little more than 'exploitation, veiled by religious and political illusions' (Marx and Engels, 1972: 337; orig. 1848).

Gradually, new productive forces undermined the feudal order. Commerce grew steadily throughout the Middle Ages as trade networks expanded and the power of guilds increased. Merchants and skilled crafts workers in the cities formed a new social category, the *bourgeoisie* (a French word meaning 'of the town'). Profits earned through expanding trade brought the bourgeoisie increasing wealth. After the mid-eighteenth century, with factories at their command, the bourgeoisie became true capitalists with power that soon rivalled that of the ancient, landed nobility. While the nobility regarded this upstart 'commercial' class with disdain, the latter's increasing wealth gradually shifted the control of European societies to the capitalists.

Industrialisation also fostered the development of the proletariat. English landowners converted fields once tilled by serfs into grazing land for sheep to secure wool for the prospering textile mills. Forced from the land, serfs migrated to cities to work in factories, where they joined the burgeoning industrial proletariat. Marx envisaged these workers one day joining hands across national boundaries to form a unified class, setting the stage for historic confrontation, this time between capitalists and the exploited workers.

Capitalism and class conflict

Much of Marx's analysis centres on destructive aspects of industrial capitalism – especially the ways in which it promotes class conflict and alienation. In examining his views on these topics, we will come to see why he advocated the overthrow of capitalist societies.

'The history of all hitherto existing society is the history of class struggles.' With this declaration, Marx and his collaborator Friedrich Engels began their best-known statement, the *Manifesto of the Communist Party* (1972: 335; orig. 1848). The idea of social class is at the heart of Marx's critique of capitalist society. Industrial capitalism, like earlier types of society, contains two major social classes – the dominant people and the oppressed – reflecting the two basic positions in the productive system. Capitalists and proletarians are the historical descendants of masters and slaves in the ancient world and of nobles and serfs in feudal systems. In each case, one class controls the other as productive property. Marx used the term **class conflict** (and sometimes *class struggle*) to refer to *antagonism between entire classes over the distribution of wealth and power in society*.

Class conflict, then, dates back to civilisations long gone (see Figure 4.3). What distinguishes the conflict in capitalist society, Marx pointed out, is how it has come out into the open. Agrarian nobles and serfs, for all their differences, were bound together by long-standing traditions and a host of mutual obligations. Industrial capitalism dissolved those ties so that pride and honour were replaced by 'naked self-interest' and the pursuit of profit in a blatant exercise of oppression. Marx believed that the proletariat, with no personal ties to the oppressors, had little reason to stand for its own subjugation.

But, though industrial capitalism brought class conflict out in the open, Marx realised that fundamental social change would not come easily. First, he claimed, workers must *become aware* of their shared oppression and see capitalism as its true cause. Second, they must *organise and act* to address their problems. This means workers must replace false consciousness with **class consciousness**, *the recognition by workers of their unity as a class in opposition to capitalists and, ultimately, to capitalism itself*. Because the inhumanity of early capitalism was plain for him to see, Marx concluded that industrial workers would inevitably rise up *en masse* to destroy industrial capitalism.

And what of the workers' adversaries, the capitalists? The capitalists' formidable wealth and power, protected by the institutions of society, might seem invulnerable.

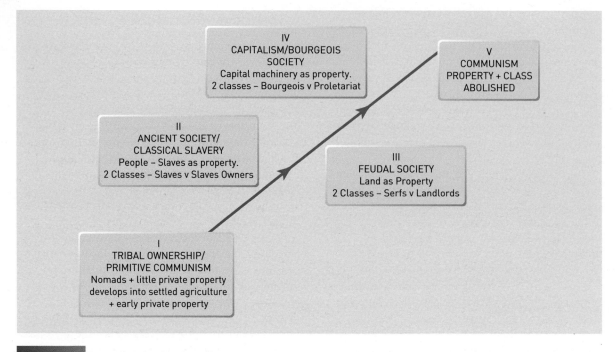

Figure 4.3   Marx's conflict model of change

But Marx saw a weakness in the capitalist armour. Motivated by a desire for personal gain, capitalists fear the competition of other capitalists. Thus Marx thought that capitalists would be reluctant to band together, even though they too share common interests. Furthermore, he reasoned, capitalists keep employees' wages low in their drive to maximise profits. This strategy, in turn, bolsters the resolve of workers to forge an alliance against them. In the long run, Marx surmised, capitalists would only contribute to their own undoing.

Capitalism and alienation

Marx also condemned capitalism for producing **alienation**, *the experience of isolation resulting from powerlessness*. Dominated by capitalists and dehumanised by their jobs (especially monotonous and repetitive factory work), proletarians find little satisfaction in, and feel individually powerless to improve, their situation. Herein lies another contradiction of capitalist society: as human beings devise technology to gain power over the world, the productive process increasingly assumes power over human beings.

Workers view themselves as merely a commodity, a source of labour, bought by capitalists and discarded when no longer needed. Marx cited four ways in which capitalism alienates workers:

1 *Alienation from the act of working.* Ideally, people work both to meet immediate needs and to develop their long-range personal potential. Capitalism, however, denies workers a say in what they produce or how they produce it. Furthermore, much work is tedious, involving countless repetitions of routine tasks. The modern-day replacement of human labour by machines would hardly have surprised Marx; as far as he was concerned, capitalism had turned human beings into machines long ago.

2 *Alienation from the products of work.* The product of work belongs not to workers but to capitalists, who dispose of it for profit. Thus, Marx reasoned, the more workers invest of themselves into their work, the more they lose.

3 *Alienation from other workers.* Marx saw work itself as the productive affirmation of human community. Industrial capitalism, however, transforms work from a cooperative venture into a competitive one. Factory work often provides little chance for human companionship.

4 *Alienation from human potential.* Industrial capitalism alienates workers from their human potential. Marx argued that a worker 'does not fulfil himself in his work but denies himself, has a feeling of misery rather than well-being, does not freely develop his physical and mental energies,

In the twentieth century, Marxism became one of the world's most influential social movements: at its peak it was shaping the economic and political life of nearly a third of the world's people, including those of China, the Soviet Union and eastern Europe. But the socialist regimes of eastern Europe and the former Soviet Union collapsed in the late 1980s. The political transformation of this world region is symbolised by the removal of statues of Vladimir Lenin (1870–1924), architect of Soviet Marxism, in city after city during the last few years

Source: Frank Spooner/Gamma.

but is physically exhausted and mentally debased. The worker, therefore, feels himself to be at home only during his leisure time, whereas at work he feels homeless' (1964b: 124–5; orig. 1844). In short, industrial capitalism distorts an activity that should express the best qualities in human beings into a dull and dehumanising experience.

Marx viewed alienation, in its various forms, as a barrier to social change. But he hoped that industrial workers would eventually overcome their alienation by uniting into a true social class, aware of the cause of their problems and galvanised to transform society.

Revolution

The only way out of the trap of capitalism, contended Marx, was deliberately to refashion society. He envisaged a more humane and egalitarian productive system, one that would enhance rather than undermine social ties. He called this system *socialism*. Marx knew well the obstacles to a socialist revolution; even so, he was disappointed that he never lived to see workers in England overthrow industrial capitalism. Still, convinced of the basic immorality of capitalist society, he was sure that in time the working majority would realise that they held the key to a better future in their own hands. This transformation would certainly be revolutionary, perhaps even violent. What emerged from the workers' revolution, however, would be a cooperative socialist society intended to meet the needs of all.

The discussion of social stratification in Chapter 8 reveals more about changes in industrial–capitalist societies since Marx's time and why the revolution he championed has not taken place. Later chapters also delve into why people in the societies of eastern Europe recently revolted against established socialist governments. But, in his own time, Marx looked towards the future with hope (Marx and Engels 1972: 362; orig. 1848): 'The proletarians have nothing to lose but their chains. They have a world to win.'

Max Weber: the rationalisation of society and the disenchantment of the world

With a broad understanding of law, economics, religion and history, Max Weber (1864–1920) produced what many regard as the greatest individual contribution to sociology. He generated ideas that were very wide ranging. Here, we limit ourselves to his vision of how modern society differs from earlier types of social organisation.

As we saw in Chapter 1, Weber's sociology can be seen as an action theory. Weber understood the power of the economic and technological, but he departed from Marx's materialist analysis. For him, ideas – especially beliefs and values – have transforming power. Thus he saw modern society as the product not just of new technology and capitalism, but of a new way of thinking. Growing out of changes in religious belief, the modern world can be characterised as an increasingly rational world. We have seen too that Weber also used **ideal types**, contrasting the ideal 'Protestant' with the ideal 'Jew', 'Hindu' and 'Buddhist'. We have already compared 'hunting and gathering societies' and 'industrial societies' as well as 'capitalism' and 'socialism'. Much of Weber's analysis focused upon the ideal types of rationality.

Tradition and rationality

Rather than categorise societies in terms of technology or productive systems, Max Weber highlighted differences in the ways people view the world. In simple terms, Weber concluded that members of pre-industrial societies cling to *tradition*, while people in industrial–capitalist societies endorse *rationality*.

By **tradition**, Weber meant *sentiments and beliefs passed from generation to generation*. Thus traditional societies are guided by the past. Their members evaluate particular actions as right and proper precisely because these actions have been accepted for so long.

People in modern societies take a different view of the world, argued Weber, embracing **rationality**, *deliberate, matter-of-fact calculation of the most efficient means to accomplish a particular goal*. Sentiment has no place in a rational world-view, which treats tradition simply as one kind of information. Typically, modern people choose to think and act on the basis of present and future consequences, evaluating jobs, schooling and even relationships in terms of what we put into them and what we expect to receive in return.

Weber viewed both the Industrial Revolution and capitalism as evidence of a historical surge of rationality. He used the phrase **rationalisation of society** to denote *the historical change from tradition to rationality as the dominant mode of human thought*. Modern society, he concluded, has been 'disenchanted', as scientific thinking and technology have swept away sentimental ties to the past.

The willingness to adopt the latest technology, then, is one good indicator of how rationalised a society is.

Drawing on Weber's comparative perspective, we deduce that various societies place different values on technological advancement. What one society might herald as a breakthrough, another might deem unimportant, and a third might strongly oppose as a threat to tradition. Inventors in ancient Greece, for instance, devised many surprisingly elaborate mechanical devices to perform household tasks. But since elites were well served by slaves, they viewed such inventions as mere entertainment. In Europe today, many small communities are guided by their traditions to staunchly oppose modern technology.

Rationality, Calvinism and industrial capitalism

Is industrial capitalism a rational economic system? Here again, Weber and Marx were in debate. Weber considered industrial capitalism as the essence of rationality, since capitalists pursue profit in eminently rational ways. Marx, however, was critical of capitalism, arguing that it was the antithesis of rationality, and claiming that it failed to meet the basic needs of most of the people (Gerth and Mills, 1946: 49).

But, to look more closely at Weber's analysis, how did industrial capitalism emerge in the first place? Weber contended that industrial capitalism was the legacy of Calvinism – a Christian religious movement spawned by the Protestant Reformation. Calvinists, Weber explained, approached life in a highly disciplined and rational way. Moreover, central to the religious doctrine of John Calvin (1509–64) was *predestination*, the idea that an all-knowing and all-powerful God has preordained some people for salvation and others for damnation. With everyone's fate set before birth, Calvinists believed that people could do nothing to alter their destiny. Nor could they even know what their future would be. Thus the lives of Calvinists were framed by hopeful visions of eternal salvation and anxious fears of unending damnation.

For such people, not knowing one's fate was intolerable. Calvinists gradually came to a resolution of sorts. Why shouldn't those chosen for glory in the next world, they reasoned, see signs of divine favour in *this* world? Such a conclusion prompted Calvinists to interpret worldly prosperity as a sign of God's grace. Anxious to acquire this reassurance, Calvinists threw themselves into a quest for success, applying rationality, discipline and hard work to their tasks. This pursuit of riches was not for its own sake, of course, since self-indulgently spending money was clearly sinful. Calvinists also were little moved to share their wealth with the poor, because they saw poverty as a sign of God's rejection. Their ever-present duty was to carry forward what they held to be their personal *calling* from God (see Figure 4.4).

As they reinvested their profits for greater success, Calvinists built the foundation of capitalism. They

An elective affinity between		Figure 4.4	The Protestant ethic and the spirit of capitalism
The Protestant ethic	**The spirit of capitalism**		
Working hard as a sign of grace	Relentless profit and hard work		
The 'Calling' and Earthly Duties	Rationality		
Salvation and predestination via 'good works'	Time is money – invest for profit		
Self-monitoring and self-control	Hard work profit motive		
Sins of waste and idleness	Importance of hard work and saving		

piously used wealth to generate more wealth, practised personal thrift, and eagerly embraced whatever technological advances would bolster their efforts.

These traits, Weber explained, distinguished Calvinism from other world religions. Catholicism, the traditional religion in most of Europe, gave rise to a passive, 'otherworldly' view of life with hope of greater reward in the life to come. For Catholics, material wealth had none of the spiritual significance that so motivated Calvinists. And so it was, Weber concluded, that industrial capitalism became established primarily in areas of Europe where Calvinism had a strong hold.

Weber's study of Calvinism provides striking evidence of the power of ideas to shape society (versus Marx's contention that ideas merely reflect the process of economic production). But always sceptical of simple explanations, Weber knew that industrial capitalism had many roots. In fact, one purpose of this research was to counter Marx's narrow explanation of modern society in strictly economic terms.

As religious fervour weakened among later generations of Calvinists, Weber concluded, success-seeking personal discipline remained strong. A *religious* or, more precisely, *Protestant ethic* became simply a '*work* ethic'. From this point of view, industrial capitalism emerged as 'disenchanted' religion, with wealth now valued for its own sake. It is revealing that 'accounting', which to early Calvinists meant keeping a daily record of moral deeds, now refers simply to keeping track of money.

Rational social organisation

Weber contended that, by unleashing the Industrial Revolution and sparking the development of capitalism, rationality had defined the character of modern society. Rational social organisation confers the following seven traits on today's social life.

1 *Distinctive social institutions.* Among hunters and gatherers, the family was the centre of virtually all activities. Gradually, however, other social institutions, including religious, political and economic systems, broke away from family life. In modern societies, institutions of education and healthcare have also appeared. The separation of social institutions – each detailed in a later chapter – is a rational strategy to address human needs more efficiently.

2 *Large-scale organisations.* Modern rationality is exemplified by a proliferation of large-scale organisations. As early as the horticultural era, political officials oversaw religious observances, public works and warfare. In medieval Europe, the Catholic Church grew larger still with thousands of officials. In modern, rational societies, the employees of national governments may number in the millions, and most people work for a large organisation.

3 *Specialised tasks.* Unlike members of traditional societies, individuals in modern societies pursue a wide range of specialised activities. The enormous breadth of occupations can be seen in any city's *Yellow Pages*, which typically runs to more than 1,000 pages.

4 *Personal discipline.* Modern society puts a premium on self-directed discipline. For early Calvinists, of course, such an approach to life was rooted in religious belief. Although now distanced from its religious origins, discipline is still encouraged by cultural values such as achievement, success and efficiency.

5 *Awareness of time.* In traditional societies, people measure time according to the rhythm of sun and seasons. Modern people, by contrast, schedule events precisely by the hour and minute. Interestingly, clocks began appearing in European cities some 500 years ago, just as commerce was starting to expand; soon, people began to think

(to borrow Benjamin Franklin's phrase) that 'time is money'.

6 *Technical competence.* Members of traditional societies evaluate one another largely on the basis of *who* they are – how they are joined to others in the web of kinship. Modern rationality, by contrast, prompts us to judge people according to *what* they are – that is, with an eye towards their skills and abilities.

7 *Impersonality.* Finally, in a rational society, technical competence takes priority over close relationships, rendering the world impersonal. Modern social life can be viewed as the interplay of specialists concerned with particular tasks, rather than people broadly concerned with one another. Weber explained that we tend to devalue personal feelings and emotions as 'irrational' because they are often difficult to control.

Rationality and bureaucracy

Although the medieval church grew large, Weber argued that it was never entirely rational because its goal was to preserve tradition. Truly rational organisations, with the principal focus on efficiency, appeared only in the last few centuries. The organisational type that Weber called *bureaucracy* became pronounced along with capitalism as an expression of rationality.

Chapter 6 explains that bureaucracy is the model for modern businesses, government agencies, trade unions and universities. For now, note that Weber considered this organisational form to be the clearest expression of a rational world-view because its chief elements – offices, duties and policies – are intended to achieve specific goals as efficiently as possible. By contrast, the inefficiency of traditional organisation is reflected in its hostility to change. In short, Weber asserted that bureaucracy transformed all of society in the same way that industrialisation transformed the economy.

Still, Weber emphasised that rational bureaucracy has a special affinity to capitalism. He wrote:

> **Today, it is primarily the capitalist market economy which demands that the official business of public administration be discharged precisely, unambiguously, continuously, and with as much speed as possible. Normally, the very large capitalist enterprises are themselves unequalled models of strict bureaucratic organisation.**

(1978: 974; orig. 1921)

Rationality and alienation

Max Weber joined with Karl Marx in recognising the unparalleled efficiency of industrial capitalism. Weber also shared Marx's conclusion that modern society generates widespread alienation, though for different reasons. For Weber, the primary problem is not the economic inequality that so troubled Marx, but the stifling regulation and dehumanisation that comes with expanding bureaucracy. It leads to an increasing 'disenchantment with the world'.

Bureaucracies, Weber warned, treat people as a series of cases rather than as unique individuals. In addition, working for large organisations demands highly specialised and often tedious routines. In the end, Weber envisaged modern society as a vast and growing system of rules seeking to regulate everything and threatening to crush the human spirit.

An irony found in the work of Marx reappears in Weber's thinking: rather than serve humanity, modern society turns on its creators and enslaves them. In language reminiscent of Marx's description of the human toll of industrial capitalism, Weber portrayed the modern individual as 'only a small cog in a ceaselessly moving mechanism that prescribes to him an endlessly fixed routine of march' (1978: 988; orig. 1921). Thus, knowing well the advantages of modern society, Weber ended his life deeply pessimistic. He feared that the rationalisation of society would end up reducing people to robots.

Emile Durkheim: the bonds that tie us together – from mechanical to organic

'To love society is to love something beyond us and something in ourselves.' These are the words of Emile Durkheim (1858–1917), another architect of sociology. This curious phrase (1974: 55; orig. 1924) distils one more influential vision of human society.

Structure: society beyond ourselves

First and foremost, Emile Durkheim recognised that society exists beyond ourselves. Society is more than the individuals who compose it; society has a life of its own that stretches beyond our personal experiences. It was here long before we were born, it makes claims on us while we are alive, and it will remain long after we are gone. Patterns of human behaviour, Durkheim explained, form established *structures*; they are *social facts* that have an objective reality beyond the lives and perceptions of particular individuals. Cultural norms, values, religious beliefs – all endure as social facts.

And because society looms larger than individual lives, it has the *power* to shape our thoughts and actions, Durkheim noted. So studying individuals alone (as psychologists or biologists do) can never capture the essence of human experience. Society is more than the sum of its parts; it exists as a complex organism rooted in our collective life. A reception class in a primary school, a family sharing a meal, people milling about a country auction – all are examples of the countless situations that set an organisation apart from any particular individual who has ever participated in them.

Once created by people, then, society takes on a momentum of its own, confronting its creators and demanding a measure of obedience. For our part, we experience society's influence as we come to see the order in our lives or as we face temptation and feel the tug of morality.

Function: society in action

Having established that society has structure, Durkheim turned to the concept of *function*. The significance of any social fact, he explained, extends beyond individuals to the operation of society itself.

To illustrate, consider crime. Most people think of lawbreaking as harmful acts that some individuals inflict on others. But, looking beyond individuals, Durkheim saw that crime has a vital function for the ongoing life of society itself. As Chapter 17 explains, only by recognising and responding to acts as criminal do people construct and defend morality, which gives necessary shape to our collective life. For this reason, Durkheim rejected the common view of crime as 'pathological'. On the contrary, he concluded, crime is quite 'normal' for the most basic of reasons: a society could not exist without it (1964a, orig. 1895; 1964b, orig. 1893).

Personality: society in ourselves

Durkheim contended that society is not only 'beyond ourselves', it is also 'in ourselves'. Each of us, in short,

builds a personality by internalising social facts. How we act, think and feel – our essential humanity – is drawn from the society that nurtures us. Moreover, Durkheim explained, society regulates human beings through moral discipline. Durkheim held that human beings are naturally insatiable and in constant danger of being overpowered by our own desires: 'The more one has, the more one wants, since satisfactions received only stimulate instead of filling needs' (1966: 248; orig. 1897). Having given us life, then, society must also instil restraints in us.

Nowhere is the need for societal regulation better illustrated than in Durkheim's study of suicide (1966; orig. 1897), detailed in Chapter 1. Why is it that, over the years, rock stars have been so vulnerable to self-destruction? Durkheim had the answer long before anyone made electric music: it is the *least* regulated categories of people that suffer the *highest* rates of suicide. The greater licence afforded to those who are young, rich and famous exacts a high price in terms of the risk of suicide.

Modernity and anomie

Compared to traditional societies, modern societies impose fewer restrictions on everyone. Durkheim acknowledges the advantages of modern freedom, but he warned of a rise in **anomie**, *a condition in which society provides little moral guidance to individuals*. What so many celebrities describe as 'almost being destroyed by their fame' is one extreme example of the corrosive effects of anomie. Sudden fame tears people away from their families and familiar routines, disrupting society's support and regulation of an individual, sometimes with fatal results. Durkheim instructs us, therefore, that the desires of the individual must be balanced by the claims and guidance of society – a balance that has become precarious in the modern world.

Evolving societies: the division of labour

Like Marx and Weber, Durkheim witnessed at first hand the rapid social transformation of Europe during the nineteenth century. Analysing this change, Durkheim saw a sweeping evolution in the forms of social organisation.

In pre-industrial societies, explained Durkheim, strong tradition operates as the social cement that

Table 4.2	**The classic theorists briefly contrasted**		
	Marx	**Weber**	**Durkheim**
Type of society	Capitalism	Capitalism/rational bureaucratic	Organic solidarity
Source of change	Economic conflicts	Religion and ideas	Population density
The future	Revolutionary change – communism – optimistic	Disenchantment of the world – pessimistic	Breakdown and anomie, search for new guilds/communities

binds people together. In fact, what he termed the *collective conscience* is so strong that the community moves quickly to punish anyone who dares to challenge conventional ways of life. Durkheim called this system **mechanical solidarity**, meaning *social bonds, based on shared morality, that unite members of pre-industrial societies*. In practice, then, mechanical solidarity springs from *likeness*. Durkheim described these bonds as 'mechanical' because people feel a more or less automatic sense of belonging together.

Durkheim considered the decline of mechanical solidarity to be a defining trait of modern society. But this does not mean that society dissolves; rather, modernity generates a new type of solidarity that rushes into the void left by discarded traditions. Durkheim called this new social integration **organic solidarity**, defined as *social bonds, based on specialisation, that unite members of industrial societies*. In short, where solidarity was once rooted in likeness, it now flows from *differences* among people whose specialised pursuits make them rely on one another.

For Durkheim, then, the key dimension of change is a society's expanding **division of labour**, or *specialised economic activity*. As Max Weber explained, modern societies specialise in order to promote efficiency. Durkheim fills in the picture by showing us that members of modern societies count on the efforts of tens of thousands of others – most of them complete strangers – to secure the goods and services they need every day.

So modernity rests far less on *moral consensus* (the foundation of traditional societies) and far more on *functional interdependence*. That is, as members of modern societies, we depend more and more on people whom we trust less and less. Why, then, should we put our faith in people we hardly know and whose beliefs may differ radically from our own? Durkheim's answer:

'Because we can't live without them'. In a world in which morality sometimes seems like so much shifting sand, then, we confront what might be called 'Durkheim's dilemma': the technological power and expansive personal freedom of modern society come only at the cost of receding morality and the ever-present danger of anomie.

Like Marx and Weber, Durkheim had misgivings about the direction society was taking. But, of the three, Durkheim was the most optimistic. Confidence in the future sprang from his hope that we could enjoy greater freedom and privacy while creating for ourselves the social regulation that had once been forced on us by tradition.

Reviewing the theories

How have societies changed?

We started with a view – sociocultural evolution, furthest developed by the North American sociologists Gerhard and Jean Lenski (Lenski and Nolan, 2010) – in which societies differ primarily in terms of changing technology. Modern society stands out in this regard because of its enormous productive power. Karl Marx also stressed historical differences in productive systems, yet pointed to the persistence of social conflict throughout human history (except perhaps among simple hunters and gatherers). For Marx, modern society is capitalist, and is distinctive because it brings that conflict out in the open.

Max Weber looked at this question from another perspective, tracing evolving modes of thought. Pre-industrial societies, he claimed, are guided by tradition, while modern societies espouse a rational world-view. Bureaucracies take on a key role. Finally, for Emile Durkheim, traditional societies are characterised by mechanical solidarity based on moral consensus. In industrial societies, mechanical solidarity gives way to organic solidarity based on productive specialisation.

Why do societies change?

Marx's materialist approach pointed to the struggle between social classes as the 'engine of history', pushing societies towards revolutionary reorganisation. Weber's idealist view argues that modes of thought also contribute to social change. He demonstrated how rational Calvinism bolstered the Industrial Revolution, which in turn reshaped much of modern society. Finally, Durkheim pointed to an expanding division of labour as the key dimension of social change.

What holds societies together?

Marx spotlighted social division, not unity, treating class conflict as the hallmark of human societies throughout history. From his point of view, elites may force an uneasy peace between the classes, but true social unity would emerge only if production were to become a truly cooperative endeavour. To Weber, members of a society share a distinctive world-view. Just as traditional beliefs joined people together in the past, so modern societies have created rational, large-scale organisations with their own organisational cultures that fuse and guide people's lives. Finally, Durkheim made solidarity the focus of his work, contrasting the morality-based mechanical solidarity of pre-industrial societies with modern society's more practical organic solidarity.

WORLD WATCH

What is European society?

Marx, Weber and Durkheim – discussed in this chapter – were not just seeking to understand the nature of industrial societies; they were Europeans largely in search of understanding industrial Europe. But it is hard to know quite what 'Europe' is. Before going on, make a list of ways you might define Europe, and ponder what are its common elements and what are its differences.

In one sense it is hard to see Europe as anything coherent. There are over 40 countries, and even more languages. They are scattered over diverse climates – from Scandinavia to the Mediterranean – and diverse cultures – from 'Spanish' to 'Nordic'. There are diverse histories, rituals, politics, economic systems and religions. Northern Europe has more individualistic values than southern Europe and Ireland (where religious values are

stronger). It is hard to see what the Nordic cultures of Denmark, Finland, Sweden and Norway have in common with the cultures of Spain, Italy or Portugal. And within each of these countries there are internal splits and differing ethnic groups (France has Algerians; Germany has guest workers; and the United Kingdom has Scots, Welsh and Irish alongside people of Asian and Afro-Caribbean descent). It is easy to ignore the diversity of this Europe and focus on the one voice of England (often with a diluted voice from North America). But clearly the English voice is not unanimous, and it is certainly not the French voice or the Norwegian one. Yet despite this, people speak of a European society. What can be meant by this?

One way is to search for some common elements. Maybe there are a few? A common history, common lands and geography and – perhaps – some broad common, cultural elements that could be seen as similar. It may indeed be what Benedict Anderson has called an 'imagined community', held together by a

common sense of history and culture (Anderson, 1989). In part this may be because most of these cultures have deep values that link to being the first industrialising countries, the first modern democratic cultures and the first Christian cultures. As we will see, these values are pervasive. Taken together, it may be, as Agnes Heller argues, that 'European culture is modernity – cumulative knowledge and progress, technology and wealth – along with nation states and ideas of freedom and equality' (Wintle, 1996: 11). It defines others through this 'own sense'.

Another way is to approach them as countries themselves seeking to be united. Since the Second World War (itself a curiously unifying factor), there have been persistent attempts to create a European Union. Starting with the Congress of Europe in 1948 at The Hague, the European Union has grown through many stages, as shown in Table 4.3. In 1951 Jean Monnet called the European Coal and Steel Community 'the first expression of the Europe that is being born'. But this involved

Table 4.3   Some landmarks in the making of the European Union

1945–1959 THE BEGINNINGS OF COOPERATION

April 1951 Treaty of Paris establishes the European Coal and Steel Community (with France, West Germany, Italy, Belgium, the Netherlands and Luxembourg). The UK does not join.

March 1957 Treaties of Rome, signed again by the above six, establish the European Economic Community and the European Atomic Energy Community. Also includes new parliament and new court and eliminates customs duties among member states.

1 January 1958 Treaties of Rome become law. In effect, this is the start of the European Economic Community (EEC).

1960–1969 A PERIOD OF ECONOMIC GROWTH

1964 Common agricultural policy established with uniform prices to start in 1967.

1970–1989 A GROWING COMMUNITY – THE FIRST ENLARGEMENT

22 January 1972 The United Kingdom, Denmark, Ireland and Norway admitted to membership from January 1973. Conservative government in the UK with Prime Minister Edward Heath takes the UK into the EEC, but a referendum in Norway rejects membership.

June 1975 Labour government in UK wishes to withdraw and holds a referendum: 67% of voters decide they want to stay in.

December 1975 Elected European Parliament planned to start in 1979. No powers to introduce legislation, but powers to advise.

1978 Members agree to ECU (European Currency Unit).

1 January 1981 Greece becomes tenth member.

January 1983 Common fishing policy.

January 1985 First European passports issued. Jacques Delors is first president of European Commission.

January 1986 Spain and Portugal join.

February 1986 The Single Act; streamlining, with legalisation now passed by a majority.

1989–2000 THE FALL OF THE BERLIN WALL – A EUROPE WITHOUT FRONTIERS

October 1990 Former East Germany becomes part of the Community.

Maastricht Treaty signed (see 1992 below).

October 1991 European Free Trade Association (EFTA – Austria, Finland, Iceland, Liechtenstein, Norway, Sweden, Switzerland) agrees an extended cooperation project – the European Economic Area (EEA) – within the Community and EFTA, creating an integrated trade area.

November 1991 Associations with Poland, Hungary and Czechoslovakia (but stopping short of full membership).

1992 The Treaty of Maastricht ratified. A key step in the integration of the EU with a timetable for the single currency, the new status of EU citizenship, a single internal market and a common foreign and security policy.

1 January 1995 Austria, Finland and Sweden join the EU, bringing membership to 15.

June 1997 The Treaty of Amsterdam concluded and launched in 1999: gave more power to the EU Parliament and 'tidied up' Maastricht 1990 (see above).

March 1998 EU opens negotiations with Cyprus, Czech Republic, Estonia, Hungary, Poland and Slovenia. New agricultural policy – a ban on member states subsidising their own farmers.

1 July 1998 European Central Bank inaugurated in Frankfurt.

1 January 1999 Single monetary policy – the euro; responsibility of European System of Central Banks. Launched by participating countries: all EU except Denmark, Sweden and the UK.

March 1999 The Amsterdam Treaty: EU's new constitution.

2000–NOW: CONTINUING EXPANSION

1 January 2000 Circulation of euro banknotes and coins.

Early 2002 Legal tender of national currencies withdrawn in most EU member states; the euro becomes the currency. UK, Denmark and Sweden do not adopt euro.

1 May 2004 Enlargement of EU with ten new members, seven of which had lived under the Third Reich or Stalinist communism. Estonia, Latvia and Lithuania were part of the former Soviet Union. Poland, Hungary, Slovakia and the Czech Republic were satellites under the Warsaw Pact. Slovenia had been part of socialist Yugoslavia. In addition, there are the islands of Malta and Cyprus (EU25).

2007: 50th anniversary of EU: now has over 400 million people.

2007 Romania and Bulgaria join (EU27). Croatia, the former Yugoslavic Republic of Macedonia and Turkey are current candidates to be accepted in the EU in the future.

2009 The Treaty of Lisbon: major changes updating Maastricht (finally approved in a second referendum in 2009).

Source: http://europa.eu.

only six countries: Belgium, France, Italy, West Germany, Luxembourg and the Netherlands. Map 4.3 aims to give some sense of the European Union's growth in the past, and also the projected plans for the future. Some now suggest that this is the most advanced and unified economic and political 'region' in the world, and that the twenty-first century may become the European Century. Others – as we shall see – strongly disagree.

Britain has always been a slightly 'awkward partner' in Europe. Until the election of a Labour government on 1 May 1997, successive Conservative governments were the embodiment of 'euroscepticism'. But since then, the UK government has adopted a more favourable stance.

A note on Turkey

In 2005 historic talks started on the incorporation of Turkey into the EU. This would bring a much larger Muslim culture into the dominant European culture. As well as bridging to the East and being the only Muslim and non-Christian country, Turkey would add one of the largest populations and one of the poorest economies of the region. It would answer critics who see the EU as purely Christian. But initially some countries – such as Austria – have been opposed. The arrival of Turkey would bring about some striking changes but it will take some 10–15 years of discussion, with many hurdles in its way (for example, there is an 'absorption capacity' test to decide if the EU can fit Turkey in).

See: Alex Warleigh, *European Union: The Basics* (2nd edn, 2008); Gerard Delanty and Chris Mumford, *Rethinking Europe* (2005).

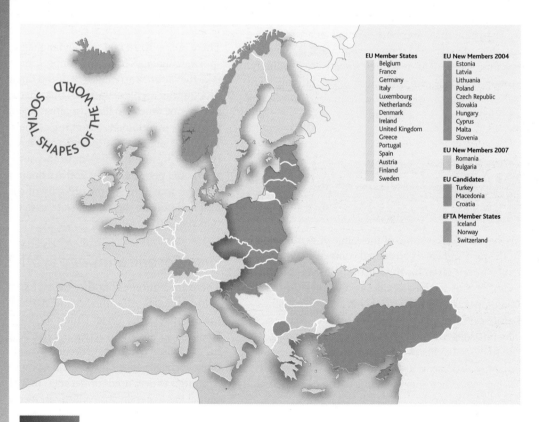

EU Member States	EU New Members 2004
Belgium	Estonia
France	Latvia
Germany	Lithuania
Italy	Poland
Luxembourg	Czech Republic
Netherlands	Slovakia
Denmark	Hungary
Ireland	Cyprus
United Kingdom	Malta
Greece	Slovenia
Portugal	
Spain	**EU New Members 2007**
Austria	Romania
Finland	Bulgaria
Sweden	

EU Candidates
Turkey
Macedonia
Croatia

EFTA Member States
Iceland
Norway
Switzerland

Map 4.3 Greater Europe: the new enlarged European Union in 2007

Where are societies heading?

Finally, there is the question of where society may now be headed (see the *Big debate* at the end of this chapter). For Marx, capitalism would generate the seeds of its own destruction: revolutionary change should bring about a new communist social order. In general, however, attempts to bring about a communist order during the twentieth century in the old Soviet Union and China were not successes. For Weber, there was a strong pessimistic streak: he saw the world as an Iron Cage, with growing rationality creating an ever-spreading 'disenchantment with the world'. Durkheim held out hope for new forms of association to emerge that would bind people together through their differences and resolve the problem of anomie. We will evaluate these views as we move through the book.

Like a kaleidoscope that shows us different patterns as we turn it, these approaches reveal an array of insights into society. Yet no one approach is, in an absolute sense, right or wrong. Society is exceedingly complex, and we gain the richest understanding from using all of these visions, as we do in the *Thinkers and theory* box on p. 135 and Map 4.4.

The contemporary shape of world societies

We have looked at some of the range of world societies in the past and have considered some of the main explanations given for the rise of the modern industrial world. In this section, we take a very quick tour of the contemporary world, introducing a few key themes before exploring them more fully in later chapters. The box suggests some of the terms that sociologists use to describe this twenty-first century world, and you may also like to look at the map on the inside back cover, which suggests some of the major social regions of the world.

The early twenty-first-century world

The world population reached 6.7 billion in mid-2007 and is projected to peak at 9 billion in 2070. At the start of the twenty-first century, world societies could be divided in several ways. (To update the population figures at any time search: popclocks at www.census/gov/main/gov/popclock.)

Nation-states

There are around 200 well-identified nation-states (one indication of a society). There have been major shifts in power. The end of the 'Cold War', which dominated politics in the last half-century, led to the break-up of four multi-ethnic states: the USSR, Czechoslovakia, Yugoslavia and Ethiopia: over 20 new independent states emerged. But along with break-ups and fragmentations also came reunification: East Germany with West Germany, and Hong Kong with the People's Republic of China, as well as the growth of a much more unified Europe through the European Union (see the *World watch* box, above).

Languages

There are up to 10,000 spoken languages. Since spoken languages indicate groups, it may be better to take the latter as an indicator of the range of societies functioning on planet earth. Thus, there are still a number of much smaller, usually indigenous, peoples who have maintained something of their own society. Thus, the languages of the native American Indians (numbering around 300), or of the Australian aboriginal peoples (about 250 are documented), help us sense something of the diversity of societies of the past and outside the 'nation state' systems of today (Crystal, 2010).

First, Second and Third Worlds

There are a number of other ways of approaching world societies. After the Second World War, and until the collapse of the Soviet Union in 1991, it became a tradition to classify societies as 'First World' (the rich, industrialised countries), 'Second World' (less rich and often socialist) and 'Third World' (poor, 'developing'). Although widely used for decades, this 'three worlds' model has generally lost validity in recent years. It was a product of Cold War politics by which the capitalist West (the First World) confronted the socialist East (the Second World), while the rest of the world (the Third World) remained more or less on the sidelines. But the sweeping transformation of eastern Europe and the former Soviet Union in the early 1990s meant that there no longer existed a distinctive Second World. Just as important, the superpower opposition that defined the Cold War has faded in recent years.

ancestors. Living without industrial technology, peasants are not very productive. Hunger, minimal housing and frequent disease all frame the lives of the world's poorest people.

This broad overview of global economic development gives us a foundation for understanding the problem of global inequality. For people living in affluent nations, the scope of human want in much of the world is difficult to grasp. From time to time, televised scenes of famine in very poor countries such as Ethiopia and Bangladesh give us a shocking glimpse of the absolute poverty that makes every day a life-and-death struggle. Behind these images lie cultural, historical and economic forces that we shall explore in the remainder of this chapter.

Note: To classify a country as 'low income' does not mean that only poor people live there. On the contrary, the rich districts of poor countries testify to the high living standards of some. Indeed, given the low wages paid to most urbanites in these countries, the typical well-to-do household is staffed by several servants and served by a gardener and chauffeur. But for the majority in the world's poor countries, poverty is the rule. Moreover, with incomes of only several hundred pounds a year, the burden of poverty is greater than it is among the poor in high-income societies.

A key reason for marked disparities in quality of life is that economic productivity is lowest in precisely the regions of the globe where population growth is highest. High-income countries are by far the most advantaged with 80 per cent of global income supporting just 22 per cent of the world's people. Middle-income nations contain about 58 per cent of the global population; these people earn about 12 per cent of the world's income. This leaves about 20 per cent of the planet's population with a scant 2 per cent of total global income (see Chapter 9, p. 287).

Newly industrialising countries and China rising

The map of the world is constantly changing, and one of the most significant recent developments is the emergence of **newly industrialising countries** (often called NICs), *lower-income countries that are fast becoming high-income ones*. A cluster of (mainly) south-east Asian countries are making rapid economic progress. These countries include Hong Kong, Singapore, South Korea, Thailand and Taiwan. Some commentators have suggested that this new 'Asian Way' has been adopting different industrialisation patterns

from those traditionally found in the West, and that they are indeed likely to become the trailblazers for the twenty-first century (Naisbitt, 1997). Above all, as we saw in the box on p. 110, China has moved out of its recent communist past to become a world player on the economic stage.

The Human Development Index

To focus on the economic alone, however, is to give a very skewed view of the world, and sociology is always interested in a wider array of factors. Some recent analysts, for example, have developed ways of classifying societies based upon a wider conception of how well a society works – how 'happy' it is, and how good its environmental track record is. These are often contentious debates and we return to them in the final chapters of this book (see Chapters 25 and 26).

The most significant new way of classifying and understanding societies has been through the development of the Human Development Index (or HDI). The HDI was first used in 1990 by the United Nations Development Programme (and is subsequently published annually in its *Human Development Report*). It is a composite figure bridging three main issues across all the countries for which relevant data are available:

- *longevity* – life expectancy at birth
- *knowledge and education* – adult literacy rate and enrolment in schooling
- *decent standards of living* – adjusted income per head.

Index values are decimals that fall between hypothetical extremes of 1 (highest) and zero (lowest). By this calculation, Norwegians enjoy the highest quality of life (HDI value 0.938), with residents of Australia, New Zealand and the USA close behind; at the other extreme, people in Zimbabwe and the Democratic Republic of the Congo have the world's lowest quality of life (0.140 and 0.239 respectively) (*Human Development Report*, 2010).

Of course, there are many critical problems in using such composite figures. Statistics need very careful interpretation, especially across cultures, and we discuss this more fully in Chapter 9. Bearing this in mind, some major points can be made from the 2010 listing.

- Of the 169 countries listed, 42 score very high HDIs, 43 score high HDIs, 42 have medium HDIs and 42 have low HDIs.
- Norway, Australia, New Zealand, the United States and Ireland rank as the top five; Zimbabwe, Congo, Niger, Burundi and Mozambique rank at the bottom.

(a) **The World Bank** ranked by income (gross national income, GNI, per capita)

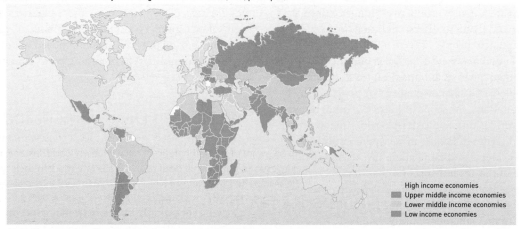

High income economies
Upper middle income economies
Lower middle income economies
Low income economies

(b) **UNDP** (UN Development Program) ranked by Human Development Index

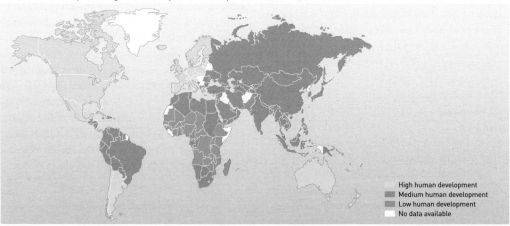

High human development
Medium human development
Low human development
No data available

(c) **UNICEF** (UN Children's Fund) ranked by under-five mortality rate (per 1,000 live births)

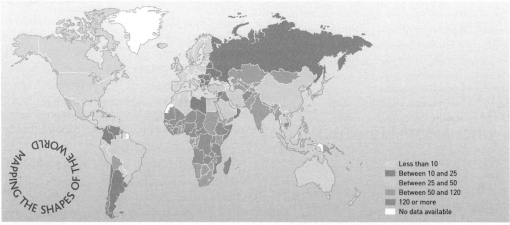

MAPPING THE SHAPES OF THE WORLD

Less than 10
Between 10 and 25
Between 25 and 50
Between 50 and 120
120 or more
No data available

Map 4.4   The world according to . . .
(a) the World Bank: ranked by income (gross national income, GNI per capita)
(b) UNDP (UN Development Programme): ranked by Human Development Index
(c) UNICEF (UN Children's Fund): ranked by under-five mortality rate (per 1,000 live births)

Source: The World Guide, 2007, 11th edn, Oxford: New Internationalist Publications, p. 60. Reprinted by kind permission of the New Internationalist. Copyright © New Internationalist, www.newint.org.

- The Netherlands is seventh; Japan is tenth; Israel is fifteenth; Denmark is nineteenth; Hong Kong is twenty-first; and the United Kingdom is twenty-sixth.
- China, Oman, Nepal, Indonesia and Saudi Arabia have made the most sustained advances in development over the past 40 years, but much of sub-Saharan Africa still lags far behind.

 For more critical comments on the Human Development Index, see Chapter 9. For a summary table of all recorded countries, see Chapter 9, p. 284. For the latest *Human Development Report* online, access: http://hdr.undp.org/en/reports/global/hdr2010.

Multiple modernities: theorising the twenty-first-century society

Over the past 50 years, sociologists have regularly claimed that we are moving into a new kind of society. How are we to characterise the times we live in? In Table 4.1 we refer to 'post-industrial societies'. Throughout this book, we use the terms 'postmodern' and 'late modern' most regularly – and often we will be using the term 'twenty-first century'. It is descriptive of the time period we are now in. But there are many different terms and concepts that can be used, and this box aims to introduce you to some of them. Each brings its own account of the new world we are moving into.

These are all controversial, and usually come from male theorists. They bring with them a high level of generalisation and suggest that very strong changes are happening. A general problem with most of them is that they write *apocalyptically*: that is, they talk of radical major changes that are coming our way and which are usually heralding 'the end of the world as we know it'. (Indeed, this is the title of one such book: Immanuel Wallerstein's *The End of the World as We Know it: Social Science for the Twenty*

First Century (1999)!) We need to be aware of these theoretical suggestions, but they all need to be seen as just that: suggestive – giving you ideas to think with – rather than conclusive.

- *The post-industrial society.* The first major suggestion and used widely between 1960 and 1990. Used by Daniel Bell, it refers to a productive system based on service work and high technology.
- *The post-history society.* Controversially put forward by Francis Fukuyama. In the wake of the collapse of communism, he argued that society had now reached its historical end point in the worldwide triumph of liberal capitalism. It was much criticised, and Fukuyama has now largely changed his position and argument.
- *The postmodern society.* Seen as a direct challenge to Enlightenment thinking and modernity. It takes many forms – especially in culture, where ideas of fragmentation, difference and pluralism are stressed. In a weaker form, it embraces nearly all the ideas below and recognises that the traditional, modern and postmodern worlds all live alongside each other.
- *Late modernity.* Associated with Anthony Giddens, David Harvey and Jürgen Habermas. Generally they do not agree with the ideas of the postmodernists, as they do

not see a break with the past modern world. Instead, they see late modern society as an intensification and speeding up of themes well developed in the modern world.

- *Reflexive modernity.* Closely linked to ideas of late modernity, but here the stress is on a society in which people become more aware (reflexive) about what is going on around them. For example, science no longer simply leads the way: people want to know more about what it means. They want to know about the environment, and about the risk generated by new technologies and the like.
- *Multiple modernities.* An idea developed by Eisenstadt to suggest that there are many past routes into the present world and many forms that contemporary modernity can take. There is no one way.
- *Liquid society.* A new form of society that is much more fluid than previous modern and traditional ones. Everything changes, everything flows, mobility is key. Zygmunt Bauman highlights the uncertainty (*Unsicherheit*) of this world; John Urry is concerned with its global flow and complexity.
- *Late capitalism.* A continuation of the themes first analysed by Marx and which can still be seen at work in so-called modern societies. But Marx's concerns have now become

amplified and are speeding up on a worldwide stage.

- *The information age/the network society* (Castells). A new form of society dependent upon new information technologies and networking (see Chapter 6).

- *The risk society.* This is Ulrich Beck's term for a new form of risk where uncertainty permeates society because of changes in technology, globalisation and the environment. These risks are not like the old natural risks (which still continue) (see Chapter 23).

- *The surveillance society* (Foucault, Cohen). A new form of society dependent on communication and information technologies for administration and control processes, and which result in the close monitoring of everyday life (see Chapter 17).

The list is really getting quite long. Other terms you may come across include:

- post-national (Habermas)
- post-honour (Ahmed)
- world risk (Beck)
- the global age (Albrow)
- the cyber-society (Haraway)
- the human rights society
- the citizenship society
- the cosmopolitan society (Appiah, Beck)
- the mobile society (Urry)

- individualised society (Beck)
- empathic civilisation (Rifkin)

And more: you may also want to note more specific processes that are discussed throughout the book. Consider, for instance, 'The McDonaldsisation of society' (Ritzer), and the 'Disneyisation of society' (Bryman) in Chapter 6.

All these theories suggest a new world that is emerging full of rapid change, uncertainty, risk, openness and individualism. They have different emphases. Some are dark, pessimistic dystopias and others provide more optimistic, positive utopian images. We will return to all this throughout the book.

Conclusion: change and societies

This chapter has aimed to introduce you to a range of different kinds of society from both the past and the present, and to suggest how they have come about and how they might be changing. For much of history, world societies have been dominated by hunting, gathering, horticultural and agrarian societies. What we have witnessed over the past few centuries has been a major shift into a capitalist, technological and 'modern' world. Such societies were the key focus of early sociologists such as Marx, Durkheim and Weber. Recently, many industrial societies seem to be entering yet another phase of society linked to computer technologies and globalisation.

As the book moves along, we shall try to appraise just what some of the more recent changes mean: whether indeed they do signpost a major new form of society in the making. The final chapter of this book will return to a further assessment of this issue.

Aborigines with a laptop

Source: © Robert Essel NYC/Corbis.

Note: Look at the art and culture of the Australian aboriginals through www.aboriginalaustralia.com.

Q Do these children really have laptops? Why are they smiling so much? Why are they marked the way they are? Do they have images of themselves on the laptop? Is this a fake photo just posed for the camera by child actors? Or are the aboriginals in some way being exploited here? What is going on?

SUMMARY

1 In the work of the Lenskis, five kinds of society have been outlined as linked to sociocultural evolution and technology. The earliest *hunting and gathering* societies were composed of a small number of family-centred nomads. Horticulture began some 12,000 years ago as people devised hand tools for the cultivation of crops. *Pastoral* societies domesticate animals and engage in extensive trade. *Agriculture*, about 5,000 years old, is large-scale cultivation traditionally using animal-drawn ploughs. This technology allows societies to grow into vast empires, making them more productive, more specialised and more unequal. *Industrial* societies began 250 years ago in Europe as people harnessed advanced energy sources to power sophisticated machinery. In *post-industrial*, *information* societies, enterprise shifts from the production of material things to the creation and dissemination of information; computers and other information-based technology replace the heavy machinery of the industrial era.

2 Karl Marx's materialist analysis pointed to historical and contemporary conflict between social classes. Conflict in 'ancient' societies involved masters and slaves; in agrarian societies, it places nobles and serfs in opposition; in industrial–capitalist societies, capitalists confront the proletariat. Industrial capitalism alienates workers: from the act of working, from the products of work, from fellow workers, and from human potential. Once workers had overcome their own false consciousness, Marx believed they would overthrow capitalists and the industrial–capitalist system.

3 Max Weber's idealist approach reveals that modes of thought have a powerful effect on society. Weber drew a sharp contrast between the tradition of pre-industrial societies and the rationality of modern, industrial societies. Weber feared that rationality, embodied in efficiency-conscious bureaucratic organisations, would stifle human creativity.

4 Emile Durkheim explained that society has an objective existence apart from individuals. His approach relates social elements to the larger society through their functions. Traditional societies are fused by mechanical solidarity based on moral consensus; modern societies depend on organic solidarity based on the division of labour or productive specialisation.

5 The contemporary world is composed of around 200 societies, which can be classified in various ways, including North and South, East and West, and low-, medium- and high-income societies.

6 The Human Development Index (HDI) has become one way of looking at world societies. This is a United Nations measurement which collates three issues: longevity, knowledge (or education) and standard of living.

7 Many terms have been introduced to discuss the nature of twenty-first-century societies. Amongst these are postmodern, post-history, post-industrial, late capitalism, late modern, self-reflexive, liquid, surveillance and information society.

CONNECT UP: Turn to Part 6 of this book for key resources and link up
with the book's website, which links to these resources
SEE: www.pearsoned.co.uk/plummer

MYTASKLIST

Ten suggestions for going further

1 Connect up with Part Six and the Sociology Web Resources

As you work through ideas and think about the issues raised in this chapter, look at the accompanying website and the resource centre at the end of this book which connects to it. There is a lot here to help you move on. To link up, see: www.pearson.co.uk/plummer.

2 Review the chapter

Briefly summarise (in a paragraph) just what this chapter has been about. Consider: (a) What have you learned? (b) What do you disagree with? Be critical. And (c) How would you develop all this? How could you get more detail on matters that interest you?

3 Pose questions

(a) Draw up a balance sheet of the pros and cons of various technologies, and then discuss whether technological change amounts to 'progress' (hint: see Gray, 2004).
(b) Examine the situation of any one contemporary indigenous people – such as the Innu. Is their way of life likely to survive into the future? (hint: see Samson, 2003).
(c) Contrast the theories of Marx, Durkheim and Weber on the emergence of the modern world. Which do you find most helpful – and why?
(d) Discuss some of the major features of contemporary world societies. What seem to be the major conflicts and issues for the twenty-first century?
(e) Which term do you think most adequately helps you describe and understand the world we live in at the start of the twenty-first century?

4 Explore key words

Many concepts have been introduced in this chapter. You can review them from the website or from the listing at the back of this book. You might like to give special attention to just five words and think them through – how would you define them, what are they dealing with, and do they help you see the social world more clearly or not?

5 Search the Web

Be critical when you look at websites – see the box on p. 940 in the Resources section. Some useful sources for this chapter are:

Indigenous and tribal peoples

Indigenous Peoples: Issues and resources
http://indigenouspeoplesissues.com

Survival International
www.survivalinternational.org

The movement for tribal peoples – many of whom are in decline

Europe

Eurostat
http://epp.eurostat.ec.europa.eu/portal/page

European statistics can be found in Eurostat, who also produce a Eurostat yearbook.

Europa
http://europa.eu

Europa is the European Union's server to the Parliament, the Council, the Commission, the Court of Justice, the Council of Auditors and other EU bodies. This server offers news, simple answers to key questions, the history of the EU, information on policies and institutions, and links to Eurostat, which is a great source of statistics. It is available in all EU languages.

China

China Perspectives
http://chinaperspectives.revues.org

China country profile at the BBC
http://news.bbc.co.uk/1/hi/world/africa/country_
profiles/1287798.stm

China Daily newspaper
www.chinadaily.com.cn

Statistics on world societies

The most general source here is provided by the CIA and
details every country in the world. See its World Fact
Book at:
www.cia.gov/library/publications/the-world-factbook

See also:
The *Human Development Report*
http://hdr.undp.org/en/reports/global/hdr2010
This is a major source for world society statistics, and will
have the most up-to-date Human Development Index results.

The theories of Marx, Durkheim and Weber can be explored
further through the websites listed in Chapter 2 (see p. 57).

6 Watch a DVD

- James Cameron's *Avatar* (2009): this is currently the
  world's top film. In it we visit Pandora which is inhabited
  by the Na'vi, a humanoid race with their own language
  and culture. Those from earth find themselves at odds
  with each other and the local culture. It is seen by many
  as a metaphor for the invasion of capitalism over tribal
  life.
- Ingmar Bergman's *The Seventh Seal* (1956–57):
  looks at the forces of life and death through a medieval
  knight returning from the crusades. See also his *Wild
  Strawberries* (1957), which examines the meanings of life
  in society.
- Satyajit Ray's trilogy *The World of Apu* (1959) – *Pather
  Panchali, Aparajito* and *Apur Sansar*: examines the growth
  of a young Indian boy through childhood, rural youth and
  city adult life.
- Luis Buñuel's surrealist films – especially *The Discreet
  Charm of the Bourgeoisie* (1972), *The Phantom of Liberty*
  (1974) and *That Obscure Object of Desire* (1977): turn
  many of the assumptions about society on their head.
- Nicolas Roeg's *Walkabout* (1971): contrasts white and
  aboriginal children's world-views in the Australian
  outback.
- Bernardo Bertolucci's *The Last Emperor* (1987): tells the
  tale of Pu Yi, born in 1906 and the last absolute monarch
  of China.

7 Think and read

Patrick Nolan and Gerhard Lenski, *Human Societies:
An Introduction to Macrosciology* (2010, 11th edn).
A text which reviews different kinds of society.

The anthropologist Jared Diamond has written a number
of books which compare the history and evolution of
societies and which have become very popular. They are
very readable. See his *Guns, Germs, and Steel: The Fates
of Human Societies* (1979), *The Third Chimpanzee* (1992)
and *Collapse: How Societies Choose to Fail or Succeed*
(2005).

Krishan Kumar, *From Post-industrial to Post-modern Society:
New Theories of the Contemporary World* (1995; 2nd
edn, 2004). Reviews three current debates on the future
of societies: the information society, post-Fordism and
postmodernity.

Gary Browning, Abigail Halci and Frank Webster (eds),
*Understanding Contemporary Society: Theories of the
Present* (2000). Provides 33 short articles to introduce
the reader to all the key aspects of modern and
postmodern societies.

Eric Hobsbawm, *Age of Extremes: The Short Twentieth
Century*, 1914–1991 (1994). This is a full account of
the history of the world during the twentieth century,
and leaves one at the very least being cautious about
any simple view of progress.

Europe

Alex Warleigh, *European Union: The Basics* (2nd edn,
2008). A handy quick tour of evolution, policies and
controversies in the European Union.

Goran Therborn, *European Modernity and Beyond: The
Trajectory of European Societies, 1945–2000* (1995).
The most important sociological study of Europe to
date by a leading Swedish sociologist.

Gerard Delanty and Chris Rumford, *Rethinking Europe:
Social Theory and the Implications of Europeanization*
(2005). A major attempt to understand Europe as a
cosmopolitan world.

8 Relax with a novel

On China, see Jung Chang's *Wild Swans* (1993).

9 Connect to other chapters

- The work of Marx, Durkheim and Weber is discussed
  in many chapters of the book and themed on the
  website.

- Discussion on low-, medium- and high-income societies is developed in Chapter 9.
- Discussions on Europe feature in boxes throughout the book.

- Jump to the China box on p. 902 in Chapter 26. Review various discussions of China in Chapters 1 (suicide), 14 (economy), 16 (family) and 17 (prisons).

10 Engage in THE BIG DEBATE

Progress: is society getting better or worse?

In Europe, generally, burdened by the sense of a long and troubled history, the fate of humankind is often looked upon with foreboding. Much of its intellectual tradition highlights critique, disenchantment, cynicism, despair and pessimism. Weber, for instance, wrote of the 'disenchantment of the world'. Freud, introduced in Chapter 7, saw civilisation as advancing at the cost of human happiness. And, perhaps most significant, the last 100 years have been the tragic century that witnessed two world wars and the Holocaust. Now, in the twenty-first century, we have entered the age of terror and the world remains in crisis.

A highly influential sociologist, Robert Nisbet (1989), once argued that one of the defining features of modernity had been a belief in progress, often in spite of problems. Indeed, the contemporary Swedish sociologist Goran Therborn also sees this as the key in distinguishing between premodernity, modernity and postmodernity. Progress is the definer of the modern world. He writes:

> Pre-modernity is looking back over its shoulder, to the past, to the latter's example of wisdom, beauty, glory, and to the experiences of the past. Modernity looks to the future, hopes for it, plans for it, constructs it, builds it. Post-modernity has lost or thrown away any sense of direction . . . Modernity ends when words like progress, advance, development, emancipation, liberation, growth, accumulation, enlightenment, embetterment, avant-garde, lose their attraction and their function as guides to social action.

> (Therborn, 1995: 4)

So can we see progress in the twenty-first century? Are we approaching a utopia or is a dystopia fast descending upon us?

To begin, we can point to some good reasons for society's belief in progress. Since the beginning of the twentieth century, for example, the scope of education has expanded to an unprecedented level. Moreover, even taking account of inflation, average income and national productivity have grown significantly. In addition, back in 1900, it was a rare home that had a telephone and, outside large cities, none had access to electricity. No one had even heard of television, and cars were still on the drawing boards. Today, almost every Western home is served by a telephone, a host of electric appliances, one or more television sets, and a DVD player; many also are equipped with satellite or cable TV. Most important of all, people born in 1900 lived an average of just 47 years; children born today can look forward to 30 additional years of life.

But some trends, especially during the last 25 years, have been troubling. It is true that some countries seem to be enjoying higher standards of living, and so on, but is this at the expense of others? Contrasts of inequality are massive, as Chapters 8–14 (Part Three) show. To give one figure from these chapters: 20 per cent of the world (some 1 billion people) lack the nutrition to work regularly, and 800 million are at risk for their lives. Add to this problems of cities, of pollution, of media, of environment, of risk, of crime, and so on. Rising crime rates have undermined people's sense of personal safety, even in their own homes. Our relative affluence, coupled with our capacity to move further and faster than ever before, seems to have eroded our sense of responsibility for others, unleashing a wave of individualism that often comes across as unbridled selfishness. As a result, not only is pessimism on the rise, but many people have been losing confidence in the direction of society.

So, which is it? Is society getting better or worse?

The theorists whose ideas we have examined in this chapter shed some light on this question. It is easy to equate 'high tech' with 'progress'. But we should make such assumptions cautiously, the Lenskis maintain, because history shows us, that while advancing technology does offer real advantages, it is no guarantee of a 'better' life. Marx, Weber and Durkheim also acknowledged the growing affluence of societies over time; yet each offered a pointed criticism of modern society because of a dangerous tendency towards individualism. For Marx, capitalism is the culprit, elevating money to godlike status and fostering a culture of selfishness. Weber's analysis claims that the modern spirit of rationality wears away traditional ties of kinship and neighbourhood while expanding bureaucracy, which, he warned, both manipulates and isolates people. In Durkheim's view, functional interdependence joins members of modern societies, who are less and less able to establish a common moral framework within which to judge right and wrong.

In the end, what human societies gain through technological advances may be offset, to some extent, by the loss of human community. We return to all these issues throughout the book, and make a further appraisal in the conclusion in Chapter 26.

Continue the debate

1 Draw up a balance sheet of 'progress' in the modern world. Do you think life in the (post)modern world is getting better or worse? What evidence can you produce for your argument?

2 Is our society's increasing level of affluence good? What might Marx, Weber and Durkheim say?

3 Do you think people in low-income countries are aware of the 'advances' in the Western/Northern/rich/high-income societies? Would they see them as advances?

A recent polemic on the idea of progress is the very readable book by John Gray, *Heresies: Against Progress and Other Illusions* (2004).

CHAPTER 5

CULTURE

WE WERE FLYING INTO HONG KONG. The air stewardess welcomed us to the land, but with a cryptic message. She informed us that Hong Kong was the land where half the people had mobile phones but the other half believed in ghosts! And here, in a nutshell, is the clash of two cultures – a 'modernising' West touching a 'superstitious' East.

Everywhere one turns in Hong Kong the contrast is visible. The bustling, dirty old temples where women cry and wail at the altars of their ancestors, offering money to their gods; the glittering, elaborate shopping malls soaring to the skies – some of the largest in the world – where consumerist capitalism is at its most spectacular. Spirituality versus materialism. Or the Chinese schoolchildren elaborately dressed in their formal 'Western' school uniforms complete with satchels – clambering over the ill-equipped peasant boats in the harbour to their own overcrowded houseboat homes. Or the Bank of Hong Kong – a monument to modern architecture, but built with full regard to *feng shui* (pronounced 'fung shway', Chinese words that mean 'wind and water') and potential 'evil spirits' and designed to keep them at bay. Here are rich and vibrant cultures pushing against each other.

Or consider another example: New York real-estate broker Barry Lewen, after six months of tough negotiations with a group of Taiwanese investors, is on the verge of signing what any broker would regard as a dream deal – the sale of a $14 million building on New York's Madison Avenue. But the investors soberly informed Lewen of 'one final concern'. Before any sale would go through, they explained, they would have to enlist the services of a master of *feng shui*. After flying to New York from Taiwan, this practitioner of the ancient Chinese art would inspect the building; only if he declared the structure to be acceptable would the sale be completed.

Several days later, a jet carrying the *feng shui* master landed at a New York airport and a car whisked him directly to the Madison Avenue building. A small crowd of anxious onlookers had assembled and they watched intently as he surveyed the setting, took account of the surrounding buildings, and, for 30 tense minutes, walked through the structure noting the shape and length of hallways, the location of doorways and lifts, and the presence of mirrors, fountains and even air conditioners. 'I can tell you there were a lot of sweaty palms,' recounts Barry Lewen. In the end, the master turned to the apprehensive audience, smiled, and formally approved the building. A wave of relief broke over the group.

To the West's way of thinking, the merit of a building is a matter of its location, its size and the state of its plumbing and other systems. Such concerns are also of great importance to the Chinese. But, historically, members of south-east Asian societies have also considered how physical space affects human feelings and emotions. From this point of view, a 'life force' or *qi* (pronounced 'chee') flows through all of nature – including buildings – so that the physical design of a home or office building will either help or hinder this flow. A 'good' building – that is, one that stands in harmony with nature – will enhance the luck, health and prosperity of the people living or working inside (Dunn, 1994). Understanding how such cultural differences work is a crucial part of sociology, and this chapter sets out to explore them.

There is no such thing as a human nature independent of culture. Men without culture . . . would be unworkable monstrosities with very few useful instincts, fewer recognisable

sentiments, and no intellect: mental basket cases.

Clifford Geertz

There is no way out of the game of culture.

Pierre Bourdieu

In this chapter, we ask:

- **What is the meaning of 'culture' and its major components?**
- **What are the key features of Muslim cultures?**
- **What is cultural studies?**
- **How is globalisation shaping culture?**

(Left) *The Tribunal of the Inquisition*, detail from mural cycle (mural), Rivera, Diego (1886–1957)/Palacio Nacional, Mexico City, Mexico/Index/The Bridgeman Art Library. © 2011 Banco de Mexico Diego Rivera Frida Kahlo Museums Trust, Mexico D.F. DACS

Diego Rivera (1886–1957) is often seen as Mexico's most important artist and became a folk hero in Latin America. He led a passionate life devoted to art and communism. He is most famous for his large-scale political murals where he critically examines social and political issues relating to the working class. This image is an extract from a large mural which depicts the past sufferings and joys of the Mexican people and the ways the masses have built a great civilisation. It suggests they can and will build glorious civilisations in the future.

Source: Index/The Bridgeman Art Library.

Look at: The Diego Rivera Virtual Web Museum: http://www.diegorivera.com/.

See: Luis-Martin Lozano and Juan Coronel Rivera *Diego Rivera: The Complete Murals* (2008).

Q Rivera can be seen as a Marxist artist. Think how artists try to capture a sense of their own societies, often vast civilizations? Can you find parallels to Rivera's depiction of Mexico in the artists of other cultures around the world?

While the 7 billion-plus people on the earth today are members of a single biological species, *Homo sapiens*, we display remarkable differences. Some differences may be arbitrary matters of convention – the Chinese, for example, wear white at funerals while people in European countries prefer black. Similarly, Chinese people associate the number 4 with bad luck, in much the same way that people in England think of the number 13. Or take the practice of kissing: most people in Europe kiss in public, most Chinese kiss only in private; the French kiss publicly twice (once on each cheek), while Belgians kiss three times (starting on either cheek); for their part, most Nigerians don't kiss at all. At weddings, moreover, North American couples kiss, Koreans bow, and a Cambodian groom touches his nose to the bride's cheek! If you have travelled much, you will know that it really helps to be aware of these differences.

Other cultural differences, however, are more profound. The world over, people wear much or little clothing, have many or few children, venerate or shunt aside the elderly, are peaceful or warlike, embrace different religious beliefs, and enjoy different kinds of art, music, food and sport. In short, although we are all one biological species, human beings have developed strikingly different ideas about what is pleasant and repulsive, polite and rude, beautiful and ugly, right and wrong. This capacity for startling *difference* is a feature of our species: the expression of human culture.

What is culture?

Sociologists define **culture** as '*designs for living*': *the values, beliefs, behaviour, practices and material objects that constitute a people's way of life.* Culture is a toolbox of solutions to everyday problems. It is a bridge to the past as well as a guide to the future. One classic account puts it like this:

> Believing, with Max Weber, that *man is an animal suspended in webs of significance he himself has spun*, I take *culture to be those webs*, and the analysis of it to be therefore not an experimental science in search of law but an interpretative one in search of meaning . . .

(Geertz, 1995: 5, our italics)

To begin to understand what culture entails, it is helpful to distinguish between thoughts and things. What sociologists call **non-material culture** is *the intangible world of ideas created by members of a society*

that span a wide range from altruism to zen. **Material culture**, on the other hand, constitutes *the tangible things created by members of a society*; here again, the range is vast, running from armaments to zips, from mobile phones to pottery. They both involve cultural **practices** – *the practical logics by which we both act and think in a myriad of little encounters of daily life* (Bourdieu, 1990). Human beings make culture and it in turn 'makes us'. It becomes part of us – what we often (yet inaccurately) describe as 'human nature'. For sociologists, there is no such thing as human nature in itself: 'nature' is produced through our varying histories and cultures. This is often hard for students to grasp, but it is another example of where common sense gets challenged by sociology.

No cultural trait is inherently 'natural' to humanity, even though most people around the world view their own way of life that way. What is crucial to our human species is the capacity to create culture in our collective lives. Every other form of life – from ants to zebras – behaves in more uniform, species-specific ways. But to a world traveller, the enormous diversity of human life stands out in contrast to the behaviour of cats and other creatures, which is more or less the same everywhere. Most living creatures are guided by instincts, a biological programming over which animals have no control. A few animals – notably chimpanzees and related primates – have the capacity for limited culture: researchers have observed them using tools and teaching simple skills to their offspring. But the creative power of humans far exceeds that of any other form of life; in short, *only humans generate and then rely on culture rather than instinct to ensure the survival of their kind*. To understand how this came to be, we must briefly review the history of our species on earth.

Culture, intelligence and the 'dance through time'

In a universe some 15 billion years old, our planet is a much younger 4.5 billion years of age. For a billion years after the earth was formed, no life at all appeared on our planet. Huge geological upheavals kept changing the earth's surface. Billions more years went by before dinosaurs ruled the earth and then disappeared. And then, some 65 million years ago, our history took a crucial turn with the appearance of the creatures we call primates.

What sets primates apart is their intelligence, based on the largest brains (relative to body size) of all living creatures. As primates evolved, the human line diverged from that of our closest relatives, the great apes, about 12 million years ago. But our common lineage shows through in the traits humans share with today's chimpanzees, gorillas and orangutans: great sociability, affectionate and long-lasting bonds for child-rearing and mutual protection, the ability to walk upright (normal in humans, less common among other primates), and hands that manipulate objects with great precision.

Studying fossil records, scientists conclude that, about 2 million years ago, our distant ancestors grasped cultural fundamentals such as the use of fire, tools and weapons, created simple shelters, and fashioned basic clothing. Although these Stone Age achievements may seem modest, they mark the point at which our ancestors embarked on a distinct evolutionary course, making culture the primary strategy for human survival.

To comprehend that human beings are wide-eyed infants in the larger scheme of things, Carl Sagan (1980) came up with the idea of superimposing the 15-billion-year history of our universe on a single calendar year. The life-giving atmosphere of the earth did not develop until the autumn, and the earliest beings who resembled humans did not appear until 31 December – the last day of the year – at 10.30 at night! Yet not until 250,000 years ago, which is mere minutes before the end of Sagan's 'year', did our own species finally emerge. These *Homo sapiens* (derived from Latin meaning 'thinking persons') have continued to evolve so that, about 40,000 years ago, humans who looked more or less like we do roamed the earth. With larger brains, these 'modern' *Homo sapiens* produced culture at a rapid pace, as the wide range of tools and cave art from this period suggests. (You can see Carl Sagan and his account visually on *YouTube*).

Still, what we call 'civilisation' (see below) only began in the Middle East (in what is today Iraq and Egypt) and China about 12,000 years ago. In terms of Sagan's 'year', this cultural flowering occurred during the final *seconds* before midnight on New Year's Eve. Our modern, industrial way of life, begun a mere 300 years ago, amounts to less than a second in Sagan's scheme. It is with this fraction of a second that most of this book is concerned. We are:

> latecomers to a global party that has been in progress for at least 3.5 billion years, since life began, and will continue till the death of the planet itself. It is a fabulous party, with billions of participants from all walks of life.

(Tudge, 1995: 76)

Human culture, then, is very recent and was a long time in the making. As culture became a strategy for survival, our ancestors descended from the trees into the tall grasses of central Africa. There, walking upright, they discovered the advantages of hunting in groups. From this point on, the human brain grew larger, allowing for greater human capacity to create a way of life – as opposed to simply acting out biological imperatives. Gradually, culture pushed aside the biological forces we call instincts so that humans gained the mental power *to fashion the natural environment for themselves*. Ever since, people have made and remade their worlds in countless ways, which explains today's extraordinary cultural diversity.

What is civilisation?

Civilisations refer to *the broadest most comprehensive cultural entities*. Although there are many cultural groupings – 'Spanish culture', 'nudist culture', 'religious culture', 'gay culture', 'musical culture' – the idea of civilisation suggests the highest possible cultural grouping of peoples. A civilisation is a culture writ large. These have no clear-cut boundaries but are very long lived. They are totalities sensed over long periods (*the longue durée*, as it is often called).

Civilisations of the past include Ancient Sumerian, Egyptian, Classical, Mesoamerican, Christian and Islamic. Contemporary civilisations are often identified as:

- Chinese (or Sinic)
- Japanese (sometimes combined with China as Far Eastern civilisation)
- Indian or Hindu
- Islamic (originating in the Arabian peninsula in the seventh century CE) and including Arab, Turkic, Persian and Malay cultures
- Orthodox, centred in Russia and separate from western civilisation
- Western (emerging about 700 CE) in Europe, North America and maybe Latin America, although the latter is increasingly seen on its own as:
- Latin American (Catholic and more authoritarian)
- African

Religions are one of the key defining features of civilisations. Christianity, Islam, Hinduism and Confucianism are four leading religions linked to civilisations, and these are discussed in Chapter 19. In the twenty-first century, some social scientists talk about a new global culture emerging which will be seen as a 'universal' civilisation, but this is a hotly contested idea (Braudel, 1995; Huntington, 1996).

Table 5.1	The quick history of world societies: only seconds before midnight in Sagan's schema

The Contemporary World (1989–)

The Short Twentieth Century (1914–1989)

The Modern Era (1789–1914)

The Early Modern World (16th–18th centuries)

The Middle Ages (5th–15th centuries)

The Ancient World (2500 BCE–900 CE)

First Empires (circa 7000 BCE–200 CE)

Prehistory: from the beginning to around 4000 BCE

Source: National Geographic Visual History of the World (2005).

The major components of culture

Although the cultures found in all the world's nations differ in many ways, they all seem to be built on five major components: *symbols, language, values, norms and material culture*. In this section, we shall consider each in turn.

1 Symbols

Human beings not only sense the surrounding world as other creatures do, we build a reality of meaning. In doing so, humans transform elements of the world into **symbols**, *anything that carries a particular meaning recognised by people who share culture*. A whistle, a wall of graffiti, a flashing red light and a fist raised in the air all serve as symbols. We can see the human capacity to create and manipulate symbols reflected in the very different meanings associated with the simple act of winking the eye. In some settings this action conveys interest; in others, understanding; in still others, insult.

We are so dependent on our culture's symbols that we take them for granted. But entering an unfamiliar society also reminds us of the power of symbols; culture shock is nothing more than the inability to 'read' meaning in one's surroundings. We feel lost and isolated, unsure of how to act, and sometimes

Here are some well-known symbols. How do you make sense of them?
Human beings are symbol-manipulating creatures and the discipline that studies the nature of signs and symbols is semiotics. Since symbols are so important in understanding cultures, sociologists often have to draw from ideas in semiotics
Source: The Creative Symbol Collection, Ingram Publishing.

frightened – a consequence of being outside the symbolic web of culture that joins individuals in meaningful social life.

Culture shock is a two-way process. On the one hand, it is something the traveller experiences when encountering people whose way of life is unfamiliar. On the other hand, it is also what the traveller inflicts on others by acting in ways that may well offend them. For example, because the English consider dogs to be beloved household pets, travellers to northern regions of the People's Republic of China might well be appalled to find people roasting dogs as a wintertime meal. On the other hand, visitors to England from much of

south-east Asia can be shocked to find how much alcohol they consume! Indeed, global travel provides almost endless opportunities for misunderstanding. When in an unfamiliar setting, we need to remember that even behaviour that seems innocent and quite normal to us may be anathema to others.

Symbolic meanings vary even within a single society. A fur coat, prized by one person as a luxurious symbol of success, may represent to another the inhumane treatment of animals. Cultural symbols also change over time. Jeans were created more than a century ago as sturdy and inexpensive clothing for workers. In the liberal political climate of the 1960s, this working-class

LIVING IN THE C21ST

Texting: the making of a new language

Languages are always changing and information technology has brought many new forms of communication and language: computing languages, message texting, tweeting. Here we consider briefly the case of texting.

Texting has developed as a new universal language over the past 20 years. The first text message (or 'telenote', as it was originally called) was sent on 3 December 1992 by Neil Papworth to colleagues at Vodafone and said 'Merry Christmas'. The commercial launch of SMS (short service messages) took place in 1995, and the first recorded monthly text message total was 5.4 million in April 1998. Ten years on – in 2009 – there was a daily average of 265 million text messages and 1.6 million picture messages being sent in the UK alone. The text message total was 96.8 billion, while over 600 million picture messages were sent across the whole year. It has been estimated that on average, some 4.7 million text messages are currently sent

every hour in Britain. (Tweeting has had a similar success story, having grown to around 50 million world users.)

Are texters the modern vandals of our languages? From many quarters, the new language is roundly condemned. It is seen as a language for the lazy and the illiterate, and masks – even encourages – dyslexia, poor spelling and laziness. David Crystal, one of the world's leading linguists defends it. He argues that all languages are living and changing things and that this new language is just part of this. He goes further in seeing it a positive and exciting development. He writes:

Ever since the arrival of printing – thought to be the invention of the devil because it would put false opinions into people's minds – people have been arguing that new technology would have disastrous consequences for language. Scares accompanied the introduction of the telegraph, telephone, and broadcasting. But has there ever been a linguistic phenomenon that has aroused such curiosity, suspicion, fear, confusion, antagonism, fascination, excitement and enthusiasm all at once as

texting? And in such a short space of time. Less than a decade ago, hardly anyone had heard of it.

There is now growing research on texting which is exploring such issues as:

Does texting erode young people's ability to write and read? Does texting result in lazy and sloppy writing? Does it mark the end of the long history of the formal languages? Does texting reduce creativity?

David Crystal's review leads him to conclude that:

Some people dislike texting. Some are bemused by it. But it is merely the latest manifestation of the human ability to be linguistically creative and to adapt language to suit the demands of diverse settings. There is no disaster pending. We will not see a new generation of adults growing up unable to write proper English. The language as a whole will not decline. In texting what we are seeing, in a small way, is language in evolution.

See www.text.it; David Crystal, txtng: thegr8 db8, Oxford University Press (2008).

aura made jeans popular among affluent students –
many of whom wore them simply to look 'different' or
perhaps to identify with working people. A decade later,
'designer jeans' emerged as high-priced 'status symbols'
that conveyed quite a different message. In recent years,
jeans remain as popular as ever; many people choose
them as everyday clothing. Still others seek out designer
labels to establish their difference from others. Jeans
do not have a fixed symbolic meaning. In sum,
symbols allow people to make sense of their lives, and
without them human existence would be meaningless.
Manipulating symbols correctly allows us to engage
others readily within our own cultural system.

The *study of the symbols and signs* is called
semiotics. Broadly, semiotics suggests that meanings
are never inherent in objects but are constructed
around them through a series of practices. The
American pragmatist Peirce, the French language
specialist de Saussure and the French philosopher
Roland Barthes have made special studies of the ways
in which any sign – a T-shirt, a flag, a pop song,
a menu, a word – can be given different meanings.
We return to this in Chapter 22.

2 Language

Language, the key to the world of culture, is *a system of
symbols that allows members of a society to communicate
with one another*. These symbols take the form of
spoken and written words, which are culturally variable
and composed of the various alphabets and ideograms
used around the world. Even conventions for writing
differ: in general, people in Western societies write
from left to right, people in northern Africa and
western Asia write from right to left, and people in
eastern Asia write from top to bottom. We cannot be
sure how many world languages there are but a good
estimate is that there are around 6,900 languages across
the world (Table 5.2).

There are three major world languages: Chinese,
English and Spanish (Table 5.3). Chinese is the official
language of 20 per cent of humanity (about 1.2 billion
people). English is the mother tongue of about 10 per
cent (600 million) of the world's people, with Spanish
the official language of 6 per cent (350 million). While
these are major languages, there are thousands of
minor ones – estimates usually vary from 5,000 to
6,000. About 3,000 are endangered: 473 of the
languages listed in the *Ethnologue* are classified as
nearly extinct – classified this way when 'only a few
elderly speakers are still living'. Linguists predict that

Table 5.2	Distribution of languages by area of origin		
Area	Living languages		No. of people
	No.	%	
Africa	2,110	30.5	726,453,403
Americas	993	14.4	50,496,321
Asia	2,322	33.6	3,622,771,264
Europe	234	3.4	1,553,360,941
Pacific	1,250	18.1	6,429,788
Totals	6,909	100.0	5,959,511,717

Source: Used by permission, © S.I.L., adapted from *The Ethnologue*, 16th
edn, M. Paul Lewis (ed.), pub. 2009.

Table 5.3	Major world languages		
Rank	Language	No. of countries	No. of speakers (millions)
1	Chinese*	31	1,213
2	Spanish	44	329
3	English	112	328
4	Arabic*	57	221
5	Hindi	20	182
6	Bengali	10	181
7	Portuguese	37	178
8	Russian	33	144
9	Japanese	25	122
10	German, Standard	43	90

* There are varieties of language within these languages too.

Source: As Table 5.2.

half of our known living languages will die out during
this century, and 80–90 per cent will die off in the next
200 years. Large languages dominate smaller ones.

 tip   Have a look at the websites on world languages
and the endangered languages. The *Ethnologue*
is the most detailed: www.ethnologue.com.

The United Nations has a website which
monitors the loss of culture – including endangered
languages – in countries around the world. See
UNESCO Intangible Cultural Heritage Site and its
Atlas of the World's Languages in Danger:
www.unesco.org/culture/ich/index.

At the same time languages are always changing and developing. There are small signs of some languages resisting extinction – language revivals aiming to rekindle interest in languages such as Welsh take place. And new forms start to appear: the growth of texting through the wide use of mobile phones has suggested – controversially – that a new kind of language may be appearing (see *Living in the twenty-first century*, p. 147).

English is also becoming a global tongue: it is a favoured second language in many of the world's nations. It is used as an official or semi-official language in over 60 countries, and is the main language of the World Wide Web, air traffic control, business conferences and pop music. But in many countries there is considerable concern about this. So much so that there is now a European Bureau of Lesser Used Languages (EBLUL) which tries to promote and conserve these less used languages (with a bulletin, *Contact*, published three times a year and a website at www.//eblul.org). And some countries, such as France and Wales, are trying hard to resist the weakening of their language by challenging English words. In any event, Chinese remains the most popular language and is likely to triple its number of speakers by 2050. The European Union itself is a Tower of Babel. The European Commission in Brussels employs 400 full-time staff to deal with translation problems. In 2007, there were 23 official languages.

Dead language and ethnicity booms

In 2000, of the 262 or so million people in the USA aged 5 or over, some 215 million spoke only one language: English. But nearly 50 million spoke other languages at home (17.9 per cent of the population): 28 million spoke Spanish, 10 million spoke Indo-European languages, and about 6 million spoke Asian and Pacific Rim languages. There were nearly 12 million who were linguistically isolated (US Census, 2000).

Despite the dominance of the English language, from the mid-1960s onwards, North America and western Europe experienced something of an 'ethnicity boom' – a widespread awareness of different ethnicities having their own languages (the Census Bureau lists 25 languages, each of which is favoured by more than 100,000 people). In Europe, there are wide variations in language too, often generating conflicts. In Spain, Basque (Euskera) was banned during Franco's dictatorship from the mid-1930s: books written in it were publicly burnt. In the 1960s, policy changed, and

by March 1980 the first Basque Parliament was elected and Euskera became its official language. In Britain, although English dominates, both Welsh and Gaelic are more widely spoken than many presume and are given full support regionally, and there are speakers of Punjabi, Bengali, Urdu, Gujarati and Cantonese, not to mention German, Polish, Italian, Greek and Spanish. There is also 'Black English Vernacular' (BEV) linked to the use of a Creole English, used by the first blacks in America (Crystal, 2010).

Language and cultural reproduction

For people everywhere, language is the major means of **cultural reproduction**, *the process by which one generation passes culture to the next*. Just as our bodies contain the genes of our ancestors, so our symbols carry our cultural heritage. Language gives us the power to gain access to centuries of accumulated wisdom.

Throughout human history, people have transmitted culture through speech, a process sociologists call the **oral cultural tradition**, *transmission of culture through speech*. Only as recently as 5,000 years ago did humans invent writing, and even then, just a favoured few ever learned to read and write. It was not until the twentieth century that nations (generally the industrial high-income countries) boasted of nearly universal literacy (see Chapter 22). Even so, in many industrial countries there are still a large number of people who are functionally illiterate – approximately one in five people in the UK have literacy and numeracy problems, which is an almost insurmountable barrier to opportunity in a society that increasingly demands symbolic skills. In low-income countries of the world, illiteracy rates range from 30 per cent (People's Republic of China) to as high as 80 per cent (Sierra Leone in Africa).

Language skills not only link us with others and with the past, they also set free the human imagination. Connecting symbols in new ways, we can conceive of an almost limitless range of future possibilities. Language – both spoken and written – distinguishes human beings as the only creatures who are self-conscious, mindful of our limitations and aware of our ultimate mortality. Yet our symbolic power also enables us to dream of a better world, and to work to bring that world into being.

Is language uniquely human?

Creatures great and small direct sounds, smells and gestures towards one another. In most cases, these signals are instinctive. But research shows that some animals have at least a rudimentary ability to use symbols to communicate with one another and with humans.

Consider the remarkable achievement of a 12-year-old pygmy chimp named Kanzi. Chimpanzees lack the physical ability to mimic human speech. But researcher E. Sue Savage-Rumbaugh discovered that Kanzi was able to learn language by listening and observing people. Under Savage-Rumbaugh's supervision, Kanzi has amassed a vocabulary of several hundred words, and has learned to 'speak' by pointing to pictures on a special keyboard. Kanzi has correctly responded to requests like 'Will you get a nappy for your sister?' and 'Put the melon in the potty.' More intriguing, Kanzi's abilities surpass mere rote learning because he can respond to requests he has not heard before. In short, this remarkable animal has the language ability of a human child aged two years six months (Linden, 1993).

Despite such accomplishments, the language skills of chimps, dolphins and a few other animals are limited. And even specially trained animals cannot, on their own, teach language skills to others of their kind. But the demonstrated language skills of Kanzi and others caution us against assuming that humans alone can lay claim to culture.

Does language shape reality?

Do the Chinese, who think using one set of symbols, actually experience the world differently from Swedes who think in Swedish or English who think in English? The answer is yes, since each language has its own, distinct symbols that serve as the building blocks of reality.

Edward Sapir (1929, 1949) and Benjamin Whorf (1956; orig. 1941), two anthropologists who specialised in linguistic studies, noted that each language has words or expressions with no precise counterparts in other tongues. In addition, all languages fuse symbols with distinctive emotions. Thus, as multilingual people can attest, a single idea often 'feels' different if spoken in, say, German rather than in English or Chinese (Gerhard Falk, personal communication to J. J. Macionis, 1987).

Formally, then, what we now call the **Sapir–Whorf hypothesis** states that *people perceive the world through the cultural lens of language*. Using different symbolic systems, a Filipino, a Turk and a Brazilian actually experience 'distinct worlds, not merely the same world with different labels attached' (Sapir, 1949: 162). They

combine two principles, **linguistic determinism**, which suggests that *language shapes the way we think*, and **linguistic relativity**, which states that *distinctions found in one language are not found in another*. Whorf's classic case studies involved the Hopis, who had only one word for everything that flies – insects, planes, pilots – except birds; and the Inuit, who had many different words for snow.

The capacity to create and manipulate language also gives humans everywhere the power to alter how they experience the world. For example, many African Americans hailed it as a step towards social equality with white people when the word 'negro' was replaced by the term 'black' and, more recently, by 'African American' or 'person of colour'. Likewise, homosexuals redefined themselves as 'gay' during the 1970s, creating a more forceful, positive self-definition.

In short, a system of language guides how we understand the world but does not limit how we do so.

3 Values and beliefs

Values are *the standards people have about what is good and bad*, which vary from culture to culture. They are prescriptive: statements about what ought to exist in a language of ethical and moral terms, and are the broad principles that underlie **beliefs**, *specific statements that people hold to be true*. While values are abstract standards of goodness, beliefs are particular matters that individuals consider to be true or false.

Cultural values and beliefs not only colour how we perceive our surroundings, they also form the core of our moral world-view. We learn from families, schools and religious organisations to think and act according to approved principles, to pursue worthy goals, and to believe a host of cultural truths while rejecting alternatives as false.

European values?

In a continent as large and diverse as Europe, of course, few cultural values and beliefs are shared by everyone. In fact, with a long history of immigration from the rest of the world, Europe may be seen as a cultural mosaic. Even so, there may be some broad shape to European life.

First, European values can be seen as the long accumulation of what might be called 'the Age of the Enlightenment' (Gay, 1970). That is, they hold broadly to the values of rationality, science and progress that came with the philosophers – the great writers and thinkers, mainly of the eighteenth century (for example, Voltaire, Hume, Diderot). This was a period marked by significant improvements in some lives due to reason, science and medicine. People started to sense that they were the makers of their own futures, that they could exert some rational control over their world, that they could bring about change and make it a better place.

Second, Europe has been dominated by versions of the Judaeo-Christian religion, and its subsequent struggle with secularisation. Much of its heritage cannot be understood without grasping the long struggles between Catholic groups and emerging Protestant ones, and the more recent weakening of both. The very calendar year and most of its key holidays – Christmas, Easter – are bound up with Christian values, culture and identity: 'To be a European is to celebrate Christmas and Easter' (Therborn, 1995: 234). Thus core Christian values might suggest:

> **You should love the Lord your God with all your heart, and with all your soul, and with all your mind. This is the first and great commandment. And a second is like it. You should love your neighbour as yourself. On these two commandments depend all the law and the prophets.**
>
> (Matthew, 22: 37–40)

Third, European values have been structured by the development of nation-states, and their belief in 'citizenship'. Here core values of rights and obligations can be laid out to suggest what a good citizen – a 'Spaniard', a 'German', a 'Scot' – is expected to do.

And finally, Europe may be seen as a culture that has generally highlighted a principle of hierarchy – that people should recognise their superiors and inferiors. Europe has deep roots in the values of a feudal and aristocratic system that turns into a class system (Therborn, 1995: 273).

Asian values

At the turn of the twentieth century, a key global debate appeared which considered whether there were distinctive values in Asia. Some have argued that the 'East' differs from the 'West' over a number of key values such as:

- Belief in strong families
- Reverence for education

- Hard work a virtue
- Virtue of saving and frugality
- A social contract between the people and the state
- East Asians practise national teamwork
- Governments should maintain a morally wholesome environment
- Collective values and rejection of extreme forms of individualism.

Often these so-called Asian values have been used to justify authoritarian states, and critics say they are not in any sense 'distinctively Asian'. Asia is a region where about 60 per cent of the world's population lives – and it harbours many contrasting values deriving from sources as different as Confucianism and Islam (Mahbubani, 2004).

World values?

The political scientist Ronald Inglehart has produced an important, if somewhat controversial, body of evidence about the different kinds of values held across the six continents in some 97 different countries throughout the world over the past 30 years (Inglehart, 2000). He clusters societies on a number of different value dimensions, but two take prominence: what he calls traditional versus secular-rational, and survival versus self-expression.

- Traditional societies appeal to an authority rooted in the past – often via religion or through autocratic leaders. Secular-rational societies tend to be much less religious and can be seen to have values that are much more individualistic.
- The survival/self-expression dimension involves themes which link to the arrival of so-called postmodern or postmaterialist societies.

Some cultures – usually what we have called low-income societies – emphasise *survival values*. For Inglehart, this means they report low levels of subjective well-being, relatively poor health, low interpersonal trust, relative intolerance towards outgroups, low support for gender equality, emphasis on materialist values, relatively high levels of faith in technology and science, relatively low concern with environmental activism, and relatively favourable attitudes to authoritarian government. *Self-expression values*, by contrast, focus on the reverse of these.

In industrial societies, one of the main variations was found between age groups. Among the oldest, top priority was given to economic and physical security, but the younger birth cohort espouses what Inglehart calls a post-materialist view, where matters such as the environment and feminism become more important. Such younger groups give more importance to belonging and self-expression.

 If you want to look at different attitudes across cultures, here are some sources:

- *World Values Surveys (WVS)*, first conducted in 1981. A new wave of surveys will be carried out in 2010–11. This will provide a 30-year time series for the analysis of social and political change. See: www.worldvaluessurvey.org.

- *Eurobarometer*, conducted in the expanding European countries since 1973. This is the website for the Public Opinion Analysis sector of the European Commission. See: http://ec.europa.eu/public_opinion/index_en.htm.

- More specific studies, such as *British Social Attitudes*. The 26th annual survey of British attitudes can be accessed at: www.natcen.ac.uk/study/british-social-attitudes-26th-report.

Values: inconsistency and conflict

Cultural values can be inconsistent and even outright contradictory (Lynd, 1967; Bellah et al., 1985). For example, we sometimes find ourselves torn between the 'me first' attitude of an individualistic way of life and the opposing need to belong and contribute to some larger community. Similarly, we affirm our belief in equality of opportunity, only to turn around and promote or degrade others because of their ethnicity, gender or sexual preference. Value inconsistency reflects the cultural diversity of society and the process of cultural change by which new trends supplant older traditions.

4 Norms

In China, people curious about how much money colleagues are paid readily ask about their salaries. In Europe, people consider such a question rude. Such patterns illustrate the operation of **norms**, *rules and expectations by which a society guides the behaviour of*

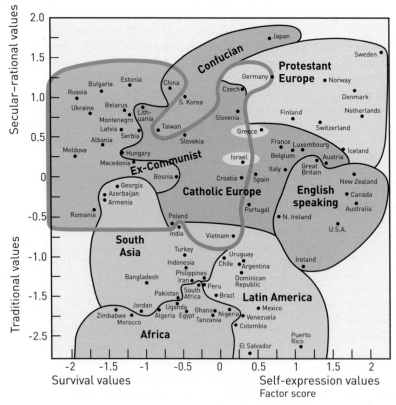

Map 5.1   World values: cultural map of the world

The World Values Surveys were designed to provide a comprehensive measurement of all major areas of human concern, from religion and politics to economic and social life. Two dimensions dominate the picture: (1) traditional/secular–rational and (2) survival/self-expression values.

Source: Inglehart-Weizel Cultural Maps of the World, www.worldvaluessurvey.org/statistics/some_findings.html.

For update: see www.worldvaluessurvey.org.

its members. Some norms are *proscriptive*, mandating what we should not do, as when Chinese parents scold young lovers for holding hands in public. *Prescriptive* norms, on the other hand, spell out what we *should* do, as when some European schools teach practices of 'safe sex'.

Most important norms apply virtually anywhere and at any time. For example, parents expect obedience from children regardless of the setting. Many normative conventions, by contrast, are situation-specific. In Europe, we expect audience applause at the end of a musical performance; we discourage it when a priest or a rabbi finishes a sermon. But, then, normative conventions change: increasingly, audiences at a rock concert can clap throughout the performance,

and fundamentalist religious leaders expect a clapping congregation (happy-clappy!). Indeed, postmodern societies seem to change a considerable informalisation of norms. They are still there, but become more complicated.

Mores and folkways

William Graham Sumner (1959; orig. 1906), an early US sociologist, recognised that some norms are more crucial to our lives than others. Sumner used the term **mores** to refer to *a society's standards of proper moral conduct*. Sumner counted among the mores all norms essential to maintaining a way of life; because of their importance, he contended that people develop an

PUBLIC SOCIOLOGY

Cultural difference, value conflicts?

Many social scientists argue that culture is the key to understanding how societies grow and change. They explain the fact that some have become advanced industrialised nations and others have not by considering their core values. Core values are seen to shape society. We have already seen how Weber saw the rise of capitalism as having a strong affinity with Protestantism through the 'Protestant ethic'.

To have an effective public sociology, 'values' need to be made explicit. They often are not. Once values are openly on the table, they can be discussed and debated.

For example, Lawrence Harrison overtly states that there are real cultural value differences between what he terms 'progressive' and 'static' societies. Progressive societies are the more industrialised societies; static ones are those which have not changed a great deal.

Among the value differences he notes are:

1 *Education*: a key to progress for progressive cultures, but of marginal importance except for the elites in static cultures.

2 *Time orientation*: progressives look to the future, statics look to the past or the present.

3 *Work*: central for progressive societies, but often a burden in static cultures.

4 *Frugality*: a major value for progressive societies – leading to investment and financial security; often a threat to static cultures.

5 *Merit*: central to advancement in progressive cultures; connections and family are what count in static cultures.

6 *Community*: in progressive cultures, community extends beyond the locality and the family; in static cultures, the family circumscribes community.

7 *Ethics*: more rigorous in advanced societies;

corruption is greater in static societies.

8 *Justice and fair play*: universal impersonal expectations in progressive cultures; in static societies, justice is often a function of who you know and how much you can pay.

9 *Authority*: dispersed in progressive societies; concentrated in static societies.

10 *Secularism*: progressive societies find that religious influence on civic life dwindles; in static societies, religion has a substantial influence.

Source: Harrison and Huntingdon (2000: 299).

Capturing general values like this is fraught with difficulties. They are far too general and suggest a moral split between 'Modern Societies' (progressive) and much of the rest of the world (static). You may like to ponder the weaknesses and strengths of such a depiction. Is the author being ethnocentric? How might culturalist explanations of change differ from materialist ones?

emotional attachment to mores and defend them publicly. In addition, mores apply to everyone, everywhere, all the time. Violation of mores – such as our society's prohibition against sexual relations between adults and children – typically brings a swift and strong reaction from others.

Sumner used the term **folkways** to designate *a society's customs for routine, casual interaction*. Folkways, which have less moral significance than mores, include notions about proper dress, appropriate greetings and common courtesy. In short, while mores distinguish between right and wrong, folkways draw a line between right and *rude*. Because they are less important than mores, societies afford individuals a measure of personal discretion in matters involving folkways, and punish infractions leniently. For example, a man who does not wear a tie to a formal dinner party is, at worst, guilty of a breach of etiquette. If, however, the man were to arrive at the dinner party wearing *only* a tie, he would be challenging the social mores and inviting more serious sanctions.

5 Material culture

In addition to intangible elements such as values and norms, every culture encompasses a wide range of tangible human creations that sociologists term *artefacts*. The Chinese eat with chopsticks rather than knives and forks, the Japanese place mats rather than rugs on the floor, and many men and women in India prefer flowing robes to the tighter clothing common

in much of Europe. An unfamiliar people's material culture may seem as strange to us as their language, values and norms.

Cultural diversity: many ways of life in one world

When contractors and estate agents in New York take account of the Chinese art of *feng shui*, as noted in the opening to this chapter, we can see a nation of striking cultural diversity. In fact, between 1980 and 1990, the number of people in the United States with Chinese or other Asian ancestry more than doubled. Historical isolation makes Japan the most *monocultural* of all industrial nations; heavy immigration over centuries, by contrast, makes the United States the most *multicultural* of all industrial nations.

Between 1820 (when the US government began keeping track of immigration) and 2001, more than 67 million people travelled to the United States from other countries. At the end of the nineteenth century, as shown in Figure 5.1, most immigrants hailed from Europe; by the end of the twentieth century, a large majority of newcomers were arriving from Latin America and Asia.

Cultural variety has characterised most of the world, and not just the United States. We return to this in Chapter 11. In this section, we look at some ways of approaching these diversities and differences.

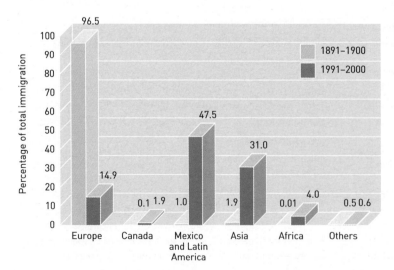

Figure 5.1 Recorded immigration to the United States, by region of birth, 1891–1900 and 1991–2000

Source: Adapted from US Immigration and Naturalization Service (2000).

The tool box of culture: ten ways to start a research investigation of culture

	Think about	Question	Discipline linkage
1	Symbols	Examine key symbols. Look at the chain of signs and the process of signification.	Semiotics
2	Language	What are the words, the slang, the special meanings of terms in this culture?	Social linguistics
3	Values	Know the values that inform cultures and guide lives.	Attitude and value measurement and surveys
4	Norms	Look for taken-for-granted rules, as well as wider, more public laws.	Sociology of law, ethnomethodology
5	Material Cultures	See material objects as acting in relational networks with consequences.	ANT theory
6	Stories and narrative	Listen to the stories (narratives, myths, accounts, etc.) that people tell.	Narrative theory
7	Verstehen Role Taking	Understand the ways people come to see others: see the world through others' eyes.	Max Weber used the term 'Verstehen'; G. H. Mead developed the idea of role taking
8	Emotions & Empathy	Appreciate what others are feeling.	Sociology of emotion – Cooley, Scheler, Hochschild
9	Identities and roles	How do people come to see themselves (who are they) and what roles do they perform?	Dramaturgy – see Goffman; role/performance theory; modern identity theory
10	Bodies	What are the key projects in which people use their bodies?	Mind/body dualism debates; the new 'body theory'

It is the challenge of ethography, field research and participant observation to examine these areas.

Source: Adapted from Plummer (2010: 108).

High culture and popular culture

Much cultural diversity is seen to have roots in social class. In fact, in everyday life, we often reserve the term 'culture' for sophisticated art forms such as classical literature, music, dance and painting. We praise some people as 'cultured', because they presumably appreciate the 'finer things in life'. The term 'culture' itself has the same Latin root as the word 'cultivate', suggesting that the 'cultured' individual has cultivated or refined tastes. By contrast, we speak less generously of ordinary people, assuming that everyday cultural patterns are somehow less worthy. In more concrete terms, Mozart is seen as 'more cultured' than Rap,

French 'cuisine' as better than fish fingers, and polo as more polished than ping pong!

Such judgements imply that many cultural patterns are readily accessible to some but not all members of a society. Sociologists use the shorthand term **high culture**[1] to refer to *cultural patterns that distinguish a society's elite*; **popular culture**, then, designates *cultural patterns that are widespread among a society's population*.

[1] The term 'high culture' is derived from the more popular term 'highbrow'. Influenced by phrenology, the bogus nineteenth-century theory that personality was determined by the shape of the human skull, people a century ago contrasted the praiseworthy tastes of those whom they termed 'highbrows' with the contemptible appetites of others whom they derided as 'lowbrows'.

Common sense might suggest that high culture is superior to popular culture. After all, history chronicles the lives of elites much more than those of ordinary women and men. But sociologists are uneasy with such a sweeping evaluation: they generally use the term 'culture' to refer to *all* elements of a society's way of life. However, they do recognise too that culture is also used to define people's social standing – their tastes, their distinction. Indeed, the term **cultural capital** (invented by sociologist Pierre Bourdieu – see Chapter 8, p. 254) is often used to designate *the practices where people can wield power and status because of their educational credentials, general cultural awareness and aesthetic preferences*. It is an idea which helps reinforce class distinctions – setting apart those who are 'cultured', who have 'travelled a lot', who know about their good wines and the latest 'art works'. 'Cultural' capital is distributed very unevenly in societies. Its acquisition starts in families and schools. But its impact continues through life as a major marker of distinction (Swartz, 1997: 76).

Subcultures and countercultures

Another set of differences are caught in the terms **subculture** (*cultural patterns that set apart some segment of a society's population*) and **counterculture** (*cultural patterns that strongly oppose those widely accepted within a society, contraculture*).

Rastafarians, young gays and lesbians, frequent-flyer executives, jazz musicians, old people in residential homes, homeless people, campus poets and offshore powerboat racers all display subcultural patterns. It is easy – but often inaccurate – to place people into subcultural categories. Almost everyone participates simultaneously in numerous subcultures, and we often have little commitment to many of them.

In some cases, however, important cultural traits such as ethnicity and religion do set off people from one another – sometimes with tragic results. Consider the former nation of Yugoslavia in south-east Europe. The turmoil there was fuelled by astounding cultural diversity. This *one* small country (which, before its break-up, was about half the size of England, with a population of 25 million) made use of *two* alphabets, professed *three* religions, spoke *four* languages, was home to *five* major nationalities, was divided into *six* political republics, and absorbed the cultural influences of *seven* surrounding countries. The cultural conflict that plunged this nation into civil war reveals that subcultures are a source not only of pleasing variety

but also of tensions and outright violence (see Chapter 16 and Sekulic et al., 1994).

Cultural diversity involves not just *variety* but also *hierarchy*. Too often, what we view as 'dominant' or 'highbrow' cultural patterns are those favoured by powerful segments of the population, while we relegate the lives of the disadvantaged to the realm of 'subculture'. This dilemma has led some researchers to highlight the experiences of less powerful members of our society in a new approach called multiculturalism (see the *Big debate* at the end of this chapter).

Youth cultures

Cultural diversity also includes outright rejection of conventional ideas or behaviour – countercultures. An example of this would be the youth-orientated counterculture of the 1960s that rejected the cultural mainstream as too competitive, self-centred and materialistic. Instead, hippies and other counterculturalists favoured a cooperative lifestyle in which 'being' took precedence over 'doing' and the capacity for personal growth – or 'expanded consciousness' – was prized over material possessions such as homes and cars. Such differences led some people at that time to 'drop out' of the larger society. Counterculture may involve not only distinctive values, but unconventional behaviour (including dress and forms of greeting) as well as music. Many members of the 1960s counterculture, for instance, drew personal identity from long hair, headbands and blue jeans; from displaying a peace sign rather than offering a handshake; and from drug use and the energy of ever-present rock and roll music. We look at these further in Chapter 13.

Cultural change

A wise human axiom suggests that 'All things shall pass'. Even the dinosaurs, which thrived on this planet for some 160 million years, exist today only as fossils. Will humanity survive for millions of years to come? No one knows. All we can say with certainty is that, given our reliance on culture, for as long as we survive, the human record will be one of continuous change.

Change in one dimension of a culture usually accompanies other transformations as well. For example, women's rising participation in the labour force has paralleled changing family patterns, including later age at first marriage, a rising divorce rate, and a growing share of children being raised in households without fathers. Such connections illustrate the principle of **cultural integration**, *the close relationship among various elements of a cultural system.*

But all elements of a cultural system do not change at the same speed. William Ogburn (1964) observed that technology moves quickly, generating new elements of material culture (such as 'test-tube babies') faster than non-material culture (such as ideas about parenthood) can keep up with them. Ogburn called this inconsistency *cultural lag*, the fact that cultural elements change at different rates, which may disrupt a cultural system. In a culture with the technical ability to allow one woman to give birth to a child by using another woman's egg, which has been fertilised in a laboratory with the sperm of a total stranger, how are we to apply the traditional notions of motherhood and fatherhood?

Cultural changes are set in motion in three ways. The first is *invention*, the process of creating new cultural elements. Invention has given us the telephone (1876), powered aircraft (1903) and the aerosol spray can (1941), all of which have had a tremendous impact on our way of life. The process of invention goes on constantly, as indicated by the thousands of applications submitted annually to the European Patent Office.

Discovery, a second cause of cultural change, involves recognising and understanding something not fully understood before – from a distant star, to the foods of another culture, to the athletic prowess of US women. Many discoveries result from scientific research. Yet discovery can also happen quite by accident, as when Marie Curie left a rock on a piece of photographic paper in 1898 and serendipitously discovered radium.

The third cause of cultural change is *diffusion*, the spread of cultural traits from one society to another. The technological ability to send information around the globe in seconds – by means of radio, television, facsimile (fax) and computer – means that the level of cultural diffusion has never been greater than it is today.

Certainly, our own society has contributed many significant cultural elements to the world, ranging from computers to jazz music. But diffusion works the other way as well: for example, much of what we assume is inherently 'British' actually comes from other cultures. Ralph Linton (1937) explained that many commonplace elements of our way of life – most clothing and furniture, clocks, newspapers, money, and often the food we eat – are derived from other cultures.

Ethnocentricity and cultural relativity

We think of childhood as a time of innocence and freedom from adult burdens such as regular work. In poor countries throughout the world, however, families depend on income earned by children. So what people in one society think of as right and natural, people elsewhere find puzzling and even immoral. Perhaps the Chinese philosopher Confucius had it right when he noted that 'All people are the same; it's only their habits that are different.'

Just about every imaginable social habit is subject to at least some variation around the world, and such differences cause travellers excitement and distress in about equal measure. The tradition in Japan is to name road *junctions* rather than streets, a practice that regularly confuses Europeans, for example, who do the opposite; Egyptians move very close to others in conversation, irritating any foreign visitors who are used to maintaining several feet of 'personal space'; bathrooms have a water tap but lack toilet paper throughout much of Morocco, causing great agitation among Westerners unaccustomed to using one's left hand for bathroom hygiene!

Because a particular culture is the basis for everyone's reality, it is no wonder that people everywhere exhibit **ethnocentrism**, *the practice of judging another culture by the standards of one's own culture.* On one level, some ethnocentrism is inevitable if people are to be emotionally attached to a cultural system. On another level, however, ethnocentrism generates misunderstanding and sometimes conflict.

For example, take the seemingly trivial matter of people in Europe referring to China as the 'Far East'. Such a term, which has little meaning to the Chinese, is an ethnocentric expression for a region that is far east *of Europe*. For their part, the Chinese refer to their country with a word translated as 'Middle Kingdom', suggesting that, like us, they see their society as the centre of the world.

Is there an alternative to ethnocentrism? The logical alternative is to imagine unfamiliar cultural traits from the point of view of *them* rather than *us*. The casual observer of an Amish farmer in Pennsylvania tilling hundreds of hectares with a team of horses rather than a tractor might initially dismiss this practice as hopelessly backward and inefficient. But, from the Amish point of view, hard work is a foundation of religious discipline. The Amish are well aware of tractors; they simply believe that using such machinery would be their undoing.

This alternative approach, called **cultural relativism**, is *the practice of judging a culture by its own standards*. Cultural relativism is a difficult attitude to adopt because it requires that we not only understand the values and norms of another society but also suspend cultural standards that we have known all our lives. But, as people of the world come into increasing contact with one another, so we confront the need to understand other cultures more fully.

The world may need greater cultural understanding, but cultural relativity introduces problems of its own. Virtually any kind of behaviour is practised somewhere in the world; does that mean that everything is equally right? Just because Indian and Moroccan families benefit from having their children work long hours, does that justify such child labour? It is hard to appreciate and understand other cultures and yet maybe maintain some sense of a universal standard. There are no simple answers to such dilemmas.

Resist making a snap judgement, so that you can observe unfamiliar cultural surroundings with an open mind. Try to imagine the issue from *their* point of view rather than *yours*. After careful thought, try to evaluate an unfamiliar custom. After all, there is no virtue in passively accepting every cultural practice. But, in reaching a judgement, bear in mind that – despite your efforts – you can never really experience the world as others do. Then turn the argument around and think about your own way of life as others might see it. What we gain most from studying others is insight into ourselves.

Muslim cultures: an example

Well over 1 billion people live in Muslim cultures across some 60 countries. They can be found in many Arab (e.g. Iraq, Egypt), Asian (e.g. Indonesia, Pakistan) and African (e.g. Algeria, Morocco) societies, as illustrated in Map 5.2. They can also be found partially almost everywhere else in the world (with large and growing minorities in Europe and America). Table 5.4 gives some indication of this. Muslim cultures are religion based and take on a wide variety of forms. All in all they serve around a quarter to a fifth of humanity.

Table 5.4	Approximate Muslim population in different countries
Saudi Arabia	100% of 27.6 million
Turkey	99.8% of 71 million
Afghanistan	Sunni Muslim 80%, Shi'a Muslim 19% of 31.88 million
Algeria	Sunni Muslim (state religion) 99% of 33 million
Morocco	98.7% of 33.75 million
Iran	98% of 65 million
Pakistan	97% of 164.7 million
Iraq	97% of 27 million
Egypt	90% of 80 million
Syria	Sunni Muslim 74%, other Muslim (includes Alawite, Druze) 16% of 19 million
Indonesia	86.1% of 234.7 million
Bangladesh	83% of 150 million
Malaysia	60.4% of 24.8 million
Lebanon	59.7% of 3.9 million
Nigeria	50% of 135 million
Kazakhstan	47% of 15 million
India	13.4% of 1.129 billion
UK	2.7% of 60.77 million
Australia	1.5% of 20 million
USA	1% of 301 million

Source: CIA, *The World Factbook*, www.cia.gov/library/publications/the-world-factbook.

Core cultural elements

What are Muslim cultures? As we have seen, all cultures suggest languages, world-views, norms, rituals and rules as well as material artefacts (like dress). Religion is the core of Muslim culture (indeed, religion has frequently been a major tool for building dominant cultures throughout world history – see Chapter 19). At the heart of its orthodoxy is complete submission to the will of Allah.

The *key text* is the Koran, Quran or Qur'an – the non-negotiable authority in Muslim life and belief. It literally means 'recitation' and it is taken to be the Word of God. It tells the life of Muhammad, and speaks of the *sunna* – his behaviour, sayings, values – and the *Shariah* – the 'path' for Muslims. 'God is Great.' 'There is no god but God.'

Understanding *language* is crucial for all cultures. Not understanding the language will inevitably bring major misunderstandings. Much discussion by

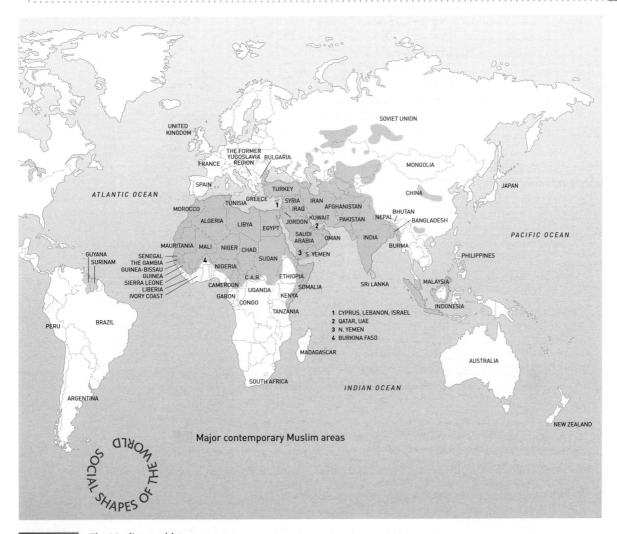

Map 5.2 The Muslim worlds

Source: Ahmed (1988: 146–7). *Discovering Islam*, Akbar S. Ahmed. Copyright © 1986 Routledge. Reproduced by permission of Taylor & Francis Books.

Westerners fails because there is a lack of comprehension – there is no speaking across cultures.

There are strong *rules* that tell Muslims what they must do (as in all cultures). Here they rest on the five pillars (a little like the Ten Commandments in Judaic and Christian religions – see Chapter 19). These are:

1 *The Shahada* – the affirmation: there is no god but God, and Muhammad is the messenger of God.
2 *Salat* – the set prayers to be said five times a day facing the Ka'ba (the shrine at the centre of the mosque at Mecca).
3 *Sawn* – daily fasting at Ramadan.
4 *Zakat* – almsgiving, contributing wealth for the poor and charitable causes (usually one-fortieth of their annual income).

5 *Hajj* – the pilgrimage to Mecca (the birthplace of Muhammad), which all healthy Muslims should try to do at least once in their life.

The *law* embodies four major different legal schools – the *Malaski*, *Hanafi*, *Shafi'I* and *Hanbali*. Most Muslims today relate to one or other of these, and this can be seen in contrasting ways: for example, performing prayer, conducting personal relations or treating criminals.

As with all cultures, rituals are very important to the conduct of daily life. There should be regular almsgiving (Zakat) and daily prayer (Salah). There is fasting during the month of Ramadan, and there should be a pilgrimage to Mecca during one's life (Hajj).

Muslim cultures are also replete with their own **material cultures**. These can be found in art (see the

(a)

(b)

(a) White-veiled East Timorese Muslim women pray at Ramadan's end
East Timorese Muslim women attend a mass prayer celebrating Eid al-Fitr at An-Nur mosque. Muslims around the world celebrate Eid al-Fitr, which marks the end of the fasting month of Ramadan.
(b) Veiled model presents a creation by Bahrain designer Maryam Wadlee
A model takes to the catwalk in an outfit by Bahrain designer Maryam Wadlee during the Gulf Night fashion show.

Source: (a) Corbis/Antonio Dasiparu/Epa; (b) Corbis/Wael Hamzeh.

opening image to Chapter 19, p. 658), calligraphy, books (the Koran), architecture (such as the mosques – the place of prostration), and in typical cultural dress and appearance: men bearded, women veiled.

Islam is a monotheistic religion. It combines holy law, a sacred text (the Koran), a prophet (Muhammad, 570–632 CE) and a prophetic revelation of individual salvation that is all-embracing over daily life. We look at it a little in Chapter 19. It began in the seventh century CE with the prophet Muhammad, born in the town of Mecca in what is now known as Saudi Arabia. Islam means entering into a condition of peace and security with God through allegiance and surrender to him. Muhammad – like Christ for Christians – is seen as the perfect example of living a life. Islam grew out of two declining empires – the Byzantine and the Sassanian – and Islam spread through the Middle East and Northern Africa.

Variation and divisions

Muslim cultures do have common themes, as suggested above. But they are also very different. There is Morrocan Islam, Pakistani Islam, Malay Islam and so on. South Asian Muslim cultures are not always at home with Arab cultures. To suggest only one Muslim culture, then, would be like suggesting there is only one Christian culture: that Christians in England are the same as Christians in Brazil, or that Methodist Christians in England are like Catholic Christians in Italy! Common themes, yes; but great variety.

After the death of the Prophet Muhammad (632 CE), the Muslim community split between the Sunni and the Shi'ite. This is a key divide that is present in many Muslim cultures and still works into conflicts today.

Sunni Muslims follow the customs of Muhammad. They originally thought that Muhammad's successor or caliph should be the best-qualified man. Today they base their lives on his sayings and actions. In contrast, the Shi'at Ali – the party of Ali – thought Muhammad's nearest relative should become their Imam. Sunni sees Islamic leadership in the consensus of the community rather than religious and political authorities. In general, they have more tolerant views based on the Koran (sometimes a parallel is drawn with Protestants in Christianity, as being a more flexible and less traditional approach). Shia – the 'partisans of Ali' – are the majority in Iran; there are more than 165 million and they generally hold strong views based on history and a strict interpretation of the Koran.

Politically too there are major splits across Muslim cultures. There are, for example, many radical groups that have appeared to fight the jihad (or holy war) across the world: the Muslim Brotherhoood in Egypt, the Islamic Revolution Front in Algeria, Hizbolllah in Lebanon, Hamas in the West Bank, and the now very well known Al Quaeda in Afghanistan. These more militant paths all have their own distinctive cultures – language, world-views, identities, knowledge.

Asabiyya: understanding Muslim cultures

Living in a culture brings deep understanding that is not always easy to see with an outsider's eyes. Yes, we can look at the rules, see the buildings and dress, read the Koran. But cultures are much more finely grained than this – they rest on hidden assumptions and rules, items that go much deeper than the surface observables. Akbar Ahmed suggests that a key idea to grasp is that of Asabiyya – an honour found through group loyalty. The loss of honour may be a key idea to understanding the workings of Muslim culture (Ahmed, 2003: 14). Indeed, it is so important that he talks about the modern world as 'the post-honour society' (Bowker, 2006; Ahmed, 1988; 2003; Rosen, 2004).

Understanding culture

Through culture, we make sense of ourselves and the surrounding world. Sociologists and anthropologists, however, have the special task of comprehending culture. They do so by using various theoretical paradigms.

The classic approach from anthropology: the functions of a culture

The reason for the stability of a cultural system, as functionalists see it, is that core values anchor its way of life (Parsons and Bales, 1955; Parsons, 1964; orig. 1951; Williams, 1970). The assertion that ideas (rather than, say, the system of material production) are the basis of human reality aligns functionalism with the philosophical doctrine of *idealism*. Core values give shape to most everyday activities, in the process binding together members of a society. New arrivals, of course, will not necessarily share a society's core orientations. But, according to the functionalist melting-pot scheme, immigrants learn to embrace such values over time.

Thinking functionally is also helpful in making sense of an unfamiliar way of life. Recall, for example, the Amish farmer ploughing hundreds of acres with a team of horses. This practice may violate the more widespread cultural value of efficiency; however, from the Amish point of view, hard work functions to generate discipline, which is crucial to Amish religious life. Long days of teamwork, along with family meals and recreation at home, not only make the Amish self-sufficient but unify families and local communities.

Of course, Amish practices have dysfunctions as well. Farm living is hard work, and some people find strict religious discipline too confining, ultimately choosing to leave the community. Then, too, different interpretations of religious principles have generated tensions and sometimes lasting divisions within the Amish world (Hostetler, 1980; Kraybill, 1989; Kraybill and Olshan, 1994).

Because cultures are strategies to meet human needs, we would expect that societies the world over would have some elements in common. The term **cultural universals** refers to *traits that are part of every known culture*. Comparing hundreds of cultures, George Murdock (1945) found dozens of traits common to them all. One cultural universal is the family, which functions everywhere to control sexual reproduction and to organise the care and upbringing of children. Funeral rites, too, are found everywhere, because all human communities cope with the reality of death. Jokes are also a cultural universal, acting as a relatively safe means of releasing social tensions.

WORLD WATCH

Disneyland: old cultures and new cultures in Europe

However unified Europe may or may not seem, it is clear that it harbours many different cultures with different ways of life and ways of doing things. Think of the following:

- *Breakfasts.* While in the UK it is cereals or a fry-up, in France they have croissants and in the Netherlands, cheese and ham.

- *The working day.* While in the UK to have a 'siesta' would be looked upon as outrageously lazy, in most Mediterranean countries the whole system shuts down after lunch for a couple of hours. Workers in Spain or Italy tend to be very casual and relaxed, even chaotic; in Germany, everything is much more formal.

- *Consuming.* The English tend to form queues, but this is not so in many European Union (EU) countries. Further, the English tend to accept the prices of goods from street sellers; not so in most of Europe. In UK bars you order drinks at the bar, pay straight away and do not tip; in most of the EU, you are served, pay at the end and leave a tip.

Yet these cultural differences – many and small – are starting to change. Increasingly, for instance, breakfasts offered at hotels throughout Europe would give a choice of cereals, fry-ups, croissants, cheese and ham, and even Japanese noodles. Cultural differences both are recognised and are breaking down.

And the new cultures

Nowhere was this clearer than when Disney came to Paris. Disneylands all over the world have been a favourite topic of cultural studies (see Bryman, 1995: 81–2, for a listing). EuroDisney, covering about 1,500 acres 20 miles east of Paris and housing six themed hotels, opened on 12 April 1992. EuroDisney was derided by French intellectuals as a cultural Chernobyl, and the unions objected to an almost fascist concern with uniformity that is anathema to the French. 'No one on the Disney payroll is allowed to smoke, wear flashy jewellery, chew gum, tint their hair an unnatural shade, possess a visible tattoo, be fat or fail to subdue their sweat glands. Men must wear their hair short, and may not have a beard or a moustache' (B. Bryson, 1993: 17).

In its opening years it was a significant failure, losing as much as $60 million in one three-month period and raising fears of closure. Many reasons were put forward for this, including the high costs and the poor weather. But at the heart of the complaints was a fear that Disney had come to the wrong place. It was out of culture.

Thus, while the French value food, here it was all fast food. While the French have a lugubrious and nonchalant manner, here the workers had to be cheery and efficient. The French could not easily play the smiling hosts. There was a cultural resistance and cultural contagion. Slowly, EuroDisney has become more successful: there is a lot of money in it, after all. And traditional cultures look less and less stable in the light of McDisney Worlds.

In 2005, Disneyland opened its first Asian Experience on Lantau Island in megapolis Hong Kong. After more than a decade of negotiations, Disney has now received clearance to build its second Disneyland in China, this one in Shanghai. In 2010, it celebrated its 55th anniversary.

See Alan Bryman, *Disney and His Worlds* (London: Routledge, 1995); and *The Disneyization of Society* (London: Sage, 2004).

EuroDisney, Paris
Source: Corbis/Peter Turnley.

Critical comment

The functional paradigm shows how culture operates as an integrated system for meeting human needs, yet by emphasising cultural stability, this approach downplays the extent to which societies change. Similarly, functionalism's assertion that cultural values are embraced by every member of a society overlooks the range of cultural diversity. Finally, the cultural patterns favoured by powerful people often dominate a society, while other ways of life are pushed to the margins. Thus, cultures typically generate more conflict than functional analysis leads us to believe.

New developments: the cultural turn and cultural studies

Over the past 40 years, sociology has been challenged by a number of newer disciplines. One of these has been 'cultural studies'. In this section, we will briefly consider a number of routes into this.

Early foundations of cultural studies: the culture industry and hegemony

Cultures are usually unequal, and some traits may benefit some members of society at the expense of others. Why do certain values dominate a society in the first place, and what are the ways in which people come to create their own alternative 'cultures of resistance'? Sociologists, often influenced by Marx, argue that values reflect a society's system of economic production. 'It is not the consciousness of men that determines their existence,' Marx proclaimed. 'It is their social existence that determines their consciousness' (1977: 4; orig. 1859).

The tradition of 'critical theory' was developed by the Frankfurt School in the 1930s. Theodor Adorno (1903–69), a leading proponent, suggested that the emerging 'mass culture' – of popular music and film, for example – weakened critical consciousness and manipulated the working masses. He studied the workings of the 'culture industry' and the ways in which it standardised culture, made people passive and served to make people uncritical. For Adorno, the 'culture industry perpetually cheats its consumers of

what it perpetually promises' (Adorno and Horkheimer, 1972: 120–3).

Another Marxist tradition was spearheaded by the Italian Antonio Gramsci (1891–1937). A militant in the Italian Communist Party, he spent ten years imprisoned by Mussolini. During this time he wrote his famous *Prison Notebooks* which developed the idea of **hegemony**, *the means by which a ruling/dominant group wins over a subordinate group through ideas*. 'Culture' in its many forms may thus serve as a mechanism for encouraging people to accept the existing social order uncritically – as a means of 'winning consent'. Through culture, coercive power may not be needed to maintain dominance. Watching a regular diet of soaps, daytime TV and sports programmes may be sufficient! This argument has been taken further by an English group of sociologists stimulated by the work of Stuart Hall (see *Thinkers and thinking* on p. 164).

The UK tradition: class and resistance

The UK tradition can be (roughly) dated from three important books written by socialist historians and literary critics. They differ from much of the discussion of this chapter, which focuses upon 'culture' as an anthropological and sociological term. Instead, each of these books switched attention to the study of the values, beliefs, behaviour and material culture of the working class in England. The three books are Richard Hoggart's *The Uses of Literacy* (1957), Raymond Williams's *Culture and Society* (1987; orig. 1958), and E. P. Thompson's *The Making of the English Working Class* (1963). What each of these books does is show that working-class culture is an intelligible, active, even coherent and vibrant culture that has historical roots. These authors highlighted the active nature of the working class – how they made their culture.

The Uses of Literacy looks at both traditional working-class culture (and Hoggart's own experiences in Leeds as a child) and the wider development of 1950s popular culture among the young – magazines, jukebox coffee bars – suggesting problems with the latter over the former as a new 'mass culture' emerged. *Culture and Society* formulated 'a theory of culture as the study of relationships in a whole way of life' (Williams, 1987; orig. 1958). *The Making of the English Working Class* traced 'the growth of class consciousness, especially through trade unions, friendly societies, educational and religious movements, political organisations and periodicals – working-class intellectual traditions, working-class community pattern, and a working-class structure of feeling' (Thompson, 1963). What this tradition highlighted, then, was the way in which working-class groups both created their own cultures and resisted other (dominant) ones. Cultures were active, and there was a worry that 'mass culture' was swamping this long-time 'active' nature.

This tradition was taken up and pushed further in the work of Stuart Hall. With Stuart Hall, 'cultural studies' comes into its own. Drawing from Hoggart and others, Hall makes culture a much more political idea. Indeed, as he says, popular culture is 'an arena of consent and resistance. It is partly where hegemony arises, and where it is secured. It is not a sphere where socialism, a socialist culture – already fully formed – might be simply expressed. But it is one

---

THINKERS & THEORY

Stuart Hall: from culture to cultural studies

Born in Jamaica in 1932, Stuart Hall came to England in the early 1950s and eventually became director of the Birmingham Centre for Contemporary Cultural Studies (CCCS) and Professor of Sociology at the Open University. He retired in 1997. He has been one of the world's leading shapers of cultural studies, and has influenced a whole generation of young scholars studying class, race, gender and national cultures. We will see the impact of his work throughout this book, especially when we look at ethnicity, media, identity and class. His students have looked at the ways media 'represent' gender; how ethnic groups battle over their identities; and how dominant political forces – such as 'Thatcherism' – have been resisted through the creation of alternative cultures, rituals and identities. He was indeed a key intellectual to recognise the importance of 'Thatcherism', *a political belief grounded in economic individualism and the free market*, and showed how this political philosophy was part of an 'authoritarian populism' which gained wider support in the culture by appealing to materialist

Stuart Hall (1932–)
Source: Eamonn McCabe.

and individualist (populist) as well as traditional (Victorian) values. He produced a model of communication with four key moments: production, circulation, use (consumption) and reproduction (see Chapter 21).

His earliest work was explicitly drawn from Marx, but most of his later work does not look to the economy so much as culture. He sees always the importance of people's lived ideas, as they turn them into everyday cultures, though he always sees these cultures enmeshed in the wider workings of the state. Much of his earlier work draws from Althusser and Gramsci, and his more recent work from **poststructuralism** – we introduce this term later (but see the Glossary at the end of the book now).

In one of his key books, *Policing the Crisis* (Hall, 1978), he

and his colleagues looked at the crime of 'mugging' in England in the early 1970s (1972–3) and showed how black youth were scapegoated for such crimes as part of wider state responses to changes in the organisation of capitalism and the state. He was one of the first to suggest that the growth of new immigrant groups in the UK in the 1950s and 1960s, combined with the recession of the early 1970s, had hit immigrant groups hard. The attacks being made on them were part of a new kind of racist response, deflecting attention away from growing unemployment and declining wages.

One of his key themes has been the ways in which cultures are hybrids, which encourage a fusion of different forms. Hybrid cultures no longer have one form or one set of values, but are much more contradictory and complex. Likewise, people do not have one unitary identity or one sense of who they are. Rather, they speak from many positions, with ethnicity, gender, sexuality and class all coming into it. Globalisation has generated more extreme forms of racism as people try to defend their own national identity.

Stuart Hall Hall retired from the Open University in 1997 and is now a Professor Emeritus. The British newspaper *The Observer* called him 'one of the country's leading cultural theorists'. For a brief tour of his work, see James Procter, *Stuart Hall* (2004).

of the places where socialism might be instituted. That is why "popular culture" matters' (Hall, in Storey, 1996: 3).

The North American tradition of cultural studies

A little after the development of the UK tradition, a distinctive US pattern of research started to develop from within mainstream sociology during the late 1980s and early 1990s. In general, it is much less abstractly theoretical and more empirically grounded in middle-range research – and usually with a much more scientific claim for its position. It deals more concretely in case studies – with much less concern for class analysis or taking critical stances. Its prime concern is with the analysis of meanings and symbols. It studies key objects like art collections, computers, AIDS, nuclear power and war memorials in order to grasp their place in the symbolic order (for examples, see Smith, 1998).

The study of the global cultural industries

One important aspect of culture in the contemporary world is the development of commercial industries. David Hesmondhalgh (2007) has outlined seven core industries which constitute large parts of the economy and employ many people. They are:

1 *Broadcasting*: the radio and television industries.
2 *Film industries*: which include the dissemination of films on video and DVD.
3 *The content aspect of the internet industry* (i.e. that which is not simply to do with electronics).
4 *Music industries*: recording, publishing and live performance.
5 *Print and electronic publishing*, including books, newspapers and CD-Roms.
6 *Video, computer and digital games.*
7 *Advertising and marketing.*

Table 5.5 shows some of the biggest corporations that are directly involved in the production and dissemination of products and services that shape contemporary culture in many countries, if not worldwide. Sony produces a wide variety of cultural objects, from music to films to video games consoles. Microsoft and Apple are responsible for computer technology, software and computer entertainment

Table 5.5	10 Large corporations with cultural industry interests (financial year 2010)	
Company	Total revenue (UK £m; approximate)	Gross profit (UK £m; approximate)
Sony Corp.	54,000	11,000
Apple	40,000	15,000
Microsoft	38,000	30,000
Vivendi	25,000	12,000
Walt Disney Co.	23,000	4,000
Coca Cola Co.	21,000	13,000
News Corporation CDI	20,000	7,000
Christian Dior SA	18,000	11,000
Time Warner Inc.	16,000	6,000
Google	18,000	11,000

Source: Adapted from: http://money.msn.com/stocks; Access date: 20 May, 2011. Currency conversion according to exchange rates published on www.xe.com; 20 May, 2011.

products that have had a defining impact on electronic cultures in the Western world and beyond for several decades. Disney cartoons began to shape the imagination of children (and many adults) in the USA in the first half of the twentieth century, and since then they have spread rapidly around the globe. News Corporation owns newspapers and TV channels that shape the political attitudes of many people in the Western world. Vivendi is involved in television, music, film and videogame production, and Time Warner is active in television, cinema and news publications. Christian Dior is regarded as a leading provider of luxury fashion, while L'Oréal produces a wide range of cosmetics and hygiene items. Google, finally, has become one of the most successful internet search engines and providers of online content worldwide. We look more at this in Chapter 22.

A recent study by Scott Lash and Celia Lury (2007) has examined a range of these 'texts' or things as they have 'moved' across the world. They are interested in the ways in which these objects have become brands which almost take on a social life of their own. Their concern is with the biography of objects – with following them through the shifting and multiple journeys they follow.

Circuits of culture: doing cultural studies research

In a celebrated discussion, Stuart Hall, Paul du Gay and others have suggested that any cultural item or object can be analysed through a circuit of culture which has five key features. Look at Figure 5.2, and then pick any cultural object that interests you. This can be a film like *Avatar*; a TV channel like Sky Arts; a TV programme like *The X Factor*; an item of clothing like a Nike shoe; or even a technology like an iPhone or iPad. Then think how you can present an analysis of it, following the questions below.

There are five moments in the process of the life of any cultural object – from fashion and food to houses and holidays. These five moments serve to establish:

- *Production*. How are raw materials, labour, time and technologies combined to create an object? This may include the inventor and founder of the object, but also the economics of its making as well as the cultures of work, the organisation of businesses and so on that generate it.

- *Representation*. What are the ways in which meanings are presented around the object (for example, images in magazines, on television and film, through logos)? This may be through spoken and written words, but also through photographs, videos, drawing, music and painting – in fact, any way of representing the 'object'.

It now becomes a set of signs and symbols, open to interpretation and the creation of meanings.

- *Identities*. What are the roles or positions from which people are recruited to buy this object? Certain styles of fashion (or houses, or food) appeal to certain kinds of people. Consuming certain items and not others may enhance style, create a sense of difference and allow for a new identity to be found.

- *Consumption*. What is involved in the exchange of services at the moment when objects are bought and consumed? It is very closely linked to production (but then, as we have shown, they are all linked), where we are concerned in part with marketing strategies, market research, advertising and design features. But the prime concern here is with the accumulation of material goods and the proliferation of spaces for consumption – shops, malls, mail order, e-markets, etc. It is linked with social differentiation (how different groups consume different items) and the ways that consumption may change people's consciousness and perceptions.

- *Regulation*. What are the ways in which the public and private spheres of life are linked in the governance and control of production and consumption? This means looking at the employment rules, and any censorship rules, laws which may regulate the way it can be produced and consumed.

The study of culture circuits often leads especially to the study of cultural industries.

Source: Paul Du Gay, Stuart Hall, L. Janes, H. MacKay and K. Negus (eds), *Doing Cultural Studies: The Story of the Sony Walkman* (Buckingham: Open University Press, 1997).

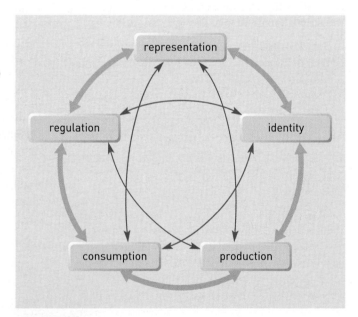

Figure 5.2   The circuit of culture

They take a range of 'objects' and follow them through the 'circuit of culture' (see Figure 5.2). Thus, they examine *Toy Story*, *Trainspotting* and the *Wallace and Grommit* animated films; the European Football Championship of 1996; the art movement BA of a group of British artists; and two major retail brands, Swatch and Nike. They devote a chapter to each and ask about its life history.

Postmodernism and the new culture

If modernism suggests the need to 'make it new', then postmodernism suggests it has all been done, and all we can do is 'play with the pieces'. In recent times, and despite its controversial nature, postmodernism has become an influential world-view, and is heavily shaped by North America. A key to the postmodern is a sense of the fragments and the loss of any one unifying theme. Postmodern culture is usually seen to (a) celebrate the surface rather than depth; (b) be eclectic and pastiched; and (c) adopt ironic and even cynical tones.

Postmodern culture is usually seen to originate in the provinces of architecture and art. Thus, postmodern architecture borrows colourfully from past styles and is less concerned with obvious function. It is found in the work of Robert Venturi, Richard Rogers, I. M. Pei and Charles Moore. The Bonaventura Hotel in Los Angeles is perhaps the classic example. Here is a massive hotel in the heart of the downtown city area whose lobby seems to serve like a gigantic aircraft hanger-come-shopping mall!

Postmodernism suggests a wide variety of pastiched and differing styles. In art it is often linked to new playful forms, such as video art, body art and 'art installations'. Many of the new art galleries, such as the Tate Modern in London, the Guggenheim at Bilbao and the new Getty in Los Angeles, are also seen as prime examples. In literature, postmodernism becomes what writer John Barth has called 'the literature of exhaustion': it is often indulgently self-reflective and is often linked to contradiction, permutation, discontinuity, randomness and excess (Lodge, 1977: 228). Likewise, postmodern films (found in the work of directors such as Jim Jarmusch and David Lynch) often engage with a radical reordering of what are seen as traditional narrative forms. And in postmodern music (John Cage, John Adams, Michael Nyman) the form is usually bare and minimalist yet with striking technosonic effects.

Looking ahead: globalisation, global cultures and hybridity

We have looked at a wide range of cultural phenomena in this chapter: culture is the stuff of our everyday life experience and sociology has found a major collaborator in its study. More than this, we also showed the impact of our concern with globalisation on cultures worldwide. We will conclude this chapter with a brief tour of the implications of globalising cultures.

Today, more than ever before, we can observe many of the same cultural patterns the world over. Walking the streets of Seoul (South Korea), Kuala Lumpur (Malaysia), Chennai (India), Cairo (Egypt) and Casablanca (Morocco), we find familiar forms of dress, hear well-known pop music, and see advertising for many of the same products we use at home. Just as important, English is rapidly emerging as the preferred second language of most of the world. So are we witnessing the birth of a global culture?

Yet as we have seen, the world is still divided into around 200 nation-states and thousands of different cultural systems. Many of these are in deep conflict. As recent violence in the former Soviet Union, the former Yugoslavia, the Middle East, Sri Lanka and elsewhere attests, many people are intolerant of others whose cultures differ from their own. Yet, looking back through history, we might sense that societies around the world now have more contact with one another, and enjoy more cooperation, than ever before. These global connections involve the flow of goods, information and people.

1 *The global economy: the flow of goods*. The extent of international trade has never been greater. The global economy has introduced many of the same consumer goods (from cars to TV shows to T-shirts) the world over.

2 *Global communications: the flow of information*. A century ago, communication around the world depended on written messages delivered by boat, train, horse and wagon, or, occasionally, by telegraph wire. Today's satellite-based communication system enables people to experience sights and sounds of events taking place thousands of miles away – often as they happen.

3 *Global migration: the flow of people*. Knowledge about the rest of the world motivates people to

move where they imagine life will be better. Moreover, today's transportation technology – especially air travel – makes relocating easier than ever before. As a result, most countries now contain significant numbers of people born elsewhere, and tourism has become one of the leading world industries.

These global links have partially made the cultures of the world more similar, at least in superficial respects. But they have also generated awareness of deep contrasts in world peoples. Some – usually poor and in low-income cultures – remain heavily restricted to a local world. But others have developed a much more flexible, global character. Ulf Hannerz describes this as a *cosmopolitan character*, who adopts:

> **a stance towards diversity . . . towards the coexistence of cultures in the individual experience . . . a willingness to engage with the other . . . a stance of openness towards divergent cultural experiences . . . a search for contrasts rather than towards uniformity . . . a state of readiness, a personal ability to make one's way into other cultures, through listening, looking, intuiting and reflecting . . .**

(Hannerz, 1990: 239)

Sociologists also talk of the hybridisation of cultures. Just as in plant biology, a hybrid is a crossover between different species, so **cultural hybridisation** refers to *the ways in which parts of one culture (language, practices, symbols) get recombined with the cultures of another*. Dutch sociologist Jan Nederveen Pieterse puts this strikingly:

> **How do we come to terms with phenomena such as Thai boxing by Moroccan girls in Amsterdam, Asian rap in London, Irish bagels, Chinese tacos and Mardi Gras Indians in the United States, or Mexican schoolgirls dressed in Greek togas dancing in the style of Isadora Duncan? How do we interpret Peter Brook directing the Mahabharata, or Ariane Manouchkine staging a Shakespeare play in Japanese Kabuki style for a Paris audience in the Théatre Soleil?**

(Pieterse, 1995: 53)

But there are three important limitations to the global culture thesis. First, the flow of goods, information and people has been uneven throughout the world. Generally speaking, urban areas (centres of commerce, communication and people) have stronger ties to one another, while rural villages remain more isolated. The greater economic and military power of North America and western Europe means that these regions influence the rest of the world more than the other way around.

Second, the global culture thesis assumes that people everywhere are able to afford various new goods and services. The grinding poverty in much of the world deprives millions of even the basic necessities of a safe and secure life.

Third, although many cultural traits are now found throughout the world, we should not conclude that people everywhere attach the same meanings to them. Do teenagers in Tokyo understand rap music the way their counterparts in New York or Los Angeles do? Similarly, we mimic fashions from around the world with little knowledge of the lives of people who first came up with them. In short, people everywhere look at the world through their own cultural 'lenses' (Featherstone, 1990). This process has been identified as **glocalisation**, *the ways in which global phenomena are responded to differently in local cultures*. Karaoke may have been sent round the world from Japan, but it takes on different meanings, songs and rituals when it is done in Thailand, London or San Francisco.

All this said, a hallmark of twenty-first century life is its hybridic and increasingly cosmopolitan nature.

SUMMARY

1 Cultures are 'designs for living' and refer to ways of life. They are partly material (tangible things like telephones or pottery), partly non-material (for example, ideas) and involve practices (the practical logics through which we act and think in everyday life). Several species display a limited capacity for culture, but only human beings rely on culture for survival.

2 As the human brain evolved, the first elements of culture appeared some 2 million years ago; the development of culture reached the point we call 'the birth of civilisation' approximately 12,000 years ago.

3 Humans build culture on symbols by attaching meaning to objects and action. Language is the symbolic system by which one generation transmits culture to the next. Values represent general orientations to the world around us; beliefs are statements that people who share a culture hold to be true. Cultural *norms* guide human behaviour: mores consist of norms of great moral significance; *folkways* guide everyday life and afford greater individual discretion. *Material culture* refers to tangible human creations.

4 High culture refers to patterns that distinguish a society's elites; popular culture includes patterns widespread in a society. Subculture refers to distinctive cultural patterns adopted by a segment of a population; counterculture means patterns strongly at odds with a conventional way of life.

5 Invention, discovery and diffusion all generate cultural change. When parts of a cultural system change at different rates, this is called cultural lag.

6 Because we learn the standards of one culture, we evaluate other cultures ethnocentrically. An alternative to ethnocentrism, cultural relativism, means judging another culture according to its own standards. The conflict perspective envisages culture as a dynamic arena of inequality and conflict. Cultural patterns typically benefit some categories of people more than others.

7 Cultures may be approached functionally (as a relatively stable system built on core values, cultural traits function to maintain the overall system). They may also be approached conflictually as webs of inequality, mass culture and hegemony.

8 The past 30 years have seen the growth of cultural studies and the study of cultural industries.

9 Increasingly we live in global cultures that generate hybrids and cosmopolitan characters.

CONNECT UP: Turn to Part 6 of this book for key resources and link up
with the book's website, which links to these resources
SEE: www.pearsoned.co.uk/plummer

MYTASKLIST

Suggestions for going further

1 Connect up with Part Six and the Sociology Web Resources

As you work through ideas and think about the issues raised in this chapter, look at the accompanying website and the resource centre at the end of this book which connects to it. There is a lot here to help you move on. To link up, see: www.pearson.co.uk/plummer.

2 Review the chapter

Briefly summarise (in a paragraph) just what this chapter has been about. Consider: (a) What have you learned? (b) What do you disagree with? Be critical. And (c) How would you develop all this? How could you get more detail on matters that interest you?

3 Pose questions

(a) Imagine you are a stranger arriving for the first time in your culture. Look at it with a stranger's ideas and try to see just how its values, symbols, languages, etc. give it a distinctive feel. Look at the book by Kate Fox: *Watching the English: The Hidden Rules of English Behaviour* (2005), which provides a fascinating account of the oddities of the English!

(b) Give instances of Eurocentrism found in this textbook (if you can find them!). Are there European values at work? Do you think European cultural values are changing? If so, how and why?

(c) Using some of the key concepts developed in this chapter – language, values, material culture, etc. – present an analysis of any one cultural group you know (such as a religious culture, a sports culture, a youth culture or a 'deviant' culture). (*Hint*: look back at Chapter 3 on ways of doing research, and do a web

search for different groups, scenes.) The chapter uses Muslim culture as an example and you could use this as your example too.

(d) What is cultural studies? How does it differ from sociology? Which might be more helpful in studying human societies?

(e) Is the world becoming more culturally hybridic and cosmopolitan? Discuss clear examples.

4 Explore key words

Many concepts have been introduced in this chapter. You can review them from the website or from the listing at the back of this book. You might like to give special attention to just five words and think them through – how would you define them, what are they dealing with, and do they help you see the social world more clearly or not?

The classic book here is Raymond Williams, *Keywords* (1975). Also see Chris Barker, *The Sage Dictionary of Cultural Studies* (2004).

5 Search the Web

Be critical when you look at websites – see the box on p. 940 in the Resources section. For this chapter look at the following.

Languages

The Ethnologue
www.ethnologue.com
Site for the study of all the world's known living languages.
The UNESCO endangered languages site
www.unesco.org/culture/ich/index.php?pg=00136

Cultural attitude surveys

World Values Survey
www.worldvaluessurvey.org
Global Voice of the People
www.voice-of-the-people.net

British Social Attitudes
www.britsocat.com/Body.aspx?control=HomePage
European Social Survey
www.europeansocialsurvey.org
http://ec.europa.eu/public_opinion/standard_en.htm

Cultural studies

Theory.org.uk
www.theory.org.uk
A well-established site for cultural theory fans (do not confuse it with theory.org).
Cultural Studies Central
www.culturalstudies.net
Another large and well-established site.

Cultural anthropology

Human Relations Area Files
www.yale.edu/hraf
A major resource on different cultures.
Society for Cultural Anthropology
www.aaanet.or/sca/index.htm
Site for the American Anthropological Society, focusing on culture.

6 Watch a DVD

Wim Wender's *Buona Vista Social Club* (1991) ostensibly looks at the making of music in Cuba, but conveys much more about culture.

This may be a good time to watch some class DVDs that display youth cultures and look for their language, values, symbols, etc. Have a look at Nicholas Ray's *Rebel without a Cause* (1955), Dennis Hopper's *Easy Rider* (1969), John Badham's *Saturday Night Fever* (1977), Michael Lehman's *Heathers* (1989) and Catherine Hardwicke's *Thirteen* (2004). These are just a few and span some 50 years. Bring them up to date with *High School Musical* (parts 1–3) or *The Twilight Trilogy* (parts 1–3). All are based on US culture, have been very influential in their time and show the drifting cultural forms of youth cultures. Search for more and maybe think of drawing up a comparison.

7 Think and read

Martin J. Gannon, *Understanding Global Cultures: Metaphorical Journeys through 23 Nations* (4th edn, 2009) provides a series of short case studies of different cultures through an organising image such as 'The Japanese Garden', 'The Brazilian Samba', 'American Football', 'The Spanish Bullfight' and 'The Swedish *Stuga*'.

Ken Gelder, *Subcultures* (2008) provides a clear and historical account of subcultures.

Ken Gelder and Sarah Thornton (eds), *The Subcultures Reader* (2005, 2nd rev. edn) and D. Muggleton and R. Weinzierl (eds), *The Post-subcultures Reader* (2004) provide both classic readings around subcultures and the different forms of youth cultures and up-to-date challenges to classical work.

Akbar Ahmed, *Discovering Islam: Making Sense of Muslim History and Society* (1988), alongside his *Islam Under Siege* (2003), provides a good guide to Muslim culture and its contemporary conflicts.

The new field of cultural studies should not be confused with 'culture', which generally has a much broader set of concerns. Jeff Lewis, *Cultural Studies: The Basics* (2nd edn, 2008) and Chris Rojek, *Cultural Studies* (2007) are two useful short guides to the whole field. The latter suggests that the field of inquiry has moved through four 'moments': the 'National/Popular', the 'Textual/Representational', 'Global/Post Essentialism' and 'Governmentality/Policy'. Simon Duhring (ed.), *The Cultural Studies Reader* (2nd edn, 2006) includes articles by Adorno, Hall, Williams, Bourdieu and many others.

The essential reading on the culture industries is David Hesmondhalgh, *The Cultural Industries* (2nd edn, 2007), which gives detailed accounts of each industry.

Finally, Scott Lash and Celia Lury, *Global Culture Industry: The Mediation of Things (2007)* examines a range of cultural products.

8 Relax with a novel

You might read some books on 'culture clash'. E. M. Forster's *A Passage to India* (1924), also a film by David Lean (1985), and Henry James's *The Europeans* (1978 edn), also a Merchant-Ivory film (1978), would be interesting starts. And for a complete contrast, Gautam Malkani's coming-of-age novel *Londonstani* (Fourth Estate, 2005) captures modern youth culture – a mix of English, street cred, Punjabi, Urdu, profanity, mobile texting and 'gangsta rap'.

9 Connect to other chapters

- For more on semiology and how to do a mass media analysis, see Chapter 22.
- For more on cultural studies, see Bourdieu in Chapter 20.
- For more on religion and culture, see Chapter 19.

10 Engage with THE BIG DEBATE

Whose culture is this? The problem of Eurocentrism, multiculturalism and postcolonialism in sociology

For some, Europe can be seen as the cradle of the modern world. Indeed, for the Swedish sociologist Goran Therborn:

> There is no doubt that Europe was the pioneer of modernity and the centre of it. Neither the Islamic, the Black African, the Hindu nor the East Asian Confucian world seems to have discovered the future as a new place, attainable but never visited before . . . Europe became the undisputed centre of modernity in terms of knowledge as well as in terms of power.
>
> (Therborn, 1995: 19)

It was the 'chief organiser' of this modern world. For Therborn, there are many features of this. Europe's 'modernity' brought new knowledge, new settlements around the world, new technologies and capital investment, as well as the development of all the 'isms' – socialism, communism, anarchism, liberalism, Protestantism, etc.

But 'a sense of Europe' can go back a long way. Some writers suggest that European culture can be defined by four elements that mark it off from the rest of the world:

- The Hellenistic and Roman Empires – rediscovered through the Renaissance – which helped establish a sense of art, politics and philosophy that shapes a characteristic 'humanistic' temper.
- Christianity, which for two millennia, and despite oppositions and internal schisms, has pervaded the European idea (and at times the very words 'Europe' and 'Christendom' were synonymous).
- The Enlightenment – the creation of a scientific, sceptical, creative intellectual climate helps to define it – as does the 'Europabild' literature.
- Industrialisation: while not alone, and these days overtaken by many other countries, it was the first region to foster the industrial world (Hay, 1968).

Yet there are serious problems with this commonly held 'Eurocentric' view. Taking a European view of the world often minimises the importance of other cultures: Asian, Latin American, African, etc. It also cultivates a view of Europe as an entity with a history of continuity, which on closer inspection is hard to sustain. Greek history, for example, is as much connected to the Middle East and the Orient. Indeed, the eminent historian Arnold Toynbee saw this continuity as a 'thoroughgoing misinterpretation of the history of Mankind' – a dangerous tendency that minimised the contribution of many other cultures. These days, this is recognised as the twin problem of 'multiculturalism' and 'postcolonialism'.

Originally emerging as an education policy in the United States, **multiculturalism** *recognises past and present cultural diversity and promotes the equality of all cultural traditions*. This movement represents a sharp turn from the view where cultures are defined through their European links. **Postcolonialism** *recognises how many cultures have been made through oppressor–subject relationships and seeks to unpack these, showing how cultures are made*.

For more than two centuries, historians have highlighted people of English and other European ancestry and chronicled events from their point of view. In the process, little attention has been paid to the perspectives and accomplishments of other cultures. Multiculturalists condemn this pattern as **Eurocentrism**, *the dominance of European (particularly English) cultural patterns*. Molefi Kete Asante, a leading advocate of multiculturalism, draws a historical analogy. Like the fifteenth-century Europeans who could not let go of the idea that the earth was the centre of the universe, many today find it difficult not to view European culture as the centre of the social universe (Asante, 1988: 7).

The European flag
Source: Corel Flags of the World

Few deny that our culture has wide-ranging roots. But multiculturalism is controversial because it demands that we rethink the norms and values at the core of our society. Not surprisingly, battles are now raging over how to describe culture. Some claim that Western thought has been dominated by **Orientalism** – *a process by which the West (Europe and America) has created an image of the East – or Orient – as a stereotype* (Said, 1978). Thus the Orient becomes 'mysterious', Turks become 'lustful', and Asians become 'inscrutable'. The others – Asians, Arabs – are seen through Western eyes in ways that are demeaning and dehumanising.

Frantz Fanon analysed the impact of white colonialism on blacks. He aimed through his writings to liberate the consciousness of the oppressed. In the first phase he sees how blacks may become assimilated to dominant white culture; a second phase sees the black writer disturbed; and a third sees the native writers turning themselves into awakeners of the people. But labels such as African, Muslim, American, 'Chinese' or, worse, 'Chineseness' are no more than starting points. The object then is to 'deconstruct' them – to take them apart and see what lies behind them.

Although multiculturalism and postcolonialism have found widespread favour in the last several years, they have provoked criticism as well. Opponents think they encourage divisiveness rather than unity by urging individuals to identify with their own category rather than with common elements. Similarly, rather than recognise any common standards of truth, say critics, multiculturalism maintains that we should evaluate ideas according to the race (and sex) of those who present them. Common humanity thus dissolves into an 'African voice' an 'Asian voice' and so on.

Critics say that multiculturalism and postcolonialism may not end up helping minorities, as proponents contend. They argue that multiculturalist initiatives (from African-American studies to all-black college accommodation) seem to demand precisely the kind of racial segregation we do not want. Then, too, an Asiacentric curriculum may well deny children a wide range of crucial knowledge and skills by forcing them to study only certain topics from a single point of view. Whose voices are to be heard?

Is there any common ground in this debate? Virtually everyone agrees that all people in Europe need to gain greater appreciation of the extent of cultural diversity. Eurocentric views distort an appreciation of the emergent global cultures, all with their differing languages, symbols, countercultures, etc.

Throughout much of history the world has been colonised by other countries and nations. Many countries have been invaded by others and had their cultures uprooted, transformed, even destroyed. And today, whenever we look at cultures, we tend to see them from the point of our own. This is now a burning issue for a new generation of sociologists: how to grasp the range of varying cultural perspectives that can be taken and to incorpoarte them into understanding. Some have referred to this as **cosmopolitanism** – *the philosophy that all people, despite their great differences, can still share a common humanity and community*.

Continue the debate

1 Do you think there is a truly distinctive 'European' culture with history and roots? What does it look like, and what is its history? Does it have a coherence, or does it conceal many voices?

2 How does the multiculturalism debate shape our views on school curricula and language learning? What are the pros and cons of different curricula and languages?

3 Whose voices are being heard once you adopt a 'postcolonial' voice?

4 Explore the idea of 'cosmopolitanism' through websites, and see if you think it just might provide a solution.

CHAPTER 6

GROUPS, ORGANISATIONS AND THE RISE OF THE NETWORK SOCIETY

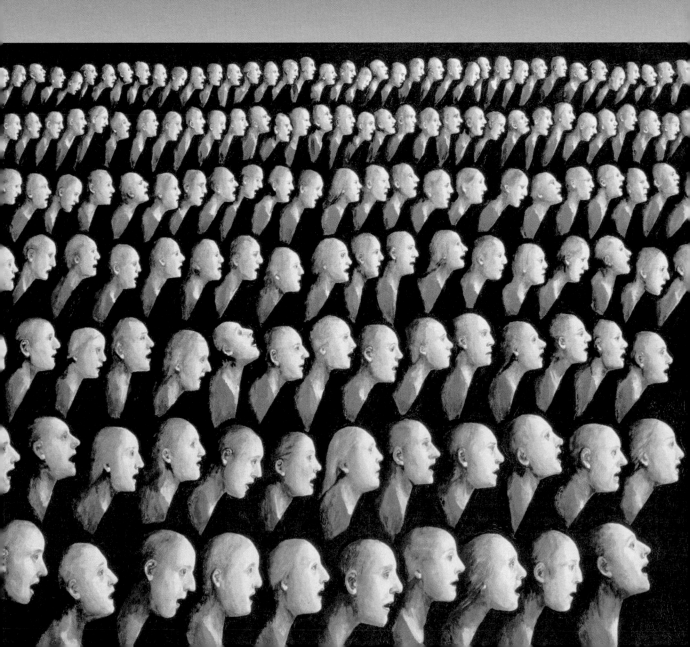

2008 SAW THE 40TH ANNIVERSARY CELEBRATION OF THE BIG MAC AND A CONTINUING EXPANSION OF MCDONALD'S ECONOMIC SUCCESS AROUND THE WORLD. The business began in 1940, with a restaurant opened by brothers Richard and Maurice McDonald in San Bernardino, California. By 1948, they had their 'Speedee Service System' and the fast-food industry had been born. Initially, it attracted little attention from the local community and went unnoticed by the world as a whole. Yet this seemingly insignificant small business would eventually spark a revolution in the restaurant industry and provide a global organisational model that would be copied by countless other businesses and even schools and churches.

The basic formula the McDonald brothers put into place – 'fast food' – was to serve food quickly and inexpensively to large numbers of people. They trained employees to perform highly specialised jobs, so that one person grilled hamburgers, while others 'dressed' them, made French fries, whipped up milkshakes, and presented the food to the customers in assembly-line fashion.

As the years went by, the McDonald brothers prospered, and they moved their single restaurant from Pasadena to San Bernardino. It was there, in 1954, that events took an unexpected turn when Ray Kroc, a travelling blender and mixer merchant, paid a visit to the McDonalds. Kroc was fascinated by the brothers' efficient system, and, almost immediately, he saw the potential for a greatly expanded system of fast-food restaurants. Initially, Kroc launched his plans in partnership with the McDonald brothers. Soon, however, he bought out their interests and set out on his own to become one of the greatest success stories of all time.

Today, over 32,000 McDonald's restaurants serve more than 58 million customers a day across 119 countries. One in 200 people across the world visit a McDonald's daily. In the UK, more than 2.5 million people eat at a McDonald's everyday. It is the best-known 'brand' in the world – its major world markets being in the USA (34 per cent), Europe (42 per cent) and Asia/Pacific, Middle East and Africa (APMEA), which account for 18 per cent of revenues. In 2008, its annual revenue was $22.79 billion.

But McDonald's has been much criticized. In 1990, activists in London distributed leaflets entitled *What's wrong with McDonald's?*, criticising its environmental, health and employment record – resulting in a major live trial; and in 2001, Eric Schlosser's book *Fast Food Nation* alleged that McDonald's profited at the expense of people's health and its workers. Morgan Spurlock's 2004 documentary film *Super Size Me* said that McDonald's food was contributing to the epidemic of obesity in society

Despite criticisms from many, especially in the environmental movement, McDonald's continues to grow and adapt. The McPuff has been pioneered in China, McRice can be found in Indonesia and the McCafé developed in Australia is popular in Hong Kong, France and Germany. The Big Mac Index has been invented as a way of comparing a Big Mac's cost in various world currencies to informally assess a currency's purchasing power parity.

The disease which inflicts bureaucracy, and what they usually die from, is routine.
J. S. Mill

Bureaucracy is a giant mechanism operated by pygmies.
Honore de Balzac

Every revolution evaporates and leaves behind only the slime of a new bureaucracy.
Franz Kafka

In this chapter, we ask:

- How do social groups shape our conduct?
- How are groups changing?
- What is the nature of organisations and the 'McDonaldisation' of society?
- How is social life changing in an age of mobile phones and Facebook?

(Left) Evelyn Williams, *Face to Face*, 1994 (oil on canvas)

Source: Face to Face, 1994 (oil on canvas) (pair of 173317), Williams, Evelyn (Contemporary Artist)/Private Collection/ The Bridgeman Art Library.

See: www.evelynwilliams.com.

 Is this conformity or individuality?

From a sociological point of view, the success of McDonald's reveals much more than the popularity of hamburgers. As this chapter will explain, one larger importance of this story lies in the extent to which the principles that guide the operation of McDonald's are coming to dominate much of social life in very many parts of the world. So much so, that sociologists have started to talk of the **McDonaldisation of society**, *a process by which the principles of the fast-food industry come to be applied to more and more features of social life*. Close, intimate groups are giving way to fast, efficient but distant ones. At the same time, the way that people communicate and get close to others is changing. No longer living in stable or well-bounded groups and communities, as we like to think people did in the past, many people now live their lives increasingly through networks. Through standard phones, mobile phones, the car, the email, the fax, we can now develop close relations with a complex network of people scattered over a wide area, even the globe. Often, people living on the other side of the world, and whom we have never seen, can become our 'friends'!

In this chapter, we will begin by examining one of the oldest ideas of sociology: that we live in *social groups*, the clusters of people with whom we associate in much of our daily lives. As we shall see, the scope of group life expanded greatly during the twentieth century. From a world built on kin and community – usually small, local, face-to-face and intense – the structure of many societies now turns on the operation of vast businesses, bureaucracies and formal organisations – usually large, impersonal and fleeting. And even more recently, we can 'log on' to our computer and surf, and we can Facebook and Twitter with a vast array of known (and unknown) individuals across the world. By 2011, 500 million people were using Facebook. In many parts of the world, social networking has become commonplace. Understanding how this changing and expanding scale of life has come to dominate society, and what it means for us as individuals, are the chapter's key objectives.

Social groups

Virtually everyone moves through life with a sense of belonging; this is the experience of group life. A **social group** refers to *two or more people who identify and interact with one another*. Human beings continually come together to form couples, families,

circles of friends, gangs, neighbourhoods, churches, businesses, clubs, communities, transnational corporations and numerous large organisations. Whatever the form, groups encompass people with shared experiences, loyalties and interests. In short, while maintaining their individuality, the members of social groups also think of themselves as a special 'we'. In what follows, we shall introduce a few terms that help clarify our thinking about groups: primary and secondary groups, group conformity, reference groups and group size.

A basic distinction: primary and secondary groups

Acquaintances commonly greet one another with a smile and the simple phrase 'How are you?' The response is usually a well-scripted 'Fine, thanks. How are you?' This answer, of course, is often more formal than truthful. In most cases, providing a detailed account of how you are really doing would prompt the other person to beat a hasty and awkward exit.

Sociologists classify social groups by measuring them against two ideal types based on members' level of genuine personal concern. This variation is the key to distinguishing *primary from secondary groups*.

Charles Horton Cooley (1864–1929) was a pioneering North American sociologist. He is most famed for his idea of the looking-glass self, discussed in Chapter 7. According to Cooley, a **primary group** is a *small social group whose members share personal and enduring relationships*. Bound together by primary relationships, individuals in primary groups typically spend a great deal of time together, engage in a wide range of common activities and feel that they know one another well. Although not without periodic conflict, members of primary groups display sincere concern for each other's welfare. This is the world of family and friends. The strength of primary relationships gives people a comforting sense of security. In the familiar social circles of family or friends, people feel they can 'be themselves' without constantly worrying about the impressions they are making.

Members of primary groups generally provide one another with economic and other forms of assistance as well. But, as important as primary ties are, people generally think of a primary group as an end in itself rather than as a means to other ends. In other words, we prefer to think that kinship or friendship links people who 'belong together', rather than people who expect to benefit from each other. For this reason, we readily call on family members or close friends to help us move into a new apartment, without expecting to pay for their services. And we would do the same for them. A friend who never returns a favour, by contrast, is likely to leave us feeling 'used' and questioning the depth of the friendship.

Moreover, this personal orientation means that members of a primary group view each other as unique and irreplaceable. We typically do not care who cashes our cheque at the bank or takes our money at the supermarket checkout. Yet in the primary group – especially the family – we are bound to specific others by emotion and loyalty. So even though brothers and sisters do not always get along, they always remain siblings.

In contrast to the primary group, the **secondary group** is *a large and impersonal social group whose members pursue a specific interest or activity*. In most respects, secondary groups have precisely the opposite characteristics of primary groups. *Secondary relationships* usually involve weak emotional ties and little personal knowledge of one another. Secondary groups vary in duration, but they are frequently short term, beginning and ending without particular significance. Students following a university course, for instance, who may not see one another after the term ends, exemplify the secondary group.

Weaker social ties permit secondary groups to include many more people than primary groups do. For example, dozens or even hundreds of people may work together in the same office, yet most of

them pay only passing attention to one another. Sometimes the passing of time will transform a group from secondary to primary, as with co-workers who share an office for many years. Generally, however, the boundary separating members of a secondary group from non-members is far less clear than it is for primary groups.

Secondary groups lack strong loyalties and emotions because members look to one another only to achieve limited ends. So while members of primary groups display a *personal orientation*, people in secondary groups reveal a goal orientation. Secondary ties are not necessarily always aloof or cold, of course. Social interactions among students, co-workers and business associates are often quite pleasant, even if they are rather impersonal. The goal orientation of secondary groups encourages individuals to craft their behaviour carefully. In these roles, we remain characteristically impersonal and polite. The secondary relationship, therefore, is one in which the question 'How are you?' may be asked without really expecting a truthful answer.

In primary groups, members define each other according to *who* they are – that is, in terms of kinship or unique, personal qualities. Members of secondary groups, by contrast, look to one another for *what* they are or what they can do for each other. In secondary groups, in other words, we are always mindful of what we offer others and what we receive in return. This 'scorekeeping' comes through most clearly in business relationships. Likewise, the people next door typically expect that a neighbourly favour will be reciprocated. Table 6.1 summarises these characteristics. (Keep in

Table 6.1	Primary groups and secondary groups: a summary	
	Primary group	**Secondary group**
Quality of relationships	Personal orientation	Goal orientation
Duration of relationships	Usually long term	Variable; often short term
Breadth of relationships	Broad; usually involving many activities	Narrow; usually involving few activities
Subjective perception of relationships	As ends in themselves	As means to an end
Typical examples	Families; circles of friends	Co-workers; political organisations
New technologies	Mobile phones can keep family and close friends in perpetual contact	Facebook can provide more 'loose' contacts and friends than ever before possible

mind that these traits define two types of social group in ideal terms; actual groups in our lives may well contain elements of both.) By placing these concepts as ends of a continuum, sociologists have devised a basic but useful scheme for describing and analysing group life.

A long-standing sociological view suggests that rural areas and small towns tend towards a greater emphasis on primary relationships while large cities are typically more secondary. While this holds some truth, some urban neighbourhoods – especially those populated by people of a single ethnicity, religion or even sexual orientation – can be quite tightly knit. 'Jewish neighbourhoods', 'Polish communities' or 'gay communities' are usually strong in primary orientation, with local meeting places or bars to facilitate this.

Primary relationships may well predominate in low-income pre-industrial societies throughout Latin America, Africa and Asia, in which people's lives still often revolve around families and local villages. Especially in rural areas, strangers stand out in the social landscape. But even many of these countries now find that more and more of their populations live in cities where secondary relations have become much more common. In high-income industrial societies, in which people assume highly specialised social roles, secondary ties usually take precedence. Most people in England, for example, routinely engage in impersonal, secondary contacts with virtual strangers – people about whom they know very little and whom they may never meet again.

Group conformity

In most of the Western world, people do not like to think they are 'conformists', that they follow the group. Most people like to think they are unique individuals, that they in some way stand out from the crowd. But think for a minute of the main groups you belong to – at school, university, in sport, at home. Think of your peer group and how you want (or even need) to be accepted by them. Maybe you do stand out as a less conformist person, but many social psychological studies have shown that group conformity is very likely. This section looks at two classic yet still widely cited social psychological studies that suggest this. Social scientists confirm the power of group pressure to shape human behaviour and report that it remains strong in adulthood as well as in adolescence.

Asch's classic research

Solomon Asch (1952) conducted a classic investigation that revealed the power of group conformity. Asch recruited students for an alleged study of visual perception. Before the actual experiment, however, he revealed to all but one member in each small group that their real purpose was to impose group pressure on the remaining subject. Placing all the students around a table, Asch asked each, in turn, to note the length of a 'standard' line, as shown on Card 1 in Figure 6.1, and match it to one of three lines on Card 2.

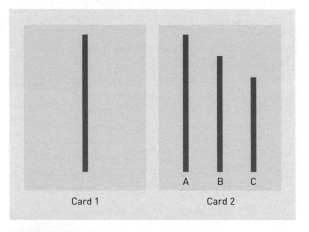

| Figure 6.1 | Cards used in Asch's experiment in group conformity (Asch, 1952) |

Anyone with normal vision could easily see that the line marked 'A' on Card 2 was the correct choice. Initially, as planned, everyone made the matches correctly. But then Asch's secret accomplices began answering incorrectly, making the naive subject (seated at the table in order to answer next to last) bewildered and uncomfortable.

What happened? Asch found that one-third of all subjects placed in this situation chose to conform to the others by answering incorrectly. His investigation indicates that many people are willing to compromise their judgements to avoid the discomfort of being different from others, even from people they do not know. Think about yourself for a minute: do you think you would conform like this?

Milgram's classic research

In an equally famous (even notorious) set of experiments, Stanley Milgram – a former student of Solomon Asch – conducted conformity experiments that were even more surprising. In Milgram's initial

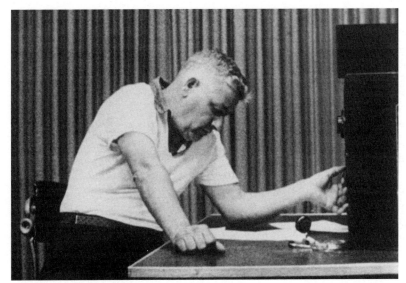

Stanley Milgram's electric shock experiment is the most famous of all social psychological experiments. Conducted in the early 1960s, you can now download it on YouTube (search: Milgram experiment). There have also been many replications (see for example The Milgram Re-enactment (2002): http://www.roddickinson.net/pages/milgram/project-synopsis.php

Source: Manuscripts and Archives, Yale University Library, Stanley Milgram Papers (MS 1406). From the film *Obedience* copyright © 1968 by Stanley Milgram; copyright renewed 1993 by Alexandra Milgram, and distributed by Penn State Media Sales.

study (Milgram, 1963, 1965; Miller, 1986), a researcher explained to male recruits that they were about to engage in a study of how punishment affects learning. One by one, he assigned them the role of 'teacher' and placed another individual – an insider to the study – in a connecting room as the 'learner'.

The teacher saw the learner sit down in an ominous contraption resembling an electric chair with an electrode attached to one arm. The researcher then had the teacher read aloud pairs of words. In the next step, the teacher repeated the first word of each pair and asked the learner to recall the corresponding second word.

As mistakes occurred, the researcher instructed the teacher to shock the learner using a 'shock generator', a bogus but forbidding-looking piece of equipment with a shock switch and a dial marked to regulate electric current from 15 volts (labelled 'mild shock') to 300 volts (marked 'intense shock') to 450 volts (marked 'Danger: Severe Shock' and 'XXX'). Beginning at the lowest level, the researcher told the teacher to increase the shock by 15 volts every time the learner made a mistake. The shocks, explained the researcher, would become painful but cause no permanent damage. And so it went. At 75, 90 and 105 volts, the teacher heard audible moans from the learner; at 120 volts, shouts of pain; at 270 volts, screams of agony; and, after 330 volts, deadly silence.

The results show just how readily authority figures can obtain compliance from ordinary people. None of 40 subjects assigned in the role of teacher during the initial research even questioned the procedure before 300 volts had been applied, and 26 of the subjects – almost two-thirds – went all the way to 450 volts.

Milgram (1964) then modified his research to see if Solomon Asch had documented such a high degree of group conformity only because the task of matching lines seemed trivial. What if groups pressured people to administer electrical shocks? To investigate, he varied the experiment so that a group of three teachers, two of whom were his accomplices, made decisions jointly. Milgram's rule was that each of the three teachers would suggest a shock level when the learner made an error and they would then administer the lowest of the three suggestions. This arrangement gave the naive subject the power to lessen the shock level regardless of the other two teachers' recommendations.

The accomplices called for increasing the shock level with each error, placing group pressure on the third member to do the same. Responding to this group pressure, subjects applied voltages three to four times higher than in control conditions in which subjects acted alone. Thus Milgram's research suggests that people are surprisingly likely to follow the directions not only of 'legitimate authority figures', but also of groups of ordinary individuals.

Zimbardo's research: the Stanford experiment

Back in August 1971, a somewhat scary and very controversial social psychological experiment was conducted on a group of students at Stanford University. It is now very well known, even notorious.

The experiment invited some 'normal' students to take part in a study which aimed to simulate prison conditions. In a basement in the psychology department at Stanford University in California, rooms were made out to be like prison cells. 'Normal' average students were divided into two groups: guards and inmates. They were then asked to live these roles for a couple of days – and were provided with 'uniforms' appropriate to their parts. Zimbardo wanted to see what they would do, but soon found he was horrified at the degree to which seemingly normal students turned seriously abusive to each other. The guards were extremely violent – physically, verbally and mentally – to the inmates. Yet previously the students had related well and had been their normal-time friends. They fell into their roles with the greatest of ease. And 'the guards' were so abusive to the 'inmates' that Zimbardo had to call the experiment off.

His study was part of a general concern and interest at that time (especially in the wake of the Nazi holocaust, where millions had been exterminated by seemingly normal people: see *European eye*, p. 186) with the ways in which people would follow authority. (Milgram's study, raised above, was another prime example of research with this interest.) What he found was scary. Normal people will do terrible things to other people if the situation demands it (Zimbardo, 2007).

Reference groups

How do we assess our own attitudes or behaviour? Frequently, we make use of a **reference group**, *a social group that serves as a point of reference in making evaluations or decisions.*

A young lad who imagines the response of his 'mates' to a girl he is going out with is using his friends as a reference group. Similarly, a banker who assesses her colleagues' reactions to a new loan policy is using her co-workers as a standard of reference. As these examples illustrate, reference groups can be primary or secondary. In each case, the motivation to conform to a group means that the attitudes of others can greatly affect us. We also use groups that we do not belong to for reference. People preparing for job interviews typically notice how those in the company they wish to join dress and act, adjusting their personal performances accordingly.

Stouffer's classic research

Samuel A. Stouffer (1949) and his associates conducted a classic study of reference group dynamics during the

Second World War. In a survey, researchers asked soldiers to evaluate the chances of promotion for a competent soldier in their branch of the service. One might guess that soldiers serving in outfits with a high promotion rate would be optimistic about their future advancement. Yet survey results supported the opposite conclusion: soldiers in branches of the service with low promotion rates were actually more optimistic about their own chances to move ahead.

The key to this paradox lies in sorting out the groups against which the soldiers measured their progress. Those in branches with low promotion rates looked around them and saw people making no more headway than they were. That is, they had not been promoted, but neither had many others, so they did not feel unjustly deprived. Soldiers in service branches with high promotion rates, however, could easily think of people who had been promoted sooner or more often than they had. With such people in mind, even soldiers who had been promoted themselves were likely to feel short-changed. So these were the soldiers who voiced more negative attitudes in their evaluations.

Stouffer's research demonstrates that we do not make judgements about ourselves in isolation, nor do we compare ourselves with just anyone. Instead, we use specific social groups as standards in developing individual attitudes. Whatever our situation in *absolute* terms, then, we assess our well-being subjectively, *relative* to some specific reference group (Merton, 1968).

Group size: form over content

If you are the first person to arrive at a party, you can observe some fascinating group dynamics. Until about six people enter the room, everyone generally shares a single conversation. But as more people arrive, the group divides into two or more smaller clusters. It is apparent that size plays a crucial role in how group members interact. Numbers matter.

To understand why, consider the formal (and here, mathematical) connection between the number of people in a social group and the number of relationships among them. As Figure 6.2 shows, two people form a single relationship (a dyad); adding a third person generates three relationships (a triad); adding a fourth person yields six. Increasing the number of people one at a time, then, boosts the number of relationships much more rapidly, since every new individual can interact with everyone already there. Thus, five people produce ten

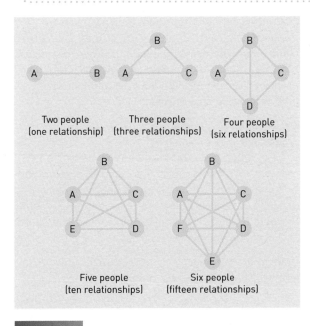

Two people
(one relationship)

Three people
(three relationships)

Four people
(six relationships)

Five people
(ten relationships)

Six people
(fifteen relationships)

Figure 6.2 Group size and relationships

relationships and, by the time six people join one conversation, 15 'channels' connect them. This leaves too many people unable to speak, which is why the group usually divides at this point.

The dyad

The German sociologist Georg Simmel (1858–1918), profiled in the *Thinkers and theory* box, built a sociology of forms in which he explored social dynamics in the smallest social groups. He used the term **dyad** to designate *a social group with two members*. Throughout the world, most love affairs, marriages and the closest friendships are dyadic.

What makes the dyad a special relationship? First, explained Simmel, social interaction in a dyad is typically more intense than in larger groups since, in a one-to-one relationship, neither member shares the other's attention with anyone else. Thus dyads have the potential to be the most meaningful social bonds we ever experience.

Second, Simmel explains, like a stool with only two legs, dyads have a characteristic instability. Both members of a dyad must actively sustain the relationship; if either one withdraws, the group collapses. Because of the importance of marriage to society, the marital dyad is supported with legal, economic and often religious ties. By contrast, a large group such as a charity run by volunteers is inherently much more stable, as it can survive the loss of many members.

Marriage in our society is dyadic; ideally, we expect powerful emotional ties to unite husbands and wives. As we shall see in Chapter 18, however, marriage in other societies may involve more than two people. In that case, the household is usually more stable, though many of the marital relationships are weaker (Simmel, 1950; orig. 1902).

The triad

Simmel also probed the **triad**, *a social group with three members*. A triad encompasses three relationships, each uniting two of the three people. A triad is more stable than a dyad because, should the relationship between any two members become strained, the third can act as a mediator to restore the group's vitality. This process of group dynamics helps explain why members of a dyad (say, a married couple) sometimes seek out a third person (a counsellor) to air tensions between them.

Nonetheless, two of the three can form a coalition to press their views on the third, or two may intensify their relationship, leaving the other feeling like a 'third wheel'. For example, two members of a triad who develop a romantic interest in each other will understand the old saying 'Two's company, three's a crowd'.

As groups grow beyond three members, they become progressively more stable because the loss of even several members does not threaten the group's existence. At the same time, increases in group size typically reduce the intense personal interaction possible only in the smallest groups. Larger groups are thus based less on personal attachments and more on formal rules and regulations. Such formality helps a large group persist over time, though the group is not immune to change. After all, their numerous members give large groups more contact with the outside world, opening the door to new attitudes and behaviour.

Does a social group have an ideal size? The answer depends on the group's purpose. A dyad offers unsurpassed emotional intensity, while a group of several dozen members is more stable, capable of accomplishing larger, more complex tasks, and is better able to assimilate new members or ideas. People typically find more *personal pleasure* in smaller groups, while deriving greater *task satisfaction* from accomplishments in larger organisations (Slater, 1958).

Social diversity

Social diversity affects group dynamics, especially the likelihood that members will interact with someone of another group. Peter Blau (Blau, 1977; Blau et al., 1982) points out four ways in which the composition of social groups affects intergroup association.

1 *Large groups turn inwards.* Extending Simmel's analysis of group size, Blau explains that the larger a group, the more likely its members are to maintain relationships exclusively among themselves. The smaller the group, by contrast, the more members will reach beyond their immediate social circle.

   To illustrate, consider the efforts of many universities to include a wider range of students from overseas. Increasing the number of international students may add important dimensions to a campus, but, as their numbers rise, these students are eventually able to maintain their own distinctive social group. Thus intentional efforts to promote social diversity may well have the unintended effect of promoting separatism.

2 *Heterogeneous groups turn outwards.* The more internally heterogeneous a group is, the more likely its members are to interact with members of other groups. We would expect, for example, that campus groups that recruit members of both sexes and people of various ethnic and geographic backgrounds would promote more intergroup contact than those that choose members of only one social type.

3 *Social parity promotes contact.* An environment in which all groups have roughly equal standing

Georg Simmel: a sociology of forms

THINKERS & THEORY

When students encounter sociology, they invariably hear of the three giants – Marx, Durkheim, Weber – who have already been introduced several times in this book. They may hear of a fourth 'founding theorist', Georg Simmel (1858–1918), but rarely will they ever consider him in any detail. Yet his influence has been very profound.

Simmel adopted a distinctive and wide-ranging approach to sociology, studying many things from money and gender to cities and 'strangers'. He viewed society as interaction, and believed the task of the sociologist was to study the interactive webs into which people entered. He was keen to depict the ways in which changing numbers and scales of interactions brought about profoundly different relationships. In the text, you see how he contrasted simple dyads with triads and the difference this makes.

But he also looked at how social relations changed as cities emerged and relationships became more and more impersonal. He provided a sociological portrait of people's changing consciousness under **modernity**, and especially cities. He saw there was a downside to this: people kept their distance from each other. But there was also an upside: people became more tolerant and even sophisticated (see Chapter 24).

Simmel invented a style of sociology known as **formal sociology**: a sociology which studies the underlying forms of interaction in society. To do this, he distinguished between *content* and *form*. Social life is about content in so far as it studies such things as marriage, war, education and drug-taking. But for sociology to be systematic it needed more than studies of little areas of social life and their contents: instead it also needed to piece together the underlying social processes that they have in common.

Georg Simmel (1858–1918)

Thus, for instance, one common process found in social life is conflict: you can look at marriages, wars, education and drug taking and you will usually find elements of social interaction involving conflicts. Sociologists needed to study not just contents, then, but also forms.

A brilliant essayist, Simmel left his mark on much contemporary sociology which looks at forms of interaction.

For a short guide to Simmel's work, see David Frisby, *Georg Simmel* (London: Routledge, 2nd edn, 2002).

encourages people of all social backgrounds to mingle and form social ties. Thus, whether groups insulate their members or not depends on whether the groups themselves form a social hierarchy.

4 *Physical boundaries foster social boundaries.* Blau contends that physical space affects the chances of contacts among groups. To the extent that a social group is physically segregated from others (by having its own accommodation or dining area, for example), its members are less apt to engage other people.

Organisations

Throughout human history, most people lived in small groups of family members and neighbours; this pattern was still widespread in Europe and the United States a century ago. Today, families and neighbourhoods persist, of course, but our lives revolve far more around **formal organisations**, *large, secondary groups that are organised to achieve their goals efficiently.*

Formal organisations, such as corporations and government agencies, differ significantly from families and neighbourhoods: their greater size renders social relationships less personal and fosters a planned, formal atmosphere. In other words, formal organisations operate to accomplish complex jobs rather than to meet personal needs.

When you think about it, organising a continent like Europe, with some 500 million members, is a remarkable feat. Countless tasks are involved, from collecting taxes and delivering the mail to the production and distribution of consumer goods. To meet most of these tasks, we rely on large, formal organisations. From national governments to private corporations, millions of people are employed in them. Such vast organisations develop lives and cultures of their own, so that as members come and go, the statuses they fill and the roles they perform remain unchanged over the years. Consider the following figures, which give some indication of the numbers of major organisations that now *exist across the world*: that is, are global. (Even this excludes hundreds of others, such as global religious organisations and global social movements.) There are:

- 77,200 major transnational corporations/companies (TNCs) such as Shell, Coca-Cola, Nestlé and Microsoft
- 10,000 single-country non-governmental organisations (NGOs) such as Médecins sans

Frontières (France) and Population Concern (UK) which have significant international activities
- 246 intergovernmental organisations (IGOs) such as the United Nations, NATO and the European Union
- 7,300 international non-governmental organisations (INGOSs), such as Amnesty International and the International Red Cross (Baylis and Smith: 2008: 332).

Types of formal organisation

There are a number of classifications of organisations. A classic one was presented by Amitai Etzioni (1975), who identified three types, distinguished by why people participate: utilitarian organisations, normative organisations and coercive organisations.

Just about everyone who works for income is a member of a *utilitarian organisation*, which provides material rewards for its members. Large business enterprises, for example, generate profits for their owners and income in the form of salaries and wages for their employees. Joining utilitarian organisations is usually a matter of individual choice, though most people must join one or another utilitarian organisation to make a living.

People join *normative organisations* not for income but to pursue goals they consider morally worthwhile. Sometimes called *voluntary associations*, these include community service groups such as the Boy Scouts and Girl Guides (the Boy Scouts, with some 360,000 members in the UK aged between 6 and 25, celebrated its centenary in 2007; the Guide Movement had 477,000), political parties, religious organisations, and numerous other confederations concerned with specific social issues (such as Greenpeace and Liberty). In 2005, nearly half of adults aged 16 and over in England participated in some form of volunteering activity, and over two-thirds participated in an informal voluntary activity (*Social Trends*, 2007: 180). About 10 per cent of adults in Britain belonged to an environmental organisation or charity – the National Trust and the Royal Society for the Protection of Birds are the largest; Greenpeace comes a respectable third with 380,000 members.

In Etzioni's typology, *coercive organisations* are distinguished by involuntary membership. That is, people are forced to join the organisation as a form of punishment (prisons) or treatment (psychiatric hospitals). Coercive organisations have extraordinary physical features, such as locked doors and barred windows, and are supervised by security personnel (Goffman, 1961). These are settings that segregate people as 'inmates' or 'patients' for a period of time and sometimes radically alter their attitudes and behaviour. *Total institutions* transform a human being's overall sense of self.

From differing vantage points, any particular organisation may fall into all these categories. A psychiatric hospital, for example, serves as a coercive organisation for a patient, a utilitarian organisation for a psychiatrist and a normative organisation for a part-time hospital volunteer.

The nature of bureaucracy

Formal organisations date back thousands of years. Elites who governed early empires relied on government officials to extend their power over millions of people and vast geographical regions. Chinese civilisation provides many examples of large formal organisations, allowing rulers to collect taxes, undertake military campaigns and construct monumental structures such as the Great Wall of China. In many countries a system known as 'oriental despotism' created huge administrative systems to build major public structures – such as the pyramids of Egypt.

The power of these early organisations was limited, however, not because elites lacked grandiose ambition, but by the traditional character of pre-industrial societies. Typically, cultural patterns placed greater importance on preserving the past or carrying out 'God's will' than on organisational efficiency. Only in the last few centuries did there emerge what Max Weber called a 'rational world-view', as described in Chapter 4. In the wake of the Industrial Revolution, the organisational structure called *bureaucracy* became commonplace in Europe and North America.

Weber and bureaucracy

We have already seen how Max Weber introduced the idea of **bureaucracy** (see p. 41) – *an organisational model rationally designed to perform complex tasks efficiently*. In a bureaucratic business or government agency, officials deliberately enact and revise policy to make the organisation as efficient as possible. What specific traits promote organisational efficiency? Weber (1978; orig. 1921) identified six key elements of the ideal bureaucratic organisation.

1   *Specialisation.* Through most of human history, everyone pursued the basic goals of securing food

and shelter. Bureaucracy, by contrast, assigns to individuals highly specialised duties.

2   *Hierarchy of offices.* Bureaucracies arrange personnel in a vertical hierarchy of offices. Each person is thus supervised by 'higher-ups' in the organisation while, in turn, supervising others in lower positions.

3   *Rules and regulations.* Cultural tradition holds scant sway in bureaucracy. Instead, operations are guided by rationally enacted rules and regulations. These rules control not only the organisation's own functioning but, as much as possible, its larger environment. Ideally, a bureaucracy seeks to operate in a completely predictable fashion.

4   *Technical competence.* A bureaucratic organisation expects officials to have the technical competence to carry out their official duties. Bureaucracies regularly monitor the performance of staff members. Such impersonal evaluation based on performance contrasts sharply with the custom, followed through most of human history, of favouring relatives – whatever their talents – over strangers.

5   *Impersonality.* In bureaucratic organisations, rules take precedence over personal whim. This impersonality encourages uniform treatment for each client as well as other workers. From this detached approach stems the notion of the 'faceless bureaucrat'.

6   *Formal, written communications.* An old adage states that the heart of bureaucracy is not people but paperwork. Rather than casual, verbal communication, bureaucracy relies on formal, written memos and reports. Over time, this correspondence accumulates into vast files. These files guide the subsequent operation of an organisation in roughly the same way that social background shapes the life of an individual.

These traits represent a clear contrast to the more personal character of small groups. Bureaucratic organisation promotes efficiency by carefully recruiting personnel and limiting the unpredictable effects of personal tastes and opinions. In smaller, informal groups, members allow one another considerable discretion in their behaviour; they respond to each other personally and regard everyone as more or less equal in rank. Table 6.2 summarises the differences between small social groups and large formal organisations.

Table 6.2	Small groups, formal organisations and networks: a comparison		
	Small groups (e.g. family)	Formal organisations (e.g. school)	Networks (e.g. Facebook)
Activities	Members typically engage in many of the same activities	Members typically engage in distinct, highly specialised activities	Members again have common focus
Hierarchy	Often informal or non-existent	Clearly defined, corresponding to offices	Largely non-existent – web-like
Norms	Informal application of general norms	Clearly defined rules and regulations	Emergent norms over time (e.g. 'netiquette')
Criteria for membership	Variable, often based on personal affection or kinship	Technical competence to carry out assigned tasks	Self-selecting
Relationships	Variable, typically primary	Typically secondary, with selective primary ties	Fragmented, focused
Communications	Typically casual and face-to-face	Typically formal and in writing	Digitalised
Focus	Person orientated	Task orientated	Communications oriented

The informal side of bureaucracy

Weber's ideal bureaucracy deliberately regulates every activity. In actual organisations, however, human beings have the creativity (or the stubbornness) to resist conforming to bureaucratic blueprints. Sometimes informality helps to meet a legitimate need overlooked by formal regulations. In other situations, informality may amount to simply cutting corners in one's job (Scott, 1981).

In principle, power resides in offices, not with the people who occupy them. Nonetheless, the personalities of officials greatly affect patterns of leadership. For example, studies of corporations document that the qualities and quirks of individuals – including personal charisma and interpersonal skills – have a tremendous impact on organisational outcomes.

Authoritarian, democratic and *laissez-faire* types of leadership also reflect individual personality as much as any organisational plan. Then, too, in the 'real world' of organisations, leaders and their cronies sometimes seek to benefit personally through the abuse of organisational power. And perhaps even more commonly, leaders take credit for the efforts of their subordinates. Many secretaries, for example, have far more authority and responsibility than their official job titles and salaries suggest.

Communication offers another example of how informality creeps into large organisations. Formally, memos and other written communications disseminate information through the hierarchy. Typically, however, individuals cultivate informal networks or 'grapevines' that spread information much faster, if not always accurately. Grapevines are particularly important to subordinates because high officials often attempt to conceal important information from them.

Throughout the hierarchy, employees modify or ignore rigid bureaucratic structures for a host of reasons. A classic study of the Western Electric factory in Chicago revealed that few employees reported fellow workers who violated rules, as the company required (Roethlisberger and Dickson, 1939). On the contrary, workers took action against those who *did* blow the whistle on their colleagues, shunning them as 'squealers'. Although the company formally set productivity standards, workers informally created their own definition of a fair day's work, criticising those who exceeded it as 'rate-busters' and those who fell short as 'chisellers'.

Such informal social structures suggest that people act to personalise rigidly defined social situations. This leads us to take a closer look at some of the problems of bureaucracy.

EUROPEAN EYE

Bureaucracy's darkest hour: killing 11 million people in the Nazi genocide

One of the most significant events of twentieth-century history was Hitler's Final Solution: the mass extermination of over 11 million people – 6 million Jews, often called 'The Holocaust', along with millions of others (gypsies, gays, 'impure races') – throughout the Second World War. There have been many other genocides in history. The book *Century of Genocide* (Totten et al., 1997) looks at eyewitness accounts of large numbers of people slaughtered during the twentieth century in Armenia, Bangladesh, Burundi, Cambodia, East Timor, Indonesia, Rwanda, south-west Africa and the Ukraine. Some have involved larger numbers of people – Rummel (1996) suggests that over 60 million people were killed in the Soviet Gulag state. But the Holocaust must be seen as unique because it involved the systematic, huge-scale extermination of large numbers of people through bureaucratic means in concentration camps such as Auschwitz in a mechanical way. People were 'rounded up'; trains took them to the death camps; there they were stripped, numbered, herded and led, finally, to the gas chambers or other execution.

Zygmunt Bauman, in his powerful sociological study *Modernity and the Holocaust* (1989), shows that 'we live in a type of society that made the Holocaust possible' (p. 88). For him, the modern world facilitated the mass exterminations.

The numbers slaughtered in the Holocaust are hard to calculate, but figures of at least 11 million deaths are common. These deaths reveal the inhumanity of people to people, and the power of social organisation and social groups. It is also a major test case for those who believe in human progress. There are approximately 250 Holocaust museums and centres around the world where you can learn more

Source: © World History Archive/Alamy.

Drawing from Max Weber's analysis of bureaucracy and Durkheim's analysis of the division of labour, he suggests that these very characteristic features of modern society made the Holocaust possible. People could exterminate large numbers of others simply because they were distant links in a work chain, following the abstract rules that most jobs now dictate. There was an abrogation of personal responsibility, fostered by bureaucracy that made it all possible then – and indeed possible again now.

People become dehumanised, and moral standards become irrelevant to the success of the technical operation.

When society seemed to be at its most advanced, and most civilised, the dark atrocities of mass extermination became a routine, bureaucratic commonplace. The challenge for sociology is to see this extreme horror – even 'evil' – as part of the routine workings of modern societies. The twentieth century was, in fact, a century of genocides.

See: Bauman (1989); Rummel (1996); Totten et al. (1997); Mann (2005) and Goldhagen (2009).

Problems of bureaucracy

Despite our reliance on bureaucracy to manage countless dimensions of everyday life, many members of our society are ambivalent about this organisational form. The following sections review several of the problems associated with bureaucracy, ranging from its tendency to dehumanise and alienate individuals to the threats it poses to personal privacy and political democracy.

1 Bureaucratic alienation

Max Weber saw that bureaucracy could be a model of productivity. Nonetheless, he was keenly aware of bureaucracy's potential to *dehumanise* those it purports to serve. That is, the same impersonality that fosters efficiency simultaneously denies officials and clients the ability to respond to each other's unique, personal needs. On the contrary, officials must treat each client impersonally as a standard 'case'.

The impersonal bureaucratic environment, then, gives rise to *alienation*. All too often, Weber contended, formal organisations reduce the human being to 'a small cog in a ceaselessly moving mechanism' (1978: 988; orig. 1921). The trend towards more and more formal organisation, therefore, left him deeply pessimistic about the future of humankind. Although formal organisations are designed to benefit humanity, he feared that humanity might well end up serving formal organisations.

2 Bureaucratic inefficiency and ritualism

Then there is the familiar problem of inefficiency, the failure of a bureaucratic organisation to carry out the work it was created to perform. Perhaps the greatest challenge to a large, formal organisation is responding to special needs or circumstances. Anyone who has ever tried to replace a lost driving licence, return defective merchandise to a discount store or change an address on a magazine subscription knows that bureaucracies can sometimes be maddeningly unresponsive.

The problem of inefficiency is captured in the concept of *red tape* (a phrase derived from the red tape used by eighteenth-century English administrators to wrap official parcels and records). Red tape refers to a tedious preoccupation with organisational routines and procedures. Sociologist Robert Merton (1968) points out that red tape amounts to a new twist on the already familiar concept of group conformity. He coined the term **bureaucratic ritualism** to designate *a preoccupation with rules and regulations to the point of thwarting an organisation's goals*. Ritualism impedes

individual and organisational performance as it stifles creativity and imagination. In part, ritualism emerges because organisations, which pay modest, fixed salaries, give officials little or no financial stake in performing efficiently. Then, too, bureaucratic ritualism stands as another expression of the alienation that Weber feared would arise from bureaucratic rigidity (Whyte, 1957; Merton, 1968).

3 Bureaucratic inertia

If bureaucrats sometimes have little motivation to be efficient, they certainly have every reason to protect their jobs. Thus, officials typically strive to perpetuate their organisation even when its purpose has been fulfilled. As Weber put it, 'once fully established, bureaucracy is among the social structures which are hardest to destroy' (1978: 987; orig. 1921).

Bureaucratic inertia refers to *the tendency of bureaucratic organisations to perpetuate themselves*. Formal organisations, in other words, tend to take on a life of their own beyond their formal objectives. Occasionally, a formal organisation that meets its goals will simply disband; more commonly, an organisation stays in business by redefining its goals so that it can continue to provide a livelihood for its members.

For example, consider the history of the US National Association for Infantile Paralysis, the sponsor of a fundraising campaign known as the March of Dimes (Sills, 1969). This organisation came into being as part of the drive to find a cure for polio. The goal was accomplished in the early 1950s when Dr Jonas Salk developed the polio vaccine. Subsequently, however, the March of Dimes did not close down; rather, it redirected its efforts towards other medical problems, such as birth defects, and continues to this day.

4 Bureaucratic abuse of power: oligarchy

Early in the twentieth century, Robert Michels (1876–1936) pointed out the link between bureaucracy and political **oligarchy**, *the rule of the many by the few* (1949; orig. 1911). According to what Michels called 'the iron law of oligarchy', the pyramid-like structure of bureaucracy places a few leaders in charge of vast and powerful government organisations.

Max Weber credited bureaucracy's strict hierarchy of responsibility with increasing organisational efficiency. By applying Weber's thesis to the organisation of government, Michels reveals that this hierarchical structure concentrates power and thus endangers democracy. While the public expects organisational officials to subordinate personal interests to organisational goals, people who occupy powerful positions can – and often do – use their access to information and the media, plus numerous other advantages, to promote their personal interests. Furthermore, bureaucracy also insulates officials from public accountability, whether in the form of a corporate president who is 'unavailable for comment' to the local press or a national president seeking to control information by claiming 'executive privilege'. Oligarchy, then, thrives in the hierarchical structure of bureaucracy and undermines people's control over their elected leaders (Tolson, 1995).

The 'total institution' as a specific form of organisation

A specific form of organisation involves being confined – often against a person's will – in prisons, concentration camps or mental hospitals. But parallels can also be drawn to life in (many) army camps, boarding schools, old people's homes, homes for the disabled, etc. These are specific forms of bureaucracies in that they are **total institutions**, *settings in which people are isolated from the rest of society and manipulated by an administrative staff*.

Erving Goffman (1961), whose work we will look at in more detail in the next chapter, observed life in a mental hospital in the early 1960s. He saw broad similarities with life in the mental hospital and other kinds of organisation. From his research, he suggested that total institutions have a number of key characteristics. First, staff members supervise all spheres of daily life, including where residents ('inmates') eat, sleep and work. Second, a rigid system provides inmates with standardised food, sleeping quarters and activities. Third, formal rules and daily schedules dictate when, where and how inmates perform virtually every part of their daily routines. Life regulated, lived in common, creates a major divide between inmate and staff.

Most of all, inmates may well experience what Goffman calls a 'mortification of the self'. Total institutions impose such regimentation often with the goal of a radical resocialisation, altering an inmate's sense of self through deliberate manipulation of the environment. The power of a total institution to resocialise is also enhanced by its forcible segregation of inmates from the 'outside' by means of physical barriers such as walls and fences topped with barbed wire and guard towers, barred windows and locked doors. Cut off in this way, the inmate's entire world can be manipulated by the administrative staff to produce lasting change – or at least immediate

compliance – in the inmate. Goffman's work can be read in tandem with the work of Zimbardo, described above.

Parkinson's Law and the Peter Principle

Finally, and on a lighter note, we acknowledge two additional insights concerning the limitations of bureaucratic organisations. The concerns of C. Northcote Parkinson and Laurence J. Peter are familiar to anyone who has ever been a part of a formal organisation.

Parkinson (1957) summed up his understanding of bureaucratic inefficiency with the assertion: *Work expands to fill the time available for its completion.* There is enough truth underlying this tongue-in-cheek assertion that it is known today as Parkinson's Law. To illustrate, assume that a bureaucrat working at the Driver and Vehicle Licensing Centre processes 50 driving licence applications in an average day. If one day this worker had only 25 applications to examine, how much time would the task require? The logical answer is half a day. But Parkinson's Law suggests that if a full day is available to complete the work, a full day is how long it will take.

Because organisational employees have little personal involvement in their jobs, few are likely to seek extra work to fill their spare time. Bureaucrats do strive to *appear* busy, however, and their apparent activity often prompts organisations to take on more employees. The added time and expense required to hire, train, supervise and evaluate a larger staff make everyone busier still, setting in motion a vicious cycle that results in *bureaucratic bloat*. Ironically, the larger organisation may accomplish no more real work than it did before.

In the same light-hearted spirit as Parkinson, Laurence J. Peter (Peter and Hull, 1969) devised the Peter Principle: *Bureaucrats rise to their level of incompetence.* The logic here is simple: employees competent at one level of the organisational hierarchy are likely to earn promotion to higher positions. Eventually, however, they will reach a position where they are in over their heads; there, they perform poorly and thus are no longer eligible for promotion.

Reaching their level of incompetence dooms officials to a future of inefficiency. Adding to the problem, after years in the office they have almost certainly learned how to avoid demotion by hiding behind rules and regulations and taking credit for work actually performed by their more competent subordinates.

A 'total institution'?
Children with shaved heads and yellow uniforms sit in rows in a classroom of an orphanage for juvenile delinquents in Bucharest, Romania

Source: © Bernard Bisson/Sygma/Corbis.

PUBLIC SOCIOLOGY

Social science and the problem of 'evil'

One of the most persistent questions asked by all societies concerns the nature of good and evil. Usually this takes us into the realm of religion – and, as we shall see in Chapter 17, one of the key functions of religion is indeed to define the good life and mark out the boundaries of the bad. But in the twenty-first-century world, social scientists also have contributions to make to this debate.

They can *first* help to show the enormous relativity of what is considered 'good and bad', 'saintly and evil' by different societies at different times, and even different groups in the same societies. 'Evil terrorists' for some countries are the saviours and heroes of others. *Second*, social scientists can document the widespread existence of seemingly bad acts: the My Lai massacre in Vietnam, the genocide in Rwanda, the bombing of the New York Twin Towers on 9/11, and a host of day-to-day nasty things that people do to each other. *Third*, they can publicly discuss the

nature of the origins of evil – a debate which is often raised in everyday discussions in the media, in pubs, at meetings of all kinds around the world. Can social science help us understand 'evil'?

Public sociology takes the works of social scientists considering these issues into public life. For example, the works of Zygmunt Bauman (see *European eye*, p. 186) and the social psychologist Philip Zimbardo (see p. 179) are two relevant observers. Bauman shocks us by telling us that the horrendous horrors of something like the Holocaust, where

PUBLIC SOCIOLOGY

millions were exterminated in the gas chambers by ordinary people (surely an evil?), were really fostered by the routine conditions of modern technology and bureaucracy. Modern societies can dehumanise and impersonalise personal relations in such terrible ways that ordinary, everyday folk can routinely slaughter their fellow citizens. Mass murder becomes banal. Good people become bad people.

And this is what Zimbardo has shown us in the more controlled situation of a social psychological experiment. It shows us how ordinary folk – you and us – if put into difficult situations may well also abuse, damage and possibly even kill each other. Again, bad things can be easily done by good people. Here, dehumanisation and moral disengagement happen both in the social laboratory and in social life.

The sociological suggestion, then, is that we should not focus on people as evil, but rather we should look at the situations and contexts that facilitate bad acts. We could all do it. This insight might help us look at the world differently. Zimbardo, for example, became a witness for the trials around the abuses by the American Military Police at the Abu Ghraib Prison in Iraq in 2004.

Many will recall the photos of extreme abuse of Iraqi prisoners

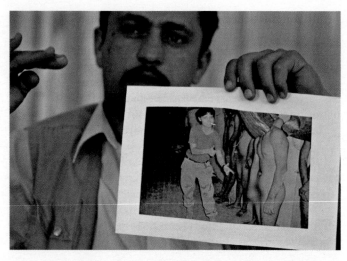

This image, obtained by The Associated Press, shows Pfc. Lynndie England holding a leash attached to a detainee in late 2003 at the Abu Ghraib prison in Baghdad, Iraq. The photo generated worldwide controversy at the start of the UK/US war with Iraq
Source: © Oleg Popov/Reuters/Corbis.

that became prominent in newspapers and on television (see the image above: but they are all online). The Iraqi prisoners were stripped, beaten, put on leashes and made to have (simulated) sex with their captives. Photos, surprisingly, were taken of these acts and eventually were leaked to the global media. It is clear these Muslims were thoroughly degraded and abused by the US Army. People around the world asked just how could such dreadful acts be perpetrated and photographed by seven normal and likeable young men and women. Was it simply a matter

of rogue soldiers and bad apples? Was it simply an isolated incident by bad people? Zimbardo thought not. It was neither an isolated incident, nor due to just a few freakish soldiers. He suggests it was built into the very command chain of the army. He saw his Stanford experiment being replicated in Abu Ghraib, and said so loud and clear to the US courts prosecuting the young soldiers. This is an important social role for social scientists to play.

See: Philip Zimbardo, *The Lucifer Effect: How Good People Turn Evil* (2007).

See also: Baumeister (2001); Lemert (1997).

Weber revisited: the 'McDonaldisation' of society

Weber's discussion of organisation was written in the early part of the twentieth century. Some 80 years on, the North American sociologist George Ritzer suggested that the 'bureaucratisation of society' has proceeded further and deeper. He took the case of

McDonald's restaurants as his illustration, but drew much wider implications.

Consider for a moment the nature of McDonald's, introduced at the start of this chapter. Have you ever eaten in one? Chances are the answer is 'yes'. Indeed, everywhere in the world your authors have travelled, they have not been far from a McDonald's! And sometimes in the most surprising of places. While visiting Hong Kong, both of us visited the former

with 744 opening in 2006. There are more than 850 pairs of golden arches in Japan, for example, and the world's largest McDonald's opened for business in China's capital city of Beijing in April 1992, with some 700 seats, 29 cash registers and 40,000 customers on its first day! (In 2006, it took a $21.6 billion revenue.)

But while McDonald's may be everywhere and has become a symbol of the modern world, this is not Ritzer's point. For him, McDonaldisation suggests that the organisational principles that underlie McDonald's are steadily coming to dominate our entire society. Our culture is becoming 'McDonaldised' – a way of saying that we now model many aspects of life on the famous restaurant chain. Parents buy toys at worldwide chain stores such as Toys R Us; more vacations take the form of resort and tour packages; television presents news in the form of ten-second sound bites; sports become packaged into ever larger stadia and broadcasts; and religion is to be found in megachurches and cyberchurches. McDonaldisation has even had an impact on education: universities devise mass courses based on pre-packaged 'modules'; admissions officers size up students they have never met by glancing over their grades; lecturers assign ghost-written textbooks and evaluate students with tests mass-produced for them by publishing companies; and even sociology may start to become McDonaldised – as McSociology! (B. Smart, 1999). The list goes on and on.

McDonald's is well known throughout the Western World, but it is also a global phenomenon. The restaurant chain had 1,135 outlets across mainland China by the end of 2009. In 2010, there were 130 McDonald's restaurants in South Africa. There is also now McDonald's Arabia

Source: © Iain Masterton/Alamy.

Portuguese colony of Macau – a little nub jutting from the Chinese coast. Few people here speak English, and life on the streets seems a world apart from the urban rhythms of London, Amsterdam or Los Angeles – where you would certainly expect to find a McDonald's. But strolling the old streets, we turn the corner and stand face to face with the famous McDonald's logo! But the most amazing thing is that the food – the burger, fries and drinks – looks, smells and tastes (almost) the same as it does thousands of miles away in Sydney!

As noted in the opening to this chapter, McDonald's has enjoyed enormous success. From a single store in the mid-1950s, McDonald's now operates over 33,000 restaurants throughout much of the world,

McDonaldisation: four principles

What do all these developments have in common? According to George Ritzer, the 'McDonaldisation of society' involves four basic organisational principles:

1 *Efficiency*. Ray Kroc, the marketing genius behind the expansion of McDonald's, set out with the goal of serving a hamburger, French fries and a milkshake to a customer in 50 seconds. Today, one of the company's most popular items is the Egg McMuffin, an entire breakfast in a single sandwich. In the restaurant, customers clear their own trays or, better still, drive away from the pickup window taking the packaging and whatever mess they make with them.

   Efficiency is now a value virtually without critics in our society. Almost everyone believes that anything that can be done quickly is, for that reason alone, good.

2 *Calculability*. The first McDonald's operating manual declared the weight of a regular raw hamburger to be 1.6 ounces, its size to be

3.875 inches across, and its fat content to be 19 per cent. A slice of cheese weighs exactly half an ounce. Fries are cut precisely nine-thirty-seconds of an inch thick.

Think about how many objects around the home, the workplace or the university campus are designed and mass-produced uniformly according to a calculated plan. Not just our environment but our life experiences – from travelling on motorways to sitting at home watching television – are now more deliberately planned than ever before.

3 *Uniformity and predictability*. An individual can walk into a McDonald's restaurant anywhere and receive the same sandwiches, drinks and desserts prepared in precisely the same way. Predictability, of course, is the result of a highly rational system that specifies every course of action and leaves nothing to chance.

4 *Control through automation*. The most unreliable element in the McDonald's system is human beings. People, after all, have good and bad days, sometimes let their minds wander, or simply decide to try something a different way. To eliminate, as much as possible, the unpredictable human element, McDonald's has automated its equipment to cook food at fixed temperatures for set lengths of time. Even the cash register at a McDonald's is little more than pictures of the items so as to minimise the responsibility of the human being taking the customer's order.

The scope of McDonaldisation is expanding throughout the world. Automatic banking machines are replacing banks, highly automated bakeries now produce bread with scarcely any human intervention, and chickens and eggs (or is it eggs and chickens?) emerge from automated hatcheries. In supermarkets, laser scanners are phasing out (less reliable) human checkout operators. Much shopping now occurs in large precincts, in which everything from temperature and humidity to the kinds of store and product are subject to continuous control and supervision (Ritzer, 1993; 2010). Recently the term 'Starbucksisation' has been introduced to update their idea.

Can rationality be irrational?

No one would challenge the popularity or the efficiency of McDonald's and similar organisations (although there has been a lot of critical comment of late and its sales are falling in parts of the world). But there is another side to the story. Max Weber viewed the increasing rationalisation of the world with alarm, fearing that the expanding control of formal organisations would take away spontaneity and human creativity – crushing the human spirit. As he saw it, rational systems were efficient, but at the terrible cost of dehumanisation and disenchantment. Each of the four principles noted above depends on controlling human creativity, discretion and autonomy. George Ritzer contends that McDonald's food is not particularly good for people; nor is the company's extensive use of packaging good for the natural environment. Taking a broader perspective, Ritzer echoes Weber's concern, asserting that 'the ultimate irrationality of McDonaldization is that people could lose control over the system and it would come to control us' (1993: 145). In his book he therefore spends some time discussing ways in which people could resist the McDonaldisation process. This includes avoiding daily routines as much as possible, avoiding classes where tests are short answer and graded by a computer, and eating in local, non-standardised restaurants.

Changing organisational forms

After the Second World War, most formal organisations in Europe were typically conventional bureaucracies, run from the top down according to a stern chain of command. Today, especially as businesses face growing global competition, rigid structures are breaking down. One important element of this trend is the increasing use of the *self-managed work team*. Members of these small groups have the skills necessary to carry out tasks with minimal supervision. By allowing employees to operate within autonomous groups, organisations enhance worker involvement in the job, generate a broader understanding of operations and raise employee morale. A few corporations (such as Procter & Gamble) have had autonomous work units since the 1960s. In recent years, many more are following suit.

Even though it is difficult to compare the performance of organisations with disparate goals and operations, research indicates that self-managed work teams do boost productivity while heading off some of the problems – including alienation – of the traditional bureaucratic model. In the business world, many companies have found that decentralising responsibility in this way also raises product quality and lowers rates of employee absenteeism and turnover.

The audit culture

Management has been among the fasting-growing occupations over the past century. More and more work requires more and more administration and management. Frederick William Taylor (1856–1915) heralded the growth of what was called *scientific management* – where, it was argued, the 'best ways' of organising work would be practised: a systematic matching of pay, abilities, tasks and rules in the work process. This 'Taylorism' established the 'time and motion' studies of work life. (It was much criticised by the Human Relations School for its lack of concern with actual work process and human experience.)

Total quality management (TQM) takes up where Taylorism left off. It started in Japan, was introduced in the USA in the 1970s and quickly became a major movement – by the 1980s entering most government agencies and travelling to the United Kingdom where it was widely adopted. *Quality assurance* (QA) depends upon a full-scale rationalisation of the work process; aims and objectives spelled out with targets and ways of evaluating their success. Strengths, weaknesses, opportunities and threats should be examined.

Feedback from customers should be monitored regularly and with corrective actions following. To do all this, major departments of evaluation and monitoring – the inspectorates – should be established with carefully trained and skilled assessors. This new public management has come to organise education, health and policing in the late twentieth and early twenty-first centuries. Thus Ofsted was formed in 1992, QAA in 1996, and the Commission for Health Improvements and the Commission for Social Care Inspectorate in 2004. They have led to national Audit Commissions, Cycles of Inspections, and an elaborate new terminology: performance indicators, audits, benchmarks, methodologies, SWOTs, feedback forms, accreditation, baseline inspections, annual monitoring, best values, best practice. Such procedures are put in place to improve the performance of education, medicine and policing. TQM makes organisations work more efficiently and effectively.

Yet critics of TQM make five major observations. They argue that it is:

- *Bureaucratic.* All the problems that Max Weber raised about the dysfunctionality of bureaucracies, discussed in the text, come into play.

- *Demoralising.* Those who experience this constant monitoring feel that their workload has been taken over by matters that are not connected to their professional concerns. Teachers want to teach; nurses want to nurse; police want to police: nobody wants to administer. Dejection happens because people are not doing the work they wish to be doing.

- *Deskilling.* The experience of work now becomes rigidly ruled by 'assessments'. Practitioners in various areas complain that this robs them of their own creativity, originality and spontaneity. Lecturers, nurses and the police are required to follow rules.

- *Disciplining and controlling.* Increasingly, management gets people to write things down, making them conform to certain clear norms, and then gains access to all this self-commenting. It becomes what some have called a 'technology of government' – a way of regulating social life.

- *Costly.* Direct costs can be high but tell little of the costings in time and skill from the professionals who have to incorporate this as part of their workload (for example, teachers get no extra money but have to devote hundreds of hours to this extra work).

See: Strathern (2000); Travers (2007); Power (1997).

Humanising bureaucracies

Humanising bureaucracy means *fostering a more democratic organisational atmosphere that recognises and encourages the contributions of everyone.* Research by Kanter (1989) and others suggests that 'humanising' bureaucracy produces both happier employees and healthier profits. Based on the discussion so far, we can identify three paths to a more humane organisational structure.

1 *Social inclusiveness.* The social composition of the organisation should, ideally, make no one feel 'out of place' because of gender, race or ethnicity.

The performance of all employees will improve to the extent that no one is subject to social exclusion.

2 *Sharing of responsibilities.* When organisations ease rigid organisational structures, they spread power and responsibility more widely. Managers cannot benefit from the ideas of employees who have no channels for expressing their opinions. Knowing that superiors are open to suggestions encourages all employees to think creatively, increasing organisational effectiveness.

3 *Expanding opportunities for advancement.* Expanding opportunity reduces the number of employees stuck in routine, dead-end jobs with little motivation to perform well. The organisation should give employees at all levels a chance to share ideas and try new approaches, defining everyone's job as the start of an upward career path.

Kanter's work takes a fresh look at the concept of bureaucracy and its application to business organisations. Rigid formality may have made sense in the past, when organisations hired unschooled workers primarily to perform physical labour. But today's educated workforce can contribute a wealth of ideas to bolster organisational efficiency – if the organisation encourages and rewards innovation.

There is broad support for the idea that loosening up rigid organisations improves performance. Moreover, companies that treat employees as a resource to be developed rather than as a group to be controlled stand out as more profitable. But some critics challenge Kanter's claim that social heterogeneity necessarily yields greater productivity. In controlled comparisons, they maintain, it is homogeneous work groups that typically produce more, while heterogeneous groups are better at generating a diversity of ideas and approaches. Optimal working groups, then, appear to be those that strike a balance: team members bring to the decision-making process a variety of backgrounds and perspectives, yet are similar enough in outlook and goals to coordinate their efforts effectively.

The Japanese situation and the drift to postmodern organisations

We have described efforts to 'humanise' formal organisations. Interestingly, however, organisations in some countries have long been more personal than those in others. For instance, organisations in Japan, a

nation that had remarkable economic success in the mid-twentieth century, developed within a culture of strong collective identity and solidarity. For much of the mid-twentieth century, Japanese companies were built on personal relationships, resembling primary groups, and reflected that society's more collective orientation. Most Japanese companies hired employees for life and played a broad role in their life – helping with mortgages, sponsoring social activities and planning social events for them. They would train employees in all phases of the work operations, and give them a much closer involvement with managers in decision making. They worked through a collective 'group' structure, unlike the more individual and competitive achievement found in the USA or the UK. They were also amazingly productive.

This has come to an end. When the Japanese economy faltered in the 1990s, employees were loathe to lay off their workers, whom they saw more as 'family'. Bit by bit, the system changed – and organisationally it is now more like the American one. Maybe a third or so of Japanese employees are now temporary, are paid lower wages and have less secure work conditions.

Stuart Clegg (1990) has taken this argument further, suggesting that the early Japanese firms approximated to what he calls the 'postmodern firm'. Such organisations were much more flexible and fluid than firms of the past. Strict demarcations were weakened, and they employed the 'just in time' (JIT) system of production. Here, goods are produced as required – there is no mass stocking of parts. And this in turn makes the system more adaptable and flexible. Postmodern organisations break with traditional models, adopting new, creative patterns of operation. In a sense they are usually hybrids of modern and postmodern modes of organising (see Table 6.3).

| Table 6.3 | Contrasting organisational forms: from modern to postmodern |

Modern organisations	Postmodern organisations
More mechanical	More organic
Hierarchical	Network
Specialised	Unspecialised
More rigid	More flexible

Declining communities and rising networks: the rise of the network society

Groups and organisations have proved to be very useful concepts for sociologists to develop. But as relationships change – from primary groups to secondary groups, from secondary groups to formal organisations, from formal organisations to postmodern organisations – so many sociologists have claimed that these changes have been detrimental. Many argue that there has been a decline in traditional communities – the *Gemeinschaft* of Toennies that we discussed in Chapter 1 (see p. 19) – along with a growth in impersonal relations through organisations and the audit culture. There has been a marked decline in small face-to-face groups.

Robert Putnam: bowling alone

This view has recently been put forward most forcefully by Robert Putnam. Surveying the lives of North Americans over the past 25 years, he notes that there has been a significant decline in social bonding within families, friends and community: a decline in church membership, a fall in membership of recreational and volunteer groups, and less engagement with team sports groups. This is what he means by **social capital** – an important sociological concept which captures *those connections among individuals over time which create social bonds*. These are our friendships and social networks, and being generally well integrated into these enhances our sense of well-being and belonging. For Putnam, societies depend on a kind of 'generalised reciprocity' where bonds link each other and there is a concern for each other's welfare. I may help someone today, and tomorrow someone may help me.

But Putnam argues (from a lot of data) that US society has shown a serious decline in social capital since the 1950s. Many people have become more and more disconnected from society, feeling less and less involved. Communities with less social capital generally have lower educational performance, more suicide, more crime, poorer health and a lesser sense of well-being (see also Chapters 8 and 21 on health and inequalities). This is an old story repeated by many sociologists for over a century. Many facts have

contributed to this, including urban sprawl, the increased number of women working and the rise of a new consumer generation. But, all in all, he claims that Americans have been 'pulled apart from one another and our communities' (Putnam, 2001: 180).

New developments: personal communities and social networks

Others, however, are less sure. Human relationships are always changing as societies change, and what we are now starting to see are new forms of social bonds that might better be viewed as personal communities and social networks. Formally, a personal community may be seen as people's intimate and active ties with friends, neighbours and workmates as well as kin (Wellman, 1988), while social networks may be seen as webs of social ties that link people who identify with one another. Liz Spencer and Ray Pahl, in a study of friendships, see friends and friend-like ties as an important (and neglected) source of social glue. From intensive interviews with people, they have developed a set of ideas around friendships – their repertoires (the range of friendships people have); their modes (the way people make and maintain friendships over time); and their patterns of suffusion (the extent to which boundaries between friends and family become blurred). From this they have explored the idea of personal communities and they ways in which such groupings give a sense of solidarity and belonging to social life (Spencer and Pahl, 2006). In their book they spend some time looking at the ways in which these personal communities can be mapped; they get their interviewees to follow these maps. You may like to try their instructions (see the *Methods and research* box) and draw your own friendship map.

Social networks

Think of a network as a 'fuzzy' group that brings people into contact without a group's sense of boundaries and belonging. If we consider a group as a 'circle of friends', then we might describe a network as a 'social web' expanding outwards, often reaching great distances and including larger numbers of people. The most basic pattern of a network – between only two people, such as two people who are merely standing in the same room – can be represented as in Figure 6.4. People are now increasingly bonding differently.

Mapping your personal community, social network and frienships circle

Spencer and Pahl (2006) asked people to list those who were important to them now, and to arrange their names in order of importance on a map, placing them in an appropriate place in relation to the centre. Two contrasting personal communities (where P is the participant) are shown in Figure 6.3.

Figure 6.3   Two contrasting personal communities (P = participant)

Source: Spencer and Pahl (2006: 52).

(a) Basic social network

(b) More complicated social network

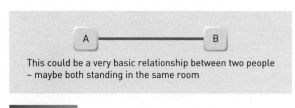

This could be a very basic relationship between two people – maybe both standing in the same room

Figure 6.4   A basic social network

Social networks go beyond ideas of groups, or even organisations. Groups and organisations usually presume some kind of boundary, often with face-to-face interactions going on within them. Networks, by contrast, envisage a field of connections and relations: a set of *nodes* (key points) and a set of *ties* (or links) that connect some or all of these nodes. The nodes could be people, or groups, or even nation-states. A more complex social network is represented in

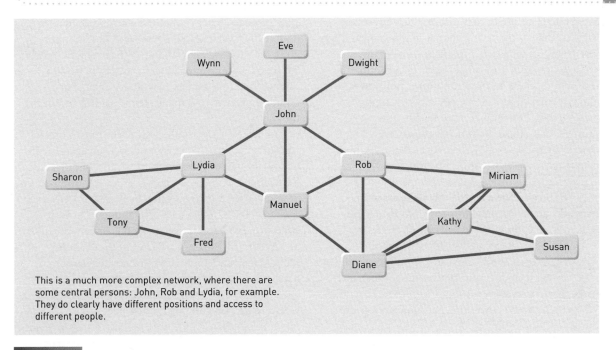

This is a much more complex network, where there are some central persons: John, Rob and Lydia, for example. They do clearly have different positions and access to different people.

Figure 6.5   A more complex social network

Figure 6.5. Here there are some central people – John, Rob and Lydia, for example – but they have different positions and access to different people.

Social network analysis, then, looks at underlying patterns and links that shape such social networks. For example, we could look at the *number* of ties, the *diversity* of ties, the *frequency* and *intensities* of interactional ties, the *directions* of interactional ties, the *content* of the ties, and the *quality* of ties. We could build up maps of friendships which interconnect; see how bounded communities or families relate beyond themselves; or even locate patterns of people who have been part of the same network of sexual partners (an area of research that has been of value in studying AIDS: see Chapter 21).

Some such networks may then be seen as densely knit (most nodes are connected) and tightly bounded (most stay within the same subset of nodes). Or by contrast they may be seen as very thin and loose (Wellman, 1999). 'Contemporary Western communities rarely are tightly bounded, densely knit groups of broadly based ties. They usually are loosely bounded, sparsely knit, ramifying networks of specialised ties' (Wellman, 1999: 97). From this, we can now talk of network communities. Living in a specific geographical area or space no longer defines your community of personal interactions – instead it is now defined through phones, cars, the internet, public transport

systems and the like. These can connect you to a wide range of people. Living in a residential community may now mean that you are not really living in a specific, geographically bounded community but in an altogether wider network community. As you connect more and more through your network, so the older style of direct face-to-face communications ceases to have the same kind of meaning. And as a result of this, each of us may well come to live in our own network. We come to live with our own personal maps of the spaces we inhabit.

All this may signify important changes in patterns of contact and communication, which we discuss further in Chapters 8 and 22. Some network contacts are solid, traditional and regular, as among college friends who, years later, stay in touch (by personal contact, or mail and telephone). But, more commonly, a network includes people we *know of* – or who *know of us* – but with whom we interact infrequently, if at all. Social networks amount to 'clusters of weak ties' (Granovetter, 1973).

Network ties may be weak, but they serve as a significant resource. For example, many people rely on their networks to find jobs. Even the scientific genius Albert Einstein needed a hand in landing his first job. After a year of unsuccessful interviewing, he obtained employment only when the father of one of his fellow students put him in touch with an office manager who hired him. This use of networks to one's advantage suggests that, as the saying goes, *who you know* is often just as important as *what you know.*

Networks are based on people's colleges and universities, clubs, local communities, political parties and informal cliques. Some networks encompass people with considerably more wealth, power and prestige than others do, which is the essence of describing someone as 'well connected'. And some people have denser networks than others – that is, they are connected to more people, which is also a valuable social resource. Typically, the most extensive social networks are maintained by people who are young, well educated and living in urban areas.

Gender, too, shapes networks. Although the networks of men and women are typically the same size, women include more relatives in their networks, while those of men are filled out with more co-workers. Women's networks, therefore, may not carry quite the same clout as the 'old boy' networks do. Even so, research indicates that, as gender inequality lessens, this difference is diminishing over time.

Technology and networks: mobile phones and network groups

Technologies have played a major role in the changing shape of networking. Just how have the telephone, email, mobile phones and SNS (social networking sites) shifted our networks and communication styles?

Take the mobile telephones as a key example. To appreciate networking, just consider that any one of the millions and millions of phones in the world can connect anybody, within seconds, to any other phone – in homes, businesses, automobiles, even in the middle of a football field. Such instant communication is beyond the imagination of those who lived in the ancient world. Of course, the telephone system depends on technological developments such as electricity, fibre optics and computers. But the system could not exist without the organisational capacity to keep track of every telephone call – noting which phone called which other phone, when and for how long – and presenting all this information to billions of telephone users in the form of regular bills. So it is connected to bureaucracies too. But it starts to enable a very different mode of building up relations.

Mobile phones make for even more complex networks and they are the fastest-spreading technology of all time. Within just a few years, many people have come to take them for granted. Mobile networks in 2007 covered 80 per cent of the world's population; double the level in 2000. There were 1 billion users by 2004, 2 billion by 2006, and in 2010 there were nearly 5 billion – approaching 70 per cent of the world's population. This is an extraordinary change in a decade and a half and many claim that it is reworking the way we live.

Consider the case of the UK. According to official statistics, in 2005, 82 per cent of children aged 12–15 had their own mobile phones (the most popular reason for having a phone was 'texting'); and some 85 per cent of adults used mobile technology regularly (*Social Trends*, 2007: 172–3). A survey conducted as early as 2006 suggested that in fact some 90 per cent of children had a mobile by the time they went to secondary school at 12, and it 'provides them with a social network, a sense of security and access to entertainment. But most importantly it provides them with a sense of belonging to their peer group' (*Mobile Life Youth Report*, 2006). 'Texting' was already a major activity: the average 11- to 17-year old received or made an average of 9.6 texts a day (in contrast, for adults the figure is 3.6). By 2010, mobiles (and texting) are firmly and ubiquitously embedded in the lives of the young (and most of the older), and are not likely to go away in their lifetimes unless a new technology replaces them (which, of course, probably will happen).

The impact of the mobile phone has been worldwide. Even in low-income and poorer countries, mobile phones have become widespread. Whereas landline telephones were costly and inaccessible, mobile phones are much cheaper. In 2010, some 40 per cent of Nigerians and 30 per cent of Bangladeshis had mobile phones, whilst India had the fourth largest uptake in the world – with some 650 million mobile phones in operation (around 60 per cent of the population – and many more than have a good sanitation!). (Sources: *Social Trends*; *GSM Statistics, 2010*; *indiatelecom*.)

Mobiles signify a shift in patterns of contact and communication. We can now have relationships on the phone anywhere, anytime. Of course, it depends a great deal whether you carry the phone around with you all the time, and whether it is switched on or off! But when it is both these things (on and with you), we shift to a new mode of contact probably unique in our history: that of *perpetual contact*. Slowly, new rules for conducting phone calls are emerging. Just as you have access to everyone on the phone, so they have access to you. This means that several things have happened in networking contacts. First, there has been a breakdown of the old split between home and street, etc. – people can now talk anywhere. Secondly, it is intrusive – it can interrupt other streams of life. Thus while going shopping, being in lectures, eating in a restaurant, having sex, or simply talking with someone else, the mobile can ring or you can ring it and the network of interaction abruptly shifts. Thirdly, it is fast: people are on tap and online for any time. All this and more has meant that new rules are having to be evolved as to how we can manage this perpetual contact (Katz and Aakhus, 2002). More than this: sociologists are now arguing that *mobile communication is reshaping social cohesion.* Keeping phones with us permanently by our side keeps us in touch with significant others all the time. Families may even be strengthened as children are always in touch with parents (Ling, 2008).

Social networking: Facebook and our internet friends

Along with mobile phones, another new technology to shift group organisation and personal life significantly has been the rise of the social networks group (SNG). Social networking websites started as early as 1985, bringing together communities to interact with each other and share information through chat rooms. Mail bulletin boards helped to stretch out to various kinds of web groups (and friendship sites such as Friends Reunited). Friends support networks started out with My Space in 2003, but this was soon overtaken by Facebook, which had over 500 million active users in July 2010. Facebook, Bebo and Twitter are widely used

worldwide; but there are many different sites for different countries: Orkut and Hi5 in South America and Central America, and Friendster, Mixi, Multiply, Orkut, Wretch, Renren and Cyworld in Asia.

In the UK, social networking doubled between 2007 and 2009. The proportion of users rose for all age groups, but the largest rises were among those aged 25 to 34 (38 percentage points) and those aged 35 to 44 (28 percentage points). Women were more likely than men to have set up a social networking site profile. Users of social networking sites reported that they used them to talk to friends and family whom they see a lot (78 per cent), those they rarely see (75 per cent), and to look for old friends and people they have lost contact with (47 per cent) (*Social Trends*, 2010). On a global scale, Facebook claims that 50 per cent of active users log on to the site each day. This would mean at least 175 million users every 24 hours. Twitter also claims that it now has 75 million user accounts, but only around 15 million are active users on a regular basis. In the first quarter of 2010, 4 billion tweets per quarter were posted.

Social network groups have certainly changed the meaning of personal relationships and, indeed, the meaning of communities (for they are often called online *communities*). Unlike traditional communities, they do not involve direct face-to-face communication but are mediated through technology. We will see later the importance of what are increasingly called *mediated lives.* Unlike traditional communities, they are not local and bound to a place but usually global and break down any firm sense of place. And unlike

Mobile phones can be used anywhere – even in the most surprising places
Source: © Al Rod/Corbis.

Manuel Castells: the network society and the Information Age

Manuel Castells (1942–)
Source: Permission from Manuel Castells.

Manuel Castells is Emeritus Professor of Sociology at the University of California, Berkeley. Born in Spain in 1942, he studied law and economics at the University of Barcelona from 1958 to 1962. He was a student activist against Franco's dictatorship and had to escape to Paris, where he eventually gained his PhD in Sociology from the University of Paris in 1967. His first book, *La Question Urbaine*, was translated into ten languages and became a classic around the world, and he became known as one of the intellectual founders of the 'New Urban Sociology'.

Castell's trilogy, *The Information Age*, is considered to be one of the most sustained and readable accounts of the rise of the information society and the new networks that come with it. He analyses the ways in which economic and social transformations in capitalism connect to the information technology revolution, and have brought about a new world social order in the twenty-first century.

His three books look at the rise of new communications, the creation of new identities, and the shifting political contours of the world in the twenty-first century – especially the role of social movements. Long and detailed as the books are, Castells tries to make himself intelligible (he does not use incomprehensible jargon) and provides much data, evidence and illustration for his arguments (it is not a work of abstract theory). The volumes have come to be regarded as one of the major statements of changing times and what sociology in the twenty-first century should have to deal with. Unlike Marx's view of the mode of production, for Castells it is the new telecommunications – the informational mode of development – that is reordering our very sense of time and space. It creates a capitalist network economy.

Crucial to Castell's work is the idea of networks and flows. Networks provide a series of hubs and points – people, cities, businesses, states – connected by flows of different sorts – information, money, people. With these 'flows' time changes: there is a speeding up of time but also a lack of standard sequencing. Time becomes a 'perpetual present' – the past comes back to us in sound bites, and the future arrives almost before we've experienced it. In this new world, our sense of space and time becomes dramatically reordered: the local now goes global; the past and the future are the present. We can be everywhere and nowhere at the same time – sitting at our computers. All this has great importance for the way we think about ourselves (our identities), our political actions (through social movements), and our ways of living (through work and families). International forms of money, international forms of crime, environmental issues – all change under this new order and Castells discusses each. The Information Age touches all globally.

A very useful guide to all this can be found in David Bell's *Cyberculture Theorists* (2007).

most traditional communities, they are unrestricted in numbers – friendships and communities usually have some kind of restricted size, but social network groups can be very large (often Facebook leads to thousands of new friends) and seemingly unbounded. As a result of these differences, many critics claim these social network sites are not communities at all, but can instead lead to 'impoverished communication'.

In contrast, defenders claim that social networks bring personalised 'methodologically individuated communities'. In many ways, they take on the characteristics of the subcultures we described in Chapter 5 (see p. 155). They generate their own languages, values, rules and norms; they build their own software and programs if needed; they provide shared resources – emotional and informational. They give members a sense of self and esteem – indeed, they become major mechanisms for creating common, shared identities and social bonds. Wellman refers to this as a 'networked individualism' in which each person sits at the centre of their own personal community. From this community they can engage with others, including involvement in local or even global politics. Defenders of SNGs would see them as simply the evolution of another form of group and social solidarity – another ingenious way of bringing people together in a large and complex world (Baym, 2010).

An uncontrolled matrix?

The new information technology has generated a global network of unprecedented size in the form of the internet, mobile phones and networking groups. We now dwell in this. Its origins seem right out of the 1960s Cold War film *Dr Strangelove*: its character demonstrated in the 1990s trilogy *The Matrix*. Five decades ago, US government officials and scientists were trying to imagine how to run the country after an atomic attack, which, they assumed, would instantaneously eliminate telephones and television. The brilliant solution was to devise a communication system with no central headquarters, no one in charge and no main power switch – in short, an electronic web that would link the country in one vast network. But by 1999, when the first part of *The Matrix* was released, this vast network has indeed taken over. The machines now run everything and use humans merely as an energy source. An illusory simulated reality constructs the world of 1999 and all people can do is try to resist it, or 'unplug' it.

Looking ahead: the network society

Spanish sociologist Manuel Castells (1996) uses the term 'network society' to capture the new kind of society we are moving into – one based on computers and information technologies, and characterised by new networks of relating (see *Thinkers and theory* above).

In the twenty-first century, we can clearly see how older patterns of group life and communication are being partially replaced by 'networking'. This brings with it a potential for self-expansion and a new logic of thinking (think of how you read a book and how you search the Web to capture the different logics at work here). It also, of course, means that life gets lived at a faster pace and in a more fragmented way. Real changes in our ways of relating to each other may be taking place. For Castells the new information technology brings five features:

1 Information as the raw material to act on: our access to information and our use of it starts to change.
2 The pervasiveness of information technologies: scarcely an item in daily use is not touched by it – from hand-held 'palm top' computing to automobile satellite technology mapping. Every institution – from medical recording to educational processes – requires the new technologies.
3 The network logic of any system using them: no longer simply linear and straightforward.
4 Flexibility: open to rapid changes and adjustments.
5 Convergence of technologies: the ways in which computers etc. can now connect to photo, sound, time and personal technologies. Complete interconnected systems may soon scan whole bodies, settings and areas (Castells, Vol. 1, 1996: 21).

Power is no longer concentrated in institutions like the state: it now diffuses through global networks. We shall return to this regularly and in more detail in later chapters (see Chapters 8, 15 and 23 especially). All the themes touched upon in this book must now be placed alongside this new 'culture of virtuality' in a globalising world. Thus, we shall see in later chapters how this is shaping the economy, power, all forms of media, and even issues like class, gender and education. We will take stock of this idea of a 'network society' in the closing chapters of this book.

SUMMARY

1 Social groups – important building blocks of societies – foster personal development and common identity as well as performing various tasks. Primary groups tend to be small and person orientated; secondary groups are typically large and goal orientated. The process of group conformity is well documented by researchers. Because members often seek consensus, work groups do not necessarily generate a wider range of ideas than do individuals working alone. Individuals use reference groups to form attitudes and make decisions.

2 Georg Simmel characterised the dyad relationship as intense but unstable; a triad, he noted, can easily dissolve into a dyad by excluding one member.

3 Peter Blau explored how the size, internal homogeneity, relative social parity and physical segregation of groups all affect members' behaviour. Formal organisations are large, secondary groups that seek to perform complex tasks efficiently. According to their members' reasons for joining, formal organisations are classified as utilitarian, normative or coercive. Bureaucratic organisation expands in modern societies to perform many complex tasks efficiently. Bureaucracy is based on specialisation, hierarchy, rules and regulations, technical competence, impersonal interaction and formal, written communications. Ideal bureaucracy may promote efficiency, but bureaucracy also generates alienation and inefficiency, tends to perpetuate itself beyond the achievement of its goals and contributes to the contemporary erosion of privacy.

4 The trend towards the 'McDonaldisation of society' involves increasing automation and impersonality. It is defined by growing efficiency, predictability, calculability and control through automation.

5 Humanising bureaucracy means recognising people as an organisation's greatest resource. To develop human resources, organisations should spread responsibility and opportunity widely. One way to put this ideal into action is through self-managed work teams. Reflecting the collective spirit of Japanese culture, formal organisations in Japan are based on more personal ties than are their counterparts in the United States and Europe.

6 We are now living in the network age. Mobile phones, social networking and the internet are relational webs that link people. The internet is a vast electronic network linking millions of computers worldwide. Mobile phones and social networking groups are starting to change group relations.

CONNECT UP: Turn to Part 6 of this book for key resources and link up
with the book's website, which links to these resources
SEE: www.pearsoned.co.uk/plummer

MYTASKLIST

Suggestions for going further

1 Connect up with Part Six and the Sociology Web Resources

As you work through ideas and think about the issues raised in this chapter, look at the accompanying website and the resource centre at the end of this book which connects to it. There is a lot here to help you move on. To link up, see www.pearson.co.uk/plummer.

2 Review the chapter

Briefly summarise (in a paragraph) just what this chapter has been about. Consider: (a) What have you learned? (b) What do you disagree with? Be critical. And (c) How would you develop all this? How could you get more detail on matters that interest you?

3 Pose questions

(a) Identify various (i) primary and secondary groups, (ii) formal and informal organisations, and (iii) networks in your own life. What do you like or dislike about each type of setting?

(b) Examine the nature of bureaucracies in the worlds you live in. Are they essentially male worlds? Are they really dehumanising? Can you write 'in praise' of them?

(c) What is the 'McDonaldisation of society'? Discuss whether it can be seen as a sign of a progressing society, or whether it should be resisted. Should it nowadays perhaps be called the 'Starbucksisation of society'?

(d) Draw up your own social network and contrast it with that of a friend. How might such networks differ across different cultures?

(e) Does the 'network society' suggest a really different way of relating to people than that found in the past? Consider how you use your mobile phone and

Facebook. How does this differ from interaction in the past?

4 Explore key words

Many concepts have been introduced in this chapter. You can review them from the website or from the listing at the back of this book. You might like to give special attention to just five words and think them through – how would you define them, what are they dealing with, and do they help you see the social world more clearly or not?

5 Search the Web

Be critical when you look at websites – see the box on p. 940 in the Resources section. For this chapter look at:

The McDonaldisation website
www.mcdonaldization.com
This gives a very good overview of the issues, but has not been kept up to date.

Social psychological experiments: Milgram
www.stanleymilgram.com
The purpose of this website is to be a source of accurate information about the life and work of the social psychologist Stanley Milgram.

Zimbardo
www.zimbardo.com
The homepage of Professor Phillip G. Zimbardo. An extremely useful website devoted to Zimbardo's work. When we looked at it in July 2007, it was very up to date. It also includes a slideshow of the famous experiment (as well as the video).

The Holocaust
www.history1900's.about.com/library/holocaust/blholocaust.htm
A clear and simple site which would lead you to many others.

On information technology, see the sites listed in Chapter 23.

6 Watch a DVD

Look at a range of films that have different kinds of group relations as their key backdrop and compare them. Why not look at:

- Frank Darabont's *The Shawshank Redemption* (1994): life in a prison.
- Nunally Johnson's *Man in a Grey Flannel Suit* (1957): life as an organisation man in the mid-1950s.
- Walter Hill's *The Warriors* (1979): life in a gang in New York.
- Steven Spielberg's *Schindler's List* (1993): life in the Holocaust.
- Larry and Andy Wachowki's *The Matrix* (1999): the Matrix is an all-engulfing simulated reality which pacifies and subdues the human population. It generated two follow-up films made in 2003, a cult following and a huge games industry around it. It suggests a life through cyber-relations at the end of the twentieth century.
- Morgan Spurlock's *Super Size Me* (2004): chronicles a month in the life of Morgan Spurlock, who eats nothing but McDonald's food and becomes dangerously ill as a result.
- David Fisher's *The Social Network* (2010): charts the rise of facebook.

7 Think and read

George C. Homans, *The Human Group* (1992; orig. 1950). This is the classic sociological investigation of the group, the setting for much of our lives.

Robert Putnam, *Bowling Alone: The Collapse and Revival of American Community* (2001). This is the most recent significant study in the USA to discuss the changing nature of groups and communities.

Philip Zimbardo, *The Lucifer Effect: How Good People Turn Evil* (2007). The controversial study described in the chapter, and here it is applied to Abu Ghraib.

George Ritzer, *The McDonaldization of Society* (1st edn, 1993; 6th edn, 2010). A highly readable and lively account of the McDonald's phenomenon and how it provides a blueprint for contemporary organisational life. The book has spawned a number of linked books. Later editions discuss 'Starbucksisation'.

Stuart R. Clegg, *Modern Organisations: Organisation Studies in the Postmodern World* (1990). An important review of

earlier studies of organisations which also suggests the postmodern organisation. There are some intriguing case studies too of the French bread industry, the Italian fashion industry and 'post-Confucian' Asian enterprises.

Max Travers, *The New Bureaucracy: Quality Assurance and Its Critics* (2007). Readable account of quality management and the audit culture, applied to health, education and policing in the UK.

John Scott, *Social Network Analysis: A Handbook* (2nd edn, 2000a). Reviews the whole field of network research.

Manuel Castells, *The Rise of the Network Society*, Vol. 1 of *The Information Age* (1996). The now classic study mentioned in the chapter. There is a new introduction to the 2nd edition published in 2010.

Frank Webster, *Theories of the Information Society* (3rd edn, 2006). An important and critical evaluation of major information society theorists, including Daniel Bell, Manuel Castells and Jürgen Habermas.

Nancy K. Baym, *Personal Connections in the Digital Age* (2010). A useful overview of the ways in which digital media are changing our lives.

8 Relax with a novel

If Weber is the great theorist of bureaucracy, then the early twentieth-century Czech novelist Franz Kafka (1883–1924) is its poet laureate. See Franz Kafka, *The Trial* and *The Castle* (both originally published in English in 1937). The word 'Kafkaesque' suggests society as a pointless and irrational organisation into which a bewildered individual has strayed.

This may also be a good time to read William Golding's *The Lord of the Flies* (1954), which has also been made into a film, twice.

9 Connect to other chapters

- For more on genocide, see Chapters 11 and 16.
- Cyberworlds and new technologies are featured further in Chapters 7, 22 and 23.
- For more on Goffman, see Chapter 7.
- For educational bureaucracies, see Chapter 20.
- For prisons, see Chapter 17.

10 Engage with THE BIG DEBATE

Mobile phones and Facebook: what are they doing to our personal life?

It would seem that the intimate face-to-face relationships of the primary group have long been breaking down. We have all been familiar with the more impersonal and transitory relationships of the secondary group for a long time. Indeed, most of us have come to accept that, while there is a part of our life where the primary group matters most, for much of our daily activities, from work to shopping to entertainment, we depend more and more on secondary groups. The ways of relating in the world have changed.

But it may well be that this is radically changing again. Indeed, many of the themes found in this text suggest that a new set of relationships are starting to happen. We now personally communicate with each other and relate to each other in ways that contrast sharply with the past. Perhaps you should start your discussion by considering what these changes have been.

One way of thinking about these is to look at your relationships with the world of high-tech gadgetry: Facebook, mobiles, texting, iPods, games, your PC. Now think about how much time you spend doing these things, usually away from face-to-face contact with people. For many, this will be a lot of time (studies have suggested that young people spend 7 hours a day on electronic gadgets!). Indeed, look around any city and you are likely to see people rushing somewhere while 'on their mobile phone'. Sit in a café and out comes the laptop. Everybody on trains seems to have ears plugged – they are all wired up. People have eyes down and are busy texting – or playing the latest game. Watch increasingly for those who get out their iPhones and iPads. More and more people (in the rich world, of course) do their work, their play, their shopping and their relationships all through computing technologies. Our daily lives are digitalised.

But think for a minute how this is changing our personal lives and group involvement. Consider some of the changes:

- Personal face-to-face talking relationships are replaced by distanced writing relationships on the screen or in texting: face-to-face contact ceases in this medium.
- Close primary groups and even secondary groups give way to global groups: providing you are connected up to the Web or your mobile, you can talk with anybody in the world. Intimacy can now spread across the globe (and it does, literally, through computer sex lines – or cybersex).
- Straightforward linear thinking – as in most writing – becomes taken over by 'hypertext' where the reader jumps around, splices the text, and moves in and out of different 'MUDS' (multi-user domains). Ways of thinking start to shift.
- Identities are no longer given in face-to-face interaction (for example, as a man or a woman), but assembled through the machine. In a literal sense, you can make yourself anybody you wish. You can become your email address, your 'facebook', or your new 'second life'.

This is just a preliminary list. You may like to continue it and we will look at it a little more in the next chapter. But the big question becomes: what will happen when we all start to conduct our lives like this, as many argue we already do? A new generation is arriving which will know nothing else.

There may be many downsides to this. What happens when people cannot afford a computer (and most of the world not only cannot afford it, but also remain illiterate)? Surely this will divide the world into a new form of stratification – the cyberclasses and the non-cyberclasses?

There again, what happens when people can afford it? Some researchers are starting to suggest that there has been an increase in shyness and an inability to communicate with others since the computer has arrived. We avoid primary groups and face-to-face relationships, and are only comfortable with machines and text talk. We can do so much more in virtual reality than we can do in 'real life'!

So there are pluses and minuses to the arrival of this new technology.

Continue the debate

1 How might the new information technology change our relationships? Have mobile phones, for example, provided more and better relationships than the past could offer? Draw up a list of the dangers and merits.
2 What is cybersex? How can people have sex with or on a computer? Is this the way ahead for all our sexual problems? (See Chapter 23, p. 818)
3 Does the new technology lead to a growing inequality?

See: Nancy Baym, *Personal Connections in the Digital Age* (2010).

CHAPTER 7

MICRO-SOCIOLOGY: THE SOCIAL CONSTRUCTION OF EVERYDAY LIFE

ON A COLD WINTER DAY IN 1938, a social worker walked anxiously to the door of a rural Pennsylvania farmhouse. Investigating a case of possible child abuse, the social worker soon discovered a five-year-old girl hidden in a second-floor storage room. The child, whose name was Anna, was wedged into an old chair with her arms tied above her head so that she could not move. She was dressed in filthy garments, and her arms and legs – looking like matchsticks – were so frail that she could not use them.

Anna's situation can only be described as tragic. She was born in 1932 to an unmarried and mentally impaired woman of 26 who lived with her father. Enraged by his daughter's 'illegitimate' motherhood, the grandfather did not even want the child in his house. Anna therefore spent her first six months in various institutions. But her mother was unable to pay for such care, so Anna returned to the hostile home of her grandfather.

At this point, her ordeal intensified. To lessen the grandfather's anger, Anna's mother moved the child to the attic room, where she received little attention and just enough milk to keep her alive. There she stayed – day after day, month after month, with essentially no human contact – for five long years.

Upon learning of the discovery of Anna, sociologist Kingsley Davis (1940) travelled immediately to see the child. He found her at a county home, where local authorities had taken her. Davis was appalled by Anna's condition. She was emaciated and feeble. Unable to laugh, smile, speak or even show anger, she was completely unresponsive, as if alone in an empty world.

After four years of care, Anna learned to walk, talk in short phrases and care a little for herself. She died on 6 August 1942 at the age of 10.

If we had a keen vision and feeling of all ordinary human life, it would be like hearing the grass grow and the squirrel's heart beat, and we should die at the roar which lies on the other side of silence.

George Eliot, *Middlemarch*, 1872

We dwell in the minds of others even when we do not know this.

Charles Horton Cooley, *Human Nature and the Social Order*, 1902

In this chapter, we ask:

- **What is micro-sociology?**

- **How do we become social and develop biographies across the life course?**

- **How is everyday life constructed and negotiated?**

- **How is everyday life changing in the twenty-first century?**

- **How are our identities, bodies and emotions socially formed?**

(Left) Painting of a masked ball by Lincoln Seligman that features on a wall of the Berkley Hotel, London

Source: Berkley Hotel Mural – 1, Seligman, Lincoln (Contemporary Artist)/Private Collection/The Bridgeman Art Library.

See: www.lincolnseligman.co.uk.

 What does the nature of the masked ball suggest about social life? Read on . . .

This classic story of Anna is a sad but instructive case of a human being deprived of virtually all social contact. Although physically alive, Anna hardly seemed human. Her plight reveals that, isolated in this way, an individual develops scarcely any capacity for thought, emotion and meaningful behaviour. In short, without social experience, an individual is not a social human being.

This chapter explores what Anna was deprived of – the means by which we become fully human. It looks at how we become social; how our bodies and emotions become social; how identities are formed; and how we assemble our everyday lives. In doing this, we move to a different kind of problem and a different level of analysis from those encountered so far. Up till now our discussions have been looking at the big picture: of society, cultures and organisations, along with the broad changes that have been taking place in them as first industrialisation and more recently the information revolution have brought new forms of society. This is **macro-sociology** – *the study of large-scale society*.

By contrast, we now turn to what may be seen as the building blocks of a society – the human actions in little social worlds that enable social life to get done. We are interested here in everyday life – how people go shopping, make breakfasts, go to work, use mobile phones, make love, fight wars, lie, cheat and steal! All the wonders of daily life are here. This is **micro-sociology** – *the study of everyday life in social interactions*. We will start by seeing just how our everyday realities are 'socially constructed'. From this, we will look at the ways in which we come to assemble our sense of who we are through what can be called the socialisation process. We will then look at five key ideas that help organise our everyday lives: *interaction*, *identity*, *bodies*, *emotion* and *biography*.

The social construction of reality

Nearly 100 years ago, the Italian playwright Luigi Pirandello (1867–1936) skilfully applied the sociological perspective to social interaction. In *The Pleasure of Honesty*, Angelo Baldovino – a brilliant man with a chequered past – enters the fashionable home of the Renni family and introduces himself in a most peculiar way:

Inevitably we construct ourselves. Let me explain. I enter this house and immediately I become what I have to become, what I can become: I construct myself. That is, I present myself to you in a form suitable to the relationship I wish to achieve with you. And, of course, you do the same with me.

(Pirandello, 1962: 157–8)

This curious introduction suggests that each human being has some ability to shape what happens from moment to moment. 'Reality', in other words, is not as fixed as we may think.

The phrase **social construction of reality** was introduced by Peter Berger and Thomas Luckmann (1967) to identify *the process by which people creatively shape reality through social interaction*. Human worlds are socially produced, changed and modified. This idea stands at the foundation of the symbolic-interaction paradigm, as described in earlier chapters, and is the hallmark of what is now called the social constructionist perspective. As Angelo Baldovino's remark suggests, especially in an unfamiliar situation, quite a bit of 'reality' remains unclear in everyone's mind. So as Baldovino 'presents himself' in terms that suit his purposes, and as others do the same, a complex reality emerges, though few people are so 'up front' about their deliberate efforts to foster an impression.

Social interaction, then, amounts to negotiating reality. Most everyday situations involve at least some agreement about what is going on, but participants perceive events differently. We have to take seriously people's different perspectives on the world, and how they come to define the situations they are in. One core issue to consider here is how the way in which people define situations helps shape the world they live in. W. I. Thomas, the founding sociologist from the University of Chicago (1966: 301; orig. 1931), succinctly expressed this insight in what has come to be known as the **Thomas theorem**: *situations we define as real become real in their consequences*.

Becoming social: the process of socialisation

How do we come to be social beings, acquiring our own perspectives on the world? Sociologists suggest that it is through a process of **socialisation**, *a lifelong social experience by which individuals construct their personal biography, assemble daily interactional rules and come to terms with the wider patterns of their* *culture.* Unlike other living species whose behaviour may be largely biologically set, human beings rely on social experience to learn the nuances of their culture in order to survive.

Questions for an account of socialisation

Socialisation theory can ask five broad questions, which may be summarised as follows:

1 *Who is being socialised?*
2 *By whom?*
3 *How?*
4 *Where?*
5 *When?*

The first question raises the issue of the nature of the person being socialised and ultimately asks about *human nature.* Is this something people are born with or are they the product of their environment? This is the classic 'nature/nurture' argument. The second question looks at the role of *agents of socialisation.* This might start out with the formative role of mothers, fathers and siblings as *primary* socialisers, but it soon moves on to other agents such as friends, peers, teachers, significant others and indeed even the mass media (see Chapter 22). The 'how' question asks about the processes through which people become socialised. *These are development theories,* which look at the many mechanisms through which we become human, and include what is known as psychodynamic and interactionist approaches. Finally, the last questions aim to locate the life in time and place – at how socialisation varies across different cultures and across history. We look at some of these questions in more detail below.

How do we develop – nature, nurture or both?

Virtually helpless at birth, the human infant depends on others for care and nourishment as well as learning. Although Anna's short life makes these facts very clear, most people mistakenly believe that human behaviour is the product of biological imperatives: for many, instincts, evolution and genes are seen as the core of human behaviour. 'It's genetic' is one of the most common claims made these days. But sociologists cast much doubt on the overstated power of the gene, as we shall see.

Initially it was Charles Darwin who argued, plausibly, that each species evolves over thousands of generations as genetic variations enhance survival and reproduction. Biologically rooted traits that enhance survival emerge as a species' 'nature'. As Darwin's fame grew, people assumed that humans, like other forms of life, had a fixed, instinctive 'nature' as well.

Such notions are still with us. People sometimes claim, for example, that our economic system is a reflection of 'instinctive human competitiveness', that some people are 'born criminals', or that women are more 'naturally' emotional while men are 'inherently' more rational. Indeed, almost anything social – from race differences to illness, from wealth to intelligence – is explained by some as genetic. We often describe familiar traits as *human nature,* as if people were born with them, just as we are born with five senses. More accurately, however, our human nature leads us to create and learn cultural traits, as we shall see.

People trying to understand cultural diversity also misconstrued Darwin's thinking. Centuries of world exploration and empire building taught western Europeans that people around the world behaved quite differently from themselves. They attributed such contrasts to biology rather than culture. It was a simple – although terribly damaging – step to conclude that members of technologically simple societies were biologically less evolved and, therefore, less human. Such a self-serving and ethnocentric view helped justify colonial practices, including land seizures and slavery, since it is easier to exploit others if you are convinced that they are not truly human in the same sense that you are.

In the twentieth century, social scientists launched a broad attack on naturalistic explanations of human behaviour. Psychologist John B. Watson (1878–1958) devised a theory called **behaviourism**, which held that *specific behaviour patterns are not instinctive but learned.* Thus people the world over have the same claim to humanity, Watson insisted; humans differ only in their cultural environment. In a classic observation, Watson remarked that 'human nature' was infinitely malleable:

> **Give me a dozen healthy infants . . . and my own specified world to bring them up in, and I will guarantee to take any one at random and train him [or her] to become any type of specialist that I might select – doctor, lawyer, artist, merchant, chief, and yes, even beggar-man and thief – regardless of his [or her] talents, penchants, tendencies, abilities, vocations, and race of his [or her] ancestors.**

(Watson, 1930: 104)

Anthropologists weighed in on this debate as well, showing how variable the world's cultures are. An outspoken proponent of the 'nurture' view, anthropologist Margaret Mead summed up the evidence:

> The differences between individuals who are members of different cultures, like the differences between individuals within a culture, are almost entirely to be laid to differences in conditioning, especially during early childhood, and this conditioning is culturally determined.

(Mead, 1963: 280; orig. 1935)

Today, social scientists (and many biologists who specialise in genetics too) are cautious about describing any type of behaviour as *simply* instinctive or genetic. Of course, this does not mean that biology plays no part in human behaviour. Human life, after all, depends on the functioning of the body. We also know that children share many biological traits with their parents, especially physical characteristics such as height, weight, hair and eye colour, and facial features. Intelligence and various personality characteristics (for example, how one reacts to stimulation or frustration) have some genetic component, as does the potential to excel in such activities as art and music. But whether a person develops an inherited potential depends on the opportunities associated with social position.

Sociologists generally work from the assumption that nurture is far more important than nature in determining human behaviour. We should not think of nature as opposing nurture, though, since we express our human nature as we build culture. For humans, then, nature and nurture are inseparable. A useful term to deal with all this is *human capabilities*. These suggest *the features which are central to a human life to function well*. In some ways they should be seen as our basic entitlements. Without them, we cannot function well in social life. They can be seen as 'opportunities for functioning' in the world (see the box on Martha Nussbaum, Chapter 14, p. 471).

Feral children/isolated children

For obvious ethical reasons, researchers cannot subject human beings to experimental isolation. Consequently, much of what we know about this issue comes from rare cases of abused children like Anna. After her discovery, Anna benefited from intense social contact and soon showed improvement. Visiting her in the county home after ten days, Kingsley Davis (1940) noted that she was more alert and even smiled with

obvious pleasure. During the next year, Anna made slow but steady progress, showing greater interest in other people and gradually learning to walk. After a year and a half, she could feed herself and play with toys.

But it was becoming apparent that Anna's five years of social isolation had left her permanently damaged. At the age of eight her mental and social development was still less than that of a two-year-old. Not until she was almost ten did she begin to grasp language. Of course, since Anna's mother had learning difficulties, perhaps Anna was similarly disadvantaged. The riddle was never solved, because Anna died at the age of ten from a blood disorder, possibly related to her years of abuse (Davis, 1940, 1947).

A second, quite similar case involves another girl, found at about the same time as Anna and under strikingly similar circumstances. After more than six years of virtual isolation, this girl – known as Isabelle – displayed the same lack of human responsiveness as Anna. Unlike Anna, though, Isabelle benefited from a special learning programme directed by psychologists. Within a week, Isabelle was attempting to speak, and a year and a half later, her vocabulary included nearly 2,000 words. The psychologists concluded that intensive effort had propelled Isabelle through six years of normal development in only two years. By the time she was 14, Isabelle was attending sixth-grade classes, apparently on her way to at least an approximately normal life (Davis, 1947).

A final case of childhood isolation involves a 13-year-old California girl victimised in a host of ways by her parents from the age of two (Curtiss, 1977; Pines, 1981; Rymer, 1994). Genie's ordeal included extended periods of being locked alone in a garage. Upon discovery, her condition mirrored that of Anna and Isabelle. Genie was emaciated (weighing only 59 pounds) and had the mental development of a one-year-old. She received intensive treatment by specialists and thrived physically. Yet even after years of care, her ability to use language remains that of a young child, and she lives today in a home for developmentally disabled adults.

The story of Victor is also a famous film, *L'Enfant Sauvage* by Francois Truffaut (1970).

All the evidence points to the crucial role of social experience in personal development. Human beings are resilient creatures, sometimes able to recover from even the crushing experience of abuse and isolation. But there is a point – precisely when is unclear from the limited number of cases – at which social isolation in infancy results in irreparable developmental damage.

Victor, often known as the wild boy of Aveyron, is probably the most discussed case of a feral child. He was first sighted in 1797 in woods near Toulouse (in the Aveyron region of France). He lacked speech and it is thought that he had grown up wild in the woods. He came to live with the French doctor Jean Marc Gaspard Itard, who attempted to teach him to speak, but Victor only ever learnt two words: milk and God. He died in 1828. Truffaut has made a very famous film about him: *L'enfant sauvage (The Wild Boy)* (1970). Extracts can be found on YouTube. See also http://www.imdb.com/title/tt0064285/

Source: artwork from *Education d'un homme sauvage* (J. M. G. Itard, Paris, 1801). CCI Archives/Science Photo Library.

Becoming biographies? Two theories of socialisation

Socialisation results in a personal **biography**, *a person's unique history of thinking, feeling and acting* (see Interlude 4, pp. 823–6). We build a biography through interacting with others throughout all our lives: as biography develops, we participate in a culture while remaining, in some respects, distinct individuals. But in the absence of social experience, as the case of Anna shows, a biography can hardly start to emerge at all.

Social experience is vital for society just as it is for individuals. Societies exist beyond the life span of any person, and thus each generation must teach something of its way of life to the next. Broadly speaking, then, socialisation amounts to the ongoing process of cultural transmission. Socialisation is a complex, lifelong process. In what follows, we highlight two major theories of human development. There are many others (which can be accessed via the website).

Sigmund Freud: the importance of the unconscious and emotional structuring

Sigmund Freud (1856–1939) lived in Vienna at a time when most Europeans considered human behaviour to be biologically fixed. Trained as a physician, Freud gradually turned to the study of personality and eventually developed the celebrated theory of psychoanalysis.

The cornerstone of this theory is the workings of the repressed **unconscious**: people's lives are partly shaped by emotional *experiences*, traumas and 'family romances' *which then become too difficult to confront and so become hidden from the surface workings of life, while still motivating our actions*. The unconscious goes deep: it is repressed and cannot be easily recovered. (Psychoanalysis and 'dream analysis' are two 'roads to the unconscious'.) In any event the unconscious often means that we really do not know why we do certain things.

Many aspects of Freud's work bear directly on our understanding of how we become social.

Life and death

Freud contended that biology is diffuse but plays an important part in social development, though not in terms of the simple instincts that guide other species. Humans, Freud theorised, respond to two general needs or drives. We have a basic need for pleasure and bonding, which Freud called the life instincts, or *eros* (from the Greek god of love). Second, opposing this need, are aggressive drives, which Freud termed the death instincts, or *thanatos* (from the Greek meaning 'death'). Freud postulated that these opposing forces, operating primarily at the level of the unconscious mind, generate deeply rooted inner tensions.

Sigmund Freud (1856–1936). Freud is the great theorist of the unconscious, but with a few exceptions (such as Parsons, the Frankfurt School and some feminisms) he has not had a major impact on sociology

Source: Pearson Education Ltd/The Illustrated London News Picture Library/Ingram Publishing/Alamy.

Id, ego, superego

These basic drives need to be controlled and Freud incorporated them and the influence of society into a model of personality with three parts: id, ego and superego. The **id** (Latin for 'that') represents the *human being's basic drives*, which are unconscious and demand immediate satisfaction. Rooted in our biology, the id is present at birth, making a newborn a bundle of needs demanding attention, touching and all kinds of nervous and sexual experience. They are a 'cauldron of seething excitation' and they seek the release of their desires. But society does not tolerate such a self-centred orientation, so the id's desires inevitably encounter resistance. Because of this cultural opposition, one of the first words a child comprehends is 'no'.

To avoid frustration, the child learns to approach the world realistically. This accomplishment forms the second component of the personality, the **ego** (Latin for 'I'), which is *a person's conscious efforts to balance innate, pleasure-seeking drives with the demands of society*. It is dominated by what Freud calls the reality

principle. The ego arises as we gain awareness of our distinct existence; it reaches fruition as we come to understand that we cannot have everything we want. We start to adjust and adapt to the vagaries of everyday life.

Finally, the human personality develops the **superego** (Latin, meaning 'above' or 'beyond' the ego), which is the *operation of culture within the individual*. With the emergence of the superego, we can see *why* we cannot have everything we want. The superego consists of cultural values and norms – internalised in the form of conscience – that define moral limits. The superego begins to emerge as children recognise parental control; it matures as they learn that their own behaviour and that of their parents – in fact, everyone's behaviour – reflects a broader system of cultural demands. It is a conscience and it creates new tensions, generating guilt and guilty thoughts.

Personality development

The id-centred child first encounters the world as a bewildering array of physical sensations and need satisfactions. With the gradual development of the superego, however, the child's comprehension extends beyond pleasure and pain to include the moral concepts of right and wrong. Initially, in other words, children can feel good only in the physical sense; but, after three or four years, they feel good or bad as they evaluate their own behaviour according to cultural standards.

Conflict between id and superego is ongoing, but, in a well-adjusted person, these opposing forces are managed by the ego. Unresolved conflicts, especially during childhood, typically result in personality disorders later on.

As the source of superego, culture operates to control human drives, a process that Freud termed *repression*. Some repression is inevitable, since any society must coerce people to look beyond themselves. Often the competing demands of self and society are resolved through compromise. This process, which Freud called *sublimation*, transforms fundamentally selfish drives into socially acceptable activities. Sexual urges, for example, may lead to marriage, just as aggression gives rise to competitive sports.

Freud and the Oedipus Complex

Central to Freud's thought, and to his theory of socialisation, is his concept of the Oedipus Complex: a metaphor for the emotional and psychic struggles and conflicts that a young child experiences with its mother and father. The term is derived from the Greek tragedy in which Oedipus marries his mother and murders his father, and looks at the passionate 'little love affairs' that children have with their families in the earliest years of life.

Broadly, Freud suggests that newborn children initially feel a strong closeness and attachment to the mother, and that the father is experienced as something of a threat to this attachment. The child thus starts to harbour hostile feelings towards the father, for which it feels increasingly guilty. This little dilemma can be experienced very profoundly. Freud uses the term 'castration complex' to suggest a powerful threat to the child. And in order to resolve this threat, the child starts to identify with the father instead.

The Oedipus Complex is the key to getting the id and all its desires under control: the father becomes part of the superego as an authority figure. Freud is outlining a basic predicament in becoming social: how to cope with all our desires and become a socialised adult with a conscience. And he does this through seeing a struggle in emotional identification.

Critical comment

Freud's work sparked controversy in his own lifetime, and some of that controversy still smoulders today. The world he knew vigorously repressed human sexuality, so that few of his contemporaries were prepared to concede that sex is a basic human need. More recently, Freud has come under fire for his depictions of humanity in allegedly male terms, thereby devaluing the lives of women. But Freud also provided a foundation that influenced virtually everyone who later studied the human personality. Of special importance to sociology is his notion that we internalise social norms and that childhood experiences have a lasting impact on socialisation. More than this, in his book *Civilisation and its Discontents* (2004; orig. 1930), he saw a distinct parallel between social and individual developments. Just as human beings develop through instinctual repression, so civilisation as a whole advances through controls. Civilisation, then, depends upon repression but in the process it generates many problems.

tip Freud is considered an intellectual giant of the twentieth century – probing deeply the dynamics of the repressed unconscious human life. He is not a sociologist but his ideas have shaped many aspects of sociology. You will find a lot about his work on the internet, but a straightforward guide is: Sigmund Freud: His Life and Work, at: www.freudfile.org.

George Herbert Mead and the social self

Our understanding of socialisation stems in large part from the life work of George Herbert Mead (1863–1931), who is introduced in the *Thinkers and theory* box on p. 214. Mead (1962; orig. 1934) described his approach as *social behaviourism*, calling to mind the behaviourism of psychologist John B. Watson described earlier. Both recognised the power of the environment to shape human behaviour. But Watson focused on outward behaviour, while Mead highlighted inward *thinking*, which he contended was humanity's defining trait.

The self

Mead's central concept is the self, *the human capacity to be reflexive and take the role of others*. Mead's genius lay in seeing that the self is inseparable from society, and bound up with communication. It is a connection explained in a series of steps.

First, Mead claims that *the self emerges from social experience*. The self is not part of the body in itself, and it does not exist at birth. But it emerges through communication with others and this is distinctly what makes us human. Mead rejected simple ideas about biological drives, and argued that the self develops *only* through social experience. In the absence of social interaction, as we saw above in the cases of isolated children, the body may grow but no self will emerge.

Secondly, Mead explained how *social experience involves communication and the exchange of symbols*. Using words, a wave of the hand or a smile, people create meaning, which is a distinctively human experience. We can use reward and punishment to train a dog, after all, but the dog attaches no meaning to these actions. Human beings, by contrast, make sense of actions by inferring people's underlying intentions. In short, a dog responds to *what you do*; a human responds to *what you have in mind* as you do it. People have to 'take the role of the other' in order to make sense of action.

Return to our friendly dog for a moment. You can train a dog to walk to the porch and return with an umbrella. But the dog grasps no meaning in the act, no intention behind the command. Thus, if the dog cannot find the umbrella, it is incapable of the human response: to look for a raincoat instead.

Thirdly, says Mead, *to understand intention, you must imagine the situation from another person's point of view.* Using symbols, we can imaginatively place ourselves in another person's shoes and thus see ourselves as that person does. This capacity allows us to anticipate how others will respond to us even before we act. A simple toss of a ball requires stepping outside ourselves to imagine how another will respond to our throw. Social interaction, then, involves seeing ourselves as others see us – a process that Mead called *taking the role of the other.* The self, then, is reflective and reflexive.

The looking-glass self

In social life, other people represent the mirror or looking glass in which we perceive ourselves. Charles Horton Cooley (1864–1929), one of Mead's contemporaries, used the phrase **looking-glass self** to designate *the image people have of themselves based on how they believe others perceive them* (1964; orig. 1902). He claimed that we can only live social lives through entering the minds of others. Whether we think of ourselves as clever or clumsy, worthy or worthless, depends in large measure on what we think others think of us. This insight goes a long way towards explaining Carol Gilligan's (1982) finding that young women lose self-confidence as they come of age in a society that discourages women from being too assertive.

The I and the Me

Our capacity to see ourselves through others implies that the self has two components. First, *the self is subject* as we initiate social action. Humans are innately active and spontaneous, Mead claimed, dubbing this subjective element of the self the *I* (the subjective form of the personal pronoun). But secondly, *the self is object* because, taking the role of another, we form impressions of ourselves. Mead called this objective element of the self the *Me* (the objective form of the

George Herbert Mead: the self is born of society

George Herbert Mead (1863–1933) was a leading US philosopher and some of his key ideas are described here. Based at the University of Chicago, he has been identified as a leading pragmatist. His work *Mind, Self and Society* (1962; orig. 1934) was published after his death from notes taken by students, and provides his major theory of the self.

Few people were surprised that Mead became a college professor. He was born to a Massachusetts family with a strong intellectual tradition, and both his parents were academics. His father was both a preacher and a teacher at a number of colleges, and his mother served for a decade as president of Mount Holyoke College.

But Mead also had a hand in shaping his own life, rebelling against the strongly religious atmosphere of his home and community. After completing college, he restlessly travelled throughout the Pacific Northwest, surveying for the railroad and reading voraciously. He gradually settled on the idea of studying philosophy, an academic endeavour he pursued at Harvard and in Europe.

Mead took a teaching position at the new University of Chicago. But his outlook still veered from the conventional. He rarely published, going against a long-standing tradition among academics. Mead's reputation and stature grew only after his death, when colleagues and former students collected and published his lecture notes. Mead drew together a wide range of ideas to help launch the new field of social psychology.

Never content with life as it was, Mead was an active social reformer. To him, the course of

George Herbert Mead (1863–1933)

Source: The Granger Collection, New York.

an entire society was as ongoing and changeable as the life of any individual. This insight follows from his basic contention: society may have the power to shape individuals, but people also have the capacity to mould their society.

For an up-to-date guide to Mead's work, see Filipe Carreira da Silva, *G. H. Mead* (2007).

personal pronoun). All social experience begins with someone initiating action (the I-phase of self) and then guiding the action (the Me-phase of self) by taking the role of the other. Social experience is thus the interplay of the I and the Me: our actions are spontaneous yet guided by how others respond to us.

Mead stressed that thinking itself constitutes a social experience. Our thoughts are partly creative (representing the I), but in thought we also become objects to ourselves (representing the Me) as we imagine how others will respond to our ideas. Table 7.1 draws out some of these contrasts.

Table 7.1	The Meadian 'I' and 'ME'
The I phase	**The ME phase**
Subject	Object
Impulsive	Determined
Knowing	Known
Acts in world	Attitudes of others
Social experience is the interplay of I and Me in process	

Development of the self

According to Mead, gaining a self amounts to learning to take the role of the other. Like Freud, Mead regarded early childhood as the crucial time for this task, but he did not link the development of the self to biological maturation. Mead maintained that the self emerges over time with increasing social experience.

Infants respond to others only in terms of *imitation*. They mimic behaviour without understanding underlying intentions. Unable to use symbols, Mead concluded, infants have no self.

Children first learn to use language and other symbols in the form of *play*, especially role playing. Initially, they model themselves on key people in their lives – such as parents – whom we call *significant others*. Playing 'mummy and daddy', for example, helps children imagine the world from their parents' point of view.

Gradually, children learn to take the roles of several others at once. This skill is the key to moving from simple play (say, playing catch) involving one other to complex *games* (like baseball) involving many others. Only by the age of seven or eight have most children acquired sufficient social experience to engage in team sports that demand taking the role of numerous others simultaneously.

Figure 7.1 shows the logical progression from imitation to play to games. But a final stage in the development of the self remains. A game involves taking the role of others in just one situation. But members of a society also need to see themselves as others in general might. In other words, we recognise that people in any situation in society share cultural norms and values, and we begin to incorporate these general patterns into the self. Mead used the term **generalised other** to refer to *widespread cultural norms and values we use as references in evaluating ourselves*.

Of course, the emergence of the self is not the end of socialisation. Quite the contrary: Mead claimed that socialisation continues as long as we have social experience, so that changing circumstances can reshape who we are. The self may change, for example, with divorce, disability or unexpected wealth. And we retain some control over this process as we respond to events and circumstances and thereby play a part in our own socialisation. Mead's theory was really the start of the perspective we introduced in Chapter 2: symbolic interactionism.

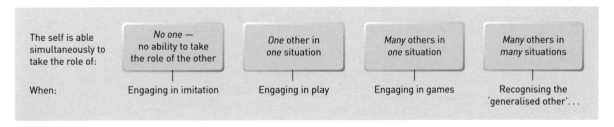

The self is able simultaneously to take the role of:	*No one —* no ability to take the role of the other	*One* other in *one* situation	*Many* others in *one* situation	*Many* others in *many* situations
When:	Engaging in imitation	Engaging in play	Engaging in games	Recognising the 'generalised other'...

Figure 1.2   Building on social experience

George Herbert Mead described the development of the self as the process of gaining social experience. This is largely a matter of taking the role of the other with increasing sophistications, broadening out from specific others to greater complexity.

Will the real Cindy Sherman reveal herself?
Cindy Sherman (b. 1954) is a leading postmodern, feminist photographer. Starting in 1977 Cindy Sherman has photographed herself dressed up and playing the roles of others. In early works she often focused on B star celebrities and fairytale characters; in more recent works she focuses on older women. But always, she dresses up and then captures herself as another self. She shows a play of selves – using her own body and photographing it as a wide array of women; and is a lively example of role playing and identity changing in life and art (though she does not cite either Erving Goffman or Judith Butler). Her art embodies two developments in the art world: the impact of postmodern theory on art practice; and the rise of photography and mass-media techniques as modes of artistic expression. For more on her work, see her website at: http://www.cindysherman.com/
Source: © Louie Psihoyos/Corbis.

Critical comment

The strength of Mead's work lies in exploring the nature of social experience itself. He succeeded in explaining how symbolic interaction is the foundation of both the self and society. Yet some critics disparage Mead's view as radically social because it acknowledges no biological element in the emergence of the self (in fact this is false criticism, as he certainly did highlight bodily processes and 'impulses'). Mead's concepts of the I and the Me are often confused with Freud's concepts of the id and the superego. But Freud rooted the id in the biological organism, while Mead saw the I as impulsive and the Me as regulative. Freud's concept of the superego and Mead's concept of the Me both reflect the power of society to shape personality. But for Freud, superego and id are locked in continual combat. Mead, however, held that the I and the Me work closely and cooperatively together, in a dialectical process (Meltzer, 1978).

The life course and generations

While both Freud and Mead focus on the earlier (or primary) socialisation stages of lives, 'life course' is a term that enables us to look right across the whole structure of a person's life – and the secondary socialisation that this usually involves. Although each stage of life is linked to the biological process of ageing, the life course itself is largely a social construction. People in different societies may experience a stage of life quite differently, or not at all. Yet each stage of any society's life course presents characteristic problems and transitions that involve learning something new and unlearning familiar routines. Note, too, that just because societies organise human experience according to age, this in no way negates the effects of other features of stratification we are examining, such as class, race, ethnicity and gender. Thus, the general patterns we have described are all subject to further modification as they apply to various categories of people.

Understanding life course development

The most basic feature of development is the changing sequencing and phasing of a life course. We are all familiar with *chronological age* and its common sequencing from babyhood, through childhood, youth, middle age, old age and so on. These have commonly been called the 'seasons of a life' (Levinson et al., 1978, 1996; Kortre and Hall, 1999), as illustrated in Figure 7.2. But these categories are themselves a problem – ageing, for example, is now quite frequently broken into a 'third age' (65–74) and a 'fourth age'

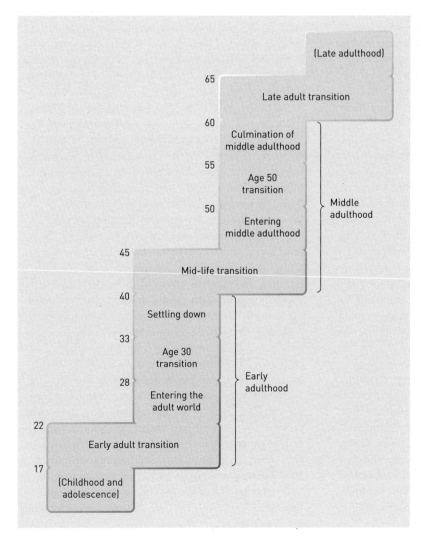

Figure 7.2 The seasons of life Daniel Levinson's research into human development depicts the lifespan as a series of critical transitions

Source: Adapted from Levinson et al. (1978: 57).

(Late adulthood)

65

Late adult transition

60

Culmination of middle adulthood

55

Age 50 transition

50

Entering middle adulthood

Middle adulthood

45

Mid-life transition

40

Settling down

33

Age 30 transition

28

Entering the adult world

Early adulthood

22

Early adult transition

17

(Childhood and adolescence)

(75+), or into the younger elderly (65–75), the older elderly (75–85), and the very old (see Chapter 13). Indeed, as we find more and more people living longer and longer, the category of 'centenarian' will become more and more common. So we must note that age phase categories themselves change: 'childhood', 'middle age' and 'youth' are now seen by sociologists and historians to be recent historical inventions – they are certainly not found in all societies (for example, Shweder, 1998). We understand now that 'life phases' themselves change across history.

Lives also need to be located on a *historical timeline* and through their demographic features. A life occurs within a definite historical time span. A line of key world events (a bit like the timeline which opens this book) can be drawn which 'situates' a life firmly within its specific cultural history. South African lives, Australian lives and Peruvian lives will have a differing sense of key dates and experiences within their cultures. In Figure 7.3, we have listed just a few Anglo-American themes: clearly a life that has been through two world wars (those born before 1914) has a different historical matrix from one that has not been through any (those born after 1945). Likewise, lives that have grown up with the key singers of their time – for example, Bing Crosby, Elvis Presley, Take That or Eminem – may use these figures and their works as a way of thinking about their lives in the future.

From this we can locate *birth cohorts*: people born in the same year, or in a cluster of named years. A **cohort** is *a category of people with a common characteristic, usually their age.* Age cohorts are likely to have been influenced by the same economic and cultural trends, so that members typically display similar attitudes and values (Riley et al., 1988). The lives of women and men born early in the twentieth century, for example, were framed by an economic depression and two world wars – events unknown to their children or grandchildren. For their part, younger people today are living in a world where Playstations, high-tech information and websites have become taken for granted in their lives (in ways which older cohorts cannot really grasp). An *age cohort generation*, then, is a group of people born in a specified period of years, who are hence tied together through a particular shared historical time period. The most obvious examples would include the 'children of the Great Depression' (see Elder, 1974), the 'baby boomers', the 'hippy generation', 'Thatcher's children', 'Generation X' and the 'digital kids' (Rushkoff, 1999) and the 'millennial generation'. This is a most important way of locating a group of people – akin to

locating them in class and gender (see Chapter 13). With some tongue in cheek, we might call today's generation the high-tech Harry Potter generation'!

A *generation cohort perspective* is the more subjective sense that people acquire of belonging to a particular age reference group through which they may make sense of their 'memories' and 'identities' (they share a common perspective and say things like 'We all lived through the war together', 'In our days, feminism was more active', 'I was part of the Peace Movement in Vietnam', 'I am an older gay – part of the Stonewall generation'). The former category is structural – it locates a person in the society overall; the latter is more subjective – it shows who people identify with over time. Both nevertheless take the researcher into an important awareness of historical time – and how different lives are shaped throughout by different historical baselines and different historical roots. To put it bluntly: a child of the Thatcher or Reagan Generation cannot have experienced the Second World War at first hand as their grandparents inevitably would have; and such factors need to be located in looking at a life. Often these critical locations are to be found in a person's 'youth' period. Shared generational and historical experiences come to play a key role in a *life history* approach.

All this is closely linked to mapping lives as a 'life trajectory' or as a 'life course' – 'a pathway defined by the ageing process or by movement across the age structure' (Elder, 1985). It is common here to see a tripartite life course, characterised by an early period of preparation, a middle part of work (including domestic work), and a final part for 'retirement'. We used to be able to think very straightforwardly of this – long periods of work were followed by retirement, punctuated by raising children, maturation and growth, followed by disengagement and decline. For men the emphasis was most on work; for women the emphasis most on raising children. But nowadays the shape of life courses is changing: heterogeneity, fragmentation and discontinuities have happened for many and the sequencing is no longer quite so clear. Not all cultures have the same 'shape' to this life course; again, it can change historically.

Some contemporary writers are talking about the postmodernisation of the life course – how the formal patterns found in the past are breaking down, with people 'dipping in and out' of phases in a much less regularised and institutionalised fashion. We have what German sociologist Ulrich Beck refers to as the 'individualisation of the life course'. As traditional industrial ways of life become destroyed, so individuals

(a) Life cohorts

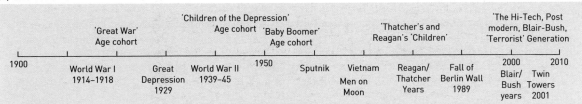

(b) Life stages

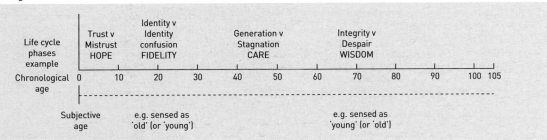

(c) 'Eight Stages of Man' – Erik Erikson

		1	2	3	4	5	6	7	8
Old Age	VIII								Integrity vs. Despair, disgust. WISDOM
Adulthood	VII							Generativity vs. Stagnation. CARE	
Young Adulthood	VI						Intimacy vs. Isolation. LOVE		
Adolescence	V					Identity vs. Identity confusion FIDELITY			
School Age	IV				Industry vs. Inferiority. COMPETENCE				
Play Age	III			Initiative vs. Guilt. PURPOSE					
Early Childhood	II		Autonomy vs. Shame, doubt. WILL						
Infancy	I	Basic trust vs. Basic mistrust. HOPE							

Figure 7.3   Mapping a life: life cohorts and life stages: (a) life cohorts; (b) life stages; (c) Erikson's (1980) 'Eight Stages of Man'

Source: Adapted from Plummer (2001a: 126–7).

The high-tech Harry Potter generation

The Harry Potter series of seven novels by English author J. K. Rowling can be seen as a sociological phenomenon. The books are long. They chronicle the adventures of Harry Potter and his friends Hermione Granger and Ron Weasley at the Hogwarts School of Witchcraft and Wizardry. The books are about 'schooldays', 'growing up', 'magic and reality' and 'death'. First published in 1997, the books have gained enormous worldwide popularity – and have led to a spin-off series of films, merchandise and recently a theme park. The books have been translated into over 67 languages, selling well over 400 million copies (Rowling is one of the most translated and fastest-selling authors in history); and the films are listed among the top grossing films of all time.

Sociologists are very interested in the ways in which 'childhood' can be constructed in different ways in different cultures. Children make sense of their social worlds through all the artefacts they find around them – from parents, friends and schools to literature and other media forms. Children's stories, children's television and children's films often provide 'keys' to understanding the experiences of different generations. The books and films that children grow up with can tell a great deal about the adult worlds that children later move into. The modern world has witnessed the experience of children and young people growing up with 'media' events. The film *Miss Potter* (2006) shows the success of the author Beatrice Potter, and her illustrated books – which became the best-sellers of their time. In the 1950s, Enid Blyton became a key author of children's books for a whole generation. And across cultures, different children's stories come into being.

Cohorts of different generations come to identify certain events (wars, depressions, coronations, prime ministers) and certain cultural objects (books, films, music, sports, celebrities) with their own specific generations. We can speak of the 'Beatles generation', the 'Star Trek generation', the 'Thatcher generation' and so on. It identifies a group of people who move through their lives with a common experience. The Harry Potter generation may well become an identifiable tag for those who experience a critical life stage between 1997 and 2007. It is high-tech because this same generation is also the first generation to completely assimilate and take for granted the world of high technology that could only be imagined or struggled with before. Harry Potter is not just a book: he comes in multiple digital forms, websites, games and DVDs. A book is no longer a straightforward book. The reality of this generation is different from those before it.

See: Wikipedia entry on Harry Potter; Plummer (2001a); Edmunds and Turner (2002). The writings of George Beahm provide tours of youthful cult reading – including more recently *Bedazzled: The Stephenie Meyer's Twilight Phenomenon* (2009).

---

find they have to construct their own life plans and course: the routines and rituals of the past have gone too. As Beck says: 'individuals must produce, stage and cobble together their biographies themselves . . . the individual is actor, designer, juggler and stage director of his own biography, identity, social networks, commitment and convictions' (Beck, 1997: 95).

Within a life trajectory, we can then go on to identify *critical life events* and *life cycle crises*. These may range from major events such as death and divorce to less significant ones. There is a very substantial amount of writing and analysis of these themes, spearheaded by

Erik Erikson's classic work on the Eight Stages of Man, but now developed in many directions. Again, though, we must distinguish between scientific accounts which try to capture some sense of an 'objective' series of phases lying, so to speak, within a life; and the more subjective awareness of subjects of their own sense of crises, their subjective identification with age, and the process of subjective reminiscences.

 Move on to Chapter 13 to examine childhood, youth and the elderly as the stages of the life cycle; look too at Interlude 4 (p. 823).

Constructing situations: Erving Goffman and drama

Erving Goffman (1922–1982), profiled in the *Thinkers and theory* box on p. 222, was the twentieth century's leading micro-sociologist. He studied what he called the **interaction order** – *what we do in the immediate presence of others* (Goffman, 1982: 2). One of the major ways he enhanced our understanding of everyday life was by noting that people routinely behave much like actors performing on a stage. By imagining ourselves as directors scrutinising what goes on in some situational 'theatre', we engage in what Goffman called **dramaturgical analysis**, *the investigation of social interaction in terms borrowed from theatrical performance*. Everyday social life becomes theatre. Dramaturgical analysis offers a fresh look at two now-familiar concepts. In theatrical terms, people come to play parts and roles as if in a play, and scripts emerge to supply dialogue and action for each of the characters. Moreover, in any setting, a person is both actor and audience. Goffman described each individual's 'performance' as the **presentation of self**, *an individual's effort to create specific impressions in the minds of others*. Presentation of self, or *impression management*, contains several distinctive elements (Goffman, 1959, 1967). We can see daily life as a series of stagecraft rules.

Performances

As we present ourselves in everyday situations, we convey information – consciously and unconsciously – to others. An individual's performance includes dress (costume), any objects carried along (props) and tone of voice and particular gestures (manner). In addition, people craft their performance according to the setting (stage). We may joke loudly in the street, for example, but assume a more reverent manner upon entering a church. In addition, individuals design settings, such as a home or office, to enhance a performance by invoking the desired reactions in others.

Consider, for example, how a doctor's surgery conveys information to an audience of patients. Doctors enjoy prestige and power, a fact immediately grasped by patients upon entering the surgery or health centre. First, the doctor is nowhere to be seen. Instead, in what Goffman describes as the 'front region' of the setting, the patient encounters a receptionist who functions as a gatekeeper, deciding if and when the patient can meet the doctor. A simple survey of the waiting room, with patients (often impatiently) awaiting their call to the inner sanctum, leaves little doubt that the medical team controls events.

The doctor's private examination room or surgery constitutes the 'back region' of the setting. Here the patient confronts a wide range of props, such as medical books and framed degrees, which together reinforce the impression that the doctor has the specialised knowledge necessary to be in charge. In the surgery, the doctor may remain seated behind a desk – the larger and grander the desk, the greater the statement of power – while the patient is provided with only a chair.

The doctor's appearance and manner convey still more information. The common hospital doctor's costume of white lab coat may have the practical function of keeping clothes from becoming soiled, but its social function is to let others know at a glance the doctor's status. A stethoscope around the neck or a black medical bag in hand has the same purpose. A doctor's highly technical terminology – frequently mystifying – also emphasises the hierarchy in the situation. The use of the title 'Doctor' by patients who, in turn, are frequently addressed only by their first names, also underscores the physician's dominant position. The overall message of a doctor's performance is clear: 'I will help you only if you allow me to take charge.'

Non-verbal communication

Novelist William Sansom describes a fictional Mr Preedy – an English holidaymaker on a beach in Spain:

> He took care to avoid catching anyone's eye. First, he had to make it clear to those potential companions of his holiday that they were of no concern to him whatsoever. He stared through them, round them, over them – eyes lost in space. The beach might have been empty. If by chance a ball was thrown his way, he looked surprised; then let a smile of amusement light his face (Kindly Preedy), looked around dazed to see that there were people on the beach, tossed it back with a smile to himself and not a smile at the people . . .
>
> . . . [He] then gathered together his beach-wrap and bag into a neat sand-resistant pile (Methodical and Sensible Preedy), rose slowly to stretch his huge frame (Big-Cat Preedy), and tossed aside his sandals (Carefree Preedy, after all).

(1956; quoted in Goffman, 1959: 4–5)

THINKERS & THEORY

The dramatic world of Erving Goffman

Erving Goffman (1922–82)
Source: © American Sociological Association. www.asanet.org.

Universal human nature is not a very human thing. By acquiring it, the person becomes a kind of construct, built up not from psychic propensities but from moral rules that are impressed from without . . .

Erving Goffman, *Interactional Ritual* (1967: 45)

Erving Goffman (1922–82) is generally considered to be the most influential of twentieth-century micro-sociologists and carved out a world of analysis that was distinctly his. A Canadian, he was trained at the University of Chicago and his first major field trip was to the Shetland Isles in Scotland for his PhD – for the book that eventually became his first classic, *The Presentation of Self in Everyday Life* (1959). Observing life closely on those islands, he started to develop a framework for seeing social life as a kind of drama. Just like people on a stage, people in everyday life could be seen as actors playing out roles and giving impressions

to others that enabled the others to make sense of what was going on. This was the *drama-turgical perspective*.

Throughout his work – which often changed direction and was idiosyncratically written – his main concern was with *the interaction order*: what people do in the presence of others. He studied how behaviour in public places works – how people walk through doors and down streets. He looked at how people develop 'interaction rituals': 'the world in truth is a wedding' is one of his famous lines, in which he suggests that much of the most routine everyday interaction has important ritual elements to it.

He looked at the ways in which identities became spoilt – how some people became stigmatised and had to work hard to present themselves as 'normal'.

Along the way, Goffman literally produced a new language for thinking about the everyday. He produced an array of 'mini-concepts' which help us see how daily life is composed, terms such as 'face-work', 'cooling the mark', front and back regions, moral careers, information control, impression management, passing, own and wise, frames, keying, role distance, role playing, role attachments, civil inattention, situational adjustments, people as 'vehicular units', total institution, avoidance rituals, presentation rituals, tie signs.

In the light of this, and your reading of some of Goffman's work, you might like to write your own 'dramaturgical handbook'. Think about who are the key players in your life and where you interact with them, and map out some of your own ways of presenting yourself and making 'interaction rituals'. Is this a useful framework for thinking about how life is constructed?

See: Greg Smith, *Erving Goffman* (2006).

Through his conduct, Mr Preedy offers a great deal of information about himself to anyone caring to observe him. Notice that he does so without uttering a single word. This illustrates the process of **non-verbal communication**, *communication using body movements, gestures and facial expressions rather than speech.*

Virtually any part of the body can be used to generate *body language*: that is, to convey information to others. Facial expressions form the most significant element of non-verbal communication. Smiling and other facial gestures express basic emotions such as pleasure, surprise and anger the world over. Further, people project particular shades of meaning with their

faces. We distinguish, for example, between the deliberate smile of Kindly Preedy on the beach, a spontaneous smile of joy at seeing a friend, a pained smile of embarrassment and a full, unrestrained smile of self-satisfaction that we often associate with the 'cat that ate the canary'.

Eye contact is another crucial element of non-verbal communication. Generally, we use eye contact to initiate social interaction. Someone across the room 'catches our eye', for example, sparking a conversation. Avoiding the eyes of another, on the other hand, discourages communication. Hands, too, speak for us. Common hand gestures in our culture convey, among other things, an insult, a request for a lift, an invitation for someone to join us, or a demand that others stop in their tracks. Gestures also supplement spoken words. Pointing in a menacing way at someone, for example, intensifies a word of warning, just as shrugging the shoulders adds an air of indifference to the phrase 'I don't know', and rapidly waving the arms lends urgency to the single word 'Hurry!'

But, as any actor knows, the 'perfect performance' is an elusive goal. In everyday performances, some element of body language often contradicts our intended meaning. A teenage boy offers an explanation for getting home late, for example, but his mother doubts his words because he avoids looking her in the eye. The movie star on a television talk show claims that her recent flop at the box office is 'no big deal', but the nervous swing of her leg belies her casual denial. In practical terms, carefully observing non-verbal communication (most of which is not easily controlled) provides clues to deception, in much the same way that a lie detector records tell-tale changes in breathing, pulse rate, perspiration and blood pressure.

Yet detecting lies is difficult, because no single bodily gesture directly indicates deceit in the way that, say, a smile indicates pleasure. Even so, because any performance involves so many expressions, few people can confidently lie without allowing some piece of contradictory information to slip through, arousing the suspicions of a careful observer. Therefore, the key to detecting deceit is to scan the whole performance with an eye for inconsistencies and discrepancies.

In sum, lies are detectable, but training is the key to noticing relevant clues. Another key to spotting deception is knowing the other person well, the reason that parents can usually pick up deceit in their children. Finally, almost anyone can unmask deception when the liar is trying to cover up strong emotions.

Gender and personal performances

Because women are socialised to be less assertive than men, they tend to be especially sensitive to non-verbal communication. In fact, gender is a central element in personal performances. Based on the work of Nancy Henley, Mykol Hamilton and Barrie Thorne (1992), we can extend the present discussion of personal performances to spotlight the importance of gender.

Demeanour

Demeanour – that is, general conduct or deportment – reflects a person's level of social power. Simply put,

powerful people enjoy far greater personal discretion in how they act; subordinates act more formally and self-consciously. Off-colour remarks, swearing or casually removing shoes and putting feet up on the desk may be acceptable for the boss, but rarely for employees. Similarly, people in positions of dominance can interrupt the performances of others with impunity, while others are expected to display deference by remaining silent (Smith-Lovin and Brody, 1989; Henley et al., 1992).

Since women generally occupy positions of lesser power, demeanour is a gender issue as well. As Chapter 12 explains, about half of all working women in Europe and the United States hold clerical or service jobs that place them under the control of supervisors who are usually men. Women, then, craft their personal performances more carefully than men and display a greater degree of deference in everyday interaction.

Use of space

How much space does a personal performance require? Here again, power plays a key role, since using more space conveys a non-verbal message of personal importance. According to Henley et al. (1992), men typically command more space than women do, whether pacing back and forth before an audience or casually lounging on the beach. Why? Our culture traditionally has measured femininity by how *little* space women occupy (the standard of 'daintiness'), while gauging masculinity by how *much* territory a man controls (the standard of 'turf').

The concept of **personal space** refers to *the surrounding area to which an individual makes some claim to privacy*. In the United Kingdom, for example, people typically position themselves several feet apart when speaking; throughout the Middle East, by contrast, individuals interact within a much closer space.

Throughout the world, gender further modifies these patterns. In daily life, men commonly intrude on the personal space of women. A woman's encroachment into a man's personal space, however, is likely to be construed as a sexual overture. Here again, women have less power in everyday interaction than men do.

Staring, smiling and touching

Eye contact encourages interaction. Typically, women employ eye contact to sustain conversation more than men do. Men have their own distinctive brand of eye contact: staring. By making women the targets of stares, men are both making a claim of social dominance and defining women as sexual objects.

Although frequently signalling pleasure, *smiling* has a host of meanings. In a male-dominated world, women often smile to indicate appeasement or acceptance of submission. For this reason, Henley, Hamilton and Thorne maintain, women smile more than men; in extreme cases, smiling may reach the level of nervous habit.

Finally, *touching* constitutes an intriguing social pattern. Mutual touching conveys feelings of intimacy and caring. Apart from close relationships, however, touching is generally something men do to women (though rarely, in our culture, to other men). A male doctor touches the shoulder of his female nurse as they examine a report, a young man touches the back of his woman friend as he guides her across the street, or a male skiing instructor looks for opportunities to touch his female students. In these examples – as well as many others – touching may evoke little response, so common is it in everyday life. But it amounts to a subtle ritual by which men express their dominant position in an assumed hierarchy that subordinates women.

Idealisation

Complex motives underlie human behaviour. Even so, according to Goffman, we construct performances to *idealise* our intentions. That is, we try to convince others (and perhaps ourselves) that what we do reflects ideal cultural standards rather than more selfish motives.

Idealisation is easily illustrated by returning to the world of doctors and patients. In a hospital, consultants engage in a performance commonly described as 'making the rounds'. Approaching the patient, the doctor often stops at the foot of the bed and silently examines the patient's chart. Afterwards, doctor and patient converse briefly. In ideal terms, this routine involves a doctor making a personal visit to enquire about a patient's condition.

In reality, something less exemplary is usually going on. A doctor who sees several dozen patients a day may remember little about most of them. Reading the chart gives the doctor the opportunity to rediscover the patient's identity and medical problems. Openly revealing the actual impersonality of much medical care would undermine the culturally ideal perception of the doctor as deeply concerned about the welfare of others.

Idealisation is woven into the fabric of everyday life in countless ways. Doctors, university lecturers and other professionals typically idealise their motives for entering their chosen careers. They describe their work as 'making a contribution to science', 'helping others', 'answering a calling from God', or perhaps 'serving the community'. Rarely do such people concede the less honourable, though common, motives of seeking the income, power, prestige and leisure that these occupations confer.

Taking a broader view, idealisation underlies social civility, since we smile and make polite remarks to people we do not like. Such small hypocrisies ease our way through social interactions. Even when we suspect that others are putting on an act, rarely do we openly challenge their performance, for reasons we shall explain next.

Embarrassment and tact

The eminent professor consistently mispronounces the dean's name; the visiting dignitary rises from the table to speak, unaware of the napkin that still hangs from her neck; the president becomes ill at a state dinner. As carefully as individuals may craft their performances, slip-ups of all kinds frequently occur. The result is *embarrassment*, which, in dramaturgical terms, means the discomfort that follows a spoiled performance. Goffman describes embarrassment simply as 'losing face'.

Embarrassment looms as an ever-present danger because, first, all performances typically contain some measure of deception and, secondly, most performances involve a complex array of elements, any one of which, in a thoughtless moment, may shatter the intended impression.

Interestingly, an audience usually overlooks flaws in a performance, thereby allowing an actor to avoid embarrassment. If we do point out a mis-step ('Excuse me, but do you know that your fly is open?'), we do it discreetly and only to help someone avoid even greater loss of face. In Hans Christian Andersen's classic fable *The Emperor's New Clothes*, the child who blurts out that the emperor is parading around naked is telling the truth, yet is scolded for being rude.

But members of an audience usually do more than ignore flaws in a performance, Goffman explains; typically, they help the performer recover from them. *Tact*, then, amounts to helping another person 'save face'. After hearing a supposed expert make an embarrassingly inaccurate remark, for example, people may tactfully ignore the comment as if it were never spoken at all. Alternatively, mild laughter may indicate

LIVING IN THE C21ST

Researching everyday life

For over a century, the main task of anthropologists has been to visit and live with different cultures around the world so that the intricacies of their daily routines and 'ways of living could be understood'. In *Watching the English* (2005), the anthropologist Kate Fox turned the tables and conducted some fieldwork on the English. She became the observer of the quaint ways of these strange people – showing how they form queues, drink in pubs, talk about social class all the time. Like all cultures, the English have developed very distinctive patterns of everyday life.

The sociologist Susie Scott is interested in examining all the everyday things we do in a society. She looks at our eating and drinking habits, how we fill in our days, how we shop and develop leisure interests, how we become embarrassed, fall in love – and do a thousand mundane things in our everyday life. Again, what she finds is that most of these everyday things have a broad pattern. She suggests that a number of theories are useful in approaching everyday life – some of these we have mentioned in this chapter (dramaturgy, symbolic interactionism, psychoanalysis) and others we have discussed elsewhere (functionalism, structuralism and cultural studies).

In one chapter, for example, she looks at the meanings and rituals we employ when we go shopping. What are the different meanings of shopping? There are many: it can be duty or a pleasure, a virtue or a vice. It can be an escape from the norms of everyday life. It can serve as a site of identity performance – whereby we 'demonstrate who we are, what we like, and with whom we identify' (Scott, 2009: 141). For some shopping becomes a lifestyle; for others it is a very practical means to an end.

The inspiration for much contemporary study of everyday is Erving Goffman, who is discussed in the text and in the box on p. 222.

See: Susie Scott, *Making Sense of Everyday Life* (2009); Kate Fox, *Watching the English* (2005).

---

that they wish to dismiss what they have heard as a joke. Or a listener may simply respond, 'I'm sure you didn't mean that', acknowledging the statement but not allowing it to destroy the actor's performance.

Why is tact such a common response? Because embarrassment provokes discomfort not simply for one person but for *everyone*. Just as the entire audience feels uneasy when an actor forgets a line, people who observe awkward behaviour are reminded of how fragile their own performances often are. Socially constructed reality thus functions like a dam holding back a sea of chaotic possibility. Should one person's performance spring a leak, others tactfully assist in making repairs. Everyone, after all, jointly engages in building culture, and no one wants reality to be suddenly swept away.

In sum, Goffman's research shows that, while behaviour is spontaneous in some respects, it is more patterned than we like to think. Almost 400 years ago, William Shakespeare captured this idea in memorable lines that still ring true:

All the world's a stage,
And all the men and women merely players:
They have their exits and their entrances;
And one man in his time plays many parts . . .

(*As You Like It*, II)

Ethnomethodology and conversational analysis

Rather than assume that reality is something 'out there', the symbolic-interaction paradigm posits that reality is created by people in everyday encounters. But how, exactly, do we define reality for ourselves? What is the logic through which we make sense of everyday life? Answering this question is the objective of other theoretical approaches: *ethnomethodology* and *conversational analysis*.

Ethnomethodology

The term itself has two parts: the Greek *ethno* refers to people and how they understand their surroundings; 'methodology' designates a set of methods or principles. Combining them makes **ethnomethodology**, *the study of the way people make sense of their everyday lives*. Ethnomethodology is largely the creation of the Californian-based sociologist Harold Garfinkel (1967), who challenged the then-dominant view of society as a broad, abstract 'system' (recall the approach of Emile Durkheim, described in Chapters 1, 2 and 4). Garfinkel wanted to explore how we make sense of countless familiar situations by looking at the practical reasoning we employ in everyday situations. On the surface, we engage in intentional speech or action; but these efforts rest on deeper assumptions about the world that we usually take for granted.

Think, for a moment, about what we assume in asking someone the simple question, 'How are you?' Do we mean physically? Mentally? Spiritually? Financially? Are we even looking for an answer, or are we 'just being polite'?

Ethnomethodology, then, delves into the sense-making process in any social encounter. Because so much of this process is ingrained, Garfinkel argues that one effective way to expose how we make sense of events is purposely to *break the rules*. Deliberately ignoring conventional rules and observing how people respond, he points out, allows us to tease out how people build a reality. Thus, Garfinkel (1967) directed his students to refuse to 'play the game' in a wide range of situations. Some students living with their parents started acting as if they were boarders rather than children. Others entered stores and insisted on bargaining for items. Some recruited people into simple games (like tic-tac-toe or noughts-and-crosses), only to intentionally flout the rules. Still others initiated conversations while slowly moving closer and closer to the other person. It was a matter of making the everyday 'strange', of 'breaching' commonsense assumptions; and this was done to show just how everyday life depends upon our ongoing sense of 'trust' with each other. Life is fragile, yet it has a rule- and game-like quality which human beings daily recognise, produce and reproduce.

Conversational analysis

Taking this one step further, some sociologists argue that the guiding feature of everyday interaction is language (see Chapter 5). To understand society and the everyday life through which it is made, we need to look at language and the rules through which we speak. In a sense, societies are languages.

Conversational analysis provides *a rigorous set of techniques to technically record and then analyse what happens in everyday speech*. It sets about listening to and observing language, recording it, transcribing it, often videotaping it. Everywhere people are talking, conversational analysts are interested in understanding their talk. Thus they look everywhere – at courts,

hospitals, street conversations, political speeches, suicide notes, statistics making, children's play, television – to see how people construct their daily talk. They see this talk and conversation as a *topic* to investigate in its own right: they are not interested in what people actually say in terms of its contents (which they call resource). Rather, they are interested in its forms and rules, which they see as the underlying feature of social interaction. Human realities are accomplished through talk.

As one example, conversational analysts are concerned with the *sequencing* of talk: sentences generally follow on from one another. 'Normal' interaction depends upon this, and everyday life can only really be accomplished if people are willing to follow certain 'sequencing rules'. One of these, for instance, is *turn taking*: people bide their time, and take turns at being hearers and tellers to talk to others. Another is the *adjacency pair* through which most greetings, openings and closings of conversations have an unstated rule that as one speaks a line, so another makes the most appropriate conventional response to it. Thus, for example, a standard opening line may be: how are you? And this requires a response, usually of the form: very well, thank you. Everyday life is in this way deeply regulated by social rules (Heritage, 1987).

Digitalised life: new features of daily interaction

We have already seen how pervasive the technologies of computers and mass media are in the twenty-first century (see Chapter 1, Table 1.4 for an overview). Here we suggest that these technologies have had growing and very significant influences on how the several billions of people now live their everyday lives on planet earth. Here as a quick illustration are some ways that everyday life has changed in the recent decades because of the new media. You may want to think how much you now take for granted these changes which were unknown features of life to your grandparents in their youth. *Amongst the new feature of interaction are:*

1   Being in *perpetual contact* with a wide range of people – mainly because of mobile phones which can be close to the body all the time. This means we can gain access to people and information at great

speed. Whereas tasks used to take weeks or months, now everything seems capable of being done in an instance. People get irritated when people do not reply to their emails for a day or so; a Google search is expected to deliver an immediate answer to any problem at once; and books, flowers and shopping of all kinds have to be delivered at the latest by the following day. Everyday life has been speeded up. (We now live in a *High Speed Society* (Hartmut and Scheuerman, 2009), and a *Fast Food Nation* (Schlosser, 2002), and it has generated a response in the 'go slow movement').

2 Being able to have *immediate global access* to people all over the world and get a response through phone, email, twitter and web cam. Daily life becomes potentially global: families at other ends of the earth can speak and even see each other on a daily basis. Wherever you are, you are never alone with a mobile phone. This has not only shifted the closeness of families and friends, but also brought strangers from all over the world into close proximity. People need never be far away from other people.

3 Being able to access friends, new communities, shared networks of interest – and complete strangers – at the click of a mouse. A massive global world of other people and friends has become possible for those who want it. *New patterns of community, friendship, dating – and sex – are all in the making* (see Chapter 6).

4 *New modes of speaking and communicating* are appearing with texting, tweeting, photograph sharing and YouTube/web cam presentations. None of these was possible before the 1990s.

5 Being able publicly to *display identities* to others through the new media, often *making public what used to be held to be very private*. The Goffman presentation of self we discussed earlier now becomes an online self. People can make up new identities online (though there does seem to be a lot of evidence that large numbers choose *not* to do this).

6 Closely linked to all of the above, our lives become – more and more – *mediated lives*. We live lives through the media, the internet, the mobile phone; and the technologies become in a sense 'our lives'.

7 Being able to *manage all kinds of everyday practical matters* from home and online: managing bank accounts, travel and holiday bookings, and shopping of all kinds. New technologies change the routines of everyday life.

8 The development of new status systems both in terms of who owns what technologies (owning the latest gadget can become very important to status), but also in terms of being able to present oneself properly online (through blogs, web pages, photos, etc). Status may now be achieved by the numbers of friends we have on Facebook!

9 The development of new rules and behaviour patterns – what Maria Bakardjieva has called the 'little behavior genres' of the internet – appear, alongside 'the micro-regulation of the internet'. New worlds of everyday habits appear which we are only just beginning to grasp.

(On all this, see Baym, 2010; Bakardjieva, 2005; Katz and Aakhus, 2002; Ling, 2008; Miller and Slater, 2000.)

The sociologies of identity, emotion and the body

In recent years, three subjects have become 'hot topics' for some sociologists to study: the body, identity and emotions. Each of these topics takes an area of life that we have typically taken for granted and almost seen as natural: of who we are, what our bodies are, and what our feelings are – and then challenges them to a sociological analysis. Typically in the past these topics have been the concerns of psychologists, doctors, psychiatrists: but this recent research now clearly shows that all three are also profoundly shaped by the social. The social invades the personal. In the following section, we look at each briefly in turn.

A sociology of identity

Identity has become a key concept within contemporary sociology, although it is far from new. For Richard Jenkins, **social identity** is '*our understanding of who we are and of who other people are, and, reciprocally, other people's understanding of themselves and of others*' (Jenkins, 1996). As a sociological concept, it serves as a crucial bridge in social life between human beings and wider cultures. Identity refers to sameness (from Latin *idem*, the same; after the Latin *identitas*, and similar to the word 'identical'); the word entered the English language around 1570. It highlights the quality or condition of being the same; of oneness and continuity. As Jeffrey Weeks says:

Identity is about belonging, about what you have in common with some people and what differentiates you from others. At its most basic it gives you a sense of personal location, the stable core to your individuality. But it is also about your social relationships, your complex involvement with others.

(Weeks, 1991: 88)

Far from being a new idea, then, it implies a sense of meaning and a sense of categorisation and difference: we mark out our identity and sameness with some by highlighting the differences between ourselves and others. It implies a necessary 'other' who is not 'us'. Zygmunt Bauman, a leading contemporary theorist, puts this strikingly when he says:

woman is the other of man, animal is the other of human, stranger is the other of native, abnormality the other of norm, deviation the other of law abiding, illness the other of health, insanity the other of reason, lay public the other of expert, foreigner the other of state subject, enemy the other of friend . . .

(Bauman, 1991: 8)

Identity as a concept, then, looks both inwards and outwards. On the one hand, it speaks to the most microscopic of events – the inner world of how we feel about ourselves. (Freud may be our partial guide here.) It suggests that there is an inner flow of being that is social. On the other hand, it also looks outwards to the most macro of organisations – to the nation-state and the global world. We can speak of Catholic identity through our identification with the Catholic Church, or Celtic identity through our identity with Ireland. Communities of many different kinds – Catholic, Celtic, Chinese – provide meanings from which we can come to fashion our sense of who we are and who we are not.

By its very terminology, then, identity theory implies some sense of sameness, commonality, continuity: if not actually present, the search is nevertheless at least on for an identity – a project of knowing who one is or what one's nation is. At the strongest extremes this is a jingoistic, brazen, self-assertive 'I am this: British, Black, Gay, and Male'. The category behind the identity is presumed and is often stridently clear. I am what I am. At the opposite extreme, the identity has so far dissolved that it is permanently unsettled, destabilised, under provisional construction, very much a project and never a thing. We are not quite sure who we are, or at any event who we are is open to frequent change.

But even in this most extreme form it has to recognise the need for and the power of categories and boundaries in the organisation of the social: it is just that these continuities and sameness are much more pluralised, shifting and fragmented than they were previously thought to be. In what follows, we will look a little more at some of these key contrasts.

Changing meanings of identity

In the past, small, homogeneous and slowly changing societies provided a firm (if narrow) foundation for building meaningful identity. In many societies throughout history, the idea of identity has not really been a problem. In traditional worlds, 'premodern identities' may often be taken for granted. People know who they are, and often define themselves through traditions and religion. They find what seems to be 'a natural place' in the order of things. Identities are shared and communal, given as part of the world, the cosmos and nature. Such identities remain quite common today. For example, in the tight-knit Amish communities that flourish in parts of the United States (well depicted in the film *Witness*, 1985), young people are taught 'correct' ways to think and behave. Not everyone born into an Amish community can tolerate these demands for conformity, but most members establish an identity that is well integrated into the community (see Hostetler, 1980; Kraybill and Olshan, 1994).

As capitalism developed, there appeared an increased concern with human individuality, which starts to make the issue of individual identity more and more important. The modern (industrial, capitalist) period becomes a time of enormous self-reflection upon just who one is. An individual identity starts to emerge which seems a unified, singular and unique, integral individual, endowed with reason and a possible essential core of human beingness. This is what has been seen as the 'birth' of the modern human subject with a quest for personal self-understanding and identity.

But modern societies, with their characteristic diversity and rapid change, offer only shifting sands on which to build a personal identity. Left to make our own life decisions, many of us – especially those with greater affluence – confront a bewildering array of options. Autonomy has little value without standards for making choices, and people may find one path no more compelling than the next. Not surprisingly, many people shuttle from one identity to another, changing

The 'who am I?' test

Sociologists working in the 1950s devised the simplest of tools for measuring self and identity, which has been called the 'Who am I?' or 'Twenty Statements' test. The authors – Kuhn and McPartland (1954)

– suggest to students that they should write the first 20 statements that come to mind in answer to the question 'Who am I?' They stress that there are no right and wrong answers. You might like to try it.

There are 20 numbered blanks in the table below. Please write 20 answers to the simple question 'Who am I?'

in the blanks. Just give 20 different answers to this question. Answer as if you were giving the answers to yourself, not to somebody else. Write the answers in the order they occur to you. Don't worry about logic or 'importance'. Go along fairly fast, for time is limited. Now look at *The big debate* on p. 239.

1	6	11	16
2	7	12	17
3	8	13	18
4	9	14	19
5	10	15	20

their lifestyle, relationships and even religion in search of an elusive 'true self'. Beset by the widespread 'relativism' of modern societies, people without a moral compass have lost the security and certainty once provided by tradition.

To David Riesman (1970; orig. 1950), pre-industrial societies promote what he calls **tradition-directedness**, *rigid conformity to time-honoured ways of living*. Members of traditional societies model their lives on what has gone before, so that what is 'good' is equivalent to 'what has always been'. Tradition-directedness, then, carries to the level of individual experience Toennies' *Gemeinschaft* and Durkheim's mechanical solidarity (see Chapters 1 and 4). Culturally conservative, tradition-directed people think and act alike because everyone draws on the same solid cultural foundation. Amish people exemplify tradition-direction; in Amish culture, tradition ties everyone to ancestors and descendants in an unbroken chain of righteous living.

Many members of diverse and rapidly changing societies define a tradition-directed personality as deviant because it seems so rigid. Modern people, by and large, prize personal flexibility, the capacity to adapt and sensitivity to others. Riesman describes this type of social character as **other-directedness**, *a receptiveness to the latest trends and fashions, often expressed in the practice of imitating others*. Because their socialisation occurs within societies that are constantly in flux, other-directed people develop fluid identities marked by superficiality, inconsistency and

change. They try on different 'selves', almost like so many pieces of new clothing, seek out 'role models' and engage in varied 'performances' as they move from setting to setting (Goffman, 1959). In a traditional society, such 'shiftiness' marks a person as untrustworthy, but in a changing, modern society, the chameleon-like ability to fit in virtually anywhere stands as a valued personal trait.

In societies that value the up-to-date rather than the traditional, people anxiously solicit the approval of others, looking to members of their own generation rather than to elders as significant role models. 'Peer pressure' can sometimes be irresistible to people with no enduring standards to guide them. Our society urges individuals to be true to themselves. But when social surroundings change so rapidly, how can people determine to which self they should be true? This problem lies at the root of the identity crisis so widespread in industrial societies today. 'Who am I?' is a nagging question that many of us struggle to answer. In truth, this problem is not so much psychological as sociological, reflecting the inherent instability of modern mass society.

Most recently, we have seen the arrival of postmodern identities. These are altogether less unified identities and much more fragmented. Identity now becomes **decentred**, *a process by which a centre, core or essence is destabilised and weakened*. This connects to many of the changes we have already identified – globalisation, feminism, proliferating new voices – and generates the search for 'new frameworks' of self-understanding. Giddens talks about all this as a reflexive self-identity:

> . . . because of the 'openness' of social life today, the pluralisation of contexts of action and the diversity of 'authorities', life style choice is increasingly important in the constitution of identity and daily activity. Reflexively organised life planning . . . becomes a central feature of the structuring of self-identity.
>
> (Giddens, 1991: 5)

What we find is that the very idea of personal identity can be thrown into doubt.

As we shall see later (Chapters 22 and 23), the presence of the new information technologies and the new media also leads to what has been called a 'culture of simulation'. This is a kind of virtual reality through which we come to live increasingly in worlds of media images and cyberspaces. The question now being asked is in what way this might be leading to new kinds of 'simulated identity' and 'cyber identity', as even the modern boundaries get eroded. On the internet, it is suggested, people can – if only for a while – become whoever they wish.

Table 7.2 briefly charts some of these shifts in the meanings of identities.

The sociology of bodies

Bodies – perhaps more than anything else – seem to be straightforwardly biological, 'natural' and given. Indeed, at first sight, bodies do not seem to be the most obvious area for sociologists to study. After all, so the argument goes, bodies are biological and individual:

Table 7.2	The shifting nature of identities	
Traditional	**Modern**	**Postmodern**
Given	Determined and structured	Chosen
Taken-for-granted	Polarised/dichotomous	Multiple/fragmenting
Powerful but hidden	Predictable	Chaotic
Essential	Essentialising	De-essentialising

sociologists are surely only interested in the cultural and the social. But if we think about our own bodies for a bit and use our newly discovered sociological imagination (see Chapter 1), we will soon discover that our bodies are indeed social (see Figure 7.4).

The social body

Traditionally, we may look at bodies through what has been called a 'Cartesian dualism' that divides bodies from non-bodies and mind from matter. René Descartes (1591–1650) is often considered the founder of modern philosophy, and at the heart of his arguments was the conclusion that mind is a non-corporeal substance, distinct from a material or bodily substance. The taken-for-granted assumption is that of the 'natural body'. True, it may become weakened in all sorts of ways (and medicine is largely there to help repair it), but the body is 'natural'.

This view is no longer tenable for sociologists. The boundaries and borders of bodies with nature and technologies have significantly dissolved. We are instead, according to the sociologist Chris Shilling, involved in **body projects**, *the process of becoming and transforming a biological entity through social action*. We work on our bodies in myriad ways – from clothing, washing and hygiene to medical and fitness regimes.

The scaling and commodification of bodies – poor bodies/rich bodies

Bodies change across space and time, and much of this may also be linked to bodies in poor and rich countries. What we could call 'poor bodies' may be linked to dirt (sanitation), disease, death, danger and diet (or lack of it), while bodies in high-income countries ('rich bodies') engage with 'body projects' such as dieting, exercise, training, body modification – from tattoos and haircuts to plastic surgery, transgender surgery and on to cyborgs (Shilling, 2003). If intimacies are grounded in bodies, then the scaling of bodies give very different meanings and responses in rich and poor worlds.

Linked to globalisation is the growth of trafficking in body parts. Everything from skin, bone and blood to organs and genetic materials of 'the other' is now up for sale, and this global trafficking is almost invariably in one direction: from the poorest to the richest. Often justified in terms of 'choices', this is part of a process of bodily commodification. As two people remarked in seeming desperation:

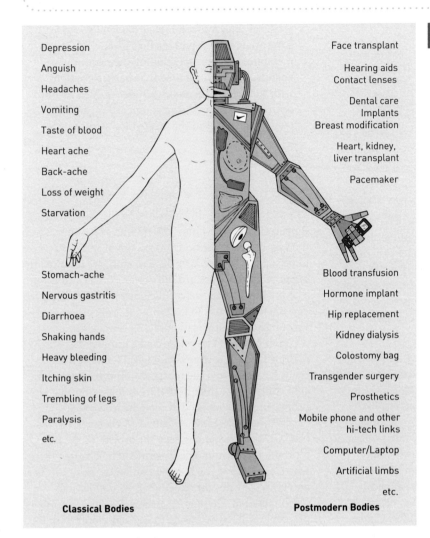

Classical Bodies   **Postmodern Bodies**

Depression
Anguish
Headaches
Vomiting
Taste of blood
Heart ache
Back-ache
Loss of weight
Starvation

Stomach-ache
Nervous gastritis
Diarrhoea
Shaking hands
Heavy bleeding
Itching skin
Trembling of legs
Paralysis
etc.

Face transplant
Hearing aids
Contact lenses
Dental care
Implants
Breast modification
Heart, kidney,
liver transplant
Pacemaker

Blood transfusion
Hormone implant
Hip replacement
Kidney dialysis
Colostomy bag
Transgender surgery
Prosthetics
Mobile phone and other
hi-tech links
Computer/Laptop
Artificial limbs
etc.

Figure 7.4   The social body: from classical bodies to postmodern bodies

I am willing to sell any organ of my body that is not vital to my survival and which could help save another person's life in exchange for an amount of money that will allow me to feed my family.

(Ad placed in the *Diaro de Pernambuyco*, Recife, Brazil, by Miguel Correira de Oliveira, aged 30)

Please, I need money to get dentures, and am a senior desparet [sic] for money. Want to sell a very good kidney. Am desparet for money for teeth. Am a senior citizen in excellent medical shape, but need $ for dentures. My husband and I have no dental plan.

(Email from E. B., Oak Hills, California, cited in Scheper-Hughes and Wacquant, 2002: 42)

Nancy Scheper-Hughes has chronicled the rise in this process of bodily commodification and the sale of organs, and puts it dramatically:

Continuous throughout these transactions across time and space is the division of society into two populations, one socially and medically included and the other excluded, one with and one utterly lacking the ability to draw on the beauty, strength, reproductive, sexual, or anatomical power of the other . . . Commercialised transplant medicine has allowed global society to be divided into two decidedly unequal populations – organ givers and organ receivers. The former are an invisible and discredited collection of anonymous suppliers of spare parts; the latter are cherished patients, treated as moral subjects and as suffering individuals. *Their* names and their biographies and medical histories are known, and their proprietary rights over the body parts of the poor, living and dead, are virtually unquestioned.

(Scheper-Hughes and Wacquant, 2002: 4)

Open and closed bodies

Sociologist Deborah Lupton (1998: 72) has indeed suggested a movement from a body that was predominantly 'open' in premodern times to one that has become increasingly 'closed' and regulated in modern times. Basically, what she means to capture with this idea is a major shift from societies where the body was ever present to one where we increasingly try to regulate and control it. In an analysis of medieval and early modern German culture, the historian Christel Roper describes how the body was seen as:

> a container for a series of processes: defecation, sexual pollution, vomiting. Fluids course about within the body, erupting out of it, leaving their mark on the outside world. The body is not so much a collection of joints and limbs, or a skeletal structure, as a container of fluids, bursting out in every direction to impact on the environment.
>
> (Roper, 1994: 23)

This was a messy world of strange fluids, smells and diseases – the body an ever-present source of chaos.

But with the enlightenment (see Chapter 1), the sociologist Norbert Elias (see the box on p. 233) suggests that we became increasingly preoccupied with taming and regulating our bodily functions and processes. They became increasingly civilised and under control. The most apparent examples of this today would be dieting, fitness regimes, medical regimes for the elderly and sick as well as plastic surgery. On this latter concern alone, Adele Clarke estimates that it is a $1.75 billion a year industry in the United States, with about 1.5 million people undergoing plastic surgery of some kind (Clarke, 1995: 147).

But there are more extreme examples which are becoming of interest. Thus, the Human Genome Project – discussed in Chapter 23 – raises the issue of genetics and the body. Basically, when every gene in the body has been identified, will this lead to radical transformations of our bodies as we undergo gene replacement?

Sociologists are also starting to discuss **cyborgs**, *creatures which connect human and biological properties to technological ones*. Anyone drugged to feel better, reprogrammed to resist disease or given an artificial organ or limb, is technically a cyborg. By this definition, currently some:

> 10% of the US population are estimated to be cyborgs in the technical sense, including people with electronic pacemakers, artificial joints, drug implant systems, implanted corneal lenses and artificial skin. A much higher percentage participate in occupations that make them into metaphoric cyborgs, including the computer keyboard operator joined in cybernetic system with the screen, the neurosurgeon guided by fibre optic microscopy during an operation, and the teen game player in the local video arcade.
>
> (Hayles, 1995: 321)

Health and illness

The sociology of health and illness – discussed more fully in Chapter 21 – may also be seen as looking at the way in which the body breaks down and needs to be socially repaired. Medical regimes are required to organise all this work around disease, decay and death. The final inability to repair the body results in death, and the need then is to find some socially organised way of dealing with dead bodies.

Sarah Nettleton has suggested a number of reasons for the growing sociological interest in the body. First has been the recent attempts by women to gain control over their bodies from male-dominated professionals (evidenced in the Boston Women's Health Book Collective, *Our Bodies, Ourselves* (1978; orig. 1971)). Second has been the growth of the new reproductive technologies (described in Chapter 18), which are shifting the meaning of foetus, birth and body. Thirdly, the 'greying of the population' (highlighted in Chapter 13) means that larger numbers of people will have to come to terms not only with the 'ageing body' but also the possibility of taking their own life. Fourthly, consumer patterns (see Chapter 15) are increasingly concerned with body products: everything from 'the fitness industry' to the 'cosmetics industry'. Fifthly, the arrival of AIDS in the early 1980s served to remind us of the limits of medical technology. And finally, ethical issues around the body – from abortion to research on embryos – are opening up debates about the boundaries between life and death (Nettleton, 1995: 102–3).

The sociology of emotions in everyday life

Emotions would seem to be another one of those topics that is far removed from sociological analysis. Emotions, after all, are something we feel within; they are personal, psychological, private. But think about it again. For in recent years, sociologists have turned their

Norbert Elias: the civilising of bodies and societies

The German–English sociologist Norbert Elias (1897–1990) made important contributions to the study of both sociology and social change. A refugee from Hitler's Germany, his studies of *The Civilizing Process* (originally published in Germany in 1939) suggest how from the Middle Ages onwards in most of Europe, people came to exert greater self-control over their behaviour and their bodies. Through a series of studies of ways of eating, sleeping, dressing, spitting, having sex, defecating, dying and

eliminating, he charts the changing ways of life.

Medieval life was unpredictable, highly emotional, often chaotic and indulgent, and there were few codes around bodily functions. Court society slowly started to change all this, by bringing about etiquette for body management, locations for defecation, and sleeping. Restraint appeared in codes such as those managing table manners. The state developed side by side with a 'civilised' system of self-control. The civilised society has self-discipline, self-control, higher shame and embarrassment, etc.

Chris Shilling (1993) summarises three key processes involved in civilising: socialisation, rationalisation and individualisation. People are

taught to hide natural functions – like defecating and urinating; rationalisation makes us less emotional; individualisation suggests that we come to see ourselves and our bodies as distinctively separate.

All of this is part of Elias's wider approach to sociology, developed in his *What is Sociology?* (1978b; orig. 1970), and known as 'figurational sociology'. Interactions between individuals and societies are his area of study: 'the network of inter-dependencies among human beings is what binds them together' (1978a: 261; orig. 1939).

Elias's work has been influential on a range of scholars who study everyday life processes. Stephen Mennell, for instance, has studied food.

Source: Elias (1978a; orig. 1939).

---

attentions to a full array of feelings, and suggested that there may indeed be social patterns to these too.

Think for a moment about your own emotions and those of your friends. Do you show them with ease, or do you perhaps try to conceal them? Do you talk about your feelings at all? And do you show different patterns of feeling from those of your friends? Maybe boys show aggression more than girls? There are surely moments when you are permitted to cry (at weddings and funerals) and moments when you may want to but know it is not appropriate (at job interviews or in gang conflicts). There are places when it seems right to 'disclose' your feelings (to loved ones, in therapy groups) and other times when it would be clearly odd to do so (perhaps to shop assistants or public officials). There is once again a certain social pattern around our feelings, and it is this which sociologists look for.

Arlie Hochschild (1983) has been prominent in introducing an important way of thinking about emotions in sociology. One of her early studies was concerned with the everyday work of airline stewardesses. This is becoming an increasingly common job – and it requires working under great pressure. Global traffic, tight confinements, 'air rage passengers', 'waitressing' and the like make it quite a taxing job. But as Hochschild spends time observing

the training of these flight attendants, she realises that they are being trained to do a different kind of job. She comments:

> The young trainee sitting next to me wrote on her notepad, 'Important to smile. Don't forget to smile'. The admonition came from the speaker in the front of the room, a crew-cut pilot in his early fifties, speaking in a Southern drawl: 'Now girls, I want you to go out there and really *smile*. Your smile is your biggest asset. I want you to go out there and use it. Smile, *really* smile. Really *lay it on*.'

(Hochschild, 1983: 4)

A core of their training, she found, was that they should be 'nice to people'. This is one of many jobs which involve service work where a central task is to smile, to be courteous, and to show your 'niceness' to others. Indeed, so basic is it that if a stewardess was not nice to you, she might well lose her job (unless, of course, there were very good reasons for this behaviour: for example, you had attacked her!) From this study, Hochschild introduces several key ideas. First, she shows how emotions are socially constructed and presented. In this she continues to draw upon the work of Goffman, mentioned above. Here we are dealing not so much with self-management as with

Arlie Hochschild's *The Managed Heart* (1984) helped shape the new sociology of emotions. Her fieldwork was amongst air hostesses where she observed them being trained to look cheerful and be happy. These days many forms of work require that we sell our emotions and smiles: we are paid to be nice

Source: Pearson Education Ltd/Photodisc/Jack Hollingsworth.

emotional management. But in any event, how you present your feelings also plays a role in forming and showing your self and identity. Secondly, she suggests that the task for a sociologist is to locate the *feeling rules* that are found in specific situations and that enable people to match their feelings with the expectations of a situation; feeling rules act as guides as to how to perform. Finally, she pioneered an important new concept: **emotional labour**, *the management of feeling to create a publicly observable facial and bodily display* (Hochschild, 1983: 7). In a way this is a new form of work involving more and more people. It involves the selling not of a skill or a craft, but of a particular emotional style. Emotion work is another form of emotional labour, but it is done in private: caring, for example, within the home; or sometimes maybe during sex with a partner (Duncombe and Marsden, 1993).

In Duncombe and Marsden's (1993) study of love and intimacy in heterosexual coupledom, they stress the importance of emotional work inside relationships. From their findings, they report the unhappiness of women at men's general unwillingness to do the emotional work needed to sustain a relationship. The women felt 'psychically deserted'. Rather pessimistically, they conclude that 'men's difficulties in expressing intimate emotions will emerge as a major source of the "private troubles" underlying the "public issues" of rising divorces and family breakdown, or the instability of cohabitation among couples who may often be parents' (Duncombe and Mardsen, 1993: 233).

Concluding reflection: the puzzles of individual and society – again

In sociology, a continuous (and endless) tension exists between the individual and society. We have already seen it in the debate over action and structure (see the *Big debate* at the end of this chapter) and it haunts much of sociological research. The social, as we have seen, implies some sense of collective life, of togetherness, whilst the individual implies that in some sense individual people can become cut off, and separate from, other 'individuals'. And the puzzle is how they can be brought together.

So here are some big questions. How can there be individuals within society and a society with individuals? How can the individual dwell in the social and the social dwell in the individual? How can individuals function as individuals within a society that must take away their individuality if it is to run well for all the other individuals too, and in an orderly fashion? How can a society develop a cohesion and a collectivity whilst fostering an individuality and cultivating a unique humanity? How can we have communities and bonding which do not overreach themselves into totalitarianisms and despotism? How can we have creative and caring individuals who do not overreach themselves into selfish, narcissistic egoists? How, in short, can we develop and maintain a balance of individuality and sociality in life and society? Most sociologists ultimately address this issue in some way or another; it is the big social question. If 'individuals' triumph, we can so often sense a crumbling anarchy of egoism and selfishness taking over; if the 'social' triumphs, we can so often sense a painful loss of individuality as we are stalked by collective terrors.

A good starting point might be to think about the balance of the individual and the social in a personal life – even your own. Individual human beings are quite likely to follow their own personal desires and interests – will be selfish – unless there are good reasons not to. There is a huge amount of evidence from biology and history of the selfish gene or of self-interest. We can challenge the details, but with everything equal I follow my self-preservation and interests. I want what is best for me. But – and this soon dawns on any thinking individual – to get this requires a bonding with others. To be on my own will be to *not* function. Without others, social life as we know it cannot function. One of the first features of becoming social is the development of the awareness of others. Our lives are henceforward shaped by these others. Following our own interests requires, in fact, that we attend to others – not all others, but some: and usually those nearest and dearest. Life becomes a struggle of attaching to others and then rejecting and losing them. At a small-scale level of social life, we are constantly bonding and breaking away. It is this making of bonds and their dissolution as we create our own individuality which is a key preoccupation of sociology.

Conclusion: micro-sociology

This chapter has served as only the briefest of introductions to a number of issues that are often termed micro-sociology, and which focus on everyday life and its social construction. We have suggested the importance of a lifelong socialisation process in helping to shape who we become during our lives; and of the importance of situations in building up the social notions of identity, body and emotion. Even as we may like to think of ourselves as 'free individuals', micro-sociology shows us how, even in the smallest moments of everyday feelings and encounters, the social is present, helping to shape the outcomes.

SUMMARY

1 The phrase 'social construction of reality' conveys the important idea that we all build the social world through our interaction. The Thomas theorem states: 'Situations defined as real become real in their consequences.'

2 For individuals, socialisation is the process of building our humanity and particular identity through social experience. For society as a whole, socialisation is the means by which one generation transmits culture to the next. The permanently damaging effects of social isolation reveal the importance of social experience to human development.

3 A century ago, people thought most human behaviour was guided by biological instinct. Today, the nature–nurture debate has tipped the other way as we understand human behaviour to be primarily a product of a social environment. So-called human nature is actually the capacity to create variable cultural patterns.

4 Sigmund Freud envisaged the human personality as composed of three parts. The id represents general human drives (the life and death instincts), which Freud claimed were innate. The superego embodies cultural values and norms internalised by individuals. Competition between the needs of the id and the restraints of the superego are mediated by the ego. To George Herbert Mead, socialisation is based on the emergence of the self, which he viewed as partly autonomous (the I) and partly guided by society (the Me). Mead contended that, beginning with imitative behaviour, the self develops through play and games and eventually recognises the 'generalised other'. Charles Horton Cooley used the term 'looking-glass self' to underscore that the self is influenced by how we think others respond to us.

5 Dramaturgical analysis studies how people construct personal performances. This approach casts everyday life in terms of theatrical performances, noting the settings of interaction, the use of body language and how performers often idealise their intentions. Ethnomethodology seeks to reveal the assumptions and understandings that people have of their social world.

6 The life course itself is largely a social construction. People in different societies may experience a stage of life quite differently, or not at all. Lives can be located through such ideas as a 'historical timeline' and birth cohorts. Life stages may be changing as the formal patterns found in the past are breaking down, with people 'dipping in and out' of phases in a much less regularised and institutionalised fashion.

7 Identity concerns our understanding of who we are. Identity refers to sameness and serves to link a sense of who we are to a wider culture. Identities change across time and space, from traditional societies where identities are shared and communal, given as part of the world, the cosmos and nature, to postmodern societies where identities are seriously questioned and challenged. Bodies were predominantly 'open' and ever present in premodern times, whereas they have become increasingly 'closed' and regulated in modern times. The body is social and 'body projects' involve the process of becoming and transforming a biological entity through social action.

8 Sociologists look at body projects – and consider the ways in which a biological entity is transformed through social actions. Some examples would include the ways in which bodies may be scaled, open or closed, and civilised.

9 Emotions are socially constructed and presented. The sociologist looks at *feeling rules* that are found in specific situations and that enable people to match their feelings with the expectations of a situation; and at emotional labour.

CONNECT UP: Turn to Part 6 of this book for key resources and link up with the book's website, which links to these resources
SEE: www.pearsoned.co.uk/plummer

MYTASKLIST

Ten suggestions for going further

1 Connect up with Part Six and the Sociology Web Resources

As you work through ideas and think about the issues raised in this chapter, look at the accompanying website and the resource centre at the end of this book which connects to it. There is a lot here to help you move on. To link up, see: www.pearson.co.uk/plummer.

2 Review the chapter

Briefly summarise (in a paragraph) just what this chapter has been about. Consider: (a) What have you learned? (b) What do you disagree with? Be critical. And (c) How would you develop all this? How could you get more detail on matters that interest you?

3 Pose questions

(a) Using the questions raised about the socialisation process as your guide, consider your own life experiences of socialisation.

(b) Take any social situation – a meeting with friends, a visit to the doctor, a shopping trip, a fight – and using ideas from this chapter, suggest how it is 'socially constructed'.

(c) Starting with your hair, move down your body to your feet – considering each body part. How far is each of these body parts made 'social'?

(d) Examine the ways in which the body is being changed by machines of all kinds.

(e) Are men less emotional than women, or do they just construct their emotions in different ways?

(f) Look at the table, which names many 'meanings of the self'. Look at them and see if you can guess what they mean. Then think of your own self and which terms if any apply to you. How do you come to make sense of your own self?

The multiple meanings of the self: where do you fit?

Essential	Core	Unified	Stable
Substantial	Spiritual	Material	Social
Dramaturgical	Presented	Impression management	Constructed
Working	Distancing	Embracing	Engulfing
Narrated	Embodied	Emotional	Multiple
Narcissistic	Contradictory	Fragmented	'In crisis'
Saturated	Mediated	Consumerised	Global
Individualised	Cyborg/ digitalised	Disciplined	Regulated
Political	Moral	Hybridic	Diasporic
Traditional	Modern	Postmodern	Homeless

4 Explore key words

Many concepts have been introduced in this chapter. You can review them from the website or from the listing at the back of this book. You might like to give special attention to just five words and think them through – how would you define them, what are they dealing with, and do they help you see the social world more clearly or not?

5 Search the Web

Be critical when you look at websites – see the box on p. 940 in the Resources section. Some useful sources for this chapter are as follows:

Freud

The Freud Archives
http://users.rcn.com/brill/freudarc.html

There are many websites on Freud, but this one contains a biography, his writings, photos, and libraries and museums.

Symbolic interactionism

Society for the Study of Symbolic Interaction
www.espach.salford.ac.uk/sssi/index.php
The website of the Society for the Study of Symbolic
Interaction. A good source for developing ideas about
symbolic interactionism.

Feral children

www.feralchildren.com/en/index.php
The website 'feral children' provides a detailed listing of all
known feral children, including links to original documents.

Ethnomethodology and conversational analysis

http://www2.fmg.uva.nl/emca
Information, resources, event listings, and weblinks on
ethnomethodology and conversation analysis.

6 Watch a DVD

Case studies of extremely deprived children

- François Truffaut's *The Wild Boy of Aveyron* (1970): a
  delightful film about a French 'wolf boy' named Victor.
- Werner Herzog's *The Enigma of Kasper Hauser* (1974):
  a classic about a German boy.
- The story of Helen Keller is told in her *The Story of My
  Life* (1902) and in Arthur Penn's film *The Miracle Worker*
  (1962) and William Gibson's play *The Miracle Worker*
  (1962) (with Anne Bancroft and Patty Duke – both of
  whom won Oscars).

Interaction issues

- Hal Ashby's *Being There* (1979): a comedy in which Peter
  Sellers plays an illiterate gardener, unable to present
  himself properly, eventually coming to be seen as some
  kind of hero.
- Harold Ramis's *Groundhog Day* (1993): life lived over and
  over again in the same way. This really is an interaction ritual.
- Woody Allen's *Zelig* (1983): like most of Woody Allen
  films this one raises the problems of human interaction.
  Zelig is good on multiple identities and the film is full of
  technical trickery to achieve this.
- Sacha Baron Cohen's *Borat: Cultural Learnings of America
  for Make Profit* (2006): outrageously challenges all
  everyday assumptions.

The body

- David Cronenberg's *The Fly* (1986): a classic horror film
  remade to be even more gruesome, but interesting concerning
  the social body, as a man's body becomes that of a fly.
- James Glickenhaus's *The Exterminator* (1970) and later
  spin-offs with Arnold Schwarzenegger were popular in
  the early 1990s and bring to the screen the issues of
  cyborgs, as does Fritz Lang's *Metropolis* (1926).

7 Think and read

Alfred R. Lindesmith, Anselm L. Strauss and Norman K.
Denzin, *Social Psychology* (8th edn, 1999; orig. 1949).
This is a classic textbook to introduce this whole field,
with strong links to symbolic interactionism.

John P. Hewitt and David Shulman, *Self and Society* (10th edn,
2010). Provides an account of the symbolic-interactionist
tradition on which much of this chapter is based.

Erving Goffman, *The Presentation of Self in Everyday Life*
(1959). Goffman's first and best-known book.

Peter L. Berger and Thomas Luckmann, *The Social
Construction of Reality: A Treatise in the Sociology of
Knowledge* (1967). A more advanced study that
elaborates on the argument that individuals generate
meaning through their social interaction.

Susie Scott, *Making Sense of Everyday Life* (2009). Useful
introduction to the sociology of everyday life – briefly
discussed in the box on p. 225.

Anthony Giddens, *Self Identity and Late Modernity* (1991).
An important study that suggests how socialisation
processes are changing in the modern world.

Robin Woofitt and Ian Hutchby, *Conversational Analysis:
Principles, Practices and Applications* (1998) and Celia
Kitzinger, *Feminism and Conversational Analysis* (2003).
Two useful guides to conversational analysis with
different emphases.

Nancy Scheper-Hughes and Loic Wacquant (eds),
Commodifying Bodies (2002). A lively collection of essays
that details the ways in which bodily parts and bodies
are sold or turned into sellable commodities.

Anthony Elliott and Charles Lemert, *The New Individualism*
(2009, rev. edn). An account of contemporary selves –
worth a look.

8 Relax with a novel

Read also Luke Rheinehart's *The Dice Man* (1971, reissued
2000) for an account of a man who creates his identity
based upon the throw of a dice. The work of George Eliot,
especially *Middlemarch* (1871–2), conveys a great deal
about emotion and interaction. See also Candace Clark's
Misery and Company: Sympathy in Everyday Life (1977).

9 Connect to other chapters

- Discussions on the body connect to many chapters, but
  see Chapter 12 on gender, Chapter 13 on ageing and
  Chapter 21 on health.
- Link the discussion of Mead to that of symbolic
  interactionism in Chapter 2.

10 Engage in
THE BIG DEBATE

Who am I? identity crisis in our time

To start: Ask yourself the question: **Who am I?** The table on p. 229 provides a very simple 'Who am I?' test (also known as the Twenty Statement test). You might like to start this discussion by privately indicating twenty answers to yourself. Just who are you? How do you define yourself?

Let's now think about some of your responses.

- Did they indicate your membership in a particular country (Australian), or a particular culture (Muslim, Goth)? These are identities we have touched upon in this part of the book.
- Did they indicate your class ('stinking rich', 'bottom billion'?), your gender (female, transgendered?), your sexuality (gay?), your ethnicity (black, Muslim?), your disablement (blind, educational difficulties?), your age (centenarian or child?)? These are identities connected to the inequalities which we discuss in Chapters 8–14.
- Did they indicate your work situation, your politics, your family position, your religion, your educational position (e.g. student), your health (e.g. a person with AIDS), or even science and technology (you may be a 'test tube baby' or a 'person with a liver transplant'). These are identities connected to the central institutions of society and which we discuss in Chapters 15–23.

All these could be seen as pretty clear and strong identities which people often have and which are linked to key concerns in society.

Consider, though, what other identities you may have that do not fit this. Here is a rag-bag of identities that people may have:

I am what I am. I am a happy person. I am an angst-ridden person in deep despair. I am in love. I am a Jewish queer. I am a Muslim atheist. I am a feminist man. I am an Asian Australian. I am a Catholic abortionist. I am a cyberspace queen.

In the modern world, the claim is that we came to develop new but strong identities. When we faced difficult times – as in our youth – we might have faced an 'identity crisis', but most of the time we roughly knew who we were and could, over a bit of time, sort out our identity. But now, as we drift into the new social order of the twenty-first century, it is claimed that our identities are much less stable, clear or coherent. Indeed, many are now living in a permanently unsettled identity crisis. Indeed, they are de-decentred and fragmented (see Table 7.2). As you provided your list of identities, did you find that you were more 'modern' or 'postmodern' in your identity list?

Many sociologists have addressed these kinds of concern. For the whole of the twentieth century, books were being written that tried to characterise the sorts of identity and identity crises we were facing. There are books that talk of *the narcissistic self* (Lasch), *the protean self* (Lifton), *the mutable self* (Zurcher), *the saturated self* (Gergen), *the abstract self* (Ziejerderveld). We also have *the cosmopolitan self, the homeless self, the individualised self, the fragmented self* and many more. Some writers have also taken to hyphenating identities: Asian-gay, Muslim-British, feminist-man. These immediately suggest some kind of tension within the identity. Other writers suggest global identities: global souls (Picolo), global citizens, people with global human rights, etc. Some talk of hybridic identities. Just who are the Japanese hip hop people we met in Chapter 2? (see Condry, *Hip Hop Japan*, 2006). Just who are the European queers in the European Song Contest that we will meet briefly in Chapter 22? And, perhaps more significant than any other at the start of the twenty-first century, just who are the identities we present and fashion on the net? Who and what are our cyber-identities?

A closing thought: the sociologist Zygmunt Bauman once said: 'If the modern "problem of identity" was how to construct an identity and keep it solid and stable, the post-modern "problem of identity" is primarily how to avoid fixation and keep the options open' (Bauman, 1996: 19).

Continue the debate

1 In what ways do you think notions of self and identity have really changed over the past 100 years?
2 Is it possible for you to be identity-less?
3 Consider how many of the new social movements discussed throughout this book (see Chapter 16, p. 565) raise issues of identity – or what has been called 'the politics of identity'.

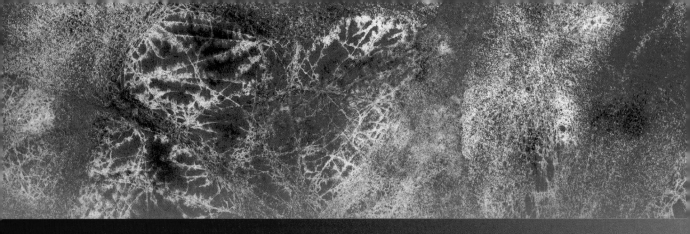

Researching food

From macro to micro

The history of the world, my sweet, is who gets eaten and who gets to eat.

Stephen Sondheim's *Sweeney Todd*

Part Two of this book has been looking at some building blocks for doing sociology: *society*, *culture*, *organisations* and *interaction*. There has been a move *from macro to micro* as we move from the widest social processes to the smallest. Any social phenomena can be analysed through these building blocks – crime, families, wars, bicycling. In this interlude we have selected one issue: food. There can be a sociology of anything – so why not food?

A *sociology of food* examines how food connects to the macro–micro flow, and how all life depends on this. It examines how food is enormously varied across societies, cultures, organisations and interactions. Among the questions it asks are:

1 *Society*. How has 'food' changed across societies – past and present? How can we understand these food changes in societies? We might even ask if societies today are 'progressing' in their eating habits!

2 *Culture*. How does food become a 'design for living' with its own values, beliefs, behaviour practices and material objects that constitute a people's way of life? What meanings, values and practices are linked to it?

3 *Organisation and network*. What are food networks? How does 'food' get organised in social life? How is it produced, distributed, sold and consumed through networks and organisations?

4 *Interaction*. How does food change across the life cycle? How does food involve the presentation of a self? How does it link to language, body and emotion? What role does it play in the story of our lives?

You will not be surprised by now to learn that there is a vast amount of writing and research on the sociology of food. Here there is only space to get you going, and to introduce just a few of these issues.

1 Food and society

Food is usually seen as very high on a basic list of items needed to survive (and so it should be: nutritionists today tell us that our bodies need some 1,300 calories a day to live: but Western societies usually take in much more than that in a day). High on the list of real human needs has to be 'food' – without food we die (*needs* are necessities that people require in order to live – usually food, shelter and clothing; *wants* are our socially generated desires – things that people would like to have but which are not necessary).

The history of societies can, in part, be seen as the evolution of food – no food, no society. The classic descriptions of major societies given in Chapter 4 are in reality partial descriptions of food production. In early societies, one key task involved roaming around the earth to find food sources (hunter-gatherers). Once food stocks were depleted, there was a need to move on. But once the idea of cultivating food was struck upon, societies could become more settled. Geographic differences in local vegetation systems and animals were more or less available for 'domestication'. Water systems needed to be developed; plants needed to be grown in settled areas; animals reared. The rise of food production varied around the world. But where food production was developed and advanced, many other skills could be developed: writing, germ control, technology, political systems.

Many writers have examined the history of food, and suggested that the evolution of industrial society can be seen as part of a wider civilising process (see the box on Elias, p. 233). Stephen Mennel, *All Manners of Food* (1984) has traced this history.

Think and discuss

Are there stages in the evolution of food?

1 Hunting and gathering.
2 Horticultural and pastoral – domestication of animals.
3 Agrarian – large-scale farming.
4 Industrial – the rise of mass production/ technological food.
5 Post-industrial – postmodern fusion and McDonaldsisation.

For a fascinating full account of the rise of food chains in society and the emergence of different kinds of societies, see Jared Diamond's *Guns, Germs and Steel: The Fates of Human Societies* (1997). You can also download much of it on YouTube. Food for Jared is a key shaper of evolution. He is not a sociologist, and sociologists are often critical of his view.

Food in late modern society

Most recently, food has taken on ever new forms. Tim Lang and Michael Heasman, in their book *Food Wars* (2004), comment that 'the 20th century witnessed arguably one of the most significant food revolutions since settled agriculture began around 10,000 years ago' (p. 139). Since then we have seen radical changes in the ways food is grown, processed, distributed and consumed.

We can see this in such changes as:

1 *Growing food* (agro-farming and biotechnology): much food is now grown with the aid of chemicals and hybrid plants, and animals are reared on factory farms.

2 *Processing food*: food is processed through high technologies and cheap labour across the world.

3 *New distribution systems across the world* (e.g. airfreight, heavy-lorry networks and satellite tracking).

4 *Retailing and marketing*: increasingly in the hands of monopolies and large **transnational corporations** (for more on TNCs, see Chapter 15).

5 *Consumption*: the creation of new tastes and brands. We now eat breakfast bars, pick at taco crisps from a bag and Mexican dips in jars, slurp alco-pops, and eat a wide variety of global food that comes pre-packed and chilled or frozen in the supermarket. And all foods

now come 'branded' through advertising. In 2002 alone, there were 13,600 new food products introduced to the world (75 per cent were sweets, breakfast cereals, bakery products, dairy products, beverages and condiments – Lang and Heasman, 2004: 140). Stand in your local supermarket and just try to count the number of foods available to you in one aisle! Eating is shopping.

In all of this we can see the growth of large TNCs dominating the organisation of food (see Chapter 15) and the significance of the globalisation of food. A worldwide food economy of considerable size and economic power has been created. And with this has come a major set of concerns about 'food' in our diets and the environment – many Western diseases are linked to modern eating problems.

TOP 10
Food companies, 2008

Ranking	Previous ranking	Company name	2008 food sales
1	4	**Nestle** (USA and Canada)	$26.477
2	1	**Tyson Foods Inc.**	26,325
3	2	**Pepsico Inc.**	25,346
4	3	**Kraft Foods Inc.**	23,956
5	5	**Anheuser-Busch InBev**	15,571
6	6	**Dean Foods Co.**	12,455
7	7	**General Mills Inc.**	12,100
8	8	**Smithfield Foods Inc.**	10,726
9	10	**Kellogg Co.**	8,457
10	13	**Coca-Cola Co.**	8,205

Source: Based on Foodprocessing.com, August 2009.

Following on from this, it is now suggested that there is a 'nutrition transition' taking place in high-income societies (linked to rising wealth). High-income societies have generated a series of health problems for themselves through their eating habits. But now it seems that these problems are starting to spread to low-income societies – because of the ways in which global marketing trends have been established. We discuss some of these problems in Chapter 21.

To conclude: food, then, is bound up with the processes and development of societies and may even be seen to underlie the creation of societies.

LIVING IN THE C21ST

Still starving – as we get fatter

According to the United Nations Food and Agriculture Organization (FAO), which measures 'undernutrition', 1.02 billion people are undernourished. That means that roughly one in six people do not get enough food to be healthy and lead an active life. Hunger and malnutrition are in fact the number-one risk to the health worldwide – greater than AIDS, malaria and tuberculosis combined. Nearly all of the undernourished are in developing countries. This hunger, which we discuss further in Chapter 9, pp. 313–14, is seen to be due to a mix of the neglect of agricultural development, increases in prices of food, political conflicts and war, and economic crises. But whatever the reasons, there are dire consequences and children are its most common 'victims'. One out of four children – roughly 146 million – in developing countries are underweight and poor nutrition plays a role in at least half of the 10.9 million child deaths each year – 5 million deaths. Under-nutrition magnifies the effect of every disease, including measles and malaria.

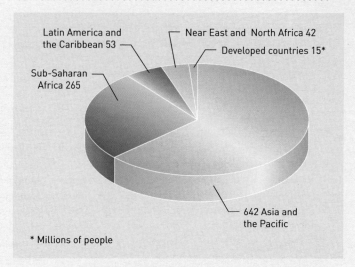

Latin America and the Caribbean 53

Near East and North Africa 42

Developed countries 15*

Sub-Saharan Africa 265

642 Asia and the Pacific

* Millions of people

More than 1.02 billion hungry people

Source: http://www.fao.org/hunger, Food and Agriculture Organization of the United States.

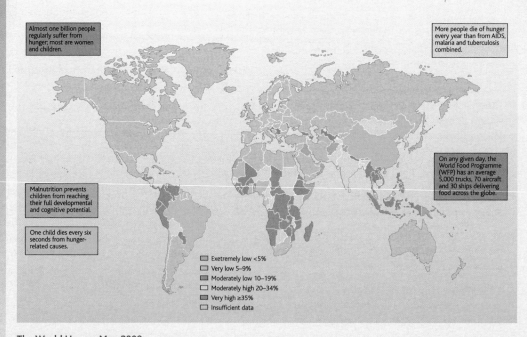

Almost one billion people regularly suffer from hunger; most are women and children.

More people die of hunger every year than from AIDS, malaria and tuberculosis combined.

On any given day, the World Food Programme (WFP) has an average 5,000 trucks, 70 aircraft and 30 ships delivering food across the globe.

Malnutrition prevents children from reaching their full developmental and cognitive potential.

One child dies every six seconds from hunger-related causes.

- Exetremely low <5%
- Very low 5–9%
- Moderately low 10–19%
- Moderately high 20–34%
- Very high ≥35%
- Insufficient data

The World Hunger Map 2009

Note: for the latest edition, click www.wfp.org/hunger/map.

Source: United Nations World Food Programme.

LIVING IN THE C21ST

The Western problems of obesity and anorexia

By stark contrast, the Western world has very different concerns linked to eating. Here the problems of 'obesity' and 'anorexia' are widely recognised, and Western governments increasingly talk about them and initiate health education programmes around them. Some 60 per cent of the US population and two-thirds of men and over half of women in the UK are estimated to be *overweight*. In England, the proportion of the adult population classified as obese increased from 16 per cent in 1994 to 25 per cent in 2008 (*Social Trends*, 2010). At the same time, there has been a growth of the problem of chronic *underweight* – though not through malnutrition. Found especially among the young, and girls in particular (though it is increasing among boys), underweight issues affect 5–7 per cent of the UK population.

Weight problems also bring serious health issues: being overweight can pose problems of diabetes, heart disease, hypertension and some forms of cancer; being underweight can pose problems of emaciation and diarrhoea, and in extreme cases the symptoms can lead to starvation and a cessation of menstruation. Both can ultimately be life-threatening. The most extreme forms of being underweight are anorexia (a sustained and deliberate restriction of food intake) and bulimia (where food may be consumed in binges but is subsequently 'thrown up'). The most extreme form of being overweight is obesity.

Obesity

The International Obesity Task Force (IOTF) revealed that 1.7 billion of the world's population was overweight or obese. In the UK, obesity levels have trebled in the past 20 years. In 2007, 24 per cent of adults (aged 16 or over) in England were classified as obese (www.ic.nhs.uk/pubs/opad09). In Europe, one in four adults will be obese by 2010 (*Tackling Obesity in England*, National Audit Office, 2001). In the United States, nearly two-thirds of adults (64.5 per cent) are overweight, with three in ten (30.5 per cent) being obese.

Several social factors seem to be shaping the 'crisis of obesity'. First, Western society is increasingly sedentary. Many people sit for long hours at work with a subsequent decline of exercise. Rising affluence has brought the growth of conveniences such as cars, computers and televisions, all of which remove activity and generate passivity. Secondly, we have witnessed the development of fast foods. Each year, billions of meals are eaten at 'quick service' catering outlets around the world; each day one in five Americans eats in a fast-food restaurant (Millstone and Lang, 2003: 95) and the consumption of fizzy drinks has almost doubled in the past 15 years. These foods are high in fats and sugar. There are, however, signs that this is beginning to change.

Curiously, obesity is not restricted to industrialised or high-income societies. In 1999 a United Nations survey found that in Brazil and Colombia the figure was around 40 per cent – comparable to much of Europe. In China, the consumption of high-fat foods has soared. Traditional diets feature grains and vegetables, but as incomes in developing societies rise, these give way to meals high in fat and sugar, which is the main source of the problem. It is a bitter irony that as low-income societies are trying to reduce hunger, the World Health Organization estimates that over 115 million people in low-income societies also suffer from obesity (and 300 million overall).

Anorexia and bulimia

Anorexia and bulimia bring an abnormally low bodyweight. In the UK about 1 per cent of female adolescents have anorexia and about 4 per cent of college-aged women have bulimia. Only about 10 per cent of people with anorexia and bulimia are male. This gender difference may reflect our society's different expectations for men and women. Men are supposed to be strong and powerful; they feel ashamed of skinny bodies.

Many have suggested that these eating disorders are part of a wider preoccupation with the body and 'looking good'. The impact here is especially on younger women and girls, who may feel the need to look attractive and slender (though younger men are increasingly being influenced too). Susan Bordo (1993) sees these women as in some ways protesting against the cultural ideals of femininity.

2 Food and culture

Food is certainly a material resource necessary for living. But in all cultures it plays a very important role in shaping a 'way of life'. Just think for a moment of cultures and you may well think of their foods. The Italians and their pasta, the Indians and their curries, the British and their fish and chips, the Scottish and their haggis, and the Swedes with their herrings! These are all stereotypes; but they flag the fact that the world is made of a multiplicity of different forms of ethnic eating. Food is built into cultural systems. Interestingly, in a postmodern, global world, we might say that the traditional forms of ethnic cuisine may be breaking down and being modified, becoming more and more blended together. This is 'fusion food' – implying the fusion of global cultures. Sociologists might call this the **hybridisation of food** (we have encountered the idea of hybridisation before: see Chapter 2).

Food as distinction

In looking at food in culture, sociologists look for the symbolic role of food. It often stands for much more than simple eating. The French sociologist Pierre Bourdieu, for instance, discusses it as a major way of establishing class and 'distinction' in French society.

Bourdieu was a leading French sociologist whom we consider later in the book (see Chapter 20). His prime interests were social class and French society. In his book *Distinction* he uses statistical data to examine both the material and the cultural dimensions of food and eating. The working class, he suggests, treat food as it is, while the bourgeoisie give it all kinds of value and significance – way beyond its basic nutrition For the bourgeoisie, food requires skilful presentation; it is an aesthetic, and it is part of the 'art of living'. He also suggests that 'It is part of men's status to eat and to eat well (and also to drink well); it is particularly insisted that they should eat on the grounds that "it won't keep", and there is something suspect about a refusal.' Women put the food on the table and eat less. In much of social life, Bourdieu suggests, the primary function of food – nutrition – is replaced by a social and aesthetic ritual (Bourdieu, 1984: 197–200).

Food as rules and regulations

We can also see that food is bound up with rules and regulations. All societies have food rules on what can or cannot be eaten, and often just how (and just when, where and why) food can be eaten. Usually this is bound up with religious codes and norms (see Chapter 19). Consider as a striking example the range of different foods that become prohibited in different cultures, and usually because of religious symbolism. The pig, for instance, is a taboo in Judaism and Islam. Here there is a sense of the violation of boundary categories (which we return to in Chapter 13 when we discuss the boundaries of 'normal bodies'). Some animals can be eaten, but some others are wholly taboo. Few Westerners eat horse or insects or snakes. But these can be common foodstuffs for some cultures at some times (Harris, 1968). Most religions also provide rules and rituals around when we should eat – there are 'fasts' and 'festivals' that are prescribed. There are 613 rules in Leviticus and Deuteronomy about eating food.

Media food and foodways

Food, then, is built into cultural practices and materials – what we might call 'foodways'. In the modern/postmodern world, food enters our magazines, newspapers, television programmes, films, arts and literature. An interesting example in recent times has been the growth of the television chef and the cookbook. Of course, cookery books have been around for a long time, and they provide fascinating accounts of the cultures of their time. The books of today – and there are many of them – are also a key to changes in our mores. Modern food cultures inhabit worlds of mass marketing, mass media and highly 'spectacular' entertainment formats.

Jamie Oliver is a UK 'celebrity chef' who started in 1998 with his own book and television programme, *The Naked Chef*. With a cheerful 'Essex-lad' style, he moved from being a cheeky young male cook to being a cook guru with an MBE. During the 2000s, his television programmes dealt more and more with social issues. First, he developed a programme for unemployed youth whom he trained up for his Fifteen restaurant; and then he waged war on the 'bad diets' of school dinners in *Jamie's School Dinners*. Most recently he has taken his campaign to the USA, where diets seem even worse than with UK children (and his reception even more strained). Probably each culture now has to have its own Jamie Oliver. His cookbooks regularly top the best-sellers, and his programmes are shown in over 40 countries, including the USA's Food Network, where he became the second most popular presenter.

Food in most Western countries is moving from being a necessity to a 'hobby pastime'. Everyday food is more and more 'bought out' through restaurants, fast-food chains, chilled foods and frozen food. It is bought and eaten 'on the go'. One in five Americans eat in a fast-food restaurant every day. Food has become fast and convenient. But, at the same time, for some, an interest in cooking and eating has grown as a hobby. We may not spend a lot of time in our kitchens, but we love buying cookery magazines and books,

TV chef Jamie Oliver deals with social issues as well as menus. His TV series *Ministry of Food* revealed both the class nature of food and the poor diets of many people in the UK. For a while he became the government's adviser on school food and nutrition

See: www.jamieoliver.com/tv.

Source: Corbis SRC/Peter Dench.

'Foodies' on TV

Notes for a history of food programmes on UK television

1950s: In the UK, Fanny (and Johnny) Craddock were the first noted 'telecooks'. They were very formal, adopting aristocratic principles, elegance and evening dress (see also Philip Harben). Marguerite Patten, in her history of food in the twentieth century, calls them 'television cookery demonstrations' (2001: 160): the cooks toured provincial theatres and city halls.

1960s: Graham Kerr, 'The Galloping Gourmet', brought a 'loosening of earlier formality', joking a lot and sometimes behaving a little naughtily. He was the breakthrough from Fanny Craddock's formality. 'Good food' and 'eating out' were also celebrated by Robert Carrier, Jane Grigson and Elizabeth David.

Late 1970s: Widespread growth of interest in international cuisines. To help you cook your Indian meal or Chinese meal at home, there were Ken Hom (a Chinese cookery programme and book) and Madhur Jaffrey (with Indian cookery). Keith Floyd displayed 'drunken masculinity' and an altogether more relaxed style of cooking, light years away from the Fanny Craddock of the 1950s. Delia Smith maintained standards and a degree of formal elegance. The best-selling cookbook blockbuster became well established, along with the growth of 'Cookery Book Clubs'.

1980s: The age of *Masterchef* and the tele 'chef contest', along with *The Food and Drink Show*. Cookery series have tie-in books, courses, and food and drink promotions of all kinds. There are very informal 'magazine style' television programmes on every aspect of food and drink.

1990s: Celebrity chefs galore. Television now comes of age with many celebrity chefs, and eventually its own TV food channels. Two Fat Ladies, Ainsley Harriott, Rick Stein and Gary Rhodes.

And onwards: Jamie Oliver, Gordon Ramsey, Nigella Lawson, Nigel Slater and James Martin. Television food has been fully postmodernised. Food is entertainment and has become very informal, much more personal and full of reflection and personalities. It is also very commercial. Cookbooks usually top the best-sellers for weeks. Television food is also fragmented, fusioned and global. The earlier formats have broken down completely. You can now watch 24 hours-a-day food channels. 'Food' has come a long way from the formal, elegant and tightly measured world of Fanny Craddock to the informal, chatty, 'throw-it-all-in-as-easily-as-you-can' sensuality of Nigella Lawson.

watching food programmes on the 'food channel', going on cookery courses, and knowing the latest styles of food and the latest talking points. Many people see cooking now as a 'de-stressing activity' (Lang and Heasman, 2004: 208).

To conclude, food is a key to culture. It performs crucial symbolic roles and helps give meaning to our lives. In the contemporary world, it is embedded in our languages, our rituals, our media worlds and even our politics and values.

3 Food and organisation

The production and use of food always involves some kind of chain – or network – of people who produce, distribute and ultimately consume food. As we have seen, these networks may be changing in the modern world – and they are for food.

The networks or social worlds of food include the obvious: food shops, restaurants, bars. But they also link to chains involved in the full range of production, distribution and consumption of food. To give just a few interconnecting networks: we need to understand the networks and social organisation of the world of work, agriculture and farming, food manufacturers, scientists working on food, health and

nutrition experts, transport systems that carry food around, law-makers who regulate foods, and educational policies around good nutrition and eating. We inhabit multiple networks of food.

A feature of the modern organisation of food is its required speed. This really is the time of fast food. It has been suggested that one in five Americans eat in a fast-food restaurant each day and that in the UK, the use of pre-prepared meals has become ubiquitous. An entirely new food system is being introduced in the modern world. We now eat fast, on the hoof; and we shop in hypermarkets: in the UK, it has been estimated that half the food consumed by the country's 60 million mouths is sold from just 1,000 stores. Although in Chapter 6 we have used the term 'McDonaldisation' to refer to a process in which the principles of the McDonald's food company are applied to many things that are not linked to food (like schools, clothes and business), it does of course also apply to food. As we have seen, McDonald's restaurants are found in over 100 countries, serving millions of people every day.

Of course, along with this are a wide range of eating problems and disorders. Much of our eating – fast and convenient as it may be – brings nutrition problems (Lang and Heasman, 2004: 210).

 Here are two films which are very critical of the food industry. You can also watch selections of them on YouTube.

Eric Schlosser, *Fast Food Nation* (book, 2001; film, 2006).

Robert Kenner, *Food, Inc.* (2008) – and several accompanying books with this title.

The global food chain and you

Think about what you have eaten in the last few days. Hamburgers, curries, apples, orange juice, coffee, tea, coke, beans, bread, chocolates, cod, chips, chicken, muesli, a Chinese take-away? Do you know where each item was produced? The chances are that many minimally processed products that you may have eaten, such as fresh fruit and vegetables, were imported from countries on the other side of the globe. More heavily processed products, from chocolates to frozen meals, probably included ingredients produced and processed by many groups of people from many different countries, some of whom have prospered by selling the product you ate, and some of whom themselves are worrying about when they might get their next meal. If you were to trace the processes of producing each of the items you consumed in your last meal, Harvey reflects, you would discover:

a relation of dependence upon a whole world of social labour conducted in many different places under very different relations and conditions of production. That dependency expands even further when we consider the materials and goods used in the production of goods we directly consume. Yet we can in practice consume our meal without the slightest knowledge of the intricate geography of production and the myriad social relationships that puts it upon our table

(Harvey, 1989)

For better or worse, the food products we use each day have become part of a cycle of international exchange that is reshaping the way people around the world live and work.

For a series of special issues on 'foods', see *New Internationalist* (1998): on coffee, 271; on cocoa, 304; on bananas, 317; on fish, 325.

4 Food and interaction

Food is a central feature of everyday life. In all societies and at all times, food is biologically necessary, but at the same time it also emerges into our daily social interactions. Consider any day and think of the number of times you simply engage with food. Think of breakfast: these days people eat their breakfast 'on the hop', but they haven't always done this; nor did they always have cereals. Nowadays we think nothing of 'snacking' our way through the day. Think of the junk food you eat (or not), the drinks you choose (a coffee from Starbucks or diet coke), the dinners, the meals out. Consider how this might differ across history, and country, and even your own life cycle. Indeed, how does food change across the life cycle? Consider the rituals of baby eating, through to teen junk food, and on, finally, to 'food for the elderly'. Consider your daily encounters around food: how do you share food with others, what are the spaces in which you do this, how do you pace your food and what kinds of conventions – even rituals – guide you along? Food may also become a part of our identity – we define ourselves as certain kinds of 'eaters' and by what kinds of 'food' we like. In the twentieth century there are an array of labels available that we can apply to ourselves: as vegetarians, vegans, anorexics, binge drinkers, gourmets. Food can help to define who we are, and who we are not. And we can link our eating to our ethnicity, gender and class. There is Indian food, Chinese food, fusion food. There is 'posh food' and 'bad food'. Food also plays a role in the social meanings of our bodies: indeed, some say 'we are what we eat'. How we eat is reflected in the way we look. And food can even be an emotion: for some,

food is the new sex. Here are three aspects of food to consider when thinking about this.

Food as interaction ritual

This can be most clearly seen in 'the meal'. Here people share food with each other. We sit with other people, share food, take turns in speaking around food, and sometimes use meals as a major way of celebrating. And if not actually celebrating a birthday, a wedding or the like, then it is tacitly celebrating life and living together. 'The family that eats together stays together.' 'Sharing food' has a long history (over half a million years), and a wide variety of forms, from family meals to large public banquets, from TV dinners to the 'dining out' experience, from the 'take-away' to the 'night out with friends' (Jones, 2007). But it goes beyond the meal: consider, for example, kitchens. Here we can look at the complicated interactions among kitchen workers – servers, dishwashers, pantry workers, managers, restaurant critics and customers. Kitchens show the effects of organisational structure on individual relations (Fine, 1995).

The body and food

Food and eating interactions are also at the centre of the new concern in many Western societies about the body, self-control, health and identity. We give meanings to food from the earliest years of our life. Deborah Lupton has explored the many ways in which we construct sociocultural and personal meanings of food and eating: in the context of childhood and the family, as well as in the social construction of foodstuffs as being linked to 'being a man' and 'being a woman' – male food and girlie food (Lupton, 1996). We shall see in Chapter 21 how obesity has become a major public issue, which in turn may be linked back to the meanings of the body, and especially that of the beautiful woman's body. And this in turn may well link to the issues of gender we discuss in Chapter 12, where we talk about the 'beauty myth'.

The food biography

Consider the story of your life which includes food. Just how has food changed over your life, from childhood to now, and who has helped you fashion those changes? Nigel Slater, the English cook, has written a lovely little book called *Toast: The Story of a Boy's Hunger* (2003), where he recalls his childhood involvements in ice cream, jam tarts, 'cheese on toast', crisps – and hundreds more foods.

Looking ahead

Over time, sociologists and others have outlined a number of key factors that affect food. These include:

- Environment (see Chapter 25) – using (and abusing) natural resources.
- Health (see Chapter 21) – many foods become acceptable because they are considered 'healthy' (yogurts, berries, food supplements). These are links between diet, nutrition, disease and public health.
- Economics and business (see Chapter 14) – poverty and the work of producing food, from inputs to consumption.
- Family dynamics (see Chapter 18) – from family meals to fast foods; shifts in the arrangements for food.
- Politics (see Chapter 16) – governance; regulations of the food economy.
- Religion (see Chapter 19) – a prime concern: religions nearly always lay down food taboos, and build food rituals into their religious ceremonies. Protestantism is quite weak on this, but consider the rules for orthodox Jews, Hindus, etc. Food is always bound up with taboos.

We will not return to food in this book. But as you read further and think more, you should be able to draw upon the analysis started here and build your own deeper understanding of the sociology of food. Maybe it generates good topics for projects?

Food: going further

Here are some of the classic academic studies on food:

- Claude Levi Strauss, *The Raw and the Cooked* (1983). Classic cultural anthropology. Food is taken as symbolic of the division between the 'natural' and the 'cooked', i.e. products of human creation. The book is not just about food!
- Stephen Mennel, *All Manners of Food* (1985). The classic historical/sociological study of food in Western history and its role in the civilising process.
- Deborah Lupton, *Food, Body and the Self* (1996). A more recent account of the role of food in our bodies, emotions and identities.
- George Ritzer, *The McDonaldization of Society* (6th edn, 2010). In fact, not so much about food as about the ways in which the process of McDonaldisation applies to much of contemporary social life.
- Gary Alan Fine, *Kitchens* (1995). Ethnography of what goes on behind the scenes.

See also: Tim Lang and Michael Heasman, *Food Wars* (2004); Eric Millstone and Tim Lang, *The Atlas of Food: Who Eats, What, Where, When, Why* (2003); James Watson and Mellisa Caldwell, *The Cultural Politics of Food and Eating* (2004). These are all lively accounts of the contemporary 'politics of food' debate.

PART 3

THE UNEQUAL WORLD

DIFFERENCE, DIVISION AND SOCIAL STRATIFICATION

CHAPTER 8

INEQUALITY, SOCIAL DIVISIONS AND SOCIAL STRATIFICATION

IT IS A CENTURY SINCE ON 10 APRIL 1912 the ocean liner *Titanic* slipped away from Southampton docks on its maiden voyage across the North Atlantic to New York. A proud symbol of the new industrial age, the towering ship carried 2,300 passengers, some enjoying more luxury than most travellers even today could imagine. By contrast, poor immigrants crowded the lower decks, journeying to what they hoped would be a better life in the USA.

Two days out, the crew received radio warnings of icebergs in the area but paid little notice. Then, near midnight, as the ship steamed swiftly and silently westwards, a lookout was stunned to see a massive shape rising out of the dark ocean directly ahead. Moments later, the *Titanic* collided with a huge iceberg, almost as tall as the ship itself, which split open its starboard side as if the grand vessel were nothing more than a giant tin can.

Sea water surged into the ship's lower levels, and within 25 minutes people were rushing for the lifeboats. By 2 a.m. the bow of the *Titanic* was submerged, and the stern reared high above the water. Clinging to the deck, quietly observed by those in the lifeboats, hundreds of helpless passengers solemnly passed their final minutes before the ship disappeared into the frigid Atlantic.

The tragic loss of more than 1,600 lives made news around the world. Looking back dispassionately at this terrible accident with a sociological eye, however, we see that some categories of passengers had much better odds of survival than others. In an age of conventional gallantry, women and children boarded the boats first, so that 80 per cent of the casualties were men. Class, too, was at work. Of people holding first-class tickets, more than 60 per cent were saved, primarily because they were on the upper decks, where warnings were sounded first and lifeboats were accessible. Only 36 per cent of the second-class passengers survived, and of the third-class passengers on the lower decks, only 24 per cent escaped drowning. On board the *Titanic*, class turned out to mean much more than the quality of accommodation: it was truly a matter of life or death.

Years later, the story of the *Titanic* still fascinates. In 1997 it was filmed (for the third time) and became the biggest box office success of all time. It was also staged as a musical. There are many threads to be analysed in the *Titanic* story: but one of them is always the extreme divisions of social class that destroyed many lives.

All animals are equal, but some are more equal than others.

George Orwell, *Animal Farm* (1945)

In this chapter, we ask:

- **What is social stratification and inequality?**

- **How are inequalities patterned through divisions of economy, gender, sexuality, age and ethnicity?**

- **How do we explain the prevalence and persistence of these divisions?**

- **What is the future of inequalities – especially the emerging digital divide?**

(Left) *Abandoned* Luigi Nono (1850–1918)

Luigi Nono (1850–1918) was an Italian painter of the Venetian school. (He was also grandfather of the celebrated avant-garde composer Luigi Nono). His works often captured the tragic element of life, with paintings of *Sick child*, *Burial of a child* and here, *Abandoned*. He died at the end of the first world war.

Source: Abandoned, 1903 by Nono, Luigi (1850–1918) Museo d'Arte Moderna di Ca'Pesaro, Venice, Italy/Bridgeman Art Library.

See: Lilie Chouliaraki *The Specatorship of Suffering.* London: Sage, 2006

Q How do we relate to images of the distant sufferer – here 'the abandoned'? How might art cultivate a disposition of care for and engagement with the sufferings of others?

The fate of the *Titanic* dramatically illustrates the consequences of social inequality for the ways in which people live and die. Social diversity and differences are everywhere part of society. But when such differences start to become socially significant – as we can see on the *Titanic* – sociologists start to speak of **social divisions**: human *differences that are rendered socially significant*. While differences may be found everywhere and can often be inconsequential (such as the differences between stamp collectors, sports people and cooks), differences between people that are given strength and made significant start to play crucial roles in the shaping of a society. The chapters in this part of the book will be examining different aspects of these differences; this chapter starts with a more general look.

Introduction: what is social stratification and inequality?

Most (and probably all) societies exist with systems of social division and social stratification, through which entire categories of people are elevated above others, providing one segment of the population with a disproportionate amount of money, power and prestige. Sociologists use the concept of **social stratification** to refer to a *system by which a society ranks categories of people in a hierarchy*. Five basic principles tend to organise them everywhere.

1 *Social stratification is a characteristic of society, not simply a reflection of individual differences*. It is a system which confers unequal access to resources. Members of industrial societies consider social standing as a reflection of personal talent and effort, though we typically exaggerate the extent to which people control their destinies. Did a higher percentage of the first-class passengers survive the sinking of the *Titanic* because they were smarter or better swimmers than the second- and third-class passengers? Hardly. They fared better because of their privileged position on the ship. Similarly, children born into wealthy families are more likely than those born into poverty to enjoy health, achieve academically, succeed in their life's work and live well into old age. Neither rich nor poor people are responsible for creating social stratification, yet this system shapes the lives of them all.

2 *Social stratification persists over generations*. To understand that stratification stems from society rather than individual differences, note how inequality persists over time. In all societies, parents confer their social positions on their children, so that patterns of inequality stay much the same from generation to generation.

Some individuals do experience **social mobility**, *change in one's position in a social hierarchy*. Social mobility may be upwards or downwards. Our society celebrates the achievements of a David Beckham or a Madonna, who rose to prominence from modest beginnings. But we also acknowledge that people move downward as a result of business setbacks, unemployment or illness. More often, people move *horizontally* when they exchange one occupation for another that is comparable. For most people, however, social standing remains much the same over a lifetime.

3 *Social stratification is universal but variable*. Social stratification seems to be found everywhere. At the same time, *what* is unequal and *how* unequal it is varies from one society to another. Among the members of technologically simple societies, social differentiation may be minimal and based mostly on age and sex (though these factors still matter in most societies today as well).

4 *Social stratification involves not just inequality but beliefs*. Any system of inequality not only gives some people more resources than others but defines certain arrangements as fair. Just as what is unequal differs from society to society, so does the explanation of why people should be unequal. Sociologists have introduced ideas such as ideology and hegemony to help us understand this. Virtually everywhere, however, people with the greatest social privileges express the strongest support for their society's system of social stratification, while those with fewer social resources are more likely to seek change.

5 *Social stratification engenders shared identities* as belonging to a particular social category different from others. Identity serves to mark off one social division from another, often being closely linked to different kinds of culture as well. In all systems of social division, people have a sense of their location – and may accept, negotiate or even resist it. For Marx, for example, a sense of class consciousness was very significant; and class identities could have been harbingers of major social change (Payne, 2000; Braham and Janes, 2002).

Types of inequality

Goran Therborn (2006: 6–9) suggests that there are three fundamental kinds of inequality. These are:

1 *Inequalities of health, life and death*. These are basically linked to the biological organism – sometimes called *vital inequality*. Birth and death rates – as well as illness and disease – are significantly shaped by social factors (see Chapter 21).

2 *Existential inequalities*. These involve the differential recognition of human individuals as persons. Stigma is the opposite of positive esteem and recognition, and this kind of inequality is linked to the study of stigma.

3 *Resource inequalities*. These are the differences between people in their capacity to act. Humans are very different in their capabilities and abilities to act in the world. Having adequate resources – money, knowledge, friends and family – helps shape life opportunities.

The intersecting forms of social divisions and the processes of inequality

For a long time, sociologists focused primarily upon one major system of stratification: that which dealt with social and economic positions. Broadly, this is how people are ranked in terms of their economic position, their power and their prestige. It included systems of slavery, caste and the modern class system. But more recently, sociologists have also recognised that social divisions and their linked inequalities are organised through a range of key social structures, such as gender, ethnicity, sexuality, disability and age. It is constructive in any sociological analysis to examine the structures of inequalities through which social life gets organised. Whatever social thing you are looking at – schools, social work or senility – always try and ask questions about how it interconnects with at least some of the inequalities shown in Table 8.1.

Within such divisions and stratification systems, Iris Marion Young has identified a number of key processes at work. These include:

Table 8.1	The intersecting orders of inequalities		
	Social structures and social orders (channels of opportunities)	Supporting ideas and identities (discourses/positionalities)	Chapter where more fully discussed
1	Class order: how does work, income, wealth shape life?	Classism and class consciousness	See Chapters 9 and 10
2	Gender order (and patriarchy): how does being a man or woman shape social life?	Sexism and gender identity	See Chapter 12
3	Racial formation (ethnicity and race): the role of ethnic and cultural difference in social life	Racialisation, racism and ethnic identity	See Chapter 11
4	Age stratification and generational orders: how are lives stratified by generation and age?	Ageism and generational self	See Chapter 13
5	Nations: what is the significance of local and national cultures?	Nationalism and national identity	See Chapter 16
6	The sexual order	Heterosexism, homophobia and heteronormativity: sexual identity	See Chapter 12
7	The disability and health order	Sickness and 'disablement' ideologies: health/ability identity	See Chapter 14

Source: Adapted from Plummer (2010) Table 7.3.

- *Social exclusion and marginalisation*: a process by which 'a whole category of people is expelled from useful participation in social life' (Young, 1990: 53). Here, people are pushed from the mainstream of participation in society. We will see this when we talk about the idea of the exclusive and inclusive society in Chapter 10.

- *Exploitation*: a process by which there is 'the transfer of the results of the labour of one social group to benefit another' (Young, 1990: 49).

- *Powerlessness*: a process by which people come to lack the authority, status and sense of self that many professionals tend to have (Young, 1990: 57).

- *Cultural imperialism*: 'the universalization of a dominant group's experience and culture, and its establishment as the norm' (Young, 1990: 59). We will see this when we discuss ideas around the postcolonial in Chapter 11.

- *Violence*: directed at members of a group simply because they belong to that group (Young, 1990: 62). Thus, we will discuss violence against women and homophobia against gays in Chapter 12.

Overview

Part Three of this book looks at aspects of these systems, gives examples and raises some debates around them.

This chapter considers some contrasting patterns of social-economic stratification and ponders why it is so widespread. Chapter 9 then looks at the wider world, raising such issues as global poverty, widening inequalities and the uneven development of societies across the globe. Chapter 10 then examines how social and economic stratification works in specific 'high-income' countries such as the UK and the United States (where poverty, for example, curiously continues to exist on a massive scale). Chapter 11 turns to the ethnic stratification system and discusses matters of race and migration. While it will focus specifically on Europe, we will also see that 'race stratification' goes deep in all cultures of the world. Chapter 12 will draw from feminist and queer sociology to introduce the ideas of patriarchy and heterosexism and see how gender acts as a major system of stratification. Chapter 13 looks at age stratification, focusing especially on children as well as the social exclusion of those in later life. As populations skew to more and more older people, a major change is in the air. Finally, Chapter 14 looks at disablement, focusing on a range of ways in which people are excluded and stereotyped through their bodies, mental faculties and general health.

Of course, one key problem with these varying systems of stratification is how they all interconnect. Sociologists have recently started to call this the problem of **intersectionality**: *the ways in which different forms*

METHODS & RESEARCH

On interviews and suffering

Pierre Bourdieu (1930–2002) was one of the leading French sociologists of the late twentieth century (he is featured in the *Thinkers and theory* box on p. 263 and will be often mentioned during this book). Although much of his research may be described as theoretical, one of his major books, *The Weight of the World* (1999) (originally published in 1993 as *La Misère du Monde*) is a remarkable instance of the sociological interview at work. The book contains around 70 interviews and commentaries with men and women who have confided 'their lives and the

difficulties they have had in living those lives'. In general, they have been denied a socially respected and valuable existence – suffering from racism, or poverty, or marginalisation; and they have not been able to adjust to rapid changes around them. We could say they lead 'damaged lives' because of inequalities.

These are no ordinary social science interviews, which can be flat, dull and overly structured. Instead, these interviews are more detailed and are often reproduced in the book as direct interviews with the interview questions included. They are placed side by side with interviews from people who hold different social positions – even though they live on the same

housing estate or work at the same place. Each interview is also given an interpretation, in which the interview has been examined and listened to repeatedly by the researcher(s) in order to make sense of it.

Complex and multilayered representations, unlike those found in the press and much journalism, can often lead the reader to sense some kind of social explanation of the social sufferings that many people experience. They also lead us to see the 'multiplicity of co-existing, and sometimes directly competing, points of view' (Bourdieu et al., 1999: 3). This study is a fine example of the interview at work in tracking the personal experience of inequalities.

of inequality and division interact with each other. We will discuss this as we go along. It is one of the major issues of current sociology to learn how to make these linkages adequately.

Closed and open systems of stratification: slavery, estate, caste and class

Here we locate four of the major systems of stratification which have been found throughout history. In describing social stratification in particular societies, sociologists often stress the degree of social closure and mobility that is allowed in the society. 'Closed' systems allow little change in social position, while 'open' systems permit some mobility (Tumin, 1985).

Slavery

Slavery is *a form of social stratification in which people are owned by others as property*. Chattel slavery turns human beings into things to be bought or sold. Many early civilisations such as Egypt and Persia (now Iran), as well as the ancient Greeks and Romans, relied heavily on slave labour. Slaves could be worked to death in the building of huge pyramids or in massive public works such as irrigation systems.

But it was not just a pervasive feature of 'classical worlds'. Between the fifteenth and nineteenth centuries, there was a major slave trade into the New World. It has been estimated that the total population of the African continent in 1500 was 47 million. As S. I. Martin chronicles:

> Over the next 350 years, between 10 and 15 million Africans arrived in chains in the New World. Four to six million more are believed to have died during their capture or the rigours of the Atlantic crossing – a total of between 14 and 21 million people. This excludes the 17 million Africans thought to have been abducted as a result of the trans-Saharan slave trade. History has seen few disruptions on such a scale.

(Martin, 1999: 21)

The forms that slavery has taken have been highly variable. The legal rights and autonomy of slaves varied. In classical Athens, for example, slaves could often hold positions of great responsibility even though they were owned by their masters. But the slaves who worked building pyramids, or excavating mines, or on plantations, were much more regulated and treated as less than human. People captured in warfare often became slaves.

Modern slavery

The British Empire abolished slavery in 1833, and the American Civil War brought slavery in the United States to an end in 1865. Although slavery no longer exists in its classical forms, it does still persist in a variety of forms in many parts of the world today (the United Nations has investigated claims that some 100,000 people in Mauritania in West Africa were being kept in slavery). However, English social scientist Kevin Bales (2004) suggests that traditional and modern slavery differ. For him, one key difference is that modern slavery is not about direct ownership but about control through violence, usually with major elements of economic exploitation. This could include:

- *Forced labour*, where governments forcibly recruit labour. This often involves children who may be forced to leave home.
- *Debt bondage*, where people labour to pay off a debt that they will probably never be able to repay and which may be inherited by subsequent generations.
- *Prostitution*, where women (and children) may move between countries in the hope of work, only to find themselves part of the human chain of sex traffic from which it may be hard to escape.
- *Servile marriage*, where women are given in marriage without the right to refuse.

It is estimated that there are 27 million slaves alive today – probably more than at any point in history. This number is also greater than the total population stolen from Africa during four centuries of the transatlantic slave trade (Bales, 2009). As other forms of slavery appear through the selling of immigrants to other countries, and the selling of body parts – usually from those in poorer countries to those needing body parts in the richer countries (see Scheper-Hughes, 2000), so estimates of modern slavery are indeed increasing. Indeed, some agencies working in this field suggest that numbers may well be much greater than Bales estimates – with perhaps more than 200 million people in modern slavery. Sometimes slavery can appear in the most unlikely places: one estimate has suggested that there are some 3,000 households in Paris holding slaves!

Usually, modern slaves are found among the poor, the uneducated and the low-status groups

(a)

(b)

(c)

Slavery: past and present
(a) Slavery in Africa in the past, when people were rounded up and shipped off to work on plantations, is not very different from the slavery that some people still face today. **(b) Present day Dinka slave trade in Sudan. (c) New Delhi, India,** 18 February: a sweeper, one of India's reported hundreds of millions of untouchables and lower-caste Hindus who perform menial labour, walks by a pig picking through garbage in New Delhi

Source: (a) Popperfoto/Getty Images; (b) David Orr/Sygma/Corbis; (c) AFP/Getty Images.

of a society: frequently, of course, these are women and children. In all cases, slavery is a closed system of stratification, robbing a life of much hope of control or change.

See *Documenting Disposable People*, a photographic essay of contemporary slavery in the world with an introduction by Kevin Bales (2010). This is an example of visual sociology.

The estate system

Medieval Europe was a feudal system based on ideas of an **estate**, *a system based on a rigidly interlocking hierarchy of rights and obligations*. Estates were created politically and supplied an orderly chain of rights and obligations throughout society. Thus, usually a chain of obligations ran through three major groups – nobility, clergy and commoners. Land was controlled by powerful lords who enlisted the military to protect their land in return for rights over a part of it. Peasants were then dominated by the local nobility, while having some control over their own pieces of land. The tenants were vassals (dependants) of the lord; the lord was linked to the monarch, and so forth.

The caste system

The **caste system** has complex meanings (Sharma, 1999) but is usually seen as a form of *social stratification based on inherited status or ascription*. A pure caste system, in other words, is 'closed' so that birth alone determines one's social destiny with no opportunity for social mobility based on individual efforts. Caste systems rank categories of people in a rigid hierarchy. Some scholars believe that the concept can only really be applied to the system found in India – a system that is now under change. Others see it as a more widespread system, one which could embrace the Deep South in America in the post-slavery period, South Africa under apartheid, elements of the system of relationships in contemporary Thailand, and even the gypsies in England.

The most frequently cited example of a caste system is that of India, or at least India's traditional Hindu villages in which most people still live. The Indian system of caste is usually discussed in terms of *varna*, a Sanskrit word that means 'colour' (see Figure 8.1). It denotes four major categories: Brahmins (priests and writers) who claim the highest status, Kshatriyas (warriors and rulers), Vaishyas (the merchants and landowners) and Sudras (artisans and servants). People outside the system become 'untouchables' and often have the most unpleasant work – handling sewage, burning corpses, scavenging. It is estimated that there are some 150 million untouchables in India (about 20 per cent of the population), whereas the Brahmins at the top make up just 3 per cent.

Each local community develops its own language and ways of building up what is, in effect, an endogamous

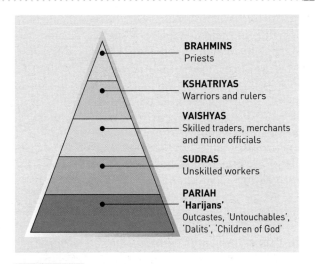

Figure 8.1   Classic depiction of the caste system

(or closed) community which lays down a very broad system of positioning. This guides people into very clear rules about washing, eating or communicating with other people. It suggests ideas of ritual purity, pollution and exclusion. In the past it was largely a fixed system – no movement between castes was possible. The most controversial group (in Western eyes at any rate) were the 'untouchables', who performed polluted work.

'Dalits' means oppressed or ground-down peoples and refers to the former 'untouchables'. Traditionally they performed 'impure' functions, – such as handling sewage and corpses, – were forced to live in the worst parts of Indian villages and towns, and were denied access to common resources like wells, shops, schools and Hindu temples. This system of savage exclusion was formally abolished over half a century ago, but today there are still some 150 million people (about 20 per cent of the population) living in around 450 castes. In the UK, research has suggested there may still be some 50,000 Dalits who suffer from 'caste' and experience discrimination in jobs, healthcare, politics, education and schools – but such figures are hard to evaluate (see Gorringe, 2006).

Race and caste

It could be argued that race is often used as a tool for the caste system (though many disagree). In the southern plantations of the USA after slavery, for example, it has been argued that the division between 'blacks' and 'whites' into strictly segregated groups was so extreme that it amounted to a version of a caste system (Dollard, 1937; repr. 1998). Likewise, it might also be argued that caste played a key role in South Africa until recently. In this nation's former policy of apartheid, the 5 million South Africans of European ancestry enjoyed a commanding share of wealth and power, dominating some 30 million black South Africans. In a middle position were another 3 million mixed-race people, known as 'coloureds', and about 1 million Asians. The *World watch* box on p. 259 details the problems of dismantling South Africa's racial caste system.

The nature of a caste system

In a caste system, birth determines the fundamental shape of people's lives in four crucial respects. First, traditional caste groups are linked to occupation, so that generations of a family perform the same type of work. In rural India, although some occupations (such as farming) are open to all, castes are identified with the work their members do (as priests, barbers, leather workers, street sweepers and so on). In South Africa, whites still hold most of the desirable jobs, with most blacks consigned to manual labour and other low-level service work.

No rigid social hierarchy could persist if people regularly married outside their own categories, as then most children would have uncertain rank. To maintain the hierarchy, then, a second trait of caste systems is mandating that people marry others of the same ranking. Sociologists call this pattern *endogamous* marriage (*endo* stems from Greek, meaning 'within'). Traditionally, Indian parents select their children's marriage partners, often before the children reach their teens. Until 1985, South Africa banned marriage and even sex between the races. Even now, interracial couples are rare since blacks and whites continue to live in separate areas.

Thirdly, caste guides everyday life so that people remain in the company of 'their own kind'. Hindus in India enforce this segregation with the belief that a ritually 'pure' person of a higher caste will be 'polluted' by contact with someone of lower standing. Often this leads to 'caste feuds', with bitter attacks and murders usually on lower-caste citizens. Apartheid in South Africa also led to much bitter conflict.

Finally, caste systems rest on powerful cultural beliefs. Indian culture is built on Hindu traditions that mandate accepting one's life work, whatever it may be, as a moral duty. Although apartheid is no longer a matter of law, South Africans still

cling to notions distinguishing 'white jobs' from 'black jobs'.

Caste and agrarian life

Caste systems are typical of agrarian societies because the lifelong routines of agriculture depend on a rigid sense of duty and discipline. Thus, caste still persists in rural India, half a century after being formally outlawed, even as its grip is easing in the nation's more industrial cities, where most people exercise greater choice about their work and marriage partners. Similarly, the rapid industrialisation of South Africa elevated the importance of personal choice and individual rights, making the abolition of apartheid increasingly likely. Note, however, that the erosion of caste does not signal the end of social stratification. On the contrary, it simply marks a change in its character, as the next sections explain.

The class system

Agrarian life relies on the discipline wrought by caste systems; industrial societies, by contrast, depend on developing specialised talents. Industrialisation erodes caste in favour of **social class**, *social stratification resulting from the unequal distribution of wealth, power and prestige*. Unlike caste, estate and slavery, it is a system that claims to be more open and based on individual achievement. A class system is seen to be more 'open' in that people who gain schooling and skills may experience some social mobility in relation to their parents and siblings. Mobility, in turn, blurs class distinctions. Social boundaries also break down as people immigrate from abroad or move from the countryside to the city, lured by greater opportunity for education and better jobs (Lipset and Bendix, 1967). Typically, newcomers take low-paying jobs, thereby pushing others up the social ladder.

People in industrial societies come to think that everyone is entitled to 'rights', rather than just those of particular social standing. This has not always been the case. The principle of equal standing before the law steadily assumes a central place in the political culture of industrial class systems. Class systems are no different from caste systems in one basic respect: people remain unequal. But social stratification now rests less entirely on the accident of birth. Class systems, for instance, may allow more individual freedom in work careers (when they are available) and in such things as the selection of marriage partners.

From 'race as caste' to social class: a report from South Africa

At the southern tip of the African continent lies South Africa. Long inhabited by black people, the region attracted white Dutch traders and farmers in the mid-seventeenth century,

Nelson Mandela, leader of the African National Congress (ANC), who was imprisoned by the white apartheid government for 27 years, at his inauguration 10 May 1994. He was elected president in South Africa's first all-race election. His ninetieth birthday was celebrated on 18 July 2008. Mandela has had a strong world moral voice, when new presidents have been elected to power. He has since become a major advocate for a variety of social and human rights organisations. Read Mandela's *Long Walk to Freedom* (1994) and see Clint Eastwood's film *Invictus* (2009)

Source: WALTER DHLADHLA/AFP/ Getty Images.

who became known as the Boers, the Dutch for farmers. Early in the nineteenth century, a second wave of colonisation saw British immigrants push the Dutch inland in the Boer Wars (1899–1902). By the early 1900s, the British had taken over the country, proclaiming it the Union of South Africa. In 1961, the United Kingdom gave up control and recognised the independence of the Republic of South Africa.

But freedom was a reality for only the white minority. Years before, to ensure their political control over the black majority, whites had instituted a policy of apartheid, or racial separation. Apartheid was made law in 1948, denying blacks national citizenship, ownership of land and any formal voice in the government. In effect, black South Africans became lower caste, receiving little schooling and performing menial low-paid jobs. Under his system, even 'middle-class' white households had at least one black household servant. The prosperous white minority defended apartheid, claiming that blacks threatened their cultural traditions or, more simply, were inferior beings. But resistance to apartheid rose steadily, prompting whites to resort to brutal military repression to maintain their power.

Steady resistance – especially from younger blacks, impatient for a political voice and economic opportunity – gradually forced change. Adding to the pressure were criticism and boycotts from many nations. By the mid-1980s the tide began to turn as the South African government

granted limited political rights to people of mixed race and Asian ancestry. Then came the right for all people to form labour unions, to enter occupations once restricted to whites, and to own property. Officials also began to dismantle the system of laws that separated the races in public places. The rate of change increased in 1990 with Nelson Mandela's release from prison. In 1994, the first national election open to all people of all races elected Mandela the president, ending centuries of white minority rule.

The suffering of people under apartheid remains one of the twentieth century's epic stories of 'man's continuing inhumanity to man'. In order that these experiences should not be easily forgotten, a Truth and Reconciliation Commission was established which compiled the evidence of over 20,000 witnesses to the regime, breaking the silence that surrounded the many gross violations of human rights committed during those years.

Despite this awareness of its past and the current dramatic political change, however, social stratification in South Africa is still partially based on race. Even with the right to own property, one-third of black South Africans have no jobs, and the majority remain poor. The worst-off are some 7 million *ukublelekka*, which means 'marginal people' in the Xhosa language. Soweto-by-the-Sea may sound like a summer getaway, but it is home to thousands of *ukublelekka* who live crammed into shacks made of packing cases, corrugated metal,

cardboard and other discarded materials. There is no electricity for lights or refrigeration. Without plumbing, people use buckets to haul sewage, and women line up to take a turn at a single water tap that serves more than 3,000 people. Any job is hard to come by, and those who do find work are lucky to earn $200 a month. Crime has become a major problem. South Africa's current president, Jacob Zuma, who was elected in 2009, leads a nation still twisted by centuries of racial caste. In 2010, however, it assumed global significance when it hosted the month-long World Cup, which attracted world attention.

Today, researchers have suggested that South Africa is probably more unequal than it was under apartheid. Jeremy Seekings and Nicoli Natrass, examining the country from the mid-twentieth century to now, conclude that there has been a shift from race to class as the key organising feature. They suggest that South Africa is now riven between 'insiders' and 'outsiders'. 'Insiders' are increasingly multiracial and enjoy access to 'good jobs' and high incomes. But 'outsiders' lack skills and employment and live 'outside' the mainstream of South African society. To make matters worse, the country now has one of the highest homicide rates in the world.

Source: Christie, 2000; Truth and Reconciliation Commission, 2000; Howarth and Norval, 1998; Seekings and Nattrass, 2006.

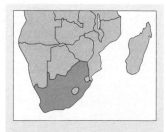

COUNTRY FACT FILE

SOUTH AFRICA

Population	49.01 million
Per capita GDP	$10,100
Life expectancy	60.4
Adult literacy	88.0
Key languages	IsiZulu 23.8%, IsiXhosa 17.6%, Afrikaans 13.3%, Sepedi 9.4%
Key religions	Zion Christian 11.1%, Pentecostal/ Charismatic 8.2%, Catholic 7.1%, Methodist 6.8%
Key city	Pretoria
Human development index	0.597 (110th, 2010)

Stratification at work: the cases of Japan and Russia

Stratification in Japan

Social stratification in Japan mixes the traditional and the contemporary. Japan is at once the world's oldest continuously operating monarchy and a modern society in which wealth follows individual achievement.

Feudal Japan

As early as the fifth century CE, Japan was an agrarian society with a rigid caste system composed of nobles and commoners and ruled by an 'imperial family'. Despite the people's belief that the emperor ruled by divine right, limited government organisation forced the emperor to delegate much authority to a network of regional nobles or *shoguns*.

Below the nobility stood the *samurai*, or warrior caste. The word *samurai* means 'to serve', indicating that this second rank of Japanese society comprised soldiers who cultivated elaborate martial skills and pledged their loyalty to the nobility. To set themselves off from the rest of the commoners, the *samurai* dressed and behaved according to a traditional code of honour.

As in Great Britain, the majority of people in Japan at this time were commoners who laboured to eke out a bare subsistence. Unlike their European counterparts, however, Japanese commoners were not the lowest in rank. The *burakumin*, or 'outcasts', stood further down in that country's hierarchy, shunned by lord and commoner alike. Much like the lowest caste groups in India, 'outcasts' lived apart from others, engaged in the most distasteful occupations and, like everyone else, had no opportunity to change their standing.

Modern Japan

Important changes in nineteenth-century Japan – industrialisation, the growth of cities and the opening of Japanese society to outside influences – combined to weaken the traditional caste structure. In 1871, the Japanese legally banned the social category of 'outcast', though even today people look down on women and men who trace their lineage to this rank. After Japan's defeat in the Second World War, the nobility, too, lost legal standing, and, as the years have passed, fewer and fewer Japanese accept the notion that their emperor rules by divine right.

Thus social stratification in contemporary Japan is a far cry from the rigid caste system in force centuries ago. Analysts describe the modern-day Japanese population in terms of social gradations, including 'upper', 'upper-middle', 'lower-middle' and 'lower'. But since classes have no firm boundaries, they disagree about what proportion of the population falls in each.

Today's Japanese class system also reveals this nation's fascinating ability to weave together tradition and modernity. Because many Japanese people revere the past, family background is never far from the surface in assessing someone's social standing. Therefore, despite legal reforms that ensure that everyone is of equal standing before the law and a modern culture that stresses individual achievement, the Japanese continue to perceive each other through the centuries-old lens of caste.

This dynamic mix echoes from the university campus to the corporate boardroom. The most prestigious universities – now gateways to success in the industrial world – admit students with outstanding scores on rigorous entrance examinations. Even so, the highest achievers and business leaders in Japan are products of privilege, with noble or *samurai* background. At the other extreme, 'outcasts' continue to live in isolated communities cut off from opportunities to better themselves.

Finally, traditional ideas about gender still shape Japanese society. Despite legal reforms that confer formal equality on the sexes, women are clearly subordinate to men in most important respects. Japanese parents are more likely to push sons than daughters towards university and the nation thus retains a significant 'gender gap' in education. As a consequence, women predominate in lower-level support positions in the corporate world, only rarely assuming leadership roles. In this sense, too, individual achievement in Japan's modern class system operates in the shadow of centuries of traditional privileges.

Class in the Russian Federation

The Russian Federation, which rivalled the USA as a superpower while it existed as the Soviet Union, was born out of revolution in 1917. The feudal system, ruled by a hereditary nobility, came to an abrupt end as the Russian revolution transferred most farms, factories and other productive property from private ownership to state control.

A classless society?

This transformation was guided by the ideas of Karl Marx, who argued that private ownership of productive property was the basis of social classes (see Chapter 4). As the state gained control of the

PUBLIC SOCIOLOGY

The Spirit Level

Richard Wilkinson and Kate Pickett are researchers with a cause. Their book *The Spirit Level* became an academic best-seller in 2009. Their research claims that inequality is socially divisive, and that inequality is the most important explanation of the prevalence of poor health and a wide range of social problems across the world. Drawing on data from the United Nations, the World Bank, the World Health Organization and the US Census, they argue that inequality causes shorter, unhealthier and unhappier lives; it increases the rate of teenage pregnancy, violence, obesity, imprisonment and addiction; and it weakens relationships. They look at research from many countries around the world and conclude that what matters in our healthy lives is where we stand in relation to others. Simply being poor is not the issue; what matters is our relative position in the society.

The USA, for example, has 'the highest homicide rates, the highest teenage pregnancy rate, comes in 28th in the league of life expectancy *and* it has the biggest income differences'. In contrast, Japan, Sweden and Norway, with much lower inequalities, also seem to have many fewer social problems. Aware that this is a simple correlation and not necessarily a cause (see p. 70), the authors spend some time developing a theory that links these facts together. For more, see: the Equality Trust at www.equalitytrust.org.uk, which includes a three-minute animated film.

See also Wilkinson's online paper, 'What difference does *inequality* make?', www.thpc. scot.nhs.uk/Presentations/ Wellbeing/Wilkinson.pdf, and Chapter 21 of this book, p. 731.

economy, Soviet officials claimed that they had engineered a remarkable achievement: humanity's first classless society.

Analysts outside the Soviet Union were sceptical about this claim of classlessness. The occupations of the people in the former Soviet Union, they pointed out, clustered into a four-level hierarchy. At the top were high government officials, or *apparatchiks*. Next came the Soviet intelligentsia, including lower government officials, university lecturers, scientists, physicians and engineers. Below them stood the manual workers and, in the lowest stratum, the rural peasantry.

Since people in each of these categories enjoyed very different living standards, the former Soviet Union was never classless in the sense of having no social inequality. But one can say, more modestly, that placing factories, farms, colleges and hospitals under state control did rein in economic inequality (although not necessarily differences of power) compared to capitalist societies such as the members of the European Union.

The 1917 Russian Revolution radically recast the society as prescribed by Karl Marx (and revolutionary Russian leader Vladimir Lenin). Then in the 1980s, the Soviet Union underwent another sweeping transformation. Economic reforms accelerated when Mikhail Gorbachev came on the scene in 1985. His economic programme, popularly known as *perestroika*, meaning 'restructuring', sought to solve a dire problem: while the Soviet system had succeeded in minimising economic inequality, everyone was relatively poor and living standards lagged far behind those of other industrial nations. Simply put, Gorbachev hoped to stimulate economic expansion by reducing inefficient centralised control of the economy.

Gorbachev's reforms soon escalated into one of the most dramatic social movements in history, as popular uprisings toppled one socialist government after another throughout eastern Europe and, ultimately, brought down the Soviet system itself. In essence, people blamed their economic plight as well as their lack of basic freedoms on a repressive ruling class of Communist Party officials.

From the Soviet Union's founding in 1917 until its demise in 1991, the Communist Party retained a monopoly of power. Near the end, 18 million party members (6 per cent of the Soviet people) still made all the decisions about Soviet life while enjoying privileges such as vacation homes, chauffeured cars and access to prized consumer goods and elite education for their children (Theen, 1984). The second Russian revolution, then, mirrors the first in that it was nothing less than the overthrow of the ruling class.

The transformation of the Soviet Union into the Russian Federation demonstrates that social inequality involves more than economic resources. Soviet society lacked the income disparity typical of European states and the United States. But elite standing in the former Soviet Union was based on power rather than wealth. Thus, even though Mikhail Gorbachev and Boris Yeltsin earned far less than a US president, they wielded great power.

And what about social mobility in Russia? Evidence indicates that during the twentieth century there was more upward social mobility in the Soviet Union than in Great Britain, Japan or the United States. Why? For one thing, Soviet society lacked the concentrated wealth that families elsewhere pass from one generation to the next. Even more important, industrialisation and rapid bureaucratisation during the twentieth century pushed a large proportion of the working class and rural peasantry upwards to occupations in industry and government. Nevertheless, this pattern has begun to change as dynasties, sometimes linked with organised crime, have formed in Russia in the last few years.

Now, with new laws sanctioning individual ownership of private property and business, some experts monitoring the changing Russian scene predict further structural social mobility along with greater economic inequality. Professionals and businessmen are being pushed aside by officials and representatives of the bureaucratic structures. Today, about a third of the country's revenues, according to Rosstat (Russia's Federal Statistic Service), are distributed to the country's richest 10 per cent of the population, and the country's poorest 10 per cent get only 1.9 per cent of total revenues.

Often, as the Russian experience attests, widespread societal changes affect people's individual social standing in a process sociologists call **structural social mobility**, a *shift in the social position of large numbers of people due more to changes in society itself than to individual efforts.* Half a century ago, industrialisation in the Soviet Union created a vast number of new factory jobs that drew rural people to cities. Similarly, the growth of bureaucracy propelled countless Soviet citizens from ploughing to paperwork. Now, with new laws sanctioning individual ownership of private property and business, some experts monitoring the changing Russian scene predict further structural social mobility along with greater economic inequality. But, equal or not, everyone hopes to enjoy a higher standard of living.

THINKERS & THEORY

Pierre Bourdieu: reproducing inequalities and dominance

Pierre Bourdieu (1930–2002)
Source: © Nogues Alain/Corbis Sygma.

For many, Pierre Bourdieu (1930–2002), a French sociologist, is considered to be one of 'the greatest sociologists of our era' (Burawoy). Although he produced at least 35 books on topics as diverse as sport, art, culture, education, photography, peasants and masculinity, he is most noted for his contribution to the study of inequality and class. His major concern was with unmasking the way domination works (what he called 'symbolic violence'). He was puzzled by the fact that whilst people live in massively unequal systems, they usually seem to come to accept them and take them for granted. He asked: how do systems of privilege, dominance and hierarchy reproduce themselves across generations – without much resistance from those below? At the heart of his work are four core ideas: *symbolic dominance and violence*, *capital*, *fields* and *habitus*. These are hard to define but briefly:

- *Symbolic dominance* means the exercise of dominance through culture and its mystification. Symbols and meanings organise our life and much class conflict is over these very symbols, languages and meanings.

- *Habitus* refers to our learned social habits: they are relatively permanent and routine ways of life which often shape our life chances. They are learned dispositions which lead people to behave in certain ways.

- *Fields* refers to relatively autonomous spaces in which social relationships get organised. Those relations are often economic, social, cultural and symbolic (but this does not exhaust the type). They are the arenas where competition and conflicts of social life get worked through.

- *Capital* refers to the resources we have to live with. Forms of capital can be exchanged. Bourdieu is most noted for developing a typology of these resources. Economic capital is the most obvious and Marx wrote about it – it refers to our economic resources (wealth, income, work). But there are others as Table 8.2 indicates. Those with high social capital know all the right people; those with cultural capital know all the right things; those with symbolic capital have the right respect.

In Bourdieu's most central and famed book, *Distinction* (1981 originally, 1984 in English), he uses a detailed questionnaire about consumer activities on a large 1960s French sample to investigate cultural tastes. Cultural tastes are enduringly linked to class position and

Table 8.2	Bourdieu's forms of capital	
Form of capital	**Definitions and features**	**How you can recognise it**
Economic capital	Ownership of wealth (and means of production)	Wealth, income, property
Social capital	Membership and involvement in social networks and the 'unceasing effort of sociability'	Good connections
		Networking
		Patronage – who you know
Cultural capital	Gained through family and education	Educational credentials
		Knowledge of arts and culture
Symbolic capital	Prestige, status and social honour	Reputation, respect

THINKERS & THEORY

capture the profound sense of social difference and distance we often feel when faced with different cultures. In particular, he is concerned with our tastes for particular music (whether popular or classical, for instance), foods, art and so forth, and with the ways items may move into and out of our scale of tastes. These can all be seen as *ways of maintaining social distance and reproducing class relations*. Each family teaches its children a certain cultural capital and a certain ethos. Starting in the pre-school years, children have different access to cultural capital. For instance, children taken by parents around the world have experiences of many different cultures with their different languages, manners, foods, arts and etiquettes. They build up experiences of travel, diversity and languages which other children may never know. Cultural capital, then, is much more than formal education; it is found often in personalities who 'know things', about art or food or films or history – who have a stock of cultural knowledge. Different tastes are cultivated in different groups – it all depends upon the groups you hang around with. It is found in the reproduction of everyday life.

We will encounter Bordieu in several places in this book. His ideas have been 'used' by many contemporary sociologists, but he is not always easy to understand. There are many guides to him: try Richard Jenkins, *Pierre Bourdieu* (revised edition, 2002).

The persistence of inequalities in social life

Looking around the world at the extent of social inequality, we might wonder how societies persist without distributing their resources more equally. Caste-like systems in early Great Britain and Japan lasted for centuries, concentrating land and power in the hands of several hundred families. Even more striking, for 2,000 years most people in India accepted the idea that they should be privileged or poor because of the accident of birth. Many still do today. As we shall see in this section of the book, today class systems pervade the world; and in many countries, the majority of their populations still live in abject poverty. Women often live in fear of violence. Ethnic minorities everywhere are discriminated against. Everywhere one looks throughout the world, we find inequalities and stratification.

As Ken Plummer has commented elsewhere:

The history of human societies can well be read as a history of billions of people going quietly to their graves with lives of almost unspeakable suffering delivered upon them from the raging inequalities of the differences given to them by the society where they were born . . . There are always it seems the rich and the poor, the slave owner and the slave, the black and the white, the migrant and the host, the educated and the ignorant, the diseased and the healthy, the man and the woman, the gay and the straight, the able and the disabled, the terrorist and the terrorised, the pathological and the normal, us and them – indeed the good, the bad and the ugly. And sociology cannot fail to see this. In human societies, differences are used as moral markers to establish how some are better than others. Moral worth is often attached to this labeling as boundaries are established of the normal and the pathological. The elite are superior; the mass are downcast. Borders become hierarchically arranged and a ranking or pecking order is established: outsiders, underclasses, dangerous people, marginals, outcasts – the scapegoats – are invented. And sociologists ask: just how are these 'outsiders' and ranking orders created, maintained and changed? This is the problem of social exclusion, the social other; and social stratification.

(Plummer 2010: 153–5)

The question we have to ask here is just why human beings have managed to sustain such systems over long periods of history. Typically, sociologists suggest four broad and interconnected answers.

1 Ideology

A first broad explanation suggests the significance of **ideology**: *cultural beliefs that serve to legitimate key interests and hence justify social stratification*. Any beliefs – for example, the claim that the rich are clever while the poor are lazy – are ideological to the extent that they bolster the dominance of wealthy elites and suggest that poor people deserve their plight. A millennium ago, a rigid estate system in Europe rested on church teachings that such arrangements reflected the will of

God. More specifically, the church endorsed as divinely sanctioned a system by which most people laboured as serfs, driving the feudal economy with their muscles. According to the church, nobility was charged with responsibility for defending the realm and maintaining public order. To question this system meant challenging the church and, ultimately, defying God. The religious justification that supported the medieval estate system for centuries is expressed in the following stanza from the nineteenth-century English hymn 'All Things Bright and Beautiful':

> The rich man in his castle,
> The poor man at his gate,
> He made them high and lowly
> And ordered their estate.

The Industrial Revolution opened the way for newly rich industrialists to topple the feudal nobility. In the process, industrial culture advanced a new ideology. Capitalists mocked the centuries-old notion that social hierarchy should depend on the accident of birth. Under God's law, the new thinking went, the most talented and hard-working individuals should dominate society. The rise of industrial capitalism transformed wealth and power into prizes won by those who display the greatest talent and effort. Class systems celebrate individualism and achievement, so that social standing serves as a measure of personal worthiness. Thus poverty, which called for charity under feudalism, became under industrial capitalism a scorned state of personal inadequacy. The same thinking recast the poor from objects of charity into unworthy people lacking ability and ambition. The ideological shift from birth to individual achievement as the basis of social inequality was well established by the time early nineteenth-century German writer Johann Wolfgang von Goethe quipped:

> Really to own
> What you inherit,
> You first must earn it
> With your merit.

Clearly, medieval and modern justifications for inequality differ dramatically: what an earlier era viewed as fair, a later one rejected as wrong. Yet both cases illustrate the pivotal role of ideology – cultural beliefs that define a particular kind of hierarchy as fair and natural. Justifications for social stratification, then, are culturally variable across history and from place to place.

More recently, the social geographer Danny Dorling has mapped out some of our contemporary ideologies in detail (Dorling 2010). Amongst the key ideological themes which prop up systems of inequality are the views that:

1. *Elitism is efficient.* For example, children and adults are divided into types and their education is funded differently. Glittering prizes are awarded for the best because they are the best. Behind this lurk ideas about IQ potential, genius children and the genetic foundations (superiority) of elite groups.

2. *Exclusion is necessary.* For example, the exclusions of certain groups in societies (typically 20 per cent of society or so – the foreigners, scroungers, criminals, etc.) can always be justified as necessary in protecting the lifestyles and wishes of the majority. Prisons, for example, can become major dumping grounds; cities can develop 'no-go' areas.

3. *Prejudice against 'the lower orders' is natural*: suspicions against immigrants, the feckless poor, security scroungers, etc. are justifiable.

4. *Greed is good:* wanting to make a lot of money is a good thing and ruthlessness is even encouraged (as seen in the current success of the television programme *The Apprentice*).

As these ideas circulate and reproduce themselves widely in contemporary culture, so we become unknowingly immersed in a culture where inequalities become widened, deepened and acceptable. At the heart of each of these statements, Dorling claims, is a justification of the perpetuation of inequalities.

2 Habitualisation

A second explanation of the perpetuation of inequalities highlights the habitualisation of inequalities in everyday life. This is a central idea of Bourdieu, as discussed in the box. For him, cultural reproduction does not involve the reproduction of the culture of all segments of society, only that of the dominant classes. People in each class transmit a distinctive 'habitus' (classifications, perceptions, ways of talking, moving and generally carrying oneself) down the generations, but schools pick up only on the habitus of the most powerful classes. He argues that the educational system has systematic biases against working-class knowledge and skills. Bourdieu observed underlying patterns of class domination in education, art and 'culture' generally. He suggested that the primary roles of education are **social reproduction**, *the maintenance of power and privilege between social classes from one generation to the next*, and **cultural reproduction**, *the process by which a society transmits dominant knowledge from one generation to another.*

A research measure for inequality: the Gini coefficient

This is the most popular of several measures of inequality because it provides a simple single summary statistic to show a pattern of income distribution. In a fully equal society, the poorest 25 per cent would earn 25 per cent of the total income, the poorest 50 per cent would receive 50 per cent of the total income – and so on. In an unequal society like ours, the richer groups earn as much as 80 per cent of the total income, whilst the poorest 25 per cent may earn as little as 1 or 2 per cent. These discrepancies are measured by the Gini coefficent. This measures incomes for different groups in a society and then matches them with an ideal 'equal pattern' like above. A rank can then be provided so that we can compare societies or groups on how 'equal' their income distribution is. Having a Gini coefficient value of 0.00 indicates that each household has the same income; a coefficient of 1.00 indicates perfect inequality. This measure is used in Wilkinson's study (see Public sociology, p. 261).

3 Subjugation

A third explanation suggests that the subjection of many subordinate groups makes them too downtrodden to challenge the dominant orders. Truly poor and socially excluded people often lack the power and resources to challenge the existing social order. They have to bear the burdens of the poor, which ill equips them for change and action. Economic deprivation defines their existence and leaves a mark. Marx, of course, believed that these exploited groups would become the revolutionary challenge; that they would rise up against their rulers. But he overlooked just how weak and disempowered such groups generally become. At the very least, as we shall see, outcast groups may also be more likely to suffer from illness, physical and mental.

4 Coercion and violence

A final but major explanation suggests the role of coercion, power and violence: we should not overlook the coercive power of ruling groups. Ultimately, elites have a lot at stake – a lot to lose – and one way or another they play a key role in regulating the poor through armed forces, police and prisons. The ultimate regulation of the unequal order is the power of the coercive state (more on this in Chapter 16).

Explaining social stratification

Why are societies stratified at all? In the next few sections we look at a few rival theories – one which suggests stratification may be functional; another which claims that societies work through exploitation and conflict; and a third – Weberian – which sees stratification as multidimensional. There are others.

1 Stratification as functional

One answer, consistent with the functional perspective, is that social inequality plays a vital part in the operation of all societies. It is, so to speak, 'needed'. Over 50 years ago, Kingsley Davis and Wilbert Moore (1945) set out such an argument by asserting that social stratification has beneficial consequences for the operation of a society. How else, asked Davis and Moore, can we explain the fact that some form of social stratification has been found everywhere? Davis and Moore described our society as a complex system involving hundreds of occupational positions of varying importance. Certain jobs – say, changing spark plugs in a car – are fairly easy and can be performed by almost anyone. Other jobs, such as transplanting a human organ, are quite difficult and demand the scarce talents of people who have received extensive (and expensive) education. Positions of high day-to-day responsibility that demand special abilities are the most functionally significant.

In general, Davis and Moore explained, the greater the functional importance of a position, the more rewards a society will attach to it. This strategy pays off, since rewarding important work with income, prestige, power and leisure encourages people to do these things. In effect, by distributing resources unequally, a society motivates each person to aspire to the most significant work possible, and to work better, harder and longer. The overall effect of a social system of unequal rewards – which is what social stratification amounts to – is a more productive society.

Davis and Moore conceded that every society could be egalitarian. But, they cautioned, rewards could be equal only to the extent that people were willing to let *anyone* perform *any* job. Equality also demands that someone who carries out a job poorly be rewarded on a par with another who performs well. Logic dictates that such a system offers little incentive for people to make their best efforts, and thereby reduces a society's productive efficiency.

Meritocracy

The Davis–Moore thesis implies that a productive society is a **meritocracy**, *a system of social stratification based on personal merit*. Such societies hold out rewards to develop the talents and encourage the efforts of everyone. In pursuit of meritocracy, a society promotes equality of opportunity while, at the same time, mandating inequality of rewards. In other words, a pure class system would be a meritocracy, rewarding everyone based on ability and effort. In addition, such a society would have extensive social mobility, blurring social categories as individuals move up or down in the social system depending on their performance.

For their part, caste societies can speak of 'merit' (from Latin, meaning 'worthy of praise') only in terms of persistence in low-skill labour such as farming. Caste systems, in short, offer honour to those who remain dutifully 'in their place'.

Although caste systems waste human potential, they are quite orderly. And herein lies a clue to an important question: why do modern industrial societies resist becoming pure meritocracies by retaining many caste-like qualities? Simply because, left unchecked, meritocracy erodes social structure such as kinship. No one, for example, evaluates family members solely on the basis of performance. Class systems in industrial societies, therefore, retain some caste elements to promote order and social cohesion.

Critical comment

The Davis–Moore thesis is a conservative one (as most functional arguments are). While Davis and Moore pointed out that *some* form of stratification exists everywhere, they could not explain why these systems can be so very different – from harsh and rigid ones, to much more flexible ones. Nor did Davis and Moore specify precisely what reward should be attached to any occupational position. They merely pointed out that positions a society deems crucial must yield sufficient rewards to draw talent away from less

important work. Can we even measure functional importance? Surgeons may perform a valuable service in saving lives, but a related profession, nursing, is vastly less well paid. Many popular footballers, pop singers and 'stars' can earn more in a few nights than most primary school teachers and childminders earn in their working lives – and the latter are responsible for raising the next generation!

Further, the Davis–Moore thesis exaggerates social stratification's role in developing individual talent. Our society does reward individual achievement, but we also allow families to transfer wealth and power from generation to generation in caste-like fashion. Additionally, for women, ethnic groups, the disabled and others with limited opportunities, stratification still raises barriers to personal accomplishment. Social stratification functions to develop some people's abilities to the fullest while barring others from ever reaching their potential.

Thirdly, by contending that social stratification benefits all of society, the Davis–Moore thesis ignores how social inequality promotes conflict and, sometimes, even outright revolution. This assertion leads us to the social-conflict paradigm, which provides a very different explanation for the persistence of social hierarchy (Tumin, 1953).

2 Marxist and neo-Marxist ideas on stratification and conflict

Conflict analysis argues that, rather than benefit society as a whole, social stratification provides major advantages to some people at the expense of others. This theoretical perspective draws heavily on the ideas of Karl Marx (whose approach to understanding social inequality was introduced in Chapter 4).

Writing (with Engels) in the original manifesto of the Communist Party (1848), Marx identified two major social classes corresponding to the two basic relationships to the means of production: individuals either (1) own productive property or (2) labour for others. In medieval Europe, the nobility and the church owned the productive land; peasants toiled as farmers. Similarly, in industrial class systems, the capitalists (or the *bourgeoisie*) own and operate factories, which utilise the labour of workers (the *proletariat*). Figure 4.3 on p. 120 suggests that these polarities occur throughout history.

Marx noted great differences in wealth and power arising from the industrial–capitalist productive system, which, he contended, made class conflict inevitable. In time, he believed, oppression and misery would drive the working majority to organise and, ultimately, to overthrow capitalism. A process would take place in which the poorer classes would become more pauperised, polarised and aware of their class position. This would lead to a class consciousness of their true economic exploitation.

Marx's analysis was grounded in his observations of capitalism in the nineteenth century, when great industrialists dominated the economic scene. In North America, for example, Andrew Carnegie, J. P. Morgan and John Jacob Astor (one of the few very rich passengers to perish on the *Titanic*) lived in fabulous mansions filled with priceless art and staffed by dozens of servants. According to Marx, the capitalist elite draws its strength from more than the operation of the economy. He noted that, through the family, opportunity and wealth are passed down from generation to generation. Moreover, the legal system defends this practice through inheritance law. Similarly, exclusive schools bring children of the elite together, encouraging informal social ties that will benefit them throughout their lives. Overall, from Marx's point of view, capitalist society *reproduces the class structure in each new generation*.

Critical comment

Exploring how the capitalist economic system generates conflict between classes, Marx's analysis of social stratification has had enormous influence on sociological thinking in recent decades. Because it is revolutionary – calling for the overthrow of capitalist society – Marxism is also highly controversial.

One of the strongest criticisms of the Marxist approach is that it denies one of the central tenets of the Davis–Moore thesis: that motivating people to perform various social roles requires some system of unequal rewards. Marx separated reward from performance, endorsing an egalitarian system based on the principle of 'from each according to ability; to each according to need' (1972: 388; orig. 1845). Critics argue that severing rewards from performance is precisely the flaw that generated the low productivity characteristic of the former Soviet Union and other socialist economies around the world.

Defenders of Marx rebut this line of attack by pointing to considerable evidence supporting Marx's general view of humanity as inherently social rather than unflinchingly selfish. They counter that we should not assume that individual rewards (much less monetary compensation alone) are the only way to motivate people to perform their social roles. Table 8.3 compares the functional and conflict paradigms.

In addition, although few doubt that capitalist society does perpetuate poverty and privilege, as Marx asserted, the revolutionary developments that he considered inevitable have failed to materialise. The next section explores why the socialist revolution that Marx predicted and promoted has not occurred, at least in advanced capitalist societies.

Table 8.3	Two explanations of social stratification: a summary
Functional paradigm	**Conflict paradigm**
Social stratification keeps society operating.	Social stratification is the result of social conflict.
The linkage of greater rewards to more important social positions benefits society as a whole.	Differences in social resources serve the interests of some and harm the interests of others.
Social stratification encourages a matching of talents and abilities to appropriate positions	Social stratification ensures that much talent and ability within society will not be utilised at all.
Social stratification is both useful and inevitable.	Social stratification is useful to only some people; it is not inevitable.
The values and beliefs that legitimise social inequality are widely shared throughout society.	Values and beliefs tend to be ideological; they reflect the interests of the more powerful members of society.
Because systems of social stratification are useful to society as a whole and are supported by cultural values and beliefs, they are usually stable over time.	Because systems of social stratification reflect the interests of only part of society, they are unlikely to remain stable over time.

Source: Adapted in part from Stinchcombe, 1963: 808.

Why no Marxist revolution?

Despite Marx's prediction, capitalism is still thriving. Why have workers in the UK and other industrial societies not overthrown capitalism? Some while ago, Ralf Dahrendorf (1959) pointed to four reasons:

1 *The fragmentation of the capitalist class.* The 120 years since Marx's death have witnessed the fragmentation of the capitalist class in Europe. A century ago, *single families* typically owned large companies; today, *numerous stockholders* fill that position. The diffusion of ownership has also stimulated the emergence of a managerial class, who may or may not be major stockholders (Wright, 1985; Wright et al., 1992). We will find more evidence of this in the next chapter (see Scott, 1991).

2 *White-collar work and a rising standard of living.* A 'white-collar revolution' has transformed Marx's industrial proletariat. As Chapter 15 details, the majority of workers in Marx's time laboured either on farms or in factories. They had **blue-collar or manual occupations**, *lower-prestige jobs involving mostly manual labour*. By contrast, most workers today hold **white-collar occupations**, *higher-prestige work involving mostly mental activity*. These occupations include positions in sales, management and other service work, frequently in large, bureaucratic organisations.

While many of today's white-collar workers perform repetitive tasks like the industrial workers known to Marx, evidence indicates that most do not think of themselves in those terms. Rather, most white-collar workers now perceive their social positions as higher than those of their blue-collar parents and grandparents. One key reason is that workers' overall standard of living in Europe rose fourfold over the course of the twentieth century, even as the working week decreased. As a result of a rising tide of social mobility, society seems less sharply divided between rich and poor than it did to people during Marx's lifetime (Wright and Martin, 1987).

3 *More extensive worker organisation.* Employees have organisational strengths that they lacked a century ago. Workers have won the right to organise into trade unions that can and do make demands of management backed by threats of 'working to rule' and strikes. Although union membership started to decline seriously in the 1980s, research suggests that well-established unions can still enhance the economic standing of the workers they represent.

Further, today's negotiations between labour and management are typically institutionalised and peaceful, a picture quite different from the often-violent confrontations common before the mid-twentieth century.

4 *More extensive legal protections.* Since Marx's death, the government has extended laws to protect workers' rights and has given workers greater access to the courts for redressing grievances. Government programmes such as National Insurance, health and safety, disability protection and social security also provide workers with substantially greater security and financial resources than the capitalists of the nineteenth century were willing to grant them.

Taken together, these four developments mean that, despite persistent stratification, many societies have smoothed out some of capitalism's rough edges. Consequently, social conflict today may be less intense than it was a century ago.

We could also add that Marx's time was starting to see the growth of the mass press, but he could hardly have foreseen the major escalation in all media forms. As Chapter 22 will suggest, we increasingly live our lives in a 'mediated society' where the media infuses all we do. Of course, some of this adopts a critical and reflective stance. But the growth of pop music, mass film, television, gameboys, computer games and the like can mean that we have started to 'amuse ourselves to death' (Postman, 1986). As we have become media-saturated with entertainment, so many people have lost the critical edge for thinking about the nature of their class position.

The critical case

Many sociologists continue to find value in Marx's analysis, often in modified form (Miliband, 1969; Domhoff, 1983; Stephens, 1986). They respond with their own set of five key points, defending Marx's critical analysis of capitalism but suggesting ways in which it needs to be modified over a hundred years later.

1 *Wealth remains highly concentrated and inequalities have increased.* Capitalism remains an extensively exploitative system with wealth in the hands of the few. In Europe, about half of all privately controlled corporate stock is owned by just 1 per cent of individuals, who persist as a capitalist class. Why does such extreme inequality continue to grow?

2 *The global system of capitalism.* Tellingly, much of the production of goods in the twenty-first century

has shifted from the high-income countries to low-income countries. As we will see in the next chapter, it is in these low-income countries that workers can be paid very little for their labour. The sweatshops of nineteenth-century England are now, literally, 'the sweatshops of the world'. Marx's model may still hold for societies once the global dimension is taken into consideration.

3 *Work remains degrading and dehumanising.* Not only has the white-collar revolution delivered little in the way of higher income, but also much white-collar work remains monotonous and routine, especially the low-level clerical jobs commonly held by women. But many new jobs have arrived which are temporary, low paid and lacking a career structure (see Chapter 15, pp. 513–17).

4 *Labour activity has been weakened.* Trade unions may have advanced the interests of the workers during the earlier twentieth century, and regular negotiation between workers and management may now be a frequent activity. Many of the concessions won by workers in the past came about precisely through the class conflict that Marx described. But by the late twentieth century, union activity had been weakened and much labour throughout the world in now non-unionised (see Chapter 15, p. 516).

5 *The law still favours the rich.* Workers have gained some legal protections over the course of the twentieth century. Even so, the law still defends the overall distribution of wealth in Europe. Just as important, 'average' people cannot use the legal system to the same advantage as the rich do.

3 Max Weber: class, status and power

Max Weber, whose approach to social analysis is described in Chapter 4, agreed with Karl Marx that social stratification sparks social conflict, but differed from Marx in several important respects. Weber considered Marx's model of two social classes too simple. Instead, he viewed social stratification as a more complex interplay of three distinct dimensions. First is economic inequality – the issue so vital to Marx – which Weber termed 'class position'. Weber's use of 'class' refers not to crude categories but to a continuum on which anyone can be ranked from high to low. A second continuum, *status*, measures

social prestige. Finally, Weber noted the importance of *power* as a third dimension of social hierarchy.

The socioeconomic status hierarchy

Marx believed that social prestige and power derived from economic position; thus he saw no reason to treat them as distinct dimensions of social inequality. Weber disagreed, recognising that stratification in industrial societies has characteristically low status consistency. An individual, Weber pointed out, might have high standing on one dimension of inequality but a lower position on another. For example, bureaucratic officials might wield considerable power yet have little wealth or social prestige.

So while Marx viewed inequality in terms of two clearly defined classes, Weber saw something more subtle at work in the stratification of industrial societies. Weber's key contribution in this area, then, lies in identifying the multidimensional nature of social rankings. Sociologists often use the term **socioeconomic status** (SES) to refer to *a composite ranking based on various dimensions of social inequality.*

A population that varies widely in class, status and power – Weber's three dimensions of inequality – creates a virtually infinite array of social categories, all of which pursue their own interests. Thus, unlike Marx, who focused on conflict between two overarching classes, Weber considered social conflict as highly variable and complex.

Inequality in history

Weber also made a key historical observation, noting that each of his three dimensions of social inequality stands out at a different point in the evolution of human societies. Agrarian societies, he maintained, emphasise status or social prestige, typically in the form of honour or symbolic purity. Members of these societies gain such status by conforming to cultural norms corresponding to their rank.

Industrialisation and the development of capitalism level traditional rankings based on birth, but generate striking material differences in the population. Thus, Weber argued, the crucial difference among people in industrial–capitalist societies lies in the economic dimension of class.

In time, industrial societies witness a surging growth of the bureaucratic state. This expansion of government, coupled with the proliferation of other types of formal organisation, brings power to the fore in the stratification system. Power is also central to the organisation of socialist societies, as we see in their extensive government regulation of many aspects of life. The elite members of such societies are mostly high-ranking officials rather than rich people.

This historical analysis underlies a final disagreement between Weber and Marx. Looking to the future, Marx believed that social stratification could be largely eliminated by abolishing private ownership of productive property. Weber doubted that overthrowing capitalism would significantly diminish social stratification in modern societies. While doing so might lessen economic disparity, Weber reasoned, the significance of power based on organisational position would only increase. In fact, Weber imagined, a socialist revolution might well *increase* social inequality by expanding government and concentrating power in the hands of a political elite. Recent popular uprisings against entrenched bureaucracies in eastern Europe and the former Soviet Union lend support to Weber's argument.

Critical comment

Weber's multidimensional analysis of social stratification retains enormous influence among sociologists, especially in Europe. Some analysts (particularly those influenced by Marx's ideas) argue that while social class boundaries have blurred, striking patterns of social inequality persist in the industrial world.

As we shall see in Chapter 10, the enormous wealth of the most privileged members of our society contrasts sharply with the grinding poverty of millions who barely meet their day-to-day needs. Moreover, the upward social mobility that historically fuelled optimism in this country all but came to a halt in the 1970s, and evidence points to an increase in economic inequality during the 1980s. Against this backdrop of economic polarisation, the 1990s were marked by a renewed emphasis on 'classes' in conflict rather than on the subtle shadings of a 'multidimensional hierarchy'.

PUBLIC SOCIOLOGY

Inequalities and The Equality Act 2010

Inequalities cover a wide range of social life and, in the contemporary world, some governments have been concerned about the problems it raises. As sociologists have mapped out the intersecting grounds of inequalities (Table 8.1 on p. 253), so some governments have tried to take seriously the idea of inequality in legislation. In 2010, the then Labour government in the UK passed a major new piece of legislation called The Equality Act. Bringing together the majority of existing equality laws, it also aimed to increase protection for minority groups and victims of discrimination by strengthening the law in some areas. (It is estimated that 90–95 per cent of the new legislation simply consolidates previous legislation.)

Previously, each area of social division, such as class, race and gender, had its own separate legislation and support organisation (such as the Race Equality Commission, disbanded in 2007). Now all the various forms of discrimination have been brought together under the heading 'protected characteristics'. Here the issues of age, disability (which includes mental health and people diagnosed as clinically obese), race, religion or belief, sex, sexual orientation, gender reassignment (people who are having or who have had a sex change, transvestites and transgender people), marriage and civil partnership, and pregnancy and maternity are all brought together in one Act. Seven different types of discrimination are included: from direct discrimination and victimisation to harassment and 'associative discrimination'. This latter category is discrimination against someone because they

are associated with another person with a protected characteristic – such as carers of disabled people and elderly relatives, who can claim they were treated unfairly because of duties that they had to carry out at home relating to their care work. It also covers discrimination against someone because, for example, their partner is from another country.

Age is still the only protected characteristic by which you can justify direct discrimination, because you can argue that treating someone differently because of their age is necessary to meet a legitimate aim. You can also still have a default retirement age of 65 (unless/ until the retirement age legislation changes, which it may do in the coming years).

 Full details of this new legislation can be found at: www.legislation.gov.uk/ uksi/2010/2317/pdfs/uksi_20102317 _en.pdf and a summary at: www.equalities.gov.uk/equality_bill.aspx.

Pedestrian passing a beggar and children, Durban, South Africa
Source: © David Turnley/Corbis.

Inequality theory as normative theory?

This chapter's explanations of social stratification also involve value judgements. The Davis–Moore thesis, which cites universal social stratification, interprets this pattern as evidence that inequality is a necessary element of social organisation. Class differences, then, reflect both variation in human abilities and the importance of occupational roles. From this point of view, the spectre of equality is a threat to a society of diverse people, since such uniformity could exist only as the product of the relentless and stifling efforts of officials like Vonnegut's fictitious 'Handicapper General' (see the *Big debate*, p. 277).

The conflict theory of Marx interprets universal social inequality in a very different way. Rejecting the notion that inequality is in any sense necessary, Marx condemned social hierarchy as a product of greed and exploitation. Guided by egalitarian values, he advocated social arrangements that would enable everyone to share all important resources equally. Rather than undermining the quality of life, Marx maintained that equality would enhance human well-being.

Everyday wealth? A man with a mobile phone and laptop on a tropical beach
Source: © Strauss/Curtis/Corbis.

Stratification and technology in global perspective

We can weave together a number of observations made in this chapter by considering the relationship between a society's technology and its type of social stratification. Gerhard and Jean Lenski's model of sociocultural evolution, detailed in Chapter 4, puts social stratification in historical perspective and also helps us to understand the varying degrees of inequality found around the world today (Nolan and Lenski, 2010).

Hunting and gathering societies

Simple technology limits the production of hunting and gathering societies to only what is necessary for day-to-day living. No doubt some individuals are more successful hunters or gatherers than others, but the group's survival depends on all sharing what they have. With little or no surplus, therefore, no categories of people emerge as better off than others. Thus social stratification among hunters and gatherers, based simply on age and sex, is less complex than among societies with more advanced technology.

Horticultural, pastoral and agrarian societies

Technological advances generate surplus production, while intensifying social inequality. In horticultural and pastoral societies, a small elite controls most of the surplus. Agrarian technology based on large-scale farming generates even greater abundance, but marked inequality means that various categories of people lead strikingly different lives. The social distance between the elite hereditary nobility and the common serfs who work the land looms as large as at any time in human history. In most cases, lords wield god-like power over the masses.

Industrial societies

Industrialisation reverses the historical trend, prompting some decrease in social inequality. The eclipse of tradition and the need to develop individual talents gradually erode caste rankings in favour of greater individual opportunity. Then, too, the increasing productivity of industrial technology steadily raises the living standards of the historically poor majority. Specialised, technical work also demands the expansion of schooling, sharply reducing illiteracy. A literate population, in turn, tends to press for a greater voice in political decision making, further diminishing social inequality. As already noted, continuing technological advances transform much blue-collar labour into higher-prestige white-collar work. All these social shifts help to explain why Marxist revolutions occurred in agrarian societies – such as Russia (1917), Cuba (1959) and Nicaragua (1979) – in which social inequality is most pronounced, rather than in industrial societies, as Marx predicted more than a century ago.

Initially, the great wealth generated by industrialisation is concentrated in the hands of a few – the pattern so troubling to Marx. In time, however, the share of all property in the hands of the very rich declines somewhat. According to estimates, the proportion of all wealth controlled by the richest 1 per cent of US families peaked at about 36 per cent just before the stock market crash in 1929; during the entrepreneurial 1980s, this economic elite owned one-third of all wealth (Williamson and Lindert, 1980; Beeghley, 1989).

Finally, industrialisation diminishes the domination of women by men, a pattern that is strongest in agrarian societies. The movement towards social parity for the sexes derives from the industrial economy's need to cultivate individual talent as well as a growing belief in basic human equality.

The Kuznets curve

The trend described above can be distilled into the following statement. *In human history, technological progress first sharply increases but then moderates the intensity of social stratification.* So if greater inequality is functional for agrarian societies, then industrial societies benefit from a more egalitarian climate. This historical shift, recognised by Nobel Prize-winning economist Simon Kuznets (1966), is illustrated by the Kuznets curve, shown in Figure 8.2.

Current patterns of social inequality around the world generally square with the Kuznets curve. Industrial societies have somewhat less income inequality – one important measure of social stratification – than nations that remain predominantly agrarian. Specifically, mature industrial societies, such as those in the European Union, Australia and the United States, exhibit less income inequality than the less industrialised countries of Latin America, Africa and Asia.

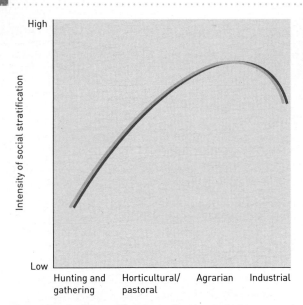

Figure 8.2 Social stratification and technological development: the Kuznets curve

The Kuznets curve reveals that greater technological sophistication is generally accompanied by more pronounced social stratification. The trend reverses itself, however, as industrial societies gradually become more egalitarian. Rigid caste-like distinctions are relaxed in favour of greater opportunity and equality under the law. Political rights are more widely extended, and there is even some levelling of economic differences. The Kuznets curve may also be usefully applied to the relative social standing of the two sexes.

Yet income disparity reflects a host of factors beyond technology, especially political and economic priorities. Societies that have had socialist economic systems (including the People's Republic of China, the Russian Federation and the nations of eastern Europe) display relatively little income inequality. Keep in mind, however, that an allegedly egalitarian society such as the People's Republic of China has an average income level that is quite low by world standards; further, on non-economic dimensions such as political power, China's society reveals pronounced inequality.

And what of the future? Although the global pattern described by the Kuznets curve may be valid, this analysis does not necessarily mean that industrial societies will gradually become less and less stratified. In the abstract, members of our society endorse the principle of equal opportunity for all; even so, this goal has not been and may never become a reality. The notion of social equality, like all concepts related to social stratification, is controversial, as the final section of this chapter explains.

Looking ahead: inequalities, stratification and divisions in the twenty-first century

Social scientists have long taken an interest in inequalities. They seem to have been present in almost all societies throughout all of history, be this through class or caste or slavery, or be it through race or sexuality or gender. Apart, perhaps, from a few very early traditional societies, it is hard not to conclude that the history of society is indeed the history of inequality.

Today, the twenty-first century is no different. Some suggest that inequalities are greater now than ever – and growing. In the long course of history, this seems unlikely. But certainly in recent times, where the measurement of such issues has become a little more reliable, we can find evidence that inequalities have indeed grown.

We can perhaps see the world most basically as split into three kinds of experience. One is that of the truly wealthy and high-status groupings – a few million or so in a world of seven billion, who fly way above most ordinary mortals with incomes that top the GDP of many of the smaller countries, and lifestyles that are hermetically sealed off from the everyday lives of the rest of us. Few sociologists have ever been seriously allowed to enter these worlds, and we know little about them.

Then, at the other extreme, there are a billion or so (somewhere between a fifth and a sixth of the world's population) – one writer calls them 'the bottom billions' – who live on incomes that amount to less than one US dollar a day. They are truly low on most social indicators such as health, literacy, political engagement, access to communications and, of course, wealth. Often homeless and living lives in the most desperate of situations, these are damaged lives, brutalised lives, even 'wasted lives' (Bauman, 2004). Sociologists have not written as much about these experiences as cultural anthropologists and developmental theorists have. Most sociology stays relatively safely away from them.

And then there are a third grouping: 'us' if you like, maybe in one sense 'the majority'. But within our social world, major social divisions continue to exist too. There are huge demonstrable inequalities across it. And it is these inequalities which sociologists seem mainly to study: the organisation of social class in modern relatively high-income societies. But all of this is heavily 'intersected' with ethnicity, gender, age, sexuality and disability. We will look at these 'intersections' in Chapters 11–14.

SUMMARY

1 Sociologists are never far away from issues of stratification and inequality, since they so seriously shape social life. The following chapters pick up on a range of these issues. Social stratification refers to categories of people ranked in a hierarchy. There are four major stratification systems: socioeconomic, ethnic, gender and age. Stratification is (a) a characteristic of society, not something that merely arises from individual differences; (b) persistent over many generations; (c) universal, yet variable in form; and (d) supported by cultural beliefs.

2 Slavery, estate and caste are major forms of stratification. Slavery still exists today. Caste systems, typical of agrarian societies, are based on ascription and rest on strong moral beliefs, shaping a person's entire life, including occupation and marriage. Class systems, common to industrial societies, reflect a greater measure of individual achievement. Because the emphasis on achievement opens the way for social mobility, classes are less clearly defined than castes.

3 Historically, socialist societies have claimed to be classless, based on their public ownership of productive property. While such societies may exhibit far less economic inequality than their capitalist counterparts, they are notably stratified with regard to power.

4 Social stratification persists for two reasons – support from various social institutions and the power of ideology to define certain kinds of inequality as both natural and just.

5 The Davis–Moore thesis states that social stratification is universal because it contributes to the operation of society. In class systems, unequal rewards motivate people to aspire to the occupational roles most important to the functioning of society. Critics of the Davis–Moore thesis note that (a) it is difficult to assess objectively the functional importance of any occupational position; (b) stratification prevents many people from developing their abilities; and (c) social stratification often generates social conflict.

6 Marx recognised two major social classes in industrial societies. The capitalists, or bourgeoisie, own the means of production in pursuit of profits; the proletariat, by contrast, offer their labour in exchange for wages. The socialist revolution that Marx predicted has not occurred in industrial societies such as Germany or the United States. Some sociologists see this as evidence that Marx's analysis was flawed; others, however, point out that our society is still marked by pronounced social inequality and substantial class conflict.

7 Max Weber identified three distinct dimensions of social inequality: economic class, social status or prestige, and power. Taken together, these three dimensions form a complex hierarchy of socioeconomic standing.

8 Gerhard Lenski and Jean Lenski explained that, historically, technological advances have been associated with more pronounced social stratification. A limited reversal of this trend occurs in advanced industrial societies, as represented by the Kuznets curve.

9 Social stratification is a complex and controversial area of research because it deals not only with facts but with values that suggest how society should be organised. Two ideas of the twentieth century may help to reorganise stratification in the twenty-first century: cyberpower and human rights.

MYTASKLIST

Ten suggestions for going further

1 Connect up with Part Six and the Sociology Web Resources

As you work through ideas and think about the issues raised in this chapter, look at the accompanying website and the resource centre at the end of this book which connects to it. There is a lot here to help you move on. To link up, see: www.pearson.co.uk/plummer.

2 Review the chapter

Briefly summarise (in a paragraph) just what this chapter has been about. Consider: (a) What have you learned? (b) What do you disagree with? Be critical. And (c) How would you develop all this? How could you get more detail on matters that interest you?

3 Pose questions

(a) Look at Table 8.1. How are social divisions and social stratification evident in your university or college? Locate your own position in the stratification system. Compare it with those of friends and family.
(b) Consider the mix of class, ethnicity, gender, sexuality, disability and age as systems of stratification. Are they all equally important? Can they be usefully combined?
(c) Compare some slavery systems from the past (like the plantation system of the USA) with those at work in the world today. (*Hint*: see Bales, 2000.)
(d) Discuss systems of stratification found in any two countries today.
(e) In what respects have the predictions of Karl Marx failed to materialise? In what respects does his analysis ring true?

4 Explore key words

Many concepts have been introduced in this chapter. You can review them from the website or from the listing at the back of this book. You might like to give special attention to just five words and think them through – how would you define them, what are they dealing with, and do they help you see the social world more clearly or not?

5 Search the Web

Be critical when you look at websites – see the box on p. 940 in the Resources section. For this chapter look at the following:

General sites concerned with inequalities

Global Policy Forum on Inequality
www.globalpolicy.org/social-and-economic-policy/global-injustice-and-inequality.html

The Equality Trust (mainly UK)
www.equalitytrust.org.uk/about

Working Group on Extreme Inequality (mainly USA)
http://extremeinequality.org

Focus on the Global South
www.focusweb.org

Online Atlas of the Millennium Development Goals
http://devdata.worldbank.org/atlas-mdg

Slavery

On modern slavery, see Anti-Slavery International:
www.antislavery.org

Contemporary 'Sexual Slavery' Links
www.brandeis.edu/projects/fse/slavery/slav-index.html
which connects to the Feminist Sexual Ethics Project

For websites on Marx, look back to Chapter 2.

6 Watch a DVD

• Von Stroheim's silent classic *Greed* (1924): about lives ruined by the desire for money.

- Les Blair's *Jump the Gun* (1997): looks at the working class in Johannesburg.
- Arthur Howes' *Nuba Conversations* (1999): looks at poverty, refugees and the Sudan.
- Srdjan Dragojevic's *The Wounds* (1999): portrays two of the most horrifically memorable under-age criminals amidst the devastating backdrop of the war in Bosnia.

7 Think and read

A short tour of the whole field is to be found in Ken Plummer, *Sociology: The Basics* (2010: Ch. 7).

Evelyn Kallen, *Social Inequality and Social Injustice* (2004). A very valuable account that looks at the links between inequalities and rights, and discusses a series of major cases such as the rights of children, women's rights, lesbian and gay rights and aboriginal rights.

Goran Therborn, *Inequalities of the World* (2006). A good general introduction is followed by a series of country case studies.

Daniel Dorling, *Injustice: Why Social Inequality Persists* (2010). Looks at key reasons why we cannot get rid of inequalities.

Geoff Payne (ed.), *Social Divisions* (2006). Introduces the idea of social divisions and has major chapters on each kind, including some not discussed here.

Shaun Best, *Understanding Social Divisions* (2005). An extensive discussion of different theories and findings around a wide range of social divisions.

Jodi O'Brien and Judith Howard (eds), *Everyday Inequalities: Critical Inquiries* (1998). A useful collection of empirical readings which show how inequalities of gender, class and race permeate everyday life.

Peter Braham and Linda Janes (eds), *Social Differences and Divisions* (2002). Covers a wide range of divisions from class to ethnicity in a lively Open University text.

Kevin Bales et al., *Modern Slavery* (2009). A major contemporary account of slavery: readable and also very disturbing to those who thought slavery was a thing of the past. This is an update of his earlier work and is supported by the 'reader', *Understanding Global Slavery: A Reader* (2005) and a photographic exhibition, *Documenting Disposable People* (2008).

8 Connect to other chapters

- Connect to Marx and Weber in Chapter 4.
- Connect to discussion of class in Chapter 10.
- Link Davis and Moore back to functionalism in Chapter 2.
- Link slavery to ideas on sexual slavery in Chapter 12.

9 Relax with a novel

- Maxim Gorky, *Mother* (1907)
- Toni Morrison, *Beloved* (1987)
- Benjamin Disraeli, *Sybil or the Two Nations* (1845)
- Edmund Wilson, *To the Finland Station* (1940)

10 Engage with THE BIG DEBATE

Are the rich worth what they earn?

For an hour of work, a residential care worker in southern England can earn about £5.80 an hour and a 16-year-old care worker, maybe £4.00; a university teaching assistant can earn a little more at about £13; and a computer programmer earns between £15 and £30. These wages seem insignificant in comparison to the hundreds of thousands of millions earned annually by television celebrities like Simon Cowell (£165 million), actors like Rowan Atkinson (Mr Bean) (£70m), celebrity hosts like Jonathan Ross (18m for a three-year contract), sports stars like David Beckham (£145m), Lewis Hamilton and Joe Lewis, and music chart-toppers like Sir Paul

McCartney (valued at £475m), Madonna (valued at £275m) and Sir Elton John (at £185m). Newcomers like Keira Knightley and Orlando Bloom have already amassed around £15 million. A few years back, the Duchess of York paid off a personal debt in excess of £1 million (a debt greater than the lifetime earnings of many Britons) by writing children's stories and working the talk show and lecture circuits in the United States.

The Davis–Moore thesis states that rewards reflect an occupation's value to society. But are the activities of pop stars and celebrity hosts really worth as as much to our society as the work of all teachers in several primary schools? In short, do earnings really reflect people's social importance?

Salaries in industrial–capitalist societies such as the UK are a product of the market forces of supply and demand. In simple terms, if you can do something better than others, and people value it, you can command greater rewards. According to this view, movie stars, top athletes, skilled professionals and many business executives have rare talents that are much in demand; thus, they may earn many times more than the typical worker in the UK.

But critics claim that the market is really a poor evaluator of occupational importance. First, they claim, the British economy is dominated by a small proportion of people who manipulate the system for their own benefit. Corporate executives pay themselves multi-million-pound salaries and bonuses even in years when their companies flounder. Japanese executives, by contrast, earn far less than their counterparts in this country, yet most Japanese corporations have comfortably outperformed their rivals in the UK.

A second problem with the idea that the market measures people's contributions to society is that many people who make clear and significant contributions receive surprisingly little money for their efforts.

Hundreds of thousands of teachers, counsellors and healthcare workers contribute daily to the welfare of others for very little salary.

Using social worth to justify income, then, is hazardous. Some defend the market as the most accurate measure of occupational worth; what, they ask, would be better? But others contend that what is lucrative may or may not be socially valuable. From this standpoint, a market system amounts to a closed game which only a handful of people have the money to play.

Continue the debate

1 Track down *The Sunday Times Rich List*, published each year, and discuss its contents. Find out the earnings of your favourite sports and media stars.

2 Look around you and consider how much cleaners and even teachers are likely to be earning.

3 Debate the significance of these disparities. Is inequality inevitable? Do you lead a 'privileged life' or an 'excluded life'? In what ways? Whither the growing inequalities?

CHAPTER 9

GLOBAL POVERTY/GLOBAL INEQUALITY

(Above) Yellow houses: a street in Sophiatown, South Africa 1940

Source: Yellow Houses: a street in Sophian town, *c.* 1940 (board), Sekoto, Gerald (1913–93)/© Johannesburg Art Gallery, South Africa/The Bridgeman Art Library. Courtesy of the Gerald Sekoto Foundation.

See: www.art.co.za/gerardsekoto/default.htm; http://the-artists.org/artist/Gerard_Sekoto.html.

Q Sekoto was a prominent artist in South Africa. Look at the websites and then consider how his art must have been shaped by his social situation. Do you think it is generally true that art is shaped by social situations? (And if so, might this also be true of sociology?)

AFGHANISTAN IS ONE OF THE POOREST AND MOST CONFLICT-RIDDEN COUNTRIES IN THE WORLD. **It has the highest rate of emigration of anywhere in the world – as people try to get out of it.** Some 70 per cent of its 28 million people live below the international poverty line. Its life expectancy of 45 years is among the lowest in the world. Its literacy rate is 28 per cent. It ranks low in the United Nations ranking of human development – at position 155 (in 2010). And its progress over time has been measured as at the bottom of many world league tables – it comes next to bottom in gender equality, child poverty, freedom and democracy measures, and health. The only league table it tops is that of drugs: 80 per cent of western Europe's heroin comes from Afghanistan!

What kind of country is Afghanistan? Eighty per cent of the country is mountainous, housing many clans, tribes and ethnic groups. Ethnically, the largest group is Pashtun (42 per cent), but there are many others with long histories of disagreements: Tajik (27 per cent), Hazara (9 per cent) Uzbek (9 per cent) and many others. For 300 years the Pashtun ruled Kabul but they lost this in 1992. Violence and civil war followed – but then civil war between tribes and wars with neighbours has long been part of Afghanistan's history. Basically Afghanistan is a pre-industrial tribal society which has been at war with it neighbouring countries for centuries. It is now also at the heart of the world conflict over terrorism.

Yet because of its geographical location, it is strategically important for many countries. Landlocked and lying at the heart of central Asia, it is bordered by Pakistan, Iran, India, China and the former Soviet republics of Turkmenistan, Uzbekistan and Tajikistan. For 2,500 years it has been the crossroads of many countries, conflicts and armies. It still is. For example, between 1842 and 1880, the British twice invaded Afghanistan to force Kabul to subordinate its foreign policy to British interests – both times with heavy losses. Britain gradually withdrew and subsequently, for much of the middle twentieth century, Afghanistan was under the influence

of the Soviet Union. In 1973, it became a republic. After a violent struggle, the communist Democratic Republic of Afghanistan was proclaimed in 1978 – attempting to modernise rapidly. This was followed by a 10-year Soviet occupation, resulting in the killing of between 600,000 and 2 million Afghans, mostly civilians. Many further conflicts followed. In 1992, the Islamic State of Afghanistan was established. Today, it is the prime home of the Taliban – a leading Islamic revolutionary organisation.

These days we hear a great deal about Afghanistan. After the 9/11 New York attack on the Twin Towers in New York, where 2,995 were killed, including the 19 hijackers, British and American troops invaded. By spring 2002, the Afghan Taliban regime had been officially defeated – the terrorists it harboured were supposedly on the run. But since then a long, drawn-out conflict has continued with thousands being killed on all sides. The last thing a poor country like this needed was such conflict, increasing its poverty day by day. It now has more people fleeing it than any other country in the world.

On 1 December 2009, US President Barack Obama announced that he would escalate US military involvement by deploying an additional 30,000 soldiers over a period of six months. He also proposed to begin troop withdrawals 18 months from that date. Several elections have also been held in Afghanistan since 2001, most recently in September 2010. There were around 2,500 candidates for the Afghan Parliament but there was severe disruption from the Taliban, who attacked all involved in the elections, including voters, killing 11 civilians and 3 Afghan National Policemen.

This is one of the poorest countries in the world: it is also one of the most conflict-ridden ones. We will return to this issue in Chapter 16. But we begin this chapter with Afghanistan as a key illustration of world inequalities and poverty.

See: Ceri Oeppen and Angela Schlenkhoff (eds), *Beyond the 'Wild Tribes':* *Understanding Modern Afghanistan and Its Diaspora* (2010).

COUNTRY FACT FILE

AFGHANISTAN

Population	29m (2009)
Per capita GDP	–0.4 (2009)
Life expectancy	44.19 male 44.61 female
Adult literacy	43.1%
Key languages	Afghan Persian or Dari (official) 50%, Pashto (official) 35%
Key religions	Sunni Muslim 80%, Shia Muslim 19%
Key city	Kabul
Human development index	0.349 (155th, 2010)

Source: World Bank and Human Development Report (2010).

Poverty is an awful, eventually degrading thing and it is rare that anything good comes from it. We rise in spite of adversity, not because of it . . .

The letters of Thomas Wolfe

Eradicating poverty is an ethical, social and economic imperative of mankind.

Copenhagen Declaration, World Summit for Social Development, 1995

In this chapter, we ask:

- **What is the nature of the unequal world we live in now? What is the scale of poverty and inequality across the world?**

- **How can we understand and measure such poverty and inequality?**

- **Who are the key groups involved in this inequality?**

Global stratification

Social stratification is found in all countries across the world. Everywhere, there are pronounced economic inequalities. There are major gender divisions. There is social exclusion based on ethnicity and race, which often results in displaced persons and refugees. There is an age stratification system at work by which both the young and the old can experience inequality. And there are processes excluding all manner of people with difference and disability. These are the key components of global stratification and we touch on them all throughout the book. In this chapter, however, the main focus will be on the poverty and economic inequalities found across the world. Why does nearly half the world still live in deep poverty? Why, in the face of great wealth in some countries and the extraordinary lives of a few million 'truly rich', do such huge discrepancies persist in the twenty-first century? Table 9.1 documents in stark form the global discrepancies.

The inequalities of the world we live in

1 Life cycle and population

Infant mortality

- 1 pregnant woman in 5,000 each year dies in the UK, but 1 in 10 pregnant women will not survive in the poorest countries.

Childhood

- 240,000 children under the age of 5 die each day due to poverty.
- 'Child labour' involves some 250 million working children (61 per cent in Asia, 32 per cent in Africa and 7 per cent in Latin America).
- Child marriage is pervasive: in some countries over half of all girls are married by the time they reach age 18 (the figure is 74 per cent in the Democratic Republic of the Congo, 70 per cent in Niger, and around 50 per cent in Bangladesh and Afghanistan).
- There are some 100 million children who work on the streets.
- There are some 10 million refugees and 5 million internally displaced people.

Old age

- In 2010, one out of every ten persons was 60 years or above; by 2050, one out of five will be 60 years or older. There were roughly 759 million people aged 60 or above, projected to rise to 2 billion by 2050.
- Throughout the world, older people often face discrimination in hiring, promotion and access to job-related training.
- In OECD countries, an average of 13.3 per cent of persons aged over 65 are poor, compared to 10.6 per cent of the general population, according to data for the mid-2000s (OECD, 2009).
- Older women are more likely to be poor than are older men.

2 Income, wealth and poverty

- 1.4 billion people (one in four) in the developing world were living on less than US$1.25 a day in 2005 (down from 1.9 billion (one in two) in 1981, but still huge).
- Over 3 billion (almost half the world) live below the World Bank's $2.50/day poverty line.
- Some 80 per cent of the population lives on less than $10 a day.
- The gross domestic product of the 41 heavily indebted poor countries (567 million people) is less than the wealth of the world's seven richest people combined.

3 City and environment

- In 2010 there were around 800,000 living in slum conditions.

4 Health, nutrition, AIDS, sanitation and disability

Disease

- Some 35,000 children die each day from preventable or easily treatable diseases.

AIDS

- An estimated 40 million people are living with HIV/AIDS (with 3 million deaths in 2004).

Sanitation

- Some 2.4 billion people lack basic sanitation.

Nutrition

- Over 20 per cent of the world's population (about 1.3 billion people) lack the nutrition they need to work regularly, living in absolute poverty.
- Most people in low-income countries not only do more physical labour, but also consume less than 2,000 calories daily.

5 Education and literacy

- 72 million children of primary school age in the developing world were not in school in 2005.
- Nearly a billion people entered the twenty-first century unable to read a book or sign their name.

6 Gender, family and sexuality

Gender

- Across the world, at least one in every three women has been beaten, coerced into sex or abused – usually by someone she knows.
- As many as 5,000 women and girls are killed annually in so-called 'honour' killings (many of them for the 'dishonour' of being raped).
- An estimated 4 million women and girls are bought and sold worldwide each year, into marriage, prostitution or slavery.
- Worldwide, some 130 million girls and young women have undergone female genital mutilation (FGM).
- Each year, women undergo an estimated 50 million abortions, 20 million of which are unsafe, and some 78,000 women die and millions suffer in the process.

Sexuality

- Around 70 countries have laws which criminalise homosexual acts, and a number of these – Iran, Afghanistan, Saudi Arabia and Chechnya among them – have the death penalty for gay sex.
- Torture is common to extract confessions of 'deviance', gays are raped to 'cure them of it', and they are sometimes killed by death squads.

7 Ethnicity, migration, hybridity, war and displaced people

- At the end of 2008 there were some 42 million displaced people worldwide. These included 15.2 million refuges, 827 asylum seekers and 26 million internally displaced persons (IDPs).
- Children make up about half of war refugees, while millions die and are often the main targets in war (being seen as the next generation of 'enemies'). Many are used as mine sweepers or spies and for kamikaze attacks. And many others are recruited or coerced into being soldiers: some 300,000 minors are recruited as active combatants by rebel groups and armies in some 41 countries – especially in Asia and Africa.
- Some 27 million people across the world live in modern slavery.

8 Crime, drugs, abuse, trafficking and violence

- Organisations combating child poverty in the world estimate that poverty forces some 100 million city children in poor countries to beg, steal, sell sex or serve as couriers for drug gangs in order to provide income for their families.

Keeping up to date with the world's inequalities through the internet

Statistics like the above soon become outdated. Here is a small selection of key words to add to your 'favourites' list, which will help you keep up to date. The links can be found on the book's website. Always be aware, though, that *all statistics bring problems*, and need thinking about critically.

- For general data on all of the world's societies: search *The World Bank*; *The CIA Factbook*; *United Nations*; *NationMaster*; *New Internationalist*.
- Size of populations and their growth: search *United Nations World Population Reports (UNFPA)*.
- Size of cities and rural areas: search *The State of the World's Cities*; *Urban agglomerations*; *United Nations urban agglomerations*.
- Basic economic development of the world's countries: search *United Nations*; *OECD*.
- World poverty statistics: search *World Bank poverty net*; *Global issues*.
- The Human Development Index for each country in the world: search *UN Human Development Index*.
- World poverty: search *Poverty*; *One world*; *Human development*; *Global issues*.
- Environmental damage and degradation: search *World Watch*; *People Planet*; *UN climate change*; *World Environment Organization*; *DEFRA UK*.
- Human rights and abuse across the world: search *Amnesty International*; *Human Rights Watch*.
- Genocides across the world: search *Genocide Watch*.
- Migrations, refugees and displaced people across the world: search *United Nations High Commissioner for Refugees (UNHCR)*.
- Political freedom and democracy across the world: search *Freedom House*.
- Diverse religions, their sizes and beliefs across the world: search *Adherents*.
- Different languages across the world: search *Ethnologue*.
- Different values across the world: search *World Values Survey*.
- Maps of the world: search *World atlas*; *Google maps*; *Worldmapper*.

| Table 9.1 | Human Development Index (HDI): 2010 rankings |

Very high human development	High human development	Medium human development	Low human development
1 Norway	43 Bahamas	86 Fiji	128 Kenya
2 Australia	44 Lithuania	87 Turkmenistan	129 Bangladesh
3 New Zealand	45 Chile	88 Dominican Republic	130 Ghana
4 United States	46 Argentina	89 China	131 Cameroon
5 Ireland	47 Kuwait	90 El Salvador	132 Myanmar
6 Liechtenstein	48 Latvia	91 Sri Lanka	133 Yemen
7 Netherlands	49 Montenegro	92 Thailand	134 Benin
8 Canada	50 Romania	93 Gabon	135 Madagascar
9 Sweden	51 Croatia	94 Suriname	136 Mauritania
10 Germany	52 Uruguay	95 Bolivia (Plurinational State of)	137 Papua New Guinea
11 Japan	53 Libyan Arab Jamahiriya		138 Nepal
12 Korea (Republic of)	54 Panama	96 Paraguay	139 Togo
13 Switzerland	55 Saudi Arabia	97 Philippines	140 Comoros
14 France	56 Mexico	98 Botswana	141 Lesotho
15 Israel	57 Malaysia	99 Moldova (Republic of)	142 Nigeria
16 Finland	58 Bulgaria	100 Mongolia	143 Uganda
17 Iceland	59 Trinidad and Tobago	101 Egypt	144 Senegal
18 Belgium	60 Serbia	102 Uzbekistan	145 Haiti
19 Denmark	61 Belarus	103 Micronesia (Federated States of)	146 Angola
20 Spain	62 Costa Rica		147 Djibouti
21 Hong Kong, China (SAR)	63 Peru	104 Guyana	148 Tanzania (United Republic of)
	64 Albania	105 Namibia	149 Côte d'Ivoire
22 Greece	65 Russian Federation	106 Honduras	150 Zambia
23 Italy	66 Kazakhstan	107 Maldives	151 Gambia
24 Luxembourg	67 Azerbaijan	108 Indonesia	152 Rwanda
25 Austria	68 Bosnia and Herzegovina	109 Kyrgyzstan	153 Malawi
26 United Kingdom	69 Ukraine	110 South Africa	154 Sudan
27 Singapore	70 Iran (Islamic Republic of)	111 Syrian Arab Republic	155 Afghanistan
28 Czech Republic	71 The former Yugoslav Republic of Macedonia	112 Tajikistan	156 Guinea
29 Slovenia		113 Viet Nam	157 Ethiopia
30 Andorra	72 Mauritius	114 Morocco	158 Sierra Leone
31 Slovakia	73 Brazil	115 Nicaragua	159 Central African Republic
32 United Arab Emirates	74 Georgia	116 Guatemala	160 Mali
	75 Venezuela (Bolivarian Republic of)	117 Equatorial Guinea	161 Burkina Faso
33 Malta		118 Cape Verde	162 Liberia
34 Estonia	76 Armenia	119 India	163 Chad
35 Cyprus	77 Ecuador	120 Timor-Leste	164 Guinea-Bissau
36 Hungary	78 Belize	121 Swaziland	165 Mozambique
37 Brunei Darussalam	79 Colombia	122 Lao People's Democratic Republic	166 Burundi
38 Qatar	80 Jamaica		167 Niger
39 Bahrain	81 Tunisia	123 Solomon Islands	168 Congo (Democratic Republic of the)
40 Portugal	82 Jordan	124 Cambodia	
41 Poland	83 Turkey	125 Pakistan	169 Zimbabwe
42 Barbados	84 Algeria	126 Congo	
	85 Tonga	127 São Tomé and Príncipe	

Source: The HDI rankings featured above were published in the *Human Development Report 2010*. You can access the full report at: http://hdr.undp.org/en/reports/global/hdr2010.

See also: pp. 133–4 and 287–8.

As this table shows, and the chapter will amplify, the human toll of global poverty is enormous. Consider three contrasts. At the end of the Second World War, the United States obliterated the Japanese city of Hiroshima with an atomic bomb. The worldwide loss of life from starvation reaches the Hiroshima death toll *every three days*. Given the magnitude of this problem, easing world hunger is one of the most serious responsibilities facing the world today. Secondly, the annual loss of life stemming from poverty is ten times greater than that resulting from all the world's current armed conflicts. In what follows, we look at this problem of world poverty in more detail. Thirdly, one author, Thomas Pogge, claims that world poverty produces substantially more harm than the fascists ever did (more each year, and this over much longer periods), and that the cost of ending poverty is tiny in comparison to the cost of ending fascist rule. He claims:

The problem is so large that it causes one third of all human deaths and blights well over half of all human lives with hunger, disease, oppression, exclusion, and abuse. Yet global inequality has increased to such an extent that such poverty is now avoidable at a cost that would barely be felt in the affluent countries.

(Pogge, 2010: 72)

The most basic starting point for thinking about global inequality is the issue of world poverty. Depending on how poverty is defined, somewhere between 1.3 billion and 3 billion people live in poverty – nearly half of the world's population. Furthermore, although many countries are indeed becoming wealthier, in general inequalities between countries seem to have been growing. Figure 9.1(a) divides the total global *income* by fifths of the population: the richest 20 per cent of the global population receive some 74 per cent of all income. At the other end of the social scale, the poorest 20 per cent of the world's people, by contrast, struggle to survive on just 1 per cent of global income. Because global income is so concentrated, the average member of a rich society (such as most people in Europe) lives extremely well by world standards. In fact, the living standard of most people below the poverty threshold far surpasses that of the majority of the earth's people. In terms of *wealth*, as Figure 9.1(b) shows, global inequality is even greater. A rough estimate suggests that the richest 20 per cent of the world own more than 90 per cent of the planet's wealth. About half of all wealth is owned by just 2 per cent of the world's population; about 40 per cent, by the richest 1 per cent.

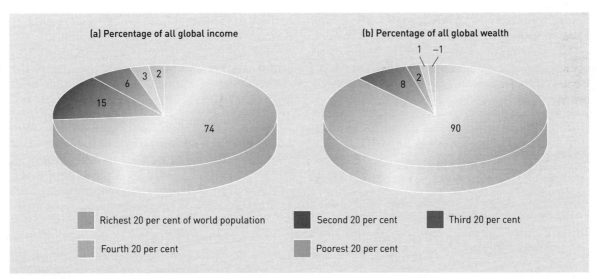

Figure 9.1   Distribution of global income and wealth
Global income is very unequal, with the richest 20 per cent of the world's people earning almost 40 times as much as the poorest 20 per cent. Global wealth is even more unequally divided, with the richest 20 per cent owning 90 per cent of private wealth and the poorest half of the world's people having barely anything at all.

Source: Macionis, John J., *Sociology, 13th*, © 2010. Printed and electronically reproduced by permission of Pearson Education, Inc., Upper Saddle River, New Jersey. Based on UNDP (2008) and Davies et al. (2006, 2008).

How can inequalities be measured?

Measuring inequalities across cultures is no easy task and in this section we look at a range of ways in which poverty and inequality have been studied. As we saw in Chapter 4, there have been a number of ways to classify societies – and many have been based on wealth and income. Throughout much of the twentieth century the major divide was seen to be the First, Second and Third Worlds. This has now been superseded by two major measures. The first is based on economic factors and depends largely on measuring the gross national product (GNP) and the gross domestic product (GDP); the latter depends on a complex series of scales which aim to measure the quality of life, known as the Human Development Index.

Poverty as money: economic measures of poverty

GNP and GDP

The standard way of measuring a country's economic productivity is through GNP and GDP. GDP or **gross domestic product** refers to *all the goods and services on record as produced by a country's economy in a given year*. Income earned outside the country by individuals or corporations is excluded from this measure; this is the key difference between GDP and **gross national product** (GNP), which *includes foreign earnings*.

For countries that invest heavily abroad, GDP is considerably less than GNP; for countries in which other nations invest heavily, GDP is much higher than GNP. For countries that both invest heavily abroad and have considerable foreign investment at home, the two measures are roughly comparable.

Purchasing power parity

It is possible to measure per capita GDP in terms of what the United Nations Development Programme (UNDP, 2001) calls 'purchasing power parities' (PPP), the value of people's income in terms of what it can buy in a local economy. For a long while, the measure of poverty was fixed at $1 a day. Currently, it is fixed at $1.5 a day. However, living on $1.5 a day does not mean being able to afford what $1.5 would buy when converted into a local currency, but the equivalent of what $1.5 would buy in the United States: for example, a newspaper, a local bus ride or a small bag of rice. Per capita PPP figures for rich countries such as Norway, Australia and Canada are very high – in the range of $40,000. For middle-income countries, including Iran, China and Ukraine, it is much lower – in the $4,000–8,000 range. And in the world's low-income countries, per capita annual income is no more than just a few hundred dollars (the average is $1,400 – but in Niger, the poorest country in the world, it is $680). In the African nations of Zaïre or Ethiopia, a typical person labours all year in order to earn what the average worker in the United States reaps in just several days. These are huge discrepancies (*World Development Report*, 2010). Figure 9.2 shows different levels of income by economic development.

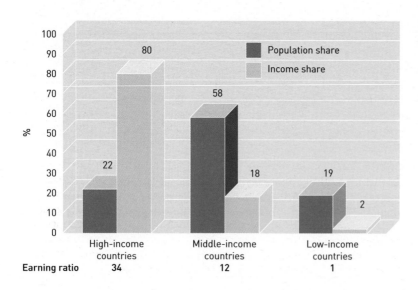

| **Figure 9.2** | Relative share of income and population by level of economic development |

Note: For every dollar earned by people in low-income countries, people in high-income countries earn $34.

Source: Macionis, John J., *Sociology, 13th*, © 2010. Printed and electronically reproduced by permission of Pearson Education, Inc., Upper Saddle River, New Jersey. Based on United Nations Development Programme (2008).

High to low incomes

Ranking countries on the basis of their economies has led to a more general distinction between high income, medium income and low income societies. **High-income countries** are defined as *the nations with highest overall standards of living* (there are roughly 65 of them); **middle-income countries** are not as rich: they are *nations with a standard living which is about average for the world as a whole* (about 75); and the remaining countries are **low income**: nations with a *low standard of living in which most people are poor* (about 40). We looked at this in Chapter 4 (see p. 131).

Poverty and the measurement of life quality: the Human Development Index

Measurements that focus only on income and wealth can ignore many other factors that play a crucial role in life. Low income is a key feature of poverty: but inequalities can also range on such things as housing, literacy and health. What we are talking about here is the very controversial subject of quality of life, and how that can be measured. For the Nobel Prize-winning economist Amartya Sen, we need to take into account human capabilities for living fulfilled and even flourishing lives. As he says: 'poverty must be seen as the deprivation of basic capabilities rather than merely as lowness of incomes' (Sen, 1999: 20). This 'capabilities' approach underpins the human development model which we introduced briefly in Chapter 4, and it suggests that if the people of a country are healthier and better educated, and have access to public services without discrimination, that country is making progress in reducing poverty. Poverty is linked to a sense of entitlement to a well-functioning life (Sen, 1999: 162). More and more, then, researchers try to go beyond the economic. The Human Development Index (HDI) brings together measures of income, education and life expectancy as a composite measure. We introduced this in Chapter 4 and it would be useful to revise it here (see pp. 133–4).

Relative versus absolute poverty

The members of rich societies typically focus on the *relative poverty* of some of their members, highlighting how those people lack resources that are taken for granted by others. Relative poverty, by definition, cuts across every society, rich or poor.

But especially important in a global context is the concept of **absolute poverty**, a lack of resources that is life threatening (often measured as a per capita income equivalent to less than one international dollar a day). Human beings in absolute poverty commonly lack the nutrition necessary for health and long-term survival. To be sure, some absolute poverty exists in Europe. Inadequate nutrition that leaves children or elderly people vulnerable to illness and even outright starvation is a reality in the UK. But such immediately life-threatening poverty strikes only a small proportion of the population. In low-income countries, by contrast, one-third or more of the people are in desperate need.

Relative or absolute poverty? By and large, rich nations such as the United Kingdom wrestle with the problem of *relative poverty*, meaning that poor people get by with less than we think they should have. In poor countries such as Somalia, absolute poverty means that people lack what they need to survive. Here people gather in Baidoa, Somalia, to bury in a common grave family members who died from starvation
Source: © Chris Steele-Perkins/Magnum Photos.

Since absolute poverty places people at risk of death, we can see the extent of this problem by examining the median age at death around the world. In other words, by what age have half of all people born in a society died? Map 9.1 shows that death in high-income countries, on average, occurs among the elderly beyond the age of 75.

Death occurs somewhat earlier in middle-income nations, reflecting a lower standard of living. But in many low-income countries of Africa and western Asia, the greater extent of absolute poverty is brought home by the fact that half of all deaths occur among children under the age of ten.

PUBLIC SOCIOLOGY

Problems with poverty and inequality measurement: what does a statistical table mean?

Throughout this book you will regularly come across aggregate statistics and league tables, such as the Human Development Index produced by the United Nations Development Programme. In this chapter, you have the figures for the HDI given in Table 9.1 as well as a vast number of statistics collated for the box on pp. 282–3, which draws from many sources. Look at them. Similar statistics are used all the time by social scientists. You have already been warned to look at statistics cautiously and carefully (see Chapter 3, pp. 94–5).

In using sociology in public debate, it is important to have some skill in handling statistics. Here are four tips:

1   *Know what the statistic claims to measure* – it is rarely simple. Think whether it really measures what it says. Thus, the Human Development Index is complex. Invented in 1990, it is these days seen as a very important measurement and is widely used. But it is a composite measure of (a) *longevity* – life expectancy at birth; (b) *knowledge* – adult literacy rate and enrolment in schooling; and (c) *decent standards of living* – adjusted income per head. Each one of these rates brings its own problems of measurement (discussed in the appendix of the Human Development Reports).

2   *Consider the population sample to which the statistic applies*. Is it a statistically representative sample, or a very special selected one? If it is national statistics, is it part of a national census – or not?

3   *Then consider the times when the data were gathered*. Often when international statistics are composed, the data come from different years. And they are invariably 'out of date' by the time they reach publication. Since social changes can be very rapid, statistics can get out of date very quickly. Meanwhile populations grow, economies go into crisis, governments fail.

4   *Can the statistics of different countries really be compared?* Different countries very often have differing degrees of sophistication in measurement. Statistics cannot be so easily produced in many low-income societies, which may be in famine or suffer a natural disaster or civil conflict. Just how can statistics be fully reliable when produced under these circumstances?

5   *Watch out for spurious accuracy*. Many statistics sound very precise – they often give numbers that are very large and precise: for example, that the population of a country is 4,789,872. This is rubbish and the pseudo precision is nonsense. It might have been the population for a few seconds once, but numbers are never accurate and things change. By the time they reach this textbook, statistics are all wildly out of date as well. So look for general trends rather than specifics. Equally common are glib generalisations – using statistics which are really based on inadequate samples and bad measurements.

In any event, *statistics must always be used with care*. Challenge just what statistics mean and how they were produced. Most of the statistics used in this book have been produced by so-called 'reliable sources'; even so, they need careful and critical scrutiny. (See: *UNDHP Human Development Report*, annual.)

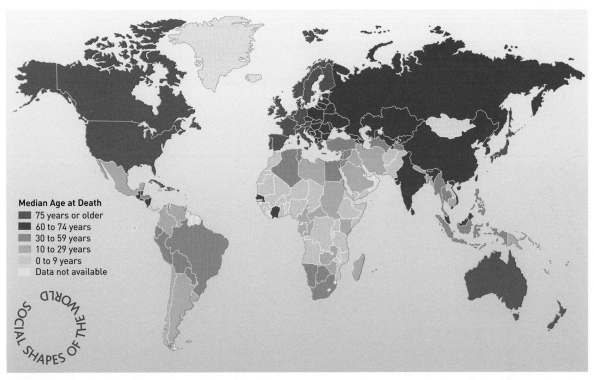

Median Age at Death
- 75 years or older
- 60 to 74 years
- 30 to 59 years
- 10 to 29 years
- 0 to 9 years
- Data not available

SOCIAL SHAPES OF THE WORLD

Map 9.1   Median age at death in global perspective
This map identifies the age below which half of all deaths occur in any year. In high-income countries, it is the elderly who face death – that is, people aged 75 or older. In middle-income countries, including most of Latin America, most people die years or even decades earlier. In low-income countries, especially in Africa and parts of Asia, it is children who die, with half of all lives ending before individuals reach 10 years of age.

Source: Based on World Bank (1993).

The globalisation of the 'super rich' and the localisation of the 'bottom billion'

The super rich

There are around 1,000 billionaires in the world. In 2010, the business magazine *Forbes* could list 937 of them – about 500 of them worth over $2 billion each (see Table 9.2). This may amount to an estimated combined wealth of $3.6 *trillion*. Surprisingly, after the financial crisis of 2009, the numbers of billionaires shot up! The average worth of the world's billionaires is now $3.5 billion. These figures are hard to imagine but, simply put, a billionaire is someone with wealth of at least a thousand million US dollars. It is wealth that most minds on the planet cannot even begin to comprehend. Many billionaires are wealthier than whole countries. Often they live lives that are cut off from the rest of the world – with private homes on private islands reached by private planes and mega yachts. The most striking inequality of the world lies in the fact that the *richest 1 per cent of adults in the world own 40 per cent of the planet's wealth*.

Billionaires can be found all over the world. The United States used to account for nearly half the names on the billionaire list, but now its share is just 40 per cent – or 403 billionaires. China (including Hong Kong) has the most billionaires outside the USA with 89. Russia has 62 (*Forbes*, 'The world's billionaires', 3 October 2010).

Table 9.2	The richest people in the world: the top 20 billionaires, 2010				
Rank	Name	Citizenship	Age	Net worth ($bn)	Residence
1	Carlos Slim Helu and family	Mexico	70	53.5	Mexico
2	William Gates III	USA	54	53.0	USA
3	Warren Buffett	USA	79	47.0	USA
4	Mukesh Ambani	India	52	29.0	India
5	Lakshmi Mittal	India	59	28.7	UK
6	Lawrence Ellison	USA	65	28.0	USA
7	Bernard Arnault	France	61	27.5	France
8	Eike Batista	Brazil	53	27.0	Brazil
9	Amancio Ortega	Spain	74	25.0	Spain
10	Karl Albrecht	Germany	90	23.5	Germany
11	Ingvar Kamprad and family	Sweden	83	23.0	Switzerland
12	Christy Walton and family	USA	55	22.5	USA
13	Stefan Persson	Sweden	62	22.4	Sweden
14	Li Ka-shing	Hong Kong	81	21.0	Hong Kong
15	Jim Walton	USA	62	20.7	USA
16	Alice Walton	USA	60	20.6	USA
17	Liliane Bettencourt	France	87	20.0	France
18	S. Robson Walton	USA	66	19.8	USA
19	Prince Alwaleed Bin Talal Alsaud	Saudi Arabia	55	19.4	Saudi Arabia
20	David Thomson and family	Canada	52	19.0	Canada

Source: Forbes, www.forbes.com/lists/2010/10/billionaire. This provides the full list of the world's 937 billionaires in March 2010.

The troubles in Africa

Africa is a vast continent housing many different societies and cultures. After Asia, it is the second largest and most populous continent in the world, and in 2005 it had more than 900 million people living in 46 countries (53 including all the island groups). It has a very long history, and is widely considered to be the country of human origins: the land of the earliest discovered human skeletal remains.

But throughout the world, it is often seen as 'the other' – a dark, mysterious continent, a 'black hole' and a land of great poverty and tragedy. This is, of course, a dangerous stereotype in itself, for Africa is a continent with many different countries, each with its own history and concerns. But most of these countries were colonised in the eighteenth and nineteenth centuries and were dominated by European civilisations (see Map 9.2). Many were at the heart of the 'slave trade'. Today, most

African countries harbour deep poverty, widespread starvation and famine, economic stagnation and an AIDS crisis. It is also the most aid-dependent region in human history (Lockwood, 2005).

On the Human Development Index (HDI) scale, most of Africa's countries are at the lowest end (see Table 9.1). It has the ten poorest countries in the world. And indeed the $-a-day headcount measure of poverty has been rising in recent years: almost 75 million more people in Africa were living in poverty at the end of the 1990s than a decade earlier (Lockwood, 2005: 6). There are, nevertheless, huge disparities within countries: Ghana and Tanzania are generally doing much better than others. Four issues can be highlighted:

- For many African countries, *poverty* is extreme, as this chapter shows in more detail.
- Many African countries are *torn with internal conflicts and wars*. This makes them highly unstable and also prone to corruption. On average, all low-income countries face a 14 per cent chance of falling into civil war in any five-year period; the economist Paul Collier notes: 'Young men, who are the recruits for rebel armies, come pretty cheap in an environment of hopeless poverty. Joining a rebel movement gives these young men a small chance of riches.'

- Most African economies are *economically marginalised*. While it is not cut off from global trade (indeed, it is large and important), Africa has not shared in the global boom in higher-value trades. Its markets are in primary commodities, not 'richer

ones'. It is always at the low end of world economic systems. On top of this, much of Africa is highly aid dependent. Economist Matthew Lockwood comments that Africa has a long history of low growth and failed development, and has come

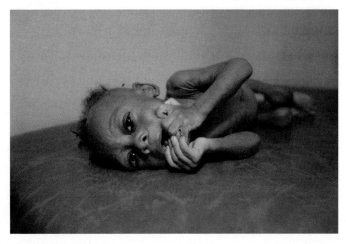

Starving African child
Source: © Picture Contact BV/Alamy.

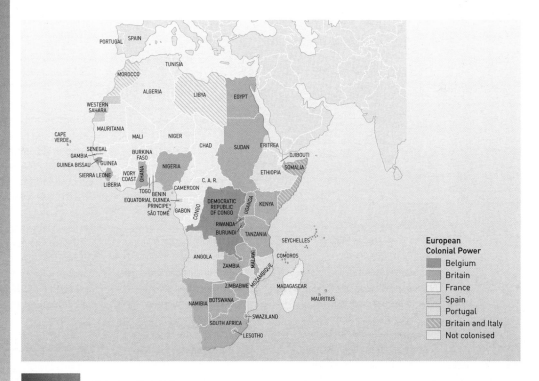

| | **Map 9.2** | Africa's colonial history |

European Colonial Power

- Belgium
- Britain
- France
- Spain
- Portugal
- Britain and Italy
- Not colonised

WORLD WATCH

Table 9.3	How many children have been orphaned by AIDS?

Number of orphans due to AIDS, alive in 2007		AIDS orphans as a percentage of all orphans, 2005	
South Africa	1,400,000	Zimbabwe	77%
Uganda	1,200,000	Botswana	76%
Nigeria	1,200,000	Swaziland	66%
Zimbabwe	1,000,000	Lesotho	64%
Tanzania	970,000	Malawi	57%
Ethiopia	650,000	Zambia	57%
Zambia	600,000	South Africa	49%
Malawi	560,000	Kenya	46%
Côte d'Ivoire	420,000	Uganda	45%

Source: www.avert.org/aids-orphans.htm.

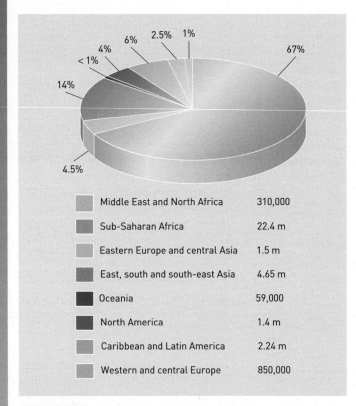

	Middle East and North Africa	310,000
	Sub-Saharan Africa	22.4 m
	Eastern Europe and central Asia	1.5 m
	East, south and south-east Asia	4.65 m
	Oceania	59,000
	North America	1.4 m
	Caribbean and Latin America	2.24 m
	Western and central Europe	850,000

Figure 9.3	Distribution of people living with HIV around the world, 2008

Source: www.avert.org/worldstatinfo.htm.

TOP 10
Poorest countries

	GDP per capita (US$)
Burundi	90
Ethiopia	110
Congo	120
Liberia	140
Malawi	150
Myanmar	160 (est.)
Guinea-Bissau	190
Sierra Leone	210
Eritrea	220
Rwanda	220

Source: Adapted from *Pocket World in Figures*, Profile Books: 18.

As the *Top 10* list and Figure 9.3 illustrate, the poorest countries in the world and the highest rates of HIV/AIDS in the world are both found in Africa. There is also a widespread problem of AIDS orphans. Table 9.3 shows the numbers of African AIDS orphans, by country. In some countries, children who have been orphaned by AIDS comprise half or more of all orphans nationally.

See: Matthew Lockwood: *The State They're In: An Agenda for International Action on Poverty in Africa* (2005); Susan Hunter *Who Cares? AIDS in Africa* (2003).

to develop 'an extraordinary dependence on aid for physical and human investment'.
• Most African countries – especially those in the sub-Saharan region – have very high rates of *HIV/AIDS* (discussed also in Chapter 21). AIDS is a massive burden.

It is firmly established across the continent and it has an impact on nearly every aspect of society. As we shall see in Chapter 21, life expectancy has plummeted. In some countries, 60 per cent of 15-year-olds cannot expect to live to 60.

The bottom billion

The United Nations can claim that global poverty has been falling in a lot of countries. In China and India there is growth, and substantial poverty reduction seems to be under way (United Nations, 2007). But alongside this welcome trend, the UN notes that there is uneven and unequal development – some are getting richer, but others are getting poorer. In general, the economic crisis which started in 2008 has made the situation much worse. There are about 50 or 60 'failing' or 'trapped' countries – around 1 billion people, one-sixth of the world (Collier, 2007). These are generally small nations and include Afghanistan, Haiti, Malawi and countries in central Asia. But 70 per cent of these 'failing states' are in Africa. Sub-Saharan Africa alone has some 450 million people living in poverty.

Key dimensions of global poverty

In this section, we briefly outline some of the key factors that correlate highly with poverty. Many poorer countries have a tendency towards:

1 *Less technology.* Almost two-thirds of people in low-income countries farm the land; the productive power of industrial technology is all but absent in these poorest nations. Energy from human muscles or beasts of burden falls far short of the force unleashed by steam, oil, gas or nuclear fuels – the power sources that propel complex machinery. Moreover, the focus of poor societies on farming, rather than on specialised production, inhibits development of human skills and abilities.

2 *High population growth.* As Chapter 24 explains in detail, countries with the least-developed economies have the world's highest birth rates. Despite the death toll from poverty, the populations of poor countries in Africa, for example, double every 25 years. There, more than half the people have yet to enter their child-bearing years, so the wave of population growth will roll into the future. Even an expanding economy cannot support vast population surges. During 1993, for example, the population of Kenya swelled by 4 per cent; as a result, even with some economic development, living standards actually fell.

3 *Traditional cultural patterns.* Poor societies are typically very traditional. Kinship groups pass folkways and mores from generation to generation. Adhering to long-established ways of life, people resist innovations – even those that promise a richer material life. The members of poor societies often accept their fate, although it may be bleak, in order to maintain family vitality and cultural heritage. Such attitudes bolster social bonds, but at the cost of discouraging development.

4 *Great inequalities.* While most societies distribute their wealth very unequally, in low-income societies the consequences are severe. In the farming regions of Bangladesh, for example, 10 per cent of the landowners own more than half the land area, while almost half of farming families hold title to little or no land of their own (Hartmann and Boyce, 1982). As another example, the richest 10 per cent of Central Americans control about three-quarters of that region's land.

5 *High gender inequality.* As we have already explained, poor societies subordinate women even more than industrial societies do. Moreover, women with few opportunities typically have many children and the needs of a growing population, in turn, restrain economic development. As a result, many analysts conclude that raising living standards in much of the world depends on improving the social standing of women.

6 *Colonised global power relationships.* A final cause of global poverty lies in the relationships among the nations of the world. Historically, wealth flowed from poor societies to rich nations by means of **colonialism**, *the process by which some nations enrich themselves through political and economic control of other countries.* Historical patterns of trade, some analysts claim, spurred certain nations to prosper economically while others simultaneously were made poor. The societies of western Europe colonised much of Latin America for more than 300 years and also controlled parts of Asia, notably India, for centuries. Africa, too, endured up to a century of colonisation.

During the twentieth century, about 130 former colonies gained their independence, leaving only a small number of countries as colonies today. As we shall see, however, a continuing pattern of domination has emerged. **Neocolonialism** (*neos* is a Greek word for 'new') amounts to *a new form of global power relationship that involves not direct* *political control but economic exploitation by multinational corporations*. **Multinational corporations**, in turn, are *large corporations that operate in many different countries*. As Chapter 15 explains, the power of today's multinational corporations to dominate a poor nation often rivals that of colonial countries in centuries past.

Poverty traps: the structural bases of poverty

The economist Stephen C. Smith sees poverty as 'a cruel trap: A billion human beings today are bound in poverty traps, in almost unrelenting misery' (Smith, 2005: ix). A poverty trap arises from the structure of the society – it cannot be escaped without sustained and deep effort to change that society. Sociologists often call this 'structural poverty'. It is not that people are lazy or foolish. Rather, the society is structured in a way that makes it very hard for them to get out of their poverty. Smith suggests that there are many such traps. Among them are:

1   *Family child labour traps*: children often have to work to support their families (more than 100 million in 2003).

2   *Illiteracy traps*: there is little access to the resources that could educate, and hence improve working chances.

3   *'Working capital' traps*: the poor have no credit and no money. This means that no plans can be made for the future. Every 'crisis' is in the current moment and has to be dealt with in the here and now.

4   *'Unsuitable risk' traps*: the poor pay more. The poor cannot afford to pay for any kind of insurance – and their work is often chaotic, dependent on the vagaries of weather, etc. Any purchases in markets can be expensive because the poor have no power to 'shop around'.

5   *'Debt bondage' traps*: when credit is given, it often comes from unscrupulous money-lenders who make the situation worse, which means they can never get out of debt.

6   *'Information' traps*: long hours of work mean little time or energy to look for other work.

7   *Under-nutrition and health traps*: which can easily lead to being laid off work, and can also create the need for women and children to act as carers, who cannot then work or study.

8   *Low skill traps*: the problems are compounded. With little education, poor health, etc. there is little opportunity for training and hence better jobs.

9   *High fertility traps*: more children are a likelihood; but children often die early. So women can spend much time in pregnancy.

10 *Farm erosion traps*: whatever land they work on, or own, is subject to climate problems.

Many of these problems are common to all the poor across the world, not just among those in low-income societies. Stephen Smith's list of these traps is relentless. To the above he adds more: for instance, criminality traps, mental health traps and powerlessness traps.

Puzzles for dealing with world poverty

1 Trade

Economies are expanding through globalisation and this generates expansion.

But: protectionism is needed so that economies can develop with their own strengths.

2 Debts and aid

Countries need more funds from rich countries. The HIPC (Heavily Indebted Poor Countries) programme considers ways in which debts can be written off.

But: aid often feeds corruption and does not reach true needs.

3 Governance and corruption

Political systems need to become more and more open and democratic.

But: the countries have such deep ethnic hatreds that this is hard to achieve.

Dealing with world poverty: the UN Millennium Development Goals

The world is galvanised into action about world poverty, although there never really seems to be enough. Action occurs through government aid programmes, through the work of non-governmental organisations (NGOs), and through direct action groups. Among the key international organisations are the International Monetary Fund (IMF) and the World Bank. Through the Bretton Woods Agreement, 184 organisations seek to maintain stability in the financial world. The World Bank has major programmes to fight poverty and improve the living standards of people in low-income societies. Together they run the HIPC (Heavily Indebted Poor Countries) programme. The United Nations runs many programmes around poverty – including UNICEF, WHO and the UN Development Programme (see Chapter 16). But at the heart of its current programme is the UN Millennium Development Goals: adopted by 189 nations at a summit in 2000, it had eight targeted goals including halving extreme poverty, universal education for children, ending child and maternal mortality and stopping the spread of HIV/AIDS (see Table 9.4, p. 296).

 For up-to-date commentaries on the Millennium Development Goals, see: www.guardian.co.uk/global-development/ millennium-development-goals.

 There are also many campaigns for specific 'issues around poverty', such as:

- the Campaign for Child Survival: www.childsurvivalcampaign.org
- the Global Alliance for Vaccines and Immunisation: www.gavialliance.org
- the Campaign against Malaria, and Malaria No More: www.malarianomore.org
- AIDS Orphans: www.avert.org/aidsorphans.com.

Problems with the UN Millennium Development Goals

The core goal among the Millennium Development Goals (MDG) – to which 191 member states of the UN committed themselves in 2000 – was: 'to halve, by the year 2015, the proportion of the world's people whose income is less than one dollar a day and the proportion of people who suffer from hunger'. Regarding eight issues, clear targets have then been set for success (see Table 9.4). A large amount of money and energy has been put into the MDG project and it has become the flag-bearer of the wish for a better and more equal world in the twenty-first century.

Yet many critics suggest that the MDG project has become aexpensive window dressing and is not dealing adequately with the deep problems of global inequality. For the critic Thomas Pogge, behind the 'pro-poor rhetoric', we find *Politics as Usual* (2010). He claims that a close scrutiny shows that goals have been diluted. Four outstanding problems can be raised here.

- First, it is claimed that the targets of the MDG have been set far too low. The global international poverty level (IPL), for example, was initially set at US$1 a day (raised in 2005 to $1.25). Most of the key statistics have been based on this and it was calculated initially on the basis of the same purchasing power as $1 had in the USA. But that $1 buys very little indeed. More than that: it defines poverty as primarily a matter of income. There are many other factors – such as sanitation, housing and literacy – that move way beyond income. Living with good sanitation, housing and literacy but with below $1 of income is living in a very different kind of poverty from living with $1 but none of these things. (In fairness, however, the MDG is concerned with these things too.)

- Second, there are real problems about measuring poverty. The project thinks we can 'count the poor'. However, many of the countries we are looking at cover large masses and huge populations, many of whom are illiterate and living in desperate conditions with little food and sanitation. How can good measurement and recording practices go on under these circumstances?

	Goal	Sample targets	2010 Progress report
Table 9.4	**The Millennium Development Goals: A sample of targets and progress, 2010**		
	1 Eradicate extreme *poverty and hunger*	Halve, between 1990 and 2015, the proportion of people whose income is less than $1 a day	The global economic crisis has slowed progress, but the world is still on track to meet the poverty reduction target (see Figure 9.4 as an example)
		Halve, between 1990 and 2015, the proportion of people who suffer from hunger	Financial crisis has reduced progress in ending hunger in most regions
	2 Achieve universal *primary education*	Ensure that, by 2015, children everywhere, boys and girls alike, will be able to complete a full course of primary schooling	Hope is dimming for universal education by 2015, even as many poor countries are making tremendous strides
	3 Promote *gender equality* and *empower women*	Eliminate gender disparity in primary and secondary education, preferably by 2005, and in all levels of education no later than 2015	For girls in some regions, education remains elusive
	4 Reduce *child mortality*	Reduce by two-thirds, between 1990 and 2015, the under-five mortality rate	Child deaths are falling, but not quickly enough to reach the target
	5 Improve *maternal health*	Reduce by three-quarters, between 1990 and 2015, the maternal mortality ratio	Data show signs of progress, with some countries achieving significant declines in maternal mortality ratios. However, the rate of reduction is still well short of the 5.5 per cent annual decline needed to meet the target
	6 Combat *HIV/AIDS, malaria and other diseases*	Halt by 2015 and begin to reverse the spread of HIV/AIDS	The spread of HIV appears to have stabilised in most regions, and more people are surviving longer
	7 Ensure *environmental sustainability*	Integrate the principles of sustainable development into country policies and programmes and reverse the loss of environmental resources	The rate of deforestation shows signs of decreasing, but is still alarmingly high
		Halve, by 2015, the proportion of the population without sustainable access to safe drinking water and basic sanitation (see the box on p. 298)	The world is on track to meet the drinking water target, though much remains to be done in some regions
	8 Develop a global partnership for development	Address the special needs of the least developed countries, landlocked countries and small island developing states	Aid continues to rise despite the financial crisis, but Africa is short-changed; only five donor countries have reached the UN target for official aid

Note: 8 goals, 21 targets and 60 official indicators are being monitored.

Source: Compiled by the authors from UN, *The Millennium Goals Report 2010*. For the full report, see: www.unfpa.org/webdav/site/global/shared/documents/publications/2010/mdg_report_2010.pdf.

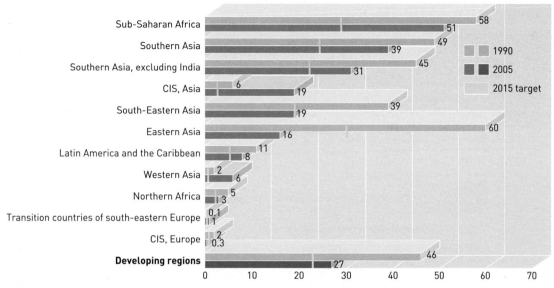

Region	1990	2005	2015 target
Sub-Saharan Africa	58	51	
Southern Asia	49	39	
Southern Asia, excluding India	45	31	
CIS, Asia	6	19	
South-Eastern Asia	39	19	
Eastern Asia	60	16	
Latin America and the Caribbean	11	8	
Western Asia	2	6	
Northern Africa	5	3	
Transition countries of south-eastern Europe	0.1	1	
CIS, Europe	2	0.3	
Developing regions	46	27	

Figure 9.4 Proportion of people living on less than $1.25 a day, 1990 and 2005 (%)
Source: UN Millennium Development Report 2010, p. 6.

Official agencies spend fortunes on their statistical work in poorer countries, but much of it lies in the sophisticated handling of data in faraway government offices. The nitty-gitty data themselves simply may not be very good.

- Closely allied to this is the time problem. As world expectations change, and indeed as conditions in countries change with various economic crises, can measurement measures easily hold across time? Most significantly, populations over the 15 years of the project will all increase significantly, and as the goal is for a proportion rather than an absolute number of people to escape poverty, it seems likely that even if the proportion goal is met, the actual numbers in poverty may increase significantly due simply to rising populations.

- Fourthly, there is an ideological element to all of this. Time and time again in reading the reports, we can be led to a sense of celebration that progress is being made on most objectives (at least until the financial crisis of 2008–9). It is in the interest of funders and career developers to tell good stories of progress with the project. But critics are sceptical.

Some 40 per cent of people have no access to sanitation. This lack of hygienic facilities experienced by 2.6 billion people is a fundamental cause of disease which leads to 2 million deaths – mainly children – each year (see over)
Source: © HJB/Alamy.

How the other half shits

Across the world of nearly 7 billion people, some 40 per cent of people have no access to sanitation. This lack of hygienic facilities experienced by 2.6 billion people is a fundamental cause of disease which leads to 2 million deaths – mainly of children – each year. Every year, around 60 million children in the developing world are born into households without access to sanitation; and children living in such households are twice as likely to get diarrhoea as those with a toilet. It is the seventh Millennium Development Goal to halve, by 2015, the proportion of the population without sustainable access to safe drinking water and basic sanitation.

Table 9.5   The worst places in the world for sanitation provision

As a percentage of population lacking access

Country	Ranking	Percentage lacking sanitation
Afghanistan	1	92
Chad	2=	91
Eritrea	2=	91
Burkina Faso	4=	87
Ethiopia	4=	87
Niger	4=	87
Cambodia	7	83
Ghana	8=	82
Guinea	8=	82
Namibia	10=	75

As a total number of people lacking access to sanitation (above 10 million)

Country	Ranking	Total population lacking sanitation
China	1	732,480,000
India	2	728,357,000
Indonesia	3	99,045,000
Bangladesh	4	84,912,000
Nigeria	5	72,072,000
Ethiopia	6	65,772,000
Pakistan	7	63,468,000
Brazil	8	45,975,000
Democratic Republic of Congo	9	39,130,000
Vietnam	10	32,409,000

Source: Water Aid, *The State of the World's Toilets*; www.wateraid.org/uk.

See also: *New Internationalist*, 'We need to think about toilets', August 2008.

Organisations combating child poverty in the world estimate that poverty forces some 100 million city children in poor countries to beg, steal, sell sex or serve as couriers for drug gangs in order to provide income for their families. Such a life almost always means dropping out of school and places children at high risk of illness and violence. Many street girls, with little or no access to medical assistance, become pregnant – a case of children who cannot support themselves having still more children.

Some 100 million of the world's children have deserted their families altogether, sleeping and living on the streets as best they can. Roughly half of all street children are found in Latin America. Brazil, where much of the population has flocked to cities in a desperate search for a better life, has millions of street children – many not yet teenagers – living in makeshift huts, under bridges or in alleyways. The public response to street children is often anger directed at the children themselves. In Rio de Janeiro, police try to keep the numbers of street children in check. When this unrealistic policy fails, however, death squads may sweep through a neighbourhood, engaging in a bloody ritual of 'urban cleansing'. In Rio, several hundred street children are murdered each year. Often, too, children can become orphaned at an early age. Some may also be sold into slavery. We look at this further in Chapter 13.

Boy scavenging on rubbish dump, Manila
Source: Pearson Education Ltd/Digital Vision.

Who are the global poor?

Figure 9.4 (p. 297) suggests the areas where inequalities can be found to have made most impact. In this section, we highlight four key groups who become most vulnerable to poverty. Although there are others, our main focus will be on children, women, refugees and the elderly.

1 Children and poverty

Poverty hits children hardest, and the extent and severity of child poverty are greatest in low-income countries. As we have already explained, death often comes early in poor societies, where families lack adequate food, safe water, secure housing and access to medical care. In many cases, too, children in poor countries leave their families because their chances to survive are better on the streets.

2 Refugees and the displaced

There are a large number of people who have no 'home' in the world – who have been displaced. In 2009, the United Nations estimated that there were:

- 43.3 million forcibly displaced people worldwide
- 15.2 million who were refugees
- 983,000 asylum seekers
- 27.1 million internally displaced persons (IDPs).

Displaced peoples are *those who often find themselves homeless in their own land*. This may be due to civil war, or to some environmental catastrophe through which they lose whatever home and possessions they may have had. An estimated 50 million people live off land that is rapidly deteriorating. After a time they will be unable to live or work off it, requiring them to move on. In 2009, there were estimated to be some 27 million people in this situation worldwide. **Refugees** are people who '*flee their own country for political or economic reasons, or to avoid war and oppression*' (*New Internationalist*, 1998: 221).

Muddy brown floodwaters by shanty town huts, Dhaka, Bangladesh, South Asia
Source: Pearson Education Ltd/Digital Vision.

They are a central feature of the global world, and they usually experience a well-founded fear of persecution (Marfleet, 2006). In leaving their 'home', often with no choice, they leave behind most of their worldly possessions.

Asylum seekers flee their own country and seek sanctuary in another state. The number of claims has been increasing in recent years, but in 2009 there were nearly a million seeking asylum whose claims had not yet been adjudicated. Many came from Afghanistan, Colombia, Ethiopia, Myanmar and Zimbabwe seeking international protection.

Table 9.6 shows where the refugees are most likely to come from and go to. Most stay within their region of origin and by far the largest movements are in Asia and Sub-Saharan Africa. Afghanistan has – for over 30 years – been the country with the greatest numbers leaving: one in four of all refugees and nearly 3 million in 2009. Neighbouring Pakistan is the country which received most refugees. Many are children (around 40 per cent in 2009). About a third live in camps and half flee to new urban areas.

There are also large movements from Iraq, Somalia, the Sudan and the Democratic Republic of Congo (DRC). Renewed armed conflict and human rights violations in DRC and Somalia led to new refugee outflows and the movement of 277,000 people primarily to the Republic of the Congo (94,000) and Kenya (72,500).

Refugees are always politically controversial. On the one hand, they symbolise humanitarian need; and on the other, they raise in potent ways issues of racism and the symbolic boundaries of a nation-state (see Chapter 11). Refugees test the willingness of governments and their people to provide asylum. They can also lead to human trafficking, where people are sold their illegal passage into a new country. Some have estimated this to be the largest industry in the world (see Chapter 16).

The United Nations High Commission for Refugees (UNHCR) was established in 1950–1 to provide a major world structure for responding to the needs of refugees and to provide standards of protection under international law. Initially it

Table 9.6	The world flow of refugees, 2010		
WHERE THE REFUGEES GO TO . . .		**WHERE THE REFUGEES COME FROM . . .**	
Country/territory of asylum	Total refugees and people in refugee-like situations	Country of refugee/asylum seeker	Total refugees and people in refugee-like situations
Pakistan	1,740,711	Afghanistan	2,887,123
Iran (Islamic Rep. of)	1,070,488	Iraq	1,785,212
Syrian Arab Rep.	1,054,466	Somalia	678,309
Germany	593,799	Dem. Rep. of the Congo	455,852
Jordan	450,756	Sudan	368,195
Kenya	358,928	Viet Nam	339,289
Chad	338,495	Myanmar	406,669
China	300,989	Eritrea	209,168
United States of America	275,461	Serbia	195,626
United Kingdom	269,363	China	180,558

Source: This is a simplified table of figures based on data in UNHCR, Global Trends, 2010.

focused on the displacement of Europeans caused by the Holocaust, the Second World War and the onset of the Cold War. It employed 33 staff and had a budget of $300,000. Over the years it has come to deal with the displacement of large groups of the world's population. It now has a budget of over $1 billion, employs 5,000 staff, has offices in 120 countries around the world and produces a major annual report (see, for example, *2009 Global Trends Refugees, Asylum-seekers, Returnees, Internally Displaced and Stateless Persons* (online).

3 The ageing

We will see in Chapter 13 how the twenty-first century is confronting a major increase in elderly people. It is often believed that this 'age explosion' is predominantly to be found in Western societies. But in fact the figures are substantial for low-income societies. They are often ignored and rendered invisible in debates about international policy and aid: and if noticed, they can be seen as unproductive, uncreative, sick, dependent and passive. But ageing is occurring at a far greater pace in low-income societies and it raises severe problems. We consider this in Chapter 13 (see Harper, 2006: Ch. 8).

4 Women and poverty

Women in Sikandernagar, one of India's countless rural villages, begin work at 4.00 in the morning, lighting the fires, milking the buffalo, sweeping floors and walking to the well for water. They care for other family members as they rise. By 8.00, when many people in Europe are just beginning their day, these women move on to their 'second shift', working under the hot sun in the fields until 5.00 in the afternoon. Returning home, the women gather wood for their fires, all the time searching for whatever plants they can find to enrich the evening meal. The buffalo, too, are ready for a meal and the women tend to them. It is well past dark before their 18-hour day is over.

In rich societies, the work women do is typically unrecognised, undervalued and underpaid; women receive less income for their efforts than men do. In low-income countries, this pattern is even more pronounced. Women do most of the work in poor societies, and families depend on women's work to provide income. At the same time, just as tradition keeps many women from school, it also accords them primary responsibility for child-rearing and maintaining the household. In poor societies, the United Nations estimates, men own 90 per cent of the

What the poor say

According to the World Bank, 'the poor are the true poverty experts'. In a major study, *Voices of the Poor* (2000), Deepa Narayan heard the voices of approximately 60,000 poor men and women from over 60 countries around the world. With striking similarity, poor people describe repeatedly and in distressing detail the impact of poverty. The large majority of poor people included in *Voices* said they are worse off now, have fewer economic opportunities, and live with greater insecurity than in the past. Here are a few of the things they said (look at the website for full details):

Poverty is pain; it feels like a disease. It attacks a person not only materially but also morally. It eats away one's dignity and drives one into total despair. A poor woman, Moldova

Children are hungry, so they start to cry. They ask for food from their mother and their mother doesn't have it. Then the father is irritated, because the children are crying, and he takes it out on his wife. So hitting and disagreement break up the marriage. Poor people in Bosnia

A group of young men in Jamaica ranked lack of self-confidence as the second biggest impact of poverty: *Poverty means we don't believe in self, we hardly travel out of the community . . . so frustrated, just locked up in the house all day.*

My children were hungry and I told them the rice is cooking, until they fell asleep from hunger. An older man, Egypt

Poor people cannot improve their status because they live day by day, and if they get sick then they are in trouble because they have to borrow money and pay interest. Tra Vinh, Vietnam

Security is knowing what tomorrow will bring and how we will get food tomorrow. Bulgaria

There is no control over anything, at any hour a gun could go off, especially at night. A poor woman in Brazil

The rich is the one who says: 'I am going to do it' and does it. The poor, in contrast, do not fulfil their wishes or develop their capacities. A poor woman in Brazil

Poverty is like living in jail, living under bondage, waiting to be free. A young woman in Jamaica

It is neither leprosy nor poverty which kills the leper, but loneliness. Ghana

When you are poor, nobody wants to speak with you. Everyone's sorry for you and no one wants to drink with you. You have no self-esteem and that's why some people start drinking. A middle-aged man in Bulgaria

Now there are hungry children, and before it was not so evident. There are children that knock on your door and ask for bread, children without shoes. This one would never see before. La Matanza, Argentina

If we knew that there would be an end to this crisis, we would endure it somehow. Be it for one year, or even for ten years. But now all we can do is sit and wait for the end to come. A woman from Entropole, Bulgaria

In slums in Malawi, the physical conditions were so bad and hopeless that the poor said *the only way we can get out of poverty is through death.*

The sewage runs in your front door, and when it rains, the water floods into the house and you need to lift the things . . . the waste brings some bugs, here we have rats, cockroaches, spiders, and even snakes and scorpions. A resident of Nova California, a slum in Brazil

In the Kyrgyz Republic, poor people said that they were forced to take many risks to survive, including stealing (with the risk of getting caught) or borrowing money (with the risk of becoming indebted). *The rich do not have to take this risk, they have money to protect themselves, and they also have power.*

You grow up in an environment full of diseases, violence and drugs . . . you don't have the right to education, work or leisure, and you are forced to 'eat in the hands of the government' . . . so you are easy prey for the rulers. You have to accept whatever they give you. A young woman, Padre Jordano, Brazil

Poor people describe four pervasive and systemic problems that affect their lives adversely almost everywhere: *corruption, violence, powerlessness* and *insecure livelihood*.

Source: www.worldbank.org/poverty/data/trends/poorsay.htm.

Woman on rubbish dump, Manila
Source: Pearson Education Ltd/Digital Vision.

land, representing a far greater gender disparity in wealth than is found in industrial nations. Clearly, multilayered systems of tradition and law subordinate women in poor societies. Caught in a spiral of circumstance that promises little hope for change, women are disproportionately the poorest of the poor. More than 500 million of the world's 800 million people living in absolute poverty and at risk for their lives are women.

Women in poor countries have limited access to birth control (which raises the birth rate), and they typically give birth without the assistance of any trained health personnel. There is a stark contrast between high- and low-income countries in this regard. Overall, gender inequality is strongest in low-income societies, especially in Asia where cultural traditions overwhelmingly favour males. This pattern of denigrating women affects virtually every dimension of life and has produced a stunning lack of females in some regions of the world (Kishor, 1993) (see Chapter 13). We look a little more at this below.

Global gender issues

In global perspective, gender inequalities are usually found at their most extreme where people are poorest. Although there is great variation across countries, many women face subordination and discrimination in many areas of life. On most measures of development, low-income women fare worse than men (Seager, 2009). Briefly:

- *Education*: two-thirds of illiterates in the world are women; 60 per cent of children deprived of education are girls. Girls have much less opportunity to move beyond a primary education.

- *Wealth*: the majority of the world's women do not equally own or inherit property or land. In African countries, widespread discrimination exists against women inheriting or owing land and wealth – and this is supported by religion, law and custom.

- *Travel*: often the state restricts travel for women, who frequently need the permission of a male relative. At the same time, low-income women are the prime target for sex trafficking.

- *Reproduction*: women in low-income societies face serious problems through pregnancy. Pregnancy kills and harms as the box summarises.

Transformations into modernity

In recent decades, the situation of low-income women has been changing. To start with, most of the world's governments are now committed – on paper at last – to full equality for women: 185 countries are signatories to the UN Convention on the elimination of all forms of discrimination against women (as of January 2008). In many areas of social life, change has been taking place: families are changing (they are getting smaller, with more families headed by women), mothers are having

Spotlight
Birth and its control in low-income societies

- *Pregnancy kills*. Maternal health disparities between rich and poor countries and between the rich and poor within countries is very great. The risk of a woman dying in sub-Saharan Africa as a result of pregnancy or childbirth is 1 in 22, as compared to 1 in 7,300 in developed regions. Every year, 536,000 women die from pregnancy-related causes.

- *Pregnancy harms*. Over 300 million women worldwide suffer from complications of pregnancy and delivery. At least 2 million women live with obstetric fistula in the developing world, and more than 50,000 new cases occur each year. Obstetric fistula is a key example of inequitable access to maternal health care and, until recently, one of the most hidden. Caused by obstructed labour, it generally presents itself in the early post-partum period. Fistula tends to affect the most marginalised members of society: young, poor, illiterate women living in remote areas.

- *Contraceptives save lives*. Fulfilling the unmet need for modern family planning in the developing world would reduce unintended pregnancies from 75 to 22 million. Having fewer children reduces the economic burden on poor families, and when fertility rates fall, more women join the labour force.

Source: UNFPA, www.unfpa.org/public/home/factsheets (accessed 2010).

fewer children, and increasingly women work outside the home for pay (though typically paid much less than men). The rise of a 'third world women's movement' has also become prominent in campaigning for the rights of women.

Still, even when economic development takes place, it does not follow that women do better. There may be new opportunities to attend school and to work outside the home, to reduce birth rates and to weaken traditional male domination, but along the way new problems occur. Labour is often the only resource at the disposal of poor women to meet their basic needs, and a lack of access to decent work is a major cause of poverty. Data on the gender division of paid and unpaid work in high-income countries revealed that in all the countries covered, men spent a longer period of their working day in market-oriented work, while women spent more time than men in cooking, cleaning and childcare (UNDP, 1995; Razavi and Staab, 2008).

As economic opportunity draws men from rural areas to cities in search of work, women and children must fend for themselves. Some men sell their land and simply abandon their wives, who are left with nothing but their children. More: the waning strength of the family and neighbourhood leaves women who are deserted in this way with little assistance. The same holds true for women who become single through divorce or the death of a spouse. In the past, kin or neighbours readily took in a woman who found herself alone. But today old ties may start to get weakened and consequently the number of poor households headed by women is increasing. Rather than enhancing women's autonomy, a new spirit of individualism has actually eroded the social standing of women.

Economic development – as well as the growing influence of Western movies and mass media – may well undermine women's traditional roles as wives, sisters and mothers in favour of defining women as objects of men's sexual attention. The cultural emphasis on sexuality, familiar to most Westerners, now encourages men in poor countries to abandon ageing spouses for younger, more physically attractive partners. The same stress on sex contributes to the world's rising tide of sex trafficking prostitution, noted in Chapter 12 (see the box on pp. 396–7).

Transformation into a modern world, then, does not affect men and women in the same ways. In the long run, the evidence suggests, it does give the sexes more equal standing. In the short run, however, the economic position of many women actually declines, as women are forced to contend with new problems that were virtually unknown in traditional societies.

Crisis for women

V. Spike Peterson and Anne Sisson Runyan, in their textbook on *Global Gender Issues* (3rd edition, 2010), outline and discuss three critical issues that women in developing/low-income societies confront. They call these the *crisis of representation*, the *crisis of insecurity* and the *crisis of sustainability*.

- The *crisis of representation* suggests that women are devalued in the way they are presented: 'third world women' are constructed in Western eyes as victims and robbed of a sense of agency and activity in their lives. Here is the challenge of thinking about the ways in which poor women are framed and discussed in public media.

- The *crisis of insecurity* is related to the violence and threats that women experience – from conflicts and wars (locally and internationally – where 'war rape' becomes commonplace) to the dangers experienced in unemployment, crime, domestic and sexual violence, and the starkness of brutal poverty. Over and over again, the stories women tell of their lives in poverty are ones of massive insecurity and a sense of risk and danger.

- Finally, the *crisis of sustainability* refers to the ways in which women's households and communities are often under threat. The ability to care for their children and reproduce their communities is under the severe threats of poverty and the violence that often surrounds it. More, today, there is a significant international migration of poor women for caregiving work, as both domestic and public-sector workers, across the world. The high demand for global care workers thereby becomes a threat to their own families, as they leave to look after the families of rich mothers in the West.

Political responses

We can detect a range of responses to women's crises in low-income society. One, the modernist response, has aimed to incorporate women directly into the process of modernisation – increasing women's productivity, helping to strengthen their households. A second has aimed to develop women's projects – building women-centred projects. In most such projects, men are more or less excluded. A third approach has aimed to bring men and women together to discuss ways of enhancing their lives and creating equalities between them.

 On international projects, the Women's Development Programme and 'gender mainstreaming', see: Womenwatch: www.un.org/womenwatch.

Spotlight
The Global Gender Gap Index

Across the globe, women do not fare as well as men. To try to capture this, social scientists speak of the **gender gap index (GGI)**: *a measure of the levels of inequality between men and women in access to resources*. This is measured by a combination of four key indicators:

1 economic participation and opportunity
2 educational attainment
3 health and survival
4 political empowerment.

Recent research has measured this 'gap' for 115 countries (about 90 per cent of the world's population), and the highest and lowest are shown below. Out of the 115 countries covered in the report since 2006, more than two-thirds have posted gains in overall index scores, indicating that the world in general has made progress towards equality between men and women, although there are countries that continue to lose ground.

For more details on the gender gap, look at: World Economic Forum Gender Gap.

Table 9.7	The Global Gender Gap Index: 2009 rankings	
Top 10 countries		
1	Iceland	0.8276
2	Finland	0.8252
3	Norway	0.8227
4	Sweden	0.8139
5	New Zealand	0.7880
6	South Africa	0.7709
7	Denmark	0.7628
8	Ireland	0.7597
9	Philippines	0.7579
10	Lesotho	0.7495
Bottom 10 countries		
125	Qatar	0.5907
126	Eygpt	0.5862
127	Mali	0.5860
128	Iran	0.5839
129	Turkey	0.5828
130	Saudi Arabia	0.5651
131	Benin	0.5643
132	Pakistan	0.5458
133	Chad	0.5417
134	Yemen	0.4609

Notes: The UK is ranked 15th, the USA 31st, China 60th, Greece 86th, Japan 101st and India 114th. Note that the differences are often very small and the measurements are far from precise. So tight rankings like this are open to much doubt. Nevertheless, they do provide an overall indication. See World Economic Forum, *The Global Gender Gap Report 2009*, Table 3a, p. 8 (www.weforum.org).

Global inequality: how is it to be explained?

What accounts for the severe and extensive poverty in low-income countries? There have been many attempts to understand the shape and experiences of world inequalities – often called 'development theory' in the past. All of these also have major implications for social change and social policy. Here we briefly outline six major arguments; Table 9.8 provides a simple summary chronology with some names and key concepts to look out for.

Modernisation theory is possibly the most common and commonsensical explanation. It is a basic progress theory which suggests that uneven world development can be linked to the advance of industrial societies overtaking traditional life. It imports many assumptions about progress and evolution, and argues that as we have acquired more scientific knowledge, developed new technologies and made economic advances through capitalism, so some societies have left behind ways of life that have inhibited their growth. Some cultures and their traditions cause societies to lag behind. In this sense, traditional societies can be seen as 'underdeveloped'. As they become more modernised, so their uneven development and inequalities will decline. The most famous and widely known theory of this form was Rostow's 'limits of growth', which suggested that societies moved through four key phases: a traditional stage, a take-off stage, a drive to technological maturity and a stage of high mass consumption.

Extreme contemporary versions of this are contemporary *neoliberal theories of development*. Here the free market of capitalism effectively means that money goes where it will – the motor engine of social change is profit. As we have seen before (Chapter 2; see also Chapter 16), neoliberal capitalism fosters an open, competitive market, in which the profit motive is prime. And as some countries advance, they gain advantages over others. This open competition inevitably means that some go to the wall – and in this case, even the largest of nation-states can fall behind. We see a version of the 'survival of the fittest' with the rich getting richer and the poor getting poorer. Aware of some of the human problems this brings – mass poverty, world hunger, bad sanitation for the vast majority of the world, damaged lives – many of these accounts also suggest the need for international organisations which will provide international programmes of aid and support to 'undeveloped' countries. But in the end, according to these theories it is only economic growth – and the success of capitalism – which will save the poor.

Both these accounts have been strongly criticised and have led to *dependency and underdevelopment theories*. The kernel of these theories is exploitation. So-called 'underdeveloped' countries have become underdeveloped not because of failure – with technology, or in the market – but because of a long history in which they have been colonised, exploited and excluded by other more dominant countries. Africa is a very good example. Here is a continent that was ravaged by both slavery and colonialism during the seventeenth and eighteenth centuries, from which it has taken centuries to recover. The ravages of the colonial past and slavery have left deep scars. Much of the world has been enslaved to the market dominance of successful capitalist countries – England and Europe especially in the nineteenth century, and the United States in different ways in the twentieth century. They have remained underdeveloped precisely because they have been made dependent upon the dominant markets of capitalism. This theory has been most identified with Andre Gunder Frank's *Capitalism and Underdevelopment in Latin America* (1967).

Closely connected to this is the wider approach of **world systems theory**. This draws from a key distinction of core and periphery – an idea which is also found in underdevelopment theories. It suggests that there is only one world connected by a complex network of economic exchange relationships. It also draws heavily from Marxist ideas, suggesting a 'world-economy' (with its origins in sixteenth-century western Europe and the Americas) in which the 'dichotomy of capital and labor' and an endless 'accumulation of capital' by competing agents lead to conflict and change. In this world system, many societies have remained at the 'periphery' with an unequal share in the market structure. There is *unequal international division of labour* at its heart. Thus the relations of periphery societies with core societies place them in positions of great inequality and differences in economic power. Core societies are developed countries, and the periphery are the dependent developing countries. The leading Marxist theorist Immanuel Wallerstein is the author of *The Modern World System* (1974).

These theories dominated thinking during between the 1960s and 1980s and still have a major in influence. But more recent accounts of the contemporary unequal world have turned to

Children stand outside their small home in the impoverished El Pantonal neighbourhood in Tegucigalpa, Honduras, on 11 October 2001. United Nation figures show that 74% of the Honduran population live below the poverty line. Today, the World Bank officially approves a $75 million package that aims to reduce poverty by 25% over fifteen years in the Central American nation

Source: © Reuters/Corbis.

some version of *globalisation*. As we have seen before (e.g. in Chapter 2), this word means many things, and for some it is actually little more than a new version of neoliberalism and the 'flattening' of the world (Friedman, 2006). The world is now seen as thoroughly interconnected with capitalism, and the new technologies have played a key role here. Old barriers and borders between nations have broker down to facilitate the flow of goods, capital, services, labour and outsourcing. There is global trade, international flows of capital and foreign investments, the mass migration of workers, and the integration of national and regional economies into the international economy through international agencies like the International Bank for Reconstruction and Development (World Bank), the International Monetary Fund (IMF) and the World Trade

Organization (WTO). It brings large trading blocks and huge global economic giants like China and the USA. And with it there is a continuing apparent downside: the great financial crisis of 1998–9, growing inequalities, continuing global poverty, the creation of sweatshops and international labour trafficking, continuing slavery, mass waste and dumping, and environmental crisis. Side by side with the construction of lush hotels and holiday resorts and the billionaire lifestyle nestles the world of slums and abject poverty.

Key elements in each of the above theories can help you try to make sense of the global inequalities around you. Ultimately, the contemporary world – with its 7 billion people and 200 states – is a web of *global complexity*: it is becoming harder and harder to make strong generalisations about it, and it is

Table 9.8	A summary of changing theories of development and inequalities	
Starting period	**Perspectives**	**Influential ideas**
1700s	Classical early political economy	Free market capitalism and Adam Smith's guiding hand
1800s	Evolutionism	Social Darwinians Progress and evolution
1850s	Colonial economics	Trusteeship/exploitation
1850s	Marxist analysis	Exploitation, colonialism, imperialism
1950s	Modernisation theory	Stages of growth: Rostow, p. 306
1970s	Dependency theory (neo-Marxist)	Gunder Frank, p. 306 Decolonisation, anti-imperialism, indigenisation Unequal division of labour: Wallerstein
1970s	World systems theory	
1980s	Neoliberalism	Global finance, economic growth, trickle down, deregulation, privatisation Market cultures, consumerism
1980s	Globalisation	Interconnectedness of world Often linked to latest phase of neoliberalism
1980s	Human development	Capabilities, human flourishing Key example: East Asia: Nussbaum and Sen, p. 417
1990s	ICT4D (Information and Communication Technology for Development)	The tele-centre and the mobile phone Digital divide, cyber-apartheid
2000s	Millennium Development Goals	Structural and eclectic reforms: p. 296
2010s	Normative theories – global complexities	Human rights, capabilities and complexities of global worlds

Source: Modified from an idea by Jan Nederveen Pieterse, 2009a: 7).

necessary to see the deep interconnectedness of a range of multiple social processes, working within a (now) global capitalist process, which are always moving and always changing.

A normative theory of inequality and global change

What is missing from all of the above theories of development is an explicit moral and evaluative stance on the world we would like to see. What kind of future world do we wish to see in the future? It is at this point, of course, that many sociologists and social researchers hand their work over to the philosophers and the politicians. They do not see it as part of their work to make value judgements. But in some ways this is slightly dishonest. Do we simply want to understand the massive world inequality so that we can leave it as it is; or do we study it because we want to make the world a better place? And if we want a better place, what might this better place look like?

Some recent theories have also brought a growing concern in development theories for specifying the kind of world we want to live in: they are normative theories. They come in various forms. Some specify that all societies should meet basic human needs (Paul Streeten). Some seek to enable *human capabilities and human rights* to flourish (in the work of Sen and Nussbaum and the development of the Human Development Index). Others have established target goals for developing societies, as in the United Nations project of establishing the *Human Millennium Goals* (HMG).

Two approaches to poverty reduction

Jonathan Sachs – in his book *The End of Poverty: How We Can Make It End in our Lifetime* (2005) – has called for 'on the ground solutions for ending poverty' (p. 23). He sees the lack of capital, resources and support for the poor as the key issues. The extreme poor lack 'health, nutrition and skills for work along with access to any kind of business, knowledge or public institutional structures which could alleviate their conditions' (p. 245). For Sachs, the solutions to world poverty require key investments – in people and infrastructure – that can give impoverished communities around the world, rural and urban, the tools for **sustainable development**. He suggests listening to the poor, hearing what they want and what they do. He argues that for a small

cost (a tiny cost to the world – but too high for the villagers), poverty could be severely reduced. He asks about local ways to handle such issues as: nutrition-depleted soils, malaria, lack of access to safe drinking water and latrines, and the unmet need for basic transport, electricity, cooking fuels and communications. He argues for funding agricultural inputs; investments in basic health; investments in education; power, transport and communications; and safe drinking water and sanitation. These can all be specific local projects which would radically change the lives of the poor.

In contrast, Paul Collier, in his book *The Bottom Billion* (2007), argues that aid is often ineffective, globalisation can make the situation worse, and what is needed is a strong plan (from the G8) of preferential trade policies, new laws against corruption and new international charters. He stresses Africa's history of repeated coups d'état and civil wars. He cites studies which show how cash

earmarked by the government for spending on poverty can disappear before it reaches its targets. The abundant natural resources in Africa do not lead to a 'trickle down' – the theory that the spending power of the rich benefits the poor. Rather more frequently, growth leads to corruption and theft. Collier concludes:

> The politics of the bottom billion is not the bland and sedate process of the rich democracies but rather a dangerous contest between moral extremes. The struggle for the future of the bottom billion is not a contest between an evil rich world and a noble poor world. It is within the societies of the bottom billion.

The real solutions to the struggles of the world's poorest people are more complex, and harder to sell to enthusiastic campaigners, than the aid-solves-everything, 'Make Poverty History' approach.

See: Sachs, 2005; Collier, 2007.

Global inequality: looking ahead

Among the most important trends of recent decades is the development of a global economy. While some see this as generating markets of increased wealth and productivity, others see it as simply exacerbating inequality around the world. Profitable investments, many of them in poor nations, and lucrative sales have brought greater affluence to those who already have substantial wealth. And increasing industrial production abroad has cut factory jobs, exerting downward pressure on wages. The net result: gradual economic polarisation.

It is true that in some regions of the world, such as the 'Pacific Rim' of eastern Asia, market forces are raising

living standards rapidly and substantially. Many Latin American nations (such as Colombia and Chile) have also recorded strong economic growth in recent years. Meanwhile, however, other poor societies, especially in Africa, are experiencing economic turmoil that frustrates hopes for market-based development.

The poor countries that have surged ahead economically have two factors in common. First, they are relatively small. Combined, the Asian nations of South Korea, Taiwan, Hong Kong, Singapore and Japan cover only about one-fifth of the land area and population of India. The economic problems that smaller countries face are more manageable; consequently, small societies more effectively administer programmes of development. Secondly, these 'best-case' nations have cultural traits in common, especially traditions emphasising individual achievement and economic success.

In other areas of the world, where powerful cultural forces inhibit change and individualism, even smaller nations have failed to turn economic opportunities to their advantage. Social inequality is striking in this global context. The concentration of wealth among high-income countries, coupled with the grinding poverty typical of low-income nations, may well constitute the most important dilemma facing humanity in the twenty-first century. To some analysts, globalisation holds the keys to ending world poverty; to others, it is the cause of this tragic problem.

SUMMARY

1 The chapter provides many statistics on world poverty and inequality. Depending on how poverty is defined, somewhere between 1.3 billion and 3 billion people live in poverty – nearly half of the world's population. The richest 20 per cent of the global population receives some 74 per cent of all income. At the other end of the social scale, the poorest 20 per cent of the world's people, by contrast, struggle to survive on just 1 per cent of global income.

2 Two major measures of inequality are widely used. The first is based on economic factors and depends largely on measuring the gross national product (GNP) and the gross domestic product (GDP); the latter depends on a complex series of scales which aim to measure the quality of life, known as the Human Development Index.

3 Absolute poverty refers to a lack of resources that is life threatening (often measured as a per capita income equivalent to less than one international dollar, or one and a half dollars, a day). Human beings in absolute poverty commonly lack the nutrition necessary for health and long-term survival.

4 The UN Millennium Development Goals were adopted by 189 nations at a 2000 Summit. The eight goals targeted include halving extreme poverty, universal education for children, ending child and maternal mortality, and stopping the spread of HIV/AIDS.

5 Four groups of world poor are given special attention: children, women, the elderly and refugees.

6 Across the globe, women do not fare as well as men. The gender gap is a measure of the levels of inequality between men and women.

7 The poverty found in much of the world is a complex problem reflecting limited industrial technology, rapid population growth, traditional cultural patterns, internal social stratification, male domination and global power relationships.

8 There are many theories to explain the problem of world poverty and inequalities. Modernisation theory maintains that successful development hinges on acquiring advanced productive technology and sees traditional cultural patterns as the key barrier. Dependency theory claims that global wealth and poverty are directly linked to the historical operation of the capitalist world economy. The dependency of poor countries on rich ones is rooted in colonialism.

9 Both modernisation and dependency approaches offer useful initial insights into the development of global inequality. Recent theories have stressed globalisation, global complexity and the development of human capabilities.

MYTASKLIST

Ten suggestions for going further

1 Connect up with Part Six and the Sociology Web Resources

As you work through ideas and think about the issues raised in this chapter, look at the accompanying website and the resource centre at the end of this book which connects to it. There is a lot here to help you move on. To link up, see: www.pearson.co.uk/plummer.

2 Review the chapter

Briefly summarise (in a paragraph) just what this chapter has been about. Consider: (a) What have you learned? (b) What do you disagree with? Be critical. And (c) How would you develop all this? How could you get more detail on matters that interest you?

3 Pose questions

(a) For all the advances of globalisation and industralisation, it seems that poverty is still with us on a massive scale and inequalities still seem to be growing. Why do you think this is? What could (or should) be done about it? Do you think that more economic aid from high-income societies will help low-income societies?

(b) Do you think advertising (for coffee from Colombia or exotic vacations to Egypt or India) provides an accurate picture of life in low-income countries? Why or why not? Do you think most people in Europe have a realistic understanding of the extent and severity of poverty in the world?

(c) Using website resources, chart the range of refugees and displaced people in the world, looking at the cause of their displacement, where (if anywhere)

they have relocated, the problems they experience as 'asylum seekers', and what their future looks like.

(d) Read the quotes in the *Speaking lives* box on p. 302 and, if you can, watch one of the films listed below. Now engage in a *verstehen* exercise: try to understand the meanings and experiences of what it is like to be severely poor.

4 Explore key words

Many concepts have been introduced in this chapter. You can review them from the website or from the listing at the back of this book. You might like to give special attention to just five words and think them through – how would you define them, what are they dealing with, and do they help you see the social world more clearly or not?

Try looking at *The A to Z of World Development* – a very useful illustrated dictionary, compiled by Andy Crump and edited by Wayne Ellwood (New Internationalist, 1998). It is now a little out of date.

5 Search the Web

Be critical when you look at websites – see the box on p. 940 in the Resources section. Some useful sources for this chapter are as follows:

World Bank
www.worldbank.org

United Nations
www.undp.org/poverty

These are two major world resources for looking at poverty. They are updated with the latest figures, articles and plans for action, as well major sections in which the poor speak for themselves.

Global Monitoring Report
www.un.org/millenniumgoals
Keeps an up-to-date check on the Millennium Development Goals.

Oxfam
www.oxfam.org.uk
Oxfam is a development, relief and campaigning organisation that works with others to overcome poverty and suffering around the world.

United Nations Refugee Agency
www.unhcr.org/basics
A really useful website on all matters linked to refugees and displacements of peoples.

On Africa and its neglect in cyberspace, see:
AllAfrica Internet Guide
www.goafrica.co.za
AllAfrica aggregates and indexes content from over 125 African news organisations, plus more than 200 other sources, which are responsible for their own reporting and views.

6 Watch a DVD

- Ermanno Olmi's *The Tree of Wooden Clogs* (1978): a stunning depiction of poverty in rural Italy in the nineteenth century.
- Jibril Diop's Mambety's *Hyenas* (1992): a classic allegory of international aid.
- Soraya Mire's *Fire Eyes* (1993): a documentary about female genital mutilation.
- Tsitsi Dangarembga's *Everyone's Child* (1996): this film is a call for action on behalf of Africa's millions of parentless children.
- Soulymane Cissé's *Yeelen* (1987): film about traditional African culture.
- Miguel Littin's *The Promised Land* (1973: Chile), Hector Babenco's *Pixote* (1981: Brazil) and Victor Gaviria's *Rodrigo D: No Future* (1989: Medellin, Columbia): all vividly capture poverty.

7 Think and read

Vandana Desai and Robert B. Potter, *The Companion to Development Studies* (2nd edn, 2008). A very useful collection of short pieces on every aspect of the developing world.

York W. Bradshaw and Michael Wallace, *Global Inequalities* (1996). Discusses basic data region by region, as well as the major explanations of global inequalities. A new edition is promised for 2009.

Peter and Susan Calvert, *Politics and Society in the Third World* (3rd edn, 2007). A comprehensive tour.

Deepa Narayan, *Voices of the Poor: Can Anyone Hear Us?* (2000). A highly readable introduction, brimming with personal experiences of poverty and inequalities in low-income countries.

Jeffrey Sachs, *The End of Poverty: How We Can Make it Happen in our Life time* (2005); Stephen Smith, *Ending Global Poverty: A Guide to What Works* (2005); Paul Collier, *The Bottom Billion* (2007); Amartya Sen, *Development as Freedom* (1999). Four contrasting books that examine the issues around poverty and what should be done.

Paul Marfleet, *Refugees in a Global Era* (2006). A useful text which looks at the global disordered world of people making long, risky journeys to flee their own countries.

More information

Two annual publications provide a wide range of data on the comparative economic development of the world's nations:

United Nations Development Programme, *Human Development Report*. This is published annually.

The World Bank, *World Development Report*. This is published annually.

The magazine *New Internationalist*, published in Oxford, provides a wealth of data on inequalities and the global situation. *The World* CD-Rom and book are also available from New Internationalist. The 11th edition was published in 2007. A new website version seems to be forthcoming.

8 Relax with a novel

There is a wide-ranging and important literature on the tensions and conflicts found in 'developing' or low-income societies. See the following:

Ben Okri, *The Famished Road* (1991)
Alan Paton, *Cry, The Beloved Country* (1948)
Chinua Achebe, *Things Fall Apart* (1958)
V. S. Naipul, *A Bend in the River* (1979)
Isabel Allende, *Of Love and Shadows* (1987)
Vikram Seth, *A Suitable Boy* (1993).
Gabriel Garcia Marquez, *One Hundred Years of Solitude* (1967).
And at a different level: see Joseph Conrad, *Heart of Darkness* (1902).

9 Connect to other chapters

- Poverty is discussed further in Chapter 10.
- The discussion of refugees should also be linked to migration and racism in Chapter 11.
- Consider women's situation more fully in Chapter 12.
- More on children and poverty in Chapter 13.
- Link to AIDS in Chapter 21.

10 Engage with THE BIG DEBATE

Will the world starve?

Hunger casts its menacing shadow not only over regions of Asia, but also over much of Latin America, most of Africa and even parts of North America. Throughout the world, hundreds of millions of adults do not consume enough food to enable them to work. And some 10 million of the world's children die each year because they do not get enough to eat. Meanwhile, in the Western world, many people suffer from obesity and spend their money on slimming aids! (See pp. 242–3.)

At the start of a new century, what are the prospects for eradicating the wretched misery of so many human beings enduring daily hunger?

It is easy to be pessimistic. For one thing, the population of poor countries is currently increasing by 90 million people annually – equivalent to adding another Mexico to the world every year. Poor countries

Hunger in the developing world 2010: World Food Programme headlines

Total in hunger	1.2 billion people go hungry every day
Total undernourished	In Asia and the Pacific, 642 million are suffering from chronic hunger; in Sub-Saharan Africa, 265 million.
Developed countries	15 million hungry in total

Source: United Nations World Food Programme, www.wfp.org/about.

can scarcely feed the people they have now; looking ahead a generation into the future, how will they ever feed double their current populations?

In addition, as detailed in Chapter 25, hunger forces poor people to exploit the earth's resources by using short-term strategies for food production that will lead to long-term disaster. For example, to feed the swelling populations of poor tropical countries, farmers are cutting down rainforests in order to increase their farmland. But, without the protective canopy of trees, it is only a matter of time before much of this land turns to desert.

Taken together, rising populations and ecological approaches that borrow against the future raise the spectre of hunger and outright starvation escalating well beyond current levels. Regarded pessimistically, the world's future is bleak: unprecedented hunger, human misery and political calamity. But there are also some grounds for optimism. Thanks to the Green Revolution, food production the world over is up sharply over the last 50 years, even outpacing the growth in population. Taking a broader view, the world's economic productivity has risen steadily, so that the average person on the planet has more income now to purchase food and other necessities than ever before.

This growth has increased daily calorie intake as well as life expectancy, access to safe water and adult literacy, while infant mortality is going down. In fact, looking at these social indicators, we can see the gap between rich and poor countries actually narrowing. So what are the prospects for eradicating world hunger – especially in

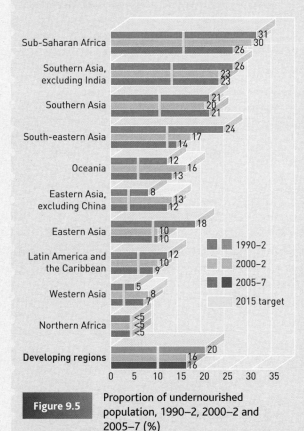

Figure 9.5 Proportion of undernourished population, 1990–2, 2000–2 and 2005–7 (%)

Source: United Nations (2010: 12).

low-income nations? Overall, we see less hunger in both rich and poor countries: that is, a smaller share of the world's people faces starvation now than, say, in 1960. But as global population increases, with 90 per cent of children born in middle- and low-income countries, the number of lives at risk is as great today as ever before. Moreover, even though living standards are rising, there has not been any narrowing of the economic gap between rich and poor countries.

Also bear in mind that aggregate data mask different trends in various world regions. The 'best case' region of the world is eastern Asia, where incomes (controlled for inflation) have tripled over the last generation. It is to Asia that the 'optimists' in the global hunger debate typically turn for evidence that poor countries can and do raise living standards and reduce hunger. The 'worst case' region of the world is Sub-Saharan Africa, where living standards have actually fallen over the last decade, and more and more people are pushed to the brink of starvation. It is here that high technology is least evident and birth rates are highest. Pessimists typically look to Africa when they argue that poor countries are losing ground in the struggle to keep their people well nourished.

Television brings home the tragedy of hunger every year or so when news cameras focus on starving people in places such as Ethiopia, Somalia and Afghanistan. But hunger – and the early death from illness that it brings on – is the plight of millions all year round. The problem is not that there is too little food in the world – there is, in principle, enough food for the world to eat (Smith, 2005: 5). Indeed, there are more people in the world suffering from being overweight than those experiencing calorie deprivation. Rather, the issue is: 'How to give the poor enough command over resources to meet their nutrition and other basic needs on a regular basis?' (Smith, 2005: 5).

The world does have the technical means to feed everyone; the question is: do we have the moral determination to do so?

Continue the debate

1 What are the primary causes of global hunger?
2 Do you place responsibility for solving this problem on poor countries or rich ones? Why?
3 Do you expect the extent of global hunger to increase or decrease? Why?

See: United Nations World Food Programme: www.wfp.org.

CHAPTER 10

CLASS, POVERTY AND WELFARE: THE CASE OF THE UK

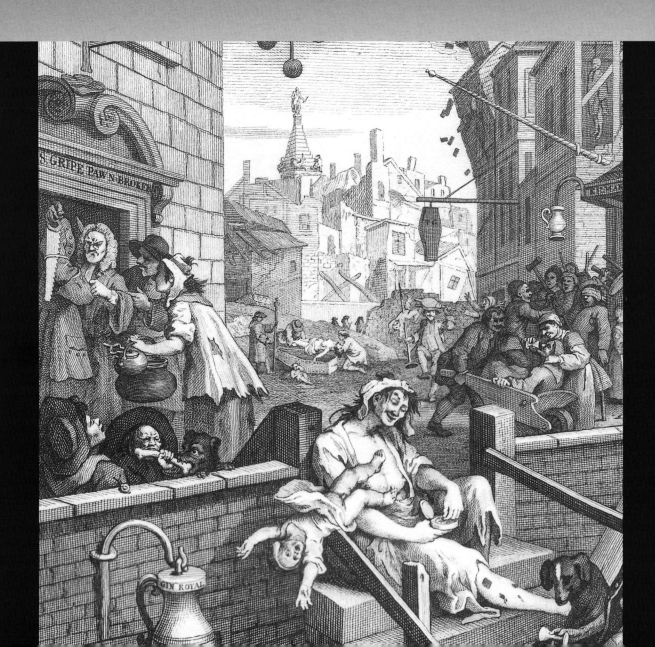

ALL CONTEMPORARY SOCIETIES HAVE CLASS STRUCTURES, though not every society treats class as an issue of premium social importance. In the United States, racial divides are often foremost in people's minds and people tend to see themselves as being much less class bound. Any visitor to the UK, by contrast, will soon hear people talk about class. Indeed, they may soon see it: with elite educational institutions from public schools to Oxford and Cambridge universities, gentlemen's clubs, and the famous houses of the landed aristocracy. At the other extreme, the homeless sleeping in streets and slum housing can mark out 'the lower classes'. As Valerie Walkerdine and her colleagues (2001) suggest:

> Class is not something that is simply produced economically. It is performed, marked, written on minds and bodies. We can 'spot it a mile off' even in the midst of our wish for it no longer to be there.
>
> (cited in Roberts, 2001: 9)

To get a good idea of what class is all about, consider two extremes in the UK. First consider the election of the new UK government (the Conservative–Democratic Alliance) in 2010. Under the co-leaders David Cameron and Nick Clegg, the cabinet of 29 was established as usual to provide the key group of people to run the country. In that cabinet, some 23 of them had wealth well over a million pounds and some 20 of them had been to the same university group – Oxford and Cambridge. They are in a sense a distinctly privileged group – with more wealth than most people in the country, but also have a different social and cultural capital, being from the UK's most prestigious (and elite) universities. What class would you put them in?

Next try to watch some episodes of Paul Abbott's semi-autobiographical Channel 4 drama about a wayward Manchester family, the Gallaghers, in the series *Shameless*. Very funny and very shocking, it displays a dysfunctional, working-class family running wild on a modern housing estate. It relentlessly and unapologetically depicts them as a 'horrifying, irredeemable bunch of work-shy, Asbo-inviting chavs, hooked on handouts, the neighbours from hell'.

Yet *Shameless* seems to have universal appeal. David Threlfall, who plays Frank Gallagher, has suggested that we all experience an excitement in seeing this dysfunctional family go into places that we, in our safe homes, would never dare enter. 'People love the Gallaghers because they know they're not them. They think, "There but for the grace of the Gallaghers go I." '

'It doesn't just attract the lower end of society,' Threlfall says. 'I've had people from right across the social spectrum tell me they get it. Sometimes reporters ask, "Don't you think you're being a bit patronising about working-class people?" To which I say, "Bollocks, you middle-class journalist!" If it was condescending, I'd know because people on the estates where we film would come and tell me.' *Shameless* has already been commissioned for an eighth series (to transmit in 2011). What class would you put these people in? (*Source*: James Rampton, 'Still Shameless', *Independent*, 21 December 2007).

In this chapter, we will examine the nature of classes, wealth and poverty in industrial capitalist societies, with a major focus on the UK. The chapter will ask how we can identify classes, present a brief 'portrait' of class life as it is lived in the UK, and examine

poverty. Finally, we will consider the emergence of 'welfare states' as a means of dealing with some of the problems that inequalities generate.

It's the same the whole world over
It's the poor what gets the blame
It's the rich what gets the pleasure
Ain't it all a bloody shame.

Billy Bennett, Traditional English Music Hall, 1930.

In this chapter, we ask:

- **What is the nature of class and its measurement?**

- **How can we 'measure' poverty in the UK?**

- **What is the nature of 'welfare states' and citizenship as means of dealing with some of the problems that inequalities generate?**

(Left) William Hogarth's engraving *Gin Lane* shows the depravity of the poor of London when trying to forget their situation by turning to drink
Source: The Art Archive.

Q William Hogarth's engravings are major social comments on life in eighteenth-century England, and his work is worth a sociological study of its own. Examine this image carefully and look up a wide range of his work at: http://exhibits.library.northwestern. edu/spec/hogarth/index.html and www.artchive.com/artchive/H/ hogarth.html. The entry in Wikipedia is also helpful and locates this image

The nature of social class

In this chapter, social class is the key issue. To give it a firmer focus, the prime concern will be with the system of class found in the United Kingdom – long considered one of the most class-ridden societies in the world. It has also been of great interest to sociologists. As we shall see, modern class systems are dynamic, fluid, always changing. An underlying split amongst sociologists here is between those who focus upon class as primarily economic (linked to income, wealth, work and poverty) and those most concerned with status and culture (linked to lifestyles, symbols and identity). Traditionally, the former take a *Marxist view* and the latter a *Weberian view* which looks more at class, status and power and is multidimensional. But as we will see, the divisions are more complicated than this.

Marx: the economic position

Karl Marx defined class in terms of those who own the means of production and those who do not (with a residual class in between). Any Marxist definition of class must give a priority to the ownership of capital and patterns of work. Thus, the leading North American class theorist Erik Olin Wright (1985, 1992) elaborated on Marx's model by dividing ownership into three categories: those *controlling resource allocation*; those *controlling the means of production*; and those *controlling labour power*. Wright defines all low-level employees as working class, and suggests that the rest in the middle occupy a contradictory position in which they may identify with either the capitalists or the

working classes. Others break down Marx's original distinctions further into six (Warner and Lunt, 1941) or even seven (Coleman and Rainwater, 1978) categories. The separation of management and 'capital', and the failure of radical class consciousness to emerge among working people, have made such class definitions difficult to translate into numbers that we can meaningfully measure and compare.

Weber: the multidimensional position

Other scholars endorse Max Weber's contention that, rather than clear-cut classes, people are ranked in a multidimensional status hierarchy. Those elaborating on Weber often examine socioeconomic status (SES) as a composite measure of social position. This can involve class, status and power, embracing work, wealth and income, status dimensions (lifestyle), consciousness and identity as well as where a person stands politically.

This is clearly a complex equation; and such definitions run into many problems because of the relatively low level of status consistency in societies. Especially around the middle of hierarchies, ranking on one dimension may often contradict one's position on another. A government official, for example, may have the power to administer a multimillion-pound budget, yet earn only a modest personal income. Similarly, members of the clergy typically enjoy ample prestige but only moderate power and low pay.

Perhaps most commonly, class these days is defined through people's *work situation* (their work tasks and the degree of control they have over their working timetables

Five elderly women onlookers are lined against a wall outside the famous Ascot race course on Ladies' Day, an annual event on the English sporting and social calendar in June. Each are standing and watching as two posh couples arrive for the day's racing dressed in showy dresses for the ladies and formal top hat and tails for the men. Each wears their red Ascot badge allowing them entry to this exclusive event attended by the Royal Family and the hoi polloi of English society. Here we see the two sides of the class system but in a humorous scene. See also the photo that opens Chapter 20
Source: © Richard Baker/In Pictures/Corbis.

and methods) and *market situation* (people's life chances, which depend upon such things as their income and opportunity for promotion). John Scott (1997), for example, breaks down capitalist classes into three types: entrepreneurs, who own and control their own businesses; internal capitalists (top career managers); and finance capitalists, who own and manage big finance companies and big business (Scott, 1997).

Key dimensions of class and social inequality in the UK

The most direct way into thinking about class is to examine three key features of the economic system: work, income and wealth. Here we look only at the last two (work is examined in Chapter 15 on the economy).

Income

A first important dimension of inequality involves **income**, *occupational wages or salaries and earnings from investments*. There are enormous discrepancies here, as Figure 10.1 suggests. Here we see a table of percentiles ranked at ten per cent intervals. The lowest 1 per cent of the population have incomes of £5,668 per year; the top 1 per cent highest are paid well over £1,200,000 a year and 90 per cent earn less than £46,488 a year. The chart shows an enormous inequality of incomes.

Average and low incomes

In more detail, between April 2008 and April 2009, the average weekly pay for employees in the UK grew by 2 per cent, reaching £489 (£531 for men; £426 for women). There were major discrepancies: health professionals and corporate managers earned median weekly pay of £1,031 and £745 respectively, while employees in sales occupations only reached a median income of £278. Likewise, available data show notable discrepancies between men's and women's full-time weekly earnings, with women earning up to £100 less than men in similar positions. If one had a degree, then average earnings were much higher. There were also regional differences. Median full-time weekly earnings reached £627 in London, but ranged from only £436 to £514 in other parts of the country. At

the time of going to press this income was falling: in April 2010, the average total pay (including bonuses) in the UK had dropped to £455 per week. The lowest income in the UK is formally fixed by the minimum wage which came into being in April 1999. Set initially at £3.60 in 1999 for those aged 22 and over (£3.00 for those aged 18–21), there are currently four levels of minimum wage. From 1 October 2010, these were:

- £5.93 – the main rate for workers aged 21 and over
- £4.92 – the 18–20 rate
- £3.64 – the 16–17 rate for workers above school leaving age but under 18
- £2.50 – the apprentice rate, for apprentices under 19, or 19 or over and in the first year of their apprenticeship.

The age at which you become entitled to the main rate was reduced from 22 to 21 on 1 October 2010. The apprentice rate was introduced on the same date.

Even so, many get less than this outside of the legal system. And you may also like to contrast this income with earnings in low-income societies that we discussed in the previous chapter, where a routine weekly income is rarely above £20). Table 10.1 shows weekly earnings by occupational group. (Note too the differentials for women.)

The rich

At the other extreme are the rich. Since 1988, the *Sunday Times* has produced an annual Rich List. This shows that the number of millionaires in the UK increased by more than 80 per cent between 2001 (230,000) and 2004 (425,000). In 2004 it reached 425,000, but the global recession of 2008 and 2009 led to the number of millionaires shrinking to 242,000. In 2010 the list suggested a major recovery: in just one year there had been a 30 per cent increase in the collective wealth of the 1,000 multimillionaires – the biggest annual improvement in the 22 years of the Rich List.

Inequalities

As some people are getting significantly richer, many others are on very low wages and getting poorer. It is not just that actual incomes in a major industrial country are often very low indeed, but also the fact that the gap between high incomes and low incomes is growing. This gap bodes badly for concerns about equality and class. In the UK in the 1980s, inequalities were growing faster than in any other country in the

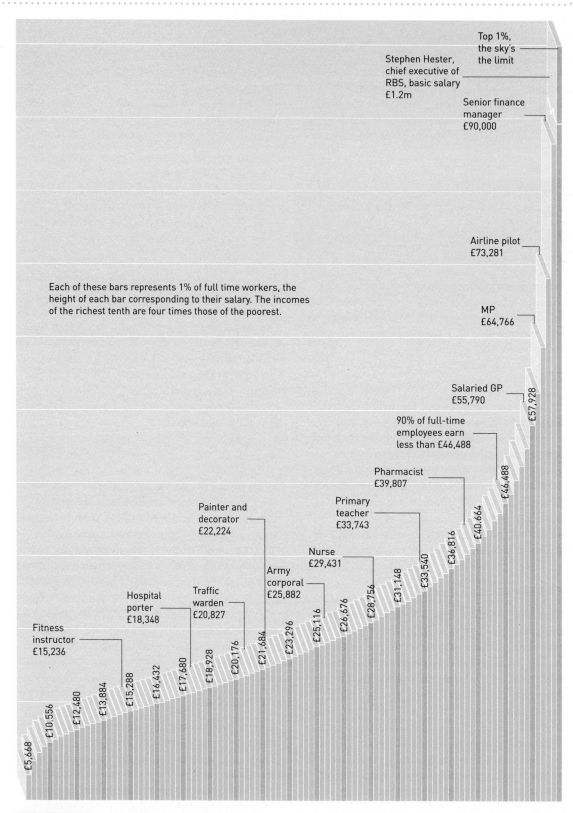

Top 1%, the sky's the limit

Stephen Hester, chief executive of RBS, basic salary £1.2m

Senior finance manager £90,000

Airline pilot £73,281

Each of these bars represents 1% of full time workers, the height of each bar corresponding to their salary. The incomes of the richest tenth are four times those of the poorest.

MP £64,766

Salaried GP £55,790

£57,928

90% of full-time employees earn less than £46,488

£46,488

Pharmacist £39,807

£40,664

Primary teacher £33,743

£36,816

Painter and decorator £22,224

£33,540

£31,148

Nurse £29,431

£28,756

Army corporal £25,882

£26,676

Traffic warden £20,827

£25,116

Hospital porter £18,348

£23,296

£21,684

Fitness instructor £15,236

£20,176

£18,928

£17,680

£16,432

£15,288

£13,884

£12,480

£10,556

£5,668

Figure 10.1 Income disparities in the UK

Source: The Guardian, 20 November 2010. Copyright Guardian News & Media Ltd 2010.

Table 10.1	Median gross weekly earnings by occupation: employees on adult rates, whose pay was unaffected by absence		
	Full time		
April 2009	**Men**	**Women**	**All**
£ per week			
All employees	**531.1**	**426.4**	**488.7**
1 Managers and senior officials	773.4	602.7	712.9
2 Professional	733.1	655.1	695.6
3 Associate professional and technical	581.5	516.0	551.1
4 Administrative and secretarial	409.3	363.6	373.7
5 Skilled trades	459.7	323.0	452.1
6 Personal service	364.6	316.8	325.8
7 Sales and customer service	311.0	285.9	296.2
8 Process, plant and machine operatives	427.8	305.7	414.0
9 Elementary occupations	344.0	271.3	322.5

Source: ONS, *Annual Survey of Hours and Earnings*, 2009, p. 10.

OECD except New Zealand. By the early 1990s growth was more stable, but since then the gap has started to grow again. The research of the Joseph Rowntree Foundation and the Child Poverty Action Group (CPAG) suggests that a great deal of poverty still exists in the UK. The number of people living in low-income households rose by 1.3 million between 2007 and 2009 and has remained constant in comparison with the year 2000. The number of children in low-income households with at least one employed adult, at 2.1 million, is the largest ever measured. We will look at this further below. (See websites for Joseph Rowntree Foundation, Child Poverty Action Group and the Department of Work and Pensions; see also *Social Trends*, 2010).

While the UK may have less income inequality than, say, Venezuela, Kenya or Sri Lanka, income inequality in these countries is higher than in many other industrial societies. Figure 10.2 shows a comparison of incomes within the EU in 2007 (see also Chapter 9).

Wealth

Income is one component of a person's **wealth**, *the total value of money and other assets, minus outstanding*

debts. Assets contributing to wealth include such items as houses, property, jewels, cars, artworks, boats, shares in a stock market, deposited money and racehorses. While the richest 1 per cent of Britons controlled 69 per cent of the national wealth in 1911, today the wealthiest 1 per cent of individuals own between one-fifth and one-quarter of the total wealth, and one-quarter of the adult population owns nearly three-quarters of the total wealth. By 2009, the Office for National Statistics found that the less wealthy 50 per cent of households in Britain only held 9 per cent of wealth. In contrast, the most affluent 20 per cent of households had accumulated 62 per cent of wealth (*Social Trends*).

Even though the wealth base has broadened, the wealthiest people still command considerable resources. According to the Sunday Times Rich List 2010, the wealth of the 1,000 richest individuals in Britain rose by more than £77 billion in 2009, in spite of a global economic crisis. Some examples among the richest 25 people in Britain include the industrialist Lakshmi Mittal and family (at £22.4 billion in 2010), Sir Richard Branson (the entrepreneur who founded the various Virgin companies, with a personal fortune estimated at between £2 billion and £3 billion; and the Duke of Westminster, wielding wealth of £6.7 billion.

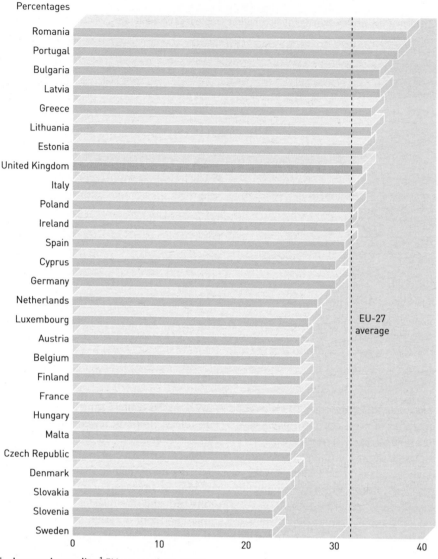

Percentages

Romania
Portugal
Bulgaria
Latvia
Greece
Lithuania
Estonia
United Kingdom
Italy
Poland
Ireland
Spain
Cyprus
Germany
Netherlands
Luxembourg
Austria
Belgium
Finland
France
Hungary
Malta
Czech Republic
Denmark
Slovakia
Slovenia
Sweden

EU-27 average

0   10   20   30   40

Figure 10.2   Income inequality:[1] EU comparison, 2007

[1] As measured by the Gini coefficient, which can take values between 0 and 100, with 0 representing complete equality and 100 representing complete inequality.

Source: EU Survey of Income and Living Standards, Eurostat in *Social Trends*, 40 (2010), Fig. 5.15, p. 69.

Author J. K. Rowling has assets of £519 million, and former Beatle Sir Paul McCartney has some £475 million. Such wealth gives the mega-rich considerable influence, from the field of national politics to minor business transactions.

The super-rich also tend to reinforce and protect each other's interests. As John Scott notes (Scott, 1991, 1996, 1997), the elite 0.1 per cent of industrial populations often share similar backgrounds, swap directorships of high-performing companies, and are dominant shareholders in the leading businesses.

 You can update information on the minimum wage online. See: www.hmrc.gov.uk/nmw/#b.

You can update on the rich through the *Sunday Times* Rich List, published annually, usually in April. Just search online for Sunday Times Rich List.

Inequalities, resources and social class

The study of inequalities and social class is ultimately about our access to different resources (or capital) to live with. Some people have an abundance of access to these resources; while others have almost no access. The most obvious 'resource' is capital or wealth or economic resources. But it goes beyond this, and these days (often following the influence of the French sociologist Pierre Bourdieu, who we met in Chapter 8), sociologists locate a wider array of resources. Below is a list of key resources and you might like to think about your own opportunities in relation to them:

- **Economic resources**: how much income, wealth, financial assets and inheritance do you have access to? How much does your work provide for your needs?

- **Social resources**: how much support do you have from family, friends, community and networks?

- **Cultural resources**: how much access do you have to the knowledge, information, skills, education of your society?

- **Symbolic resources**: how much access do you have to people giving you legitimacy and privileging your life over others?

- **Political resources**: how much autonomy do you have in your life? Are you able to control much of your day or do others control it for you?

- **Bodily resources**: in what ways does your body seem to limit or control your life? How far do others regulate your body?

- **Personal resources**: how much has your own unique life and life history helped you generate the personal skills needed for you to move easily in the world?

Source: Adapted from Plummer, 2010: 175.

Social class in the UK

Goran Therborn has suggested that *social class is one of the key defining features of modern Europe*, as Europe was the first major arena of industrialisation. More than anywhere in the world, class is to be found here (1995: 68). Europe as a whole, he contends, first experienced the rise of a manual working class through the industrialisation period, followed much more recently by a decline in this section of the population. Nowadays, 'less than a third of the economically active population is engaged in industrial labour' (1995: 76), marking the shrinking size of the working-class population. And there is a widespread view – amongst both politicians and the public – that class is less important than it was.

Yet, all main political parties in the UK, at least rhetorically, claim to want to create conditions for upward social mobility – a world where we can all 'make it'. Indeed, both of the last two Conservative prime ministers, John Major (1990–7) and Margaret Thatcher (1979–90), came from 'humble' origins: he, the son of a circus acrobat and garden gnome salesman; she, the daughter of a grocer from Grantham. The current Con–Lib coalition in the UK, by contrast, brings leaders David Cameron and Nick Clegg to power, with much more obviously privileged backgrounds.

There are various ways of visualising these class patterns. Most conventionally, the class structure is seen as a ladder – here the steps suggest mobility as people move upwards. More often it is seen as a pyramid – here the base would be a large working class, a smaller middle class and a tiny upper class. But recent class studies suggest this is not an adequate image. It may be better to see class through the image of a ball – with a large middle class in the centre and smaller working and upper classes at the ends. The middle class may account for around 50 per cent of western European societies – but it is growing as traditional manual occupations decline. Figure 10.3 provides an image of this.

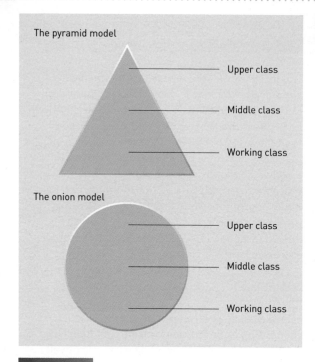

The pyramid model

Upper class

Middle class

Working class

The onion model

Upper class

Middle class

Working class

Figure 10.3   The shapes of class

Table 10.2	The likely shape of class in the UK?
Upper class	0.2–0.1%
Lower upper class	Less than 10%
Upper middle and service class	15%
Lower middle class	20%
Skilled working class	20%
Unskilled working class	30%
Underclass	5%

Source: Based on Runciman (1990).

Runciman (1990) has produced such a map. He has documented that the approximate proportions of people at the different levels of the British class structure are as shown in Table 10.2. In the next sections, we will examine some of these distinctions and groups.

1 The upper classes

In industrialised countries, the upper classes make up anything from 5 to 10 per cent of the population, and include a small cadre of the super-rich (around 0.2 per cent). Traditionally, the upper classes have been linked to old aristocratic traditions and to significant ownership of property (especially land). But this 'old' money is increasingly being joined by 'new' money. We might distinguish two groups: the upper-uppers and the lower-uppers.

Upper-uppers

Membership of the upper-upper class is almost always the result of ascription or birth. In much of Europe, many large landed estates have passed from generation to generation for centuries. The British aristocracy owns 40 per cent of British land: with the monarch at the head, they include dukes, marquesses, earls and viscounts. These families possess enormous wealth, primarily inherited rather than earned. Most of them have *old money*. Set apart by their wealth, members of the upper-upper class live in a world of exclusive affiliations. Children typically attend private schools with others of similar background, completing their formal education at high-prestige colleges and universities.

Europe remains highly stratified. Not only do the rich have controlling stakes in most businesses, but they also benefit from the most schooling, enjoy the best healthcare and consume the greatest share of almost all goods and services (Scott, 1991). Such privileges contrast sharply with unemployment throughout much of Europe, and the poverty of millions of people who struggle from day to day simply to buy food and keep a roof over their heads.

Sociologists have long debated just what social class is, and we have encountered some of these debates in Chapter 8. Some are very theoretical – building on the ideas of Marx and Weber developed in the previous chapter. Some adopt the large-scale survey approach – attempting to measure 'classes'. Still others provide descriptive case studies. We will look at some of this research as we go along. In what follows, we will show some of the major ways in which class has been measured, discuss broad features of different classes and consider whether people are generally moving between classes. We will not, however, be concerned with the detailed complexities of the debates. It will be sufficient for our purposes to provide the broadest contours.

METHODS & RESEARCH

Measuring social class through your postcode

Market research seems to be taking over from sociology in its ability to identify social class groups. Using postcodes and examining spending patterns, market research has developed ever complex but clear systems of classifying different social–economic groups. *Mosaic* is based on analysis of the latest trends in UK society: it suggests 155 Mosaic person types aggregate into 67 household types and 15 groups, to create a three-tier classification that can be used at the individual, household or postcode level. Here we see a few of the new categories emerging.

For more details of this emerging methodology, see: Mosaic UK 2009 http://strategies.experian.co.uk/ Products/Demographic%20 Classifications/~/media/Files/ Brochures/Mosaic%20UK%20 2009%20brochure.ashx

Source: Optimise the value of your customers and locations, now and in the future – Mosaic UK – the consumer classification of the United Kingdom, © 2010 Experian Ltd. All rights reserved.

Group	Description	%↑	%🏠	Type	Description	%↑	%🏠
A	Alpha Territory	4.28	3.54	A01	Global Power Brokers	0.32	0.30
				A02	Voices of Authority	1.45	1.18
				A03	Business Class	1.83	1.50
				A04	Serious Money	0.68	0.56
B	Professional Rewards	9.54	8.23	B05	Mid-Career Climbers	2.90	2.30
				B06	Yesterday's Captains	1.80	1.84
				B07	Distinctive Success	0.48	0.48
				B08	Dormitory Villagers	1.81	1.29
				B09	Escape to the Country	1.41	1.31
				B10	Parish Guardians	1.14	1.00
C	Rural Solitude	4.84	4.40	C11	Squires Among Locals	1.01	0.85
				C12	Country Loving Elders	1.32	1.31
				C13	Modern Agribusiness	1.61	1.36
				C14	Farming Today	0.53	0.53
				C15	Upland Struggle	0.36	0.34
D	Small Town Diversity	9.21	8.75	D16	Side Street Singles	1.21	1.17
				D17	Jacks of All Trades	2.60	1.99
				D18	Hardworking Families	2.87	2.63
				D19	Innate Conservatives	2.53	2.96
E	Active Retirement	3.41	4.34	E20	Golden Retirement	0.52	0.67
				E21	Bungalow Quietude	1.42	1.79
				E22	Beachcombers	0.57	0.60
				E23	Balcony Downsizers	0.90	1.29
F	Suburban Mindsets	13.16	11.18	F24	Garden Suburbia	2.82	2.14
				F25	Production Managers	2.31	2.63
				F26	Mid-Market Families	3.75	2.70
				F27	Shop Floor Affluence	2.82	2.73
				F28	Asian Attainment	1.45	0.98
G	Careers and Kids	5.34	5.78	G29	Footloose Managers	1.11	1.67
				G30	Soccer Dads and Mums	1.34	1.34
				G31	Domestic Comfort	1.24	1.09
				G32	Childcare Years	1.46	1.52
				G33	Military Dependants	0.19	0.17
H	New Homemakers	3.99	5.91	H34	Buy-to-Let Territory	1.08	1.79
				H35	Brownfield Pioneers	1.13	1.38
				H36	Foot on the Ladder	1.48	2.37
				H37	First to Move In	0.30	0.37
I	Ex-Council Community	10.60	8.67	I38	Settled Ex-Tenants	2.08	2.06
				I39	Choice Right to Buy	1.90	1.72
				I40	Legacy of Labour	3.46	2.68
				I41	Stressed Borrowers	3.15	2.20
J	Claimant Cultures	4.52	5.16	J42	Worn-Out Workers	1.82	2.30
				J43	Streetwise Kids	0.90	1.05
				J44	New Parents in Need	1.80	1.80
K	Upper Floor Living	4.30	5.18	K45	Small Block Singles	1.26	1.77
				K46	Tenement Living	0.62	0.80
				K47	Deprived View	0.36	0.50
				K48	Multicultural Towers	1.09	1.11
				K49	Re-Housed Migrants	0.97	0.99
L	Elderly Needs	4.04	5.96	L50	Pensioners in Blocks	0.89	1.31
				L51	Sheltered Seniors	0.67	1.12
				L52	Meals on Wheels	0.51	0.86
				L53	Low Spending Elders	1.98	2.68
M	Industrial Heritage	7.39	7.40	M54	Clocking Off	2.18	2.25
				M55	Backyard Regeneration	2.40	2.06
				M56	Small Wage Owners	2.81	3.09
N	Terraced Melting Pot	6.54	7.02	N57	Back-to-Back Basics	2.50	1.97
				N58	Asian Identities	1.06	0.88
				N59	Low-Key Starters	1.60	2.72
				N60	Global Fusion	1.38	1.44
O	Liberal Opinions	8.84	8.48	O61	Convivial Homeowners	1.74	1.68
				O62	Crash Pad Professionals	1.41	1.09
				O63	Urban Cool	1.25	1.10
				O64	Bright Young Things	1.36	1.52
				O65	Anti-Materialists	1.12	1.03
				O66	University Fringe	1.10	0.93
				O67	Study Buddies	0.87	1.14

Lower-uppers

Most upper-class people actually fall into the *lower-upper class*. From most people's point of view, this group is every bit as privileged as the upper-upper class. The major difference, however, is that lower-uppers are the 'working rich' who depend on earnings rather than inherited wealth as the primary source of their income. They include what we have come to call the 'fat cats', whose incomes often rise to extraordinary heights. The lower-upper class also includes 'the jet-set rich' – the very visible and very famous, such as the footballer who accepts a million-pound contract to play in the Premiership; the computer whiz who designs a program that sets a standard for the industry; or the musician whose work tops the charts – these are the lucky and talented achievers who reach the level of the lower-upper class. Celebrities such as Elton John and Andrew Lloyd Webber are included here, but there are also the entrepreneurial rich, including such people as Richard Branson, Alan Sugar, the Guinness family (the brewers) and the Sieff family (Marks & Spencer). Entrepreneurial capitalists, rentiers, executive and finance capitalists generally make the majority of their money through wise investments of stocks and bonds.

Especially in the eyes of members of 'society', the lower-upper class are merely the 'new rich' who can never savour the status enjoyed by those with rich and famous grandparents. Thus, while the new rich typically live in the biggest homes, they often find themselves excluded from the clubs and associations of old-money families.

2 The middle classes

The middle classes used to be the 'middle group' between poor and rich, who gained income through trade and manufacturing. Weber predicted their growth and Marx their demise. In fact, however, the middle classes have made up a larger and larger proportion of most of the class structure of Europe. Middle-class occupations have material and cultural advantages over working-class employment, generally offering more security, higher pay and higher prestige. The middle class encompasses far more racial and ethnic diversity than the upper class. While many upper-class people (especially upper-uppers) know each other personally, such exclusiveness and familiarity do not characterise the middle class. We can identify three general shades of middle class: the upper (or traditional) middle class, the service class and the lower middle class. It is a large and highly fragmented group, characterised by considerable lifestyle diversities (see Savage et al., 1992).

Class measurements in the UK

So far we have looked at a number of variables and issues in identifying class. To examine the challenges of defining class more directly, we will now look at three classifications in use in the UK.

1 The Registrar General's Index of Social Class

This provided a straightforward classification of social classes which was widely used in the twentieth century. Originally introduced in the census of 1911, this scale ranked occupations and skills of similar social standing, from 'professionals'

to 'unskilled manuals'. Table 10.3 illustrates the six categories in this scale. It ceased to be used, however, with the arrival of the new NS-SEC scale which was introduced into the 2001 census and which is discussed below.

Although the index has been very widely used, it does bring a great many problems. Among the most prominent have been:

- A huge chunk of the population is now in classes 3a and 3b, mainly because of occupational changes in the twentieth century.
- Pay scales and prestige within the same category are often quite different, or again have changed over time. For example, a starting teacher may earn £20,000 or a major lawyer £300,000-plus. It makes the category nonsensical.

- Women were allocated class based on their nearest male relative, but large numbers of women now work (there were fewer when the 1911 classification was introduced).

For these and other reasons, in the latter part of the twentieth century, sociologists in the UK struggled to find better measurements such as the Essex University Class Scale (Marshall et al., 1988) and the Surrey Occupational Scale (1986).

2 John Goldthorpe's modification

John Goldthorpe, one of the most prominent British class analysts of the late twentieth century, modified the Registrar General's scale. Goldthorpe groups workers into three

METHODS & RESEARCH

Table 10.3	**The twentieth-century Registrar General scale categories**		
Class	**Letter**	**Name of class**	**Examples**
1	A	Professional	Solicitors, accountants, surgeons, university lecturers
2	B	Managerial and technical	Managers, teachers, nurses
3a	C1	Skilled non-manual	Estate agents, secretaries, sales clerks
3b	C2	Skilled manual/craft	Bricklayers, electricians, drivers
4	D	Partly skilled manual	Postal carriers, pub/bar staff
5	E	Unskilled manual	Cleaners, labourers

main categories of work, and further subdivides each group. He suggests that there are the following broad groupings:

- A *service class* made up of (a) professional and managerial workers; (b) supervisors of non-manual workers.
- An *intermediate class* made up of (a) routine non-manual workers; (b) small proprietors; (c) supervisors of manual workers; (d) lower-grade technicians.

- A *working class* made up of (a) skilled; (b) semi-skilled; (c) unskilled manual workers.

Such a 'class scale' makes allowances for three factors that determine the general social power that people gain from their occupation: prestige, income and wealth.

3 The National Statistics Socio-Economic Classification (NS-SEC)

This is a more recent classification system. It was announced in December 1998 and was used for the first time in a major way in the UK census in 2001. It draws upon a number of features from the Goldthorpe scale above. Instead of just ranking occupations, it highlights (a) job security, (b) promotion opportunity, and (c) ability and opportunity to work on one's own and make decisions. It is shown in Table 10.4.

Table 10.4	**Eight-, five- and three-class versions of the NS-SEC scale, and their nested relationship**	
Eight classes	**Five classes**	**Three classes**
1 Higher managerial and professional occupations	1 Managerial and professional occupations	1 Higher occupations
1.1 Large employers and higher managerial occupations		
1.2 Higher professional occupations		
2 Lower managerial and professional occupations		
3 Intermediate occupations	2 Intermediate occupations	2 Intermediate occupations
4 Small employers and own account workers	3 Small employers and own account workers	
5 Lower supervisory and technical occupations	4 Lower supervisory and technical occupations	3 Lower occupations
6 Semi-routine occupations	5 Semi-routine and routine occupations	
7 Routine occupations		
8 Never worked and long-term unemployed	Never worked and long-term unemployed	Never worked and long-term unemployed

Note: The number of classes used depends upon both the analytical purposes at hand and the quality of available data.

Source: Based on Office for National Statistics.

The upper-middle class

The more powerful end of this category, also dubbed the traditional middle class, earns above-average incomes. Family income may be even greater if both wife and husband work. High income allows upper-middle-class families gradually to accumulate considerable property, a comfortable house in a fairly expensive area, several cars and investments. A majority of upper-middle-class children receive university educations, and postgraduate degrees are common. Many go on to high-prestige occupations (as doctors, engineers, lawyers, accountants or business executives). Lacking the power of the upper class to influence national or international events, the upper-middle class nonetheless often plays an important role in local political affairs.

The service class

The service class includes people who provide highly valued and well-paid services to employers, including middle-level bureaucrats, management of health, welfare and education services, technically trained secretaries and business consultants. This group also

LIVING IN THE C21ST

The parade of class: what a difference a class makes

Imagine an hour-long parade of people with heights matched to income. What a parade it would be! For more than 25 minutes, all the toddlers and 'vertically challenged' would march by. Three-quarters of an hour would pass before we saw people of average height or taller. Suddenly, for the last minute we would be stunned to see people who would be 20 metres or so tall. Then in the final seconds, huge, colossal figures would start to emerge, their heads lost in the clouds. Just a few massive people, and yet such vast numbers of small ones. One of the world's richest men, Bill Gates, could stand as tall as 10 miles.

This is an example of the colourful language used in several recent reports on inequality. It makes a point. More prosaically, we can say that most Western societies are characterised by extremes of inequality: huge numbers with low incomes and a few with large incomes. But statistics conceal the experiences. At one end there is the life of luxury – a level of wealth that most of us can only imagine. But at the other extremes are what

sociologist Richard Sennett has called 'the hidden injuries of class'. These are the deep scars often thrust upon a life because of no work or demeaning work over which one has little control; because of poor housing or no housing; because money is tight and there are no assets; and, maybe worst of all, because of a deep sense of being outside society, at the bottom of the heap.

Why do sociologists spend so much time talking about class? The answer is that there is little doubt that *social class has a major impact on nearly every dimension of our lives*. While class alone does not define our sense of place in society, class is one of the most significant influences on our lives. Our class impacts us *objectively*: that is, in our health, our education, our possessions and our lifestyle. But it also impacts us *subjectively*: that is, in the way we see ourselves, our language, our values, our ideas, our 'cultural capital'. Here are a few examples of the impact of class on various aspects of life in the UK:

- *Infant mortality* (see also Chapter 24). Working-class children may be three times more likely to die in their first year of life than children of professional parents.
- *Health* (see also Chapter 21). Working-class people may be three times more likely to have long-term serious illness than people of the higher classes.

- *Death* (see also Chapters 21 and 24). A child of an unskilled manual worker may well die around seven years earlier than a counterpart born to professional parents.
- *Divorce* (see Chapter 18). The risk of divorce is four times higher among manuals than among professionals.
- *Education* (see Chapter 20). Just 1 per cent going to university come from the unskilled manual class, while some 78 per cent come from social class I.
- *Public safety* (see Chapter 21). Crime rates were lowest in affluent suburban and rural areas and highest in council estates and low-income areas.
- *Job security*. There is much less job security for working-class occupations than for middle-class professions.
- *Unemployment*. While around 14 per cent in social class V may be out of work, unemployment is much smaller in class I (around 3 per cent).
- *Home ownership*. While some 90 per cent of professionals were owner-occupiers, only around 40 per cent of unskilled manual workers were.

Note: The above is only a schematic and is meant only to provide a general sense that there are differences; the list does not specify years or detail. For further discussion, see the relevant chapters.

Source: Social Trends (2007); Acheson (1998); Scott (2000b).

includes many people who work in media, teaching, fashion and therapy professions. Service-class people enjoy a lot of autonomy in their work, usually exercise and delegate authority, and tend to have secure careers (see Goldthorpe, 1982; Lash and Urry, 1987). David Lockwood (1992) further subdivides this group into professionals, who rely on cultural capital (knowledge); managers; and petty bourgeois (traders and small property owners). People in this class also tend to own property (though in less fashionable districts), to own vehicles (though less expensive models) and to have relatively high levels of education, though they are more likely to work to pull maximum advantage from state-sponsored education and to have attended second-tier colleges and universities.

The lower-middle class

The rest of the middle class falls close to the centre of the class structure. People in the lower-middle class typically work in less prestigious white-collar occupations (such as bank clerks, middle managers or sales clerks) or in highly skilled blue-collar jobs (including electrical work and carpentry). Commonly, lower-middle-class households earn incomes around the national average. Income at this level provides a secure, if modest, standard of living. Lower-middle-class people generally accumulate some wealth over the course of their working lives, mostly in the form of a house. People in this class generally complete some post-secondary school qualifications, though not necessarily university degrees. They are sometimes seen as 'intermediate classes': that is between the working and middle class.

3 The working classes

Two distinct phases have marked out the working class. What we might call *traditional* working-class life used to be defined in terms of strong identities based in communities associated with a particular field of labour, such as were found in traditional mining communities (Dennis et al., 1956), steel communities (Beynon et al., 1991), fishing communities, and so forth. But to name these communities is to sense their demise. In the UK, the old coalfields around Durham or the steel furnaces blasting out around Middlesbrough have gone and the fishing communities around the country are rapidly shrinking. With them went jobs, income, security and communities. After long periods of unemployment and demoralisation, some people benefit from new patterns of work that

emerge. But these patterns are very different, often involving relocation and work that is much more fragmented. We have moved from work in the mine to work in McDonald's. And with that, traditional working-class communities are in steep decline.

But a new working class has also emerged. This is one that will own their own homes, live in suburbs and be more affluent, with cars and DVD players. It is even unlikely that they will see themselves as working class. Indeed, Beverley Skeggs' ethnographic research on young women from working-class backgrounds in a northern town suggests that being working class now carries a stigma and the concern is to be seen as respectable (Skeggs, 1997).

Working-class occupations generally yield a household income somewhat below the national average. Working-class families thus find themselves vulnerable to financial problems, especially when confronted by unemployment or illness. Besides generating less income, working-class jobs typically yield less personal satisfaction. Tasks tend to be routine, requiring discipline but rarely imagination, and workers are usually subject to continual supervision. Such jobs also provide fewer benefits, such as private medical insurance and pension schemes. About half of working-class families own their homes, usually in lower-cost districts.

Social exclusion and the idea of an underclass

Social exclusion

In recent years, an important concept has entered the sociological language: that of social exclusion. The term probably has its origins in France, *les exclus* (the excluded) being those who fell though the net of social protection in the 1970s – lone parents, disabled, the uninsured unemployed (Burchard, 2000: 385). It is related in part to ideas of the underclass, as it highlights people being cut off from the mainstream of society. It has been used both in the United Nations (where it highlights a lack of access to the basic institutions of civil society, a lack of citizenship) and in Europe, where it has been widely adopted.

There have been several attempts to chart the main indicators of social exclusion. The Rowntree/New Policy Institute developed a substantial listing – embracing income, children, young adults, adults and the elderly, and whole communities (Gordon and

Townsend, 2000: 367). The Institute for Public Policy Research (IPPR) highlighted exclusion over four domains – income poverty, exclusion from the labour market, exclusion in education, and health. The Poverty and Social Exclusion (PSE) Survey distinguished four dimensions of exclusion: impoverishment, or exclusion from adequate income or resources; labour market exclusion; service exclusion; and exclusion from social relations.

In 1997, in the UK, a Social Exclusion Unit or Task Force (SEU) was set up under the Labour government to focus on specific groups, such as street homeless and pregnant teenagers. It closed in 2006, and created a tighter unit to focus on a much more specific and smaller group that had been identified in its work. This smaller group was identified as 'high harm, high risk and high lifetime cost'. The aim of the new policy was to intervene in the lives of these people as soon as they appeared at risk of exclusion, breakdown or criminal behaviour (*Guardian*, 13 June 2006).

The underclass

The **underclass** is a more difficult term. For some sociologists, it comprises those people '*under the class structure*', *those who are economically, politically and socially marginalised and excluded*. Typically, these people live between unemployment and the labour market of casual and temporary work. They usually live on state benefits or charitable aid. Encompassing frail pensioners, single 'trapped' parents and the long-term unemployed, the term covers those who are in a sense 'outside' the system of work and even class. In 1987, Dahrendorf estimated that about 5 per cent of the British population fell within the underclass – and that this percentage was growing rapidly.

The idea of an underclass has a long and controversial history. Marx spoke of the *lumpenproletariat* (the social scum of vagrants, misfits, dregs). Booth (1901–2), Rowntree (1902) and Mayhew (1861) described the 'dangerous classes' of 'paupers, beggars and outcasts with a repugnance to regular labour'. There is a long history of distinguishing undeserving, disreputable poor from 'respectable' people trapped in a 'cycle of deprivation' (Morris, 1994). This is discussed in the *Big debate* at the end of this chapter. All these writings point to a heavily stigmatised group at the bottom of the heap, excluded from work, living in dire poverty. The least generous observers suspect the underclass of turning to crime and, as we shall discuss more later, this view often associates racial and underclass issues.

The novel *Angela's Ashes* depicts the harrowing childhood of Frank McCourt in the 1930s and 1940s in Limerick, Ireland. Later turned into a film, the starkness of poverty is dramatically conveyed – the overcrowded and basic housing, the lack of sanitation, the deprivation of food. Such stark poverty has often been depicted in literature

Source: Ronald Grant Archive. Courtesy Dirty Hands Prods/RGA.

The American sociologist Charles Murray has been a recent champion of the idea of 'underclass'. Looking at the United States, in his book *Losing Ground* (1984) he charted what he saw as the failure of welfare policies, where he argued that more and more people had become dependent on the state. In the late 1980s he brought these ideas to the UK and they became serialised in The *Sunday Times* (26 November 1989). For Murray, this underclass lived in a different world, raised its children differently and had different values. He pondered: 'How is a civilised society to take care of the deserving without encouraging people to become undeserving? How does it do good without engendering vice?'

In Europe, the problem of the underclass is often linked to problems of migration. Workers who cannot find work in their own countries want to go to others where work may be found. But in this process – as new arrivals, often with different ethnic backgrounds – all they can find is casual work. Algerians in France, Turks in Germany, Moroccans in Spain and Bangladeshis in the UK often confront both formal and informal barriers against their entering the regular labour market. People who have illegally joined family and friends in the European Union face an even more tenuous position, as they cannot even apply for benefits to meet basic needs. The drive for daily survival focuses the attention of underclass people more on the present. Without much prospect of work, people in the underclass live on the margins of society.

Although many people experience the conditions implied by the term 'underclass', the academic use of this term is problematic. 'Underclass' is often used as an abusive 'catch all' phrase that lumps together many different kinds of experience, and then proceeds to stigmatise them. It is the most recent term – in a long line – for blaming the poor for their poverty. So sociologists have to be very careful how they come to use it.

Poverty: the lower ends of inequality in capitalist society

Sociologists address the concept of poverty in two different ways. **Relative poverty** refers to *the deprivation of some people in relation to those who have more*. Relative poverty is universal and unavoidable; even a rich society has some members who live in relative poverty. It depends on the values and standards of living that a particular society sets; those falling below it are 'poor'. In contrast, absolute poverty is a deprivation of resources that is life threatening. It depends upon a universally agreed minimum for adequate nutrition and living. Much of the poverty we discussed in the previous chapter – the lives of perhaps 800 million people, one in seven of the earth's entire population – is like this.

Yet even in Europe, one of the most affluent regions in the whole world, as defined by its gross domestic product, people still go hungry, become homeless, live in poor housing and endure poor health because of the wrenching reality of poverty.

Measuring poverty

Some of the earliest attempts to measure poverty were conducted in Britain in the latter part of the nineteenth century. Aware of the shocking conditions brought about through rapid industrialisation in major cities such as Manchester and London, the philanthropist and businessman Charles Booth set about a door-to-door survey in large areas of London, enumerating the numbers of people occupying each dwelling and measuring poverty in terms of their income. Poverty, for Booth, was taken to be absolute and objective: it was the amount of money people had to live on. If it fell below a certain breadline of nutritional needs, it meant that people were poor.

A little later, Seebohm Rowntree conducted three surveys between 1899 and 1951 in the city of York and concluded in the last study that poverty had more or less been eradicated in the UK by 1951. He defined absolute poverty in subsistence terms: 'nothing must be bought but that which is absolutely necessary for the maintenance of physical health and what is bought must be of the plainest and most economical description'. Subsequent researchers developed more sophisticated modes of measurement (see Scott, 1994, for an excellent review of the work of Booth and Rowntree).

Since the mid-1950s, poverty in the UK has been studied by Peter Townsend, who defines it as 'the lack of the resources necessary to permit participation in the activities, customs and diets commonly approved by society' (Townsend, 1979: 81). After a major survey, using a national random sample, Townsend concluded that poverty and deprivation almost certainly begin to occur at a level which is over 50 per cent above the official government definition of poverty for means-tested social assistance rates. Social assistance rates are fixed by governments at minimum levels;

(b)

(a) New York: keeping warm is always a problem to those living in the street and fashionable Fifth Avenue is no different. With her legs wrapped in newspaper, a woman enjoys the warmth from the grating. The fashions in the window have little meaning for her; (b) Doré's London in Victorian times

Source: (a) © Bettmann/Corbis; (b) plate from Doré: *A London Pilgrimage*.

(a)

Townsend and many subsequent researchers see this as far too low and basic, failing to take into account the relative need for 'participation' in a society.

A little later, Mack and Lansley took Townsend's ideas of relative poverty one step further. For a television series called *Breadline Britain*, they investigated the 'British standard of living' by conducting a public opinion poll. They asked people what they regarded as necessary for a good standard of living. Then, documenting the level of missing necessities experienced by a national quota sample of over 1,000 people (see Table 10.5), they defined the poor as those 'excluded from the way of life that most people take for granted' (Mack and Lansley, 1985: 15). They found that the number of poor people, especially children, increased in Britain between 1983 and 1990.

The Mack and Lansley approach consistently moves the poverty line upwards over time, as expectations of living standards shift (Table 10.5). These days, for instance, students increasingly need computers for their

work. You might ask yourself whether a student who is unable to afford to buy a computer is poor. This approach has recently been developed further and applied across Europe (Gordon and Townsend, 2000).

Given the complexities of these more sophisticated sociological approaches, it is most common, these days, for poverty to be measured relatively through income. Until 1987, poverty was measured as living below whatever was the government's current supplementary benefit level. (It moves under various names in various countries. Currently, in the UK it is the income support level/employment support level.) Nowadays, households below-average income (HBAI) is the most common measure.

As we have seen, in the measurement of world poverty the most common indicator is to measure those who live below an income of US$1 a day (recently changed to $1.50); and this itself is a problem for analysts (see pp. 286–8). In the UK (and much of Europe) the standard measurement is 60 per cent

Table 10.5	Mack and Lansley's 'lack of necessities' as a poverty measure		
Necessity	1983 Percentage of households unable to afford	Necessity	1990 Percentage of households unable to afford
1 Holiday	21	1 Regular savings	30
2 Two pairs of shoes	9	2 Holiday	20
3 Meat or fish every other day	8	3 Decent decoration	15
4 Hobby	7	4 Outing for children	14
4 Damp-free house	7	5 Insurance	10
4 Warm coat	7	5 Out-of-school activities	10
4 Weekly roast	7	7 Separate bedrooms	7
8 Leisure equipment for children	6	7 Hobby	7
8 New clothes	6	7 Telephone	7
8 Washing machines	6	10 Best outfit	8
		10 Entertaining of children's friends	8

Source: Adapted from Frayman (1991: 6), reprinted in Scott (1994).

below median income. The most commonly used data in the UK are at the *Households Below Average Income (HBAI)* data source (which you can find at www.dwp.gov.uk). In the UK, the **poverty line** is defined in terms of *60 per cent of the median household income*. This means that in 2003–4, the poverty line could be calculated at the following (note though that this does not include housing costs):

Single person	£98
Couple	£178
Couple with two children (5–11)	£262
Lone parent with two children	£182

Given the complexities of measuring poverty, estimates of it are notoriously variable and 'poverty figures' can be quite wide ranging. Rowntree in 1950 found only 1.5 per cent of York living in poverty, but he was applying very strict absolute standards. Under the more lenient relative standards of recent times, poverty is found to be anywhere between a tenth and a third of the population. Thus, Townsend's major study of 1969 (published in 1979) found that 21.8 per cent of the population were below 140 per cent of the Supplementary Benefit line, and 22.9 per cent below his deprivation standard. In 1993, the Low Pay Unit estimated that a third of the population lived in poverty; the OECD suggested there were 12 million poor in the UK (a quarter of Europe's 50 million people living in poverty); and 10 per cent of

people claimed income support (5.6 million people) (Skellington, 1996: 105–11).

The Labour governments of 1997–2010 set themselves a series of major targets to radically reduce relative poverty. At the time they came to power, research suggested that around a quarter (26 per cent) of the British population were living in poverty (as measured in terms of low income and multiple deprivation necessities). For a while, poverty seemed to decline, through such measures as a national minimum wage, working families tax credit, pension credit and winter fuel payments. In 2003, the Joseph Rowntree Foundation could declare that 'poverty fell by about a million'. By the time labour lost office in 2010, however, poverty had surged back upwards. The Rowntree Foundation found that the number of low-income households had risen continuously during the latter part of the 2000s, returning to numbers previously measured ten years before. Likewise, the Institute for Fiscal Studies has pointed out that poverty levels have risen continuously since 2005 and now slightly exceed the numbers measured at the beginning of the past decade. According to the Child Poverty Action Group, in 2008 13.5 million people in the UK, or 23 per cent of the population, were considered poor, in the sense that their income amounted to less than 60 per cent of the national median income after housing costs had been paid.

Spotlight

Poverty in the UK, 2010

Poverty in the UK is usually measured as households with below 60 per cent of contemporary median net disposable income. Between 1945 and the early 1970s there was a narrowing of the gap between richest and poorest. Since then there has been a widening of the gap (with a slight narrowing in the early 2000s).

- *Children*. In 2008/9, there were 2.8 million children living in UK households with below 60 per cent of contemporary median net disposable household income before housing costs and 3.9 million after housing costs.

- *Working-age adults*. In 2008/9, there were 5.8 million working-age adults living in UK households with below 60 per cent of contemporary median net disposable household income before housing costs, and 7.8 million after housing costs.

- *Pensioners*. In 2008/9, there were 2.3 million pensioners living in UK households with below 60 per cent of contemporary median net disposable household income before housing costs, and 1.8 million after housing costs.

So, officially in 2008/9 between 10.9 and 13.5 million people were likely to be living at 60 per cent below the average income of the country (around 23 per cent of the population). This is the official poverty line. This comprises:

- 53 per cent who are in households which include at least one child
- 34 per cent who are in households of people of working age without children
- 13 per cent who are in pensioner households.

The cost to UK society of poverty and the many other social problems to which it is related is huge. While it is not easy to quantify all the consequences of poverty, here are some of the annual costs directly or indirectly connected to child poverty:

- £3 billion spent on children by local authority services
- more than £500 million to support homeless families with children
- around £300 million on free school dinners
- around £500 million on primary healthcare for deprived children
- knock-on costs in lost taxes and extra benefits claimed by adults with poor job prospects, linked to educational failure at school.

Source: Department of Work and Pensions, http://research.dwp. gov.uk/asd/hbai.asp (released 20 May 2010). For updates see: Joseph Rowntree Foundation, www.jrf.org.uk/reporting-poverty/ facts-figures; Child Poverty Action Group www.cpag.org.uk. More generally, see: Pat Thane (ed.), *Unequal Britain* (2010).

A note on poverty in Europe

In the European Union, poverty and social exclusion have generally been rising, despite a series of programmes to combat them. In 1975, poverty was recorded at some 38 million people and by the 1990s at some 50 million. In 2007 around 17 per cent of people in the EU-27 lived in a household with less than 60 per cent of the respective national median income and were considered to be 'at risk of poverty'. As Figure 10.2 on p. 322 shows, the highest levels of inequality were recorded in Romania, Portugal and Bulgaria, while the lowest were recorded in the Nordic states, the Czech Republic, Slovakia, Slovena and Hungary. In the majority of countries, social benefits reduce the proportion of people at risk of poverty by between 25 and 60 per cent. Thus, benefit payments were instrumental in lifting approximately 35 per cent of persons with low income above the poverty line. The household types most at risk of poverty are single parents with dependent children, single elderly people and single females.

Overall, there are significant inequalities in Europe. Broadly, the 20 per cent of the EU with the highest incomes received five times the income of those 20 per cent with the lowest incomes.

Who are the poor?

Although no single description covers all poor people, poverty is pronounced among certain categories of the population. In particular, it is likely to hit people who are disadvantaged in other ways: low-wage earners, the unemployed, disabled people. With this in mind, who are the poorest groups in the UK? In summary, for 2007/8, the risk of income poverty was highest for:

1 Children: more than 30 per cent of children are facing the risk of poverty.
2 Ethnicity: 19 per cent of white people were poor; in contrast, the risk of poverty among Bangladeshi, Pakistani, and Black non-Caribbean people lay at between 50 and 60 per cent.
3 Lone parents: approximately 50 per cent were income poor.
4 Pensioners: more than 20 per cent of single pensioner households faced the risk of poverty.
5 Disabled: the poverty risk for households with one or more disabled members ranged from nearly 30 to more than 50 per cent.

Age: children and the elderly

A generation ago, the elderly were at greatest risk of poverty. They still remain at risk, but studies now conclude that a 'new poverty' has emerged among the young and children. In the UK, the number of elderly needing assistance fell from 1.8 million in 1974 to 1.4 million in 1991. Today, the burden of poverty falls most heavily on children. Thus, numbers of children under 16 needing assistance in the UK rose from 800,000 in 1974 to 2.3 million in 1991 and 3.9 million in 2007. According to the Child Poverty Action Group, more than 30 per cent of children in 2008 lived in households considered poor after housing costs were accounted for. The Rowntree study suggested that the poverty rates of children were higher among those:

- in households without any workers
- in lone-parent families
- with a larger number of siblings
- with household members suffering a long-standing illness
- of non-white ethnicity
- living in local authority housing
- in households in receipt of Job Seeker's Allowance or Income Support.

The same story is true in much of the rest of Europe. In the United States, it is even more extreme. In 2008, 14.1 million children or 19 per cent of all children were poor. Among Hispanic and African American children, more than 30 per cent were living in poverty. According to the National Poverty Center, children represent a disproportionately large share of the poor in the USA. They account for 35 per cent of the poor population, while only representing 25 per cent of the country's population in general.

Race and ethnicity

Studies also strongly suggest that 'multiple deprivations' affect ethnic minorities, leading to significantly higher levels of poverty. The Joseph Rowntree Foundation's (1995) study of poverty in the UK was 'particularly concerned . . . at what is happening to the non-white population'. One in three of the non-white population was in the poorest fifth of the population. Most significant here were alarming rates of unemployment (worst of all among people of Pakistani and Bangladeshi origin) and the difficulties of ethnic women and children, not least Afro-Caribbean single-parent families. Many of these groups were contributing to an emerging underclass (see above). Recent work by Lucinda Platt (2002; 2007) suggests little change.

Ethnicity is important across the world when looking at poverty. In the United States, for example, in absolute numbers, two-thirds of all poor people are white. But in relation to their overall numbers, African-Americans are almost three times as likely as white people to be poor. In 2008, 24.7 per cent of African-Americans (8.7 million people) lived in poverty, compared to 21.2 per cent of Latinos (9.4 million), 10.6 per cent of Asians (1.3 million), and 9.2 per cent of non-Hispanic white people (21.4 million). Thirty per cent of African-American children are poor (US Census Bureau, 2008).

Gender and family patterns

The term **feminisation of poverty** describes *the trend by which women represent an increasing proportion of the poor*. Many years ago, Peter Townsend (1987) identified four groups of women that made up the 'female poor'. These are:

- single (including divorced) women with children
- elderly women pensioners
- 'carers' who look after children or other dependants
- women with low earnings.

This *feminisation of poverty* is part of a larger change: the rapidly increasing number of households – at all class levels – headed by single women. This trend, coupled with the fact that households headed by women are at high risk of poverty, explains why women (and their children) represent an increasing share of the European poor. Black women appear in all these categories, and for them poverty becomes even more likely.

Disablement

Disabled people may be severely affected by poverty. Often they have been excluded from the routine activities of everyday life – they may be less likely to have (well-paid) employment. They usually have lower average income levels and in addition have to meet the 'extra costs' of impairment (Townsend, 1979; Barnes et al., 1999: 134).

The 'Death of Class' debate

The past 50 years or so have seen so many changes in the socioeconomic environment that it would be surprising if there had not also been changes in the nature of class. Sociologists have for a long time disagreed about both its importance and how it should be studied. While some argue that 'class remains the sociological key to understanding the structure of society' (Scott, 1994: 19) and have argued that its significance is still central, others have contended that 'class as a concept is ceasing to do any useful work for sociology' (Pahl, 1989). Which is it?

The end of class?

Some sociologists argue that we have become more and more of a classless society and that the concept of class cannot incorporate the scope of the changes that are happening in the (post)modern world. It is not a question of whether inequalities persist – all agree that they do (and many suggest they are widening). But it is often more a matter of whether and how these inequalities can be traced back to class as *the* key issue.

For instance, as we have previously seen, in so much early sociology, women were excluded. Much of 'class theory' naively ignored gender, and much of it may well therefore be misconceived. Certainly, bringing women into the picture shifts the focus of class questions, such as how child-bearing, child-rearing, and 'domestic labour' and housework fit into the labour structure. Moreover, women as a group generally earn less than men – even at comparable levels of education and experience. While overt sex discrimination is illegal in the European Union (as well as in most other industrialised countries), women remain more likely to be 'ghettoised' into lower-paid occupations such as social work, auxiliary nursing, child care and routine secretarial roles (see Chapter 12 for further details). All this means, at the very least, that gender has to be an important factor in understanding inequality. And, as we shall see in the next chapter, the same can also be said of ethnicity.

One (ex?) Marxist, André Gortz (1982), significantly called his book *Farewell to the Working Class*. If class is seen as primarily economic, involving some sense of class awareness and consciousness, and if it is seen as an important force for bringing about social change, then critics argue it has clearly declined in significance. Thus, the power (or lack of it) linked to different groups and social movements – ethnic groups, the disabled, women, the elderly, etc. – has become much more prominent. Matters of consumption and lifestyle have become more and more important in people's lives. The role of new social movements in bringing about social change (see Chapter 16) also now seems

more important generally than class in shaping change (Waters, 1997). Further, wider changes in society – the spread of share ownership, the growth of social mobility through education, the flexibility of what has been called post-Fordist production (see Chapter 15) – have all contributed to a reworking of the class order.

Perhaps the most widespread argument on the 'death of class' is that there has been a general 'levelling-up' of the classes. Traditional working-class communities such as those associated with mining or the steel industry have vanished and new working-class lives have become heavily shaped by home ownership and consumerism. The 'working class' no longer harbours the strong community that it once did. Indeed, there has been a clear failure of working-class-based action and a decline of working-class identity and trade unionism. During the Thatcher period, there was a major dealignment of politics, so that there is no longer even a clear working-class vote attached to the Labour Party (Crewe, 1992).

The embourgeoisement thesis

One of the first major studies in the UK to examine the shifting nature of class was in the work of David Lockwood, John Goldthorpe, Frank Beckhoffer and Jennifer Platt, who looked at the changing nature of class among Luton car workers in the 1960s (Goldthorpe et al., 1968). Their study was explicitly designed to examine the so-called 'embourgeoisement' thesis that 'we are all in the middle class now'. It examined an early version of the theory of the decline of class: that the traditional 'proletarian' working class was losing its old identity, becoming more affluent and looking more and more like the middle classes. In the main, this study rejected such a thesis. True, it certainly showed major changes in class: the car factory workers were comparatively well paid, could spend money on major consumer goods, and were becoming home-owners. But the middle class had advanced in line with this. Further, the car workers still usually voted Labour and did not really adopt middle-class lifestyles. They had become a new kind of working class – much more private and home-centred, seeing their work as a means to make money but with little sense of the job satisfaction found in middle-class work (Goldthorpe et al., 1968). So the argument to be made here is not that class was weakening or vanishing, but that it was changing with the times.

This study, however, was conducted over half a century ago. The world has moved on. More recent studies have suggested that key divides now occur around *consumption* and *lifestyles* which cut right across old class lines. In the 1980s, Ray Pahl, looking at working-class households in Kent, saw the working class as becoming more and more divided – often between those in regular work and those drifting in and out of unemployment. Strikingly, he suggests that 'if the cathedral of the nineteenth century was the factory chimney, that of the twentieth century is the shopping mall' (Pahl, 1984; J. Pahl, 1989).

More important, perhaps, are the new divides between those who rely on the market and those who rely on the state; between those who own their houses and those who rent them; between those who work and those who are unemployed; between 'work-rich' and 'work-poor' households. Classes now need to be linked to the 'texture' of cultures and the key role of (largely middle-class) social movements, such as the Green Movement.

In this view, then, class analysis has become so complicated that the nature of what we are studying ceases to be clear. Myriad variables are important to studying inequality, and 'class' as a concept can no longer handle this range. 'Class' can no longer be simply linked to the workplace as it is being replaced by 'lifestyle', 'differences' and all sorts of other inequalities linked to ethnicity, gender, sexuality, age and disability (see subsequent chapters). The failure of class analysis to seriously incorporate these concerns made it weaker and weaker. Indeed, some argue that 'class analysis' has become an area of academic study, of restricted relevance to only a few ivory tower academics! Others take a very different view.

The continuing importance of class

Indeed, many sociologists – John Goldthorpe, John Scott, David Rose and many others – still take class as the central feature of societies. The nature of class may be changing, they claim, but it remains the central organising feature of industrial countries. John Scott argues that 'Class differences persist and have in many respects become sharper' (Scott in Payne, 2000: 38). Class here is not in dispute, but its changing character may be. These class theorists often point to a number of key changes, including the following:

1 The decreasing importance of the manual/ non-manual labour distinction as manual work declines.

2 The collapse of a very traditional working class (for example, around mining communities).

3 The growth and diversity of the middle class, including the expansion of the service sector.

4 The identification of an underclass who are largely outside the class system and, indeed, society.

5 The introduction of both gender and ethnicity into various class schemas as a complicating factor.

While these sociologists do try to incorporate many of the issues raised by those who have suggested the end of class, they conclude that class is still the most important factor. Class, and class analysis, are far from dead. Indeed, this chapter should have clearly shown that although class patterns are changing, they are deep and widespread. 'Classlessness' may have been exaggerated, for there remains a very clear, powerful and strong upper class. People still strongly identify with class groups; and new divisions and polarisations continue to appear.

The cultural turn and fractured identities

Many of the newer theorists try to take a conciliatory role between the older theories of class and newer accounts. Sympathetic to postmodernism and cultural studies, they suggest that the idea of any one overarching 'truth' about class is now unlikely. Older theorists of class sometimes placed a belief in the importance of class and class consciousness that may have made it too central, restricting their vision. Now class needs to be seen as cultural as well as economic, and closely linked to the wider social divisions found in contemporary society. In the work of Harriet Bradley, Beverley Skeggs and Mike Savage, the way ahead lies in the idea of recognising that we all now inhabit complex and changing cultures (see Chapter 5), embodying fractured identities (see Chapter 7) – identities that are not unitary or essential, but variable and changing and plural. People's sense of social location in social worlds is no longer simply a matter of class: their lives are bound into all the variations of inequality that this section of the book is discussing – class, yes, but also ethnicity, gender, age and other factors such as disability or sexuality. Bradley, Skeggs and Savage suggest that identities around class are now highly fractured.

Class, then, remains an important area of sociological analysis. Recent analyses and research, however, suggest that it continues to change its forms, and must be considered alongside a whole array of new identities and social changes.

Citizenship and the rise of welfare states

An important development of modern, industrial capitalist societies has been the evolution of welfare states. A narrow definition of this would be 'the involvement of the state in social security and social services' (Cochrane and Clarke, 1993: 4). More broadly, some definitions of the welfare state include a commitment to full employment and a whole arena of welfare policies to do with education, health and families. Welfare states are therefore very much bound up with improving the quality of life for a society's citizens and reducing the problems generated through inequalities.

Most modern industrialised nations are welfare states – they increasingly have to deal with public problems and deal with them through public expenditure. In Britain, in 1981, 56.3 per cent of the government's budget was spent on welfare; in 1993, it was 64.1 per cent. This was despite having an anti-welfare government for much of this time. (Much of the rise, though, was due to costs of increased unemployment, etc.)

Some industrial societies, such as Sweden, have highly developed welfare states, while others, such as the United States, have only minimal ones. Nevertheless, it is a characteristic feature of modern societies that they have to devote large sums to welfare.

A central question in understanding the workings of welfare states concerns the extent to which they are run by governments or through markets (see Chapter 15). When the market dominates, we often talk of the **marketisation** of the welfare state – here it is run by *an economic system based on the principles of the market, including supply, demand, choice and competition.* Thatcherism (discussed in Chapter 16) attempted to bring marketisation into all spheres of life, including much of the welfare state. Thus, as we shall see, both education (Chapter 20) and health (Chapter 21) were to move to the principles of the market. Even prisons, as we shall see in Chapter 17, have moved towards markets and privatisation.

The citizenship approach

The growth of state involvement with the 'welfare' of its citizens parallels the growth of industrial societies. In the optimistic version, this is a story of growing 'citizenship rights'. The key thinker in this area is the British sociologist T. S. Marshall (1893–1981), who argued that with industrialisation, citizenship emerged in three ways. These were:

1 *Civil*: the rights necessary for individual freedom – liberty of the person, freedom of speech, thought and faith, the right to own property and to conclude valid contracts, and the right to justice. The key institutions to implement this would be the civil and criminal courts of justice.

2 *Political*: the right to participate in the exercise of political power, as a member of a body invested with political authority or as an elector of such a body. This included such institutions as parliament and local elective bodies, along with the extension of political suffrage.

3 *Social*: the whole range from the right to a modicum of economic welfare and security, to the right to share to the full in social heritage and to live the life of a civilised being according to the standards prevailing in the society. Educational and social welfare institutions are the key here.

For Marshall, each of these sets of rights appears in distinct periods. In the Middle Ages, they were 'wound together' but weak. Civil rights emerged most clearly in the eighteenth century, political rights in the nineteenth and social rights in the twentieth century.[1] Many do not agree with the precise periodisation and remark that Marshall's model was developed through one case study only – that of the UK. When applied to other countries it does not fit so well. Bryan Turner (1990), for example, has suggested that the foundations of citizenship differ for France, Germany and Sweden. Marshall's model does raise a series of key issues about the emerging rights and responsibilities in modern societies.

A Marxist approach

Marxists see the welfare state differently: instead of seeing it as a benign set of institutions that foster security and equality, they argue that it helps contribute to the smooth running of the capitalist order. In order for capitalism to work, it needs a well-trained labour force that is reasonably healthy and secure. The welfare state ensures this. Marxists suggest that advanced capitalism needs welfare to 'buy off' working-class dissent and maintain social order with a secure workforce (Piven and Cloward, 1972).

[1] There is talk, at the beginning of the twenty-first century, of the emergence of a fourth cluster of citizen rights centred around 'intimate citizenship' (Plummer, 2003).

The three worlds of welfare capitalism

In 1990, Costa Esping-Andersen published a much-discussed study of different kinds of welfare regime. For him, 'The welfare system is not just a mechanism that intervenes in . . . inequality; it is, in its own right, a system of stratification' (1990: 23). He argued that there were three major kinds of welfare system, though they are a little like ideal types (see Chapter 1). They can be evaluated as systems of **decommodification**, whereby the focus is on *the degree to which welfare services are free from the market*. (Commodification, by contrast, turns welfare issues into sellable things and needs markets.) The three main 'worlds' he locates are:

1 *Social democratic*. This argues for universal rights, equality and a kind of 'universal solidarity' in favour of the welfare state. It is largely anti-market. It takes on many family responsibilities and is a universalist model. Scandinavian countries largely adopt this approach.

2 *Corporatist/'Bismarck'*. Here, welfare is mainly organised through work itself, through business, tradition, church and existing powers. This approach does not enourage redistribution. While the state may deliver welfare, its aim is the maintenance of traditional families. This is a conservative model, found in Austria, France, Germany and Italy.

3 *Liberal*. This intervenes in the market as little as possible and gives benefits that are subject to strict entitlement rules. It is a basic safety-net approach, showing a direct line of inheritance from the old Poor Laws. It leads to market-based insurance for the wealthy and means testing for the poor. Private schemes are encouraged. Examples are the United States, Australia and Canada. The UK used to be close to the social democratic model, but under Thatcherism moved closer and closer to the market/liberal model.

Esping-Andersen derived this classification from his own research into pensions, unemployment insurance and sickness benefits. He examined levels of benefit, protection against risks and strictness of rules that govern access across a number of countries. It was on this basis that he could classify societies thus:

- Lowest scores for welfare – liberal: the USA and UK.
- Intermediate scores for welfare – corporatist: France, Germany, Italy and Switzerland.
- Highest scores for welfare – social democratic: Scandinavia, Belgium and the Netherlands.

More recently, Leibfreid (2001) has added a fourth group: the 'Latin Rim countries' – Spain, Greece, Portugal, southern Italy and part of France – which have 'rudimentary welfare states'.

The welfare state in the UK

The UK is quite close to the liberal model but is, at least historically, a bit of a mixture of all three. Its roots go back to the Poor Law in Elizabethan and Tudor England, where government started to impose an elementary framework on what had previously been the task of churches and charities. But this rudimentary care of the sick broke down with mass industrialisation and the arrival of capitalism. In 1834 the Poor Law Amendment Act set up a national Poor Law Commission to oversee the development of a system with links eventually growing to state education and healthcare. All this shapes the 'state' links to a society's population, and especially its 'poor' and 'working class'.

Bit by bit, a system that was heavily *laissez-faire* gave way to a system that is more central and state controlled. By the start of the twentieth century, legislation such as the Pensions Act of 1908 and the National Insurance Act of 1911 provided cover for sickness and unemployment for some workers, introducing the 'insurance principle' into British social security.

The period 1945–75 may be seen as the years of the 'classic welfare state'. It was spearheaded by the work of William Beveridge in several major reports. Waging war on the 'five great evils' of 'Want, Disease, Ignorance, Squalor and Idleness', his plan for social security was to abolish Want – but only if the others could simultaneously be abolished (Beveridge, 1942: paragraph 8). This was a time when there was a commitment to a mixed economy, to full employment and to a welfare state that would provide universal rights. At this stage, the welfare state in the UK was closest to the social democratic model described above. In education, health, childcare and welfare provisions, the UK seemed to be moving towards this social democratic welfare state. There were 'means-tested' systems, but the broad principles stressed universality.

This was also the period when the National Health Service came into existence – a time very different from our own, when most people rented their houses, nobody had televisions but instead listened to the wireless, few had overseas holidays, only a minority had telephones, nobody had computers, and few had cars so most were dependent upon public transport. Social democratic thinkers believed the welfare state

The Social Charter: social policies in the European Union

In May 1989, the European Community Charter of the Fundamental Social Rights of Workers – commonly known as the Social Charter – was approved. It was subsequently incorporated as the 'Social Chapter' into the Maastricht Treaty in 1991 (see Chapter 4). The Charter's main provisions included the following rights and guarantees of workers who hold citizenship in EU countries.

The rights were:

- to work in the EU country of one's choice
- to a fair wage
- to continuing improvements in living and working conditions
- to adequate social protection and social security
- to belong to a trade union (or professional body) and to be represented in collective bargaining
- to satisfactory healthcare and safe working conditions.

The guarantees were:

- equal treatment for men and women in the workplace, and 'enabling men and women to reconcile their occupational and family obligations'
- consultation between employers and workers
- protection of children and adolescents; with a minimum working age of 15, fair pay and reasonable hours
- a minimum decent standard of living for the elderly
- changes to make it easier for the disabled to become part of the workforce.

Until 1997, the UK opted out of the Social Chapter. In practice, the UK did recognise many of the conditions, but the former Conservative government objected to the regulations of maximum hours and minimum wages, as well as to fathers being given a statutory three months' unpaid leave after the birth of a child. The Conservatives argued that these provisions would increase industrial costs to a level that would make the UK less competitive with the United States, Japan and the newly industrialising countries. The Labour government elected in 1997 rejected these arguments and signed up to the Social Chapter.

Like most such mission statements, these ideal goals are not always followed in practice. Although there is a clear statement that men and women should be treated equally, in practice there remain significant pay and opportunity differentials. Additionally, the charter does not always allow for consistent enforcement. Some issues, including a 48-hour maximum working week and a common retirement age for men and women, are laid down centrally, but other matters, including the power to set the age of retirement, remain at the discretion of national governments.

Through the Social Protection in Europe Directive (1993), all EU countries must provide a basic level of support in unemployment benefits, pensions, cover for work accidents, health cover and maternity benefits. A predictable pattern emerges: a high level of protection in Sweden, as is the case for Luxembourg and the Netherlands; a low level of protection in Spain, Portugal, Ireland, Greece and the UK; and middle levels of support in France, Germany, Finland, Denmark, Belgium and Austria.

would create citizenship for all and would combat inequality. But by the mid-1970s – as unemployment surged forward and huge economic changes were in the offing – it was clear that it had not been especially successful in redistribution. Indeed, a number of commentators saw most of the benefits of the system going to the middle classes (Le Grand, 1982).

A new period was ushered in from the mid-1970s onwards. Most notably, from 1979 there emerged a much more 'anti-welfare state' approach. It was, as Prime Minister Margaret Thatcher bluntly put it, a rejection of the Nanny State. Monetarist theory (to be outlined in Chapter 15) was put into practice

and at the same time the 'classic' welfare state began to be 'marketised'.

When the New Labour government was elected in 1997 with a landslide majority, many believed that it would reverse the marketisation policies of the Thatcher years. While it set up a Social Exclusion Unit which aimed to target specific groups in need (such as the homeless) and to provide integrated services for them, in the main it continued with a policy in which the market was given a major focus. The new Coalition government elected in 2010 showed clear signs of accelerating this marketisation strategy.

Looking ahead: class in the twenty-first century

This chapter has raised many problems about class and its role in modern industrial societies. We have seen that there are many problems involved in knowing just what it is; and at the same time we have heard both from sociologists who regard it as the key feature of modern societies and from others who see it as a factor in decline.

For the authors of this book, it seems impossible to deny the continuing role that class plays in social life. It is tangibly present through poverty, low incomes, extremes of wealth, prestige systems and status, and differing degrees of control over work and life. However, it is changing and new patterns of class are in the making.

At the same time, one of the most important lessons of recent times is that class on its own is a weak concept. It needs to be placed in specific circumstances and connected to other key issues such as social exclusion, gender, ethnicity and age: it is these which the subsequent chapters will examine.

SUMMARY

1 Social inequality involves disparities in a host of variables, including income, wealth and power. Marxists would adopt an approach to measuring class that focuses upon the ownership of the means of production, while Weberians tend to focus on a range of variables, including work and market situation.

2 Occupation is a common way in which class is measured. The Registrar General's classification is the most commonly used such classification in the UK. This has recently been updated to the National Statistics Socio-Economic Scale (NS-SES). Income and wealth are other ways in which social class is often measured.

3 The upper class, which is small (about 5 per cent), includes the richest and most powerful families. Members of the upper-upper class, or the old rich, derive their wealth through inheritance over several generations; those in the lower-upper class, or the new rich, depend on earned income as their primary source of wealth. The middle class includes 40–45 per cent of the population. The upper-middle class may be distinguished from the rest of the middle class on the basis of higher income,

higher-prestige occupations and more schooling. The working class, sometimes called the lower-middle class, includes about one-third of the UK population. With below-average income, working-class families have less financial security than those in the middle class. Only one-third of working-class children reach college and most eventually work in blue-collar or lower-prestige white-collar jobs. There is a growing 'underclass' – people outside society and the class system.

4 Social class affects nearly all aspects of life, beginning with health and survival in infancy and encompassing a wide range of attitudes and patterns of family living.

5 Since the early 1970s, changes in the economy have reduced the standard of living for low- and moderate-income families. One important contemporary trend is a decline in manufacturing industries, paralleling growth in low-paying, service-sector jobs.

6 An important aspect of modern capitalist societies has been the development of welfare states alongside the idea of 'citizenship'.

CONNECT UP: Turn to Part 6 of this book for key resources and link up
with the book's website, which links to these resources
SEE: www.pearsoned.co.uk/plummer

MYTASKLIST

Ten suggestions for going further

1 Connect up with Part Six and the Sociology Web Resources

As you work through ideas and think about the issues raised in this chapter, look at the accompanying website and the resource centre at the end of this book which connects to it. There is a lot here to help you move on. To link up, see: www.pearson.co.uk/plummer.

2 Review the chapter

Briefly summarise (in a paragraph) just what this chapter has been about. Consider: (a) What have you learned? (b) What do you disagree with? Be critical. And (c) How would you develop all this? How could you get more detail on matters that interest you?

3 Pose questions

(a) Assess your own social class. What factors would you have to take into account? Look at measurements that sociologists have invented. How well do you fit with these? Does your family have consistent standing on various dimensions of social stratification? Why do most people find talking about their own social position awkward?

(b) Identify some of the effects of social stratification on health, values, politics and family patterns.

(c) Is class dead? If so, why?

(d) What categories of people are at high risk of poverty in Europe? Does any evidence support the assertion that the poor are responsible for their situation? Does any evidence suggest that society is primarily responsible for poverty?

(e) Compare three 'welfare states'. Why is public assistance for the poor more controversial in some countries than in others?

4 Explore key words

Many concepts have been introduced in this chapter. You can review them from the website or from the listing at the back of this book. You might like to give special attention to just five words and think them through – how would you define them, what are they dealing with, and do they help you see the social world more clearly or not?

5 Search the Web

Be critical when you look at websites – see the box on p. 940 in the Resources section. For this chapter look at the following:

The Poverty Site
www.poverty.org.uk
This site monitors what is happening to poverty and social exclusion in the UK. The material is organised around 100 statistical indicators covering all aspects of the subject, from income and work to health and education. It is run by the Joseph Rowntree Foundation.

Child Poverty Action Group
www.cpag.org.uk
CPAG provides information about low-income families and the policies that affect them. It produces regular newsletters and fact lists.

Low Pay Commission
www.lowpay.gov.uk
This provides commentary, debate and the most recent figures, especially on the minimum wage.

Policylibrary.com
www.policylibrary.com/welfare
A useful guide to social policy issues.

6 Watch a DVD

Daryll Zanuck's *The Grapes of Wrath* (1940) is a classic film about the Depression and Alan Parker's *Angela's Ashes* (2000) is a striking depiction of poverty in Ireland. There is a fascinating cluster of early films about social class in Britain set in the 1950s – often seen as 'kitchen sink dramas' from 'angry [working class] young men'. These include: *Look Back in Anger*, *The Loneliness of the Long Distance Runner*, *Saturday Night and Sunday Morning*, and *Taste of Honey*. The films of Mike Leigh, such as *High Hopes* (1988), *Secrets and Lies* (1996) and *Vera Drake* (2004), convey both the humour and desperation of working-class life.

7 Think and read

General sociology texts on class

Wendy Bottero, *Stratification: Social Division and Inequality* 9 (2005). A readable and comprehensive introduction to the UK class system examining all the key debates.

Tony Bennett, Mike Savage, Elizabeth Bortolaia Silva, Alan Warde, Modesto Gayo-Cal, David Wright, *Culture, Class, Distinction* (2009). Engages head-on with the recent critiques of class from postmodernist and other angles, and provides a replication of Bourdieu's classic study.

Fiona Devine and Mary C. Waters, *Social Inequalities in Comparative Perspective* (2004). A valuable recent series of essays on class systems in a range of (mainly Western) countries.

Tim Butler and Paul Watt, *Understanding Social Inequality* (2007). Uses contemporary theories to make sense of class, poverty and inequality in the UK.

Discussions on poverty

Ruth Lister, *Poverty* (2004) A very valuable overview.

Tess Ridge and Sharon Wright (eds), *Understanding Inequalities, Poverty and Wealth: Policy and Prospects* (2008). A useful collection of readings and arguments in a student-friendly text.

Lucinda Platt, *Understanding Inequalities* (2011). The most recent critical overview of inequalities in the UK.

The rich

George Irwin, *Super Rich: The Rise of Inequality in Britain and the United States* (2008).

Exclusion, inclusion and welfare states

Ruth Levitas, *The Inclusive Society? Social Exclusion and New Labour* (2nd edn, 2005). Good on social exclusion.

C. Esping-Andersen, *The Three Worlds of Welfare Capitalism* (1990). Now the classic study of modern welfare which distinguishes three types (and clearly favours the Scandinavian model).

James Russell, *Double Standards: Social Policy in Europe and the United States* (2nd edn, 2010).

8 Relax with a novel

- Alan Parker's *Angela's Ashes* (2000): the compelling novel by Frank McCourt about grinding poverty in early-twentieth-century Ireland is also a vivid and striking film depiction of poverty.
- *The Grapes of Wrath* (1940): John Steinbeck's classic novel of the Depression. It was turned into a major, moving and classic film by John Ford in 1940.
- *Down and Out in Paris and London* (1933): George Orwell's classic account of tramps and derelicts working in kitchens and out of them. In a way, it is an early example of a kind of participant observation study.

9 Connnect to other chapters

- Link discussion of poverty and its measurement back to Chapter 9.
- Think about links to ethnicity, gender and age to be discussed in Chapters 11–13.
- Return to Marx and Weber in Chapters 2 and 4 and think of how this links to class.
- Think about issues of method. See Chapter 3 and ask: how do you know you are measuring class and poverty in a valid and reliable way?
- Link class to issues of identity, as discussed in Chapter 7.

10 Engage with THE BIG DEBATE

Why does poverty still exist in high-income countries?

That the richest regions on earth – Europe and North America – are home to tens of millions of poor people and massive inequalities raises serious questions. Of course, many of the people counted among the officially poor in industrialised countries are better off than the poor in other countries – in the UK 30–40 per cent of people own their homes and nearly 30 million (half the population) own cars. But it is also the case, as noted earlier, that malnutrition and outright hunger are quite widespread, along with violence, illness and a host of other problems that accompany economic deprivation.

Debate these two approaches to the problem of poverty.

Position 1: Blaming the poor – cycles of deprivation and cultures of poverty

One side of the issue is based on the following view: *The poor are primarily responsible for their own poverty*. Since the creation of the English Poor Laws, some thinkers in industrial nations have drawn distinctions between the 'deserving' and the 'undeserving' poor. Believing that social standing primarily reflects talent and individual effort, these people contend that industrial societies offer considerable opportunities to anyone able and willing to take advantage of them. The poor, then, are those who cannot or will not work, people with fewer skills, less schooling or simply lower motivation. While some people (historically, widows, orphans and the disabled) command our compassion as 'worthy poor', this line of reasoning leads us to condemn many people as, in one way or another, responsible for their own fate, and hence undeserving.

Some researchers have offered a different view, suggesting that a *culture of poverty* holds down the poor, fostering resignation to poverty as a matter of fate. Anthropologist Oscar Lewis (1961), who investigated the poor *barrios* of Latin American cities, is one of the early proponents of this view. Although Lewis doubted that most poor people could do much about their plight, he did not blame them individually for their poverty. Instead, he claimed that the *barrio* environment socialised children to believe that there is little point in aspiring to a better life. The result is a self-perpetuating cycle of poverty, as one generation transmits its way of life to the next. In the UK, this has been a widely influential model too.

Research in the United States led Charles Murray (1984) to much the same conclusion. Especially in areas of intense poverty such as the inner cities, claims Murray, a lower-class subculture has taken hold, eroding personal ambition and achievement. One element of this subculture, as he sees it, is a present-time orientation that encourages living for the moment. While a future orientation guides most better-off people to study, plan, work hard and save, Murray saw poor people as failing to look beyond the moment. In living for the present, he concluded, the poor perpetuate their own poverty and, therefore, reap what they deserve.

Position 2: Blaming society – social exclusion and structural divisions

The other side of the issue can be summed up as follows: *Society is primarily responsible for poverty*. This alternative position, argued by William Ryan (1976), holds that social structures – not people themselves – distribute the resources unequally and are, therefore, responsible for poverty. Looking at societies around the world from this point of view, we see that those that distribute wealth very unequally (such as the United Kingdom) also have high levels of relative poverty, while societies that strive for more economic equality (such as Sweden and Japan) lack such extremes of social stratification.

Poverty, Ryan insists, is not inevitable. Low income, not personal deficiencies, cause the problem. Ryan interprets any lack of ambition on the part of poor people as a consequence rather than a cause of their lack of opportunity. He therefore dismisses Lewis's analysis as little more than 'blaming the victims' for their own suffering. In Ryan's view, social policies that empower the poor would give them real economic opportunity and yield more economic equality.

Weighing the evidence

Each of these explanations of poverty has won its share of public support, and each has advocates among policy-makers. As Murray sees it, society should pursue equality of opportunity, especially for the young, but otherwise people should take responsibility for themselves, and their success will correspond to their talents and interests.

Ryan takes a more activist approach, asserting that public policy should reduce poverty through more equitable redistribution of income. Programmes such as comprehensive child care, for example, could help poor mothers gain job skills; indeed, the living standard of every poor person could be raised by a tax-funded, guaranteed minimum income for every family.

Certainly, both of these views could be put into practice, and many societies periodically lean towards one or the other. Typically, conservative policies are sympathetic towards the first, while left-leaning and liberal strategies are usually more in tune with the second.

Continue the debate

1 What are the major groups in the communities of poor people? Is it reasonable to divide some of them into 'deserving' and some into 'undeserving' categories?
2 Why do you think poverty in Europe seems to be constantly on the increase?
3 Discuss strategies for reducing poverty.

CHAPTER 11

RACISM, ETHNICITIES AND MIGRATION

BOSNIA, A FEDERAL STATE OF THE FORMER YUGOSLAVIA, is a country marked by multicultural and ethnic differences. Its chronicler, Noel Malcolm, has said: 'There is no such thing as a typical Bosnian face: there are fair-haired and dark-haired Bosnians, olive-skinned and freckled, big-boned and wiry-limbed. The genes of innumerable people have contributed to this human mosaic' (1996: 1). In its 1,000-year history it has been touched by all the great empires of the European past: Rome, Charlemagne, the Ottomans and the Austro-Hungarians. It has harboured most of the major faiths: Western Christianity, Eastern Christianity, Judaism and Islam. And it has been home to migrants from all over Europe bringing their own languages and culture. It has long been home to Slavs (who arrived 1,000 years ago), and Muslims and Croats whose own states bordered it (Croatia and Serbia). In 1991, the three main groups were Muslims (44 per cent), Serbs (31 per cent) and Croats (17 per cent).

Yet 1992 marked Bosnia's destruction. A bloody civil war erupted between the Serbs (Orthodox Christians), the Croatians (Catholics) and the Bosnian Muslims. Estimated to have cost the lives of some 500,000, unleashing some three and a half million refugees, it also involved the systematic rape of thousands of Muslim women, the destruction of much of the country's infrastructure, and the desecration of its great ancient mosques and churches. Whole cities were destroyed, as each group claimed its territories and aimed to 'cleanse' other ethnic groups. The biggest and most hideous ethnic cleansing was of the Bosnian Muslims, attacked by the Serbs. After much humanitarian intervention, a settlement was reached in 1995 (known as the Dayton Agreement).

Although it was a 'local war', it eventually provoked international intervention. But even this could not prevent a large and devastating civil war. It has come to symbolise the modern 'ethnic' war complete with its horrendous atrocities and ethnic cleansings. Neighbouring groups hate each other and are willing to do the most terrible things. Today, most wars are not between nation-states. They are tribal conflicts between different ethnic groupings. It may be that the days of the big wars are over. What we are seeing is a proliferation of civil wars and 'tribal conflicts'. Currently there are some 30 civil wars taking place all over the world and the map later in the chapter documents some of these (see p. 370). This chapter probes both the differences of peoples and the hatreds that this generates.

See: Noel Malcolm, *Bosnia* (2002); pp. 368–9 and 553.

(Left) Ron Waddams, *We the Peoples . . .* 1984 (acrylic on board)

Source: We the Peoples . . . 1984 (acrylic on board), Wadams, Ron (Contemporary Artist)/Private Collection,/The Bridgeman Art Library.

See more of Waddams' work online at: http://www.larrenart.org.uk.

Q What do you see here? The artist uses elements from the near and distant past to create contemporary expression of spiritual and humanitarian concerns. Many of the works are reflections on living without conflict, and refer to the aims of the United Nations Charter.

Race, as a meaningful criterion within the biological sciences, has long been recognised to be a fiction. When we speak of 'the white race' or 'the black race', 'the Jewish race' or 'the Aryan race', we speak in biological misnomers and, more generally, in metaphors . . .

Henry Louis Gates

In this chapter, we ask:

- **What are the meanings of race, ethnicity and racialisation?**

- **How can we start to explain prejudice and racism?**

- **What are the major patterns and problems around migration?**

- **What is the ethnic situation in the UK?**

Globally, the pattern of inequality and conflict based on colour, ethnicity and culture is becoming ever more pronounced. The extermination of Jews and other minorities, such as gypsies and homosexuals, in the Holocaust may mark the twentieth century's extreme low point (see Chapter 8), but ethnic strife still continues. Indeed, with the collapse of the former Soviet empire, Ukrainians, Moldavians, Azerbaijanis and a host of other ethnic peoples in eastern Europe are struggling to recover their cultural identity after decades of Soviet subjugation. In the Middle East, deep-rooted friction divides Arabs and Jews, while blacks and whites strive to establish a just society in South Africa. In Turkey there is conflict between the government and Kurdish nationalists; in Sudan between north Muslim Arabs and southern blacks, both Christian and animist – going on since the 1950s; in Sri Lanka between Hindu Tamils and Buddhist Sinhalese; in Rwanda between Hutus and Tutsis (see below); in Iraq between Sunni and Shi'ite. And, of course, in Israel between

Jews and Palestinians. The list goes on and on (see the map in Chapter 16 on conflict zones).

In the African nations, the Asian countries, the Arab states, in the Balkans, and elsewhere in the world, racial and ethnic rifts frequently flare into violent confrontation. Every year or so we hear of new conflicts. There are, for example, major ethnic tensions in most large, urban cities, exploding intermittently as with the Los Angeles 'riots' of 1992 or, more recently, in the autumn of 2005, with the conflict waged in many French suburbs for over two weeks. In just two nights, over 2,000 cars were burned in large and small towns – Nantes in the west, Avignon in the south, and Evreux in Normandy (*Guardian*, 7 November 2005: 20). It was suggested that some 6,000 cars were destroyed in 12 nights. This was seen mainly as a conflict between black African youths aged 14–25, along with others from poor big-city suburbs, and the state: it was conflict between marginalised youth and France as a society. Between 7 and 10 per cent of France is ethnic and

The Rwandan Genocide was the 1994 mass murder of an estimated 850,000 people in the small East African Nation of Rwanda. The Rwandan military and Hutu militia groups systematically set out to murder all the Tutsis they could reach, regardless of age or sex, as well as the political moderates among the Hutu. Here a man looks at photographs of genocide survivors (see pp. 363–5)

Source: © Radu Sigheti/Reuters/Corbis.

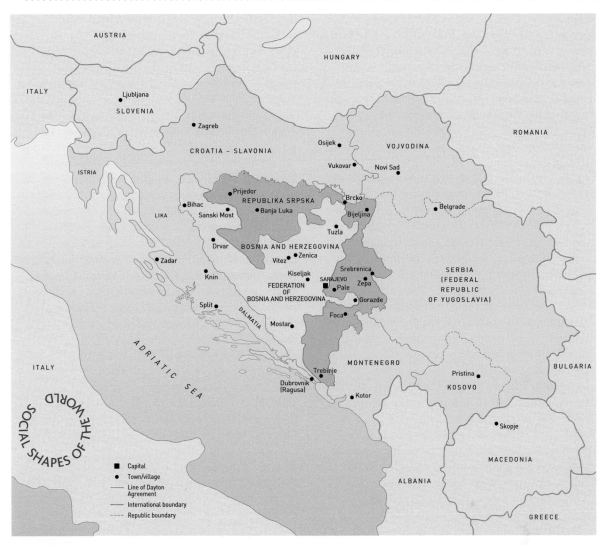

SOCIAL SHAPES OF THE WORLD

Map 11.1   **The former Yugoslavia**
Yugoslavia as a country dissolved in the early 1990s into five independent countries and has been a site of many conflicts. We now have: Bosnia and Herzegovina (1992), Croatia (1992), Macedonia (1991–4), and Serbia and Montenegro (also known as the Federal Republic of Yugoslavia) which separated in 2006. Kosovo unilaterally declared its independence from Serbia in 2008.

See the introduction to this chapter and page 553.

70 per cent of this is Muslim. The national policy is generally assimilationist and integrationist, but this policy was seen to be not working. Further, the migration of displaced peoples everywhere across the globe nearly always generates cultural conflicts. Worldwide, ethnic antagonisms remain, fomenting hatred and mistrust, and propelling violence and war.

This chapter examines the meaning of ethnicities, and the racism and conflicts that often accompany them. It critically examines how these social constructs have shaped our history and suggests why they continue to play such a central part – for better or worse – in the world today.

The social significance of nation, race and ethnicities

Most people living on the earth today live in nation-states. But this is a phenomenon of recent history. Ethnic groups made claims to their territories and right up to the sixteenth century people lived with these territorial limits. But between the sixteenth and nineteenth century, as we shall see later in more detail, nation-states as we now know them started to congeal (see Chapter 16, p. 545). Little by little, people came to identify themselves as belonging to 'nations'. In the words of Benedict Anderson, nation-states started to develop as **imagined communities**: *a socially constructed community, one which is imagined by the people who perceive themselves as part of that group.* The trouble is that behind this 'imagined community' lie many old ethnic divisions and conflicts seething away.

Ethnicity refers basically *to a shared historical and cultural heritage.* People frequently use the terms 'race' and 'ethnicity' imprecisely and interchangeably. Using the 'correct' language in the study of race and ethnicity can be very difficult. Some commentators prefer the language used by different ethnic groups themselves: the word 'black' (in the UK) or 'people of colour' (in the United States). The trouble here is that there is no agreement within these groups: some, often more political, people prefer one word; others may prefer another. For example, 'Asian' English-American black feminist Indian Kum-Kum Bhavnani suggests that 'black' is used in Britain as a political category for racialised groups – all those non-white groups who experience racism. This would include Pakistani, Bangladeshi and Indian groups. The word would then become a unifying force for a 'black movement'. But others do not agree. Tariq Modood argues that 'black' is not suitable for Asians in the UK because it generates a false sense of essential unity and is itself used inconsistently (it sometimes means only people of African descent). Indeed, he argues that most Asians do not use the term, and that what is really needed is a language of Asian pride with its own historical and cultural roots (Bhavnani, 1993; Modood, 1994). Using the 'right' language can be very difficult.

Race and racialisation

'Race' itself is a very muddled, and even dangerous, concept. The idea of **race** came into use between the latter part of the eighteenth and the mid-nineteenth centuries: it is thus a modern idea. It usually refers to *a category of people who share biologically transmitted traits that members of society deem socially significant.* People may classify each other into races based on different physical characteristics, such as skin colour, facial features, hair texture and body shape. These differences are superficial; individuals of all races are members of a single biological species. People the world over display a bewildering array of racial traits. This variety is the product of migration and intermarriage over the course of human history, so that many genetic characteristics once common to a single place are now evident throughout the world. The most striking racial variation appears in the Middle East (that is, western Asia), which has long served as a 'crossroads' of human migration. Striking racial uniformity, by contrast, characterises more isolated peoples such as the island-dwelling Japanese. But no society lacks genetic mixture, and increasing contact among the world's people will ensure that racial blending accelerates in the future.

Nineteenth-century thinkers, such as A. de Gobineau (1816–82) in his *Essay on the Inequality of the Human Races* (1915; orig. 1853), developed a three-part scheme of racial classification. Labelling people with relatively light skin and fine hair as *Caucasian*, those with darker skin and coarser, curlier hair *Negroid*, and those with yellow or brown skin and distinctive folds on the eyelids *Mongoloid*, a 'race science' was established, in which, for example, Caucasians were seen as people of greater intelligence and higher morality! Sociologists consider such theories and categories not just as very misleading (since we now know that no society is composed of biologically pure individuals) but also politically dangerous (in fuelling the fires of racism). Indeed, this has led most sociologists to reject the very idea of race and to look elsewhere for better concepts to understand these issues.

Nevertheless, people around the world do seem quick to classify each other racially. This *process of ranking people on the basis of their presumed race* sociologists now call **racialisation**: it is at the heart of this system of inequality and social exclusion. As will be explained later, people may also defend racial hierarchy with assertions that one category is inherently 'better' or more intelligent than another, though no sound scientific research supports such beliefs. But, because so much is at stake, it is no wonder that societies strive to make racial labelling much clearer than the 'facts' permit. Early in the twentieth century, for example, many southern states in the United States legally defined as 'coloured' anyone who had as little as one-thirty-second African ancestry (that is, one African-American great-great-great-grandparent). Today, with less of a caste distinction in the United States, the law enables parents to declare the race of a child, if they wish to do so at all.

Ethnicity and its problems: ten key words to think with

1 *Race/ethnicity*: race usually refers to a *presumed* significant biological difference between groups, whereas ethnicity refers to differences based on cultural, religious and historical heritage which confer distinctive identities. All societies are composed of cultures linked to many different ethnic histories.

2 *Racialisation*: refers to the social processes by which people are ranked, sorted and classified on the basis of their presumed race. Often such rankings devalue certain 'race' groups over others and are organised through political processes.

3 *Racial formation*: refers to a social structure which is organised around race, ethnicity and racialisation, although they change across history and across lives. It involves language and material conditions – and in lives we can see speak of racial projects: ways of organising and dealing with resources along racial lines (see Omi and Winant, 1995).

4 *Racism*: refers to the belief that *the genetic factors* which constitute race are a primary determinant of human traits and capacities, and that racial differences produce an inherent superiority of a particular race. The *new racism* suggests that *cultural factors* may also be the basis of this superiority and discrimination.

5 *Multiculturalism*: recognises both past and present cultural diversity and promotes the potential equality of all cultural traditions (see the *Big debate* in Chapter 5, p. 172). It refers to differences found across a culture based on race and ethnicity, and more generally, cultural differences. It is applied as a policy in a range of areas of social life, but especially in education. It argues for an ability to live with difference and to promote different cultural traditions as equally acceptable within a culture.

6 *Diaspora*: the movements (and scatterings) of different cultures and ethnicities across the world. Most nations (see Chapter 16) can be seen as composed of many different groups who have migrated and moved from country to country throughout history.

7 *Othering*: a process in which groups come to define themselves through the recognition of people outside their group as 'the other' – which usually means they are outsiders to be stigmatised.

8 *Politics of recognition*: a politics which gives priority to the importance of acknowledging human differences and according equal respect to these differences. It is often contrasted with a politics of redistribution, which is more concerned with equality. They are not in fact incompatible.

9 *Colonialism*: the process by which some countries/ nations enrich themselves through political and economic control of other countries.

10 *Intersectionality*: the connections between race and other forms of domination and exclusion, such as class, gender, sexuality, age and disability (as discussed in this section of the book).

For a full and lively collection of readings on all these issues, see Les Back and John Solomos (eds), *Theories of Race and Racism: A Reader* (2nd edn, 2009).

Ethnicity, multiculturalism and the diaspora

Ethnicity is a valuable term, but not when it is applied only to groups that differ from us: everybody on the planet is part of a complex ethnicity. Members of an *ethnic category* have common ancestors, a language or a religion that, together, confer a distinctive social identity. The forebears of Pakistani, Indonesian, Caribbean, Hong Kong or Chinese Europeans – to name just a few – may well retain cultural patterns rooted in particular areas of the world. There are over a million foreign students in French schools (and three-quarters of a million in Germany) where German, English, Spanish, Italian, Portuguese, Arabic,

Hebrew, Russian, Japanese, Dutch, Chinese and Turkish are taught. In Britain, there exist around 100 minority languages – about a quarter of them taught in English schools, and in the United States, more than 30 million people speak a language other than English in their homes (Crystal, 2010).

But it goes deeper than just language. Most Europeans and Americans of Spanish, Italian and Polish ancestry are Roman Catholic, while others of Greek, Ukrainian and Russian ancestry are members of the Eastern Orthodox church. There are more than 6 million Jewish Americans (with ancestral ties to various nations) who share a distinctive religious history. Similarly, several million women and men in Europe have a Muslim heritage. Almost every country in the world is composed of multiple ethnicities, each harbouring its own culture and history. Chapter 5 has given you a more detailed discussion of this for Muslim cultures (see p. 158). In a loose sense, **multculturalism** is a term used to indicate an awareness of this range of different cultures (see below).

Race and ethnicity may overlap, but one has a firm sense of biological difference (now very muddled) and the other relies on understanding cultural heritage. The two can sometimes go hand in hand. Gujarati Hindus, for example, can have distinctive physical traits and – for those who maintain a traditional way of life – cultural attributes as well. But ethnic distinctiveness should not be viewed as racial. For example, Jews are sometimes described as a race although they are distinctive only in their religious beliefs as well as their history of persecution (Goldsby, 1977).

Finally, ethnicity involves even more variability and mixture than race does, for most people identify with more than one ethnic background (a person might claim to be, say, German and English). Many Asians in the UK, for example, identify with quite specific ethnic cultures in Asia, as well as 'being British'. Often this leads to hyphenated identities such as 'Asian-British', 'Afro-Caribbean' or 'Black-African' (see Chapter 7 on identities). Ethnic communities can also vary greatly: from Punjabi Hindus (who speak Punjabi) and Gujarati Muslims (who speak Gujarati) who come from Indian states (Punjab and Gujarat); to those from Pakistan (such as Mirpuri Muslims), Bangladesh (such as Bengali Muslims) and East Africa (such as Uganda or Kenya). Table 11.1 provides a listing of key groupings.

Moreover, people may intentionally modify their ethnicity over time. Many West Indian immigrants to England have gradually shed their cultural background, becoming less 'West Indian' and absorbing new ethnic traits from others. In a reversal of this pattern, others have highlighted their background through 'Rastafarianism' (see below). Likewise, many people with native Irish ancestry have recently taken a renewed interest in their traditional ethnicity, enhancing this dimension of their identity. In short, ethnicity is about varying cultures (see Chapter 5) which are themselves changeable and fluid. Much of this leads to discussions of migration patterns, hybridities and diasporas – so we understand the paths along which different ethnicities have travelled in the world.

Studying these different ethnicities and cultures leads us to an awareness of diasporas. **Diaspora** refers to *the dispersal of a population from its 'homeland' into other areas.* Table 11.2 helps clarify what this term means.

Minorities

A racial or ethnic **minority** is *a category of people, distinguished by physical or cultural traits, who are socially disadvantaged.* Distinct from the dominant 'majority', in other words, minorities are set apart and subordinated. The breadth of the term 'minority' has expanded in recent years beyond people with particular racial and ethnic traits to include people with physical disabilities; as the next chapter explains, some analysts view all women as minorities as well. Gays and lesbians have also been placed in a minority framework.

Minorities have two major characteristics. First, they share a *distinctive identity*. Because race is highly visible (and virtually impossible for a person to change), minority men and women typically have a keen awareness of their physical distinctiveness. The significance of ethnicity (which people can change) is more variable. Some people (many Reform Jews among them) have downplayed their historic ethnicity, while others (including many Orthodox Jews) have retained their cultural traditions and have lived in distinctive ethnic enclaves.

A second characteristic of minorities is *subordination*. As the remainder of this chapter will demonstrate, racialised minorities typically have less income, lower occupational prestige and more limited schooling than their counterparts in the majority. Class, race and ethnicity, as well as gender, are not mutually exclusive issues but are overlapping and reinforcing dimensions of social stratification.

While not all members of any minority category are disadvantaged, race or ethnicity often serves as *a master status or core identity* that overshadows personal accomplishments.

Table 11.1   'Asians in Britain': contrasting groups

Place of origin	Religion	First language	Community known as
(a) Indian subcontinent			
(i) India			
Punjab State	mainly Sikhs some Hindus	Punjabi	Punjabi Sikh Punjabi Hindu
Gujarat State	mainly Hindus some Muslims	Gujarati (some Kutchi)	Gujarati Hindu Gujarati Muslim (Kutchi Muslim)
(ii) Pakistan			
Punjab	Muslims	Punjabi (some Urdu)	Punjabi Muslim
Mirpur (Azad Kashmir)	Muslims	Punjabi (Mirpuri dialect)	Mirpuri
NW Frontier Province (very few)	Muslims	Pashto	Pathan
(iii) Bangladesh			
Sylhet District	Muslims	Bengali	Bengali Muslim
(b) East Africa			
Most have come from Uganda, Kenya, Tanzania, some from Malawi, Zambia; the families of most East African Asians originated in:			
(i) Gujarat State (main group)	Hindus some Muslims	Gujarati (some Kutchi)	EA Gujarati Hindu EA Gujarati Muslim (EA Kutchi Hindu) (EA Kutchi Muslim)
(ii) Punjab State (India)	Sikhs Hindus	Punjabi	EA Punjabi Sikh EA Punjabi Hindu
(iii) Punjab (Pakistan)	Muslims	Punjabi (some Urdu)	EA Punjabi Muslim

Source: Based on Coombe and Little (1986: 38).

Table 11.2   Some key features of diasporas

1 A dispersal and scattering of people from an original 'homeland'.

2 A strong ethnic consciousness around the homeland and strong empathy with co-members.

3 This consciousness includes a collective memory and idealisation of an imagined community.

4 There is a discontent with the host land.

5 Frequently, a social movement is built with the idea of 'returning to the homeland'.

6 There is the possibility of a good life in the new land if it has a tolerance of pluralism.

Source: Based on Robin Cohen, *Global Diasporas* (2008: 17).

Prejudice and racism

We have to ask why people hold such negative views of others based on their race or ethnicity. Three ideas help here: prejudice, stereotyping and racism.

Prejudice

Prejudice is *a rigid and irrational generalisation about an entire category of people*. A prejudice is an attitude – a prejudgement – that one applies indiscriminately and inflexibly to some category with little regard for the facts. People commonly hold prejudices about individuals of a particular social class, sex, sexual orientation, age, political affiliation, race or ethnicity.

Prejudices can be positive or negative. Our positive prejudices tend to exaggerate the virtues of people like ourselves, while our negative prejudices condemn those who differ from us. Negative prejudice runs along a continuum, ranging from mild aversion to outright hostility. Because attitudes are rooted in culture, everyone has at least some measure of prejudice. Most people recognise that white people commonly hold prejudiced views of minorities, but minorities, too, harbour prejudices, sometimes of whites and often of other minorities.

Stereotypes

Prejudices combine to form a **stereotype** (*stereo* is derived from Greek meaning 'hard' or 'solid'), described as *a prejudicial, exaggerated description applied to every person in a category of people*. Because many stereotypes involve emotions such as love and loyalty (generally towards members of in-groups) or hate and fear (towards out-groups), they are exaggerated images that are hard to change even in the face of contradictory evidence. For example, some people have a stereotypical understanding of the poor as lazy and irresponsible spongers who would rather rely on welfare than support themselves (NORC, 1994). As Chapter 10 explained, however, this stereotype distorts reality because most poor people tend to be children, women, working adults or elderly people.

Stereotypes have been devised for virtually every racial and ethnic minority, and such attitudes may become deeply rooted in a society's culture. In the United States, for example, half of white people stereotype African-Americans as lacking motivation to improve their own lives (NORC, 1994: 236). Such attitudes assume that social disadvantage is a matter of personal deficiency, which, in most cases, it is not. Moreover, stereotypes of this kind ignore the fact that most poor people in the United States are white and that most African-Americans work as hard as anyone else and are not poor. In this case the bit of truth in the stereotype is that black people are more likely than white people to be poor (and slightly more likely, if poor, to receive welfare assistance). But by building a rigid attitude out of a few selected facts, stereotypes grossly distort reality.

Racism

A powerful and destructive form of prejudice, **racism** refers to *the belief that one racial category is innately superior or inferior to another*. Racism has pervaded world history. The ancient Greeks, the peoples of India and the Chinese – despite their many notable achievements – were all quick to view 'others' as inferior. Racism has also been widespread in our own history: indeed, it is probably found in every society in the world today. Thus in Australia, targeted groups include aboriginals, Pacific Islanders and Chinese, while in Denmark the Somalians and other refugee groups are objects of racism. It is hard to find cultures that do not have some form of race tension or conflict.

Racism and social domination

Historically, the assertion that one specific category of people is innately inferior to another has served as a powerful justification for subjecting the targets of these taunts to *social* inferiority. By the end of the nineteenth century, European nations and the United States had forged vast empires, often ruthlessly and brutally subjugating foreign peoples with the callous claim that they were somehow less human than the explorers who enslaved them.

In the twentieth century, racism was central to the Nazi proclamation that a so-called Aryan super-race of blond-haired, blue-eyed Germans was destined to rule the world. Such racist ideology encouraged the systematic slaughter of anyone deemed inferior, including some 6 million European Jews and millions of Poles, gypsies, homosexuals and people with physical and mental disabilities.

More recently, racial conflict has intensified in western Europe with the immigration of people from former colonies as well as from eastern Europe seeking a higher standard of living. In Germany, France, Britain and elsewhere, growing public intolerance of immigrants has fuelled a resurgence of Nazi-style rhetoric and tactics. The United States, too, is experiencing increasing racial tensions in cities and on college campuses. Racism – in thought and deed – remains a serious social problem everywhere as people still contend that some racial and ethnic categories are 'better' than others.

Explaining racism

If prejudice does not represent a rational assessment of facts, what are its origins? Social scientists have come up with various answers to this vexing question, citing the importance of frustration, personality, culture and social conflict.

W. E. B. Du Bois: race and conflict

One of sociology's pioneers, who has not received the attention he deserves, is William Edward Burghardt Du Bois (1868–1963). Born to a poor Massachusetts family, Du Bois showed extraordinary aptitude as a student. After graduating from

William Edward Burghardt Du Bois (1868–1963). As well as being a founding sociologist, he was an intellectual leader of the black community in America, a civil rights activist, a historian and a Pan-Africanist. He helped shape a black standpoint sociology. Note that many sociologists have been actively involved in social movements for change

See: Edward J. Blum. *W. E. B. Du Bois, American Prophet*. Philadelphia, University of Pennsylvania Press, 2007.

Source: africanpictures/akg-images.

high school, he went to college, one of only a handful of the young people in his small town (and the only person of African descent) to do so. After graduating from Fisk University in Nashville, Tennessee, Du Bois realised a childhood ambition and enrolled at Harvard, repeating his junior and senior years and then beginning graduate study. He earned the first doctorate awarded by Harvard to a person of colour.

Du Bois believed that sociologists should direct their efforts to contemporary problems, and for him the vexing issue of race was the paramount social concern. Although he was accepted in the intellectual circles of his day, Du Bois believed that US society consigned African-Americans as a whole to an existence separate and apart. Unlike white people, who can make their way in the world simply as 'Americans', Du Bois pointed out, African-Americans have a 'double consciousness', reflecting their status as Americans who are never able to escape identification based on colour.

Politically speaking, his opposition to racial separation led Du Bois to serve as a founding member of the National Association for the Advancement of Colored People (NAACP). Du Bois maintained that his research, too, should attempt to address pressing racial problems. Later in his life, Du Bois reflected (1940: 51):

I was determined to put science into sociology through a study of the condition of my own group.

I was going to study the facts, any and all facts, concerning the American Negro and his plight.

After taking a position at the University of Pennsylvania in Philadelphia, Du Bois set out to conduct the research that produced a sociological classic, *The Philadelphia Negro: A Social Study* (1967; orig. 1899). In this systematic investigation of Philadelphia's African-American community at the turn of the century, Du Bois chronicled both the strengths and weaknesses of people wrestling with overwhelming social problems. Running against the intellectual current of the times (especially Spencer's social Darwinism), Du Bois rejected the widespread notion of black inferiority, attributing the problems of African-Americans to white prejudice. But his criticism extended also to successful people of colour, whom he scolded for being so eager to win white acceptance that they abandoned all ties with those still in need. 'The first impulse of the best, the wisest and the richest', he lamented, 'is to segregate themselves from the mass' (1967: 317; orig. 1899).

At the time *The Philadelphia Negro* was published, Du Bois was optimistic about overcoming racial divisions. By the end of his life, however, he had grown bitter, believing that little had changed. At the age of 93, Du Bois left the United States for Ghana, where he died two years later.

Source: Based, in part, on Baltzell (1967; orig. 1899) and Du Bois (1967; orig. 1899).

1 Scapegoat theory of prejudice

Scapegoat theory holds that prejudice springs from frustration. Such attitudes, therefore, are common among people who are themselves disadvantaged (Dollard et al., 1939). Take the case of a white woman frustrated at the low wages she earns working in a textile factory. Directing hostility at the powerful people who operate the factory carries obvious risks; therefore, she may well attribute her low pay to the presence of minority co-workers. Prejudice of this kind may not go far towards improving the woman's situation, but it serves as a relatively safe way to vent anger and it may give her the comforting feeling that at least she is superior to someone.

A **scapegoat**, then, is *a person or category of people, typically with little power, whom people unfairly blame for their own troubles*. Because they are often 'safe targets', minorities are easily used as scapegoats. The Nazis blamed the Jewish minority for all of Germany's ills in the 1930s. And today some Europeans attribute troubles at home to the presence of Turkish, Pakistani or other immigrants from abroad.

2 Authoritarian personality theory

Theodore W. Adorno and his colleagues (1950) claimed that extreme prejudice was a personality trait of particular individuals. They based this conclusion on research showing that people who displayed strong prejudice towards one minority were usually intolerant of all minorities. Such people exhibit *authoritarian personalities*, rigidly conforming to conventional cultural values, envisaging moral issues as clear-cut matters of right and wrong, and advocating strongly ethnocentric views. People with authoritarian personalities also look upon society as naturally competitive and hierarchical, with 'better' people (such as themselves) inevitably dominating those who are weaker.

By contrast, Adorno found, people tolerant towards one minority were likely to be accepting of all. They tend to be more flexible in their moral judgements and believe that, ideally, society should be relatively egalitarian. They feel uncomfortable in any situation in which some people exercise excessive and damaging power over others.

According to these researchers, authoritarian personalities tend to develop in people with little education and harsh and demanding parents. Raised by cold and insistent authority figures, they theorised,

children may become angry and anxious people who seek out scapegoats whom they come to define as their social inferiors.

3 Cultural theory of prejudice

A third approach holds that, while extreme prejudice may be characteristic of certain people, some prejudice is common to everyone because such attitudes are embedded in culture.

For more than 40 years, Emory Bogardus (1968) studied the effects of culturally rooted prejudices on interpersonal relationships. He devised the concept of *social distance* to gauge how close or distant people feel in relation to members of various racial and ethnic categories. Interestingly, his research shows that people throughout the United States share similar views in this regard, leading Bogardus to conclude that such attitudes are culturally normative.

Bogardus found that members of US society regarded most positively people of English, Canadian and Scottish background, welcoming close relationships with and even marriage to them. There was somewhat less of a premium on interactions with people of French, German, Swedish and Dutch descent. The most negative prejudices, Bogardus discovered, targeted people of African and Asian descent.

If prejudice is widespread, can we dismiss intolerance as merely a trait of a handful of abnormal people, as Adorno asserted? A more all-encompassing approach recognises that some bigotry is within us all as we become well adjusted to a 'culture of prejudice'.

4 Oppression of minorities

A fourth view claims that powerful people utilise prejudice as a strategy to oppress minorities. To the extent that the public looks down on Turkish guest workers in Germany, illegal Latino immigrants in the southwest United States, or refugees in the UK, employers are able to pay these people low wages for hard work. Similarly, elites benefit from prejudice that divides workers along racial and ethnic lines and discourages them from working together to advance their common interests (Geschwender, 1978).

5 The postcolonial plight and the new 'cultural' racism

While older forms of 'scientific' racism (with their focus on biological races as inferior) still continue, an important theory to have an impact upon race thinking recently has been **postcolonial theory**. This refers to *the wide critiques of (usually 'white') Western cultures that are made by people who have been colonised in the past.* As is well known, from the sixteenth century onwards (but especially during the nineteenth century) European colonial empires such as those of the British, Portuguese, Spanish, French, Belgian and Dutch were established all over the world. The indigenous peoples of Asia, Africa and the Americas became subject to cultural conquest – often enslavement and genocide, too. But in an even wider sense, postcolonialism can bring an understanding of the wider world historical process by which people have invaded other cultures throughout history. It is a feature of many societies that as one culture invades another, so it attempts to settle its own values and beliefs over it – from the Incas, the Ottomans and the Chinese through to the British in North America with the native Indian tribes. It is a major world process that leads to the blurring and fragmentation of different groups across the world, each of which generally creates its own sense of the threatening 'other' within its midst.

Postcolonialism challenges the superiority of 'white' or dominant thinking and listens to the voices of peoples who have been hidden from sight through this process of colonialisation. These are people who, in effect, have 'lost their voice' (see Chapter 2). At the heart of this critical position is the recognition of just how much 'the West' (in this case, principally western Europe and the United States) came to dominate the world throughout the nineteenth and early twentieth centuries. As Edward Said, a leading figure in the postcolonial movements, has commented:

> By 1914 . . . Europe held a grand total of roughly 85% of the earth as colonies, protectorates, dependencies, dominions and commonwealths. No other set of colonies in history was as large, none so totally dominated, none so unequal in power to the Western metropolis.

(Said, 1993: 3)

Such colonisation has left its mark on the world.

What these newer ideas highlight are the ways in which ethnicities depend upon different senses of collectivity and belonging among groups. They stress the ways in which boundaries – often defined as 'the nation' or 'us' – are created, maintained, challenged and transformed between different ethnic groups (Jenkins, 1997: 16–24). State policies (for example, on immigration) are often closely connected to identifying these groupings, which are frequently identified through 'race' and 'colour', and then made the source of boundary definition. Nationalism often takes on an importance in such discussions: just what does 'being British', 'being German', 'being Scandinavian' or even 'being European' mean?

The categories are far from simple. Take the case of 'being British'. Although claims may be made by some about the purity of the category, sociologist Stuart Hall has suggested that it is very much a 'mongrel category': 'Our mongrel selves and most cultures are inextricably multicultural – mixed ethically, religiously, culturally and linguistically' (Hall, 1992a). Thus, 'being British' – historically encompassing descent from many waves of European immigrants as well as peoples of the 'Celtic fringe' of Scotland, Ireland and Wales – must at the very least engage with major migrations from Asia, the West Indies, etc., with the history of the Commonwealth, and with many countries across the world that have some legacy of colonisation. To quote Paul Gilroy, a leading sociologist of ethnicity and race:

> **We increasingly face a racism which avoids being recognized as such because it is able to line up 'race' with nationhood, patriotism, and nationalism. A racism which has taken a necessary distance from crude ideas of biological inferiority now seeks to present an imaginary definition of the nation as a unified cultural community. It constructs and defends an image of national culture – homogeneous in its whiteness yet precarious and perpetually vulnerable to attack from enemies within and without.**

(Gilroy, 1987: 87)

Discrimination

Closely related to prejudice is the concept of **discrimination**, *any action that involves treating various categories of people unequally.* While prejudice refers to attitudes, discrimination is a matter of behaviour. Like prejudice, discrimination can be either positive (providing special advantages) or negative (placing obstacles in front of particular categories of people). Discrimination also varies in intensity, ranging from subtle to blatant.

Prejudice and discrimination often – but not always – occur together. A personnel manager prejudiced against members of a particular minority may refuse to employ them. Robert Merton (1976) describes such a person as an *active bigot*. Fearing legal action, however, another prejudiced personnel manager may not discriminate, thereby becoming a *timid bigot*. What Merton calls *fair-weather liberals* may be generally tolerant of minorities yet discriminate when it is expedient to do so, such as when a superior demands it. Finally, Merton's *all-weather liberal* is free of both prejudice and discrimination.

Not all kinds of discrimination are wrong. Individuals discriminate all the time, preferring the personalities, favouring the looks or admiring the talents of particular people. Discriminating in this basic sense of *making distinctions* is necessary to everyday life and rarely causes problems. But discriminating on the basis of race or ethnicity is another matter.

All societies praise some forms of discrimination: in other words, while condemning others. Universities, for example, systematically favour applicants with greater abilities over those with less aptitude. This kind of discrimination is entirely consistent with our culture-based expectation that the greatest rewards go to people with more ability or those who work harder.

But what if a university were to favour one category of people (Christians, say) over another (Jews), regardless of individual talent? Unless the university had a religious mission (making a specific religion directly relevant to performance in school), such a policy would discriminate in a manner both morally wrong and against the law.

In historical terms, principles of fair play change along with economic development. In low-income countries, people routinely favour members of their families, clans, religious groups and villages. Traditional people typically recognise a moral duty to 'look after their own'. In high-income industrial societies, by contrast, cultural norms elevate the individual over the group, so that achievement rather than ascription guides our code of fairness. Many organisations, therefore, seek out the most qualified applicant while forbidding 'nepotism' or 'conflict of interest', by which employees would favour a relative or reject someone based on race or sex.

Institutional discrimination

We typically think of prejudice and discrimination as the hateful ideas or actions of specific individuals. But far greater harm results from **institutional**

discrimination, which refers to *bias in attitudes or action inherent in the operation of society's institutions*, including schools, hospitals, the police and the workplace. Until the US Supreme Court's *Brown* decision in 1954, the principle of 'separate but equal' legally justified the institutional discrimination by which black and white children in the United States attended different schools. In effect, the law before *Brown* upheld institutional racism in the form of an educational caste system. Institutional discrimination remains one of US society's most intractable problems. Despite the *Brown* decision, relatively little has changed since 1954: while no US schools remain officially 'black' or 'white', most students still attend schools in which one race or the other predominates overwhelmingly. Indeed, in 1991, a court decision recognised that neighbourhood schools would never provide equal education as long as the US population was divided into racially segregated neighbourhoods, with most African-Americans living in city centres and most white people (and Asian-Americans) living in geographically and politically separate suburbs.

In the UK, the report by Sir William Macpherson into the murder of Stephen Lawrence suggested that police conduct during the case had been seriously lacking and that institutional racism was at work in the British police. On 22 April 1993, a young black man, Stephen Lawrence, was murdered by a gang of white youths as he waited at a bus stop. After the murder, there were complaints from the family that the murder had not been properly investigated and that indeed the police had behaved in a racist fashion. The Macpherson Report was a detailed investigation of the events around the crime, and concluded that although individual police officers may not have been deliberately prejudiced, the Metropolitan Police Service itself was 'institutionally racist'. Macpherson defined this as:

> **The collective failure of an organisation to provide an appropriate and professional service to people because of their colour, culture, or ethnic origin. It can be seen or detected in processes, attitudes and behaviours which amount to the discrimination through unwitting prejudice, ignorance, thoughtlessness and racist stereotyping which disadvantage minority ethnic people.**

(Macpherson, 1999: 6.43)

The report has been influential in generating public debate on police policy and racism in the UK.

Oppression, prejudice and discrimination: the vicious cycle

Oppression, prejudice and discrimination frequently reinforce each other. W. I. Thomas offered a simple explanation of this fact, noted in Chapter 7. The Thomas theorem states: *if situations are defined as real, they are real in their consequences* (1966: 301; orig. 1931). Because people socially construct reality, stereotypes become real to those who believe them and sometimes even to those who are victimised by them. Power also plays a role here, since some categories of people have the ability to enforce their prejudices to the detriment of others.

Prejudice by whites against people of colour, for example, does not produce *innate* inferiority but it can produce *social* inferiority, consigning minorities to poverty, low-prestige occupations and poor housing in racially segregated neighbourhoods. If white people interpret social disadvantage as evidence that minorities do not measure up to their standards, they unleash a new round of prejudice and discrimination, giving rise to a *vicious cycle* whereby each perpetuates the other, as illustrated in Figure 11.1, even from generation to generation.

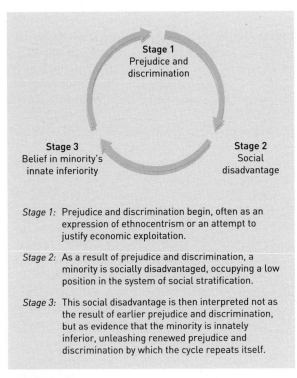

Stage 1
Prejudice and discrimination

Stage 2
Social disadvantage

Stage 3
Belief in minority's innate inferiority

Stage 1: Prejudice and discrimination begin, often as an expression of ethnocentrism or an attempt to justify economic exploitation.

Stage 2: As a result of prejudice and discrimination, a minority is socially disadvantaged, occupying a low position in the system of social stratification.

Stage 3: This social disadvantage is then interpreted not as the result of earlier prejudice and discrimination, but as evidence that the minority is innately inferior, unleashing renewed prejudice and discrimination by which the cycle repeats itself.

Figure 11.1 Prejudice and discrimination: the vicious cycle

Majority and minority: patterns of interaction

Social scientists describe patterns of interaction among racial and ethnic categories in terms of four models: multiculturalism, assimilation, segregation and genocide.

1 Multiculturalism and pluralism

Pluralism is *a state in which racial and ethnic minorities are distinct but have social parity*. In a pluralist society, categories of people are socially different, but they share basic social resources more or less equally. Most Western societies are – to differing degrees – pluralistic in several respects. They provide schooling and other services to all categories of people, and generally promise them equal standing before the law. Moreover, large cities contain dozens of 'ethnic villages' where people proudly display the cultural traditions of their immigrant ancestors. In London there are Arab, Chinese, Maltese, Greek, Italian, Jewish, 'West Indian' and, of course, differing Asian communities. In New York there is Spanish Harlem, Little Italy and Chinatown; in Philadelphia, Italian 'South Philly'; in Miami, 'Little Havana'; in Chicago, 'Little Saigon'; as well as Latino East Los Angeles.

Pluralism – living with difference – is one goal of the recent trend towards multiculturalism. As described in Chapter 5, this scholarly and political initiative seeks to promote an ability to live with difference and to accept as equal the many cultural traditions that make up our national life.

But, in other respects, much of the West remains far from pluralistic. In the United States, for instance, while most people appreciate and value their cultural heritage, only a small proportion of minorities want to live and interact only and exclusively with their 'own kind' (NORC, 1994). Further, in many cases, racial and ethnic identity is forced on people by others who shun them as undesirable. For example, people in many communities in the Appalachian Mountains of the eastern United States remain culturally distinctive because others snub them as 'hillbillies'. And worse: in recent years, rising levels of immigration have stretched many people's tolerance for social diversity. One reaction against the new immigrants has been a social movement seeking to establish English as the official language of the United States – hardly a strategy to bolster pluralism.

Switzerland presents a much sharper example of pluralism. In this European nation of almost 7 million people, German, French and Italian cultural traditions run deep. The Swiss have been relatively successful in maintaining pluralism (albeit, but critically, involving little difference in colour), officially recognising all three languages. Just as important, the three categories have roughly the same economic standing (Simpson and Yinger, 1972).

2 Assimilation

Assimilation is *the process by which minorities gradually adopt patterns of the dominant culture.* Assimilation involves changing modes of dress, values, religion, language or friends. This is the so-called 'melting pot' model in which various nationalities have fused into an entirely new way of life. At the turn of the nineteenth century, one immigrant expressed this perception in these words:

> **America is God's Crucible, the great melting-pot where all races of Europe are melting and reforming. Here you stand, good folks, think I, when I see them at Ellis Island [the historical entry point for many immigrants in New York], here you stand with your fifty groups, with your fifty languages and histories, and your fifty blood-hatreds and rivalries. But you won't be long like that, brothers, for these are the fires of God . . . Germans and Frenchmen, Irishmen and Englishmen, Jews and Russians, into the Crucible with you all! God is making an American!**

(Zangwill, 1921: 33; orig. 1909)

The melting-pot image is misleading as a matter of historical fact. Rather than everyone 'melting' into some new cultural pattern, minorities typically adopt the traits (the dress, accent and sometimes even the names) of the dominant culture established by the earliest settlers.

Not surprisingly, elites tend to favour the assimilation model, since it holds them up as the standard to which others should aspire. Many immigrants, too, have been quick to pursue assimilation in the hope that it will free them from the prejudice and discrimination directed against distinctive foreigners and encourage upward social mobility. But multiculturalists find fault with the assimilation model because it tends to paint minorities as 'the problem' and define them (rather than the elites) as the ones who need to do all the changing.

Certainly some assimilation has occurred. In the UK, while Afro-Caribbean and Asian cultures may be strong, they have also taken on many key features of British society. In the United States, as fast as some urban 'ethnic villages' disappear, new ones emerge, the product of a steady and substantial stream of immigrants. Almost 30 per cent of today's New Yorkers are foreign born – the highest percentage in 50 years. No wonder some analysts argue that race and ethnicity endure as basic building blocks of US society (Glazer and Moynihan, 1970).

As a cultural process, assimilation involves changes in ethnicity but not in race. For example, many Americans of Japanese descent have discarded their traditional way of life but still maintain their racial identity. However, racial traits do diminish over generations as the result of **miscegenation**, *biological reproduction by partners of different racial categories.* Miscegenation (typically outside marriage) has occurred throughout US history despite cultural and even legal prohibitions. Norms against miscegenation are now eroding and, while the share of officially recorded interracial births in the United States is still just 4 per cent, it is rising steadily.

3 Segregation

Segregation refers to *the physical and social separation of categories of people.* Some minorities, especially religious orders like the Amish of Pennsylvania, have voluntarily segregated themselves. Mostly, however, majorities segregate minorities involuntarily by excluding them. Various degrees of segregation characterise residential districts, schools, occupations, hospitals and even cemeteries. While pluralism fosters distinctiveness without disadvantage, segregation enforces separation to the detriment of a minority.

South Africa's system of apartheid (described in Chapter 8) illustrates racial segregation that has been both rigid and pervasive. Apartheid was created by the European minority it served, and white South Africans historically enforced this system through the use of brutal power. All this is changing dramatically, as the *World watch* box in Chapter 8 (p. 259) indicated. Likewise, in the United States, racial segregation has a long history. Centuries of slavery gave way to racially separated lodging, schooling and transportation. Decisions such as the 1954 *Brown* case have reduced overt and *de jure* (Latin meaning 'by law') discrimination in the United States. However, *de facto* ('in fact') segregation continues.

Greater London poster
Promoting an image of London's multicultural diversity

Source: Equality and Human Rights Commission. This poster was originally published by the Commission for Racial Equality, which is now part of the new Equality and Human Rights Commission: www.equalityhumanrights.com.

Only a full century after the abolition of slavery did the US government take action to dismantle the 'Jim Crow' laws that continued to separate people of European and African ancestry. Until the early 1960s, these laws formally segregated hotels, restaurants, parks, buses and even drinking fountains. More than three decades later, de facto racial segregation in housing and schooling remains a reality for millions of people of colour in the United States

Source: © Bettmann/Corbis.

A woman looks at a burned house, site of the slayings of five Turkish immigrants by Neo-Nazis in Germany
Source: © Peter Turnley/CORBIS.

In the 1960s, Karl and Alma Taeuber (1965) assessed the residential segregation of black people and white people in more than 200 cities in the United States. On a numerical scale ranging from zero (a mixing of races in all neighbourhoods) to 100 (racial mixing in no neighbourhoods), they calculated an *average* segregation score of 86.2. Subsequent research has shown that segregation has decreased since then, but only slightly; even African-Americans with high incomes continue to find that their colour closes off opportunities for housing (Wilson, 1991; NORC, 1994).

We associate segregation with housing but, as Douglas Massey and Nancy Denton (1989) point out, racial separation involves a host of life experiences beyond neighbourhood composition. Many African-Americans living in inner cities, these researchers concluded, have

little social contact of any kind with the outside world. Such *hypersegregation* affects about one-fifth of all African-Americans but only a small fraction of comparably poor whites (Jagarowsky and Bane, 1990).

In short, segregation generally means second-class citizenship for a minority. For this reason, many minority men and women have struggled valiantly against such exclusiveness. Sometimes the action of a single person can make a difference. On 1 December 1955, Rosa Parks boarded a bus in Montgomery, Alabama, and sat in a section designated by law for black people. When a crowd of white passengers boarded the bus, the driver asked Parks and three other African-Americans to give up their seats. The three did so, but Rosa Parks refused. The driver left the bus and returned with police, who arrested her for violating the racial segregation laws. A court later convicted

Spotlight

The ways we exclude others: processes of social division

Throughout this part of the book we are discussing many processes in which people get excluded from society. Here are some key processes to think about, find illustrations of and discuss:

1 Social exclusion
2 The dominance and subordination of groups
3 Exploitation
4 Marginalisation
5 Stereotyping
6 Discrimination
7 Stigmatisation
8 Ghettoisation
9 Segregation
10 Colonisation
11 Violence
12 Pauperisation
13 Disempowerment
14 Silencing of voices
15 'Othering'
16 Dehumanisation
17 Genocide

Parks and fined her $14. Her stand (or sitting) for justice sparked the African-American community of Montgomery to boycott city buses, ultimately bringing this form of legal segregation to an end (King, 1969).

4 Genocide

Genocide is *the systematic annihilation of one category of people by another.* A more recent term for this is **ethnic cleansing**, a term used especially in the Bosnian conflict **described** at the start of this chapter. Some prefer **eliminationism** (Goldhagen, 2009). This racist and ethnocentric brutality violates nearly every recognised moral standard; nonetheless, it has occurred time and again in the human record.

Genocide figured prominently in centuries of contact between Europeans and the original inhabitants of the Americas. From the sixteenth century on, the Spanish, Portuguese, English, French and Dutch forcefully colonised vast empires. These efforts decimated the native populations of North and South America, allowing Europeans to gain control of the continent's wealth. Some native people fell victim to calculated killing sprees; most succumbed to diseases carried by Europeans, to which native peoples had no natural defences (Matthiessen, 1984).

History in sociology: examining genocide

One strand of ways of doing sociology requires a critical inspection through history. Michael Mann's book *The Dark Side of Democracy* (2005) traces the history of genocides, and provides case studies of state murder such as the Nazis, Stalin and Mao. He tries to piece together these cases into a broader theory – an explanation of these atrocities.

Although murderous ethnic 'cleansing' is found throughout history (he describes the conflicts in the Assyrian, Greek and Roman societies, Goths, Mongols, Chinese and the Middle East, along with Ghenghis Khan, Attila and Ivan

the Terrible), Mann suggests that it is distinctly modern – it has become a routine feature of the democratic process. Built largely out of ethnic conflicts, in the twentieth century he suggests it led to some 70 million refugees.

In 2003, to different degrees, these conflicts could be found in Bosnia, Kosovo, Macedonia, Algeria, Israel, Iraq, Chechnya, Azerbaijan, Afghanistan, Pakistan, India, Sri Lanka, Kashmir, Burma, Tibet, Chinese Xinjiang, the Southern Philippines, Indonesia, Bolivia, Peru, Mexico, the Sudan, Somalia, Senegal, Uganda, Sierra Leone, Rwanda, Nigeria, Congo, the Basque Country and Burundi. Inter-ethnic conflicts were multiple: Russians and Chechens, Sunni and Shi'ite Muslims, various Afghan tribes. Many involve substantial killings. It is estimated that in the last four years of its 12-year life, the Nazi regime killed some 20 million.

Mann highlights four linked networks of power which organise this terrorism and tyranny. He calls these ideological (concerned with value and rituals), economic (concerned with material interests), military (concerned with lethal violence) and political (central and concerned with the territorial regulation of life). He outlines those societies that are changing to democratisation as being in greater turmoil. Here enemy minorities – fairly old ethnic groups – are more easily found. These are largely in the South. Those in the North have become much more stable, though they have been through a major period of conflict in the past (between Catholics and Protestants, for example). These days such conflicts are less common.

See: Michael Mann, *The Dark Side of Democracy: Explaining Ethnic Cleansing* (2005).

Claims of genocides continue in the twenty-first century. In 2008–2010, a crisis emerged between Georgia and Russia. Both countries accused each other of military build up near the separatist regions of South Ossetia and Ankhazia. Increasing tensions led to the outbreak of the 2008 South Ossetia war. In this photo, a South Ossetian woman looks at the bodies of Georgian soldiers on August 13, 2008 in Tskhinvali. Georgians accused Russian tanks still present inside the Georgian town of Gori of destroying buildings and shooting at people. The president accused the opposing forces of setting up 'internment camps' inside South Ossetia to carry out a policy of 'ethnic cleansing' of the local population. The tem 'genocide' is possibly now overused: the numbers dead in this situation have been very hard to estimate

Trace current debates on: Genocide Watch: http://www.genocidewatch.org/.

Source: AFP/Getty Images.

R. J. Rummel, in his book *Death by Government* (1996), has coined the concept of **democide** to capture *mass murders by governments*. He argues that 'democracies commit less democide than other regimes' but shows how during the twentieth century some 169 million people have been the victims of state murders. He suggests that the Soviet Gulag state murdered the most – some 61 million – closely followed by the communist Chinese (35 million), the Nazi genocide state (21 million) and the Chinese Nationalist regime (some 10 million). Unimaginable horrors befell large numbers of outcast people. But Rummel's calculations do not stop here. He suggests that 5 million were murdered by Japan's military; 2 million were slaughtered by Pol Pot in Cambodia between 1975 and 1980: a quarter of the population perished in the Cambodian 'killing fields'; nearly 2 million were murdered in Turkey; and many more in Vietnam, Poland, Pakistan, North Korea and Mexico.

Migration, ethnicity and race

We live in a world of some 200 million migrants – maybe 10–14 million of them refugees. About 3 per cent of the world's population are on the move (UN Development Report, 2009). Migration patterns – the movements of people in and out of societies – offer crucial clues to the workings of

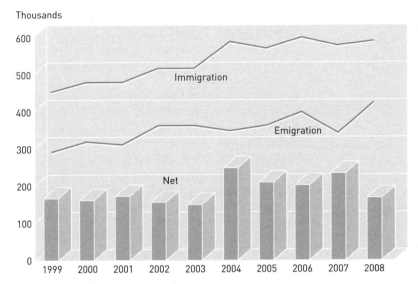

Figure 11.2 Long-term international migration, UK, 1999–2008

Source: Long-Term International Migration (LTIM), International Passenger Survey (IPS), www.statistics.gov.uk.

societies. Not only do they help in understanding demographic patterns (discussed in Chapter 24), they focus attention upon the dynamics of different groups in a society. They highlight some of the major global inequalities across countries and the world. Often these 'migratory' groups become singled out in the processes of racialisation and discrimination. Bauman (1998) has distinguished between two major forms of global mobility. The *Vagabonds* are the mass of impoverished travellers who are on the move because they have to be (through government genocide, poverty or finding their country inhospitable). In contrast, the *Tourists* are those on the move because they want to be – who want to travel and who can afford to do so. In this chapter our main concern is with the former grouping.

There have always been migratory movements: sometimes voluntary, sometimes planned, sometimes forced. There has been exile, forcible repatriation and evacuation thoughout history. In the past, the distances travelled were often short, but with new modes of travel, vast distances have often been covered. Sometimes there have been enforced geographical dispersals of a people (for example, Jews). These are the **diasporas**. Sometimes peoples have been assimilated and absorbed into a host culture. Sometimes there is a refusal to have permanent settlers.

Until recently, four main patterns of migration have been identified:

- The *classical model*, which fits the United States, Canada and Australia. Generally such countries encourage migration and see immigrants as future citizens.

- The *colonial model*, which fits France, the Netherlands and the UK. Generally, migration to these countries has been heavily skewed to their colonies, giving them a kind of privileged position in as much as immigrants have potential citizenship rights.

- The *'guest worker' model*, which fits Germany and Belgium. Generally, migration here is temporary and without potential citizen rights. As with the other models, migration is usually for work – but in this case, conditions of employment and potential security of work are much weaker.

- The *'illegal' models*. Most countries have some illegal migration. It is characterised especially by people living outside the official society – and often, therefore, being forced to take the lowest-paid, most temporary and demanding work.

Traditionally, sociologists have suggested various phases through which migrants may pass. These phases of migration hold best for the classical pattern outlined above, but they are common in the others too. In phase 1 there is temporary labour migration of young workers who send their earnings back home, and have a strong feeling that they still belong to the homeland. In phase 2 there is often a prolonging of stay and the development of some new social networks. In phase 3 there is often a family reunion – issues of long-term settlement can now start to appear, along with the development of new ethnic communities. And in phase 4 (and depending on government policies) there is permanent settlement. This model is only an ideal type: it is much less relevant to certain groups of migrants, such as refugees or the highly skilled.

Contemporary trends in migration

Recently Castles and Miller have suggested that migration is rapidly changing its forms in the twenty-first century. They suggest six key developments (2009: 10–12):

- *The globalisation of migration*: more and more countries are affected by migratory movements.

- *The acceleration of migration*: there are growing numbers in all major regions.

- *The differentiation of migration*: a wide array of types are found – refugees, labour migrants, permanent settlers – all at the same time. Sex trafficking has also become prominent.

- *The feminisation of migration*: many more women are playing a much larger role (until recently, it was mainly men who migrated in the first instance). Examples are Filipinos to the Middle East and Thais to Japan.

- *The politicisation of migration*: raising many issues from religious belief to domestic politics, as well as issues of national and international security. Migration raises political controversies all round the world.

- *The proliferation of migration transition*: traditional lands of emigration become lands of transit migration and immigration as well (e.g. Spain, Mexico, Turkey and South Korea).

This growth in global migration results in many cultures confronting more and more ethnic diversity. And as ethnic diversification grows, we find an increase in levels of racism.

European patterns of migration

The history of Europe is the history of its migratory peoples. These migratory peoples may rapidly become outsider ethnic groups. So it is as well to remember that people originating from places as far flung as Africa, India and the Caribbean have lived in Europe for hundreds of years.

During the twentieth century, the European pattern may be seen as occurring in three main waves. Wave 1 was the 'European Exodus'. In the decades surrounding the turn of the nineteenth and twentieth centuries, it is estimated that 'around 52 million Europeans left their

countries and 72 per cent of them settled in North America' (Soysal, 1994: 17).

Wave 2 was the 'European Inflow', shortly after the Second World War, which saw a large number of immigrants in Europe. There were two main kinds of recruitment: one was of colonial workers – the inflow from former colonies – usually for work. This was true of the UK (with immigrants coming from Ireland, the West Indies and parts of southern Asia and East Africa). France experienced migration from former Southern colonies: by 1970, there were 90,000 Tunisians, 140,000 Moroccans and over 600,000 Algerians. In the Netherlands, some 300,000 Indonesians (formerly the Dutch East Indies) resettled (Castles and Miller, 1993: 72). The second kind of flow was from guest workers – they were 'guests' visiting temporarily and not, strictly speaking, immigrants seeking to become permanent citizens. They were expected to leave when their work came to an end and they had no political or economic rights: they were not citizens. Migrant workers constituted large portions of the manual working population in many European countries.

These workers may be seen as an **industrial reserve army** – *a disadvantaged section of labour that can be supplied cheaply when there is a sudden extra demand*. Throughout much of Europe, such migrant workers were brought in to swell the labour force and were central to the reconstruction of Europe.

Wave 3 came after 1973, when there was a marked decline in migration to Europe. In the UK, for instance, new legislation started to restrict migration. Currently, about 15 million migrants in Europe are 'foreigners' – that is, they have no formal citizenship status (Soysal, 1994: 22). Foreign workers vary greatly: in 1990, they made up 2 per cent of the labour force in Denmark but 18 per cent in Switzerland. The Swedish have classically lacked much migration. In 1975, a new policy emerged that stressed equality between immigrants and Swedes, freedom of cultural choice for immigrants and cooperation between the native Swedish majority and various ethnic minorities (Soysal, 1994: 47).

More recently there have been significant changes in the migration patterns in the EU. The Maastricht Treaty (see Chapter 4, p. 128) meant that less developed nations such as Poland, Bulgaria and Romania entered the EU between 2004 and 2007; and that the whole area became a *borderless* continent for its members. This meant that EU members were free to move from country to country.

In the UK, for instance, it was estimated that some half a million new migrants arrived from within the EU (mainly from Poland) – often seeking low-paid work.

Refugees and migration in crisis

Throughout the world, through wars, genocides, conflicts and disasters, people are compelled to leave their homes. Sometimes this leads to refugee settlements, and sometimes long journeys to find a 'new home' – at least for a while. The photos below indicate some of the most recent humanitarian crises.

Afghanistan has a population of around 28 million – with several million living in refugee camps in Pakistan and Iran. From the 1930s to the 1970s it had a stable monarchy. This was overthrown by Marxist rebels and the USSR in the 1970s, which in turn were overthrown in 1992 through the establishing of an Islamic republic. In 1996, this was overthrown by the Taliban – a fundamentalist faction of Islam.

(a) An Afghan refugee family waits at a refugee camp before their departure from Islamabad to Afghanistan, 6 May 2004. Thousands of Afghan refugees have returned to their homeland as part of the UNHCR repatriation programme
(b) Members of five families from Fallujah rest at a relative's home after fleeing the American siege of their city. They brought 39 people in all and among them was 17-year-old Sajidah Hameed, who was to be married in four days. Her fiancé was among the estimated 600 people from Fallujah, Iraq, who were killed in fighting with American troops (April 2004)
(c) Médecins Sans Frontières hospital on the Sudanese border. Nutrition centre for children, Tine, Chad, April 2004
(d) Iraqi Kurds on Isik Veren Mountain, Turkey

Source: (a) © Faisal Mahmood/Reuters/Corbis; (b) © Ed Kashi/Corbis; (c) © Patrick Robert/Corbis; (d) © Peter Turnley/Corbis.

Living through ethnic cleansing

Stevan Weine spent many years talking with Bosnians who had witnessed ethnic cleansing. Below is one of the testimonies he gathered.

For the first ten days they didn't give us any food. Then they fed us once a day at 6.00. They gave us three minutes to come from our building to the kitchen. Some of us were more than 50 metres away, and we had no chance to reach the kitchen. Those who came had three minutes to eat. Those who did not had no food. The guards formed a line that we had to run through to get to the kitchen. As we ran they beat us with guns, wheels, and tools.

After eleven days I asked them to let me go to the washroom just to wash my face. When I got there I didn't see that two men from Kolarac also came inside along with some soldiers from special units. The soldiers started to beat them. When they saw me they took me to a place with a big sink and started to beat me. They told me to lick the floor of this washroom for 20,000 people which was dirty with urine and sewage. They broke my ribs. I vomited for one month. I vomited blood.

Sometimes they put us in a 4 × 4 meter room – 700 people. They told us to lie down and they closed the windows and the doors. It was summer.

We lay like sardines in a can. Those on top were in the best position. Every morning, some on the bottom were dead. Every morning a guard came with a list and called people's names. Those they brought out never came back.

One day they came at 3 a.m. and they brought out 174 people. I was one of them. They lined us up behind a building they called the White House. Ten soldiers came with automatic weapons and they started to shoot us. Only three of us survived.

The worst event was when I watched one young man as they castrated him. Right now I can hear his cry and his prayers to be killed. And every night it wakes me. He was a nice young man. His executioner was his friend from school. He cut his body and he licked his blood. He asked him just to kill and to stop all that suffering. All day and all night we heard his prayers and his crying until he died. This is something that I cannot forget. It gives me nightmares and makes sleep almost impossible. I can't remember the people who were the executioners. For me all of them in those uniforms were the same. I can't remember who was who.

At the end of our first meeting, H. said I am all tears. When I speak about that even though my eyes are open I see all those images in front of me.

The second meeting begins tentatively, with H. saying, it is difficult to talk about anything when all the days were similar. So we review the last meeting's testimony with him and ask some questions to restart the dialogue.

Here in my neighborhood there is a man who was with me in the camp. He was a prisoner, like me, but he had the duty to beat us in order to save his own skin. And he did that very well. He wasn't alone. I know many examples of people like him. They had to do that just to survive. But I preferred it when he beat me. I always stayed on my feet. He didn't beat as hard as the others. I remember also one other man. He was a Muslim. He was very violent. He killed many prisoners. Finally we prisoners killed him by our own hands.

'You were there when that happened?'

Yes I was there. They moved him from our camp but then after some time they brought him back. And they pushed him inside a crowd of prisoners because they knew what would happen. All of us participated in that. One thousand people. And nobody could say 'I killed him' because all of us did. I didn't directly participate in the killing. But I was in the same room. I do not feel guilty. I wished to be in that group – the execution group – and I wished to participate in killing him. But I was really very weak.

I have to say something about the first prisoner who beat us and any other person who had to do the same job he did. Some people came to my house in Chicago to ask me to sign a note condemning him. I didn't do that because I do not think he is guilty. He helped many people. He didn't beat us like the Serbs did. He saved many, many lives. He needed to do that to save his own life.

SPEAKING LIVES

Our region had very rich soil, and we had many farm animals. Day after day the Serbs brought our animals, and Muslim butchers had to slaughter them and put them in freezer trucks. Every day for two and a half months freezer trucks took that meat somewhere. Almost everything went into Serbia. The Serbs passed through our region especially to find gold and money. If someone wished to take all your property,

he came and asked you to sign a paper that was something like a will, and you left him everything you had – car, truck, house, and everything inside. And for that he gave you a piece of bread. But if he went to your house and he couldn't find everything you signed over to him, he would then kill your family and come back into the camp and kill you.

I want to tell you something else. We had a special platoon. About a hundred prisoners had the duty of taking the bodies of

murdered people, putting them in trucks, and bringing them to a special place with pits to dispose of them. They knew where they put all the Muslim bodies. One day before our camp was closed, before the Red Cross came, the soldiers killed all of them. Serbs killed all one hundred Muslims just to wipe out all witnesses. I was not in that group because I was too weak and too thin.

Source: Weine (1999: 35–6).

The events of 11 September 2001 identified the Taliban as protecting Osama bin Laden and a bombing campaign was started by US and British forces. By 2010, the country was one of the poorest and most conflict-torn countries on earth. It is not surprising that it had generated the largest number of refugees (see Table 9.6 on p. 301).

Sudan has a population of 38 million and is the largest country in Africa. The majority of its population are Arab Muslims (22 million – over 50 per cent), who are in the north; by contrast, groups in the south (rich in oil) (and rival groups including the Dinka (11.5 per cent), the Nuba (8.1 per cent), the Zande and the Nuer) tend to be Christian or Animist. From 1898 to 1956, the British colonised much of the area. Since that time there has been constant strife/war between the non-Muslim 'black' population of the south and the Arab Muslim-controlled government of the north; 30,000 people are believed to have died in the war, and several million from the south are now homeless. It is considered to be one of the worst humanitarian crises the world has seen.

Rwanda is quite a small country (population 7 million) tucked away in east central Africa (bordered by Uganda, Tanzania, Burundi and the Congo). It has a life expectancy of around 38.5. It was originally inhabited by the Twa, and became home to the Hutu. The Tutsi appeared in the fourteenth century and came to rule in the fifteenth. There is a long history of periodic rules first by Hutu and then by Tutsi. In 1962 the Hutu took rule again, and waged wars and

genocide, massacring over 500,000 Tutsi. And then as the Tutsi fought back, it left some 2 million refugees, mainly Hutu, to flee to neighbouring countries.

North America: who is the majority in the land of migration?

Although Europe may be seen as a continent of migration, the figures of ethnic groups present in Europe are small when compared with those found in the United States, truly the modern land of migration. Table 11.3 shows just how many groups have settled in the United States, and any visit to Ellis Island off New York – the place where most of the migrating people first arrived – would soon confirm the enormity of this migration pattern.

With such a vast pattern of migration, the argument is now made that 'white' groupings are becoming a minority. During the 1980s, Manhattan, the central borough of New York City, gained a minority-majority. This means that people of African, Asian and Latino descent, together with other racial and ethnic minorities, became a majority of the population. The same transformation has taken place in 186 counties across the United States (some 6 per cent of the total). As early as 2050, according to some projections, minorities will represent a majority of the country.

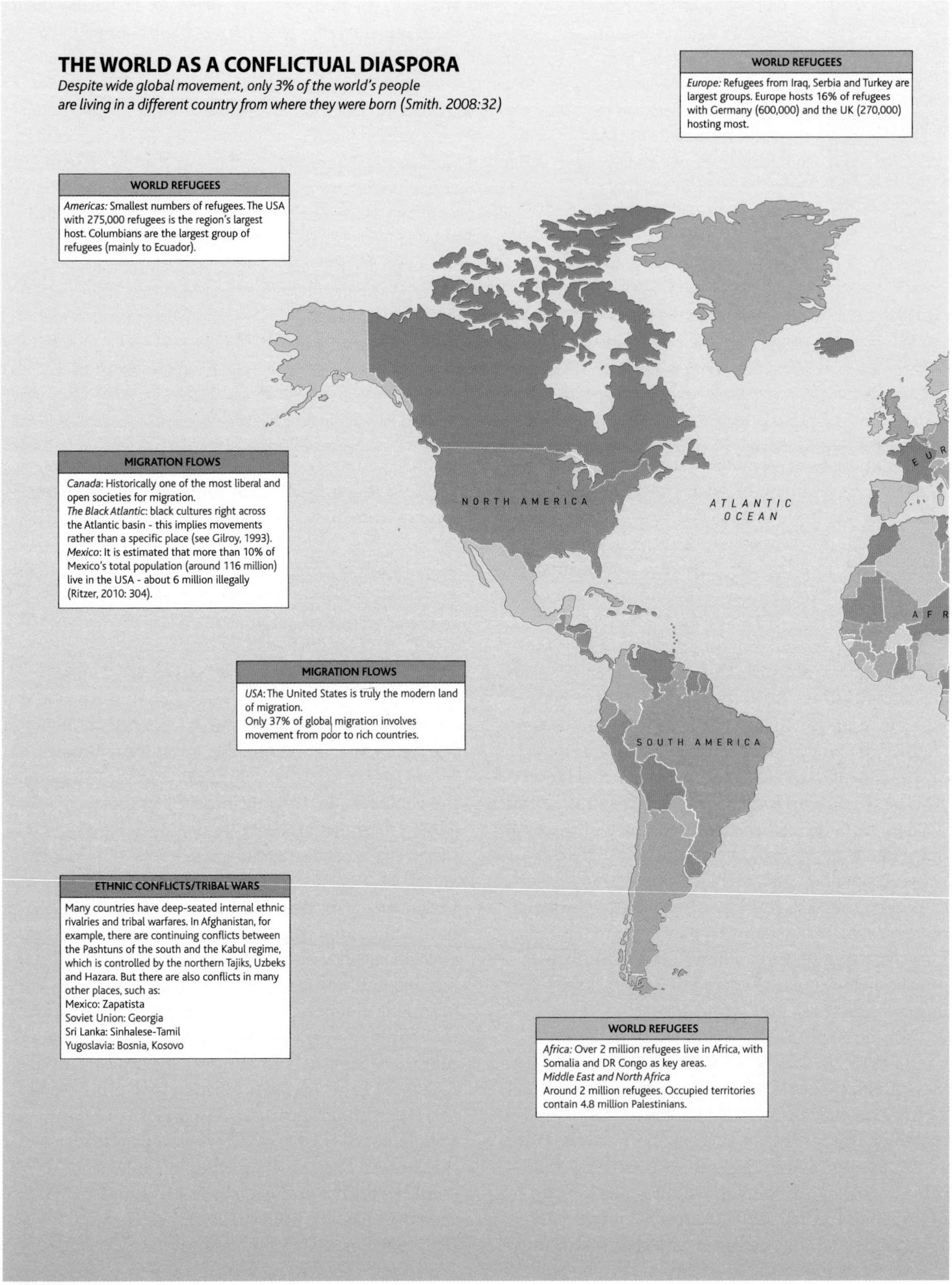

THE WORLD AS A CONFLICTUAL DIASPORA

Despite wide global movement, only 3% of the world's people
are living in a different country from where they were born (Smith. 2008:32)

WORLD REFUGEES

Europe: Refugees from Iraq, Serbia and Turkey are largest groups. Europe hosts 16% of refugees with Germany (600,000) and the UK (270,000) hosting most.

WORLD REFUGEES

Americas: Smallest numbers of refugees. The USA with 275,000 refugees is the region's largest host. Columbians are the largest group of refugees (mainly to Ecuador).

MIGRATION FLOWS

Canada: Historically one of the most liberal and open societies for migration.
The Black Atlantic: black cultures right across the Atlantic basin - this implies movements rather than a specific place (see Gilroy, 1993).
Mexico: It is estimated that more than 10% of Mexico's total population (around 116 million) live in the USA - about 6 million illegally (Ritzer, 2010: 304).

MIGRATION FLOWS

USA: The United States is truly the modern land of migration.
Only 37% of global migration involves movement from poor to rich countries.

ETHNIC CONFLICTS/TRIBAL WARS

Many countries have deep-seated internal ethnic rivalries and tribal warfares. In Afghanistan, for example, there are continuing conflicts between the Pashtuns of the south and the Kabul regime, which is controlled by the northern Tajiks, Uzbeks and Hazara. But there are also conflicts in many other places, such as:
Mexico: Zapatista
Soviet Union: Georgia
Sri Lanka: Sinhalese-Tamil
Yugoslavia: Bosnia, Kosovo

WORLD REFUGEES

Africa: Over 2 million refugees live in Africa, with Somalia and DR Congo as key areas.
Middle East and North Africa
Around 2 million refugees. Occupied territories contain 4.8 million Palestinians.

NORTH AMERICA

ATLANTIC OCEAN

SOUTH AMERICA

EUR

AFR

Map 11.2   The world as a conflictual diaspora

MIGRATION FLOWS

Europe: The Maastricht Treaty (see Chapter 4) set out a timetable for European integration and the new status of EU citizenship. It created a borderless community with members having citizenship across member countries. Large numbers moved from poorer countries to richer ones in search of work.

WORLD REFUGEES

Afghanistan: In 2010, some 2.9 million refugees were living in 71 host countries.

RUSSIA

O P E

CHINA

I C A

ARABIA   INDIA

PACIFIC OCEAN

INDONESIA

AUSTRALIA

MIGRATION FLOWS

Arab countries: In most Arab Gulf countries the labour force consists of up to 80% migrant workers. The major sending countries are the Philippines, Indonesia, Sri Lanka, Nepal and Bangladesh. These countries also supply labour for Japan, South Korea, Taiwan, Malaysia and Thailand. About 10% of the population of Philippines, 8 million people, are engaged in work away from their home country.

WORLD REFUGEES

General figures
In 2010, 43.3 million people were forcibly displaced around the world, including 27.1 million internally displaced people (IDP) and 15.6 million refugees. This is the highest number of displaced people worldwide since the 1990s.
Key movements
The key drivers of these trends are continuing conflicts in countries such as Afghanistan, Somalia and the Democratic Republic of Congo. Conflicts in places such as Iraq and Sudan are also prominent. Colombia's 3.3 million internally displaced persons are the highest number in the world. African nations account for 40% of the world's internally displaced population.
Resettlement
Four out of every five refugees are housed in the developing world, with Europe only accounting for the resettlement of 16% of the global population.
The internally displaced
27.1 million people were displaced in their own country in 2009. Columbia, Congo and Pakistan have witnessed the largest numbers.

GLOBAL ETHNICITIES

The USA is a land of migration and ethnic diversities: the Rainbow Coalition (see Table 11.3).
China, Australia and mainland Europe are the most homogenous (under 10% diversity: Smith, 2008: 23).
India, many central African states and Indonesia have 50% ethnic diversity: non-single ethnic or national groups are more than 50% of the population. Indonesia identifies over 300 ethnic groups speaking some 700 languages (see Smith, 2008: 22-3).

Table 11.3	The Rainbow Coalition: racial and ethnic categories in the United States, 2007	
Racial or ethnic classification*	**Approximate US population**	**Share of total population (%)**
Hispanic descent	**45,427,437**	**15.1%**
Mexican	29,166,981	9.7
Puerto Rican	4,120,205	1.4
Cuban	1,611,478	0.5
Other Hispanic	10,528,773	3.5
African descent	**38,756,452**	**12.8**
Nigerian	225,284	0.1
Ethiopian	159,809	0.1
Somalian	90,363	<
Other African	38,280,996	12.7
Native American descent	**2,365,347**	**0.8**
American Indian	1,922,043	0.6
Alaska Native Tribes	110,556	<
Other Native American	332,748	0.1
Asian or Pacific Island descent	**13,667,962**	**4.4**
Chinese	3,045,592	1.0
Asian Indian	2,570,166	0.9
Filipino	2,412,446	0.8
Vietnamese	1,508,489	0.5
Korean	1,344,171	0.4
Japanese	803,092	0.3
Cambodian	218,624	0.1
Other Asian or Pacific Islander	1,765,382	0.6
West Indian descent	**2,231,842**	**0.7**
Arab descent	**1,545,982**	**0.5**
Non-Hispanic European descent	**198,696,006**	**65.9**
German	50,756,529	16.8
Irish	36,495,800	12.1
English	28,178,670	9.3
Italian	17,849,848	5.9
Polish	9,976,358	3.3
French	9,616,662	3.2
Scottish	6,019,281	2.0
Dutch	5,071,425	1.7
Norwegian	4,655,711	1.5
Two or more races	**6,509,013**	**2.2**

* People of Hispanic descent may be of any race. Many people also identify with more than one ethnic category. Therefore, figures total more than 100 per cent.

< indicates less than 1/10 of 1 per cent.

Source: US Census Bureau (2008).

Ethnicity in the UK

So far, we have drawn a rather broad map, suggesting that racism is a continuing feature across the world. We will now consider the specific case of the UK. Table 11.4 below presents the broad sweep of racial and ethnical diversity in the UK, as recorded by the 2001 Census. Every country in the world can be analysed in terms of its ethnic dimensions.

Brief history: ethnicity, migration and conflict

The timeline on p. 374 outlines some of the significant developments and conflicts in ethnic relations in the UK over many years. We can go back a long way. Since the Anglo-Saxon invaders of the sixth and seventh centuries drove Celtic-speaking Britons into Wales, Cornwall and the Scottish highlands, England has been more ethnically homogenous than most of the rest of Europe. Nevertheless, there have been 'blacks' in England for hundreds of years (as many as 20,000 in the eighteenth century), who were often sailors or

servants of white masters. Black communities often grew around seaports such as Liverpool. In the nineteenth century, migrants to the cities were from the less wealthy or developing areas of the UK, such as Ireland, Wales and Scotland. London, Manchester, Liverpool and Glasgow had large settlements from Ireland (by 1851, half a million Irish had settled in England and Wales). Jews started migrating in significant numbers around the time of the First World War and there was an acceleration during the 1930s. Nearly all the major migration during this latter period came from western European countries.

In modern times, the critical period for migration to the UK followed the Second World War. This was a part of massive immigration into Europe from all over the world – estimated to involve around 30 million people. At this time, after the war, there was a marked labour shortage which made many countries seek new reserves of labour. It was also a time when the colonies – so critical at an earlier period – were coming to an end. In England, the new Commonwealth (India, Pakistan and the West Indies) was important and provided a major recruiting base for migration and labour.

Initially, the largest postwar immigrant group coming to Britain were the Irish – nearly 900,000.

Table 11.4	Population of Great Britain by ethnic group and age, 2008 (%)			
	Under 16	16–64	65 and over	All people
White				
White British	18	65	17	100
White Irish	7	68	25	100
Other White	14	75	12	100
Mixed	51	47	2	100
Asian or Asian British				
Indian	20	72	8	100
Pakistani	34	62	4	100
Bangladeshi	36	61	4	100
Other Asian	23	73	5	100
Black or Black British				
Black Caribbean	20	66	13	100
Black African	33	64	2	100
Other Black	37	57	6	100
Chinese	12	83	5	100
Other ethnic group	20	75	4	100
All ethnic groups	19	65	16	100

Source: *Social Trends*, 40 (2010), Table 1.4, p. 4.

Timeline Ethnic divides in the UK

Prior to the 1950s

1066	Norman invasion of Britain from northern France.
1362	English language legally recognised.
1707	Union of Scotland and England.
1807	Slave trade abolished in the British Empire.
1834–8	Slavery abolished in the British Empire.
1892	Dadabhai Naoroji is the first Asian elected to the House of Commons.
1919	Anti-black riots in Liverpool.
1921	Anglo-Irish Treaty established Eire; six northern counties with a Protestant majority to remain as part of the UK.
1930–40s	Around 60,000 Jews come to Britain to escape Nazis and the war.

The modern period: from the 1950s

1948	British Nationality Act: distinguished British subjects who were citizens of the UK, and those from the Commonwealth and colonies. Both groups could enter and work in the UK; the arrival of the ship *Empire Windrush* with 492 West Indians on board.
1955	Churchill wanted slogan 'Keep Britain white'.
1958	First 'race riots' in Notting Hill, London.
1962	Commonwealth Immigrants Act: withdrew right of entry to Commonwealth immigrants under most considerations.
1965	Race Relations Act (under the Labour government): an early attempt to ban discrimination in public places, or to incite racial hatred; Race Relations Board set up.
1968	'Troubles' start in Northern Ireland; the Provisional Irish Republican Army (IRA) formed. Commonwealth Immigrants Act; Race Relations Act extended the 1965 Act to employment and housing, but not to police. Enoch Powell's 'Rivers of Blood' speech.
1971	Immigration Act: aliens could now enter only with a work permit; aliens could apply for citizenship after four years; distinctions between patrials and non-patrials.
1972	Expulsion of Ugandan Asians: 27,000 accepted by Britain.
1976	Race Relations Act: Commission for Racial Equality formed and indirect discrimination (e.g. via advertising) made illegal; Anti-Nazi League formed. Notting Hill Carnival formed.
1981	British Nationality Act: British citizenship could pass to children only if their parents were born in the UK.
1980s	Inner-city 'race conflicts' at Brixton, Merseyside, Hackney; Lord Scarman reported on these conflicts in 1982, identifying key tension between police and local black youth; police relations with young black people were identified as significant.
1983	Black sections in Labour Party.
1985	More inner-city clashes. Conflict in Tottenham led to death of a policeman (Broadwater Farm Estate).
1988	Immigration Act: dependants of men who settled before 1973 could no longer join them, unless evidence of non-dependency.
1991	Census questions on ethnicity (3 million people, 5.5 per cent of population identified).
1993	Asylum and Immigration Act: certain countries to be refused asylum automatically; murder of black teenager Stephen Lawrence.
1997	Nine Black and Asian MPs returned at general election.
1999	Macpherson Report in the wake of the inquiry into Stephen Lawrence, who was murdered in 1995.
2000	The Race Relations (Amendment) Act: strengthened duty to promote race and equality.
2000–1	More race tensions in Bradford, Burnley and Oldham.

The new millennium: multiethnic Britain in terrorist times?

2000 The Commission on the Future of Multi-Ethnic Britain (Parekh Report) from Runnymede Trust. Suggested we should – among other things – understand the transitional nature of all identities; achieve a balance between cohesion, difference and equality; address and eliminate all kinds of racism; and build a 'human rights culture'.

2001 '9/11' terrorists attacks (and later 7/7): created new climate of racism linked to terrorist fears, which especially impacted the Muslim communities. New migrant groups from Iraq, Afghanistan and Zimbabwe: 'victims' of internal conflicts, and harbingers of world conflicts to come.

2002 Highest figure of 'asylum applications' to the UK (103,000 people: 24 per cent of EU total).

2004 Workers' Registration Scheme: required new migrants to register for work on arrival.

2005 Suicide bombings in London by four British Muslims intensified debates about multiculturalism.

2006 The Terrorism Act: latest in a line of legislation since '9/11' which centred on terrorism and the growth of terrorist fears. This legislation authorised 28 days' detention without trial for terrorist suspects. An array of new offences around terrorism were created.

2006 New eastern European migrants: around 375,000 people from eastern Europe came to the UK to work. Six out of ten are Polish. Most have stayed in the south of England and work in construction, agriculture, catering, retail and healthcare.

2007 Exacerbated by the attacks of 9/11 and 7/7: background of forced migration, global terrorism and social segregation. Equality and Human Rights Commission took over from the Commission for Racial Equality.

Note: The Equality and Human Rights Commission can be found at: www.equalityhumanrights.com.

New Commonwealth immigrants came independently during the 1950s. Often, their arrival in England was a shock: the 'Mother Country' was grey and dreary, and very, very cold! Added to this was an unexpected turn towards racism, as UK society encountered, for the first time in its modern history, a 'mass' migration of 'black' workers. Famously, in 1948, the first of many ships, the *Empire Windrush*, carrying many Commonwealth immigrants, arrived in Britain. Many others followed. London Transport had directly recruited large numbers of these new immigrants. Many immigrants subsequently followed from Pakistan and India. From this time on, racism became a much more visible feature of the English landscape, with debates about the colour bar and the need to ban migrants from certain jobs. From the 1960s onwards, starting with the Commonwealth Immigrants Act of 1962, much stricter controls were introduced to regulate immigrant entry. The past 50 years in the UK can be depicted as a constant series of conflicts and tensions, as the timeline shows.

Cultures of ethnicities: generations and movements

The number of people from ethnic minorities in the UK has grown from a few tens of thousands in 1950

to more than three million now. The population of Great Britain is made up predominantly of people from a White British ethnic background: in 2008, around 83 per cent of the population belonged to this ethnic group. The pattern of migration into Great Britain from the 1950s onwards has produced a number of distinct ethnic minority groups within the general population. In 2008, the second largest ethnic group was Other White (5 per cent) – for example, those born overseas – followed by Indian (2 per cent) and Pakistani (also 2 per cent). The remaining ethnic minority groups accounted for around 8 per cent of the population.

Table 11.4 shows the age structure of the population, which varies across the different ethnic groups. The Mixed ethnic group – for example, people who identify with both of their parents' differing ethnicities, had the youngest age profile in Great Britain in 2008, with more than half (51 per cent) of people in this group aged under 16. Only 2 per cent of people in the Mixed ethnic group were aged 65 and over. The Other Black group also had a young age profile, with 37 per cent of people in this group being aged under 16. The majority of people in the Chinese group in Great Britain in 2008 were aged between 16 and 64 (83 per cent). Only 12 per cent of people in the Chinese group were under 16, and 5 per cent were aged 65 and over.

Understanding *multiple ethnic diversities* accompanied by *multiple different racisms* is usually a key to grasping an ethnic situation anywhere: there is never one unitary racism or one unified ethnic group. Still, in the UK ethnic groups are commonly divided into crude groupings such as 'South Asian', 'Caribbean' 'Polish' or 'Irish' – even though these terms are crude and conceal a wealth of further differences (and conflicts). Within these groupings there are many subgroupings of class, age, gender and sexual orientation. Some ethnic groupings develop their own strong communities and identities; others do not.

Ethnic groupings bring elements of their culture of origin to a hybrid arrangement of other cultures. This is a growing, and crucial, feature of modern global societies which mix and transform earlier cultural elements with newer ones. There are now a great many studies that document diverse aspects of these cultures.

South Asian communities may be seen in many parts of the UK, but they are often structured by their roots in religion. Most Bangladeshis and Pakistanis are Muslim; Indians may be Sikh, Hindu or Muslim. Much as in the migration model outlined above, we can trace various phases of development. A pioneer phase sees a small number of early migrants arriving and establishing small south Asian communities. Despite the major culture shock from the confrontation with UK culture, the old culture is maintained. From this there follows a phase of mass migration, where the diverse cultural patterns from home are imported and developed. Family, religious codes and dress all play a key solidifying role. There follows a major phase of family reunion, with a substantial second generation being born into the community. Throughout, there is a tension between the old culture and the new. New divisions start to appear: Sikhs from one region (such as Jullunder Doab) with Muslims from another (such as Mirpur district in Kashmir). By now, we have a third generation – and even a fourth generation is starting to appear. Here the realities of 'being Asian' and 'being British' become very different: new generations create new cultural responses – new music styles, new dress codes, new responses to religion compared to their parents (and grandparents) – even as they face new kinds of racism.

One key part of some Asian cultures is the Muslim faith (discussed in Chapter 5). In recent years, since the New York terrorist attack on 9/11, tensions have been heightened in Muslim communities in the UK and the world as they are perceived to be involved in terrorist activities. A new pattern of racism has emerged: *Islamophobia* (see the *Big debate* at the end of the chapter) along with new controversies such as the debate on the Muslim veil (see the *Public sociology* box on p. 377). Here again we find multiple splits within the community and many new responses (some younger women now wear the very veils that their parents had fought to reject).

The same is true of Caribbean cultures: again, there is a mix of elements. Religion plays a strong role, but so too do elements of recovering an earlier culture. At the same time, much of this is mixed with elements from the dominant cultures. There are several notable strands, including Pentecostal culture and Rastafarianism.

Pentecostal culture has its roots in the Caribbean and the United States, and grew in England from the 1950s onwards. The first assemblies were in 1954 in Wolverhampton. There is a strong regard for the British way of life, while at the same time a strong moral system is imposed that is slightly at odds with much of the contemporary culture. Pentecostalists are not allowed to drink, swear, have any kind of sex outside marriage or even wear jewellery.

Rastafarian culture has its origins in Jamaica in the early 1930s after the demise of Marcus Garvey, who suggested 'Africa for the Africans'. 'Rastas' adopted Haile Selassie, one-time Emperor of Ethiopia, as the messiah and argued that Babylon was the system of European colonialism that enslaved Africans. There was a conspiracy to keep blacks suppressed. The culture surfaced in the UK in the 1970s and is easily distinguished by its dreadlocks hairstyle; many white youths copied the style during the 1970s and 1980s.

In practice, there is a diversity of culture. Early sociological studies depicted this diversity: in a now classic study of male youth in the St Paul's area of Bristol, the late Ken Pryce (1986; orig. 1979) looked at six lifestyles, with a mix of Afro-Caribbean and UK culture. This was a participant observation that indicated, above all, the range of male youth forms that were developing. Broadly, he distinguished between those who held an expressive-disreputable orientation and those who valued a stable, law-abiding orientation.

Six types were identified at that time. In the first groupings were:

- Hustlers: males, marginal and hedonistic (Yardies are a more recent and tougher version).
- Teenyboppers: delinquents and/or Rastafarians.

In the second (more law-abiding) grouping were:

- Proletarian respectables: those who adopt more conventional lifestyles.
- Saints: the Pentecostals, as defined above.
- Mainliners: white-collar black people.
- In-betweeners: an older, law-abiding group, who also have a passion about their 'black culture'.

Debating the Muslim veil

In 2010 the French government passed a bill to make it illegal to wear garments such as the niqab or burka, which incorporate a full-face veil, anywhere in public. It envisaged fines of €150 (£119) for women who break the law and €30,000 and a one-year jail term for men who force their wives to wear the burka. The niqab and burka are widely seen in France as threats to women's rights and the secular nature of the state.

The debate over women and 'the veil' has achieved an almost central role in many Western cultures. There have been controversies about it in schools and the workplace; in the UK, government minister Jack Straw urged a 'public debate' in 2006; and it has featured in press, news and TV talk shows as a major issue.

How can a sociologist help in such a passionate public debate? Does a sociologist have helpful things to say? Consider that a sociologist could bring to work (a) some evidence (empiricism); (b) some critical thoughts (theory); and (c) a systematic standpoint (analysis).

Empiricism

What are the social facts of the veil? Most religions prescribe some dress for women: in Judaism, Christianity and Islam the concept of covering the head is or was associated with propriety. The veil has a long history, and fieldwork suggests that the veil is a very important, though not the most essential, feature of contrasting Muslim cultures across the world. Since there are over a fifth of the world's population engaged in this practice, it cannot be lightly dismissed. Veiling is far from one simple act. There are many kinds of veil – the *khimar* is a type of

headscarf while the *niqāb* and *burqa* are two kinds of veil that cover most of the face except for a slit or hole for the eyes. The sociologist can document the history and the different cultures in which it is used. Very often the kind of veiling practice depends on the kind of culture it is lodged in – and it is often linked to Sunni/Shi'ite divides.

Theory

One debate concerns the ways in which the veil fits into Muslim lives – what does it mean to Muslim women, and men? What too does it mean to a European? Research shows multiple and ambiguous meanings. There are major diversities of practice, meaning and significance across different Muslim cultures and the challenge for sociologists is to make clear these multiple histories and meanings. To some it is crucial, to others marginal; some even deny its role. For some it is a deep religious expression; for some it signifies what a woman must do; for some it may be seen as a personal threat, a fear or a danger; for some a sign of subordination, even slavery; to yet others a means of Muslim identity; to yet more a sign of resistance to the 'West'. There is a wide range of dress – from dark and total, to light and almost 'fashionable'. And different groups respond in different ways. What is clear to the sociologist is that there is no absolute fixed meaning on which all agree. Veiling is multiply symbolic and contested. Part of the sociologist's job is to see what this contest is about.

Analysis

The contest strikes in at least three key areas:

1 *The gender debate*: here it can be seen as part of the struggle

about the Western view of men and women that is strongly linked to Western feminism. The veil represents women's subordination, and is the iceberg tip of this subordination. More deeply, Islam is a religion which regulates women's lives and keeps women out of public space, public life, etc. Some Muslim women argue to the contrary – that the veil helps them to assert their identity. Still others organise major campaigns against it. So there is conflict across many groups which needs to be grasped.

2 *The modernity debate*: part of the struggle here is the divide between tradition, symbolised by the veil, and the West – a modern view of individualism and freedom. The veil symbolises a 'clash of cultures' and their views of where the future is headed. It symbolises being a Muslim woman in a Western-dominated world.

3 *The assimiliation/minority debate*: here the concern is whether different groups should be assimilated into a culture and whether it helps for them to make themselves stand out through their differences.

What is important throughout this is the sociological recognition that things are not quite what they seem – that there is no one simple account of this social phenomenon and that it is indeed a critical symbol of our times. Carefully unpacking these ideas – and bringing rich complexity and awareness of differences – is one task for sociological analysis which could help informed citizen debate and critical thinking.

See: Joan Wallach Scott: *The Politics of the Veil* (2007). There is plenty to see on YouTube on this: for example, French Muslim woman denied citizenship for wearing the veil, www.youtube.com/watch?v=JoKOVjIM2_Q.

More recent studies such as those by Les Back (1996) and Rupa Huq (2006) trace the new emerging styles and growing diversities of ethnic cultures. They show how new generations of 'Brits' generate Asian-styled bhangra and post-bhangra cultures (bhangra is a dance which originated in the Punjab region) and Afro-Caribbean-styled rap and hip hop cultures, even as they mix and merge with 'Brit culture'. Ethnic cultures now criss-cross class, gender, sexuality and age, and become an everyday feature for many of 'British cultures', having one foot in a 'culture of origin' and another foot in 'diverse British cultures'. Ethnic cultures are dynamic: they are always changing and on the move. Each generation pushes its culture on in different ways and, as young generations become older generations, so the culture moves again. We can see some of this in films like Ayub Khan-Din's *East is East* (1999) and the sequel *West is West* (2010).

Ethnicity and class

In general, those of Caribbean, Pakistani and Bangladeshi descent tend to occupy the lowest position in the labour market and to experience the highest levels of unemployment (Mason, 2000a: 106).

We have seen that, although there is no official poverty line in the UK (Chapter 10), something like 15–25 per cent of the population may well be living in poverty. There are few specific data on ethnicity, but one commentator has remarked that:

> **Every indicator of poverty shows that black people and other ethnic minorities are more at risk of high unemployment, low pay, shift work and poor social security rights. Their poverty is caused by immigration policies which have often excluded people from abroad from access to welfare, employment patterns which have marginalised black people and other ethnic groups into low paid manual work, direct and indirect discrimination in social security and the broader experience of racism in society as a whole.**

(Oppenheim, 1993: 130)

Ethnicity and age

A Joseph Rowntree Foundation report of 1995 (see Chapter 10) was alarmed at the disparities that were appearing between ethnic youth and others. In the late 1980s, while 12 per cent of young whites were unemployed, the figure was higher for young ethnic groups: 25 per cent of Afro-Caribbeans, 16 per cent of

Indians, 27 per cent of Pakistanis and Bangladeshis (aged 16–24) (Skellington, 1996: 102).

Ethnicity and gender

If stratification systems appear across race, class and gender lines – which this book suggests they do – then black women are more likely to be at the centre of all three systems of stratification (if age is added, then elderly black women may be the most vulnerable of all).

There has been a growing amount of research on black women in the UK in recent years, which suggests among other things that black women:

- make up something like a quarter of the minority labour force (Phizacklea, 1995)
- are often heavily concentrated in the worst work: poorly paid, bad conditions, temporary, hard work, long hours, often unregistered home work, often subject to unemployment (Allen and Walkowitz, 1987)
- are often unpaid workers in family businesses (Anthias and Yuval Davis, 1993)
- are often in single households – over 30 per cent of British West Indian households are single parents (Anthias and Yuval Davis, 1993: 117)
- may perform well in school and university, only to find they have less access to work and are less well paid
- are over-represented in the prison population.

White feminism is often critical of the family, and the subordination of women within it. This can mean an implicit attack on Muslim women, whose lives are often circumscribed by the family, and on Afro-Caribbean women, who are often seen to be single mothers. This has resulted in a significant debate amongst black women, who sometimes feel they have become the objects of white feminism, which is critical of their family life and their subordination to it.

Racisms and ethnic antagonisms in Europe

Racism, of various kinds and under various names, runs deep throughout history. We have examined some of its complex roots above. It is not really suprising, then, that racism is found throughout Europe. As Figure 11.2 shows, Europe is a culture in which there are many ethnic diversities. And much of this diversity makes for distinct antagonism. There are five features to note.

First, racism is generally on the increase. Nearly all countries in the European Union report increased numbers of racist incidents and attacks on foreigners and individuals belonging to ethnic, racial or linguistic minorities. In France, this has involved numerous attacks on people of North African origin, as well as anti-Semitism. In Germany, the objects have mainly been Turkish, as well as gypsies (the Sinti and Roma). There also appears to be a worrying resurgence of anti-Semitism and 'Holocaust denial' spearheaded by new skinhead gangs. In part, the latter is explained through the growing tensions arising from the reunification of East and West Germany. Further, European football matches regularly produce concern about the levels of racist violence. And each year there are many deaths across Europe that are caused by racism (see the box below on skinheads and Roma).

Secondly, problems of displaced people throughout Europe have led to many issues around 'asylum seekers'. Leaving their home countries because of intolerable social, economic and political conditions, such asylum seekers may then find themselves confronting further racism and discrimination in the country of destination. Often, they are placed in camps that resemble prisons, and find themselves without family, support or funds. Governments, which are cautious of the political implications of allowing too many asylum seekers into their countries, often deploy subtle and tacit racist selection procedures.

A third development is the extremes of ethnic purging and cleansing that have been taking place across eastern Europe. The horrors of the events of Bosnia (which were told at the start of this chapter) are but one of many such conflicts which have been taking place over religions and borders as the old cultures of Russia and Yugoslavia break down. In Europe we now have the 'Serbian Question', the 'Albanian Question', the 'Macedonian Question', the 'Hungarian Question' and the 'Roma Question' (Kocsis, 2001).

A fourth development is the emergence of a more sophisticated kind of racism, one often called the 'new racism' or 'cultural racism'. This new racism no longer makes the old (and not very respectable) arguments (usually about biological inferiority), but highlights instead *cultural* differences as those that really matter. Just how incompatible this 'different culture' is with the dominant one becomes a key issue. Closely allied with this is the recognition of multi-racisms: for example, white people who are racist to some groups can like or even admire other ethnic groups. There are then racisms or plural racisms (Modood, 2005).

Finally, there is an emerging mentality that is specific to Europe. In England, it takes the form of 'little England'; in Europe more generally, it is 'Fortress Europe'. There is a growing concern to exclude the poorer countries on the fringe of Europe, which includes some of the eastern European countries, as well as those in Africa and eastern Asia. And there has been a growing intolerance of migrating groups – especially what have become known as 'bogus asylum seekers'.

Contemporary conflict across Europe

Two concerns have driven much racism in Europe so far in the twenty-first century. One has been the rise of and scare about terrorism. The other has been the scares over immigration. Both connect to issues of racism.

Since the 9/11 bombings at the World Trade Center in New York, the world has been alerted to 'terrorists'. But much of this scare is also linked to issues of racism. After all, the main perpetrators of the Trade Center outrage were Muslim, and this has led to conflicts about Muslims and their religion. Across the world, there have been recurrent attacks and fears about more. In addition to this, there has also been a growing tide of concern over immigration. By 2002, electoral rebellion over the issue of immigration was threatening the party systems of Austria, Belgium, Denmark, France and the Netherlands.

The Dutch were also incensed by the 2002 assassination of Pim Fortuyn, a gay anti-immigration politician. The Netherlands has been proud for a long while of its 'tolerance' of minorities. It has welcomed tens of thousands of Muslim asylum seekers allegedly escaping persecution. But in 2004, the killing of Theo van Gogh (a famous and polemical film-maker – and a descendant of the painter Vincent van Gogh) raised the possibility of assassinations as part of the European jihad and al Qaeda. Osama bin Laden, the leader, now facilitates actions from European jihadist networks across Europe that assemble for specific missions. The Dutch General Intelligence and Security Service (AIVD) says that radical Islam in the Netherlands encompasses 'a multitude of movements, organisations and groups'. Some are non-violent and share only religious dogma and a loathing for the West. But AIVD stresses that others, including al Qaeda, are also 'stealthily taking root in Dutch society' by recruiting estranged Dutch-born Muslim youths.

According to Robert S. Leiken, two types of jihadist can be found in Europe. *Outsiders* can be seen as typically referring to asylum seekers or students, who gained refuge in liberal Europe from crackdowns against Islamists in the Middle East. *Insiders* are a group of demoralised, cut-off, marginalised citizens – often second- or third-generation children of immigrants. They are often unemployed and form something like an underclass – in Paris or Marseilles, in Amsterdam or Bradford. All have grievances against their society, and the current crisis of terrorism fuels their passions.

With the Muslim headscarf controversy raging in France and England, talk about the connection between asylum abuse and terrorism rising in the United Kingdom, and the Dutch outrage over the van Gogh killing, western European racism now raises many issues. A major concern is the debate over liberalism and multiculturalism. Many of the new ethnic cultures that have become settled within European borders in recent decades are now feeling unsettled by some of the challenges of the new century.

Ethnic antagonisms in the UK

Britain is now two entirely different worlds, and the one you inherit is determined by the colour of your skin.

(Salman Rushdie, 1982: 418)

There has been a long history of ethnic antagonisms in the UK, but several main issues can be highlighted.

First, *public conflicts* – even riots. In the 1950s, shortly after the arrival of a major wave of West Indians, there were the Notting Hill Riots – in this case, with whites attacking blacks. But by the 1980s the rioting and conflicts had changed. Now it was the blacks themselves who protested, in a series of riots throughout the 1980s, mainly involving young people against the police – in Brixton (April 1981), St Paul's in Bristol, Handsworth, and Toxteth in Liverpool. They were considered serious enough for a committee of inquiry, chaired by Lord Scarman. In an influential report, he located the problems of black inner-city youth whose lives had become marginalised. He noted the tension between black youth and the police, the plight of inner-city

Patricia Hill Collins: standpoints at the intersections of gender and race

Patricia Hill Collins (born 1 May 1948) is Distinguished University Professor of Sociology at the University of Maryland, College Park, and former President of the American Sociological Association Council. She is a prominent thinker on race, gender and inequality. She was one of the first sociologists to point simultaneously to the *intersections* of gender and race (see this chapter), and to develop what has

come to be called *standpoint theory* (see Chapter 3). She draws on her own experience as an African-American woman and makes a key sociological point about connecting sociological theory to personal life. Both of these help to shape a different kind of sociology. Her key ideas are published in her classic book *Black Feminist Thought: Knowledge, Consciousness and the Politics of Empowerment*, originally published in 1990.

Her work is striking because in addition to her personal experiences, she uses a wide range of sources such as fiction, poetry, music and oral history – which is relatively unusual for sociologists. She sees contributions to social theory coming from poets and writers like Alice Walker and Audre Lorde. The core of her book focuses upon case studies of 'black womanhood' and black women's historical oppression

in family, motherhood and work. Throughout she places black women's experience at the centre of her analysis and is concerned with the ways in which black women can empower themselves through a deeper understanding of their situation. In later books, she has examined discrimination against women in black communities and the role of black women as 'outsiders within'; the relationship between black nationalism, feminism and women in the hip-hop generation; and the problems of public education.

See also: Fighting Words: Black Women and the Search for Justice (1998); *Black Power to Hip Hop: Racism, Nationalism, and Feminism* (2006); and *Another Kind of Public Education: Race, Schools, the Media and Democratic Possibilities* (2009).

WORLD WATCH

The Roma in Europe

Around 8 million gypsies or Roma live in Europe. They pose major issues of human rights. They are largely scattered in small communities throughout the former communist societies and around the Mediterranean. For example, in Slovakia they make up as much as 10 per cent of the population; in Hungary and the Czech Republic it is estimated that they comprise around 3 per cent; and in Romania they number some 2 million people – the largest national population in the world.

The terms used to describe them are often hard to define: 'pikeys', 'travellers', 'Gypsies', 'Roma', 'Bohemians', 'Manush' and 'Burugoti' can be used, though they do not all mean the same thing. One thing they have in common is that wherever they are found, they are usually badly treated. They also figure low on most social indicators – usually among the very poorest of a society, under-educated, short-lived, dependent on welfare, segregated, in poor health, and removed from political life. They are also among the most imprisoned. They are hugely discriminated against – from where they can live, to life in school, to being the victims of neo-Nazi thugs.

In one major incident, a Romani teenager, Mario Goral, was attacked by a group of skinheads in the central town of Slovakia, Ziar nad Hronom. Some 30 skinheads attacked a pub frequented by Roma with Molotov cocktails, crowbars and knives. They doused Mario with gasoline and polystyrene and set him on fire. He died a few days later. Only after his death did the Slovak government condemn the attack. And writing anonymously in the Presov evening newspapers, the skinheads explained who they were to the general public:

The skinheads wanted to protect Presov against Gypsies – Roma. Who else

Romanian Roma women Julieta Moise, left, and Maria Bacanu, right, stand with children in Barbulesti, Romania, September, 2010. The European Union had just announced that it will take legal action against France over its expulsion of more than 1,000 gypsies in recent weeks after their improvised settlements were destroyed and they were rounded up to be flown home. But as France carries out mass expulsions in a broadly condemned policy of ethnic targeting, some returnee gypsies are saying home-grown poverty is better than the seething hostility they face on French streets

Source: AP/Press Association Images.

WORLD WATCH

but the Gypsies create a mess in the city, steal, and participate in the black market? Now you can think that we are very racist. But you can hardly find a man who would not be ashamed of a Gypsy ... We want Slovaks to live in Presov, in Slovakia. We want a white Slovakia, because if nothing changes, then it will be a catastrophe for Presov and for Slovakia.

(*The Economist*, 12 May 2001: 29–32)

Anti-Roma violence continues. Since January 2008, in Hungary, the Czech Republic and the Slovak Republic, such violence has gained significant prominence in the media. The attacks involve firebombing, shooting, stabbing, beating and other acts of violence. They have taken the lives of eight people and have left dozens of others with serious injuries. Many of the attacks have targeted families and children. They are happening in an increasingly racist climate. These countries have seen a

strengthening of extremist and openly racist groups, which spread hate speech and organise anti-Romani marches through the very same villages where people are being attacked. Breaking EU rules, in September 2010, the French government deported some 1,000 Roma to Romania and Bulgaria. The controversies continue for one of Europe's most stigmatised minorities.

For updates: see European Roma Rights Centre, www.errc.org.

living, and the exclusion experienced by black youth. Troubles erupted again in the summer of 2001, when further conflicts broke out in the north of England – in Bradford, Oldham, Leeds and Burnley. As usual, these conflicts primarily involved young men, but this time they flared up mainly in poor Muslim communities where there was also a menacing threat from right-wing campaigners such as the National Front.

A second issue is *racial attacks*. There is a long history of violence directed towards 'blacks' – what will be described in Chapter 17 as **hate crimes**. Many instances of these crimes have involved young people again, and the police. The Runnymede Trust estimated that between January 1970 and November 1989, some 74 people died as a result of racial attacks (Skellington, 1996: 83). Since then it has documented a further 61 cases (and each case is discussed on its website). The level of violence on the street appears to have escalated.

Third, has been the widespread existence of *racial discrimination*. Formally, this is now illegal in the UK and in many other countries. In practice, it often works on a more informal and covert level. A number of surveys have found discrimination in the work situation. Studies from the Policy Studies Institute (formerly Political and Economic Planning, PEP) have regularly documented high levels of discrimination (see Daniel, 1968; Modood et al., 1997). Often, the studies show blatant discrimination – with white and black stooges applying for similar jobs, only to find that the black population is more discriminated against.

All of the above signals a long-term and growing series of complex problems. Migration and ethnic diversity can bring fears, prejudice, racism – and the possibilities of more and more ethnic conflict and ethnic cleansing, even ethnic war. Stuart Hall

(1992b: 308–9) has suggested three main responses to ethnic divides in a multicultural society. These are:

- A defensive strengthening of local/dominant cultural identities. People feel threatened and resolve this through a reassertion of absolute values. In the UK, this can mean an 'aggressive little Englandism'.
- A defensive strengthening of the minority culture identities. With the experience of racism and exclusion, the culture of origin is used to construct a strong counter-identity. This can be found in the UK as Rastafarianism (reasserting 'Africa' and the Caribbean) and the revival of Muslim fundamentalism (in the Pakistani community).
- The creation of new 'mixed' identities – a possible consequence of globalisation, giving a broader sense of identity. In the UK, the identity 'black' can be used by both Afro-Caribbean and Asian communities. Paul Gilroy (1994) talks of 'the Black Atlantic' as a cultural network spanning many countries (Africa, the Caribbean, the Americas, the UK) where people may have African descent even though they have come to modify it greatly in new cultures.

The future of ethnic relations: multiple racisms, multiple ethnicities

This chapter has highlighted the multiple ethnicities – each taking generational forms – across all cultures. Often these are connected to deep conflicts and hostilities between groups. Most societies have their ethnic tensions, and in some that tension leads to the death of thousands, even millions.

We started by reviewing a number of major explanations of prejudice and discrimination. Often, such prejudices are seen as the individual quirks of a few people in prejudiced cultures. But this chapter has tried to show that these processes are deeply social and work right across the world: they are based upon shifting patterns of ethnic migration, the creation of diasporas and the existence of multiple ethnic cultures organised on generational, class and gender lines which are struggling to defend their own ways of life. Each culture comes to identify some people as different from and outside the culture. These are often connected to economic problems, and these 'others' come to serve major scapegoating functions and can mark out boundaries of national identities. They can be used to reassert the importance and dominance of majority populations.

Ethnic divides seem wide and deep. As we saw in the opening story of Bosnia, many contemporary wars are connected to such divides. In the twenty-first century, new patterns of racism are being generated around new migration patterns and the ubiquitous growth of 'terrorist fears' after the 9/11 attacks. An understanding of the social processes at work in the construction of these hostilities – and of the ways we may transcend them to live together with our differences – seems ever more urgent.

SUMMARY

1 Race involves a presumed cluster of biological traits. A century ago, scientists identified three broad, overarching racial categories: Caucasians, Mongoloids and Negroids. However, there are no pure races and these categories are in disrepute. Ethnicity is a matter not of biology but of shared cultural heritage. Racialisation is the process of naming different races. Minorities, including those of certain races and ethnicities, are categories of people who are socially distinctive and who have a subordinate social position.

2 A prejudice is an inflexible and distorted generalisation about a category of people. Racism, a powerful type of prejudice, is any assertion that one race is innately superior or inferior to another. Discrimination is a pattern of action by which a person treats various categories of people unequally. Institutional discrimination refers to the fact that the law and other social institutions, in contrast to individuals, can treat different categories of people unequally.

Pluralism refers to a state in which racial and ethnic categories, although distinct, have equal social standing. Assimilation is a process by which minorities gradually adopt the patterns of the dominant culture. Segregation means the physical and social separation of categories of people. Genocide involves the extermination of a category of people.

3 Migration patterns have played a significant role in shaping most cultures. Future patterns of migration are likely to be more global, and involve more women.

4 The main ethnic groups in the UK number about 7 per cent of the population. They are an ethnically heterogeneous group but include south Asians (from India, Bangladesh and Pakistan) and Afro-Caribbeans. Forty-eight per cent are under the age of 24.

5 Ethnic antagonisms are widespread and increasing in Europe. Attacks, harassment and discrimination are features of minority ethnic living in Europe.

MYTASKLIST

Ten Suggestions for going further

1 Connect up with Part Six and the Sociology Web Resources

As you work through ideas and think about the issues raised in this chapter, look at the accompanying website and the resource centre at the end of this book which connects to it. There is a lot here to help you move on. To link up, see: www.pearson.co.uk/plummer.

2 Review the chapter

Briefly summarise (in a paragraph) just what this chapter has been about. Consider: (a) What have you learned? (b) What do you disagree with? Be critical. And (c) How would you develop all this? How could you get more detail on matters that interest you?

3 Pose questions

(a) Discuss patterns of ethnic inequality in any one European culture.
(b) What is meant by 'racialisation'? How does it connect to the idea of 'race'?
(c) What are the major patterns of migration in postwar Europe? Should there be limits on immigration?
(d) Examine what is meant by the 'new racism'. Give examples.

4 Explore key words

Many concepts have been introduced in this chapter. You can review them from the website or from the listing at the back of this book. You might like to give special attention to just five words and think them through – how would you define them, what are they dealing with, and do they help you see the social world more clearly or not?

5 Search the Web

Be critical when you look at websites – see the box on p. 940 in the Resources section. For this chapter look at the following:

Minority Rights International
www.minorityrights.org
An international NGO, based in London, which promotes the rights of ethnic, religious and other minorities. Contains a great deal of information.

Migration

Two main (United Nations) agencies acting on behalf of the world's refugees and migrants are:

United Nations High Commissioner for Refugees (UNHCR)
www.unhcr.ch

Global Commission for International Migration
www.gcim.org

See also:

Centre of Migration
www.compass.ox.ac.uk

The Age-of-migration website for the book by Castles and Miller (see below) has a useful set of links at:
www.age-of-migration.com/uk/resources/weblinks.html

History of International Migration
www.let.leidenuniv.nl/history/migration
www.swap.ac.uk/Links/links.asp?sid=__Jacsb21&screen=2
A major source of links on issues of migration and refugees.

Race and racism

Institute of Race Relations
www.irr.org.uk
The Institute of Race Relations (IRR) was established as an independent educational charity in 1958 to carry out research and publish and collect resources on race relations throughout the world.

Runnymede Trust
www.runnymedetrust.org
The Runnymede Trust is an independent policy research organisation focusing on equality and justice through the promotion of a successful multi-ethnic society.

European Network Against Racism
www.enar-eu.org/en

European Monitoring Centre on Racism and Xenophobia
http://eumc.eu.int

European Commission against Racism and Intolerance (ECRI)
www.coe.int/T/e/human_rights/ecri/1-ECRI

6 Watch a DVD

There are many films to see on racism. Here is a list of some classics worth seeing:

- Udayan Prasad's *My Son the Fanatic* (1997): a father is confronted by his Islamic fundamentalist son in Bradford.
- Tony Gatlif's *Gadjo Dilo* (1999): gives an ethnographer's eye on gypsy life and racism in Romania.
- Robert Mulligan's *To Kill a Mockingbird* (1962): the classic novel of racism in the Deep South of the United States came to be a major film.
- Stephen Frear's *My Beautiful Laundrette* (1985): Asian community in the UK meets gay life in a laundrette. Controversial in its day.
- Damien O'Donnell's *East is East*: very funny but telling look at discrimination within Asian communities in the UK.
- Alan Parker's *Mississippi Burning* (1988) tells the true story of the Ku Klux Klan and the murders of civil rights workers.
- John Singleton's classic *Boyz N the Hood* (1991): about surviving the pressures of family and street life in south-central Los Angeles. Set a model for black American films.
- Wayne Wang's *Chan is Missing* (1982): a 1982 film of two taxi drivers searching the streets of San Francisco. Something of a cult film.
- Gurinda Chadas' *Bend it like Beckam* (2002): fusion of Hindi culture meets Western culture meets feminism and gay, and all through football!
- Terry George's *Hotel Rwanda* (2004): harrowing account of the Tutsi conflict in Rwanda.
- Nick Broomfield's *Ghosts* (2007): the Chinese immigrants discussed at the start of Chapter 15 are here 'documented' to show the abuses of the global migrant worker's life.

7 Think and read

Tariq Modood, *Multicultural Politics* (2005). A foremost UK sociologist engaged with the debate over multiculturalism raises many of the key issues.

The Parakh Report, *The Future of Multi-Ethnic Britain* (2000). A sustained analysis of a modern multi-ethnic society with key recommendations for a 'human rights culture'.

David Mason, *Race and Ethnicity in Modern Britain* (2nd edn, 2000a). A short, clear introduction to the whole field. Now a little out of date.

Christian Karner, *Ethnicity and Everyday Life* (2007). Examines ethnicity as a structure of action, a way of seeing and a structure of feeling.

Patricia Hill Collins, *Black Feminist Thought* (2nd edn, 2000). A now classic and important statement of theoretical issues concerning black feminism.

Stephen Castles and Mark J. Miller, *The Age of Migration: International Population Movements in the Modern World* (4th edn, 2009). A major textbook which discusses migration movements on a global level, and shows how they lead to ethnic minorities.

Philip Marfleet, *Refugees in a Global Era* (2006). A critical review of the whole social process of migration.

Martin Shaw, *What is Genocide?* (2007). An important book that builds a sociology of the most extreme form of discriminating hatred and scapegoating: genocide.

Finally: three recent books that will help you engage with current debates are: Paul Gilroy, *After Empire: Melancholia or Convivial Culture* (2004); Kwame Anthony Appiah, *Cosmopolitanism: Ethics in a World of Strangers* (2006); Akbar Ahmed, *Journey into Islam: The Crisis of Globalization* (2007).

More information

Internationally, the Minority Rights Group publishes the *World Directory of Minorities*, which details 1,000 minorities (and their various persecutions). *The International Migration Review* (Center for Migration Studies, New York) is a regular and valuable source of information on migration patterns. *Race Today*, *Ethnic and Race Relations*, and *Race and Class* are all journals that highlight matters of race; the first is the most accessible to students. For up-to-date 'briefing papers' on issues of concern to the multi-ethnic society in the UK, look at the Runnymede Trust's website (see above).

8 Relax with a novel

Four good classic US novels on race and racism are Ralph Ellison's *Invisible Man* (1999); Maya Angelou's *I Know Why the Caged Bird Sings* (1993); James Baldwin's *Giovanni's Room* (1956); and Alice Walker's *The Colour Purple* (1982).

9 Connect to other chapters

- For links to culture and language, see Chapter 5.
- For links to world poverty, see Chapter 9.
- For links to religion, see Chapter 19.
- Ethnicity is also discussed in the chapters on crime (17), family (18) and education (20).

10 Engage with THE BIG DEBATE

Dangerous extremists: Islamic fundamentalists or Islamophobes?

As we have seen in Chapter 5, Muslim cultures are widespread in the world and involve around a sixth of the world's population. Further, as we shall see in Chapter 19, Islam is the dominant faith in some 40 states throughout the world, and is seen by many to be the fastest-growing religion. In the UK, there has been a significant growth over the past decade to around 2.4 million Muslims – partly due to the birth rate and immigration, but also because of 'conversions' to the faith. Overall, Muslims account for some 3 per cent of European faith.

In the twenty-first century, Islam has come to symbolise key questions about ethnicity, prejudice and tolerance. This can be seen from the prominence given to the debate over the Salman Rushdie affair and the Iranian *fatwah* (death threat) imposed upon him (see the opening vignette to Chapter 19). It is seen in the controversy in France and elsewhere over the veil (see the box on p. 377). And it is seen in the Gulf Wars waged against Iraq in 1992 and 2003. Some have even claimed that this is a new 'Holy War' between East and West, where the traditional forces of the anti-Western, anti-rational and anti-modern Islamic religions are in spiritual and moral combat with the modernising but decadent West. Benjamin Barber (1995), for one, sees this as a clash of civilisations, a conflict between the *jihad* (holy war) and the materialism symbolised by McDonaldisation (see Chapters 5, 6 and 19). It is a conflict which may also be linked to ethnicity and some see it as the major world conflict in the twenty-first century. In the aftermath of the World Trade Center bombings in 2001, such tensions have become more and more acute.

And with it has arrived Islamophobia. On the one hand, some Westerners argue that Islam is a dangerous force in the world. It is seen as a fundamentalist religion (see Chapter 19), holding strongly to traditionalist views, emphasising religious texts and looking back to its past to affirm its puritan vision. It is seen to hold particular prejudices against many modern concerns of the West: the liberation of women, the 'open and free society', the decline of religion, the acceptance of diversity such as homosexuality and 'sexual freedom'. And it is seen to favour an absolutist religious state where nothing can exist outside the religion. Indeed, of the 40 or so states where Islam is dominant, few can be called democratic. All of this clashes with the modern values of the Western state.

Such claims certainly do have some basis in fact, but the critics argue that such statements are extreme: the Islamic faith actually comes in a number of varieties, and many of its supporters do not adopt these extreme positions. Just as Christianity has a number of its own divides, so too do the Muslims. Most are not extreme. Indeed, as we have seen, a key divide lies between Shi'ism and the Shi'ites (who hold more traditional and rigid views) and the Sunnis (who accept more diversity and change). In the UK, for instance, the majority of Muslims must be distinguished from small extreme groups like Al-Muhajiroun which calls for Islamic government in the UK (*Khilafah*).

It is the more extreme views which get reported most often, and it is these ideas which form the basis of a new form of prejudice called 'Islamophobia' – *a hatred of all things Muslim*. Where once the Jews or blacks or 'Asians' were prime objects of attack, increasingly Muslims have become the new objects of prejudice and discrimination. Not only is the incidence of violent attacks against Muslims increasing, but prejudicial views are being widely held. Few, for example, blamed the Catholics for IRA bombings in Ireland: the IRA was recognised as a more extreme group. So why blame Muslims for much of what is, in fact, only an extreme edge?

In 1996, the Runnymede Trust – a major organisation which promotes and researches a multicultural society in the UK – announced a commission to look into what it considered as the most rapidly growing form of prejudice. It was concerned to look at such things as anti-Islamic and anti-Muslim attitudes; the relations between Islam and secular outlooks and other world faiths; the treatment of Islam and Muslim concerns in the media; and the contributions of British Muslims to government and society. The Trust highlighted a major emerging form of prejudice in Western societies, one that is likely to become more and more recognised. Since then the term has come into wide use.

These divides raise serious issues around prejudice and discrimination. How far can a multicultural society which claims to accept religious and ethnic diversity pursue such outright attacks upon different religions? At the same time, how far can a religious strand which rejects tolerance and diversity be allowed to propagate its views? This is a classical dilemma of freedom for those who may advocate unlimited freedom.

Continue the debate

1 What is Islamophobia, and what might cause it?
2 Consider some possible scenarios of what might happen in Europe and the West in the future.
3 Will more and more Muslims be co-opted into Western secular individualism? Will more and more Muslims stay with their own faith, while accepting multicultural values? Or will a strong defence of Islamic fundamentalism lead to growing ethnic conflicts?
4 What is multiculturalism? Does it work?

See: Tariq Modhood, *Multicultural Politics* (2005), especially Part II: The Muslim Challenge; Runnymede Trust (1997); Barber (1995). Visit Islamophobia Watch: www.islamophobia-watch.com.

CHAPTER 12

THE GENDER ORDER AND SEXUALITIES

IN THE NEW GUINEA SOCIETY OF THE SAMBIA, boys aged 7 to 10 are taken from their mothers to a special place outside the village. Here they experience powerful homosexual fellatio activities. For a number of years, they daily fellate, for some years as fellator and then later as fellated. Elders teach that semen is absolutely vital; that it should be consumed daily since it is the basis of biological maleness; and that their very masculinity depends on it. At the same time, they must avoid women, who are seen to be contaminating. When they are young men, they are returned to society, where they settle down and marry women. With fatherhood, their homosexuality ceases. But then the cycle starts all over again when the men steer their own young sons into this erotic pattern. 'Homoeroticism is the royal road to Sambia manliness.' This is a ritualised form of homosexuality, and for the Sambia it is absolutely essential that men engage in these fellating activities in order to establish both their masculinity and, ultimately, their heterosexuality. Masculinity, here, is the outcome of a regime of ritualised homosexuality leading into manhood.

Some may find such research a little unsettling. Masculinity is often said to be the very opposite of homosexuality. Life among boys and men in the Sambia is clearly not like life among boys and men in modern Europe. In Europe, there is no ritualised homosexuality among all young boys in order for them to become men. Quite the opposite. If boys are found to be involved in sex with other boys, they are often presumed to be passing through a brief homosexual phase, or they are seen as being effeminate and queer. It is certainly not seen as 'manly'.

This is just one area of research that the field of gender studies has been developing for the past 25 years, and it has come up with all kinds of interesting research findings and theories. Once again we find that gender is not an automatically biological thing, but a phenomenon that involves a great deal of social activity. This chapter provides an introductory exploration of this area (Herdt, 1981).

He is the Subject, he is the Absolute – she is the Other.

Simone de Beauvoir, *The Second Sex*, 1997 introduction

Every time we liberate a woman, we liberate a man.

Margaret Mead

No society treats its women as well as its men.

United Nations Development Programme, 1997

In this chapter, we ask:

- How can we distinguish between sex, gender, sexism, patriarchy and gender stratification?

- How do we become gendered and learning gender identities?

- How does feminism and the Women's Movement challenge gender stratification?

- How can sociologists approach the study of sexualities?

- How are gay, lesbians and queers reacted to in societies?

(Left) Lynn Randolph, *Cyborg* (1989)
Source: With kind permission from Lynn Randolph.

Lynn Randolph's work has been discussed by Donna Haraway, and debates and ideas on it can be found at her excellent website at: http://www.lynnrandolph.com/

Q This image is quite prominent in the world of cyber-art. What does it suggest to you about the human body and its transformation? What is the human being?

We tend to think that 'becoming a man' or 'becoming a woman' is a straightforward process of 'natural' development. But sociologists and anthropologists have long shown quite otherwise. The Sambia described in the opening to this chapter are a case in point. Cultural meanings about what is considered masculine and feminine, and what is not, vary from one society to another and from one historical period to another. Not only do such meanings vary, but so do the sexual activities in which people engage. This is all part of a **gender order**, *the ways in which societies shape notions of masculinity and femininity into power relationships*. When applied to smaller groups such as school classrooms, families or bars, we can talk of the workings of a **gender regime**, *the gender order as it works through in smaller settings*.

What it means to be masculine or feminine differs across cultures and history. Research suggests that 'our concept of masculinity seems to be a fairly recent historical product, a few hundred years old at most' (Connell, 1995: 68). Indeed, a leading sociologist of masculinity, R. W. Connell, suggests that the way we think about masculinity today was closely linked to the rise of individualism in early modern European society. Prior to this, while women were regarded as different from men (they were seen as 'incomplete' men), there was not the clear split into masculinity and femininity we have today.

Many people claim that what it is to be a man or a woman, a heterosexual or a homosexual, reflects basic and innate differences between the sexes. But, as we shall see, the different social experiences of women and men are the creation of society far more than biology. Connell, for example, is very clear that there are a whole array of different masculinities at work in different societies. It is true that some become dominant – *the main ways of being a man in a society*, or what he called **hegemonic masculinity**. But others (which he calls subordinated)

(a)

(b)

Drag queens, illustrated here, are further examples of 'performing' or 'playing' with gender

Source: From a sociological study of drag queens by Leila Rupp and Verta Taylor (2003). *Drag Queens at the 801 Cabaret*, © Leila Rupp and Verta Taylor, 2003, pub. University of Chicago Press.

can be very different, emphasising femininity, or homosexuality, or being highly resistant to gender.

 A useful guide to the world of transgender is Susan Stryker and Stephen Whittle, *The Transgender Studies Reader* (2006). At the last count there were some 12 million transgender internet hits! A helpful starting point is www.transgenderzone.com.

In this chapter, then, we shall look at this gender order. To begin, we shall distinguish between the key concepts of sex and gender. We will then examine how people become gendered, before moving on to an analysis of sexism, patriarchy and gender stratification. We will see how the women's movement emerged to challenge gender stratification. Finally, we will look at some recent accounts of sexuality.

The gender order

Key terms and basic distinctions: sex and gender?

Typically, sociologists make a number of key distinctions. **Sex** refers to *the biological distinction between females and males*, and is usually taken to have six major components: chromosome make-up, reproductive organs, external genitals, hormonal states, internal genitals and secondary sex characteristics. In general, we can speak of a female as having XX chromosomes, clitoris and vagina, ovaries, oestrogen and breast development; and the male as having XY chromosomes, penis and testicles, gonads, testosterone and a beard. There are, however, enormous variations within the two sexes in genetic and hormonal endowment. For example, an infant may be born with too few or too many X or Y chromosomes, giving it the chromosome make-up of one sex and the genitals of another.

LIVING IN THE C21ST

Testing for gender?

In 2009, Caster Semenya won the 800 metres at the world championships in a world-leading 1 minute, 55.45 seconds. Coming from a very poor

Source: Michael Steele/Staff/Getty Images.

background in South Africa she developed an interest in sports science and went on to become a world champion. But something about 'her' did not seem quite right. She appeared to be a bit too masculine for a woman racer. After she won her race, the world track and field federation requested she take a gender test. They were concerned that she did not meet the requirements to compete as a woman. Was she cheating – with drugs perhaps? Or did she have a rare medical advantage?

This 'gender test' requires a physical medical evaluation, and reports from a range of experts: an endocrinologist, a psychologist, a gynecologist, an internal medicine specialist and an expert on gender. Her family was upset; South African leaders thought it racist; and gender specialists had a field day. What is this 'gender test' that can determine what the sex or gender of a person is?

Surely for most people sex or gender is obvious. Clearly not so: the tests were many and it took months to reach a decision. But for privacy reasons the results have not been made public.

Despite controversy and major human rights issues, all did not go badly for Caster. In November 2009 South Africa's sports ministry issued a statement that Caster Semenya had reached an agreement with the IAAF to keep her medal and the prize money. In December 2009, she was voted the Number One Woman's 800 metre runner of the year. And after 11 months of exile, she returned in July 2010 to win another race in Finland and the Commonwealth Games in October in India – as a woman.

But many were left wondering about some of the issues that are the key to this chapter. What is a gender test? How do you know a gender?

By contrast, the term **gender** refers to *the social aspects of differences and hierarchies between male and female*. Gender is evident throughout the social world, shaping how we think about ourselves, guiding our interaction with others and influencing our work and family life. But gender involves much more than difference; it also involves power and hierarchy, because in most societies men enjoy a disproportionate share of most social resources.

Thus, whereas sex may be male or female, gender refers to the social meaning of masculinity and femininity. Since this stresses the social aspects, you will note that it is gender that sociologists are interested in: 'sex' would be more appropriate for a course in biology. But in any event, 'sex' itself is not always a clear-cut matter. A hormone imbalance before birth can produce a **hermaphrodite** (a word derived from Hermaphroditus, the offspring of the mythological Greek gods Hermes and Aphrodite, who embodied both sexes), *a human being with some combination of female and male internal and external genitalia*. Because our culture is uneasy about sexual ambiguity, we often look upon hermaphrodites with confusion. By contrast, the Pokot of eastern Africa are indifferent to what they consider a simple biological error and the Navajo regard hermaphrodites with awe, viewing them as the embodiment of the full potential of both the female and the male (Geertz and Geertz, 1975).

THINKERS & THEORY

Judith Butler: gender is what you do

Judith Butler is one of the world's leading feminist philosophers, who has written widely. She has been most influential in sociology through her book *Gender Trouble* published in 1990 (translated into 20 languages). She has played a major role in rethinking the divides between sex and gender, and the categories

Judith Butler has become one of the world's leading post-structural, feminist and queer philosophers. She can be found on YouTube, and an engaging film on her work is *Judith Butler: Philosophical Encounters of the Third Kind* (2007). (*See*: http://icarusfilms.com/new2007/judi.html)

Source: © ullsteinbild/Topfoto Topfoto.co.uk.

of lesbian, gay and transgender, and has turned the very notion of identity into a problem. Her work can be seen as part of the way in which intellectual ideas connect to social movements and has been prominent in shaping queer theory.

Butler is concerned with the ways in which human subjectivity is created – and, in particular, with how humans come to submit themselves to definitions handed to them through the norms of the powerful. In effect, they become subjects against themselves. Butler does not see a presence or essence behind a self; rather the self is constituted through the doing (see Chapter 7). Doing gender comes before being gender. For her, gender is *performative*. It is certainly not biological. For her even the distinction sex/gender should be dissolved: there are no biological foundations to gender. Gender depends upon the repetition of certain stylised acts. As she famously claims: 'Gender is a stylised repetition of acts. The effect of gender is produced through the stylization of the body' (p. 140). Gender is not who you are but what you do.

Drawing on a heady mix of Freudian, Derridean and Foucauldian theory (she is no easy read), Butler has highlighted how the gendered body is subjected in a regime of power. Her key idea is *performativity*. Simple performance is not performativity. As she says: 'it is important to distinguish performance from performativity: the former presumes a subject, but the latter contests the very notion of a subject'. Performativity, in short, brings into being that which it names.

She used 'drag' as a key example. Drag and cross dressing show that men and women can challenge gender by appearance: subverting the taken-for-granted. Transsexuals are a prime case for gender study, suggesting how much the life of transgender depends upon performing gender appropriately.

Although Butler's work is most noted in sociology for her approach to gender performativity, her later work covers a wide range of topics from mourning and censorship/'injurious speech' to biography and war. You can find her speaking on YouTube. For a review of her work see, Moya Lloyd, *Judith Butler: From Norms to Politics* (2007).

Gender concepts

Under the term 'gender' are several key linked concepts. **Gender identity** refers to the *subjective state in which someone comes to say 'I am a man' or 'I am a woman'* (look back at Chapter 7). It is perfectly possible – and not uncommon – to believe that one is a woman while having all the biological sex attributes of a male. Currently, such experiences are often designated as either *transsexualism* or *transgenderism*. Surgery is common for **transsexuals**, *people who feel they are one sex though biologically they are the other.* Tens of thousands of transsexuals across the world have medically altered their genitals to escape the sense of being 'trapped in the wrong body'. Over the past 30 years a major social movement has appeared around transgenderism, arguing that gender

has been too narrowly defined as a dichotomous male and female and claiming that gender needs to be much more broadly conceived and approached (Bornstein, 1998).

Gender role refers to *learning and performing the socially accepted characteristics for a given sex.* The content of this may differ enormously across cultures and even within a culture. Again, it is possible to hold a gender identity (such as 'I am a man') that crosses with a gender role (for example, 'I am a man and I wear a dress'). This is the case of what contemporarily is referred to as *transvestism*. A variant of this can be drag. Transgenderism is usually seen as the word that encompasses transexuality and transvestism and much else besides.

Finally, **gender performance** refers to ways of 'doing gender', *the ways in which masculinities and*

Margaret Mead and Samoa

Margaret Mead (1901–78) was an intellectual polymath and giant of the twentieth century, and one of the world's leading anthropologists. Although her

Margaret Mead (1901–78)
Source: © Bettmann/Corbis.

work has been criticised, she produced a number of classic studies in the earlier part of the twentieth century that radically helped us see cultures and sex in new ways. Her passion was to gather accurate information and she used a range of fieldwork strategies (including film) to do this. She was also a passionate early feminist. Famously, she claimed to 'Never doubt that a small group of thoughtful, committed citizens can change the world.'

In one of her studies (1963; orig. 1935), Margaret Mead studied three societies of New Guinea. Trekking high into the mountains, Mead observed the Arapesh, whose men and women were remarkably similar in attitudes and behaviour. Both sexes, she reported, were cooperative and sensitive to others – what our culture would label 'feminine'.

Moving south, Mead then studied the Mundugumor, whose culture of headhunting and cannibalism stood in striking contrast to the gentle ways of the Arapesh. Here, Mead reported, females and

males were again alike, though they were startlingly different from the Arapesh. Both Mundugumor females and males were typically selfish and aggressive, traits defined as more 'masculine' in Europe and the United States.

Finally, travelling west to survey the Tchambuli, Mead discovered a culture that, like our own, defined females and males differently. Yet the Tchambuli reversed many of our notions about gender: females tended to be dominant and rational, while males were submissive, emotional and nurturing towards children.

Based on her observations, Mead concluded that what one culture defines as masculine another may consider feminine. Further, she noted that societies can exaggerate or minimise the importance of sex. Mead's research, then, makes a strong case that gender is a variable creation of culture. It can be sharply distinguished from sex, which is the biological substratum of gender.

See a key website on her work at: www.interculturalstudies.org.

femininities are acted out. Candace West and Don Zimmerman have argued that:

> A person's gender is not simply an aspect of what one is, but, more fundamentally, it is something that one does, and does recurrently in interaction with others.

(West and Zimmerman, 1987: 125)

All the above issues of sex and gender need to be distinguished from the sexual and the erotic. Whereas sex and gender involve languages of 'male' and 'female', and 'masculinity' and 'femininity' respectively, the sexual and the erotic involve a language of desire: of heterosexuality, homosexuality, bisexuality, sadomasochism and more. This language is much more concerned with types of sexual desire, experience and partner. Again this has a biological substratum – of orgasms and physiological changes around arousal – but most of what is distinctive about human sexuality comes from the fact that it is hugely symbolic and social. Gender identity – 'I am a man' – often becomes the basis for organising the erotic – 'therefore I am a heterosexual interested in women'. But it does not have to. Most male homosexuals have no doubt that they are men, but have a sexual interest in the same sex. In that sense, it is quite mistaken to see male homosexuality as necessarily linked to effeminacy.

Table 12.1	Traditional notions of a polarised gender identity	
Feminine traits	**Masculine traits**
Submissive	Dominant
Dependent	Independent
Unintelligent and incapable	Intelligent and competent
Emotional	Rational
Receptive	Assertive
Intuitive	Analytical
Weak	Strong
Timid	Brave
Content	Ambitious
Passive	Active
Cooperative	Competitive
Sensitive	Insensitive
Sex object	Sexually aggressive
Attractive because of physical appearance	Attractive because of achievement

Patriarchy, gender stratification and sexism

Gender goes to the heart of social organisation and three terms will help clarify this. First, the concept of **gender stratification** refers to *a society's unequal distribution of wealth, power and privilege between the sexes*. In most countries throughout the world, societies allocate fewer valued resources to women than to men. Second, **sexism** is *the belief that one sex is innately superior to the other*. Historically, many societies have rested upon a belief in the innate superiority of males who, therefore, legitimately dominate females. Sexism has much in common with racism: both are ideologies that support the social domination of one category of people by another. As we shall see presently, *institutionalised sexism* pervades the operation of the economy, with women highly concentrated in jobs that are less challenging and that offer relatively low pay. Similarly, the legal system has historically turned a blind eye towards violence against women, especially violence committed by boyfriends, husbands and fathers.

A third and perhaps most telling concept is that of **patriarchy** (literally, 'the rule of fathers'), *a form of social organisation in which men dominate, oppress and exploit women*. While some degree of patriarchy may be universal, there is significant variation in the relative power and privilege of females and males around the world. In Saudi Arabia, for example, the power of men over women is as great as anywhere on earth; in Norway, by contrast, the two sexes approach equality in many respects.

Patriarchy at work

For women, there are two important areas of work: *paid employment* and *work done at home* (domestic labour). The relationship between the two is also important.

The dark side of gender: gender violence

The Declaration on the Elimination of Violence Against Women, adopted by the United Nations

Sylvia Walby: unequal global gender

Sylvia Walby OBE is UNESCO Chair in Gender Research at Lancaster University and is one of the leading theorists of a macro global sociology of gender inequality. Her early work in the 1970s and 1980s focused on the workings of the core elements of patriarchy across societies, which she saw as being comprised of six overlapping and changing structures:

1 *Paid work*: women are likely to be paid less (see below and Chapter 15).

2 *The household*: women are likely to do the housework and raise the children (see below and Chapters 15 and 18).

3 *The state*: women are much less likely to have access to formal power (see Chapter 16).

4 *Violence*: women are much more likely to be abused (see below and Chapters 9, 17, 18 and 21).

5 *Sexuality*: women's sexuality is more likely to be treated negatively (see below and Chapter 21).

6 *Culture*: women are more misrepresented in media and public culture (see above and Chapter 22).

In her book *Theorising Patriarchy* (1990), she argued that these elements take on different forms in different cultures and at different times: in particular, that the twentieth century in the West saw a move from private patriarchy (where men regulate in the home) to public patriarchy (where the state and the labour market shape women's lives). She claimed that the case for this was strongest in the Scandinavian countries.

She has subsequently linked her founding work into developments in recent theory to develop a wide analysis of forces shaping global futures. She is influenced by a number of strands briefly introduced elsewhere in this book: theories of modernity and change (see Chapter 4), globalisation (see Chapter 2), intersectionality (see Chapters 8 and 12) and the flows and waves of global complexity (see Chapter 26). From this she builds an account of the modern world which highlights the workings of class, gender and race regimes that organise the complexities of the modern world. Using measures such as the Human Development Index (see Chapters 4 and 9), she charts the transformations in inequalities in the modern world.

Her work is wide ranging, complex but also schematic. For the more advanced sociology student, it brings together a wealth of ideas and data that are worth considering in the analysis of contemporary global inequalities.

See: Sylvia Walby, *Globalization and Inequalities: Complexity and Contested Modernities* (2009).

Sylvia Walby is a leading feminist sociologist. She is the UNESCO chair of Gender Research at Lancaster University and in 2008 was awarded an OBE for services to equal opportunities and diversity. See her website at: http://www.lancs.ac.uk/fass/sociology/profiles/34/

Source: Courtesy Sylvia Walby.

General Assembly in 1993, defines violence against women as 'any act of gender-based violence that results in, or is likely to result in, physical, sexual, or psychological harm or suffering to women, including threats of such acts, coercion or arbitrary deprivation of liberty, whether occurring in public or private life'. It encompasses, but is not limited to:

physical, sexual and psychological violence occurring in the family, including battering, sexual abuse of female children in the household, dowry-related violence, marital rape, female genital mutilation and other traditional practices harmful to women, non-spousal violence and violence related to exploitation; physical, sexual

and psychological violence occurring within the general community, including rape, sexual abuse, sexual harassment and intimidation at work, in educational institutions and elsewhere; trafficking in women and forced prostitution; and physical, sexual and psychological violence perpetrated or condoned by the state, wherever it occurs.

(UNFPA, 2000: 25–6)

According to the United Nations, 'At least one in five of the world's female population has been physically or sexually abused by a man or men at some time in their life' (UNFPA, 2000: 25). Figures vary across countries and for differing kinds of abuse, but that such abuse is both widespread and frequently condoned makes it a crucial area for understanding patriarchy. Some of its findings are given below.

Across the world, there are many social practices and institutions which actively work to regulate women's lives and often keep them in subordinate positions. The ultimate strategy is that of violence and fear of violence. **Gender violence** is *all those practices of domestic and sexual violence directed at maintaining gender hierarchies and punishing femininities* (Peterson and Runyan, 2010: 166). Here we briefly mention a wide range of these practices, each of which has been studied by feminists (they have also been major areas of social movement campaigns globally).

- *Domestic violence* (IPV – Intimate Partner Violence). The women's movement directed attention to this in the 1970s, setting up women's refuge centres and shifting public and official attitudes to a previously accepted and hidden practice. Possibly one in four women in the UK will experience battering and domestic violence and need help (85 per cent of domestic violence cases are men against women). In the United States, a woman is battered, usually by her intimate partner, every 15 seconds. Across the world, at least one in every three women has been beaten, coerced into sex or abused, usually by someone she knows (UNFPA, 2000: 4–5; Chapter 3). We say a little more about this in Chapter 18.

- *Child abuse.* Concern about this goes back to the women's movement's concern in the nineteenth century, and nowadays it has become widely recognised as an issue. The UK Home Office estimates that around 21 per cent of girls (and 11 per cent of boys) experience some kind of child sex abuse. Maybe as many as 30 per cent of women are abused with men making up 95 per cent of perpetrators.

- *Rape.* Across half the world marital rape is not even recognised (and it was not recognised generally at all until the 1970s). Most rape victims are known by their attacker and most are not reported (in the UK the rate of reporting is estimated to be about 15 per cent). We can ask: why is it so low? Of those reported, few come to court and even fewer are convicted. Despite years of feminist campaigning, rape remains a crime where the victim is frequently blamed. Major new interventions – changes in rape legislation, the development of rape crisis centres and helplines, Reclaim the Night rallies, rape counselling and the like – were all a product of the women's movement in the 1970s. Many are now in decline. Rape is a major global issue and rape rates differ across countries. Genocidal rape refers to the systematic programme of raping women and girls in order to humiliate enemies. It is also widespread in wars (Allen, 1996).

- *Abortion.* Each year women undergo an estimated 50 million abortions, 20 million of which are unsafe; some 78,000 women die and millions suffer (UNFPA, 2000: 4–5; Chapter 3).

- *Sexual harassment.* This is another area defined by feminists in the 1970s and from which significant legal changes were brought about in many workplaces.

- *Coerced marriage.* This is often associated with early marriage, dowry price and early pregnancy.

- *Honour killings.* This is practised when a women is said to have brought shame on her family for a disapproved partner or in some cases for the 'dishonour' of being raped. As many as 5,000 women and girls are killed annually in so-called 'honour' killings.

- *Female genital mutilation (FGM).* This involves the removal of all or part of the female genitalia – usually before the girl is 15. It is widely practised across Africa and some Middle Eastern countries. Worldwide, some 130–40 million girls and young women across the world *have undergone* female genital mutilation (possibly 2,000 a year in the UK alone).

- *Sex work.* This ranges from pole dancing to prostitution, and sex slavery to trafficking.

- *Sexual slavery.* An estimated 4 million women and girls are bought and sold worldwide each year, into marriage, prostitution or slavery.

Spotlight

Female genital mutiliation

Throughout the world, there are between 8 and 10 million women and girls in 28 countries in Africa and many in the Middle East (India, Pakistan, Malaysia) who are *at risk* of undergoing one form or other of female genital mutilation (FGM). The rate is 98 per cent in Somalia. Quite frequently it results in death. Reasons for the practice are cultural: cleanliness, a conformity to norms, the enhancing of male pleasures, and chastity. Many Western feminists have protested against this practice for several decades; yet some feminists in countries where it is practised can also recognise that it is part of a culture's heritage and it brings with it enormous ritual significance. A woman's identity and life can be destroyed if she does not submit to the practice. It cannot therefore be easily changed. So although the United Nations has led efforts against it, and it has been outlawed in some 15 of the 28 countries where it existed, the practice often continues due to its deep roots.

Medically, the consequences of genital mutilation are more than loss of sexual pleasure. Pain is excruciating and may persist, along with the danger of infection, infertility and even death. This is a system that distorts medicine into a brutal form of political and sexual control.

For more details of countries involved and the practices and politics of FGM, see the Female Genital Cutting Education and Networking Project at: www.fgmnetwork.org.

- *Pornography and dehumanisation.* The pornography industry is estimated to be worth $97 billion worldwide (Banyard, 2010: 154) and is overwhelmingly directed against women. Recent accounts suggest that with the rise of the internet there has been a massive increase in the volume of imagery and the growth of extreme images (for some descriptions of this pornography, see: Banyard, 2010; Walker, 2010). Much of pornography is now also DIY. See the *Big debate* at the end of the chapter.

- *Regulation of dress and demeanour.* This is a highly contentious area but it includes debates about footbinding in China, high heels in the fashion industry, and the sexualisation of women's bodies as younger girls are willing (or want) to wear less clothing in public.

- *Sexual murder.* Half of all female murder victims are killed by their partners, and serial murders are usually against women.

Of course, as we know (Chapters 3 and 9) such figures are not always reliable and are often hard to interpret. Nevertheless the cumulative evidence suggests that there is a major issue of violence against women across the world. The core of understanding these issues is to see them not as 'women's issues' but as part of a gender regime in which patriarchy plays a key organising role. We need to see women and men through their relationships with each other: beatings and sexual violence are often just woven into the texture of a man and a woman's relationship.

Is patriarchy inevitable?

Technologically simple societies have little control over biological forces. Thus, men's greater physical strength, as well as women's common experience of pregnancy, combine to bolster patriarchy. Technological advances, however, give members of industrial societies a wider range of choices about gender. Industrial machinery has diminished the primacy of muscle power in everyday life, just as contraception has given women control over pregnancy. Today, then, biological differences provide little justification for patriarchy.

Categorical social inequality – whether based on race, ethnicity or sex – also comes under attack in the more egalitarian culture of industrial societies. In many industrial nations, law mandates equal employment opportunities for women and men and equal pay for comparable efforts. Nonetheless, in all industrial societies, the two sexes continue to hold different jobs and receive unequal pay, as we will explain presently. So does the persistence of patriarchy mean that it is inevitable? Some sociologists contend that biological factors underlie sex-based differences – especially a greater level of aggressiveness on the part of males. If this is so, of course, the eradication of patriarchy would be difficult and perhaps even impossible (Goldberg, 1974, 1993; Rossi, 1985; Popenoe, 1993). However, most sociologists believe that gender is primarily a social construction, subject to change. Simply because no society has yet eliminated patriarchy, then, does not mean that we must remain prisoners of the past.

To understand why patriarchy has persisted throughout human history, we need to see how gender is rooted and reproduced in society, a process that begins with the way we learn to think of ourselves as children and continues through the work we perform as adults.

Asking 'Where are the women in all this?'

In every account of society, and every discussion of it, an important question to ask is: Where are the women in all this? Is there a different pattern of social life for men and women? What are the different issues raised here for men and women?

Some sociologists claim that, in the past, when the word 'society' was used it always meant 'male society', and this masked what a different experience society can be for men and women. More recently, some postmodern work tries to suggest that even using the terms 'men' and 'women' reinforces gender segregation. We need to be aware of this, but at the same time public sociology needs to keep on asking: *Just where are the 'women' in all this?*

For example, when you discuss:

- *Global life*: ask how women fare in different contries around the world. In some – like the Scandinavian countries – they fare much better than others (see Chapter 9 for details of the world gender gap).

- *The economy*: ask about the likelihood of: lower pay, fewer opportunities to achieve (the glass ceiling), different kinds of work ('shift work' and care), and the balance of unpaid work – raising children, domestic labour and caring work. How many women are in the Rich List? (look at Chapter 15).

- *The polity*: ask about the rights to vote in a society (and when women got them), the number of women in official positions of power, the women who are world leaders, the numbers of women at war and the numbers in the peace movement (look at Chapter 16).

- *Crime*: ask about how many women commit crimes – compared to men? How many

women go to prison? How many are violent and kill? How are women's problems with the law handled? (look at Chapter 17)

- *Religion*: ask about the number of world religions that have female gods, or women spokespeople. How are women treated by their religions? Are they prohibited from certain gatherings, spaces or positions? (look at Chapter 19)

- *Family*: ask about the roles of men and women in raising children – psychologically, materially, socially and for life (look at Chapter 18).

- *Health*: ask about women's illnesses – and men's. Just how do the patterns differ?

The 'answers' to all these questions can be found in the relevant chapters of this book, and you may like to dig them out! Or you can look at: Geoff Payne (ed.), *Social Divisions* (2006), which gives evidence and discusses the issues for the UK (look at Chapter 21).

Sex trafficking, tourism and the sex trade in Thailand

One form of modern slavery that reveals the exploitation and abuse of women across the world is sex trafficking. This involves the recruitment, transportation, and then 'holding' of women, girls and boys by force (or abduction and fraud) – usually people in positions of great vulnerability. Large sums of money change hands for sex.

For example, Thailand is one of many countries across the world involved in this. In some cases, parents sell female infants to agents who pay others to raise them, then 'harvest their crop' when the girls approach their teenage years and are old enough to work the sex trade. In other cases, girls who see little future in a rural village make their own way to the city, only to fall into the hands of pimps who soon have them working in brothels, soliciting in bars or performing in sex shows. Pimps provide girls with clothes and housing, but at a price that exceeds the girls' salaries. The result is a system of debt bondage that keeps

women virtual prisoners of their unscrupulous employers. Those who run away are pursued by agents and forced to return.

The future for these girls, women and boys may be very bleak. Most experience violence and degradation; they suffer from a host of diseases brought on by abuse and neglect; and 40 per cent are now infected with the virus that causes AIDS. It has been suggested that there are at least 2 million prostitutes in Thailand; but a figure like this would mean that one in four Thai women between the ages of 15 and 29 would be a prostitute. This claim needs careful reflection. Reliable

WORLD WATCH

'Sex trafficking' is now a major industry all around the world. Here sex workers sit on steps in India awaiting trade
Source: © Jeffrey L. Rotman/Corbis.

statistics on sexual trafficking are notoriously hard to find. Meanwhile, the government of Thailand protests about its country being internationally identified with sex trafficking (Bangkok is often seen as the sex capital of the world) and it has put measures in place to control sex work.

In any event, it is quite wrong to isolate one country like Thailand. Sex trafficking is a global issue and a multi-billion-dollar global business. It is not the same as sex tourism – which is 'sexual intercourse while away from home', but it can be, and often is, linked. Basically, sex trafficking involves the degrading move of women from the poorer countries to the richer countries for sexual purposes: from Latin America to the USA, from eastern Europe and Africa to western Europe; from Vietnam to Thailand; and from Thailand to Japan. Governments are trying to

create an international response, but it is difficult. This is a worldwide phenomenon. The 2003 UN Trafficking Protocol is an attempt to create an international response.

You can find details about sex trafficking on the websites of organisations like Human Trafficking.org (www.humantrafficking.org) and the Coalition Against Trafficking in Women (www.catw-ap.org/facts.htm). See also: Kempadoo and Doezema (1998); Davidson (1998); and the film written by Abu Morgan, *Sex Trafficking* (2004), which looks at the global business of young women being forced into prostitution in European and American cities. Laura María Agustín (2007) provides a more critical view.

 Films on sex trafficking can be found at: http://children.foreignpolicyblogs.com/human-trafficking-and-slavery-related-movies-and-documentaries.

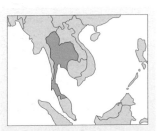

COUNTRY FACT FILE

THAILAND

Population	65,000,000 (2005)
Per capita GDP	$9,200 (2006)
Life expectancy	71.7 years (2006)
Literacy	around 93% (1995)
Language	Thai or Siamese
Religions	Buddhism (94%)
Main city	Bangkok: 1.6 million in 1958, 5.6 million in 1999, and now nearly 7 million (2007)
Urban population	33% of total (2007)
Human development index	0.702 (70th, 2010)

Becoming gendered: the case of gender socialisation

The first question people usually ask about a newborn (and nowadays a pre-born too!) – 'Is it a boy or a girl?' – looms large because the answer involves not just sex but the likely direction of the child's entire life. In fact, gender is at work even before the birth of a child, since in many parts of the world parents generally hope to have a boy rather than a girl. In China, India and other strongly patriarchal societies, female embryos are at risk because parents may abort them, hoping later to produce a boy, whose social value is greater.

There is a huge amount of research and theorising on gender development, but three broad traditions can be briefly distinguished.

1 *Social learning theories*. These suggest that differences in gender behaviour are learnt, in the same way as all behaviours, through a mixture of rewards, reinforcements and punishments. From its earliest day the baby boy is rewarded for behaving in 'boyish' ways and punished for being 'girl-like'. Often, this theory suggests how boys come to model themselves upon or imitate the behaviour of other men and boys, as this will be most highly praised and rewarded. The boy, in effect, thinks, 'I want rewards. I am rewarded for doing boy things, therefore I want to be a boy.' It is a very widely held theory, and a very simple one.

2 *Cognitive theories*. These suggest that differences in gender emerge through a categorisation process in which boys come to place themselves in a 'masculine' category and proceed to organise their experiences around it. Here the boy, in effect, says 'I am a boy, therefore I want to do boy things.' Some of these theories suggest that there may be preformed stages at which such identifications can take place, while others suggest that the identities emerge out of social contexts. Kohlberg (1981) is a major proponent of this view. Go to any primary school and you will soon see how boys and girls seem to sort themselves into groups of their own sex, and this continues a lifelong process of being reinforced within particular gender patterns.

3 *Psychodynamic theories*. These, derived from Freud (introduced in Chapter 7), suggest that differences in gender emerge out of emotional struggles between the infant and its caretakers in the earliest years of life. Most classically, a boy's emotional structure emerges from the conflict between the love of his mother and the fear of his father which, if resolved successfully, will eventually lead the boy to identify strongly with his father and hence with masculinity. Psychodynamic theorists disagree with each other over the nature of this conflict and its timing, but it is basic to this theory that gender is structured 'unconsciously' into a deep emotional form in early childhood.

Each of these theories has many variants, is very widely held and has spawned a massive research and analytical literature. In general, the virtues of one theory are the weaknesses of the others, and each theory has its own emphasis, behaviour, cognition or emotion. It is far beyond the scope of this book to review all this material, but here we will focus on the Freudian tradition.

Nancy Chodorow and the reproduction of mothering

How do little girls grow up to become mothers? Why don't boys? Chodorow (1978) starts her analysis by criticising some of the most popular explanations of gender differences – those that stress biology, social learning and role learning. Although such theories may be partially correct, they all fail to deal adequately with the way in which gender differences are organised into the deep psychic structuring of individuals. She prefers to use a Freudian theory (introduced in Chapter 7). For her, masculinity and femininity are rooted in strong emotional structures established very early in life and are very hard to transform. Men in Anglo-Saxon culture tend, on the whole, to become more emotionally restricted yet more independent, and more work- and achievement-orientated than women, who seem to 'connect better'. Men often lack a 'connectedness' to relate to loved ones, while girls tend to develop stronger attachments and reproduce this in mothering. Of course, these are generalisations. (They are not that dissimilar to Talcott Parsons's distinctions between expressive and instrumental roles, discussed below.)

Chodorow (1978) argues that, in order to understand the development of these strong emotional structures, we have to go back to the intense connections between child and mother in which both baby boy and baby girl are overwhelmingly dependent upon the mother. (Note that this is true of Western culture; it is by no means true of all.) From the beginning of life there is a process of forming strong attachments and dependencies with the mother, and an accompanying sense of anxiety and fear when she is absent. There is a massive identification of both boy and girl with the 'mother' – the primary caregiver who suckles, shelters and comforts the baby. The image of the mother is incorporated and internalised by the child.

So far, the description holds for both boys and girls. Bit by bit, the child has to break away from the strong identification with the carer, to test its competence against the outside world. Although both the baby girl and baby boy are primarily attached to the mother, the girl remains attached while the boy breaks away. The little girl does not outgrow her dependency, she does not develop a strong sense of separateness and boundaries, and this leads her ultimately to identify with the needs of others more than boys. In later life this asserts itself as the need for mothering. 'The basic feminine sense of self is connected to the world, the basic masculine sense of self is separate' (Chodorow, 1978: 169).

While the little girl stays in close identification with the mother and ultimately attains a less separate, more connected sense of identity, the little boy is pushed into a sharper, stronger and earlier separation. This rupture may be experienced as an abandonment and generate lifelong anxieties around rejection. For many boys, so the story goes, this leads to a turning to the outer world (especially of hitherto relatively insignificant fathers) and the establishment of a separate, autonomous identity – one fearful of connecting in case of abandonment, and often open to rage against the long-lost love object, the mother. In one swoop male autonomy, male inexpressiveness and male hostility towards women are explained!

Critical comment

Although this theory is influential, critics have worried that the evidence for it is inadequate: it depends on a few clinical cases for generalisations. Feminist critics have also accused the theory of 'blaming the victim', of ultimately blaming mothers for the reproduction of male power in their sons (see Trebilcot, 1984). Other critics also see the theory as presenting a model of development that is too unchangeable. These days, for example, we see many 'modern' 'new' men who

are very seriously involved in 'mothering' – or 'parenting', as it is increasingly called. Chodorow responds by saying that, although gender identity is established in early lives, it is only a provisional structure and one that is open to change in later life. Indeed, she advocates fathers being much more involved in raising children, so that it breaks the cycle of motherhood and both boys and girls find nurturance in fathers as well as mothers (Chodorow, 1978).

Gender across the life cycle

Chodorow's theory needs supplementing by looking at both wider influences on the child (peer group, school, workplace), and transformations over the life cycle. There is, for instance, a considerable body of research that suggests that childhood worlds are highly segregated by gender and that this segregation works to structure gender identity. Likewise, there is research on the male life cycle that suggests that as men become older they often change into more emotionally responsive and less powerfully autonomous people than was evidenced in their youth and childhood. Gender emerges over the entire life cycle through a series of ever-changing encounters in which meaning is built up, modified and transformed. Gender is not something fixed at any time, but is a process constantly open to historical changes in the wider world, local changes in situation and biographical shifts over the life cycle.

Gender and work

Andrew Tolson in a pioneering English study of masculinity, *The Limits of Masculinity* (1977), suggested that in addition to early family experiences there are three major sites for boys and men in which gender is formed and structured: the peer group, the school and the workplace. He was particularly keen to emphasise the *importance of the workplace* in reinforcing male identity. Just as adult female lives often become swamped by thinking about 'their children', so male lives become overwhelmed by 'their work' – seeking success in it, dealing with boredom from it, finding alternatives to it, being humiliated by lack of it. In many ways this concern with work as a key to male identity simply reflects the earlier experiences of childhood – the quest for power, autonomy and the concomitant anxiety about failure and rejection.

'It's only natural': are gender and sexuality really socially constructed?

Some of the most popularly held assumptions in society are about gender and sex. 'Everybody' seems to believe that men are biologically men, women are biologically women, and sex is natural. To put it bluntly: 'Motherhood is natural to women', 'sex is a naturally powerful drive', 'men are naturally more aggressive', 'some men can't help rape – it's their sex drive that is too strong', 'men are naturally promiscuous' – these and hundreds of similar observations (perhaps you could list some more) are pervasive 'commonsense' assumptions found in everyday life. Sexual differences are – after all – 'only natural'.

Turning to the scientific literature, it is easy to find a large amount of research to justify this 'only natural' view of the world. From the writings of the early social Darwinians to contemporary sociobiologists, from research on 'hormones' to research on 'sex differences in the brain', from theories of 'aggression' to theories of 'male bonding', many writers who claim the authority of science have been concerned with laying out the biological foundations for gender.

Now, although nobody would wish to deny the role of the biological substratum in human activities – it clearly sets constraints on what is humanly possible – many social scientists suggest that some of these biological claims are extravagant and overstated. They have conducted a large amount of research on gender and sexuality, and done a great deal of thinking about it, and argue that human sexualities and human gender are always and everywhere socially constructed. That is, the social shapes of gender and sexuality are bound up with the economic, religious, political and cultural times people live in. This is, again, not to deny the biological. But it is to stress what many people refuse to acknowledge. Sexualities and genders are always humanly produced in social contexts and we must look at these if we are to understand them.

Among the main observations that sociologists make are:

- *The importance of history, culture, the social and the symbolic.* Whatever the biological substratum of human life, there is much evidence from the humanities and the social sciences that suggests significant variations in human experience across cultures and history – from classic anthropological work which claims to show that men may be 'feminine' and women may be 'masculine' (see the box on Margaret Mead, p. 393) to historical research which suggests how living arrangements such as 'the family' can be organised very differently. The 'biological' always has to be mediated by the symbolic in order for it to be social. Imagine, for instance, what human sexuality would be like if it were unmediated by meaning – a world of uncoordinated erections and lubrications, of sexuality without rule or fantasy, of fumbling inabilities to interpret acts, orgasms, objects or people as sexual. Biology may provide cues, impulses and constraints, but all of this has to be interpreted through history and culture. Human beings are symbol manipulators who make and inhabit worlds of meaning which can be transmitted and modified from generation to generation. We have 'culture' and a 'history' in ways that other animals do not.

- *The issue of reductionism.* Biological arguments have a tendency to be overly simple, reducing vastly complex human civilisations and historical epochs to a chromosome, a hormone, a gene. It is suggested by some sociobiologists (for example, Goldberg, 1974, 1993) that all the complexities of long historical processes and variations can be squashed into one hormone. Often, such claims are used to capture not only the past and the present, but also the future. Consider a famous observation by one of the world's leading sociobiologists, E. O. Wilson:

  In the hunter-gatherer societies, men hunt and women stay at home. This strong bias persists in agricultural societies and on that ground alone appears to have a genetic origin. The genetic basis is intense enough to cause a substantial division of labour even in the most free and most egalitarian of future societies.

  (Quoted in Sayers, 1982: 29)

Even without any training in sociobiology, you can probably see some criticisms which might be made. Would it be fair to say it is reductionist and oversimple – that is, does it reduce complex social phenomena to unitary biological ones? Wilson is one of the most sophisticated sociobiologists and there is much of value in his work, but he is still capable of making generalisations that pay no attention to the complex variations of human societies.

- *Problems of science and refutation*. Although there are many biological explanations of most social phenomena, from crime and race relations to the family and gender, in most cases there are strong disagreements among biologists. Claims of truth are made prematurely. There are endless controversies even within biology over the role of hormones, chromosomes and genes. Those interested in reading a biologist's analysis of the evidence on gender might find Anne Fausto-Sterling's *Myths of Gender: Biological Theories about Men and Women* (1992) to be valuable. She is a biologist, and reviews the evidence on such issues as hormones and aggression,

menstruation and female behaviour, intelligence and men, and in all cases she finds little evidence of straightforward biological causation of human behaviour. And others such as Donna Haraway (a 'scientist' who is highlighted in the box in Chapter 23, p. 810) refute any such simple biological ideas.

- *Problems of ideology*. It is important to ask just why the 'it's only natural' types of argument are so popular when the world is more complex and the explanations it provides are too simple. The answer to this may well lie not in the truth of the biological claims but in the ways in which they can be socially used. They come to serve ideological functions – in providing simple, uncomplicated answers that typically reaffirm the existing social order and the division of gender roles.

- *Problems of the future and change*. Many social scientists demonstrate the ways in which genders and sexualities keep on changing. But much of biological arguing persists in telling us how we stay the same. But, however biological sex may be, we are also moral

and political animals living in societies that change. And we thus need to be wary of the ways in which biological arguments can be produced to legitimate the social order: and in this case biological male dominance and biological male aggression. The moral dimension is not the same as the biological. As Janet Richards, a 'sceptical feminist', has put it:

> And suppose that men are naturally dominant because of the miraculous testosterone of which we hear so much these days. Why should feminists be reluctant to admit or anti-feminists to think that it clinches their case? Even if men are naturally inclined to dominance it does not follow that they ought to run everything. Their being naturally dominant might be an excellent reason for imposing special restrictions to keep their nature under control. We do not think that the men whose nature inclines them to rape ought to be given free rein to go around raping, so why should the naturally dominant be allowed to go around dominating?
>
> (Richards, 1982: 64)

Traditional sociological understandings of gender

Although they come to differing conclusions, the functional and conflict paradigms can again help us here: each points up the importance of gender to social organisation.

Functional analysis

As Chapter 4 suggested, members of hunting and gathering societies had little power over the forces of biology. Lacking effective birth control, women experienced frequent pregnancies, and the responsibilities of childcare kept them close to home. Likewise, to take advantage of greater male strength, norms guided men towards the pursuit of game and other tasks away from the home. Over many generations, this sexual division of labour became institutionalised and largely taken for granted (Lengermann and Wallace, 1985).

Industrial technology opens up a vastly greater range of cultural possibilities. Human muscle power no longer serves as a vital source of energy, so the physical strength of men loses much of its earlier significance. At the same time, the ability to control reproduction gives women greater choice in shaping their lives. Modern societies come to see that traditional gender roles waste an enormous amount of human talent; yet change comes slowly because gender is deeply embedded in social mores.

Talcott Parsons: gender and complementarity

In addition, as Talcott Parsons (1942; 1964, orig. 1951; 1964, orig. 1954) explained, gender differences help to integrate society – at least in its traditional form. Gender, Parsons noted, forms a *complementary* set of roles that links men and women together into family units that carry out various functions vital to the operation of society. Women take charge of family life, assuming primary responsibility for managing the household and raising children. Men, by contrast, connect the family to the larger world, primarily by participating in the labour force.

Parsons further argued that distinctive socialisation teaches the two sexes their appropriate gender identity and skills needed for adult life. Thus society teaches boys – presumably destined for the labour force – to be rational, self-assured and competitive. This complex of traits Parsons termed *instrumental*. To prepare girls for child-rearing, their socialisation stresses what Parsons called *expressive* qualities, such as emotional responsiveness and sensitivity to others.

Society, explains Parsons, promotes gender-linked behaviour through various schemes of social control. People incorporate cultural definitions about gender into their own identities, so that failing to be appropriately feminine or masculine produces guilt and fear of rejection by members of the opposite sex. In simple terms, women learn to view non-masculine men as sexually unattractive, while men learn to avoid unfeminine women.

Critical comment

Functionalism advances a theory of complementarity by which gender integrates society both structurally

(in terms of what people do) and morally (in terms of what they believe). Although influential in the mid-twentieth century, this approach is rarely used today by researchers exploring the impact of gender.

For one thing, the analysis assumes a singular vision of society that is not shared by everyone. Poor women, for example, have always worked outside the home as a matter of economic necessity; today, more and more women at all social levels are entering the labour force for various reasons. A second problem, say the critics, is that Parsons' analysis minimises the personal strains and social costs produced by rigid, traditional gender roles (Giele, 1988). Third, and finally, to those whose goals include sexual equality, what Parsons describes as gender complementarity amounts to little more than male domination. As is often the case, we find that functionalist analysis has a conservative cast.

Conflict analysis

It is a different story from a conflict point of view: gender now involves not just differences in behaviour but disparities in power. Conventional ideas about gender have historically benefited men while subjecting women to prejudice, discrimination and sometimes outright violence, in a striking parallel to the treatment of racial and ethnic minorities (Hacker, 1951; Collins, 1971; Lengermann and Wallace, 1985). Thus, conflict theorists claim, conventional ideas about gender promote not cohesion but tension and conflict, with men seeking to protect their privileges while women challenge the status quo.

As earlier chapters noted, the conflict paradigm draws heavily on the ideas of Karl Marx. Yet Marx was a product of his time in so far as his writings focused almost exclusively on men. His friend and collaborator Friedrich Engels, however, did explore the link between gender and social class (1902; orig. 1884).

Friedrich Engels: gender and class

Looking back through history, Engels noted that in hunting and gathering societies the activities of women and men, though different, had comparable importance. A successful hunt may have brought men great prestige, but the vegetation gathered by women constituted most of a society's food supply (Leacock, 1978). As technological advances led to a productive surplus, however, social equality and communal sharing gave way to private property and, ultimately, a class hierarchy. At this point, men gained pronounced power over women. With surplus wealth to pass on to heirs, upper-class men took a keen interest in their children. The desire to control property, then, prompted the creation of monogamous marriage and the family. Ideally, men could be certain of paternity – especially who their sons were – and the law ensured that wealth passed to them. The same logic explains why women were taught to remain virgins until marriage, to remain faithful to their husbands thereafter and to build their lives around bearing and raising children.

According to Engels, capitalism intensifies this male domination. First, capitalism creates more wealth, which confers greater power on men as wage earners as well as owners and heirs of property. Second, an expanding capitalist economy depends on defining people – especially women – as consumers and convincing them that personal fulfilment derives from owning and using products. Third, to allow men to work, society assigns women the task of maintaining the home. The double exploitation of capitalism, as Engels saw it, lies in paying low wages for male labour and no wages for female work (Eisenstein, 1979; Barry, 1983; Vogel, 1983).

Critical comment

Conflict analysis highlights how society places the two sexes in unequal positions of wealth, power and privilege. As a result, the conflict approach is decidedly critical of conventional ideas about gender, claiming that society would be better off if we minimised or even eliminated this dimension of social structure.

But conflict analysis, too, has its limitations. One problem, critics suggest, is that this approach casts conventional families – defended by traditionalists as morally positive – as a social evil. Second, from a more practical standpoint, conflict analysis minimises the extent to which women and men live together cooperatively and often quite happily. A third problem with this approach, for some critics, is its assertion that capitalism stands at the root of gender stratification. Agrarian countries, in fact, are typically more patriarchal than industrial–capitalist nations. And socialist societies, too – including the People's Republic of China – remain strongly patriarchal.

 See Rosemarie Tong, *Feminist Thought: A More Comprehensive Introduction* (3rd edn, 2008).

Spotlight
Theories of gender in summary

Scattered through this chapter you will find many key theories of gender mentioned. Here is a brief summary guide to what are often identified as some key theoretical positions:

- *Classical functionalism*: gender flows from gender roles and creates the smooth running of society.
- *Early socialist Marxism*: gender is a basic form of exploitation in the family between men and women.
- *Learning theories*: gender is socially learnt.
- *Psychodynamic theories*: gender is learnt through emotional crisis in early life.
- *Symbolic interactionist theories*: gender brings multiple symbolic meanings negotiated in everyday life.
- *Labour market theory*: gender is structured through the public sphere (low pay for women) and the private sphere (women's exploited domestic labour and child-rearing)
- *Radical feminism and sexual control*: gender is organised through male dominance, their sexuality and sexual needs, and the regulation of women's bodies.
- *Performative theory*: gender is a stylised repetition of acts.
- *Social constructionism*: gender is historically produced, socially organised and contextually changed.
- *Postmodernism*: gender is one of a flow of differences, never fixed and stable, and always fragmented and changing.
- *Intersectionality theories*: gender is one part of a matrix of inequalities including race, class, age, sexuality and nation.
- *Queer theory*: gender is organised through heterosexuality and a clear gender binary, both of which need 'deconstructing' and 'destablising'.

Resisting patriarchy: the women's movement and new theories of feminism

Feminism is *the advocacy of social equality for the sexes, in opposition to patriarchy and sexism.* With roots in the English Revolution and the French Revolution – each with its concern over equality – the 'first wave' of the feminist movement was initiated with Mary Wollstonecraft's *A Vindication of the Rights of Woman*

(1992; orig. 1792) and continued with the liberal classic by John Stuart Mill and Harriet Taylor Mill, *The Subjection of Women* (1869). They argued against women's perceived (biologically) inferior status and argued for improved education and equality before the law. Many of the initial campaigns centred on morality and sexuality, and an end to slavery. Perhaps the primary objective of the early women's movement was securing the right to vote, which British women first exercised in the general election on 14 December 1918 (Banks, 1981; Rowbottom, 1997). But other disadvantages persisted and a 'second wave' of feminism arose in the 1960s. More recently, some suggest a third – maybe postmodern – wave has arrived.

Basic feminist ideas

Although people who consider themselves feminists disagree about many things, most would probably support five general principles:

1 *The importance of change.* Feminist thinking is decidedly political; it links ideas to action. Feminism is critical of the status quo, advocating social equality for women and men.

2 *Expanding human choice.* Feminists maintain that cultural conceptions of gender divide the full range of human qualities into two opposing and limited spheres: the female world of emotion and cooperation, and the male world of rationality and competition. As an alternative, feminists pursue a 'reintegration of humanity' by which each person develops all human traits (French, 1985).

3 *Eliminating gender stratification.* Feminism opposes laws and cultural norms that limit the education, income and job opportunities of women.

4 *Ending sexual violence.* A major objective of today's women's movement is eliminating sexual violence. Feminists argue that patriarchy distorts the relationships between women and men and encourages violence against women in the form of rape, domestic abuse, sexual harassment and pornography (Millet, 1970; Dworkin, 1987; L. Kelly, 1988).

5 *Promoting sexual autonomy.* Finally, feminism advocates women's control of their sexuality and reproduction. Feminists support the free availability of birth control information. Most feminists support a woman's right to choose whether to bear children or to terminate a pregnancy, rather than allowing men – as husbands, doctors and legislators – to regulate sexuality. Many feminists also align with the gay and lesbian movement to overcome homophobia and heterosexism (which will be discussed later) (Vance, 1984; Segal, 1997).

Variations within feminism

As one would expect, feminism is not cut from one cloth. Indeed, it has many internal conflicts and much variety. We consider a few below.

Variations by country

One way in which feminism varies is simply by country. While 'North American feminism' has

Reproductive politics
The battles over fertility, pregnancy and contraception

A key change in women's situation centres on their control over their reproductive ability. In many societies, women spend most of their lives reproducing large families of children and often also experiencing high infant mortality. Sociologists have documented a major decline in fertility and the rise of smaller families. Women's movements have been important in transforming fertility rates and in the development of reproductive politics – despite many groups being opposed. A major opposition, for example, comes from the Vatican. Look at:

- *Development*: Chapter 9 raises the issue of pregnancy, the importance of contraceptives and fertility control in poor societies where morbidity from pregnancy is high yet family size is also often larger.
- *Families*: Chapter 18 suggests the significance of the decline in size to the new '2 to 3' size of family.
- *Science*: Chapter 23 discusses the technologies, ethics and growth of new assisted conceptions and 'test tube babies'.
- *Populations*: Chapter 24 looks at different fertility rates across the world, the demographic transition, the decline in numbers of children, the empowering of women and the growth of the elderly.

probably become the most organised, public and vocal in the world, it has also bred what might be called a 'superstar feminism' whereby a number of women become very prominent through their writing and media work (for example, Betty Friedan, Susan Brownmiller, Susan Faludi, Naomi Wolf).

In Europe, feminists are less likely to be so media focused, and each country develops its own 'style' and set of conflicts. Angela Glasner has observed that:

Feminism in Europe exhibits a wide variety of forms ... the political context has ... been important in determining the specific form, and indeed in prescribing or proscribing feminism altogether. In Italy, Holland, Denmark and Norway, the second wave has been strongly influenced by left wing politics and has been predominantly led by middle class women. In France, the movement has been largely contained within the academic community, and in Germany it has been significantly diluted by conservatism.

(Glasner, 1992: 76–7)

We can also say that in Italy, Britain, Holland, Denmark and Norway it has been a more broadly based movement with alliances to the left. In Sweden the initiatives for change came much earlier: as a result, a strong collectivist culture emerged with women as a notable presence. Hence, there was little second-wave feminism as such. In the new democracies, by contrast (Spain, Portugal), hindered by both past authoritarianism and the Roman Catholic background, the women's movement has been slower to develop.

Theoretical and political divisions in feminism and feminist sociology

People pursue the goals of both understanding and eliminating gender inequality in different ways. Classically, three major distinctions have been found within feminism, though recently many others have been noticed. Although the distinctions among them are far from clear-cut, each describes the problem of patriarchy in somewhat different terms and calls for correspondingly distinctive strategies for social change (Banks, 1981; Barry, 1983; Stacey, 1983; Vogel, 1983).

Table 12.2	100 years of feminist campaigns	
The six demands of the Suffragettes 1919	**The seven demands of the 1970s Women's Liberation Movement**	**Feminist wants in 2010**
• Equal pay for equal work. • An equal standard of sex morals as between men and women, involving a reform of the existing divorce law which condoned adultery by the husband, as well as reform of the laws dealing with solicitation and prostitution. • The introduction of legislation to provide pensions for civilian widows with dependent children. • The equalisation of the franchise and the return to Parliament of women candidates pledged to the equality programme. • The legal recognition of mothers as equal guardians with fathers of their children. • The opening of the legal profession and the magistracy to women.	• Equal pay. • Equal education and job opportunities. • Free contraception and abortion on demand. • Free 24-hour nurseries. • Financial and legal independence. • End to all discrimination against lesbians; a woman's right to define her sexuality. • Freedom from intimidation by threat or use of violence or sexual coercion regardless of marital status, and an end to all laws which perpetuate male dominance and men's aggression to women.	• Liberated bodies. • Sexual freedom and choice. • An end to violence against women. • Equality at work and home. • Politics and religion transformed. • Popular culture free from sexism. • Feminism reclaimed.

Note: There is no simple agreement about the aims of the feminist movement. The above are provisional statements: the first in 1919 were the six major demands of the National Union of Women's Suffrage Societies; the second were produced out of regular Women's Liberation Conferences at Ruskin College, Oxford between 1970 and 1978; and the last is from Catherine Redfern and Kristin Aune's book on *The New Feminist Movement* (2010).

1 Liberal feminism

Liberal feminism is grounded in classic liberal thinking that individuals should be free to develop their own talents and pursue their own interests. Liberal feminists accept the basic organisation of our society but seek to expand the rights and opportunities of women. Liberal feminists support equal rights and oppose prejudice and discrimination that block the aspirations of women.

Liberal feminists also endorse reproductive freedom for all women. Some respect aspects of the family as a social institution, calling for widely available maternity leave and childcare for women who wish to work. Others are critical of the way in which the family reproduces gender and argue that freedom is not possible for women until families are dramatically changed (Okin, 1989).

With their strong belief in the rights of individuals, liberal feminists do not think that all women need to march in step towards any political goal. Both women and men, working individually, would be able to improve their lives if society simply ended legal and cultural barriers rooted in gender.

2 Socialist feminism

Socialist feminism evolved from Marxist conflict theory, in part as a response to how little attention Marx paid to gender, in part as a strategy to challenge both patriarchy and capitalism. Engels claimed that patriarchy (like

(a)

(a) Bella Abzug (1920–1998) ran for Congress and was one of the chief organisers of the Women's Liberation Day parade in New York, on the fiftieth anniversary of women winning the vote in the United States. She is carrying an anti-motherhood sign reading 'Free the female body from pain and inequality. Put motherhood in a test-tube.'
(b) The London suffragettes demonstrate and are arrested, 1910

Source: (a) Hulton Archive/Getty Images;
(b) Popperfoto/Getty Images.

(b)

class oppression) has its roots in private property; thus, capitalism intensifies patriarchy by concentrating wealth and power in the hands of a small number of men.

Socialist feminists view the reforms sought by liberal feminism as inadequate. The bourgeois family must be restructured, they argue, to end 'domestic slavery' in favour of some collective means of carrying out housework and childcare. The key to this goal, in turn, is a socialist revolution that creates a state-centred economy operating to meet the needs of all. Such a basic transformation of society requires that women and men pursue their personal liberation together, rather than individually, as liberal feminists maintain. (Further discussion of this view can be found in Chapter 18 and in Barrett, 1980.)

3 Radical feminism

Radical feminism, too, finds the reforms called for by liberal feminism inadequate and superficial. Moreover, radical feminists claim that even a socialist revolution would not end patriarchy. Instead, this variant of feminism holds that gender equality can be realised only by eliminating the cultural notion of gender itself. Fundamentally, say radical feminists, patriarchy rests on the subordination of women through sexuality and reproduction. Men exert power over and through women's bodies. We will consider this view in more detail below, when we discuss sexuality. Radical feminists seek to overthrow 'male sexuality', heterosexual parenting and the family.

There are many disagreements from within, however. Thus, some would support the new reproductive technologies – conception here can take place outside the body, so that there is no necessary link between women's bodies, men and child-bearing. With the demise of motherhood, radical feminists reason, the entire family system (including conventional definitions of motherhood, fatherhood and childhood) could be left behind, liberating women, men and children from the tyranny of family, gender and sex itself (Dworkin, 1987). But others see the new reproductive technologies as based on patriarchy and male science – a way of robbing women's rights over their own wombs. Further, they celebrate women's key role as mothers (see Richardson, 1993).

In general, radical feminists seek a revolutionary overthrow of the patriarchal order. Andrea Dworkin is a leading North American feminist who has suggested the centrality of male power and outlined its seven key dimensions. She writes as follows:

The power of men is first a metaphysical assertion of self – an I am that exists a priori, bedrock, absolute, no embellishment or apology required, indifferent to denial or challenge. Second, power is physical strength used over and against others less strong or without the sanction to use strength as power. Third, power is the capacity to terrorise, to use self and strength to inculcate fear – fear in a whole class of persons. The acts of terror run the gamut from rape to battery to sexual abuse of children to war to murder to maiming to torture to enslaving or kidnapping to verbal assault to cultural assault to threats of death to threats of harm backed up by the ability and sanction to deliver. The symbols of terror are commonplace and utterly familiar – the gun, the knife, the bomb, the fist, and so on. Even more significant is the hidden symbol of terror – the penis. Fourth, men have the power of naming, a great and sublime power. This power of naming enables men to define experience, to articulate boundaries and values, to designate to each thing its realm and qualities, to determine what can and cannot be expressed, to control perception itself. Fifth, men have the power of owning. Historically, this power has been absolute, denied to some men by other men in times of slavery and other persecution, but in the main upheld by armed force and law. In many parts of the world, the male right to own women and all that issues from them, children and labour, is still absolute. Sixth, the power of money is a distinctly male power. Money speaks, but it speaks with a male voice. In the hands of women, money stays literal, count it out, it buys what it is worth or less. In the hands of men, money buys women, sex, status, dignity, esteem, recognition, loyalty, all manner of possibility. In the hands of men, money does not only buy – it brings with it qualities, achievements, honour, respect. On every economic level, the meaning of money is significantly different for men than for women. Seventh, men have the power of sex. They assert the opposite, that this power resides in women, whom they view as synonymous with sex. He fetishises her body as a whole and in its parts. He exiles her from every realm of expression outside the strictly male-defined sexual or male-defined maternal. He forces her to become that thing that causes erection, then holds himself helpless and powerless when he is aroused by her. His fury when she is not that thing, when she is either more or less than that thing, is intense and punishing.

(Dworkin, 1981: 1)

4 Other feminisms

Although liberal, socialist and radical feminisms are seen as the basic divides among feminists – and ones that have quite a long history – many others are seen to exist. Among these are:

- *Psychoanalytic feminism*. This comprises those who draw from or respond to Freud and the work of psychoanalysis. We have seen something of this in the work of Nancy Chodorow cited earlier in this chapter. But there are a great many other feminists who draw upon various psychoanalytic traditions, focusing upon the formation of sexual identities. Some have been especially influenced by the work of the French thinker Jaques Lacan, who has reworked many of Freud's ideas to give a greater focus on the ways in which gender becomes encoded in language from the earliest years of childhood (see Beasley, 1999: Chapter 6).

- *Black feminism*. Some feminists are very critical of any 'unified' or 'essential' sense of what it means to be a woman, and make their argument clear by highlighting the fragmented and different positions of women who come from different backgrounds. They often adopt a 'black standpoint' and bring a critique to the (predominantly) white and middle-class women's movement. Often these groups (themselves split) can be linked to postcolonial struggles and the women's movement in countries all over the world (for example, Patricia Hill Collins, 1990).

- *Postmodern feminism*. Some feminists take the 'black' standpoint even further and, along with postmodernism, declare that there is no grand narrative of gender across all time and space. They challenge all universal categorisations of women (as well as other categories such as class and race) (Beasley, 1999).

- *The new international women's politics*. The main strands of feminism as located above have usually been seen as 'Western' and have sometimes been in tension with the aims of women from low-income or Third World societies. For them, struggles over religion, poverty and housing may take greater priority. And they may have organisational forms that are less confrontational and more collective than those found in the West. Recognising diversity and the different needs of women in contrasting cultures, a large international network of women has appeared globally. Notably, in 1995 many women were present at the United Nation's Women's Conference in Beijing, only to find a parallel amorphous grassroots conference for women from all over the world developing in Huairou, 60 kilometres away. As Christa Wichterich writes in her account of it:

> **It was a rainbow encompassing the most diverse structures and politics, from local rank and file and self help groups to well-funded lobbies and umbrella organisations: Women's World Banking alongside Canadian pro-life activists, the National Council of German Women's Organisations opposite Kuwait women widowed by the Iraqi invasion, Latin American lesbians and Indian peasants. And all conceivable shades between participant and representative politics were there in the marketplace.**
>
> (Wichterich, 2000: 145)

Sexualities

Sexuality and stratification

We start to see in the quote from Andrea Dworkin cited earlier, as well as in women's struggles over human rights, just how closely linked gender and sexuality may be, and how power may work to connect them. In this section, the focus now turns to **sexuality**: with those *aspects of the body and desire that are linked to the erotic*. This is usually seen as such a personal area of life that sociologists have not spent a great deal of time studying it. Indeed, most of our contemporary understanding of sexuality comes from the work of biologists, medical researchers and sexologists. They tend to look at hormones, brain structures, drives and instincts. From the writings of the earliest social Darwinians to the contemporary sociobiologists (see Chapters 2 and 23) and more recent research on hormones and differences in the brain, most researchers have been concerned with laying out the biological foundations of sexuality. This is also true of much common sense, too. People tend to assume that 'sex is only natural'. But recall from Chapter 1 that sociologists tend to challenge these natural, taken-for-granted views.

Thus, when sociologists started to study human sexuality, they soon realised that it is profoundly unlike that found in other animals. As the *Public sociology* box on p. 402 suggests, sociologists generally find problems with the overstatement of biological factors. Most sociologists who study sexuality argue that what is distinctive about human sexuality is that it is both (a) symbolic and meaningful, and (b) linked to power. We will consider some of these theories later, but here it will be helpful to start asking questions about the ways in which sexuality links to social stratification and social exclusion. At least five elements are important.

Sex control and negativism

All cultures have mechanisms to organise sexuality and no society allows a 'sexual free-for-all'. Human sexualities are patterned through law, religion and a range of social institutions such as kinship and family systems and economic and social organisation. Nevertheless there is great variation in the levels of control: some religions, for example, seek to regulate sexuality very strictly (for example, much of Islam); others less so. There are those who are positive about it, and those who are extremely sex-negative (Davis, 1983).

The hierarchy of sex

Closely linked to the above, Gayle Rubin (1984) talks of the ways in which societies come to classify and sort their different patterns of sexuality, such that some are valued, others are not. Figure 12.1 shows Rubin's sex hierarchy and provides a striking visual image of these evaluations. Rubin devised this hierarchy in the early 1980s and it is interesting to consider whether the items on it have shifted over the past 30 years.

The institutions and identities of heterosexuality

Heterosexuality is usually seen as the 'natural' foundation of society, but once again sociologists often approach this as a social construction of power in which men are forceful, driven by sex, and active, while women are usually believed to be more passive. Heterosexuality helps structure inequalities between the sexes and undermines a gender hierarchy – of what it is to be a man and a woman – along with a series of assumptions about what it means to 'have sex'. As an institution, heterosexuality fosters cultural forms such as heterosexual courtship and romance, and generates what is called a binary way of thinking: the world gets divided into heterosexual and homosexual. It also frequently embraces what has traditionally been called a 'double standard', where boys and men are seen as naturally more sexually active ('driven by drives') and girls and women less so. Indeed, once girls and

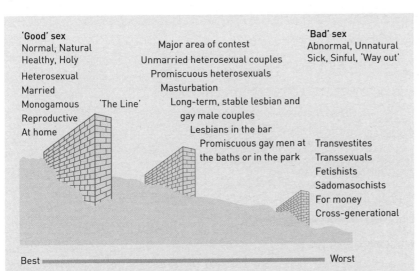

Figure 12.1 Rubin's sex hierarchy: the struggle over where to draw the line

Source: Adapted from Rubin (1989: 282). Reproduced from *Pleasure and Danger: Exploring Female Sexuality*, edited by Carol S. Vance (London: Pandora Press, 1989).

women do become more sexually active, they are often labelled by the boys and men as 'slags' and 'tarts' (Lees, 1993; Holland et al., 1998). The term 'compulsory heterosexuality' was introduced by the poet Adrienne Rich. Stevi Jackson is one of the UK's leading feminist sociologists to write about sexuality. She combines key themes around heterosexuality, patriarchy and power. Her work has recently been brought together in *Heterosexuality in Question* (Jackson, 1999).

The continuum of violence

Central to much feminist thinking (as we have already seen and will see further below) are the ways in which many women's lives are engulfed in violence perpetrated by men. Much of this is sexualised. Think of the sheer range of sexual experiences that can affect women – from the little wolf-whistles in the street to the pornographic photograph hanging in the office, from flashing and obscene phone calls to stalking and on to harassment, assault and pressurised sex. Liz Kelly speaks of 'pressurised sex' – when the woman (it could sometimes be a man) is expected to have sex even when she does not really want to: no direct force is involved. More apparent is coercive sex and, at the most extreme, rape, murder and genocide. These all exist alongside major systems of exclusion: class, race and gender.

Heterosexism and homophobia

Heterosexism – like racism and sexism – describes an ideology that categorises and then unjustly dismisses as inferior a whole group of fellow citizens; in the case of heterosexism, the group are people who are not heterosexual. It has been institutionalised in laws, education, religions and language across the world. Attempts to enforce heterosexuality are as much a violation of human rights as racism and sexism, and are now increasingly challenged with equal determination.

Homophobia is the fear of and resulting contempt for homosexuals. The term was coined in the early 1970s by an American psychiatrist George Weinberg, who defined it as *the dread of being in close quarters with homosexuals* (Weinberg, 1973). Table 12.3 lists a number of questions Weinberg introduces in his book in order to construct what he called the standard homophobia scale. A number of researchers have suggested that people intolerant of homosexuals are likely to be more authoritarian, more dogmatic, more cognitively rigid, more intolerant of ambiguity, more status-conscious, more sexually rigid, more guilty and negative about their sexual impulses, and less accepting of others in general (Morin and Garfinkle, 1978).

Even a major organisation for human rights such as Amnesty International came to recognise the problem of homophobia only in the last decade of the twentieth century (previously refusing to see it as a problem).

Table 12.3	Questions for Weinberg's standard homophobia scale	Yes	No
Homosexuals should not be allowed to hold government positions		☐	☐
It would be upsetting for me to find out I was alone with a homosexual		☐	☐
Homosexuals should not be allowed to hold government positions		☐	☐
I would not want to be a member of an organisation which had any homosexuals in its membership		☐	☐
I find the thought of homosexual acts disgusting		☐	☐
If laws against homosexuality were eliminated, the proportion of homosexuals in the population would probably remain about the same		☐	☐
A homosexual could be a good President of the United States		☐	☐
I would be afraid for a child of mine to have a teacher who was homosexual		☐	☐
If a homosexual sat next to me on the bus I would get nervous		☐	☐

Source: Adapted from Weinberg (1973).

Nevertheless, in a recent report, it showed that there are more than 70 countries with laws that criminalise homosexual acts, and a few of these – including Iran, Afghanistan, Saudi Arabia and Chechnya – have the death penalty for gay sex. Torture is common to extract confessions of 'deviance', gays are raped to 'cure them of it', and they are sometimes killed by death squads (Amnesty International, 2001).

Understanding sexualities: critical sexualities studies

As we saw in Chapter 5, language, symbols and communications are vital to human beings: it is through these that we become distinctively social beings. It should not therefore be surprising to find that this is what sociologists highlight.

It may be an interesting exercise to think about all the ways in which human sexuality differs from animal sexuality. Being firmly embedded in language and communication, we become the 'talking' and 'thinking' sex. That is, we can talk and think about sex in elaborate ways which animals cannot. We can write books about it, develop pornographic representations of it, discuss it, create fantasies about it and ultimately develop a highly sophisticated language of sex (Weeks, 2011). Animals do not. Further, we often tend to use sex for social ends, not just biological goals such as reproduction. When asked why they have sex, they rarely just say 'I was driven by my biology'. Instead they see it as an expression of love, as a means to establish bonding, as a way of being clear about manliness or womanliness, or indeed our maturity. It can be used to show our aggression (as in rape) or to fill up our boredom or as a kind of hobby. It can be used as play, as performance, as power and as a form of work (for example, prostitution). One recent article suggested that there are some 237 reasons that people give for having sex (Merton and Buss, 2007)!

In what follows, we look at three major theoretical approaches that work from a social view of sexualities.

1 Social constructions and scripting theory

Drawing on this, William Simon and John Gagnon were the founders of what has now become commonly known as the 'social constructionist' approach to sexuality. Both worked at the Kinsey Institute for Sexual Behavior in the 1960s, collecting and unearthing mounds of empirical data. And yet in the midst of this, both felt the need to look at what was happening in a more sociological way. To do this, they suggested that the metaphor of *script* was much more useful in understanding sexuality for humans than was biology (Gagnon and Simon, 1973). In scripting theory, human sexualities are best seen as drama. In Chapter 7, we saw how Erving Goffman viewed social life as drama. This idea can also be applied to sexuality. An elaborate set of stagecraft rules and performance guides our sexualities and brings them into action. Sex, for human beings, is not a matter of automatic sexual release; instead sexuality must have life breathed into it through drama. **Sexual scripts**, then, are *guidelines that help define the who, what, where, when and even why we have sex.*

Think for a minute of any sexual act, from that of 'a man and wife engaged in coitus inside marriage' to 'a woman engaged in prostitution' to 'a gay man meeting another in a gay bar'. In all cases, what has to be distinctive about these encounters is that they do not just happen 'out of the blue'. They depend upon rituals, signs and symbols to make sense of it all. In each case, certain people are defined as appropriate partners (the *who*). The activities can take place only in certain places (the *where*) – they cannot take place anywhere: places are limited. They define more or less what can be done – prostitutes set agreements and limits, partners know what is expected and do not usually go beyond boundaries (the *what*). Likewise, we cannot just do sex whenever we wish to – it is bounded into certain times (the *when*). And finally, when we come to talk about it – or just privately reflect on it – we start to tell ourselves the reasons why we did these things (the *why*).

Gagnon and Simon suggest that sexual scripts are crucial to human sexualities and they outline three major forms they can take. *Personal scripts* are those within our heads – telling us, for instance, what turns us on. *Interactive scripts* are those which emerge between partners or groups, telling what each person is expected to do. *Historical–cultural scripts* are those scripts which exist in the wider culture and which tell us what is expected of us sexually. Fieldwork studies have been conducted of sexual encounters, ranging from situations of rape and striptease to those of homosexual 'cruising' and 'sadomasochism', which attempt to unravel these scripts.

2 Discourses of sexualities

Closely linked is the 'discourse' approach to sexuality. Following on from the work of Michel Foucault (introduced in Chapter 17), many sociologists see sexuality as being located within an elaborate language structure that organises power relations. They are concerned with seeing the ways in which language shapes the way we see sex. A language approach to sex might, for instance, look at the ways in which 'chat shows' like *Oprah* let people talk about sex on television, and how this has some influences in the wider society. Or it may look at the ways in which new categories of sexual problems – sex addiction, AIDS, child sex abuse – come to be constructed and how they develop a language of their own. Much of our sexual life is lived through these discourses, and sociologists have increasingly turned their attention to them.

Foucault's study, *The History of Sexuality* (1979; orig. 1976), provides a major entrance to this way of thinking about sex and has been very influential. He suggests that the nineteenth century was not a time when sex was silenced and repressed, as was once commonly thought. On the contrary, he argues that it was a time when people were encouraged to talk more and more about it – usually in very negative ways. There was what he called 'an incitement to discourse' – people were encouraged to talk. Thus it was a time when scientists started to study sex (the psychiatrists and the sexologists); a time when new categories of sexuality came into being (like 'the hysterical woman', the 'masturbating child', 'the pervert' and the Malthusian Couple); and a time when sexualities became reorganised through all this talk into new forms of power relationships (Foucault, 1979; orig. 1976).

3 Feminist theories of sexuality

A third important impetus for the sociological study of sexuality has come from feminists, though as we might expect from the different positions outlined above there has been little agreement on a common approach. We will look briefly at two: the radical feminists and the libertarian socialists.

(a) Radical feminism

In the radical feminist version, sexuality is seen to be one of the key mechanisms through which men have regulated women's lives. The nineteenth-century feminists recognised this when they waged war on prostitution, venereal disease, the low age of consent and immorality of all forms. They saw this as generated by men: as Frances Swiney wrote: 'women's redemption from sex slavery can only be achieved through man's redemption from sex-obsession'. The solution to the problem was

'votes for women and chastity for men' (see Jeffreys, 1987). Through establishing anti-vice organisations, their aim was to stop men's debauchery.

Late-twentieth-century radical feminists have taken these arguments even further. They characterise the central features of sexuality as being male. Thus sexuality is centred on the penis, is aggressive, takes place devoid of emotional sensitivity and is often extremely fixated and fetishistic. It is men who rape, abuse and harass. It is men who buy and use pornography and pay sex workers. It is men who become serial sex offenders and sex killers.

Radical feminists argue that it is through men's sexuality exerting control over women's bodies that women are subordinated. Rape is the clear symbol here: it is not about sexual release, so much as about male power and violence. It is a mechanism through which 'all men keep all women in a constant state of fear'. Out of this wing of the women's movement have grown the campaigns over pornography, the battles against child sex abuse and over violence against women in the home, and the development of new arguments about rape and the setting up of rape crisis centres. Two of these will be briefly considered below.

The case of sexual harassment

Sexual harassment refers to *comments, gestures or physical contact of a sexual nature that are deliberate, repeated and unwelcome*. During the 1990s, sexual harassment became an issue of national importance that has already significantly redefined the rules for workplace interaction between the sexes.

Most victims of sexual harassment are women. This is because, first, our culture encourages men to be sexually assertive and to perceive women in sexual terms; social interaction in the workplace, on campus and elsewhere, then, can readily take on sexual overtones. Second, most individuals in positions of power – including business executives, doctors, assembly-line supervisors, university lecturers and military officers – are men who oversee the work of women. Surveys carried out in widely different work settings confirm that half of women respondents report receiving unwanted sexual attention (Loy and Stewart, 1984; Paul, 1991).

Sexual harassment is sometimes blatant and direct, as when a supervisor solicits sexual favours from a subordinate, coupled with the threat of reprisals if the advances are refused. Behaviour of this kind, which not only undermines the dignity of an individual but prevents her from earning a living, is widely condemned. Courts have declared such *quid pro quo* sexual harassment (the Latin phrase means 'one thing in return for another') to be an illegal violation of civil rights.

However, the problem of unwelcome sexual attention often involves subtle behaviour – sexual teasing, off-colour jokes, pin-ups displayed in the workplace – none of which any individual may *intend* as harassing to another person. But, using the *effect* standard favoured by many feminists, such actions add up to creating a *hostile environment* (Cohen, 1991; Paul, 1991). Incidents of this kind are far more complex because they involve very different perceptions of the same behaviour. For example, a man may think that showing romantic interest in a co-worker is paying the woman a compliment; she, on the other hand, may deem his behaviour offensive and a hindrance to her job performance.

Women's entry into the workplace does not in itself ensure that everyone is treated equally and with respect. Untangling precisely what constitutes a hostile working environment, however, demands clearer standards of conduct than exist at present. Creating such guidelines – and educating the public about them – is likely to take some time (Cohen, 1991; Majka, 1991). In the end, courts (and, ultimately, the court of public opinion) will draw the line between what amounts to 'reasonable friendliness' and behaviour that is 'unwarranted harassment'.

Rape and date rape

Another important area of action is that of rape. For a long time, the academic study of rape was mainly the province of male criminologists, who saw rape through two main lenses. The first argued that rapists were pathological people and few and far between. The second suggested that many women said 'no' to sex when they actually wished to participate; further, it was often precipitated by them.

Such arguments have been roundly condemned by feminists over the past 30 years, and through their campaigns they have brought about change. Critical here has been the growth of rape crisis centres, offering both support to rape victims and campaign materials that have worked to change police and court practice, as well as the law.

(b) Libertarian and socialist perspectives

Not all feminists agree on the analysis of sexuality and men provided by radical feminists. These feminists – who count liberals and socialists in their number – charge that radical feminism is too extreme and too fixed in its conceptions of what male sexuality is, and ultimately adopts a position that makes heterosexuality impossible.

It is also too sex-negative. Many feminists are trying to develop an account of sexuality that recognises that, while there is often *danger* in (male) sex, there can also be *pleasure* (Vance, 1984). Of course, acts of rape and coercive degradation remain unacceptable to all feminists, but they argue there should also be explorations about what it is that women desire, how women can have sexual relations with men that are not degrading, and how new patterns of positive sexuality can be developed (see Segal, 1994).

Key elements of sexual stratification: gay and lesbian relations

Although same-sex erotic experiences exist across cultures and throughout history with varying degrees of acceptability and frequency, it was not until the nineteenth century in Europe and America that homosexuality was invented as an object of scientific investigation. The term itself was introduced by a sympathetic Hungarian doctor, Benkert, in 1869 amidst a flurry of attempts at classifying sexuality. From this time until the 1970s, the dominant mode of thinking about homosexuality was clinical – it was primarily viewed through a medical framework as a pathology, its causes were located in biological degeneracy or family pathology, and treatments ranging from castration to psychoanalysis were advocated. Although such an approach still continues among a few, since 1973 the American Psychiatric Association has officially removed homosexuality from its clinical listing of pathologies, seeing it as non-pathological in itself. Ironically, some of the leading clinicians, and notably Freud, had never viewed it as a pathology: in 1935 Freud could write in a famous 'letter to a mother' that 'whilst homosexuality is assuredly no advantage, it is nothing to be classified as an illness; we consider it to be a variation of the sexual development'.

While the nineteenth century saw the ascendancy of the clinical model of homosexuality, it also saw the growth of writing and campaigning that challenged the orthodox heterosexual assumptions. Thus Magnus Hirschfield established the Scientific Humanitarian Committee and the Institute for Sexual Science in Germany in 1897 and campaigned through scientific research for the acceptance of homosexuality up until the 1930s, when the Nazi movement stopped such advocacy and started a policy of extermination instead. Others, such as Edward Carpenter in England and André Gide in France, pursued a more literary defence. It was not, however, until the period after the Second World War that a substantial body of published research suggested the ubiquity and normality of homosexual experience. Pivotal to this enterprise was the publication of the Kinsey Report in 1948 and 1953, which contained the findings of interviews with well over 12,000 American men and women. Among the men, Kinsey found that 37 per cent had experienced some post-adolescent homosexual orgasm and 4 per cent had a preponderance of such experience; among the women, the figures were around 13 per cent and 3 per cent respectively. When Kinsey added that such responses were to be found among all social groups and in all walks of life, he created a social bombshell. He concluded that homosexual behaviour was neither unnatural nor neurotic in itself, but an 'inherent physiologic capacity'.

Throughout this period, however, homosexuality was strongly condemned by law in most European countries and in all American states. It was not until the 1960s, and a decade or so after proposals for change made in the British Wolfenden Report and the American New Model Code, that the legal situation changed. Despite the progressive growth of organised groups during the 1950s, it is the New York 'Stonewall Riots' of 1969 that are generally taken to symbolise the birth of the modern international 'Gay Movement' (Weeks, 1977). The scientifically imposed term 'homosexual' was shifted to the self-created term 'gay'; medical rhetoric was converted to political language; organisations for gays became widespread in most large cities, and millions of gay men and women started to 'come out' and positively identify with the term 'gay'. The 1970s therefore started to demonstrate a real change in gay experiences in most high-income societies.

Throughout much of the world, same-sex relations are becoming more acceptable. But there are certain parts of the world – especially in some Muslim societies – where homosexuality can be punished by death. Map 12.1 shows the current world legal situation for gays (see *World Guide 2007*: 29–32 for a country by country survey). The timeline illustrates some landmark events in the progress of homosexual acceptance.

Queer theory

As lesbians, gays and bisexuals have 'come out', and become both more visible and more accepted within the mainstream of many Western societies, so their voices have increasingly entered sociology and social

Timeline Landmarks in 'the homosexual's progress'

1869	The idea of 'the homosexual' defined
1895	The three trials of Oscar Wilde
1928	Radclyffe Hall's *The Well of Loneliness* published
1930s	Small-scale growth of homophile movement
1948	The Kinsey Report: found a high incidence of homosexual behaviour
1949	1950s Homophile Movements in the USA
1957	The Wolfenden Report: law change proposed Homosexual Law Reform Society in the UK
1967	Sexual Offences Act partially decriminalised homosexuality
1969	Stonewall and the emergence of the Gay Liberation Front
1970	Gay Liberation in the UK
1980s	Growth and spread of the commercial gay scene – the pink pound
1981	AIDS first identified
1987	Queer theory and queer politics, civil partnerships in Scandinavia and Netherlands
1988	Anti-gay UK legislation; repealed in 2003
2005	Civil partnership laws in the UK

Source: Jeffrey Weeks, *The World We Have Won*, Routledge, 2007.

science debates. There has been a growth of lesbian and gay studies, which have been especially influential in the sociological study of sexualities (Plummer, 1992).

In the late 1980s a new approach, **queer theory**, argued that *most sociological theory still has a bias towards 'heterosexuality' and that non-heterosexual voices need to be heard.* Such theorists would argue that all the topics discussed in this book – from stratification and ethnicity, to religion and economy – would be greatly enhanced if the position of 'non-heterosexual voices' were placed at the centre. For example, it suggests that many religions have been organised around 'homophobic' persecutions; that a new form of economy is emerging that is based upon the spending power of young middle-class gay men – the pink economy; and that the experience of being lesbian or gay can differ significantly across different ethnic minority communities (Seidman, 1996). New insights can be provided for all the traditional concerns of sociology once we give a focus to a different group such as 'queers'. Queer theory started to emerge around the mid to late 1980s. The roots of queer theory are

ILLEGAL

Death penalty in 5 countries
Imprisonment in 75 countries

AFRICA

Nigeria: in Sharia areas, up to death for men and 50 lashes and 6 months in prison for women

Afghanistan: maximum death penalty (no known cases since end of Taliban rule)

Uganda: up to life imprisonment

Malawi: illegal for men – up to 14 years in prison

Malaysia: fine, prison sentence up to 20 years, whippings

Zimbabwe: fine; up to a year in prison

Africa has become a home for Evangelical Christians from North America

South Africa: legal since 1944

IRAN

Death for men, 100 lashes for women

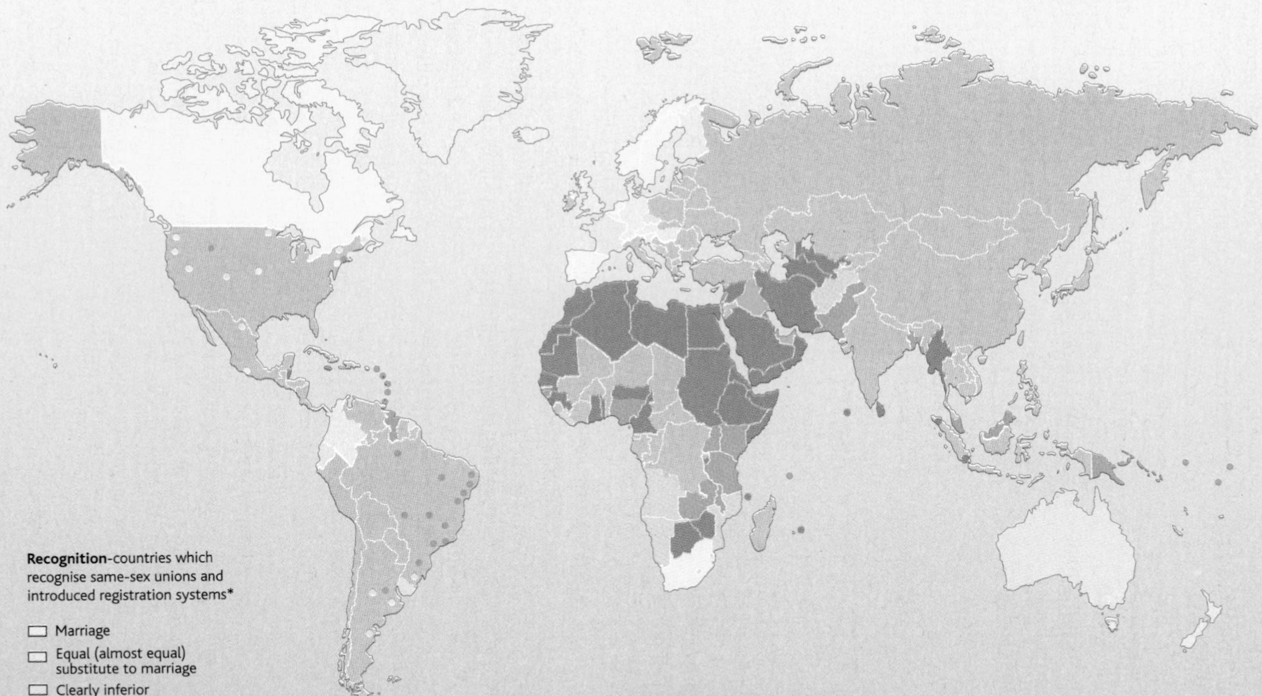

Persecution-death penalty or imprisonment for same-sex acts:

Death penalty

Imprisonment from 11 years to a life-long sentence

Imprisonment from 1 month to 10 years

Imprisonment, no precise indication of the length

Unclear

No specific legislation

• **Protection** – countries which introduced laws prohibiting discrimination on the grounds of sexual orientation (in some countries such bans included in national constitutions and in some countries in other laws; areas of protection from discrimination vary)

Recognition-countries which recognise same-sex unions and introduced registration systems*

Marriage

Equal (almost equal) substitute to marriage

Clearly inferior substitute to marriage

* this category also includes some Australian entities which have no registration systems

MARRIAGE AND PARTNERSHIPS

Denmark was the first country to have legal partnerships in 1989. In 2001, the Netherlands became the first nation to grant same-sex marriage.

Recognition of same-sex union in 26 countries and 30 entities (parts of a territory). While six countries in Europe (the Netherlands, Belgium, Spain, Norway, Sweden and Portugal) have legalised same-sex marriages, a number of other countries have legalised registered partnerships or civil unions in the last 20+ years as well.

In July 2010, Argentina became the first Latin American country to legalise same-sex marriage. Mexico City (but not the rest of Mexico) has similar legislation. The Catholic Church is vehemently opposed.

Look out for: Slovenia is expected to legalise same-sex marriage within the next year; the matter is being addressed by its Parliament at this time. It has had same-sex registered partnerships since 2006.

Albania's Parliament is also working on granting its LGBT citizens full marriage equality; it is not known when this will occur.

Ireland published a same-sex registered partnership bill in June 2009; proponents expect registered partnerships to be fully legalised soon, although additional forces are presently fighting for full marriage equality instead.

The USA: In Connecticut, Iowa, Massachusetts, New Hampshire, Vermont and Washington, DC, marriages for same-sex couples are legal and currently performed. In New York, Rhode Island and Maryland, same-sex marriages are recognised, but not performed. In California, same-sex marriages were performed between 16 June 2008 and 4 November 2008, then outlawed and are now under dispute.

PROTECTION

Anti-discrimination laws exist in at least 53 countries.

World homosexuality laws

Source: Wikipedia: http://en.wikipedia.org/wiki/Image:World_homosexuality_laws.svg, accessed 18 September 2007. This article is licensed under the GNU Free Documentation Licence. It uses material from the Wikipedia article 'Homosexuality laws of the world'; Lesbian and Gay Rights in the World, http://ilga.org/ilga/en/article/1161.

Map 12.1

usually seen to lie in the work of Eve Kasofsky Sedgwick, who argued that:

> many of the major nodes of thought and knowledge in twentieth-century Western culture as a whole are structured – indeed fractured – by a chronic, now endemic crisis of homo/heterosexual definition, indicatively male, dating from the end of the nineteenth century . . . An understanding of any aspect of modern Western culture must be, not merely incomplete, but damaged in its central substance to the degree that it does not incorporate a critical analysis of modern homo/heterosexual definition.
>
> (Sedgwick, 1990: 1)

The feminist philosopher Judith Butler has also suggested there can be no kind of claim to any essential gender: it is all 'performative', slippery, unfixed. She sees gender as never essential, not innate, never natural but always constructed through performativity – as a 'stylized repetition of acts' (Butler, 1990: 141). Much of the interest in queer theory has been concerned with playing around with gender. Initially fascinated by drag, transgender and transsexualism, with divas, drag kings, and key cross genderists such as Del LaGrace Volcano and Kate Bornstein (1995), some of it has functioned almost as a kind of subversive terrorist drag. It arouses curious, unknown queered desires, emancipating people from the constraints of the gendered tyranny of the presumed 'normal body' (Volcano et al., 1999). Others have moved out to consider a wide array of playing with genders, from 'faeries' and 'bears', leather scenes and the Mardi Gras, and on to the more commercialised/normalised drag for mass consumption: RuPaul, Lily Savage, Graham Norton.

If there is a heart to queer theory, then it must be seen as a radical stance around sexuality and gender that denies any fixed categories and seeks to subvert any tendencies towards normality within its study. Certain key themes are worth highlighting. Queer theory is a stance in which:

- The polarised splits between both the heterosexual and the homosexual and the sex and gender are challenged.
- Identity – a sense of who one is – is no longer seen as stable or fixed.

Queer ethnography

Using queer theory, Sasho Lambevski (1999), for instance, attempts to write 'an insider, critical and experiential ethnography of the multitude of social locations (class, gender, ethnicity, religion) from which "gays" in Macedonia are positioned, governed, controlled and silenced as subaltern people' (1999: 301). As a 'gay' Macedonian (the terms must be a problem in this context?) who had spent time studying HIV in Australia, he looks at the sexual conflicts generated between the gay Macedonians and gay Albanians (never mind the Australian connection). Lambevski looks at the old cruising scenes in Skopje, known to him from before, that now take on multiple and different meanings bound up with sexualities, ethnicities, gender playing, clashing cultures. Cruising for sex here is no straightforward matter. He describes how in approaching and recognising a potential sex partner as an Albanian (in an old cruising haunt), he feels paralysed. Both bodies are flooded with ethnic meaning, not simply sexual ones, and ethnicities reek of power. He writes: 'I obeyed by putting the (discursive) mask of my Macedonicity over my body.' In another time and place he might have reacted very differently.

Lambevski is overtly critical of much ethnography and wishes to write a queer experiential ethnography, not a confessional one (1999: 298). He refuses to commit himself to what he calls 'a textual lie', which 'continues to persist in much of what is considered a real ethnographic text'. Here bodies, feelings, sexualities, ethnicities, religions can all be easily left out. Nor, he claims, can ethnography simply depend on site observation or one-off interviewing. There is a great chain of connection: 'the gay scene is inextricably linked to the Macedonian school system, the structuring of Macedonian and Albanian families and kinship relations, the Macedonian state and its political history, the Macedonian medical system with its power to mark and segregate "abnormality" (homosexuality)' (1999: 299). There is a chain of social sites; and at the same time his own life is an integral part of this (Macedonian queer, Australian gay). Few researchers have been so honest as to the tensions that infuse their lives and the wider chains of connectedness that shape their work.

The commercialisation of sex

As we will see in Chapter 15, consumption has become one of the major activities of the twenty-first century. And it will come as no surprise to find that contemporary human sexualities have come to be marketed, commodified, distributed and consumed across the world. Contemporary sexualities are structured more and more in global capitalist markets (Altman, 2000). This is no minor observation, although it is a much neglected one.

We can find the commercialisation and selling of sex in five major ways. These are:

1 *Selling bodies*. This is the most obvious: in 'prostitution' and sex work, trafficking of bodies, stripping, table dancing/lap dancing, sex tourism and sex parties. 'Real sex' is on sale. Much of this is global, and in rich/First World countries large numbers of men are purchasers of sex.

2 *Selling images*. Money (often big money) is involved in the selling of erotica, pornography and internet messaging. Not only is there a huge industry of pornography for men (straight and gay), but there are also now substantial markets for women. The widespread nature of this has been called the 'pornographication' of culture (McNair, 2002).

3 *Selling sex objects*. Most prominent here are 'sex toys' – from s/m costumes, nitrate inhalants ('poppers') and whips/harnesses to dildos, vibrators, inflated blow-up dolls and lingerie – organised through shops like Ann Summers. Parties are organised: the 'circuit party' organises sex parties (usually gay) on a national and international scale (see Storr, 2004).

4 *Selling new technologies*. Much of sex is also marketed through medical aid – from Viagra to contraceptives, and cosmetic and transgender surgery.

5 *Selling relationships*: including marriage (such as mail-order brides) and meeting places, such as gay bars, singles bars or indeed almost any bar which can facilitate sexual relationships. Likewise, relationships can become subject to expensive therapy and standardised self-help books which can sell, for example, the 12 steps needed for a perfect relationship. Increasingly, relationships can be found in the marketplaces of cyberspace.

See: Dennis Altman, *Global Sex* (2001); Feona Attwood (ed.), *Mainstreaming Sex: The Sexualization of Western Culture* (2009); Merl Storr, *Latex and Lingerie: Shopping for Pleasure at Ann Summers Parties* (2004).

Under the George W. Bush Adminstration (2001–9), most American public schools taught abstinence as the most effective form of birth control and protection from sexually transmitted diseases. A strong pro-abstinence discourse developed. It was linked to core agendas of conservative Christians – like creationism, parental rights or the culture wars – and enabled them and the Bush administration to both preserve traditional hierarchies and at the same time generate a fear of sexual panic. Fears continue today with the current anxiety over the 'sexualisation of young people'
Source: Gail Burton/AP/APA Photos.

• All sexual categories are open and fluid (which means modern lesbian, gay identities, bisexual and transgender identities are fractured along with all heterosexual ones).

• Its most frequent interests include a variety of sexual fetishes, drag kings and drag queens, gender and sexual playfulness, cybersexualities, polyamory, sadomasochism and all the social worlds of the so-called radical sexual fringe.

Social change and sexuality

AIDS and the gay movement are but one instance of major changes taking place in sexuality. The English sociologist Anthony Giddens, in his book *The Transformation of Intimacy* (1992), talks about a number of other recent changes. Most important here is the arrival of 'plastic sexuality' and the 'pure relationship'. By the former he means that modern sexuality has broken away from its long historical connection to reproduction and has opened up into a much wider array of ways of doing sex. This is closely connected, of course, to the widespread availability and acceptability of contraceptive techniques. He also sees this 'plastic sex' as closely linked to the idea of the 'pure relationship', by which communication is enhanced between men and women and greater equality happens around sexual and emotional experiences. Giddens recognises that there is also room for danger in contemporary developments. For as women gain more and more equality, so some men feel more and more threatened. Modern times thus bring a growing potential for both an increasing democratisation of personal relationships and at the same time a growing potential for a gender war between men and women. We return to this thorny issue in Chapter 18, when we consider changes in the family.

Looking ahead: gender and sexuality in the twenty-first century

On the surface, recent changes in the gender and sexuality spheres have been remarkable. Two centuries ago, women in the West occupied a position that was clearly and strikingly subordinate. Husbands controlled property in marriage, laws barred women from most jobs, women were excluded from holding political office and even from voting. Although women today often do remain in subordinate positions, especially when linked to class or ethnicity, the movement towards equality has brought many changes. Further, homosexuality was against the law and decried as a sickness. Today, in most Western countries, being gay,

lesbian or queer has become a lifestyle choice and, as we shall see in Chapter 18 on families, the key debates now centre on the rights to have gay families and raise children. In Europe gay partnerships are now widespread through legislative changes. There are also other significant changes in sexuality: the growth of a general openness, the possibility of more democratic relationships between men and women, the more ready acceptance of birth control. The sociologist historian Jeffrey Weeks describes this major 'progress' as 'the world we have won' (2007).

And yet, in a world context, the position of women and sexual minorities remains poor. As many chapters in this book suggest, women are more likely to experience poverty, to experience violence and sexual violence, to be forced into early marriages, to encounter genital mutilation and to be forced to work for very low incomes in sweatshop conditions. A worldwide women's movement is challenging much of this, but there is also much resistance. Likewise, in many countries throughout the world, lesbians and gays are persecuted and may even be executed. Again, an international gay movement attempts to bring about changes in these areas.

But in the West, too, a clear 'backlash' against feminism and queer politics persists. Traditionalists argue that gender still forms an important foundation of personal identity and family life and that it is deeply woven into the moral fabric of our society. They see feminism as a threat to social stability. Traditionalists have also been arguing for a more conservative return to sexual values of the recent past, such as virginity and chastity (see the photo on p. 419). For example, in the United States, new organisations such as the Silver Ring Thing have been set up to counter the twin problems of teenage pregnancy and sexually transmitted disease among teenagers. Opposing sex education, it attempts to attract the young to Christianity, encouraging teens to pay $15 for a bible and a silver (chastity) ring and to make a chastity pledge. By contrast, in Sweden and Holland, which have low rates of teen pregnancy, thorough programmes of sex education are championed (*The Week*, 22 May 2004).

But others recognise the variability of genders throughout cultures and history, and sense that there are now many ways of being men and many ways of being women. Still others argue even more radically for the need to transcend all gender boundaries. On balance, however, changes across the boundaries of sexuality and gender seem likely to continue.

SUMMARY

1 Sex is a biological concept; a human foetus is female or male from the moment of conception. Hermaphrodites represent rare cases of people who combine the biological traits of both sexes. Transsexuals are people who feel they are one sex when biologically they are the other.

2 Heterosexuality is the dominant sexual orientation in virtually every society in the world, though people with a bisexual or exclusively homosexual orientation make up a small percentage of the population everywhere.

3 Gender involves how cultures assign human traits and power to each sex. Gender varies historically and across cultures. Some degree of patriarchy, however, exists in every society.

4 Through the socialisation process, people link gender with personality (gender identity) and actions (gender roles). Three theories dominate socialisation theory: behavioural learning, cognitive learning and psychodynamic learning. Learning to mother is an important part of this socialisation process. The major agents of socialisation – the family, peer groups, schools and the mass media – reinforce cultural definitions of what is feminine and masculine.

5 Gender stratification entails numerous social disadvantages for women. Although most women are now in the paid labour force, a majority of working women hold low-paying clerical or service jobs. Unpaid housework also remains predominantly a task performed by women.

6 Women earn less than men do. This disparity stems from differences in jobs and family responsibilities as well as discrimination.

7 Women now earn a slight majority of all bachelor's and master's degrees. Men still receive a majority of all doctorates and professional degrees.

8 The number of women in politics has increased sharply in recent decades. Still, the vast majority of people elected are men.

9 Minority women encounter greater social disadvantages than white women.

10 Violence against women is a widespread problem in the UK. Our society is also grappling with the issues of sexual harassment and pornography.

11 Functional analysis holds that pre-industrial societies benefit from distinctive roles for males and females, reflecting biological differences between the sexes. In industrial societies, marked gender inequality becomes dysfunctional and slowly decreases. Talcott Parsons claimed that complementary gender roles promote the social integration of families and society as a whole.

12 Conflict analysis views gender as a dimension of social inequality and conflict. Friedrich Engels tied gender stratification to the development of private property. He claimed that capitalism devalues women and housework.

13 Feminism endorses the social equality of the sexes and actively opposes patriarchy and sexism. Feminism also strives to eliminate violence against women, and to give women control over their sexuality.

14 There are three variants of feminist thinking. Liberal feminism seeks equal opportunity for both sexes within current social arrangements; socialist feminism advocates abolishing private property as the means to social equality; radical feminism aims to create a gender-free society.

15 There are three central approaches to the sociological study of sexuality: social constructionism, which highlights scripts, languages and symbols; discourse theory, which emphasises language structures and power; and feminism, which highlights power and gender and has two major variants – radical feminist and libertarian socialist.

16 Same-sex relations – gay and lesbian relationships – have undergone profound changes in the last 100 years.

17 Queer theory suggests the need to deconstruct or abolish the binary gender systems of male and female, gay and straight.

18 'Plastic sex' and 'pure relationships' may be future patterns of sexuality. They both indicate a growing flexibility, openness and potential equality in relationships.

CONNECT UP: Turn to Part 6 of this book for key resources and link up
with the book's website, which links to these resources
SEE: www.pearsoned.co.uk/plummer

MYTASKLIST

Ten suggestions for going further

1 Connect up with Part Six and the Sociology Web Resources

As you work through ideas and think about the issues raised in this chapter, look at the accompanying website and the resource centre at the end of this book which connects to it. There is a lot here to help you move on. To link up, see: www.pearson.co.uk/plummer.

2 Review the chapter

Briefly summarise (in a paragraph) just what this chapter has been about. Consider: (a) What have you learned? (b) What do you disagree with? Be critical. And (c) How would you develop all this? How could you get more detail on matters that interest you?

3 Pose questions

(a) What are the most significant changes in gender and sexuality over the past 20 years? Why have they happened? Look at Rubin's sexual hierarchy (Figure 12.1 on p. 411); this was her description in the early 1980s. In what ways has it changed in the twenty-first century? Look at Jeffrey Weeks's book *The World We Have Won* (2007). Do you see signs of a backlash?

(b) Why is gender a dimension of social stratification? How does gender interact or intersect with inequalities based on race, ethnicity and class?

(c) What problems do you find with biological explanations for men and women's differences? Suggest some examples of how gender roles vary cross-culturally, historically and contemporaneously.

(d) How valuable do you find the idea of 'patriarchy'? Even Sylvia Walby, whom we discuss in the chapter,

has now forsaken it for ideas of the gender order. So what are its major components, how far have they changed in the twentieth and twenty-first centuries, and is it still a useful idea?

(e) How would you define 'queer' sociology?

4 Explore key words

Many concepts have been introduced in this chapter. You can review them from the website or from the listing at the back of this book. You might like to give special attention to just five words and think them through – how would you define them, what are they dealing with, and do they help you see the social world more clearly or not?

See: Jane Pilcher and Imelda Whelman (eds), *50 Key Concepts in Gender Studies* (2004); Jo Eadie, *Sexuality: The Essential Glossary* (2004).

5 Search the Web

Be critical when you look at websites – see the box on p. 940 in the Resources section. For this chapter look at the following:

Women Watch
www.un.org/womenwatch/directory
A United Nations website which monitors the position of women across the world on many dimensions.

Global gender gap:
www.weforum.org/en/Communities/Women%20 Leaders%20and%20Gender%20Parity/GenderGapNetwork/ index.htm

Women's/feminist sites

The Feminist Majority Foundation
www.feminist.org
Women's web world! Homepage of Feminist Majority Online, which links to plenty of information concerning women, such as news and events, political actions, publications, arts and entertainment. US based.

International women's sites
A detailed listing of women's sites can be found at:
http://userpages.umbc.edu/~korenman/wmst/links_intl.html

Queer and gay sites

International Gay, Lesbian, Bisexual, Trans and Intersexual Association
www.ilga.org
Provides useful data on the situation of lesbians, and others across the world.

Queer Resource Directory
www.qrd.org
Links to various issues concerning 'queer' people, such as education, health, family, youth, religion, cultures, law and politics by regions. At last view it had not been updated since 2009.

Stonewall
www.stonewall.org
Stonewall is the major campaign organisation for lesbians and gays in the UK.

Violence and women

Violence Against Women Online Resources (USA)
www.vaw.umn.edu

End Violence Against Women
www.endviolenceagainstwomen.org.uk/pages/the_facts.html

World Health Organization: Violence Against Women factsheet
www.who.int/mediacentre/factsheets/fs239/en/UN

Women's Aid (UK)
www.womensaid.org.uk

6 Watch a DVD

- Bryan Forbes' *The Stepford Wives* (1974): classic story of computerised women pleasing their men. It was remade as a film for a 2004 audience. It might be interesting to compare the 30-year difference!
- Rob Reiner's *Stand by Me* (1985): 1950s childhood, friendships and masculinity.
- Peter Cattaneo's *The Full Monty* (1997): unemployed men in Sheffield take to stripping, and say a lot about their masculinity.
- Stephen Daldry's *Billy Elliot* (2000): a miner's son wants to be a ballet dancer.
- Lasse Halstrom's *Cider House Rules* (1999): abortion, incest, ethnicity and history!
- Robert Rosenberg et al.'s *Before Stonewall* (1985): narrated by Rita Mae Brown, it offers a unique portrait of the history of the homosexual experience in America.

- Patricia Rozema's *I've Heard the Mermaids Singing* (1987): lesbian romance.
- Jennie Livingston's *Paris is Burning* (1990): extraordinary film documenting the Harlem transsexual ball circuit of the mid-1980s.
- Claudia Weil's *Critical Choices* (1996): abortion clinic drama, raising a lot of issues.
- Andrew Jarecki's *Capturing the Friedmans* (2003): award-winning and controversial documentary on an upper-middle-class Jewish family whose world is changed when father and son are arrested for child abuse. Much of the film is made from the family's own documentary video.

7 Think and read

Momin Rahman and Stevi Jackson, *Sexuality and Gender* (2010). Stimulating and wide coverage.

Jennifer Marchbank and Gayle Letherby, *Introduction to Gender: Social Science Perspectives* (2008). Wide introductory coverage of gender issues in a straightforward fashion.

Rosemarie Tong, *Feminist Thought: A Comprehensive Introduction* (3rd edn, 2008). Introduces a full range of feminist perspectives.

Sylvia Walby, *Theorizing Patriarchy* (1990). A classic that provides a detailed analysis of the workings of patriarchy, now the gender order. The figures provided now need a little updating. It can be supplemented with her much more ambitious and difficult *Globalization and Inequalities* (2009).

Catherine Redfern and Kristin Aune (2010) *Reclaiming the F Word: The New Feminist Movement (2010)*. An up-to-date review of the state of women through a feminist lens.

Raewyn Connell, *Gender* (2nd edn, 2009). A short guide by one of the leaders in the field who transgendered from male scholar to woman scholar.

Jeffrey Weeks, *Sexuality* (3rd edn, 2009). A classic short guide to the field, now updated.

Joni Seager, *The Atlas of Women in the World* (4th edn, 2009): a good visual overview of the state of women in the world.

Teela Sanders, Maggie O'Neill and Jane Pitcher, *Prostitution* (2009). A textbook guide to the issues.

8 Relax with a novel

For a starting novel on gender, see Margaret Atwood's *The Handmaid's Tale* (1985). On gay and lesbian writing, see Edmund White's *A Boy's Own Story* (1982) and Jeanette Winterson's *Oranges Are Not the Only Fruit* (1985).

9 Connect to other chapters

- The issue of gender is raised in most chapters, but see gender and work in Chapter 15, gender and crime in Chapter 17, and gender and education in Chapter 20.
- Sexual violence is also considered in Chapter 18, and in the opening story of Chapter 21; see also hate crimes in Chapter 17.

- Link the women's movement to feminism and social movements in Chapter 16.
- Link to HIV and AIDS, discussed in Chapter 21.
- Connect back to class, poverty and ethnicity in Chapters 10 and 11, and forward to age in Chapter 13.
- Link gay rights to gay and lesbian couples in Chapter 18.

10 Engage with THE BIG DEBATE

Does 'porn' degrade women? Gender, sexuality and the continuing politics of pornography

The issue of pornography in the twenty-first century has been anticipated by a century of controversy. 'Porn' has long generated heated debates about the nature of sexuality, gender and censorship.

In the 1980s, some feminists made strong attacks on pornography, picketed porn stores, and tried to have it outlawed; while yet other feminists took a different critical stance which was more 'pro-sex', fearing that attack on porn could also work to repress women's sexuality. Still others – like Madonna – 'celebrated' women's sexualities. They placed women's previously hidden sexuality at the forefront of their acts. Madonna's videos, for instance, introduced audiences to female sadomasochism, masturbation, lesbianism and leather fetishism; and all are celebrated (see her book *Sex*, published in 1990). 'Strike a (erotic) pose' was her theme.

We can therefore see two main camps which are still around today. On one side, radical feminists and others argue that pornography should be a major issue because it strikes at the core of gender and sexuality. Indeed, it shows the very nature of what men desire and what male sexuality is. They argue that pornography is really a power issue because it fosters the notion that men should control both sexuality and women. Both Andrea Dworkin (see above) and Catharine MacKinnon (1987) castigated pornography as one foundation of male dominance because it portrays women in dehumanising fashion as the subservient playthings of men. Worth noting, in this context, is that the term 'pornography' is derived from the Greek word *porne*, meaning a harlot who acts as a man's sexual slave. Among the key arguments marshalled by feminists against pornography are:

- Pornography – like most of male sexuality – degrades and abuses women. It is violent, voyeuristic, objectificatory, dehumanising and designed to satisfy the male's concern with masturbation.
- Pornography is about male power. It shows how men seek to control women, not only in the porn itself – the male eye takes the woman over, the woman is represented as being there for the man – but also in the making of the porn: here women have often been turned into abuse objects and actually become prostitutes and whores for men.
- Pornography is an ideology that promotes sexual violence in society. By encouraging an objectificatory and abusive approach to women, it actually encourages rape and sexual violence. In the words of the famous epigram: 'pornography is the theory, rape is the practice'.

Many feminists did not agree with these arguments and set up movements to challenge the above. They argue:

- The pornography issue gives too much weight to sexuality as a source of women's oppression and deflects attention from other more important sources, such as their weak position in the labour market, how racism compounds their problems, exploitation at home in the domestic labour market, and so on.
- The pornography issue encourages censorship, and this works against women's interests. Indeed, in some places where porn has been banned, so have all kinds of women's publications, especially those for lesbians.
- The pornography issue side-steps the issue of women's sexuality and their growing desire for their own erotica. Women make pornography for themselves; it is not all male. And anti-porn feminists make women seem to be passive, asexual victims of male desire. They are not.
- Finally, the representations of pornography do not have one clear meaning. They have different meanings to different groups and, while they can be about male power and violence, this is certainly not their only meaning.

In the twenty-first century, and with the pervasive growth of porn accessible to most, there has been renewed concern. Online pornography is available to all at the click of a button – and its imagery has become more and more plentiful, diversified and extreme. It is part of the widespread commercialisation of sex and what some have called the sexualisation of society. Dail Gines, a sociologist based in the USA, has developed a strong critique of porn in her book *Pornland* (2010), where she argues that porn affects men in the following ways:

- It makes them want to emulate the sex they see in porn.
- It makes them think that women in general enjoy porn sex.
- It makes them feel like sexual losers because they cannot perform like the men in porn.
- It makes them angry at the women in their lives who refuse to perform porn sex.
- It makes them less interested in real human beings and more interested in using porn.
- It gets in the way of connection when they are having sex with their partners.

- It cultivates a taste for harder and harder porn, since they become desensitised and bored.

There are many positions in this ongoing dialogue and we suggest that you do some online research into how easy or not it is to access pornography, and then organise a debate on the pros and cons of what you see.

Continue the debate

1 Has there been a growth in pornography with the rise of the internet, and has this started to create a different sexual environment – a sexualised one? What might be meant by sexualisation?

2 Do you think sexuality is largely defined by men for their own needs? What might a non-male sexuality look like?

3 What kinds of image in pornography would not be sexist, and would not subordinate women?

4 Can the world of high-tech computer sex be regulated? What do you think of the development of xxx categories to regulate porn and sex lines?

5 Where do we draw boundaries? Is there never a case for censorship?

CHAPTER 13

AGE STRATIFICATION: CHILDREN, YOUTH AND LATER LIFE

THERE IS A TENDENCY TO THINK of 'age' as something 'wired into our bodies'. It is biological. Yet, as you will be aware by now, the sociologist is always looking for the social patterns – for the more social side of life, of how everything gets socially organised. So it is also true that how we create and respond to age categories are also social events.

First, consider two small societies. The Sherpas are a Tibetan-speaking, Buddhist people in Nepal. In this society, there is almost an idealisation of old age. Old people here usually live in their own homes, and most are in good health. The old here are held in esteem and valued. By contrast, the Fulani of Africa move older people to the very edge of their communities and families – indeed, very near to their future graves. They may already be seen as socially dead and are held in low regard. Social expectations towards the elderly differ widely across societies (Schaefer, 2001: 319).

Now consider some of those growing older in the contemporary West. We now have rock stars from the 1960s like Sir Mick Jagger (of the Rolling Stones), Sir Paul McCartney (of the Beatles) or even Sir Cliff Richard 'growing old'. They seem to be trying to resist what a few decades ago would have been seen as 'old age'. They are really part of the 'young growing older' – despite their chronological age, they do not see it as anything to do with being old. And indeed, they are not old *in the same ways* that people were at their age some 50 years ago. Each generation in every society has to find its own social meanings of age.

Think of the 'old' today. Think of the millions who now follow new consumption patterns for those growing old. In the UK, they go on Saga holidays, winter retreats to the Costa del Sol (O'Reilly, 2000), join the University for the Third Age. Across the Western world we see the growth of retirement colonies, surgical reconstructions for the ailing body, new political movements – the so-called 'Grey Power Movement'. Growing old is not what it used to be. It has become a 'lifestyle enclave' (Bellah et al., 1985). We also have a new group who are living longer and longer: the centenarians. Several decades ago, living to be over a hundred was really quite rare. But over the last 30 years, the number of centenarians in the UK has more than quadrupled from 2,600 in 1981 to 11,600 in 2009. The estimated number of centenarians in the UK has increased by 70 per cent since 2000.

Future numbers of centenarians will depend on both the numbers of people at younger ages in the population today and their future survival. Current population projections suggest the number of centenarians in the UK will reach almost 80,000 by mid-2033. This is a five-fold increase from the 2009 figure, an average annual increase of 8 per cent.

In this chapter we give a key focus to this ageing issue; but we start by also looking a little at children and young people.

Source: Office for National Statistics, UK, May 2011.

Old age will only be respected if it fights for itself, maintains its rights, avoids dependence on anyone and asserts control over its own to its last breath.

Cicero

In this chapter, we ask:

- **What is age stratification? – examining three key stages of life: childhood, youth and old age**

- **What is the sociology of childhood?**

- **How can we make sense of youth cultures across the world?**

- **What are the problems and implications of an ageing society?**

(Left) Felicitas, 99 years 364 days old, and Maria (2001)

This is an example of Cathy Greenblat's work combining sociology with photography, which was introduced in Chapter 3. Looking at the dependent elderly across the world, she shows how they are far from empty shells but come alive in diverse ways.

Source: © Cathy Greenblat 2001.

 What do you see as the advantages – and disadvantages – of using photography in sociology?

Age divisions are found across all societies as a major means of differentiating peoples. Although all societies have systems of **age stratification**, whereby there is *an unequal distribution of wealth, power and privileges among people at different stages in the life course*, the nature of this varies across societies and history. And our twenty-first century is no exception. The historian Peter Laslett first suggested that we need *A Fresh Map of Life* (1989), which should be approached through Four Ages. The First Age coincides broadly with childhood, and the second with adulthood and learning. A Third Age has grown in recent years and marks the period bounded between the end of work and the arrival of the Fourth Age of 'dependence, decrepitude and death' (Laslett, 1989: 90).

Others, more controversially, suggest that the postmodern world is seeing a breakdown of clear age bands, that chronological age patterns are becoming less crucial to people's lives. Social divisions around age are different from other divisions in so far as we are all likely to move through them: today's children are tomorrow's pensioners. But attached to each age band comes a series of socially produced assumptions about what it should be like to be in that age group. In this chapter we will look briefly at children (and the emerging new field known as the sociology of children), youth cultures and the increasing numbers of people who are 'growing older'.

What is the sociology of childhood?

There is a lot of evidence that ideas about children change remarkably across cultures and over the centuries, and that the experience of children across the world today can be very different indeed. Charles Dickens' classic novel *Oliver Twist* is set in London early in the nineteenth century, when the Industrial Revolution was rapidly transforming English society. Oliver's mother died in childbirth and, barely surviving himself, he began life as an indigent orphan, 'buffeted through the world, despised by all, and pitied by none' (Dickens, 1886: 36; orig. 1837–9). As was typical for a poor child of his time, Oliver Twist was soon facing the toil and drudgery of a workhouse, labouring long hours to pay for filthy shelter and meagre food. Global figures for child poverty today are shown in Figure 13.1.

Today we think of *childhood* – roughly, the first 12 years of life – very differently: it is supposed to be a time of freedom from the burdens of the adult world. But until about a century ago, as *Oliver Twist* testifies, children in Europe and North America shouldered most of the burdens of adults. According to historian Philippe Ariès (1965), once children were able to survive without constant care, medieval Europeans expected

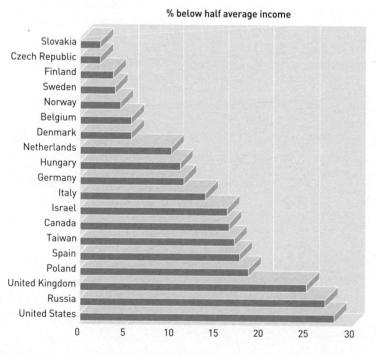

% below half average income

Figure 13.1 Population of children living in households in poverty

Note: The Luxembourg Income Study began in 1983 and looks at 25 countries across four continents: Europe, America, Asia and Oceania. See www.lisproject.org.

Source: Adapted from Luxembourg Income Study.

them to take their place in the world as working adults. Likewise, as we look at the world's population of children in different countries today, we find that many of them take on responsibilities and concerns we associate with adult life. 'Being a child' is therefore a very different experience across cultures (and indeed even within one culture, according to the class, gender and ethnicity of the child). Consider just four dimensions: *work, marriage, war and death*. The most obvious feature of contemporary Western childhoods is that most children are 'protected' from most of these most of the time. But this is far from true of most children across the world today, as we briefly discuss below.

Spotlight

The state of the world's children

- 8.8 million children worldwide died before their fifth birthday in 2008.
- 4 million newborns are dying in the first month of life.
- 4 million under-fives die each year from just three causes: diarrhoea, malaria and pneumonia.
- 2 million children are living with HIV.
- 15 million children have lost one or both parents due to AIDS; 14 million are AIDS orphans.
- 64 million women aged 20–4 in the developing world were married before the age of 18.

For a full account of *The State of the World's Children* (2009), see the United Nation's Special Report on this. It is accessible on PDF at: www.unicef.org/publications/files/SOWC_Spec._Ed._CRC_Main_Report_EN_090409.pdf.

Child labour

'Child labour', often scorned in high-income countries (though in fact there are some 2.5 million children working in the developed economies) is a routine fact of everyday daily life in many poorer societies, especially in Africa and Asia. There are a few children under 5 who work, but most child labour is between 5 and 17; and the International Programme for the Elimination of Child Labour (IPEC) reports that the global number of child labourers declined from 222 million to 215 million, or 3 per cent, over the period 2004 to 2008, representing a 'slowing down of the global pace of reduction'. Table 13.1 provides a summary of world figures (see: International Labour Organization, 2010 and www.ilo.org/ipec).

Child marriage

As with work, so with marriage: many children across the world get 'married' – often for economic reasons. Early marriages are pervasive in parts of Africa and south Asia. In some countries over half of all girls are married by the time they reach age 18 (United Nations Children's Fund, March 2001: press release). The figure is 74 per cent in the Democratic Republic of the Congo, 70 per cent in Niger, and around 50 per cent in Bangladesh and Afghanistan.

Poverty is one of the major factors underpinning child marriage. In Bangladesh, for example, poverty-stricken parents may be persuaded to part with their daughters through a promise of marriage, or by false marriages, which are used to lure girls into prostitution abroad. There can be serious downsides to all this.

Table 13.1	Regional estimates of child labour, 2008 (5–17 age group)						
	Total children	Children in employment		Child labourers		Children in hazardous work	
	(000s)	(000s)	%	(000s)	%	(000s)	%
World	1,586,288	305,669	19.3	215,269	13.6	115,314	7.3
Asia and the Pacific	853,895	174,460	20.4	113,607	13.3	48,164	5.6
Latin America and the Caribbean	141,043	18,851	13.4	14,125	10.0	9,436	6.7
Sub-Saharan Africa	257,108	84,229	32.8	65,064	25.3	38,736	15.1
Other regions	334,242	28,129	8.4	22,473	6.7	18,978	5.7

Source: ILO (2009) *Accelerating Action Against Child Labour*, Table 1.4, p. 10. Copyright © International Labour Organization 2009.

Child labour
Source: © Robert van der Hilst/Corbis.

Child marriage may serve as a major life restriction and can have a serious impact on health. It can cut off educational opportunities, and for girls in particular (and the rate of child marriage is very much higher for girls) it will almost certainly mean premature pregnancy – with higher rates of maternal mortality and a lifetime of domestic and sexual subservience. According to a UNICEF report on child spouses, domestic violence is common and causes some girls to run away in desperation. 'Those who do so,' the report says, 'and those who choose a marriage partner against the wishes of their parents, may be punished, or even killed by their families. These girls run the risk of "honour killings" that occur in Bangladesh, Egypt, Jordan, Lebanon, Pakistan, Turkey and elsewhere' (*Early Marriages, Child Spouses:* UNICEF Report, March 2001: 13). Child prostitution is closely linked to this, with a current estimate that at least a million of the earth's children are forced into it.

Children at war

Children are often the main targets in war (being seen as the next generation of 'enemies'). Many are used as mine sweepers or as spies, and for kamikaze attacks

There are an estimated 300,000 child soldiers around the world. Every year the number grows as more children are recruited for use in active combat. See Coalition to Stop the Use of Child Soldiers http://www.child-soldiers.org/home

Source: © John Warburton-Lee Photography/Alamy.

across the world. Children make up about a half of war refugees, while millions die. But of growing concern has been the many children who are recruited or coerced into being soldiers. Figures are hard to estimate: maybe some 300,000 minors have been recruited as active combatants by rebel groups and armies in some 36 countries, especially in Asia and Africa. The problem is most critical in Africa, where up to 100,000 children, some as young as 9, were estimated to be in armed conflict in mid-2004. In 2002, the United Nations raised the minimum age for recruiting soldiers from 15 to 18.

tip There is a website to learn about the plight of child soldiers and to hear their own voices.
See: Coalition to Stop the Use of Child Soldiers, www.child-soldiers.org/home. This organisation also produces regular *World Reports* which are downloadable. The 3rd edition was published in 2008.
Look out for the film *Johnny Mad Dog* (2009) about child soldiers fighting a war in an unnamed African country.

Child illness and mortality

For many children around the world, the early years of life are times of sickness and morbidity. As we shall see in later chapters, low-income societies are frequently societies with high infant mortality and morbidity.

Take the issue of AIDS, to be discussed more fully in Chapter 21. Of the 21.8 million people who had died from AIDS by 2000, 4.3 million were aged under 15 years old. Approximately 50 per cent of all new infections are occurring among young people. In Botswana and South Africa, it is estimated that one-half of today's 15-year-olds will die of AIDS. But more than this, many of the children in sub-Saharan Africa find their parents dying of HIV/AIDS and this makes for large numbers of what have been called 'AIDS orphans'.

Spotlight
The rights of the child

According to the Convention on the Rights of the Child (1989), every child has the right to:

- family relations and parental guidance
- life, survival and development
- registration, name, nationality, care and preservation of identity
- access to appropriate information
- health and access to healthcare services
- benefit from social security
- a decent standard of living
- education.

Source: Derived from the Convention on the Rights of the Child (1989). For more information: see www.unicef.org/crc.

Thinking about children

Traditionally, children have been seen as 'little innocents' (whose innocence needs protecting), as 'little devils' (whose naughtiness needs taming) or as adults-in-the-making (what has often been called the child development approach, as children move through stages on their way to adulthood). More recently, sociologists have come to reject all these views and have started to approach children as *actively creating and living in their own complex worlds*. In their book *Constructing Childhood*, Alison James and Adrian James have argued that seeing 'childhood as a natural state' works to subordinate children and place them in worlds 'protected' by adult worlds; it robs the child of what might be called his or her 'agency', and it obscures the power and dependency relations created by adults over children. Childhood may be seen as another socially constructed social division.

Allison James, Chris Jenks and Alan Prout have suggested four key ways in which sociologists can approach children. The first is *the socially constructed approach*. Here childhood does not exist in a fixed or essential form: instead we have to show how it is built up in specific groups and societies. It simply does not mean the same thing at different times. Thus, for instance, it may be thought of as exploitation to our minds to hear about children having to work; for much of history and in many societies today, it is simply considered the normal thing to do to help the family survive. Likewise, if we described a mixed family of children all huddled up in the same bed, we would probably consider this to be a form of child abuse and call in social services! But again, in many societies today and of the past, the separate spaces for children that Western societies now consider natural for children were in fact unknown.

A second approach is that of *the tribal child*. Here children's own worlds are seen as 'real places and provinces of meaning in their own right' (James et al., 1998: 28). Their own worlds are honoured, whether this is a world of play in the schoolyard, the club, the gang or even computer games. This approach is mainly an ethnographic project of mapping what the child's actual worlds are like to live in for them, and not as seen through the eyes of adults.

A third approach sees the child as part of a *minority group*. This is a political form of analysis which looks at the ways in which power works in children's lives. It senses that often the child is one of the least equal members of a social group; that children are often excluded from adult activities and treated in ways that minimise their agency and autonomy. It is a position which can have a lot in common with children's rights arguments. Thus, in 1989 almost all countries in the world signed the United Nations Convention of the Rights of the Child. According to this, all children across the world should have the right to be protected by laws which would aim for their survival and development, as well as protection against harmful influences and exploitation. The laws urge full participation in family, cultural and social life, as well as access to healthcare, education and services for children. Within this view, child labour, marriage and violence are all forms of childhood oppression to be overcome.

Finally, a fourth approach sees the child as *relational and structural*. Here childhood is seen as part of the life course (see Chapter 7) and the lives of children share common characteristics as a collectivity which indicate relationships to other collectivities like families, work and education.

The voices of child soldiers

The army was a nightmare. We suffered greatly from the cruel treatment we received. We were being constantly beaten, mostly for no reason at all, just to keep us in a state of terror. I still have a scar on my lip and sharp pains in my stomach from being brutally kicked by the older soldiers. The food was scarce and they made us walk with heavy loads, much too heavy for our small and malnourished bodies. They forced me to learn how to fight the enemy in a war that I didn't understand why was being fought.

(Emilio, recruited by the Guatemalan army at the age of 14)

One boy tried to escape [from the rebels], but he was caught. His hands were tied, and then they made us, the other new captives, kill him with a stick. I felt sick. I knew this boy from before. We were from the same village. I refused to kill him and they told me they would shoot me. They pointed a gun at me, so I had to do it. The boy was asking me: 'Why are you doing this?' I said I had no choice. After we killed him, they made us smear his blood on our arms. . . . They said we had to do this so we would not fear death and so we would not try to escape.

(Susan, abducted by the Lord's Resistance Army in Uganda)

In May 2000, the United Nations established a new protocol for stopping the use of child soldiers. By April 2004, 115 countries had signed it and 71 countries had ratified it. The protocol argued that governments must ensure that nobody under the age of 18 should take part in hostilities or be conscripted into armies.

(Human Rights Watch on Children's Rights)

The killing of the children: infanticide in India

Rani, a young woman living in a remote Indian village, returned home from the hospital after delivering a baby girl. There was no joy in the family. On the contrary, upon learning of the birth, the men sombrely filed out of the mud house. Rani and her mother-in-law then set about the gruesome task of mashing oleander seeds into several drops of oil to make a poisonous paste, which they forced down the baby's throat. The day came to an end as Rani returned from a nearby field where she had buried the child.

As she walked home, Rani felt not sadness at losing her daughter but bitterness at not bearing a son. Members of her village, like poor people throughout the world (and especially Asia), favour boys while defining girls as an economic liability. Why? Because, in poor societies, most power and wealth falls into the hands of men. Parents recognise that boys are a better investment of their meagre resources, since males who survive to adulthood will provide for the family. Then, too, custom dictates that parents of a girl offer a dowry to the family of her prospective husband. In short, given the existing social structure, families are better off with boys and without girls.

One consequence of this double standard is the high rate of sex-selective abortion throughout rural India, China and other Asian nations. Curiously, in India, even villages that lack running water typically have a doctor who performs high-tech amniocentesis or ultrasound to determine the sex of a foetus. The woman's typical response, upon hearing the results of the test, is either elation at carrying a boy or resolve to terminate the pregnancy quickly so that she may 'try again'. Although there are no precise counts of abortion and female infanticide, analysts point out that, in some rural regions of Asia, men outnumber women by as many as ten to one.

For girls who manage to survive infancy, gender bias presents overwhelming barriers. Generally speaking, parents provide girls with less food, schooling and medical care than they give to boys. In times of drought or other crisis, families may leave girls to die while they channel what little resources they have towards the survival of a son.

Female infanticide was outlawed in India more than a century ago, but it still continues, and local authorities often collude in the slaughter of girls. 'It is just not possible not to notice that perhaps up to four out of ten baby girls are being killed soon after birth: it shows in the sex ratio of the children in their villages' (Calvert and Calvert, 2001: 242).

Youth: their cultures and tribes

Although all societies have age grades which must include the young, the recognition of a category called 'youth' is relatively new. 'Youth' as a distinct social category seems to have appeared alongside the Industrial Revolution (Musgrove, 1968). In the chaos of mass urbanisation in the nineteenth century (brilliantly depicted in the writings of Charles Dickens, and the more academic writings of Mayhew and Booth), young people were often found to be 'in trouble'. There were street gangs in New York, Fagin's pickpockets in the London of *Oliver Twist*, Parisian hoodlums known as Apaches, and regular battles between street gangs in England. Indeed, a number of studies have shown how we can find 'Hooligans' throughout recent history (Pearson, 1983). By the late nineteenth century, poverty and lack of education were soon recognised by many early social researchers like G. Stanley Hall in the United States and John Barron Mays in Liverpool to play a key role in the lives of the young. In 1889, Hall named a new life stage 'adolescence' which he saw as characterised by paternal conflict, moodiness and risk taking (Savage, 2007). So, in some ways, 'youth' came to exist because of the rise of the modern world. They are part of it. And in it they often come to signify 'trouble'.

But even more specifically, the concept of 'teenagers' started to appear in the post-Second World War of the United States, and was transported rapidly around the 'Western world' – linked to the rise of a new music and commercial/consumer market. New styles, dress and fashion, accessories, magazines and music became more and more important until now, in the Western world, youth culture is almost dominated by the notions of 'music' and styles (Savage, 2007). These styles and their cultures have been one main focus of sociological research.

Youth culture studies

During the twentieth century, sociologists started to investigate the nature of subcultures and gangs in cities. At one level, these sociologists simply described what they saw: Frederick Thrasher's study of *The Gang*, which looked at over 1,000 youth gangs in Chicago in the 1920s, is a good example. They conducted participant observation and ethnographies to capture the symbols, languages, values and material cultures in which young people lived.

Widespread youth cultures only started to appear in very distinctive form in the period after the Second World War. Here was a period of relative affluence in the West, the extension of schooling, and the emergence of a pervasive consumer market. Relatively disconnected from the responsibilities of adult family life, young people became a noticeable consumer market. Many new products – from records and films, to sports gear and clothing styles – could be directed at them. From these 'material conditions', youth cultures started to appear with their own 'ways of life', their own 'webs of meaning'. In the United Kingdom, for instance, a string of cultural styles developed: Teddy Boys came first in the 1950s (in the wake of the first rock 'n' roll record and film – Bill Haley's *Rock around the Clock*); the mods and rockers followed in the 1960s and adopted distinctive and contrasting dress, music styles and values. In the UK, contemporary youth culture research started in the 1960s with the study by David Downes, Stan Cohen and others. Key concerns of this work were the issues of delinquency and social class. They connected to major strands of criminological theory – anomie, labelling, differential association (see Chapter 17) – and in fieldwork studied the styles of emerging youth groups. The 'mods' in the 1960s set up a mode of aspiring working-class youth, whereas the 'rocker' style set up a mode for traditional working-class youth. The later multitude of youth styles with their rich diversities of music, fashion, language and style continue to be significantly shaped across class, gender and ethnic lines. In all of this, young people – often willingly – are separated out as a distinct and separate group. Some sociologists claim that youth has become a major scapegoat, and is frequently socially excluded and stereotyped.

Later work during the 1970s and 1980s was shaped by the cultural studies tradition (see *Thinkers and theory*, p. 164) and the researches of Stuart Hall (*Policing the Crisis*), Dick Hebdidge (*Subcultures*) and Paul Willis (*Learning to Labour*: see Chapter 29) amongst many others. Here 'youth styles' became more

and more important. These sociologists argued that such cultures 'express and resolve, albeit magically, the contradictions which remain hidden or unresolved in the parent culture' (Cohen, 1980: 82–3; orig. 1972). Thus youth cultures were seen as active ways of dealing with the problems generated by both the wider cultures (with their different pushes towards getting jobs, consuming goods, getting on in school, becoming men and women) and the immediate 'adult' culture of the parents. These were stressful times, and young people had to develop and negotiate their own responses. Youth styles came to be seen as forms of resistance, in which the young worked up their own cultures as a way of handling a string of problems. Social class, gender and ethnicity played key roles in this. Youth cultures often parodied the wider consumer culture they were part of: to put it generally, punks, bikers, Goths, crusties, hippies dressed down; mods, soul boys, home boys dressed up!

Youth culture theory has successively paraded a long variety of youth types. It delights in studying Goths and grunge, chavs and scranners, 'emo skaters' and 'indie bohos', along with older styles – skinheads, hippies, punks, rastas, acid heads and New Age travellers – which keep reworking themselves. It is a world of postmodern cultures and shows how class, gender and ethnicity intersect in 'style' (Thornton, 2006; Muggleton and Weinzierl, 2003).

This more recent wave of youth research have been influenced by a more postmodern and fluid approach. The postmodern language of youth refuses to see any kind of unified coherence amongst the contemporary young. Indeed, it is now much less inclined to talk of youth subcultures or contracultures at all, which sounds much too uniform and fixed. Instead, more recent research and theory sees tribes, neo-tribes, taste cultures, lifestyles and hybridity. Thus Anoop Nayak uses the term 'youth scapes' (2003: 19) to indicate the potential diversity and movement of youth forms orbiting around different identities and values. Youth cultures are to be found moving through specifically geographical sites – there are a diverse array of 'geographies of youth': clubbing, local music scenes, urban landscapes, dance cultures, lifestyles, night-time economies and 'cool places' (Skelton and Valentine, 1998). Boundaries are fluid and switchable. Nevertheless, there may be key themes. Paul Hodkinson's study of Goths (2002), for example, suggested four key indicators of the new youth movements: identity, commitment, consistent distinctiveness and autonomy. All in all, youth cultures have been popular topics to study in sociology and in recent years there has been a major revival in ways of thinking about them. Chapter 5 has shown a little of this diversity (Muggleton and Weinzierl, 2003; Hebdidge, 1979).

Underemployed youth? Disconnected youth?

The sociology of youth has many other concerns. A key concern here is with the transitional years of education and the passage into work. How do young people get, or not get, jobs? Here, researchers often find a great deal of 'leisure poverty'. A real lack of money prohibits (much, if any) participation in nightclubs, drinking, dressing up or going to the movies. As a 17-year-old said in a study of Teesside Youth in England:

'We just sit in watching the TV, or if it's pay day [i.e. benefit payment day] we get a few cans and a video' (Louise, 17, unemployed). Disengaged young men and single mothers have even fewer opportunities. 'Hanging around' can become a major life activity, and trying to fill up time becomes a major problem (MacDonald and Marsh, 2005). Ken Roberts, in a major study of youth in eastern Europe and the West highlights what he calls 'underemployment': a condition which has been normalised, where large numbers of youth are unemployed, have less than permanent work or take jobs which are way below their qualifications. It has become a feature of depressed labour markets across the world but notably in eastern Europe. This is a major problem to be dealt with in the future and strikes a much more troubled note

These days, youth cultural styles are among the most global in the world. Partly because of a widely common youth language of pop music, cable and satellite TV, film and the like, much of youth culture depends on borrowing from many sources. Young people play around with the dominant culture, creating a collage of diverse bits in their own lives, mixing styles of fashion, music and consumption. These photographs capture some of the different dress styles of youth. Why do young people wear such clothes, and adopt values and languages to go with them?

Young people across the world like to differentiate themselves by the clothes they wear or the activities they perform, although some would find this difficult if not impossible, as these examples show: (a) London skateboarders; (b) Breakdance at skate park; (c) A morning commuter train speeds through the Tanah Abang slum near downtown Jakarta, Indonesia, as two residents sleep alongside the railway line; (d) Saharan horse race followers.

Source: (a) © Roger Cracknell 01/classic/Alamy; (b) © Howard Barley/Alamy; (c) PA Photos; (d) Magnum Photos © Chris Steele-Perkins.

when contrasted with the fun-seeking youth of the postmodern youth culture tradition.

Youth in low-income societies

This 'underemployment' becomes more and more serious when we consider the issue of youth in low-income societies. Here youth cultures take on different dimensions from those in the richer West. In much of the world, young people live in severe poverty, experience unemployment on a mass scale, are illiterate, get bound up with drugs and youth crime, and have very poor health. Of course, these issues are found in high-income societies too – the news is constantly full of the horror stories of the young. But in low-income societies we are talking on a different scale. Consider some findings from *The United Nations World Youth Report*, 2005. It claimed:

- Over 200 million young people (18 per cent of all youth) live in poverty (that is, on less than $1 a day); and 515 million live on less than $2 a day. That is getting on for an eighth of the world's population.
- World youth unemployment is high and, at a total of 88 million, it is highest in western Asia, north Africa and sub-Saharan Africa.
- As in the Western world, young people are reaching adolescence at earlier ages and marrying later, with premarital sex increasing.
- There are growing problems of drug use, youth crime and sexuality (with HIV/AIDS being a prime cause of mortality – 10 million young people were living with HIV/AIDS, mostly in Africa and Asia).
- More: 130 million young people are illiterate. And while information and communication technologies have proliferated, the digital divide between the young of the rich world and the poor world is huge.
- And in the midst of all this a great many young people, especially in African states, are disproportionately involved in conflicts – local and national. They become young soldiers, fighters, guerrilla activists. Violence and injuries are a common cause of death. This is more common for young men than young women, but women also have their problems. Women in low-income societies have a much higher likelihood of being drawn into sexual trafficking (UN (2005), www.un.org/youth).

Parallels can be found in many of the cities of high-income countries. For example, sociologists have studied similar experiences in the United States. In Philadelphia, for instance, and many inner cities in North America, a pervasive street violence exists. Many young people come to live tormented lives in the midst of drugs, death and a decaying environment. Discount stores open up, along with graffiti and very run-down buildings – many no longer inhabited. It is here that groups of black youths start to appear, hanging around on street corners, outside stores, in the street and at major complexes. The air is thick with danger and potential violence. It is the world of *Boyz'n the Hood* and, indeed, *Favella Rising*. Street families seem to show a lack of consideration for others. And at the heart of the problem is the issue of respect – being treated 'right' or being granted one's 'props' (or proper due) or the deference one deserves.

Global youth cultures

Finally, we can mention an emerging phenomenon that some sociologists have called 'Generation Global'. Gathering in 'global cities' throughout the world where work and lifestyles are available in plenty – Dublin, Cape Town, Prague, Saigon, Shanghai, Tel Aviv, London and New York – they find a world of young people travelling and going overseas in record numbers. Here, middle-class and relatively rich kids find themselves on gap years abroad; travelling through international corporations; or simply surfing in cyberspace. Their social networks become global. They make friends all over the world. But once again we can speak of a global divide being created. Most youth of the world cannot even begin to aspire to this.

Western influences have frequently created major concerns for young people in much of the world. Youth in many non-Western cultures may well gain knowledge about the lifestyles of 'Western youth', and can often gain access to some of the artefacts of Western youth culture – music, dress, film. Growing numbers can communicate via some access to ICT. DVDs, music, dance and the internet set up a kind of international youth culture. Witnessing global mass media and some migrating (sometimes in exile) from their own countries, young people in non-Western countries become more and more exposed to the consumerism and 'lifestyle' issues of young people in the West. But all of this sets up major tensions.

For example, one examination of youth in Tehran found that growing numbers of young Iranians were gaining access to all kinds of modern commodities. Everything from DVDs and CDs to large-scale use of the internet – often illegally – are part of Iranian youth life. But at the same time, much of it involves risking jail for things their counterparts in the West take for granted: everything from wearing make-up to slow

Youth films as documenting lives

There are an enormous number of films that can be used for sociological study. Here we look at two made about youth. There are a great many such films, which are usually made for the teen movie market (young people are the largest cinema goers). But here are two very different films that became popular in the first years of the twenty-first century.

First is the award-winning film *City of God*, by Katia Lund and Fernando Meirelles and released worldwide in 2003, which takes us into the world of two young people living in Rio de Janeiro over a ten-year period. It tells us the story of being young and growing up in a lower-class slum (favela), *Cidade de Deus* (Portuguese for 'City of God'). This is not an easy life – far from it; and it is a far cry from the 'youth cultures' of the West, which sociologists more commonly have studied. It is full of violence, drug use and deep poverty. Both the film and the book are based on a true story, the war between Rocket (Knockout Ned) and Li'l Dice (characters based on their real-life counterparts).

Rocket comes from a fishmonger's home, where his family sell fish in the quarter, while Li'l Dice grows up in a gang of hoodlums who kill and steal. The film begins close to the end of the story and moves back a decade. The whole story is told against a background of violence, despair and drugs. As the kids grow up in this environment, they take different paths and

go through many changes. Li'l Dice becomes a violent gangster with his own gang, killing his rivals. Rocket wants to escape all this – though he witnesses it. He develops an interest in photography and wishes to use it to escape the violence of his environment. The tagline of the film is: 'Fight and you'll never survive . . . Run and you'll never escape.'

A few years later, a second film, *Favela Rising* (by Jeff Zimbalist and Matt Mochary, 2006) returned to similar favellas of the poor in Rio de Janeiro. And, again, this film vividly tells another (real) story of the gang life of the young in the Brazilian city. This time we are told the story of Anderson, a drug dealer who turns good citizen, but not without a lot of trouble on the street. The young here live amidst street violence, shootings, gun running, drugs and street crime. The police are under-trained, underpaid and corrupt. The documentary tracks a number of street deaths (proclaiming at the start that over 1,000 children were killed in just one year). But, and this seems to be the film's point, there is an escape: many young people who are

surrounded by this life do not want it. In this story, they actively trace a new life through the styles and culture of music – in this instance, Afro-Reggae. They dance away in large concerts and the film turns from a story of despair to a story of hope. It is here in the music, the film seems to suggest, that utterly marginalised youth find their own systems of respect.

Both these films have a focus on poor 'black' male youths in the city. These environments are found all over the world. And always we can view them through the lenses of class, gender, sexuality and ethnicity. The films act as ethnographies of urban life in low-income societies. In them we see the social divisions of a society at work. Here you can start to apply these ideas to a specific group.

 Other recent films to analyse are: Warwick Thornton's *Samson and Deliah* (2010) which tells the tale of a teenage boy on an aboriginal settlement who plays in a reggae band; Larry Clark's *Kids* (1995) (kids in downtown USA); Ken Loach's *Sweet Sixteen* (2001) (problems of Scottish youth); and Shane Meadows' *This is England* (2006) (troubled youth in Thatcher's Britain of 1983).

Are these fair representations of youth in the Western world today?

Guns are part of the youth culture in the cities of the world's low-income societies

Source: Kobal Collection Ltd/Globo Films.

dancing at parties can be seen as 'moral crimes', and anxious parents have to bail their children out of courts (Basmenji, 2005).

Likewise, ever since the break-up of the old Soviet Union, people in central Asia (or eastern Europe) – those in Tajikistan, Kazakhstan, Kyrgyzstan, Turkmenistan and Uzbekistan – have experienced Western influences that stress individualism at the expense of central Asian traditions of family and communalism. As we saw in Chapter 5, Islam has historically played a powerful force in their lives. When anthropologist Collette Harris looked at the lives of Muslim youth in Tajikistan, she found that the dominant Islamic culture still framed the lives of the young, but beneath the surface youth often modified, shifted and resisted it. Young central Asians today confront a complex mixture of the old and the new that strains personal relations, especially within the family, between generations and between spouses. For many 'global youth', the old worlds of tradition have become increasingly unsettled (Harris, 2006).

Growing older

We turn now to the main topic of this chapter – growing older. A quiet but powerful revolution is reshaping the world: the number of people growing older is increasing dramatically.

Global trends

One striking feature of the modern world is the ageing of the population. The latest UN projections suggest that the number of people aged 60 and over will double by the middle of this century. The 80-plus year group is growing faster than any other age group. Indeed, they are projected to increase fourfold over the next 50 years. Centenarians (aged 100 years or older) are likely to increase 15-fold, from roughly 145,000 in 1999 to 2.2 million by 2050. While through much of its history the world has had an ageing population that is relatively small, the United Nations predicts that most of the world will soon have an ageing population well above 20 per cent, and for about a third of the world it will be well over 30 per cent. This shift in the age structure of a population will have marked implications for the organisation of society. After all, for most of history we have had 'young populations'. Table 13.2 shows the societies which currently have the largest numbers of people who are elderly and Figures 13.2–13.5 show the countries and regions where the percentage population above 65 is greatest.

Table 13.2	Rank order of the world's largest older populations 2008 (millions)	
Rank	Country	Population 65 and over
1	China	106.1
2	India	59.6
3	United States	38.7
4	Japan	27.5
5	Russia	19.9
6	Germany	16.5
7	Indonesia	13.9
8	Brazil	12.3
9	Italy	11.7
10	France	10.4
11	United Kingdom	9.7
12	Ukraine	7.4
13	Spain	7.3
14	Pakistan	7.2
15	Mexico	6.7
16	Thailand	5.5
17	Bangladesh	5.4
18	Poland	5.1
19	Turkey	5.1
20	Vietnam	5.0
21	South Korea	4.9
22	Canada	4.6
23	Argentina	4.4
24	Nigeria	4.3
25	Philippines	3.9

Source: US Census Bureau, International Data Base, accessed on February 19, 2008.

Low-income/developing societies

Yet while the so-called 'greying of society' is commonly seen as a feature of Western industrialised societies and not one of the poorer, low-income societies, nothing could be more wrong. Sarah Harper, writing in her review of the situation in 2006, commented that:

Currently almost two-thirds of the world's older population live in developing societies, with the absolute numbers of people in these regions estimated to more than double to reach some 1 billion in 2030. The numbers are truly staggering – there are 47 million Africans over the age of 60, 49 million live in Latin America and the Caribbean and already 370 million live in the Asian Pacific region. Perhaps most significant is the speed at which these countries are ageing. The demographic transition which took place between 100 and 150 years in the developed world will occur in less than 50 years in these countries.

(Harper, 2006: 30)

Figure 13.2 The world's 25 oldest countries, 2008 (% of population aged 65 years and over)

Source: US Census Bureau, International Data Base, accessed 28 January 2008. See www.census.gov/prod2009pus/p95-09-1.pdf.

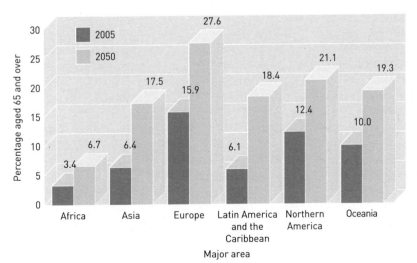

Figure 13.3 A demographic revolution: the changing world profile of ageing, 2005–50

Source: United Nations Programme on Ageing, 2007.

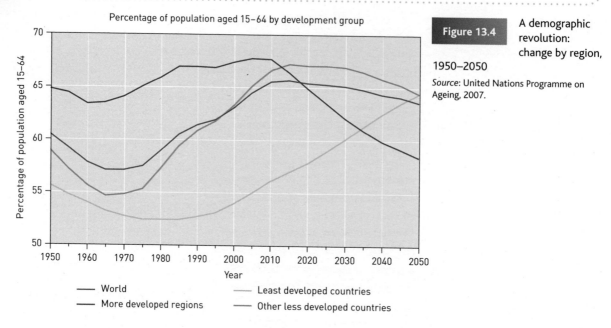

Figure 13.4 A demographic revolution: change by region, 1950–2050

Source: United Nations Programme on Ageing, 2007.

Table 13.2 shows this trend. It is important to stress the social implications of this (highlighted too in Chapter 9). These are mainly very poor countries, with low incomes, very poor health and little social provision. In general, the main focus of humanitarian concern in these countries lies with children and the young: the fact that there are millions of poverty-stricken elderly in these countries is sometimes (even often) ignored. These are the severely neglected. Often having just managed to survive poverty, wars, genocides, famine, migration, the dissolution of their families and widespread disease, they now have to confront getting old and dying. Their lives are among the most 'damaged' in the contemporary world. They are a prime example of what the sociologist Baumann has called 'Wasted Lives' (2004). Bear them in mind as a group while you read some of the tendencies of the world to become a postmodern high-tech place for the young and the wealthy.

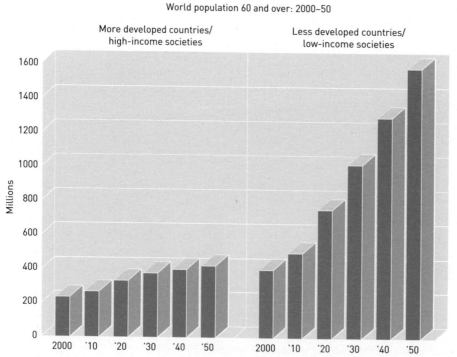

Figure 13.5 Number of older people in developed and developing regions

Source: Nugent, J. B. (2006) The old-age security motive for fertility, *Population and Development Review*, II, 1, pp. 75–97.

TOP 10
10 largest populations aged 80 and over

		%
1	Japan	6.1
2	Italy	5.8
3	Sweden	5.4
4	France	5.3
5	Germany	5.0
6	Belgium	4.9
7	Spain	4.9
8	Switzerland	4.9
9	Austria	4.7
10	UK	4.7

Note: Portugal is ranked 13 with 4.4 per cent of the population over 80 and Estonia is ranked 15 with 4.0 per cent.

Source: Pocket World in Figures, Profile Books, 2010.

 The weekly magazine *The Economist* provides an annual publication which digests many of the major world statistics. It first started publication in 1991, and the 2011 edition was published in the autumn of 2010:

The Economist, *Pocket World in Figures: 2011 edition.* London: Profile Books, 2010.

The Western world: the case of Europe and the UK

Consider the case of Britain. In 1880 fewer than 5 per cent of the population was *over 65*; in 2001, this was roughly 16 per cent and by mid-2008 it was 19 per cent, equivalent to 11.8 million people. At the same time, the number of people *over 85* in the UK reached 1.3 million, accounting for 2 per cent of the population, compared with 1 per cent in 1971. There were more than twice as many women aged 85 and over as men: 914,000 compared with 422,000. The proportion of people aged 85 and over is projected to increase further, to reach 4 per cent by 2031 (*Social Trends*, 2010).

The European situation

Similar change is occurring right across the rest of Europe. Within the EU, the average percentage of people over 65 rose from 10.6 per cent in 1960 to 14 per cent in 1991, and is predicted to rise to approximately 30 per cent by 2020. But there are differences across countries, with Ireland having the youngest population of EU countries and Sweden having the oldest (followed closely by Germany, France and the UK). Italy had the highest proportion of the elderly in the Europe – in 2005, people over 65 accounted for 19.5 per cent of the population out of a population of 57 million: that is, over 10 million were over 65.

Gender variations

Women outnumber men in the elderly population (due to their greater longevity) and the discrepancy increases with advancing age: at ages 70–4 there are roughly four women for every three men; at 80–4 there are two women for every man; and by 95, the ratio becomes three to one (Walker and Maltby, 1997: 11). However, the ratio of men to women is growing – what has been called the 'diminishing feminisation of later life' (*Social Trends*, 2004: 3). We can soon expect to see many more men in old age.

The dependency ratio

The growth in ageing populations is to be found in nearly all societies in the twenty-first century: it is a major, if not frequently discussed, social trend. Typically, rich nations have low birth rates, coupled with increasing longevity. This is sometimes called the 'demographic time bomb' and it highlights the **dependency ratio**: *the numbers of dependent children and retired persons relative to productive age groups* (Coleman and Salt, 1992: 542). This has been hovering around 58 and 53 over the past 25 years. Recently, because of falling fertility and family size it has been declining; it is not a problem yet. But changes predicted for this century suggest a growth in the dependency ratio – there will be fewer and fewer people of working age, and more and more will be dependants.

The past two centuries have witnessed a remarkable increase in life expectancy (see Figure 13.6). Neither men nor women born in England and Wales in 1821 had a life expectancy of much more than 40. Today, most women born today can look forward to 80 years of life; and men to just over 75 years (*Social Trends*, 2001: 127). This represents an increase of roughly 100 per cent in less than two centuries. Since 1971, the proportion of the population aged 65 and over has increased from 15.9 per cent to 18.0 per cent for women and from 10.5 per cent to 13.7 per cent for men (though it should be noted that this is a much slower rater of increase than in many other countries) (*Social Trends*, 2004: 1).

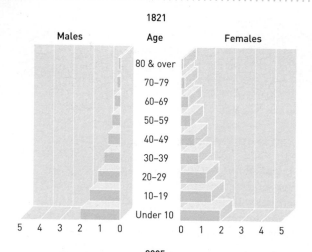

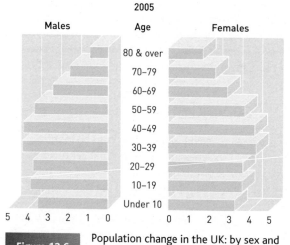

| Figure 13.6 | Population change in the UK: by sex and age, 1821 and 2005 |

Source: Office for National Statistics; General Register Office for Scotland.

Underlying this gain in life span are medical advances that have virtually eliminated infectious diseases such as smallpox, diphtheria and measles, which killed many infants and young people in the past, as well as more recent medical strides which fend off cancer and heart disease – afflictions common in the elderly. Looking beyond the elderly population, a rising standard of living during the twentieth century has promoted the health of people of all ages.

Consider the consequences of this massive increase in the elderly population. As elderly people steadily retire from the labour force, the proportion of non-working adults will generate ever-greater demands for social resources and programmes. Indeed, as the ratio of elderly people to working-age adults, which analysts call the *old-age dependency ratio*, almost doubles in the next 50 years (rising from 20 to 37 elderly people

per 100 people aged 18 to 64), this could shift the tax burden to the young, who will not be able to afford it. Some suggest that this may well lead to a major conflict between the generations (Kotlikoff and Burns, 2004). For instance, one key area of concern is the healthcare system because the elderly today account for a quarter of all medical expenditures. With the skyrocketing costs of medical care, tens of millions of additional elderly men and women could place an unprecedented demand on healthcare systems throughout the world (see Table 13.3).

The diversity of ageing

In terms of everyday experience, interacting with elderly people will become commonplace in coming decades. In recent history, our society has been marked by a considerable degree of age segregation. The young rarely mingle with the old, so that most young people know little about ageing. In the twenty-first century, as the elderly population increases, this pattern will probably change. But tomorrow as well as today, how frequently younger people interact with the elderly depends a great deal on where in the country we live. A lot of strands of research conducted in the early 2000s in the UK suggests that the diversity of the elderly is much greater than any other group. Yet there is a tendency to stereotype and lump all 'the old' together. At the very least there are, obviously, many different cultural, gender, class and race subgroups (Dean, 2004: 6).

Finally, the elderly represent an open category in which all of us, if we are lucky, end up. But the category represents great diversity, representing all cultures, classes, sexes, sexual orientations and ethnic groups. Even so, several broad distinctions between the elderly have become common. One of these distinctions is that between the **third age** (50–74) – *a period of life often free from parenting and paid work when a more active, independent life is achieved* – and a **fourth age** – *an age of eventual dependence* (Laslett, 1996). Another distinction is between a very large group – the 'young old' (65–75) – who enjoy good health and financial security, are typically autonomous and are likely to be living as couples, and the 'older old' (75–85) who become increasingly dependent on others because of both health and money problems. Finally, there is a growing group of 'very old'. Both these ways of grouping the elderly suggest a move from periods of increased activity and autonomy to one of growing dependency.

Table 13.3	Issues and implications for the worlds of older people: a summary
Issue	**Implication**
1 Health and disabilities	Growing need for health services and finance to support
2 Work and retirement	Changing shape of life course
	New patterns of both 'work' and leisure in later life
	Changing incomes of elderly:
	pension needs (linked to 3 below)
3 Income and poverty	Greater strain on finances for some groups in old age – living longer
	Major 'poverty' group – need to be reduced or eliminated
4 Care, family and community	New relations between home, community and residential institutions – needing finance and a clearer focus on the nature of care and caregivers
	Problems of elder abuse and neglect
	Recognition of new roles: the young old look after the old old!
	New retirement colonies for different groups, e.g. lesbian and gay communities in Palm Springs
5 Personal adjustment	Problems of isolation through bereavement, etc.
	Need for new meanings of later life and communities of support
	New identities for the ageing?
6 Ageism and discrimination	The rise of the 'grey vote'; a new politics of ageing
7 Culture	'Culture' has a vivid youth imagery and value base towards youth, and the old easily get 'written out'.
	Shifting images of ageing as more and more people fit the category, and hence more facilities have to become available
8 Well-being	Growing concerns about 'well-being' at all stages of life
9 Politics, resistance and fighting back	Rejection of the elderly as passive and the rise of new movements for the old

The social implications of ageing

1 Health and disability

Getting older inevitably brings some decline in biological functioning and, to put it bluntly, there can be a decline in limb and liver, bowel and bladder, heart and brain. All the illnesses – cancer, heart attacks, disabilities, etc. – are more common, and the chances of getting these illnesses increase as people age. In the West, this may not be too significant for the 'young old', but by the time we face the 'old old' (over 85) it usually becomes

very pronounced. There is, nevertheless, evidence of declining ability and growing disease among all the elderly, and in low-income societies, it appears quite early on and is even more severe.

As populations age, non-communicable diseases (see Chapter 21) become more and more common. In Western countries at least, more and more older people see themselves as ill and report illness (as Table 13.4 suggests).

2 Work and retirement

The transition from working life to retirement poses some problems for many older people. As the pattern of work changes in industrial societies, so there is a

Table 13.4	Self-reported illness: by sex and age, 2005	
Great Britain	**Rates per 1,000 population**	
	Long-standing illness	Limiting long-standing illness
Males		
0–4	140	45
5–14	181	72
15–44	175	90
45–64	401	233
65–74	554	342
75 and over	583	402
All ages	273	150
Females		
0–4	93	28
5–14	160	67
15–44	209	114
45–64	407	245
65–74	589	370
75 and over	545	401
All ages	282	163

Source: Adapted from *General Household Survey* (Longitudinal), Office for National Statistics. *Social Trends* 37, 2007, Table 7.3.

pronounced tendency for people to retire at earlier and earlier ages – sometimes by choice, sometimes through compulsory redundancies. Although the idea of retirement is familiar to us, it is actually a recent creation, becoming commonplace only in industrial societies during the nineteenth century (Atchley, 1983).

In the industrialised world, 'retirement' is often seen as a significant marker of getting older: it marks a change in the life/work routines and is signified by an 'old age pension'. Most significantly, it can shift you into a more dependent position.

Pensions and the coming pension crisis

Throughout Europe a major source of income for the elderly is the pension. Generally, this is a two-tier system: public and private (usually an occupational pension). The latter is much more available to men, once again reinforcing the weaker position of women in old age. As the value of this often decreases over time, so the elderly become relatively poorer.

German Chancellor Otto von Bismarck first introduced retirement pensions in 1889, setting the age then at 70 (in 1916, it was lowered to 65). Denmark followed suit in 1892 with New Zealand and Australia soon following. In the UK the old age pension was introduced in 1908. The United States and Canada were slower to introduce comprehensive schemes – in 1935 and 1927 respectively. Today, nearly all industrialised countries have pension schemes, with the minimum age set most commonly at 65.

A key issue here concerns the economics of just how much private companies are to be involved in paying out (through insurance schemes) and how much the government contributes (often through workers' pay-as-you-go systems over their working life). It is the problem of state provision versus private provision that we have encountered before (see Chapter 10).

In Europe generally, we can find two major systems of pension: those where statutory provisions provide a universal basic pension which can then be supplemented by an earnings-related pension (as in Denmark, Sweden, Finland, the UK and Ireland); and those where occupational pensions are provided by employers, which are supplemented by universally minimum benefits (as in Germany, Austria, France, Belgium, Luxembourg, Italy, Spain and Portugal).

As the ageing population grows in size, governments have become increasingly concerned about the future of pensions – the 'pension debate' is now with us. Two critical problems now appear. One concerns the so-called crisis in the dependency ratio. The other is the continuing problem of redistribution. The claim is usually made that many countries have placed too great a reliance on personal savings and public pay-as-you-go systems; not enough emphasis has been placed on the development of capital markets to fund private pension arrangements. There are major needs to reform retirement income systems (pensions). A key worry seems to be that the cost of pay-as-you-go public pensions will escalate in the face of ageing populations.

The crisis in the dependency ratio

Earlier in the chapter we discussed the **dependency ratio** (*the numbers of dependent children and retired persons relative to working, productive age groups*) and some of the social consequences of shifts in this. Here is a major example of such potential shifts. The costs of looking after the elderly may increase the tax burdens of the working group that pays taxes. As the needs of the growing older population increase, so younger people in work may have to pay more for their provision. Some commentators think this is leading to a 'coming generational storm' (Kotlikoff and Burns,

PUBLIC SOCIOLOGY

Talking about Alzheimer's and dementia

Dementia describes 'a collection of symptoms, including a decline in memory, reasoning and communications skills, and a gradual loss of skills needed to carry out daily activities' (Alzheimer's Society, 2007: 1). In the UK, there are currently 700,000 people with dementia (since at least 15,000 of these are younger people, it should not be seen as just a disease of the old). This is about one person in 88 of the UK population. Estimates suggest that it could be over a million by 2025, nearly two million by 2051, and it will continue to grow. Two-thirds are women, and typically the older you grow,

the greater the chance of getting it (one-third of people over 95 have dementia). Some 60,000 deaths a year are directly linked to it. Two-thirds of people with dementia live in the community, while one-third live in a care home. In 2007, dementia cost around £17 billion a year (Alzheimer's Society, 2007).

In 2007 the Alzheimer's Society: Dementia Care and Research produced a research report (*The Rising Cost of Dementia in the UK*) commissioned through King's College London and the London School of Economics to provide a report on the state of Alzheimer's in the UK. It called for:

- making dementia a national health and social care priority
- increasing funded research

- improving care skills and carer support
- establishing a national debate on dementia.

Sociology is such a wide area of study that it cannot look at everything equally. But here is an important public issue, generally neglected in public talk, yet experienced very widely in silence. A 'public sociology' could see this as an issue, conduct more social research on it – especially perhaps on the social conditions that would enhance the lives of those experiencing dementia – and help to find a public voice to establish this debate. At present the public voice has to rely on novels (like John Bayle's *Iris* (1998), later made into a moving film). See also the film *Away From Her* (2008).

See: Anthea Innes *Dementia Studies* (2009).

Hilda is not lost at the piano. Another example of Cathy Greenblat's photography on dementia and long term care (see Chapter 3)
Source: © Cathy Greenblat.

2004) where the young will increasingly resent the old. Others think that the debate is an 'imaginary time bomb' (Mullan, 2002), a crisis that is being stirred up by media but which in fact is not likely to happen.

Robin Blackburn's *Banking on Death* (2003) argues that an ageing 'pension crisis' has been spread by financial interests, alarmist media and right-wing politicians to help develop private systems of pensions. He suggests the rise of a 'grey capitalism' and shows

how badly the financial services industry performs as a custodian of savings and pension funds. Attempts by companies to meet the costs of the ageing society through a proliferation of new financial products, which provide a host of new investment and financial arrangements, have often failed. They have wiped billions from the savings of employees and allowed corporations to escape taxation, while allowing a new breed of chief executive to accumulate extravagant fortunes at the expense of shareholder and employee alike. Robin Blackburn calls this an *'Age Shock'* (2007). In this later work he identifies new sources of pension finance.

The continuing problem of redistribution

People who have been poor all their life are likely to remain poor in old age; and wealthier people will, in most cases, have better pension provision which will see them as old people still enjoying the pleasures of higher incomes. Those in lower-paid occupations often do not have occupational pensions, which in any case are not always 'safe' and protected, and are thus dependent upon state pensions. And their relative value to earnings has been declining since 1982. The poverty of many old people is in part connected to poor pension provision more generally.

As a public issue, the critical sociologist John Vincent puts it well: 'Why do we hear more about the future cost of state pensions or healthcare than, for example, the long term cost to future generations of disposing of nuclear waste, or in terms of global warming for today's consumption of hydrocarbon fuels?' (Vincent, 2006: 210). As always, sociological analysis is closely connected to political observation.

Shifts in work

Advancing technology reduces the need for everyone to work, as well as placing a premium on up-to-date skills. Retirement permits younger workers, who presumably have the most current knowledge and training, to predominate in the labour force. Some of the lowering of retirement ages may be linked to the growth of unemployment – stimulating early retirement policies in many countries. The establishment of private and public pension schemes provided the economic foundation for retirement. In poor societies that depend on the labour of everyone, and where no pension schemes exist, most people work until they become incapacitated.

Work not only provides earnings, but also figures prominently in our personal identity. Hence, retirement from paid work usually brings a significant reduction in income and sometimes entails a diminished status and even a loss of purpose in life.

Class differences are often important in retirement. Working-class retirement may often lack 'an active concept of retirement', whereas middle-class retirement – with better resources – has led to an expanding

consumer market and culture (Fennell et al., 1988: 83; Blaikie, 1999). For many older people, fresh activities and new interests minimise the personal disruption and loss of prestige brought on by retirement. They join 'the third age' – a time of active leisure. Volunteer work can be personally rewarding, allowing individuals to apply their career skills to new challenges and opportunities. But for others, and especially older women, this might be little more than a 'bourgeois option, unavailable to those who have low incomes and poor health' (Arber and Ginn, 1995: 8).

Around the world, there is little agreement as to when (or even if) a person should retire from paid work. In the light of such variability, one might wonder if a society should formally designate any specific age for retirement. Vast differences in the interests and capacities of older people make the notion of a fixed retirement age controversial. In the United States, as a result, Congress began phasing out mandatory retirement policies in the 1970s and virtually ended the practice by 1987. The United States is one of the few countries that have legislated against age discrimination – France, Spain, Canada, New Zealand and Australia being others (Walker and Maltby, 1997: 80).

In Europe, men more than women have faced the transition of retirement. Elderly women who spend their lives as homemakers do not retire *per se*, though the departure of the last child from home serves as a rough parallel. As the proportion of women in the labour force continues to rise, of course, both women and men will experience the changes brought on by retirement (Laczo and Phillipson, 1991).

3 Income and inequalities: poverty and the elderly

For most people in Europe, retirement leads to a significant decline in income. While some of the elderly are quite affluent, many lack sufficient savings or pension benefits to be self-supporting. John A. Vincent has argued that:

> The inequalities in the rest of society are reproduced in old age, and appear to be amplified. After retirement, the inequalities resulting from low pay, unemployment, disability, ill health, sex discrimination and racial discrimination are carried through into old age. The decline in the value of savings and pensions . . . means the worst off are the very old.

(Vincent, 1996: 23–4)

He argues that the elderly are the most disadvantaged in society, and yet they are often excluded from mainstream studies of class and inequality. Simple matters such as income invariably decrease. There is a systematic curve that shows that income starts low in early life, increases until middle age and then declines through later years.

More close inspection shows certain trends in the UK. Citing evidence from the General Household Survey, Vincent shows that the income of men over age 74 in the UK may drop by an average of £80 per week, while a woman's may drop nearly £60 (Vincent, 1996: 22). More of their income has to be spent on the 'bare necessities' of life: food, fuel, housing. And the older one gets, the poorer one becomes. Poverty rates rise significantly as people enter old age, making an increasing gap between the wealthy elderly and the poor elderly. Nevertheless, the proportion of pensioners living in low-income households has been falling throughout the last decade, from 29 per cent of all pensioners in 1996/7 to 17 per cent in 2005/6. Among single pensioners, the rate has halved over the period, from 40 per cent to 20 per cent. Pensioners now account for about one-sixth of all the people in poverty (poverty.org, 2007).

Although the living standards of older people have generally been rising in recent years, there are wide differences across countries. In general, there are low poverty rates in Denmark, Germany, Ireland and Luxembourg; medium poverty rates in Belgium, France, Italy and the Netherlands; and the countries with the highest poverty rates are Greece, Portugal, Spain and the UK. This said, however, when compared with the poverty rates found in the United States, all these levels are relatively low. One study ranking poverty levels gives Norway an index of 4.8 (low), the UK an index of 8.8 (middling) and the United States an index of 16.9 (high) (Vincent, 1996: 28).

In Europe, then, although many elderly are faring better than ever before, growing old (especially among women and minorities) still means a growing risk of poverty, one that is feminised (more women experience it) and polarised (there is a sharp divide between the poor old and the wealthy old). What is distinctive about the deprivation of the elderly, however, is that it is often hidden from view. Because of personal pride and a desire to maintain the dignity of independent living, many elderly people conceal financial problems, even from their own families. It is often difficult for people who have supported their children for years to admit that they can no longer provide for themselves, even though it may be through no fault of their own.

4 Care, family and community

Elderly people are also more likely than the whole population to experience social isolation, poverty and abuse. One of the most apparent concerns of the elderly is being 'old and alone' (Tunstall, 1966): there is a problem of both potential isolation and loneliness. Retirement may cut the old off from friends and workmates; the death of a spouse may leave the old on their own; and illness may bring limited mobility and a reduced chance to meet others. In Europe, '15% of those aged 60–4 live alone. This percentage doubles for those 70–4 and is almost 48% for those aged over 80' (Walker and Maltby, 1997: 13). This is much more likely to happen in the northern countries (the UK, the Netherlands, France and Belgium) and less likely in the southern (Greece, Portugal and Spain). But living alone is not the same as feeling lonely. Indeed, in the European survey, loneliness almost runs in reverse to living alone. The elderly in Portugal and Greece are more likely to feel lonely, and those living in Germany, the UK and Denmark are least likely (Walker and Maltby, 1997: 26). One recent UK study suggested that only a minority of older people were lonely (7 per cent) and a relatively small group (11–17 per cent) felt isolated (Dean, 2004: 13). While many do live alone, most old people seem to keep regular contact with their children – either by phone or by living near them. This has been called 'intimacy at a distance'.

One of the greatest causes of social isolation is the inevitable death of significant others. Few human experiences affect people as profoundly as the death of a spouse or family member. Widows and widowers must rebuild their lives in the glaring absence of people with whom, in many instances, they spent most of their adult lives. Some survivors choose not to live at all. One study of elderly men noted a sharp increase in mortality, sometimes by suicide, in the months following the death of their wives (Benjamin and Wallis, 1963).

The 'old' – or at least what we have called the 'old old' – can easily be cut off from the 'mainstream' of society. One study by Scharf et al. (2001) found that 70 per cent of the people studied in deprived areas felt some kind of exclusion, and 40 per cent suffered multiple exclusions. Living in poverty was a key factor here, but there were many others. They were socially isolated, fearful of their neighbourhoods and potential crime, afraid of going out, and excluded from wider activities.

The issue of care

Who looks after the old as they become more frail and dependent upon others? Traditionally the answer to this in many societies has been 'families'. As 'mums' and 'dads' grow older, their offspring repay their earlier debts – emotionally and economically – to their parents. They look after them. In some societies, the elderly become elevated in their communities – their achievements celebrated, their presence honoured.

Although this continues today in modern and postmodern societies, families have themselves changed and so have the baselines of support and care. Increasingly, in many societies people come to live on their own as they get older and older. As problems compound, some also become isolated.

In the UK, personal care for the dependant can come in one of three ways:

- *Residential care or nursing ('residential care')*: this is usually very expensive in the UK. Help comes to about 60 per cent in the UK (with assets less than £21,000); about a third are self-funders. The cost of a care home averages between £400 and £500 per week.

- *At home, with paid professionals ('home care')*: depends on provision of local governments. It can be expensive and variable in quality. But in the UK, services are supposed (at least) to meet essential needs.

- *At home, with unpaid family members ('informal care')*: full-time carers (over 35 hours a week) can get an allowance of £45 if they are not claiming other benefit.

In the UK, the Wanless Review (*Securing Good Care for Older People: Taking a Long-Term Review*, 2006) suggested that the costs of older people's social care will increase to £29.5 billion in 2026. The report suggested a free package of basic care, topped up by personal contributions matched by the state. The need for universal benefits like the NHS would continue.

Fear of crime

Many surveys across the world (including the *British Crime Survey 2007*) have suggested that the elderly have a great 'fear of crime'. They fear abuse and mugging, and are very sensitive to any reported incidents of elderly crime. This fear restricts their movements and makes them fearful of going out of their homes after dark: they can become trapped in

their own homes. In the Netherlands, more than half of those aged 65 or over no longer go out after dark; in Denmark, two-fifths of women aged 60 or over are afraid of being exposed to violence in the evening. Large numbers of old people are thus becoming stranded in their own homes.

Yet the reality is quite often different. Criminal statistics (see Chapter 16) strongly suggest that people aged 60 or over are much less likely to become victims of crime than those of other age groups. To take one quick example, while 12.6 per cent of young men were victims of violent crimes in 2005/6, only 0.4 per cent of those over 65 were such victims (*Social Trends*, 2007: 119).

Gender issues

The problems of social isolation fall most heavily on women, who typically outlive their husbands. Over 40 per cent of older women (especially the 'older elderly') live alone, compared to 16 per cent of older men. As with everything to do with old age, it is strongly structured by gender (Arber and Ginn, 1995).

The family and abuse

Problems of family violence became increasingly recognised in Europe during the 1970s and 1980s. First came 'wife battering', then 'child abuse' (see Chapter 17). Most recently, an increasing number of researchers have noticed the phenomenon of 'granny battering' – or elder abuse. Abuse of older people takes many forms, from passive neglect to active torment, and includes verbal, emotional, financial and physical harm. Research suggests that between 3 and 4 per cent of elderly people (mainly women) suffer serious maltreatment each year, and three times as many sustain abuse at some point. Like family violence against children or women, it is difficult to determine how widespread abuse of the elderly is because victims are understandably reluctant to talk about their plight. But as the proportion of elderly people rises, so does the incidence of abuse (Payne, 2005; Pillemer, 1988; Glendenning, 1993).

A research study in the UK, published in 2007, suggested that more than 700,000 elderly people are subjected to abuse in their own homes or private nursing homes in the UK (based on a sample of 2000: *UK Study of Abuse and Neglect*, June 2007). Violence, bullying and neglect – along with verbal abuse that lowers the esteem of old people and makes them feel bad, incompetent and inadequate – is very common. This is a quiet but pervasive problem, not raised very often and not producing large amounts of public concern.

What motivates people to abuse the elderly? Often the cause lies in the stress of caring – financially and emotionally – for ageing parents. Today's middle-aged adults represent a 'sandwich generation' who may well spend as much time caring for their ageing parents as for their own children. This care-giving responsibility is especially pronounced among adult women, who not only look after parents and children but hold down jobs as well.

5 Personal adjustment and quality of life

Although physical decline in old age is often less serious than most younger people think, this change can cause emotional stress. Older people can endure more pain, become resigned to limited activities, adjust to greater dependence on others and see in the death of friends or relatives frequent reminders of their own mortality. Moreover, because our culture places such a premium on youth, ageing may spark frustration, fear and self-doubt. Psychiatrist Erik Erikson (1963, 1980), whose work has looked at the life cycle (see Chapter 7), suggests that in the final stages of life elderly people must resolve a tension that springs from 'integrity versus despair'. No matter how much they may still be learning and achieving, older people recognise that their lives are nearing an end. Thus the elderly spend much time reflecting on their past accomplishments and disappointments. To retain their personal integrity, Erikson explains, older women and men must face up to past mistakes as well as savour their successes. Otherwise, this stage of life may turn into a time of despair – a dead end with little positive meaning.

Despite these worries, research indicates that most people cope fairly well with the challenges of growing old. One of the earliest studies of this was that by Bernice Neugarten (one of North America's leading social gerontologists), in which she suggested four main adaptations:

- Some people develop *disintegrated and disorganised personalities* because they find it nearly impossible to come to terms with old age. Despair is the common thread in these lives, sometimes to the point of making them passive residents of hospitals or nursing homes.

- Another segment of Neugarten's subjects, those with *passive-dependent personalities*, were only slightly better off. They had little confidence in their abilities to cope with daily events, sometimes seeking help even if they did not actually need it. Always in danger of social withdrawal, their level of life satisfaction remained relatively low.

- A third category of people had *defended personalities*, living independently but fearful of advancing age. Such people tried to shield themselves from the reality of old age by valiantly fighting to stay youthful and physically fit. While concerns about health are certainly positive, setting unrealistic standards for oneself can only breed stress and disappointment.

- Most of Neugarten's subjects, however, fared far better, displaying what she called *integrated personalities*. As she sees it, the key to successful ageing lies in maintaining one's dignity, self-confidence and optimism while accepting the inevitability of growing old. This seems by far the most common pattern (Neugarten and Neugarten, 1996).

6 Discrimination and ageing

In earlier chapters, we explained how ideology – including racism and sexism – seeks to justify the social disadvantages of minorities. Sociologists use the parallel term **ageism** to designate *prejudice and discrimination against the elderly*. Like racism and sexism, ageism can be blatant (as when individuals deny elderly women or men a job simply because of their age) or subtle (as when people speak to the elderly with a condescending tone, as if they were children). Also, like racism and sexism, ageism builds physical traits into stereotypes; in the case of the elderly, people consider greying hair, wrinkled skin and stooped posture as signs of personal incompetence. Negative stereotypes picture the aged as helpless, confused, resistant to change and generally unhappy (Butler, 1975). Even sentimental notions of sweet little old ladies and charmingly eccentric old gentlemen gloss over older people's individuality, their distinct personalities and their long years of experience and accomplishment (Bytheway, 1995).

Ageism, like other expressions of prejudice, may have some foundation in reality. Statistically speaking, old people are more likely than young people to be mentally and physically impaired. But we slip into ageism when we make unwarranted generalisations about an entire category of people, most of whom do not conform to the stereotypes.

7 Culture

In high-income societies, the twenty-first century is bringing some radical changes to ways in which the elderly live. Some market researchers have distinguished between the 'new age' elderly (who have considerable disposable income) and the traditional elderly (who have very little). The generation that brought about change in the 1960s – the baby boomers – is now reaching its old age, and again new institutions are appearing to deal with their changing needs. At present and over the next decade or so, a new cohort of elderly is arriving that is very different from that of the past. Many are better educated, wealthier and keener to be very active than the majority of the past (though that may well make the problems of the many poor and isolated even greater). The 'new age' elderly are willing to spend money on products and services to make that happen. Some signs of this can already be seen in such developments as:

1 The growth of commercial markets for the leisure activities of the elderly – SAGA in the UK now employs some 3,000 people with an annual budget of some £350 million.
2 The growth of internet use among the young elderly. Although the new technologies are largely in the hands of the young, new cohorts of the elderly will have general skills for surfing and for access to such things as social networking (like sagazone.co.uk and cyberhealth (see Chapter 21).
3 The growth of self-help groups for the elderly. New movements like the University of the Third Age (U3A) have been emerging since the early 1980s to provide a wide range of the new elderly 'leisure classes'. The rapid growth of gardening centres all over the UK, for instance, may be related. (See www.u3a.org.uk)
4 The development of new retirement communities and the migration of the elderly to the 'sun'.
5 The growing political organising of the elderly. There is a wing of the elderly that is highly political. The National Pensioners Convention (NPC) in Britain represents over 1,000 local, regional and national pensioner groups with a total of 1.5 million members. The NPC has its roots back in the early twentieth century with the trade union movement. (See NPC at www.npcuk.org.)

8 Well-being

Given the youth orientation of most European societies, it may be easy to imagine that the elderly are generally unhappy. But research suggests that, while personal adjustments and problems are inevitable, the experience of growing old may also provide positive experiences – many old people do not even see themselves as old. As they say, 'I don't feel old' (Thompson et al., 1990). Indeed, a European survey of the elderly found that only one in five were not satisfied with their lives, while two out of three reported they were very busy or leading full lives (Walker and Maltby, 1997: 23, 122). More recent research in the UK has looked at the quality of life and concluded that:

> **most men and women rated their quality of life as good in varying degrees, as opposed to just alright or bad. Quality of life deteriorated with older age, but almost three quarters of the group aged 65–69 rated their lives overall as 'so good it could not be better' or 'very good' compared to a third to a half of those in older groups. It concluded the main drivers of quality of life in older age were: people's standards of comparison; their sense of optimism; good health and physical functioning; engaging on a large number of social activities; feeling supported; and living in safe communities with good community facilities and services.**
>
> (Dean, 2004: 7)

9 Politics, resistances and fighting back

Poets have often seen the damaging ways in which the old have been treated, and have shown ways to 'fight back'. Thus Dylan Thomas says:

> **Do not go gentle into that good night,**
> **Old Age should burn and rave at close of day;**
> **Rage, rage against the dying of the light**
>
> (Dylan Thomas, 1951)

The French philosopher Simone de Beauvoir and the American author Betty Friedan were two leading feminist thinkers in the mid-twentieth century. De Beauvoir was famed for *The Second Sex* (orig. 1949 in France) in which she argued that women were defined in and through men as 'the other'. Ten years later, Friedan achieved celebrity status for her book *The Feminine Mystique* (1963) which showed that

Table 13.5	The two faces of growing older in the 21st century	

The positive face of growing old (often linked to 'young old' or third age)	The negative face of growing old (often linked to 'old old' or fourth age)
Longevity: people live much longer	Over-prolonged life: keeping alive against will
Body, emotion and mind still flourishing	Body, emotion and mind in steep decline
Active social life and engagements: new cultures of the elderly	Loss of active life: isolation as friends die
Fitness, health and body enhancements	Loss of health: dementia and Alzheimer's
Mobility and travel	Loss of mobility, often residential care
Positive self and forward looking	Demeaned self and loss of dignity
Resilience: ability to cope with later life problems	Failures in capacities to deal with problems and increasing dependency on others

See: Marie de Hennezel, *The Warmth of the Heart Prevents Your Body from Rusting: Ageing without growing* (2011).

Western societies defined women only in sexual relation to men – as wives, mothers or sex objects. Thirty years later, having long established their feminist voices, both Friedan and de Beauvoir issued another call for change, this time in the way we view the elderly.

De Beauvoir, in *The Coming of Age* (*La Vieillesse*, 1970), rallied against the injustices shown to the old and the ways in which they had been silenced. Friedan loooked at the media in the USA and showed that the old were largely ignored, concluding that elderly people were conspicuous by their absence; only a small percentage of television shows, for example, feature central characters who are over 60. In addition, when members of many Western societies do think about older people, it is in negative terms: the elderly lack jobs, have lost their vitality and look back to their youth. In short, the 'ageing mystique' is that we define being old as little more than a disease, marked by decline and deterioration, for which there is no cure.

Describing the denial of elderly, the discriminations that were pervasive in culture, they claimed it was time we started seeking the 'fountain of ageing' by highlighting the potential and possibilities of this stage of life. In many societies, older people are now discovering that they have more to contribute than others give them credit for. Playing in orchestras, assisting small business owners, designing housing for the poor, teaching children to read – there are countless ways in which older people can enhance their own lives by engaging people around them. The bottom line, concludes Friedan, is that people do not stop living when they grow old; they grow old when they stop living.

Depending on class, old age comes at different times and has different impacts. It should remain a time of creative and meaningful projects, and have positive instead of the negative cultural meanings it is usually shrouded within. The value of life should be nowhere clearer, but instead society may be guilty of treating the elderly with disdain, dehumanising them.

Researching ageing

Each of sociology's major theoretical paradigms sheds light on the process of ageing in Europe. We examine each in turn.

Functional analysis: ageing and disengagement

One of the earliest accounts came in the 1960s from Cumming and Henry (1961), borrowing some ideas from the leading functionalist Talcott Parsons. They argued that as ageing threatens society with disruption as physical decline and death take their toll, society's response is to *disengage* the elderly – to gradually transfer statuses and roles from the old to the young so that tasks are performed with minimal interruption.

Thus, disengagement theories suggest that it is functional to remove ageing people from traditional work roles – as they confront diminishing capacities for work, and look forward to relinquishing some of the pressures of their jobs in favour of new pursuits of their own choosing. Society also grants older people greater freedom, so that unusual behaviour on their part is construed as harmless eccentricity rather than dangerous deviance.

Such disengagement has an added benefit in a rapidly changing society because young workers typically have the most up-to-date skills and training. Formally, then, **disengagement theory** is *the proposition that society enhances its orderly operation by disengaging people from positions of responsibility as they reach old age.*

Although this is an old theory, it is still widely cited because some see it as explaining why rapidly changing, industrial societies typically define their oldest members as socially marginal. But it is largely rejected, and for four reasons. First, many workers cannot readily disengage from paid work because they do not have sufficient financial security to fall back on. Second, many elderly people – regardless of their financial circumstances – do not wish to disengage from their productive roles. Disengagement, after all, comes at a high price, including loss of social prestige and social isolation. Third, there is no compelling evidence that the benefits of disengagement outweigh its costs to society, which range from the loss of human resources to the increased care of people who might otherwise be able to fend better for themselves. Indeed, as the numbers of elderly people swell, devising ways to help seniors remain independent is a high national priority. Then, too, any useful system of disengagement would have to take account of the widely differing abilities of the elderly themselves. But fourth, and perhaps most significant, it makes the elderly appear too passive and too much like victims. And many studies show this is not true.

Humanistic analysis: activity and biography

This latter criticism is picked up from within symbolic interactionism and becomes almost a mirror image. Instead of disengagement (which would undermine the satisfaction and meaning many elderly people find in their lives), what we find are ageing people actively reconstructing the meanings of their lives. What seniors need, in short, are productive and recreational activities that imbue their retirement with meaning and joy. Activity theory proposes that, to the extent that elderly people do disengage, they substitute 'new lives' for the ones they leave behind. The elderly pursue active lives as much as the young do. Indeed, study after study suggests the importance to the elderly of

following their interests, remaining engaged with daily activities and relationships, etc. (Havighurst et al., 1968; Neugarten and Neugarten, 1996). Activity theory thus shifts the focus of analysis from the needs of society (as stated in disengagement theory) to the needs of the elderly themselves. This second approach also highlights social diversity among elderly people.

Functionalists might say this tends to exaggerate the well-being and competence of the elderly and even ask if we really want elderly people actively serving in crucial roles, say, as physicians or airline pilots. From another perspective, activity theory falls short by overlooking the fact that many of the problems that beset older people have more to do with how society, not any individual, operates.

The biographical approach

An important part of this activity theory is the role of telling the story of our lives. Of growing interest to both gerontologists and sociologists in recent times has been a biographical approach to ageing. This is a humanistic approach that aims to listen to the stories of the lives of the elderly. Three types can be distinguished.

First is the *reminiscence* story. In the 1960s, Butler and others started to suggest the importance of 'reminiscence' and 'life reviews' in the lives of the elderly (Butler, 1963). The act of purposely remembering can play a significant role in helping to create a coherent and unitary self (see, for example, Meyerhoff, 1992). Gerontologists have found that a characteristic of many elderly is their desire to tell, and tell again, some key highlights of their life. These can perform important functions both practically for the researcher, in providing key jumping-off points for further questions, but also therapeutically, since the telling of these stories is often an important part of the elderly person's adjustment process. With the 'greying of the population' and the growing tendency of the elderly to end their lives inside nursing homes, getting their life stories told can perform many valuable functions. The recognition of this has recently had something of the momentum of a social movement. A pioneer in this field, Joanna Bornat, has traced the origins of this movement in the UK to three sources: the academic growth of oral history; the spread of community publishing – such as the Centerprise Publishing Project in Hackney, London (with books such as Dot Steran's *When I Was a Child*, published in 1973); and the development of ideas in psychology around recall and memory, enabling almost everyone to become an oral historian of some kind (Bornat, 1994). (The UK organisation Help the Aged produced a type slide show in 1981 called *Recall* to facilitate this.)

Second is the *oral history*. Here the life is told in order to throw light on the times of the elderly person: stories of the Second – or First – World War; stories of the Depression; stories of illegitimate children and the problem this led to. All this and more help the oral historian to fill out the portraits of the historical past (see Thompson et al., 1990). Closely allied to this is the gathering of a family history. (These days, many bookshops provide rather elaborate 'family history' albums that facilitate this.)

Third is the *sociological life history*. Here the life is told through a series of stages and themes which help us understand the workings of a life over the life course. Does the life, for instance, fit into the stages discussed in Chapter 7 of this book? What might be the life's major organising themes – possibly linked to power, intimacy, work, play and love? Does it, in the end, achieve some kind of coherence around the life? Jaber Gubrium, for instance, while listening to the life stories of elderly people in 'Florida Manor', can sense, tellingly, that many lives never achieve a coherence – that many 'elderly faces' may reveal the fragments of stories past while being unable to find connections with the (often diseased) present. As Gubrium says at the close of his book of life stories:

> **There is little overall evidence that affairs are ultimately settled, sundered ties finally repaired, transgressions at last righted or accounted for, or preparations of the future or the afterlife completed.**

(Gubrium, 1993: 188)

Critical gerontology: ageing and inequality

Conflict theories highlight how different age categories compete for scarce social resources, a fact that contributes to age stratification. By and large, middle-aged people in Europe enjoy the greatest social privileges, while the elderly (as well as children) contend with less power and prestige and face a higher risk of poverty. Employers often shunt elderly workers aside in favour of younger men and women as a means of keeping down wages. As a consequence, conflict theorists note, older people become second-class citizens (Phillipson, 1982; Atchley, 1983).

To conflict theorists, age-based hierarchy is inherent in industrial–capitalist society. Capitalist culture has an overriding concern with profit, and hence facilitates the devaluation of those categories of people who are economically unproductive. Viewed as mildly deviant because they are less productive than their younger counterparts, the elderly are destined to be marginal members of a society consumed by material gain. In recent years, a cluster of British sociologists – Townsend, Walker, Phillipson and Vincent – have all highlighted the links between old age, dependency, divisions of labour and structures of inequality. The key to their work is the idea of **structured dependency**, *the process by which some people in society receive an unequal share in the results of social production* (Vincent, 1996: 186). Originally, in the work of Townsend and Walker, this referred to material dependency and focused upon the ways the elderly were structured out of work and into low incomes and poverty, and how this was reflected in welfare, health and care policies generally. More recently, it has become concerned with interpersonal

Living over a hundred years – immigrants in time

Elizabeth 'Lizzie' Bolden died in December 2006 at the age of 116, leaving 40 grandchildren, 220 great-great-grandchildren and 75 great-great-great-great grandchildren. Lizzie was born in Memphis on 15 August 1890, the daughter of freed slaves. For most of her life she lived through the 'Jim Crow' laws of segregation in the southern states of America; lived in poverty (though not seeing it as that); and became the 'mother' of her Missionary Baptist Church (founded in 1927). Her life – with her husband Lewis – remained relatively unchanged from that of her slave parents – cotton farming the land but in very limited ways (Pilkington, *Guardian*, 16.12.06: 25).

Imagine if your memory might be able to take in some of the events over the past hundred years:

from minor things like clothes and meals to bigger ones like wars, deaths and births. The shifts in technology alone are astounding. And as more and more people hit the hundred mark (and become centenarians), so the span of generations grows and grows. Whole groups of people become 'immigrants in time' – not really knowing anything or much about the 'new culture' that has emerged around them.

Websites can guide you to the names and details of the world's longest-living people.

dependence; with the ways the elderly are often infantilised into a form of helplessness, and how they may become segregated not only in institutions but also in the growing practices of keeping the elderly 'off the streets'. New dependencies can exclude the old from an autonomous 'normal' life.

Conflict analysis also draws attention to social diversity in the elderly population. Differences of class, ethnicity and gender splinter older people as they do everyone else. Those in higher social classes have far more economic security, greater access to top-flight medical care and more options for personal satisfaction in old age than others do. Likewise, elderly WASPs (white, Anglo-Saxon Protestants) typically enjoy a host of advantages denied to older minorities. For ethnic groups, ageing is confounded by 'triple jeopardy': because they are old, usually poor and also black. And throughout this chapter we have seen how women, who represent an increasing majority of the elderly population with advancing age, experience the social and economic disadvantages of both ageism and sexism (Arber and Ginn, 1995).

Critical comment

Social conflict theory adds to our understanding of the ageing process by underscoring age-based inequality and explaining how capitalism devalues elderly people who are less productive. The implication of this analysis is that the aged fare better in non-capitalist societies.

One shortcoming of this approach goes right to its core contention: rather than blame *capitalism* for the lower social standing of elderly people, critics hold that *industrialisation* is the true culprit. Thus, they claim, socialism does little to lessen age stratification. Furthermore, the notion that capitalism dooms the elderly to economic distress is challenged by the steady rise in the income of the elderly population in recent decades.

Looking ahead: ageing in the twenty-first century

This chapter has explored a remarkable trend: the 'greying' of the Western world. We can predict with confidence that the ranks of the elderly will swell dramatically in the decades to come. As this chapter has shown, not only will numbers increase, so too will those living to older and older ages. It will not

be uncommon to find centenarians. Within the next 50 years, society's oldest members will gain unprecedented visibility and perhaps influence in our everyday lives. As this prediction is realised, gerontology, the study of the elderly, will also grow in stature as part of an expansion of research in all fields directed towards ageing and the elderly.

The reshaping of the age structure of our society raises many serious concerns. With more people living to an advanced age (and living longer once they reach old age), will the support services they need be available? As the elderly make more demands on services, the population will comprise proportionately fewer younger people to meet their needs. And what about the spiralling healthcare costs of an ageing society? As the baby boomers enter old age, some analysts paint a doomsday picture of the modern world as a 'twenty-first century Calcutta', with desperate and dying elderly people everywhere (Longino, 1994: 13). For many the future will be bleak, as they face problems of poverty, lack of integration, fear of crime and the like.

But not all the signs are so ominous. For one thing, the health of tomorrow's elderly people (that is, today's young and middle-aged adults) is better than ever: smoking is down and the consumption of healthy foods is up. Such trends probably mean that the elderly of the end of this twenty-first century will be more vigorous and independent than their counterparts are today. Moreover, many of tomorrow's old people will enjoy the benefits of steadily advancing medical technology, though the elderly can prove costly in these areas.

Another positive sign may be the financial strength of the elderly. Costs of living are certain to rise, but tomorrow's elderly will confront them with unprecedented affluence. Note, too, that the baby boomers will be the first cohort of the elderly in which the vast majority of women have been in the labour force, a fact reflected in their more substantial savings and pensions.

On balance, there are reasons for both concern and optimism as we look ahead. But there can be no doubt that younger adults will face a mounting responsibility to care for ageing parents. Indeed, as the birth rate drops and the elderly population grows, our society is likely to experience a retargeting of care-giving from the very young to the very old.

Finally, an ageing population will almost certainly bring change to the way we view death. In all likelihood, death will become less of a social taboo and more a natural part of the life course, as it was in centuries past. Should this come to pass, both young and old alike may benefit.

SUMMARY

1 All societies have systems of *age stratification*, whereby there is an unequal distribution of wealth, power and privileges among people at different stages in the life course. This varies across societies and history.

2 Childhoods are socially constructed and organised differently across cultures and throughout history. Consideration of how children are linked to work, marriage, war and death in both high-income and low-income societies reveals these differences. The most obvious feature of contemporary Western childhoods is that most children are 'protected' from most of these for most of the time. But this is far from true of most children across the world today.

3 The proportion of elderly people in the world is rising rapidly. By the middle of the twenty-first century, 20 per cent of our society will be elderly.

4 The age at which people are defined as old has varied through history. Until several centuries ago, old age began as early as the age of 30. In poor societies today, in which life expectancy is substantially lower than in Europe, people become old at 50 or even 40.

5 In global perspective, industrialisation fosters a decline in the social standing of elderly people.

6 As people age, they commonly experience social isolation brought on by retirement, physical disability and the death of friends or spouse. Even so, most elderly people look to family members for social support.

7 Since 1960, poverty among the elderly has dropped sharply. The aged poor are categories of people, including single women and people of colour, who are likely to be poor regardless of age.

8 Ageism – prejudice and discrimination against old people – serves to justify age stratification.

9 Although many seniors are socially disadvantaged, the elderly encompass people of both sexes, and all races, ethnicities and social classes. Thus older people do not qualify as a minority.

10 Disengagement theory, based on structural functional analysis, holds that the elderly disengage from positions of social responsibility before the onset of disability or death. In this way, a society accomplishes the orderly transfer of statuses and roles from an older to a younger generation.

11 Activity theory, based on symbolic-interaction analysis, claims that a high level of activity affords people personal satisfaction in old age.

12 Age stratification is a focus of social conflict analysis. The emphasis on economic output in capitalist societies leads to a devaluing of those who are less productive, including the elderly.

13 Modern society has set death apart from everyday life, prompting a cultural denial of human mortality. In part, this attitude is related to the fact that most people now die after reaching old age. Recent trends suggest that people are confronting death more directly and seeking control over the process of dying.

CONNECT UP: Turn to Part 6 of this book for key resources and link up
with the book's website, which links to these resources
SEE: www.pearsoned.co.uk/plummer

MYTASKLIST

Ten suggestions for going further

1 Connect up with Part Six and the Sociology Web Resources

As you work through ideas and think about the issues raised in this chapter, look at the accompanying website and the resource centre at the end of this book which connects to it. There is a lot here to help you move on. To link up, see: www.pearson.co.uk/plummer.

2 Review the chapter

Briefly summarise (in a paragraph) just what this chapter has been about. Consider: (a) What have you learned? (b) What do you disagree with? Be critical. And (c) How would you develop all this? How could you get more detail on matters that interest you?

3 Pose questions

(a) Compare the experiences of either (i) children, (ii) youth or (iii) the old in a high-income society and a low-income society. How does this reveal the social construction of age?

(b) Discuss the evolution of youth cultural styles and the explanations that sociologists have given of them.

(c) Why are the populations of industrial societies getting older? What are some of the likely consequences of this demographic shift?

(d) Keep a record of different age groups who use public spaces like buses, shopping centres and parks. Watch how different age groups come to dominate at different times. How often do you see older people on buses, tubes, etc. alone at night?

(e) Make a list of contrasting ageing experiences through ethnicity, class, gender, sexual orientation and disability. Consider what they have in common and how they may differ.

4 Explore key words

Many concepts have been introduced in this chapter. You can review them from the website or from the listing at the back of this book. You might like to give special attention to just five words and think them through – how would you define them, what are they dealing with, and do they help you see the social world more clearly or not?

5 Search the Web

Be critical when you look at websites – see the box on p. 940 in the Resources section. For this chapter look at the following:

Children

UNICEF
www.unicef.org/sowc96/contents.htm
This is the UNICEF 'State of the World's Children' site, and provides information and statistics on children around the world.

Centre for Working Families
www.bc.edu/bc_org/avp/wfnetwork/berkeley/index.html
This site produces an excellent guide to reading in children.

Youth

United Nations Youth Assembly
www.faf.org/unyouthassembly/ya_home.htm

The United Nations website on youth which provides a great deal of information across the world.
www.un.org/youth

The 'Voices of Youth' page of the UNICEF website.
www.unicef.org/voy

World Youth Alliance
www.wya.net/ourwork/advocacy.html?catid=75

Ageing

UN Programme on Ageing: Towards a Society for All Ages
www.un.org/esa/socdev/ageing

National Council on Ageing
www.ace.org.uk
This agency works to improve the quality of life for older people in the UK, publishing books and research on the elderly via the Age Concern Institute of Gerontology at King's College London.

Centre for Policy on Ageing
www.cpa.org.uk
Has a state-of-the-art database, held on CD-Rom.

Research into ageing

Age UK
www.ageuk.org.uk

National Council on Ageing
www.ncoa.org

American Society on Ageing
www.asaging.org

Retirement World
www.retirenet.com

6 Watch a DVD

Children

- Jan Sverak's *Kolya* (1997): film of a five-year-old boy set against the Prague revolution.
- Nicolas Roeg's *Walkabout* (1971): classic set in the Australian outback.
- Tsitsi Dangarembga's *Everyone's Child* (2000): a call for action on behalf of Africa's millions of parentless children.
- Iguel Arteta's *Chuck and Buck* (2000): an unnerving film about childhood friendships and perpetual 'childishness'.
- Jean-Stephane Sauvaire's *Johnny Mad Dog* (2008): award-winning drama about child soldiers.

Youth cultures

The classics to watch are:

- *Rebel Without a Cause*, Nicholas Ray (1955)
- *Saturday Night Fever*, John Badham (1977)
- *The Leather Boys*, Sidney J. Furie (1964)
- *Les Quatre Cent Coups*, François Truffaut (1959)

See also:

- *Samson and Delilah*, Warwick Thorton, 2010

Ageing

- *The Alan Bennett Collection*: Bennett's observations on the old are always insightful.
- Mike Leigh's film *High Hopes* is not about old age, but a key feature of the film is the 'old mother' – forgetting, downtrodden, neglected, silenced – whose visible presence throughout the film is haunting and disturbing. Is this the way the elderly get treated?
- Ron Howard's *Cocoon* (1985), Bruce Beresford's *Driving Miss Daisy* (1989), Mark Rydell's *On Golden Pond* (1981) and Peter Marteson's *Trip to Bountiful* (1985) are very dated, somewhat romantic Hollywood films that featured issues around people growing older in the 1980s.

On reverse ageing, see:
David Fincher's *The Curious Case of Benjamin Button* (2008): features Brad Pitt in a short story by F. Scott Fitzgerald, telling the story of a man growing backwards in time.

7 Think and read

Children

Allison James, Chris Jenks and Alan Prout, *Theorizing Childhood* (1998). The classic text to establish the field of the sociology of childhood.

Alison James and Adrian James, *Key Concepts in Childhood Studies* (2008). A quick and readable tour.

Karen Wells has provided a lively account of *Childhood in a Global Perspective* (2009).

Youth

Jon Savage, *Teenager: The Creation of Youth Culture 1875–1945* (2007).

Ken Roberts, *Youth in Transition: Eastern Europe and the West* (2009).

Robert MacDonald and Jane Marsh, *Disconnected Youth: Growing Up in Britain's Poor Neighbourhoods* (2005).

David Muggleton and Rupert Weinzierl (eds), *The Post-subcultures Reader* (2003).

James Farrer, *Opening Up: Youth Sex Culture and Market Reform in Shanghai* (2002).

United Nations World Youth Report: The Global Situation of Young People (2005).

Ageing

Sarah Harper, *Ageing Societies* (2006) and Virpi Timonen's *Ageing Societies: A Comparative Introduction* (2008). Provide excellent and up-to-date accounts of the elderly and their plight in a global context.

Pat Thane (ed.), *The Long History of Old Age* (2005). A marvellously illustrated account of 'age' in different times and places. An absolute must for any budding 'gerontologist'.

On the new cultures and bodies, see Christopher Gilleard and Paul Higgs, *Cultures of Ageing* (2000) and *Contexts of Ageing* (2005).

John Vincent, Chris Phillipson and Murna Downs (eds), *The Futures of Old Age* (2005). Looks at key contemporary themes such as pensions, health, gender and identity in later life.

Jan Baars, Dale Dannefer, Chris Phillipson and Alan Walker, *Aging, Globalization and Inequality? The New Critical Gerontology* (2006). Provides an important review of the field of critical gerontology with a focus on globalisation.

8 Relax with a novel

Look at William Golding's *Lord of the Flies* (1954) and Mark Twain's *The Adventures of Tom Sawyer* (1876) and *The Adventures of Huckleberry Finn* (1884). Of recent interest has been the book by a child soldier, Ishmael Beah, *A Long*

Way Gone (2007), which documents a different kind of childhood.

There are many interesting writings about ageing and being old. As with all sociological concerns, a good novel on the topic can help you feel your way into the issues. A very selective listing is Julian Barnes, *The Lemon Table* (2005); John Bayley, *Iris* (1998), where the author 'copes' with his (famous) wife's Alzheimer's disease.

9 Connect to other chapters

- Link to Chapter 4 on the shapes of society.
- For more on women and poverty, see Chapter 12; and on children and the elderly and poverty, see Chapter 10.
- For more on demographic trends, see Chapter 24.

10 Engage with
THE BIG DEBATE

A sad or happy old age: what are the social implications of living longer?

Demographers seem quite sure that Western industrialised societies are changing their age 'shape': older people (including very old people, over 85, over 100) are becoming more and more prevalent. All manner of sociological implications come with this.

One group of scholars think this is very good news. It is because of our control of health and the body that people can now live longer, being able to live healthy lives, retire from work and have a rich and rewarding life. There are suggestions that the 'new old' have more money and income than any previous generation and that this can be spent on vacations, hobbies such as sport and cooking, new second homes and the like. Many of the new elderly seem to have more opportunities ahead. Indeed, researchers looking into this group have found much more variety and happy living. One example is the growth of cosmetic surgery among older women so that they can look good (and possibly have new relationships and new sexual encounters). Older men too may be becoming more sexually active than in the past with the introduction of Viagra. Yet, once again, we must be careful. Although this may be true for some, critics note that this is only true for some: those on low incomes will not have these often costly new opportunities, so there will be clear issues of social

class shaping this. But after the experience of being the 'new or young old' (roughly 65–85), moving beyond (roughly) 85 will bring many more extended problems of health, income and isolation, as discussed in the chapter. It is caught in one striking phrase: 'Everyone I once knew is now dead.'

Other scholars pursue a different line. For them, the new ageing is in fact a biological time bomb, with dire consequences. With so many old, there will be fewer people to look after them and less and less money available from public funds to support them. *Work structures* would have to change – with people needing to work much longer to support their later years. Indeed, 'if older people are healthier than ever, could or should they remain in work longer?' (Macnicol, 2006). *Family structures* could also become very complex, and the younger old may find themselves more and more looking after the 'elderly old'. Intergenerational relationships may start to change dramatically. And the broader *culture* may change its codes and meanings: the focus on youth, dynamism and new achievements so common in contemporary times may give rise to growing concerns with 'older wisdoms' and indeed could ultimately lead to a culture being preoccupied with death, dying and looking after self and others.

Other views are even more extreme. Some doctors and their supporters believe we are well on our way to extending life in multiple ways, even to banishing death. The new 'immortalists' believe that healthy bodies will become more and more the norm as people live longer and longer and adopt new lives – lives which are inconceivable to us as we are at present. Research in intensive care units, for instance, can give us knowledge on how to 'beat death' and live much longer. And so we can start to ask questions that would have seemed absurd half a century ago: just what would society look like if we were to live to 300 or more? This sounds like science fiction to most, but there are many scientists who suggest that it is coming. They argue that we can transcend all our limitations, and the biggest of all these is 'death'. Commonly death is seen as natural, inevitable, one of the very few (if the only) absolutes of life. Brian Appleyard's book *How to Live Forever or Die Trying* (2007) discusses this new immortality movement, such as the Immortality Institute (Imminist) founded in 2002 by Bruce Klein.

Continue the debate

Devise a balance sheet for the different stages of ageing – the young old, the old old, the 'living forever' old – and consider whether being old could well be 'the best time of your life': something to look forward to increasingly.

CHAPTER 14

DISABILITIES, CARE AND THE HUMANITARIAN SOCIETY

STEPHEN WILLIAM HAWKING was born on 8 January 1942 in Oxford, England. He is renowned as one of the world's leading mathematicians and cosmologists, writing a worldwide best-selling book *A Brief History of Time* (1988). Since 1979 he has been the Lucasian Professor of Mathematics at Cambridge University. He studies the basic laws which govern the universe and is world renowned: he has 12 honorary degrees, was awarded the CBE in 1982, and was made a Companion of Honour in 1989. He is the recipient of many awards, medals and prizes and is a Fellow of the Royal Society and a Member of the US National Academy of Sciences. Professor Hawking has three children and one grandchild, and he continues his research with an extensive programme of travel and public lectures. He is a worldwide academic success story.

He is also a person with motor neurone disease (MND). He is severely physically impaired and has no voice. Although he was never especially active as a child or youth, he functioned reasonably well. But at 21, he went into hospital for tests and was eventually diagnosed. Over stages he became severely 'disabled' – he found his body poorly coordinated, had difficulty walking, couldn't climb stairs. Bit by bit, he took to a wheelchair. Up to 1974, he was able to feed himself, and get in and out of bed. But then these became difficult – indeed, impossible. Community and private nurses looked after him for a few hours each day. But in 1985 he caught pneumonia and had to have a tracheotomy operation, which removed his ability to speak. After this, and to this day, he needed 24-hour nursing care. But all the time he continues to work and have a hugely successful career.

His voice has been aided by a technology which allows Hawking to select words from a series of menus on the screen, by pressing a switch in his hand. These can then be sent to a speech synthesiser and emerge as Stephen's words. He can manage up to 15 words a minute. As he says:

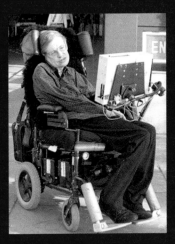

Stephen Hawking
Source: Corbis/Prashant Nadkar/Reuters.

I can either speak what I have written, or save it to disk. I can then print it out, or call it back and speak it sentence by sentence. Using this system, I have written a book, and dozens of scientific papers. I have also given many scientific and popular talks. They have all been well received. I think that is in a large part due to the quality of the speech synthesiser. One's voice is very important. If you have a slurred voice, people are likely to treat you as mentally deficient: Does he take sugar? This synthesiser is by far the best I have heard, because it varies the intonation, and doesn't speak like a Dalek. The only trouble is that it gives me an American accent.

Disability is a difference that exists only to be undone.

Sharon L. Snyder and David T. Mitchell

Motor neurone disease is comparatively rare – there are about 5,000 people in the UK living with MND. The mind continues to be active while the body starts to give up. It is a highly impaired experience that can happen at any age. There is no known cure at present.

Source: www.hawking.org.uk. For more information on motor neurone disease and amyotrophic lateral sclerosis (ALS), as well as other progressive conditions, look at the website of the Motor Neurone Disease Association (UK), www.mndassociation.org.

(Left) Pieter Breughel the Elder, *The Cripples*, sixteenth century
See: Web Gallery of Art at www.wga.hu.
Source: Bridgeman Art Library Ltd/Louvre, Paris/France/BAL.

Q What does this painting say to you? Little is known of the artist's politics or religion, so the exact nature of the moral is open to interpretation.

In this chapter, we ask:

- **What is disability and how should we think about it?**

- **What have been the cultural, historical and contemporary responses to disability?**

- **What are the features of the disability movement?**

- **How have disability rights been globalised?**

- **What is meant by the growth of the compassionate temperament and the humane society?**

Stephen Hawking is an extraordinary celebrity of the 'disability world' – famous just because he combines such excellence of mind with such frailty of body. His image is known throughout the world, and his books are best-sellers. In this chapter we delve a little into the wider social processes of disablement. The World Health Organization (WHO) estimates that disabled people make up 10 per cent of the world's population – around 650 million people. We go on to close this part by looking at the ways in which care and aid are being developed for the disabled and others.

Clarifying disabilities and differences

First, who is and who should be called disabled? What does the term mean? Two strikingly different, but not necessarily incompatible, approaches can be recognised from the outset (though there is no reason that they cannot be linked). One is the concern with **impairment**. A person is blind, or deaf, physically or mentally 'handicapped'. There may be physical or mental impairments, but they are features in which individual lives become incapacitated or impaired from their full functioning. Often these impairments can be directly linked to biology, genetics and 'medicine'.

In contrast, another approach sees these impairments as differences surrounded by social reactions, which are usually forms of social discrimination that may well exclude people from normal life. These are usually called **disabilities** – they disable from society, rendering people less able than they are or could be, and they are social. It is disability rather than impairment that is the province of the sociologist.

Although the two approaches are interconnected, they do seem to generate quite different ways of thinking about the issues. Table 14.1 suggests some of these contrasts. In reality, we blend both models.

Social workers and health providers have had a tendency to use the individual models in thinking about disability, while sociologists and disability activists (see below) have had a tendency to use the latter. But in fact the 'social' and the 'individual' model are only ways of thinking: they cannot be so clearly separated in practice. Everyday life combines elements of both. But as a thinking tool for sociologists, these distinctions can help show what some of the major issues may be for a sociology of disability.

Table 14.1	Definitions and pure/ideal models of disability
Individual model	**Social model**
Impairment	Disability
Personal tragedy	Social oppression
Personal problem	Social problem
Individual treatment	Social action
Medicalisation	Self-help
Professional dominance	Individual and collective responsibility
Expertise	Experience
Individual identity	Collective identity
Prejudice	Discrimination
Care	Rights
Control	Choice
Policy	Politics
Individual adjustment	Social change

Source: Oliver (1996: 34).

In this chapter we discuss a wide variety of differences and impairments which come to be identified as 'disabilities' (see Table 14.2 and Figure 14.1). These can be seen as violations of some rules or expecations

Table 14.2	Types of 'disablement'/'impairment'
Normative violations	Body stigmas
Body size	Giants, dwarfs
Body weight	Anorexia, bulimia, obesity
Body movement	Paraplegic/quadriplegic/wheelchair
Body image	Disfigurement
Senses:	
Visual	Blind – visually impaired
Aural	Deaf – hard of hearing
Speech	Stutterers
Learning	'Educationally subnormals', 'learning difficulties'
Emotional	'Autism'
Mind	'The mentally ill'
Wider health	AIDS and other illnesses (see Chapter 21)

England
Percentages

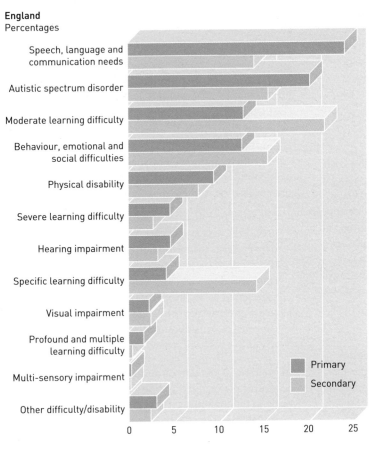

Figure 14.1 Pupils with statements of special educational needs (SEN):[1] by type of need, 2009[2]

[1] As a proportion of all children with statements of SEN in maintained primary and secondary schools, respectively.

[2] Data are at January.

Source: Department for Children, Schools and Families in *Social Trends*, 40 (2010), Fig. 3.5, p. 31.

which then become social stigmas. Disabilities usually involve the social processes of norm violation, labelling and, often, dehumanisation.

The classical social theories and disability

Here we briefly reintroduce the three main traditional theoretical issues in sociology and link them to disability. We then take some of these ideas a little further.

Functionalism and disability

Functionalism examines the ways in which social orders function. It looks at how parts of societies function or fit (or not) into the wider social order. In this account, disability is examined as a social role – in this case, a 'sick role', which we discuss

further in the chapter on medicine (Chapter 21). It could easily see disability as simply a dysfunction and consider the way it disrupts social life. But it could also think about the ways in which the disabled perform crucial functions for society. For example, the existence of 'disabled people' in a society can help mark out the boundaries of the 'disabled' and the 'normal'. Most commonly, disability becomes a role which serves a number of functions. Functionalism, in looking at the smooth running of society, often highlights social control.

This process has been discussed for a long time by sociologists. Indeed, one of our earliest sociologists, Emile Durkheim (see Chapters 1, 2 and 4), suggested that this kind of division – into the normal and the pathological – seems to be bound up with the conditions for social life. For him the simple classification of the normal and the pathological served to mark out moral boundaries, and unite people against common enemies. It establishes that there is a 'we' and the 'other', and it is hard to find instances of societies that do not do this. It could be that some societies need 'others' to know who they are, and hence to function well.

An interesting connection can be made to the theories of Mary Douglas. Disability here can be seen as a threat to the social order and responses to it help to mark out the boundaries of order (see the *Thinkers and theory* box on p. 465).

Interactionism and disability

Interactionism looks at the processes through which meanings are constructed, and its close ally is labelling theory – which examines the role of social labels or categories in social life. In this account, disability appears as a social category and as an emerging meaning, and sociologists examine the ways in which it works in societies: how it emerges in situations and what it might do to people who are labelled as 'disabled'. The key concerns here focus upon the meanings that are given to disabilities, and the ways in which many of these are stigmatising.

The sociologist Erving Goffman has been influential in understanding stigma. He suggests an array of problems that happen when people are confronted with stigmas. Stigmas break down normal and routine interaction. They challenge and threaten what we take for granted. Hence disabled people often come to find their disability as threatening routine order. The blind challenge the sighted world; the deaf challenge the world of hearing; the physically disabled challenge the ways in which we routinely move around the world. Disabilities generate interaction problems.

Conflict theory and disability

Conflict theory looks at the different interests in a society and how frequently some interests come to dominate, oppress or exploit others. In this account, disability is located within a system of different conflicts and interests, and it is seen most commonly as an experience which is discriminated against and oppressed.

We return to the wider issues of class, ethnicity, gender and sexuality again here. Mark Hyde has reviewed some of these divisions and concluded:

> **Disabled people experience profound levels of economic disadvantage, resulting in intense deprivation, and ultimately, a poor quality of life . . . they are particularly dependent on state social services and benefits . . . are often segregated by welfare programmes . . . are subject to a significant level of state regulation . . . and experience considerable discrimination.**
>
> (Hyde, 2006: 270)

In the UK, 50 per cent of disabled people are economically inactive and disabled women are more likely to be unemployed than disabled men (Office for National Statistics, 2001). Mike Oliver's *The Politics of Disablement* suggests that disability must be linked to the working of capitalism. The difficulties, subordination and conflicts of disabled people take on different patterns in different societies, and within capitalism they are often seen as threatening to the routine world of hard work and money making. In its earlier days, capitalism

Dancing wheels
Source: Getty Images AFP.

 Discuss the meanings of wheelchair dancing.

Mary Douglas: danger, disability and purity

Dame Mary Douglas (1921–2007) was a leading English anthropologist initially conducting fieldwork in the Belgian Congo, where she examined male control of access to younger women (in her book *The Lele of the Kasai*, 1963). Her maxim was that 'as a social animal, man is also a ritual animal'; and it was these rituals which fascinated her. Even in apparently secular societies, human beings have rituals and symbols embodied in meals, dress and especially the body. Much of her work thus focused on food, risks, drinking, consumption and the taboos. She works in what we could call a 'Durkheimian tradition'.

Her most distinctive work is on purity, pollution and the moral order. Rules establish classificatory systems in societies, which lead to societies being systems of codes and conventions embedded in social life. Sanctions are imposed on transgressions. Her model can be dramatically applied to those who have physical stigmas and disabilities. They become outsiders and society needs ritual purifications around them.

In our zeal to classify and categorise, we fail. The world is too complex to manage this effectively. And so in the process of classifying, we find the need to search out more and more forms of classification. This may be true of all societies, though maybe it is more intense in modernist ones, for as Mary Douglas says in *Purity and Danger* and other works:

> Dirt is the by-product of a systematic ordering and classification of matter, in so far as ordering involves rejecting inappropriate elements . . . Dirt . . . appears a residual category, rejected from the normal scheme of classification.
>
> (Douglas, 1966/1970: 48)

And the existence of 'dirt' leads to the zeal to classify more and more, and expunge and annihilate the dirt that this may leave. In short, classification systems are needed in order to make sense of the world and boundaries are needed to mark out 'group belonging' (the we) from others.

See: Mary Douglas, *Purity and Danger* (1966) and *Natural Symbols* (1970).

---

was a major tool for regulating people in general, but especially the disabled. They found themselves in prisons, asylums, workshops, industrial schools and colonies. It was a period when the disabled were seen as 'less than human' and placed under regulatory systems. While this may be helpful in examining the past, it does not help us see just how and why the current situation has been changing. Feminist writers have also shown great concern for the differences of the disability experience for men and women. Private issues to do with marital relationships, housework, abuse, violence and care come more to the focus.

Stigma and outsiders: cultural responses to disabilities

Labelling theory suggests the importance of categorising and labelling in social life. When people define situations as real, they become real in their consequences. We have met them before (in Chapter 7) and discuss some of these ideas further in Chapter 17. Here we just introduce a long history of words and practices that stigmatise, shame and exclude people from the normal world. Sociologists have taken a keen interest in this, asking just what these words and practices are, and why they have come about.

Let's start with a sample of words. Throughout history, the experiences we are talking about in this chapter have been variously called:

> **Cripples. Idiocy, feeble mindedness, mental subnormality, cretins. Lepers, blind with canes, the deaf and dumb. A world of 'freaks' – giants, dwarfs, siamese twins, fat ladies and living skeletons (Fiedler, 1981: 13). They are also lunatics, nut cases, wierdos, sad people. Sometimes they are monsters. They are the handicapped, the subnormal, the retarded . . .**

We are sure you can think of many others.

All of these images construct ideas of some people being 'the other'. Whatever they are, they are not you. Over time, we may debate and change the words that we call 'others'. But beneath terminology there is still a sense that there are 'others' – people who are 'out there', who are something else, radically different from 'us'. They are not 'normal' and often they are very dangerous.

It is important to see that our responses help to shape the very phenomenon we are looking at: the words help to bring into being particular kinds of reality for the 'impaired' and 'disabled'. Labelling may be a key to understanding the process of disablement.

Sociologists find that stigmatising labels seem to function widely in most societies. They facilitate the hierarchy, division and ordering of society by making it clear that some people are most surely not in the society. They are excluded, and made to sit on their borders and boundaries.

Now some borders can be perfectly tame, harmless and useful. A garden fence can be a helpful marker. But they can also be harbingers of hatred. Many have commented upon this: Thomas Szasz, a social psychiatrist, once said: 'the first law of the jungle is kill or be killed', while 'the first law of human society was stigmatize or be stigmatized'. It is precisely because the inside/outside debate so often leads to enemies – with all the mocking injury and terrorist exterminations they can bring – that it is especially potent. In many ways, as Beck (1997: 81) says, 'enemy stereotypes empower'. The invention of the other galvanises animosity. In a telling phrase, Bauman remarks:

> woman is the other of man, animal is the other of human, stranger is the other of native, abnormality the other of norm, deviation the other of law abiding, illness the other of health, insanity the other of reason, lay public the other of expert, foreigner the other of state subject, enemy the other of friend.

(Bauman, 1991: 8)

A short history of responses to disabilities

We can trace the history of varying responses to what we now call disabilities from earliest links to religion and magic through to other responses where disabilities have been denied, mocked, excluded, institutionalised or even killed. A quick history of disablements would show that our responses in the past have embraced religious demonisation, medical pathologisation and social discrimination. Consider:

- The slaughtering of the innocents: the frequent killing at birth of deformed children.
- The entertainment of the freaks: amusement for the bored rich in many societies, found in the popularity of 'circus freaks' in the nineteenth century.

- The locking away and banishing from sight of the disabled: in workhouses, asylums and institutions.
- The applications of science: the categorisation of differences as disorders and dysfunctions.
- The perpetuation of 'eugenic beliefs': the search for ideal people and the reductions of faults and others who display these faults (the racial 'hygiene' of Nazi Germany led to mass deaths, of which as many as 275,000 may have been disabled).
- The medicalisation of the disabled: the search for treatments and cures.
- The growth of an ideology of benevolence: the creation of 'charity systems'.
- The normalisation of disabilities: attempts to correct much of the above from the 1970s onwards through deinstitutionalisation, inclusion and normalisation.

Disablements are also to be found in art and literature and contemporary film (you might like to look again at the painting which starts this chapter). In 'children's books' (also much read by adults) we see 'disabilities' in *Gulliver's Travels* (with its Lilliputians and Brobingnagians), *Alice in Wonderland* or even *The Wizard of Oz* with the little people of Munchkinland (and never mind the tale of what they get up to in the film version!). The adult world of literature is also full of somewhat scary deformed monsters (Dracula, Mr Hyde, Wolf Man, King Kong, etc.).

In Western twentieth-century societies, one stream of 'imagining/representing disabilities' came to us from the mass media (see Chapter 22). In the modern film disabled people stagger around being mocked, scaring people and often even slashing, mutilating and engaging in cannibalism.

Several stages appear in the history of films representing disability. A first stage (roughly 1890s–1930s) continued the 'freak show' tradition. Earlier films of interest here might include *Quasimodo, the Hunchback of Notre Dame* (Lon Chaney film, 1923) and Todd Browning's *Freaks*, which shows a circus world of (actual) bearded ladies, human caterpillars and the dancing pinhead. Between the 1930s and the 1970s a more exploratory 'personal tragedy' approach was often taken. Often this was combined with some kind of mysterious intrigue or crime (*The Snake Pit, The Lost Weekend*, etc.). Developing in parallel there is a 'shock-horror' tradition which appears with *The Mummy, Dracula* and *Frankenstein* films and is exemplified in more recent films like *The Texas Chain Saw Massacre* through to all the *Halloween*

Image from Todd Browning's film *Freaks*

Source: The Kobal Collection Ltd/MGM.

 The film *Freaks* was controversial when made in 1932. Look at parts of it on YouTube. Was this an exploitation film? Why?

and Wes Craven films. Here, monsters are at work (cf. Norden, 1994).

While the older traditions may still continue, there has been a more recent tendency to incorporate – even 'normalise' – the disabled in mainstream films, such as Robert Zemecki's *Forrest Gump* (1994) or, more startlingly and controversially, David Cronberg's *Crash* (1996).

This has also given rise to an alternative, radical representation – often in films made by the disabled themselves, or else by 'radical film-makers', such as Frederick Wiseman's *Blind*, and *Adjustment and Work* (1986).

There is now a new Disability Cinema and annual International Film Festival (see www.disabilityfilm.org.uk).

The Elephant Man: Joseph Carey Merrick (1862–1890)

Joseph Merrick (often referred to as John Merrick and popularly called the Elephant Man) is a reasonably well-documented nineteenth-century (Victorian) case study of a man with what is often called 'neurofibromatosis' (some think it was Proteus Syndrome). In any event, he was a hugely disfigured man, and this started in his childhood. Born into a middle-class family, his condition led to him being cast out of his home and being sent to the Leicester Union workhouse. Seriously ill, he would probably have died on the streets, had he not been 'rescued' by circus showmen who paid for his necessary surgery and then turned him into a successful museum freak show exhibit. He may have made a reasonable sum of money from this but it was later stolen from him by robbers and less scrupulous showmen. He was eventually taken to Whitechapel Hospital by Dr Frederick Treves, where, after initially being cared for, he eventually became what could now be called a 'medical freak'. He went before medical classes as a 'case study', subjected to humiliating public examinations (often naked), was visited by the rich and famous who wanted to see him, and was even taken out 'to be seen' in public life.

Here we can see a life that is turned into an object of derision and amusement, of benevolence and hate, of medical inspection and seemingly humanitarian compassion. We like to think these days that the many 'physically different' are treated much better than this. But are they?

In 1980, David Lynch's film *The Elephant Man* became a critical success and it is worth seeing. But ironically, the depiction of disabilities like this in film can also bring its own problems. On the one hand, such a film may be seen as critically educational and designed to make us think about the different responses to disability. But on the other hand, there is a worry that it panders to some kind of lower interest in 'the odd'.

Joseph Carey Merrick (1862–90), Victorian England's famous 'Elephant Man', is shown in a photo from the Radiological Society of North America

Source: PA Photos.

See: www.phreeque.com for a series of photos and 'stories' about similar 'freaks' and perhaps monitor your own responses. See also: Robert Bogdan, *Freak Show* (1990); Michael Howard and Peter Ford, *The Elephant Man* (2001). Extracts from the 1980 film can be found on YouTube.

Contemporary disabling responses: legal responses and social policy

In recent years, and across the world, there have been major changes in the reactions to disabilities. In much the same way as there have also been major changes in social reactions to 'women', 'gays' or 'blacks', these new attitudes and policies have been generated largely by disabled people themselves. Of course, as with all change, these shifts have been limited and partial. But that said, there have been significant shifts in laws, policies and practices in many parts of the world. The castigating of the outsider disabled person becomes less and less acceptable; and new laws and planning help facilitate the environment for people with disabilities.

For example, in May 2001, the World Health Organization formally changed its official definition of disability and introduced the International Classification of Functioning, Disability and Health (ICF). In this, it moved away from a purely physical model of impairment and adopted more of the social model (see above). It explains:

> Functioning is an umbrella term encompassing all body function, activities and participation; similarly disability serves as an umbrella term for impairment, activity limitations or participation restrictions. ICF also lists environmental factors that interact with all these constructs. In this way

it enables the user to record useful profiles of individuals' functioning, disability and health in various domains.

(WHO, 2001: 2)

The ICF has two domains: classified body function and structure, along with activities and participation, within environmental and personal factors; it hence uses a multidimensional approach. You could say this is a little vague, and that it suggests the social model was only partially introduced. More recently, campaigners on disability issues have worked from a more developed social model, and yet others who once championed it (like Tom Shakespeare) have suggested the social model was too strong, and what was required was an interactionist model looking at the interaction between social and individual factors.

In the UK, the 1995 Disability Discrimination Act (DDA) made it illegal to discriminate against disabled persons in three areas: (a) employment; (b) access to goods, facilities and services; and (c) buying or renting land and property. A new legal definition of disability in the DDA is provided as any person who has a physical or mental impairment or long-term health condition, which has a substantial and long-term adverse effect on their ability to carry out normal day-to-day activities. Normalisation is a key guide, and it rejects refusal of employment on grounds of disability (Best, 2006: 85).

In 1999, a Disability Rights Commission Act established a new body that would monitor the elimination of discrimination against disabled people and promote equal opportunities (a little like the Committee for Racial Equality set up in 1976 under the Race Relations Act). A little later, the Special Educational Needs and Disability Act 2001 enhanced the rights of parents of children with disabilities. If parents wish it, then Local Education Authorities now have a responsibility to educate children with special educational needs in mainstream schools.

But these laws are not just happening in the UK. Similar legislations, bodies and practices are now found around the world.

Despite all these developments, critics argue that they have amounted to very little. One says: 'Despite major changes in legislation . . . the dominant picture remains one of discrimination, prejudice, injustice and poverty, often rationalised on the grounds of supposed progress for disabled people' (Swain et al., 2004: 1).

Contemporary disabling attitudes

Whatever recent legal changes may have occurred, there is still substantial evidence that there remains a prejudice against disabled people today. In a recent study of *British Social Attitudes* (2007), for example, while only 25 per cent of the population think that there is a lot of prejudice towards the disabled, many survey respondents indicated the opposite. Around half, for example, would not be comfortable with a relative marrying a blind person and only 19 per cent say they would feel comfortable were a person with schizophrenia to marry a close relative of theirs. As is common with many prejudices, familiarity with disabled experiences usually reduces the levels of stigmatisation.

Although quite a small-scale study, one look in the UK at the attitudes of people to disability outlined five types of response:

1 Traditionalists (about 15 per cent) who had stereotyped views.
2 Followers (26 per cent) who were mainly non-disabled and have little interest in disability issues.
3 Progressives (36 per cent), mainly non-disabled, middle-class educated – normalising.
4 Transformers (9 per cent), younger, often disabled, who want normalisation.
5 Issue-driven respondents (14 per cent) – usually disabled or disabled identified – who were 'vocal and active on behalf of disabled groups'.

The reactions from social science

The diagnostic social sciences have a long history of classifying, examining and suggesting responses (often treatments) to disabilities – which two authors have recently called 'an obscene curiosity disguised beneath the neutral veil of empirical inquiry' (Snyder and Mitchell, 2006: 193). They are critical of the rise of 'people based research practices' where disabled people start speaking back about their experiences – but often at their own expense of time, energy and liberty. They describe their own experiences, tell of their own stories (and subjectivities), and make public their interior worlds. This may have a dramatic policy function – to make services better fit their needs. But it may also serve as a tool which further exaggerates their differences and works to set them apart. Whether they are correct in this analysis remains to be seen.

The disability movement

How do human beings deal with their impairments, disabilities and stigmas? We could see four main patterns:

1 *Denial*: some try to deny their disabilities. Mild disabilities can simply be avoided – they do not seem serious enough to make an issue. Some impairments can be concealed, and even when they cannot, some try to pass them off as 'normal'. A person with a speech defect, for example, may learn that they can hide their defect by not exposing themselves to certain situations (avoiding new people and strangers where they lack confidence) or not saying certain words or sounds (some sounds and words are often much harder to say than others). Sometimes they solicit the support of others. They adopt a cloak of competence. They avoid situations which would be threatening. They deny and disavow their stigma.

2 *Normalisation*: here the disability comes to be incorporated routinely into daily life. It becomes habitual, accepted. This does not mean the process is trying to make the disabled 'normal' – like everybody else. It means, rather, the means by which the disabled come to lead lives that are routine and normal for themselves, and that society in turn assists in this by providing conditions of everyday living which are as close as possible to the regular circumstances and ways of life or society.

3 *Disengagement*: here the disabled withdraw from social groups and society. This can often be seen in the institutional response – not only when disabled people are placed in institutions and hence are made to withdraw from the wider society, but also when they become even more isolated and cut off within institutions.

4 *Fighting back*: here the response is to use their disability actively – in both their personal life and also for wider social change. This can be done in small personal ways (rebelling, resisting), but it can also be seen as part of a wider social movement, which is discussed below.

The Disability Movement is worldwide and plays an increasing role for disabled people. Some organisations are national; others are international like Disabled People's International. Some are for specific groupings like the World Federation of Deaf, or the World Blind Movement. The movement gives a voice to disabled people, allowing them to challenge more traditional views and make their own decisions about their lives. No longer hidden away or patronised, the movement encourages a much more visible and active role.

Disability organisations can be yet another example of the **new social movements**, which *transform identities and society, creating new political awareness in the post-industrial society* (we discuss this further in Chapter 16).

Types of disability organisation

Three main types of organisation stand out (adapting the work of Mike Oliver, 1990):

1 *Umbrella/coordinating organisations of many groups*. The United Kingdom's Disabled People's Council (UKDPC) is the UK's national organisation of the worldwide Disabled People's Movement. Set up in 1981 by disabled people to promote full equality and participation in UK society, it now represents some 70 groups run by disabled people in the UK at national level. Between them, member groups have a total membership of around 350,000 disabled people. It is run by disabled people, works on issues of human rights, and claims to have been the main body behind the changes which led to the Disability Discrimination Act (see www.bcop.org.uk).

In general, these are the oldest and most established of organisations. In the past, they have been linked to charitable bodies and have provided a range of services and consultations. They were often not very inclusive: grass-roots activism was not on their agenda. But this has changed a lot in recent years.

2 *Consumerist/self-help*. The 'Independent Living Movement' (De Jong, 1979) is a prime example of this. In the 1970s it signalled a major shift from the biomedical view of disability to a social concept model. The goals shifted from the cure, maintenance and safekeeping of the disabled – with disabled people being in a kind of childlike dependency – to goals of inclusion and full participation within society. The movement grew in North America along with other counter-cultural groups of the late 1960s (like the women's, black, gay and student movements). It was developed in the Scandinavian countries during the 1970s.

With this approach, the disabled role and all the stereotypes associated with it are now rejected. Key ideas now become the normalisation of the disabled, their 'mainstreaming' and their deinstitutionalisation. Society should change to

Martha Nussbaum: human capabilites and human rights

Martha Nussbaum (1947–) is a leading contemporary social philosopher. Originally a 'classical scholar' interested in the work of Aristotle, most of her recent work considers contemporary social issues where she is seen as a major champion of human rights. She has looked at disability rights along with many other issues: women in developing countries, the issues surrounding gays and lesbians, animal rights, the problem of shame in many cultures, and most recently social change and religious conflict in India. She argues from a position that we would call liberal, feminist, humanist and cosmopolitan. Her work seeks to develop ideas about the free, dignified and equal social human being, the 'just society', 'well-being' and a good quality of life. Many of her arguments lead her to the field of 'human rights'.

Her core thesis centres around what she calls 'human capabilities', an idea she developed with the economist Amartrya Sen. Human **capabilities** are *'opportunities for functioning'* in the world. They are, in her view, basic human entitlements. We cannot flourish as human beings without these 'entitlements'. The disabled cannot flourish without these capabilities being recognised and cultivated. One of her key questions concerns the activities which are central to a human life, so central that without them we could not consider this life 'truly human'. She suggests a number of human capabilities which include:

1 *Life*: being able to live to the end of a 'normal human life'.

2 *Bodily health and integrity*: being able to have good health, be adequately nourished and have adequate shelter.

3 *Bodily integrity*: being secure and able to move from place to place in safety; and having opportunities for sexual satisfaction and for choice in matters of reproduction.

4 *Senses, imagination and thought*: being able to imagine, think and reason – cultivated by an adequate education.

5 *Emotions*: being able to have attachments and care for things outside oneself, and to love those who love and care for us.

6 *Practical reason*: being able to plan a conception of a good life for one's self in critical reflection.

7 *Affiliation*: being able to live for and in relation to others; having self-respect and being able to be treated as a dignified being whose worth is equal to that of others.

8 *Other species*: being able to live with concern for and in relation to animals, plants and the world of nature.

9 *Play*: being able to laugh and enjoy recreational activities.

10 *Control*: over one's environment.

For Nussbaum, 'all citizens should have a basic threshold of each of these capabilities'. They are all important and interrelated. Applied to disability, there is a clear raising of issues which must be considered for the functioning and even flourishing of all lives.

See: Martha Nussbaum, *Creating Capabilities* (2011), *Frontiers of Justice: Disability, Nationality and Species Membership* (2006), as well as *Sex and Social Justice* (2001). See YouTube 'Conversations with History', Martha Nussbaum.

Martha Nussbaum (1947–)
Source: Permission from Martha Nussbaum.

provide an environment for the disabled. Bit by bit, over the past 40 years many of these arguments have become rather mainstream in themselves. Most Western governments now incorporate disability voices in their planning and programmes.

Independent Living Centres are staffed by persons with disabilities and usually entirely run by them. Hundreds of groups have been established. They argue for environmental change: accessible housing, curb cuts, audible pedestrian signals, accessible transportation and accessible public buildings. They work for rights and specific legislation. They change the wider culture – making an impact on transport systems, toilet facilities, recreation, shopping, education and employment (see: www.ilusa.com and www.ncil.org.uk).

3 *Populist/activist.* In the UK, one of the major groups was UPIAS – the Union of Physically Impaired Against Segregation, established in 1974. Michael Oliver, in work with the Open University, produced a book, *Handicap in a Social World* (1981), which started to formulate a much clearer social model, distinguishing 'personal tragedy theory' from 'social oppression theory' (as outlined in Table 14.1). His main concern was with neither medical models nor social science models, but ones that came from the experiences of disabled people themselves.

Disability activism grew during the 1970s and it now plays a major role in shaping policies for the disabled. It engages in direct political action and consciousness-raising. In the UK, the Direct Action Network engages in some civil disobedience. It adopts a much more direct, in-your-face approach:

Direct action is in your face. Disabled people are supposed to be invisible: they are not supposed to go out and be seen. Direct action has changed this. We are noticed!

(A disabled activist, cited by Hyde, 2006: 266)

The activist groups are the most radical of the groups. They usually provide a more complex analysis of 'disability politics' and generate heated debates about the future of disability. They not only offer a critique of the responses to disability but also find the whole society lacking. Disability Identity Politics provides a new consciousness.

A recent development here has been the arrival of 'crip theory' (McRuer, 2006). This takes queer theory as its model of thinking (see Chapter 12) and uses the idea of 'the cripple' to threaten the general view of the normal body. They urge a radical rethinking of the ways in which we think about disability and disabled people. Bodies and disabilities are fluid, ever changing. The enemy is the idea of 'compulsory able-bodiness' (McRuer, 2006).

Finding a voice

The importance of self-activism was highlighted in 1995 at the World Summit on Social Development, when the World Disability Movement presented its own position paper (*The Disability Movement: A Joint Statement*). It argued:

In any situation people find the best solution for themselves. And disabled people have come up with solutions, the solutions of advocacy, independent living, income generation and self help within our own organisations. All these solutions are based on the principles of integration

Great Britain's Danny Crates celebrates winning the Gold Medal in the men's T46 800 metres at the Paralympic Games in Athens, Greece, 25 September 2004
Source: PA Photos.

and equalisation of opportunities and the implementation of human rights ... These solutions are all effective, low-cost and do not require setting up tiers of professionals to run them. They do not include expensive building that has to be maintained and refurbished. They are the grass-roots solutions which can be employed everywhere – in rural and urban areas – which will benefit everybody and which include everybody. They are solutions that not only apply to all disabled people but to the rapidly growing numbers of elderly people, to children, to the poor, to refugees, to ethnic minorities

(Hurst, 1999: 28)

And:

We've begun to realize that the disabilities aren't the problem that needs to be fixed. Just as some people are black or fat or short or tall or wear glasses, persons with disabilities have unique physical or mental characteristics which simply don't meet (and often never can) society's standard of normal. Experts trained in biomedical knowledge, and counsellors who understand the psycho-social dynamics of deviation, are not the ones who can solve the problems. Rather, it is other disabled persons who've lived, experienced, and found solutions on how to live with and manage disabilities in the so called 'normal' standardized world who are the 'real' experts who can best share the knowledge and experience required.

(Disabled person)

Disability sport

Sports activities have, over the past few decades, provided a major worldwide arena where disabled people have been able to demonstrate to themselves and the wider world their functional abilities. The 'Special Olympics' started in 1968. It treated everyone who participated as a winner, and it now involves around 2.5 million children and adult athletes in more than 165 countries. The International Paralympics is more competitive. It started in England in 1948, being staged as an Olympic-style competition in Rome in 1960. The number of athletes participating in the Paralympics has increased from 400 athletes from 23 countries in Rome in 1960 to 3,806 athletes from 136 countries in Athens in 2004. From the 2012 bid process onwards, the host city chosen to host the Olympic Games will

be obliged also to host the Paralympics. (On disability sport, see: the English Federation of Disability and Sport at www.efds.net; the International Paralympic Committee at www.paralympic.org/release; and the Special Olympics at www.specialolympics.org.)

Globalisation: differences and disabilities

Globally, the World Health Organization estimates that disabled people make up 10 per cent of the population – around 650 million people. Eighty per cent of persons with disabilities live in developing countries. This figure is increasing through population growth, medical advances and the ageing process.

On all our dimensions of inequality, the disabled feature prominently. Disabled people account for 15 to 20 per cent of the world's poorest people. Women with disabilities are recognised to be multiply disadvantaged, experiencing exclusion on account of their gender and their disability. In Bangladesh, 97 per cent of disabled women are unemployed. They are also particularly vulnerable to abuse. A small 2004 survey in Orissa, India, found that virtually all of the women and girls with disabilities were beaten at home, 25 per cent of women with intellectual disabilities had been raped and 6 per cent of disabled women had been forcibly sterilised.

According to UNICEF, 30 per cent of street youths are disabled. Disabled people of working age in developed and developing countries are three times more likely to be unemployed and live in real poverty; 90 per cent of children with disabilities in developing countries do not attend school.

The disabled are also 'excluded' from many key social institutions. In many countries, disabled people are unable to place their vote. While an estimated 386 million of the world's working-age people are disabled, unemployment is as high as 80 per cent in some countries. Often employers assume that persons with disabilities are unable to work. Most low-income societies lack transport systems with accessibility; they usually have little or no free medical care or social protection services; and the idea of disability rights is only beginning to be placed on an agenda that often seems to have much more pressing needs. But disability levels are often very high in low-income countries – and not least because of many civil conflicts which can lead to severe disabilities. The UN suggests that for every child killed in warfare,

WORLD WATCH

The global politics of disability

The UN Convention on the Rights of Persons with Disabilities, 2007

Initially proposed by Mexico in 2001, the UN Convention on the Rights of Persons with Disabilities was signed by 102 countries in 2007. It aims 'to promote, protect and ensure the full and equal enjoyment of all human rights and fundamental freedoms by all persons with disabilities, and to promote respect for their inherent dignity.'

People with disabilities are here seen to include 'those who have long-term physical, mental, intellectual or sensory impairments which in interaction with various barriers may hinder their full and effective participation in society on an equal basis with others'.

It is based on eight key principles:

1 Respect for inherent dignity, individual autonomy including the freedom to make one's own choices, and independence of persons.
2 Non-discrimination.
3 Full and effective participation and inclusion in society.
4 Respect for difference and acceptance of persons with disabilities as part of human diversity and humanity.
5 Equality of opportunity.
6 Accessibility.
7 Equality between men and women.
8 Respect for the evolving capacities of children with disabilities and respect for the right of children with disabilities to preserve their identities.

The signatories will have to enact laws and other measures to improve disability rights and also agree to get rid of legislation, customs and practices that discriminate against disabled people. The thinking behind the convention is that welfare and charity should be replaced by new rights and freedoms. At the time of the convention being passed, only 45 countries in the world had already passed disability legislation.

See: www.un.org/disabilities/convention.

A Mexican example

Los Discapacitados of the city of Oaxaca, Mexico, is a grass-roots cosmopolitan advocacy group which campaigns for rights, access and opportunities for people with disabilities in the city and region of Oaxaca. It is just one of thousands of such groups found all over the world.

Disabled people were in the recent past primarily dealt with by rehabilitation agencies. But now groups are creating a new culture for disabled people. Working with local and international groups, using the internet creatively, they want the voices of the disabled to be heard.

German Lopez and his friend Pedro Flores (both of whom had contracted polio in their infancy) set up major events for the local disabled. They spend numerous hours partying, often dancing the night away – some use their crutches while they dance, others dance in their chairs. They spent hours in sporting activities – basketball, tennis, track and swimming – leading to national and international tournaments.

In the past, the family was the core for looking after the disabled. Now there are many community groups which create strong identities for disabled people, as well as positive life styles.

Source: Michael James Higgins and Tanya L. Coen, *Streets, Bedrooms and Patios: The Ordinariness of Diversity in Urban Oaxaca* (2000) (Chapter 5).

---

three are injured and permanently disabled (see the brief discussion on child soldiers in Chapter 13). (The source for all these figures is a United Nations factsheet on disabilities where you can find much more: www.un.org/disability/convention/facts. It is important to bear in mind that facts are very hard to obtain, as so many disabled people are hidden and anonymous with regard to official statistics.)

Disability World

One example of globalisation is the creation of the US webzine *Disability World*. Originally funded by the National Institute on Disability and Rehabilitation

Research as the cornerstone of the IDEAS for the New Millennium Project (1999–2005), *Disability World* was managed by the World Institute on Disability (WID), based in Oakland, California, and conducted as a collaborative effort with the participation of three other US-based disability groups: the Independent Living Research Utilization Project, the Inter-American Institute on Disability (IID), and Rehabilitation International (RI).

Disability World covers seven key areas: independent living; employment; arts and media; technology and accessibility; governance and legislation; women; children and youth. It focuses on ten countries each year, holds international meetings on specific themes (like independent living, employment, media and disability governance), and is developing a portrait of the status of people with disabilities in each of the countries targeted for coverage. The first 23 issues were published in both English and Spanish. It houses a literature database of more than 800 abstracts of articles primarily covering employment, independent living, governance, disabled women, disabled children, technology and appropriate technology, community-based rehabilitation and rehabilitation in developing countries, all searchable by topic or country. This is all accessible on its website: www.wid.org/publications.

Mental disorders, mental health and well-being

Alongside these physical disablements, there are also global concerns about mental abilities – mental health, well-being and mental illness. According to the WHO, mental health is:

> . . . a state of well-being in which the individual realizes his or her own abilities, can cope with the normal stresses of life, can work productively and fruitfully, and is able to make a contribution to his or her community. [It] is the foundation for well-being and effective functioning for an individual and for a community. This core concept of mental health is consistent with its wide and varied interpretation across cultures.

There are hundreds of millions of people across the globe who do not experience this well-being:

depressions, schizophrenia, bipolar disorder and all kinds of other mental disorders are to be their experience – an experience which often works to socially exclude them. In this section we will introduce some sociological ideas on this.

Nature and incidence of global mental disorder

People who lack sound mental health have been called many things – lunatics, the mad, the mentally ill. Just like the disabled, throughout history and around the world they have been exposed to a wide range of responses. And as with the stigmas attached to the physically disabled, the mentally disabled often face stigma too. They have been banished to the edge of town where they are left semi-naked or in rags, tied up, beaten and left to go hungry. Millions of patients in many mental hospitals fared little better. The WHO has claimed that around 14 per cent of the **global burden of disease** (GBD: see Chapter 21, p. 727) is attributed to mental disorders. Estimates made by WHO in 2002 showed that 154 million people globally suffer from depression and 25 million people from schizophrenia; 91 million people are affected by alcohol use disorders and 15 million by drug use disorders. A further 50 million people suffer from epilepsy and 24 million from Alzheimer's disease and other dementias. In addition to the above figures, a WHO study in 2005 suggested that 326 million people suffer from migraine, 61 million from cerebrovascular diseases and 18 million from neuroinfections. Finally, nearly a million people die from suicide every year. One in four patients visiting

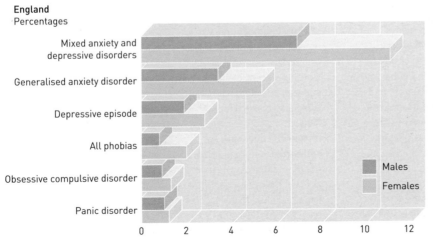

England
Percentages

Mixed anxiety and depressive disorders

Generalised anxiety disorder

Depressive episode

All phobias

Obsessive compulsive disorder

Panic disorder

0   2   4   6   8   10   12

Males
Females

Figure 14.2 Prevalence of common mental disorders: [1] by sex, 2007

[1] In the week prior to interview.

Source: McManus, S. et al., *Adult psychiatric morbidity in England, 2007*, p. 31.

Data supplied by

NHS

The Information Centre
for health and social care

Social explanations of mental problems

Broadly, contemporary explanations of mental disorders fall into two broad clusters. The first (and most common) locate these mental problems firmly within the individual body and are studied by biologists, psychologists and psychoanalysts. Illness is explained through neurological disorder, genetics, brain disorders and psychic breakdowns of various kinds. The second – and much less common – locate mental problems arising from the social environment and often even challenge the very idea of 'mental illness' that is usually taken for granted by the former.

The social theories come in four main varieties:

- *Social causation theories*: there is a long tradition of seeing mental problems as arising from environmental changes. Thus, for example, rates of mental disorder rise during times of war, financial crisis and experience of violence. War and other major disasters have a large impact on mental health and psychosocial well-being. Rates of mental disorder tend to double after emergencies. Here are to be found shell-shock and rape trauma syndrome, which have identifiable sources from experience in the environment. In addition, many sociologists have studied the correlations between mental problems and social class, showing

potential links to disadvantaged neighbourhoods, poverty and financial stress, casual work and unemployment, poor accommodation and homelessness (see: Rogers and Pilgrim, 2010; Wilkinson and Pickett, 2009; Graham, 2007). Such studies also take seriously the fact that women and their social experiences seem to be overrepresented in pyschiatric diagnosis.

- *Labelling theories*: theories which look at the ways in which social reactions help shape and organise the things that are being labelled. Here chaotic behaviour, stressful experiences, 'problems in living' and even 'residual rule breaking' come to be identified by friends, families, communities, professional and even strangers as symptomatic of disorders. The influential and important work of Erving Goffman on asylums and the moral career of the mental patient is the classic instance of this work (see Chapter 7). Goffman suggests that mental patients suffer from the contingencies of everyday life, are identified as ill by a 'circuit of agents' like family and doctors, and then embark upon a career of ritual degradations which reorganise their sense of self. Deprived of their own clothing, decent bedding and proper toilet facilities, subject to abuse and neglect and sometimes restrained with shackles and confined in caged beds, the mentally ill, in the past at least, have been degraded through labels. Many studies have shown the significance of this ritual labelling

(e.g. Rosenhan, 1973; Scheff, 1967).

 See the video on Rosenhan's work at: www.psychblog.co.uk/video-being-sane-in-insane-places-163.html.

- *Constructionist theories*: theories closely linked to labelling theory and which make the very category of mental illness a problem to be studied. This approach often adopts the ideas of Foucault (see Chapter 17, p. 593) on power and surveillance, and both charts the history of the idea of mental illness and demonstrates the ways in which power works its way through the language, science and psychiatric workings of the idea of mental illness. This challenges the often presumed universal nature of the category of mental illness and disorder, and shows its regulatory role.

- *Structural realist theories*: these theories try to locate mental illness in a full, embodied material environment and social structure. They do not 'reduce' mental illness to simple bodily breakdown, but neither do they see it as simple label and construction. Instead, they argue that material conditions which cause mental breakdown need to be considered alongside the material and symbolic categories of mental illness that happen within specific contexts and historical times. An illustration of this approach is claimed by Anne Rogers and David Pilgrim in their textbook: *A Sociology of Mental Health and Illness* (4th edn, 2010).

a health service has at least one mental, neurological or behavioural disorder, but most of these disorders are neither diagnosed nor treated (see www.who.int/mental_health/mhgap/en/index.html).

The problem here, though, is that different mental disorders may have different meanings in different societies. The responses of others may help define and shape them. A belief in being possessed by the 'Zar' spirit is widespread in east and central Africa, particularly in Sudan and Ethiopia where it is associated with episodes of random laughing, shouting and singing. In Malaysia and Indonesia, people suffer from *latah*, a 30-minute panic of screaming, dancing, and hysterical laughter, punctuated by shouted obscenities. In some southeast Asian cultures, men have been known to experience what is called *amok* – an episode of murderous rage followed by amnesia. *Brainfag* is experienced by stressed-out students in Nigeria and other parts of Africa – a reaction, it is said, to the alien pressures of Western-style book learning.

Responses to mental disorders

Most of the people affected – 75 per cent in many low-income countries – do not have access to the treatment they need. There is huge inequity in the distribution of skilled human resources for mental health across the world. Shortages of psychiatrists, psychiatric nurses, psychologists and social workers are among the main barriers to providing treatment and care in low- and middle-income countries. Low-income countries have 0.05 psychiatrists and 0.16 psychiatric nurses per 100,000 people, compared to 200 times more in high-income countries.

Therapy culture

During the twentieth century, a major new industry and several professions developed around the world of therapy and the self. The goal of this therapy culture was to analyse and treat the personal problems and mental health of individuals. It is to be found in:

- The rise of self-help books and groups such as those which give advice (often providing 12 steps for recovery) on 'losing weight' or giving up alcohol (Weightwatchers, Alcoholics Anonymous, etc.).
- The development of counsellors – with many different groups and varieties trained in different theories and ideologies, such as 'mo directive counselling', 'crisis counselling' and 'bereavement counselling'. They work over a wide range of problems from 'deficit disorders' to 'sexual addiction', and find their homes in schools, workplaces, prisons, etc.
- The fostering of a psychodynamic profession wth an ideology of the world in various psychoanalytic strategies drawing from the work of Freud, Jung, etc. – and which aim to unravel the unconscious workings in individual psyches (e.g. psychoanalysis).

All of this resulted in the spread of a new language and categorisation to locate the personal life – and the individual and their identities (see Chapter 7). A wide array of new terms started to appear to help us 'understand ourselves' and probe who we are. These include such newly labelled phenomena as:

anorexia, alcoholism, bulimia, attention deficit disorders, bipolar disorders, eating disorders, antisocial personality disorder, Asperger's disorder, attention-deficit hyperactivity disorder, avoidant personality disorder, dependent personality disorder, depression (major depressive disorder), generalised anxiety disorder, narcissistic personality disorder, obsessive–compulsive disorder, panic disorder, posttraumatic stress disorder, separation anxiety disorder and phobias of all kinds.

The Diagnostic and Statistical Manual of Mental Disorders (DSM)

Many of these professions and terms help large numbers of people with their problems. At the same time, we see two key social processes at work. These are:

1 *The medicalisation of everyday life*: these are the new ways in which we accept medicine routinely into our lives and accept that it has a role in regulating the lives of children, our deviances like drinking and eating too much, as well as in many areas of life – such as anger management and bereavement counselling – which for most of history have not really been seen as medical problems.

2 *The individualisation of social problems*: the ways in which problems which may well have their origins in relationships (e.g. family breakdown, adult–child interaction) or wider social structures (unemployment, war, greed and violence) are turned into individual problems.

Some key books analysing the rise of the therapeutic culture are:

Philip Rieff, *The Triumph of the Therapeutic* (1966)
Paul Halmos, *The Faith of the Counsellors* (1965)
Maurice North, *The Secular Priests* (1972)
Peter Berger, *The Homeless Mind* (1974)
Edwin Schur, *The Awareness Trap* (1977)
Christopher Lasch, *The Culture of Narcissim* (1979)
Frank Furedi, *Therapy Culture* (2003)

Humanitarianism, care and the humane society

In this concluding section of Part Three (social divisions and inequalities), we turn to another characterisation of society that deals with many of the issues we have been discussing throughout these chapters. You have already seen many accounts of the arrival of a new postmodern world (see Chapter 4). Here we introduce the idea of an emerging society which tries to remove inequalities and divisions and to foster humane responses to social life. We call this the 'humane society' and below we consider briefly its origins and some of its key concerns.

The growth of the 'compassionate temperament'

Natan Sznaider has characterised the development of modernity (and into postmodern times) as one which sees the growth of 'the compassionate temperament'. For Sznaider, 'compassion is the moral organization of society'. It is about pain – 'about sensing other people's pain, about understanding pain, about trying to do something about it' (Sznaider, 2001: 25). And this has not always been the case. As he says:

> It is the first moral campaign not organized by the church or the state. The structures of modernity are what make this self organization possible. And the moral sentiments that result from this process constitute qualitatively new social bonds.

(Sznaider, 2001: 1)

Sznaider, rather boldly, suggests that it is exactly the modern world which fosters 'compassion'. It was not present before. And by compassion, he means the development of 'moral sentiments'. Usually sociologists say almost the opposite: that modern society has

corroded moralities and fostered breakdown. But Sznaider takes an alternative stance, which he tries to document through recent history. Of course, he agrees with sociologists who say that major changes are taking place, but he interprets the many changes in a different way. He says:

> What they see as discipline, I see as compassion. Where they see power, I see moral sentiments. And where they see social control as the state's control over society, I see social control as society's control over itself – a kind of control explicitly different from state control or religious control.

(Sznaider, 2001: 2)

This is a radically different statement about society from that which has informed much 'critical sociology'. In this view, a 'humanitarian consciousness' developed during the eighteenth and nineteenth centuries. Cruelty and pain came to be seen as social evils, and compassion becomes organised to protest against it. It is not shaped by divine will but through an abstract and rational idea of 'humanity'. Prior to modern times, cruelty and suffering were more likely just to be accepted. In modern times, cruelty and suffering became – to put it bluntly – unacceptable.

Public compassion involves the ability to sense and imaginatively reconstruct others' sufferings, along with a desire to do something about it. Modern humanitarianism implies universal sympathy, an equality of sentiment and a striving for universal happiness. The past did not. Medieval charity and its precursors lacked this empathy and moral sentiment.

Of course, Sznaider does not deny that modern times have also been times of unspeakable cruelty, holocausts and other horrors. But as he says: 'this has been the century of cruelty, and it has also been the century of compassion' (Sznaider, 2001: 99). (See also: Rifkin, 2010.)

Looking for the signs of an emerging compassionate society

Much of sociology has looked at the sufferings of people in humanly constructed social worlds – of how, in a way, they make 'hell on earth' for each other. If you read this introductory book carefully, you will find a long list of troubles: genocides, wars, environmental crises, suicide, inequalities of many kinds, and world and local poverty. No wonder that the social sciences (especially economics) are called the dismal and the sad sciences!

Recently, however, some social scientists are starting to look more for the signs of a better society – taking a more positive interpretation. They look for 'well-being' across the world; at their most extreme they try to measure 'happiness' (Layard, 2007). Sometimes, this kind of work is ridiculed by more critical social science as utopian and, indeed, for closing its eyes to the terrible things that are going on in the world. But, of course, this approach is not denying the existence of terrible things happening in society – it just wants to redress the balance a little, and show signs of betterment.

To close this part of the book, then, you might like to consider the following issues as 'signs of an emerging compassionate society'.

1 Welfare states and social protection

Over the past hundred years, many societies have come to accept that the state has a major role to play in the well-being of its members. It cannot just leave them and their lives to their own disasters. It needs policies for welfare – to fight the problems of poverty, ignorance, poor health and so on. It needs to provide money that will facilitate the protection of its more vulnerable societal members – the child, the elderly, the disabled and others. It needs to establish legislative frameworks in which this can be done. Hence we have seen the growth of the welfare state and social protection, and the rise of health services and education systems. The big issue, of course, is whether this should be the final responsibility of the government or whether it should be placed in a system of capitalist markets.

Social protection is the *help available to people who are in need or are at risk of hardship for reasons such as illness, low income, family circumstance or age.* The most basic aim is to provide healthcare and income security for all. To this end, central governments, local authorities and private bodies (commercial and voluntary) can provide help and support in four major areas:

- direct cash payments – social security, benefits
- payments in kind – bus passes, free prescriptions
- provision of service
- unpaid care.

In the UK in 2010, total government expenditure on social protection was £196 billion – equivalent to 27 per cent of total government expenditure. For 2003, it was calculated out at £4,710 per person (which was higher than the EU average). Luxembourg, Sweden and Denmark spend the most (at around £5,000–£6,000 per head); Spain and Portugal spend the least (at around £3,000). In other words, we spend a great deal on these acts of benevolence and are willing to be taxed to support them. In the UK, social security benefits cost around £115 billion in 2010. The personal social services (social work) cost £33 billion (2010).

Figure 14.3 suggests some of the key ways in which the new Coalition government elected in the UK in May 2010 expected to spend money on public services in 2011 in a climate of major cuts. Although it is never 'enough', many governments now spend vast sums of money on caring for and protecting their members.

2 Social care

In recent years, and especially because of the works and research of feminist writers, there has been a growing recognition of the importance of 'care' as a feature of social life. The nature of social care and its provision is now a 'hot topic' in sociology, and governments increasingly take it into account as a major organising principle of society.

In the latter decades of the twentieth century, some sociologists have become more and more interested in 'care'. An early example was the study by Janet Finch, who looked directly at the ways in which daughters often look after – 'care' for – their elderly parents. Why was it daughters that mainly did this? What did they actually do? What did it do to them?

Care can mean two things, but they are often linked. Care (as in caring person) can mean a kind of mental state, usually viewed positively. We say 'they are such a caring person'. But it can also mean an act of labour (see Chapter 15), a practice in which a person does certain things to assist others. We say 'she' is a 'carer'. These two ideas often hang together, and they may even be a sequence: from a caring thought comes a caring action. Hilary Graham (1983) suggests there is also a *caring about*, which suggests a more general concern for others, and a *caring for*, which concerns the more specific work employed in looking after someone. The former tendency can lead to an interest in 'an ethics of care'; the latter has been neatly called 'a labour of love' (1983).

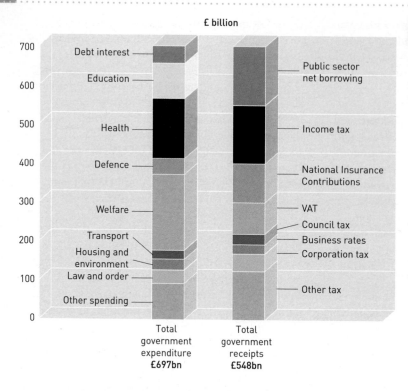

£ billion

Figure 14.3 Total government expenditure and receipts by function, 2010–11

Source: Based on HMSO, *Spending Review*, October 2010.

Total government expenditure **£697bn**

Total government receipts **£548bn**

Joan Tronto, in developing her ideas of care, does, however, note just how much ideas of care are often devalued in society. 'Carers' tend to be at the bottom of the hierarchy. Care workers are unpaid, underpaid, devalued and often marginalised. Put like this, ironically it comes to appear that 'care' really may not be one of the core assumptions on which we can agree – who cares about the low-status workers? Who cares about the carers?

Australian sociologist Michael D. Fine has provided us with a very nuanced account of care in the twentieth century. His concern is with care in all its forms, but notably the distinction between private care and formal care. He sketches a basic model, as shown in Table 14.3.

3 Rights and equality frameworks

Many contemporary societies have come to take for granted that people have rights and that they should be treated, roughly, equally. Much contemporary legislation, for instance, seeks to provide frameworks that will facilitate:

- a broad equality of people before the law
- the idea of people having human rights
- the idea of what it is to be a good citizen.

These ideas have been debated for centuries (Ishay, 2004) but have come to prominence in the modern world. The human rights movement is worldwide; and the debate over citizenship is currently ubiquitous (Isin and Turner, 2004). See Chapter 16, pp. 569–73.

4 Self-care and global activism

One of the most striking developments in the late twentieth century, with roots back into Samuel Smiles

Table 14.3   Modes of care provision: a basic schema

	Informal Care of particular individuals	*Formal* Care of strangers
Unpaid	Family care (at home)	Volunteers
Paid	Paid domestic help (private)	Human service facilities and institutions care professionals

Source: Fine (2007: 200).

Senior citizens in Brighton, England, carrying signs, which say 'The British Pensioner, Living or Existing?' and 'The Battlers of Britain Still Fighting!', in protest for better pension rights in the United Kingdom

Source: © Howard Davies/Corbis.

Self Help etc., has been the widespread growth of self-help groups and global social movements of care which aim to promote the health and well-being of their members. They range from patient and patient support groups to radical action groups. These days they often have to be media aware in order to bring their concerns to a wider public.

Some are geared towards research and education, some are fund-raising organisations, some are politically active – from lobbying governments to challenging general perceptions – some provide general mutual support for their members, some offer treatment: many offer all or most of these things. They can be looked at as social movements, pressure groups, resistance to

Disability politics in action
Source: Getty Images/News.

professional power, charities and philanthropic groups and as models of new selves. In general, they divide between those which are assimilationist (i.e. those that want improvements and support within the terms of the existing society) and radical (i.e. those that see the need for fundamental changes before the issues around the problem can be resolved) (Robinson and Henry, 1977).

Movements that 'care' about rights, illness, education, the environment and health are widespread. Just as we have seen, in this chapter, the rise of disability activism, so we can find – elsewhere in this book – an environmental movement (Chapter 25), a women's movement (Chapter 12), a gay and lesbian rights movements (Chapter 12), a health movement (Chapter 21), a minority rights movement (Chapter 11), AIDS activism (Chapter 21) and many others. These days they are more and more facilitated in their organising through websites.

5 A sociology of philanthropy?

In the early twenty-first century there are some signs that charity and the 'not for profit sector' is growing. The number of UK registered charities doubled in 30 years, with 76,000 in 1970 and some 187,000 by 2002. According to the Charity Commission, the number of registered charities was 182,042 in early 2010, and in the previous year, the UK population donated some £9.9 billion to charities. Approximately 54 per cent of individuals in the UK, i.e. 26.8 million persons, made donations. The average amount per donor was £31 (see Figure 14.4). Charities' total annual income was around £52.6 billion per annum – half of which comes from government funding. Some studies suggest that relatively little of this charitable money from big spenders actually goes to low-income groups (CAF, www.cafonline.org and www.charity-commission.gov.uk).

According to the Sunday Times Giving List, the top 100 leading philanthropists in the UK distributed around £2.5 billion in 2009. Some gave to major and international charitable organisations (AIDS, worldwide humanitarian relief, helping Africa feed itself). Many see this as social investment rather than charity. Some find their names in the newspapers for their acts – Elton John gave around £23 million to AIDS causes, J. K. Rowling some £4 million; and Jaimie Oliver (see p. 245) gave £2.7 million – mainly to his Fifteen Foundation for young cooks. Often the celebrities are deeply involved in their charities. In the USA, Bill Gates alone has given some £36 billion to health and education causes through the Bill & Melinda Gates Foundation; and he is pioneering new ways of engaging the charity world – with larger funding supports given in more infornal ways. Likewise, Warren Buffett, currently the third richest man in the world, made endowments of £24 billion. Table 14.4 suggests that high-level donors are more likely to give money to religious and artistic causes than to those charities that support low-income groups (see Sunday Times Giving Index, 2010).

The continuing search for new ways of developing 'charity' and philanthropy is often given bad press by social science – charity and benevolence are often seen as masks of self-interest and as sops for the consciences of the rich. When Madonna adopts a child from Africa, she is wide open to criticism. As we saw in Chapter 9, much of the aid funding to poorer countries can be costly and misplaced. That said, charity and philanthropy do appear to be widespread social practices helping large numbers of people.

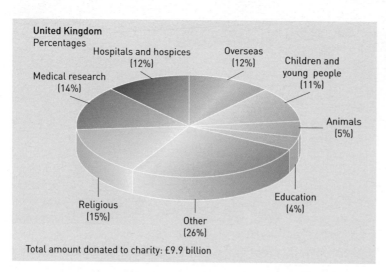

United Kingdom
Percentages

Hospitals and hospices (12%)
Overseas (12%)
Children and young people (11%)
Medical research (14%)
Animals (5%)
Religious (15%)
Other (26%)
Education (4%)

Total amount donated to charity: £9.9 billion

| **Figure 14.4** | Proportion of total amount given to charity: by cause, 2008/09 |

Source: Charities Aid Foundation; National Council for Voluntary Organisations in *Social Trends*, 40 (2010), p. 197, Fig. 13.18.

Table 14.4	Charities by fundraising income, 2009 (£m, rounded down)	
		£m
1	Cancer Research UK	353
2	Oxfam	207
3	RNLI	141
4	NSPCC	124
5	British Red Cross Society	123
6	Macmillan Cancer Support	106
7	Salvation Army Trust	106
8	RSPCA	99
9	British Heart Foundation	93
10	Save the Children UK	87
11	Tate	79
12	National Trust	74
13	PDSA	73
14	Marie Curie Cancer Care	71
15	Christian Aid	66
16	Sightsavers International	65
17	RSPB	62
18	Guide Dogs for the Blind	60
19	RNIB	55
20	World Vision UK	54

Source: Charity Market Monitor 2009.

Nowhere can this be seen more clearly than in the assistance given to many low-income societies. Philanthropic practices are hardly new, but they do seem to be taking new forms and playing a key role in twenty-first-century societies.

 tip The Charities Aid Foundation produces an annual report on charities in the UK downloadable at www.cafonline.org/pdf/UK_Giving_2009.pdf.

6 Volunteering and the third sector

The **voluntary sector** is the *sphere of social activity undertaken by organisations that are for non-profit.* It is non-governmental and sometimes called the third sector. Two types of volunteering are often distinguished: with the *informal*, unpaid help is given to people who are not relatives (over half the population), whilst with the *formal*, unpaid help is given to others through organisations and clubs (about 40 per cent of the UK population) (see *Social Trends*, 2010: 195). Table 14.5 shows the range of voluntary work found in a UK survey in 2007/8. According to this, the most common types of voluntary work involve raising money or taking part in sponsored events – these activities were undertaken by just over

Table 14.5	Selected types of voluntary work undertaken in the UK: by sex, 2007/08[1]			
England				Percentages
		Men	Women	All aged 16 and over
Raising or handling money or taking part in sponsored events		33	36	34
Organising or helping to run an activity or event		31	32	32
Member of a committee		26	21	23
Coaching or tuition		22	11	15
Leading a group		15	10	13
Giving advice, information or counselling		13	11	12
Secretarial, administrative or clerical work		11	12	12
Befriending or mentoring people		10	13	12
Visiting people		10	12	11
Providing transport or driving		12	8	10

[1] As a proportion of all who had done voluntary work in the 12 months prior to interview.

Source: *Taking Part: The National Survey of Culture, Leisure and Sport*, Department for Culture, Media and Sport, in *Social Trends*, 40 (2010), Table 13.16, p. 196.

a third (34 per cent) of volunteers. Just under a third (32 per cent) helped to run an event, and almost a quarter (23 per cent) were members of a committee. Most types of voluntary work were performed by similar proportions of men and women.

 See the work of the Institute for Volunteering Research: www.ivr.org.uk/aboutus; and the organisation Volunteering England: www.volunteering.org.uk.

7 International governance

It is possible that societies have always dreamed of living in global harmony. At the start of the twenty-first century, there are now major international organisations firmly in place to provide global governance and care. One hundred years ago we had neither the United Nations nor the thousands of international non-governmental bodies that strive for the care and protection of citizens on a global scale.

These movements monitor progress in the world, set major targets for social improvements and galvanise actions for change. Already in this textbook, for example, we have met measurement devices like the Human Development Index and the gender gap. For all their problems (see Chapter 9), these are useful in trying to see 'the state of the world' (see Chapter 26). Likewise, the Millennium Development Goals attempt to provide goals for eliminating world poverty (see Chapter 9), while the Kyoto Agreement establishes international agreements of carbon emissions (see Chapter 25). Table 14.6 shows the number and range of major human rights protocols that the UN has established to date. Engaged in all of these activities are hundreds of thousands of people from across the world who are fighting to make the world a better and more equal place. These organisations can be criticised on many grounds; but that this is a start in the development of major worldwide institutions of care and compassion cannot easily be denied. Sociologists need to study their workings.

8 The cultivation of cosmopolitanism

Finally, accompanying all this has not just been a compassionate temperament, but also a growing cosmopolitan attitude. This is not a new idea – the

Table 14.6	**The core United Nations Human Rights Conventions are:**

The core United Nations Human Rights Conventions are:

- International Covenant on Civil and Political Rights
- International Covenant on Economic, Social and Cultural Rights
- Convention on the Elimination of all Forms of Racial Discrimination
- Convention on the Elimination of all Forms of Discrimination against Women
- Convention against Torture and other Cruel, Inhuman and Degrading Treatment or Punishment
- Convention on the Rights of the Child
- International Convention on the Protection of the Rights of All Migrant Workers and Members of their Families
- Convention on the Rights of Persons with Disabilities

All can be consulted on the internet at the Office for the Commissioner of Human Rights at: www.unhchr.ch/html/menu.

history of cosmopolitanism is long, going back to at least the ancient Greeks and Romans. The term *cosmos* speaks to the world as a whole, whilst *polis* speaks to a self-governing political community. Taken overall, **cosmopolitanism** suggests that *all people, despite their great differences, can share a common humanity*. It has taken on many diverse meanings and forms – the sociologist Robert Holman has listed over 30 (Holman, 2009). Three major distinctions might help us:

- *Political cosmopolitanism*: this is usually associated with discussions about global citizenship, global human rights and global governance (Fine, 2007).

- *Cultural cosmopolitanism*: here the focus is on the great differences that exist both within and between cultures (Benhabib, 2002).

- *Ethical cosmopolitanism*: this focuses on the vision of cosmopolitanism as a way in which people accept each other's differences and come to live together.

Cosmopolitanism has become a major talking point in recent times. As Appiah (2006) puts it, cosmopolitanism means a 'universal concern and respect for legitimate difference'.

Looking ahead: disability, difference and change

Differences and disabilities have been responded to throughout history in a multitude of fashions. For much of the twentieth century, many differences – including people with disabilities – were stigmatised, medicalised and regarded as 'victims' of their condition and a 'burden' on society. But what we have also started to see in this chapter is the ways in which people of difference have started to change the conditions in which they live. More and more, and across the world, there is a growing 'disability awareness' and a rejection of the old discrimination. This is part of a more general trend towards rights

and care. Disabilities are now increasingly seen as distinctive forms of social inequality, discrimination and social exclusion which require social changes in order to be rectified.

We have seen (Chapter 4) that the idea of progress is a difficult one. Over the past few chapters you have read a lot about exclusion, discrimination and inequality. The bad news is that it pervades all of social life and that, in some of its forms, inequalities are growing wider and the potential for conflicts is growing. But the good news is that, over the last century or so, we have experienced new social structures of empathy and compassion which argue for change and bring about new practice of care. The notion of the growth of a compassionate, caring society does give some room for hope in a world that is so often seen as being in terminal decline.

SUMMARY

1 We need to distinguish between impairments and disabilities and social and medical models. Disability rather than impairment, and social models rather than medicine, is the province of the sociologist.

2 Main social theories of disability include the functionalist, interactionist and conflict theories. The first examines the social role of disability. The second looks at the social meanings of disability. And the third looks at the inequalities that surround disablement.

3 The category of disabled often functions to mark out the normal and the outsider in society.

4 There is a long history of stigmatising the disabled. They have been demonised, medicalised and turned into objects of fun. Looking at both literature and film shows shifts in the ways the disabled are being portrayed in contemporary societies.

5 The disabled can deal with their impairments in four ways: as denial, as 'normalisation', through disengagement and in resisting and fighting back.

6 Disability movements divide into (a) coordinating, (b) self-help and (c) activist.

7 Disability movements and the rights around disability have now become global issues.

8 The 'humane society' is one that tries to reduce inequalities and divisions and to foster humane responses to social life.

9 The modern world has strands of development that seem to foster 'compassion' and the development of 'moral sentiments'.

10 Signs of this emerging society include: welfare states, social protection, social care, rights and equality frameworks, self-care and global activism, charity and philanthropy, international governance and the cosmopolitan attitude.

CONNECT UP: Turn to Part 6 of this book for key resources and link up with the book's website, which links to these resources
SEE: www.pearsoned.co.uk/plummer

MYTASKLIST

Ten suggestions for going further

1 Connect up with Part Six and the Sociology Web Resources

As you work through ideas and think about the issues raised in this chapter, look at the accompanying website and the resource centre at the end of this book which connects to it. There is a lot here to help you move on. To link up, see: www.pearson.co.uk/plummer.

2 Review the chapter

Briefly summarise (in a paragraph) just what this chapter has been about. Consider: (a) What have you learned? (b) What do you disagree with? Be critical. And (c) How would you develop all this? How could you get more detail on matters that interest you?

3 Pose questions

(a) Trace the history of changing attitudes to disabilities and impairments. Could you argue that the twenty-first century has shown some signs of progress?

(b) 'The first law of the jungle is kill or be killed', while 'the first law of human society was stigmatize or be stigmatized' (Szasz). In what ways are the disabled at the forefront of the stigma process? Analyse the work of disability activist movements as part of a wave of new global social movements.

(c) In what ways, if at all, can the twenty-first century be seen as a 'compassionate' and 'caring' society?

4 Explore key words

Many concepts have been introduced in this chapter. You can review them from the website or from the listing at the back of this book. You might like to give special attention to just five words and think them through – how would you define them, what are they dealing with, and do they help you see the social world more clearly or not?

5 Search the Web

Be critical when you look at websites – see the box on p. 940 in the Resources section. For this chapter look at the following:

WHO disability page
www.who.int/topics/disabilities/en/

Disability Alliance
www.disabilityalliance.org
Produces the very useful annual *Disability Rights Handbook*, and works to break the link between poverty and disability.

Disability World
www.disabilityworld.org
Produced by the World Institute of Disability, this site provides a wealth of worldwide information on all aspects of disability. Strongly recommended.

Disability Now
www.disabilitynow.org.uk
Published regularly online by Scope. Very useful for up-to-date information.

International websites

World Health Statistics 2007
www.who.int/whosis/en/index.html

Disability Tables
www.icdi.wvu.edu/disability/pages/World_Contents.htm

International Disability Alliance
www.internationaldisabilityalliance.org

Human functioning and disability – statistical definitions and guidelines
http://unstats.un.org/unsd/demographic/sconcerns/disability/

UK websites

Arthritis Care
www.arthritiscare.org.uk/Home

British Polio Fellowship
www.britishpolio.org.uk

Scope – about cerebral palsy
www.scope.org.uk

Multiple Sclerosis Society
www.mssociety.org.uk

Cystic Fibrosis Trust
www.cftrust.org.uk

Learning Disability Statistics
www.learningdisabilities.org.uk/information/learning-disabilities-statistics

Mind: mental distress statistics
www.mind.org.uk

6 Watch a DVD

- Julian Schnabel's *The Diving Bell and the Butterfly* (2007): tells the story of French fashion designer who becomes almost wholly paralysed – except for his eyes which can still blink and through which we can access his consciousness. Also a biography.
- Damien O'Donnell's *Inside I'm Dancing* (2004): two young men – with cerebral palsy and muscular dystrophy – struggling against a residential home for the disabled.
- Peter Bogdanovich's *Mask* (1985): a mother, played by Cher, fights for the rights of a badly disfigured boy.
- Milos Forman's *One Flew Over the Cuckoo's Nest* (1975): a classic on surviving life in a mental hospital. It is a good accompaniment to Erving Goffman's *Asylums: Essays on the Social Situation of Mental Patients and Other Inmates* (1961).
- Mike Nichol's *Regarding Henry* (1991): a tough lawyer is seriously injured and makes a slow recovery.
- David Lynch's *The Elephant Man* (1980): the classic story told with John Hurt in the lead role.
- Henry Alex Rubin and Dana Adam Shapiro's *Murderball* (2005): follows teams of paraplegics to the 2004 Paralympics. Much of the film is shot via the wheelchair, and there's no preaching.
- Kirby Dick's *Sick: The Life and Death of Bob Flanegan, Supermasochist* (1997): controversial example of 'crip theory' at work as a man with cystic fibrosis performs dramatic sexual acts!

7 Think and read

Disability

Colin Barnes and G. Mercer, *Disability* (2nd edn, 2010) and Lennard J. Davis (ed.), *The Disability Studies Reader* (3rd edn, 2010) continue to be two very useful guides to the whole field.

Mike Oliver, *Understanding Disability* (2nd edn, 2009) and Tom Shakespeare, *Disability Rights and Wrongs* (2006). Important critical reviews of the state of disability studies which promote new agendas.

Erving Goffman, *Stigma* (1962). The classic and field-shaping text. It is short, fairly easy to read and helped change the way the world sees disabilities.

Sharon L. Snyder and David T. Mitchell, *Cultural Locations of Disability* (2006). Important recent study of different discourses and responses to disabilities.

Anne Rogers and David Pilgrim, *A Sociology of Mental Health and Illness* (4th edn, 2010). Textbook overview of the mental health field of study.

Paul Higgins, *Outsider in a Hearing World* (1980) and Robert Edgerton's *The Cloak of Competence* (1972) are two early fieldwork studies of disabilities.

Suffering and the humanitarian society

Iain Richardson, *Suffering: A Sociological Introduction* (2005). An important book which needs to be read alongside Natan Sznaider's *The Compassionate Temperament* (2001). A short but important history of the rise of compassion in society. For a wide-ranging introduction to cosmopolitanism, see Robert J. Holton's *Cosmopolitanism* (2009). See also Jeremy Rifkin's *The Empathetic Civilization* (2010).

8 Relax with a novel

- Blake Morrison, *And When Did You Last See Your Father?* (2007)
- John Bayley, *Iris* (1999).
- C. S. Lewis, *A Grief Observed* (1961/1963).

9 Connect to other chapters

- Link to Chapter 17 on theories of labelling and deviance.
- Link to Chapter 21 on health and medicine.
- Link to Chapter 16 on social movements.
- Link to Chapter 26 on the state of the world.

10 Engage with THE BIG DEBATE

Do the disabled have the right to a flourishing life? Bio-ethics and disability rights

As we shall see in Chapter 21, medicine plays a major role in contemporary social life and it has played a significant role in the cultural response to all kinds of disability. Recent trends have looked more and more to moral, ethical and ultimately political debate about differences. This is not to reduce the significance of medicine, but simply to note that many of the decisions around lives are moral ones. And in a society that is called 'reflexive modernity' (see Chapter 4), people are increasingly reflecting on the nature of their differences and disabilities.

Medical ethics have been around for a long time. The Hippocratic oath (from the Greek physician Hippocrates) is famously cited – even though nowadays this is much disputed – as a key source for what became 'medical ethics' in the seventeenth century. (The first code of medical ethics that appears to have been adopted by a professional organisation was written by English physician Thomas Percival (1740–1804) in 1794; it was adapted and adopted by the American Medical Association (AMA) in 1846.)

Modern bio-ethics is mainly a response to, and product of, concerns around the new technologies. Bio-ethics grew from the 1970s and is now a huge specialism with major journals, books and conferences covering a vast field of issues. Among these are:

long-term and end-of-life care, cloning, life support, surrogacy, medical torture, euthanasia, cryonics, contraception, eugenics and medical research(!), abortion, animal rights, artificial insemination, assisted suicide, body modifications, circumcision, female genital mutilation, gene therapy, genetically modified foods, human cloning, genetic engineering, population control, drug use and life extension.

There are important case studies, wide philosophical debates, 'world expert' pressure groups campaigning around the issues, books, leaflets, publications, conferences and significant social worlds organised around all of these issues. There are charters of rights, research centres, ethics committees, websites and international organisations. Bio-ethics is now a major industry.

Several values guide much of the debate, including:

1 *Best interest*: a practitioner should act in the best interest of the patient.
2 *Minimal harm*: 'first, do no harm'.
3 *Rights*: the patient has the right to refuse or choose their treatment.
4 *Dignity and respect*: the patient (and the person treating the patient) have the right to dignity and respect.
5 *Truthfulness and honesty*: there should be informed consent, and people must be fully informed of their situation.
6 *Justice*: this concerns the distribution of scarce health resources, and the decision of who gets what treatment. People should be treated fairly.

Values such as these do not give answers as to how to handle a particular situation, but provide a useful framework for understanding conflicts.

The disability debate

Ethics appears at three critical junctures for the disabled. New ethical issues are raised by disability and disability activists which often go against the grain of much contemporary ethical trends. They centre on the ethics of living a disabled life. So much research, policy and law making seems to work from the view that in some ways 'disability' is not good, and needs to be cured or removed. But behind this is a coded message to all who live with disabilities: in some ways your life is not really worth living. Many ethical issues bring to the fore the devaluation of disabled lives. These are thorny issues. Tom Shakespeare, a disabled activist and researcher, suggests three main areas for scrutiny.

The first concerns prenatal diagnosis (PND). It raises the question: if you learnt in advance that your child is likely to be born with a serious impairment, would it be right to abort this child? This re-raises the issue that the eugenics movement was confronted with some 100 years ago. It also raises key issues for those concerned more generally with the abortion debate.

The second concerns the new cures and remedies that are fast becoming available for the disabled. The Human Genome Project, gene therapy and stem cell research (see Chapter 23) are now key features of medical research. But they all work with ideas about the 'perfect' or 'better' body. Their research will lead to a decline of bodily impairments of all kinds. With an eye on the future, this may be very good news. But for those living with disabilities in the present, it can serve to reinforce their problems. Medicine can never solve all problems.

The third concerns the wider issue of death and the autonomy of the end of life (which we discuss in Chapter 21). These issues of disability rights at the end of life are dramatically portrayed in films like *Million Dollar Baby* (2004) and *The Sea Inside* (2004). Increasingly, there are many issues to confront at the end of a life: living wills, assisted suicide, voluntary euthanasia and resuscitation. One danger for the disabled in much of this is that their lives may be prematurely ended.

On all these issues, Shakespeare (2006: 131) concludes that:

> Listening to the voices of disabled people and those directly affected is an important principle in bio-ethics. It is dangerous for non-disabled people to project their own fears and misconceptions as to what it might be like to be impaired.

With this comment in mind, discuss each of the three debates above. Gather data from disability rights groups on their position and try to hear their voice on these issues.

See: Tom Shakespeare, *Disability Rights and Wrongs* (2006).

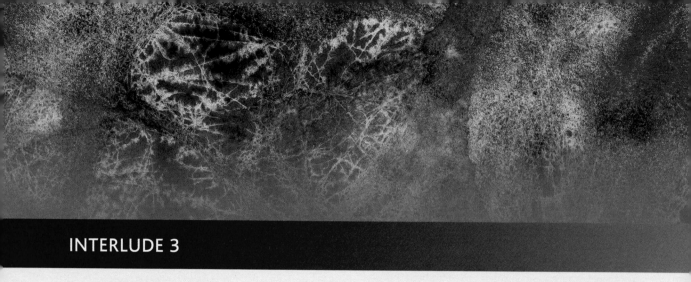

Researching music and inequalities

Nothing more clearly affirms one's class, nothing classifies more infallibly than tastes in music.

(Bourdieu, 1984: 18)

Part Three of this book has examined the nature of inequalities. At first glance, a turn to music as an illustration of inequalities might seem an odd choice of topic. Since, however, there is little in social life that is untouched by the inequalities we have been looking at, we should not really be surprised to find that it even shapes our musical lives. Inequalities are a central concern of sociological analysis precisely because they deeply invade every aspect of social experience. And music is no different. Once you start to think about it, we hope you will soon see that music is also embedded in worlds of inequality.

So in this interlude, we ask: Just how is music connected to the inequalities of:

· social class
· race, nation and ethnicity
· gender
· age?

We can as usual only provide brief entrances to these topics.

A sociology of music?

But first, before we turn to inequalities, we ask: what is meant by a sociology of music? Music can be found across societies and large numbers of people engage with it. People live musical lives and do musical things. Music is found across nature, of course — birds whistle, wolves howl, hyenas laugh, hens cluck and whales even 'sing'. But other animals do not develop musical instruments like pianos, write songs and symphonies, sing in choirs, stage operas and musicals, set up rock bands. They certainly do not develop national anthems. Nor do they develop technologies like iPods so they can move round the social world with music

as their daily backdrop. For many human animals, music is a central feature of life — we are the music-making animal busy making musical worlds.

Music is social — usually we do it with other people. It is not surprising that sociologists have studied it: here is a short list of examples of the kinds of studies that sociologists have conducted.

1 *The workings of musical groups of all kinds*: brass bands, rock group, jazz ensembles, orchestras. All have been studied and of special interest is the way they demonstrate collective behaviour, cooperative role taking across people, and how people do things together. To play together is a distinctly social thing (Faulkner and Becker, 2010).

2 *The role of music in town, village and community life.* In a marvellous study, Ruth Finnegan's *The Hidden Musicians* (2007) examined a wide range of local music groups — from classical to folk, from musical theatre to rock and pop — and suggests the roles they play in sustaining human life and its humanities.

3 *The study of specific music forms, from punk and rap to musicals and opera.* Debbie Weinstein in *Heavy Metal* (revised edn, 2000) lived in a world of heavy metal, whilst Paul Atkinson mixed in more elite circles studying opera (2006).

4 *The role that music plays in everyday life.* DeNora in her study *Music in Everyday Life* (2000) examines the ways in which music becomes a backdrop for daily life and surveys the ways we listen to music, the situations we listen in, why we listen and ultimately our emotional responses to music.

5 *The social role of composers.* Norbert Elias's classic *Mozart: The Sociology of a Genius* (1994) can be seen as a study of the sociology of genius.

6 *The historical evolution of different musical forms.* In Max Weber's *The Rational and Social Foundations of Music* (1958), he traces the role of harmony and melody in Western music and the break with atonality.

7 *The critique of music as mass culture.* Theodore Adorno, the Frankfurt sociologist, saw mass music as part of the deadening hand of *The Culture Industry*.

8 *The varieties of world music and the links to globalisation and othering.* See Laurent Aubert, *The Music of the Other* (2007).

Musical divisions

Here are some routes into starting to think about just how our music is bound up with our social divisions and inequalities.

Class: music as cultural capital and mark of distinction – or not

Social class plays a significant role in the shaping of musical tastes and often music helps symbolically to display and locate our class position. We have referred to Pierre Bourdieu's much celebrated book in the 1980s on taste in French society, where he conducted a large-scale survey asking people to specify their preferences on a huge range of things: their personal tastes in music, art, theatre, home decor, social pastimes, literature and so on. (It was based on a large survey carried out in 1963 and 1967–8, with a total of 1,217 subjects.) One feature of this study was to examine how social location, position and rank – distinctions – appear to be related to the kinds of music people know and like. And broadly he found this to be the case.

It is an old study, so more recently, it has been reworked in the UK and again class differences in music taste have been brought out. Tony Bennett, Mike Savage and a number of colleagues investigated people's musical tastes in an attempt to map then with social class. Many people are now prone to a wide range of music and have become 'cultural omnivores' – new radio programming, the ability to create one's own playlists and the general mixing of music have made music genres much more mixed and blended than it was in the past. At the same time, there is a kind of gravitation of certain classes to certain kinds of music. Respondents are given eight different types of music (rock, classical, jazz, heavy metal, etc.) and various examples (Mahler's Symphony No. 5, Eminem's 'Stan') and they are asked about their knowledge and preference. The researchers conclude, though with some caution: 'No working-class interviewees show significant knowledge of, or participation in, classical music. By contrast amongst our elite interviews all but two say they like classical music' (Bennett et al., 2009: 84).

This is not really surprising. Many music studies point in the same direction. For example, Paul Atkinson's ethnographic study of the opera (*Everyday Arias*, 2006), looking at both performances and audiences, soon shows the ways in which this form of music works as a clear cultural marker. Much of the opera works to mark out higher boundaries: 'The Opera company is itself a source of symbolic value. It can offer cultural capital. It provides a highly valued and legitimated form of "high" culture.' More than this: for the audience it 'helps reflect and reinforce one's position within the economic and cultural marketplace' (Atkinson, 2006: 150).

Ethnicity and nation: music as marker of the 'other' – who is in and out?

Music also plays a significant role in making out cultural boundaries and ethnic identities. At the simplest level, most cultures in the world have their own national anthem and every culture develops its own styles and rhythms: the Mexican bamba, the Spanish volero, the Brazilian bossa nova and Black music from be bop to hip hop. Each of these styles in turn helps define and maintain a sense of who people are. Music can serve as a major symbolic boundary marker between groups. It is both a way of creating a symbolic identity for groups and a way of keeping races apart – giving identity, shaping fashions, developing group styles and creating outsiders.

Rupa Huq's *Beyond Subcultures* (2006), a study of shifting youth music styles over the past several decades, makes very clear the role of music in establishing identity as she looks at how Bhangra, post-bhrangra and rai in part help create a generational culture for a new generation of Asian youth, and how rap and hip hop in turn essentially come to define black music. Rap becomes a 'black cultural expression that prioritises black voices from the margins of America' (citing Rose, 1994: 111). Ironically, this also brings sexism, homophobia and anti-racism.

What Ruq also stresses – in these postcolonial and postmodern times – is the hybridity and mix of the so-called authentic ethnic purity, as white kids borrow these music styles. We have seen this earlier in our case study of Japanese hip hop (Chapter 2). What is happening here is a drift to multiple musical identities that shift the boundaries of ethnic categories even as they are being maintained.

Gender: music as conservativism or rebellion?

Tracing the history of Western music – from say the fourteenth century to now – it is very hard to find any 'famous' women who were composers, musicians or performers (until very recently). It is an oddly male world.

Of course, there are many women composers throughout this history, but as is common, they have been lost from sight and from the popular histories. We know of Vivaldi, Mozart and Beethoven but not (usually) of their wives. We know of Robert Schumann but not Clara Schumann, Felix Mendelsohn but not Fanny Mendelsohn. And when women musicians start to appear in the nineteenth century, they inhabit an oddly gendered world where their work becomes sexualised (as divas, as whores). It is only very recently that women have entered the public world of music – and especially the world of popular music.

Popular music largely followed the same way. It has been described as 'an exclusively masculine world steeped in male ritual' (Cosgrove, in Huq, 2006). For a long while, men overwhelmed the music scene in every aspect: performance, writing, production, management. Of course, there were exceptions but it was a man's world. It was perhaps Madonna in the 1980s who challenged the position of women in music in a symbolic way. She showed both on stage and off stage the diversity and strength of women, and along the way generated an enormous anount of scholarship that debated 'The Madonna Connection'. Since her there has been an array of spicey girls, riot grrrls and chick rock, along with a spectrum of stars from Britney Spears to Lady Gaga. Sheila Whiteley in her book *Women and Popular Music* (2000) asks why 1960s pop cultures marginalised female performers like Dusty Springfield and Marianne Faithfull; considers how women artists like Annie Lennox responded to changing debates within feminism; and starts to consider the role of new wave girl bands in the noughties.

Age as schism or solidarity

A fourth connection between music and inequality can be found in the differences of age: music is always bound up with generations. The operas of the past were once identified more with the masses; now they have become the music of older elites at their expensive 'opera houses'. Rock and roll – harbinger of youth in the 1950s – is now identified with a much older generation. 'Elvis' and 'Cliff' have long ceased to symbolise rebellious youth and now signify the dying generations of grandparents. The 'youth culture' styles which started in the twentieth century now bring their own youth and dance music, marking out differences and separation from other age groupings. Thus in the twentieth century groups moved rapidly through college dances, big bands, rock and roll, the Beatles and the Stones, Flower Power, Abba, Glam Rock, Progressive, Punk, Rap, New Age, Pop, Grunge, Heavy Metal, Brutalism, Garage and Techno: the music styles ceaselessly parade through different age groups, serving as markers for their age generation differences and identities.

Often the popular music of a historical time can be seen to be in opposition to the older generation (with their dance bands, swing and crooners). As the youth of one time grows into the middle age and the old age of another time, so they stay with their interests in their own kind of popular music. Music has now become a way of identifying generations. At the same time, these days the music styles of each generation have now become widely available across different age groups and accessible to all. This has started to result in much contemporary music 'blending' into a much wider range of music styles connecting across generations. There are still distinctive generational varieties, but age has become much more complicated. In more and more ways, music is becoming cosmopolitan and is being used as ways of crossing over age and generation boundaries. Sometimes even music becomes a way of creating bonds across the age groups.

Musical differences

Music is social and connects to our differences in many ways. In this interlude, we have taken another everyday topic and tried to convince you of just how deeply interconnected it is with matters of social difference and inequalities.

Select reading

Paul Atkinson, *Everyday Aria: An Operatic Ethnography* (2006)
R. Tia DeNora, *Music in Everyday Life* (2000)
Ruth Finnegan, *The Hidden Musicians: Music Making in an English Town* (1989)
Rupa Huq, *Beyond Subculture* (2006)
Thomas Turino, *Music as Social Life* (2008)

PART 4

SOCIAL STRUCTURES, SOCIAL PRACTICES AND SOCIAL INSTITUTIONS

CHAPTER 15

ECONOMIES, WORK AND CONSUMPTION

ON A HOT SUMMER'S DAY IN 2000, a large sealed container lorry arrived at Dover in the UK. As the lorry door was opened by immigration inspectors, it was clear that something terrible had happened. For a start there was no chilled air – which would have been usual for a lorry full of food. Indeed, there seemed to be no air at all. And there was a very strange smell. Soon the worst was uncovered: the lorry contained 58 dead young illegal Chinese migrants. Only two had survived the journey.

Kei Su Di, aged 20, was one of the two survivors. He had left his family in China 11 days earlier, having paid the first installment of a £20,000 fee. Travelling in groups, he and his hopeful companions flew from Beijing to Belgrade, and eventually reached Rotterdam where they were all packed tightly into a lorry for the concealed and illegal journey to the UK. Tomato racks were placed at the front to conceal the illegal travellers. Each person had no more space than the size of a newspaper; they had no food or water; there were little bags for excrement; and the ventilation was off so that any noise from within the lorry could not be heard. In the end, their silenced screams as they suffocated to death are hard to imagine.

Of the 58 dead found in the container lorry, 23 came from one county (Changle) in China, and the rest from neighbouring counties. In search of a better life, they had found the equivalent of 10 years' pay to give to organised criminals (the 'Snakeheads') to 'export' them to a land of opportunity. Full of hope, their families had waved them goodbye . . .

On a cold winter's night in 2004, a group of illegal Chinese immigrants trawled the wild and unruly beach at Morecambe (near Blackpool) in search of cockles to be sold on the market. They worked nine hours for a pound in the bitter cold. The beach was notoriously dangerous – even experienced fishermen would not use it. Suddenly, they found themselves engulfed by the incoming tide and 19 of them were drowned in the darkness – not knowing which way to run or turn, or how to escape. It was subsequently found that they were living 40 to a house in the most squalid conditions.

Here are two tragic incidents involving crime and illegal migration. But odd as this may seem, this is also now part of the economy. Behind both tragedies there appears to have been a gang – The Snakeheads (named after the sliding movement of a snake) – that preys on poor migrants. In the case of the illegal lorry, they charged migrants around £20,000 each to transport them across Russia to Europe, and in 2000 it was estimated they netted some £4 billion. This is human trafficking on a large scale. It has become a hugely profitable industry, probably worth US$30 billion each year. Europe may well account for some 6–7 million illegal immigrants each year. Likewise, the migrant cockle workers were desperate for some money and, although they earned very little and they put their lives at great risk, they seemed to have no other options. Here is the rough side of our economy at work (see the film *Ghosts* (2007) and www.guardian.co.uk/refugees).

Source: *Guardian*, 19 June 2000, 6 April 2001; *The Week*, 1 July 2000; *Sunday Telegraph*, 8 February 2004.

Global capitalism affects whatever it touches, and it touches virtually everything . . .

Arlie Hochschild

In this chapter, we ask:

- **What is the economy and how is it changing?**

- **What are the key different kinds of economic system?**

- **How does capitalism work?**

- **What is the nature of work and corporations in post-industrial capitalist economies?**

- **What is the nature of consumption in modern capitalism?**

Ford Madox Brown, *Work*, a detail

Source: Preliminary study for *Work*, 1863, 1852–65 (oil on canvas) (see also 62924 & 100701), Brown, Ford Madox (1821–93)/ © Manchester Art Gallery, UK/ The Bridgeman Art Library.

Discover more about the painter and his works at: www.european-artgallery.com/artist_page.cfm?painter=105 and www.manchestergalleries.org/the.collections/search-the-collection.

Q This painting shows a whole range of people from various social strata going about their daily tasks. How many kinds of work can you see in this painting, how are they organised, and does the painting have much to say about social class?

It may seem odd to start a chapter on economies with two curious accounts of the death of Chinese illegal immigrants. But economies, for sociologists, are not simply about economics. For while **economies** may comprise of *social institutions that organise the production, distribution and consumption of goods and services*, such goods and services are diverse (such as here, the illegal sale of immigration) and connected to all the other social institutions, such as families (who raised money for the migrants to travel and then had to cope with their deaths), politics (where governments restrict migration and the flow of peoples), crime (where illegal immigrants were forced to work for nine hours for £1 by gang leaders) and media (which turned the deaths into a major issue). They are all interconnected. *Economies are never just economies.*

Hence in this chapter, we will explore the social significance and workings of economies, investigating the changing character of work in today's world, showing how economies are interdependent with other features of societies, suggesting that they are now more closely interconnected internationally than ever before. An opening section will look at the emergence of modern economic systems – and highlight the growth of capitalism. The chapter is then organised though the three key phases of economic organisation: (a) production, (b) distribution and (c) consumption of goods (such as food, clothing and shelter) and services (such as the work of religious leaders, doctors, police officers and telephone operators). Throughout the chapter, we will keep a close eye on social change and life in the twenty-first century.

Table 15.1 shows the largest and smallest economies of 2010. Of great interest is the rapid rise of China to second place in the world's economies. As we have suggested elsewhere (Chapters 4 and 26), this is perhaps a sign of the world to come.

Table 15.1	The largest and smallest economies in the world, by GDP, for 2009/10						
The largest economies in the world, by GDP (US$bn)				The smallest economies in the world, by GDP (US$bn)			
Rank	Country	Human development rank 2010	GDP 2010	Rank	Country	Human development rank 2009	GDP 2010
1	USA	4	14,799.56	1	Kiribati	Not ranked	0.152
2	China	89	5,364.87	2	São Tomé and Príncipe	127	0.203
3	Japan	11	5,272.94	3	Tonga	85	0.301
4	Germany	10	3,332.80	4	Dominica	88	0.375
5	France	14	2,668.79	5	Samoa	Not ranked	0.54
6	UK	26	2,222.63	6	Comoros	140	0.564
7	Italy	23	2,121.12	7	St Kitts and Nevis	60	0.565
8	Brazil	73	1,910.50	8	St Vincent and the Grenadines	93	0.581
9	Canada	8	1,556.035	9	Grenada	74	0.645
10	Russia	65	1,507.59	10	Democratic Republic of Timor-Leste	162	0.659

Source: Human development data adapted from HDR Statistical Tables, downloadable at http://hdr.undp.org/en/statistics/data; access date 4 September 2010. GDP data adapted from IMF World Economic Outlook database, at www.imf.org/external/ns/cs.aspx?id=28; access date 7 September 2010.

Changing economies: the 'Great Transformations' and the development of capitalism

As Chapter 4 explained, members of the earliest human societies relied on hunting and gathering to live off the land. In these societies, production, distribution and consumption of goods were all usually primarily dimensions of family life. What is distinctive about the modern world is the growth of technologies, and with it the accompanying development of a capitalist economic system. It is part of the 'Great Transformation' we discussed in Chapter 1.

The Agricultural Revolution

The development of agriculture about 5,000 years ago brought change to these societies. Agriculture emerged as people harnessed animals to ploughs, increasing the productive power of hunting and gathering more than tenfold. The resulting surplus freed some people in society from the demands of food production. Individuals began to adopt specialised economic roles: forging crafts, designing tools, raising animals and constructing dwellings. A division of labour started to become more and more important as size increased.

With the development of agriculture under way, towns emerged, soon to be linked by networks of traders dealing in food, animals and other goods. These four factors – agricultural technology, productive specialisation and division of labour, permanent settlements and trade – were the keys to an expansion of the economy.

In the process, the world of work became less obviously bound up with families, though production still occurred close to home. In medieval Europe, for instance, most people farmed nearby fields. Both country and city dwellers often laboured in their homes – a pattern called *cottage industry* – producing goods sold in frequent outdoor 'flea markets' (a term suggesting that not everything was of high quality).

The Industrial Revolution

By the middle of the eighteenth century, a second technological revolution was proceeding apace, first in England and soon afterwards elsewhere in Europe and North America. The development of industry was to transform social life even more than agriculture had done thousands of years before. Industrialisation introduced five notable changes to the economies of Western societies.

1 *New forms of energy*. Throughout history, people derived energy from their own muscles or those of animals. Then, in 1765, James Watt pioneered the development of the steam engine. Surpassing muscle power 100 times over, steam engines soon operated large machinery with unprecedented efficiency.

2 *The centralisation of work in factories*. Steam-powered machinery soon rendered cottage industries obsolete. Factories – centralised and impersonal workplaces separate from the home – proliferated. Work moved from the private sphere to the public sphere – that is, people 'went out to work'.

3 *Manufacturing and mass production*. Before the Industrial Revolution, most work involved cultivating and gathering raw materials, such as crops, wood and wool. The industrial economy shifted most jobs into manufacturing, which turned raw materials into a wide range of saleable products. For example, factories mass-produced timber into furniture and transformed wool into clothing.

4 *Division of labour and specialisation*. Typically, a single skilled worker in a cottage industry fashioned a product from beginning to end. Factory work, by contrast, demands division of labour and specialisation so that a labourer repeats a single task over and over again, making only a small contribution to the finished product. Thus as factories raised productivity, they also lowered the skill level of the average worker. Despoiling occurred.

5 *Wage labour*. Instead of working for themselves or joining together as households, industrial workers entered factories as wage labourers. They sold their labour to strangers, who often cared less for them than for the machines they operated. Supervision became routine and intense. Incomes were usually pitifully low and workers were hence subject to great exploitation.

The impact of the Industrial Revolution gradually rippled outwards from the factories to transform all of society. While working conditions were very poor for many, greater productivity steadily raised the standard of living as countless new products and services filled an expanding marketplace. The benefits of industrial technology were shared very unequally. Some factory owners made vast fortunes, while the majority of industrial workers hovered perilously close to poverty. Children, too, worked in factories or deep in coal mines for pennies a day. Women factory workers, among the lowest paid, endured special hardships.

In Europe and North America, workers gradually formed trade unions to represent their collective interests in negotiations with factory owners. From the late nineteenth century onwards, governments in the West were forced to outlaw child labour, push wages upwards, improve workplace safety and extend schooling and political rights to a larger segment of the population.

The Information Revolution and the post-industrial society

The nature of production itself also started to change. By the middle of the twentieth century, many Western countries were being transformed. Automated machinery reduced the role of human labour in production, while bureaucracy simultaneously expanded the ranks of clerical workers and managers. Service industries – such as public relations, healthcare, education, media, advertising, banking and sales – started to employ the bulk of workers. Distinguishing the post-industrial era, then, is a shift from industrial work to service jobs.

Driving this economic change was a third technological transformation: the development of the computer and the new technologies we have encountered in previous chapters (see Chapters 1, 3, 4 and 6). The *Information Revolution* in Europe, the United States, much of newly industrialising Asia and elsewhere started to generate new kinds of information and new forms of communication, changing the character of work just as factories did two centuries ago. This Information Revolution unleashed three key changes.

1 *Tangible products to ideas.* The industrial era was defined by the production of goods; in the post-industrial era, more and more work revolves around creating and manipulating symbols. Computer programmers, writers, financial analysts, advertising executives, architects and all sorts of consultants represent the workers of the Information Age.

2 *Mechanical skills to literacy skills.* Just as the Industrial Revolution offered opportunities to those who learned a mechanical trade, the Information Revolution demands that workers have literacy skills – the ability to speak, write and use computer technology. People who can communicate effectively enjoy new opportunities; those who cannot face declining prospects.

A street cleaner sweeps a road near a coal-fired power plant at an industrial park in Shizuishan, China's northern Ningxia Hui Autonomous Region, 7 December 2009, just before the biggest climate meeting in history, with 15,000 participants from 192 nations, took place in Copenhagen seeking to agree curbs on greenhouse gas emissions and raise billions of dollars for the poor in aid and clean technology
Source: Corbis/REUTERS/Jason Lee.

3 *Decentralisation of work away from factories.* Just as industrial technology (steam power driving massive machines) drew workers together into factories, computer technology now permits many people to work almost anywhere. Indeed, laptop computers and facsimile (fax) machines linked to telephone lines now make the home, a car or even a plane a 'virtual office'. New information technology, in short, is reversing the industrial trend and bringing about a return of home-based 'cottage industries'. The virtual workplace and 'telecommuting' is becoming a reality for many.

The need for face-to-face communication as well as the availability of supplies and information still keep most workers in the office. On the other hand, today's more educated and creative labour force no longer requires – and often resists – the close supervision that marked yesterday's factories.

Sectors of the economy

The three 'revolutions' just described also reflect a shifting balance among the three sectors of a society's economy. The **primary sector** *generates raw materials directly from the natural environment* and includes agriculture, animal husbandry, fishing, forestry and mining. It predominates in pre-industrial societies. The **secondary sector** *transforms raw materials into manufactured goods* and includes the refining of petroleum and the use of metals to manufacture tools and automobiles. It grows quickly as societies industrialise. The **tertiary sector** *generates services rather than goods* and includes teachers, shop assistants, cleaners, solicitors, IT experts and media workers.

The tertiary sector grows with industrialisation and dominates the economies of high-income nations as they enter the post-industrial era. Now accounting for some 70 per cent of economic output in high-income countries, it accounts for only 48 per cent in low-income societies. This marks one of the most significant changes in modern economies.

Figure 15.1 shows these differences strikingly. Here we see that in low-income countries 25 per cent of the workforce is engaged in the primary sector, compared to just 2 per cent in high-income societies. When it comes to the tertiary sector of services, some 72 per cent of the labour force is 'in service' in high-income societies, but only 47 per cent in much poorer ones. Old economic patterns of agriculture and even manufacturing are giving way to an increasingly service and information-based economy (World Bank, 2008). Table 15.2 gives the detailed breakdown for the UK and the changes between 1978 and 2008. You can see the significant growth in financial, health and education services – and a massive decline in the manufacturing base.

The nature and variety of capitalism

As we have seen, the contemporary world is predominantly **capitalist**. It is *an economic system in which resources and the means of producing goods and services are privately owned*. It brings three key features (see the Timeline on p. 501):

1 Private ownership of property.
2 Pursuit of personal profit.
3 Free competition, consumer sovereignty and markets.

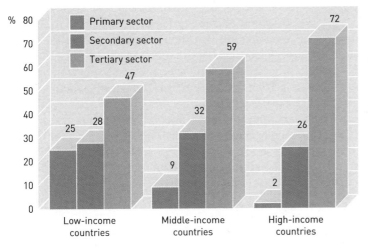

Figure 15.1 The size of economic sectors, by income level of country

Source: Macionis, John J., *Sociology, 13th*, © 2010. Printed and electronically reproduced by permission of Pearson Education, Inc., Upper Saddle River, New Jersey. Estimates based on World Bank (2008).

| Table 15.2 | Employee jobs: by industry[1] in the UK |

United Kingdom — Percentages

	1978	1988	1998	2008	2009	Change 1978 to 2008	Change 2008 to 2009
Agriculture and fishing	1.7	1.4	1.3	1.0	1.0	−0.7	–
Energy and water	2.8	1.8	0.8	0.7	0.7	−2.1	–
Manufacturing	28.5	20.7	17.0	10.5	10.0	−18.0	−0.6
Construction	5.7	5.1	4.4	4.8	4.8	−0.8	–
Distribution, hotels and restaurants	19.5	21.3	23.8	23.6	23.5	4.1	−0.1
Transport and communications	6.5	5.9	5.7	5.9	5.8	−0.7	−0.1
Finance and business services	10.5	14.8	18.1	21.4	20.8	10.9	−0.6
Public administration, education and health	21.1	24.5	24.2	26.9	28.1	5.8	1.2
Other services[2]	3.8	4.5	4.7	5.3	5.4	1.5	0.1
All industries (=100%) (millions)	24.3	23.7	24.7	27.2	26.5	2.9	−0.7

[1] Date are at June each year and are not seasonally adjusted. See Appendix, Part 4: Standard Industrial Classification 2003 (SIC2003).
[2] Community, social and personal services including sanitation, dry cleaning, personal care, and recreational, cultural and sporting activities.

Source: *Short-Term Employment Surveys*, Office for National Statistics in *Social Trends*, 40 (2010), p. 49.

The shape of capitalism has shifted across time and across countries. Capitalism has a long history. We can find evidence of merchants making money through investing in goods in Genoa and Venice during the twelfth century. But the arrival of a distinctively modern capitalism is usually linked to the rise of the industrial world, first in the cotton mills in England at the turn of the eighteenth century, and then throughout Europe and the United States. In this factory-based capitalism, workers sold their labour for wages and in the process capitalist owners made profits.

It was the eighteenth century thinker Adam Smith (now featured on English banknotes) who argued that the market system is dominated by consumers, who select goods and services that offer the greatest value. He developed ideas around what has come to be called 'market capitalism' and which is indentified with neoliberalism. Producers compete with one another by providing the highest-quality goods and services at the lowest possible price. Thus, while entrepreneurs are motivated by personal gain, everyone benefits from more efficient production and ever-increasing value. In Smith's time-honoured phrase, from narrow self-interest comes the 'greatest good for the greatest number of people'. Smith claimed that a free market and a competitive economy would regulate themselves by the 'invisible hand' of the laws of supply and demand. Government control of an economy would inevitably upset the complex market system, reducing producer motivation, diminishing the quantity and quality of goods produced, and short-changing consumers.

Pure, ideal capitalism is non-existent. The United States may have the purest form – private markets are more extensive than in Europe – yet even there the guiding hand of government does play a role in economic affairs. Through taxation and various regulatory agencies, the government influences what companies produce, the quality and costs of merchandise, the products that businesses import and export, and the consumption and conservation of natural resources. The federal government also owns and operates a host of businesses, including the US Postal Service, the Amtrak railway system and the Nuclear Regulatory Commission (which conducts atomic research and produces nuclear materials). The entire US military is also government-operated. Federal officials may step in to prevent the collapse of businesses, as in the 'bailout' of the savings and loan industry. Further, government policies mandate minimum wage levels, enforce workplace safety standards, regulate corporate mergers, provide farm price supports, and funnel income in the form of social security, public assistance, student loans and veterans' benefits to a majority of people.

Capitalism comes in many forms: Japan and the United States, for instance, work very differently. Generally, modern capitalism has moved through three phases. The first was a *liberal capitalism*, which dominated Britain and the United States in the early and middle nineteenth century and involved a free market, a 'facilitative' state and a legal framework which helps to maintain capitalism. Second was an *organised capitalism*, which involved an administered market and a more 'directive state'. There was, for example, in the UK between 1946 and 1979 much

more 'state' intervention as governments often shaped economic policies. More recently a *disorganised/ post-Fordist capitalism* has emerged, which involves an increase in the service sector, more global and dispersed operations and a decline of nation-states (Lash and Urry, 1987). Throughout the short modern history of capitalism it has been persistently subject to periods of booms and bust (see *Timeline*).

Disorganised capitalism: Fordism and post-Fordism

Fordism was associated with the American car manufacturer Henry Ford, who, at the start of the twentieth century, developed the assembly line to produce cheap cars that could be purchased by the

Timeline Twentieth-century modern capitalism and its crises

Capitalism takes many forms and the last 200 years have seen a varying history of booms, depressions and crises of different scales. There is nothing new about this cycle of 'boom and bust' – in 1720 there was the famous South Sea Bubble. It is often seen to approach a ten-year cycle.

The 'Roaring Twenties'

- leading to the Wall Street Crash of 1929 and the Great Depression of the 1930s. It led ultimately to 'New Deal capitalism', which focused on the '3 Rs': *relief* for the unemployed and poor; *recovery* of the economy to normal levels; and *reform* of the financial system to prevent a repeat depression.

Postwar prosperity

- starting in the 'You never had it so good' 1950s (a phrase of UK Prime Minister Harold Macmillan) and carrying on through the 'swinging sixties'.

The 'stagflation' of the 1970s

- accompanied by the neoliberalism of UK Prime Minister Margaret Thatcher (Thatcherism) and President Ronald Regan (Reaganism). Here the free market became the dominant force, with officially less and less state intervention. Despite changes of governments it set a pattern of social life which influenced much of the world and continued until the 'bust' of 2008.

Fall of Soviet Union in 1991 and global capitalism

- the rise of China, India and the newly industrialised countries of southeast Asia (NICs) and the boom years of the 1990s and the early twenty-first century. This was a period of conspicuous consumption, living on credit, substantial loans and debts, a belief in economic growth – and massive inequalities.

2008 financial crisis

- the credit crunch, the crisis of subprime mortgages; banks had to be bailed out with massive debts; recession followed.

For a straightforward account of these booms and busts, see Andrew Gamble (2009).

masses. **Fordism** is *an economic system based on mass assembly-line production, mass consumption and standardised commodities.* It depends upon dedicated machinery and tools producing identical components; centralised unskilled labour used intensively on specific tasks; and low-cost production of vast quantities of goods. Workers do repetitive work over long periods: the work is usually of mind-blowing tedium. They are paid reasonably well and this increases their consumer spending. Fordism is technically limited and not very flexible. A classic study by Huw Beynon looked at the Ford motor plant in Liverpool in the late 1960s and documented this moving assembly line where about 16,000 different components had to be 'screwed, stuck or spot welded' as the car moved and slipped down the line (Beynon, 1973: 105). The relentless pressure is more amusingly documented in Charlie Chaplin's classic silent film *Modern Times*.

While Fordist production techniques continued through much of the twentieth century, newer and more flexible ones emerged alongside them (especially in Japan and southeast Asia). This newer process involved:

- shifts in production: more flexible systems of production
- more flexible time: part-time, temporary and self-employed workers
- decentralisation of labour into smaller, less hierarchical units
- the 'casualisation of labour', where work becomes less stable and secure
- 'just-in time' (that is, last-minute) rapid production
- movement from standardised goods to goods including options

- gradual replacement of 'mass marketing and advertising' by 'niche marketing', targeted at specific 'style' groups
- globalisation, with a new international division of labour.

Often called **post-Fordism**, this *new economic system is based on flexibility (rather than standardisation), specialisation and tailor-made goods* (see Table 15.3 for comparison). We have already seen some of this at work in organisational forms in Chapter 6 (where they were identified as 'postmodern'). These modes are not just to be found in work practices, but in consumption in the home as well. As we shall see, much of this new pattern has meant a system which is much more casual in its employment of workers.

The global revolution: globalisation and the global economy

As technology draws people around the world closer together, another important economic transformation seems to be taking place. As we saw in Chapter 2, globalisation has become a key feature of the late modern world: we have witnessed the emergence of a **global economy**, *economic activity spanning many nations of the world with little regard for national borders*. The development of a global economy has six main consequences.

First, we are seeing a global division of labour by which each region of the world specialises in particular kinds of economic activity. Agriculture occupies more than 70 per cent of the workforce in low-income

Table 15.3	A comparison of ideal types of production system: from Fordist to post-Fordist	
	Fordist	**Post-Fordist**
Product	Standardised – all the same	Specialised – better quality?
Labour	Fragmented	Integrated
	Few tasks	Many tasks
	Little discretion	Flexible
Management	Centralised	Decentralised
Technology	Fixed machines	Multi-purpose/electronic
Contracts	Relatively secure	For most: insecure

countries, while industrial production is concentrated in the middle- and high-income nations of the world. The economies of the richest nations, including Europe, now specialise in service-sector activity.

Secondly, we are seeing workers in the poorer countries working long hours for little pay in what have been called 'the sweatshops of the world'. They produce goods that can be sold in high-income countries. In a single day, workers may produce hundreds of garments in poor working conditions. Just one garment sold to high-income societies would sell for the equivalent of their wages for five days (Klein, 2000: 353). Often, too, these workers are compelled to travel long distances, leaving families behind, in order even to find such opportunities for work. Note, too, that very frequently this labour is that of children. The International Labour Organization suggests that some 250 million children work in low-income societies, a number that excludes child work hidden from the statisticians, such as domestic labour (often by girls). This brings the total nearer 500 million, and this does not include the children who work in high-income societies.

Thirdly, an increasing number of products pass through the economies of more than one nation. Consider, for instance, that workers in Taiwan may manufacture shoes, which a Hong Kong distributor sends to Italy, where they receive the stamp of an Italian designer; another distributor in Rome forwards the shoes to New York, where they are sold in a department store owned by a firm with its headquarters in Tokyo.

A fourth consequence of the global economy is that national governments no longer control the economic activity that takes place within their borders. In fact, governments cannot even regulate the value of their national currencies, since money is now traded around the clock in the financial centres of Tokyo, London and New York. Global markets are one consequence of satellite communications that forge information links among the world's major cities. Indeed, this gives rise to *global cities* (see Chapter 24).

The fifth consequence of the global economy is that a small number of businesses, operating internationally, now control a vast share of the world's economic activity. One estimate concludes that the 600 largest multinational companies account for fully half of the earth's entire total economic output (Kidron and Segal, 1991). The world is still divided into approximately 200 politically distinct nations. But, in light of the proliferation of international economic activity, 'nationhood' has lost much of its former significance.

Finally, a major consequence of this modern global capitalist system is the *extraordinary inequality of wealth* – the top few against the bottom billion. Look back to Chapter 9 to review the wealth of the super-rich when compared with the abject poverty of over half the world.

Capitalism and its alternatives

Contemporary economies of the world have conventionally been seen through two abstract models – *capitalism* and *socialism*. Few societies have economies that are purely one or the other: most European countries are, to varying degrees, *mixed economies*. Sweden and the other Scandinavian countries are generally seen as a version of a more socialist approach – interventionist, corporatist and planned. But they are in the process of being pulled towards the German model, which is more inclined towards a social market. The system in the UK was mixed until the advent of Thatcherism in 1979, since when it has moved more and more towards a privatised market system (the neoliberal model).

Socialism

Socialism is *an economic system in which natural resources and the means of producing goods and services are collectively owned*. In its ideal form, a socialist economy opposes each of the three characteristics of capitalism we have described above. Thus, socialism brings:

1   *Collective ownership of property*. An economy is socialist to the extent that it limits the right to private property, especially property used in producing goods and services. Laws prohibiting private ownership of property are designed to make housing and other goods available to all, not just to those with the most money. Karl Marx asserted that private ownership of productive property spawns social classes, as it generates an economic elite. Socialism, then, seeks to lessen economic inequality while forging a classless society.

2   *Pursuit of collective goals*. The individualistic pursuit of profit also stands at odds with the collective orientation of socialism. Socialist values and norms condemn what capitalists celebrate as the

entrepreneurial spirit. For this reason, private trading is branded as illegal 'black market' activity.

3 *Government control of the economy.* Socialism rejects the idea that a free-market economy regulates itself. Instead of a *laissez-faire* approach, socialist governments oversee a *centrally controlled* or *command economy.* Socialism also rejects the idea that consumers guide capitalist production. From this point of view, consumers lack the information necessary to evaluate products and are manipulated by advertising to buy what is profitable for factory owners rather than what they, as consumers, genuinely need. Commercial advertising thus plays little role in socialist economies.

The People's Republic of China and a number of nations in Asia, Africa and Latin America – some two dozen in all – model their economies on socialism, placing almost all wealth-generating property under state control. But the extent of world socialism has declined in recent years as societies in eastern Europe and the former Soviet Union have forged new economic systems increasing the sway of market forces.

Socialism and communism

Some people equate the terms *socialism* and *communism.* More precisely, as the ideal spirit of socialism, **communism** is *an economic and political system in which all members of a society are socially equal.* Karl Marx viewed socialism as a transitory stage on the path towards the ideal of a communist society that had abolished all class divisions. In many socialist societies today, the dominant political party describes itself as communist, but nowhere has the pure communist goal been achieved.

Why? For one thing, social stratification involves differences of power as well as wealth. Socialist societies have generally succeeded in reducing disparities in wealth only through expanding government bureaucracies and subjecting the population to extensive regulation. In the process, government has not 'withered away' as Karl Marx imagined. On the contrary, socialist political elites have usually gained enormous power and privilege. Marx would probably have agreed that a communist society is a *utopia* (from Greek words meaning 'not a place'). Yet Marx considered communism a worthy goal and might well have disparaged reputedly 'Marxist' societies such as North Korea, the former Soviet Union, the People's Republic of China and Cuba for falling far short of his ideal.

Capitalism and socialism: the big issues

Which economic system works best? In practice, most societies now work from a mix of capitalism and socialism to different degrees, although capitalism has become stronger and stronger. In 1989 and 1990, the nations of eastern Europe (seized by the Soviet Union after the Second World War) rejected their socialist regimes. And today, China is also moving towards a market economy. But what was it like before these dramatic changes? We can look at this through three dimensions: economic productivity (or GDP), economic equality and civil liberties.

1 Economic productivity

Important elements of GDP, such as the proportion of the international export market a country controls, varied dramatically among capitalist countries. As a group, however, capitalist countries generated more goods and services than socialist countries. Averaging the economic output of industrialised nations at the end of the 1980s yielded a per capita GDP of about US$13,500. The comparable figure for the former Soviet Union and the nations of eastern Europe was about $5,000. This means that capitalist countries outproduced socialist nations by a ratio of 2.7 to 1 (United Nations Development Programme, 1990). Recent comparisions of the differences between capitalist South Korea (at $22,985 per capita GDP) and socialist North Korea (at $1,700) finds an even sharper contrast (United Nations Development Programme, 2008).

2 Economic equality

How resources are distributed within a society stands as a second crucial issue. A comparative study completed in the mid-1970s calculated income ratios by comparing the earnings of the richest 5 per cent of the population and the poorest 5 per cent (Wiles, 1977). This research found that societies with predominantly capitalist economies had an income ratio of about 10 to 1; the corresponding figure for socialist countries was 5 to 1. This comparison of economic performance reveals that *capitalist economies produced a higher overall standard of living but also generated greater income disparity.* Or, put otherwise, *socialist economies created less income disparity but offered a lower overall standard of living.*

3 Civil liberties and personal freedom

A third issue to consider in evaluating socialism and capitalism is the personal freedom and civil liberties that each offers its citizens. Capitalism emphasises *freedom to* pursue one's self-interest. It depends on the freedom of producers and consumers to interact in a free market, with minumum interference by the state. By contrast, socialist societies emphasise *freedom from* basic wants. Equality is the goal which requires state intervention in the economy, and this in turn limits some of the choices of citizens. There are, then, major tensions between freedom from and freedom to, between freedom and equality.

This tension has not been resolved between the two systems. In the capitalist West, many freedoms are ostensibly guaranteed, but are these freedoms worth as much to a poor person as a rich one? On the other hand, in Cuba or North Korea – two of the last remaining socialist states – economic equality is bought at the expense of the rights of people to express themselves freely.

Varieties of twenty-first century capitalism

At the start of the twenty-first century, capitalism is to be found throughout the world. Although it is in crisis, it is usually seen as the dominant contemporary form of economic organisation. It does, however, take on a range of different forms, shaped by history, governments (see Chapter 16) and cultures (see Chapter 5). For example, three kinds are regularly distinguished as:

- *Neoliberal market capitalism*: decentralised, open markets; an anti-trust or union tradition; fluid capital markets; individualism; minimum state involvement and planning; maximising returns to owners of capital; linked with the 'liberal democracy' political system (e.g. predominantly the United States, and the United Kingdom to a lesser extent, as it is also shaped by the EU – see social market capitalism, below).

- *Social market capitalism*: social partnerships, more organised markets, dedicated bank-centred capital markets; state interventions; linked with 'social democracy' (e.g. much of western Europe and the Scandinavian countries).

- *Developmental capitalism*: guided markets, tight business networks, strong bureaucracy, highly technological, reciprocity between state and firms; state plays quite a strong role; linked with 'developmental democracy' (e.g. Japan, the NICs and the Association of South-East Asian Nations) (Dicken, 2010).

Many of the nations of western Europe – including Sweden and Italy – have merged socialist economic policies with a democratic political system. Analysts call this **democratic socialism**, *an economic and political system that combines significant government control of the economy with free elections*. Under democratic socialism, the government owns some of the largest industries and services, such as transportation, the mass media and healthcare. In Sweden and Italy, about 12 per cent of economic production is state controlled or 'nationalised'. That leaves most industry in private hands, but nevertheless subject to extensive government regulation. High taxation (aimed especially at the rich) funds various social welfare programmes, transferring wealth to less advantaged members of society.

Along the Pacific Rim, in Japan, South Korea and Singapore, yet another blend of capitalism and socialism is found: **state capitalism**: *an economic and political system in which companies are privately owned, although they cooperate closely with the government*. Systems of state capitalism are all capitalist nations, but their governments work closely with large companies, supplying financial assistance or controlling imports of foreign products to help businesses function as competitively as possible in world markets. During this century, China has also conspicuously opened itself to the market system – while still keeping central state control (see Chapter 26).

Since the fall of the old socialist regimes in the late 1980s, eastern Europe (including the German Democratic Republic (GDR), Czechoslovakia, Hungary, Romania and Bulgaria) has also moved towards market-led or capitalist systems. In 1992, the Soviet Union itself dissolved. Ten years later, three-quarters of its state enterprises were partly or entirely under private ownership. There were many reasons for these sweeping changes. In part, socialist economies underproduced compared to capitalist societies, and living standards were often very low. And while members were formally equal, they often experienced large restrictions on freedom and heavy-handed states which regulated the media. New elites based on power usually appeared.

So far the market reforms in eastern Europe are very uneven. Some countries (Slovakia, the Czech Republic)

The degradation and alienation of work in the Western world

Many people have spoken up about the conditions of work in all countries of the world. In film, in novels and in many autobiographies, you can find the voices of people talking about their work experiences. In this chapter, we have two boxes to capture this. Here we look at two studies of Western voices. In the next box (p. 509), we look at the voice of a Guatemalan girl worker. Look on the internet to find many other voices.

Oral history

In the 1970s, the oral historian Studs Terkel conducted many interviews about the experience of work. Many of these showed how dull, repetitive jobs can generate alienation for men and women.

Phil Stallings was a 27-year-old car worker in a Ford assembly plant in Chicago.

> I start the automobile, the first welds. From there it goes to another line, where the floor's put on, the roof, the trunk, the hood, the doors. Then it's put on a frame. There is hundreds of lines. . . .
>
> I stand in one spot, about two- or three-feet area, all night. The only time a person stops is when the line stops. We do about thirty-two jobs per car, per unit. Forty-eight units an hour, eight hours a day. Thirty-two times forty-eight times eight. Figure it out. That's how many times I push that button.
>
> The noise, oh it's tremendous. You open your mouth and you're liable to get a mouthful of sparks. [Shows his arms.] That's a burn, these are burns. You don't compete against the noise. You go to yell and at the same time you're straining to manoeuvre the gun to where you have to weld.
>
> You got some guys that are uptight, and they're not sociable. It's too rough. You pretty much stay to yourself. You get involved with yourself. You dream, you think of things you've done. I drift back continuously to when I was a kid and what me and my brothers did. The things you love most are what you drift back into.
>
> It don't stop. It just goes and goes and goes. I bet there's men who have lived and died out there, never seen the end of the line. And they never will – because it's endless. It's like a serpent. It's just all body, no tail. It can do things to you . . .
>
> (Terkel, 1977: 151)

Twenty-four-year-old Sharon Atkins was a college graduate working as a telephone receptionist for a large midwestern business.

> I don't have much contact with people. You can't see them. You don't know if they're laughing, if they're being satirical or being kind. So your conversations become very abrupt. I notice that in talking to people. My conversation would be very short and clipped, in short sentences, the way I talk to people all day on the telephone . . .
>
> You try to fill up your time with trying to think about other things: what you're going to do on the weekend or about your family. You have to use your imagination. If you don't have a very good one and you bore easily, you're in trouble. Just to fill in time, I write real bad poetry or letters to myself and to other people and never mail them. The letters are fantasies, sort of rambling, how I feel, how depressed I am . . .
>
> I never answer the phone at home.
>
> (Terkel, 1977: 60)

Participant observation

More recently, Barbara Ehrenreich (2001) in the USA and Polly Toynbee (2003) in the UK have experimented with going undercover in the world of low-paid women's work. They worked in cafés and fast-food restaurants, acted as cleaners and maids, as well as working in factories. Both were highly educated middle-class women, but on low incomes they did not fare well. They felt stigmatised; they had difficulty finding a place to live or ways of getting to work; and of course they worked long hours, often with gruelling work. And there was more to the work than they thought. Barbara Ehrenreich remarks towards the end of her book:

> How did I do as a low-wage worker? If I may begin with a brief round of applause: I didn't do half bad at the work itself, and I claim this as a considerable achievement. You might think that unskilled jobs would be a snap for someone who holds a Ph.D. and whose normal line of work requires learning entirely new things every

couple of weeks. Not so. The first thing I discovered is that no job, no matter how lowly, is truly 'unskilled.' Every one of the six jobs I entered into the course of this project required concentration, and most demanded that I master new terms, new tools, and new skills – from placing orders on restaurant computers to wielding the backpack vacuum cleaner. None of these things came as easily to me as I would have liked; no one ever said, 'Wow you're fast!' or 'Can you believe she just started?'

Whatever my accomplishments in the rest of my life, in the low-wage work world I was a person of average ability – capable of learning the job and also capable of screwing up.

(Ehrenreich, 2001: 193–4)

are faring well; others (such as the Russian Federation itself) have brought out many of the weakest points of capitalism, with growing poverty and inequality, high competitiveness and social decline (Burawoy, 1997).

To conclude: countries in eastern Asia, western Europe, eastern Europe and elsewhere illustrate that there are many ways in which governments and companies can work cooperatively. Blends of socialism and capitalism are becoming a common pattern.

Global capitalism: triumph or crisis?

For many, then, it looks as if capitalism is here to stay: it is seen as the dominant (and for many, the only way) of organising the economy across the world. There are now very few societies that support a strict socialist/communist model (North Korea, Cuba and a few states in Africa and Latin America). All rivals are usually dismissed. Nowhere is this view clearer than in Francis Fukuyama's much discussed book *The End of History* (1989). For him, history came to an end with the triumph of Western capitalism. The Soviet bloc had collapsed and we are now living in an age of permanent capitalism.

By contrast, the political philosopher John Gray in his book *False Dawn* (2002) argues that the unfettered global free market economy is not likely to stay. In the long run of world history, contemporary capitalism will be seen as a mere blip. With modern capitalism we increasingly find social instability, growing social inequalities and economic unpredictability across the world. This may not be tenable into the distant future. Indeed, Gray argues that 'the free market is a rare, short-lived phenomenon', a specific product of English nineteenth-century social engineering, from whose cycles of boom and bust we still have much to learn.

Gray does not, however, see the future as bringing a return to the socialist models of the past. Indeed,

at present, he offers few solutions to 'the deepening international anarchy' in which free markets spiral out of control. At the start of the twenty-first century, it is unclear to Gray and many others in which direction our economies are now heading.

The changing nature of work

Work seems to be a precondition of social life. Three billion people on this planet labour for wages. They sell their labour for money. And most spend some 70 to 80 per cent of their lives working in order to meet their everyday needs and wants. They live and work in every imaginable place – from the salt mines of Russia to the most remote Chilean village. Their work conditions and their work experiences vary enormously. Men and women, old and young, work – but their experiences may be hugely different. Yet at the same time, others are unemployed – around 160 million are seeking employment. And many millions (as we saw in the opening stories) travel from their homeplaces to find employment and are often stigmatised 'migrant workers'. A much smaller number of people employ these people. The wealthiest of these 'business people' and employers – like Bill Gates and Rupert Murdoch – control finances that are equal to that of small countries (cf. Castree et al., 2004: xi). In this section, we look at some of the basic characteristics of work and just how it may be changing in the twenty-first century.

Work in Europe and the UK

First, here are a few details about the numbers who work. In 2009, about 65 per cent of the EU-27's population aged between 15 and 64 were employed. In 12 member states, over 67 per cent were employed (in

Germany, Denmark, Cyprus, the Netherlands, Austria, Slovenia, Finland, Sweden, the United Kingdom, Iceland and Norway). But the employment rate remained below 60 per cent in Spain, Italy, Hungary, Malta, Poland, Romania and Croatia. Table 15.4 shows a detailed breakdown of this for you to consider – showing also the gender differences between employment for men and women. Across Europe, the working week in 2007 approximated 42 hours – but there were variations, the number of hours being lowest in Norway, Luxembourg, Lithuania, Ireland and Denmark, and highest in the UK, Austria, the Czech Republic, Poland and Slovenia.

Looking at the UK in 2009, there were 31.4 million people over 16 in work. Around 18 million people were economically inactive. Figure 15.2 shows the ways this was patterned over the life cycle (age) and between men and women. Across the country, there are also large variations: in 2008, working-age employment rates were highest in Scotland, at 76 per cent, while in Northern Ireland only 70 per cent of working-age persons were employed. In England, London had a

relatively low employment rate of 70 per cent, while the highest employment rate was to be found in the southeast, at 79 per cent.

Contrary to a popular stereotype, the number of hours worked per week has been going up in recent years – we are not becoming a 'leisure society'. Looking at Europe, people working full time in Italy worked 37 hours per week (the lowest in the EU), whilst those in the UK worked 42 hours (one hour less than the countries with the highest number of hours worked) (*Social Trends*, 2004: Chapters 4 and 5).

Age clearly also affects labour force participation. Typically, both women and men join the workforce in their teens and early twenties. During their child-bearing years, however, women's participation lags behind that of men. After about the age of 45, the working profiles now differ, with women more likely to continue in work and men less likely. There is a marked withdrawal from the labour force as people approach the age of 65. After that point in life, only a small proportion of each gender continues to perform steady income-producing work.

Table 15.4		Employment rates: by gender, EU comparison, 2008						
								Percentages
	Men	**Women**	**All**			**Men**	**Women**	**All**
Denmark	81.9	74.3	78.1	Spain		73.5	54.9	64.3
Netherlands	83.2	71.1	77.2	Lithuania		67.1	61.8	64.3
Sweden	76.7	71.8	74.3	Bulgaria		68.5	59.5	64.0
Austria	78.5	65.8	72.1	Luxembourg		71.5	55.1	63.4
United Kingdom	77.3	65.8	71.5	Belgium		68.6	56.2	62.4
Finland	73.1	69.0	71.1	Slovakia		70.0	54.6	62.3
Cyprus	79.2	62.9	70.9	Greece		75.0	48.7	61.9
Germany	75.9	65.4	70.7	Poland		66.3	52.4	59.2
Estonia	73.6	66.3	69.8	Romania		65.7	52.5	59.0
Slovenia	72.7	64.2	68.6	Italy		70.3	47.2	58.7
Latvia	72.1	65.4	68.6	Hungary		63.0	50.6	56.7
Portugal	74.0	62.5	68.2	Malta		72.5	37.4	55.2
Ireland	74.9	60.2	67.6					
Czech Republic	75.4	57.6	66.6	EU-27 average		72.8	59.1	65.9
France	69.8	60.7	65.2					

Source: Eurostat, *Labour Force Survey*, © European Union, 2008.

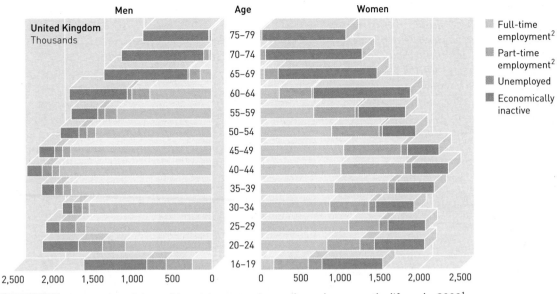

| Men | Age | Women |

United Kingdom
Thousands

2,500   2,000   1,500   1,000   500   0   0   500   1,000   1,500   2,000   2,500

Legend:
- Full-time employment[2]
- Part-time employment[2]
- Unemployed
- Economically inactive

Figure 15.2   Economic activity and inactivity status: by gender and age over the life cycle, 2009[1]

[1] Data are at Q2 and are not seasonally adjusted.
[2] The *Labour Force Survey* asks people to classify themselves as full or part time, based on their own perceptions.
Source: *Labour Force Survey*, Office for National Statistics in *Social Trends*, 40 (2010), Fig. 4.2, p. 45.

SPEAKING LIVES

The story of an eight-year-old agricultural worker in Guatemala

The story of Rigoberta Menchú has become a famous life story in social science. She tells the story of her life in her book *I, Rigoberta Menchú* – the life of a Guatemalan peasant who experiences revolutionary change. After the success of her book, she went on to become a leading political figure. In the extract below, she talks of her early work experiences in the family and on the fields.

I worked from when I was very small, but I didn't earn anything. I was really helping my mother because she always had to carry a baby, my little brother on her back as she picked coffee. It made me very sad to see my mother's face covered in sweat as she tried to finish her load, and I wanted to help her. But my work wasn't paid, it just contributed to my mother's work. I either picked coffee with her or looked after my little brother, so that she could work faster. My brother was two at the time . . . I remember that, at the time, my mother's work was making food for forty workers. She ground maize, made tortillas, and put the nixtamal on the fire and cooked beans for the workers' food. That's a difficult job . . . All the dough made in the morning has to be finished the same morning because it goes bad. My mother had to make the number of tortillas the workers would eat. She was very appreciated by the workers because the food she gave them was fresh.

I was five when she was doing this work and I looked after my little brother. I wasn't earning yet. I used to watch my mother, who often had the food ready at three o'clock in the morning for the workers who started work early, and at eleven she had the food for the midday meal ready. At seven in the evening she had to run around again making food for her group. In between times, she worked picking coffee to supplement what she earned. Watching her made me feel useless and weak because I couldn't do anything to help her except look after my brother. That's when my consciousness was born. It's true. My mother didn't like the idea of me working, of

earning my own money, but I did. I wanted to work, more than anything to help her, both economically and physically. The thing was that my mother was very brave and stood up to everything well, but there were times when one of my brothers or sisters was ill – if it wasn't one of them it was another – and everything she earned went on medicine for them. This made me very sad as well . . .

When I turned eight, I started to earn money on the finca. I set myself the task of picking 35 pounds of coffee a day . . . my brothers and sisters finished work at about seven or eight in the evening and sometimes offered to help me, but I said: 'No, I have to learn because if I don't learn myself, who's going to teach me?' I had to finish my

Rigoberta Menchú

Source: I, Rigoberta Menchú: An Indian Woman in Guatemala, Verso, New Left Books, designed, illustrated and reprinted by permission of Sophie Herxheimer.

workload myself. Sometimes I picked barely 28 pounds because I got tired, especially when it was very hot. It gave me a headache. I'd fall asleep

under a coffee bush, when suddenly I'd hear my brothers and sisters coming to look for me.

In the mornings we'd take turns to go off into the scrub to do our business. There are no toilets in the finca. There was only this place up in the hills where everyone went. There were about 400 of us living there and everyone went to this same place. It was the toilet for all those people. We had to take it in turns. When one lot of people came back, another lot would go. There were a lot of flies on all that filth up there and everyone went to this same place. There was only one tap in the shed where we lived, not even enough for us to wash our hands.

Source: Menchú (1984); see also Menchú (1998).

The decline of agricultural work

When the twentieth century began, about 40 per cent of the industrial world's labour force were engaged in farming. By its end, the figure was nearer 2 per cent, and many agricultural workers worked part time. Even though today's agriculture involves fewer people, it is often more productive. A century ago, a typical farmer grew food for five people; today, one farmer feeds 75. This dramatic rise in productivity also reflects new types of crop, pesticides that increase yields, more efficient machinery and other advances in farming technology. While in southern Europe holdings remain small (4 to 7 hectares in Greece, Portugal and Italy), in the north the holdings are much larger (in the UK, the average is 68 hectares).

This process signals the eclipse of 'family farms', which are declining in number and produce only a small part of our agricultural yield, in favour of large *corporate agribusinesses*. But, more productive or not, this transformation has wrought painful adjustments for farming communities across the country, as a way of life is lost.

From factory work to service work

Industrialisation swelled the ranks of factory workers during the nineteenth century, but by 1911 more than 45 per cent of the United Kingdom workforce had service jobs (with 40 per cent in industry and some 15 per cent in agriculture) (Coleman and Salt, 1992: 375). Jobs in the service industries have continued to increase: between 1978 and 2000 by 36 per cent, from 15.6 million in 1978 to 21.2 million (and those in manufacturing industry fell by 39 per cent from 7.0 million to 4.2 million). Overwhelmingly, then, jobs in the industrialised world have moved to the service sector.

'Teleworking' has become well established as a form of work. Between 1997 and 2002, the number of such workers grew by 70 per cent and in spring 2001 there were 2.2 million teleworkers (equivalent to 7.4 per cent of the total UK workforce). Some of these work mainly in their own home or in various locations using home as a base, but others work at 'call centres'. In the second quarter of 2009, 84,000 people worked as call centre agents and operators in the UK, and 52,000 worked as telephone salespersons.

Not surprisingly, workers are often young and female, and the conditions in such call centres can be the modern equivalent of the old steel mills, with 'customer service representatives' (CSRs) being expected to take as many as 20 calls an hour, or even two calls a minute. It is a new service industry that is relentless. And as with so much work in high-income countries, much of this work is farmed out to low-income countries such as India.

In addition, note the growth of the new information technology (IT) sector. The trend towards a 'knowledge society' signposts a real shift in patterns of work. By mid-2009, the IT sector was prevalent and pervaded all forms of work: 189,000 persons worked as IT technicians in the UK, and 141,000 were employed as IT strategy and planning professionals. An additional 297,000 were working as managers in fields related to information and communications technology.

The growth of service occupations is one reason for the widespread description of Europe as a middle-class society. Nevertheless, as explained in Chapter 10, much service work – including sales positions, secretarial work and jobs in fast-food restaurants – yields little of the income and prestige of professional white-collar occupations, and often provides fewer rewards than factory work. In short, more and more jobs in this post-industrial era provide only a modest standard of living. This is illustrated in Table 15.5.

The dual labour market

The change from factory work to service jobs represents a shifting balance between two categories of work. The **primary labour market** includes *occupations that provide extensive benefits to workers*. This favoured segment of the labour market contains the traditional white-collar professions and high management positions. These are jobs that people think of as *careers*. Work in the primary labour market provides high income and job security and is also personally challenging and intrinsically satisfying. Such occupations require a broad education rather than specialised training, and offer solid opportunity for advancement.

But few of these advantages apply to work in the **secondary labour market**, *jobs providing minimal benefits to workers*. This segment of the labour force is employed in the low-skilled, blue-collar type of work found in routine assembly-line operations, and in low-level service-sector jobs, including clerical positions. The secondary labour market offers workers much lower income, demands a longer working week and affords less job security and opportunity to advance. Not surprisingly, then, workers in the secondary labour market are most likely to experience alienation and dissatisfaction with their jobs. These problems most commonly beset women and other minorities, who are over-represented in this segment of the labour force. In spring 1996, only 8 per cent of male employees worked part time, while some 45 per cent of women did (*Social Trends*, 1997: 71).

Most new jobs in our post-industrial economy fall within the secondary labour market, and they involve the same kind of unchallenging tasks, low wages and poor working conditions characteristic of jobs in factories a century ago. Moreover, job insecurity is on the rise as the economy shuttles an unprecedented share of workers from one temporary position to another.

Gender, women and work

One of the most striking features of the modern world is that more and more women are working across the world, accounting for around 36–40 per cent of the world's labour force. Men, by contrast, become increasingly unemployed, both when young and as they get older.

In the UK, for example, working men and women have different patterns of work at most ages. Young men (16–19) are least likely to be in work; men in their thirties and forties are most likely to work, with around 82 per cent employed full time in 2009; and at later ages, men's work activity sharply declines. For women, full-time employment was at its highest for women aged 25 to 29, with 53 per cent in full-time employment in 2009, and fell to 42 per cent for women aged 35 to 39. Part-time employment then becomes more common. There has been a steady growth of women in the labour market, from roughly 30 per cent in 1945 to 45 per cent by the end of the twentieth century. Over the last 40 years the numbers have grown from 10 million (in 1971) to 13 million in 1999. By 2009 employment rates for men and women had significantly converged, but they had not equalised (*Social Trends*, 2009). Part-time employment continues to be more common among women than among men, particularly in younger age groups. Indeed, the characteristics of women's work are often very different from those of men:

Table 15.5   Highest- and lowest-paid occupations, and average hourly pay (£), excluding overtime, for employee jobs, United Kingdom, 2009

Lowest paid	£
1 Sales occupations	7.46
2 Elementary administration and service occupations	7.55
3 Elementary trades, plant and storage-related occupations	8.39
4 Caring personal service occupations	8.72
5 Textiles, printing and other skilled trades	8.86
6 Customer service occupations	8.95
7 Skilled agricultural trades	8.98
8 Transport and mobile machine drivers and operatives	9.58
9 Leisure and other personal service occupations	9.62
10 Process, plant and machine operatives	10.30

Highest paid	£
1 Health professionals	31.89
2 Corporate managers	23.19
3 Teaching and research professionals	21.27
4 Business and public service professionals	21.12
5 Science and technology professionals	19.66
6 Culture, media and sports occupations	16.45
7 Business and public service associate professionals	16.38
8 Protective service occupations	16.05
9 Managers and proprietors in agriculture and services	15.67
10 Health and social welfare associate professionals	14.97

Source: Adapted from Annual Survey of Hours and Earnings 2009, Table 2.6a; www.statistics.gov.uk/downloads/theme_labour/ASHE-2009/tab2_6a.xls, access date 4 September 2010.

- They work more often for wages (as opposed to salaries).
- They are usually paid less than men.
- Often their work has less status.
- Job insecurity is greater.
- They are more likely to become unemployed in many countries.
- Advances into administrative and managerial positions are often blocked by what has been called 'the glass ceiling'.

Further, a process of **occupational gender segregation** *works to concentrate men and women in different types*

of job. According to *Social Trends*, men in 2009 were most likely to be employed as managers or senior officials, while women were most likely to be employed in administrative and secretarial work; 16 per cent of women worked in personal service occupations, such as hairdressing and childcare, and 11 per cent worked in customer service occupations. These occupations were much less likely to be found among men (3 and 5 per cent, respectively). Women's work is also often characterised by what Arlie Hochschild has called a 'second shift' (maybe even more precisely, a triple shift). After a day's work in the factory or the office, the woman usually returns home to do the domestic work, raise the children and cook the meals (we consider this in Chapters 12 and 17). All this is unpaid work.

'Doing the dirty work'

This unpaid and often hidden work – domestic labour – has another aspect. There is also a significant amount which is paid and visible: largely that which is performed by women employed by middle-class men and women. Such work is often disproportionately performed by racialised groups and migrant workers.

Bridget Anderson (2000), in her study of migrant domestic workers in five European cities (Athens, Barcelona, Bologna, Berlin and Paris) in the mid-1990s, found that such work not only brought low pay and long hours, it could amount to a kind of 'slavery'. Women from poor countries would be asked to do impossible lists of work tasks; to care for children and families; to have very little time away from the home where they worked; and to be treated in subservient ways. Often they found it difficult to break away from the middle-class family that 'bought' them.

The sweatshops of the world

This global labour goes further. In lower-income countries, women are often compelled to work in the 'sweatshops of the world'. The term 'sweatshop' was introduced around the 1880s during the Industrial Revolution to describe the subcontracting system of labour. Miriam Ching Yoon Louie comments:

> Sweatshop workers toil at the bottom of a pyramid of labour exploitation and profit generation. Workers' immediate bosses are subcontractors, often men of their own ethnicity. Manufacturers and retailers sit at the top of the pyramid over the contractors who act as buffers, shock absorbers and shields . . . Like the nineteenth-century sweatshop middle-men, many of today's subcontractors survive the competition by 'sweating' their workers out of wages, hours, benefits and safety rights.

(Louie, 2001: 4)

In the poorer countries all over the world, workers are exploited to produce goods for the richer nations, as in this Korean enterprise where many Burmese work on textile production

Source: Richard Vogel/AP/PA Photos.

Such sweatshops are especially common in the garment industry. With exceptionally low incomes (much less than a pound a day), work conditions are subject to little or no regulation, are casual and temporary, and are often hazardous. Much of women's work here is uncounted, so official figures can mean very little. These women are also 'on the move', migrating to where the work is. For example, each year about 100,000 women leave Asia's developing countries to work in newly industrialising economies. Although the world's agricultural force is shrinking rapidly, it is also becoming feminised – some 40 per cent of agricultural workers worldwide are women. For many women around the world, globalisation is a concrete process of exploitation. As Christa Wichterich writes in *The Globalized Woman*:

> **Female textile-workers from Upper Lusatia in Eastern Germany are losing their jobs to women in Bangladesh; Filipinas clean vegetables and kitchens in Kuwait; Brazilian prostitutes offer their services around Frankfurt's main railway station; and Polish women look after old people at rock-bottom prices in various parts of Germany. Women in the Caribbean key in commercial entries for North American banks. In the Philippines, families who make a living by sorting through refuse cannot sell their plastic wares whenever a shipment of unbeatably cheap waste, collected by Germany's recycling scheme, arrives. And what is for the next meal is decided not by local women, but by multinationals specialising in novelty food and genetically modified crops.**

(Wichterich, 2000: viii)

Business process outsourcing

A rapidly growing sector of work has been the spreading of industries from high-income societies to lower-income societies: we have already seen this in the manufacturing of many commodities above, but we also find it now in the re-routing of telephone calls to call centres set up in poorer parts of the world where educated workers can be paid much less. In India, business process outsourcing (BPO) has grown by 60 per cent a year since 2000 and employs over a million people. It employs graduates for long hours, having trained them in English to answer calls. Workers make about £140 in a month, way below the UK or US salaries for equivalent work, but more than a farm worker in India would make in six months.

Female telephone operator working in a call centre, giving advice over the phone.
Source: Pearson Education Ltd/Eyewire.

The spread of part-time and flexible work

Over the past decade, part-time work has become more common – especially for women. In the UK in 2009, there were some 7.5 million part-time jobs, of which 5.6 million were done by women. One consequence of this can be the undermining of job security. Several decades ago, workers could confidently assume that hard work and playing by the rules all but guaranteed that their jobs would be there until they were ready to retire. This is no longer the case.

In the short run, at least, the dislocation for workers is tremendous. Companies scrambling to 'remain competitive' in the global economy are 'downsizing' and decentralising to gain 'flexibility'. These trends mean not only cutting the number of people on the payroll – managers as well as secretaries – but also replacing long-term employees with temporary workers. By hiring 'temps', companies no longer have to worry about providing insurance, paid vacations or pensions. And, if next month workers are no longer needed, they can be released without further cost.

Self-employment

Self-employment – *earning a living without working for a large organisation* – was once commonplace in Europe. Families owned and operated farms, and self-employed urban workers owned shops and other small businesses or sold their skills on the open market. With the onset of the Industrial Revolution, however, the economy became more centralised so that self-employment diminished. But more recently this has been changing. The number of self-employed people in the UK increased throughout the 1980s to peak at 3.6 million in 1990. In spring 1996 there were 3.3 million, three-quarters of whom were men. By 2009, the rate of self-employment was 13.7 per cent. In the European Union as a whole, 18.8 per cent of all employment was self-employment. Particularly high rates of self-employment were found in Greece and Romania, at more than 30 per cent. In contrast, in Sweden, Estonia, Luxembourg and Denmark, rates of self-employment lay below 10 per cent.

Most self-employed workers work in agriculture, fishing and construction, and are more likely to perform blue-collar than white-collar work. Society has always painted an appealing picture of working independently: no time clocks to punch, no one looking over your shoulder. For minorities who have long been excluded from particular kinds of work, self-employment has been an effective strategy for broadening economic opportunity. Further, self-employment holds the potential – though it is rarely realised – of earning a great deal of money. But for all its advantages, self-employment is vulnerable to fluctuations in the economy, which is one reason that only one-fifth of small businesses survive for more than ten years. Another common problem is that the self-employed generally lack pension and healthcare benefits provided for employees by large organisations.

The underground economy

Running parallel with the economic activity monitored and regulated by governments is the **underground economy**, *economic activity generating income that is unreported to the government as required by law*. On a small scale, most people participate in the underground economy on a regular basis. One family makes extra money from a car boot sale; another allows its teenage children to baby-sit for the neighbours without reporting the income received. Taken in total, such activities amount to millions of pounds in lost taxes annually. But much of the underground economy (or 'black economy') is attributable to criminal activity, which can run into billions of pounds. We opened with the story of 'people trafficking', which may well be a hidden economy of many billions of pounds, but to this we can add the sale of illegal drugs and weapons, trafficking of stolen goods, bribery, extortion, illegal gambling and money laundering. Some countries, including parts of the Russian Federation and parts of Latin America, face larger problems with illicit activity than others. But the dimensions of this form of work are also clearly global: there is a globalised underground economy.

Non-work

In 2009, 72.7 per cent of the working-age population were employed. This means that nearly 1 in 5 of those of working age were unemployed. Some 37 per cent of working-age individuals in the UK (18 million people) were economically inactive: that is, not working because of being a student, having a disability, retirement, or having duties of care towards family members. The main reasons for economic inactivity were being a student and long-term sickness or disability. Together, these reasons covered nearly two in three of the economically inactive population.

In 2009, 16.9 per cent of UK households (3.3 million) were workless. According to the Office for National Statistics, this is the highest rate measured since 1999. About 4.8 million people lived in these households, among them 1.9 million children. Some sociologists have started to suggest that a future trend may well be the rise of the workless society, but others suggest that a main trend is rather towards increasingly fragmented and casual work patterns.

Recent trends are undoing workplace bonds with remarkable speed and at all levels of the labour force. Like workers at the dawn of the industrial era centuries ago, many of today's secretaries, engineers, bank staff and even corporate executives are finding their job security vanishing before their eyes. For the foreseeable future, there is probably no going back to the traditional notion of lifetime employment with one company.

Changes in trade unions

The changing economy has been accompanied by a declining role for **trade unions**, *organisations of workers collectively seeking to improve wages and working conditions through various strategies, including negotiations and strikes.* Membership in trade unions increased rapidly in Europe through the earlier part of the twentieth century, peaking at 13 million people in the UK in 1979 (around 55 per cent). But by the mid-1990s it had dropped to 9 million (around 35 per cent); by 2000 it had fallen to 29 per cent. In 2009, there were 7.1 million trade union members in the UK (*Social Trends*, 2010). Figure 15.3 maps the rise and fall of the unions in the UK – a pattern repeated in many countries of the world.

During the 1980s, the British government under Margaret Thatcher was firmly committed to weakening the power of trade unions. Blaming unions for strikes and industrial unrest, the Thatcher government introduced much legislation (like the 1980 Employment Act and the 1984 Trade Union Act) which made secret ballots on industrial action compulsory, prohibited 'secondary picketing' by restricting union members to picket only at their own place of work, and made industrial action in support of workers employed elsewhere illegal. The Thatcher government also reduced consultation with union officials. Symbolically, too, this was the time of the 1985 miners' strike, in

which pit closures became a key issue and which was used by Thatcher as a key defining moment to bring the unions down. Add to this the increases in unemployment during this period and it is clear that the unions' strength was considerably undermined. Hyman sees all this as a process of 'coercive pacification' in which employers and government suppress and weaken union activities (Hyman, 1989).

But the decline of unions is not an isolated British phenomenon. In the United States, in absolute numbers, union membership peaked during the 1970s at almost 25 million people. Since then, it has declined steadily. In 2009, 12.3 per cent of all wage and salary workers in the USA were union members.

While a similar trend has emerged throughout Europe, in a few countries, particularly Denmark, trade union membership has actually increased. Roughly 80 per cent of workers in the Scandinavian countries belong to unions, and employer–union cooperation is high. In Europe as a whole about 40 per cent belong to unions, while in Canada and Japan the proportion is about one-third (Western, 1993, 1995).

The relative decline of unions stems from a number of trends already noted. First, industrial countries have lost tens of thousands of jobs in the highly unionised factories as industrial jobs have been 'exported' overseas. Many plant managers have succeeded in forcing concessions from workers, including, in some

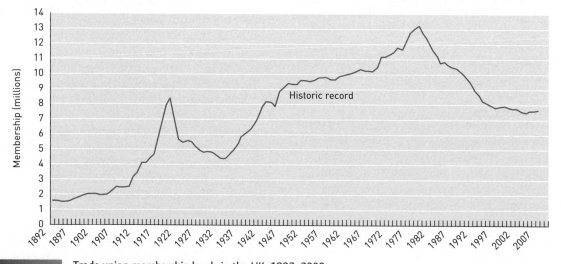

| Figure 15.3 | Trade union membership levels in the UK, 1892–2009 |

Source: Labour Force Survey, Office for National Statistics; Department for Employment (1892–1974); Certification Office (1974–2007/8) in Archur, J. (2010) *Trade Union Membership 2009*, Dept for Business, Innovation and Skills, Chart 1.1, p. 3.

cases, the dissolution of trade unions. Moreover, most of the new service-sector jobs being created today are not unionised, and hardly any temporary workers belong to a trade union. Young people are much less likely to be unionised than older workers.

Falling job security may well make union membership a higher priority for workers in the years to come. But to expand their membership, unions will also have to adapt to the new global economy. Instead of seeing foreign workers as a threat to their interests, in short, union leadership will have to forge new international alliances.

The quality and experience of work: from dehumanisation to 'decent work'

To conclude this section, it may be helpful for you to consider the nature of employment relations in the modern workplace, and to ponder the kind of work that you would like and the situation more generally of most people in the world. Among the issues to consider are:

- *Autonomy*: does the worker have some autonomy, or does management strictly control and regulate?

- *Training*: does the worker get training for specific skills, or is there no training and a presumption of no skill?

- *Wages*: does the worker get a reasonable wage? A good wage? A fair wage? An exploitative wage? A low wage?

- *Hours*: does the worker have fixed and limited hours, or are they long and variable?

- *Promotion*: good opportunities or no prospects?

- *Security*: permanence, fixed contracts, temporary or job insecurity?

- *Status*: full time or temporary?

- *Non-wage perks*: does the worker have access to a company pension (or a company car), or are there no non-wage perks?

- *Facilities*: just what is the work environment like – does it have good facilities, or are they poor?

- *Health support*: does the work environment provide 'health and safety' or not?

- *Worker representation*: does the worker have some kind of voice, a union, in which they can debate problems and grievances, or not?

Putting the questions as bluntly as this, we can see that the world is, and always has been, very divided. There are those for whom the experience of work is positive: they have autonomy, feel their work is valued, and work the hours they need. But for others (and this is probably most of the world's population), work overwhelmingly brings low skills, low wages, long hours, no autonomy and insecurity; it is short lived and has no supports or prospects. This work is often described as degraded and dehumanised – people become objects of work and lose their human dignity. It was a major theme of Marx's theory that under capitalism the condition of labourers and their work would become increasingly unbearable. Looking around the world today, there is plenty of evidence that much work is indeed dehumanised and degraded.

At the simplest level, consider yet more statistics. There are about 200 million children (below 15) who work. Some 12.3 million people endure 'forced labour'. Only 20 per cent of the world's population get any kind of social security. About 86 million people have to leave their home countries for work. And for around one in five of the world, the hours worked in a week are over 48, and many work a seven-day week.

In the light of all this, the idea of 'decent work' as a worldwide goal for labour systems has been introduced. The International Labour Organization (originally founded in 1919 and now a branch of the United Nations) comments:

> **Decent work sums up the aspirations of people in their working lives. It involves opportunities for work that is productive and delivers a fair income, security in the workplace and social protection for families, better prospects for personal development and social integration, freedom for people to express their concerns, organize and participate in the decisions that affect their lives, and equality of opportunity and treatment for all women and men'.**

(www.ilo.org/global/Themes/Decentwork)

THINKERS & THEORY

Ulrich Beck: a brave new world of work in a globalised risk society

German sociologist Ulrich Beck (1944–) is a Professor of Sociology at Munich University and the London School of Economics. Since 1986, when he published his key first book *The Risk Society* in German, he has produced a large volume of influential work around the new world order.

For Beck, old work society is going. The old order – first modernity – was characterised by 'collective lifestyles, full employment, the national state and the welfare state, and an attitude of heedless exploitation of nature' (Beck, 2000a: 18). The new world order sees the decline of paid employment, globalisation, and new crises around the environment, gender and technologies.

He characterises this newly emerging society variously as:

(a) A 'second modernity' which is replacing the age of simple modernity linked to capitalist industrialisation.

(b) A 'global risk society' which brings growing uncertainty. Risk now derives less from the natural dangers of the past (like earthquakes or floods) and more from the new technologies that we have created (from computer dependency to new genetic modification) (see Chapter 19). Life becomes insecure, uncertain and risky.

(c) A 'reflexive modernity', in which people become more and more aware of the

problems inherent in the first modernity. Life becomes more aware of the problems of living. The idea of 'sustainability', discussed in Chapter 24, is an example.

(d) An 'individualised society'. Whereas the safe structures of modernity had involved stable families, protected and stable jobs, strong local communities and class loyalty, now the world becomes much less stable and thoroughly individualised. The world becomes more individualised rather than collective, life now becomes a 'do-it-yourself' biography, work becomes more 'chopped up' and consumption becomes pervasive.

(e) A 'cosmopolitan society' is one which looks beyond the borders and boundaries of nation-states and fixed identities. Beck looks towards a future where 'in a radically insecure world, all are equal and everyone is different'.

He has books on each of these themes.

Much of Beck's writing anticipates the way experiences of work will change in this new society. Life in the 'second modernity' can be characterised by an increase of global capitalism, a decline of unions and a major shift in the flexibility of the labour process. In one book, *The Brave New World of Work* (2000a), he discusses eleven different scenarios of work, all of which flag the end of full employment as we have thought about it in the first modernity (see Beck, 2000: Chapter 4). This is a world where standard work is increasingly being replaced by non-standard forms of work. He suggests that the situation of work in Brazil anticipates much of what the

Ulrich Beck (1944–)
Source: Permission from Ulrich Beck.

rest of the Western world may soon come to experience. He sees such a society as having four main groups: the super-rich, the overworked middle class, the working poor and those with no work at all, who live in local poverty. This is the blueprint for relations in the future. A significant group will be the 'super-rich'. But a huge group will have little work: they will have time in abundance – but no resources. Work is not available to them. They live in localised poverty. Many may well live in prisons. So Beck asks: *What happens when the work society runs out of work?* (2000: 62).

He suggests that with the decline of unionism, we can now look to the start of a new politics to emerge outside the formal realm of politics. Women's perspectives will become increasingly important (as their experience of work is very different); and we could expect a move from paid work to what he calls 'civil labour' – forms of work that are self-organised and which develop art, culture and politics.

As he concludes: 'Cosmopolitans of the World Unite!' (2000: 176).

Unemployment

Every industrial society has some unemployment. Much of it is temporary. Few young people entering the labour force find a job right away; some workers temporarily leave the labour force while seeking a new job, to have children or because of a strike; others suffer from long-term illnesses; still others may lack skills to work.

But the economy itself also generates unemployment, often called structural unemployment. Jobs disappear as occupations become obsolete, as businesses close in the face of foreign competition and as recessions force layoffs and bankruptcies. Since 1980, for example, the 'downsizing' of US businesses has eliminated some 5 million jobs – a quarter of the total – in that country's 500 largest corporations.

Unemployment rates vary over time, as they do from country to country. The number of unemployed people worldwide reached 212 million in 2009, up 34 million or an unprecedented 19 per cent since 2007. The unemployment rate in the 27 countries of the European Union was 8.9 per cent, US unemployment stood at around 9.3 per cent and in Japan it was 5.1 per cent.

Unemployment in Europe

Unemployment rates and experiences both differ and fluctuate greatly across Europe, as Table 15.6 shows.

Overall, in 2009, the EU-27 had an average unemployment rate of 8.9 per cent, high in Slovakia, Estonia, Lithuania, Spain and Ireland, much lower in Denmark, Cyprus, Luxembourg, the Netherlands, Austria and Slovenia. The long-term unemployed are much more prominent in the eastern European countries. In absolute terms, Russia had a large rate of unemployment, at between 8 and 9 per cent in early 2010, while Norway has a much more modest 3.3 per cent. Figure 15.4 also shows the greater likelihood of women to be unemployed.

Unemployment in the UK

From the late 1940s to the 1970s in the UK, it was generally assumed that unemployment should never rise above 1 million. But since that time there have been quite dramatic swings: 3 million by 1985, down again to 1.5 million by the early 1990s, up again to 2.5 million people (8.5 per cent of the workforce) in 1994, and in 2001 the Blair government formally announced that it had fallen below the symbolic figure of 1 million. This figure crept up again so that in spring 2003 there were 1.48 million unemployed. Of course, this unemployment rate reflected large regional differences, with the lowest rate in the southeast and southwest (around 3.8 per cent) and the highest in the north of England (around 6.5 per cent) and Greater London (7 per cent) (*Social Trends*, 2003: 63). In 2009 and early 2010, the number of unemployed individuals in the UK continuously surpassed 2.3 million (at 7.6 per cent).

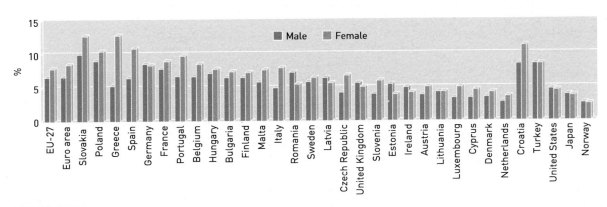

Figure 15.4   Unemployment rates, 2007
Note: The figure is ranked on the average of male and female.
Source: Eurostat *Europe in Figures: Eurostat Yearbook 2009*, © European Union, 2009.

Table 15.6	Unemployment rates in Europe, 1999–2009										
	1999	2000	2001	2002	2003	2004	2005	2006	2007	2008	2009
EU-27	:	8.7	8.5	8.9	9.0	9.1	8.9	8.2	7.1	7.0	8.9
Euro area	9.3	8.4	8.0	8.4	8.8	9.0	9.0	8.3	7.5	7.5	9.4
Belgium	8.5	6.9	6.6	7.5	8.2	8.4	8.5	8.3	7.5	7.0	7.9
Bulgaria	:	16.4	19.5	18.2	13.7	12.1	10.1	9.0	6.9	5.6	6.8
Czech Republic	8.6	8.7	8.0	7.3	7.8	8.3	7.9	7.2	5.3	4.4	6.7
Denmark	5.2	4.3	4.5	4.6	5.4	5.5	4.8	3.9	3.8	3.3	6.0
Germany	8.2	7.5	7.6	8.4	9.3	9.8	10.7	9.8	8.4	7.3	7.5
Estonia	:	13.6	12.6	10.3	10.0	9.7	7.9	5.9	4.7	5.5	13.8
Ireland	5.6	4.2	3.9	4.5	4.6	4.5	4.4	4.5	4.6	6.3	11.9
Greece	12.0	11.2	10.7	10.3	9.7	10.5	9.9	8.9	8.3	7.7	9.5
Spain	12.5	11.1	10.3	11.1	11.1	10.6	9.2	8.5	8.3	11.3	18.0
France	10.4	9.0	8.3	8.6	9.0	9.3	9.3	9.2	8.4	7.8	9.5
Italy	10.9	10.1	9.1	8.6	8.4	8.0	7.7	6.8	6.1	6.7	7.8
Cyprus	:	4.9	3.8	3.6	4.1	4.7	5.3	4.6	4.0	3.6	5.3
Latvia	14.0	13.7	12.9	12.2	10.5	10.4	8.9	6.8	6.0	7.5	17.1
Lithuania	13.7	16.4	16.5	13.5	12.5	11.4	8.3	5.6	4.3	5.8	13.7
Luxembourg	2.4	2.2	1.9	2.6	3.8	5.0	4.6	4.6	4.2	4.9	5.2
Hungary	6.9	6.4	5.7	5.8	5.9	6.1	7.2	7.5	7.4	7.8	10.0
Malta	:	6.7	7.6	7.5	7.6	7.4	7.2	7.1	6.4	5.9	7.0
Netherlands	3.2	2.8	2.2	2.8	3.7	4.6	4.7	3.9	3.2	2.8	3.4
Austria	3.9	3.6	3.6	4.2	4.3	4.9	5.2	4.8	4.4	3.8	4.8
Poland	13.4	16.1	18.3	20.0	19.7	19.0	17.8	13.9	9.6	7.1	8.2
Portugal	4.5	4.0	4.1	5.1	6.4	6.7	7.7	7.8	8.1	7.7	9.6
Romania	7.1	7.3	6.8	8.6	7.0	8.1	7.2	7.3	6.4	5.8	6.9
Slovenia	7.3	6.7	6.2	6.3	6.7	6.3	6.5	6.0	4.9	4.4	5.9
Slovakia	16.4	18.8	19.3	18.7	17.6	18.2	16.3	13.4	11.1	9.5	12.0
Finland	10.2	9.8	9.1	9.1	9.0	8.8	8.4	7.7	6.9	6.4	8.2
Sweden[1]	6.7	5.6	5.8	6.0	6.6	7.4	7.6	7.0	6.1	6.2	8.3
United Kingdom	5.9	5.4	5.0	5.1	5.0	4.7	4.8	5.4	5.3	5.6	7.6
Croatia	:	:	:	14.8	14.2	13.7	12.7	11.2	9.6	8.4	9.1
Turkey	:	:	:	:	:	:	9.2	8.7	8.8	9.7	12.5
Norway	3.0	3.2	3.4	3.7	4.2	4.3	4.5	3.4	2.5	2.5	3.1
Japan	4.7	4.7	5.0	5.4	5.3	4.7	4.4	4.1	3.9	4.0	5.1
United States	4.2	4.0	4.8	5.8	6.0	5.5	5.1	4.6	4.6	5.8	9.3

[1] Break in series, 2001.

Source: Eurostat, http://epp.eurostat.ec.europa.eu/statistics_explained/index_php/File:Table_unemployment_rates.PNG, © European Union, 2010.

Who are the unemployed?

Writing of the UK (but the data are probably generalisable across Europe), Adrian Sinfield (1981) suggests that five major groups are more likely to become or remain unemployed:

- those who experience redundancies due to economic change
- unskilled youth trying to make the transition from school to work
- older workers who face enforced retirement
- unemployed women
- the long-term unemployed.

Experiencing unemployment

Unemployment can wreak havoc on lives and families. Many studies have suggested that there is an initial shock, followed for a short while by denial and optimism (in which there may be a sense of being on holiday for a little while), but this is soon followed by distress and anxiety. If the unemployment continues for a long time, it may lead to resignation and adjustment. It has also been linked to ill health, premature death, attempted and actual suicide, marriage breakdown, child battering, racial conflicts and football hooliganism. A subculture of despair can emerge, sometimes linked to the development of an underclass (see Chapter 10). For women who see work as an escape from the home, unemployment can be especially harsh (Jahoda et al., 1972; orig. 1933). Generally, unemployment affects those with least resources most.

Problems of measuring unemployment

Measuring unemployment is no easy task. Although there are official figures, they can conceal the difficulties in recording practices and the major differences within countries. In many countries, but especially lower-income ones, it can be almost impossible to count the numbers out of work.

Government unemployment statistics, based on monthly national surveys, generally understate unemployment for three reasons. First, to be counted among the unemployed, a person must be actively seeking work; 'discouraged workers', those who have given up looking for a job, are omitted from the statistics. Second, many people unable to find jobs for which they are qualified settle, at least for a while, for 'lesser' employment: a secretary works as a 'temp' several days a week, or a former university lecturer drives a taxi while seeking a new teaching position. Such people are counted among the employed, though they might better be described as *under*employed. Third, changes in policies towards the unemployed or in the procedures for measuring unemployment can conceal and distort the 'true picture'. In the UK, for instance, between 1982 and 1996 there were at least 14 changes that tended towards lowering the figures. For example, since 1982, only those eligible for benefits are included in the unemployment figures; and since 1988, most people in the UK under the age of 18 have been ineligible for benefits (income support), resulting in 90,000 being taken off the register. There are many tricks that can conceal unemployment – such as youth training schemes which conceal unemployment by taking young people out of the unemployment statistics. On the other hand, statistics also overlook the fact that many people officially out of work receive income 'under the table' from odd jobs or even from illegal activity. But, even considering off-the-books income, the actual level of unemployment is probably several percentage points above the official figure.

The world of corporations

At the core of today's capitalist economy lies the market, which is composed centrally of **corporations**, *organisations with a legal existence, including rights and liabilities, apart from those of their members.* By incorporation, an organisation becomes an entity unto itself, able to enter into contracts and own property. More and more these corporations transcend nation-states: as we have seen, they are transnational corporations (or TNCs) and they are the primary 'movers and shapers' of the world economy. A **transnational corporation** is *a firm which has the power to coordinate and control operations in more than one country, even if it does not own them* (Dicken, 2010).

The practice of legal incorporation accelerated with the rise of large businesses a century ago because it offered company owners two advantages. First, incorporation shields them from the legal liabilities of their businesses, protecting personal wealth from lawsuits arising from business debts or harm to consumers. Second, profits earned by corporations receive favourable treatment under the tax laws of Europe. The largest corporations are typically owned not by single families but by millions of stockholders, including other corporations. This dispersion of corporate ownership has spread wealth to some extent, making more people small-scale capitalists. Moreover, day-to-day operation of a corporation falls to white-collar executives, who may or may not be major stockholders themselves. Typically, however, a great deal of corporate stock is owned by a small number of the corporation's top executives and directors (Dicken, 1998).

Capitalist markets

Capitalist economies can vary greatly in their approach to the market. In the purest form, the market is simply a situation where there is private ownership of companies competing freely and equally with other companies. But as many commentators have noted, such a fully free system is rare. There are many reasons for this. Among these are the facts that governments often intervene in markets; some companies can become so large that they dominate certain markets; and companies can become heavily bureaucratic so that they are not open to quick adjustment to market situations.

Economic concentration

While many companies are small, with assets worth less than £750,000, the largest corporations dominate the global economy (see Table 15.7). In 2010 for example, Wal-Mart employed well over 2 million people across the world, while the largest world corporation was car maker General Motors (GM), with more than £413 billion in revenue (*Fortune*, 2010). This one company has higher revenue than many countries. It may also have more influence!

Spotlight
Global corporations

The world's dominant corporations are clustered in very few countries – the top 50, for example, originate from only 12 countries (China, USA, Spain, the UK, Netherlands, France, Russia, Brazil, Germany, Italy, Switzerland and Japan). There are two major lists of the world's biggest corporations. In the US, *Fortune* magazine ranks the top 500 by *revenue*. In the UK, the *Financial Times* ranks them on *shareholder value*. (You can also rank companies by country, work force, or industry.)

- *The World Top 10* in *Fortune* regularly highlights: Wal-Mart, Royal Dutch Shell, Exxon Mobil, BP, Toyota Motor, Japan Post Holdings, Sinopec, State Grid, AXA, China National Petroleum, Chevron, General Electric.

- *The World Top 10* in the *Financial Times* highlights: Petro China, Exxon Mobil, Apple Inc., Microsoft, Wal-Mart, BHP Billiton, General Electric, and the Industrial and Commercial Board of China.

- *The UK Top 10* in the *Financial Times* (with the London Stock Exchange) regularly feature: BHP Billiton, Royal Dutch Shell, HSBC, Vodafone, BP, Rio Tinto, GlaxoSmithKline, Unilever, British American Tobacco and BG Group.

- *Green Lists.* Note that there are also Green Lists – companies that have the best environmental credentials. This frequently includes for the UK: Kingfisher, the BT Group, Biffs, BP, Unilever, Severn Trent, BSkyB Group, BHP Billiton, M&S Group. Across the world, the highest ranked include: Vestas Wind Systems, Ericsson, MTR, and Svenska Cellulosa, Kingfisher, BT and Westpac Banking.

The latest details on all these companies can usually be found easily through a Google search. Company reports are usually quite obscure but can be found online too.

The capitalism of Wal-Mart

A number of mega-companies rival each other for top place in the world market. Wal-Mart is one of these. It is one of the largest companies in the USA, and is fast becoming one of the largest in the world (in the UK it trades as ASDA). It is seen by many as one 'template' for the modern capitalist organisation (Lichtenstein, 2006: 3).

Wal-Mart is today one of the largest profit-making enterprises in the world. It operates more than 5,000 stores worldwide, has sales of over $400 billion a year (with revenues larger than those of Switzerland), employs more than 2 million workers, has sales around $1 trillion a year, and its owners – the Walton family – own shares and assets of over $120 billion. It is to be found all over the US landscape, and it is now opening up stores everywhere around the world.

It can be found in Mexico City and Tokyo, China and Germany. Its biggest claim for success is that it provides low prices, cheap enough for poor families to survive on. But it also claims to serve its communities: revitalising the community, creating 'happy workers' and doing good philanthropic works. On the surface, it looks like a model of 'happy' capitalism – providing work and cheap goods for average and poor families.

But Wal-Mart is not without its critics. They ask: at what hidden costs do these 'cheap' prices come? The film *Wal-Mart: The High Cost of Low Price* (2005) (and the book that accompanies it by Gregg Spott (2006)) sets out to reveal the global problems of this mega transnational corporation. Indeed, it shows how Wal-Mart is at the centre of a number of court cases, legal conflicts and protest movements across the globe. If you look at the criteria for 'decent work' outlined in this chapter,

Wal-Mart itself would claim that it meets these. But critics suggest that very few are met. They suggest there is a 'high cost' to pay for the 'low prices'. The critics claim, among other things, that 'associates' (workers) earn low wages for long working hours. Across the world, conditions of work can be particularly bad by Western standards. In China, for example, workers often work seven days a week for long hours and pay of $3 a day. They also live in 'dorms'. Both gender and race discrimination takes place in the workplace. Little (or no) health insurance is provided. And often Wal-Mart is claimed to lead to the breakdown of small communities (local shops inevitably close), while also creating dangerous areas (the car parks of the malls are not adequately monitored and can become the scenes of crimes).

See: Nelson Lichtenstein (ed.), *Wal-Mart: The Face of 21st Century Capitalism* (2006).

Conglomerates and corporate linkages

Economic concentration has spawned **conglomerates**, *giant corporations composed of many smaller corporations*. Throughout much of the twentieth century, small companies were gobbled up by larger ones. Some industries, such as tobacco, came to be dominated by three or four major firms. Since the 1980s, however, there has been some shift in this process, as some companies have decided to downsize and shift some of their functions to other firms.

Conglomerates emerge as corporations, enter new markets, spin off new companies or carry out takeovers of existing companies. Forging a conglomerate is also a strategy to diversify a company, so that new products can provide a hedge against declining profits in the original market. Faced with declining sales of tobacco products, for example, R. J. Reynolds merged with

Nabisco foods, forming a conglomerate called RJR–Nabisco. Coca-Cola's soft drinks market is still growing, but this company now produces fruit drinks, coffee and bottled water, as well as movies and television programmes. Besides conglomerates, corporations are also linked through mutual ownership, since these giant organisations own each other's stock. In today's global economy, many companies have invested heavily in other corporations commonly regarded as their competitors. Chapter 22 looks a little more at how big media corporations such as Disney and TimeWarner link and diversify.

One more type of linkage among corporations is the *interlocking directorate*, a social network of people serving simultaneously on the boards of directors of many corporations. These connections give corporations access to valuable information about each other's products and marketing strategies. Laws forbid linkages of this kind among corporations that compete directly with one another. Yet beneficial linkages persist among non-competing corporations with common interests – for example, a corporation building tractors may share directors with one that manufactures tyres. Indirect linkages also occur when, for example, a member of General Motors' board of directors and a director of Ford both sit on the board of Exxon/Esso (Weidenbaum, 1995).

Corporate linkages do not necessarily run counter to the public interest, but they certainly concentrate power and they may encourage illegal activity. Price fixing, for example, is legal in much of the world (the Organisation of Petroleum Exporting Countries (OPEC) meets regularly to try to set oil prices), but not in Europe. By their nature, however, corporate linkages invite price fixing, especially when only a few corporations control an entire market.

Corporations and competition

The capitalist model assumes that businesses operate independently in a competitive market. But while smaller businesses and self-employed people may indicate a competitive sector, they are usually at considerable disadvantage since the corporate core is largely non-competitive. Large corporations are not truly competitive because, first, their extensive linkages mean that they do not operate independently and, second, a small number of corporations come to dominate many large markets.

With the exception of some public utility providers (in the UK this used to include water), no large company can establish an actual **monopoly**, *domination of a market by a single producer*. The law does permit lesser economic concentration called **oligopoly**, *domination of a market by a few producers*. Oligopoly results from the vast investment needed to enter a new market such as the car industry. Certainly, the successful entry of foreign-owned corporations into the European car markets shows that new companies can successfully challenge the biggest corporations. But all large businesses strive to limit competition simply because it places profits at risk.

Although capitalism favours minimal government intervention in the economy, corporate power is now so great – and competition among corporations sometimes so limited – that government regulation may be the only way to protect the public interest. Yet, governments are also the corporate world's single biggest customer, and national governments frequently intervene to bolster struggling corporations. In short, corporations and governments typically

work together to make the entire economy more stable and profitable.

Corporations and the global economy

Corporations have grown in size and power so fast that they are now responsible for most of the world's economic output. In the process, the largest corporations – centred in Europe, Japan and the United States – have spilled across national borders and now view the entire world as one vast marketplace. As noted in Chapter 9, multinationals are large corporations that produce and market products in many different nations.

Corporations become multinational in order to make more money, since most of the planet's resources and three-quarters of the world's people are found in less developed countries. Worldwide operations, then, offer access to plentiful materials and vast markets. In addition, labour costs are far lower in poor countries of the world. A manufacturing worker in Taiwan labours all week to earn what a German worker earns in a single day or less.

The impact of multinationals on poor societies is controversial, as Chapter 9 explained in detail. On one side of the argument, modernisation theorists argue that multinationals unleash the great productivity of the capitalist economic system, which will boost economic development (Rostow, 1978; Berger, 1986). Cadbury-Schweppes alone, for example, far out-produces any one of the least-productive nations in the world. Corporations offer poor societies tax revenues, capital investment, new jobs and advanced technology – taken together, what modernisation theorists call a certain recipe for economic growth.

On the other side of the argument, dependency theorists who favour a socialist economy claim that multinationals only intensify global inequality (Wallerstein, 1979). Multinational investment, as they see it, may create a few jobs in poor countries but it also stifles the development of local industries, which are a better source of employment. Further, critics charge, multinationals generally push developing countries to produce expensive consumer goods for export to rich nations rather than food and other necessities that would bolster the standard of living in local communities. From this standpoint, multinationals establish a system of neo-colonialism, making poor societies poorer and increasingly reliant on rich, capitalist societies.

While modernisation theory hails the virtues of an unregulated market as the key to a future of progress and affluence for all the world's people, advocates of dependency theory call for the replacement of market systems by government regulation of economic affairs.

Consumption in modern economies

Until very recently the dominant approach to the economy taken by sociologists has concerned the production of goods, with a focus on either businesses or workers and work. So far this has been the main focus of this chapter too. But sociologists have increasingly come to recognise the importance of not just what we produce, but what – and how – we consume. Indeed, as there has been a growing move in society *from production to consumption*, so there has been the growth of *a sociology of consumption*. Shopping and consuming has now become a major social practice of everyday life; and in some markets – such as the 'youth market' – it has become almost the number one social activity. 'Going shopping', 'Born to shop', 'Shop till you drop', 'I am what I consume' are common slogans.

Throughout most of history, the shop has been the 'open air market'. In Hong Kong or in Thailand's busy street markets today, there is a sense of historical continuity, of the bustle of the market. But with the arrival of the huge department store and the rise of advertising in the nineteenth century, new worlds of conspicuous consumption were slowly created. Goods moved from being merely functional commodities such as food to eat, and became instead major markers of lifestyles and identities. The question now posed concerns whether consumers are sovereigns or dupes – *are we driven to consume through our needs and choices, or are we perhaps driven to consume through the manipulation of our needs?*

The branding of commodities

The modern capitalist world is dominated by internationally known brand names such as Nike, Starbucks, Mitsubishi, Shell, Wal-Mart, Virgin, McDonald's, Calvin Klein, Sony, IBM, Coca-Cola and Toshiba. What we find here is that brands, not products, become more and more central. Thus people no longer ask for a soft drink, they want a Coke; they

do not want trainers but Nikes; they do not want underwear but Calvin Kleins. This branding depends on promotion and advertising: the growth in global advertising spending now outpaces the growth of the world economy by one-third (Klein, 2000: 9, 11). New markets are constantly being generated – Baby Gap for Kids, for example. Overall, however, many are strongly linked to the youth market, creating what has been called 'The Global Teen':

> **Despite different cultures, middle class youth all over the world seem to live their lives as if in a parallel universe. They get up in the morning, put on their Levis and Nikes, grab their caps, backpacks and Sony personal CD players, and head for school.**
>
> (Klein, 2000: 119)

The Branded World is organised through style, logos and image. Thus 'Tommy Hilfiger pioneered a clothing style that transforms its faithful adherents into walking, talking, lifesized Tommy dolls, mummified into fully branded Tommy worlds' (Klein, 2000: 28). Brands start to have their own superstores and sometimes even their own city space and 'branded villages' (e.g. Disney's Celebration Town in Florida). They sponsor sports, arts, music, education – each time getting their brand identified with culture. And 'stars' are paid large sums to lend their names to the goods: Tiger Woods (with a $90 million contract with Nike over five years), Michael Jordan, Puff Daddy, Martha Stewart, Austin Powers, Michael Jackson.

There are major downsides to all this. Commodities become very predictable – it is a world of 'theme park shopping', and a kind of self-censorship creeps in to stop diversity. Major companies are merged till they regulate the markets, and goods are produced largely in the sweatshops of low-income countries. Here the labour force has no unions and is utterly temporary: lines of young women hunch over their hard work for a dollar a day and with no job security. There is a floating workforce where 'temps' develop an odd kind of loyalty to their 'brand'.

Further, our identities – who we are – come to be shaped by everything we buy: designer clothes (or otherwise), the 'latest' film and music band (or 'golden oldies'), the 'coolest' (or plain) food, the holiday, the car and so on. We are what we buy. And this has fuelled the worlds of logos. For some people, logos matter more than the quality of the goods (see the discussion of 'Nike culture' in Goldman and Papson, 1998). Advertising, logos and consumption serve up images of the good life to which we start to aspire.

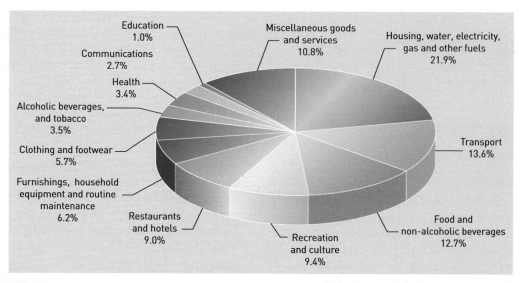

Figure 15.5   Consumption expenditure of households on goods and services, EU-27, 2006 (% of total household consumption expenditure)

Note: Figures do not sum to 100% due to rounding.

Source: Eurostat *Europe in Figures: Eurostat Yearbook 2009*, © European Union, 2009.

'Born to shop': the growth of consumer societies

Many suggest, then, that Western societies are cultivating 'consumer societies'. Indeed, shopping has become the second most popular leisure activity in Britain, after watching television (*Social Trends*, 2010). Think of your own life and how purchases – buying clothes, CDs, computers, tickets to sporting events and so forth – may play a part in it. Look at Figure 15.5. Consider the following:

- *The massive growth of shopping malls* with 'megastores' such as Virgin Records, hypermarkets like Tesco, chain stores such as Argos, retail parks and the endless proliferation of DIY stores across the country. Each Tesco store in Britain had a minimum area of 10,670 square metres in the 1990s (compared with 3,048 in the 1970s). In some parts of eastern Europe, such as Poland, there has been a massive expansion of 'hyper malls'.

- *The arrival of shopping not as a merely functional activity* (for example, to buy the necessary food for a meal) *but as a major leisure form in itself*. Malls and shopping centres are key public spaces to 'hang around' in, and shops are designed for us to wander in voyeuristically, looking and enjoying the sights. Many people often go just to look, not to purchase, and can spend hours and hours doing this.

- *The growth of more and newer forms of commodities*. We now 'need' commodities that we could not even imagine some 50 years ago: sports clothes geared to every sport; new bathroom commodities such as shower gels, foot creams and electric toothbrushes; new electronic gadgets ranging from computer toys and video games to mobile phones and multimedia computers; new forms of entertainment such as multiplex cinemas and leisure complexes; new modes of eating out, from fast-food to up-market dining; holidays that take us to theme parks, on world cruises and to 'resort hotels'; and cars owned individually.

- *The attachment of our identities to our shopping*. Especially in the major 'youth markets', our identities can be constructed around the kinds of shop we go to and the sorts of commodity we buy. Caught in early phrases such as 'conspicuous consumption' and in more recent phrases such as 'I shop, therefore I am', much consumption heralds the types of people we are.

- *The spread of credit cards*. In the UK, at least one-third of all consumption is based on credit; there were 25 million credit cards in the UK by 1998 and, in 2002, purchases of around £100 billion were made through credit cards. The figures are higher for many other countries, especially the United States (Ritzer, 1995).

Think and discuss

Debt and online shopping

We live with debt and credit cards

The volume of automated payments and debit card transactions in the UK in 2008 were both approximately nine times greater than they were in 1985. Debit card payments accounted for the largest volume of non-cash payments in 2008 with 5.3 billion transactions, followed by automated payments transactions (3.4 billion) and credit and charge card transactions (1.8 billion).

We are more and more shopping online

When interviewed in the UK between January and March 2009, 64 per cent of all recent internet users in the UK had purchased goods or services over the internet at least once. Of these, 83 per cent (26 million) had purchased items within the three months prior to interview. Men were more likely to have purchased goods and services over the internet in 2009 than women (69 per cent and 60 per cent respectively).

Source: Social Trends, 2010.

- *Teleshopping and netshopping.* Going online means that an array of armchair services become available – from shopping and banking to travel and public services. Hundreds of channels with interactive shopping services come on stream through the television and the internet, and all goods are purchasable through credit cards.

Mass consumption, cultural dopes and a shallow world

The rise of so much consumption has given sociologists much to discuss. In the first place, some argue that the 'consumerist' culture is having a deleterious effect on the quality of life. Socialist critic Jeremy Seabrook (1996) sees consumerism accelerating since 1945, and destroying traditional cultures and solidarities. The 'loads-a-money' culture promotes self-gratification, and with the market dominating, leads to a general flattening of life – destroying differences and communities. This is seen to lead to

the weakening of creativity and the decline of participatory communities as people now go to the impersonal shopping mall and not 'the corner shop', and it generates a crass materialism. We have seen something of this in our earlier discussion of George Ritzer's McDonaldisation thesis (Ritzer, 1993, and see Chapter 6). Indeed, in a later book, Ritzer has discussed more fully the dangers of what he calls 'cathedrals of consumption' (Ritzer, 2004a).

We have also seen the dangers inherent in what we could call the 'brand name society', where what is on sale is not so much a commodity as a logo. The importance of the sign – the Nike swoosh, the Virgin 'V', the Tommy Hilfiger colours – turns shoppers into walking advertising systems.

Consumption: a sovereign world of choice, distinctiveness and creativity?

Others, by contrast, argue that the new consumerism has been a major advance for most. It has become the means for a higher standard of living, as well as a chance not to deaden culture but to enhance it. Goods and brands may spread through the world, but they are used differently and become different things. With the packaging of CDs in vast megastores, for instance, global music has developed – and the sheer range of music available now has increased dramatically. The same is true of food, with supermarkets now making available ingredients and recipes unheard of 20 years ago. Far from flattening culture, consumerism has enriched it, giving us a greater choice and a better control of our lives. There has been a growing mass participation in creative activities, from DIY to music, from cooking to reading, and from painting to all kinds of 'hobby'.

Inequalities and consumption

Many years ago the sociologist Thorstein Veblen recognised what he called conspicuous consumption, through which people (usually elites) can enhance their status through commodities, from clothes and houses to cars and other material symbols of wealth (Veblen, 1953; orig. 1899). Consumption and its display are not available to all and thus can become a marker of inequality.

In Veblen's view, consumption patterns lead to three ways of excluding people. The first is through money:

The modern marketplace: shopping malls and megastores are now a common sight throughout much of the world. Asia is home to eight of the world's ten largest shopping malls, six of which have been built since 2004. See Chapter 24, p. 842
Source: © Viviane Moos/Corbis.

many people simply cannot afford to purchase new or high-quality goods and services, and suffer 'economic exclusion' as a result. Others may be excluded spatially; without a car or good public transport they cannot easily get to shopping centres and other places of consumption. Often, indeed, if restricted to using small local shops, they will find they pay more and have less choice. Finally, some people will be excluded because they lack the knowledge and skills to consume. Being a skilful consumer these days may well require knowledge of the metric system, computing or international food, for example.

Of course, many people resist these pervasive forms of consumption: they do not want to be part of a high-consumption world and may actively prefer to support local shops, while being indifferent, or in some cases even hostile, towards international brand names. To some extent, this is what the new worldwide 'anti-globalism' protests are about (for example, Klein, 2000). Still, for some, not being able to shop

and consume in this way can be experienced as a form of social exclusion.

The new consumption patterns may make life difficult for many. Elderly people, for instance, may find small local shops closing, while the new megastores – should they want to use them – are inaccessible. The elderly are less likely to drive and their state of health may make time and travel hard; and even the design of stores, with high shelves, big trolleys, masses of people and constant commotion, makes them seem very inhospitable places.

Disneyisation

One recent and useful lens through which to understand the way contemporary consumption works has been provided by an analysis of the marketing strategies of Walt Disney. Most people have some idea of what a Disney theme park is like, and indeed large numbers of people have visited one.

Alan Bryman, taking his lead from Ritzer's discussion of McDonaldisation (see Chapter 6), has suggested that **Disneyisation** is *the process by which the principles of the Disney theme parks are coming to dominate more and more sectors of American society as well as the rest of the world* (Bryman, 2004: 1). Disneyisation lies at the heart of modern consumption (and capitalism?), in that it has started to shape many shopping experiences, providing a platform for purchases. In his book, Bryman suggests that four main principles lie behind Disneyisation. These are:

- *Theming*, putting the sales object into a story line to which it is not necessarily related. Thus a restaurant takes on the theme of rock music (for example, Hard Rock Café) or movies (Planet Hollywood), a hotel takes on the theme of a place (New York, Venice, ancient Rome or Egypt in Las Vegas) or shopping takes on a historical theme (Liverpool's Albert Docks, London's Tobacco Dock, and Barcelona's Port Vaill).

- *Hybrid consumption*, in which one type of shopping becomes linked in with another very different kind, making them increasingly hard to distinguish. Airports and sports stadia, for example, become shopping malls too.

- *Merchandising*, the promotion and sale of goods which bear copyrighted images and logos. Thus films such as *Pirates of the Carribean*, *Shrek*, *Star Wars* and *Spider-Man* also generate not just DVDs, CDs and videos but T-shirts, greeting cards, toys, books, video games and tie-ins with food and clothing markets. Often the merchandise makes much more money than the original product!

- *Performative or emotional labour*, in which the frontline service industry is seen less as a job and more as a performance. Often this involves 'dressing up' and performing a role in line with the attire; usually it involves smiling and being friendly – acting as if the tasks being done are fun and friendly and not really work at all.

When you next go shopping, remember this is the most popular leisure activity, and ponder if any of this fits.

Looking ahead

This chapter has suggested that although industrial capitalism may have become the dominant economic form throughout most of the world over the past 200 years, it continues to change. The chapter has looked at the rise of fragmentation in both work and production (post-Fordism); the flow of companies across the world (globalisation); the increasing use of women's labour; the changing patterns of service work; the rise of major markets of mass consumption, which seem to be generating ever-increasing demand for consumer goods; and the ever fluctuating nature of capitalism's unstable market which led to the credit crunch of 2008–9.

Sociologists are not fortune-tellers and cannot predict the future. It would have been hard for them to predict, in the late eighteenth century, the rise of the new information economy that appears to be emerging in the early twenty-first. But this chapter does at least suggest that, just as capitalism has been flexible in the past, so it may well continue to adjust to the changes of the future.

SUMMARY

1 The economy is the major social institution by which a society produces, distributes and consumes goods and services. It is not just economic, but social.

2 In technologically simple societies, the economy is subsumed within the family. In agrarian societies, most economic activity takes place outside the home. Industrialisation sparks significant economic expansion built around new energy sources, large factories, mass production and worker specialisation. The post-industrial economy is characterised by a productive shift from tangible goods to services. Just as the technology of the Industrial Revolution propelled the industrial economy of the past, so the Information Revolution is now advancing the post-industrial economy.

3 The primary sector of the economy generates raw materials; the secondary sector manufactures various goods; the tertiary sector focuses on providing services. In pre-industrial societies, the primary sector predominates; the secondary sector is of greatest importance in industrial societies; the tertiary sector prevails in post-industrial societies.

4 Social scientists describe the economies of today's industrial and post-industrial societies in terms of two models. Capitalism is based on private ownership of productive property and the pursuit of personal profit in a competitive marketplace. Socialism is based on collective ownership of productive property and the pursuit of collective well-being through government control of the economy. Although most European economies are predominantly capitalist, the European community and national governments are broadly involved in economic life. Governments play an even greater role in the 'democratic socialist' economies of some western European nations and the 'state

capitalism' of Japan. The Russian Federation has gradually introduced some market elements into its formerly centralised economy; the nations of eastern Europe are making similar changes.

5 The emergence of a global economy means that nations no longer produce and consume products and services within national boundaries. Moreover, the 600 largest corporations, operating internationally, now account for most of the earth's economic output.

6 The nature of work is changing. Agricultural work is generally in decline and there is a move from factory work to service work. There is a spread of part-time and flexible work, a relative decline in trade union activity, and the growth of international labour markets which bring about 'sweatshop' labour. New forms of work, such as 'teleworking', are growing rapidly.

7 Unemployment has many causes, including the operation of the economy itself. The European unemployment rate is generally at least 5 per cent.

8 Transnational corporations (TNCs) form the core of the world's economies. They produce and distribute products in most nations of the world, although the distribution of wealth resulting from this activity is hugely unequal.

9 The consumer society has become crucial to the working of modern capitalism. The Western world is increasingly buying goods and services in large, centralised establishments, a pattern that has sapped the strength of small, locally based industries.

10 Disneyisation suggests four principles that help shape contemporary consumption: theming, hybrid consumption, mechandising and performative labour.

CONNECT UP: Turn to Part 6 of this book for key resources and link up with the book's website, which links to these resources
SEE: www.pearsoned.co.uk/plummer

MYTASKLIST

Ten suggestions for going further

1 Connect up with Part Six and the Sociology Web Resources

As you work through ideas and think about the issues raised in this chapter, look at the accompanying website and the resource centre at the end of this book which connects to it. There is a lot here to help you move on. To link up, see: www.pearson.co.uk/plummer.

2 Review the chapter

Briefly summarise (in a paragraph) just what this chapter has been about. Consider: (a) What have you learned? (b) What do you disagree with? Be critical. And (c) How would you develop all this? How could you get more detail on matters that interest you?

3 Pose questions

(a) Make a critical analysis of your last 'shopping expedition'. Drawing from ideas in this chapter, discuss what you bought, the processes by which those items were produced, the people and agencies that benefited from your purchases, and why you felt motivated to purchase those goods and services. Consider whether you were involved in the process described in the chapter as 'Disneyisation' and, if so, in what ways.

(b) Look at the people who work on your campus. What are their official designations – cleaners, teaching assistants, secretaries, professors, etc? From the tables in the text, guess how much they earn. What sort of contracts do they have? How much autonomy do they have over their working day?

(c) Identify several ways in which the Industrial Revolution reshaped the economies of Europe. How is the Information Revolution transforming these economies once again?

(d) What key characteristics distinguish capitalism, socialism and democratic socialism? Compare these systems in terms of productivity, economic inequality and support for civil liberties.

4 Explore key words

Many concepts have been introduced in this chapter. You can review them from the website or from the listing at the back of this book. You might like to give special attention to just five words and think them through – how would you define them, what are they dealing with, and do they help you see the social world more clearly or not?

For this chapter, a dictionary of economics would be useful. See:

John Black, *A Dictionary of Economics* (2nd edn, 2009)

Graham Bannock et al., *The Penguin Dictionary of Economics* (2004)

5 Search the Web

Be critical when you look at websites – see the box on p. 940 in the Resources section. For this chapter look at the following:

Statistics on work patterns, unemployment, consumption and the economy generally can be found in sources already mentioned: search under

Social Trends (UK)
Eurostats (Europe)
World Bank Fact Book (World)

See also:

United Nations Conference on Trade and Development (UNCTAD)
www.unctad.org
Useful for all kinds of data about global trade.

International Labour Organization (ILO)
www.ilo.org
A UN organisation devoted to advancing opportunities for women and men to obtain decent and productive work. A useful statistical resource and offers many new stories of work around the world.

International Monetary Fund
www.imf.org

New Economics Foundation (NEF)
www.neweconomics.org/about
An independent think-and-do tank that inspires and demonstrates real economic well-being and is developing the new economics.

Institute for Economic Affairs
www.iea.org.uk
The IEA's goal is to explain free-market ideas to the public, including politicians, students, journalists, business people, academics and anyone interested in public policy.

The Work Foundation
http://theworkfoundation.com
The Work Foundation is a not-for-profit organisation that brings all sides of working organisations together to find the best ways of improving both economic performance and the quality of working life.

Trades Union Congress
www.tuc.org
Information on unions in the UK.

Two useful magazines are:

Fortune Magazine
www.fortune.com
One of the world's leading business magazines. Among many other things, you can access lists of the top companies, lists of some of the best companies to work for, and a list of the 40 richest under-forties in the USA.

The Economist
www.economist.com/index.html
A weekly magazine focusing on international news and business affairs.

See also:

Interbrand
www.interbrand.com/books_papers.asp
A website devoted to discussion and details on brand names.

See also the websites of:

Naomi Klein, www.naomiklein.org/main
Paul Krugman, http://krugman.blogs.nytimes.com

6   Watch a DVD

- Park Kwang-Su's *A Single Spark* (1998): a tale of trying to improve working conditions in South Korea's garment shops, with powerful images of the sweatshops (world distribution: Fortisimo Films, Rotterdam).
- Charlie Chaplin's *Modern Times* (1936): classic silent comedy, which shows the Fordist production line.
- Joseph Santley's *Rosie the Riveter* (1944): five women who work during the Second World War.
- Ken Loach's *Bread and Roses* (2001): illegal immigrant Hispanic janitors work in Los Angeles to send money back home. On very low incomes and poor work conditions, they unionise. Strong stuff.
- *Ghosts* (2007): Chinese immigrants to the UK die on Morecombe Bay while working. A harrowing tale, which we introduced in the opening to this chapter.

7   Think and read

Geoffrey Ingham, *Capitalism* (2008) and David Harvey, *A Brief History of Neoliberalism* (2005) are good at setting the background economic scene. On the 1990s economic crisis, see Andrew Gamble, *The Spectre at the Feast* (2009).

Rudi Volti, *An Introduction to The Sociology of Work and Occupations: Globalization and Technological Change into the Twenty-First Century* (2008). Lively and global.

Noel Castree, Neil MCoe, Kevin Ward and Michael Samers, *Spaces of Work: Global Capitalism and Geographies of Labour* (2004). Critical of globalisation and capitalism, a book that brings the 'new geography' to issues surrounding work.

Peter Dicken, *Global Shift: Transforming of the World Economy* (6th edn, 2010). A major study of the world economy, now in its fifth edition. *The* classic. It is stuffed full of diagrams and charts and is very comprehensive, although it is not an easy or introductory read!

Naomi Klein, *No Logo* (2000) and *Shock Doctrine: The Rise of Disaster Capitalism* (2008). *No Logo* is a popular and very lively read on the ways in which modern economies depend upon brand names. The 'bible' of the anti-capitalist movement.

Ulrich Beck, *The Brave New World of Work* (2000a). This comes from one of the world's leading contemporary sociologists and is a polemic about where work may be heading in the future – what he calls the 'Brazilianization of work'.

Finally:

Benjamin R. Barber, *Consumed* (2007), George Ritzer, *Cathedrals of Consumption* (2004a) and Alan Bryman,

The Disneyization of Society (2004) are three useful books on consumption.

8 Relax with a novel

See: *The Ragged Trousered Philanthropists* by Robert Tressel and Peter Miles.

9 Connect to other chapters

- Link to chapters on social divisions in Part Three. How do class, gender and ethnicity link to work? What might happen if you are disabled? Or gay?
- For more on women and work, see gender in Chapter 12 and families in Chapter 18.
- For more on consumption and identity, see Chapter 5.

10 Engage with THE BIG DEBATE

The crisis and the crash: will capitalism survive?

The 2007–8 'credit crunch' was one of the more serious financial crises faced by the world. It stemmed from an unstable mortgage market in America whereby mortgage lenders approved high-risk mortgage loans to people with poor credit records. Problems ensued. When it just involved poor people, it passed relatively unnoticed. But by 2007, it was found to be a problem for major banks like Bear Stearns in the United States, and Northern Rock in England. Bit by bit, a major world financial crisis ensued, which will now shape the world for the next decade or longer. Here we suggest a full-scale debate on the nature of contemporary capitalism.

The rise of Thatcherism, Reaganism and the neoliberal model

Neoliberalism has dominated the world economic order now for over 30 years. When Margaret Thatcher came to power as Prime Minister in the UK in 1979, she started to revolutionise the way in which both the economy and the government were to be run. So influential was she that a whole ideology – **Thatcherism** – was named after her. Broadly, this is *a system of political beliefs based on free markets, individualism and minimum state intervention*. Her ideas are also known as neoliberalism, and were shaped particularly by the libertarian Milton Friedman (1912–2006), famed for the saying that 'there was no such thing as a free lunch'. (A **libertarian** is someone who *takes individual freedom as the prime political value*.) In the USA, Thatcher's leadership coincided with the presidency of Ronald Reagan (1911–2004, presidency 1981–9) and Reaganism. What they both achieved was to radically shift the grounds of government debate to a focus on the importance of market mechanisms and reduced government intervention. Between 1946 and 1979,

for example, very few people in the UK discussed health or education provision through market models (though in the USA, they did!). But it is a sign of Thatcher's influence that nowadays many countries across the world, and not just the UK, have come to stress the importance of markets in many areas of life.

The debate is not a new one, however. Thatcher just 'modernised' it, 30 years ago, for the UK. Historically, most European societies have had a mix of market and government intervention – hence, mixed economies. From 1946, and with the exception of the Thatcher years (1979–90), the British government has regularly intervened in the economy, both through the welfare state and for a while with its extensive programme of nationalisation (now ceased). The Scandinavian countries also had a pronounced 'welfare' and interventionist background. By contrast, US society has relied on 'the market' for most economic decisions: the market sets prices, as potential buyers and sellers bid for goods and services upwards or downwards in a changing balance of supply and demand.

The march of the neoliberal model

With Thatcherism all the previously nationalised industries (including telephones, water, gas, electricity and rail) were privatised, and a programme of internal markets was introduced into the welfare state (especially in healthcare and schools).

Defenders praise the market for encouraging choice, diversity and flexibility: in so doing, the market coordinates the efforts of countless people, each of whom – to return to Adam Smith's crucial insight – is motivated only by self-interest. Economists like Milton Friedman (revised edn, 1990) argue that a more or less freely operating market system has provided many members of capitalist societies with an unprecedented economic standard of living.

They also claim that virtually any task that government undertakes, it performs inefficiently. They claim that the products we enjoy – such as computers,

Table 15.8	Capitalism: for and against
Capitalism is a good force	**Capitalism is a problem**
Free markets are crucial.	There is no such thing as a free market.
Governments should not intervene in the market.	Implicitly, they always intervene – regulating international trade, fostering migration policies, passing factory and workplace Acts. When the credit crunch happened, ultimately governments bailed banks out for billions.
Free markets mean freedom of individuals to choose.	Freedom to choose is only for a few. Many and especially the poor have little choice.
Free markets generate wealth.	But the wealth is unevenly distributed and the system favours the rich getting richer and the poor getting poorer.
Everybody gets richer – as wealth trickles down to the poor.	The rich are made richer, but there is no guarantee for the poor. In fact, the poor often get poorer and inequalities increase. Why do we have so many people across the world living in abject poverty?
Markets serve personal and private interests – people get what they want.	But public goods are not private interests: the needs of all – the collective good – is not fostered under capitalism (e.g. good environment, safety and protection, travel, education, health and security).

household appliances and the myriad offerings of supermarkets and shopping centres – are primarily products of the market. By contrast, the least-satisfying goods and services available today, and Friedman places schools, public transport and health services among these, are those operated by governments. Thus, while some government presence in the economy is necessary, supporters of free markets maintain that an economy that operates with minimal state regulation serves the public interest well.

Critics of the neoliberal model

Other analysts, however, all but dismiss the market and see it as a negative force. For one thing, critics point out, the market has little incentive to produce goods and services that generate little profit, which include just about everything consumed by poor people. Government-directed public housing, for example, stands as a vital resource that no profit-seeking developer would offer independently.

Second, critics look to government to curb what they see as the market system's self-destructive tendencies. The formation of economic monopolies, for example, can threaten the public interest. Government can perform a host of regulatory functions, intervening in the market to control inflation, to enhance the well-being of workers (by creating workplace health and safety standards) and to benefit consumers (through product quality controls). Indeed, the power of global corporations is so great, conclude the critics, that even government cannot effectively defend the public interest. And as we shall see in Chapter 25, with increasing environmental degradation being heaped upon the planet, often through self-interested corporations, surely there is a need for international governments to provide regulation?

Finally, critics support government's role in curbing what they see as another market flaw: magnifying social stratification. As we have seen, capitalist economies characteristically concentrate income and wealth; a government system of taxation (which typically would apply higher rates to the rich) counters this tendency in the name of social justice. For a number of reasons, then, the market operating alone does not serve the public interest.

Does the market's 'invisible hand' feed us well or pick our pockets? Although many – perhaps most – people view the market as good, they also support some government role in economic life to benefit the public.

Indeed, government assists not only citizens but business itself by providing investment capital, constructing roads and other infrastructure, and shielding companies from foreign competition. Yet the precise balance struck between market forces and government decision-making continues to underlie much of the political debate around the world.

Look now at Table 15.8, which debates the case for and against capitalism.

Continue the debate

1 Why do defenders of the free market assert that 'the government that governs best is the government that governs least'?
2 Does a market system meet the needs of all? Does it serve some better than others?
3 What is your impression of the successes and failures of Thatcherism? Compare it with socialist economic systems.
4 Will capitalism remain the dominant economic system in the twenty-first century? What are the alternatives to capitalism?

Source: Gray (2002).

If you are interested in contemporary social-economic debate, look at:

Ha-Joon Chang, *23 Things They Don't Tell You about Capitalism* (2010)
Andrew Gamble, *The Spectre at the Gate* (2009)
David Harvey, *The Enigma of Capital* (2009)
Tim Jackson, *Prosperity Without Growth* (2009)

CHAPTER 16

POWER, GOVERNANCE AND SOCIAL MOVEMENTS

HE PEOPLE CALLED IT 'The Battle of Seattle'. It started in early December 1999 on the streets of Seattle, which was for a short while to be the home of a major political conflict over world finance. The World Trade Organization (WTO) had come to town for a major international conference, and the people were not happy with it. The WTO came into being in 1995 (originally set up under the General Agreement on Trade and Tariffs, GATT) and claimed to be the only 'global international organisation dealing with the rules of trade between nations'. The goal is to help producers of goods and services, exporters, and importers conduct their business . . . Its main function is to ensure that trade flows as smoothly, predictably, and freely as possible.' Based in Geneva, in 2000 it had around 500 staff and a budget of some $83 million. In 2010, it had over 150 nation members accounting for nearly all of world trade.

But the people said it was 'undemocratic': it had been formed from the powerful, global financial elite and did not represent the people of the world. Accused of neglecting the environment, poorer countries, child labour and exploitation, while championing free trade, it came to symbolise the new global world of high finance and transnational corporations. And the people protested. Some 30,000 protestors took to the streets. At its heart was a political attack on capitalism and the widespread global influence of corporations. There was a sense of global awareness that much of what the 'First World' consumes makes for the tragedies of the 'Third World'. But it was wider than this: in a sense it was a coming together of all the 'causes' of the late twentieth century: the Greens, animal rights, anti-slavery, disarmament and non-violence, the New Age, lifestyle politics, eco-feminism, labour rights, civil rights, human rights. There have been many critiques and movements against contemporary world capitalism – which has seen as unprecedented changes characterised variously as 'turbo-capitalism' (Edward Luttwak)

market fundamentalism' (George Soros), 'casino capitalism' (Susan Strange), 'cancer-stage capitalism' (John McMurtry) and 'McWorld' (Benjamin Barber). In this chapter we look at a range of diverse political responses to the world we live in.

See: Massimiliano Andretta and Donatella della Porta (eds), *The Global Justice Movement* (2007).

The early days of the anti-globalisation or global justice movement

1994:   Formation in Mexico of 'People's Global Action' ('Ya Basta').

1999:   Battle of Seattle; 1,200 NGOs combined.

2000s: Summits challenged in Quebec, London, Barcelona, Sweden, Genoa and New York

2005   31st G8 Summit in Edinburgh.

Man is a political animal.

Aristotle

In this chapter, we ask:

- What are the different kinds of power and the nature of democracies?

- How has politics become globalised?

- How are women excluded from power?

- What is the political organisation of Europe?

- How can we explain the workings of power?

- How does power work 'beyond the rules'? Revolutions, war and terrorism

- What is the significance of social movements in the twenty-first century?

- What is the significance of human rights regimes?

(Above) Demonstrators gather to protest against the World Trade Organization (WTO) during its 1999 conference in Seattle. What started out as a peaceful protest turned into a violent clash between demonstrators and riot police, with many injuries, over 500 arrests and major damage to the downtown area

Source: © Christopher J. Morris/Corbis.

(Left) Lenin addresses the workers to encourage them to support him

Source: Vladimir Ilyich Lenin (1870–1924) *Addressing the Red Army of Workers on 5th May 1920*, 1933 (oil on canvas), Brodsky, Isaak Israilevich (1883–1939)/Private Collection, RIA Novosti/The Bridgeman Art Library.

See: www.marxists.org/archive/lenin/index.htm as a general source on Marxism; also www.aha.ru~mausoleu; www.stel.ru/museum; http://azer.com/aiweb/categories/magazine/al142_folder/142_lenin_art.html.

 Soviet art rejected the trends of twentieth-century art in much of the Western world. What might this image tell you about Soviet power?

This chapter investigates the dynamics of power and focuses on it mainly as a process within societies and among nations. Formal **politics** is *the social institution that distributes power, sets a society's agenda and makes decisions*, and **governance** is *the exercise of political, economic and administrative authority in the management of a country's affairs at all levels*. We will be looking mainly at the more formal exercise of power in this chapter, but first we should recognise that power has much wider implications.

Power

Power is actually to be found as much in everyday encounters (see Chapter 7) as it is in formal politics and governance. This is *informal power*. You can encounter it in face-to-face interactions, inside families, between men and women, in the workings of institutions such as schools and prisons, in child–adult relations. But precisely because it can be found everywhere, sociologists often have difficulty defining it. It is most obviously seen when people take decisions that affect others' lives, but it can be more subtle: as when people prevent certain issues from ever even being discussed; or where it tacitly shapes desires and wishes, often against our will. Michel Foucault is most extreme, for he sees power as everywhere, and to be found in all relationships (Foucault, 1977). It does not simply come from the top; it is not simply about the formal institutions of power. He looks at all social life to find the power mechanisms at work in it. We look a little further at his ideas in Chapter 17.

Max Weber's classic ideas on power and authority

Perhaps the classic sociological statement on power is to be found in the work of Max Weber (1978; orig. 1921), whom we have regularly encountered before. He declared power to be the ability to achieve desired ends despite resistance from others. Force – physical might or psychological coercion – may be a basic expression of power, but no society can exist for long if power derives only from force, because people will break rules they do not respect at the first opportunity. Social organisation, therefore, depends on generating some sense of legitimacy and consensus. As we have seen earlier, sociologists use concepts such as ideology and hegemony to deal with this non-coercive power.

The key to social stability is exercising power within a framework of legitimacy. This insight led Weber to focus on the concept of **authority**, *power that people perceive as legitimate rather than coercive*. When parents, teachers or police perform their work well, their power can generally win respect as authority. The source of authority, Weber continued, differs according to a society's economy. He distinguished three types: traditional, rational–legal and charismatic.

Traditional authority is *power legitimised through respect for long-established cultural patterns*. The might of Chinese emperors in antiquity was legitimised by tradition, as was the rule of nobles in medieval Europe. In both cases, hereditary family rule within a traditional, agrarian way of life imbued leaders with almost god-like authority. In the modern world, traditional authority is being challenged more and more.

Rational–legal authority is *power legitimised by legally enacted rules and regulations*. It is legitimised by **government**, *formal organisations that direct the political life of a society*. Weber viewed bureaucracy as the organisational backbone of rational, industrial societies. Rationally enacted rules not only guide government in more and more countries today, but they also underlie much of our everyday life. The authority of classroom teachers and lecturers, for example, rests on the offices they hold in bureaucratic schools and universities. Compared to traditional authority, then, rational–legal authority flows not from family background but from organisational position. Thus, while a traditional monarch rules for life, a modern prime minister or president accepts and relinquishes power according to law, with authority remaining in the office.

Charismatic authority is *power legitimised through extraordinary personal abilities that inspire devotion and obedience*. Charisma, a concept to be detailed in Chapter 19, designates exceptional personal qualities that people take to be a sign of divine inspiration. Unlike tradition and rational law, then, charisma has less to do with social organisation and is more a trait of individual personality. The extraordinary ability of charismatics to challenge the status quo is deeply ingrained in global history: Vladimir Lenin guided the overthrow of feudal monarchy in Russia in 1917, Mahatma Gandhi inspired the struggle to free India from British colonialism after the Second World War, and Martin Luther King, Jr, galvanised the Civil Rights Movement in the United States. In more recent years, charismatic women, including Indira Gandhi of India, Benazir Bhutto of Pakistan, Golda Meir of Israel and Margaret Thatcher of the United Kingdom, have gained international political prominence.

A Theocratic State Celebrated: Iran is a major theocratic state. Here Iranians are carrying images of the late Islamic leader Ayatollah Ruhollah Khomeini and his successor incumbent leader Ayatollah Ali Khamenei at a rally celebrating the 31st anniversary of Islamic Revolution at the Azadi (liberty) Square in Tehran, capital of Iran, 11 February 2010

Source: © Ahmad Hala bisaz/Xinhua Press/Corbis.

LIVING IN THE C21ST

Religion as power: theocracy in Iran

A **theocracy** (from the Greek θεοκρατία, meaning 'the rule of God') is a *form of government where a god or religion is recognised as the supreme ruler*. The Islamic state of Iran and the Vatican in Rome are the only theocracies that are ruled by a religious figure (the Grand Ayatollah and the Pope). But there are many other countries that are partially theocratic – Saudi Arabia, Sudan, the Republic of Yemen, Afghanistan, the United Arab Emirates, Pakistan, Malaysia and Mauritania are all Islamic theocracies. The Vatican City is the only Christian theocracy. Most theocracies are usually authoritarian in nature and ruled by an absolute king (e.g. Saudi Arabia), a president (e.g. Sudan), a prime minister, or both (e.g. Pakistan). Some are called *constitutional theocracies*. Very controversially, some see Israel as a theocracy based on the Jewish faith.

Here we will briefly consider the case of Iran. Iran is one of the world's oldest civilisations: Persia and part of Mesopotamia. Its roots stretch back to the dawn of civilisation around 3,500 BCE. Today, it is a modern oil-exporting economy. And it is a theocracy: the Islamic Republic of Iran. Islam became its religion around 637 with the death of Muhammad and has continued to be so to this day. This new religion was linked with the growth of science, and Iran became for a while a leading, advanced civilisation. The invasion of Genghis Khan and the Mongols in the thirteenth century led to mass slaughter. Later, as Western industrialisation took place, its central role in the world started to decline.

Iran has had a long and difficult history of political conflict. The great split between Sunni and Shi'a took place in the lifetime of Muhammad's son-in-law. But the religious-based conflicts

LIVING IN THE C21ST

continue today. Modernisation started in the 1950s with the 'help' of the United States: Mohammad Mossadegh (1882–1967) was the democratically elected, fairly secular prime minister of Iran from 1951 to 1953, and was responsible for many reforms as well as the development of the oil industry. He was overthrown in a *coup d'état* backed by the US Central Intelligence Agency. Mossadegh resisted and was put under house arrest. The Shah returned in 1953 and became king of kings in 1976, and Americanisation proceeded until the Islamic revolution of 1979.

This was the defining moment in modern history of Iran. With serious economic problems, the people revolted and the Shah fled the country. The Khomenei returned from exile and the world's first Islamic republic was declared. Iran has remained an Islamic republic ever since. With this, the Mullahs appointed Khomenei as supreme ruler: a society was constructed through religion. The Islamic republic is a mixture of theocracy and democracy. It has presidential elections every five years or so;

and yet all government is tightly regulated by a religious council and a supreme leader (Vali-e-Faqih) who controls all branches of government, the judiciary and the revolutionary guard. Originally ruled by Ayatollah Khomeini, Iran is now ruled by Ayatollah Ali Khamenei. The religious council is composed of a number clerics.

The period 1997–2005 was marked by the presence a more liberal president, Muhammad Khtamai; but he was encircled by the religious establishment. An ultra conservative new president, Mahmoud Ahmadinejad, was elected in 2005 (and gained a much disputed second term in 2009).

Iran is generally a prospering country – doing well on the Human Development Index. Life expectancy has increased from 59 years in 1980 to 71 in 2005. It now has one of the lowest birth rates in the world. At the same time, it is a highly repressive society and fares very badly on human rights.

 A key book on Iran is Sami Zubaida: *Islam, The People and the State* (revised edn, 2009).

For a sense of the country, see Nasrin Alavi, *We are Iran* (2006). It is a patchwork of diverse Iranian voices found on Iranian blogs – telling it as it is.

An excellent documentary was produced by the BBC and Rageh Omar in 2007. It is well worth a look and you can see most of it on YouTube: search *Rageh Inside Iran*.

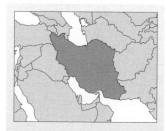

COUNTRY FACT FILE

IRAN

Population	66.4 million
Per capita GDP	$4,030
Life expectancy	69.65 male 72.72 female
Adult literacy	83.5%
Key languages	Persian, Persian dialects 58%
Key religions	Shi'a Muslims (89%) Sunni Muslims (9%)
Key city	Tehran
Human development index	0.702 (70th, 2010)

Types of political system

Political systems display marked variety. Some societies such as the Nuer in Africa, studied by the anthropologist E. E. Evans-Pritchard (1951), have been 'headless', having no leaders. But more generally, throughout much of history, imperial systems or empires – the Chinese, the Japanese, the Islamic, the Roman – have dominated politics, functioning as separate worlds having little contact with each other. Life under these systems was often capricious. It is only in the latter part of the second millennium that we start to see the emergence of what we take for granted today: the nation-state, with a clearly defined territory, military support and nationalist creed. Historically, the

idea that people imagine a community connected to their nation is probably not that common. But it has been a defining feature of the modern world.

Generally speaking, the world's major contemporary political systems fall into four categories: totalitarianism, authoritarianism, monarchy and democracy. Theocracies are often seen as fifth (see *Living in the twenty-first century* above).

1 Totalitarianism

The most restrictive political form is **totalitarianism**, *a political system that extensively regulates people's lives.* Although some totalitarian governments claim to represent the will of the people, most seek to bend people to the will of the government. As the term itself implies, such governments represent total concentrations of power and prohibit organised opposition of any kind. Denying the populace the right to assemble for political purposes and controlling access to information, these governments thrive in an environment of fear and social atomisation. Socialisation in totalitarian societies is intensely political, seeking not just outward compliance but inward commitment to the system. In North Korea, pictures of leaders and political messages over loudspeakers are familiar elements of public life that remind citizens that they owe total allegiance to the state. Government-controlled schools and mass media present only official versions of events.

Government indoctrination is especially stringent whenever political opposition surfaces in a totalitarian society. In the aftermath of the 1989 pro-democracy movement in the People's Republic of China, for example, officials demanded that citizens report all 'unpatriotic' people – even members of their own families. Further, Chinese leaders subjected all students at Beijing universities to political 'refresher' courses. Totalitarian governments span the political spectrum from the far right (including Nazi Germany) to the far left (North Korea).

2 Authoritarianism

Some nations give their people little voice in politics. **Authoritarianism** refers to *a political system that denies popular participation in government*. An authoritarian government is not only indifferent to people's needs; it lacks the legal means to remove leaders from office and provides people with little or no means even to express their opinions. Polish sociologist Wlodzimierz Wesolowski sums up authoritarianism this way: 'The authoritarian philosophy argues for the supremacy of the state [over other] organised social activity' (1990: 435). The absolute monarchies in Saudi Arabia and Kuwait are highly authoritarian, as are military juntas, found today in Congo and Ethiopia, where political dissatisfaction has been widespread. (This is not always the case, however, as the *World watch* box shows in the case of the 'soft authoritarianism' of the small Asian nation of Singapore.)

3 Monarchy

Monarchy is *a political system in which a single family rules from generation to generation*. Today's British monarchy traces its lineage back roughly 1,000 years.

During the medieval era, absolute monarchy, in which hereditary rulers claimed a virtual monopoly of power based on divine right, flourished from England to China and in parts of the Americas. In some nations, today monarchs still exercise virtually absolute control over their people. The system is legitimated by tradition.

Yet as democracies and egalitarianism have spread throughout many parts of the world, so monarchs have gradually passed from the scene in favour of elected officials. Europe's remaining monarchs – in the UK, Spain, Norway, Sweden, Belgium, Denmark and the Netherlands – now preside over *constitutional monarchies*. They serve as symbolic heads of state, while actual governing is the responsibility of elected politicians: the monarch may formally reign, but elected officials actually rule. Still, in 2003, around 30 nations were political monarchies where families passed power from generation to generation.

4 Democracies

The historical trend in the modern world has favoured **democracy**, *a political system in which power is exercised by the people as a whole*, though quite how this power is to be exercised has always been a key problem. Members of democratic societies rarely participate directly in decision-making; *representative democracy* places authority in the hands of elected leaders, who are accountable to the people (under *participatory democracy* people would represent themselves and take their own decisions). The system is legitimated by rational–legal authority, and a rational election process places leaders in offices regulated by law.

Democracy and its problems

But democratic political systems are much more than just leaders and followers; they are often built on extensive bureaucracy and economic power. Considerable formal organisation is necessary to carry out the expanding range of government activities undertaken by democratic societies. As it grows, government gradually takes on a life of its own, revealing an inherent antagonism between democracy and bureaucracy. The federal government of the United States, for example, employs more than 3 million people (excluding the armed forces), making it one of the largest bureaucracies in the world. Another 15 million people work in some 80,000 local governments. In the UK, some 2.6 million people are employed by local authorities alone.

'Soft authoritarianism' or planned prosperity? A report from Singapore

Singapore, a tiny nation on the tip of the Malay Peninsula with a population of just over 3 million, seems to many to be an Asian paradise. Surrounded by poor societies that grapple with rapidly growing populations, squalid, sprawling cities and surging crime rates, the affluence, cleanliness and safety of Singapore make the European visitor think more of a theme park than a country.

In fact, since its independence from Malaysia in 1965, Singapore has startled the world with its economic development; today, the economy is expanding rapidly and per capita income now rivals that of the United States. But, unlike Europe or the United States, Singapore has scarcely any social problems such as crime, slums, unemployment or children living in poverty. In fact, people in Singapore do not even contend with traffic jams, graffiti on underground trains or litter in the streets.

The key to Singapore's orderly environment is the ever-present hand of government, which actively promotes traditional morality and regulates just about everything. The state owns and manages most of the country's housing and has a stake in many businesses. It provides tax incentives for family planning and completing additional years of schooling. To keep traffic under control, the government slaps hefty surcharges on cars, pushing the price of a basic saloon car up to around £25,000.

Singapore made international headlines in 1994 after the government accused Michael Fay (from the United States) of vandalism and sentenced him to a caning – a penalty illegal in most Western countries. Singapore's laws also permit police to detain a person suspected of a crime without charge or trial and to mandate death by hanging for drug dealing. The government has outlawed some religious groups (including Jehovah's Witnesses) and bans pornography outright. Even smoking in public brings a heavy fine. To ensure that city streets are kept clean, the state forbids eating on the subway, imposes stiff fines for littering and has even outlawed the sale of chewing gum.

In economic terms, Singapore defies familiar categories. Government control of scores of businesses, including television stations, telephone services, airlines and taxis, seems socialist. Yet, unlike socialist enterprises, these businesses are operated efficiently and very profitably. Moreover, Singapore's capitalist culture celebrates economic growth (although the government cautions its people about the evils of excessive materialism) and this nation is home to hundreds of multinational corporations.

Singapore's political climate is as unusual as its economy. Members of this society feel the hand of government far more than their counterparts in Europe. Just as important, a single political organisation – the People's Action Party – has ruled Singapore without opposition since the nation's independence 30 years ago.

COUNTRY FACT FILE

SINGAPORE

Population	4,450,000 (2006)
Urban population	100%
Per capita GDP	$31,400 (2006 est.)
Life expectancy	79.4 years (2005–10); male 76 years, female 80 years (2000)
Literacy	Over 93% (2004)
Languages	Malay, English, Chinese (Mandarin) and Tamil (official languages)
Religions	Buddhism, Islam, Christianity, Taoism and Hinduism, Sikh and Jewish minorities
Main cities	Singapore: around 3 million
Human development index	0.846 (27th, 2010)

Clearly, Singapore is not a politically democratic country. But most people in this prospering nation seem content – even enthusiastic – about their lives. What Singapore's political system offers is a simple bargain: government demands unflinching loyalty from the populace; in return, it provides a high degree of security and prosperity. Critics charge that this system amounts to a 'soft authoritarianism' that stifles dissent and gives government unwarranted control over people's lives. Most of the people of Singapore, however, know the struggles of living elsewhere and, for now at least, consider the trade-off a good one.

Source: Based on Branegan (1993).

The great majority of these bureaucrats were never elected and are unknown to the public they purport to serve. To elect them would seem impractical, given their numbers and the need for specialised training. But, ironically, while the public focuses attention on a small number of elected leaders, most everyday decision-making is carried out by career bureaucrats who are not directly accountable to the people (Scaff, 1981).

Democracy and freedom: contrasting approaches

Despite their distinctive histories and cultural diversity, virtually all industrialised nations in the world claim to be democratic and politically free. Map 16.1 shows the countries of the world where 'free' systems exist. By the end of 2003, according to Freedom House (a New York-based organisation that tracks global political trends), more people in the world were 'free' than 'not free' for the first time in history (see Table 16.1). In 2007, its latest worldwide political survey found

that the percentage of countries designated as 'free' has remained flat. Setbacks for freedom have happened in a number of countries in the Asia-Pacific region, with a more modest decline in Africa, and a solidification of authoritarian rule in the majority of countries of the former Soviet Union. Some countries – Guyana, Haiti and Nepal – became more free; and Thailand and the Congo (Brazzaville) less free.

Table 16.1	The extent of global freedom: 30-year global trend, 1973–2003		
	Free countries	Partly free countries	Not free countries
1973	43	38	69
1983	54	47	64
1993	75	73	38
2003	89	55	48

Source: Freedom House.

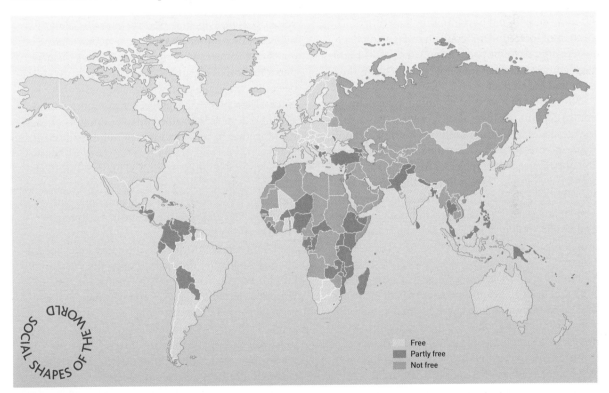

Free
Partly free
Not free

Map 16.1 Map of Freedom, 2009
Source: Map of Freedom, 2009, http://www.freedomhouse.org.

 Freedom House is an independent watchdog organisation that supports the expansion of freedom around the world. Freedom House supports democratic change, monitors freedom, and advocates for democracy and human rights. Since its founding in 1941 by prominent Americans concerned with the mounting threats to peace and democracy, Freedom House has been a vigorous proponent of democratic values and a steadfast opponent of dictatorships of the far left and the far right. Its website is a useful source of information on the extent and change of 'global freedom' – though some of its statistics are contested by other groups. See www.freedomhouse.org.

Measuring 'freedom' is always a problem: and here it is defined in terms of national ratings on political rights and civil liberties – and since countries mean different things by these terms, these are very hard to measure. So these conclusions need to be tempered, as usual, with caution. Still, overall, it looks like there is a worldwide movement towards democratisation. Again, though, we must be careful and ask just what is meant by this political freedom.

The political life of the West is largely shaped by the free-market economic principles of capitalism. Supporters argue that the operation of a market system affords individuals the personal freedom to pursue whatever they perceive as their self-interest. Thus, the argument continues, the capitalist approach to political freedom translates into personal liberty – freedom to vote for one's preferred leader or otherwise act with minimal interference from government.

Yet, as the last chapter explained, capitalist societies are marked by a striking inequality of wealth. Such economic disparity, critics counter, gives some people far more choices and opportunities than others. Thus, capitalism looks undemocratic in so far as such a system attends to the needs of only the wealthy and highlights choices that may not be available to the poor and less well off.

Supporters of a socialist economic system, by contrast, point out that socialist politics strives to meet every citizen's basic needs for housing, schooling, a job and medical care. Thus, the socialist approach to political freedom emphasises freedom from basic want. For example, there is little of the hunger and homelessness we associate with the capitalism of the United States in more socialist nations such as Norway and Sweden. Many in the Scandinavian countries would regard their systems as more free because of this.

But critics of socialism counter that such systems are more likely to be unresponsive to people's needs and aspirations as well as heavy-handed in their suppression of any political opposition. During the 1990s, for example, people living under socialist governments in eastern Europe overthrew that system in favour of a free market that would, presumably, reduce political repression (and, hopefully, raise living standards: something that is now in doubt).

These contrasting views of freedom raise an important question: are economic equality and political liberty compatible? To foster economic equality, socialism tends to infringe on individual initiative. Capitalism, on the other hand, provides broad political liberties, which, in practice, mean little to the poor.

Many of the countries of Europe may be seen generally to favour positions which can be called **social democratic**. This is *a mix of capitalist and socialist/welfare economies and politics*. Scandinavian countries pay high taxes and have strong welfare systems, middle European countries have lower commitments, southern European systems are less comprehensive, and the UK system highlights welfare and social services with quite high tax levels, but also has income-dependent benefits.

The rise of nation-states and the globalisation of politics

Most people living on the earth today live in **nation-states** – *political apparatuses over a specific territory with their own citizens backed up by military force and a nationalistic, sovereign creed*. But this is a new phenomenon of recent history. It has far from typically been the case in the past, where land masses have been ruled diversely by tribal chiefs, kings, emperors and sultans – despots who ruled by force and theocracies held together by religion. Ethnic groups made claims to their territories and, right up to the sixteenth century, people lived with these territorial limits set through land stewardship. Nation-states as we now know them congealed between the sixteenth and nineteenth centuries. Starting with the Treaty of Westphalia (1648), criteria started to be set out to demarcate local domestic territories and recognise independent nations. Thereafter the old empires – the Russian Empire, the Austro-Hungarian Empire, the British Empire – started to collapse, and new nation-states started to appear. Nationalism is hence also a new and modern phenomenon. Modern nation-states subsequently became the core of the systems of catastrophic wars built around nationalism in the twentieth century.

A nation-state sounds like a contradiction. A *state* is a political organisation with effective rule, sovereignty and governance over a limited geographic area – claiming a monopoly on authority, controlling armies and civil service, and believing it can use violence 'legitimately'. By contrast, a *nation* suggests a human and cultural community – connected often with religions, languages, ethnicities and a shared way of life. The nation is something to make sacrifice for, even lay one's life down for, and usually generates strong identities (I am German; I am Thai; I am a Maori). Often these are less real than **imagined communities** – an influential term developed by Benedict Anderson to suggest how nationalism is linked to the emergence of a 'print-capitalism' and the growing rejection of ideas of the monarchy and divine rule. (There has been much recent sociological research on the nation-state and its workings by Michael Mann, Anthony Smith and Saskia Sassen; along with a concern about the democratisation or not of these states).

Globalisation and politics

In Chapter 15, we pointed to the emergence of a global economy, meaning that finance flows routinely across national boundaries, along with products and services. In a similar way, we can point to the parallel development of a global political system. As we have seen, for the past 300 years or so, the dominant mode of governing has been through the nation-state, and we still think primarily in terms of these nation-states – such as Norway, China or Australia. At the same time, politics has clearly become part of a globalisation process. In some ways, there is a long history of 'international governance': ancient Greece and Renaissance Italy are two earlier examples. But today we can see at least five ways in which country politics have become interlinked:

1   The steady growth of political interconnectedness over large regions – notably the European Union comprising some 27 states, and the Association of South East Asian Nations (ASEAN: Indonesia, the Philippines, Malaysia, Singapore, Brunei, Thailand, Vietnam, Laos, Myanmar and Cambodia) – signposts a continuing regional interconnectedness (see: www.aseansex.org).

2   A worldwide layer of global government has been introduced since 1945, with the development of the United Nations. A major raft of political institutions, from UNICEF and UNHCR to UNESCO and WHO, have developed within it, and now play significant roles in world policies (for these and other abbreviations see the list on pp. 952–3; their website addresses are all straightforwardly found: do a Google search for the initials given above).

3   Multinational corporations (discussed in Chapter 15) now represent a political order of a quite different kind. They have enormous power to shape social life throughout the world. From this point of view, politics is dissolving into business as corporations grow larger than governments. *Of the 100 largest economies in the world, 51 today are corporations, not countries* (Brecher et al., 2000: 128).

4   The Information Revolution has put national politics on to the world stage. Even as early as 1989, hours before the Chinese government sent troops to Tiananmen Square to crush the 1989 pro-democracy movement, officials 'unplugged' the satellite transmitting systems of news agencies in an effort to keep the world from watching as events unfolded that day. Despite their efforts, news of the massacre was flashed around the world minutes after it began via the fax machines in universities and private homes. In short, just as individual nations can no longer control their own economies, so no national government can fully manage the political events that occur within its borders. And when suicide bombers attacked New York's Twin Towers on 11 September 2001, the whole world watched on more or less as it happened. Current information technology brings politics to homes and businesses across the globe in a flash.

5   New social movements have also been involved in the new Information Revolution and turned their activities into global campaigns and actions. As we shall see below, new forms of power have been developing linked to social movements. Green movements such as World Action for Rainforests (at www.rainforestweb.org) and the Women's Environmental Network (at http://web.wen.org) and hundreds of others are now global 'eco-warriors'. They are playing a significant role in putting issues of the green agenda on the actions list of international government (Scarce, 2006).

There are many recent examples of global politics. The 'Make Poverty History' campaign, which accompanied the G8 Gleneagles Summit in 2005, demanded 'trade justice', 'drop the debt' and 'more and better aid' for low-income societies. Over 500 organisations from some 84 nations participated, and a proliferation of websites for communication developed. At the time, the campaign was claimed to have been a huge political success; in practice, it closed down a year later amidst much criticism. In December 2009, tens of thousands of people staged protests in Copenhagen and around the world to push for stronger international commitments at the climate change conference in the Danish capital.

Gender and power

Throughout history, women have been excluded from most positions in the political system. Moreover, until very recently, women rarely appeared in studies or research connected to politics and governance. Simply posing the question 'where are the women?' in studies of any aspect of the political system soon reveals their lack of representation. Consider the seemingly simple issue of the right to vote: women in general acquired this right very late – sometimes a century after men had gained it. Moreover, the proportion of women in governments across the world is low, well below 40 per cent at best.

A few women, though, have risen to prominence: Indira Gandhi (in India during the 1960s through to the 1980s), Margaret Thatcher (a Conservative and very influential free marketer in England 1979–90), Mary Robinson (President of Ireland 1992–6), Sirimavo R. D. Bandaranaike (Prime Minister of Sri Lanka in the 1960s, 1970s and 1990s), Angela Merkel (Chancellor of Germany, elected autumn 2005), Ellen-Johnson-Sirleaf (first elected female president in Africa in 2006 – Liberia), Benazir Bhutto of Pakistan (assassinated in 2007) and Julia Gillard (first female prime minister of Australia in 2010). But simply to name them is to suggest how few of them there are: in 2009, there were 13 women who could be counted amongst the 200 or so world leaders.

Looking at the membership of world parliaments and national assemblies tells a similar story. Very few have any kind of equality between men and women. There has been growth, however: in 1995, national assemblies comprised, on average, 11.5 per cent women;

World leaders gather to discuss the global financial crisis at the G20 Summit in London on 2 April 2009. It is interesting to see how few women are world leaders. They are Angela Merkel (Germany) and Cristina Fernandez de Kirchner (Argentina)
Source: © Olivier Hoslet/epa/Corbis.

Table 16.2		Meetings of the global women's movement	
	Date	**Location**	**Delegates**
1st	1975	Mexico	6,000
2nd	1980	Copenhagen	7,000
3rd	1985	Nairobi	15,000
4th	1995	Beijing	8,000
5th	2000	Beijing +5	
6th	2005	Beijing +10	
7th	2010	Beijing +15	
	2 July 2010	UN Entity for Gender Equality and the Empowerment of Women established*	

* See UN Women: www.unwomen.org.

by May 2008, it was 18.4 per cent. Rwanda had nearly 50 per cent women, as did Sweden. The USA had only 15 per cent and the UK around 20 per cent. The same is true at a global level: the United Nations has not been able to achieve 50:50 equality even though it has committed to doing so. And most of its women are concentrated at lower occupational levels. In short, wherever you look, there are many fewer women than men in politics (Peterson and Runyan, 2010: 109 et seq.).

Both first- and second-wave feminism may have brought about some changes (see Chapter 12). Most significantly, we can start to see something like the emergence of a transitional women's movement in the past few decades. Often prompted by organisations such as the United Nations, a number of International Women's Conferences have been held, though these often revealed significant conflicts between 'First World' and 'Third World' women. Priorities and approaches differ greatly across cultures.

In the most general terms, these organisations have recognised that standard development models, such as the Human Development Index discussed in Chapters 4 and 9, do not reveal the extent or nature of gender imbalances in the status of women when compared to men across the world. The United Nations Development Programme (UNDP) has championed eight major areas where the position of women needs to be further equalised. These are:

1   Autonomy of the body (for example, controls over reproduction and sexuality, and the problem of violence).

2   Autonomy within family and household (for example, freedoms to marry, divorce and have custody of children in case of divorce).

3   Political power (for example, increased role in decision-making in unions, governments, parliaments, etc.).

4   Social resources (for example, access to health and education).

5   Material resources (for example, access to land, houses and credit).

6   Employment and income (for example, fair distribution of paid and unpaid labour).

7   Time (for example, relative access to leisure and sleep).

8   Gender identity (for example, problems with the rigidity of the sexual division of labour).

In all these areas, across the world, women tend to be in a strikingly less powerful position than men. As we saw in Chapter 13, there is now a global gender gap report which enables global tracking of the shifting fortunes of women's equality across the globe.

 For more on women in politics, see Websites on Women and Politics at: www.ipu.org/wmn-e/web.htm.

Political organisation in Europe

Although this has not always been the case, all the countries of western and central Europe may currently be seen as liberal democracies with a plurality of political parties and an electoral process. Spain, Germany, Greece and Italy have all at times been run by authoritarian governments. Portugal and Spain were right-wing dictatorships until the mid-1970s. The situation in eastern Europe is somewhat more complex. The Soviet Union dominated this bloc and most countries were communist until 1989. Since then, and often with much difficulty, they have been in the process of becoming democracies too.

In most countries there is usually both a national system of government and a local one. This can sometimes cause major tensions, when different parties hold the balance of power in one but not the other. But in general, the political parties of Europe have been stable.

The European Union

Most European countries are standing at the threshold of major change. They have their own (usually long-standing) political system as a nation-state. The nation-states of Europe are the independent nations – with their own territories, military forces, sense of national identity, and forms of citizenship and government, such as Parliament in the UK and the Bundestag and Bundesrat in Germany.

But increasingly important is the fact that many of the nation-states have become member states of the European Union (Norway and Switzerland are major exceptions), sending their elected representatives to the European Parliament at Strasbourg. As the map of Europe (Map 4.3) in Chapter 4 shows, there are a number of countries within Europe that have recently joined and others that are lining up to join. Figure 16.1 shows the main political parties in the European Parliament elected in June 2009. The centre-right European People's Party (EPP) remains the most powerful group in the 2009–14 European Parliament, with 263 out of the 736 MEPs (Members of the European Parliament). The Social Democrats (PES) have 163 seats; and the Liberal ALDE group has 66 seats. The Greens retained their fourth place with 52. Europe's voters generally shifted to the right: in four of the EU's six biggest nations (Germany, France, Italy and Poland), centre-right ruling parties performed unexpectedly well, whilst centre-left governments in Britain and Spain did badly. Nationalist and anti-immigration parties made gains in the Netherlands, Denmark, Finland, Austria, Greece, Romania and Hungary.

In the June 2009 elections, there was widespread apathy. The turnout continued to fall – it was 50 per cent in 1999; 45 per cent in 2004; and 43 per cent in 2009. In Britain, two-thirds of voters stayed away from the polls (Table 16.3). Voters often cast votes for fringe parties and parties in opposition to their own governments. Table 16.4 reveals this in detail.

The EU has developed a whole panoply of European institutions. Among these are:

- *The Commission*: with at least one member for each country; it proposes new laws and implements them.

- *The Council*: each country has one seat; this is the main decision-making body.

- *The Parliament*: in 2009, there were 736 MEPs; they are allocated proportionally to population.

- *The Court of Justice*: monitors the EU laws and watches member states' compliance.

- *The European Court of Human Rights*: established in 1959.

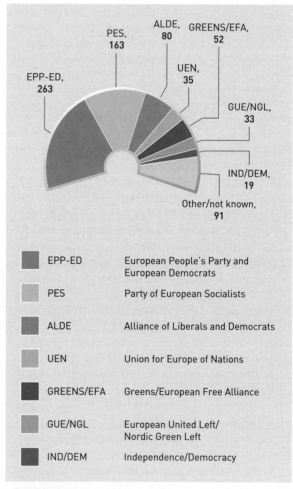

	EPP-ED	European People's Party and European Democrats
	PES	Party of European Socialists
	ALDE	Alliance of Liberals and Democrats
	UEN	Union for Europe of Nations
	GREENS/EFA	Greens/European Free Alliance
	GUE/NGL	European United Left/ Nordic Green Left
	IND/DEM	Independence/Democracy

Figure 16.1   Major political parties in the New European Parliament (Elected in June 2009)

Note: For a full breakdown of political parties, see www.parties-and-elections.de/eu.html.

Source: European Parliament Elections 2009, Research Paper 09/53, 17 June 2009, p. 25.

Table 16.3	Turnout in elections to the European Parliament, 1979 to 2009, by EU country

	1979	1981	1984	1987	1989	1994	1995	1996	1999	2004	2007	Prov. 2009
Belgium	91		92		91	91			91	91		86
Denmark	48		52		46	53			50	48		60
Germany	66		57		62	60			45	43		43
Ireland	64		48		68	44			50	59		55
France	61		57		49	53			47	43		40
Italy	86		82		81	74			70	72		66
Luxembourg	89		89		87	89			87	91		91
Netherlands	58		51		47	36			30	39		37
United Kingdom	32		33		36	36			24	39		35
Greece		81	81		80	73			70	63		52
Spain				69	55	59			63	45		44
Portugal				72	51	36			40	39		37
Sweden							42		39	38		44
Austria								68	49	42		42
Finland								58	30	39		40
Czech Rep										28		28
Estonia										27		43
Cyprus										73		59
Lithuania										48		21
Latvia										41		53
Hungary										39		36
Malta										82		79
Poland										21		27
Slovenia										28		28
Slovakia										17		20
Bulgaria											29	37
Romania											29	27
EU total	62		59		58	57			50	45		43

Source: European Parliament, www.elections2009-results.eu/_turnout_en.html. TNS opinion in conjunction with the European Parliament.

Note: In Belgium, Luxembourg, Cyprus and Malta voting is compulsory; this was also the case in Italy up to 1992.

Table 16.4	MEPs by country and political group 2009 (provisional)

*	EPP-ED	PES	ALDE	UEN	GRN/EFA	GUE/NGL	IND/DEM	Others	Total
Austria	6	5	0	0	1	0	0	5	17
Belgium	6	5	5	0	3	0	0	3	22
Bulgaria	6	4	5	0	0	0	0	2	17
Cyprus	2	1	0	0	0	2	0	1	6
Czech Rep	2	7	0	0	0	4	0	9	22
Denmark	1	4	3	2	2	1	0	0	13
Estonia	1	1	3	0	0	0	0	1	6
Finland	4	2	4	0	2	0	0	1	13
France	30	14	6	0	14	4	1	3	72
Germany	42	23	12	0	14	8	0	0	99
Greece	7	9	0	0	1	3	2	0	22

Table 16.4		continued							
*	EPP-ED	PES	ALDE	UEN	GRN/EFA	GUE/NGL	IND/DEM	Others	Total
Hungary	15	4	0	0	0	0	0	3	22
Ireland	4	2	1	3	0	1	1	0	12
Italy	34	0	7	9	0	0	0	22	72
Latvia	1	0	1	3	1	0	0	2	8
Lithuania	4	3	2	2	0	0	0	1	12
Luxembourg	3	1	1	0	1	0	0	0	6
Malta	2	3	0	0	0	0	0	0	5
Netherlands	5	3	6	0	3	2	2	4	25
Poland	28	7	0	15	0	0	0	0	50
Portugal	10	7	0	0	0	5	0	0	22
Romania	13	11	5	0	1	0	0	3	33
Slovakia	6	5	0	1	0	0	0	1	13
Slovenia	3	2	2	0	0	0	0	0	7
Spain	23	21	2	0	2	1	0	1	50
Sweden	5	5	4	0	2	1	0	1	18
United Kingdom	0	14	11	0	5	1	13	28	72
All MEPs	**263**	**163**	**80**	**35**	**52**	**33**	**19**	**91**	**736**

* For explanations of these headings, see p. 548.

Source: European Parliament, www.elections2009-results.eu/en/national_parties_en.html. TNS opinion in cooperation with the European Parliament.

Explaining power: the classic analysis of power in society

Sociologists and political scientists have long debated how formal power is distributed. Power is among the most difficult topics of scientific research because decision-making is complex and often occurs behind closed doors. It might be brutally visible in authoritarian societies, but in 'democratic' ones it is much harder to locate. From this mix of facts and values, three competing models of power have traditionally been discussed: the pluralist model, the power elite model and the ruling class (or Marxist) model (see Table 16.5).

The pluralist model

Formally, the **pluralist model** is *an analysis of politics that views power as dispersed among many competing interest groups*. This approach is closely tied to structural–functional theory. Pluralists claim, first, that politics is an arena of negotiation. With limited resources, no organisation can expect to realise all its goals. Organisations, therefore, operate as veto groups,

achieving some success but mostly keeping opponents from reaching all their goals. The political process, then, relies heavily on negotiating alliances and compromises that bridge differences among numerous interest groups and, in the process, produce policies that generate broad-based support. In short, pluralists believe that power is widely dispersed throughout society and that the political system takes account of all constituencies.

A second pluralist assertion holds that power has many sources, including wealth, political office, social prestige, personal charisma and organisational clout. Only in exceptional cases do all these sources of power fall into the same hands. Here, again, the conclusion is that power is widely diffused (Dahl, 1961, 1982).

Research results

Supporting the pluralist model, Nelson Polsby (1959) found that in New Haven, Connecticut, key decisions on various issues – including urban renewal, the nomination of political candidates and the operation of the schools – were made by different groups. Polsby also noted that few of the upper-class families listed in New Haven's Social Register were also economic leaders. Thus, Polsby concluded, no one segment of society rules all the others.

Robert Dahl (1961) investigated New Haven's history and found that, over time, power had become increasingly dispersed. Dahl echoed Polsby's judgements, concluding that 'no one, and certainly no group of more than a few individuals, is entirely lacking in [power]' (1961: 228).

The pluralist model implies that 'democracies' are indeed reasonably democratic! They grant at least some power to everyone. Pluralists assert that not even the most influential people always get their way, and even the most disadvantaged are able to band together to ensure that some of their political interests are addressed.

The power elite model

The **power elite model** is *an analysis of politics that views power as concentrated among the rich.* This second approach is closely allied with the social-conflict paradigm. The term 'power elite' is a lasting contribution of C. Wright Mills (1956), who argued that the upper class holds the bulk of society's wealth, prestige and power. The power elite constitutes the 'super-rich' or, in Marxist terms, the capitalists who own and control the lion's share of the economy. These families, broadly linked through business dealings as well as marriage, are able to turn the national agenda towards their own interests.

Mills, writing about the power elite in the United States, claimed that historically that country has been dominated by three major sectors – the economy, the government and the military. Elites circulate from one sector to another, consolidating their power as they go. Alexander Haig, for example, has held top positions in private business, served as White House chief of staff under Richard Nixon, was secretary of state under Ronald Reagan, made a bid for the White House in 1988 as a presidential candidate, and is a retired army general. Haig is far from the exception: a majority of national political leaders enter public life from powerful and highly paid positions – 10 of 13 members of the Clinton cabinet were reputed to be millionaires – and most return to the corporate world later on.

Power elite theorists challenge claims that the United States is a political democracy; the concentration of wealth and power, they maintain, is simply too great for the average person's voice to be heard. Rejecting pluralist assertions that various centres of power serve as checks and balances on one another, the power elite model contends that those at the top encounter no real opposition.

Research results

Over more than 60 years, social scientists have conducted research that helps to evaluate these opposing views of government. Supporting the power elite position, Robert and Helen Lynd (1937) studied Muncie, Indiana (which they called 'Middletown', to indicate that it was a typical city). They documented the fortune amassed by a single family – the Balls – from their business manufacturing glass canning jars and showed how the Ball family dominated many dimensions of the city's life. If anyone doubted the Balls' prominence, the Lynds explained, there was no need to look further than the local bank, a university, a hospital and a department store, which all bear the family name. In Muncie, according to the Lynds, the power elite more or less boiled down to a single family.

Floyd Hunter's (1963; orig. 1953) study of Atlanta, Georgia, provided further support for the power elite model. Atlanta, concluded Hunter, had no one dominant family, but there were no more than about 40 people who held all the top positions in the city's businesses and controlled the city's politics.

The ruling class: a Marxist model

For Marxists, political equality is 'one of the great myths of our time' (Miliband, 1969; Miliband and Panitch, 1993). Basically, the state always works in the interests of the dominant, ruling, economic class: it favours and supports 'capital'. Although there may be many different groupings – elected parliaments, judiciaries, local government, pressure groups – which create a semblance of balance, checks and equality, in practice they simply serve as masks for what is really happening. There have been many prominent sociologists who have adopted variants of this position. Three will be introduced here.

The Italian Marxist Antonio Gramsci (1891–1937) was a leader in the Italian Communist Party. Imprisoned from 1926 till his death by Mussolini's fascist government, his theory appears in his *Prison Notebooks*. For Gramsci, 'the state = political society + civil society'. The ruling class must gain the consent of the working class. No government can rule by force alone for long. He called this process **hegemony**, *the means by which a ruling/dominant group wins over a subordinated group through ideas.* To make hegemony work, dominated groups have to be taken into consideration, their interests noted and concessions given to them. Because dominated groups are always

Table 16.5	Three models of contemporary politics and society		
	Pluralist	**Power elite**	**Ruling class**
Distribution of power	Highly dispersed	Concentrated	Concentrated
Is it democratic?	Yes: every vote counts; no one group dominates	No: a small share of people dominate economy, armed services and government	No: concentration of wealth and power
Voter apathy	Some people are just not interested, but all could have a voice	How can ordinary folk stop 'big government'? Apathy is perfectly understandable	Apathy is alienation. Most people are powerless

partially aware of their subordinated position, these concessions become vital to the smooth working of the state (Gramsci, 1971).

Ralph Miliband (1969) provided a lot of detail about the social background of cabinet ministers, senior police, top judges and the like, showing how they act in the interests of capital. Either these people occupy elite positions in the bourgeoisie, or through education and culture they have come to identify with this group. Much work of the media disguises the real nature of the power, providing a process of legitimation.

Nicos Poulantzas (1969) adopts a wider (and much more abstract) approach. Individual politicians are not of interest to him. Instead, he looks at the state as part of a society, independent of people. It, so to speak, rolls on all on its own. The ruling class does not govern directly, but its interests are served through the autonomous functioning of a state which rises above sectional interests and maintains a myth of public interests and national unity. For Poulantzas, the state works through a repressive apparatus – army, police, etc. – using coercive power, and an ideological apparatus – church, schools, media and family – which 'manipulates' values and beliefs. Poulantzas's theory is very abstract, and indeed he has been criticised for being too general and for seeing too little role (or indeed no role!) for people to play in shaping their own lives. More than this: he does not provide any evidence for his theories, and some have argued that the theory is impossible to prove or disprove.

Who rules Britain?

John Scott has studied the power structures in the UK, asking: who rules Britain? He suggests that 'there is in

Britain today a ruling class' (1991: 4). While there is an economically dominant class at the top of the class structure, there is also a series of overlapping status circles at the top. Here there are strong alignments between educational backgrounds: 'private schooling remained the most important route to political success' (1991: 134). He suggests that Britain is run by an 'inner circle' of finance capitalists who represent a 'city' point of view. They fuse banking and industry, and play a key role in articulating capitalist industries within the power elite (Scott, 1991: 150–1; and see Chapter 10).

Power beyond the rules

Politics is always a matter of disagreement about goals and the means to achieve them. Yet a political system tries to resolve controversy *within* a system of rules. The most heated debates in the European Union today surround efforts to harmonise these rules across the many disparate countries. But political activity often exceeds – or tries to do away with – established practices. It goes beyond the accepted rules. Here we look at six ways this happens.

1 Revolution

Political revolution is *the overthrow of one political system in order to establish another*. In contrast to reform, which involves change within a system and rarely escalates into violence, revolution implies change of the system itself, sometimes sparking violent action.

No type of political system is immune to revolution; nor does revolution invariably produce any one kind of government. Colonial rule by the British monarchy in the United States was overthrown by the revolutionary war. The French revolutionaries in 1789 also overthrew a monarch, only to set the stage for the return of monarchy in the person of Napoleon. In 1917, the Russian Revolution replaced monarchy with a socialist government built on the ideas of Karl Marx (overturned, again, in 1992).

Despite their striking variety, revolutions share a number of traits, according to political analysts (de Tocqueville, 1955, orig. 1856; also Brinton, 1965; Skocpol, 1979):

1 *Rising expectations.* Although common sense would dictate that revolution is more likely when people are grossly deprived, history shows that revolution generally occurs when people's lives are improving. Rising expectations, rather than bitter resignation, fuel revolutionary fervour.

2 *Unresponsive government.* Revolutionary zeal gains strength to the extent that a government is unwilling or unable to reform, especially when demands for change are made by large numbers of people or powerful segments of society.

3 *Radical leadership by intellectuals.* The English philosopher Thomas Hobbes (1588–1679) observed that political rebellion is often centred in universities. During the 1960s, throughout Europe

Violence beyond the rules: a report from the former Yugoslavia

The conflicts and wars within and around Yugoslavia during the 1990s have led to a number of new, highly unstable mini-states and groupings. We have already seen what this has meant in Bosnia (see pp. 347, 349 and 367–8). In many ways the extent of destruction and displacement of peoples reached catastrophic levels during this period. This is a deeply troubled region, and Serbs, Croats and Muslims have all committed war crimes – tens of thousands of deaths, rapes and serious injuries, plus an incalculable loss of property.

War is violent, but it also has rules. Many of the current norms of warfare emerged from the ashes of the Second World War, when German and Japanese military officials were brought to trial for war crimes. Subsequently, the United Nations has added to the broad principles of fair play in war that have become known as the 'Geneva Conventions' (the first of which dates back to 1864). One of the most important principles of the rules of war is that, whatever violence soldiers inflict upon each other, they cannot imprison, torture, rape or murder civilians; nor can they deliberately destroy civilian property or wantonly bomb or shell cities to foster widespread terror. Even so, a growing body of evidence reveals that all these crimes have occurred as part of the protracted and bloody civil war in the former Yugoslavia. And they have gone 'beyond the rules'.

The United Nations and the future of interventions

Late in 1993, therefore, a United Nations tribunal convened in the Netherlands to assess the evidence and consider possible responses. After the Second World War, the Allies successfully prosecuted (and, in several cases, executed) German officers for their crimes against humanity based on evidence culled from extensive Nazi records. This time, however, the task of punishing offenders proved to be far more difficult. For one thing, there appeared to be no written records of the Balkan conflict; for another, United Nations officials feared that arrests might upset the delicate diplomatic efforts at bringing peace to the region.

Even so, since beginning their investigations in 1993, the United Nations has indicted more than 50 military officers on all sides of the conflict for war crimes. And in 2000, the former Yugoslavian president Slobodan Milosevic was arrested, and charged at the International Tribunal in The Hague with atrocities committed by troops under his command in Kosovo, and by others that linked him with atrocities in the Croatian War of 1991, and the Bosnian conflict of 1992–5. Milosevic conducted his own defence in the five-year-long trial, which ended without a verdict when Milosevic died on 11 March 2006 in the War Criminal Prison in The Hague.

Many observers suspect that – despite a staggering toll in civilian deaths – very few of those responsible will ever be convicted.

Source: Adapted from Nelan (1993) and various news reports.

and the United States, students were at the forefront of much of the political unrest that marked that tumultuous decade. Students also played a key role in China's pro-democracy movement, as they did in the toppling of socialist governments in eastern Europe.

4 *Establishing a new legitimacy*. The overthrow of a political system rarely comes easily, but it is more difficult still to ensure a revolution's long-term success. Some revolutionary drives are unified merely by hatred of the past regime and fall victim to internal division once new leaders are installed. Revolutionary movements must also guard against counter-revolutionary drives spearheaded by past leaders; frequently, revolutionaries ruthlessly dispose of these former leaders.

2 'Terrorism'

Terrorism, *violence or the threat of violence employed by an individual or a group as a political strategy*, is nothing new. But since the suicide bombings of the World Trade Center in New York and the Pentagon in Washington on 11 September 2001, terrorism has taken centre stage in international politics. The United States government, led by President Bush, declared 'war' on all forms of terrorism and in October 2001 started its major mission in bombing the Taliban regime in Afghanistan, which was suspected of protecting the prime terrorist organisation, al Qaeda, and the prime suspect, Osama bin Laden. This 'war' was followed by the invasion of Iraq in March 2003. A sense of perpetual conflict, wars and 'terrorism' has defined the first decade of the twenty-first century. It has led to heated discussion as to what is and what is not terrorism – along with growing concerns over new biological weapons of terrorism (such as anthrax) and the threat of attack on nuclear installations.

Like revolution, terrorism is a political act beyond the rules of established political systems. Paul Johnson (1981) offers four insights about terrorism. First, explains Johnson, terrorists try to cast violence as a legitimate political tactic, even though virtually every society condemns such acts. Terrorists also bypass (or are excluded from) established channels of political negotiation. Terror is thus a weak organisation's strategy to harm a stronger foe. For example, the

Wanted by Interpol
BIN LADEN, Usama

Pictures of Saudi-born Osama bin Laden are posted on Interpol's wanted list, 15 September 2001. He was the presumed architect of the suicide bombings of 11 September 2001 and became 'the world's most wanted man'. He was killed by American forces on 2 May 2011, aged 54. He was 'hiding' in Pakistan

Source: © Reuters/Corbis.

Terrorist suicide bombings, New York City, 11 September 2001
Source: © David Turnley/Corbis.

people who held Western hostages in the Middle East until 1991 may have been morally wrong to do so, but they succeeded in directing the world's attention to that region of the globe.

Second, Johnson continues, terrorism is a tactic employed not only by groups but also by governments against their own people. **State terrorism** refers to *the use of violence, generally without the support of law, against individuals or groups by a government or its agents.* While contrary to democratic political principles, state terrorism figures prominently in authoritarian and totalitarian societies, which survive by inciting fear and intimidation. From the left-wing regimes in North Korea and the former Soviet Union to the extreme right-wing regimes in Nazi Germany and Zaïre, states have routinely employed terror against their own citizens. More recently, Saddam Hussein has ruled Iraq in the same manner.

Third, although democratic societies reject terrorism in principle, democracies are especially vulnerable to terrorists because they afford extensive civil liberties to their people and have minimal police networks. This susceptibility helps to explain the tendency of democratic governments to suspend civil liberties if officials perceive themselves to be under attack. Hostage taking and outright killing provoke widespread anger, but devising an effective response to such acts poses several thorny problems. Because most terrorist groups are shadowy organisations with no formal connection to any established state, targeting reprisals may be impossible. Yet the failure to respond can encourage other terrorist groups. Then, too, a forcible military reaction to terrorism may broaden the scope of violence, increasing the risk of confrontation with other governments.

Finally, terrorism is always a matter of definition. Governments claim the right to maintain order, even by force, and may brand opponents who use violence as 'terrorists'. Similarly, political differences may explain why one person's 'terrorist' is another's 'freedom fighter'.

Old and new terrorism

We can make a distinction between old and new styles of terrorism. In the past, terrorism was linked to nationalism and the struggles over national boundaries. It is usually focused on its enemies and their destabilisation or destruction. It is fairly local.

By contrast, new-style terrorism is enhanced by the new information technology. It is much more dispersed, more global, and much less formally structured. A famous example would be the fundamentalist al Qaeda. Their object of attack is 'the world' – or 'the West'. It aims to rescue the world from the decadence of the West – its modernism – and to reconstruct it in the sight of Allah. It was created in 1989 through Osama bin Laden and others in Afghanistan. It is now said to operate in 40 to 50 countries across the world.

The new terrorism is seen to have emerged largely since 11 September 2001, and can be characterised by four key features:

1 *Organisational decentralisation.* Terrorist organisations no longer organise themelves in pyramidic, hierarchical structures. They are much more likely to take the form of loose clusterings organised through chains, hub-and-spoke networks, or a series of contact points.

2 *Operational asymmetry.* The acts of violence become unanticipated and unconventional. Objects are attacked which may, on the surface, seem to have little relevance, and attacks may happen quite unpredictably.

3 *Religious centrality.* Struggles are seen as between forces of good and evil, with religious belief and religious extremism as a core motivating factor.

4 *Weapons of mass destruction.* The stakes are raised with the new terrorism: high-yield weapons come to be employed and deaths can potentially be catastrophically large. These weapons include biological, chemical, radiological and nuclear agents (Martin, 2004).

3 Corruption and state crimes

Corruption and state crimes range from the relatively mild to the extreme and cover a wide range of abuses and crimes costing trillions of pounds. Included here are bribery, nepotism, patronage, embezzlement and cronyism. In the UK, there has been a long history of parliamentary scandals and corruption: in 2009 there was a prolonged scandal over multiple abuses by MPs which related to costs of maintaining two residences, one in the constituency and one in London. They

included renting second homes, overclaiming for tax, evading tax, claiming expenses they were not entitled to, subsidising the property balance and more generally overclaiming for food, travel and all kinds of purchases. In many countries, corruption goes much further than this and includes state involvement in organised and corporate crime, avoidable 'natural' disasters, facilitating criminal enterprises such as drug trafficking, money laundering, human trafficking, torture, criminal policing, war crimes and genocide.

Corrupt governments have enriched themselves in many ways, such as by plundering natural resources (oil and mineral) or foreign aid, which can be spent on armaments or material rewards (from extravagant buildings to clothes). A corrupt dictatorship is the extreme case: and often results in decades of suffering for the vast majority of its citizens. A classic case of a corrupt, exploitive dictator is Marshal Mobutu Sese Seko, who ruled the Democratic Republic of the Congo (which he renamed Zaire) from 1965 to 1997. Another classic case is Nigeria, especially under the rule of General Sani Abacha, who was *de facto* president from 1993 until his death in 1998. He is reputed to have stolen some US$3–4 billion.

Transparency International (TI) is an international non-governmental organisation which aims to raise public awareness in part through the annual construction of a Corruption Perceptions Index. The boxes show the top ten least and most corrupt governments in 2010. To form this index, TI compiles surveys that ask business people and analysts, both in and outside the countries they are analysing, their

---

TOP 10

Least corrupt countries

Highest score is least corrupt

1	Denmark	9.3
1	New Zealand	9.3
1	Singapore	9.3
4	Finland	9.2
4	Sweden	9.2
6	Canada	8.9
7	Netherlands	8.8
8	Australia	8.7
8	Switzerland	8.7
10	Norway	8.6

Source: Reprinted from Corruption Perceptions Index 2010. Transparency International's Corruption Perception Index measures the perceived levels of Public Sector Corruption in 178 Countries around the word.

TOP 10
Most corrupt countries

Lowest score is most corrupt

1	Somalia	1.1
2	Myanmar	1.4
2	Afghanistan	1.4
4	Iraq	1.5
5	Uzbekistan	1.6
5	Turkmenistan	1.6
5	Sudan	1.6
8	Chad	1.7
9	Burundi	1.8
10	Equatorial Gurinea	1.9

Source: Reprinted from Corruption Perceptions Index 2010. Transparency International's Corruption Perception Index measures the perceived levels of Public Sector Corruption in 178 Countries around the word.

perceptions of how corrupt a country is. Since so much corruption is hidden, the CPI has been criticised as potentially very unreliable.

A total of 178 countries are ranked in this survey on a scale from 10 to 0 with New Zealand best at 9.3 and Somalia worst at 1.1. Hong Kong is ranked 13th, the UK 20th, the USA 22nd, Poland 41st, South Africa 54th, Brazil 69th, Syria 127th, Uganda 127th, Pakistan 143rd and Russia 154th. For the full results see: www.transparency.org/policy_research/surveys_indices/cpi/2010.

4 War

Perhaps the most critical political issue is war. War is as old as humanity. In recorded history, since 3600 BCE, it has been estimated that some 14,500 major wars have been waged, killing some 4 billion people.

WORLD WATCH

War and peace: a militarised world

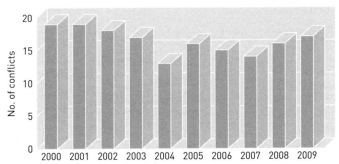

Major armed conflicts, 2000–9

Nuclear warheads (estimates), 2010

Country	Deployed warheads	Total warheads
USA	2,468	9,600
Russia	4,630	12,000
United Kingdom	160	225
France	300	300
China	nk	240
India	nk	60 to 80
Pakistan	nk	70 to 90
Israel	nk	80
Total	7,560	22,600

WORLD WATCH

The most and least peaceful states: Global Peace Index 2010

The most peaceful countries			The least peaceful countries		
Rank	Country	Score	Rank	Country	Score
1	New Zealand	1.188	145	Pakistan	3.050
2	Iceland	1.212	146	Sudan	3.125
3	Japan	1.247	147	Afghanistan	3.252
4	Austria	1.290	148	Somalia	3.390
5	Norway	1.322	149	Iraq	3.406

The five top arms-producing companies in the world, excluding China, 2008

Rank	Company	Country	Arms sales in US$
1	BAE Systems	UK	32,420
2	Lockheed Martin	USA	29,880
3	Boeing	USA	29,200
4	Northrop Grumman	USA	26,090
5	General Dynamics	USA	22,780

Source: Stockholm International Peace Research Institute, *SIPRI Yearbook 2010: Armaments, Disarmament and International Security* (Oxford University Press: Oxford 2010), Figure 2A.1, Table 8.1, Table 28.1, Table 6A.1.

In the twentieth century alone, it has been estimated that well over 100 million people died as a result of war. Many people think of war as extraordinary, yet it is periods of peace that are actually rare (*New Internationalist*, 1999: 18; Roxborough, 2004).

Mary Kaldor (2007), Martin Shaw (2003) and others have distinguished between different types of war throughout history. In the past, wars were usually waged with mercenary or conscript armies using weapons from swords to (more recently) firearms. Many of the twentieth-century wars were not like this. Funded on a large scale through the mobilisation of the whole economy, mass armies deployed massive firepower, tanks and aircraft. The two world wars of the twentieth century were sites of major destruction, including the dropping of the atomic bombs on Nagasaki and Hiroshima. A key feature of late-twentieth-century warfare, then, was the potential destructiveness of today's nuclear arsenals and the ways in which more and more civilians come to be killed. Table 16.6 suggests ways in which these 'old wars' evolved.

At present over 30 wars are being waged across the earth with millions of casualties. Most of these armed conflicts of recent times tend to take place within states rather than between them. The Bosnia–Herzegovina war described at the start of Chapter 11 is a major example of what have been called 'new wars'. They are mixtures of war, organised crime and mass violations of human rights with civilian deaths, and do not follow any obvious rules of modern warfare. Indeed, they seem almost anarchic – attacking people and property at local, private levels. Rape and genocide are commonplace. Mary Kaldor argues that these new wars require international intervention and regulations for their resolution, which she calls a 'cosmopolitan approach' (Kaldor, 2007). Martin Shaw sees them as **degenerate wars**, whereby there is '*a deliberate and systematic extension of war against an organized armed enemy to war against a largely unarmed civilian population*' (Shaw, 2003: 5). Such is typical of more and more modern wars.

The costs of war

The costs of armed conflicts extend far beyond battlefield casualties. Together, the world's nations spend some £3.5 trillion annually for military

Table 16.6	The evolution of 'old wars'			
	17th and 18th centuries	**19th century**	**Early 20th century**	**Late 20th century**
Type of polity	Absolutist state	Nation-state	Coalitions of states; multinational states; empires	Blocs
Goals of war	Reasons of state; dynastic conflict; consolidation of borders	National conflict	National and ideological conflict	Ideological conflict
Type of army	Mercenary/professional	Professional/conscription	Mass armies	Scientific–military elite/ professional armies
Military technique	Use of firearms, defensive manoeuvres, sieges	Railways and telegraph, rapid mobilisation	Massive firepower; tanks and aircraft	Nuclear weapons
War economy	Regularisation of taxation and borrowing	Expansion of administration and bureaucracy	Mobilisation economy	Military–industrial complex

Source: Based on Kaldor (2006).

U.S. soldiers carry the body of an American soldier, who was killed in a roadside bomb attack in Afghanistan's Kandahar province, to a medical evacuation helicopter. Pararescuemen and pilots from the 46th and 26th Expeditionary Rescue Squadrons responded to the attack which killed two American soldiers and wounded three others
Source: AP Photo/David Guttenfelder.

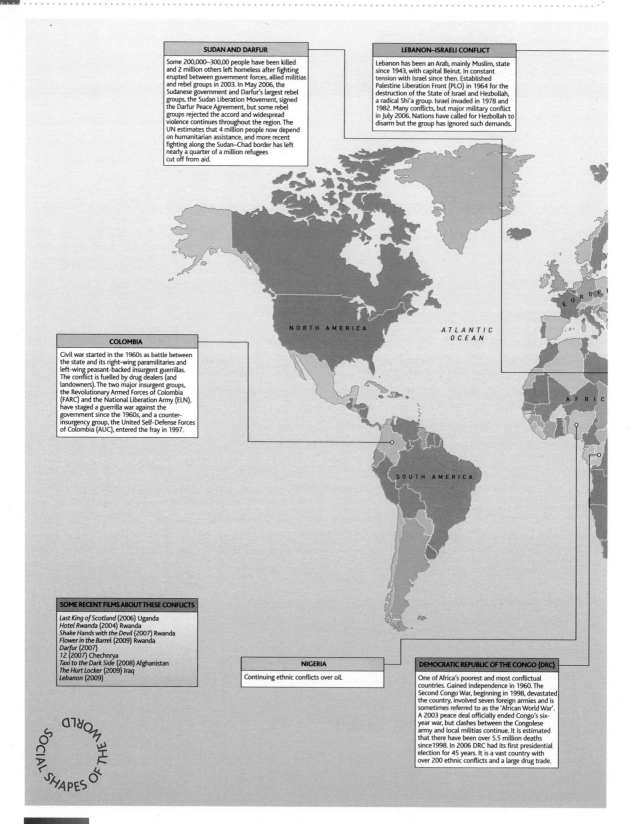

SUDAN AND DARFUR

Some 200,000–300,00 people have been killed and 2 million others left homeless after fighting erupted between government forces, allied militias and rebel groups in 2003. In May 2006, the Sudanese government and Darfur's largest rebel groups, the Sudan Liberation Movement, signed the Darfur Peace Agreement, but some rebel groups rejected the accord and widespread violence continues throughout the region. The UN estimates that 4 million people now depend on humanitarian assistance, and more recent fighting along the Sudan–Chad border has left nearly a quarter of a million refugees cut off from aid.

LEBANON–ISRAELI CONFLICT

Lebanon has been an Arab, mainly Muslim, state since 1943, with capital Beirut. In constant tension with Israel since then. Established Palestine Liberation Front (PLO) in 1964 for the destruction of the State of Israel and Hezbollah, a radical Shi'a group. Israel invaded in 1978 and 1982. Many conflicts, but major military conflict in July 2006. Nations have called for Hezbollah to disarm but the group has ignored such demands.

COLOMBIA

Civil war started in the 1960s as battle between the state and its right-wing paramilitaries and left-wing peasant-backed insurgent guerrillas. The conflict is fuelled by drug dealers (and landowners). The two major insurgent groups, the Revolutionary Armed Forces of Colombia (FARC) and the National Liberation Army (ELN), have staged a guerrilla war against the government since the 1960s, and a counter-insurgency group, the United Self-Defense Forces of Colombia (AUC), entered the fray in 1997.

SOME RECENT FILMS ABOUT THESE CONFLICTS

Last King of Scotland (2006) Uganda
Hotel Rwanda (2004) Rwanda
Shake Hands with the Devil (2007) Rwanda
Flower in the Barrel (2009) Rwanda
Darfur (2007)
12 (2007) Chechnrya
Taxi to the Dark Side (2008) Afghanistan
The Hurt Locker (2009) Iraq
Lebanon (2009)

NIGERIA

Continuing ethnic conflicts over oil.

DEMOCRATIC REPUBLIC OF THE CONGO (DRC)

One of Africa's poorest and most conflictual countries. Gained independence in 1960. The Second Congo War, beginning in 1998, devastated the country, involved seven foreign armies and is sometimes referred to as the 'African World War'. A 2003 peace deal officially ended Congo's six-year war, but clashes between the Congolese army and local militias continue. It is estimated that there have been over 5.5 million deaths since1998. In 2006 DRC had its first presidential election for 45 years. It is a vast country with over 200 ethnic conflicts and a large drug trade.

SOCIAL SHAPES OF THE WORLD

Map 16.2   'Troublespots': some world conflicts in focus

CHECHNYA

Became independent from Russia in 1991. Russia has invaded twice, recapturing the would-be breakaway republic at a cost of approximately 500,000 lives, mostly Chechen civilians. The second Russian offensive in 1999 installed a Moscow-friendly government and was a serious blow to the Chechan independence movement. Counterattacks took place at the Dubrovk Moscow Theatre in 2002, with 850 people held hostage (and 52 people killed) and the Beslan School Siege (2004), where 344 civilians were killed, of whom 186 were children.

GAZA AND PALESTINE: ISRAELI–ARAB CONFLICTS

Zionists settled in Israel in the 1880s, and after the Second World War there was mass migration (the Exodus) by Jews to the Jerusalem area. Two states in Palestine – one Jewish, one Arab – were enforced by the United Nations in 1947. Continuing tension between Arabs and Jews since then. Conflicts include Israeli-Arab wars of 1949-9, Suez (1956) and the Six Day War of 1967. Rarely out of the news as a major world troublespot, most recently with its 2006 conflict with Lebanon and the bombarding of HAMAS (Islamic resistance movement) in December 2008. 1.5 million people are packed into Gaza, many of whom have been killed.

AFGHANISTAN

Following the 11 September 2001 attacks, the USA conducted a military campaign to destroy the al Qaeda terrorist network and overthrow the Taliban government that protected it. NATO forces now occupying the country continue to face a determined Taliban insurgency. But there is continuing internal conflict between the Pashtuns of the south and the Kabul regime, which is controlled by the northern Tajiks, Uzbeks and Hazara. By mid-2010, it is estimated that well over 10,000 civilians had been killed along with 2,000 members of the armed forces. A gradual withdrawal of US and UK forces is planned.

KASHMIR

Ongoing conflict over disputed territory between India and Pakistan.

GULF/IRAQ WARS

20th March 2003: US missile attacks on Iraq (Baghdad) mark start of armed hostilities (but a long history of US military intervention before).

SRI LANKA AND THE TAMIL TIGERS

The Liberation Tigers of Tamil Eelam (LTTE), also known as the Tamil Tigers, have waged a violent secessionist campaign against the Sri Lankan government since 1970, a fight that has claimed more than 65,000 lives. The LTTE seeks independence for the northeast region of the island, the traditional home of the Tamil ethnic group. A 2002 Norwegian-brokered ceasefire is officially still in place, but international monitoring groups say it only exists on paper; the two sides have violated the agreement more than 3,000 times, but 2006 was a relatively peaceful year, at least as far as civilian casualties went.

RWANDA

Conflicts between the Tutsi tribe and the Hutu go back to the 16th century. In 1959, a Hutu revolt led to overthrow of Tutsi rule. Independence in 1962, followed by rebellions and coups. In 1944 inter-ethnic violence escalated, with an estimated 800,000 Tutsis slaughtered in ten days (10% of the population).

SOMALIA–ETHIOPIA

A long-running civil war since 1988 in which 300,000 have died. UN and US troops have been involved. Recent developments risk the war moving into neighbouring Eritrea.

MIDDLE EAST AND NORTH AFRICA UPRISINGS

In early 2011, many internal rebellions started against long-standing dominant (largely authoritarian) regimes in Arab countries of the Middle East including Egypt, Syria, Libya, Tunisia and Bahrain. In March, the UN intervened in Libya as violence escalated.

UGANDA

Former British colony gained independence in 1962. Coup led by General Odi Amin Dada in 1971 and decades-long civil war. Over 1.4 million Ugandans were uprooted in an insurgency dating back to 1987 (see the film *The Last King of Scotland*).

RUSSIA

CHINA

ARABIA

INDIA

PACIFIC OCEAN

INDONESIA

AUSTRALIA

purposes. Such expenditures, of course, divert resources from the desperate struggle for survival by millions of poor people throughout the world. Moreover, a large proportion of the world's top scientists concentrate on military research; this resource, too, is siphoned away from other work that might benefit humanity.

In recent years, defence has been the largest single expenditure of most governments. The average proportion of GDP that the world spends on defence is around 3 per cent, but many countries spend more than that. In the United States, for example, defence accounts for 18 per cent of all federal spending. By September 2010, the Iraq War was estimated to have cost $900 billion.

The United States became a superpower as it emerged victorious from the Second World War with newly developed nuclear weapons. The atomic bomb was first used in war by US forces to crush Japan in 1945. But the Soviet Union countered by exploding a nuclear bomb of its own in 1949, unleashing the 'Cold War', by which leaders of each superpower became convinced that their counterparts were committed to military superiority. Ironically, for the next 40 years, both sides pursued a policy of escalating military expenditures that neither nation wanted or could afford.

With the collapse of the Soviet Union in 1991, much of the Cold War dissipated. Even so, before the Iraq conflict started, US military expenditure remained high. Some analysts have argued that, all along, the US economy has relied on militarism to generate corporate profits (Marullo, 1987). This approach, closely allied to power elite theory, maintains that the United States is dominated by a **military–industrial complex**, *the close association among the federal government, the military and defence industries.* The roots of militarism, then, lie not just in external threats to US security; they also grow from within the institutional structures of US society.

But another reason for persistent militarism in the post-Cold War world is regional conflict. Since the collapse of the Soviet Union, for example, localised wars have broken out in Bosnia, Chechnya and Rwanda, and tensions still run high in a host of other countries, including Iraq and a divided Korea. Even wars of limited scope have the potential to escalate, involving other countries, and the danger of regional conflicts is growing as more and more nations gain access to nuclear weapons. The main cost, though, at the present time focuses on Iraq.

5 Nuclear weapons

Despite the easing of superpower tensions, the world still contains almost 25,000 nuclear warheads perched on missiles or ready to be carried by aircraft. This arsenal represents destructive power that one can barely imagine: five tons of TNT for every person on the planet. Should even a small fraction of this stockpile be detonated in war, life as we know it would cease on much of the earth. Albert Einstein, whose genius contributed to the development of nuclear weapons, reflected: 'The unleashed power of the atom has changed everything save our modes of thinking, and we thus drift toward unparalleled catastrophe.' In short, nuclear weapons have rendered unrestrained war unthinkable in a world not yet capable of peace.

At present, although the UK, France and China all have substantial nuclear capability, the vast majority of nuclear weapons are based in the United States and the Russian Federation. Other countries – Israel, India, Pakistan, North Korea – also possess some nuclear weapons, while others (including Iran) may be in the process of developing them. Some nations have stopped the development of such weapons, including Argentina, Brazil and South Africa (Shaw, 2003; Roxborough, 2004; see also Chapter 23).

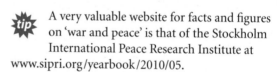 A very valuable website for facts and figures on 'war and peace' is that of the Stockholm International Peace Research Institute at www.sipri.org/yearbook/2010/05.

6 Information warfare

As earlier chapters have explained, the Information Revolution is changing almost every dimension of social life. Currently, military strategists envisage future conflict played out not with rumbling tanks and screaming aircraft but with electronic 'smart bombs' that would greatly reduce an enemy country's ability to transmit information. In such 'virtual wars', soldiers seated at workstation monitors would dispatch computer viruses to shut down an aggressor's communication lines, causing telephones to fall silent, air traffic control and railway switching systems to fail, computer systems to feed phoney orders to field officers, and televisions to broadcast 'morphed' news bulletins, prompting people to turn against their leaders.

Like the venom of a poisonous snake, the weapons of 'information warfare' can quickly paralyse an adversary, perhaps triggering a conventional military engagement. Another, more hopeful, possibility is that new information technology might not just precede conventional fighting but prevent it entirely. Yet so-called 'infowar' also poses new dangers, since, presumably, a few highly skilled operators with sophisticated electronic equipment could also wreak havoc on communications in Europe and the rest of the world.

New politics: the rise of social movements

Politics is always on the move: things change. At the start of the twenty-first century, it is often claimed that a new politics is in the making. There are many signs of this: the partial break-up of nation-states, globalised politics, the creation of major new political units such as the European Union, the arrival of 'new wars', and, as the *Big debate* at the end of the chapter suggests, the collapse of traditional divides between left and right. In addition, we could consider the seeming growth of political apathy and voter discontent; the embracing by some of what has been called 'post-materialist values'; and the potential for digital democracies, whereby voting systems are modified through the widespread use of computers. Some sociologists, such as Ulrich Beck, now believe we have entered a period of *sub-politics*, where the world of major political institutions built up in modernity is increasingly under question through a politics that takes place in everyday life. Formal politics becomes less and less effective as sub-politics develops (Beck, 1997). One feature of this may be the rise and proliferation of new social movements (NSMs), which, while having a long history, are far more common today than in the past and take on a different form.

Development of social movements

Mass mobilisation and social movements began to take shape in Western countries during the later eighteenth century – symbolised massively by the French Revolution. During the nineteenth century a durable set of elements started to appear that spread across the world (through colonisation, migration and trade), whereby more and more groups and populations engaged in new forms of political action. Charles Tilley (1929–2008) was a sociologist who spent much of his life showing the rise of social movements in parallel with the development of the ballot box. In his book *Social Movements 1768–2004* (Tilley, 2004), he suggests that these new social movements combine three things:

1 They develop public campaigns, getting organised to make collective claims on targeted audiences.

2 They combine whole repertoires of political actions, ranging from public meetings, processions and rallies through to demonstrations, petitions and the creation of special purpose associations.

3 And ultimately they display and present themselves to the public as good causes and worthy people. They are united, with large numbers of committed supporters.

Social movements have perhaps become the key feature of modern political life. What is interesting to note about them is that not only do they provide the momentum for political change, they also provide a sense of meaning in life. Very often people build their sense of who they are (their identities) from these very movements. Identity has become a basis for social action and change. The list of such organisational movements and identities is very long and very

The new social movements

The importance of NSMs is marked at the start of the twenty-first century. During the course of this book, we look at a number of them. For starting points, see:

- the women's movement: Chapter 12

- the gay and lesbian movement: Chapter 12
- the AIDS movement: Chapter 21
- the green movement: Chapter 25
- ethnic movements: Chapter 11
- the elderly movement: Chapter 13
- the disability movement: Chapter 13

- religious movements: Chapter 19
- the anti-capitalist movement: the opening to this chapter
- the human rights movement.

They all have websites. Search for them all through 'Social Movements and Culture', www.wsu.edu/-amerstu/smc/gay.htm.html.

striking. Amongst them are the women's movement, gay, lesbian, bisexual and transgender (LGBT) movements, environmental movements, student movements, anti-globalisation movements, the 'right to life' movement, the animal rights movement, the Landless People's Movement, the indigenous people's movements, the human rights and civil rights movements, the disability movement, the AIDS movement, and rights of all kinds. All these have been studied by sociologists and often made central to a grasp of contemporary political life.

Stages of social movements

Researchers have identified four phases in the life of the typical social movement (shown in Figure 16.2): emergence, coalescence, bureaucratisation and decline (Blumer, 1969; Mauss, 1975). In Stage 1, emergence, social movements build on the perception that all is not well. Some, such as the gay and lesbian rights movement and the women's movement, are born of widespread dissatisfaction. Others emerge only as a small vanguard group, which increases public awareness of some issue.

By the second stage, coalescence, the movement must define itself and develop a strategy for 'going public'. Leaders must determine policies, decide on tactics, build morale and recruit new members. At this stage, the movement may engage in collective action such as rallies or demonstrations to attract media attention in the hope of capturing public notice. Additionally, the movement may form alliances with other organisations to gain necessary resources.

To become an established political force, a social movement must bureaucratise: that is, develop formal structures (Stage 3). As procedures become formal, the movement depends less on the charisma and talents of a few leaders and relies more on a capable staff. Social movements which avoid this stage, such as the campaigns organised to produce legislation against 'dangerous dogs' and handgun ownership in Britain, have short lives, fading when leaders lose energy or even die. Bureaucratisation can also weaken a movement by blunting the radical and innovative edge. On the other hand, the well-established Greenpeace, despite its changing leadership, offers a steady voice on behalf of environmentalists.

Social movements are inherently dynamic, so a decline (Stage 4) need not signal a demise. Eventually, however, most social movements do wither. This may occur when members achieve their primary goals, or because of organisational factors, such as poor leadership or exhaustion of resources, or because hostile public or governmental reaction (sometimes literally) beats activists into submission. 'Selling out' is another possible outcome, when organisational leaders may use their positions to enrich themselves.

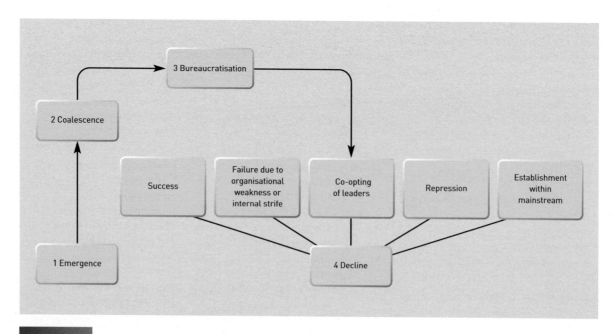

Figure 16.2   Stages in the life of social movements

New social movements and new politics

Alan Touraine, Alberto Melucci, Klauss Offe and others suggest that the new post-industrial or information societies are fostering a growing awareness of differences through subcultures and counter-cultures, and that these are generating new social movements around a wide range of public issues. In recent decades, for example, gays, lesbians, bisexuals and transgendered people have organised to combat oppression and discrimination. A green movement has emerged to challenge environmental destruction. Disability alliances have been formed to champion the rights of the disabled. There has been a powerful women's movement, a men's movement, an age-activist movement, AIDS and various health movements. More recently, as the opening story told, there has been a worldwide anti-capitalist movement bridging many different groups, from respectable lobbying groups to out-and-out anarchists. Like any social movement that challenges convention, they often spark counter-movements as others try to block their goals. In contemporary societies, almost every significant public issue gives rise to both a social movement favouring change and an opposing counter-movement to resist change and reinforce the status quo.

Although social movements have been around for a long time, the so-called 'new social movements' generally broaden the range of what is considered political. They are much less concerned with the traditional issues of politics such as class and work (and the old trade unions and class movements). Their membership tends to be younger. Organisationally, they tend to be much more informal, more fragmented, less hierarchical, with little interest in formal power. They employ a wider range of tactics for change – often illegal and direct. They do not usually pursue mainstream or conventional values, but are part of what we have already noted as 'post-materialist values' where the issue is much more the quality of life (see Chapter 5 on post-materialist cultural values). They are part of what Giddens has called the new politics of lifestyles (1990: 158).

Today's most notable social movements are concerned with global ecology, the social standing of women and gays, reducing the risks of war, animal rights, and the rejection of a worldwide global capitalism. One feature of these movements is their national and international scope. The power of the state continues to expand in post-industrial societies. Not surprisingly, then, as global political connections multiply, social movements respond by becoming international in scope. One clear strength of NSMs is their growing recognition of the global scale of response needed to deal with the development of a global economic and political system, and to spotlight the power of the mass media to unite people around the world in pursuit of political goals.

A million women rise, protest and march proclaiming 'Together we can fight male violence'. London, 2010

Source: © Janine Wiedel Photolibrary/Alamy.

Critics argue that this approach exaggerates differences between past and present social movements. The women's movement, for example, focuses on many of the same issues, including workplace conditions and pay, that consumed the energies of labour organisations for decades.

Explaining social movements

There have been many attempts to explain the nature of social movements in the contemporary world. Often they are pitched as rival explanations in opposition to each other. In this section we will briefly outline nine of these major explanations. In our view, they should not be seen as rivals. Instead, we think they can all be viewed as partial explanations focusing on different aspects or problems. Any full explanation is likely to draw upon each contribution.

1 *Conflict and suffering.* Marx's ideas have remained some of the most useful for approaching the ways social movements work. His concern, as we have seen, was with the class movement and the development of class consciousness and identity as a necessary condition for bringing about social movement. He outlined the conditions in which the working class became poorer and poorer under the new capitalist industrialisation, and how this led in turn to a growing awareness of themselves as a social class that could come together and seek radical change.

2 *Structural strain.* These early explanations often developed functional theory and suggested that social movements arise because of a problem, threat or breakdown in the social structure: for example, the French Revolution arose because of the increasing poverty of the peasants. The more recent concern over world finance or the environment can be located in the breakdown of the banking system and the ecological order respectively. The focus here is upon the breakdown in the social world to which a social movement becomes a response. Useful as this may be for a starting point, it fails actually to address the nature of social movements.

3 *Movements as process and collective behaviour.* It was the symbolic interactionist Herbert Blumer who turned his attention to the movements as a collective social process. He argued that social movements should be seen as processual, symbolic and interactive. They emerged out of collective behaviour and could be traced through definite stages. In his work, he detected five key stages which have shaped much thinking since. Figure 16.2 is a modified version of this.

4 *Symbolic politics.* Blumer's ideas also led to the view that social movements could be seen not simply as *instrumental* in bringing about change but also as performing distinct *symbolic* roles. Thus, for example, in Joseph Gusfield's study of the campaigns and temperance movements against alcohol in the United States in the 1930s, he could argue that these should not be seen simply as instrumental drives to prevent people from drinking, but as more of a symbolic mechanism to promote and enhance the status of a middle class under threat. Behind many social movements there were key issues of class and status at work, of declining elites and emerging new groups.

5 *Organisational resources and their mobilisation.* Arising in the 1970s, another major attempt to explain the rise of social movements focused sharply on the nature of their organisations. To be a successful asocial movement in effect required the successful mobilisation of good organisational resources. Resources are understood here to include: knowledge, money, media, labour, solidarity, legitimacy, and internal and external support from the power elite. A successful movement would have leaders with good skills, access to good administrative and organisational support, and of course access to funds and finance to help lobby and organise. In a sense, the more access a group had to financial support, the stronger it could grow.

6 *Identity politics.* Closely connected to this was the firm focus on the development of new identities as a basis for organising social movements. Growing in part during the time of the countercultural movements of the late 1960s and 1970s, movements emerged where a clear identity became a core focus. The black movement with a strong race identity, the women's movement with a strong identity of women, and the lesbian and gay movement with a strong sexual identity became key examples. Here the fashioning of a strong identity (usually with claims to rights attached to it) became the key organising explanation of social movements.

7 *Claims making' 'frames'.* As part of the wider social constructionist turn in social theory, social movements can be examined in terms of the kinds of claim they make for change. A key explanation now becomes the ways in which social movements develop rhetoric and languages to put their case – and how these 'claims' come to be accepted or not.

8 *Globalisation of social movements.* Most recently with the rise of theories of globalisation theories, it is becoming increasingly clear that social movements can rarely be approached in terms of simple local communities: very often their causes, organisations, identities and claims move across the globe. We see this most strikingly in the 'Make Poverty History' movement, the postcolonial movements and the worldwide environmental movements.

9 *Digitalisation of social movements.* The globalisation of movements has also involved digital developments – websites, blogging, twitter and the rest have made worldwide communications easy and widespread.

Social movements and social change

Social movements exist to encourage – or to resist – social change. Sometimes we overlook the success of past social movements and take for granted the changes that other people struggled so hard to win. Early workers' movements, for example, battled for decades to end child labour in factories, to limit working hours, to make the workplace safer and to establish the right to bargain collectively with employers. Legislation protecting the environment is also the product of successful social movements throughout the twentieth century. The women's movement has yet to attain full social equality for the sexes, but it has significantly extended the legal rights and economic opportunities of women. In fact, younger people can be surprised to learn that, early in the twentieth century, few women worked for income and none was permitted to vote.

Past social movements have shaped society in ways that people now take for granted. Just as movements produce change, so change itself sparks social movements. New social movements have been shaped by widespread dissatisfaction with the existing political system and debates. They bring new issues (especially issues linked to the environment, gender, peace, sexuality, race and world development) and a broader conception of participatory politics, and often dissolve the clear distinction between public and private (see Chapter 22). As leading German sociologist Klauss Offe says, 'the conflicts and contradictions of advanced industrial society can no longer be resolved by the state or by increasing bureaucracy' (Offe, 1985). New social movements are seen as the answer.

This broad view leads to one overarching conclusion: we can draw a direct link between social movements and change. In one direction, social transformations, such as the Industrial Revolution and the rise of capitalism, sparked the emergence of various social movements. Going the other way, the efforts of workers, women, racial and ethnic minorities and gay people have sent ripples of change throughout industrial societies. Thus social change is both the cause and the consequence of social movements.

Social movements have become a growing feature of globalised post-industrial life. The scope of social movements is likely to grow, for two reasons. First, the technology of the Information Revolution has drawn the world closer together than ever before. Today anyone with a satellite dish, personal computer or fax machine can stay abreast of political events, often as they happen. Secondly, as a consequence of new technology as well as the emerging global economy, social movements are now uniting people throughout the entire world. As we saw in the opening tale to this chapter, with the realisation that many problems are global in scope has come the understanding that they can be effectively addressed only on an international scale.

 There are many reports on human rights across the globe that are worth looking at in order to keep up to date with current concerns. Try:

Human Rights Watch: www.hrw.org

Amnesty International: http://thereport.amnesty.org and in the UK, *Annual Reports on Human Rights*: http://centralcontent.fco.gov.uk/resources/en/pdf/human-rights-reports/human-rights-report-2009 (which started in 1997 and ran until 2010: at the time of going to press, we have learned that the current UK government is thinking of scrapping it).

Anthony Giddens: the global politics of 'life choice', 'Third Way' and environmental regulation

Anthony Giddens is one of the UK's leading sociologists. In his many early books he examined the classical social theories of sociologists (Marx, Durkheim and Weber), and ultimately produced his own theory of the link between action and structure – a theory known as **structuration theory**, which we briefly introduced in Chapter 1. In his later books, starting around the late 1980s, he becomes more concerned with the arrival of globalisation and what he calls 'late modern society'. This is a society where the pace and scope of change deepens and accelerates – we break free from traditions, our sense of time and space gets reordered, and globalisation becomes a central process. Social life is lifted out ('disembedded') from local traditional contexts and becomes more open and fluid. In 1999 he summarised his major ideas for a worldwide audience in a series of talks he gave as the Reith Lectures (the BBC's most prominent annual lecture series). They were published in a short book, *Runaway World* (1999).

Giddens senses that contemporary identities are changing as we become more aware of having to choose who we are. Traditional institutions such as the family are also changing as relations between members become more equal, open and democratised. Above all, he senses a major change in the political order. What was ushered in with modernity was an 'emancipatory politics' – its main focus was on justice, freedom and equality. It was embodied in the ideals of the French Revolution and the American War of Independence. These political values remain to this day, but now they are not new but widespread. He believes they will continue. In addition a new set of concerns have arrived which make politics more concerned with questions about how we should live our lives in a late modern world. This is what he calls 'the politics of life choice', and it is this new politics which is becoming more prominent. He espouses a utopian realism in which new models of life and participation are to be evolved in helping us live in a new kind of social order (Giddens, 1990).

Giddens suggests that the old social democratic 'welfare consensus' that was found in many industrial countries till the late 1970s has collapsed. The classic distinctions of 'left' and 'right' have broken down. The changes have come about partly because of the rise of free-market philosophies associated with Thatcherism and Reaganism – capitalist neoliberalism (identified in the previous chapter and often seen as uncaring and inadequate) along with the fall of the old Soviet Union and what some claim to be 'the death of socialism' (Giddens, 1998: 3).

Giddens talks of this new politics as the **Third Way** – *a framework that adapts politics to a changed world, transcending old-style social democracy and neo-liberalism*. He identifies a number of dilemmas of the late modern world and suggests that:

> The overall aim of third way politics should be to help citizens pilot their way through the major revolutions of our time: globalization, transformations in personal life and our relationships to nature . . . third way politics should preserve a core concern with social justice.
>
> (Giddens, 1998: 64)

He outlines the new 'Third Way values' in a series of slogans: 'Equity', 'Protection of the vulnerable', 'Freedom as autonomy', 'No rights without responsibilities', 'No authority without democracy', 'Cosmopolitan pluralism' and 'Philosophic conservatism' (1998: 66). He suggests a Third Way programme which would involve a radical centre, a new democratic state, an active civil society, a democratic family, a new mixed economy, equality as inclusion, positive welfare, the social investment state, the cosmopolitan nation and cosmopolitan democracy (1998: 70).

Way beyond left and right: international environmentalism

Most recently, Giddens has become concerned about the turn to the right in politics and indeed the growth of far-right parties. In his latest writings, he suggests that the third way was a major source of change in the 1990s, but today we must go beyond this – beyond left and right. His key concern has become the politics of the environment, which is not a simple left and right issue at all. He sees climate change and

global heating as an urgent and serious problem which requires international agreements alongside effective global policy planning and action. This is a real challenge and the 'rich' governments (often the highest polluters) should foster new structures to deal with this. (We look more at this in Chapter 25.)

Unlike many sociologists, Giddens plays an active role in world politics and publishes less and less. His advice has been sought by political leaders from Asia, Latin America and Australia, as well as from the USA and Europe. He had a major impact upon the evolution of New Labour in the UK and took part

in the original Blair–Clinton dialogues from 1997 onwards. Nowadays, he is a major crusader on the need for international coordination, planning and policy around the environment.

Source: Giddens (1990, 1991, 1998, 1999, 2004, 2009).

See Giddens on YouTube – you will find many lectures by him.

The globalisation of 'human rights regimes'?

A final major development we will consider in the political landscape of the early twenty-first century is the arrival of the international language of 'human rights'. Increasingly, after the horrors of the Holocaust and other atrocities, a major trend in world politics has been towards 'rights'. Yet such a language is far from new. Three waves of human rights in recent history have been distinguished (Klug, 2000).

The *first wave* started in the late eighteenth century in the West against a background of totalitarianism and a lack of religious freedom: the search was on for liberty, justice and equality before the law. The 1789 French Declaration of the Rights of Man and Citizen spoke of 'the natural, inalienable and sacred rights of man', while the 1776 US Declaration of Independence from the colonial power of Britain claimed that:

> We hold these truths to be self evident, that all men are created equal; that they are endowed by their creator with certain inalienable Rights; that among these are life, liberty and the pursuit of happiness.

The prime task of this wave of rights was freedom from state tyranny and religious persecution, and it led to the American Bill of Rights and the French Declaration of Rights.

The *second wave* started around the Second World War and an evolving United Nations (UN). International human rights treaties and declarations came to be enacted and enforced by international courts and monitoring bodies. Rights talk here focused especially on dignity, equality and community. It is enshrined in what most would consider the central document of human rights of our times – the Universal Declaration of Human Rights (UDHR), which is built into the UN Charter. 'Human dignity' is the core value

behind such rights. The declaration established a potentially universal language of freedom and equal rights – even for those many countries like South Africa which were not able to achieve it at that time. Each of the main covenants has been ratified by some 140 out of 190 states, and the numbers are growing.

The *third wave* started to appear at the end of the Cold War (early 1990s) against a background of increasing globalisation and a new millennium looking for common values. It champions mutuality and participation. Here, more and more countries establish their own rights programmes, and 'human rights regimes' begin to seem part of a major international political network. There are now, for instance, over 200 human rights NGOs in the United States, and a similar number in the UK and Europe. They are growing fast. Political scientist Benjamin Barber (1995) can now talk of a 'world of citizens without frontiers'. Most countries – even when they are riddled with the denial and corruption of human rights – still make claims to use versions of this language (which should, of course, alert us to some of the major problems with such a language: it can and does mean all things to all people!).

British sociologist Martin Albrow, in *The Global Age*, talks of a new kind of citizenship – *global citizenship* – which 'begins in people's daily lives, is realized in everyday practices and results in collective action up to the level of the globe' (Albrow, 1996: 177). He sees the model for this as the international working-class movement in the nineteenth century, but now sees many roots into this through citizens who are, as he puts it, 'performing the state'. Here are global actions at the local level. Many of these claims now come conspicuously from new social movements – the green movement of eco-warriors, the gay/lesbian/queer/ transgender movement, the women's movement – and they are epitomised in what has come to be called the Battle of Seattle, introduced in the opening to this chapter. These may not reinforce national systems of governance and may indeed even run counter to them.

WORLD WATCH

Global governance: the United Nations

The United Nations had 191 members in 2003, and has a regular budget of about $1.25 billion. It stands, among other things, 'as a focal point for global security issues, a world forum for debate, a network for developing universal norms and standards, and a vehicle for administering humanitarian assistance around the world' (Krasno, 2004: 3). Since its inception in 1945, it has come to symbolise the long-sought-for goal of universal government and harmony. It divides into six main committees which deal with (a) politics and security issues, (b) economic and financial issues, (c) social, humanitarian and cultural issues, (d) trusteeship issues, (e) legal issues, and (f) administration and budget. The Millennium Declaration was adopted by member states in 2000, and called for the eradication of poverty, access to clean water, sanitation and access to clean energy sources (see Chapter 25).

See: Jean Krasno, *The United Nations: Confronting the Challenges of a Global Society* (2004).

US President George W. Bush addresses the 57th session of the United Nations General Assembly at the UN headquarters, New York

Source: © Brooks Kraft/Corbis.

WORLD WATCH

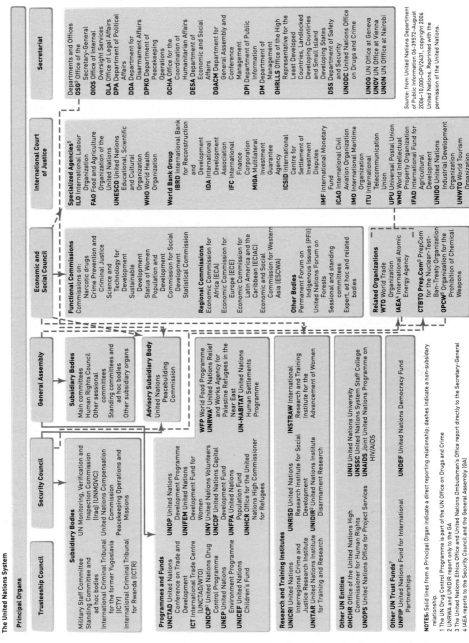

The United Nations System

Principal Organs

Trusteeship Council | Security Council | General Assembly | Economic and Social Council | International Court of Justice | Secretariat

Trusteeship Council / Security Council

Subsidiary Bodies
Military Staff Committee
Standing Committee and ad hoc bodies
International Criminal Tribunal for the former Yugoslavia (ICTY)
International Criminal Tribunal for Rwanda (ICTR)

UN Monitoring, Verification and Inspection Commission [Iraq] (UNMOVIC)
United Nations Compensation Commission
Peacekeeping Operations and Missions

Programmes and Funds
UNCTAD United Nations Conference on Trade and Development
  ICT International Trade Centre (UNCTAD/WTO)
UNDCP[1] United Nations Drug Control Programme
UNEP United Nations Environment Programme
UNICEF United Nations Children's Fund

UNDP United Nations Development Programme
  UNIFEM United Nations Development Fund for Women
  UNV United Nations Volunteers
UNCDF United Nations Capital Development Fund
UNFPA United Nations Population Fund
UNHCR Office for the United Nations High Commissioner for Refugees

WFP World Food Programme
UNRWA[2] United Nations Relief and Works Agency for Palestine Refugees in the Near East
UN-HABITAT United Nations Human Settlements Programme

Research and Training Institutes
UNICRI United Nations Interregional Crime and Justice Research Institute
UNITAR United Nations Institute for Training and Research

UNRISD United Nations Research Institute for Social Development
UNIDIR[2] United Nations Institute for Disarmament Research

INSTRAW International Research and Training Institute for the Advancement of Women

Other UN Entities
OHCHR Office of the United Nations High Commissioner for Human Rights
UNOPS United Nations Office for Project Services

UNU United Nations University
UNSSC United Nations System Staff College
UNAIDS Joint United Nations Programme on HIV/AIDS

UNDEF United Nations Democracy Fund

Other UN Trust Funds[7]
UNFIP United Nations Fund for International Partnerships

General Assembly

Subsidiary Bodies
Main committees
Human Rights Council
Other sessional committees
Standing committees and ad hoc bodies
Other subsidiary organs

Advisory Subsidiary Body
United Nations Peacebuilding Commission

Economic and Social Council

Functional Commissions
Commissions on:
Narcotic drugs
Crime Prevention and Criminal Justice
Science and Technology for Development
Sustainable Development
Status of Women
Population and Development
Commission for Social Development
Statistical Commission

Regional Commissions
Economic Commission for Africa (ECA)
Economic Commission for Europe (ECE)
Economic Commission for Latin America and the Caribbean (ECLAC)
Economic and Social Commission for Western Asia (ESCWA)

Other Bodies
Permanent Forum on Indigenous Issues (PFII)
United Nations Forum on Forests
Sessional and standing committees
Expert, ad hoc and related bodies

Related Organizations
WTO World Trade Organization
IAEA[4] International Atomic Energy Agency
CTBTO Prep.Com[5] PrepCom for the Nuclear-Test-Ban-Treaty Organization
OPCW[6] Organization for the Prohibition of Chemical Weapons

International Court of Justice

Specialized Agencies[5]
ILO International Labour Organization
FAO Food and Agriculture Organization of the United Nations
UNESCO United Nations Educational, Scientific and Cultural Organization
WHO World Health Organization
World Bank Group
IBRD International Bank for Reconstruction and Development
IDA International Development Association
IFC International Finance Corporation
MIGA Multilateral Investment Guarantee Agency
ICSID International Centre for Settlement of Investment Disputes
IMF International Monetary Fund
ICAO International Civil Aviation Organization
IMO International Maritime Organization
ITU International Telecommunication Union
UPU Universal Postal Union
WMO World Meteorological Organization
WIPO World Intellectual Property Organization
IFAD International Fund for Agricultural Development
UNIDO United Nations Industrial Development Organization
UNWTO World Tourism Organization

Secretariat

Departments and Offices
OSG[3] Office of the Secretary-General
OIOS Office of Internal Oversight Services
OLA Office of Legal Affairs
DPA Department of Political Affairs
DDA Department for Disarmament Affairs
DPKO Department of Peacekeeping Operations
OCHA Office for the Coordination of Humanitarian Affairs
DESA Department of Economic and Social Affairs
DGACM Department for General Assembly and Conference Management
DPI Department of Public Information
DM Department of Management
OHRLLS Office of the High Representative for the Least Developed Countries, Landlocked Developing Countries and Small Island Developing States
DSS Department of Safety and Security
UNODC United Nations Office on Drugs and Crime
UNOG UN Office at Geneva
UNOV UN Office at Vienna
UNON UN Office at Nairobi

Source: from United Nations Department of Public Information 06-39572–August 2006–10,000-DPI/2431, copyright 2006 United Nations. Reprinted with the permission of the United Nations.

NOTES: Solid lines from a Principal Organ indicate a direct reporting relationship; dashes indicate a non-subsidiary relationship.
1 The UN Drug Control Programme is part of the UN Office on Drugs and Crime
2 UNRWA and UNIDIR report only to the GA
3 The United Nations Ethics Office and United Nations Ombudsman's Office report directly to the Secretary-General
4 IAEA reports to the Security Council and the General Assembly (GA)
5 The CIBIO Prep.Com and ORCW report to the GA
6 Specialized agencies are autonomous organizations working with the UN and each other through the coordinating machinery of the ECOSOC at the intergovernmental level, and through the Chief Executive Board for coordination (CEB) at the inter-secretariat level.
7 UNFIP is an autonomous trust fund operating under the leadership of the United Nations Deputy Secretary-General UNDEF's advisory board recommends funding proposals for approval by the Secretary-General.

Global bureaucracy at work. Examine the organisations that have been developed within the United Nations. You can track the detailed reports of many of these through the UN website at www.un.org. You can watch the UN at work on YouTube: search 'United Nations'

| Map 16.3 | **Life after communism** |

When communism collapsed in the late 1980s, a new hope and optimism appeared for the people of the former Soviet Union and eastern Europe. They hoped for freedom, an expanding economy and an end of corruption. None of this has happened. GDP growth has declined in every country but Poland (with Russia, Georgia, Moldova, Ukraine and Tajikistan the worst). Most countries have become poorer (poverty rose from 14 million in 1989 to 147 million in 1998) – indeed the increase in people living on less than a dollar a day has grown faster in the former Soviet republics than anywhere else in the world. There are differences: Slovakia is one of the most equal countries in the world; Russia and Armenia are among the least equal. Map 16.2 charts some of the issues.

Source: Adapted from 'Life after communism: the facts', *New Internationalist*, 366, April 2004.

They challenge government to recognise key issues – often linked to how people can gain control over their (personal) lives in a 'runaway world'. They organise global conferences that establish worldwide agendas of rights. Human rights systems now appear across the world.

The trouble with rights

Although we can find talk of 'citizens and rights' everywhere in contemporary politics, a number of problems have been identified with it.

First is the claim to universalism. When the classic Universal Declaration of Human Rights was adopted, most Third World or low-income societies were still under colonial rule, and even today many remain suspicious of it. 'Human rights' can easily become a euphemism for Western intervention in other countries. It is often a universality of the privileged. Many of the rights claims just do not ring true in many parts of the world. The right to a paid vacation, for instance, makes no sense in most of the world where sweatshop labour conditions apply; and women's rights

Human Rights Bills and Acts

The Human Rights Act 1998

This came into force in the UK on 2 October 2000. It was the first time that the UK had enforceable official human rights protection. Drawing from the European Convention on Human Rights, the Act now means that old common law in the UK will have to change if it does not respect the rights enshrined in the convention, and that all legislation must now comply with these rights. The main rights are as follows.

Article

2   The right to life*
3   Freedom from torture, inhuman and degrading treatment
4   Freedom from slavery
5   Freedom from arbitrary arrest and detention
6   The right to a fair trial
7   Freedom from retrospective penalties
8   The right to privacy and family life
9   Freedom of religion
10 Freedom of expression
11 Freedom of assembly and association
12 The right to marry and found a family
13 Prohibition of discrimination
14 Restrictions on political activity of aliens
15 Prohibition of abuse of rights
16 Limitation on use of restrictions on rights

In addition, the Act stipulates, among other things:

- The right to peaceful enjoyment of property
- The right to education
- The right to free elections
- Abolition of the death penalty
- Preservation of the death penalty in times of war.

The full text can be downloaded from www.direct.gov.uk.

* Article 1 is missing as it does not list a right.

Other Bills and Acts

The Bill of Rights, 1689: www.constitution.org/eng.

The Declaration of the Rights of the Citizen, approved by the French Assembly of France, 26 August, 1789: www.hrcr.docs/index.html.

The United States Bill of Rights, 1791: www.usconstitution. net.

United Nations Universal Declaration of Human Rights: www.un.org/rights.

See: Human and Constitutional Rights Documents: www.hrcr.docs/index.html.

---

become a serious problem when there are major clashes of cultural and religious expectation around family and gender.

Secondly, even if there could be agreement, many of the rights claims are almost completely unenforceable pragmatically. There is evidence from international organisations such as Amnesty International and Human Rights Watch that these 'rights' are incessantly violated around the world. In wars of liberation, for example, one finds gross violations both by the oppressors as well as by the liberators. Rights regimes are often so private that they become unenforceable even with goodwill.

Finally, much rights talk is too individually based. There is a focus on individual rights as opposed to group rights. Collective human rights differ from individual rights. Human rights theory has traditionally focused on the rights of the individual, independent of social groupings, and advocates for individual human rights seek redress mainly through the nation-state system or through intergovernmental structures, such as the United Nations. The focus of collective human rights, on the other hand, is on the rights of social groups, and proponents seek to create an innovative framework independent of nation-states to enhance and protect these rights.

SUMMARY

1 Politics is the major social institution by which a society distributes power and organises decision-making. Max Weber explained that there are three ways to transform coercive power into legitimate authority: through tradition, through rationally enacted rules and regulations, and through the personal charisma of a leader.

2 Four clusters of government can be roughly outlined. Monarchy is based on traditional authority and is common in pre-industrial societies. Although constitutional monarchies persist in some industrial nations, industrialisation favours democracy based on rational–legal authority and extensive bureaucracy. Authoritarian political regimes deny popular participation in government. Totalitarian political systems go even further, tightly regulating people's everyday lives.

3 The world remains divided into between 190 and 200 politically independent nation-states; one dimension of an emerging global political system, however, is the growing wealth and power of multinational corporations. Additionally, new technology associated with the Information Revolution means that national governments can no longer control the flow of information across national boundaries.

4 The dramatic growth of democratic governments in much of Europe during the past two centuries goes far beyond mere population increase; it reflects wider government involvement in the economy and all of society.

5 The traditional left (socialists) and right (conservatives) take different positions on economic and social issues. The left calls for government regulation of the economy and action to ensure economic equality; conservatives believe the government should not interfere in these arenas. Conservatives, however, do support government regulation of moral issues such as abortion, while the left, along with liberals, argue that government should not interfere in matters of conscience.

6 The pluralist model holds that political power is widely dispersed; the power elite model takes an opposing view, arguing that power is concentrated in the hands of a small, wealthy segment of the population. The Marxist or ruling class model argues that this elite is in fact an economic class.

7 Revolution, terrorism, corruption and war take power outside the normal workings of a political order. Revolution aims to radically transform a political system. Terrorism uses violence in pursuit of political goals. States as well as individuals engage in terrorism. War is armed conflict directed by governments. The development and proliferation of nuclear weapons have increased the threat of global catastrophe. Enhancing world peace ultimately depends on resolving the tensions and conflicts that fuel militarism.

8 A social movement entails deliberate activity intended to promote or discourage change. Social movements vary in the range of people they seek to engage and the extent to which they strive to change society. A typical social movement proceeds through consecutive stages: emergence (defining the public issue), coalescence (entering the public arena), bureaucratisation (becoming formally organised) and decline (brought on by failure or, sometimes, success).

9 At the start of the twenty-first century, the issue of global 'human rights' has been placed firmly on the political agenda.

CONNECT UP: Turn to Part 6 of this book for key resources and link up
with the book's website, which links to these resources
SEE: www.pearsoned.co.uk/plummer

MYTASKLIST

Ten suggestions for going further

1 Connect up with Part Six and the Sociology Web Resources

As you work through ideas and think about the issues raised in this chapter, look at the accompanying website and the resource centre at the end of this book which connects to it. There is a lot here to help you move on. To link up, see: www.pearson.co.uk/plummer.

2 Review the chapter

Briefly summarise (in a paragraph) just what this chapter has been about. Consider: (a) What have you learned? (b) What do you disagree with? Be critical. And (c) How would you develop all this? How could you get more detail on matters that interest you?

3 Pose questions

(a) How is politics changing in the twenty-first century? What are the problems posed by the developing arguments around 'human rights'?

(b) In what respects do some recent social movements (those concerned with the environment or animal rights) differ from older crusades (focus on, say, civil rights and gender equality)?

(c) Do you think that the dangers of war in the world are greater or less than in past generations? In what ways has war changed? Are there 'new wars'?

(d) Examine the causes and consequences of any one 'crisis spot' in the world today. Do you have any suggestions that could lead to any kind of resolution?

4 Explore key words

Many concepts have been introduced in this chapter. You can review them from the website or from the listing a t the back of this book. You might like to give special attention to just five words and think them through – how would you define them, what are they dealing with, and do they help you see the social world more clearly or not? Maybe look at:

Martin Smith, *The New Penguin Dictionary of Politics* (2008).

Frank Barnaby, *The Future of Terror: A 21st Century Handbook* (2007): provides a quick guide to the current conflicts.

5 Search the Web

Be critical when you look at websites – see the box on p. 940 in the Resources section. For this chapter look at the following:

Political sources on the net
www.politicalresources.net
Useful worldwide listings.

Stockholm International Peace Research Institute
www.sipri.org
Details global military resources.

Freedom House
www.freedomhouse.org
Freedom House charts the state of the world's democracies in its annual volume *Freedom in the World*. It is accused of very clear Western bias.

Transparency International
www.transparency.org
Charts the corruption of governments around the world.

Parties and Elections
www.parties-and-elections.de.
The latest European political parties and parliamentary groups in the European Union.

The UK government and its cabinet
www.cabinetoffice.gov.uk
Provides insight into the workings of the UK government.

Open Democracy
www.opendemocracy.net/about
A human rights and democracy website.

Clausewitz homepage
www.clausewitz.com/index.htm
Clausewitz is seen as a major theorist of war and his book *On War* the key text.

Social movements

List of social movements
There have been a number of attempts to create a list of social movements but it is proving impossible to construct a full list. We suggest you search with the phrase '*list of social movements*' and you will soon find more than you can handle!

Human rights

On human rights, some of the key documents from the United Nations Universal Declaration of Human Rights (1948) to the Beijing Declaration on Women's Global Rights (1995) have been usefully gathered in M. Ishay, *The Human Rights Reader* (1997). A useful listing of all documents linked to human rights across the world can be found at: www.hrcr.org. See also the TIP box on *Human Rights Watch* (p. 567).

6 Watch a DVD

- Michael Moore's satire *Fahrenheit 9/11* (2004) received much praise as a critique of the Bush administration and the Iraq invasion. Some find it over the top!
- The Greek director Costa-Gravas made a reputation for himself in the 1970s with a series of probing political films, such as *Z* (1969), *The Confession* (1970) and *State of Siege* (1972). His *Missing* (1981) dealt with Allende's Chile and is a powerful moral and political drama.
- Stanley Kubrick's *Dr Strangelove: Or How I Learned to Stop Worrying and Love the Bomb* (1964), Gillo Pontecorvo's *The Battle of Algiers* (1965), Alan Parker's *Midnight Express* (1978), which deals with drugs and prison in Turkey, and Oliver Stone's *JFK* (1991) are all worth looking at.
- Classic films dealing with war include: Lewis Milestone's *All Quiet on the Western Front* (1930), Stanley Kubrick's *Paths of Glory* (1975), Michael Cimino's *The Deer Hunter* (1977), Oliver Stone's *Born on the Fourth of July* (1989), Steven Spielberg's *Saving Private Ryan* (1998) and Kathryn Bigelow's *The Hurt Locker*.

- On twenty-first-century terrorism, there are now a number of striking films. Adam Curtis's *The Power of the Nightmare* (2005) is a telling documentary from the BBC. Michael Winterbottom's (with Mat Whitecross) *The Road to Guantanamo* (2005) shows how three Muslims from Tipton in the West Midlands are arrested as al Qaeda suspects and treated barbarously in prison.

7 Think and read

John Hoffman and Paul Graham, *Introduction to Political Theory* (2nd edn, 2009). An excellent introductory text which covers the wide range of classical and contemporary accounts of politics.

John Baylis and Steve Smith (eds), *The Globalization of World Politics* (5th edn, 2010). This is a wide-ranging textbook which is kept up to date with new revisions. An excellent and much-used source book.

Anthony D. Smith, *Nationalism* (2001). Provides a succinct guide to the nature of nations and nationalism. His recent study, *The Cultural Foundations of Nations* (2008) is a lively account of the relationship between nations and modernity.

Charles Tilly, *Social Movements 1768–2004* (2004). Provides a concise history of the rise of social movements in the modern world.

Darren J. O. Byrne, *Human Rights: An Introduction* (2003). Established textbook with full discussion of all matters linked to human rights.

Penny Green and Tony Ward, *State Crime: Governments, Violence and Corruption* (2004). Details the corruption of governments.

Martin Shaw, *War and Genocide: Organized Killing in Modern Society* (2003). A very readable and important text. It is also linked to Shaw's website. See: www.martinshaw.org

The work of Mary Kaldor is also very significant here: see *New and Old Wars* (2007).

On terrorism, see Gus Martin, *Understanding Terrorism* (3rd edn, 2010).

Andrew Heywood, *Global Politics* (2011). Wide-ranging and up-to-date global account.

More information

For recent political data on the UK, see *The Guardian Political Almanac* (annually).
Key magazines include: *New Statesman* (UK) and *Foreign Policy* (USA).
See also the student magazine *Politics* (Blackwell publishers).

8 Relax with a novel

Classic works on the political world include:

George Orwell, *Animal Farm* (1945).

Edmund Wilson, *To the Finland Station* (1940).

Gunter Grass, *The Tin Drum* (1959).

Isabel Allende, *Of Love and Shadows* (1987).

J. Coetzee, *Waiting for the Barbarians* (1980).

Leo Tolstoy, *War and Peace* (1869).

9 Connect to other chapters

- Link back to Marx and Weber in Chapter 3, and clarify how their theories of power link to social change.
- For more on genocide, see Chapter 11.
- For more on wars and conflicts to science and the risk society, see Chapter 23.
- Consider how gender may be linked to power – see Chapter 12.
- To see how the ideas of the surveillance society and the work of Foucault are relevant to the discussion of power, refer to Chapter 17.

10 Engaging with THE BIG DEBATE

Are we moving beyond left and right? The politics of difference

Industrialisation, the emergence of modern nation-states and revolutionary movements on behalf of democracy have brought people together under the labels 'left' or 'right' for the past 200 years. (The terms originated in the French revolutionary assembly of the 1790s, where radicals sat on the left and moderates sat on the right.) For most of the twentieth century, the political divides have been very sharply drawn on these lines: capitalism versus communism, right versus left, the East versus the West. The demise of the Cold War between the United States and what Reagan called the 'evil empire' of the USSR (dominated by Russia) was spectacularly symbolised at the end of the 1980s by the fall of the Berlin Wall. At the time there was much jubilation. But the problem now – in the twenty-first century – is: where is all this heading? For many of the old communist countries, a kind of chaos has ensued. For much of the old West, a kind of directionlessness has happened. If the old divides are crumbling, what is politics about in the twenty-first century?

One response was to see the end of these conflicts as the end of history. The fall of the Berlin Wall symbolised the final victory of capitalist democracy: this was the way of the world from now on. Francis Fukuyama (1989) sees 'the end of history' as nothing less than the worldwide triumph of modernity, capitalism and liberal democracy. The ideological battles are now over, and there are no alternatives. Fukuyama sees the 'universalisation of Western democracy as the final form of human government' (1989): monarchism, fascism

and communism have been rendered indefensible for all but a few extreme groups.

But not all agree with Fukuyama. Many new 'politics' are being suggested. For instance, in Chapter 25 we document the degradation of our environment; here many argue for the worldwide development of a green politics. Others, such as the English social theorist Anthony Giddens, are arguing for a 'democratic life politics' – a global politics which rethinks how we are to live and how we are to revitalise democracy through dialogue in a world which is changing globally at an accelerating rate. Arguing that both 'socialism and conservatism have disintegrated' (1994: 9), Giddens champions a 'dialogic democracy' where importance is given to dialogues and the many different voices arguing for different ways to live. He seeks a radical rethinking of democracy – in opposition to fundamentalism of all kinds (see the box on p. 568).

Others see these 'fundamentalisms' as the very basis of conflicts in the future. Benjamin Barber (1995) argues that the world is no longer divided between left and right. Instead the divide has shifted globally to one between consumerist capitalism (symbolised by a global McDonald's, or McWorld) and religious and tribal fundamentalisms (symbolised by the Islamic *jihad*). The former saw rapidly dissolving nation-states and political boundaries, leading to the triumph of individualism and the marketplace all over the world. At the same time, the latter is forcing ethnic, religious and tribal conflicts into politics everywhere. This tension may be seen as one which goes to the heart of global modernity, and its manifestations in 'tribal warfare' have become increasingly apparent. Indeed, after the Twin Tower attacks in New York in September 2001, many argue that such conflicts and wars are now well under way.

Jubilation at the fall of the
Berlin Wall, November 1989

Source: Tom Stoddart/Hulton
Archive/Getty Images.

This is an important debate for contemporary sociology. Some argue that the old left and right positions of the twentieth century need a clear reasserting: they are still relevant. Others argue that we have reached 'the end of history' and we are now, more or less, stuck with capitalist liberal democracies which in the twenty-first century will rule the world. Still others see distinct dangers emerging in the continuing clashes between ethnic and religious fundamentalism and the free-for-all marketplace of consumer capitalism – the clash of civilisations. And still more are looking to the creation of new political forms with social movements and new issues – green politics, lifestyles politics, differences – at the forefront. There is a new political scene in the making at the start of the twenty-first century which is far removed from the Cold War of the twentieth.

Continue the debate

1 Have we really reached 'the end of history' and the triumph of liberal capitalism?

2 If fundamentalism is on the increase, will this not result in more and more bloody wars and conflicts?

3 How might sociological analyses of power, ethnicity (see Chapter 11) and religion (see Chapter 19) assist in understanding the war between the United States and its allies and 'terrorism'?

4 Is a politics based on lifestyle not just an indulgence of the over-rich West?

5 How central do you think social movements around 'green politics' will become in the twenty-first century?

Source: Fukuyama (1989); Giddens (1994); Barber (1995); Heywood (2011).

CHAPTER 17

CONTROL, CRIME AND DEVIANCE

GO INTO ANY EUROPEAN CITY CENTRE ON A SATURDAY NIGHT and the chances are you will find drunken revellers everywhere. And it won't be long before such drinking turns, for some, to violence and unruly behaviour. At the start of the twenty-first century, 'binge drinking' has become a way of life. Binging used to mean, clinically, a periodic bout of continual drinking by someone who was alcohol dependent, and ending only when the drinker could not continue. Nowadays, it is slang for a very high intake of drink in a single session (often defined roughly as five 'good' drinks or more – leading to drunkenness). Since 1970, alcohol consumption has increased by 50 per cent and drink has never been more accessible or cheaper in real terms. New 'designer drinks' are everywhere. European alcohol consumption is roughly double that found in the rest of the world.

There is nothing new about this heavy drinking: the history of alcohol consumption in the UK and drunken behaviour seems to go back to at least the Vikings. Across Europe, the main difference has been that in Mediterranean drinking countries, the dominant beverage was wine. In northern European and Anglo-Saxon cultures, beer and spirits have predominated. But things are rapidly changing now in the globalised world of the young.

Binge drinking seems to be highest in Ireland, the UK, Sweden and Finland; it is slightly lower – but growing – in France, Germany and Italy. Drinking is now widespread amongst both boys and girls. In Spain, young girls keep up with the boys. In Britain, there are 'ladettes' and 'vertical drinking places' (standing room-only bars), and sometimes more girls than boys, and

often very young (many are 15 years old). In Poland, girls often outnumber boys. In general, though, levels of drinking are roughly half the levels for women as men. In the UK, around a quarter of women and only 1 in 6 men aged 18–24 report never binge drinking. Quite a large proportion of children report being drunk at the age of 13 or younger (ESPAD, 1999; Plant and Plant, 2006).

Thoughout Europe, cities have become night-time 'no-go areas'. Cities are often taken over by young men in search of alcohol, drugs, sex – or a fight. Increasingly, young women do this too. These 'urban nightscapes' provide a fast-moving world of youth spaces in bars, pubs, nightclubs and music venues, where, increasingly, big business has moved in. They provide branded, themed and stylised experiences. For kids, 'consumption' (see Chapter 15) becomes a key activity and helps to establish a different style, scene and identity. A new range of alcohol products, including designer drinks, facilitate all this. Here are young professionals, students, women and gay consumers, as well as excluded groups and also alternative nightlife activity, such as squats and free parties. All this occurs against a backdrop where urban nightlife is becoming increasingly a bright life, a carefully formatted, McDonaldised world (see Chapter 6). Big branded names take over large parts of downtown areas, leaving consumers with an increasingly standardised experience.

Finally, consider the case of the UK where there has been a major relaxation of the licensing hours since November 2005. Several years on there are worries: there is real concern that the current epidemic of binge drinking will get even worse.

Crime is necessary, it is linked to the fundamental conditions of all social life and because of that it is useful; for those conditions to which it is bound are themselves indispensable to the normal evolution of morality.

Emile Durkheim

In this chapter, we ask:

- **What are the social patterns of crime?**

- **How is globalisation shaping crime?**

- **What is the changing character of social control?**

- **What are the main sociological accounts of crime?**

(Left) Artist's dark vision of life in prison
Source: Prison. © Allan E. Cober/Stock Illustration Source.

See: www.isa.umich.edu/english/pcap and www.ica.org.uk/Insider%20Art+14012.twl.

 In summer 2007, the Institute of Contemporary Arts (ICA) in London organised a show of art by prisoners and others in confinement in Britain, including inmates at young offender institutions, high-security psychiatric hospitals, secure units and immigration removal centres, as well as people supervised by probation and youth offending teams. It included painting, sculpture, drawing, ceramics, textiles and other media. This chapter opens with an image from prisoner art (though not from this exhibition). Discuss the nature and role of prison art.

One of the most striking features of living in the modern world is the sense that many people have – that we are now in a world gone mad with crime. Crime and violence (and often sex) is everywhere: in our newspapers, in films, in the soap operas. Terrible crimes of all sorts are seen to be on the increase. And many of our concerns – like drug trafficking and control – stretch across the globe. Anxieties and fears about crime are up; our changing penal responses to crime are becoming more and more repressive. Nowadays, most governments make 'crime control' one of their central political arguments in elections, and the message is to get 'tough on crime and tough on the causes of crime'. Everywhere in the world it seems to be a growing issue.

In this chapter we open up some of the many questions dealing with control, crime and deviance. We start by trying to get a sense of just what the crime and deviance issues look like across the globe. We will look, too, at the changing shapes of the social control process, which seems to be expanding considerably across modern and late-modern society. We will also look at some of the reasons behind the growth of crime, by asking what indeed causes it. The *Timeline* suggests some of the major theories and positions within the study of crime. Although we do not have space to consider them all in this chapter, you may like to review them after you have read it, and see which ones you can identify.

Timeline The development of criminology

Early modern period	Demonism, witchcraft
Late 18th century onwards	Classical School and Beccaria
1870s	Italian or Positivist School
1910 onwards	Functionalist criminology
1920s	Psychoanalytic theories
1920s	Life-story research
1930s onwards	Anomie theory
1920s/1930s	Chicago tradition
1930s/1940s	Differential association
1960s onwards	Control theory
1960s/1970s	Subcultural theory
1960s/1970s	Labelling theory
1970s onwards	Moral panic theory
1973	New criminology
1970s	Critical criminology
1970s	Birmingham School BCCCS
1970s	Political economy of crime
1976	Just deserts/the justice model
1970s onwards	Feminist criminology
Late 1970s onwards	Black and anti-racist criminology
Late 1970s onwards	Focauldian genealogies and governance
1980s	Left realism – square of crime
1980s	Resurgence of radical right
1990s	Postmodern criminology
2000s	Globalisation of crime
2000s	Human rights
	Cultural criminology
	Environmental criminology

Source: Based on Carrabine et al. (2008).

Some opening definitions

Societies may be seen as layered by norms which guide virtually all human activities, and deviance is the violation of these norms along with the recognition and labelling of such violations. **Deviance** then involves *the recognised violation of cultural norms*. There are many kinds of norm: health norms, sexual norms, religious norms. People who violate such norms are ill (health norms), perverts (sex norms) or heretics (religious norms). One distinctive category of deviance is **crime**, *the violation of norms that a society formally enacts into criminal law*. Criminal deviance is extensive, ranging from very minor traffic violations to serious offences such as murder and rape.

Some instances of deviance barely raise eyebrows; other cases command a swift and severe response. Members of our society pay little notice to mild non-conformity such as left-handedness or boastfulness; we usually take a dimmer view of drunken driving or vandalism; and

we call the police in response to a burglary. There is a continuum of responses to crime, and we do not all respond in the same ways.

Not all deviance involves action or even choice. For some categories of individuals, just *existing* may be sufficient to provoke condemnation from others. To some older people, young people may symbolise trouble; to some whites, the mere presence of 'blacks' may cause suspicion. What deviant actions or attitudes have in common is some evaluation of *difference* that prompts us to regard another person as an 'outsider' (Becker, 1966). Deviance or crime is much more than a matter of individual choice or personal failing. *How* a society defines deviance, *whom* individuals brand as deviant and *what* people decide to do about non-conformity are all issues of social organisation.

The social and global shapes of crime

All societies have crime and deviance: sociologists generally agree that there is no such thing as a crime-free society. Indeed, crime may be a necessary price to pay for a certain social freedom (and hence non-conformity). It may serve as a means of bringing about change – the political criminals of one generation can become the leaders of another – and it may mark out the moral boundaries of society – if we had no 'bad', could we have any 'good'? A society with no crime or deviance would probably have to be a very rigid and very controlled society. At the same time, societies may have very different levels or rates of crime – too much 'freedom', for example, may lead to very high levels of crime. Not all societies have the same 'social shape' of crime.

A high crime rate?

Although there is always a lot of public concern about crime, it is important to note that the broad trend in many Western countries is downwards. From roughly 1995, across 35 Western countries including the United States, crime rates have actually started to fall (Blumstein and Wallman, 2000; *British Crime Survey*, annually; *Social Trends*, annually). But this is after a long period of annual increase. In the UK, roughly 100,000 offences were recorded annually between 1876 and 1920, growing to half a million by 1950, two and a half million by 1980, and nearly six million in 2002–3. But then crimes recorded started to drop: in 2009, there were 5.2 million crimes recorded by the police across the UK, a fall of 5 per cent from 5.4 million offences in 2007–8. In 2005–6, there were 8.4 million fewer crimes in England and Wales than the peak of 19.4 million in 1995, representing a fall in the *British Crime Survey* crime rate of 44 per cent (see Table 17.1).

Table 17.1	Incidents of crime: by type of offence,[1] England and Wales, 1981–2008 (millions)						
	1981	1991	1995	2001–2	2006–7	2007–8	2008–9
Household crime							
Vandalism	2.7	2.8	3.4	2.6	3.0	2.7	2.8
All vehicle-related theft[2]	1.8	3.8	4.4	2.5	1.7	1.5	1.5
Burglary	0.7	1.4	1.8	1.0	0.7	0.7	0.7
Bicycle theft	0.2	0.6	0.7	0.4	0.5	0.4	0.5
Other household theft[3]	1.5	1.9	2.3	1.4	1.2	1.1	1.2
All household crime	6.9	10.4	12.4	7.9	7.1	6.5	6.8
Personal crime							
Theft from the person	0.4	0.4	0.7	0.6	0.6	0.6	0.7
Other thefts of personal property	1.6	1.7	2.1	1.4	1.1	1.0	1.1
All BCS violence	2.1	2.6	4.2	2.7	2.5	2.2	2.1
Assault with minor injury	0.6	0.8	1.4	0.7	0.6	0.5	0.5
Assault with no injury	0.8	1.0	1.6	1.0	1.0	0.9	0.8
Wounding	0.5	0.6	0.9	0.6	0.6	0.5	0.5
Robbery	0.2	0.2	0.3	0.4	0.3	0.3	0.3
All personal crime	4.1	4.7	6.9	4.7	4.2	3.8	3.9
All crimes reported to BCS	11.0	15.1	19.4	12.6	11.3	10.2	10.7

[1] Until 2000 respondents were asked to recall their experience of crime in the previous calendar year. From 2001/02 onwards the British Crime Survey (BCS) became a continuous survey and the recall period was changed to the 12 months prior to interview.
[2] Includes theft of, or from, a vehicle, as well as attempts.
[3] Includes thefts and attempted thefts from domestic garages, outhouses and sheds, not directly linked to the dwelling, as well as thefts from both inside and outside a dwelling.

Source: Social Trends, 40, 2010, p. 128, Table 9.3.

In the United States, the crime rate was also extremely high: during the 1990s, police tallied some 8 million serious crimes annually, but again these have started to fall in recent years.

Crime rates, then, escalated throughout most of the twentieth century but have generally fallen a little in recent times. The drop is not great, but talk of constantly rising crime rates is not – statistically at any rate – true. However, this does not stop many people saying that 'crime has never been higher and things are getting worse'. As we shall see below, there are real problems in knowing exactly what criminal statistics such as these mean, and they should always be approached with caution (see also Chapter 3, pp. 94–5).

Types of crime in the UK

From reading the newspapers you could easily believe that sexual and violent crimes were everywhere. In fact, property crimes account for the majority (72 per cent) of all offences recorded by the police in 2007–8 in England and Wales (Figure 17.1). While killings attract much attention, they account for around 600 or 700 offences a year, and well over half of these take place in the home: that is, they are 'domestic'. Sex crimes, which probably attract most attention, are among the crimes with the lowest rates of all (T. Thomas, 2000). In 2007–8, only 1 per cent of all crimes committed in England and Wales were sex crimes. Looking at criminal statistics, the following generalisations can be made:

- In 2007, the peak age for men to be found guilty of or to be cautioned for an offence was 17; 6 per cent of men in this age group were found guilty or cautioned, as opposed to 1 per cent of women in the same age group. This prevalence of male crime persists across all age groups.
- Less than 1 per cent of men in each age group over the age of 45, and of women over the age of 19, were found guilty of an indictable offence.
- The likelihood of being a victim of crime is shaped to a large extent by people's place of residence. In 2007–8, for instance, the highest levels of household crime, such as theft and burglary, occurred in Yorkshire and the Humber, whereas Londoners were most likely to become victims of personal crime, such as assault and robbery.
- Many offenders have already been convicted of an offence previously (seven out of ten males in 1994). In 2006, the reoffending rate for juveniles and adults was 39 per cent.
- A small proportion of offenders are responsible for a large proportion of offences. Two-thirds of adults released from prison in 2003 reoffended within two years. Four in ten young offenders reoffended within a year. More recent data largely confirm this trend.
- In 2008 there were 2.1 million violent offences reported in the British Crime Survey – a fall of 614,000 incidents since 2001–2.
- In 2008, there was a total of £609.9 million worth of plastic card fraud losses on UK-issued cards, the highest recorded since 1998.

England & Wales

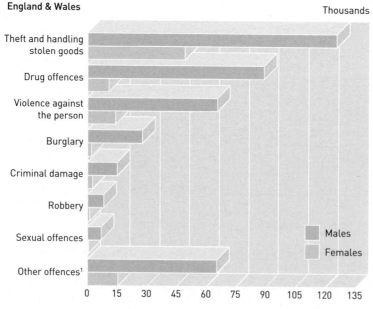

Thousands

Figure 17.1 Offenders found guilty of, or cautioned for, indictable offences: by sex and type of offence, 2008

Source: Office for Criminal Justice Reform, Ministry of Justice, in *Social Trends*, 40 (2010), Fig. 9.12, p. 133.

¹ Includes fraud and forgery and indictable motoring offences.

- The most common form of crime recorded by police in England and Wales in 2007–8 was theft and the handling of stolen goods (36 per cent).
- There were 763 homicide offences recorded in 2007–8, an increase of 3 per cent compared to the previous year.
- There were at least 69 killings in England and Wales where the victim was aged under 16 in 2007–8, accounting for around 9 per cent of all offences currently recorded as murder or manslaughter. Of these, 79 per cent were killed by someone they knew, including 43 children (62 per cent) who were killed by their parents. In comparison, ten homicide victims (14 per cent) in this age group were killed by strangers. There were 24 child homicide victims aged between 5 and 15 and 45, child homicide victims were aged 4 and under. Around 62 per cent of all children murdered were male (see *Social Trends*, 2010).

Problems of measuring crime

Criminologists and sociologists usually turn to several key sources when they want to see the patterns of crime in a society. In the UK, for instance, the key sources are the statistics gathered by the Home Office and published annually as *Criminal Statistics in England and Wales*. Most industrial societies have comparable reports, but in low-income societies these figures are much less reliable and much harder to obtain. Over the past 30 years a new system has been introduced which surveys the public's experience of crime in England. This is known as the *British Crime Survey*, and since 2001 it has been an annual survey.

1 Official statistics

Crime statistics – like all statistics – must be read with extreme caution. One way of understanding the construction of crime statistics is to see them like a flow, through which smaller and smaller numbers of offences get counted. We start with a very large pool of actual offences where the numbers are unknown and unknowable. There is then a sharp drop in numbers at each stage. It seems likely that as few as two in 100 offences result in a conviction. This is the hidden figure of crime. Figure 17.2 shows the flows through the criminal justice system, and at each stage the numbers incorporated shift.

Official statistics of 'recorded crimes' include only crimes reported to the police. (But they may not include all the crimes reported – some, for instance,

may not be crimes or may be very trivial.) So getting crimes reported is the first key issue in statistics construction. Quite clearly, not all crimes are reported, though this differs with the offence. The police learn about almost all killings, but assaults – especially among acquaintances – are far less likely to be reported. The police record an even smaller proportion of property crimes, especially when losses are small. Some victims may not realise that a crime has occurred, or they may assume they have little chance of recovering their property even if they notify the police. Reports of rape, although rising over time, still grossly understate the extent of this crime.

The majority of crimes come to police attention by being reported by the public (about 90 per cent). The public's responsiveness is shaped by such issues as:

- tolerance of certain kinds of crime (such as vandalism)
- seriousness of offence (such as very minor thefts or brawls)
- confidence in the police ('nothing can be done')
- crimes without victims (such as drug offences)
- awareness that it is a crime (for example, some fraud).

2 British Crime Survey

These official criminal statistics are not the only way of recording crime. A major alternative way is through a *victimisation survey*, in which a researcher asks a representative sample of people about their experience of crime. People do not always respond fully or truthfully to such surveys, experts acknowledge, but the results of these surveys indicate that actual criminality occurs at a rate two or three times higher than official reports suggest.

In England and Wales, since 1982, there has been a regular major victim survey of crime: the *British Crime Surveys*. Since 2001 it has been conducted annually. Here a random sample of about 5,000 adults are asked questions about being victims of crime, whether they reported the crimes or not, and their fear of crime. These studies raise further doubts about the value of crime statistics, as they have persistently shown both much higher rates and significant discrepancies for different kinds of crime. At the same time, these figures also suggest that the overall growth of crime may have been exaggerated, since crime statistics are so dependent on the vagaries of reporting. Indeed, on the basis of these studies, 'the risk of becoming a victim of any form of crime is still historically low at 27 per cent,

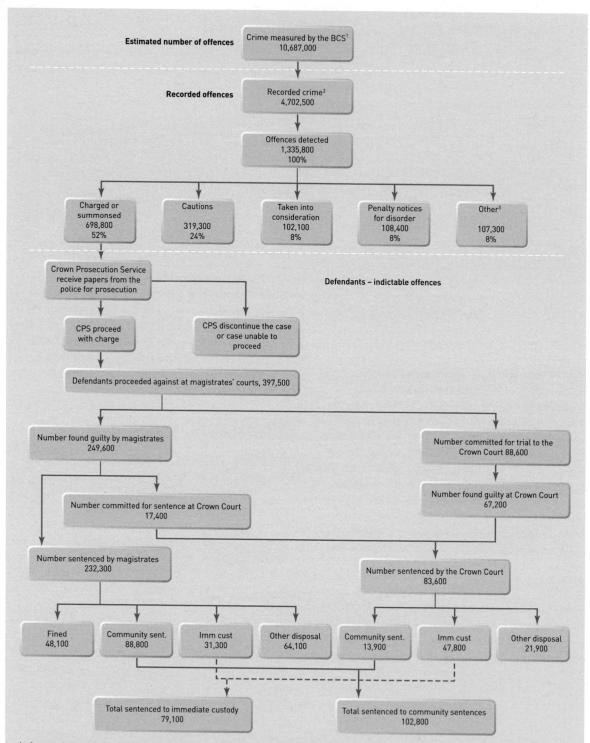

Figure 17.2 Flows through the criminal justice system, 2008

Source: *Criminal Statistics: England and Wales 2008* (Ministry of Justice, 2010) p. 17.

Is there more crime than last year?

Below is a comparison of the two major research tools for measuring crime in the UK. Their findings for the year 2008–9 have overlaps, similarities and differences. Look at them. Again think about the problems of using statistics.The BCS and police recorded crime differ in their coverage of crime. Overall, crime as measured by the BCS shows no change in most crime types compared with the 2007–8 BCS. Crimes recorded by the police show a 5 per cent decrease compared with 2007–8, with decreases in most crime types.

British Crime Survey crime
- All BCS crime stable (10.7 million crimes in 2008/09)
- Violent crime – stable
- with injury – stable
- Domestic burglary – stable
- Vehicle-related theft – stable
- Theft from the person up 25%
- Vandalism – stable
- Risk of being a victim of crime up from 22% to 23%

Police recorded crime
- All police recorded crime down 5% to 4.7 million crimes
- Violence against the person down 6%
- with injury down 7%
- Domestic burglary up 1%
- Offences against vehicles down 10%
- Theft from the person down 12%
- Criminal damage down 10%
- Robbery down 5%
- Drugs offences up 6%

Source: *Crime in England and Wales, 2008–9* (Home Office 2009) Home Office Statistical Bulletin.

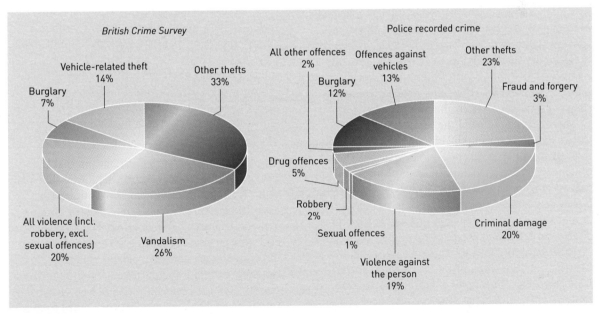

British Crime Survey

- Vehicle-related theft 14%
- Burglary 7%
- Other thefts 33%
- All violence (incl. robbery, excl. sexual offences) 20%
- Vandalism 26%

Police recorded crime

- All other offences 2%
- Offences against vehicles 13%
- Burglary 12%
- Other thefts 23%
- Fraud and forgery 3%
- Drug offences 5%
- Robbery 2%
- Sexual offences 1%
- Violence against the person 19%
- Criminal damage 20%

Figure 17.3 Which crimes are included in the British Crime Survey and the Police recorded statistics?
Source: *Criminal Statistics in England and Wales 2008* (Ministry of Justice, 2010).

around the same level as 1981, and one-third lower than the risk in 1995 (when it was 40 per cent) (*Social Trends*, 2004: 139). Personal crimes, such as assault, and robbery are consistently prevalent among young adults. For instance, in 2006, 26 per cent of men and women between 10 and 25 years of age had become victims of such offences.

The *Methods and research* box above looks at the contrasting findings of these two crime surveys in the UK for 2008–9.

The globalisation of crime

Because it is impossible to be accurate about measuring crime in any one society such as the UK, it becomes even harder to compare crimes across cultures. In many low-income countries, the data are significantly flawed anyway. Despite these problems, crime rates do appear to differ throughout the world.

Thus, although violent crime is prevalent in many countries of western Europe, the violent crime rate in the United States generally emerges as about five times greater; and the rate of property crime is twice as high. With differences as great as this, it seems reasonable to conclude that crime is more frequent in the United States than in western Europe. On the other hand, there are parts of eastern Europe where it is very hard to measure what is actually going on. Indeed, it has been suggested that some of these countries have become increasingly 'gangsterised', with very high levels of crime. Since the fall of communism in these countries, market economies have appeared which have been ill-prepared to cope with changing demands. As a result, a kind of criminal wasteland has appeared in certain areas (Castells, 1998: 180–90). All this may contrast greatly with many nations of Asia, including India and Japan, where rates of violent and property crime seem to be among the lowest in the world. Likewise, in Iran and many other Muslim countries, rates of crime are generally thought to be low.

There again, in some of the largest cities of the world, such as Manila in the Philippines and São Paulo in Brazil, crime rates do appear to be soaring. These are the cities that have rapid population growth and millions of desperately poor people (see Chapter 24). By and large, however, the traditional character of less economically developed societies and their strong family structure allow local communities to control crime informally.

As we have seen in many earlier chapters, we are experiencing 'globalisation' on many fronts, and crime is no exception. Some types of crime have always been multinational, including terrorism, espionage and arms dealing. But newer ones are appearing as crimes travel through countries and know no borders. Below we suggest eight ways in which crime has become increasingly globalised.

1 *Trafficking in commodities*: many illegal markets exist across the globe to sell a wide range of commodities. These range from arms and weapons through pornography to drugs. Even illegal nuclear weapons can be smuggled across borders for money. These are all multibillion dollar industries trading in illegal commodities. (See the box on p. 590; watch the film *Trafficking*.)

2 *Trafficking in people*: many illegal markets exist across the globe to sell people and their body parts. Women and children may be moved from low-income countries to richer ones, where they enter the new massive world of sex markets (see Chapter 12). Since the development of transplant surgery, a major new industry has developed involving the sale of organs usually from poor people to the rich (in Chapter 7, we look briefly at this). Most generally, we also find the smuggling of illegal immigrants – there is a widespread trade in people leaving their own country, desperate to find work and security elsewhere. Chapter 15 has already described the plight of 58 Chinese immigrants being smuggled into the UK who were found dead on arrival: they had been packed into a lorry with the air vent closed. The driver was sent to prison for 14 years. (See also the film *Ghosts*.)

3 *Trafficking in money*: money gained from dubious often illegal activities gets banked, lost and then reworked back into the formal system through a system of offshore banks, secrecy and confidentiality (this is known as money laundering). Money earned in illicit markets has to get back into the legitimate economy. Such activities are found extensively in drug markets, but the free markets of the neoliberal world also work to foster an increase in all kinds of financial crime.

4 *The development of cybercrimes*: the internet knows few borders, and its global character means that many crimes can be conducted across countries with ease. The internet facilitates new kinds of criminal activity (like hacking, spamming, malicious software and spyware, identity theft) as well as enabling many old crimes (such as fraud, stalking, smuggling, money laundering and pornography) to flourish (cf. Jewkes, 2007). All these new crimes have worldwide implications. You can be stalked or robbed from anywhere in the world (see also Chapter 23).

5 *Environmental crimes*: many 'new crimes' are emerging because of criminal neglect or more direct criminal activity. We include here the dumping of toxic waste by rich countries in poor countries (e.g. in Abidjan, off the Ivory Coast in 2006, where over 15,000 people sought medical attention; or Trafigura in 2009), through to the international illegal trade in wildlife, the size of which is estimated to lie between

$10 and $20 billion. (This area of globalisation has led to a whole new area of criminology – often called green criminology) (see also Chapter 25).

6 *The mediaisation of crime*: knowledge and images of crime travel the world through media images. Crime – and its control – is no longer of one country, as we see its forms and efforts to control it across the world on television, film, YouTube and the internet.

7 *Global crimes of war and the new terrorism*: here we find the massacring of civilians, the torturing of captives, the prevalence of genocide. At the same time, global surveillance and migration control increase (see Chapter 16).

8 *Globalisation of crime control*: surveillance and new crime policies have witnessed the growth of penal sanctions and the state in regulating lives across the world. In the search for a more secure society, more and more groups are being monitored (and often excluded). Social control has come to take on a more international character – examples are the Centre for International Crime Prevention in Vienna, and various United Nations programmes such as the Global Programmes against Corruption, and the Global Programme against Trafficking. Crime control programmes developed in one country can get transported to another. (On all this and more, see Katja Franko Aas: *Globalization and Crime*, 2007.)

Global drugs and their control

Trafficking in illegal commodities, especially drugs, accounts for billions of pounds and may well be the world's largest industry. The illegal drugs trade is found all over the world: cocaine in Colombia and the Andes; opium/heroin from the Southeast Asian Golden Triangle (Burma, Thailand, Vietnam, Laos); all along the troubled Mexican border; as well as in Turkey, the Balkans, Afghanistan and Central Asia. Like any economic process, the global drugs trade has three key dimensions: consumption, production and distribution (trafficking) (see Chapter 15). But this economic process gets seriously distorted because of the illegal nature of the markets. Drug use raises serious issues of social control.

Consumption

Table 17.2 indicates the global use of drugs. The 2010 UNODC Global Report on Drugs estimates that between 155 and 250 million people (3.5–5.7 per cent of the population aged 15–64) used illicit substances at

least once in 2008. Cannabis use is by far the largest category, involving 129–90 million users. Note, though, that this is an enormous range and the statistics are very unreliable.

Cultivation, production and distribution

The bulk of cultivation of drugs is carried out by very poor people on small plots of land. Drugs attract much higher prices than crops such as potatoes and hence generate hugely profitable markets. These markets often become a substantial part of the economies of poorer countries' GDP (often between 10 and 15 per cent). A chain of poverty and profit arises: the value of a drug is little when it starts out from the plant, but as it moves from hand to hand and dealer to dealer it usually acquires enormous value. As the prices rise, a massive underground economy grows. Because drugs are against the law, they are frequently controlled by criminal organisations, not the government; and huge profits can be reaped through a black or illicit economy. These drugs cannot be regulated by the usual market forces; and their marketing often generates violence, fear and corruption on a wide scale.

The Golden Triangle developed after the Second World War as a major producer of opium in Thailand, Myanmar, Laos and Vitenam, and peaked in the 1990s. The source then switched to Afghanistan, which now accounts for between 89 and 90 per cent of illicit global supplies. In Afghanistan, ending the growth of the poppy crops is not seen as a viable option because the sale of poppies constitutes the livelihood of many of Afghanistan's rural farmers. It has been claimed that as many as 3.3 million Afghans are involved in producing opium. In turn this supports the Taliban in Afghanistan. Most of the opium is processed into heroin and subsequently sold in Europe and Russia. Afghan opium kills 100,000 people every year worldwide.

Two Latin American countries – Mexico and Colombia – are also important in illicit opium supply. This trade is linked to organised crime and government corruption, and here we see the rise of the '**Narco State**': *an area that has been taken over and is controlled and corrupted by drug cartels, where law enforcement is weak or effectively non-existent.* Often the drugs trade gets an institutionalised presence in the state. Mexico is seen as a classic example. Here there are many notorious gangs: all along the US–Mexico border (more than 2,000 miles long), drugs, guns and killings are common. Between 2007 and 2010, it was estimated that some 23,000 people were killed as criminal drug cartels fought each other and 'innocent bystanders' (Vuillamy, 2010).

Table 17.2   Estimated number of illicit drug users in the past year aged 15–64 years, by region and subregion: 2008

Region/subregion	Cannabis users in the past year		Opiate users in the past year		Cocaine users in the past year		Amphetamines-group users in the past year		Ecstasy users in the past year	
	Number (lower)	Number (upper)	Number (lower)	Number (upper)	Number (lower)	Number (upper)	Number (lower)	Number (upper)	Number (lower)	Number (upper)
Africa										
North Africa	**27,680,000** 4,680,000	**52,790,000** 10,390,000	**680,000** 130,000	**2,930,000** 540,000	**1,020,000** 30,000	**2,670,000** 50,000	**1,550,000** 260,000	**5,200,000** 540,000	**350,000**	**1,930,000**
West and Central Africa	14,050,000	22,040,000	160,000	340,000	640,000	830,000	*estimate cannot be calculated*		*estimate cannot be calculated*	
Eastern Africa	4,490,000	9,190,000	150,000	1,730,000	*estimate cannot be calculated*		*estimate cannot be calculated*		*estimate cannot be calculated*	
Southern Africa	4,450,000	11,170,000	240,000	320,000	290,000	900,000	310,000	1,090,000	220,000	420,000
Americas										
North America	**38,210,000** 29,950,000	**40,030,000** 29,950,000	**2,290,000** 1,290,000	**2,440,000** 1,380,000	**8,720,000** 6,170,000	**9,080,000** 6,170,000	**4,760,000** 3,090,000	**5,890,000** 3,200,000	**3,040,000** 2,490,000	**3,280,000** 2,490,000
Central America	580,000	600,000	100,000	110,000	120,000	140,000	320,000	320,000	20,000	30,000
The Caribbean	430,000	–1,730,000	60,000	90,000	110,000	320,000	30,000	510,000	10,000	240,000
South America	7,300,000	7,530,000	840,000	870,000	2,330,000	2,450,000	1,320,000	1,860,000	510,000	530,000
Asia										
East/South-East Asia	**31,510,000** 5,370,000	**64,580,000** 23,940,000	**6,460,000** 2,830,000	**12,540,000** 5,060,000	**430,000** 390,000	**2,270,000** 1,070,000	**4,430,000** 3,430,000	**37,990,000** 20,680,000	**2,370,000** 1,460,000	**15,620,000** 6,850,000
South Asia	16,490,000	27,550,000	1,390,000	3,310,000	*estimate cannot be calculated*		*estimate cannot be calculated*		*estimate cannot be calculated*	
Central Asia	1,890,000	2,140,000	340,000	340,000	*estimate cannot be calculated*		*estimate cannot be calculated*		*estimate cannot be calculated*	
Near and Middle East	7,790,000	10,950,000	1,890,000	3,820,000	*estimate cannot be calculated*		*estimate cannot be calculated*		*estimate cannot be calculated*	
Europe										
West/Central Europe	**29,370,000** 20,850,000	**29,990,000** 20,990,000	**3,290,000** 1,090,000	**3,820,000** 1,370,000	**4,570,000** 4,110,000	**4,970,000** 4,130,000	**2,500,000** 1,600,000	**3,190,000** 1,710,000	**3,850,000** 2,180,000	**4,080,000** 2,190,000
East/South-East Europe	8,520,000	9,010,000	2,210,000	2,460,000	470,000	840,000	900,000	1,480,000	1,680,000	1,890,000
Oceania	2,140,000	3,410,000	120,000	150,000	330,000	390,000	470,000	630,000	840,000	910,000
GLOBAL ESTIMATE	**128,910,000**	**190,750,000**	**12,840,000**	**21,880,000**	**15,070,000**	**19,380,000**	**13,710,000**	**52,900,000**	**10,450,000**	**25,820,000**

Source: UNODC, *World Drug Report 2008*, United Nations, 2010.

Control: international responses: 'the war on drugs'

Responses to drugs vary enormously across the world – from intense control and legislation through to a much more relaxed attitude and decriminalisation. Typical of the former is the policy of the United States, where a major 'war on drugs' and criminalisation have been major features of its policies (and have been very influential on the policies of many allied countries from Mexico to the United Kingdom). By contrast, the policies of countries like Amsterdam and Portugal have put major areas of drug use out of the reach of law, and seen drug use as much more of a medical problem. (Often the claim is made that alcohol is actually a more serious drug than many of those which have been criminalised.) The policies of the United Nations have been to create alternative programmes of development – to eliminate drug cultivation through introducing new rural development to combat poverty. A 2010 report claims this to be a partial success; global cocaine and heroin production is in decline from all-time highs (UNODC, 2010).

In general, though, the 50-year 'war on drugs' approach has raised many serious problems and cannot be considered a success. In summary:

- There have been few signs of the global 'drugs problem' diminishing over the past 50 years – and many claim it has kept growing in scale.

- A new massive world population of imprisoned drug users has emerged – and with it a new growing prison population riddled with drug problems.
- A major development of organised crime and drug cartels has been created – with a major worldwide underground market – closely linked with government and police corruption and street violence.
- Communities have become ghettoised – whole communities have become organised through drug dealing and the threats of violence posed by gangs.

Drugs as a problem has certainly not been resolved or contained. Instead, a massive industry has now developed around drug control. In some countries, the response has become militarised as conventional law enforcement agencies have failed. These use military weapons in drug control, accompanied by massive levels of violence. There is often extreme international pressure on governments to reduce drug production – in order to get international funding and kudos. Practically, funding is often channelled to the reduction of crop production and law enforcement. Little money goes to education and treatment. Such responses allow the military into law enforcement and weaken the democratic foundations of a state. The United States and its negative approach are often seen as lying at the 'heart of the problem'. It spends $40 billion on the 'war against drugs' and imprisons some 1.5 million of its citizens (Buxton, 2006). Yet the drug problem continues.

PUBLIC SOCIOLOGY

What are the goals of a penal system? How should crime be dealt with?

Penality refers to *the institutions and agencies that compose a penal system, including the economic, political, intellectual and cultural conditions*. It is a very wide term, but part of its task is to clarify the object or target of the system. There are many ways to think about the work of the penal system, but one way is to consider the

different goals of a penal system. What is it set up to do? What does it think it is doing, why and to whom?

There is probably no single issue in society about which the public gets more heated than 'crime' (indeed, social surveys frequently show this to be so). There is widespread awareness and fear of crime. As such, the whole issue is featured regularly in media debates, and it is usual to find key public speakers in strong disagreement. Very often they speak from a number of very different standpoints, making radically different assumptions. And, of course, they are not necessarily always compatible. Malcolm Davies has

very succinctly summarised the tensions that may be found in any penal policy. It may:

> Denounce the wrongful, deter the calculating, incapacitate the incorrigible, rehabilitate the wayward, recompense the victim and punish only the culpable.
>
> (Davies, 2009: 347)

Sometimes these are not compatible. Try to identify which of the following positions experts might have as you listen to them:

- *Deterrence*: seeks to prevent crime through effective, efficient sanctions, usually ensuring that punishments are certain, clear, swiftly

PUBLIC SOCIOLOGY

applied and severe but fair. It assumes a very rational model of behaviour and an uncomplicated view of human social life. The world is usually much messier than this.

- *Rehabilitation* (and reform): seeks to bring about change in the causes of crime – economic, personal, social, often linked to treatments and community action. It assumes criminals have no or little control or responsibility over their crimes, and that changes in people or the environment can be readily engineered. In this vein, people ask which specific treatments and responses work. Which have a high impact for success and change? Often, the conclusion is that many do not work very effectively.

- *Restoration*: seeks to return to things 'as they were'. Justice aims to reconcile conflicts, heal rifts in communities and bring things together. There must be a moral response to crimes but not one that leads to rejection of criminals.

Again, it may assume a perhaps too rational model of behaviour – though this time perhaps a more benign one. People will cooperate and do right if given the right social opportunities.

- *Retribution*: the offender deserves to be 'punished'; an eye for an eye, a tooth for a tooth (what historically is the *lex talionis*, the law of the scale). Here, past behaviours are looked at, and society has a duty to punish wrongdoers. This can easily slide into 'vengeance', which many think is not a good moral basis for the law. But a version known as 'just deserts' highlights the need for a fair and recognised scale of appropriate punishments.

- *Incapacitation and social protection*: society must be protected. People are protected by simply excluding the criminal – in prison or in capital punishment. This seems to be a very popular response among the public, but not among criminologists (except as part of a wider

system of multiple aims incorporating several of the other aims outlined above).

- *Radical non-interventionism*: the minimum intervention. It may be at odds with the penal system, since it wants to run the system down. This position suggests that the penal system does not really work well and indeed may even promote a lot of crime. This may make sense for some crimes without victims, but for more serious crimes, it is not generally acceptable to the public. In some areas, however, there may be some value in cutting back the law, reducing the number of professionals working on criminals, closing down institutions where prisoners are incapacitated, and diverting criminals into other – maybe welfare – responses to crime.

Look out for these kinds of broad positions when you hear discussions in the media.

See Davies et al. (2009: chapter 1 and part D).

Changes in social control

Because societies have rules, members target each other with efforts at social control. Cases of more serious deviance may provoke a response from a formal **social control system** which involves *planned and programmed responses to expected deviance* (S. Cohen, 1985: 2). At the most visible level, this involves a **criminal justice system**, *a societal reaction to alleged violations of law utilising police, courts and prison officials* using various punishments and corrections, from prisons to probation. The criminal justice system is a society's formal response to crime. In some countries, military police keep a tight rein on people's behaviour; in others, officials have more limited powers

to respond to specific violations of criminal law. But there are also less visible networks of control: from the informal networks of families and friends, through the monitoring done by social workers and psychiatrists, to the closed-circuit surveillance in shops and shopping centres, the development of electronic tagging and the rise of private policing. Some of these will be discussed below.

Most of the key features of the modern Western control system – often called 'penality' – emerged at the end of the eighteenth century. Although, for instance, jails existed prior to this time, they were not the large-scale places with individual cells and strict rules that exist now. Instead, they were smaller and local and held crowds of people who were undifferentiated by crime and offence. Often they were just 'holding places' on the way to the gallows (Ignatieff, 1978). Likewise, policing was organised on a local basis. Only in 1829 was the Metropolitan Police force established in England.

But, with industrialisation and the emergence of the modern world, all this changed. *Control processes became subject to bureaucratisation, professionalisation and state funding.* Thus, control became organised through bureaucratic, rule-bound organisations run by new trained professionals such as prison officers and policemen, and central government started to play a significant role in legislation and in the funding of control. In 1999–2000, around £12 billion was spent on the criminal justice system in the UK (more than doubling between 1977 and 1997). Some 124,000 people were employed by the police (as well as 53,000 civilians) (*Social Trends*, 2001: 172). This scale is mirrored in most other industrial countries: everywhere social control today is a large part of public/state spending.

In his classic book *Discipline and Punish: The Birth of the Prison* (1977; orig.1975) Foucault (profiled in the box below) depicts this change dramatically. In the striking opening pages – well worth a read – he compares the earlier forms of brutal and chaotic punishment on the body with the more recent forms of surveillance and imprisonment which are intensely rule governed. As he says, it is the difference between the spectacle of a *public execution* and a *timetable*. The former leads to the following normal event in 1757:

> **. . . on a scaffold that will be erected (at the Place de Grève), the flesh will be torn from his breasts, arms, thighs and calves with red hot pincer, his right hand . . . burnt with sulphur, and, on those places where the flesh will be torn away, poured molten lead, boiling oil, burning resin, wax and sulphur melted together and then his body drawn and quartered by four horses and his limbs and body consumed by fire, reduced to ashes and thrown to the winds . . .**

(Foucault, 1977; orig. 1975: 3)

Michel Foucault: power and surveillance

The French philosopher and historian of ideas Michel Foucault (1926–84) was one of the twentieth century's most influential thinkers. He examined a number of major changes that marked out the distinctive ways in which we think in 'the modern world' when compared with the past, and he developed an important theory to link power, knowledge and discourse.

Always a radical and critical thinker, he saw dramatic ruptures with the past and suggested that these modern developments were not signs of simple 'enlightened' progress, but evidence of extending power and increasing surveillance. For Foucault, power is everywhere and works its way through

Michel Foucault (1926–84)
Source: AFP/Getty Images.

discourses – *bodies of ideas and language often backed up by institutions.* Thus, criminology is a discourse that invents or produces its own set of ideas and languages about the criminal as an object to be studied, backed up by many institutions such as the prison and the courts. Power works its way distinctly through this discourse to help shape the whole society's view of crime.

'Knowledge' in this view may act as a way of keeping people under control.

Table 17.3 below shows how Foucault's work looks at such changes as (1) the appearance of the modern prison along with the rise of criminology; (2) the 'birth of the clinic' as a distinctly modern way of handling health; (3) the development of the psychiatric discourse and modern approaches to madness, through grasping the appearance of a very distinctive modern way of reasoning; and (4) the development of our modern languages around sexuality. Very wide ranging, he even asks questions about the very idea of what it means to be an 'individual' human being in Western societies.

Many of Foucault's ideas challenge common sense. He argued, for instance, that 'sexuality' has not always existed: it is a creation of the modern world. And he suggested that prisons, far from solving the

THINKERS & THEORY

crime problem, actually extend it. His most accessible book is *Discipline and Punish* (1977; orig. 1975), in which he traced the development of the modern prison system. A brief extract from this is given in the text.

His ideas are controversial and much discussed. Some say he was one of the most brilliant figures of twentieth-century thought. Others feel that his difficult writing and complexity have detracted from engagement with what is happening in the world.

For 'easy' introductions to Foucault's work, see Geoff Danaher, Tony Schirato and Jen Webb: *Understanding Foucault* (2000) and Lisa Downing, *Cambridge Introduction to Michel Foucault* (2008).

Table 17.3	A basic guide to some of Foucault's major works (from Plummer, 2010)	
Examine the discourses of	**To show power relations inside institutions like**	**Key book**
Criminology	Prisons, courts, law, policing, surveillance	*Discipline and Punish* (1975)
Health	Hospitals	*The Birth of the Clinic* (1963)
Mental illness and psychiatry	Asylums, classification systems, welfare	*Madness and Civilization* (1961)
Sexology, psychology, social science	Therapy, prison, governmental interventions, law	*The History of Sexuality* (1976)
Humanities, literature and history	Academic life, universities	*The Archaeology of Knowledge* (1969)
Religion, politics, education	Government, schools	Found in many of his interviews and essays

Source: Plummer (2010).

while the latter leads, 80 years on, to:

> *Art. 17.* The prisoners' day will begin at six in the morning in winter and at five in the summer . . . they will work for nine hours a day . . .
>
> *Art. 18.* Rising. At the first drum-roll, the prisoners must rise and dress in silence . . . at the second drum-roll, they must be dressed and make their beds. At the third, they must line up and proceed to the chapel for morning prayer . . .
>
> *Art. 19.* The prayers are conducted by the chaplain and followed by a moral or religious reading. This exercise must not last more than half an hour . . .

(Foucault, 1977; orig. 1975: 6)

The differences in systems of control are clearly illustrated.

Control cultures in the twenty-first century

The modern control system may be characterised in three ways. First, the old system of public control (financed by the state) of prisons and policing laid down during the nineteenth century has continued to expand. New prisons are being built and in some countries prison populations have increased dramatically. Second, and starting in the period after the Second World War, a new and largely informal system of control has been grafted on to this. This brings an ever-increasing number and wider range of people into the control network. Third, starting in the early 1980s, the system overall has expanded greatly to include a wide range of newer surveillance techniques, and many of these are privately sponsored and funded.

The twenty-first century: the global prison century?

Prisons seem to be expanding and growing in nearly all countries. Nils Christie (2000) calls this the 'Prison Industrial Complex'. There has been a massive expansion in numbers going to prison, as well as numbers of prisons.

Towards the end of 2008, more than 9.8 million people were held in prisons throughout the world –

Gitarama Prison

Kigali, Rwanda, Africa

Gitarama has the most overcrowded prison in the world. In 2006, it reportedly held 7,477 detainees although its official capacity was 3,000 (and the original building design was for only 500 people). The jail is so congested that inmates have no option but to stand all day and night, and many suffer from rotting feet. The floor is moist and filled with raw faeces and the stench is unbearable. The survival rate is low due to the violence and the demeaning conditions in the building where one in eight prisoners will die from disease or violence. Many of the prisoners are locked up for genocide committed against Rwanda

See: http://www.unhcr.org/refworld/ publisher,AMNESTY,,RWA,3ae6aa0340,0.html.

Source: Reuters.

about half of these in the United States (2.29 million), Russia (0.89 million) and China (1.57 million – plus pre-trial detainees and prisoners in 'administrative detention'). The United States is frequently cited as the country with the highest prison population in the world – some 756 per 100,000 people. Japan has a conspicuously low rate of prisoners (63 per 100,000 people). In Europe, the trend may not be quite so developed. Indeed, some countries such as Sweden, Norway and the Netherlands have long been seen as having the most humane and contained prison systems in the world. But in Europe overall there are sharp contrasts: the median rate for southern and western European countries is 95 whereas for countries spanning both Europe and Asia (e.g. Russia and Turkey) it is 299. In England and Wales, it is 153 per 100,000 of the national population, as opposed to 88 in Northern Ireland and 152 in Scotland. With a couple of minor exceptions – Luxembourg and Estonia – it is the highest rate of imprisonment in Europe.

But almost everywhere the most striking feature is that in recent years, prison use is on the increase and the treatment of prisoners is getting worse. For instance, in the Netherlands in 1975, there were 2,356 prison cells and the rate of imprisonment was 17 per 100,000. In the middle of 2006, it had 21,013 prisoners comprising 128 per 100,000 of the population. In the UK the prison population was relatively stable during the 1970s and early 1990s, but in the mid-1990s it

began to increase. It rose by 79 per cent over the years from 17,435 in 1900 (when records began) to reach 82,572 in 2008. Data from the World Prison Population List 2009, compiled at King's College London, show a world pattern largely consistent with this growth pattern (see the box).

Imprisonment has become a huge industry and a system in crisis in the early twenty-first century. This may be partly due to new policies such as the 'three strikes' policy (first introduced in Washington in 1992) which produces a mandatory life sentence after three offences. It may also be due to a decisive penal shift in many countries to be 'tough on crime and on the causes of crime'. There has been a clear shift from policies of rehabilitation to policies of punishment over the past decade. The Top 10 box on page 597 shows the largest prison populations.

Privatising prisons

Since the late twentieth century, there has been a turn away from state investment in prisons towards privatisation. Although private arrangements for running prisons can be traced back for some time (for instance, to early arrangements of labour leasing – the chain gangs), since the early 1990s more and more countries have come to see privatisation as one fruitful way of handling the 'penal crisis'.

World Prison Population List

The *World Prison Population List* gives details of the number of prisoners held in 218 independent countries and dependent territories. It is published by the International Centre for Prison Studies. Its most recent report in January 2009 found the following:

- More than 9.8 million people are held in penal institutions throughout the world – an increase of 300,000 since the previous count two years before. (If prisoners in 'administrative detention' in China are included, the total is over 10.6 million.)
- Almost half of the world's prisoners are in the United States (2.29 million), China (1.57 million sentenced prisoners) and Russia (0.89 million) – countries which account for just over a quarter of the world's population.
- The United States' prison total constitutes a rate of 756 per 100,000 of the national population, making it pro rata by far the biggest user of prison in the world. Almost three-fifths of countries (59 per cent) have rates below 150 per 100,000. The overall world prison population rate

(based on 9.8 million prisoners and a world population of 6,750 million) is 145 per 100,000.

- With a prison population rate of 153 per 100,000 (a rise of 5 since the previous edition of the list), England and Wales lock up more prisoners per head of population than other countries in western Europe apart from Spain (160) and Luxembourg (155) and some 60 per cent more than countries such as Belgium, France, Germany, Ireland and Italy.
- Particularly large rises have recently occurred in Europe, in Turkey and Georgia (both up more than 50 per cent since mid-2006). The largest recent falls in prison population in Europe are in Romania (down 2 per cent since September 2006) and the Netherlands (down 22 per cent since mid-2006).
- Notable rises elsewhere include those since mid-2006 in Chile (up 28 per cent), Brazil (up 18 per cent) and Indonesia (up 17 per cent).
- The report also found that the rise in prison populations is evident in every continent. Updated information on countries included in previous editions of the *World Prison Population List* shows that prison populations have risen in 71 per cent of these countries

(in 64 per cent of countries in Africa, 83 per cent in the Americas, 76 per cent in Asia, 68 per cent in Europe and 60 per cent in Oceania).

- The list shows that rates vary considerably between different regions of the world, and between different parts of the same continent. For example:

Africa: the median rate for western African countries is 35 per 100,000 whereas for southern African countries it is 231.
The Americas: the median rate for south American countries is 154 whereas for Caribbean countries it is 324.5.
Asia: the median rate for south-central Asian countries (mainly the Indian subcontinent) is 53 whereas for (ex-Soviet) central Asian countries it is 184.
Europe: the median rate for southern and western European countries is 95 whereas for the countries spanning Europe and Asia (e.g. Russia and Turkey) it is 229.
Oceania (including Australia and New Zealand): the median rate is 102.

Source: adapted from Walmsley, R. (2009) *World Prison Population List*, 8th edn.

Initially, privatisation was applied in the United States to the 'soft end' of the control process – to small facilities for juveniles, low-security prisons and women's prisons. The first contracted-out house for juveniles was established in 1975 in Pennsylvania. A little later, Corrections Corporation of America (CCA) and Wakenhut started to get contracts for adult prisons.

Those in favour of private prisons argued that they were more economic, more flexible and more efficient

– they provided new and better facilities, and costs were reduced in both prison building and operations. Critics suggested that it was 'punishment for profit'. It was an area where markets and profits could be made against the public and individual good.

The system has grown throughout the world. It has been taken up in Australia, but most European countries take it seriously too. France has had one of the strongest involvements, with at least 17 private institutions accommodating over 10,000 prisoners.

TOP 10

Largest prison populations

1	USA	2,300,000
2	China	1,600,000
3	Russia	860,000
4	Brazil	460,000
5	India	370,000
6	Mexico	225,000
7	Thailand	212,000
8	Iran	166,800
9	South Africa	160,000
10	Ukraine	144,380

Note: Based on total prison population, latest available year; rounded values.

Source: *Pocket World in Figures*, Profile Books, 2011, p. 101.

Privatisation is also found in Germany, the Netherlands and the UK (see James et al., 1997).

Spreading the net: informal control

This massive growth of prisons has ironically been accompanied by the spread of what have been called 'alternatives to prison'. They are clearly *not* 'alternatives' but exist side by side with prison expansion, bringing an ever-increasing number of people into the control network. Young offenders, for instance, who were once cautioned may now be placed on a community care order or required to attend some form of therapy group. The British criminologist Anthony Bottoms has called these developments the *bifurcation* of the system: 'put crudely, this bifurcation is between, on the one hand, the so-called "really serious offender" for whom very tough measures are typically advocated; and on the other hand, the "ordinary offender" for whom we can afford to take a much more lenient line' (Bottoms, 1988).

The rise of the surveillance society

The penal system overall has expanded greatly to include a wide range of surveillance techniques, and many of these are privately sponsored and funded. Although surveillance has been around for a long time, its intensity has grown so much in the modern world that we can start to talk of a **surveillance society**, *a society dependent on communication and information technologies for administrative and control processes and which results in the close monitoring of everyday life* (Lyon, 2001).

In non-industrial societies, surveillance operates in an informal manner, often through primary groups (see Chapter 6). But larger organisations require much more complex monitoring of events. Since the rise of the industrial society, more and more energy has been expended on collecting records on the lives of citizens and monitoring their behaviour. Most noticeable here has been the dramatic increase in closed-circuit television (CCTV) in recent years. In shops, on motorways and in all kinds of public places, surveillance can now take place 24 hours a day, 365 days a year. The UK seems to have the highest number of surveillance cameras in Europe – with 4 million cameras throughout the UK and half a million in London alone. Indeed, an average person in London is purportedly filmed 300 times a day (Monahan, 2006: 3). Crime detection is no longer dependent upon the police being called; now they can systematically monitor and video-record crimes, sending appropriate squads to deal with them.

New digital technologies can also put faces into an electronic file of suspects so that previous shoplifters in stores can be identified as soon as they enter the shop. Developing systems are also going to be able to electronically identify people through the unique iris patterns in their eyes or through their unique voices. This could mean, for example, that passports or credit cards will become things of the past, as features of our body are digitally scanned as a unique identifying personal bar code.

But not all surveillance operates so formally. Another interesting development has been the informal operation of *Neighbourhood Watch Schemes*. Starting in 1982, there has been an enormous growth in the number of people who want to watch over their communities. By 2010, it was estimated that there were some 150,000 such schemes in the UK. Likewise, systems of electronic tagging – a system of home confinement aimed at monitoring, controlling and modifying the behaviour of defendants or offenders – have been introduced since the mid-1980s in a number of countries, including Canada, the United States, the UK, Sweden, Norway and Denmark. Here, the offender wears an electronic bracelet or anklet and is monitored for 24 hours a day. Public opinion was initially against the idea, and some governments, such as that in the UK, found it difficult to implement initially (not least

Surveillance cameras are widespread. Here is the state-of-the-art surveillance camera control centre, built and operated by Manchester (UK) police and the National Car Parks Company to control crime. Over 450 different cameras feed into the system. Since the implementation of the system they have been used to monitor 3,000 incidents and make 1,300 arrests

Source: © George Steinmetz/Corbis.

LIVING IN THE C21ST

The ever-present gaze: CCTV surveillance in Britain

Below is a fictional account by Norris and Armstrong (1999) of Thomas Kearn's day as he encounters various forms of surveillance. As you read it, spot the different kinds of surveillance technique at work (they are numbered). When you have finished, chart your own day and see if it looks at all like this.

Thomas Kearn's day starts as usual. At 7.15 a.m. the sounds of BBC Radio Four, emanating from his clock radio, penetrate his slumbering consciousness. He wakes quickly, showers and dresses in his best suit, which flatters his 38-year-old frame. His ten-year-old son and four-year-old daughter are washed and dressed by the time he joins them for breakfast. At 8.15 he kisses his wife goodbye and shuts the front door of his apartment behind him, children in tow, to dispatch them to school and nursery, before embarking on another office day. They head towards the lift along the concrete walkways and are captured on a covert video surveillance operation, set up by the local authority, aimed at identifying residents who are dealing in drugs from their premises (1) ... As they wait for the lift, their presence is monitored on the concierge's video system 12 floors below, as is their descent, for there is also a camera in the lift and their predictable daily routine is preserved on tape to be stored for 28 days, or longer if necessary (2). As they walk from the lobby of their apartment block to the car, it is not only the concierge who monitors the Kearns' departure, but Mr Adams on the fifteenth floor, who has tuned his television to receive output from the Housing Estate's cameras (3).

Thomas drives out of the estate on to the dual-carriageway and, although vaguely aware of the sign that declares 'reduce your speed now – video cameras in operation', still drives at 10 miles an hour over the speed limit and trips the automatic speed cameras (4). By 8.30 he has dropped his daughter off at the CCTV-monitored nursery (5) and is heading towards his son's school. He stops at a red light, which is as well because had he jumped it, another picture would have been taken to be used as evidence in his prosecution (6). As they wait in the playground for the buzzer to signal the start of school, they are filmed by a covert camera secreted in the building opposite to monitor the playground for signs of drug dealing (7) and their goodbye kiss is also captured on the school's internal CCTV system which monitors every entrance and exit (8). Noticing that his fuel tank is nearly empty, he drives to the petrol station and fills up. He knows that he is being filmed as a large sign at the cash desk declares: 'These premises are under 24-hour video surveillance' (9).

He leaves the garage and approaches the station, and quietly curses as he is stopped by the barriers at the railway crossing. His location is caught on one of the four Railtrack cameras monitoring the crossing specifically to ensure that the intersection of road and track is clear when the train crosses (10). A few minutes later he is parked in the car park opposite the station under the watchful eye of another set of cameras (11).

As usual, Thomas buys a newspaper at the newsagents, and is filmed by

their in-store security cameras as he does so. No one is monitoring the images from the two cameras but they are taped on a multiplex video recorder which records the images from both cameras on one tape and enables any incident to be reviewed should it be necessary (12). Before buying his ticket, he makes a telephone call from the public box on the station forecourt to remind his wife that he will be late home. Unbeknown to him he is filmed by a covert camera installed by British Telecom to try to catch those who vandalise their telephone boxes and hoax callers to the emergency services (13). His call made, he buys his ticket, walks to the platform and waits for his train, all of which has been recorded and monitored by the 32 cameras operating at the station (14). On arrival at his destination, he walks the short distance to his office and smiles at the camera monitoring the reception area (15). He is, however, unaware that his movements are being recorded by a

number of covert cameras hidden in the smoke detector housings as he walks along the corridor towards his office (16).

The story continues and leads us to consider residential surveillance, school surveillance, road traffic surveillance, telephone and cash machine surveillance, railway surveillance, retail and commercial surveillance, hospital surveillance, football stadia surveillance and police surveillance.

Continue the debate

1 Consider whether the rapid rise of CCTV is valuable. What are its chief advantages? What problems does it bring?

2 Is this the face of the future? Where might the limits of CCTV lie? Can it be checked now?

3 Read George Orwell's *Nineteen Eighty-Four* and consider whether Orwell's reality has now become a commonplace part of everyday life in the UK.

Source: Norris and Armstrong (1999: 40–2); Lyon (2001).

---

because of the technical problems). But with adequate liaison with probation committees, it is slowly becoming one more pathway open to the penal system. It is much cheaper than imprisonment and has a moderate success rate. The main reasons for failure seem to be linked to alcohol and drug misuse.

In the UK, one final recent development is that of the ASBO – the Anti-Social Behaviour Order which was introduced under the Crime and Disorder Act 1998 and strengthened by the Anti-Social Behaviour Acts in 2003. These serve restrictions on people (usually young people) committing intimidating and disruptive activities – including truancy, public drunkenness and graffiti. The number of ASBOs

issued in England and Wales increased sharply from 135 in December 2000 to 7,360 in September 2005 (*Social Trends*, 2007: 125). Once again, this heightens the level of surveillance in the community. Much of this serious government policy has been mocked (see Wallace and Spanner, *How to get an ASBO!* (2007), which suggests that ASBOs have now become almost a figure of fun among the young and a popular word now captures them – the 'chav'. See also Lee Bok, *The Chav Guide to Life*, 2007). In 2010, the new Conservative–Liberal Coalition government decided to dismantle the system.

In sum, there has been a major expansion in social control and surveillance in modern societies.

Boundaries of control are being blurred and many new deviants are being 'created' through this system. The downside of all this, of course, is a civil liberties concern: we may never quite know who is watching us, when or where. George Orwell's nightmare world of *Nineteen Eighty-Four* may finally be upon us.

Perpetuating the death penalty

Even as these newer forms of control appear in the twenty-first century, older ones continue. Not only are prisons getting fuller, as we have seen above, but the death penalty still remains in many countries. The death penalty has a long history as a response to all kinds of crime; it has now been abolished in some 130 countries (in 90 countries for all crimes, whereas other countries have kept it for exceptional crimes such as war crimes, or still have it as a law but have an established practice of not enforcing it). At the same time, countries such as the United States, China and

many African states still enforce the death penalty (see Map 17.1).

Among the advanced industrial societies, the United States retains the death penalty (it also has an oddly high homicide rate when compared with similar societies). Since 1977, when the death penalty was restored, roughly 1,057 people have been executed. Of these, 367 were black, 621 were white and 75 were Hispanic. At the start of 2007, there were some 3,300 people (only 49 of them were women) still awaiting execution on Death Row (for more information see Amnesty International's website: www.amnestyusa.org/death-penalty/death-penalty-facts).

Penal populism: tapping into the public mood of punitiveness

A key component of the 'crime problem' is the feelings and responses of the public towards crimes. For many

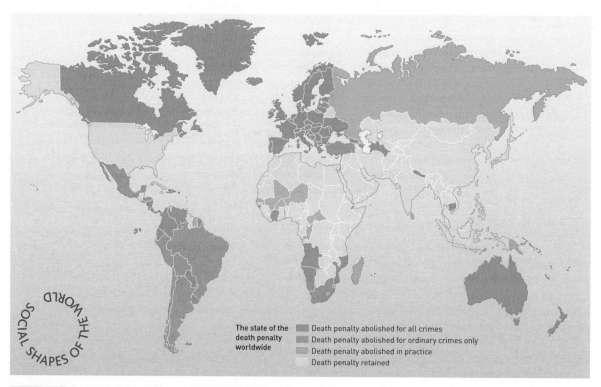

The state of the
death penalty
worldwide

☐ Death penalty abolished for all crimes
☐ Death penalty abolished for ordinary crimes only
☐ Death penalty abolished in practice
☐ Death penalty retained

Map 17.1   **The death penalty in global perspective**
This map shows the extent to which different degrees of the death penalty are still allowed in various parts of the world. Abolition of the death penalty has often been seen as the hallmark of a 'civilised' society. If this is so, what does this map suggest about the state of the world?
Source: Adapted from *Amnesty* magazine, Issue 117, Jan./Feb. 2003, www.amnesty.org.

THINKERS & THEORY

Stanley Cohen: from Mods and Rockers to states of denial

Stanley Cohen is a prominent world leader in sociology, criminology and human rights. Born in Johannesburg, he has lived in both England and Israel and was the Martin White Professor of Sociology at the London School of Economics.

Cohen's work has always shown a deep concern for the oppression and suffering of others. In South Africa as child and youth, he saw the horrors of apartheid at first hand. In England and the United States he witnessed the inhumanities of a so-called advanced criminal justice system. And in Israel he came to detest the atrocities generated through the Israeli–Palestinian conflicts. The thread that holds all his work together is a passionate preoccupation with the often unnecessary sufferings of people living under systems of social control – from the smallest regulations in our everyday lives, through the workings of courts and prisons, to mass systems of torture and genocide. An intellectual maverick, he has always been radically critical of orthodox criminology and has – over the past 40 years – been consistently at the forefront of its rethinking.

His earliest research, *Folk Devils and Moral Panics* (1972), is a classic sociology book. In it he looked at the big English youth phenomenon of the 1960s: the rise of the so-called 'Mods and Rockers'. After the teddy boys of the 1950s these were the first major youth phenomenon of the post-Second World War era, and sparked a great deal of controversy. They seemed to turn the local beaches of Clacton (near London) into a battle ground. In his work, the 'Mods' and 'Rockers' came into being, at least in part, because of the very responses of media, police and courts – who helped define and shape a moral panic. Interventions – usually in the name of benevolence or 'doing good' – can sometimes actually make situations worse, not better.

Stanley Cohen
Source: Permission from Stanley Cohen.

After this he looked explicitly at 'social control'. He researched prison life and became involved with various prison reform movements. He also started the mapping of an extensive vision of just how control systems were changing across the world (Cohen, 1985). For him, the old penal system of prisons was still getting larger, while a whole new system – surveillance, community programmes, therapies and medicalisation – was now mapped on top of it. In all of this, we were witnessing a major extension of social control over our lives.

In the most recent phase of his work, Cohen's research has taken him into the field of human rights as he charts the ways in which man's ghastly inhumanity to man – all over the world – continues. He sees a world full of sufferings: wars, torture, wrongful and dreadful imprisonment and genocide. While there are both people who are the victims of this, and others who victimise, his concern is with a third group: those who turn a blind eye and refuse to see what is going on. He asks: Why do people not see, fail to see, persistently deny the horrors that are going on all around them? Why do they say 'there is nothing I can do about it'? Across the world, millions of lives are ravaged on a daily basis; and most people simply do not want to know. In this there is an ironic twist to his research. Whereas 30 years ago he saw issues like 'Mods and Rockers' as media events that gained an exaggerated importance, his work these days looks at events like torture and genocide which seem to be given too little attention in the media.

Source: Cohen (1972; 1985).

reasons, the 'public' is generally concerned about crime – partly because they worry about being victims of crimes, partly because they are concerned that some people are not 'good citizens', and perhaps partly because they have some broad sense of retribution, fairness and punishment. Sociologists are concerned with studying these public responses.

Much contemporary response to crime has been characterised as *penal populism*: the idea that the public has a generally punitive stance towards crime and criminals, and also that politicians can benefit from exploiting this belief. 'Popular opinion' sees crime as high on social problems listings, often sees courts as doing too little, and believes the police are not doing their job properly, that crime is everywhere and 'out of control', and that we have 'gone soft'.

Penal populism is a structure of belief. Facts are largely irrelevant: it is a discourse embedded in the popular media and depends on resentment against elite groups – rulers, academic and intellectual – who seem to be 'in charge of things' and 'not doing a good job'. There is a resentment against the powerful, against experts and officials who often seem to be on the side of the criminal and not the victim. A distance from them is often encouraged by the media; and it is part of a wider decline in trust and belief in rulers and experts. It is also part of the wider processes of people finding their voice.

For John Pratt (2007), penal populism marks a key shift in what might be called 'penal power'. Beginning in the 1970s, penal populism started to give a much greater voice to victims, victims' rights movements and anti-crime movements, and often has come to have great symbolic importance. Penal populism depends on creating enemies, scapegoats and images of threatening people: welfare scroungers, the violent, gangs and strangers – the paedophiles, sex offenders, immigrants and others in our midst. Often it connects to a sense of a dangerous world. Famous media cases often galvanise this; and some press and TV treatments of crime encourage both fear and the demand for stronger sanctions.

Explaining crime and deviance

We have so far shown how crime has definite social patterns, and we have examined some of the ways in which society responds to the criminal. Now we are ready for the question that haunts most people: just what makes people criminal or deviant? How can we explain this? Too often, though, this is the only question that people ask: why do people do it, and how can we stop them? What sociologists try to make clear is that crime is bound up with the very conditions of a society.

1 The classical school

The classical school of criminology dates back to Enlightenment thinking (see Chapter 1) and highlights the nature of crime as a rational choice. People commit crimes when they can (a) maximise their gains and (b) be relatively sure of not being punished. Crime is a rational act. This means that a great deal of emphasis within this school turns to adjusting the penal system to deter people from committing crimes. Cesare Beccaria, an Italian who argued for major penal reform in 1764, is generally seen as the founder of the 'classical tradition' in criminology. He questioned the nature of severe punishment and advocated instead a system of deterrence. For him, punishments could only deter if they were 'proportional' to the crime: the more serious crimes should receive more serious punishments. Punishment must be essentially public, prompt, necessary, the least possible in the given circumstances, proportionate to the crimes and dictated by the laws (Beccaria, 1963; orig. 1764). His ideas have remained influential. What is a just sentence? In the 1970s the 'Back to Justice' model suggested by von Hirsch and his colleagues claimed that 'the severity of punishment should be commensurate with the seriousness of the wrong' (von Hirsch, 1976: 66). They argued that:

- The degree of likelihood that the offender might return to crime should be irrelevant to the choice of sentence. He should be sentenced on what he has done.
- Indeterminate sentences should be abolished. Particular crimes merit particular punishments, and offenders should know what they will get.
- Sentencing discretion should be sharply reduced. A system of standardised penalties should be introduced.
- Imprisonment should be limited to serious offences – usually for crimes of serious harm.
- Milder penalties should not claim to rehabilitate, but simply be less severe punishments (von Hirsch, 1976).

The problems with the classical model

Critics have suggested a number of problems with these classical ideas. First, they argue, it suggests that crime is a free choice and, as we shall see, many accounts of crime argue that it is determined in some way (from poor family background to unemployment). If this is so, simple deterrence will not work. Secondly, it assumes that people are rational, free and self-interested. If they can see they will be punished, they will be deterred; if they think they can get away with crime, they will. But not all human activity is like this. Finally, the theory assumes that societies work in fair and just ways, whereas often it is not possible to have justice and fairness in societies that are themselves organised in ways that are neither just nor fair. You cannot easily have 'justice in an unjust society'.

2 The positivist school

Positivist theories focus on the characteristics and causes of a criminal type. Here we will look briefly at some biological and psychological versions (but there are social versions too).

Chapter 7 explained that people a century ago understood – or, more correctly, misunderstood – human behaviour as an expression of biological instincts. Understandably, early interest in criminality emphasised biological causes as well. In 1876 Caesare Lombroso (1835–1909), an Italian physician who worked in prisons, declared that criminals have a distinctive physique – low foreheads, prominent jaws and cheekbones, protruding ears, excessive hairiness and unusually long arms that, taken together, made them resemble the ape-like ancestors of human beings. Many criminals (not all) were atavistic throwbacks to an earlier form of species on the evolutionary scale (Lombroso, 1970; 1911: 68).

But Lombroso's work was flawed. Had he looked beyond prison walls, he would have realised that the physical features he attributed exclusively to prisoners actually were found throughout the entire population. We now know that no physical attributes, of the kind described by Lombroso, distinguish criminals from non-criminals (Goring, 1972; orig. 1913).

In the middle of the twentieth century, William Sheldon and colleagues (1949) took a different tack, positing that body structure might predict criminality. Sheldon categorised hundreds of young men in terms of body type and, checking for any criminal history, concluded that delinquency occurred most frequently among boys with muscular, athletic builds. Sheldon Glueck and Eleanor Glueck (1950) confirmed Sheldon's conclusion, but cautioned that a powerful build does not necessarily cause or even predict criminality. The Gluecks postulated that parents treat powerfully built males with greater emotional distance so that they, in turn, grow up to display less sensitivity towards others. Moreover, in a self-fulfilling prophecy, people who expect muscular boys to act like bullies may provoke such aggressive behaviour.

Recent genetics research and the Human Genome Project (see Chapter 23) continue to seek possible links between biology and crime. To date, no conclusive evidence connects criminality to any *specific* genetic flaw. Yet people's overall genetic composition, in combination with social influences, may account for some variation in criminality (Rowe and Osgood, 1984; Wilson and Herrnstein, 1985; Jencks, 1987).

The key features of positivism

Despite differences, what most biological or psychological theories have in common is a particular approach or paradigm towards crime. This paradigm has been called *positivistic criminology* by the sociologist David Matza (1964) and it has three major characteristics.

First, it always focuses upon *the criminal as a specific type of person*. Thus criminology started to draw up long classification systems of different kinds of offender. Lombroso, for example, identified not just the born criminal, but also the emotional criminal, the morally insane criminal and the masked epileptic criminal.

Second, it looks for the *ways in which criminals differ from others*. The focus is upon finding the different characteristics, which may range from body parts (for example, size and weight of skulls) or body types or personality types. Long lists of ways in which offenders differ from non-offenders can be drawn up. This was advanced greatly by new technologies such as photography in the nineteenth century (which could record bodily and facial features) and fingerprint testing in the twentieth century. Most recently, chromosome typing (the XYY chromosome is said to be linked to violent offences) and DNA testing have become the focus of attention. The police now make regular use of 'criminal profiling'.

Third, positivism *seeks out explanations for criminal conduct as being in some way out of control* of the criminal who perpetrates criminal acts. Thus, crime is caused by 'feeble-mindedness', 'atavistic regression', 'unsuccessful socialisation' or 'XYY chromosomes'. Crime, says Matza, is not a free choice but is determined. Positivism is a deterministic theory.

Although this general account of crime is called positivistic criminology, it should not be confused with positivism introduced in Chapter 2, although it does have many similarities. Common to both is the belief in science. But as we have seen (Chapter 3) and shall see further (Chapter 23), science is not itself a straightforward idea.

Critical comment

At best, biological theories that trace crime to specific physical traits explain only a small proportion of all

C. LOMBROSO — *L'homme criminel.*   Pl. XXXVII.

FOUS CRIMINELS.

An example from Lombroso's study that claimed to relate physiognomy to criminal nature. This plate shows a variety of 'typical' criminals. Lombroso, 'L'homme criminel' plate xxxvii, 1895

Source: © Mary Evans Picture Library.

crimes. At this point, we know too little about the links between genes and human behaviour to draw any firm conclusions (Daly and Wilson, 1988). Likewise, although psychologists have demonstrated that personality patterns have some connection to delinquency and other types of deviance, the value of this approach is limited by one key fact: the vast majority of serious crimes are committed by people whose psychological profiles are *normal*.

The positivist approach to crime spotlights criminals as people; it offers no insight into how some kinds of behaviour come to be defined as deviant in the first place. Both biological and psychological approaches view deviance as an individual attribute without exploring how conceptions of right and wrong initially arise, why people define some rule breakers but not others as deviant, or the role of social power in shaping a society's system of social control.

3 Functionalism and the social foundations of deviance

Although we tend to think of deviance in terms of the free choice or personal failings of individuals, all behaviour – deviance as well as conformity – is shaped by society. There are three social foundations of deviance, identified below.

1 *Deviance varies according to cultural norms.* No thought or action is inherently deviant; it becomes deviant only in relation to particular norms. The life patterns of rural Icelanders, urban Californians and Welsh mining communities differ in significant ways; for this reason, what people in each area prize or scorn varies as well. Laws, too, differ from place to place. In Amsterdam, for example, the use of soft drugs is permitted, and there are even shops for their sale. In the rest of Europe, marijuana is outlawed.

2 *People become deviant as others define them that way.* Each of us violates cultural norms regularly, occasionally to the extent of breaking the law. For example, most of us have at some time walked around talking to ourselves or have 'borrowed' supplies, such as pens and paper, from the workplace. Whether such activities are sufficient to define us as mentally ill or criminal depends on how others perceive, define and respond to any given situation.

3 *Both rule making and rule breaking involve social power.* The law, Karl Marx asserted, amounts to little more than a strategy by which powerful people protect their interests. For example, the owners of an unprofitable factory have a legal right to close their business, even if doing so throws thousands of people out of work. But if workers commit an act of vandalism that closes the same factory for a single day, the workers are subject to criminal prosecution. Similarly, a homeless person who stands on a street corner denouncing the city government risks arrest for disturbing the peace; a politician during an election campaign does exactly the same thing while receiving extensive police protection. In short, norms and their application are linked to social inequality.

The functions of crime

Functionalist theory teaches us a great paradox about crime and deviance: that far from always being disruptive, it may contribute to a social system and underlie the operation of society. In his pioneering study of deviance, Emile Durkheim (1964a, orig. 1895; 1964b, orig. 1893) made the remarkable assertion that there is nothing abnormal about deviance; in fact, it performs four functions that are essential to society.

1 *Deviance affirms cultural values and norms.* Culture involves moral choices. Unless our lives dissolve into chaos, people prefer some attitudes and behaviours to others. But any conception of virtue rests upon an opposing notion of vice. Just as there can be no good without evil, then, there can be no justice without crime. Deviance, in short, is indispensable to the process of generating and sustaining morality.

2 *Responding to deviance clarifies moral boundaries.* By defining some individuals as deviant, people draw a social boundary between right and wrong. For example, a university marks the line between academic honesty and cheating by disciplining those who commit plagiarism.

3 *Responding to deviance promotes social unity.* People typically react to serious deviance with collective outrage. In doing so, Durkheim explained, they reaffirm the moral ties that bind them. For example, most US citizens joined together in a chorus of condemnation after suicide bombers hijacked several planes and crashed them into the Pentagon and the Twin Towers of the World Trade Center on 11 September 2001.

4 *Deviance encourages social change.* Deviant people, Durkheim claimed, push a society's moral boundaries, suggesting alternatives to the status quo and encouraging change. Moreover, he declared, today's deviance sometimes becomes tomorrow's morality (1964a; orig. 1895: 71). In the 1950s, for example, many people denounced rock-and-roll music as a threat to the morals of youth and an affront to traditional musical tastes. Since then, however, rock and roll has been swept up in the musical mainstream, becoming a multibillion-dollar industry.

4 Strain theories

Merton's strain theory

While deviance is inevitable in all societies, Robert Merton (1938, 1968) argues that excessive violations arise from particular social arrangements. Specifically, the scope and character of deviance depend on how well a society makes cultural *goals* (such as financial success) accessible by providing the institutionalised *means* (such as schooling and job opportunities) to achieve them. This tension or norm breakdown he called *anomie*. We have seen this term before in the writings of Durkheim (see Chapter 4).

Writing originally about North American society in the 1930s, Merton argued that the path to *conformity* was to be found in pursuing conventional goals by approved means. The true 'success story', in other words, is someone who gains wealth and prestige through talent and hard work. But not everyone who desires conventional success has the opportunity to attain it. Children raised in poverty, for example, may see little hope of becoming successful if they 'play by the rules'. As a result, they may seek wealth through one or another kind of crime – say, by dealing in cocaine. Merton called this type of deviance *innovation* – the attempt to achieve a culturally approved goal (wealth) by unconventional means (drug sales).

According to Merton, the 'strain' between a culture's emphasis on wealth and the limited opportunity to get rich gives rise, especially among the poor, to theft, the selling of illegal drugs or other forms of street hustling. In some respects, at least, a 'notorious gangster' such as Al Capone was quite conventional – he pursued the fame and fortune at the heart of the 'American dream'. But, like many minorities who find the doors to success closed, this bright and enterprising man blazed his own trail to the top. As one analyst of the criminal world put it:

> **The typical criminal of the Capone era was a boy who had . . . seen what was rated as success in the society he had been thrust into – the Cadillac, the big bankroll, the elegant apartment. How could he acquire that kind of recognisable status? He was almost always a boy of outstanding initiative, imagination, and ability; he was the kind of boy who, under different conditions, would have been a captain of industry or a key political figure of his time. But he hadn't the opportunity of going to Yale and becoming a banker or broker; there was no passage for him to a law degree from Harvard. There was, however, a relatively easy way of acquiring these goods that he was incessantly told were available to him as an American citizen, and without which he had begun to feel he could not properly count himself as an American citizen. He could become a gangster.**

(Allsop, 1961: 236)

The inability to become successful by normative means may also prompt another type of deviance that

Table 17.4	Merton's theory of anomie and its adaptations	
Mode	Institutionalised means (hard work)	Societal goal (acquisition of wealth)
Non-deviant		
Conformity	+	+
Deviant		
Innovation	–	+
Ritualism	+	–
Retreatism	–	–
Rebellion	±	±

Note: + indicates acceptance; – indicates rejection; ± indicates replacement with new means and goals.
Source: Based on Merton (1968: 194).

Merton calls *ritualism* (see Table 17.4). Ritualists resolve the strain of limited success by abandoning cultural goals in favour of almost compulsive efforts to live 'respectably'. In essence, they embrace the rules to the point where they lose sight of their larger goals. Lower-level bureaucrats, Merton suggests, often succumb to ritualism as a way of maintaining respectability.

A third response to the inability to succeed is *retreatism* – the rejection of both cultural goals and means so that one, in effect, 'drops out'. Retreatists include some alcoholics and drug addicts, and some of the street people found in cities. The deviance of retreatists lies in unconventional living and, perhaps more seriously, in accepting this situation.

The fourth response to failure is *rebellion*. Like retreatists, rebels reject both the cultural definition of success and the normative means of achieving it. Rebels, however, go one step further by advocating radical alternatives to the existing social order. Typically, they call for a political or religious transformation of society, and often join a counterculture.

What is important in this kind of explanation is that it looks at society as a whole and finds stresses and strains within the system that seem to generate 'weak spots' – crime is induced through a system which has potential for contradiction and conflict. Merton's theory has been extremely influential in the development of 'delinquent gang theory', as we shall see.

Youthful deviant subcultures

Albert Cohen's (1971; orig. 1955) study of delinquent boys pioneered the idea of boys becoming delinquent because of what he termed **status frustration**, *the process by which people feel thwarted when they aspire to a certain status*. In schools especially, Cohen noted that boys from more deprived backgrounds often found school life an alienating and frustrating experience. They wanted to be successes initially, but found that they had not developed the skills to do this in their family and community life. For example, reading books was alien, and being polite and well spoken hard. Their cultural differences had equipped them poorly for school life. Frustrated, Cohen suggests they invert the values of the school – achievement, hard work and planning for the future – and develop instead what can be called a contraculture: where values of non-achievement, playing around and not thinking of the future become deliberately, almost perversely, their goals. Cohen asserts that delinquency is most pronounced among lower-class youths because it is they who contend with the least opportunity to achieve success in conventional ways. Sometimes those whom society neglects seek self-respect by building a deviant subculture that 'defines as meritorious the characteristics they *do* possess, the kinds of conduct of which they *are* capable' (Cohen, 1971; orig. 1955: 66). Having a notorious street reputation, for example, may win no points with society as a whole, but it may satisfy a youth's gnawing desire to 'be somebody'.

Walter Miller (1970; orig. 1958) agrees that deviant subcultures typically develop among lower-class youths who contend with the least legitimate opportunity. He spotlights six focal concerns of these deviant subcultures: (1) *trouble*, arising from frequent conflict with teachers and police; (2) *toughness*, the value placed on physical size, strength and athletic skills, especially among males; (3) *smartness* (or 'street smarts'), the ability to out-think or 'con' others, and to avoid being similarly taken advantage of; (4) *excitement*, the search for thrills, risk or danger to escape from a daily routine that is predictable and unsatisfying; (5) a preoccupation with *fate*, derived from the lack of control these youths feel over their own lives; and (6) *autonomy*, a desire for freedom often expressed as resentment towards figures of authority.

Richard Cloward and Lloyd Ohlin (1966) also extended Merton's theory in their investigation of delinquent youth. They maintain that criminal deviance results not simply from limited legitimate opportunity but also from available illegitimate opportunity. In short, deviance or conformity grows out of the *relative opportunity structure* that frames young people's lives.

Consider, once again, the life of Al Capone. An ambitious individual denied legitimate opportunity, he organised a criminal empire to take advantage of the demand for alcohol in the United States during Prohibition (1920–33). As Capone's life shows, illegal opportunities foster the development of *criminal subcultures* that offer the knowledge, skills and other resources that people need to succeed in unconventional ways. Indeed, gangs may specialise in one or another form of criminality according to available opportunities and resources (Sheley et al., 1995).

But some poor and highly transient neighbourhoods may lack almost any form of opportunity – legal or illegal. Here, delinquency often surfaces in the form of *conflict subcultures* where violence is ignited by frustration and a desire for fame or respect. Alternatively, those who fail to achieve success, even by criminal means, may sink into *retreatist subcultures*, dropping out through abuse of alcohol or other drugs.

Critical comment

Derived from Durkheim's analysis, Merton's strain theory has also come under criticism for explaining some kinds of deviance (theft, for example) far better than others (such as crimes of passion or mental illness). In addition, not everyone seeks success in conventional terms of wealth, as strain theory implies. As we noted in Chapter 5, members of our society embrace many different cultural values and are motivated by various notions of personal success.

The general argument of Cloward and Ohlin, Cohen and Miller points in interesting directions, but it falls short by assuming that everyone shares the same cultural standards for judging right and wrong. Moreover, we must be careful not to define deviance in ways that unfairly focus attention on poor people. If crime is defined to include stock fraud as well as street theft, offenders are more likely to include affluent individuals. Finally, all structural–functional theories imply that everyone who violates conventional cultural standards will be branded as deviant. Becoming deviant, however, is actually a highly complex process, as the next section explains.

Four girls from 'Gang 18', Secca, Sleepy, La Gata and La Diabla, make the symbol 18 with their hands, San Salvador, El Salvador
Source: © Jérome Sessini/Corbis.

5 Learning theories

Sutherland's differential association theory

Learning any social patterns – whether conventional or deviant – is a process that takes place in groups. According to Edwin Sutherland (1940), any person's tendency towards conformity or deviance depends on the relative frequency of association with others who encourage conventional behaviour or norm violation. This is Sutherland's theory of *differential association*.

6 Labelling theory

Labelling theory claims that deviance and conformity result not so much from what people do as from how others respond to those actions; it highlights social responses to crime and deviance. Consider these situations. An office worker 'borrows' a computer from the office; a married man at a convention in a distant city has sex with a prostitute; a Member of Parliament drives home drunk after a party. In each case, 'reality' depends on the response of others. Is the first situation a matter of borrowing or is it theft? The consequences of the second case depend largely on whether news of the man's behaviour follows him back home. In the third situation, is the official an active socialite or a dangerous drunk? The social construction of reality, then, is a highly variable process of detection, definition and response. Because 'reality' is relative to time and place, one society's conventions may constitute another's deviance.

In its narrowest version, labelling theory asks what happens to criminals after they have been labelled, and suggests that crime may be heightened by criminal sanctions. Thus, sending an offender to prison may actually work to criminalise him or her further, and stigmatising minor infractions at too early an age may lead a young offender into a criminal career. In a broadest version, the theory suggests that criminology has given too much attention to criminals as types of people and insufficient attention to the panoply of social control responses – from the law and the police to media and public reactions – which help to give crime its shape.

Although the elementary understanding of the way in which criminal responses may shape crime goes back a long way – caught in popular phrases like 'give a dog a bad name', etc. – the twentieth-century origins of the theory are usually seen to lie with Frank Tannenbaum in his classic study *Crime and the Community* (1938). Here he argued that:

> **The process of making the criminal, therefore, is a process of tagging, defining, identifying, segregating, describing, emphasizing, evoking the very traits that are complained of . . . The person becomes the thing he is described as being . . . The way out is a refusal to dramatize the evil.**

(Tannenbaum, 1938: 19–20)

The theory also connects to the sociological ideas of Durkheim, G. H. Mead, the Chicago School, symbolic interactionism and conflict theory, and draws upon both the idea of a 'self-fulfilling prophecy' and the

No social class stands apart from others as being either criminal or free from criminality. According to various sociologists, however, people with less of a stake in society and their own future typically exhibit less resistance to some kinds of deviance. Here in São Paulo we see a drug addict prostitute with a client

Source: © Michael Ende/Agentur Bilderberg GmbH.

dictum of W. I. Thomas that 'when people define situations as real they become real in their consequences' (W. I. Thomas and D. S. Thomas, 1928).

It was not really until the period between the early 1960s and the late 1970s that labelling theory became a dominant sociological theory of crime, influential in challenging orthodox positivist criminology. During this heyday the key labelling theorists were usually seen to be the North American sociologists Howard S. Becker and Edwin Lemert.

Becker, whose own work focused on marijuana use and its control, outlined the broad problem of labelling when he asked: 'We [should] direct our attention in research and theory building to the questions: who applied the label of deviant to whom? What consequences does the application of a label have for the person so labelled? Under what circumstances is the label of a deviant successfully applied?' (Becker, 1963: 3). In what became the canonical statement of labelling theory, he announced that:

> **Social groups create deviance by making the rules whose infraction constitutes deviance, and by applying those rules to particular people and**

> **labeling them as outsiders ... Deviance is not a quality of the act the person commits, but rather a consequence of the application by others of rules and sanctions to an 'offender'. The deviant is one to whom that label has successfully been applied: deviant behaviour is behaviour that people so label.**

(Becker, 1963: 9)

Primary and secondary deviance

Edwin Lemert (1951, 1972) notes that many episodes of norm violation – say, truancy or under-age drinking – provoke little reaction from others and have little effect on a person's self-concept. Lemert calls such passing episodes *primary deviance.*

But what happens if other people take notice of someone's deviance and make something of it? If, for example, people begin to describe a young man as a 'boozer' and push him out of their social circle, he may become embittered, drink even more and seek the company of others who condone his behaviour. So the response to initial deviance can set in motion *secondary deviance,* by which an individual engages in repeated norm violations and begins to take on a deviant identity. The development of secondary deviance is one application of the Thomas theorem, which states: 'Situations defined as real become real in their consequences' (Thomas, 1928).

The terms *primary and secondary deviance* capture the distinction between original and effective causes of deviance: primary deviance arises from many sources but 'has only marginal implications for the status and psychic structure of the person concerned', whereas secondary deviance refers to the ways in which stigma and punishment can actually make the crime or deviance 'become central facts of existence for those experiencing them, altering psychic structure, producing specialised organisation of social roles and self regarding attitudes' (Lemert, 1972: 40–1). Deviant ascription became a pivotal or master status. It was Lemert who argued that rather than seeing crime as leading to control, it may be more fruitful to see the process as one in which control agencies structured and even generated crime.

Stigma

The onset of secondary deviance marks the emergence of what Erving Goffman (1963) called a *deviant career.* As individuals develop a strong commitment to deviant behaviour, they typically acquire a **stigma,** *a powerfully negative social label that radically changes a person's self-concept and social identity.*

Stigma operates as a master status (see Chapter 7), overpowering other dimensions of social identity so that an individual is diminished and discounted in the minds of others and, consequently, socially isolated. Sometimes an entire community formally stigmatises individuals through what Harold Garfinkel (1956) calls a *degradation ceremony*. A criminal prosecution is one example, operating much like a university graduation except that people stand before the community to be labelled in a negative rather than a positive way.

Retrospective labelling

Once people have stigmatised a person, they may engage in **retrospective labelling**, *the interpretation of someone's past consistent with present deviance* (Scheff, 1984; orig. 1966). For example, after discovering that a priest has sexually molested a child, others may rethink his past, perhaps musing, 'He always did want to be around young children.' Retrospective labelling distorts a person's biography in a highly selective and prejudicial way, guided more by the present stigma than by any attempt to be fair. This process often deepens a person's deviant identity.

The medicalisation of deviance

Labelling theory helps to explain an important shift in the way our society understands deviance. Over the last 50 years, the growing influence of psychiatry and medicine has prompted the **medicalisation of deviance**, *the transformation of moral and legal issues into medical matters.*

In essence, medicalisation amounts to swapping one set of labels for another. In moral terms, we evaluate people or their behaviour as 'bad' or 'good'. However, the scientific objectivity of modern medicine passes no moral judgement, utilising instead clinical diagnoses such as 'sick' and 'well'.

To illustrate, until the middle of the twentieth century, people generally viewed alcoholics as weak and morally deficient people, easily tempted by the pleasure of drink. Gradually, however, medical specialists redefined alcoholism so that most people now consider alcoholism a disease, rendering individuals 'sick' rather than 'bad'. Similarly, obesity, drug addiction, child abuse, promiscuity and other behaviours that used to be moral matters are today widely defined as illnesses for which people need help rather than punishment.

The significance of labels

Whether we define deviance as a moral or medical issue has three profound consequences. First, it affects *who responds* to deviance. An offence against common morality typically provokes a reaction by ordinary people or the police. Applying medical labels, however, places the situation under the control of clinical specialists, including counsellors, psychiatrists and physicians.

A second difference is *how people respond* to deviance. A moral approach defines the deviant as an 'offender' subject to punishment. Medically, however, 'patients' need treatment (for their own good, of course). Therefore, while punishment is designed to fit the crime, treatment programmes are tailored to the patient and may involve virtually any therapy that a specialist thinks will prevent future deviance (von Hirsch, 1976).

Third, and most important, the two labels differ on the issue of *the personal competence of the deviant person.* Morally speaking, people take responsibility for their behaviour, whether right or wrong. If we are sick, however, we lose the capacity to control (or even comprehend) our behaviour. Defined as incompetent, the deviant person becomes vulnerable to intense, often involuntary, treatment. For this reason alone, attempts to define deviance in medical terms should be made only with extreme caution.

Critical comment

The various symbolic-interaction theories share a focus on deviance as process. Labelling theory links deviance not to *action* but to the *reaction* of others. Thus some people come to be defined as deviant while others who think or behave in the same way are not. The concepts of stigma, secondary deviance and deviant career demonstrate how people can incorporate the label of deviance into a lasting self-concept.

The labelling perspective brought political analysis into deviancy study. It recognised that labelling was a political act and that 'what rules are to be enforced, what behaviour regarded as deviant and which people labelled as outsiders must . . . be regarded as political questions' (Becker, 1963: 7). From this it went on to produce a series of empirical studies concerning the origins of deviancy definitions through political actions (in such areas as drug legislation, temperance legislation, delinquency definitions, homosexuality, prostitution and pornography) as well as the political bias in the apprehension and adjudication of deviants.

Closely allied to this political analysis was the view of deviance as a form of resistance: people did not simply accept the labels of deviance that others placed upon them. Instead, they employed a series of secondary adjustments – rebelling, retreating, rejecting, rationalising. Here were studies of the crafting of the deviant identity, where self-labelling, deviance avowal and deviance neutralisation took place.

Yet labelling theory has several limitations. First, because this theory takes a highly relative view of deviance, it glosses over how some kinds of behaviour, such as murder, are condemned virtually everywhere. Labelling theory is thus most usefully applied to less serious deviance, such as teenage misconduct or mental illness.

Secondly, the consequences of deviant labelling are unclear. Research is inconclusive as to whether deviant labelling produces subsequent deviance or discourages further violations (Sherman and Smith, 1992). The deterrent theory of crime, for instance, would actually see sanctions as inhibiting crime rather than amplifying it.

Thirdly, the theory is seen as bringing political implications. Those on the political right often object to the theory on the ground that it seems to sympathise with the criminal and say 'hands off, leave the criminals alone'. Those on the political left, while acknowledging that the theory brings power into the analysis, suggest that it fails to look at the wider *conflictual* workings of the society. It is to these latter theories that we now turn.

7 Conflict criminologies

Conflict theory demonstrates how deviance reflects inequalities and power. This approach holds that the causes of crime may be linked to inequalities – of class, race and gender – and that who or what is labelled as deviant depends on the relative power of categories of people.

Conflict theory links deviance to power in three ways. First, the norms – and especially the laws – of any society generally bolster the interests of the rich and powerful. People who threaten the wealthy, either by seizing their property or by advocating a more egalitarian society, come to be tagged as 'common thieves' or 'political radicals'. As noted in Chapter 4, Karl Marx argued that the law (together with all social institutions) tends to support the interests of the rich. Echoing Marx, Richard Quinney makes the point succinctly: 'Capitalist justice is by the capitalist class,

for the capitalist class, and against the working class' (1977: 3).

Secondly, even if their behaviour is called into question, the powerful have the resources to resist deviant labels. Corporate executives who order the dumping of hazardous wastes are rarely held personally accountable for these acts. And, as the O. J. Simpson trial in the United States made clear, even when charged with violent crimes, the rich have the resources to vigorously resist being labelled as criminal (although this particular case – and the main reason for so much interest in it – was complicated by race: O. J. Simpson was not just wealthy, but black).

Thirdly, the widespread belief that norms and laws are natural and good masks their political character. For this reason, we may condemn the unequal application of the law but give little thought to whether the *laws themselves* are inherently fair (Quinney, 1977).

The new criminology

Although there is a long history of conflict theories of crime (from at least Marx onwards), since the 1970s there has been a significant revitalisation of interest. A key book here was by the British sociologists of crime Ian Taylor, Paul Walton and Jock Young, called *The New Criminology* (1973). This was a substantial critique of all the theories outlined above, and more. Broadly, they argued that most existing theories of crime had not looked at a wide enough range of questions (to take in the wider structural explanations of control as well as of crime, for instance), and had often ignored wider material conflicts at the root of much of the criminal process. At the time of writing, all the authors were Marxists.

Spitzer (1980), also following the Marxist tradition, argues that deviant labels are applied to people who impede the operation of capitalism. First, because capitalism is based on private ownership of wealth, people who threaten the property of others – especially the poor who steal from the rich – are prime candidates for labelling as deviants. Conversely, the rich who exploit the poor rarely are called into question. Landlords, for example, who charge poor tenants high rents and evict those who cannot pay are not considered a threat to society; they are simply 'doing business'.

Secondly, because capitalism depends on productive labour, those who cannot or will not work risk deviant labelling. Many members of our society think of people out of work – even if through no fault of their own – as deviant.

Thirdly, capitalism depends on respect for figures of authority, so people who resist authority are labelled as deviant. Examples are children who play truant or talk back to parents and teachers; adults who do not cooperate with employers or police; and anyone who opposes 'the system'.

Fourthly, anyone who directly challenges the capitalist status quo is likely to be defined as deviant. Into this category fall anti-war activists, environmentalists and labour organisers.

To turn the argument around, society offers positive labels to whomever enhances the operation of capitalism. Winning athletes, for example, have celebrity status because they express the values of individual achievement and competition vital to capitalism.

Additionally, Spitzer notes, we condemn using drugs of escape (marijuana, psychedelics, heroin and crack) as deviant, while espousing the use of drugs that promote adjustment to the status quo (such as alcohol and caffeine).

The capitalist system also strives to control threatening categories of people. Those who are a 'costly yet relatively harmless burden' on society, says Spitzer, include Robert Merton's retreatists (for example, those addicted to alcohol or other drugs), the elderly and people with mental and/or physical disabilities. All are subject to control by social welfare agencies. But those who challenge the very underpinnings of the capitalist system, including the inner-city 'underclass' and revolutionaries – Merton's innovators and rebels – come under the purview of the criminal justice system and, in times of crisis, military forces such as the US National Guard.

Note that both the social welfare and criminal justice systems apply labels that blame individuals and not the system for the control they exert over people's lives. Welfare recipients are deemed unworthy freeloaders; poor people who vent rage at their powerlessness are labelled rioters; anyone who actively challenges the government is branded a radical or a communist; and those who attempt to gain illegally what they cannot otherwise acquire are called common thieves.

Critical comment

Like other analyses of deviance, however, conflict theory has its critics. First, this approach implies that laws and other cultural norms are created directly by and exclusively for the rich and powerful. At the very least, this assumption is an oversimplification, since many segments of our society influence, and benefit

from, the political process. Laws also protect workers, consumers and the environment, sometimes in opposition to the interests of the rich.

Secondly, conflict analysis implies that criminality springs up only to the extent that a society treats its members unequally. However, as Durkheim noted, all societies generate deviance, whatever their economic system.

8 The emergence of left realism

Since the mid-1980s a new debate has appeared. One group of criminologists – from a conflict, Marxist background – have introduced the idea of left realism. Seeing crime as a serious problem, especially in inner-city areas, which has grown in recent years, they analyse what they call 'the square' of crime – the state, society and the public at large, offenders and victims (Figure 17.4). All four factors need to be looked at for all types of crime.

In their argument, a crucial fact is that the victims of crime are overwhelmingly the poor, working-class and often ethnically deprived groups – for example, unskilled workers are twice as likely to be burgled as other workers. *Much crime, then, is largely done by the working class on the working class.* They argue that the causes of crime need to be looked for in deep structural inequalities (see Chapter 10). Crime is produced by

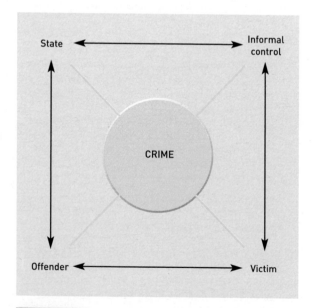

| Figure 17.4 | The 'square of crime' has become the organising framework for those theorists who call themselves the Left Realists |

Source: Adapted from Jock Young.

The Jack-Roller and criminological life stories

The gathering of life stories has been especially popular in the work of sociologists who study crime. Some of the earliest work of Henry Mayhew, for example, on the life and labour of the London poor provides rich life stories of the criminals of the Victorian underworld. Most famously, the Chicago School of Sociology gathered a great many rich life stories of delinquents in the 1920s and 1930s. The stories often follow a particular narrative convention which suggests:

- the importance of early childhood in the causes of crime
- some key stages and sequences in criminal careers
- a major epiphany or turning point initiating a life of crime
- a role in integrating the life into a story.

In this short extract, Stanley – the Jack-Roller, interviewed by Clifford Shaw in the early 1930s – speaks. In the book he tells his full story from about the age of 4, when he first gets into trouble, on to the age of 16. Here he captures some of the ideas of labelling theory discussed in the text.

Mingling in high society

The guard led me, along with other prisoners, to the receiving and discharging department, where I was stripped of my civilian clothes and ordered to take a bath. Then I was given my prison uniform and led to the Bertillon Room, where my photographs and measurements were taken, and identification marks recorded. After having my hair shaved off, given a number for a name, and a large tablespoon to eat with, I was assigned to a cell.

The cell was bare, hard, and drab. As I sat on my bunk thinking, a great wave of feeling shook me, which I shall always remember, because of the great impression it made on me. There, for the first time in my life, I realised that I was a criminal. Before, I had been a mischievous lad, a poor city waif, a petty thief, a habitual runaway; but now, as I sat in my cell of stone and iron, dressed in a gray uniform, with my head shaved, small skull cap, like all the other hardened criminals around me, some strange feeling came over me. Never before had I realised that I was a criminal. I really became one as I sat there and brooded. At first I was almost afraid of myself, being like a stranger to my own self. It was hard for me to think of myself in my new surroundings. That night I tried to sleep, but instead I only tossed on my bunk, disturbed by my new life. Not one minute was I able to sleep.

This brief passage is very suggestive. What do you sense from it and how does it link to a wider understanding of crime?

Why Stanley is especially interesting as a life story is that he was re-interviewed in his seventies by the criminologist Jon Snodgrass. He had moved from Chicago to Los Angeles, married and got divorced, and by and large lived an adult life free of crime. He had, however, been the victim of a mugging himself (see Snodgrass, 1982; on life stories and crime in general, see Bennett, 1981; Messerschmidt, 2000).

'The Jack-Roller'

Source: The Jack-Roller: A Delinquent Boy's Own Story. Photo of the cover, Shaw, Clifford R. (1966; orig. 1930), with an introduction by Howard S. Becker; cover design by James Bradford Johnson (University of Chicago Press).

relative deprivation, *a perceived disadvantage arising from a specific comparison*, and **marginalisation**, *where people live on the edge of society and outside the mainstream with little stake in society overall.*

All this calls for the pursuit of justice at a wide level. The left realists argue for fundamental shifts in economic situations, enlightened prison policies, environmental design and accountable police.

Crime in context

The claims made by left realists are to avoid over-generalised accounts of crime, and to see 'crime in context'. The specific shapes of crime, its causes and the way criminals are controlled, change across the world as society changes. New causes of crime and new patterns of crime appear worldwide. Ian Taylor, for example, argues that the strong shift to a 'market society' since the time of Thatcher and Reagan (discussed in Chapter 15) has not just tended to promote more 'ugly' crime, but also brought more 'brutish' penal responses (Taylor, 1999). He sees a number of transitions that need to be dealt with in understanding current crime, including:

- *The job crisis*. New forms of work, as described in Chapter 15, have brought much less stable working conditions, under-employment and low pay. This provides a context for many young men especially to find better opportunities for a living in crime than in ordinary employment.

- *The crisis of material poverty and social inequality.* As we saw in Chapters 9 and 10, while most countries across the globe are experiencing some levels of prosperity, inequalities are widening. The marginalisation of whole groups of people makes crime an easier option.

- *The fear of crime and 'the other'*. The world appears to have become a dangerous place to live; there is a 'fear of crime' and a 'fortress mentality'. The heightened sense of insecurity makes many unable to deal reasonably with the problem of crime.

- *Other factors* include the crisis in the family and the wider culture.

9 The rise of a feminist and gendered criminology

It is an odd irony that conflict analyses of crime discussed above long neglected the importance of gender, despite its focus on social inequality. If, as conflict theory suggests, economic disadvantage is a primary cause of crime, why do women (whose economic position is generally much worse than that of men) commit far fewer crimes than men do?

Until the 1970s, the study of crime and deviance was very much a male province. But the influential work of British sociologist Carol Smart has changed all that. In her book *Women, Crime and Criminology*, published in 1977, she documented the ways in which women had been neglected in the study of crime and deviance. But she also showed that, when they had been included, the approach had usually been highly sexist or blatantly misogynist. For instance, in one notorious case, a criminologist, Otto Pollak, proposed that women are in fact more criminal than men: it is just that they are also more devious and cunning and hence can 'cover up their crimes' better (Pollak, 1950)!

How does gender figure in some of the theories we have already examined? It is clear that Robert Merton's strain theory has a very masculine cast in that it defines cultural goals in terms of financial success. Traditionally, at least, this goal has had more to do with the lives of men, while women have been socialised to view success in terms of relationships, particularly marriage and motherhood (Leonard, 1982). A more woman-focused theory might point up the 'strain' caused by the cultural ideals of equality clashing with the reality of gender-based inequality. It could help us see that different forms of deviance may emerge for women: those that are linked to marriage and motherhood. Indeed, women who do not marry ('spinsters') and who do not have children ('childless') are often seen as 'problems' (see Hutter and Williams, 1981; Smart, 1984; Richardson, 1993).

Labelling theory offers greater insight into ways in which gender influences how we define deviance. To the extent that we judge the behaviour of females and males by different standards, the very process of labelling involves sex-linked biases. Further, because society generally places men in positions of power over women, men often escape direct responsibility for actions that victimise women. In the past, at least, men engaging in sexual harassment or other assaults against women have been tagged with only mildly deviant labels, if they have been punished at all.

But feminist criminologists have gone much further than reappraising past theories. They have opened up a whole field of new questions and issues. Among the issues have been the importance of the fear of crime in women's, and especially older women's, lives (see Chapter 13); the gendering of sexual violence, and especially the growth of domestic violence, rape and incest (see Chapter 18); and the gendering of social control.

This last topic concerns the ways in which women are handled differently by police, courts and prisons – often through a code of chivalry or through a mechanism by which women are pathologised and rendered as having medical problems. The classic debate here suggested that while men became criminals, women went mad! Feminist criminologies have thrown critical thought over such statements (see Busfield, 1997).

One further contribution of feminist criminology has been to raise the issue of men, violence and masculinity. They have suggested that since more men are involved in violent crimes, and more young men are involved in 'yob culture', there may be a link between forms of masculinity and forms of crime.

Masculinity and crime

And when you think about it, crime does seem to be a male preserve. Statistics repeatedly show that many more men than women commit crimes. Indeed, as Richard Collier notes, 'most crimes would remain unimaginable without the presence of men' (Collier, 1998: 2; see also Jefferson, 1997). Men are also more likely to come before courts and are more likely to end up in prison. Although there are women's prisons, they are greatly outnumbered by those for men. Figure 17.5 documents some of this. Given all this, then, it might seem obvious that in the past criminology should have focused upon the study of men.

But these facts alone should alert us to something very interesting going on. If there is such a skew towards men, could this mean that the whole process of crime is connected to gender? (Gender is more fully discussed in Chapter 12.) It must be a strong probability. We are not, of course, saying that all men are criminal and all women are not, but we are suggesting that there is something about 'masculinity' – or at least certain forms of it – that makes it more probable that men will commit crimes. We need, for instance, to explain why it is that men commit more crimes and women fewer. And indeed, once we start to raise these issues a whole new field of questions and problems arises.

For instance, in virtually every society in the world there would seem to be more stringent controls on women than men. Historically, our society has restricted the role of women to the home. Even in much of Europe today, many women find limited opportunities in the workplace, in politics and in the military. In many bars of Europe, women remain decidedly unwelcome: these places are men's domains. Moreover, women on their own in public places may be looked upon with some suspicion. And elsewhere in the world, the normative constraints placed on women are often greater still. In Saudi Arabia, women cannot vote or legally operate motor vehicles; in Iran, women who dare to expose their hair or wear make-up in public can be whipped.

In the 1990s, masculinity became for a while a key area of research. James Messerschmidt (1993) in the United States researched detailed life stories of

Over 20 : 1	Sexual offences	75 : 1
	Taking and driving away motor vehicles	33 : 1
	Burglary	23 : 1
	Motoring offences (indictable)	20.6 : 1
5–20 : 1	Offences under the Public Order Act 1986	17 : 1
	Criminal damage (summary/less than £2000)	16.5 : 1
	Drunkenness	16.5 : 1
	Robbery	13.5 : 1
	Criminal damage (indictable over £2000)	9.4 : 1
	Drug offences	9.4 : 1
	Common assault (summary)	7.0 : 1
	Violence against the person (indictable)	5.7 : 1
	Assault on constable	5.5 : 1
Under 5 : 1	Theft and handling stolen goods	2.8 : 1
	Fraud and forgery	2.8 : 1
Under 1 : 1 (women form majority)	TV licence evasion	1 : 2
	Offence by prostitute	1 : 100

Figure 17.5 Ratio of male to female offenders found guilty or cautioned for selected offence groupings in the UK

Source: After Coleman and Moynihan (1996: 95–6).

criminals to show how far much crime is deeply bound up with masculinity. More recently, Christopher Mullins (2006) has examined the meanings of masculinities in the streets of an American city (St Louis, Missouri), and how these shaped violence. He showed how a street-based life of violence was deeply linked to a sense of being a man – and how this played a role not only in their street violence but also in their relationships with their 'women' and families. In recent years, more and more criminologists have taken seriously the roots of crime in masculinity (see also Jefferson, 1993).

10 The importance of race and ethnicity

During the 1980s and 1990s more and more sociologists were concerned with how so much crime analysis connected to issues of ethnicity and race. Paul Gilroy, for example, was concerned with the 'black criminal' as a widespread stereotype; there was controversy over the death of Stephen Lawrence and the subsequent responses in the Macpherson Report and the development of ideas about institutional racism (see Chapter 11); there were 'race riots' in inner cities; and there was growing concern over both the higher rates of black victimisation and the much higher rate of black imprisonment – all this and more led to what has been called an 'anti-racist criminology'. This asks questions like:

- Why are so many fears about race and crime linked in with race?
- Why is there so much violence which has a race/ ethnic base? Here we can include a wide range of issues – from lynching in the United States to racist state crime in the Nazi and Rwandan genocides.
- How does institutionalised racism – or more straightforward racial prejudice – work in the police and criminal justice system?
- Why are some ethnic minorities associated with higher levels of offending?
- Are the reasons for offending and victimisation among ethnic minorities different from those among ethnic majorities?

Race and ethnicity have long been correlated both to crime victimisation and to crime rates. In the UK, for instance, ethnic minorities are more likely to be victims of crime than the white population: some 26 per cent of all black households are likely to be victims of theft compared to 20 per cent of white households. The

figures are 22 per cent for those of Indian origin, and 25 per cent for those of Pakistani/Bangladeshi origin (Morgan and Newburn, 1997: 27).

Racial bias in police work seems globally ubiquitous. Roma in Bulgaria are called 'dirty Gypsies' and threatened with violence during police stops; in Spain, Moroccan immigrants report being stopped by the police almost every day, sometimes twice a day; Blacks and Arabs in Paris complain that the police always stop the same people – them. And in the UK, it is black people and Muslims who are most commonly targeted. A recent study in 2010 suggested that black people are 26 times more likely than white people to be stopped and searched by the police in England and Wales (and Asians were 6.3 times more likely to be stopped than whites). Throughout Europe, minorities and immigrant communities routinely report discriminatory treatment by the police, particularly in police decisions about whom to stop, question, search and, at times, arrest (see: www.soros.org/initiatives/justice/focus/equality_ citizenship/projects/ethnic_profiling).

Looking at crime rates in the UK, in 1995 people of Afro-Caribbean origin made up around 1.5 per cent of the total population, but 11 per cent of males in prison. For women, the figure was of greater disparity – some 20 per cent of women in prisons are Afro-Caribbean. For other ethnic groups in the UK, the figures are different: thus south Asians account for 2.7 per cent of the population and about 3 per cent of the prison population.

In the United States, the figures are even more striking – and more alarming. Official statistics indicate that 68 per cent of arrests for crimes in 1998 involved white people. However, arrests of African-Americans were higher than for whites in proportion to their numbers: black people represent 12.7 per cent of the population and 31.9 per cent of arrests for property crimes (versus 65.3 per cent for whites) and 40.2 per cent of arrests for violent crimes (57.7 per cent for whites) (US Federal Bureau of Investigation, 1999).

What accounts for the disproportionate level of arrests among Afro-Caribbeans and African-Americans? Several factors stand out. To the degree that prejudice related to colour or class prompts white police to arrest black people more readily and leads citizens more willingly to report 'blacks' to police as suspected offenders, people of colour are overly criminalised (Holmes et al., 1993). In the UK in 1994–5, 22 per cent of people from ethnic minorities (compared with 5 per cent of the population) were stopped and searched: the figure in London was 37 per cent. This certainly suggests that 'blacks' are more likely to be placed under suspicion (ISTD Factsheet, 1997).

Secondly, race is closely linked to inequalities (see Chapter 11) and, as we have seen above, many of the categories of crime suggest that crime is linked to inequality. Criminality is promoted by the sting of being poor in the midst of affluence, as poor people come to perceive society as unjust. Looking only at the US figures, unemployment among African-American adults is double the rate among whites, two-thirds of black children are born to single mothers (in contrast to one in five white children), and almost half of black children grow up in poverty (as opposed to about one in six white children). With these patterns of inequality, no one should be too surprised at proportionately higher crime rates for African-Americans (Sampson, 1987). And the broad pattern also holds for the UK.

Thirdly, remember that the official crime index excludes arrests for offences ranging from drunk driving to white-collar violations. Clearly, this omission contributes to the view of the typical criminal as a person of colour. If we broaden our definition of crime to include driving while intoxicated, insider stock trading, embezzlement and cheating on income tax returns, the proportion of white criminals rises dramatically.

Finally, some categories of the population have unusually low rates of arrest. People of south Asian descent, who account for about 4 per cent of the population, figure in only 1.1 per cent of all arrests. As Chapter 11 documents, south Asians enjoy higher than average incomes and have established a more successful record of educational achievement, which enhances job opportunities. Moreover, the cultural patterns that characterise Asian communities emphasise family solidarity and discipline, both of which inhibit criminality (see: Webster, 2007; Bowling and Phillips, 2002; Smith, in Maguire et al., 1997).

11 Cultural criminology

This starts with a key premise: 'Mainstream criminology is an abject failure' (Ferrell et al., 2008: 204). Although the significance of culture (see Chapter 5) has been grasped since the early Chicago work on crime and hence throughout most of the twentieth century, it is only recently (largely in the wake of postmodern ideas) that a new sphere of criminology known as *cultural criminology* has been developed. Broadly it highlights:

1 *A criminology of everyday life.* Cultural criminology looks at the ways in which crime weaves its way mundanely through everyday practices and routines. Crime is never far away: there is graffiti on walls, surveillance cameras on the roofs, credit cards and mobile phones snatched from your hand. In their book, Ferrell et al. (2008) trace a day's activities to show how imbued with possible risk and crime everyday life is.

2 *The centrality of media presentations of crime* – which are pervasive in all media forms and take many angles. Thus there are television programmes reporting crime (the daily news), celebrating crime (*The Wire*, *CSI Crime Scene Investigation*) and controlling it (*Crimewatch*) (see Jewkes, 2007; Carrabine, 2008).

3 *The rejection of an overly rational view of crime and its control.* Instead it looks at crime as providing emotional 'highs' and 'kicks' which are not open to simple rational understanding. Violence, risk, danger can bring their own emotional buzz. These are 'the seductions of crime' (see Katz, 1990).

4 *Concern with the image, styles and feeling worlds of crime.* Much of this is coterminous with the imagery of violence; crime crosses the borderline with 'normality' as pop music embraces sadomasochism and the war crimes of Abu Ghraib posts digital images of abuse and violence online.

5 *New forms of crime.* Crimes known as 'edgework', for example, are based on extreme voluntary risk (such as advanced sky diving) carried to precarious and illegal extremes (e.g. illegal graffiti writing in dangerous situations). It is the basis of the film by David Fincher, *Fight Back* (1999) and typically involves men in high-risk activities (see Lyng, 2004).

6 *New methods of cultural analysis and fieldwork styles*: it brings new kinds of ethnography – variously called visual ethnography, liquid ethnography and 'instant ethnography'.

tip The book *Cultural Criminology: An Invitation* (2008) by Jeff Ferrell, Keith Hayward and Jock Young is a lively introduction to this new approach and includes a listing of many key cultural films about crime that are worth watching.

Looking ahead

The study of crime and deviance is generally one of the most popular areas that students study in sociology. In part this replicates the wider interests in crime found in society at large (witness the popularity of crime shows of all kinds on television). But often students approach this topic with a distinctly non-sociological approach: they want to explain what makes people murder, take drugs or engage in violence. For sociologists the questions are different.

Sociologists seek to show how crime and deviance are 'normal' and found in all societies. They look at the ways in which control systems grow, change and shape crime and deviance. They examine the crucial role that social inequalities play in structuring crime. And they are concerned with global dimensions: just how different crimes become more prevalent in some cultures than others, and how globalisation increasingly means that criminal worlds stretch across countries and continents. This chapter has opened up some of these topics.

SUMMARY

1 Deviance refers to the labelling of normative violations ranging from mild breaches of etiquette to serious violence.

2 Official statistics are not reliable and reflect a number of social processes. Alternatives to these statistics include victim surveys such as the *British Crime Survey*.

3 Social control has seen three major developments: the old system expands; a new one is grafted on; and surveillance increases. Modern societies are surveillance societies. There has been a significant expansion of prison populations throughout the world, along with the introduction of the privatisation of prisons.

4 Deviance has societal rather than individual roots because it (a) exists in relation to cultural norms, (b) results from a process of social definition, and (c) is shaped by the distribution of social power. Durkheim asserted that responding to deviance affirms values and norms, clarifies moral boundaries, promotes social unity and encourages social change.

5 Positivistic theories focus upon the characteristics and causes of a criminal type. Biological investigation, from Caesare Lombroso's nineteenth-century observations of convicts to recent research in human genetics, has yet to offer much insight into the causes of crime.

6 Labelling theory holds that deviance arises in the reaction of others to a person's behaviour. Acquiring a stigma of deviance can lead to secondary deviance and the onset of a deviant career.

7 Social conflict theories hold that laws and other norms reflect the interests of powerful members of society. Social conflict theory also spotlights white-collar crimes, which cause extensive social harm even though the offenders are rarely branded as criminals.

8 The square of crime suggests four dimensions that need to be considered: the state, informal control, the offender and the victim.

9 Feminist criminology has grown as a response to a neglect of gender issues in the study of crime. It has led to many new developments, including the study of masculinity and its link to criminality, and the gendering of social control processes.

MYTASKLIST

Ten suggestions for going further

1 Connect up with Part Six and the Sociology Web Resources

As you work through ideas and think about the issues raised in this chapter, look at the accompanying website and the resource centre at the end of this book which connects to it. There is a lot here to help you move on. To link up, see: www.pearson.co.uk/plummer.

2 Review the chapter

Briefly summarise (in a paragraph) just what this chapter has been about. Consider: (a) What have you learned? (b) What do you disagree with? Be critical. And (c) How would you develop all this? How could you get more detail on matters that interest you?

3 Pose questions

(a) Look at your own life and consider how far you have become part of the surveillance society.
(b) Why do you think crime rates are lower in some countries than in others? The portrait drawn of globalisation and crime by some commentators such as Manuel Castells makes crime problems in particular societies such as the UK fade by comparison. Do you think the globalisation of crime is a serious issue? In what ways? With drugs as an example, consider what might be done to alleviate the situation.
(c) Examine the ideas of Michel Foucault on crime and prisons. Do you agree with his implicit view that our 'humane treatment' of prisoners is in fact a controlling and corroding use of power?
(d) Trace the emergence of the modern control system. Does it work?

4 Explore key words

Many concepts have been introduced in this chapter. You can review them from the website or from the listing at the back of this book. You might like to give special attention to just five words and think them through – how would you define them, what are they dealing with, and do they help you see the social world more clearly or not? Look at:

Eugene McLaughlin and John Muncie, *The Sage Dictionary of Criminology* (2nd edn, 2005). A useful set of short essays on key terms and aspects of criminology.

5 Search the Web

Be critical when you look at websites – see the box on p. 940 in the Resources section. For this chapter look at:

UK Criminal Statistics
http://rds.homeoffice.gov.uk/rds/crimeew0809.html
Resources for official crime statistics for England and Wales.

United Nations Office of Drugs and Crime (UNODC)
www.unodc.org/unodc/index.html
Excellent international resource

Crime Theory
www.crimetheory.com
A useful timeline of major criminologists and their work.

Prison Reform Trust
www.prisonreformtrust.org.uk
A good website on penal matters in the UK.

Centre for Crime and Justice
www.crimeandjustice.org.uk/cjm.html

Institute of Criminology, University of Cambridge
www.crim.cam.ac.uk

International Centre for Prison Studies
www.prisonstudies.org

Death Penalty Information Centre, USA
www.deathpenaltyinfo.org

Comprehensive information on issues and debates surrounding the death penalty, with a focus on the USA.

Amnesty International
http://web.amnesty.org
The Amnesty International website provides further important information on the death penalty and surrounding issues and debates at the international level.

See also the very useful listing found in the webliography of Carrabine et al., *Criminology: A Sociological Introduction* (2008).

6 Watch a DVD

Crime and deviance is one of the most popular genres of both film and writing. This list could be very extensive. Just think of some of the films you have seen recently. Note, too, some classics:

- William Friedkin's *The French Connection* (1971): the first major film – semi-documentary in style – about drug trafficking.
- Steven Sodenbergh's *Traffic* (2000): tells a number of stories concerning drug use.
- François Truffaut's *Quatre Cents Coups (The Four Hundred Blows)* (1959): a classic film on delinquency by the celebrated French film-maker Truffaut, in which a young boy in Paris finds himself in a detention centre.
- Stanley Kubrick's *A Clockwork Orange* (1970): banned for nearly 30 years, a classic tale of 'modernity and control'.
- Louis J. Gassnier's *Reefer Madness* (1938): seemingly a warning film about the dangers of marijuana to America's youth, it now looks as if it has to be a spoof. But is it? (Also known as *Tell Your Children*.)
- Sydney Lumet's *Twelve Angry Men* (1957): the classic courtroom drama.
- Frederick Wiseman's *Law and Order* (1969): classic documentary – now there are many – on crime.

7 Think and read

Eamonn Carrabine, Pam Cox, Maggy Lee, Ken Plummer and Nigel South, *Criminology: A Sociological Introduction* (2004; 2nd edn, 2009). Provides a broad introduction to all the sociological fields of crime and deviance. A lively textbook.

Tim Newburn (ed.), *Key Readings in Criminology* (2009). All you need to know collected in short articles – an excellent reader.

Mike Maguire et al., *The Oxford Handbook of Criminology* (4th edn, 2007). This is the key comprehensive text, with very extensive coverage of all the issues. It is a 'big book' and it is quite expensive.

Roger Hopkins Burke, *An Introduction to Criminological Theory* (3rd edn, 2009). A good introduction to the different theories and approaches to crime.

Malcolm Davies, Hazel Croall and Jane Tyrer, *Criminal Justice: An Introduction to the Criminal Justice System in England and Wales* (4th edn, 2009). Especially good at introducing aspects of the criminal justice system in the UK. On global issues, see: Mick Cavadine and James Dignan (eds), *Penal Systems: A Comparative Approach* (2008).

Katja Franko Aas, *Globalization and Crime* (2007). Key text to link crime with globalisation.

Jeff Ferrell, Keith Hayward and Jock Young (2008). *Cultural Criminology*. Exciting and different approach to crime which highlights culture.

Karen Evans and Janet Jamieson (eds), *Gender and Crime: A Reader* (2008). Useful collection covering gender issues.

Stanley Cohen, *Visions of Social Control* (1985). An important – if now a little outdated – study of changes in social control in the contemporary world. Read in conjunction with David Garland, *The Culture of Control* (2002).

Jeffrey Reiman and Paul Leighton, *The Rich Get Richer and the Poor Get Prison* (9th edn, 2009). A classic statement on US prisons and crime, with its own website at http://paulsjusticepage.com/crimepays.htm.

8 Relax with a novel

The world of the thriller is everywhere. On the origins of the crime novel in eighteenth-century England, see the fascinating study by Hal Gladfelder, *Crime in Eighteenth Century England* (2001). Twentieth-century crime classics might include:

Anthony Burgess, *A Clockwork Orange* (1962)

Truman Capote, *In Cold Blood* (1965)

On deviance, madness, drugs and total institutions, see Ken Kesey, *One Flew Over the Cuckoo's Nest* (1962).

9 Connect to other chapters

- Link crime to gender debates in Chapter 12.
- Link problems of measuring crime to discussion of methods in Chapter 3.
- Link crime to groups, organisations and socialisation through Chapters 6 and 7.
- Link stigma and labelling to aspects of disability in Chapter 14.
- For the development of human rights and worldwide crime, see Chapter 16.

10 Engage with THE BIG DEBATE

Is crime really decreasing – or increasing?

The sociologist Emile Durkheim (introduced in Chapters 1, 2 and 4) suggests that crime has always existed, and indeed it is hard to find societies where no crime exists. At the same time, the rate of crime, the fear of crime and the general awareness of crime does differ sharply across different cultures, groups and historical periods (as we have shown in the chapter). So although there is clear evidence of crime going back a long way in all societies, we could still argue that crime is significantly on the increase in much of the world. Certainly this is regularly claimed in most European societies and in North American societies. We seem to live in a world of perpetual fear of crime where crime is everywhere on the rise. Yet, as we show in the chapter too, if we were to take recent crime statistics seriously, it would look as if crime is actually on the decrease.

Look at some crime statistics – national or international – and consider what they say (you may find the chapter will help you to make sense of them). Look too at Figure 17.2, which shows the complex flows involved in constructing criminal statistics. Then consider some of the following recent social changes to assess the likelihood of them having an impact upon crime growing – or not. Consider:

- As girls become more equal, they may also become more prone to being aggressive and assertive.
- As mass consumerism increases, so the desires for commodities are increased. We may see an escalation in credit card use with a potential increase in fraud.
- As labour markets become more casual and insecure, and as more people enter the informal or underground economy, so people may start to look for alternative ways to survive. Crime, especially in the informal economy, may be one of these (see Chapter 15).
- As families become less 'traditional', so older styles of parental control on behaviour become weakened (Morgan, 1978; Dennis and Erdos, 1993).
- As shifts take place in city life (brought about by cars, suburbs, commuting, gated communities, etc.), we now see the development of a 'night-time economy', and all manner of crimes that are facilitated by movement.
- As we witness the massive growth of the new information technologies, so we find new patterns of crime, from cybercrimes to mobile phone theft.
- As young people become a separate and often unsupervised age group, so their criminal activities and drug-using propensities increase.
- As the population becomes older, so there may be a growth of both crimes among the elderly and the elderly as victims of crime (at present they figure relatively low on both counts) (Rothman et al., 2000).
- As we experience changes in social ecology, so all manner of new crimes come into being connected to the environment. Some writers have called these green crimes (see Chapter 25).
- As the electronic mass media such as film and television produce more and more images of crime and violence, so people find such lives more and more plausible.

Continue the debate

1 What problems do you find in measuring crime?
2 Is the evidence for the growth or decline in crime rates? Are some crimes growing more than others? What kind of evidence do you need to support your arguments?
3 Discuss each of the above propositions about social change and crime. Attempt to find evidence for or against them.

CHAPTER 18

FAMILIES, PERSONAL LIFE AND LIVING TOGETHER

IT IS NOW 30 YEARS SINCE CHINA BEGAN implementing a strict birth control policy of one child per couple. The government argued that its policy would avoid a population explosion, and indeed it has prevented some 400 million births, which would have stretched China's resources and prevented its growth. The policy has also resulted in a skewed age structure (it is getting older: in 2009, 13 per cent were over 60) and gender structure (many more boys have been born as girls have been aborted). There has also been a proliferation of forced abortions and sterilisations; newborn children have been abandoned or killed. Heavy fines are still imposed on those with more than one family. Along with this, a hidden population of children, whose birth had to be concealed for fear of reprisals, has appeared. The average size of Chinese families has dropped from over 3 in 1980 to 1.8 in 2008. Recently, some flexibility has been brought into the system (parents outside the cities are often allowed to have a second child if the first-born was a girl).

Meanwhile, in Japan, women are simply not having children – not enough, at least, to replace adults of child-bearing age. Since 1950, in fact, the average number of children born to a Japanese woman during her lifetime has tumbled from 3.65 to 1.3. This precipitous decline is no indication that the Japanese have lost their love for children. Quite the contrary. Virtually all young Japanese couples claim to want children, and even screaming babies on a bus or train elicit smiles and sympathy from fellow travellers. The reason for the declining birth rate is that Japanese women display unprecedented reluctance to marry. Back in 1970, only 20 per cent of Japanese women reaching the age of 30 had yet to wed; today, that share has doubled to 40 per cent.

Why the second thoughts about marriage? For one thing, Japanese culture defines motherhood as a full-time responsibility, which precludes a career. Just as important, the typical Japanese husband works long hours – half are away from home at least 12 hours a day. When he is at home, moreover, the typical Japanese man performs almost no housework and spends little time with his children. To young women in Japan, therefore, marriage commonly amounts to a daily round of housework, doting on youngsters and shuttling older children to special 'cram' schools where they prepare for all-important college entrance examinations. Faced with such prospects, more women are opting to stay single, live with parents, work and enjoy plenty of free time and spending money. Business and governments are alarmed by this. New laws are being made to encourage women to have more children and some businesses are offering up to £6,000 to employees to have children.

See: Susan Greenhalgh, *Just One Child: Science and Policy in Deng's China* (2008); Marcus Rebick, *The Chinese Japanese Family* (2009).

There is no such thing as the family – only families.

Diana Gittins (1993: 8)

The normal family is not normal. Family diversity has always been normal and it is here to stay.

Judith Stacey (2011: 191)

In this chapter, we ask:

- What is personal life and the nature of family life?

- What are the key changes in modern lives and families?

- How can we explain key changes? The main theories of families

(Left) Carl Larsson, *My Loved Ones*
See: http://www.clg.se and http://www.carllarsson.se.
Source: The National Museum of Fine Arts, Stockholm © the Nationalmuseum, Stockholm.
Photographer: Sven Nilsson.

Q Carl Larsson is one of Sweden's most famous painters. Here, the image of family life perhaps anticipates the homely style indicated these days in the furnishings of IKEA. What do you think? What is his image of family life about? How might it fit with the opening quote?

The state of the family is a 'hot topic' all around the world, not just in Japan and China, where policies on families are very different. In many countries across the world, the traditional image of a married or cohabiting couple with children is less strong than it was. In the UK fewer than one in four households now conform to this standard; and the often presumed model of the traditional nuclear family is now more likely to be found in the UK among households in Bangladeshi and Pakistani communities. In the United States the situation has developed further: one sociologist has suggested that even by 1986 'only 7 per cent of households conformed to the "modern" pattern of breadwinning father, homemaking mother and one to four children under the age of eighteen' (Stacey, 1996: 133). In many countries across the world, there are new laws and key debates emerging around gay marriages, same-sex registered partnerships and queer families as well as controversies about 'arranged marriages' and 'forced marriages' and the position of women in many families. And 'assisted conception', which ranges from 'test-tube babies' to 'surrogate motherhood' and 'baby selling' on the internet (to be discussed in Chapter 23), also brings new issues (Becker, 2000). Alongside all this there has been the growth of **individualisation** as a *process which gives more and more importance to the choices we can make about the personal life we wish to have*. All taken together, an important point is made: personal life in the twenty-first century is changing dramatically; and with it the nature of our 'families'.

These various family structures and changes are the key topics of this chapter. In it we will highlight

Global patterns of marriage – and its terminologies

Cultural norms, as well as laws, identify people as desirable or unsuitable marriage partners. Some marital norms promote **endogamy**, *marriage between people of the same social category*. Endogamy limits marriage prospects to others of the same age, race, religion or social class. By contrast, **exogamy** mandates *marriage between people of different social categories*. In rural India, for example, young people are expected to marry someone of the same caste (endogamy), but from a different village (exogamy).

Throughout the world, societies pressure people to marry someone of the same social background but of the other sex. The logic of endogamy is simple: people of similar social position pass along their standing to offspring, thereby maintaining traditional social patterns. Exogamy, by contrast, helps to forge useful alliances and promotes cultural diffusion.

In industrial societies today, laws prescribe **monogamy** (from Greek meaning 'one union'), *a form of marriage joining two partners*. The high level of divorce and remarriage, however, suggests that serial monogamy is a more accurate description of much western marital practice. While monogamy is the rule throughout the Americas and in Europe, many pre-industrial societies – especially in Africa and southern Asia – prescribe **polygamy** (from Greek meaning 'many unions'), *a form of marriage uniting three or more people*. There are two types of polygamy. By far the more common is **polygyny** (from Greek meaning 'many women'), *a form of marriage uniting one male and two or more females*. Islamic societies in Africa and southern Asia, for example, permit men up to four wives. In these societies, however, most families are still monogamous because few men have the wealth needed to support several wives and even more children. **Polyandry** (from Greek meaning 'many men' or 'many husbands') is *a form of marriage joining one female with two or more males*. This pattern appears only rarely. One example can be seen in Tibet where agriculture is difficult. There, polyandry discourages the division of land into parcels too small to support a family and divides the work of farming among many men. Polyandry has also been linked to female infanticide – the aborting of female foetuses or killing of female infants – because a decline in the female population forces men to share women.

Historically, most world societies have permitted more than one marital pattern; even so, most actual marriages have been monogamous (Murdock, 1965; orig. 1949). This cultural preference for monogamy reflects two key facts of life: the heavy financial burden of supporting multiple spouses and children, and the rough numerical parity of the sexes, which limit the possibility of polygamy.

the variety of ways of living together and some of the important recent changes in personal life and the way we organise families and households. It offers some insights to explain these trends. Yet, as we shall also point out, changing family patterns and personal lives are nothing new. Nearly two centuries ago, for example, as the Industrial Revolution propelled people from farms to factories, there was much concern over the decline of the family. Today, of course, many of the same concerns surround the rising share of women working, whose careers draw them away from home. In short, changes in other social institutions, especially the economy, keep shaping ways of living together, including marriage and family life.

What are 'families'?

Let's start with the basics. What is family? For a long while in sociology, the **family** has been seen as *a key social institution, found in all societies, that unites individuals into cooperative groups that oversee the bearing and raising of children*. Most families are built on **kinship**, *a social bond, based on blood, marriage or adoption, that joins individuals into families*. Although all societies contain families, just who is included under the umbrella of kinship has varied through history, and varies today from one culture to another. During the twentieth century, most members of society regarded a **family unit** *as a social group of two or more people, related by blood, marriage or adoption, who usually live together*. Initially, individuals are born into a family composed of parents and siblings (a *family of orientation* central to socialisation) and in adulthood, people have or adopt children of their own (a *family of procreation*). Throughout the world, families form around **marriage**, *a legally sanctioned relationship, involving economic cooperation as well as normative sexual activity and child-bearing, that people expect to be enduring*. Embedded in our language is evidence of a cultural belief that marriage alone is the appropriate context for procreation: traditionally, people have

attached the label of *illegitimacy* to children born out of wedlock; moreover, *matrimony*, in Latin, means 'the condition of motherhood'. This link between child-bearing and marriage has weakened, however, as the proportion of children born to single women has increased (noted to be nearing one in four).

But sociologists – looking at history and watching the changes around them – now find the very idea of 'family' much more complicated. Many now object to defining as 'families' only married couples and children because that implies that everyone should embrace a single standard. As more and more people forge non-traditional family ties, which we will discuss later, many are now thinking of kinship in terms of *families of affinity* or **families of choice** (Weston, 1991), *people with or without legal or blood ties who feel they belong together and wish to define themselves as a family*. What does or does not constitute a family, then, is a moral and political – as well as a legal – matter that lies at the heart of the contemporary 'family values' debate, raised in box *Global families 2*.

Sociologist Christopher Carrington, however, puts this somewhat differently: 'I understand family as consisting of people who love and care for one another' (Carrington, 1999: 5). Carrington's own family research was not with conventional kin, but involved conducting participant observation research within lesbian and gay families in California. He does not approach the family through ideas of kinship or institutions (which implies something too static) but instead as a series of activities: 'People', he says, ' "do" family.' The chapters of his book reflect this as he looks at just how families are achieved through various forms of work: *feeding work* (who cooks, shops, plans); *house work* (who cleans, washes, looks after plants and pets, does the household repairs); *kin work* (looking after the children, visiting parents, etc.); *consumption work* (including watching TV, arranging holidays, purchasing clothes and household goods); and what we might also call *care work* (looking after partners, children and others). All of this implies some continuing divisions of labour within the family and we shall return to this later in the chapter.

GLOBAL FAMILIES: 2

A report from Sweden

Sweden is burdened with few of the social problems that are often identified with modern capitalism: in urban Sweden, there is little of the violent crime, drug abuse and grinding poverty that have blighted many other places. This Scandinavian nation seems to fulfil the promise of the modern welfare state, with an extensive and professional government bureaucracy that sees to virtually all human needs.

But Sweden also has very different kinds of family. Because people look to the government – not to spouses – for economic assistance, Swedes are less likely to marry than members of any other industrialised society. For the same reason, Sweden also has a high share of adults living alone (more than 20 per cent). Moreover, a large proportion of couples live together outside marriage (25 per cent) and half of all Swedish children (compared to about one in three in Europe) are born to unmarried parents. Average household size in Sweden is also the smallest in the world (2.2 persons). Finally, Swedish couples (whether married or not) are more likely to break up than partners in any other country. US sociologist David Popenoe sums up by claiming that the family 'has probably become weaker in Sweden than anywhere else – certainly among advanced Western nations. Individual family members are the most autonomous and least bound by the group' (Popenoe, 1991: 69).

Popenoe contends that a growing culture of individualism

and self-fulfilment, coupled with the declining influence of religion, began to 'erode' Swedish families back in the 1960s. The movement of women into the labour force also plays a part. Sweden has the lowest proportion of women who are homemakers (10 per cent versus about 25 per cent in Europe) and the highest percentage of women in the labour force (77 per cent versus 59 per cent in Europe).

But, most important, according to Popenoe, is the expansion of the Swedish welfare state, one of the most far-reaching schemes of its kind. The Swedish government offers citizens a lifetime of services – and high taxes. Swedes can count on the government to give them jobs, sustain their income, deliver and educate their children, provide comprehensive healthcare and, when the time comes, pay for their funeral.

Many Swedes supported this welfare programme, Popenoe explains, thinking it would strengthen families. But with the benefit of hindsight, he concludes, we see that proliferating government programmes have actually been replacing families. Take the case of childcare. The Swedish government operates public childcare centres open to all. As officials see it, this system puts care in the hands of professionals, and makes this service equally accessible regardless of parents' income. At the same time, however, the government offers no subsidy for parents who want to care for children in their own home. In effect, then, government has taken over much of the traditional family function of child-rearing.

If this system has solved so many social problems, why should anyone care about the erosion of traditional family life? For two reasons, says Popenoe. First, government can do only at great cost what families used to do for themselves. Recently, Swedes voted to cut back on their burgeoning welfare system because of skyrocketing costs.

Secondly, can government employees in large childcare centres provide children with the level of love and emotional security they would receive from two parents living as a family? Unlikely, claims Popenoe, noting that small, intimate groups can accomplish some human tasks much better than formal organisations can.

David Popenoe uses the case of Sweden as part of his claim for a return to traditional families. We return to this issue in the *Big debate* at the end of this chapter.

Source: Popenoe (1991, 1994).

COUNTRY FACT FILE

SWEDEN

Population	9.2m
Urban Pop	8.47m
Per capita GDP	$51,950
Life expectancy	Men 79.6
	Women 83.6
Major city	Stockholm
Key religions	Lutheran (87%)
Key language	Swedish
Human development index	9th (0.885)

Sources: Economist World in Figures, 2011.

Family, history and world forms

When we look at the debate among historians and sociologists over just how the family has changed over time, one thing is clear. The notion of an 'ideal' nuclear family of two parents and two children has, historically, been rare. Throughout history, there have been all kinds of combination – shaped by age cycles, class, region, ethnicity and the like – which have made families very varied and complex. And at any one historical period, we would not expect families to be all the same. Jean-Louis Flandrin (1979) has shown how, for example, a whole array of family types existed at the same time in different parts of France. And British historian Peter Laslett (1972) studied parish records of English country villages from 1564 to 1821 and found that extended families were rare because of late marriage and shorter lives. But there were also large households – where the richer would take in the poorer as labourers and domestic servants.

Lawrence Stone, in a classic study, has charted three phases of the family in western Europe between 1500 and 1800: the first was 'open lineage' and involved a lack of close relations and lack of privacy, but extensive kin. The second was 'restricted patriarchy' (1530–1640), where there were increased loyalties to state and church and less to kin and community. The final stage of 'closed domesticated' families highlights privacy, bonds between children and parents, and 'affective individualism'. It was 'an open ended, low keyed, unemotional, authoritarian institution' (Stone, 1977).

The English sociologists Michael Young and Peter Willmott have traced the changing form of families in modern Britain. In the 1950s they studied the very strong traditional family ties in 'traditional' Bethnal Green in East London and traced how they weakened as the families moved out to new housing estates such as Greenleigh in outer London (Young and Willmott, 1957). The three-generation (grandparents, parents and child) and larger family is replaced with a smaller nuclear pattern where the relationship between husband and wife becomes more intense. In a later study, Young and Willmott (1973) suggested that these newer families were becoming more 'symmetrical'. That is, the relationships were becoming increasingly equal with husband and wife spending more and more time together. These kinds of change have become a common theme in much of the writing on the family – one expects to find shifts from an extended and often patriarchal form of family to a more nuclear and symmetrical form. However, it must be remembered that this is only one pattern – a largely traditional, working-class one. Families vary and change with class and environment.

Family in the world: 1900–2000

The leading Swedish sociologist Göran Therborn has written a major account of the family and social change across the world in the twentieth century. For Therborn (2004), there are three key elements shaping family structures and he studies each in detail. These are:

1 *Degree of male dominance (patriarchy)* (see Chapter 12). In the twentieth century there has been a major weakening of patriarchy in some countries (notably Western ones), which has been accompanied by the growth of schooling and education for girls – a factor which Therborn sees as crucial (p. 74). At the same time, in many cultures this has not happened. Two key periods of change are noted: the First World War and Russian Revolution – producing a need for women to work – and the sexual revolution of the 1970s.

2 *The need for marriage in sexual regulation.* What has been found quite widely in the West, but not elsewhere, is what has been called the 'detraditionalising of the family'. Western countries have become more open and intimate, and less bound by tradition. This has led to a proliferation of new forms. But it is important to see that this is not spreading globally: there is no globalisation of the family. For example, Muslim cultures remain even more strongly committed to the holy family, and in sub-Saharan Africa polygamy remains common. In Asia, most countries are committed to monogamy.

3 *Fertility and birth control.* The core development here has been the falling birth rate in many countries – again notably in the West. And with this comes a major change in the age structure, as populations become older. All this is linked to what has been called the demographic transition and the growth of family planning. (See the box, and we discuss this further in Chapters 13 and 24.) Again, there are many variations: in the West the trend is stronger, but with major exceptions – such as population in sub-Saharan Africa.

The demographic transition

Two waves of fertility decline

1850s–1960s

The move to the 'two-to-three child norm' worldwide starts in France (by 1900), in England and Wales (by 1914), and in Australia, USA, Belgium and central Europe by 1930, and in the rest of Europe, the USSR, Japan, the USA, Australia and Canada by 1965.

1980s–2000

Initially Ireland, New Zealand, Chile, Cuba, China and Taiwan; later, by 2000: Argentina, Colombia, Cost Rica, Mexico, Israel, Iran, Thailand and Vietnam.

Source: Abridged from Therborn (2004: 238).

These three key factors are at the heart of Therborn's account. From these detailed analyses of many cultures, he is able to suggest five major family types (and a few lesser ones) that have emerged:

1 *The West Asia/North Africa Family (Islamic)* is where Islam is at the centre. Here marriage and theology are deeply interconnected. This is a patriarchy strongly engaged with the veiling and sexual control of women. Family matters are of great importance.

2 *The Sub-Saharan African Family (Animist)* combines a strong gender hierarchy but with some female autonomy. Mass polygyny is quite common with several wives serving a common patriarch. Conjugal relations are hence 'thinner' than in the Asian families, but great importance is attached to fertility.

3 *The South Asian Family* (Hindu) is more religious and shaped by religious rituals (e.g. the caste system). It is again characterised by strong patriarchy, but here also is to be found female seclusion. Marriage is regulated by strict rules of endogamy and exogamy.

4 *The East Asian (Confucian) Family* (e.g. China) is strong, central and unchanging. It has an explicitly patriarchal structure, with duty being honoured to both father and patrilineal ancestors. 'Filial piety' – the son's duty – is a core value. Marriage is universal; the husband dominates; fertility

reproduces the male bloodline. As religion is often weaker in such Confucian cultures, the family becomes the moral stronghold.

5 *European/North American (Christian)* is the least patriarchal family, even as it is regulated by the rules of the Catholic Church. Marriage is by 'consent'; monogamy is prized; fertility decisions are in the hands of the couples. In recent times, it has become the family system that is most open to change. It is the main focus of this chapter (Therborn, 2004: 297–301).

Thinking about families: theories and ideas

As in earlier chapters, several theoretical approaches offer a range of insights about the family.

1 The classic approach – the functions of the family

As we would expect, functionalism suggests we look for the functions of the family. Social scientists have produced long lists of functions, and then debated how they have changed over time. You may like to try to create your own list – what are the tasks of families? – before moving on. Below is a fairly standard listing.

1 *Socialisation*. As explained in Chapter 6, the family is the first and most influential setting for socialisation. Ideally, parents teach children to be well-integrated and contributing members of society (Parsons and Bales, 1955). Of course, family socialisation continues throughout the life cycle. Adults change within marriage, and, as any parent knows, mothers and fathers learn as much from raising their children as their children learn from them.

2 *Regulation of sexual activity*. Every culture regulates sexual activity in the interest of maintaining kinship organisation and property rights. One universal regulation is the **incest taboo**, *a cultural norm forbidding sexual relations or marriage between certain kin*. Precisely which kin fall within the incest taboo varies from one culture to another. The matrilineal Navajo, for example, forbid marrying any relative of one's mother. Our bilateral society applies the incest taboo to both sides of the family

but limits it to close relatives, including parents, grandparents, siblings, aunts and uncles. But even brother–sister marriages found approval among the ancient Egyptian, Incan and Hawaiian nobility (Murdock, 1965; orig. 1949). Reproduction between close relatives can adversely affect the mental and physical health of offspring. But this biological fact does not explain why, among all species of life, only human beings observe an incest taboo. The key reasons to control incest, then, are social. Why? First, the incest taboo minimises sexual competition within families by restricting legitimate sexuality to spouses. Secondly, it forces people to marry outside their immediate families, forging broader alliances. Thirdly, since kinship defines people's rights and obligations towards each other, forbidding reproduction among close relatives protects kinship from collapsing into chaos.

3 *Social placement.* Families are not *biologically* necessary for people to reproduce, but they do provide for the *social* placement of children. Social identity based on race, ethnicity, religion and social class is ascribed at birth through the family. This fact explains the long-standing preference for so-called legitimate birth. Especially when parents are of similar social position, families clarify inheritance rights and allow for the stable transmission of social standing from parents to children.

4 *Material and emotional security.* People have long viewed the family as a 'haven in a heartless world', looking to kin for physical protection, emotional support and financial assistance. To a greater or lesser extent, most families do provide all these things, although not without periodic conflict.

When all these functions are taken together, families are often seen as 'the backbone of society'.

Critical comment

This approach dominated thinking for much of the early part of the twentieth century – from this point of view, it is easy to see that society as we know it could not exist without families. But this approach seriously overlooks the great diversity in ways people can live together in the modern world, the frequent conflicts that families generate, and the different interests they harbour. Children now are often socialised outside the traditional family; many people now have sexual relations outside the family; and there is a lot of evidence of abuse and violence within the family that

makes it clear that families can be extremely dysfunctional places. Moreover, functionalism pays little attention to how other social institutions (say, government) could meet at least some of the same human needs. Finally, it minimises the problems of family life. Established family forms reinforce patriarchy and incorporate a surprising amount of violence, with the dysfunctional effect of undermining individual self-confidence, health and well-being, especially of women and children.

2 Inequality and the family: conflict theory

Rather than concentrating on ways that kinship benefits society, other theorists investigate how families may perpetuate social inequality. The role of families in the social reproduction of inequality takes several forms.

1 *Property and inheritance.* As noted in Chapter 12, Friedrich Engels (1902; orig. 1884) traced the origin of the family to the need to identify heirs so that men (especially in the higher classes) could transmit property to their sons. Families thus support the concentration of wealth and reproduce the class structure in each succeeding generation.

2 *Patriarchy.* Engels also emphasised how the family promotes patriarchy. The only way men can know who their heirs are is to control the sexuality of women. Thus, Engels continued, families transform women into the sexual and economic property of men. A century ago in Europe, most wives' earnings belonged to their husbands. Although this practice is no longer lawful, men still exert power over women. Despite moving rapidly into the paid workforce, women continue to be paid less, work in more marginal occupations and still have to bear major responsibility for child-rearing and housework. As we shall see from the work of Delphy and Leonard below, patriarchal families offer considerable benefits to men. They also deprive men of the chance to share in the personal satisfaction and growth derived from close interaction with children.

3 *Race and ethnicity.* Racial and ethnic categories will persist over generations only to the degree that people marry others like themselves. Thus endogamous marriage also shores up the racial and ethnic hierarchy.

A radical feminist approach to the family

Many of the arguments above have been significantly developed by many feminists who see the family as the central location of women's oppression. They argue that men generally benefit greatly from families while women often do not. Until recently, men have nearly always been head of the household and made the key decisions about the family allocating rewards (often payment in kind, such as holidays): even when women work, they often have little decision-making autonomy.

In the 1990s, Christine Delphy and Diana Leonard's *Familiar Exploitation* (1992) was very influential. It argues that the family is an economic system, where men benefit from the work of women (and in many countries the work of children too). This is not just the work in the labour market (of which they do increasing amounts), but also the work they do at home. Family members work for the head of the household. As they say, it is 'the work women do, the uses to which our bodies can be put, which constitutes the reason for our oppression'.

Many studies suggest that women still do more housework than men, still spend more time looking after the children (especially in the more mundane and humdrum ways) and are much more likely to have to look after the sick and the elderly (Finch, 1989; Hochschild, 1989). They are also much more likely to have to give moral support to men (who often make little contribution to their wife's work).

These feminist arguments are strong claims and a careful evaluation of the evidence is needed to make sense of this. For instance, in modern families, there are now many single-parent households where women are alone; further, women are increasingly choosing not to marry, to get divorced once married and not to have children. Twenty per cent of women remain childless, by choice.

Critical comment

Some sociologists show how family life maintains social inequalities. During his era, Engels condemned the family as part and parcel of capitalism. Yet non-capitalist societies have families (and family problems) all the same. Kinship and social inequality are deeply intertwined, as Engels argued, but the family appears to carry out various societal functions that are not easily accomplished by other means. And the arguments produced by radical feminists usually fail to take into account the growing trends towards equality in decision-making between men and women.

3 The family at the intersection of class, ethnicity and gender

Dimensions of inequality – social class, ethnicity and race, and gender – are powerful forces that shape marriage and family life.

Class

Families can vary enormously across social class (see Chapter 10). Not only does class shape a family's financial security and range of opportunities, it can also affect the family size and shape. For instance, in the UK, families are still likely to be larger among the working class, who also have higher rates of divorce.

In an influential North American study, Lillian Rubin (1976) found that working-class wives deemed a good husband to be one who refrained from violence and excessive drinking and held a steady job. Rubin's middle-class informants, by contrast, never mentioned such things; these women simply *assumed* a husband would provide a safe and secure home. Their ideal husband was a man with whom they could communicate easily and share feelings and experiences.

Such differences reflect the fact that people with higher social standing have more schooling, and most have jobs that emphasise verbal skills. In addition, middle-class couples share a wider range of activities, while working-class life is more sharply divided along gender lines. Conventionally masculine ideas of self-control, Rubin explains, can stifle emotional expressiveness on the part of working-class men, prompting women to turn to each other as confidantes.

Clearly, what women (and men) can hope for in marriage – and what they end up with – is linked to their social class. Much the same holds true for children in families; boys and girls lucky enough to be born into more affluent families enjoy better mental and physical health, develop higher self-confidence, and go on to greater achievement than poor children do (Komarovsky, 1967; Bott, 1971; Rubin, 1976; Fitzpatrick, 1988).

Ethnicity

But it is not just social class that shapes families. As Chapter 11 indicates, ethnicity and race are powerful social forces. The effects of both surface in family life. We must beware of stereotyping: just as there is enormous diversity behind the label 'white families', so there is great variety among ethnic families. But some differences do seem striking. Ethnic family forms in the UK have been subject to change over the past 40 years: in the early days of mass migration (1950–70), there was often a severe dislocation of family life, as patterns found in the former homes were disrupted. But subsequently new forms of stability emerged.

Asian families

The Asian population across the world generally has a very strong family system (Fukuyama, 1995). The first contact by Asians with UK culture after migration therefore often came as a culture shock. In the main, Asian culture has continued to assert the importance of family life.

The village model of India was for a while transferred to the UK, with a complex network of kin and responsibilities. In some ways this is the classic 'extended family' model. On arrival initially in the UK, these traditional family structures were disrupted: there were smaller houses, there was less support and women became more isolated from other women. Chain migration eventually restored this as families were reunited. English families were often seen as 'morally bankrupt' (Elliot, 1996: 52).

In Asian families there are usually more people per household than in white families: three-quarters of Pakistani and Bangladeshi households have an average of five members, and three-fifths of Indian households contain four or more people, compared with a quarter of white households (Skellington, 1996: 62, 49).

An ideal type would suggest a value that places family before individual self-interest, and one that is patrilineal, patrilocal and with a strong gender hierarchy. Marriage is a contract between two families, not two individuals.

It is important to recognise again major differences between Asian communities (see Chapter 11). These can be compounded by gender. For instance, while east African and Indian women often work, taking them out of the house, Bangladeshi and Pakistani women's lives – more restricted by Islamic rules which do not permit women to be in close proximity to non-family men – lead to a much stronger home-based commitment, including 'homework'. Likewise, Muslims can marry close kin but this is not permitted for Sikhs and Hindus. *Purdah* is strong in Islam and restricts Islamic women more.

Sallie Westwood and Parminder Bhachu (1988) nevertheless see these traditions as evoking changes. Again, families do not remain static, but respond to current circumstances. Some become more nuclear and a diversity of Asian families starts to appear.

Families around the world: Asian
Tibetan family dressed up for a visit to the Labrang Monastery during the Tibetan New Year
Source: © Wong Adam/Redlink/Corbis.

Afro-Caribbean families

These account for less than 1 per cent of all families in the UK (Skellington, 1996: 50). Thirty-seven per cent were headed by a female (compared with 9 per cent of white families). Marriage is often weaker, women-headed households are more common, and the husband/father role is likely to be less strong. In a curious fashion, there is a resemblance to the situation in the United States, where African-American families are also like this. Jocelyn Barrow explains this form of family by linking it to Caribbean society. Originally, while marriage is much valued in Caribbean societies, other patterns of sexual union were possible. There were common-law family households with unmarried cohabitation, as well as women-headed households (Barrow, 1982).

In the main, extended kin units have not reappeared among Afro-Caribbean families in the UK. One study suggested that fewer than 1 per cent of children are cared for by grandmothers as the 'grandmother family' disappears. The families often tend to be matrifocal, even though Afro-Caribbean women are more likely to be working and have less support than in the Caribbean. Men often become marginal to family life.

Lone-parent families are highest among West Indian families (43 per cent in the 1991 Census) but lowest for Asian: the figures were 6 per cent for Indian and Pakistani, 5 per cent for Bangladeshi and 11 per cent for white families (Skellington, 1996: 50, 60).

Gender

Among all races, Jessie Bernard (1982) asserts, every marriage is actually two different relationships: a woman's marriage and a man's marriage. Although the extent of patriarchy has diminished with time, even today few marriages are composed of two equal partners. Studies in the UK suggest that although there have been some moves towards equality, and that families do come in many forms, it remains the case that men still make most of the major decisions, and that wives generally are economically dependent upon husbands and are more likely to take responsibility for childcare and the housework within the family (Pahl, 1989; Devine, 1992).

4 Interaction and the micro-sociology of the family

We saw in Chapter 7 how some sociology works not just at the grand macro-level but at the level of the situation. Micro-sociology would explore how individuals shape and experience family life. Seen from the inside, family life amounts to individuals engaging one another in a changing collage of meanings and work. People construct family life, building a reality that differs from case to case and from day to day. As we saw in Christopher Carrington's (1999) work on lesbian and gay families above, 'people do families'. It is work – caring work, feeding work, kin work and so on (Carrington, 1999: 6).

Family living also offers an opportunity for intimacy, a word with Latin roots meaning 'sharing fears'. That is, as a result of sharing a wide range of activities over a long period of time, members of families forge emotional bonds. Of course, the fact that parents act as authority figures often inhibits their communication with younger children. But, as young people reach adulthood, kinship ties typically 'open up' as family members recognise that they share concern for one another's welfare. They also engage in emotional work (see Chapter 7 and Hochschild, 1983; Macionis, 1978a).

Social-exchange analysis

An early approach to the dynamics of the family came with social-exchange analysis. It depicts courtship and marriage as forms of negotiation (Blau, 1964). In the case of courtship, dating allows each person the chance to assess the likely advantages and disadvantages of taking the other as a spouse, always keeping in mind the value of what one has to offer in return. In essence, exchange analysts contend, individuals seek to make the best 'deal' they can in selecting a partner. Physical attractiveness is one critical dimension of social exchange. In patriarchal societies around the world, beauty has long been a commodity offered by women on the marriage market. The high value assigned to beauty explains women's traditional concern with physical appearance and their sensitivity about revealing their age. For their part, men have traditionally been assessed according to the financial resources they command. Recently, however, because increasing numbers of women are joining the labour force, they are less dependent on men to support them and their children. Thus, the terms of exchange have been converging for men and women.

Critical comments

Micro-level analysis offers a useful counterpoint to functionalist and conflict visions of the family as an institutional system. Adopting an interactional or exchange viewpoint, we gain a better sense of the individual's experience of family life and appreciate how people creatively shape this reality for themselves.

Using this approach, however, we run the risk of missing the bigger picture: namely, that family life is similar for people affected by any common set of economic and cultural forces. UK families vary in some predictable ways according to social class and ethnicity, and, as the next section explains, they typically evolve through stages linked to the life course.

5 Newer developments: 'doing families', 'family practices' and personal life

More recently, there have been a number of new ways of thinking about families and we will consider some of these here. First, the English sociologist David Morgan has suggested that families can be analysed as a set of 'practices'. At the start of the twenty-first century, most people no longer follow fixed paths for living in families. Like Carrington, he suggests that people are *doing family* rather than simply being in one. Family has come to signify a sense of intimate connections, and much less the formal legal ties of marriage. We are talking now about the multiple ways of doing families. But all this fluidity is not really random: people live their life through a regular set of practices. Rather than simply viewing the family as a fixed 'thing', it is now seen as a set of relationships built around such things as housework, caring, being a mother, being a child, or having sex. These practices highlight:

- *The doing of families*: what actually goes on and gets done in families. This is an active image of activities.

- *The everyday life of families*: we are more concerned with the relatively routine and trivial. David Morgan writes: 'what you had for breakfast today and how you consumed your breakfast may tell the observer as much about your routine understandings of family living as the more dramatic [rituals] such as weddings and funerals' (Morgan, 1999: 17).

- *The processes and fluidity of family life*: practices ebb and flow into each other and one set of practices mixes and merges with others.

- *Regularities*: even if active, people develop patterns, such as 'breakfasting', 'watching television', 'washing baby' or 'having sex'.

- *Interplay of biography and history*: lives are woven together and develop a sense of the past.

- *Interplay of positions*: there are many ways of viewing from the family – children, mothers, fathers, grandparents, visitors, friends, etc. (Morgan, 1999: 17–18).

Personal life

Carol Smart (2007) has taken all this further in a major way. She has studied families in their various patterns for a quarter of a century and has found sociology lacking. Many of the studies look at the wrong things; many of them take too pessimistic a view of change. Smart is critical of the more general and abstract theories which seem in despair about the 'individualisation' and 'chaos' of contemporary families. This is found in a lot of media reporting and gets support from the unresearched theories of Ulrich Beck, Zygymunt Bauman and others. As she says: 'their ideas run directly counter to most empirical sociological studies of family and kinship in Britain' (2007: 20). More than that, they offer very little evidence for their assertions. In particular, they ignore the continuing significance of class, gender inequality, power and intergenerational relationships which is found in the research of Jane Ribbens McCarthy, Lynn Jamieson, Graham Crow, Ros Edwards and others.

Carol Smart prefers a focus on personal life: an 'area of life which impacts closely on people and means much to them, but which does not presume there is an autonomous agency'. It does not mean an individual isolated and with free will. It is rather a term which, whilst it allows for the fact that human beings have agency and make choices, indicates that their lives are always bound up with the presence of others. A personal life charts the ways we connect and link to other people. The personal life is always 'embedded in the social' (Smart, 2007: 29). For Carol Smart, the sociologist's task is to 'map personal lives into their social context and into their specific history or spatial location'. Usually within a life, we can study the 'life projects' of how people make plans and organise their lives. This personal life is always on the move – changing, growing and evolving with all the relations around it. The study of the 'personal life' allows us to look at a whole array of areas that sociologists have hitherto neglected and to bring them to the forefront in our thinking: areas like love, emotions, sexuality, bodies, intimacies. To help in these explorations, Smart suggests five key concepts:

1 *Biography*: how we live our lives over time with many other people. We have personal histories of our own which give meaning to our lives over time, and many of these meanings – and our sense of agency and actions – are located within the family. We become individuals and tell the stories of our lives through the families we live in (and see the interlude at the end of Part Four).

2 *Memory*: how families play a key role in the shaping of 'social memories': they provide key contexts for what we know and can recall. There is now much work on the sociology of memory which suggests that it is not merely a psychological matter – of recalling something from a memory box in the brain. Rather we remember with and through other people: memory is something which is shaped and fashioned by the social. *Memories are collective, shared and social.* Family spaces are particularly important places for organising our memories – often through things such as family photographs and albums. Our social memories speak to our childhoods; they generate contexts in which we recount the meanings of our lives; and they change as our families change.

3 *Embeddedness*: how people become woven together and how this keeps changing and emerging. Here the focus is concretely on what families actually do on a day-to-day basis: from meals and holidays, to the family crises and troubles which all families confront.

4 *Relationships*: how people connect to each other. Here we are concerned with the differing and changing quality of the texture of how people relate to each other, and the emotions that are woven and constructed into these relationships.

5 *Imaginary*: how we come to think and even dream about our personal lives. Often we think more about what we want to be rather than what we actually are. This dreaming and reflection on families and personal life is a very important part of life – and, again, it is collective and cultural. And as the famous adage goes: we should be careful what we dream, for our dreams may come true.

In all of this, then, Carol Smart suggests some key features of this 'personal life' which we all know about but which have been so rarely studied and understood. This includes the 'secrets and lies' found in every family and rarely discussed. It includes the ways in which possessions and things are shared and owned. It looks at the need to understand the anxieties, disrespect and hurts that are found in most relationships and families at all ages and across all members – and, dare we say, across all cultures. These are what make personal relationships – at the extremes there is violence and abuse, but there are surely also everyday troubles in the 'families we live with'. And then there is the significance of love, sex and other kinds of emotions which are fostered in families and personal life.

At the heart of Smart's approach is the need to get close to families and personal lives, to study them in their local contexts and to use autobiographical understandings in particular. There have been sweeping statistical generalisations and quite a lot of grander theorising, but very little close attention to the close living of lives through families and what it means to people. She wants to get away from grand theories of the family and crude statistical abstractions, and wants more research on the family to get closer to real 'families' and what is actually going on. When this happens, she claims we will find that multiple different families are amazingly resilient and strong – even in the face of the many changes they have to confront.

Some practices of family life

Practising care

One of the key 'practices' of families is 'caring': caring for partners, caring for children and caring for parents. This is a three- or four-generational span of care. And there is an important distinction to be made here between *caring about*, which is about love, feelings and emotions, and *caring for*, which is an active form of work – a 'labour of love' which involves looking after someone (Ungerson, 1987). They may, of course, be deeply interwoven, but they need not be. Overwhelmingly, this latter care process falls upon the women in the family, although it is usually invisible. Although there are signs that some men are playing a small role in it, feminist research has generally shown that the caring process is closely linked in modern societies to what it means to be a woman. Recall in Chapter 12 how Nancy Chodorow suggested that the social process of becoming a woman was closely linked to the social process of becoming a mother. It is the extension of this 'social mothering' that makes women more prone to look after the array of people within the family – and also outside it.

There has been quite a lot of research on 'care'. It suggests that these commitments are rarely straightforward and always negotiated – often over long periods of time and implicitly. Sometimes there is an unwillingness to engage in care. Often the array of family members that will be carers is narrowly defined: usually from spouse, to daughter, to daughter-in-law and son. There is a hierarchy of care: sons and daughters define their care duties primarily to their own children and partners, only secondarily to their parents. Older people usually do not want to give up their independence – and so are looked after 'at a distance' ('intimacy at a distance'). Nevertheless, research strongly suggests that there is a great deal of care taking place among families today. But when governments cut back on public care, this can hit many families very hard, as they are already engaged in a great deal of unpaid care (Finch and Groves, 1983; Finch, 1989; Elliot, 1996: 122–40).

Housework practices

Closely linked to the caring tasks of the household is the challenge of who does the household work. Traditionally, and in many countries around the world today, this is usually seen as women's work. The man is the provider and the woman is the home maker. As women now routinely go out to paid employment everyday, and most women in low-income societies have always had to work, this seems a very uneven division of labour.

With the recent change in status of women in some societies, it is often claimed that men now contribute more to the housework. Research generally suggests not – and that women now do a 'double shift' (working both in and out of the home). The men do more than in the past, and women do less – but not significantly; and it varies a great deal from country to country as Table 18.1 shows.

Doing violence

In Chapter 12 we saw the significance of violence in women's lives. Much of this takes place within the family. The ideal family, of course, is seen as a haven from the dangers of the outside world; the reality is that many families are exceedingly dangerous places. From the biblical story of Cain killing his brother Abel to the horror stories of child abuse that we hear in the

Table 18.1	The percentage of people daily involved in housework across Europe			
Country	Sex respondent		Total	Female-Male difference
	Male	Female		
Finland	64%	95%	79%	31%
Sweden	65%	90%	77%	25%
Romania	60%	93%	76%	33%
Denmark	65%	86%	74%	21%
Hungary	46%	93%	70%	47%
Slovakia	47%	92%	70%	45%
Luxembourg	44%	92%	69%	48%
Belgium	44%	91%	68%	47%
Estonia	53%	84%	68%	31%
Bulgaria	33%	95%	66%	62%
Lithuania	44%	90%	66%	46%
Netherlands	47%	86%	66%	39%
Germany	36%	90%	64%	54%
Latvia	43%	85%	64%	42%
Portugal	27%	96%	62%	69%
France	32%	86%	61%	54%
Slovenia	30%	96%	61%	66%
Austria	28%	89%	59%	61%
Greece	18%	94%	59%	76%
UK	36%	80%	58%	44%
Italy	26%	88%	57%	62%
Turkey	15%	91%	57%	76%
Ireland	33%	78%	56%	45%
Malta	21%	91%	54%	70%
Cyprus	19%	80%	53%	61%
European average*	35%	88%	62%	53%

* The sample was weighted according to the population size of each country.

The sample included 26,245 respondents from 25 European societies. See http://iriss.ceps.lu/documents/irisswp75.pdf.

Source: 'Engendered housework: a cross-European analysis'; Bogdan Voicu, Malina Voicu and Katarina Strapcov No. 2007-07, IRISS Working Paper Series, from IRISS at CEPS/INSTEAD.

news regularly, we see that the disturbing reality of many homes has been **family violence**, *emotional, physical or sexual abuse of one family member by another*. Some time back, sociologist Richard J. Gelles pointed to a chilling fact:

> **The family is the most violent group in society with the exception of the police and the military. You are more likely to get killed, injured or physically attacked in your home by someone you are related to than in any other social context.**

(quoted in Roesch, 1984: 75)

How does this violence work?

Violence against women

During the 1970s a seemingly new 'family problem' was discovered: men's violence against women. The women's movement responded by actively establishing women's refuges and also through a critical analysis of men's violence towards women (which often connected it to the rape and power debate discussed in Chapter 12). In England, Erin Pizzey set up the first women's refuge in Chiswick in 1972 (Pizzey, 1974), and today they are common in many large cities throughout the world (though usually, to avoid male harassers, they are kept fairly anonymous). A study by Jayne Mooney (2000) in north London found that about half of all women surveyed had experienced threats of violence or actual violence, although many of these women had not told anybody. In the 1990s, the United Nations recognised domestic violence as a human rights abuse.

It has been claimed that between 1 in 4 or 5 women will be a victim of domestic violence in their lifetime – many of these on a number of occasions. Like most such statistics, they are notoriously difficult to verify, as such events are seriously underreported (see Chapter 17). Women may be ashamed, feel they are to blame, be too frightened to tell anyone, or love their partner and not want him to be criticised or punished for what he did. Whatever the case, we know that such violence is widespread. Reports from around the world show different rates of violence – but its presence seems to exist in families everywhere and many women live in fear because of it. In ten countries surveyed in a 2005 study by the World Health Organization, more than 50 per cent of women in Bangladesh, Ethiopia, Peru and Tanzania reported having been subjected to physical or sexual violence by intimate partners, with figures reaching a staggering 71 per cent in rural Ethiopia. Only in one country (Japan) did less than 20 per cent of women report incidents of domestic violence (Garca-Moreno et al., 2005).

There are a number of factors that help shape domestic violence across the world. The leading researchers in this area, Rebecca and Russell Dobash, highlight 'men's possessiveness and jealousy, men's expectations concerning women's domestic work, men's sense of their right to punish "their" women, and the importance to men of maintaining and exercising their authority' (Dobash, 1992: 3). At the heart of the problem is usually masculinity. The family is usually a place where certain levels of violence will be tolerated and the very intensity of family ties makes it a very emotional place. The violence of the family can become routine. Recently, there has been growing

Spotlight

What do we mean by violence against women?

The United Nations claims that 'It is estimated that one in every five women faces some form of violence during her lifetime, in some cases leading to serious injury or death.' Gender violence has been identified as a key issue of our times. Below, a United Nations report outlines its key forms.

- *Physical violence* means a woman has been: slapped, or had something thrown at her; pushed, shoved, or had her hair pulled; hit with a fist or something else that could hurt; choked or burnt; threatened with or had a weapon used against her.

- *Sexual violence* means a woman has been: physically forced to have sexual intercourse; had sexual intercourse because she was afraid of what her partner might do; or forced to do something sexual she found degrading or humiliating.

- Though recognized as a serious and pervasive problem, *emotional violence* does not yet have a widely accepted definition, but includes, for example, being humiliated or belittled; being scared or intimidated purposefully.

- *Intimate-partner violence* (also called 'domestic' violence) means a woman has encountered any of the above types of violence, at the hands of an intimate partner or ex-partner; this is one of the most common and universal forms of violence experienced by women.

Source: www.who.int/gender/documents/MDGs&VAWSept05.pdf.

research into the children of such families, who often become the 'hidden victims' of domestic violence (Harne and Radford, 2008).

In the past, the law regarded domestic violence as a private, family matter. Now, even without separation or divorce, a woman can obtain court protection from an abusive spouse. Anti-stalking laws (which prohibit people from following or threatening ex-partners), such as the 1997 Harassment Act in the UK, are now found in many countries. Finally, communities across Europe have established shelters that provide counselling as well as temporary housing for women and children driven from their homes by domestic violence. The analysis has shifted from being based on individuals, to being based on the power relations – patriarchy – between men and women (see Chapter 12).

Violence against children

Family violence also victimises children. In the United States upwards of 3 million children – roughly 4 per cent of all youngsters – suffer abuse each year, including several thousand who die as a result. Child abuse entails more than physical injury because abusive adults misuse power and trust to undermine a child's emotional well-being. Child abuse is most common among the youngest and most vulnerable children (Straus and Gelles, 1986; Van Biema, 1994).

In the UK several noticeable cases have galvanised action and thinking. In 1973, the seven-year-old Maria Colwell was beaten to death by her stepfather after social workers had allowed her to return to her family from foster care. It led both to a moral panic (see Chapter 22) and to the development of a public awareness of abuse. Later, in 1985, the death of Jasmine Beckford also served to highlight the

continuing problem. The most recent controversy was in 2009 over Baby P., a 17-month-old boy who died in London after some 50 injuries. As a consequence of such cases, social work intervention increased, and registers of children at risk (now Children's Plans) were created. In 2010, there were 46,709 children registered in the UK. Still, the plight of abused children continues: many suffer in silence, believing during their formative years that they are to blame for their own victimisation. The initial abuse, compounded by years of guilt, can leave lasting emotional scars that prevent people abused as children from forming healthy relationships as adults.

About 90 per cent of child abusers are men, but they conform to no simple stereotype. As one man who entered a therapy group reported, 'I kept waiting for all the guys with raincoats and greasy hair to show up. But everyone looked like regular middle-class people.' Most abusers, however, share one trait: they were abused themselves as children. Researchers have discovered that violent behaviour in close relationships is learned. In families, then, violence begets violence.

GLOBAL FAMILIES: 3

The modern family in the UK around 2008

Households

There are three main types: a married couple, a cohabiting couple and a lone-parent family. An increasing trend towards smaller household sizes has seen the average household size in Great Britain fall from 3.1 people per household in 1961 to 2.4 people in 2009. There are more lone-parent families, smaller family sizes and, in particular, more one-person households (see Table 18.2).

Partnerships

In 2007, the majority of the adult population in England and Wales were living as part of a couple, either cohabiting or married. Types of partnership

vary according to age group: adults aged 16 to 29 were the least likely age group to be living with a partner; in comparison, almost three-quarters (71 per cent) of adults aged 30 to 44 and just over three-quarters (76 per cent) of adults aged 45 to 64 were living with a partner, as either a married or a cohabiting couple (see Figure 18.1).

Marriages

Between 1950 and 2005, there was a marked decrease in the number of first marriages. In 1950, more than 300,000 couples married for the first time; this was less than 200,000 in 2005. But remarriage was common – more than 40 per cent of marriages are remarriages, compared with 21 per cent in 1971. People are also marrying later in life. Marriage is by far the most common partnership type. In 2007 more than half (55 per cent) of adults aged 30 and over were married. The number of

marriages in England and Wales fell for the third consecutive year in 2007, to around 231,500.

Cohabitation

This has risen significantly. Cohabitation among non-married people is now very common: in 2005, 23 per cent of men and 28 per cent of women were cohabiting. Cohabitation is often found among the divorced and frequently ends through remarriage.

Divorces

The peak period for divorce was in the 1970s. It is now more stable, at around 150,000 a year. Since 1971, marriages have fallen one-fifth and divorces have doubled. Almost half of marriages end in divorce, and most are sought by women (7 out of 10 petitions), while men are more likely to remarry. Roughly a quarter of children can now expect to find their original parents divorced by the time

GLOBAL FAMILIES:3

they are 16. The UK has the highest divorce rate in the European Union but it is not as high as it is in the United States. There were around 128,500 divorces in England and Wales in 2007, a fall of 3 per cent compared with 2006. This was the lowest number of divorces in a single year since 1976 (see Table 18.3).

Step-families

In 2000–1 step-families accounted for 8 per cent of families with dependent children.

Civil partnership

Despite hotly contested debates all over the world, gay marriages or registered partnerships now exist in many countries. In all the Scandinavian countries and most of Europe, such partnerships are now law. Registered partnerships became law in the UK in 2005. There were 18,059 civil partnerships formed in the UK between December 2005 and the end of December 2006. A fall in the number of civil partnership registrations was recorded in all four countries of the UK in 2008. The largest annual fall was in Scotland (24 per cent) where 525 partnerships were registered in 2008, followed by Northern Ireland (23 per cent) where 86 partnerships were registered. England accounted for around 88 per cent (6,276) of all civil partnerships formed in the UK, a fall of 18 per cent in registrations compared with 2007. The smallest fall was recorded in Wales (4 per cent) where 282 partnerships were registered in 2008.

Home alone

More people are now living alone. In the UK in 2002, 6.2 million adults were living alone. A quarter of all households are now one-person households. This is double what it was in 1971 (when it was 3 million). In addition, household size fell from 3.09 in 1961 to 2.46 in 1990. Many of these are elderly households (in 2000, 10 per cent of these belonged to elderly women and half of all women over 75 years live alone). A new

Table 18.2	Households in Great Britain: by type of household and family (%)					
	1961	1971	1981	1991	2001[1]	2009[1]
One person households						
Under state pension age[2]	4	6	8	11	14	14
Over state pension age[2]	7	12	14	16	15	14
One family households						
Couple[3]						
No children	26	27	26	28	29	29
1–2 dependent children[4,5]	30	26	25	20	19	18
3 or more dependent children[4,5]	8	9	6	5	4	3
Non-dependent children only	10	8	8	8	6	6
Lone parent[3]						
Dependent children[4,5]	2	3	5	6	7	7
Non-dependent children only	4	4	4	4	3	3
Two or more unrelated adults	5	4	5	3	3	3
Multi-family households	3	1	1	1	1	1
All households						
(= 100%) (millions)	16.3	18.6	20.2	22.4	23.9	25.2

[1] Data are at Q2 (April–June) each year and are not seasonally adjusted.
[2] State pension age is currently 65 for men and 60 for women.
[3] These households may contain individuals who are not family members. Couples data for 2009 include a small number of same-sex couples and civil partners.
[4] Children aged under 16 and those aged 16 to 18 who have never married and are in full-time education.
[5] These families may also contain non-dependent children.

Source: Census, Labour Force Survey, Office for National Statistics in *Social Trends*, 40 (2010), Table 2.2, p. 15.

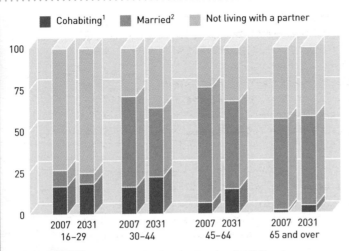

Figure 18.1 Partnerships in England and Wales (%)

¹ Includes people who are separated and cohabiting.
² Includes people who are separated but not cohabiting; projections are not available for this group.

Source: Office for National Statistics in *Social Trends*, 40 (2010), Fig. 2.9, p. 19.

trend is for younger men to live on their own (3 per cent in 1971; 10 per cent in 2000; predicted to be 14 per cent by 2021).

Lone parents

Since 1971, living in lone-parent households has become a more common experience. Almost one in five families with dependent children are lone-parent families. The figures nearly trebled in 25 years from 1 million to 2.8 million. In 1972, 6 per cent of all children grew up in Britain with a single parent, as compared to 22 per cent in 2006. The proportion of living in couple families decreased from 92 per cent to 76 per cent. A large part of this is due to divorce. About 10 per cent of lone-parent families are headed by lone fathers and 90 per cent by lone mothers. Denmark and Sweden have the highest numbers of lone parents in Europe.

Children

In 1901, 34.6 per cent of the population in the UK were under 16; in 1981 it was 22.3 per cent. The average number of children in a family was 1.8 (including adopted and stepchildren). The birth rate is 1.73 per woman. The number of families with dependent children in the UK in 2009 was around 7.6 million. Of these, 4.6 million (61 per cent) were married couple families. The second most common type was families headed by a lone mother (1.8 million), followed by cohabiting couple families (1.0 million) and lone father families (0.2 million). In the main, children still live in traditional families headed by a couple (78 per cent in spring 2002).

Birth

The number of births in England and Wales increased for the seventh successive year in 2008, rising from 690,000 in 2007 to 709,000 in 2008. The number of live births is now at its highest level since 1972, when there were 727,000 live births. During this period the average age for women giving birth for

the first time has risen from 23.8 years to 27.5 years. Since the 1970s there has been a fall in the proportion of babies born to women aged under 25, from 47 per cent in 1971 (369,600 live births) to 25 per cent in 2008 (180,700 live births).

The generational gap

There is a large difference in attitude towards 'family' between those born before 1930 and those born since 1950. Older cohorts are firmly against living together before marriage (well over 60 per cent) whereas younger cohorts born since 1950 strongly favour living together before marriage (*British Social Attitudes*, 2004).

Sexuality

The pill remains the most popular form of contraception with a quarter of all women aged 16–49 using it. In 1971, 21 per cent of births were conceived out of marriage; by 2000, it was over half. There has also been a dramatic decline in the age of first intercourse: the median for young men and women (born between 1966 and 1975) was 17 years. Gay and lesbian sexualities are much more accepted.

Life expectancy

The twentieth century has seen 25 years added to human life expectancy, shifting the shape of the life cycle.

Births outside marriage

In the UK, about one-third of all live births occur outside marriage and in nearly all European countries the rate has doubled in the last 30 years.

GLOBAL FAMILIES: 3

Table 18.3   Divorces (per 1,000 persons)

	1997	1998	1999	2000	2001	2002	2003	2004	2005	2006	2007
EU-27 (1)	1.8	1.8	1.8	1.8	1.9	1.9	2.0	2.0	2.0	:	:
Belgium	2.6	2.6	2.6	2.6	2.8	3.0	3.0	3.0	2.9	2.8	2.9
Bulgaria	1.1	1.3	1.2	1.3	1.3	1.3	1.5	1.9	1.9	1.9	2.1
Czech Republic	3.2	3.1	2.3	2.9	3.1	3.1	3.8	3.2	3.1	3.1	3.0
Denmark	2.4	2.5	2.5	2.7	2.7	2.8	2.9	2.9	2.8	2.6	2.6
Germany	2.3	2.3	2.3	2.4	2.4	2.5	2.6	2.6	2.4	2.3	:
Estonia	3.8	3.2	3.3	3.1	3.2	3.0	2.9	3.1	3.0	2.8	2.8
Ireland	0.0	0.4	0.6	0.7	0.7	0.7	0.7	0.8	0.8	:	:
Greece	0.9	0.7	0.9	1.0	1.1	1.0	1.1	1.1	1.2	1.3	1.2
Spain	0.9	0.9	0.9	0.9	1.0	1.0	1.1	1.2	1.7	:	:
France	2.0	2.0	2.0	1.9	1.9	1.9	2.1	2.2	2.5	2.2	:
Italy	0.6	0.6	0.6	0.7	0.7	0.7	0.8	0.8	0.8	:	0.8
Cyprus	1.3	1.3	1.7	1.7	1.7	1.9	2.0	2.2	2.0	2.3	2.1
Latvia	2.5	2.6	2.5	2.6	2.4	2.5	2.1	2.3	2.8	3.2	3.3
Lithuania	3.2	3.3	3.2	3.1	3.2	3.0	3.1	3.2	3.3	3.3	3.4
Luxembourg	2.4	2.4	2.4	2.4	2.3	2.4	2.3	2.3	2.3	2.5	2.3
Hungary	2.4	2.5	2.5	2.3	2.4	2.5	2.5	2.4	2.5	2.5	2.5
Malta	–	–	–	–	–	–	–	–	–	–	–
Netherlands	2.2	2.1	2.1	2.2	2.3	2.1	1.9	1.9	2.0	1.9	2.0
Austria	2.3	2.2	2.3	2.4	2.6	2.4	2.3	2.4	2.4	2.5	2.4
Poland	1.1	1.2	1.1	1.1	1.2	1.2	1.3	1.5	1.8	1.9	1.7
Portugal	1.4	1.5	1.7	1.9	1.8	2.7	2.2	2.2	2.2	2.3	2.4
Romania	1.6	1.8	1.6	1.4	1.4	1.5	1.5	1.6	1.5	1.5	1.7
Slovenia	1.0	1.0	1.0	1.1	1.1	1.2	1.2	1.2	1.3	1.2	1.4
Slovakia	1.7	1.7	1.8	1.7	1.8	2.0	2.0	2.0	2.1	2.4	2.3
Finland	2.6	2.7	2.7	2.7	2.6	2.6	2.6	2.5	2.6	2.5	2.5
Sweden	2.4	2.3	2.4	2.4	2.4	2.4	2.4	2.2	2.2	2.2	2.3
United Kingdom	2.8	2.7	2.7	2.6	2.7	2.7	2.8	2.8	2.6	:	:
Croatia	0.9	0.9	0.8	1.0	1.1	1.0	1.1	1.1	1.1	1.1	:
FYR of Macedonia	0.5	0.5	0.5	0.7	0.7	0.6	0.7	0.8	0.8	0.7	0.7
Turkey	:	:	:	:	:	:	0.7	1.3	1.3	1.3	:
Iceland	1.9	1.8	1.7	1.9	1.9	1.8	1.8	1.9	1.9	1.6	:
Liechtenstein	2.1	:	:	3.9	2.5	2.9	2.5	2.9	2.7	2.3	2.8
Norway	2.3	2.1	2.0	2.2	2.3	2.3	2.4	2.4	2.4	2.3	2.2
Switzerland	2.4	2.5	2.9	1.5	2.2	2.2	2.3	2.4	2.9	2.8	2.6

¹ Break in series, 1998.

Source: Eurostat *Europe in Figures: Eurostat Yearbook 2009*, p. 157, Table 3.14 © European Union, 2009.

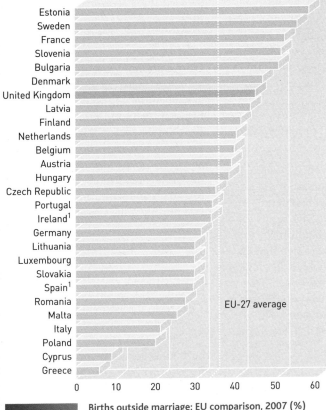

| Figure 18.2 | Births outside marriage: EU comparison, 2007 (%) |

[1] Data are for 2006.

Source: Office for National Statistics; Eurostat in *Social Trends*, 40 (2010), Fig. 2.19, p. 24.

and women are having children later in the life cycle.

Forced marriages

In 2009 the UK Forced Marriage Unity (FMU) gave advice or support in 1,682 cases; 86 per cent of these cases involved females and 14 per cent involved males. Forced marriages usually take place to prevent a young woman from marrying someone 'unsuitable' (in terms of class, race, ethnicity, religion or sect); to fulfil a betrothal to a relative; to 'fix' sexual orientation (where either of the spouses is not heterosexual); or to provide a carer for a disabled husband. They often involved abduction abroad, rape or unwanted pregnancy, and have high rates of domestic violence, divorce or abandonment. Girls are being sent at an ever younger age to the family's 'home country' and only returned to Britain once they have been married and become pregnant (see: www.fco.gov.uk/en/travel-and-living-abroad/when-things-go-wrong/forced-marriage/information-for-victims).

Adoption

The adoption rate has sharply fallen. There were 21,500 adoptions in 1971 and just under 6,000 in 2001.

Source: *Social Trends* (mainly the 2010 issue).

Yet most occur in stable relationships outside marriage (in 1992, 75 per cent of registered births included both parents as opposed to 45 per cent in 1971). Birth rate outside marriage is highest in Sweden and Estonia and lowest in Greece. (See Figure 18.2.)

Women remaining childless

While most women do have children, the number who do not has been growing (20 per cent of those born in 1954 and 25 per cent of those born in 1979 remain childless)

Twenty-first-century families?

Well into the twenty-first century, families and relationships have continued their path of change – especially in Western societies. True, many of

the older patterns persist, and often mingle with the family patterns of non-Western cultures; but there are certainly some new fashions in the making. We have seen in Chapter 12 the emergence of a new, flexible, highly individualistic, sexually 'plastic', 'pure relationship' where partners are mutually interdependent (Cancian, 1987; Giddens, 1991; Beck and Beck-Gernsheim, 1995). The suggestion is that for some (and it *may* be a blueprint for the future), relationships are emerging where men and women are more interdependent and equal; where their child-rearing is altogether part of a more egalitarian and democratic system; where sexuality and love become more 'plastic', diffuse, open. This is a relationship of choice, closely allied to individualism.

The changes we outline have been taken by many to herald a new form of family relationship. American family sociologist Judith Stacey has argued that we may be discovering the postmodern family. She writes:

> The postmodern family condition is not a new model of family life equivalent to that of the modern family; it is not the next stage in an orderly progression of stages in family history; rather the postmodern family condition signals the moment in history when our belief in a logical progression of stages has broken down ... The postmodern family condition incorporates both experimental and nostalgic dimensions as it lurches forward and backward into an uncertain future.
>
> (Stacey, 1996: 8)

The box on p. 637 details what the family looks like in one country, the UK, and suggests certain trends – many of which also hold for other Western countries. Recent findings on a range of European families show a number of features in common:

- a reduction in the number of marriages
- an increase in the average age at which people marry
- an increase in the number of divorces
- a smaller average household size
- a higher proportion of people living alone
- the highest proportion of people living alone is found among the elderly.

In what follows, we shall highlight a few features.

Marriage and divorce

One of the most striking features of modern societies has been the decline in first marriage and the rapid growth of divorce. There were 40 per cent fewer first marriages in the UK in 1994 than there were in 1971 – a steep drop. In 2001, around half of adults in the UK population were married. The age of marriage has also increased – in 2001, it was around 30.6 for men and 28.4 for women (in 1971 it was 24.6 and 22.6 respectively). By contrast, the number of divorces has more than doubled in the same period – a steep rise.

There is also a general drift towards marrying at older ages.

These are trends found throughout Europe and other industrialising societies. Most countries in the European Union have seen a decline in marriage rates, with Sweden having the lowest number of marriages. Taking Europe as a whole, the divorce rate quadrupled between 1960 and 1992, although as Figure 18.3 shows, there are significant differences across all countries. Divorce is highest in the UK and the Nordic countries, and lowest in the Mediterranean regions. US society has the highest divorce rate in the world: double that of Canada and Japan, and seven times as high as Italy (US Bureau of the Census, 2002).

Nevertheless, since the mid-1980s, these rapid rises have stabilised a little, as Figure 18.4 suggests. Although the trend of ending marriage may have slowed for the moment, it does nevertheless seem a stable Western pattern. Far from divorce being an unusual ending to a marriage, it is becoming more and more the norm.

The high UK divorce rate can be traced to a number of factors. The most common reason for women to be granted divorce in the UK is the 'unreasonable behaviour' of the man; for men, it is the adultery of the wife (*Social Trends*, 1997: 48). More broadly, we can see divorce rising because:

1 *Divorce is legally easier to accomplish.* For example, in the UK before 1857, divorces were almost impossible: they were only for wealthy men and required a private Act of Parliament. Legislation over the following century made divorce increasingly easy. But it was the Divorce Reform Act of 1969 (law from 1971) which shifted the grounds of divorce to the 'irretrievable breakdown of marriage' doctrine. Couples could now divorce after two years' separation (five years if the partner objected). From this point onwards, divorces escalated. So there is little doubt that, formally, the changes in the law have made divorce possible. The key peaks of divorces in the UK in the 1970s were almost certainly due to the release of a backlog of long-dead marriages. But since the Matrimonial and Family Proceedings Act 1984, couples no longer have to be married for three years before they can divorce. This has given further impetus for an increasing divorce rate.

2 *Demographic changes.* We commonly exaggerate the stability of marriage in the past, when the early death of a spouse ended as many marriages after a few years as divorce does now. When people lived less long, marriages were of shorter duration.

Marriages[1]   Divorces[2]

Denmark
Netherlands
Portugal
Greece
Finland
Ireland
Spain
United Kingdom
Germany
France
Italy
Austria
Luxembourg
Sweden
Belgium
EU average

Rates per 1,000 population   Rates per 1,000 population

| Figure 18.3 | Marriage and divorce rates: EU comparison, 2002 |

[1] 2001 data for Spain.

[2] 2001 data for Ireland, Spain, Germany, France, Italy and EU average.

Source: Adapted from *Social Trends* (2002: 32); Office for National Statistics; Eurostat.

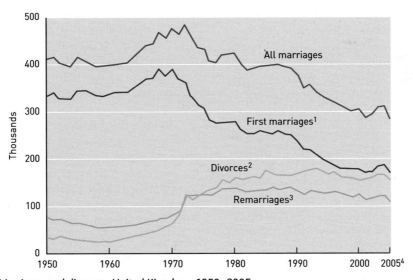

| Figure 18.4 | Marriages and divorces, United Kingdom, 1950–2005 |

[1] For both partners.

[2] Includes annulments. Data for 1950–1970 for Great Britain only. Divorce was permitted in Northern Ireland from 1969.

[3] For one or both partners.

[4] Data for 2005 are provisional. Final figures are likely to be higher.

Source: *Social Trends* (2007: Fig. 2.9), Office for National Statistics, General Register Office for Scotland, Northern Ireland Statistics and Research Agency.

These days, without divorce most people's marriages could last some 50 years or more – given current life expectancy and marriage rates.

3 *Individualisation is increasing.* Beck and Beck-Gernsheim (1995) see the rise of a modern society where both men and women expect choice and control over their lives, as well as equality. The times are a changing, and we have become more individualistic, seemingly more concerned with personal happiness and success than with the well-being of families and children. Life has become a 'planning project' for many in the West and there are no longer clear guidelines as to who should do what in a family. This makes for more tension and potential conflict as men and women become more individualised, less certain about their roles and more prone to breaking up (Beck-Gernsheim, 2002).

4 *Romantic love often subsides.* Modern cultures emphasise romantic love as a basis for marriage, rendering relationships vulnerable to collapse as sexual passion subsides. There is now widespread support for the notion that one may end a marriage in favour of a new relationship simply to renew excitement and romance.

5 *Women are now less dependent on men and have changed expectations.* Their increasing participation in the labour force has reduced wives' financial dependence on husbands. In addition, women have largely come to expect more from life than being the 'home maker' alone. They are more likely to demand equality from husbands, who may not have recognised the changing role of women. Changing expectations from women, then, may make it easier for them to walk away from unhappy marriages.

6 *Many of today's marriages are stressful.* With both partners working outside the home in most cases, jobs consume time and energy. In the past, wives looked after children, but now (and given the difficulty of securing good, affordable childcare) raising children can be more difficult. Tensions may be increasing between men and women, as women come to demand and expect more. While children do stabilise some marriages, divorce is most common during the early years of marriage when many couples have young children.

7 *Divorce is more socially acceptable.* Divorce no longer carries the powerful, negative stigma it did a century ago. Couples considering divorce typically do not receive the discouragement from family and friends they once did.

Who divorces?

There is considerable discussion of the factors that put marriages at risk. They are varied but include:

- *Age*: at greatest risk of divorce are young spouses, especially those who marry after a brief courtship and have few financial resources.

- *Class*: those in the highest social class are least likely to divorce and those in the lowest social class are most at risk.

- *Gender*: women who have successful careers are more prone to divorce, partly due to the strains that arise in two-career marriages but, more important, because financially independent women are less inclined to remain in an unhappy marriage.

- *Prior marriage*: men and women who divorce once are more likely to divorce again, presumably because problems follow them from one marriage to another.

Finally, couples who have known their partners for short periods of time before marriage, those who marry in response to an unexpected pregnancy, and people who are not religious divorce more readily than other couples (Coleman and Salt, 1992).

The experience of divorce

A series of recent studies in the UK have looked at divorce and step-parenting and have persistently found that the decisions taken in these areas are not taken lightly and bring with them major moral concerns. Thus, for instance, the research of Carol Smart and Bren Neal (1999) examines relationships of parenting that are negotiated and renegotiated following a divorce, and are especially concerned with the influence this has on the children. Through their work a complex set of 'post-divorce' relationships, processes, phases and 'practices' come into view. They sense how new roles start to appear: solo parenting, co-parenting, custodial parenting. They find how a complex flow between parenting roles and those of 'others' (grandparents, step-siblings, etc.) surrounds it. And they show new possibilities of 'step-grandparents' emerging. Firmly against the moral traditionalist position – for example, of Patricia Morgan (1995), who is cited as saying that the divorce law 'allies' itself with the spouses who want to break up marriages, and in doing so, rewards selfishness, egoism and destructiveness over altruistic commitment – their focus is much more on the daily moral struggles which are encountered through divorce.

Muslim families in Niger

Families in Muslim Africa look and feel very different from Western families. To start with, Niger is one of the world's poorest (and hottest) countries in the world, ranking near last on the United Nations Human Development Index. It is a landlocked, sub-Saharan nation, situated on a vast, arid state on the edge of the Sahara desert, and has been under military rule for much of its post-independence history. It has one of the lowest literacy rates in the world, its health system is basic and disease is widespread. A history of colonisation and slavery still shows in its culture: a controversial study suggested

that more than 800,000 people are enslaved (almost 8 per cent of the population). The major groups (90 per cent) share many Muslim beliefs and practices, though there are divides. Niger also has the world's highest infant mortality rate. At the same time, it also has the highest fertility rate in the world (7.2 births per woman). This means that nearly half (49 per cent) of the population is under age 15.

Most typically, in the rural areas, families are composed of a married father and his sons with their wives in a large extended household that is organised around traditional farming labour. Polygamy is authorised by Islam: men can have up to four wives, and more than one-third of married women in Niger are in

COUNTRY FACT FILE

THE REPUBLIC OF NIGER

Population	15.3 million (UN, 2009)
Capital	Niamey
Area	1.27 million square kilometres (489,000 square miles)
Major languages	French (official), Arabic, Hausa, Songhai
Major religions	Islam, indigenous beliefs
Life expectancy	50 years (men), 52 years (women) (UN)
GDP	$700 (2009 est.)
Human development index	182nd (lowest in list)

Families around the world: Muslim
Muslim families at dinner, South Africa.

Source: © David Turnley/Corbis.

GLOBAL FAMILIES: 4

polygamous unions. Nevertheless many men do not have the economic means to practise this. Although the minimum legal age of marriage is 15, many marry below this age. Marriages are often arranged by the parents in both rural and urban communities. Girls are frequently married off by the age of 12, with half of all girls in Niger married and pregnant by the age of 16, according to a UN report. There is a 76 per cent incidence of child marriage and it is rare to marry someone of whom parents disapprove. Much of this process might be seen by a Western observer as coercive or forced marriage. In addition,

many groups practice patrilineal Islamic-influenced inheritance. There are also bilateral inheritance practices and much informal pre-inherited property in the form of gifts.

The position of women is poor. The Nigerian family code is very unfavourable to women. Female genital mutilation is a common practice, but in decline. There are high levels of obstetric fistula, due to inadequate medical care compounded by the fact that the average age for first pregnancies is 14 years old. There is widespread and often unrecognised domestic violence, marital rape, forced marriage and trafficking in women and children.

Niger is in a process of change but stereotyped and traditional practices persist. A law has been proposed to change the legal marrying age to 18, but has yet to be adopted

See: www.unicef.org/wcaro/ WCARO_Niger_Factsheet-11.pdf; www.forwarduk.org.uk/key-issues/ child-marriage; www.antislavery.org/ includes/documents/cm_docs/2009/f/ full_english_slavery_in_niger.pdf.

tip Throughout this chapter, look at the case studies of different families. Research for more data on the internet. The families we briefly introduce come from:

1   China and Japan (introduction)
2   Sweden (p. 626)
3   UK (p. 637)
4   Niger (p. 645)
5   Mexico (p. 650)

Likewise, Jane Ribbens McCarthy and others, in their studies of step-parenting (McCarthy et al., 2000), find an overwhelming sense that 'adults must take responsibility for children in their care, and therefore must seek the needs of the children first'. 'This,' they say, 'is such a strong moral imperative that it seems to have been impossible for anyone to disagree with it in the accounts we have heard' (McCarthy et al., 2000: 16). What we see here, then, is that divorce and step-parenting may lead to a heightened sense of moral decision-making in families. It may be a long process of negotiation, but there are elements of sharedness.

Some writers are starting to suggest that what we are seeing here in families is the emergence of a postmodern morality which is not to be handed down from on high by moralists, but which is instead the very stuff of many people's everyday lives. Children may well now be exposed to a more complex set of relations from an earlier time than perhaps they were in the past. But none of this necessarily means they are open to neglect and indifference.

Custody residence and parenting

More than half of all divorcing couples must resolve the issue of child custody. Society's conventional practice is still to award custody of children to mothers,

based on the notion that women are better parents than men. A recent trend, however, is towards joint custody, whereby children divide their time between the new homes of their two parents. Joint custody is difficult if divorced parents live far apart or do not get along, but it has the advantage of keeping children in regular contact with both parents.

Because mothers usually gain custody of children but fathers typically earn more income, the well-being of children often depends on fathers making court-ordered child-support payments.

Financial support

In 1991 the UK's Conservative government of the day set up the Child Support Agency (CSA), which aimed to make absent parents (mainly fathers) contribute to their children's upbringing. An agency was set up to administer it and collect money from absent fathers, focusing especially in the first instance on low-income fathers who were easier to locate (through social security offices). It led to considerable controversy and a campaign against the CSA (APART, Absent Parents Asking for Reasonable Treatment). Partly, this was because it did not take into account the obligations a parent may have to a second family, but in addition, it was retrospective, overturning earlier court agreements. Further, if the parent with the child was already on income support, everything collected was recouped by the Benefits Agency.

Controversies still continue, and you can catch up with current controversies by looking at the Child Support Agency website at www.csa.gov.uk.

Remarriage

Despite the rising divorce rate, marriage – and remarriage – remain as popular as ever. In the UK over one-third of all marriages each year are second marriages. Most people remarry within three to five years. Men, who derive greater benefits from wedlock, are more likely to remarry than women are.

Remarriage often creates *blended families*, composed of children and some combination of biological parents and step-parents. Members of blended families thus have to define precisely who is part of the child's nuclear family (Furstenberg, 1984). Blended families also require children to reorientate themselves; an only child, for example, may suddenly find she has two older brothers. And, as already noted, the risk of divorce is high for partners in such families. But blended families also offer both young and old the opportunity to relax rigid family roles.

Lone-parent families

Lone-parent households with dependent children more than doubled from 3 per cent of households in 1971 to 7 per cent of households in 2006. As Table 18.2 shows, the number of people in lone-parent households shifted from 4 per cent in 1971 to 12 per cent in 2006. And the proportion of children living in such families more than tripled between 1972 and 2006 to 24 per cent. By any standards, this is a significant growth. Lone-parent families, over 90 per cent of which are headed by a single mother, may result from divorce, separation, death or the choice of an unmarried woman to have a child. Until the mid-1980s, most of the increase was due to divorce, but since then, the proportion of divorced mothers has remained stable, while that of single never-married mothers has doubled. Across Europe the percentage of births outside marriage has been rising significantly. The rate is highest in the Scandinavian countries and lowest in Greece. In the UK it is around 32 per cent, compared with 8 per cent in 1971.

Entering the labour force has bolstered women's financial capacity to be single mothers. But lone

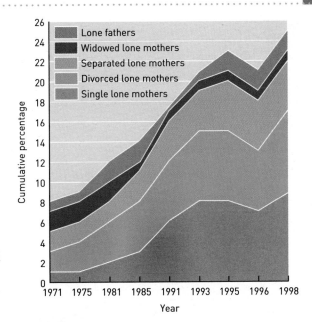

| Figure 18.5 | Lone-parent families by marital status in the UK, 1971–98 |

Source: Adapted from www.statistics.gov.uk, Office for National Statistics.

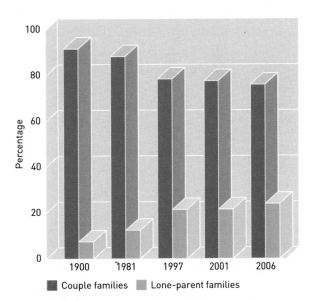

| Figure 18.6 | The shift in household structure, Great Britain, 1972–2006 |

Source: *Social Trends* 37 (2007), Office for National Statistics, www.statistics.co.uk.

parenthood – especially when the parent is a woman – greatly increases the risks of poverty, as it can limit the woman's ability to work and to further her education. Many women in Europe now become pregnant as

Great Britain
Percentages

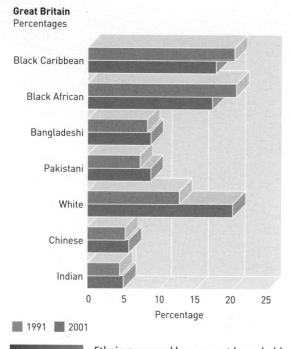

| 1991 | 2001

Figure 18.7   Ethnic group and lone-parent households, Great Britain, 1991 and 2001

Source: Census 2001, Office for National Statistics; Census 2001, General Register Office for Scotland, *Social Trends* (2007: Fig. 2.6).

unmarried teenagers, and many decide to raise their children on their own. These young women with children – especially if they have the additional disadvantage of being minorities – form the core of the rising problem of child poverty in Europe.

Some research suggests that growing up in a lone-parent family can disadvantage children. The most serious problem among families with one parent – especially if that parent is a woman – is poverty. On average, children growing up in a lone-parent family start out with disadvantages and end up with lesser educational achievement and lower incomes, and have a greater chance of forming lone-parent families themselves.

Cohabitation

Cohabitation is *the sharing of a household by an unmarried couple*. A generation ago, widespread use of terms like 'living in sin' and 'premarital sex' indicated disapproval of both cohabitation and sex outside marriage. But all this has changed. Attitude surveys find a generational difference, with older people often

disapproving of cohabitation, but younger people overwhelmingly in favour of it (*Social Trends*, 2003: 33). Between 1986 and 2005, the proportion of non-married men and women aged under 60 who were cohabiting in Great Britain doubled (from 11 per cent to 24 per cent for men; 13 per cent to 24 per cent for women) (*Social Trends*, 2007: 19). Divorced women and younger women in their twenties were the most likely to cohabit. Cohabitation rarely lasts more than two years, and frequently leads to marriage. In a sense, it has become the new form of 'engagement'.

Cohabitation is common in Europe as a whole. It is most pronounced in Sweden and other Scandinavian societies as a long-term form of family life, with or without children. By contrast, this family form is much rarer in more traditional (and Roman Catholic) nations such as Italy.

Step-parenting

In 1991 there were around half a million step-families and around 1 million children (step-children and natural children) living in such families in the UK. There were three times as many step-fathers as step-mothers, as children are more likely to stay with their natural mothers (*Social Trends*, 1997: 44). Step-families are growing fast: in 2000, there were some 2.5 million children in step-families, accounting for about 6 per cent of all families in the UK.

Gay and lesbian couples: 'families of choice', registered partnerships and marriage

Since the 1980s there has been increasing interest in gay and lesbian marriages and partnerships. Kath Weston suggests that these are 'families of choice' as opposed to the more conventional 'families of blood' (Weston, 1991). In 1989, Denmark became the first country to formally recognise homosexual marriages, thereby extending some social legitimacy to gay and lesbian couples as well as conferring legal advantages for inheritance, taxation and joint property ownership. A registered partnership gives two people of the same sex the equivalent rights to heterosexual marriages, except for the rights of adoption or a church marriage.

Versions of registered partnerships are becoming increasingly common throughout many countries

Four same-sex couples celebrate after getting married at the town hall in Mexico City March 11, 2010. The first same-sex couples tied the knot in Mexico City on Thursday under the first law in Latin America to broadly legalize gay marriage. The new law goes beyond previous legislation allowing same-sex couples the same marriage rights as straight couples

Source: © Mario Guzman/epa/Corbis.

of the world. The Nordic cultures were first and most prominent: all have registered marriages or partnerships, Denmark in 1989, Norway in 1993, Sweden in 1995, Iceland and Finland in 1996. Most other European countries have followed. In the UK, the Civil Partnership Act 2004 came into effect in December 2005 and in the first nine months, some 15,700 partnerships were formed. In other countries, such as South Africa, Mexico and a few states of the United States (Vermont, Connecticut and Hawaii) laws are being enacted. The pace of change has been significant worldwide, and the trend in public opinion is towards greater support.

Most gay and lesbian couples in households including children raise the offspring of previous heterosexual unions and some couples have adopted children. But many gay parents are quiet about their sexuality, not wishing to draw unwelcome attention to their children. In several widely publicised cases in recent years, courts have removed children from homosexual couples, claiming to represent the best interests of the children (Weeks et al., 2001).

In the United States, while gay people cannot legally marry (although they can adopt children), some cities (including San Francisco and New York) allow 'registered partnerships' that confer some of the legal benefits of marriage. However, it has been estimated that in the United States there are as many as 1 million gay and lesbian couples who are now raising one or more children (Kimmel, 2003).

While this pattern challenges many traditional notions about families in Europe, it also indicates that many gay and lesbian couples perceive the same rewards in child-rearing that 'straight' couples do. There is an irony in all this. As gays and lesbians establish the legal basis for 'marriage' around the world, more and more heterosexuals are running away from it as marriage becomes less popular and divorce increases.

Singlehood

Living alone is becoming more common in Europe. In 2005, the number of people living alone in Great Britain had more than doubled since 1971, from 3 million to 7 million (*Social Trends*, 2007: 13). Elderly widows have always represented a large share of single people. But a new group of men aged between 25 and 44 have become the second biggest group to live alone: the numbers doubled between 1986 and 2005: 7 per cent to 15 per cent. And it is projected that this group will continue to rise. In the United States, though, the story is somewhat different. Here it is younger women who are staying single. In 1960, 28 per cent of US women aged 20–24 were single; by 2003, the proportion had soared to 74 per cent. Underlying this trend is women's greater participation in the labour force: women who are economically secure view a husband as a matter of choice rather than a financial necessity.

GLOBAL FAMILIES:

The globalisation and glocalisation of Mexican families

For some time the Mexican family has been seen as a distinctive subject of study by social researchers. Their studies have pointed, for instance, to the centrality of the value of family unity as the unquestionable source of individual and social stability to the historical organisation of family life in Mexico. They have also highlighted cultural tendencies towards strict patriarchal divisions within families: for instance, with regard to fathers' authority over their wives and children, and strict role divisions between men's participation in public life and paid labour and women's confinement to housework, childcare and a largely domestic life. More recently, research has highlighted trends towards more egalitarian forms of family life based on the intimate involvement of spouses and children rather than fixed gendered hierarchies. These trends have been related to factors such as women's massive incorporation into paid labour in the context of the expansion of the modern urban service sector since the 1950s, economic crises requiring both spouses to work to provide for their families, and the advent of easy-to-use contraceptive methods and family planning campaigns reducing women's fertility rates and detaching sexuality from reproduction.

Diversity and glocalisation

Yet, in spite of these distinctive patterns, 'the Mexican family' in

Families around the world: Mexican
A family of eleven people poses outside shanty town mexico.
Source: © Barry Lewis/Alamy.

a sense does not exist. There is a need to acknowledge the diversity of family relationships that exist in contemporary Mexico (see, again, the opening quote to this chapter from Diana Gittins). In Western popular culture and media, intimate relationships among Mexicans are often portrayed as being shaped by the cultural dynamics of 'machismo'. The concept of machismo refers to extreme forms of masculinity characterised by, among other things, very assertive and

sometimes aggressive behaviour and men's imposition of their authority over their female partners and other female family members. Related to this notion is the image of Mexican families as characterised by clear gendered divisions of power and tasks between a male household head and 'breadwinner' and his submissive wife, limited in her life to housework and childcare.

This imagery has recently been criticised as stereotypical misrepresentation of the empirical diversity of family

life among Mexicans. The US anthropologist Matthew Gutmann (1996), for example, points to the complex dynamics of family interactions among the residents of a working-class neighbourhood in Mexico City. His findings provide limited empirical evidence of the men's hyper-masculine behaviour in line with notions of machismo. Rather, they point to a variety of understandings and experiences of masculinity, involving fathers actively participating in childcare and loving husbands helping their wives with housework as much as instances of domestic abuse and clear gendered divisions of power and tasks within families. Similarly, the work of the sociologist Gloria González-López (2005) suggests that family relationships among Mexicans are characterised by considerable regional variations in terms of factors such as social class, locally specific political and economic dynamics, culture, and social differences between urban and rural settings. In view of this research, it seems indicated to think about a variety of locally specific 'Mexican families' rather than 'the Mexican family', unchanging and socioculturally homogeneous.

Global trends and globalisation

Beyond this localised diversity, it is important also to see the ways in which Mexican families participate in processes of social change on a potentially global scale. For instance, in her research on US–Mexican migrant families, Jennifer Hirsch (2003) concludes that factors such as declining fertility levels, women's increasing access to education, and the propagation of egalitarian, individualistic sexual ideals and information about sexuality by the mass media, all contribute to the increasing cultural significance of the mentioned cultural ideal of love-based companionate relationships and family life. It has been concluded (Hirsch and Wardlow, 2006) that such developments reflect a global trend away from traditional patriarchal family life towards alternative modern forms of intimacy. In spite of their distinctiveness, Mexican families thus seem to some extent to be shaped by social forces that are not particular to Mexican society.

Mexican families are both global and local – they participate in social processes that reshape families around the globe in often very similar ways (global), but at the same time they are shaped in a distinctive way by historical forces particular to Mexican society at large, such as the mentioned value of family unity (global and local), and a variety of regionally specific social, economic and political conditions (local).

Look at

González-López, G. (2005) *Erotic Journeys: Mexican Immigrants and Their Sex Lives.*

Gutmann, M. (1996) *The Meanings of Macho: Being a Man in Mexico City.*

Hirsch, J. (2003) *A Courtship After Marriage: Sexuality and Love in Mexican Transnational Families.*

Hirsch, J. and Wardlow, H. (eds) (2006) *Modern Loves: The Anthropology of Romantic Courtship and Companionate Marriage.*

For a wider look, see also:

Jaipul L. Roopnarine and Uwe P. Gielen (2005) *Families in Global Perspective.*

Prepared for this book by Daniel Nehring.

Looking ahead: families in the twenty-first century

In recent decades, transformation in family life throughout much of the world has generated controversy, with advocates of 'traditional family values' locked in debate with supporters of new family forms and greater personal choice. Whatever position one takes on the merits of current family trends, change is certain to continue into the coming century. Based on current evidence, we can make five predictions about the future of family life.

First, divorce rates are likely to remain high, even in the face of evidence that divorce can harm children. There may be some erosion of support for easy dissolution of marriage, yet several generations of high divorce rates have seriously weakened the idea that marriage is a lifetime commitment. Looking back through history, marital relationships are about as durable today as they were a century ago, when many marriages were cut short by death (Kain, 1990). But more couples now *choose* to end marriages that fail to live up to their expectations. Therefore, although the divorce rate has stabilised recently, it is unlikely that marriage will regain the durability characteristic of the 1950s. One major reason is that increasing numbers of

A family poses for a very formal portrait on a garden bench, c. 1890
Source: © DaZo Vintage Stock Photos/ Images.com/Corbis.

women are able to support themselves, and traditional marriages appeal to fewer of them. Men, as well, are seeking more satisfying relationships. Perhaps we should view the recent trend towards higher divorce rates less as a threat to families than as a sign of change in family form. After all, most divorces still lead to remarriage, casting doubt on the notion that marriage itself is becoming obsolete. It is possible, too, that this trend may spread throughout parts of the non-Western world.

Secondly, family life in the twenty-first century will be highly variable. It may become increasingly 'postmodern'. We have noted an increasing number of cohabiting couples, lone-parent families, gay and lesbian families and blended families. Most families may still be based on marriage and most married couples still have children. But, taken together, the variety of family forms observed today represents a new conception of family life as a matter of choice.

Thirdly, men are likely to play changing roles in child-rearing. For much of the nineteenth and early twentieth centuries, men played limited roles in the raising of children. In the 1950s, a decade many people nostalgically recall as the 'golden age' of families, men began to withdraw from active parenting (Snell, 1990; Stacey, 1990). Since then,

the share of children growing up in homes without their fathers has passed 25 per cent and is continuing to rise. A countertrend is emerging as some fathers – older, on average, and more established in their careers – eagerly jump into parenting. There has also been the rise of the 'new man', highly involved in child-rearing. But, on balance, the high UK divorce rate and a surge in single motherhood point to more children growing up with weaker ties to fathers than ever before.

Fourthly, economic changes will continue to reform marriage and the family. In many families, both household partners must work to ensure the family's financial security. As Arlie Hochschild (1989) points out, the economy is responsible for most of the change in society, but people *feel* these changes in the family. Marriage today is often the interaction of weary men and women: adults try their best to attend to children, yet often this can become minimal parenting. There are signs, however, that parents are giving increasing attention to their children in the UK.

Finally, the importance of new reproductive technologies will increase. While ethical concerns will surely slow these developments, new methods of reproduction will continue to alter the traditional meanings of parenthood.

SUMMARY

1 All societies are built on kinship, although family forms vary considerably across cultures and over time.

2 In industrial societies such as Europe, marriage is monogamous. Many pre-industrial societies, however, permit polygamy, of which there are two types: polygyny and polyandry.

3 In global perspective, patrilocality is most common, while industrial societies favour neolocality and a few societies have matrilocal residence. Industrial societies embrace bilateral descent; pre-industrial societies tend to be either patrilineal or matrilineal.

4 Families in the past were varied, and indeed varied in the same historical period. There is no such thing as one family form.

5 Functionalist analysis identifies major family functions: socialising the young, regulating sexual activity, transmitting social placement and providing material and emotional support.

6 Conflict theories explore how the family perpetuates social inequality by strengthening divisions based on class, ethnicity, race and gender.

7 Micro-level analysis highlights the variable nature of family life both over time and as experienced by individual family members.

8 Families differ according to class position, race and ethnicity.

9 Gender affects family dynamics, since husbands play a dominant role in the vast majority of families. Research suggests that marriage provides more benefits to men than to women.

10 Today's divorce rate is much higher than a century ago; four in ten current marriages will end in divorce. Most people who divorce – especially men – remarry, often forming blended families that include children from previous marriages.

11 Family violence, victimising both women and children, is far more common than official records indicate. Adults who abuse family members most often suffered abuse themselves as children.

12 Society's family life is becoming more varied. Lone-parent families, cohabitation, gay and lesbian couples and singlehood have proliferated in recent years across the world.

13 Although ethically controversial, new reproductive technology is altering conventional notions of parenthood.

CONNECT UP: Turn to Part 6 of this book for key resources and link up with the book's website, which links to these resources
SEE: www.pearsoned.co.uk/plummer

MYTASKLIST

Ten suggestions for going further

1 Connect up with Part Six and the Sociology Web Resources

As you work through ideas and think about the issues raised in this chapter, look at the accompanying website and the resource centre at the end of this book which connects to it. There is a lot here to help you move on. To link up, see: www.pearson.co.uk/plummer.

2 Review the chapter

Briefly summarise (in a paragraph) just what this chapter has been about. Consider: (a) What have you learned? (b) What do you disagree with? Be critical. And (c) How would you develop all this? How could you get more detail on matters that interest you?

3 Pose questions

(a) How has the emerging post-industrial economy affected family life? What other factors are changing the family?

(b) Why do some analysts describe the family as the 'backbone of society'? How do families perpetuate social inequality?

(c) Do you think that lone-parent households do as good a job as two-parent households in raising children? Why or why not?

(d) On balance, are families in Europe becoming 'postmodern'? What evidence supports your contention? When you take the world picture of families, would you also find evidence of major family changes?

(e) What do you understand by David Morgan's idea of 'family practices'? Keep a diary on your own 'family practices' for a week.

4 Explore key words

Many concepts have been introduced in this chapter. You can review them from the website or from the listing at the back of this book. You might like to give special attention to just five words and think them through – how would you define them, what are they dealing with, and do they help you see the social world more clearly or not?

5 Search the Web

Be critical when you look at websites – see the box on p. 940 in the Resources section. For this chapter look at the following:

United Nations family development
www.un.org/esa/socdev/family

Introduction to the Focal Point on the Family within the United Nations Secretariat.

Single parents
http://singleparents.about.com
A US website which contains streams of information for single parents.

Gay and lesbian couples
http://buddybuddy.com/partners.html
World details and ongoing debates about gay and lesbian marriages.

Some 'family' research centres in the UK include:

Morgan Centre for the study of relationships and personal life (Manchester)
www.socialsciences.manchester.ac.uk/morgancentre

Families and Social Capital (Southbank)
www1.lsbu.ac.uk/families

Centre for Family Research (Cambridge)
www.ppsis.cam.ac.uk/CFR

Families, Life Course and Generations (FLaG) Research Centre (Leeds)
www.sociology.leeds.ac.uk/flag/about

6 Watch a DVD

- Martin Scorsese's *Alice Doesn't Live Here Anymore* (1974) was one of the first 'single mum' films which, for its time, raised a lot of issues. But it now seems a bit old-fashioned.
- There are many Hollywood treatments of classic issues, though they usually deserve very critical viewing. They include Robert Benton's Oscar-winning *Kramer vs Kramer* (1979) on divorce, Robert Redford's *Ordinary People* (1980) on neurotic mothers, and John Lithgow's *Terms of Endearment* (1983) on the importance of family bonds. They make an interesting comparison with films made nearly two decades later, such as Ang Lee's *The Ice Storm* (1997).
- In contrast with many Hollywood films, the films of Mike Leigh in the UK depict family life in tragi-comic tones: see his *Secrets and Lies* (1996), *Life is Sweet* (1990) and *Bleak Moments* (1971).
- See also: Lisa Cholodenko's *The Kids Are Alright* (2010) and Robert Benton's *The Human Stain* (2003).

7 Think and read

Jaipaul L. Roopnarine and Uwe Gielen (eds), *Families in Global Perspectives* (2005). Provides case studies of the family in Africa, Asia, the Middle East, Europe and the Americas.

David Cheal, *Families in Today's World: A Comparative Approach* (2008). Provides an introduction.

Carol Smart, *Personal Life, Relationships and Families: New Directions in Sociological Thinking* (2007). Striking new study which rethinks ideas on the ways we live together.

Goran Therborn, *Between Sex and Power: Family in the World* (2004). Major new study which traces the history and patterns of family across the world in the twentieth century.

Graham Allan and Graham Crow, *Families, Households and Society* (2001). Reviews current issues and debates, mainly in the UK.

Judith Stacey, *Unhitched: Love, Marriage and Family Values from Western Hollywood to Western China* (2011). Worldwide empirical research to challenge thinking on one major form.

David Morgan, *Family Connections: An Introduction to Family Studies* (1996). The key book for studying the family as a series of family practices.

Lynn Jamieson, *Intimacy: Personal Relationships in Modern Societies* (1998). Helps establish this as a major new area of enquiry.

Anthony Giddens, *The Transformation of Intimacy* (1992). Written in an accessible way, this book examines the major changes between men and women.

Jeffrey Weeks, Brian Heaphy and Catherine Donovan, *Same Sex Intimacies: Families of Choice and Other Life Experiments* (2001). Provides original UK data on these 'experiments in living'.

Lynne Harne and Jill Radford, *Tackling Domestic Violence* (2008). Recent guide to the issues.

8 Relax with a novel

There are many wonderful novels to read about the personal life. Here is a sample of old classics and new ones:

Jane Austen, *Pride and Prejudice* (1813).
Leo Tolstoy, *Anna Karenina* (1877).
Virginia Wolf, *To the Lighthouse* (1927).
Vladimir Nabokov, *Lolita* (1955).
Laurie Lee, *Cider with Rosie* (1959).
Alan Bennett, *Talking Heads* (1988).
Annie Proulx, *The Shipping News* (1993).
Zoe Heller, *Notes on a Scandal* (2003).
Lionel Shriver, *We Need to Talk about Kevin* (2003).

9 Connect to other chapters

- An important development – the new reproductive technologies – is discussed in Chapter 23.
- See Chapter 12 for linked discussions of both sexual violence and homosexuality.

10 Engaging with THE BIG DEBATE

What is the future of the family? The family values debate

Are 'traditional families' vital to our way of life? Or are they a barrier to progress? To begin, people typically use the term 'traditional family' to mean a married couple who, at some point in their lives, raise children. But the term is more than simply descriptive – it is also a moral and political statement. That is, support for the traditional family implies that people place a high value on getting and staying married, that parents should place more importance on raising children than on pursuing their own careers, and that society should accord special respect to two-parent families rather than various 'alternative lifestyles'.

On one side of the debate, Patricia Morgan, from a conservative view, and Norman Dennis and George Erdos from an ethical socialist view, argue that there has been a serious erosion of the traditional family since 1960. And it is not hard to see that there have indeed been changes from the figures in the *Global families* box on p. 637. There are fewer marriages, fewer children, more divorce, more singlehood, more single parents. Indeed, the number of children born out of wedlock has grown 'from one in ten in the late 1970s to over three in ten in the early 1990s' (Morgan, 1995: 4). And, because of both divorce and increasing numbers of children born out of wedlock, the share of youngsters living with a single parent at some time before age 18 has quadrupled since 1960 to half of all children. Combining the last two facts, just one in four of today's children will grow up with two parents and go on to maintain a stable marriage of their own.

In the light of such data, serious consequences follow. These include the rise of delinquency, the growth of incivility, the huge welfare burden. The family is not just changing, it is heading towards total collapse, and it does not look good for the future of society.

Patricia Morgan suggests that the traditional family of man–wife–children is being replaced by the mother–child state. She deplores the rise of lone-parent families, especially children born out of wedlock, and is very concerned about the growth of 'welfare dependency' for many of these poor lone-parent families. Norman Dennis, with similar arguments, is most concerned with the ways in which a new family without fatherhood has been created. It is this lack of a father to be an adequate role model for children which has created many problems. In sum, and drawing from research, he suggests that 'on average the life-long socially certified monogamous family of the pre-1960s pattern was better for children than any one of a variety of alternatives' (Dennis and Erdos, 1993: 34).

The same debate is found in the United States. There David Popenoe (1993) describes this breakdown as a fundamental shift from a 'culture of marriage' to a 'culture of divorce'. Traditional vows of marital commitment – 'till death us do part' – now amount to little more than 'as long as I am happy'. The negative consequences of the cultural trend towards weaker families, Popenoe continues, are obvious everywhere: as we pay less and less attention to children, the crime rate goes up along with a host of other problematic behaviours, including smoking, drinking and premarital sex.

As Popenoe sees it, then, we must work hard and quickly to reverse current trends. Government cannot be the solution (and may even be part of the problem): since 1960, as US government spending on social programmes has soared fivefold, the traditional family has grown weaker and weaker. The alternative, Popenoe reasons, is a cultural turnaround by which people will question and ultimately reject the recently popular 'me-first' view of our lives in favour of greater commitment to a spouse and children. (We have seen such a turnaround in the case of cigarette smoking.) Popenoe concludes that we should save the traditional family, and that means we need to affirm publicly the value of marital permanence as well as endorse the two-parent family as best for the well-being of children.

On the other side of the debate, many sociologists argue that the recent changes in the family have mainly been for the good. They are really simply reflections of changes in the wider social world. As people's desire for choice, individuality, freedom, etc. has grown, so has their desire for more control over their personal life. The traditional families desired by the traditionalists are described in too romantic and nostalgic terms. Families of the past often meant that wives were stuck with violent husbands and large families of children lived in abject poverty. Equality was minimal, as was choice.

Instead of returning to a mythical past, a goal now is to achieve democracy in the personal sphere. Equality and choice become key features of modern families. In any event, it is no longer possible to have only one ideal family form – even if we should want it. The world has grown too complex. As Beck and Beck-Gernsheim argue in *The Normal Chaos of Love* (1995), society has become individualised and with that 'It is no longer possible to pronounce in some binding way what family, marriage, parenthood, sexuality or love mean, what they should be or could be; rather they vary in substance, exceptions, norms and morality from individual to individual and from relationships to relationships' (Beck and Beck-Gernsheim, 1995: 5). The traditionalists are looking back to a world that has now gone, and cannot be returned to. They do not paint a rosy picture. They recognise that we are in a transition period, one in which there is likely to be 'a long and bitter battle – a war between men and women' (1995: 5).

Most of our current institutions were designed at a time when there was a sharp division between women in the home and men at work. Now this is changing: work situations, laws, town planning, school curricula all have to be changed.

For Judith Stacey, the traditional family is more problem than solution. Striking to the heart of the matter, Stacey writes (1990: 269): 'The family is not here to stay. Nor should we wish it were. On the contrary, I believe that all democratic people, whatever their kinship preferences, should work to hasten its demise.' The main reason for rejecting the traditional family, Stacey explains, is that it perpetuates and enhances various kinds of social inequality. Families play a key role in maintaining the class hierarchy, transferring wealth as well as 'cultural capital' from one generation to another. Moreover, feminists charge that the traditional family is built on patriarchy, which subjects women to their husbands' authority as well as saddling them with most of the responsibility for housework and childcare. And from a gay-rights perspective, she adds, a society that values traditional families inevitably denies homosexual men and women equal dignity and participation in social life.

Stacey thus applauds the breakdown of the family as a measure of social progress. Indeed, she views the family not as a basic social institution but as a political construction that serves to elevate one category of people, which she identifies as affluent white males, at the expense of women, homosexuals and poor people who lack the resources to maintain middle-class respectability.

Moreover, Stacey continues, the concept of 'traditional family' is increasingly irrelevant to a diverse society in which people reject singular models of correct behaviour and in which both men and women must work for income. What society needs, Stacey concludes, is not a return to some golden age of the family, but political and economic changes (including income parity for women, universal healthcare, programmes to reduce unemployment and expanded sex education in the schools) that will provide tangible support for children as well as ensure that people in diverse family forms receive the respect and dignity everyone deserves.

Continue the debate

1 To strengthen families, Popenoe urges parents to put children ahead of their own careers by limiting their joint working week to 60 hours. Do you agree? Why or why not?
2 Judith Stacey urges greater choice and equality in relationships and this means more diverse families. Do you agree?
3 What policies or programmes would you support to enhance the well-being of children?
4 Can you mount a 'defence of single parents', looking at evidence for their 'successes' and 'failures'?

Source: Stacey (1990, 1993); Abbot and Wallace (1992); Dennis and Erdos (1993); Popenoe (1993); Beck and Beck-Gernsheim (1995); Council on Families in America (1995); Morgan (1995).

CHAPTER 19

RELIGION AND BELIEF

IN 1989 SIR AHMED SALMAN RUSHDIE published his controversial novel *The Satanic Verses* in Britain. One character in the book, the Prophet Mahound, appears as a figure of debauchery, foul language and obscenity. Sensing that this was a thinly disguised, blasphemous attack on Mohammed and the Islamic faith, British Muslims soon expressed their anger and requested a publisher's apology for misrepresenting the Islamic faith. Matters rapidly escalated: the book was ritually burned in Bolton and Bradford; the media accused the Muslims of intolerance; voices were raised against Rushdie in India and Pakistan. On Valentine's Day 1989, the Iranian leader Ayatollah Khomeini issued a *fatwa* – or official call for execution – against Rushdie. Although initially a British affair, *The Satanic Verses* scandal escalated into an international one, symbolising battles between religious institutions and secular cultures, and accompanied by a resurgence of anti-Islamic feeling in the West. Fearing for his life, Rushdie went into hiding, where he stayed for over ten years. Years later, in 2007, he was knighted in the UK. And controversy – though on a much smaller scale – flamed up all over again.

In March 1995, a small group of terrorists released a poisonous gas in Tokyo's underground system, killing 12 but blinding many more and causing complete pandemonium. But this was no ordinary act of terrorism. It was conducted by Aum Shinriyko, a religious sect that claimed 10,000 Japanese members and 20,000 in Russia. Its leader Shoko Asahara had actually created a stockpile of weapons to kill around 10 million people.

In March 1997, Marshall Applewhite led 39 of his followers to commit suicide as part of the cult Heaven's Gate. Their dead bodies, laid out neatly in bunk beds, were found in Rancho Santa Fe, California. The cult was a distinctly modern group – they wore sneakers and were computer geeks – yet they looked for signs of religious meaning on their computers. They attached enormous significance to the Hale-Bopp comet as a sign that their time to go to heaven had arrived. And when it appeared, they were all led by their cult leader to drink a curious mix of vodka and barbiturates so that their 'earthly vessels' could rise to the heavens.

And on 11 September 2001, in by far the most devastating terrorist action up to that date, four civil airliners were hijacked by suicide bombers and targeted at major US buildings. Two demolished the Twin Towers of the World Trade Center in New York, the third destroyed part of the Pentagon in Washington, and the fourth crashed in Pennsylvania. These were rapidly identified with terrorist attacks, and especially with Osama bin Laden and his al Qaeda international terrorist network. Bin Laden is on record as saying that he is conducting a religious war – an Islamic *jihad* – against America.

It is often argued that religion is in decline in the modern world – in the face of rising rationality and science. And it is true that in many European countries, church going and even Christian beliefs are becoming less common. But, as the cases above well illustrate, in the contemporary world religion may play as powerful a role as it always has. This chapter will examine the nature and role of religion in the twenty-first century world.

See: Salman Rusdie discussing his book and the death sentence on YouTube at: http://fora.tv/2007/05/20/Salman_Rushdie#fullprogram

There is only one religion, though there are a hundred versions of it.

George Bernard Shaw: *Plays Pleasant and Unpleasant* (1898), vol. 2 preface

If God did not exist it would be necessary to invent him.

Voltaire

In this chapter, we ask:

- **What are the key features and forms of religion?**
- **How are religions organised and why do they exist?**
- **What is the variety of global religions?**
- **How is social change shaping contemporary religions? Is it in decline or not?**

(Left) *The Ascent of the Prophet Mohammed to Heaven* by Aqa Mirak, sixteenth-century Persian manuscript

Source: OR2265 Ascent of the Prophet Mohammed to Heaven, Mirak, Aqa (FL. c. 1520–76) British Library, London, UK, © British Library Board. All Rights Reserved/ The Bridgeman Art Library.

Q Aqa Mirak was a sixteenth-century Persian painter. Think how religious art is shaped by both history and culture.

The twenty-first century world has put religion firmly back on the agenda of sociology as a major area for analysis. For much of the twentieth century, sociologists had argued that religion was in decline, that societies were becoming secularised. But it is now clear that across the globe religion is asserting itself in many ways, and many argue that it is becoming stronger. In this chapter we ask what religion is, explore the changing face of religious belief throughout history and around the world, and examine the place of religion in today's modern, scientific, rational world – as it becomes global, postmodern and digital.

What is religion?

Throughout most of human history, human beings living in small societies attributed birth, death and even what happened in between to the operation of supernatural forces. Over the course of the last several hundred years, however, science (discussed in Chapter 23) has emerged as an alternative way of understanding the natural world, and scientific sociology offers various explanations of how and why societies operate the way they do.

Yet religion is a matter of **faith**, *belief anchored in conviction rather than scientific evidence*. For instance, the New Testament of the Bible defines faith as 'the assurance of things hoped for, the conviction of things not seen' (Hebrews 11: 1) and exhorts Christians to 'walk by faith, not by sight' (2 Corinthians 5: 7). Some people with strong faith may be disturbed by the thought of sociologists turning a scientific eye to what they hold as sacred. Since religions vary a great deal around the world, with no one thing sacred to everyone on earth, this raises in an acute form *the problem of relativity* and leads to the question: just how can billions of people across the world organise their lives with such profoundly different belief systems, each of which claims its own god or gods? Sociologists recognise that religion appears central to virtually every culture on earth, and they seek to understand just why such religious beliefs and practices assume such importance and what role they play. Because religion deals with ideas that transcend everyday experience, neither common sense nor any scientific discipline can verify or disprove religious doctrine.

The sacred and the profane

Durkheim (whose ideas were introduced in Chapter 4) claimed that the focus of religion is 'things that surpass the limits of our knowledge' (1965: 62; orig. 1915). As human beings, Durkheim explained, we organise our surroundings by defining most objects, events or experiences as **profane** (from Latin, meaning 'outside the temple'), *that which is an ordinary element of everyday life*. But we set some things apart, Durkheim

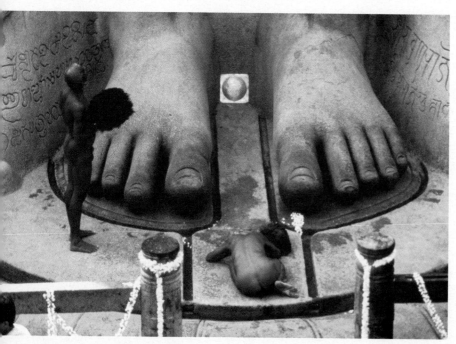

Religion is founded on the idea of the sacred, that which is set apart as extraordinary and which demands our submission. Bowing, kneeling or prostrating oneself – each a common element of religious devotion – symbolises this submissiveness
Source: Raghu Rai/Magnum Photos.

continued, by designating them as **sacred**, *that which is extraordinary, inspiring a sense of awe, reverence, and even fear.* Distinguishing the sacred from the profane is the essence of all religious belief. **Religion**, then, is *a social institution involving beliefs and practices based upon a conception of the sacred.*

Around the world, matters of faith vary greatly, with no one thing sacred to everyone. Although people regard most books as profane, Jews view the Torah (the first five books of the Hebrew Bible or Old Testament) as sacred, in the same way that Christians revere the entire Bible and Muslims exalt the Qur'an (Koran).

However, a community of believers draws religious lines, Durkheim (1965; orig. 1915: 62) claimed. People understand profane things in terms of their everyday usefulness: we sit down at a computer or turn the key of a car to accomplish various tasks. What is sacred, however, we set apart from everyday life and regard with reverence.

All religions have models of life by which people can organise their activities. Usually these include a **cosmogony**, *a tale about how the world/universe was created*; a theodicy, a tale about how evil and suffering is to be found in the world; and a broad vision of the **ethical life** – *how people should behave.* In addition they are likely to have many rituals: meditations and mantras, worship, festivals, and regulations on hygiene, diet and sex. To make clear the boundary between the sacred and the profane, Muslims remove their shoes before entering a mosque to avoid defiling a sacred place of worship with soles that have touched the profane ground outside. Similarly, every Hindu devotee must engage in ritual washings, while for Jews there are rites of passage such as bar mitzvah for boys and bat mitzvah for girls. The sacred is the focus of **ritual**, which is *formal, ceremonial behaviour.* Holy communion is the central ritual of Christianity; the wafer and wine consumed during communion symbolise the body and blood of Jesus Christ, and are never treated as food.

Religiosity

Religiosity designates *the importance of religion in a person's life.* Years ago, Charles Glock (1959, 1962) distinguished five distinct dimensions of religiosity. *Experiential* religiosity refers to the strength of a person's emotional ties to a religion. *Ritualistic* religiosity refers to frequency of ritual activity such as prayer and church attendance. *Ideological* religiosity concerns an individual's degree of belief in religious doctrine. *Consequential* religiosity has to do with how strongly religious beliefs figure in a person's daily behaviour. Finally, *intellectual* religiosity refers to a person's knowledge of the history and doctrines of a particular religion. Anyone is likely to be more religious on some dimensions than on others; this inconsistency compounds the difficulty of measuring the concept of religiosity.

Understanding religion

Although, as individuals, sociologists may hold any number of religious beliefs – or none at all – they all agree that religion has a major importance for the operation of society. Each theoretical paradigm suggests ways in which religion affects social life.

Religion as ritual: the functions of religion

Emile Durkheim (1965; orig. 1915) maintained that we confront the power of society every day. Society, he argued, has an existence and power all of its own beyond the life of any individual. Thus, society itself is 'godlike', surviving the ultimate deaths of its members whose lives it shapes. Durkheim contended that, in religious life, people celebrate the awesome power of their own society. This insight explains the practice, in every society, of transforming certain everyday objects into sacred symbols of collective life. Members of technologically simple societies, Durkheim explained, do this with the **totem**, *an object in the natural world collectively defined as sacred.* The totem – perhaps an animal or an elaborate work of art – becomes the centrepiece of ritual, symbolising the power of society to transform individuals into a powerful collectivity.

Durkheim pointed out three major functions of religion for the operation of society:

1 *Social cohesion.* Religion unites people through shared symbols, values and norms. Religious doctrine and ritual establish rules of 'fair play' that make organised social life possible. Religion also speaks eloquently about the vital human dimension of *love.* Thus, religious life underscores both our moral and emotional ties to others.

2 *Social control.* Every society uses religious imagery and rhetoric to promote conformity. Societies infuse many cultural norms – especially mores relating to marriage and reproduction – with religious justification. Looking beyond behavioural norms, religion confers legitimacy on the political system.

In medieval Europe, in fact, monarchs claimed to rule by divine right. Few of today's political leaders invoke religion so explicitly, but many publicly ask for God's blessing, implying to audiences that their efforts are right and just.

3 *Providing meaning and purpose.* Religious beliefs offer the comforting sense that the vulnerable human condition serves some greater purpose. Strengthened by such convictions, people are less likely to collapse in despair when confronted by life's calamities. For this reason, major life-course transitions – including birth, marriage and death – are usually marked by religious observances that enhance our spiritual awareness.

Critical comment

Durkheim's analysis contends that religion represents the collective life of society. The major weakness of this approach, however, is its tendency to downplay religion's dysfunctions – especially the capacity of strongly held beliefs to generate social conflict. During the early Middle Ages, for example, religious faith was the driving force behind the Crusades, in which European Christians sought to wrest from Muslim control lands that both religions considered to be sacred. Conflict among Muslims, Jews and Christians continues as a source of political instability in the world today. The long-standing social divisions in Northern Ireland (now a little abated) are also partly a matter of religious conflict between Protestants and Catholics; Dutch Calvinism historically supported apartheid in South Africa; and religious differences continue to fuel divisions in Algeria, Bosnia, India, Sri Lanka and elsewhere. The map on p. 666 demonstrates this. In short, nations have long marched to war under the banner of their god: differences in faith have provoked more violence in the world than have differences of social class. Indeed, the history of the world may well be written as a history of religious war and conflict.

Religion as constructed meaning: the power of the symbol

Max Weber's theory is usually considered a prime example of an action theory, and it is discussed elsewhere in this book. He saw religion as sometimes being a major force for change – as we saw in Chapter 3, the Protestant ethic served as a major catalyst for the development of capitalism. But there are many others. 'Society', asserts the Catholic sociologist Peter Berger

(1967: 3), 'is a human product and nothing but a human product, that yet continuously acts back upon its producer.' From an action perspective, religion (like all of society) is socially constructed (although perhaps with divine inspiration!). It is one of the chief mechanisms through which meanings are constructed and people make sense of their lives. It is also one of the areas of life most shot through with symbolism and ritual. Thus, through various rituals, from saying grace before daily meals to annual religious observances such as Easter and Passover, individuals develop the distinction between the sacred and profane. Further, Berger explains, by placing everyday events within a 'cosmic frame of reference', people confer on their own fallible, transitory creations 'the semblance of ultimate security and permanence' (1967: 35–6).

Marriage is a good example. If we look on marriage merely as a contract between two people, we assume that we can end it whenever we want to. But if partners define their relationship as holy matrimony, this bond makes a far stronger claim on them. This fact, no doubt, explains why the divorce rate is lower among people who are more religious.

Especially when humans confront uncertainty and life-threatening situations – such as illness, war and natural disaster – we bring sacred symbols to the fore. By seeking out sacred meaning in any situation, in other words, we can lift ourselves above life's setbacks and even face the prospect of death with strength and courage. Interactionists have researched the ways in which many of the newer religions such as the Moonies and Scientology give people meaning in the face of a modern world which can be deeply stressful (Lofland, 1977; Barker, 1984).

Critical comment

The action approach views religion as a social construction, placing everyday life under a 'sacred canopy' of meaning (Berger, 1967). Of course, Berger adds, the ability of the sacred to legitimise and stabilise society depends on its constructed character going unrecognised. After all, we could derive little strength from sacred beliefs if we saw them to be mere devices for coping with tragedy. Then, too, this micro-level view pays scant attention to religion's link with social inequality, to which we turn shortly.

Religion as a chain of memory

The contemporary French sociologist Danièle Hervieu-Leger (2000) sees religion as a kind of memory which provides a chain of connection between individual believers and their communities. In order to understand the changing roles of religious beliefs, we need to trace the historical chains of memory and how they become ruptured by major events (such as the Reformation). Just how the 'memory mutates' becomes of significant interest.

In traditional societies, these memories are very strong indeed. They are supported by all kinds of rituals and strong communities, and are passed from generation to generation. But in modern societies they become much weaker. Hervieu-Leger talks of 'the crumbling memory of modern societies' and sees them as 'amnesic' societies in so far as they tend to forget their traditions and their past (see Davie, 2000).

Religion as power and inequality: the conflicts of the spirit

Another sociological view of religion is that of Marx, who claimed that religion served ruling elites by legitimising the status quo and diverting people's attention from the social inequities of society. In a famous statement, he saw religion as the 'opium of the people'. It is 'the sign of an oppressed creature, the sentiment of a heartless world and the soul of soulless conditions' (1964: 27; orig. 1848). Religion works both to create and to reinforce systems of stratification, as well as dulling the awareness of it. The caste system, as we have seen in Chapter 8, is a key feature of Hinduism and stratifies into layers of priests, rulers, merchants and servants – with a large 'outcast' group that does not fit (the untouchables). The structure of the Christian church, likewise, has often created considerable wealth for its religious leaders. The extremely wealthy and powerful Vatican City State with it Papal leader has status as an independent country in many international organisations, illustrating the close alliance between religious and political elites.

Gender and ethnicity also figure in religion's tie to social inequality. Virtually all the world's major religions have reflected and encouraged male dominance of social life, as the *World watch* box explains. Many religions predominate in a specific geographical region or society. Islam commands the devotion of most (but not all) people within the Arab societies of the Middle East; Hinduism is closely fused with the culture of India, as is Confucianism with the Chinese way of life. During Marx's lifetime, powerful Christian nations of western Europe justified colonial exploitation of Africa, the Americas and Asia by claiming that they were merely 'converting heathens'. In practical terms, working for political change may mean opposing the church and, by implication, God. Religion also encourages people to look hopefully to a 'better world to come', minimising the social problems of this world.

Critical comment

Social conflict analysis reveals the power of religion to legitimise social inequality. Yet critics of religion's conservative face, Marx included, minimise ways in which religion has promoted change as well as equality. Nineteenth-century religious groups in the United Kingdom, for example, were at the forefront of the movement to abolish slavery. In the United States, religious organisations and their leaders (including the Reverend Martin Luther King, Jr) were at the core of the civil rights movement and today serve as one of the main lobbies for the needs of poor immigrants from Latin America. There has been a long-standing 'radical' Catholic movement supporting revolutionary change in Latin America and elsewhere (discussed below).

World religions and patriarchy: do gods favour men?

All world religions seem to be patriarchal. They usually have male gods at the centre of their cosmologies. They favour men to be their officials on earth. And frequently they devise ways of excluding women from their organisations, their power base and the wider society. There is a paradox in all this, though. Just as women are often excluded from the power and influence of religions, so they often display higher levels of religiosity than men. Various surveys have suggested that women are more likely to believe in God than men and that Muslim women were more likely to say that religion was important to them than men (*Social Trends*, Modood).

The pioneering feminist Simone de Beauvoir (in her important book *The Second Sex*, orig. 1949) claimed that 'Man enjoys the great advantage of having a God endorse the code he writes ... For the Jews, Mohammedans, and Christians amongst others, man is master by divine right; the fear of God will therefore repress any impulse toward revolt in the downtrodden female.' For example, while many Christians revere Mary, the mother of Jesus, the New Testament also contrasts men made in 'the image and glory of God' with

women, made for 'the glory of man', professing: 'For man was not made from woman, but woman from man. Neither was man created for woman, but woman for man' (1 Corinthians 11: 7–9). Likewise, the Qur'an, the sacred text of Islam, contends that 'men are in charge of women' (quoted in Kaufman, 1976: 163). Historically, the major world religions have barred women from serving as priests. Islamic groups, Orthodox Jews and the Roman Catholic Church continue to exclude women from the religious hierarchy.

Still, over the past 50 years many religions have begun to confront the challenges from feminist stances. A growing number of Protestant denominations have overturned historical policies and now ordain women. Since 1993, women have been ordained in the Church of England and around half of those accepted for ordination are now women. There are now 2,000 women clergy in England and around 8,000 worldwide (O'Brien and Palmer, 2007). Reform Judaism has long elevated

women to the role of rabbi (and is the largest denomination to ordain gay and lesbian people). In 1985, the first woman became a rabbi in the Conservative denomination of Judaism.

Challenges to the patriarchal structure of organised religion – from the ordination of women to the introduction of gender-neutral language in hymnals and prayers – has sparked heated controversy, delighting progressives while outraging traditionalists. Propelling these developments is a lively feminism within many religious communities today. Feminist Christians contend that the rigid patriarchal traditions in many churches stand in stark contrast to the biblical image of Jesus Christ as non-aggressive, non-competitive, meek and humble of heart – traits often linked to femininity.

Feminists argue that unless traditional notions of gender are removed from our understanding of God, women will never have equality with men in the church. Theologian Mary Daly (1928–2010) put the matter bluntly:

'If God is male, then male is God.' Mary Daly was a major outspoken feminist critic (and was herself originally a Catholic). She sees Christianity as a patriarchal myth. For her, the Christian story served to eliminate earlier 'goddess' religions and women: 'there is no female presence involved in this Monogender Male Automotherhood', she claims. She then goes on to argue that Christianity is rooted in male 'sado-rituals', with its 'torture cross symbolism', and that it embodies women-hating. This leads her to mount a full-scale critique of male religions (Daly, 1973, 1978).

World religions show few signs of changing their orthodox lines on women. In July 2010, the Pope declared the 'attempted ordination of a woman' to the priesthood as one of the most serious crimes against church law. The Catholic Church teaches that it cannot ordain women as priests because Christ chose only men as his apostles. Of course, feminists and proponents of a female priesthood reject this. The long conflict continues.

The nature of religious organisations

Sociologists have devised broad schemes to categorise the hundreds of different religious organisations in the world. The most widely used model takes the form of a continuum, with *churches* at one pole and *sects* at the other.

Church

Drawing on the ideas of his teacher Max Weber, Ernst Troeltsch (1931) defined a **church** as *a type of religious organisation well integrated into the larger society.* Church-like organisations usually persist for centuries and claim as adherents generations of the same family. Churches have well-established rules and regulations, and expect their leaders to undergo approved training before being formally ordained. They have large memberships and tend to be bureaucratic.

While concerned with the sacred, a church accepts the ways of the profane world, which gives it broad appeal. Church doctrine conceives God in highly intellectualised terms (say, as a force for good), and favours abstract moral standards ('do unto others as you would have them do unto you') over specific mandates for day-to-day living. By teaching morality in safely abstract terms, a church can avoid social controversy. For example, many churches that, in principle, celebrate the unity of all peoples, have in practice all-white memberships. Such duality minimises conflict between a church and the surrounding political landscape (Troeltsch, 1931).

A church generally takes one of two forms. Islam in Morocco represents an **ecclesia**, *a church formally allied with the state.* Ecclesias have been common in history; for centuries Roman Catholicism animated the Roman Empire; Confucianism was the state religion in China until early in the twentieth century; the Anglican church remains the official Church of England, as Islam is the official religion of Pakistan and Iran. State churches typically define everyone in the society as a member; tolerance of religious difference, therefore, is severely limited. A **denomination**, by contrast, is *a church, independent of the state, that accepts religious pluralism*. Denominations are sects that have become incorporated into mainstream society. Thus Christian denominations include Baptists, Methodists and Lutherans, among others.

Sect

At the other end of our continuum is the **sect**, *a type of religious organisation that stands apart from the larger society*. Sect members hold rigidly to their own religious convictions while discounting what others around them claim to be true. In extreme cases, members of a sect may withdraw from society completely in order to practise their religion without interference from outsiders. When cultures view religious tolerance as a virtue, members of sects are sometimes accused of being dogmatic in their insistence that they alone follow the true religion (Stark and Bainbridge, 1979).

In organisational terms, sects are less formal than churches. Thus, sect members often engage in highly spontaneous and emotional practices as they worship, while members of churches tend to be passively attentive to their leader. Sects also reject the intellectualised religion of churches, stressing instead the personal experience of divine power. A further distinction between church and sect turns on patterns of leadership. The more church-like an organisation, the more likely its leaders are to be formally trained and ordained. Because more sect-like organisations celebrate the personal presence of God, members expect their leaders to exude divine inspiration in the form of **charisma** (from Greek, meaning 'divine favour'), *extraordinary personal qualities that can turn an audience into followers*, infusing them with the emotional experience that sects so value.

Sects generally form as breakaway groups from established churches or other religious organisations (Stark and Bainbridge, 1979). Their psychic intensity and informal structure render them less stable than churches, and many sects blossom only to wither and disappear a short time later. The sects that do endure typically become more like churches, losing fervour as they become more bureaucratic and established.

To sustain their membership, many sects rely on active recruitment, or proselytising, of new members. Sects place great value on the experience of **conversion**, *a personal transformation or religious rebirth*. Members of Jehovah's Witnesses, for example, eagerly share their faith with others in the hope of attracting new members. Finally, churches and sects differ in their social composition. Because they are more closely tied to the secular world, well-established churches tend to include people of high social standing. Sects, by contrast, attract more disadvantaged people. A sect's openness to new members and promise of salvation and personal fulfilment may be especially appealing to people who perceive themselves as social outsiders. However, as we shall explain presently, many established churches in the world have lost membership in recent decades. In the process, a number of sects, often global, now find themselves with more affluent members.

Cult

A **cult** is *a religious organisation that is substantially outside a society's cultural traditions*. Whereas a sect emerges from within a traditional religious organisation, a cult represents something else entirely. Cults typically form around a highly charismatic leader who offers a compelling message of a new way of life. Because some cult principles or practices may seem unconventional, the popular view of cults pictures them as deviant or even evil. Negative publicity given to a few cults has raised suspicion about any unfamiliar religious group. As a result of such aberrant behaviour, some scholars assert that to call a religious community a 'cult' amounts to declaring it unworthy.

Many long-standing religions – Christianity, Islam and Judaism included – began as cults. Of course, not all or even most cults flourish for very long. Cults are more at odds with the larger society than sects, and many demand that members not only accept their doctrine but embrace a radically new lifestyle. As a result, people sometimes accuse cults of brainwashing new members, although research suggests that most people who join cults experience no psychological harm (E. Barker, 1981). The rise in new cults is discussed further below.

The social shapes of global religions

As we have seen, religion is found in virtually all societies, and the diversity of religious expression is almost as wide ranging as culture itself. In this section, we will look at the range of traditional religions, focusing on some of the major patterns and the societies to which they belong. Map 19.1 provides a view of global state of religions.

The global state of religions

WORLD WATCH

INDIGENOUS FAITHS

Many cultures still have their original faiths. There are many of these but they tend to be quite small in size.

CHRISTIANITY

World's largest religion. Over 2.1 billion adherents and 33,000 dominations (50% Catholic; 20% Independents)

ISLAM

20% of world's population is Muslim - around 1.4 billion. Islam is a state religion of 25 countries.

HINDUISM

Third largest world religion. Nearly a billion and primarily in south Asia.

BUDDHISM

6% of world's population, mainly in southeast Asia (Burma, Thailand, Cambodia; but also Mongolia and Bhutan). Hundreds of smaller groupings worldwide.

SIKHISM

24 million worldwide, mainly India.

JUDAISM

There are only 13 million Jews worldwide, more than 5 million live in Israel. 80% live in Israel or the USA.

NON-BELIEVERS

Both China and Russia - with large populations - have histories of non-belief; but overall the highest concentration is in northern Europe.

USA

Dominance of Christianity, and also the rise of the Militant Christian right. Dominion Theology and Pentecostalism. Plays an important role in politics with extreme wings of Christian terrorists.

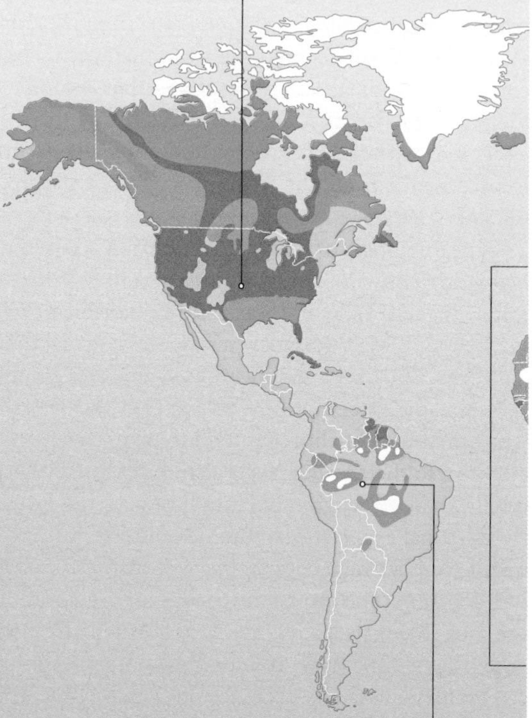

Majority of population compriesd of:

- Roman catholics
- Protestants
- Christians from various churches
- Orthodox Christians
- Churches of Eastern Christianity
- Mormons
- Muslims (Sunnis)
- Muslims (Shiites)
- Jews
- Buddhists
- Japanese Shintoists and Buddhists
- Hindus
- Sikhs
- Indigenous religions
- no dominant religion/ nonreligious
- unpopulated

Map 19.1

Source: Adapted from Ninian Smart, *World Atlas of Religions* (1999) and Joanne O'Brien and Martin Palmer, *The Atlas of Religion* (2007).

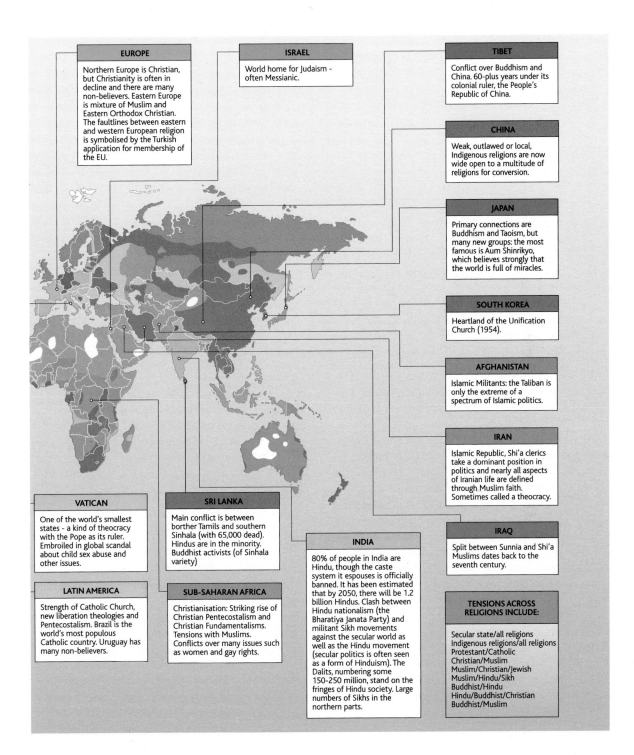

EUROPE

Northern Europe is Christian, but Christianity is often in decline and there are many non-believers. Eastern Europe is mixture of Muslim and Eastern Orthodox Christian. The faultlines between eastern and western European religion is symbolised by the Turkish application for membership of the EU.

ISRAEL

World home for Judaism - often Messianic.

TIBET

Conflict over Buddhism and China. 60-plus years under its colonial ruler, the People's Republic of China.

CHINA

Weak, outlawed or local, Indigenous religions are now wide open to a multitude of religions for conversion.

JAPAN

Primary connections are Buddhism and Taoism, but many new groups: the most famous is Aum Shinrikyo, which believes strongly that the world is full of miracles.

SOUTH KOREA

Heartland of the Unification Church (1954).

AFGHANISTAN

Islamic Militants: the Taliban is only the extreme of a spectrum of Islamic politics.

IRAN

Islamic Republic, Shi'a clerics take a dominant position in politics and nearly all aspects of Iranian life are defined through Muslim faith. Sometimes called a theocracy.

VATICAN

One of the world's smallest states - a kind of theocracy with the Pope as its ruler. Embroiled in global scandal about child sex abuse and other issues.

SRI LANKA

Main conflict is between border Tamils and southern Sinhala (with 65,000 dead). Hindus are in the minority. Buddhist activists (of Sinhala variety)

INDIA

80% of people in India are Hindu, though the caste system it espouses is officially banned. It has been estimated that by 2050, there will be 1.2 billion Hindus. Clash between Hindu nationalism (the Bharatiya Janata Party) and militant Sikh movements against the secular world as well as the Hindu movement (secular politics is often seen as a form of Hinduism). The Dalits, numbering some 150-250 million, stand on the fringes of Hindu society. Large numbers of Sikhs in the northern parts.

IRAQ

Split between Sunnia and Shi'a Muslims dates back to the seventh century.

LATIN AMERICA

Strength of Catholic Church, new liberation theologies and Pentecostalism. Brazil is the world's most populous Catholic country. Uruguay has many non-believers.

SUB-SAHARAN AFRICA

Christianisation: Striking rise of Christian Pentecostalism and Christian Fundamentalisms. Tensions with Muslims. Conflicts over many issues such as women and gay rights.

TENSIONS ACROSS RELIGIONS INCLUDE:

Secular state/all religions
Indigenous religions/all religions
Protestant/Catholic
Christian/Muslim
Muslim/Christian/Jewish
Muslim/Hindu/Sikh
Buddhist/Hindu
Hindu/Buddhist/Christian
Buddhist/Muslim

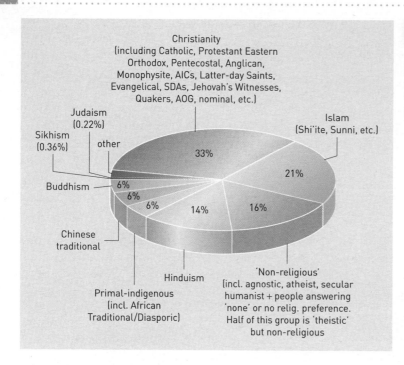

Figure 19.1 Major religions of the world: by number of adherents

Note: Total adds up to more than 100% due to rounding and because upper bound estimates were used for each group.

Source: © 2005 www.adherents.com.

Religion predates written history. Archaeological evidence indicates that our human ancestors routinely engaged in religious rituals some 40,000 years ago. Early hunters and gatherers, and some modern non-Western peoples, embrace **animism** (from Latin, meaning 'the breath of life'), *the belief that elements of the natural world are conscious life forms that affect humanity*. Animistic people view forests, oceans, mountains, even the wind as spiritual forces. Hunters and gatherers conduct their religious life entirely within the family. Members of such societies may look to a *shaman* or religious leader, but there are no full-time, specialised religious leaders. Belief in a single divine power responsible for creating the world marked the rise of pastoral and horticultural societies. The Christian view of God as a 'shepherd' may be linked to earlier religions, all of whose original followers were pastoral peoples.

As societies develop more productive capacity, religious life expands beyond the family and priests take their place among other specialised workers. In agrarian societies, the institution of religion gains prominence, as evidenced by the centrality of the church in medieval Europe. Even the physical design of the city casts this dominance in stone, with the cathedral rising above all other structures.

While many of the world's thousands of different religions are highly localised with few followers, there are a number of what we might call *global religions*. These, by contrast, span large areas and often have millions of adherents. We shall briefly describe six of the major world religions, which together claim as adherents some 4 billion people – almost three-quarters of humanity.

1 Christianity

Christianity is the most widespread religion, with nearly 2 billion followers, who constitute roughly one-third of humanity. Most Christians live in Europe or the Americas; more than 85 per cent of the people in the United States and Canada identify with Christianity. Moreover, people who are at least nominally Christian represent a significant share of the population in many other world regions, with the notable exceptions of northern Africa and Asia. The diffusion stems from the European colonisation of much of the world during the last 500 years. This dominance of Christianity in the West can be seen in the practice of numbering years on the calendar beginning with the birth of Christ.

Christianity originated as a cult, incorporating elements of its much older predecessor Judaism. Like many cults, Christianity was propelled by the personal charisma of a leader, Jesus of Nazareth, who preached a message of personal salvation. Jesus did not directly challenge the political powers of his day, calling on his followers to 'Render therefore to Caesar things that are Caesar's' (Matthew, xxii: 21). But his message was revolutionary, nonetheless, promising that faith and love would lead to triumph over sin and death.

Christianity is one example of **monotheism**, *belief in a single divine power*. This new religion broke with the Roman Empire's traditional **polytheism**, *belief in many gods*. Yet Christianity has a unique version of the Supreme Being as a sacred Trinity: God the Creator; Jesus Christ, Son of God and Redeemer; and the Holy Spirit, a Christian's personal experience of God's presence. The claim that Jesus was divine rests on accounts of his final days on earth. Tried and sentenced to death in Jerusalem on charges that he was a threat to established political leaders, Jesus endured a cruel execution by crucifixion, which transformed the cross into a sacred Christian symbol. According to Christian belief, Jesus was resurrected – that is, he rose from the dead – showing that he was the Son of God.

The apostles of Jesus spread Christianity widely throughout the Mediterranean region. Although the Roman Empire initially persecuted Christians, by the fourth century Christianity had become an ecclesia – the official religion of what later came to be known as the Holy Roman Empire. What had begun as a cult four centuries before was by then an established church.

Christianity took various forms, including the Roman Catholic Church and the Orthodox Church, centred in Constantinople (now Istanbul, Turkey). Further division occurred towards the end of the Middle Ages, when the Protestant Reformation in Europe sparked the formation of hundreds of denominations. Dozens of these denominations now command sizeable followings in Britain.

2 Islam

We have encountered Islam before in Chapter 5. Islam has some 1.1 billion followers (19 per cent of humanity), called Muslims. Like all religions, it is not uniform but made of many schisms – Sunnis, for example, are the more mystical branch of the Muslims. A majority of people in the Middle East are Muslims, which explains our tendency to associate Islam with Arabs in that region of the world. But most Muslims are *not* Arabs. Map 19.1 shows that a majority of people across northern Africa and western Asia are also Muslims. Moreover, significant concentrations of

Muslims are found in Pakistan, India, Bangladesh, Indonesia and the southern republics of the former Soviet Union.

Islam is the second largest faith in Europe, with estimates of 6 million (3 per cent of most western European populations). If eastern Europe were added in, the numbers would be significantly greater. Estimates place the number of British Muslims at 1,200,000 – most concentrated in the Midlands, London, Strathclyde, Yorkshire and Lancashire. British Muslims are predominantly Sunni, with only around 25,000 Shi'as (Storry and Childs, 1997).

As we have seen, Islam is the word of God as revealed to the prophet Mohammed, who was born in the city of Mecca (now in Saudi Arabia) around the year 570 CE. To Muslims, Mohammed, like Jesus, is a prophet, but not a divine being (as Christians define Jesus). The Qur'an (Koran), sacred to Muslims, is the word of God (in Arabic 'Allah') as transmitted through Mohammed, God's messenger. In Arabic, the word 'Islam' means both 'submission' and 'peace', and the Qur'an urges submission to Allah as the path to inner peace. Muslims express this personal devotion in a daily ritual of five prayers.

Islam spread rapidly after the death of Mohammed, although divisions arose. All Muslims, however, accept the Five Pillars of Islam (see Chapter 5). Like Christianity, Islam holds people accountable to God for their deeds on earth. Those who live obediently will be rewarded in heaven, while evil-doers will suffer unending punishment. Muslims are also obligated to defend their faith. Sometimes this tenet has justified holy wars against non-believers (in roughly the same way that medieval Christians joined the Crusades to recapture the Holy Land from the Muslims). Today, one of the world's major conflicts is between 'Western cultures' and fundamentalist Islam (Ahmed, 2007).

Many Westerners view Muslim women as among the most socially oppressed people on earth. Muslim women do lack many of the personal freedoms enjoyed by Muslim men, yet most accept the mandates of their religion. Moreover, patriarchy was well established in the Middle East before the birth of Mohammed. Some defenders of Islam's treatment of women argue that Islam actually improved the social position of women by demanding that husbands deal justly with their wives. Further, although Islam permits a man to have up to four wives, it admonishes men to have only one wife if having more than one would encourage him to treat women unjustly (Qur'an, 'The Women', v. 3). These issues have been raised before in Chapter 11.

3 Judaism

Speaking purely in numerical terms, Judaism, with only 15 million adherents worldwide, is among the smallest of the world's religions. Only in Israel do Jews represent a national majority. But Judaism has significance in many countries. The United States has the largest concentration of Jews (6 million people), and the largest European communities are found in France (500,000–600,000) and Britain (300,000) (Davie, 1994: 225).

Jews look to the past as a source of guidance in the present and for the future. Judaism has deep historical roots that extend back some 4,000 years before the birth of Christ to the ancient cultures of Mesopotamia. At this time, Jews were animistic, but this belief was to change after Jacob – grandson of Abraham, the earliest great ancestor – led his people to Egypt. Under Egyptian rule, Jews endured centuries of slavery. In the thirteenth century BCE, a turning point came as Moses, the adopted son of an Egyptian princess, was called by God to lead the Jews from bondage. This exodus (this word's Latin and Greek roots mean 'a marching out') from Egypt is commemorated by Jews today in the annual ritual of Passover. As a result of the Jews' liberation from bondage, Judaism became monotheistic, recognising a single, all-powerful God.

A distinctive concept of Judaism is the *covenant*, a special relationship with God by which Jews became a 'chosen people'. The covenant also implies a duty to observe God's law, especially the Ten Commandments as revealed to Moses on Mount Sinai. Jews regard the Bible (or, in Christian terms, the Old Testament) as both a record of their history and a statement of the obligations of Jewish life. Of special importance are the first five books of the Bible (Genesis, Exodus, Leviticus, Numbers and Deuteronomy), designated as the Torah (a word roughly meaning 'teaching' and 'law'). In contrast to Christianity's concern with personal salvation, Judaism emphasises moral behaviour in this world.

Judaism is composed of three main denominations. Orthodox Jews hold strictly to traditional beliefs and practices, maintaining historical forms of dress, segregating men and women at religious services and consuming only kosher foods. Such traditional practices set off Orthodox Jews as the most sect-like. Hasidism is the most messianic and fosters a strong spiritual devotion to Judaism. In the mid-nineteenth century, many Jews sought greater accommodation to the larger society, leading to the formation of more church-like Reform Judaism. More recently,

Two Jewish boys read the Talmud, the Jewish sacred book
Source: Gleb Garanich/Reuters.

a third segment – Conservative Judaism – has established a middle ground between the other two denominations.

All Jews, however, share a keen awareness of their cultural history, which has included battling against considerable prejudice and discrimination. A collective memory of centuries of slavery in Egypt, conquest by Rome and persecution in Europe has shaped Jewish identity. A militant Catholic Church instigated a strong separation of Christian and Jew during the Crusades. Interestingly, the urban ghetto (derived from the Italian word *borghetto*, meaning 'settlement outside the city walls') was first home to Jews in Italy, and this form of residential segregation soon spread to other parts of Europe (Sowell, 1996: Chapter 6). Substantial numbers of Jews have lived in eastern Europe since medieval times (with Poland often being the 'capital').

Around 120,000 Jews came to England as refugees from the pogroms of Russia between 1875 and 1914. Many settled in east London (Castles and Miller, 1993: 55). As larger numbers entered the country during the final decades of the nineteenth century, anti-Semitism increased. During the Second World War, anti-Semitism reached a vicious peak when Jews experienced the most horrific persecution in modern times as the Nazi regime in Germany systematically annihilated approximately 6 million Jews. The history of Judaism is a grim reminder of a tragic dimension of the human record – the extent to which religious minorities have been the target of hatred and even slaughter. Despite all this, anti-Semitism still seems widespread (and some even claim that a new anti-Semitism has emerged to attack Zionism and Israel: but this is another hot debate) (Iganski and Komin, 2003).

4 Hinduism

Hinduism is the oldest of all the world religions, originating in the Indus River Valley approximately 4,500 years ago. Hindus number some 775 million (14 per cent of humanity). Map 19.1 shows that Hinduism remains an Eastern religion, the predominant creed of India today, although it does have a significant presence in a few societies of southern Africa as well as Indonesia.

Hinduism differs from most other religions because it did not spring from the life of any single person. Hinduism also has no sacred writings comparable to the Bible or the Qur'an. Nor does Hinduism even envisage God as a specific entity. For this reason, Hinduism – like other Eastern religions – is sometimes thought of as an 'ethical religion'. Hindu beliefs and practices vary widely, but all Hindus recognise a moral force in the universe that imposes on everyone responsibilities known as *dharma*. One traditional example of *dharma* is the need to act in concert with the traditional caste system, described in Chapter 8.

A second Hindu principle, *karma*, refers to the belief in the spiritual progress of the human soul. To a Hindu, all actions have spiritual consequences and proper living contributes to moral development. Karma works through *reincarnation*, a cycle of new birth following death, so that individuals are reborn into a spiritual state corresponding to the moral quality of their previous life. Unlike Christianity and Islam, Hinduism proclaims no ultimate judgement at the hands of a supreme god, although in the cycle of rebirth, each person reaps exactly what the individual has sown. The sublime state of *nirvana* represents spiritual perfection: when a soul reaches this rarefied plateau, it exits the cycle of rebirth.

Looking at Hinduism, we see also that not all religions can be neatly labelled monotheistic or polytheistic. Hinduism may be described as monotheistic because it envisages the universe as a single moral system; yet Hindus perceive this moral order in every element of nature. Rituals, which are central to a Hindu's life, are performed in a variety of ways. Most Hindus practise private devotions, including, for example, ritual cleansing following contact with a person of a lower caste. Many also participate in public rituals, such as *Kumbh Mela*, during which pilgrims flock to the sacred River Ganges in India to bathe in its purifying waters. This ritual, which occurs every 12 years, attracts 15 to 20 million people (Pitt, 1955; Sen, 1961; Schmidt, 1980).

5 Buddhism

Some 2,500 years ago, the rich culture of India also gave rise to Buddhism. Today more than 350 million people (6 per cent of humanity) embrace Buddhism, and almost all are Asians. As shown in Map 19.1, adherents of Buddhism are concentrated in parts of southeast Asia – notably Myanmar (Burma), Thailand, Cambodia and Japan. Buddhism is also widespread in India and the People's Republic of China. Of the world religions considered so far, Buddhism most resembles Hinduism in doctrine, but, like Christianity, its inspiration springs from the life of one individual.

Siddhartha Gautama was born to a high-caste family in Nepal about 563 BCE. As a young man, he was preoccupied with spiritual matters. At the age of 29, he underwent a radical personal transformation, setting off for years of travel and meditation. His path ended when he achieved what Buddhists describe as *bodhi*, or enlightenment. Understanding the essence of life, Gautama became a Buddha. During the third century BCE, the ruler of India joined the ranks of Buddhists, subsequently sending missionaries throughout Asia and elevating Buddhism to the status of a world religion.

Energised by the Buddha's personal charisma, followers spread his teachings, the *dhamma*, across India. The Buddhist ethics are found in the five Precepts: do not kill; do not steal; do not lie; do not be unchaste; do not drink intoxicants. Central to Buddhist belief is the notion that human existence involves suffering. The pleasures of the world are real, of course, but Buddhists see such experiences as transitory. This doctrine is rooted in the Buddha's own travels throughout a society rife with poverty. But the Buddha rejected wealth as a solution to suffering; on the contrary, he warned that materialism inhibits spiritual development. Buddhism's answer to world problems is for individuals to pursue personal, spiritual transformation.

Buddhism closely parallels Hinduism in recognising no god of judgement; rather, it finds spiritual consequences in each daily action. Another similarity lies in its belief in reincarnation. Here, again, only full enlightenment ends the cycle of death and rebirth, thereby liberating a person from the suffering of the world (Schumann, 1974).

When Western people perform religious rituals, they typically do so collectively and formally as members of specific congregations. Eastern people, by contrast, visit shrines individually and informally, without joining a specific congregation. (a) Moonie wedding, South Korea; (b) Buddhist monks in Colombo protesting against the war; (c) Kumbh Mela festival in India

Source: (a) Reuters/Str Old; (b) Reuters/Str Old; (c) © David Pearson/Alamy.

People making offerings of candles, incense sticks and burning paper money to appease the spirits of their ancestors in China
Source: © Victor Paul Borg/Alamy.

6 Chinese religions and 'Confucianism'

As we saw in Chapter 4, from about 200 BCE until the beginning of the twentieth century, Confucianism was an ecclesia – the official religion of China. Following the 1949 Revolution, religion was suppressed by the communist government of the new People's Republic of China. Although officials provide little in the way of data to establish precise numbers, hundreds of millions of Chinese are still influenced by Confucianism. While almost all adherents to Confucianism live in China, Chinese immigration has introduced this religion to other societies in southeast Asia.

Confucius or, properly, K'ung-Fu-tzu, lived between 551 and 479 BCE. He shared with Buddha a deep concern for the problems and suffering in the world. The Buddha's response was a sect-like withdrawal from the world; Confucius, by contrast, instructed his followers to engage in the world according to a strict code of moral conduct. Thus it was that Confucianism

became fused with the traditional culture of China. Here we see a second example of what might be called a 'national religion'. As Hinduism has remained largely synonymous with Indian culture, Confucianism is enshrined in the Chinese way of life.

A central concept of Confucianism is *jen*, meaning humanness. In practice, this means that we must always subordinate our self-interest to moral principle. In the family, the individual must display loyalty and consideration for others. Likewise, families must remain mindful of their duties to the larger community. In this way, layer upon layer of moral obligation integrates society as a whole. Most of all, Confucianism stands out as lacking a clear sense of the sacred. We could view Confucianism, recalling Durkheim's analysis, as the celebration of society itself as sacred. Alternatively, we might argue that Confucianism is less a religion than a model of disciplined living. Certainly the historical dominance of Confucianism helps to explain why Chinese culture has long taken a sceptical attitude towards the supernatural. If we conclude that Confucianism is best thought of as a disciplined way of life, we must also recognise that it shares with religion a body of beliefs and practices that have as their goal goodness, concern for others and the promotion of social harmony (Schmidt, 1980).

7 Non-religious: sceptics, agnostics, 'seculars', atheists and humanists

Technically, these beliefs should not be included here. Durkheim and others define religion through 'the sacred', 'things set apart and forbidden'. But throughout history and across the world today, there are very large numbers of people who have doubts about or refuse the dominant worldwide institutionalised faiths. Estimates of world non-believers circulate around the 1 billion figure (i.e. about one-sixth of the world's population). In some countries, such as the former Soviet Union, atheism was the official belief. In others,

religion in general is much less organised, as we have seen for China in Chapter 4. Europe has the highest numbers of self-avowed non-religious atheists – around 41 million. Australia and New Zealand also have a relatively high proportion of non-believers. Non-believers can be seen as falling into two broad groups: those who are sceptical about the existence of God (sceptics, agnostics), and those who hold the stronger view that the existence of God can never be proved. Non-believers can be found across all the continents.

In the UK, the British Humanist Association claims that 'Humanism is the belief that we can live good lives without religious or superstitious beliefs. Humanists make sense of life using reason, experiences and shared human values' (*BHA News*, July 2007: 1). The problem with this definition is that history shows a long history of humanisms of all kinds – and that many include a belief in God. Like most religious beliefs, non-religious beliefs are also multiple and often contradictory (Zuckerman, 2005; Dawkins, 2006a; McGrath, 2004).

Society without God

Phil Zuckerman is a Californian sociologist who has been researching religions for over 20 years and has written a wonderful introduction to the sociologies of religion – looking at a wide range of them. His most recent study took him to the Nordic countries – and especially Denmark and Sweden. Here he found – as the title of his book puts it – a *Society Without God*.

In Denmark and Sweden, Zuckerman found that most people don't worship or pray, don't give much credence to any religion, and certainly don't believe in a God. He interviewed around 150 Danes and Swedes of all ages and educational backgrounds over the course of 14 months, asking them questions about what it was

like to live a life without God. And he found that most of them could lead lives without any worries about an afterlife and were quite contented. Far from being decaying societies of sin and badness, the residents in these countries score top rankings on a number of scales which measure human progress, such as the Human Development Index, which we met in Chapter 9; and the 'happiness index' (see Chapter 26). Their societies have some of the lowest rates of crime in the world, excellent health and educational systems, strong economies, as well as well-supported arts and egalitarian social policies. They stand out as better on most matters of welfare than many countries which are riddled with religious conflicts, wars and genocides. There is no guarantee, it seems, that believing in God will secure you any success on earth!

See: Phil Zuckerman, *Society without God: What the Least Religious Countries Can Tell Us about Contentment* (2008). And see an interview with him on YouTube: search *Phil Zuckerman Deadline*.

COUNTRY FACT FILE

DENMARK

Population	5.5 million
Per capita GDP	$36.00
Life expectancy	78.3
Adult literacy	100%
Key religions	Evangelical Lutheran/ non-believers
Key language	Danish
Key city	Copenhagen
Human development index	0.866 (19th)

Source: Economist World in Figures (2010).

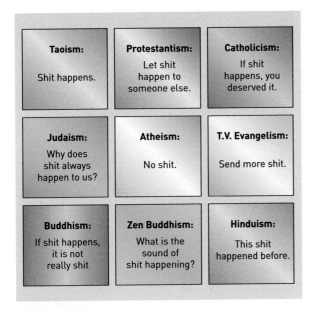

Taoism:

Shit happens.

Protestantism:
Let shit happen to someone else.

Catholicism:
If shit happens, you deserved it.

Judaism:
Why does shit always happen to us?

Atheism:
No shit.

T.V. Evangelism:
Send more shit.

Buddhism:
If shit happens, it is not really shit

Zen Buddhism:
What is the sound of shit happening?

Hinduism:
This shit happened before.

Figure 19.2 World religions, a humorous view
Source: Original design by Barbara Shoolery
© Game Plan Design.

Religion: East and West

This brief overview of world religions points up two general differences between the belief systems that predominate in Eastern and Western societies. First, Western religions (Christianity, Judaism and Islam) are typically deity-based, with a clear focus on God. Eastern religions (Hinduism, Buddhism, Confucianism) tend to be more like ethical codes that make a less clear-cut distinction between the sacred and secular. Second, the operational unit of Western religious organisations is the congregation. That is, people attend a specific place of worship with others, most of whom are members. Eastern religious organisations, by contrast, are more broadly tied into culture itself. For this reason, for example, a visitor finds a Thai or Hong Kong temple awash with people – tourists and worshippers alike – who come and go on their own schedule, paying little attention to those around them.

These two distinctions do not overshadow the common element of all religions: having a conception of a higher moral force or purpose that transcends the concerns of everyday life. In all these religious beliefs, people of the world find guidance and a sense of purpose for their lives.

Religion in Europe

Christianity is one of the foundations of European societies. For much of the past two millennia, Christianity has defined life in Europe, dignifying all major actions, from birth and baptism through marriage to death and burial. It has held out the hope of 'salvation'. In pre-Reformation feudal society, the church was unitary – supported by royalty and the entire population. Hamilton says:

> The medieval world was Christian in the sense that everybody shared a common understanding of the world in which they lived based on Christian premises. Only the very learned had full and detailed knowledge of the whole world picture, but everybody understood some part of it.

(Hamilton, 1996: 87)

Yet, while all the countries of Europe make some claim to be Christian and to have Christian values, there are significant religious divides both within and across countries. A potted history would have to include:

- The early combats with both Judaism and Islam in the struggle to establish a dominant religion.
- The fourth-century split of the European Christian Church into Roman Catholicism in the West and Greek Orthodoxy in the East. While Roman Catholicism spread to the Americas, the Eastern Orthodox lost ground in central Europe and Asia to Islam during the eleventh century.
- The long struggles between empires and the papacy. Pope Innocent III (1198–1216) finally established a papal state in central Italy.
- The conflicts within the church itself: the heretical struggles and executions of witches, etc., along with a rather dissolute clergy with an eye on wealth.
- The continuing conflicts with other religions, with high periodic violence (the Spanish Inquisition, the Crusades and the Nazi Holocaust).
- The Reformation: it started in Germany with Martin Luther (1483–1546) when reformists renounced allegiances to Rome in 1520. By 1570, Protestants had established a presence in many places – especially Scandinavia, Britain and 'Baltic Europe', moving later into the Netherlands, France, Spain and even Italy. Calvinism (formed by John Calvin, 1509–64) emerged in France, the Netherlands and Scotland.
- Migration and missionary missions to colonies in the Americas and Africa.

- The rise of science, with its claims for rationality, as a serious challenge to Christianity during the Enlightenment and the Industrial Revolution.
- The denial of religion throughout eastern Europe during its communist period, with its attendant struggles from within. (In some countries, such as Poland, religion became a major instigator of change.) Subsequently, there have been major changes: the number of active churches in Moscow, for instance, grew from 50 in 1988 to 250 in 1993.

Today, in Europe, divides and schisms continue, often based on these past conflicts and issues. Indeed, Yugoslavia, torn by divisions between Christians as well as between Christianity and Islam, has dramatically revealed the sharper edge of the continuing conflicts. There have also been deep-seated conflicts between Protestants and Catholics (as in the long conflicts within Northern Ireland) and between religion and humanism (as in the Netherlands). The Christian Democratic parties in many European governments partly base their platforms on Christian principles. In the UK, the Queen is head of both church and state and the two are interconnected. In Germany, the government collects church taxes (*Kirchensteuer*) on behalf of churches and uses it for social services.

Abortion issues continue to preoccupy those countries with a strong Catholic base. The most obvious divides are between the more religious, Catholic countries of southern Europe (Italy, Spain, Greece and Portugal) and the less religious Protestant north. France and Ireland are predominantly Catholic; Belgium, the Netherlands, Britain and the Nordic countries are generally much less religious.

There are also growing populations of Muslims throughout Europe – often with growing tensions. There are three main minority faiths in Europe, and Islam now constitutes the second largest faith in Europe, claiming millions of faithful – around 3 per cent of most European populations. In France, however, the figure is much higher at between 5 and 6 million (nearly 10 per cent of the population): 70 per cent of these have their heritage in former north African colonies of Algeria, Morocco and Tunisia. Estimates place the number of British Muslims at around 1,500,000. When eastern Europe is added in, the numbers are significantly greater. Turkey is 99 per cent Muslim.

Finally, there are possibly around 1 million Jews in post-Holocaust western Europe, concentrated mainly in France (around 500,000) and Britain (300,000). And as we shall see later, there has been a substantial increase in what we can call the new religious movements (NRMs) (Davie, 2000: 13–14).

How religious are people in the UK?

Note that the statistics in Table 19.1 have been widely quoted but they are based on the 2001 census. A new census is being produced in 2011. There is also evidence from small-scale studies that most religions have been in decline in the UK. See Steve Bruce, *God is Dead: Secularization in the West* (2002). But there is also contrasting evidence that while the Christian faith is in decline, the Muslim faith is growing: with 1,870,000 in 2004 growing to 2,422,000 by 2008 (*Social Trends*, 2010).

Table 19.1	UK population by religious identification	
	Thousands	**%**
Christian	42,079	71.6
Buddhist	152	0.3
Hindu	559	1.0
Jewish	267	0.5
Muslim	1,591	2.7
Sikh	336	0.6
Other religion	179	0.3
All religions	45,163	76.8
No religion	9,104	15.5
Not stated	4,289	7.3
All no religion/not stated	13,626	23.2
Base	58,789	100

Source: Social Trends (2004).

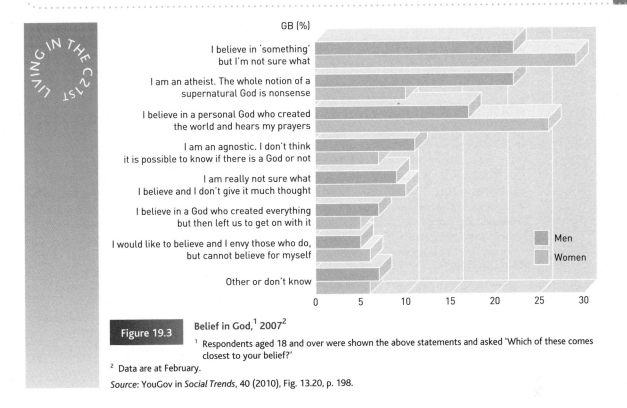

GB (%)

I believe in 'something' but I'm not sure what

I am an atheist. The whole notion of a supernatural God is nonsense

I believe in a personal God who created the world and hears my prayers

I am an agnostic. I don't think it is possible to know if there is a God or not

I am really not sure what I believe and I don't give it much thought

I believe in a God who created everything but then left us to get on with it

I would like to believe and I envy those who do, but cannot believe for myself

Other or don't know

Men
Women

0   5   10   15   20   25   30

Figure 19.3 Belief in God,[1] 2007[2]

[1] Respondents aged 18 and over were shown the above statements and asked 'Which of these comes closest to your belief?'

[2] Data are at February.

Source: YouGov in *Social Trends*, 40 (2010), Fig. 13.20, p. 198.

A note on religion in the UK: God is dead

In line with much of Europe, Britain is a relatively non-religious country: when 1,000 people were polled both in the UK and the USA and asked 'Do you believe there is a God?', less than 30 per cent in the UK said yes, compared with 80 per cent in the USA. Indeed, around 60 per cent of the population say they have no connection with any religion or church. Although we can map out the population structure by religious identification – as Table 19.1 does – research generally shows a very low number of people who participate in any kind of religious activity or believe in any kind of God. In 2000, some 60 per cent did claim to be religious and 50 per cent of the population claimed to be Christian. But by 2006 only a third seemed to believe in a God; about 6 per cent went to church; about two-thirds described themselves as not religious.

All major world religions are represented, but the numbers outside Christianity are relatively low: about 6 to 7 per cent. Nearly 40 per cent said they did not consider themselves belonging to any particular religion. The figures for Christian belief also include a lot of non-practising Christians – who may claim the religion but do not take it too seriously in their life.

In Britain, the Churches of England and Wales are formally tied to both Parliament and the monarchy, though the Church of England has shed its image as the 'Tory Party at prayer'. Membership in established, 'mainstream' churches has dwindled. Support for the Anglican, Roman Catholic, Presbyterian and Baptist churches has been declining significantly since the late twentieth century. Nominally, there are around 27 million Anglicans (nearly two-thirds claimed to associate with the Church of England), but only 2 million have officially registered. There are some 5 million Catholics, who are much more likely to attend church (Liverpool is Britain's only mainly Catholic city). Research also suggests that non-religious parents pass on their lack of faith to their children. Two religious parents have roughly a 50–50 chance of passing on their beliefs (Voas and Crockett, 2005: 11–12). That said, the churches do remain involved in the cultural life of the UK, through such activities as playgroups, youth clubs, care for the elderly and community centres. Christianity may now be more of a cultural force than a spiritual one.

As the established Christian churches lose members, however, other religious organisations are showing

LIVING IN THE C21ST

The god delusion or the twilight of atheism?

In the early twenty-first century, with a major conflict starting to appear between the West and the (fundamentalist) Muslim faith – a conflict with long historical roots – another schism became prominent. This is the divide between believers and non-believers.

There are now a number of countries where over half of the population may be seen as non-believers: Sweden, Denmark, Norway, Japan and much of Europe rank at the top. According to the 2009 *Human Development Report*, the four highest ranked nations in terms of human development were Norway, Australia, Iceland and Canada. All four have very high degrees of atheism. The Netherlands, Sweden and Japan – also with low religion – were in the top ten.

There are deep historical roots into non-believing: from Socrates' refusal to acknowledge Greek gods to Copernicus' heretical idea that the earth revolved around the sun; from Darwin's huge controversy over our evolution from the apes to Freud's understanding of our unconscious. The modern world can indeed be seen as a long battle between 'science' and 'religion' (see Chapter 23).

Recently, there have been a number of spokespeople emerging to make claims for non-belief, and to criticise religions. They have become 'best-sellers' and have attracted wide attention and a not inconsiderable 'following'. In the USA, Sam Harris has published *The End of Faith* (2006), *Letter to Christian Nation* (2007) and *The Moral Landscape* (2010). In the UK, the leading spokesperson has been the scientist Richard Dawkins with his book *The God Delusion* (2006) (as well as the commentator Christopher Hitchens' *God is not Great* (2007) and the philosopher A. C. Grayling's *Against all Gods* (2007) and *The Good Book* (2011)).

In all these books, God is seen as a superstition that the modern world can no longer afford. For progress, we must look for the evidence. We must follow the scientific road. For Dawkins, the highest impulses – empathy, charity – can be found to emerge in natural selection. We are instinctively drawn to acts of human kindness and generosity from our own interests.

As a social movement, atheism is generally quite small and moves under a plethora of names. American Atheists, for example, have only about 2,500 members and a budget of less than a million dollars. In the UK, the British Humanist Association and the National Secular Society are also quite

small. Alistair McGrath suggests that far from witnessing the growth of atheism, at the start of the twenty-first century we are experiencing its twilight (McGrath, 2004).

To most cultures, 'atheists' are seen as a threat to their established order. But for some, like John Gray, humanism is in fact simply a 'mirror image of monotheism'. Indeed, for Gray it is an episode in the decline of Christianity. Atheism has the same key features as most religions: the dogmatism of faith – though in this case it is the dogmatism of non-faith.

Amongst the core religious controversies of our times which humanists debate with believers are:

- Role of women
- Homosexuality and gay marriage
- Abortion and reproductive rights
- Euthanasia
- The family
- Contraception
- Stem cell research
- Dress codes
- Punishments

And at the broadest level: the conflict over science and religion, modernity and tradition. Atheists tend to take liberal views on most of these matters.

 On YouTube you can find Richard Dawkins and Alistair McGrath in debate with each other.

surprising strength. The UK now has substantial populations of Muslims, Sikhs, Hindus and Jews, which, in contrast to the Christian faiths, have generally grown significantly in recent years. Immigration initially underpinned the numbers of Muslims, Sikhs and Hindus, who have established large communities to be found in London, the Midlands,

West Yorkshire and Strathclyde, were born in the UK. The one religion which seems to be on the increase in the UK is the Muslim faith with 1,600,000 in 2001 growing to 2,422,000 by 2008. Britain also has the second-largest Jewish community in Europe.

Despite these general observations, measuring religious involvement in any country can be quite a

Muslim leaders in front of Britain's oldest mosque, at Earlsfield
Source: Paul Popper Popperfoto/getty Images.

Religion in the twenty-first century

The twentieth century was the age when 'the death of God' was proclaimed. And across parts of the Western world, Christianity was in notable decline. We seemed to be arriving in the Secular Age. But the twenty-first century is beginning to tell a different story. Now, from many angles, there is a resurgence of interest in religion of all kinds. In much of the world, religion is alive and well, even though it is undergoing a number of quite significant changes. In this section we will detect five major trends at work. These are:

1. A limited, partial secularisation that is continuing the twentieth century trend towards a secular age.
2. A resurgence of interest in the mainstream traditional world faiths as they take on new forms and come to attract a wider group of followers.
3. The development of a wide range of new religious movements.
4. The growth of fundamentalisms alongside 'the clash of civilisations', which results in more and more religiously linked conflict, culture wars and even genocide.
5. The development of new institutional (maybe postmodern?) forms of religion, such as cyber-churches and mega-churches.

1 Limited and partial secularisation

The first trend regularly discussed among sociologists is **secularisation**, *the historical decline in the importance of the supernatural and the sacred*. For society as a whole, secularisation points to the waning influence of religion in everyday life: we have just seen this in the description of religion in the UK above. And as religious organisations become more secular, they direct attention less to other-worldly issues (such as life after death) and more to worldly affairs (such as sheltering the homeless, feeding the hungry and raising funds). In addition, secularisation means that functions once performed mostly by the church (such as charity) are now primarily the responsibility of businesses and government. More, it means that people are less likely to view the world in spiritual terms and are more likely to see it in terms of material goods and consumption – a trend detected in Chapter 15.

difficult exercise. Peter Brierley (2000), who has studied this in the UK in some detail, suggests there are three major ways to measure it. First, there is *involvement in religious community*: this would involve anyone associated with religion – through baptism, for example. Second, there is *religious membership* – those who join a religious organisation. Finally, there is *religious attendance* – those who go to religious services. Research suggests that in the twenty-first century, very few attend church, there are declining numbers of members, but a somewhat larger number may well affiliate with religions on particular occasions.

Christianity, then, seems to be on the decline in the UK. Church membership and church attendance have been falling and many are concerned that a whole generation has now been brought up without Christian convictions – a real change over the past 50 years.

Secularisation, with Latin roots meaning 'the present age', is commonly associated with modern, technologically advanced societies (Cox, 1971). Jose Casanova has suggested that the term itself can lead to confusion, as it contains three different strands that need clarifying. The first is 'secularisation as decline of religious beliefs and practices'. This is perhaps the most popular meaning, but it conceals other hidden and deeper meanings. Thus the second is 'secularisation as differentiation of the secular spheres from religious institutions'. It is in Europe that one can find the least differentiation between state and the church. And finally, secularisation may be seen as 'marginalisation of religion to a privatised sphere' (Casanova, 1994: 211). Here, while religion may still be honoured in public, it plays less of a role in the private life of individuals.

Secularisation is often seen as one result of the increasing importance of science in understanding human affairs. Science takes over from religion. In broader terms, people perceive birth, illness and death less as the work of a divine power than as natural stages in the life course. Such events are now more likely to occur in the presence of physicians (scientific specialists) than religious leaders (whose knowledge is based on faith). With the rise of science, religion's sphere of influence has diminished. Theologian Harvey Cox elaborates:

> The world looks less and less to religious rules and rituals for its morality or its meanings. For some, religion provides a hobby, for others a mark of national or ethnic identification, for still others an aesthetic delight. For fewer and fewer does it provide an inclusive and commanding system of personal and cosmic values and explanations.

(Cox, 1971: 3)

If Cox is correct, should we expect that religion will disappear completely some day? Is there a decline in religion? The consensus among sociologists is 'no' (Hammond, 1985; Berger, 1999), for three reasons. If the world is looked at globally, then religion is still an overwhelming and dominant force. It is true that religion holds less sway in Europe (and particularly the Scandinavian countries). It is also true that secular views are common among what may be identified as an international subculture of humanists among academics, whose views do have global significance and influence. But everywhere else, religious fervour seems to be clearly rising. Peter Berger says: 'the world today, with some exceptions, is as furiously religious as it ever was, and in some places more so than ever' (1997: 32).

Even as traditional religious forms flourish and expand, modernity and postmodernity – with their growing disenchantment with the world – create an ongoing requirement for creating meanings that go beyond it. People, it is argued, are desperate for meaning in a meaningless world, and they find it in the new religions (Davie, 1998). Hence we find the development of new religions and a resurgence of interest in older religions – trying to make them sensible for today. We consider this below.

2 Resurgence of interest in the mainstream traditional world faiths

Many now argue that Christianity is in fact growing – and becoming global (Jenkins, 2007). What has often been overlooked by sociologists is the southward expansion of Christianity in Africa, Asia and Latin America. Jenkins believes that by 2050, only one Christian in five will be a non-Latino white person. In Africa, Christians grew from 10 million in 1900 to 360 million in 2000. But what is really striking about this change is the way these expanding Christian countries are much more fundamentalist – traditional, morally conservative and evangelical. They are much more inclined to deal with faith-healing, exorcism and mysticism. They often raise huge funds from the relatively poor. A new 'Christendom' is coming to the poorer world in the twenty-first century that could well have major consequences.

Pentecostalism

Starting in the early twentieth century with William J. Seymour, Pentecostals believe that Jesus will return in their lifetime. God will send a new Pentecost if only people have faith to believe hard enough. Pentecostals differ from evangelicals and others in emphasising the 'Holy Spirit' that can enter ordinary people and give them extraordinary powers. With faith, people could speak in tongues, float in the air, fall in trances: some 80 per cent believe they will be transported to heaven. Today it is estimated that there are at least 500 million 'revivalists' and that this may be one of the world's fastest-growing religions – indeed, they could represent a quarter of the world's Christian population (World Christian Database). They meet in huge arenas and buildings (as large as football stadiums), in shopping malls and 'redemption camps' all over the world. They are most significant in Africa, Latin America and the United States.

Pentecostal meetings are less hierarchical and dogmatic than the formal Christian church. They are more expressive; crowds pursue 'ecstasy' and this taps into emotion. The movement started largely with the poor and black in the USA but has now spread to a worldwide religion. It is populist (anyone can set up a church), innovative and highly emotionally charged. The sociologist Peter Berger says: 'Max Weber is alive and well and living in Guatemala City' (*Economist*, 23 December 2006: 86). Religion here is both premodern and postmodern; it is the 'fiesta', the 'encounter group' and the 'big business'.

3 The emergence of new religious movements (NRMs)

While membership in established, 'mainstream' churches may have plummeted, affiliation with other religious organisations (including Seventh-Day Adventists and Christian sects) has risen just as dramatically. Indeed, secularisation itself may be self-limiting. As church-like organisations become more worldly, some people within a religious 'marketplace' may simply abandon them in favour of more sect-like religious communities that better address their spiritual concerns and whose members seem to exhibit greater religious commitment (Stark and Bainbridge, 1981; Iannaccone, 1994). Thus, in the face of secularisation and the seeming decline in religion, many so-called NRMs have appeared. Indeed, one of the most striking developments of recent years has been the proliferation of NRMs. It is estimated that there may now be as many as 20,000 new religious groupings in Europe alone.

One way of thinking about these movements is to see their affinities with the traditional mainstream religions described above. Thus, some are linked to Hinduism (Hari Krishnas and the disciples of Bhagwan Rajneesh); others to Buddhism (various Zen groups); and others to Christianity (the Children of God). Some NRMs are eclectic (the Unification Church), while others have links with the Human Potential Movement (which advocates therapies to liberate human potential, such as transcendental meditation). Many years ago (in 1976), the late Roy Wallis (1945–90) proposed a typology of these growing groups which is still useful. He suggested three main kinds of NRM: world affirming, world rejecting and world accommodating.

World-affirming groups

The world-affirming groups are usually individualistic and life-positive, and aim to release 'human potentials'. They encourage an active participation in society. Research suggests that these are more common among middle-aged, middle-class groups, who are often disillusioned and disenchanted with material values and in search of new positive meanings. These groups generally lack a church, ritual worship or strong ethical systems. They are often more akin to 'therapy groups' than traditional religions.

A major example of this is the Church of Scientology, founded by L. Ron Hubbard. Hubbard developed the philosophy of 'dianetics', which stresses the importance of 'unblocking the mind' and leading it to becoming 'clear'. Hubbard believed in a rebirthing. His church spread throughout the world (with a base in California) and generated courses (usually expensive) and books galore (see Wallis, 1976).

A second example is transcendental meditation (TM). Brought to the West by the Hindu Mahareshi Mahesh Yogi in the early 1950s, it focuses upon building a personal mantra which is then dwelt upon for periods each day. Again, the focus is upon a good world – not an evil one – and a way of 'finding oneself' through positive thinking. Much of this mode of thinking has helped generate a major new linked movement: that of 'New Age'.

'New Age' is a hybrid mix and match of religions, therapies and astrologies, and has become increasingly important since the 1970s. It is part of what might be seen as the globalisation of modern religion – mixing as it does elements from both Eastern and Western traditions, along with the wider concerns of environment and ecology. Bruce (1996: 197) suggests that these are largely 'audience' or 'client cults'. The former have led to a major market of 'self-help therapy' books with mass distribution; the latter have led to the proliferation of new 'therapists' (from astrological to colour therapists), establishing new relationships between a consumer and a seller. Among the practices involved are tarot readings, crystals, reflexology, channelling and I Ching. Currently, many bookshops devote more shelf space to these sorts of book than to books on Christianity. The fascination with television programmes such as *The X Files* may also be seen as part of this. It brings a new science, a new ecology, a new psychology and a new spirituality. 'New Agers make the monistic assumption that the Self is sacred' (Heelas, 1996: 140).

Bulgarian Hare Krishna parade through the streets of Sofia, August 1996
Source: Reuters/Alexei Dityakin.

World-rejecting groups

The world-rejecting groups are like the sects described above. In some ways they are quite like conventional religions in that they may require prayer and the study of key religious texts, and they have strong ethical codes. They are always highly critical of the outside (material evil) world and they demand change of their members through strong communal activities. They are exclusive, share possessions and seek to submerge identities to the greater whole. They are often millenarian – expecting God's intervention to change the world and inspiring activism to make this come about ('millenarian' is derived from the millennium, the 1,000-year reign of Christ). Researchers have suggested that it may well be people who live on the margins who are most attracted to these groups.

Perhaps the most widely cited example of world-rejecting groups is the Unification Church (popularly known as the Moonies), founded in Korea by the Reverend Sun Myung Moon in 1954. It appeared in California in the early 1960s where it was studied by the sociologist John Lofland in his book *Doomsday Cult* (2nd edn, 1977). Later Eileen Barker (1981, 1984) studied it in England. The Unification Church rejects the mundane secular world as evil and has strict moral rules: monogamous heterosexual sex, no smoking, no drinking, etc.

Another example is the Hare Krishna (Children of God, or ISKON – the International Society for Krishna Consciousness). The members are distinguished by their shaved heads, pigtails and flowing gowns; Hare Krishnas repeat a mantra 16 times a day.

These sects are the movements that have come under most public scrutiny in recent years, largely because of the fear of indoctrination and the problems of severe control and even mass suicide. There is a growing list of extreme examples – the mass suicide by Jim Jones's People Temple in Jonestown, Guyana

(Hall, 1987); the Aum Supreme Truth (run by Shoko Ashara), which detonated poisonous gas canisters in the Tokyo underground in 1995, leaving 12 dead and 5,000 sick; and the more recent suicidal death of the 39 members of Heaven's Gate in California when they sighted the Hale-Bopp comet. Heaven's Gate programmers posted a message on their website saying: 'We are happily prepared to leave this world.' While these new religious forms mirror the means and powers that other religions have continued to employ, they are seen by the press and public as deviant, and hence attract more attention.

World-accommodating groups

World-accommodating religions are more orthodox. They maintain some connections with mainstream religion, but give a high premium to the inner religious life. The Neo-Pentecostals (discussed above) are a good example. The Holy Spirit 'speaks' through them, giving them the gift of 'speaking in tongues'. Such religions are usually dismayed at both the state of the world and the state of organised mainstream religions. They seek to establish older certainties and faith, while giving them a new vitality.

4 Religious fundamentalisms and the 'clash of civilisations'

The most extreme version of contemporary developments is the growth of **fundamentalism** across religions. This can be seen as *a conservative religious doctrine that opposes intellectualism and worldly accommodation in favour of restoring traditional, other-worldly spirituality.* Although it is a bit of a rag-bag word – meaning all things to all people – it generally suggests belief in a timeless and absolute value given to sacred writings in all times and places. It is applied to a wide variety of groups: from the 'Moral Majority' in the United States, to Orthodox Jews in Israel and the Islamic government in Iran. In response to what they see as the growing influence of science and the erosion of the conventional family, religious fundamentalists defend their version of traditional values. From this point of view, the liberal churches are simply too tolerant of religious pluralism and too open to change. The enemy of fundamentalism is the 'Great Satan of Modernity' (Bruce, 2000).

A number of features distinguish religious fundamentalists of various stripes.

1 *They interpret 'infallible' sacred texts literally.* Fundamentalists, who see sacred texts as infallible blueprints for life, insist on literal interpretations of the sacred texts as a means of countering what they see as excessive intellectualism among more liberal and revisionist organisations.

2 *They reject religious pluralism.* Fundamentalists maintain that tolerance and relativism water down personal faith, and they harshly judge most modern faiths as illegitimate.

3 *They find a personal experience of God's presence.* Fundamentalists seek to propagate spiritual revival. They define all areas of life as sacred. For example, fundamentalist Christians seek to be 'born again' to establish a personal relationship with Jesus that will shape a person's everyday life.

4 *They oppose secularisation and modernity.* Fundamentalists believe that modernity undermines religious conviction. Secular humanism leads to profane moral corruption.

5 *They promote conservative beliefs, including patriarchal ones.* Fundamentalists argue that God intends humans to live in heterosexual families ruled by men. They blame feminist and gay rights movements for contributing to moral decline. In particular, fundamentalists condemn abortion and decry lesbian and gay relations.

6 *They emerge in response to social inequality or a perceived social crisis.* Fundamentalists attract members by offering solutions to desperate, worried or dejected people.

Taken together, these traits have given fundamentalism a backward and self-righteous reputation. At the same time, this brief sketch also helps us to understand why adherents find such religions an appealing alternative to the more intellectual, tolerant and worldly 'mainstream' denominations.

Fundamentalist religions in the UK and across Europe have recently gained strength, but we must use the term 'fundamentalist' with care. While conservative branches of many religions have turned fundamentalist, the term is often used pejoratively to dismiss religious movements which question the status quo. In particular, as Chapter 11 noted, there has been the development of 'Islamophobia', whereby the label 'fundamentalist' is often used in the West to dismiss the claims of a range of Islamic movements. Even in cases where Islam has evolved into an extreme form, fundamentalist extremism often emerges in response to the capitalist version of modernity that has favoured the West while leaving extreme poverty elsewhere (Esposito, 1992: 14). As we have seen in Chapter 11, it is likely that issues of fundamentalism will become more and more central in the twenty-first century.

Moreover, we should not see fundamentalism as necessarily new. Indeed, Steven Bruce suggests that:

> There is nothing at all unusual in people taking religion very seriously. What we now regard as religious 'extremism' was commonplace 200 years ago in the Western world and is still commonplace in most parts of the globe. It is not the dogmatic believer who insists that the sacred texts are divinely inspired and true, who tries to model his life on the ethical requirements of those texts, and who seeks to impose these requirements on the entire society who is unusual. The liberal who supposes that his sacred texts are actually human constructions of differing moral worth, whose religion makes little difference to his life, and who is not quite happy to accept that what his God requires of him is not binding on other members of his society: this is the strange and remarkable creature.

(Bruce, 2000: 116–17)

The clash of civilisations

It is precisely this religious conviction that has been behind many historical wars. Yet one of the more dramatic potentials that arise from the spread of fundamentalism may be the increasing risk of major international conflicts based upon religion. Samuel P. Huntington, for instance, sees new fault lines of world conflict arising from religious resurgence across the world in all faiths: 'The unsecularisation of the world is one of the dominant social facts in the late twentieth century' (Huntington, 1996: 96, citing George Wigel). He sees localised 'fault line' wars breaking out all over the world, especially between Muslims and non-Muslims. At the same time, 'core state' conflicts are also appearing between the major states of civilisations. A major issue here may be between the Christian West and the Muslim world. In any event, since the breakdown of the Cold War between East and West, the major issues of conflict have returned to all those religious schisms that dominated much of earlier history too.

5 The arrival of new religious forms and organisations

One dimension of secularisation is the rise of what Robert Bellah (1975) has called **civil religion**, *a quasi-religious loyalty binding individuals in a basically secular society*. In other words, even if some traditional dimensions of religiosity are weakening, new religious qualities may be found in such things as patriotism, membership in associations, good citizenship and even sports meetings which can retain religious qualities. He conducted research in the United States, where, he argues, religious qualities appear in a range of rituals, from rising to sing the US national anthem at sporting events, to presidential inauguration ceremonies, to sitting down to watch televised public parades several times a year. In England, ceremonies linked to the royal family (coronations, royal weddings, etc.), as well as village fêtes, town parades and similar gatherings, all may serve these same functions.

The enormous outpouring of grief around the death of Diana, Princess of Wales could be taken as further evidence of civil religion. Immediately after her death in Paris on 31 August 1997, hundreds of thousands of people publicly showed their grief by sending flowers, attending the funeral and signing 'commemoration books'. These people came from all walks of life and religions, but created a strong sense of group belonging and national – even international – grief.

The electronic, 'cyber' and 'mega-church'

In contrast to the small village congregations of years past, some religious organisations – especially fundamentalists – have become electronic churches dominated by 'prime-time preachers' (Hadden and Swain, 1981). Electronic religion has been especially strong in the United States and has propelled charismatic preachers such as Oral Roberts, Pat Robertson, Robert Schuller and others to greater prominence than all but a few clergy have ever enjoyed in the past. About 5 per cent of the US television audience (around 10 million people) regularly tune into religious television, while perhaps 20 per cent (around 40 million) watch some religious programming every week (Martin, 1981; Gallup, 1982; NORC, 1994).

During the 1980s, regular solicitation of contributions brought a financial windfall to some religious organisations. Seen on 3,200 stations in

Indonesia is the world's most populous Muslim nation but Christians account for about 10 per cent of the 226 million population. This is Katedral Mesias in Jakarta, Indonesia: a Chinese–Indonesian multi-million-dollar megachurch that covers 600,000 square feet of land and has two chapels that hold a maximum occupancy of 6,300 people. Here, Christians listen to a preacher during its opening in 2008

Source: © Enny Huraheni/Reuters/Corbis.

half the countries in the world, for example, Jimmy Swaggart received as much as $180 million annually in donations. But some media-based ministries were corrupted by the power of money. In 1989, Jim Bakker (who began his television career in 1965 hosting a children's puppet show with his wife Tammy Faye) was jailed following a conviction for defrauding contributors. Such cases, although few in number, attracted enormous international attention and undermined public support as people began to wonder whether television preachers were more interested in raising moral standards or private cash.

Along with the electronic church, we can also find the growth of the 'cyber-church' and the 'mega-church'. The former is easy to find on a website, as all major world religions now have a proliferation of websites, but so too do the multitude of smaller new religious movements. The internet is a prime force for information giving, but it is also an arena for membership recruitment.

'Mega-churches' are very large worship centres – often only loosely affiliated with existing denominations, and more likely to be identified with 'born-again' religions or charismatic Christians. In the United States and all over the world, they can be found in shopping malls and parking lots. Characteristically, they are very large: they house as many as 1,000–3,000 worshippers or more. The Yoido Full Gospel Church in Seoul, South Korea, has six daily services in a facility with 13,000 seats! It has some 700,000 members and reaches 30,000 other worshippers via closed-circuit television. There are 11 choirs and a 24-piece orchestra. In the United States, the largest mega-church is the Lakewood Church, Houston, with 25,060 total weekend attenders in 2003. In 1970, there were just ten such churches; by 2003 there were 740. Many of them function like businesses with their own media (contemporary music, television) technologies and massive budgets (upwards of US$12 million).

Taking stock and looking ahead

The pace of social change is accelerating. Two contradictory processes are happening at the start of the twenty-first century. On the one hand, the process of 'secularisation' suggests a growing disenchantment with the spiritual and the supernatural and for some a turn to rationality, and science has gained increasing support with many. Secularisation has spread across much of Europe and other Western cultures, with the partial exception of the United States, but remains relatively weak in the rest of the world, where traditional religions hold stronger sway. On the other hand, the growth of religious fundamentalism, the continuing adherence of billions to the 'mainstream' religions, the continuing clash of civilisations over their passionate commitment to their faiths (as in the war in Afghanistan), and the development of more and more 'new religions' all suggest that multiple religions, with all their potential for conflicts, wars and human suffering, will remain a central element of modern society for many years to come. Religion may have been dying in the twentieth century: it seems very alive and well in the twenty-first.

SUMMARY

1 Religion is a major social institution based on distinguishing the sacred from the profane. Religion is a matter of faith, not scientific evidence, which people express through various rituals. Sociology analyses the social consequences and correlates of religion, but sociology cannot make claims about the ultimate truth or falsity of any religious belief.

2 Emile Durkheim argued that individuals experience the power of their society through religion. Religion promotes social cohesion and conformity by conferring meaning and purpose on life. Max Weber connects religion to meanings and social change: his analysis of Calvinism's contribution to the rise of industrial capitalism demonstrates religion's power to promote social change. Hervieu-Leger has come to see religion as 'chain of memory'. Societies have memories, and as this weakens, so too does religion. Peter Berger suggests that religious beliefs are socially constructed as a means of responding to life's uncertainties and disruptions. Using the social conflict paradigm, Karl Marx charged that religion is the 'opium of the people' and reinforces social inequality.

3 Churches, which are religious organisations well integrated into their society, fall into two categories – ecclesias and denominations. Sects, the result of religious division, are marked by suspicion of the larger society as well as charismatic leadership. Cults are religious organisations that embrace new and unconventional beliefs and practices.

4 Many hunter-gatherer societies are and have been generally animistic, with religious life just one facet of family life; in more complex societies, religion emerges as a distinct social institution. Followers of six world religions – Christianity, Islam, Judaism, Hinduism, Buddhism and Confucianism – represent three-quarters of all humanity. Non-religious groups are about a sixth of the world's population.

5 Five main issues are appearing in contemporary debates over religion: (a) a limited, partial secularisation that is continuing the twentieth-century trend towards a secular age; (b) the resurgence of interest in the mainstream traditional world faiths as they take on new forms and come to attract a wider group of followers; (c) the development of a wide range of new religious movements; (d) the growth of fundamentalisms alongside 'the clash of civilisations', which results in more and more religiously linked conflict, culture wars, and even genocide; and (e) the development of new institutional (maybe postmodern?) forms of religion like cyber-churches and mega-churches.

CONNECT UP: Turn to Part 6 of this book for key resources and link up
with the book's website, which links to these resources
SEE: www.pearsoned.co.uk/plummer

MYTASKLIST

Ten suggestions for going further

1 Connect up with Part Six and the Sociology Web Resources

As you work through ideas and think about the issues raised in this chapter, look at the accompanying website and the resource centre at the end of this book which connects to it. There is a lot here to help you move on. To link up, see: www.pearson.co.uk/plummer.

2 Review the chapter

Briefly summarise (in a paragraph) just what this chapter has been about. Consider: (a) What have you learned? (b) What do you disagree with? Be critical. And (c) How would you develop all this? How could you get more detail on matters that interest you?

3 Pose questions

(a) In the twenty-first century, is religion becoming more important than ever? If so, how and why?
(b) You can use the website to look at all of the world's major religions as outlined in the text. It is important to note that these 'traditional' religions are using the most up-to-date technologies to spread their word. Consider how modernist tools can be used to bring out traditional ideas of the sacred. What problems and contradictions might this raise?
(c) Using the website, track down the sites of some major new religious movements and inspect what they have to say. Consider the sheer variety of sites and why are there so many.
(d) Use the internet to look for evidence which points to a decline in religion in Europe. Discuss the rise of non-belief and atheism in some parts of the world.

4 Explore key words

Many concepts have been introduced in this chapter. You can review them from the website or from the listing at the back of this book. You might like to give special attention to just five words and think them through – how would you define them, what are they dealing with, and do they help you see the social world more clearly or not?

John Bowker, *World Religions* (2006).

John Bowker, *The Concise Oxford Dictionary of World Religions* (2005).

5 Search the Web

Be critical when you look at websites – see the box on p. 940 in the Resources section. Look at the following:

Adherents.com www.adherents.com/largecom
Seems to be getting out of date and has not recently been updated. Still, it details some of the largest religious communities of all kinds to be found in the world.

New Religious Movements database
http://religiousmovements.lib.virginia.edu/home.htm
Details more than 200 sites of new religions.

Cult Information Centre www.cultinformation.org.uk
CIC is an educational charity providing advice and information for victims of cults, their families and friends, researchers and the media.

Religious Tolerance www.religioustolerance.org
A website promoting religious tolerance and providing information on different belief systems and surrounding controversies and debates.

Some specific words to search

All the major religions have their own websites: here are some names to search for:

World Council of Churches
Islam at a glance
Judaism
Hinduism Today
Zen Buddhism
Humanism

6 Review a DVD

- Peter Mullan's *The Magdalene Sisters* (2002): shocking true drama about child abuse in the Catholic Church.
- Antonia Bird's *Priest* (1994): a young gay priest confronts his religion.
- Stanley Kramer's *Inherit the Wind* (1960): classic film based on the Scopes 'monkey' trial – science versus religion. Powerful.
- Xavier Beauvois' *Of Gods and Men* (2010): a film about faith and belief – and the murder of monks in Algeria by fundamentalists.
- There is also an online *Journal of Film and Religion* produced by the University of Nebraska, www.unomaha.edu/~wwwjrf

7 Read and think

General introductions

Phil Zuckerman, *Invitation to the Sociology of Religion* (2003). A very general and readable introduction.

Joanne O'Brien and Martin Palmer (2007) *The Atlas of Religion*. Great maps and summaries of all the world's religions.

Grace Davie, *Religion in Modern Europe: A Memory Mutates* (2000). Discusses the diversity of religion in western Europe and follows the theory that religion is a form of collective memory.

More specific readings

Lester Kurtz, *Gods in the Global Village: The World's Religions in Sociological Perspective* (2nd edn, 2006). Provides a detailed account of all the world's major religions and an analysis of how they are changing under the impact of globalisation and multiculturalism.

Steven Bruce, *Fundamentalism* (2000). Looks at the rise of fundamentalism in the face of modernity, which fundamentalists see as the 'Great Satan'.

Mark Juergensmeyer (2008) *Global Rebellion: Religious Challenges to the Secular State from Christian Militias to Al Quaeda*. Lively account of the twenty-first-century world conflicts over religion.

8 Connect and integrate

Many of the ideas in this chapter can also be developed by looking at other chapters. For example:

- For more on the theories of Marx, Durkheim and Weber, see Chapter 4.
- The controversy over ethnicity and the veil is discussed in Chapter 11 (p. 377).
- New religious movements express some of the themes of new social movements, which are discussed in Chapter 16.

9 Relax with a novel

Look at Salman Rushdie's *Satanic Verses* (1989), which caused such controversy among the worldwide Muslim community that a *fatwa* was issued on the author. New controversies continue to appear. For a recent illustration amongst Christian groups, see the story writing of Philip Pullman, especially *The Good Man Jesus and the Scoundrel Christ* (2010).

10 Engage in
THE BIG DEBATE

Is religion in decline? The death of God or the triumph of religions?

For years now, philosophers like Nietzsche (1844–1900) have proclaimed 'the death of God' and sociologists have talked about the ways in which the modern world is becoming increasingly secularised. After all, as science and rationality become more and more central to the ways in which the modern world works, so the mysteries of the universe, which religion so often had to explain, become demystified. And yet, sociologists increasingly point to the weakness of this secularisation thesis and suggest that, far from becoming less and less religious, the trends actually suggest that we are becoming more and more religious. It is not secularisation that is the issue but desecularisation.

We are talking globally. It is clearly the case that much of northern Europe is becoming less and less religious. But it seems that everywhere else in the world this is not so. Peter Berger suggests that 'on the international religious scene, it is conservative or orthodox or traditionalist movements that are on the rise almost everywhere' (1999: 6). He suggests this is so partly because they are opposed to what they see as developments in the modern world, but also because religion itself is the status quo: it has always been around, and it will continue to be so. What we are witnessing now is an 'Islamic upsurge' alongside a Christian 'Evangelical upsurge'. The Catholic impact can be found from Manila to Krakow, and from Santiago to Seoul (Berger, 1999: 19). With over 1 billion adherents, it is to be found in almost every country, served by some 4,300 bishops and some 404,500 priests. Philip Jenkins looks at the rise of Pentecostalism across the globe – and sees a new Christendom in the making: 'the coming of global Christianity' (2007). At the same time, we see religion fanning wars and civil wars on the Indian subcontinent, in the Balkans, in the Middle East and in Africa. (Look at the map on p. 666). There are disputes in every continent. Everywhere religion is on the rise.

Continue the debate

1 What evidence is there for desecularisation? For secularisation?
2 Do you believe that the modern and postmodern worlds are showing a decline in religion? Why? Why not?
3 Are the new religious revivals a response to the crises of the modern world?
4 Look at the *Living in the twenty-first century* box on p. 678 and consider the debate over atheism.
5 Look at the map on p. 666 and consider just why so many different religions are in conflict with each other. Might this suggest a coming global war of religions?

CHAPTER 20

EDUCATION

COLIN SAMSON IS A SOCIAL RESEARCHER who spent years working with the Innu in Labrador in northern Canada. For most of their history, the Innu were a nomadic people, living by hunting. They were independent and self-reliant and had a strong sense of their purpose in the world. When the Canadian government introduced a policy of assimilation, which extinguished their unique identity and their right to the land, their way of life came under severe threat. Samson documents how the changes left the Innu ashamed and confused, and precipitated high rates of suicide, gas sniffing, widespread alcoholism and child abuse. There was a failure to recognise the distinctiveness of the group and its values and history, and in attempting to assimilate them, a crisis developed.

One part of this crisis was to be found in schooling, which the Canadian authorities insisted upon. In a sense the goal was to take on a new generation of Innu and help in the transformation of their culture into a more western European one. In the West, we tend to see formal schooling as a necessity – for the transmission of culture and knowledge, and indeed the preservation of social solidarity, values and order. Education is also one of the major determinants of a person's life chances. But for the Innu, they found this experience of formal schooling an alienating one. It made them apprehensive and worried. They found that schools did not tell the truth about who the Innu were, and did not speak to their values or way of life. Instead they got linear timetables, school discipline, formal lessons and abstractions, and all were alien to them. The school worked to transform them into Akaneshaut (white children). As some Innu commented:

> It made me 'think English' and gave me 'white thoughts' . . . I lost part of my life.

The only thing that kids are able to learn in school is to be embarrassed by our culture . . .

I am ashamed to say that I went to the school at all . . . I wasted my years in school . . .

Kids now talk back to their parents. That comes from the school. They don't pay attention at all. They don't listen to parents because in school they get a lot of English. They are gradually losing their language. Kids are starting to talk to each other in English.

(Samson, 2003: 199–201)

Far from providing values and maintaining a way of life, the schools were seen to erode Innu values among the young. School is remembered as a kind of culture shock. Whereas their education before came from living with nature, the landscape and animals, and their values from the persistent need to survive, now they found themselves confronted with abstractions and formalities. More used to lived experience in the past, the abstracted education of the West made them less competent in the world. The values they were now taught were often in terms of money and success – not in terms of spirituality, the hunting way of life and animals.

Source: Samson (2003).

I have never let my schooling interfere with my education.

Mark Twain

Give a man a fish and you feed him for a day. Teach a man to fish and you feed him for a lifetime.

Chinese proverb

In this chapter, we ask:

- Is all the world becoming educated?

- What are key approaches to studying education?

- How do social divisions perpetuate themselves through education?

- What are key issues being debated in the sociology of education?

(Left) Peter Wagner, Thomas 'Tim' Dyson, George Salmon, Jack Catlin and George Young, outside Lord's, 1937; Jimmy Sime/Getty

Look at this photo and tell what you see. Most frequently, and for over 70 years, this image has been used in both popular and academic writing to tell the same story of educational inequality and social class division. It has become a popular photo – almost a cliché, used by books and newspapers when they want to make the point about inequalities. Here are the smart boys from Eton and Harrow, and the poor boys mocking them: the 'toffs and toughs' in conflict with each other. But recently, a study has suggested that all may not be as simple as the image suggests. Ian Jack researched the history of the photo and its five boys, and suggested all may well not be what it seems. The Harrow schoolboys did not come from elite backgrounds and fared badly in life (one died at 16); the rough boys were not in fact rough and fared better in life. There is, it seems, much more to this picture than meets the eye.

Source: Jimmy Sine/Stringer/Hulton Archive/Getty Images.

Look online at the account of this photo: see Ian Jack: Five Boys: The Story of a Picture. *Intelligent Life. Spring 2010.*

Downloadable at: http://moreintelligentlife.com/content/ian-jack/5-boys.

Q 'The camera never lies'. Trace the social history of this photo and show how the camera often lies.

All societies pay attention to ways of transmitting their cultures and values, and in the modern world these have increasingly become housed in schools and the broader educational process. This chapter spotlights **education**, *the social institution guiding the critical learning of knowledge, job skills, cultural norms and values.* In industrial societies, as we shall see, much education is a matter of **schooling**, *formal instruction under the direction of specially trained teachers.*

Global education, poverty and literacy

Most people in the Western world spend much of their first 20 years in various kinds of school: nursery, primary, secondary and tertiary. Until recently, formal schooling in all societies was a privilege restricted to a small elite, and so it remains in many poorer societies today.

In hunter-gatherer and small agrarian societies, people's survival depended on learning as much as they could about the plants, animals and landscape in their environment. The Innu were not unusual. Elders devoted much time to passing on both cultural beliefs and knowledge of the natural world to the younger generations. As agrarian societies grew in size and complexity, people needed to learn only specialised knowledge for their field of work, rather than general knowledge. The majority of people in such systems spent most of their time performing physical labour which required little training, while a minority with the greatest wealth and power enjoyed the spare time to study literature, art, history and science. Indeed, the English word 'school' comes from the Greek word for 'leisure'.

We find marked diversity in schooling throughout the world today. In some developing regions, including much of central Asia and central America, religious organisations play a major role in providing education to children. In other regions, particularly eastern Asia,

Open-air classroom in the Primary School, Togo. Togo is a tropical sub-Saharan country with a population of approximately 6.7 million. It ranks at 139 on the Human Development Index (2010) (see Chapter 9)
Source: © Atlantide Phototravel/Corbis.

Europe, the United States, Canada, Australia and New Zealand, the state formally coordinates and regulates the majority of schools. In most high-income societies, a growing number of young people are awarded first degrees: this is much less common in low-income societies, but the numbers are growing rapidly.

All low-income countries have one trait in common: there is limited access to formal schooling. Universal education might seem a relatively straightforward goal, but it has proved as difficult as any to achieve. In the poorest nations, more than 10 per cent of primary-aged children are out of school. At secondary levels, the number attending school is much lower. Table 20.1 provides basic data on school attendance in different regions.

By 2009, low-income countries as a whole had achieved a net enrolment in primary education approaching 90 per cent – higher in east Asia and Latin America, lower in Africa. Likewise, enrolment in secondary education worldwide has expanded tenfold over the past 50 years (from 40 million in 1950 to more than 400 million today), and tertiary education has

Table 20.1	School attendance in low-income societies				
Countries and territories	**School net enrolment rate (%) 2003–8**			**School net attendance rate (%) 2003–8**	
	Male	Female	Male	Female
(a) Primary schools				
AFRICA	79	74	69	66
Sub-Saharan Africa [Sudan, Djibouti]	76	70	65	63
Eastern and Southern Africa	83	82	69	70
West and Central Africa	68	58	63	58
Middle East and North Africa	92	88	85	81
ASIA	92	89	84	81*
South Asia	87	82	83	79
East Asia and Pacific	98	97	88	88*
Latin America and Caribbean	95	95	92	93
CEE/CIS	92	90	94	92
Industrialized countries	94	95	–	–
Developing countries	89	86	80	78*
Least developed countries	81	76	67	65
World	90	87	81	78*
(b) Secondary schools				
AFRICA	34	30	32	29
Sub-Saharan Africa [Sudan, Djibouti]	30	26	27	23
Eastern and Southern Africa	32	29	20	19
West and Central Africa	–	–	33	27
Middle East and North Africa	63	58	53	50
ASIA	–	–	55	49
South Asia	–	–	53	45
East Asia and Pacific	61	64*	61	65
Latin America and Caribbean	69	74	67	73
CEE/CIS	79	75	79	76
Industrialized countries	91	92	–	–
Developing countries	53	52*	51	46
Least developed countries	31	27	28	26
World	61	60*	51	47

* Excludes China.

Source: *The State of the World's Children Special Edition*, UNICEF, Tables 1 and 5.

grown from 6.5 million in 1950 to 88.2 million in 1997. Nevertheless, across the globe it is still the case that some 69 million school age children were not going to school in 2008 (though down from 106 million non-attendees in 1999) (United Nations, Millennium Development Goals Fact Sheet, October 2010).

The illiteracy question

Despite the world growth in education, illiteracy remains a major issue. A person can be said to be literate 'who can, with understanding, both read and write a short simple statement on his or her everyday life' (UNESCO, 2000: 23). The number of literate adults worldwide has been increasing rapidly. The figure doubled from 1.5 billion in 1970 to 3.4 billion in 2000 (see Table 20.2). This still leaves a huge proportion of the world's population as illiterate. Indeed, at the start of the twenty-first century, by 2005–6 there were an estimated 781 million illiterate adults in the world, about 64 per cent of whom are women. As a consequence, illiteracy disadvantages many.

Table 20.2	Literacy rates[1] across the world, 2000	
	Male	Female
Sub-Saharan Africa	69	53
Middle East and North Africa	74	52
South Asia	66	42
East Asia and Pacific	93	81
Latin America	90	88
CEE/CIS[2] and Baltic States	99	96
World	84	74

[1] Defined as percentage of persons aged 15 and over who can read and write.
[2] Central Eastern Europe/Commonwealth of Independent States.

Source: UNICEF (2004b: 121).

TOP 10
Lowest literacy rates

	Adult literacy (%)
1 Mali	26.2
2 Burkina Faso	28.7
2 Niger	28.7
4 Chad	32.7
5 Ethiopia	35.9
6 Guinea	38.0
7 Sierra Leone	39.8
8 Benin	40.8
9 Senegal	41.9
10 The Gambia	45.3

Note: India is ranked 25th with literacy amongst adults of 62.8% and Nigeria is ranked 23rd with a literacy rate of 60.1%.
Source: *Pocket World in Figures* (2011) Profile Books Ltd.

Even among some high-income countries, illiteracy remains a problem. While the United States opened educational opportunities to all citizens long before most other industrialised countries, some 25 million adults read and write at no more than a fourth-grade level and another 25 million have only eighth-grade language skills. This means that one in four adults in the United States is functionally illiterate, and the proportion is higher among the elderly and minorities. The problem of illiteracy in the United States is most serious among Latinos. In part this is due to a drop-out rate among 14- to 24-year-olds of almost 30 per cent, which is three times the rate among whites or African-Americans. The broader issue is that schools fail to teach many Spanish-speaking people to read and write *any* language very well (Kozol, 1980, 1985a, 1985b).

The new illiteracy

Even this conceals the real nature of what has been called the 'new illiteracy'. As societies develop and expand their information technologies, so illiteracy will increasingly come to mean the inability to use computers, word processing, email and websites. Although these skills are expanding rapidly across the world, they are still highly selective. There has however been significant growth in low-income societies in recent years, see Table 20.3 which shows the results. In 2004, while there were 750 computers per thousand people in the USA, there were fewer than five per thousand in Cambodia, Uganda, Laos, Niger, Liberia and the Congo (*New Internationalist*, 2007: 60, 6–7). Table 20.3 shows the results of a survey of computer use in primary schools in 11 countries and see Chapter 1, p. 23.

Resolving illiteracy

Observers such as Ivan Illich (1973) argue that the answer to widespread illiteracy is not to transpose Western-style schools into the rest of the world.

Table 20.3	Pupils in schools with computers: a global view 2005–6													
	Computer for administrative use		Computer-based management system		Website of the school on the Internet		Intranet site within the school		Computers for pupils to use without access to the Internet		Computers for pupils to use with access to the Internet		Pupils without computers	
	%	SE	%	SE	%	SE	%	SE	%	SE	%	SE	%	SE
Argentina	75.3	1.61	35.5	1.60	18.0	1.40	7.7	0.91	44.0	1.75	22.9	1.34	48.0	1.73
Brazil	70.4	1.91	50.0	2.46	10.7	1.66	20.1	2.22	23.4	2.09	22.8	2.13	63.5	2.29
Chile	93.4	1.07	67.7	2.08	48.6	2.42	47.3	2.58	46.4	2.38	90.2	1.49	2.7	0.82
India	12.8	1.80	9.8	1.62	2.9	1.05	5.7	1.55	9.9	1.54	8.8	1.61	85.3	1.69
Malaysia	95.2	1.10	62.2	2.49	33.9	2.73	18.9	2.20	61.8	2.55	59.4	2.62	21.1	2.25
Paraguay	29.0	1.71	12.6	1.36	5.0	0.81	3.2	0.64	10.4	1.14	6.5	0.92	86.2	1.27
Peru	52.7	2.00	28.2	1.92	12.1	1.78	7.8	1.23	33.5	2.04	22.1	1.86	54.5	1.95
Philippines	47.8	2.44	16.9	1.83	5.6	0.93	4.7	0.73	22.9	2.16	5.8	0.69	76.0	2.18
Sri Lanka	21.3	2.40	5.7	1.20	2.0	0.85	8.5	1.61	18.9	2.23	3.1	0.99	79.5	2.26
Tunisia	21.9	1.97	33.5	2.07	14.3	1.48	13.3	1.41	31.3	2.15	23.1	1.96	56.8	2.30
Uruguay	93.4	1.00	62.4	2.01	19.9	1.62	7.9	1.09	43.1	2.16	36.8	1.88	38.5	1.96

Source: *A View Inside Primary Schools* (UNESCO Institute for Statistics, 2008).

THINKERS & THEORY

Paulo Freire: empowering the poor

The Brazilian educator Paulo Freire (1921–97) used literacy programmes for the poor to enable them to take control of their own lives. He argued that formal education often enabled elites to impose their values on 'developing' peoples. In 1963 he pioneered a literacy project across Brazil for 5 million people, and was supported by a left-wing government. Later, however, he fell out of favour when a new right-wing government came to power. Freire was jailed, before going into exile in Bolivia and Chile. His key book was *Pedagogy of the Oppressed* (1972), and his key idea was conscientisation, where *education becomes a tool to transform the social order*. Ultimately, education struggles for liberation from all kinds of oppression. His work also became part of liberation theology in Latin America. Many of his ideas are used across the world to bring about social change.

Instead of formal degrees on paper, they suggest, people in developing areas need the practical knowledge and skills to provide for their basic life needs in a changing natural environment and to build small businesses that can generate wealth in ways sensitive to local cultural norms. In high-income societies, schooling for everyone serves as the means of training people to participate in democratic political life and apply the economic knowledge and technological skills that are increasingly important in the modern world. At the same time, however, schooling can also serve as a major mechanism for reproducing social inequalities.

Schooling around the world

In this section, we make a quick tour of some school systems to provide a sense of their variety.

Schooling in India

India has become a middle-income country, but there are large numbers of families who live in poverty and may depend upon the earnings of children. Many children work up to 60 hours a week and this greatly reduces the time and opportunity for schooling.

Still, about 90 per cent of children in India complete primary schools – typically in crowded schoolrooms where one teacher attends to upwards of 60 children. Children in the poorest families often begin full-time work at an early age to help supplement the family income. Fewer than half of Indian children go on to secondary education.

Pronounced patriarchy also shapes Indian education; 59 per cent of boys but only 49 per cent of girls attend secondary school. While just over one-third of the Indian population is illiterate, two-thirds of women lack basic literary skills. A large majority of the children working in Indian factories are girls. There are economic costs to raising a girl. Parents must provide a dowry, and after the marriage, a daughter's work benefits her husband's family (UNESCO, 2009).

Schooling in Japan

Before 1872, only a privileged few enrolled in school. But today, Japan is widely praised for producing some of the world's highest achievers. Early grades concentrate on transmitting Japanese traditions, especially a sense of obligation to family. By their early teens, students encounter Japan's system of rigorous and competitive examinations.

The Japanese government invests heavily in the education of students who perform well in these exams, while students performing poorly are pushed out of the system. Understandably, then, around half of Japanese students attend 'cram schools' to supplement their standard education and prepare for the exams. Japanese women, most of whom are not in the labour force, often devote themselves to their children's success in school.

Schooling in Europe

While all countries in the European Union agree that schooling is highly important, each takes a different approach to education. Luxembourg requires children to attend pre-school. In the Netherlands, primary school begins at four. While the UK introduced compulsory education in 1870, Italy and Greece did not follow suit until the 1950s, and Spain waited until the 1960s. Portugal introduced 6 years of compulsory elementary schooling in 1968, but did not fully implement this requirement until 1986. EU countries also require different minimum periods of study. Portugal, Spain and Italy require only 8 years of schooling; Ireland, Greece, Luxembourg and Denmark require 9 years; France, the Netherlands and Germany, 10 years; the United Kingdom, 11 years; and Belgium, 12 years.

Many European countries have a multi-track secondary education system which channels some students towards university and others towards various levels of vocational training. In Germany, for example, students undertake general secondary education for two years from age 12, then split into the grammar (*Gymnasium*), basic vocational (*Hauptschule*) and higher vocational (*Realschule*) groups. Some countries encourage greater educational specialisation from the secondary level onwards than others. Secondary students in Italy and Germany have more subjects to study at the post-16 level than students in the UK. As with the previous examples, European educational structures also help maintain the social power structures, as we shall now see by looking more closely at the UK.

Schooling in the UK

During the Middle Ages, schooling was a privilege of the British nobility, who studied classical subjects since they had little need for the practical skills related to earning a living. As the Industrial Revolution created a need for an educated labour force, a rising share of the population entered the classroom. In 1891, the Education Act made elementary education free to all citizens. Three major Acts shaped British education during the twentieth century. These were:

1 *The Balfour Act (1902)*, which established Local Education Authorities (LEAs), and gave these bodies powers over secondary and higher education.

2 *The Butler Act (1944)*, which established a Ministry of Education and set up the tripartite system of three different kinds of school – grammar, technical and secondary modern – to cater to the supposed differing intellectual abilities of students. The Act made education from 5 to 15 free for all people, improved equality of opportunity in education, and offered support services to students from poor families, including free milk, dental check-ups and healthcare.

3 *The Baker Act (1988)*. Following the recommendations of the previous year's Black Report, the British government enacted a series of sweeping and controversial changes in the Education Act of 1988. These included:

Table 20.4	Types of school in the U.K. 1970/1–2008/9				
	Numbers of students (thousands)				
	1970/1	1980/1	1990/1	2000/1	2008/9
Public sector schools[1]					
Nursery[2]	50	89	105	152	150
Primary	5,902	5,171	4,955	5,298	4,869
State-funded secondary[3] of which, admissions policy					
Comprehensive	1,313	3,730	2,925	3,340	3,243
Grammar	673	149	156	205	221
Modern	1,164	233	94	112	142
City technology colleges	–	–	8	17	3
Academies	–	–	–	–	122
Not applicable	403	434	298	260	197
All public sector schools	9,507	9,806	8,541	9,384	8,948
Non-maintained schools	621	619	606	609	621
All special schools	103	148	114	113	107
Pupil referral units	–	–	–	10	16
All schools	10,230	10,572	9,260	10,116	9,691

[1] Excludes maintained special schools and pupil referral units.
[2] Figures for Scotland before 1998/9 only include data for local authority pre-schools, data thereafter include partnership pre-schools. From 2005/6, figures refer to centres providing pre-school education at a local authority centre, or in partnership with the local authority only. Children are counted once for each centre they are registered with.
[3] Excludes sixth-form colleges from 1980/1 onwards.

Source: Adapted from *Social Trends*, 40, 2010, Table 3.3, p. 29.

- the introduction of the National Curriculum, with achievement targets for students at the ages of 7, 11, 14 and 16
- the right for schools to 'opt out' of the Local Education Authority system if a majority of parents voting in a secret ballot wanted to do so
- devolution of the financial management of schools from LEAs to boards of governors
- the introduction of city technology colleges (15 in 1994).

The arrival of the Labour Government of 1997, with its high priority of 'education, education, education', heralded the passing of an Education Act more or less every year. Between the 1950s and 1970s, the major divide in British education was between the grammar schools and secondary schools, with the former being both more middle class and more successful. The Labour Party of the 1960s had gradually worked to abolish grammar schools and introduce a 'comprehensive' system – ostensibly providing equality of education for all. In practice, some grammar schools remained and comprehensive schools became stratified into

'good' and 'bad'. But when the Labour government of 1997–2010 came to power in 1997, it pledged that education would be a priority. It introduced a wide range of new policies and legislation which included:

- A continuing expansion of education at all levels. In 1970/1 there were 723 state nursery schools in the UK compared with 3,209 in 2008/9. In 2007/8, there were almost 2.5 million students in higher education, nearly four times the total of 621,000 in 1970/1 (*Social Trends*, 2010).
- The development of specialist schools and city academies. These were allowed to specialise but aimed to replace 'failing schools' in disadvantaged areas. The academies programme was introduced in 2000 to promote publicly funded independent schools managed by sponsors from a range of backgrounds, including universities, businesses, faith communities and voluntary groups. These new 'city academies' were allowed to build up their own admission arrangements. There were suspicions that selection might reappear through the back door.

- Education action zones whereby additional funding was given disadvantaged areas to set up breakfast clubs, homework clubs, summer literacy and numeracy schemes.
- A major programme of school regulations through a regulatory body (Ofsted), which aimed to enhance standards by creating a programme of target and monitoring of schools alongside competitive league tables – all of which was widely disliked by teachers.

At the end of the period of Labour government, traditional social distinctions persisted in British education. Many wealthy families still sent their children to independendent *public schools*. Such elite schools not only teach academic subjects, they also convey to children from wealthy families the distinctive patterns of speech, mannerisms and social graces of the British upper class. These schools are far too expensive for most students. Indeed, many prominent members of the Labour government in 1997 sent their own children to grant-maintained schools rather than comprehensives, recognising the continuing difference in standards of education at each level. Moreover, graduates from Oxford and Cambridge, or 'Oxbridge', often enter the core of the British power elite. Research conducted in 2008 showed that although only 7 per cent of the population attended independent schools, well over half of many professions have done so. For example, 75 per cent of judges, 70 per cent of finance directors, 45 per cent of top civil servants and 32 per cent of MPs were independently schooled (Cabinet Office, 2009), as Figure 20.1 shows. More than two-thirds of the top members of the civil service and successive British governments have 'Oxbridge' degrees.

It seems that the new coalition government, which came to power in 2010, is making reforms that may well extend these inequalities; but it is too soon to be clear.

Understanding education in the modern world

The previous brief comparisons illustrate that education is shaped by other institutions and social forces. Education transmits cultural values and can also contribute to social divisions. In this section we will look briefly at some major approaches to education.

The functions of education

As we saw in Chapter 2, functionalism highlights the way the institutions of a society are interdependent and interconnect with others. It asks questions about the ways in which institutions work and function in a society – usually to maintain some sense of order (though it can also ask questions about its disruptions and breakdowns – the dysfunctions). Functionalist theories of education can be traced to Emile Durkheim. While Durkheim recognised the wide variety of education practices in all societies across the world, he believed that it usually served a major role of creating a moral bond. Education helped sustain social cohesion.

Contemporary functionalists focus on a number of key functions of schools. The most apparent functions of schools are:

- *Intellectual*: they provide basic thinking skills for analysis and evaluation.
- *Political*: they inculcate people into the norms of their society and train them to be good citizens.
- *Social*: they socialise students into the culture and values of their society.
- *Economic*: they prepare students for later occupational roles and train them for the division of labour.

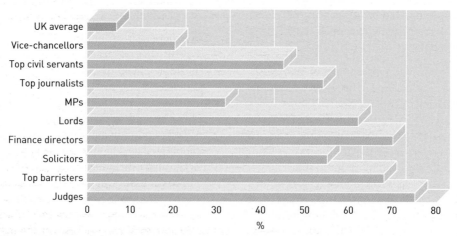

Figure 20.1 Proportion of professionals independently schooled: by profession

Source: Milsom Report, 2009, The Panel on Fair Access to the Professions, Fig. 1f, p. 18.

But functionalists often take it further than this. They suggest that modern schools are also the means by which modern democratic societies are shaped and maintained by creating conditions for students to achieve academic success. They are institutions which create opportunities for development and success and can help to lead to a more democratic and meritocratic society. Meritocracy implies that success is linked to achievements rather than accidents of birth. (The term 'meritocracy' was first used in Michael Young's 1958 satirical book *Rise of the Meritocracy*. The term was intended to be pejorative.)

The ethnographic tradition: studying classrooms and cultures

One approach to studying education is to examine first hand what is going on every day, face to face in schools, and this is where fieldwork comes into its own. Researchers, often applying symbolic interactionism (see Chapters 2 and 7) and the method of participant observation (Chapter 3), have documented the *perspectives* of teachers and students, the *labelling* mechanisms within a classroom, the general *processes* through which classes are constructed and negotiated, the different student *roles* and *cultures* which emerge within these classrooms, and the impact of *social divisions* (gender, class, disability and race) on these interactions. There have been many such studies. Good early examples of this are described in the box.

Within school cultures, an 'invisible pedagogy' (Bernstein, 1977), or hidden ranking system, emerges to shape academic performance and the long-term life chances of students. Early studies of classroom interaction in the UK suggest that, while teachers may strive to be impartial, they are culturally conditioned to assess their students' ability by ranking them on a scale

Studying schools

One focus in the sociology of education has been on the ethnography of schools and classrooms. Often a sociologist enters a school and becomes an observer of school life for a year or so, documenting teaching, the relations between children and teachers, the emergence of different school cultures and their links to the wider school, community and society. Colin Lacey's *Hightown Grammar* (1970), David Hargreaves' *Social Relations in a Secondary School* (1967), Paul Willis's *Learning to Labour* (1976) and Stephen Ball's *Beachside* (1981) were pioneers of this tradition. Stephen Ball was a participant observer of Beachside Comprehensive for three years. A typical approach was that of Colin Lacey (1970), who immersed himself in a school for 18 months, spending a year observing, doing some teaching himself, engaging staff and pupils in informal conversations, sending out questionnaires to students, and backing all this with material from school records.

Many of these studies point in the same directions. Subcultures emerge in schools for different groups. Kids might conform, rebel, withdraw or develop their own pathways (turning to sports, for example). Most common was the development of a subculture of academic achievement and a subculture of low achievers, often demoralised and bored with school. School structures emphasised competition to the detriment of low achievers (and typically low achievers can be linked to inequalities). There is often a labelling process or self-fulfilling prophecy at work – David Hargreaves and Stephen Ball notably showed how children quickly got classified into types, which are frequently based more on behaviour than ability. Children were often selected from lower streams and indentified as 'louts' and 'trouble makers'. This negative labelling led some kids to resist and fight back. Being 'bad' often gave them an inverse kind of status. Often, as Paul Willis showed, the disaffected youth of schools simply take this culture with them into the workplace (or more commonly the street culture of no work).

As this kind of study developed, other issues became important. Early work was also carried out on girl cultures (Stanworth, 1983), ethnicity (Sewell, 1996) and sexuality (Mac an Ghail, 1994). Oddly, in recent times, much less research has been conducted which uses this kind of method in the study of schools.

Classic UK school studies

David Hargreaves, *Social Relations in a Secondary School* (1967)

Colin Lacey, *Hightown Grammar* (1970)

Peter Woods, *The Divided School* (1979)

Stephen Ball, *Beachside* (1981)

Michelle Stanworth, *Gender and Schooling* (1983)

Máirtín mac an Ghail, *Making of Men: Masculinities, Sexualities and Schooling* (1994)

Tony Sewell, *Black Masculinities and Schooling* (1996)

of other characteristics, such as appearance, personality, enthusiasm and conformity, which bear little relation to actual ability (Hargreaves, 1975). In those days, teachers often favoured boys over girls (Stanworth, 1983) and white boys over Afro-Caribbean boys, by tacitly giving them much more attention and opportunities to speak. Likewise, Asian girls were also more likely to be stereotyped as 'passive' (Brah and Minhas, 1988). Here we also see the significance of labelling pupils in certain ways (as 'slow learners' or 'trouble'): this can bring about **self-fulfilling prophecies**, *a prediction that causes itself to become true*, when, for example children defined as low achievers at school actually become low achievers. It is a matter of expectations.

The social background of the students also plays a role in how they experience education. In a major classic study, Paul Willis (1977) looked at a small group of working-class boys and studied their transition from school to work. He found that they generated an anti-school culture heavily focused upon their masculinity. They had little time for the middle-class school values or for posh qualifications, seeing them as boring, effeminate and a waste of time. They castigated other boys who followed the rules as 'ear 'oles' and saw them as sissies. Similar studies found such boys associating good grades with femininity and, to keep face in the eyes of their mates, boys might hand in work that was poor and disorganised. For these 'lads', 'having a laff' was especially important, and it is a value they then took to their workplace. For instance, in class there might be 'a continuous scraping of chairs, a bad tempered "tut-tutting" at the simplest request, and a continuous fidgeting which explores every permutation of sitting or lying on a chair'. They then carried this 'anti-authority', 'anti-achievement' culture to their place of work.

There is much evidence that this pattern continues today. It can be charted from different studies over time. For instance, in the 1990s Mairtin Mac an Ghaill (1994) looked at the construction of gender in classrooms, focusing on a hierarchy of dominant and subordinate masculinities. He observed four major types (there was also a small sub-group of gay male students):

- The '*Macho Lads*' – white, working-class boys who are defiant of the school and disdainful of student achievers (similar to Willis above).

- The '*Academic Achievers*' – boys whose male identities are built out of seeing themselves as future professionals: they take their work and

school seriously, even though they are seen as effeminate 'dickheads' by the Macho Lads.

- The '*New Enterprisers*' – these are less keen on conventional A-levels, but do find a space for work in skills that interest them, such as computer sciences.

- The '*Real Englishmen*' – these see themselves as superior to the teachers, and think they are capable of effortless academic achievement.

Critical comment

Focusing on classroom interactions is valuable, but it does tend to under-emphasise the relations between the activities within schools and the wider working of society as a whole, as we shall see by looking at a different, more macro approach.

The critical and conflict traditions: education and social divisions

Another major approach to studying education is through social divisions and social conflict. Education – at all levels – becomes a means for the reproduction of society's inequalities: it can act as a means of social control, reinforcing acceptance of the status quo. In various, sometimes subtle ways, schools operate to reproduce the status hierarchy.

Thus a number of sociologists have suggested that the origins of the UK system in the nineteenth century lay in class issues and control. The public schools came very early for the elite; then in the nineteenth century came the rather limited Sunday schools to provide a basic education for the working classes – often moral education. There was a continuous fear of an insurgent working class rising up once it had too much education.

Samuel Bowles and Herbert Gintis (1976) point out that the clamour for public education in the late nineteenth century arose precisely when capitalists were seeking a literate, docile and disciplined workforce. In many countries with immigrants, but notably the United States, mandatory education laws ensured that schools would teach immigrants the dominant national language as well as cultural values supportive of capitalism. Compliance, punctuality and discipline were – and still are – part of what conflict theorists call the **hidden curriculum**, the *subtle*

SPEAKING LIVES

A self-fulfilling prophecy: from the autobiography of Malcolm X

Malcolm, a black American, went to school in Lansing, Michigan, in the 1940s. He became leader of the Black Muslims and a spokesperson for many black Americans in the 1960s, and was assassinated in 1965. This is an extract from his autobiography, in which he illustrates the self-fulfilling prophecy at work in his school: think of the power of telling someone 'you're good with your hands'. (See also the film of his life by Spike Lee – *Malcolm X* (1992) with Denzil Washington in the lead role.)

One day something happened which was to become the first major turning point of my life. Somehow, I happened to be alone in the classroom with Mr Ostrowski, my English teacher. He was a tall, rather reddish white man and he had a thick mustachio. I had gotten some of my best marks under him, and he had always made me feel that he liked me.

I know that he probably meant well in what he happened to advise me that day. I doubt that he meant

any harm. It was just in his nature as an American white man. I was one of his top students, one of the school's top students – but all he could see for me was the kind of future 'in your place' that almost all white people see for black people.

He told me, 'Malcolm, you ought to be thinking about a career. Have you been giving it thought?' The truth is, I hadn't. I never have figured out why I told him, 'Well, yes sir, I've been thinking I'd like to be a lawyer.' Lansing certainly had no black lawyers – or doctors either – in those days, to hold up an image I might have aspired to. All I really knew for certain was that a lawyer didn't wash dishes, as I was doing.

Mr Ostrowski looked surprised, I remember, and leaned back in his chair and clasped his hands behind his head. He kind of half smiled and said, 'Malcolm, one of life's first needs is for us to be realistic. Don't misunderstand me, now. We all of us like you, you know that. But you've got to be realistic about being a nigger. You need to think about something you can be. You're good with your hands – making things. Everybody admires your carpentry shop work. Why don't you plan on carpentry? People like you as

Malcolm X (1925–65)
Source: © Bettmann/Corbis.

a person – you'd get all kinds of work.'

The more I thought afterwards about what he said, the more uneasy it made me. It just kept treading around in my mind.

What made it really begin to disturb me was Mr Ostrowski's advice to others in my class – all of them white. They reported that Mr Ostrowski had encouraged what they had wanted. Yet nearly none of them had earned marks equal to mine.

It was then that I began to change – inside.

I drew away from white people, I came to class, and I answered when called upon. It became a physical strain simply to sit in Mr Ostrowski's class.

Source: Adapted from Malcolm X, *The Autobiography of Malcolm X* (1966: 35–7).

presentation of political or cultural ideas in the classroom. It teaches young people 'to know their place and sit still in it' and 'reproduces inequality by justifying privilege and attributing poverty to personal failure' (Bowles and Gintis, 1976: 114). In the next section, we will look at just how some of these social divisions work in more detail.

Class divisions

Schools routinely tailor education according to students' social background, thereby perpetuating social inequality. Indeed, out of all major Western cultures, it has been argued that 'only the Netherlands and Sweden show persistent trends of equalising access

PUBLIC SOCIOLOGY

The Bell Curve debate: are the elite more intelligent?

It is rare that the publication of a new book in the social sciences captures the attention of the public at large. But *The Bell Curve: Intelligence and Class Structure in American Life* (1994) by Richard J. Herrnstein and Charles Murray did that and more, igniting a firestorm of public controversy over why pronounced social stratification divides US society and, just as important, what to do about it. In the first several months of its release, 400,000 copies of the book were sold around the world. Several thousand reviews and commentaries have been written in the short time since the book's publication. Although the book speaks specifically about the USA, its general argument has been made for many countries.

The Bell Curve is a long (800-page) book that addresses many critical issues and resists simple summary. But its basic thesis is captured in the following propositions:

1 Something we can describe as 'general intelligence' exists; people with more of it tend to be more successful in their careers than those with less.
2 At least half the variation in human intelligence (Herrnstein and Murray use figures of 60 to 70 per cent) is transmitted genetically from one generation to another; the remaining variability is due to environmental factors.
3 Over the course of the twentieth century – and especially since the

'information revolution' – intelligence has become more necessary to the performance of industrial societies' top occupational positions.
4 Simultaneously, the best US universities have shifted their admissions policies away from favouring children of inherited wealth to admitting young people who perform best on standardised tests.
5 As a result of these changes in the workplace and higher education, US society is now coming to be dominated by a 'cognitive elite', who are, on average, not only better trained than most people but actually more intelligent.
6 Because more intelligent people are socially segregated on the university campus and in the workplace, it is no surprise that they tend to pair up, marry and have intelligent children, perpetuating the 'cognitive elite'.
7 Near the bottom of the social ladder, a similar process is at work. Increasingly, poor people are individuals with lower intelligence, who live segregated from others, and who tend to pass along their modest abilities to their children.

Resting on the validity of the seven assertions presented above, Herrnstein and Murray then offer, as an eighth point, a basic approach to public policy:

8 To the extent that membership in the affluent elite or the impoverished underclass is rooted in intelligence and determined mostly by genetic inheritance, programmes to assist underprivileged people will have few practical benefits.

The book has prompted considerable controversy. Critics

first questioned exactly what is meant by 'intelligence', arguing that anyone's innate abilities can hardly be separated from the effects of socialisation. Of course, rich children perform better on intelligence tests, they explained: these people have had all the advantages! Some critics dismiss the concept of 'intelligence' outright as phony science. Others take a more moderate view, claiming that we should not think of 'intelligence' as the sole cause of achievement, since recent research indicates that mental abilities and life experiences are interactive, each affecting the other.

In addition, while most researchers who study intelligence agree that genetics does play a part in transmitting intelligence, the consensus is that no more than 25–40 per cent is inherited – only about half what Herrnstein and Murray claim. Therefore, critics conclude, *The Bell Curve* misleads readers into thinking that social elitism is both natural and inevitable. In its assumptions and conclusions, moreover, *The Bell Curve* amounts to little more than a rehash of the social Darwinism popular a century ago, which heralded the success of industrial tycoons as merely 'the survival of the fittest'.

Perhaps, as one commentator noted, the more society seems like a jungle, the more people think of stratification as a matter of blood rather than upbringing. But, despite its flaws and exaggerations, the book's success suggests that *The Bell Curve* raises many issues we cannot easily ignore. Can a democratic system tolerate the 'dangerous knowledge' that elites (including not only rich people but also political leaders) may be just a little more intelligent than the

PUBLIC SOCIOLOGY

rest of us? What of *The Bell Curve*'s description that elites are increasingly insulating themselves from social problems such as crime, homelessness and poor schools? As such problems have become worse in recent years, how do we counter the easy explanation that poor people are hobbled by their own limited ability? And, most basically, what should be done to ensure that all people have the opportunity to develop their abilities as fully as possible?

Continue the debate

1 Do you agree that 'general intelligence' exists? Why or why not?
2 In general, do you think that people of higher social position are more intelligent than those of low social position? If you think intelligence differs by social standing, which factor is cause and which is effect?
3 Do you think sociologists should study controversial issues such as differences in human intelligence? Why or why not? Is *The Bell Curve* ideology or science – and what is the difference?

A useful summary and review of critiques can be found at: *Human Intelligence and the Bell Curve* at www. indiana.edu/~intell/bellcurve.shtml.

to education in the course of the twentieth century' (Therborn, 1995: 257). By contrast, education in countries such as the UK has reflected stratification in quality of provision both for individuals and for people of different social classes (Mackinnon et al., 1996: 173).

Table 20.5 shows the differential achievements of children at school from different class backgrounds. *There is no doubt that children from working-class homes consistently under-achieve at every level of the educational system when compared to middle-class and upper-class children.* Why should this be?

Some, like Charles Murray – discussed in the *Public sociology* box – have contended that genetic intellectual potential determines performance in school (Herrnstein and Murray, 1994). Indeed, the tripartite system in Britain gave prominence to the results of

IQ tests given to children at age 11 in helping divide students into their supposedly appropriate schools. The implication of this explanation, however, is that lower-class people generally have lower genetic intellectual abilities. Thus lower-class people could be said to deserve their status because they lack the intellectual ability to compete with people from higher classes.

Many others reject this explanation, however, pointing out that governments have tended not to invest as heavily in the schools attended by the poorest children, and that the less well off also tend to experience greater health problems, which in turn affect their performance at school. Moreover, poorer families cannot afford to send their children to nursery pre-school training and later to cram schools, to hire private tutors, or to purchase items such as books or

Table 20.5	Attainment of level 2 qualifications[1] at age 16 and 17: by socioeconomic classification of parent,[2] 2008			
England	Percentages			
	Age 16	Age 17	Proportion without Level 2 at 16 but gaining by 17	Proportion without Level 2 at 17
Higher professional	81	88	33	12
Lower professional	75	82	28	18
Intermediate	61	71	26	29
Lower supervisory	47	58	20	42
Routine	43	54	20	46
Other/not classified	37	49	19	51

[1] Attainment of five or more GCSE grades A* to C, National Vocational Qualification level 2, Vocationally Related Qualification level 2, Intermediate General National Vocational Qualification. See Appendix, Part 3: Qualifications.
[2] National Statistics Socio-economic Classification (NS-SEC) of parent.

Source: Social Trends, 40 (2010) Table 3.16, p. 38.

personal computers, which give children from more affluent backgrounds an advantage. Additionally, as the Willis (1977) study discovered, poorer children often grow up in environments where people see little hope of upward social mobility and rebel against the system rather than try to conform with it. In such an environment, adults often discourage rather than encourage success at school. To make matters worse, people in different communities within a country often develop distinct dialects and colloquial vocabularies (Bernstein, 1977). While groups across the class divides do this, the dialects and words associated with richer and middle-class communities gain status, while those associated with lower-class communities get judged as 'uneducated'. In consequence, poor children are more likely to be more regularly criticised in school for 'weak' language skills and thus to develop lower educational confidence. These many factors, which have no relation to biological potential, have contributed to the educational class divide in countries such as the UK (see Halsey et al., 1961; Jackson and Marsden, 1963; Douglas, 1964).

Education as a key reproducer of inequalities

At every level of education the evidence has suggested for a long time that working-class children tend not to do so well in schools as middle-class children. There are many reasons for this and we have already encountered a number of them in earlier chapters – especially in our discussion of education and the reproduction of class (see Chapters 8 and 10). Western educational systems tend to be white, middle-class cultures. In this they support the class and racial systems giving credence to the middle class and often alienating the working class.

In summary, five crucial factors converge in structuring and reproducing social class in education. Early research work has pointed to these processes and later work simply reinforced it.

1 The class base of the home

The family is the crucible of education and what goes on there shapes all the child's experiences. At base, working-class homes have less money, low-paid work and unemployment, and much less capital or wealth (see Chapter 10). Early research focusing on working-class families showed how often working-class homes had a lack of books and what is now called 'cultural

capital'. More recent work has shown how middle-class families – usually with more money – have a different language, a different set of values, a different knowledge base, a different set of interests. Stephen Ball has shown how:

> the middle-class family is engaged with its children's education as a family project, and the vast majority of the work is done by mothers. Middle-class parents do not want the child to be 'dragged down' or distracted. These parents fear that, in the 'wrong' context, the child will come under the influence of children with bad attitudes and 'dangerous minds'. They also want the child 'stretched'.

(Ball, 2006)

It is middle-class children who get the early piano lessons, swimming lessons, the extracurricular language lessons and the holidays in cultural places from the earliest of ages.

2 The class ecology of the local environment

The geographical catchment areas of the schools reflects a local economic and housing market, along with a local class culture. The opportunities provided by these local communities are very different, and establish different environments for their local schools. A well known 'grapevine' exists which informs parents of where the 'better' schools are; and in turn the parents of middle-class children can afford to move their children into areas with these 'better' schools. The notion of choosing your school makes sense in different ways to different class groups: without adequate financial resources it is not so easy to choose to live in the right catchment area. And this in turn leaves some areas to develop 'sink schools'.

3 The culture of the school itself

Research has long shown how the cultures of schools differ greatly – as do their outside reputations. 'Good schools' are formally defined in terms of exam results, but there are other factors at work which are often class located. There is a wealth of studies which suggest the ways in which schools become 'middle-class factories with middle-class teachers cultivating middle-class values'. For many working-class children, schools are alien environments and they cannot wait to leave. Several studies have documented the alienation of young working-class and often 'black' children from this culture (e.g. Willis, 1978).

4 The marketplace of schools

Paying for a good education is a key feature of most educational systems. Stephen Ball has studied what he calls 'circuits of schooling' which plug parents from different social classes into different circuits. In the UK, Ball describes three systems:

- a circuit of local, community, comprehensive schools, which recruit from the local community
- a circuit of cosmopolitan, high-profile elite maintained schools, which recruit from outside of the local community
- a local system of day, independent schools, which attract some parents whose children cannot enter the 'cosmopolitan elite' schools, or who are interested in the private system.

Over and above is the private fee-paying school and the public school system. The cost of these is prohibitive for average- and low-income workers: in 2010/11, the school fee at Harrow was £9,890 per term (£29,670 per annum). At the lower end of the scale, in poorer areas, 'sink schools' and slum schools appear. Educational systems depend on financial resources but these are unequally distributed across the classes. Hence more middle-class children go to private schools and the 'elite educational institutions'. They are given more resources and more support. Increasingly, schools are becoming like businesses, and with this come business values.

5 Reproducing across generations

Ultimately, this whole system is then reproduced on a daily basis – through economic, cultural and social capital (see Chapter 8). Private education in particular plays a key role in the accumulation of social capital (from private nurseries all the way up to the elite Oxbridge and Ivory Tower systems, where new friendships and networks are developed and often sustained over the cycle.

 On all this, see the work of Stephen Ball, *Education Policy and Social Class* (2006).

Disability divisions

Historically, children with all kinds of disability and special needs have been socialised into having low expectations of success in both education and work, whilst the 'academic' and the 'normal' are awarded accolades and privileges. In the UK system for many years, this took place largely through a process of exclusion in 'special schools'. There were schools for the 'deaf', schools for the 'blind' and schools for the 'physically handicapped' (all terms that are now often questioned). The 1944 Education Act encouraged disabled children to be educated in mainstream schools, but in practice Local Education Authorities made separate provision. The 1981 Special Education Act abolished the category of handicap, and introduced the category of educational special needs (SEN). Although some say that special schools are needed – how can the deaf learn British Sign Language, and how can they develop positive identities without special schools? – others suggest that special schools actually perpetuate the disabling and stigmatising process (see Chapters 14 and 17). The education experience may remain inferior: disabled students come to have narrower curricula; teachers often have lower expectations; courses are taught in life skills rather than academic knowledge. Often there are disproportionate numbers of immigrant and other 'minority' children are also overrepresented. Children with SEN are at best tolerated, but often abused and excluded. In the climate of 'league tables' introduced into British schools, the disabled seem even less likely to succeed (Tomlinson, 1982). Sustaining the balance of separation and inclusion remains a constant dilemma.

Ethnic differences

Not every country has adopted the extreme policy of racial segregation in classrooms once practised in the United States and South Africa, but racial differences in educational achievement appear in many countries, and these differences often coincide with social status differences between ethnic groups. Studies in the UK, such as the report of the Swann Committee (Swann, 1985), found that in general West Indian children perform less well than Asian children, and in both cases boys do less well than girls. Asian girls may often do better than white boys, but black boys regularly come out at the bottom of the heap. This pattern continues through higher education. Drawing on the work of David Gilborn (1995), Mairtin Mac an Ghaill (1994) and others, Gail Lewis et al. (2000) have summarised a number of key studies and concluded the following:

- Racial distinctions are applied to pupils of both African-Caribbean and Asian descent but in different ways, leading to divergent expectations of each group . . .

- Such racial distinctions are often based on racial stereotypes of Caribbean and Asian family structures and relationships as, equally but differently, pathological or dysfunctional . . .
- Pupils of Asian descent are characterised as academically able and diligent, if also quiet and docile; and African-Caribbean descent pupils are characterised as academically poor and lazy . . .
- Boys of African-Caribbean descent are assumed to be disorderly and thus to present teachers with behavioural problems.
- There is a high level of conflict between white teachers and African-Caribbean descent pupils . . .
- Teachers and schools themselves often play an active, though unintended part in the creation of this conflict . . .
- There is constant overrepresentation in school exclusions of black pupils . . . of both sexes . . .
- Levels of academic success may be achieved by pupils despite – rather than because of – teacher/ school support . . . (Lewis et al., 2000: 269–70)

Some part of all this may be accounted for through links to class – Afro-Caribbean children are more likely to have parents in manual work. Another feature may well be the workings of a self-fulfilling prophecy (described in the *Speaking lives* box, p. 701). Another contributory factor must also be some forms of racism and racialisation at work (see Chapter 11). In addition, part of the explanation may lie in what Smith and Tomlinson (1989) term 'the school effect'. While these authors argue that 'what school a child goes to makes far more difference than which ethnic group he or she belongs to' (1989: 281), they also note that people from ethnic minorities are more likely to be clustered into particular areas, and that their children's educational fate rests in the hands of the schools near where they live. For groups more likely to be poor, or immigrants clustered in poor sections of central cities to cut costs as they adjust to a new culture, this can be bad news.

Since schools tend to reinforce the dominant culture in a society, students from minority communities often face a confusing problem when trying to reconcile differences between their own original culture and that of the larger society in which they live. Children may not feel inclined to sever their roots with their cultural origins, and wish to keep their own language or religion, for example. Often this can initially spark conflict within schools, as schools expect that children should be fully assimilated into the values of the dominant society. With this approach there has often been tacit ethnic discrimination, to which a major response was the promotion of anti-racism strategies in schools, whereby discriminatory practices were more overtly condemned. More recently, multiculturalism is often promoted in the curriculum, allowing the diversity of cultures to be taken more seriously (see Giroux, 1992).

Gender differences

Peer groups socialise their members according to normative conceptions of gender. A series of feminist researchers in the UK – the late Sue Lees, Christine Griffin and Angela McRobbie among them – have interviewed girls and discovered the ways in which their 'femininity' is shaped from early years. Likewise, some male sociologists – Paul Willis, Mike O'Donnell and Mairtin Mac an Ghaill among them – have studied boys. Reading their studies, it is not hard to sense the overwhelming pressures placed on young boys and girls to conform to gender stereotypes, and to sense the sanctions they will experience if they step out of these roles.

Many of the world's societies have considered schooling more important for boys than for girls. Although the education gender gap has narrowed in Western countries in recent decades, in many low-income societies the divisions remain at a high level. Women still study traditionally feminine subjects such as literature, while men pursue mathematics and engineering. By stressing the experiences of people in traditionally masculine professions, such as the military, while ignoring the lives of other, largely female workforces, such as domestic workers, schools reinforce male dominance in society.

During the 1970s, sociologists discovered how girls were usually disadvantaged at school. Rosemary Deem demonstrated that education for girls in the past largely centred upon how it would prepare them for the family. Dale Spender found curricula riddled with 'sexism' and Sue Sharpe observed that schools steered girls towards 'feminine' subjects. Michelle Stanworth looked at a mixed group of students, finding that teachers gave more attention to boys than to girls. As a result of such experiences, girls learned to lack faith in their abilities (Deem, 1980; Spender, 1982; Stanworth, 1983; Sharpe, 1994). At the same time, Julian Wood (1984) found that there is a general, highly charged, sexual atmosphere in schools – a point that few commentators seem to have noticed before – where there is also a massive amount of sexism among the boys. Boys' cultures regularly derided girls and women as mere body parts. The *Living in the twenty-first century* box on p. 708 highlights how 'homosexuality' appears – or rather does not appear – in this context.

But this was early work. More recently, boys are doing less well and girls doing better. The achievement of girls at all levels of education has overtaken that of boys, though it is often subject-linked. Table 20.6 shows that with one small exception girls now perform better than boys in every subject at every stage of secondary education. And it continues: in 1970/1 males outnumbered females in higher education by at least 2 to 1; by 1996/7 females outnumbered males. There were almost seven times as many female higher education students in 2007/8 (1.4 million) as in 1970/1 (205,000), but only two and a half times as many male students (1.1 million compared with 416,000) (*Social Trends*, 2010). This trend has remained stable now for 20 years.

Table 20.6	Pupils reaching or exceeding expected standards in England,[1] by Key Stage and sex (%)			
	1999		**2009**	
	Boys	**Girls**	**Boys**	**Girls**
Key Stage 1[2]				
English				
Reading	78	86	81	89
Writing	75	85	75	87
Mathematics	84	88	88	91
Science	85	88	87	91
Key Stage 2[3]				
English	62	74	75	84
Mathematics	69	70	80	80
Science	75	76	85	87
Key Stage 3[4]				
English	55	73	71	84
Mathematics	63	66	79	80
Science	59	62	76	79

[1] By teacher assessment.
[2] Pupils achieving level 2 or above at Key Stage 1.
[3] Pupils achieving level 4 or above at Key Stage 2.
[4] Pupils achieving level 5 or above at Key Stage 3.

Source: *Social Trends*, 40 (2010) Table 3.14, p. 37.

How this shift can be explained is an interesting question. Some suggest that it is to do with the rising expectations placed on girls and women (in turn partly linked to the growth of feminist ideals: see Chapter 12). Girls in the 1990s became less family-focused, attaching more importance to education and work (Sharpe, 1994), whilst a feminist-inspired culture has given many women stronger motivations to succeed. Others suggest it may have much to do with 'the crisis of boys and men', whereby falling expectations are placed on some boys as they become part of what is commonly called a 'lads culture', and a culture of under-achievement has grown among boys (Willis, 1977; Mac an Ghaill, 1994). Partly too it may be a consequence of a shift in educational policies. The National Curriculum in the UK, for example, insists that all boys have to take a language and all girls have to take a science subject; and almost all schools and universities now have equal opportunities policies.

Ability or merit? Streaming and teaching

Despite continuing controversy over standardised tests, most schools use them as the basis for **streaming**, *the assignment of students to different types of educational programme*. Streaming, or tracking, is a common practice in many industrial societies, including the UK, the United States, France and Japan. The educational justification for tracking is to give students the kind of schooling appropriate to their individual aptitude. For a variety of reasons, including innate ability and level of motivation, some students are capable of more challenging work than others. Young people also differ in their interests, with some drawn to, say, the study of languages, while others seek training in art or science. Given this diversity of talent and focus, no single programme for all students would serve any of them well.

But critics see streaming as a thinly veiled strategy to perpetuate privilege. The basis of this argument is research indicating that social background has as much to do with streaming as personal aptitude does. Students from affluent families generally do well on standardised, 'scientific' tests and so are placed in university-bound streams, while schools assign those from modest backgrounds (including a disproportionate share of the poor) to programmes that curb their aspirations and teach technical trades. Streaming, therefore, effectively segregates students both academically and socially.

Most schools reserve their best teachers for students in favoured streams. Thus high-stream boys and girls find that their teachers put more effort into classes, show more respect towards students and expect more from them. By contrast, teachers of low-stream students concentrate on memorisation, classroom drill and other unstimulating techniques. Such classrooms also emphasise regimentation, punctuality and respect for authority figures.

In light of these criticisms, schools are now cautious about making streaming assignments and allow greater mobility between streams. Some have even moved

LIVING IN THE C21ST

Dude, You're a Fag: structuring homosexuality out of education

What is it like to grow up gay? In many countries across the world, it is better to keep quiet: homosexuality is against the law and can even result in the death penalty. But even in countries where homosexuality is more accepted, it can be very hard to come out or be gay at school. Many young people between 14 and 21, who generally seem to know they are gay quite early in life, find their experiences and feelings more or less completely overlooked while they are at school. There are four major ways in which schools make the situation of young gays and lesbians more difficult.

The first is through the hidden curriculum, which not only reproduces conventional gender roles in the classroom, but also reinforces heterosexuality. There have been attempts by some schools to introduce gay texts, but these attempts have caused much controversy.

A second mechanism concerns the absence of lesbian and gay role models in schools. Authorities have objected to gay teachers being 'known about' or teachers openly discussing the issue of being gay. Yet it is precisely the quality of 'being out' that is required in schools if gay teenagers are to have the heterosexual assumption at least punctured and, more practically, if they are to have access to adults who may help them

discuss their gay feelings. There have been some recent changes here, as more celebrities, like Ricky Martin, George Michael and John Barrowman, came out. Indeed, studies show that the age of young people coming out is getting lower and lower, and many schools do now recognise their gay and lesbian youth. A few even integrate 'gay' materials into their curriculums.

A third mechanism, the social operation of youth peer groups, 'structures out' homosexuality. Adolescent culture after the age of ten places much importance on going out with the opposite sex – a key way of validating one's normality.

And there is a fourth and final mechanism that comes into force if all else fails. This entails a direct homophobic response, through the harassment of gay youth by both teachers and other children. In a recent survey, Stonewall – the leading gay and lesbian campaign organisation in the UK – concluded that:

> Homophobic bullying is almost endemic in Britain's schools. Almost **two thirds (65 per cent)** of young lesbian, gay and bisexual pupils have experienced direct bullying. **Seventy-five per cent of** young gay people attending faith schools have experienced homophobic bullying.
>
> **Ninety-seven per cent of** pupils hear other insulting homophobic remarks, such as 'poof', 'dyke', 'rug-muncher', 'queer' and 'bender'. Over **seven in ten** gay pupils hear those phrases used often or frequently. Less than **a quarter (23 per cent)** of young gay people have been told that homophobic

bullying is wrong in their school. In schools that have said homophobic bullying is wrong, gay young people are **60 per cent** more likely not to have been bullied.

(Hunt and Jensen, 2007)

In her study of an American school, C. Pascoe demonstrates how the 'specter of the fag' becomes a disciplinary mechanism for regulating heterosexual as well as homosexual boys and how the 'fag discourse' is as much tied to gender as it is to sexuality.

As with each of the other mechanisms for making homosexuality invisible, this sort of direct homophobic response occurs in every setting a young person encounters. From mockery and abuse to physical violence, from being rejected by parents to losing one's job, from psychiatric treatment to imprisonment – all these remain distinct possibilities for those who dare to breach the heterosexual assumption.

Continue the debate

1 Briefly consider your own school experience. Did homosexuality get mentioned at all? If it was mentioned, was this a negative mention or a positive one?
2 Did you know any gays or lesbians when you were at school? If so, how did you respond to them?
3 Are schools changing so that the situation for lesbian and gay youth is no longer as difficult as it was?

See: C. J. Pascoe, *Hey Dude, You're a Fag: Masculinity and Sexuality in High School* (2007).

Source: Plummer, in Herdt (1989); Hunt and Jensen (2007).

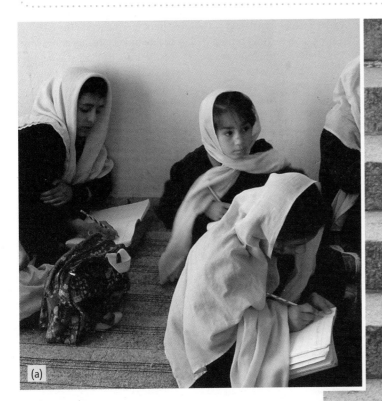

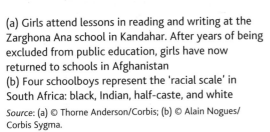

(a) Girls attend lessons in reading and writing at the
Zarghona Ana school in Kandahar. After years of being
excluded from public education, girls have now
returned to schools in Afghanistan
(b) Four schoolboys represent the 'racial scale' in
South Africa: black, Indian, half-caste, and white

Source: (a) © Thorne Anderson/Corbis; (b) © Alain Nogues/
Corbis Sygma.

away from the practice entirely. While some streaming
seems necessary to match instruction with abilities,
rigid streaming has a powerful impact on students'
learning and self-concept. Young people who spend
years in higher streams tend to see themselves as bright
and able, whereas those in lower streams develop lower
ambition and self-esteem (Rosenbaum, 1980; Oakes,
1982, 1985).

Just as students are treated differently within
schools, schools themselves differ in fundamental ways.
One key distinction separates state and public schools
in the UK. State schools often have larger class sizes,
insufficient libraries and fewer science labs. But money
alone does not magically bolster academic quality.
Even more important are the cooperative efforts
and enthusiasm of teachers, parents and students
themselves. In other words, even if school funding
were exactly the same everywhere, the students whose
families value and encourage education would still

learn more than others (Jencks et al., 1972). In short,
we should not expect schools alone to overcome the
effects of marked social inequality.

Yet, schools certainly reflect privilege and
disadvantage. As educational critic Jonathan Kozol
(1992) concludes, 'savage inequalities' in our school
system alert young children to the reality that our
society has already defined them as winners or losers.
And, Kozol continues, all too often the children go on
to fulfil this labelling.

Finally, a key theme of conflict analysis deserves to
be highlighted: *schooling transforms social privilege into
personal merit.* Attending university, in effect, is a rite
of passage for people from well-to-do families. People
are more likely to interpret university degrees as
'badges of ability' than as symbols of family affluence
(Sennett and Cobb, 1973). At the same time, people
tend to transform social disadvantage into personal
deficiency when they criticise school leavers.

Education as a major issue of our time: more questions than answers

Purpose

What is the point of education? This is 'the philosophy of education debate'. Some arguments centre on the value of education for the economy; others upon the need for a critical, thinking citizenship – informed and able to discuss ideas carefully with knowledge, information, etc.

Economy

Can we afford all this education? This is 'the public spending debate'. The costs of education in all countries throughout the world are spiralling – almost out of control. A key sub-issue here is whether the funding should be private or public, selective or universal. And more, if students are human capital, how should they be seen as investments for the future?

Hi-tech

Does the new hi-tech Information Revolution mean radically shifting the way we teach and learn? Just as we now look back in horror at the ways children were (not) taught in the nineteenth century, how might we come to see the education of the middle twentieth century? This is the 'e-debate', the educational cyber-world issue. Children will from now on just take for granted the Information Revolution. They live with it from the earliest ages. Children of two or three now use computers;

iPods, YouTube, email and texting have become central to contemporary communication. All educational systems need now to have the new technologies at the very heart of them. The days of changeover – of adjusting to a new system – are over. The new system is here. But what will it be like (Salman, 2004)?

Populations

Is education now for all across the entire life cycle? Consider the debates over special needs, higher education and third age. Education is not just for children; more and more it is seen as a lifelong process.

Audit and management

Are we maintaining – or, better still, 'advancing' – with our educational standards? This is the 'quality debate'. Education is in constant fear of being 'dumbed down' and unruly. Systems have been put in place or are being put in place so that schools and universities are well managed and well audited. But often these very systems overreach themselves and there are problems. Teachers may be stripped of their authority by managers and policed by new inspection regimes (see Chapter 6 on audit culture).

Equity

Are students being treated equally? Are we in a meritocracy? For a long while, there has been a concern over the ways in which certain groups receive such a 'better start in life' through a more priviliged educational route. This used to be the old debate between 'elite/private' education and mass/public education. And to some

extent it remains so. The old problems keep reappearing: why do the working class still fail to succeed as well as the middle class in what is mainly a middle-class institution? But now we also have to bring gender (why do girls seem to do better now than boys in schools in the Western world?), ethnicity and disability to the foreground.

Freedom

What choices do we have in education? There are two kinds of issue here. The first concerns the freedom to learn and teach – much of what is now learnt and taught is restricted to a tightly structured syllabus, and the issue is raised of how far this could or should go. The second concerns parent power – the rights of parents and students to choose their own schools and universities. How far can such 'rights' be extended without creating greater inequalities?

Local problems

What are the daily 'threats' that schools and even universities now face? Here there are a range of changing issues that confront schools on a regular basis. Day-to-day school life can be challenged by bullying, teacher harassment, unruly behaviour, school meals, truanting, violence.

Global concerns

What are the issues being posed by globalisation? Now more and more students travel the globe – both in reality and in virtuality. There are increasing concerns about the universal homogenisation of standards (for instance, the 'Europeanisation' of education, and the creation of worldwide league tables for universities).

Critical comment

This kind of analysis – allied to conflict theory – points up the connection between formal education and social inequality, and shows how schooling transforms privilege into personal worthiness, and social disadvantage into personal deficiency. Critics claim that the approach minimises the extent to which schooling has met the intellectual and personal needs of students, propelling the upward social mobility of many young people in the process. Further, especially in recent years, 'politically correct' educational curricula, closely tied to conflict theory, are challenging the status quo on many fronts.

Education in the twenty-first century: some current issues

Most Western cultures now place a high premium upon their educational systems. Education debates figure prominently at election times. Perhaps because we expect our educational institutions to do so much – pass on culture and knowledge, equalise opportunity, instil discipline, stimulate individual imagination, provide a labour force, conduct pathbreaking research – education has remained at the centre of controversy for a number of years. In this section, we look at a few recent issues.

1 Global inequalities in higher education

Educational inequalities are found at all stages of the educational system throughout the world. At higher levels it is even more marked: out of 100 adults of tertiary age, 69 are enrolled in higher education in North America and Europe, but only five are enrolled in sub-Saharan Africa and 10 in south and west Asia. Nevertheless in recent years there have been more and more students following higher education in lower-income countries and the inequalities are narrowing. Overall during the past 40 years, there has been a massive worldwide increase in the number of students in higher (or tertiary) – fivefold from 28.6 million in 1970 to 152.5 million in 2007. The expansion has been greatest since 2000, and especially in sub-Saharan Africa and much of Asia, including China. Figure 20.2 gives some detail. Figure 20.3 also shows that gender inequalities are taking a new shape. Broadly, in higher-income societies more and more women are following higher education; but they lag behind in much of the rest of the world.

Harvard University, USA
Source: © Corbis.

Higher Education Across the World

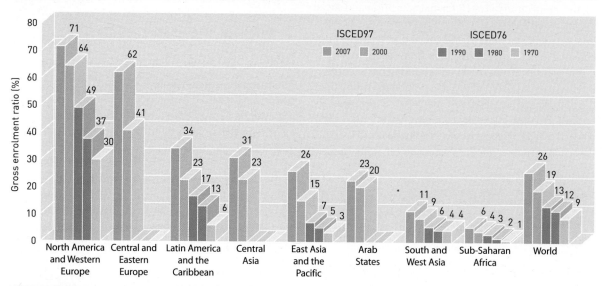

Tertiary education gross enrolment ratios: by region, 1970–2007

Notes: ISCED: International Standard Classification of Education. For the purpose of maintaining consistency across the time series, post-secondary non-tertiary (ISCED4) students were included in certain countries. This may lead to an overestimate of the tertiary gross enrolment ratio, especially for central Asia and only slightly for North America and western Europe. Regions are ranked in decreasing order of gross enrolment ratio in 2007.

Source: UNESCO Institute for Statistics, Time Series Data, Table 1. *Global Education Digest 2009*, p. 14, Fig. 3.

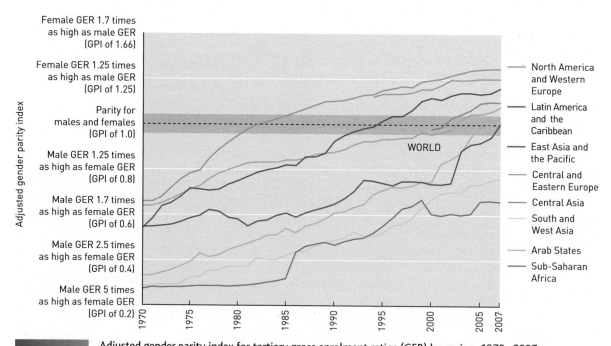

Adjusted gender parity index for tertiary gross enrolment ratios (GER) by region, 1970–2007

Note: The adjusted gender parity index provides a comparable scale for both sexes: gender parity indices favouring women are expressed as the ratio of female gross enrolment to male gross enrolment; those favouring males are expressed as the ratio of male gross enrolment to female gross enrolment. The shaded area denotes a gender parity index between 97 per cent and 103 per cent.

Source: UNESCO Institute for Statistics, Time Series Data, Table 1. *Global Education Digest 2009*, p. 16, Fig. 4.

TOP 10

Top global universities, 2010

1   Harvard University, USA
2   California Institute of Technology, USA
3   Massachusetts Institute of Technology, USA
4   Stanford University, USA
5   Princeton University, USA
6   University of Cambridge, UK
7   University of Oxford, UK
8   University of California, Berkeley, USA
9   Imperial College London, UK
10 Yale University, USA

Source: Times Higher Education World University Rankings.
http://www.timeshighereducation.co.uk/world-university-rankings.

Globalisation and education

The twenty-first century is witnessing a significant growth in 'mobile students'. In 2007, over 2.8 million students were enrolled in educational institutions outside of their country of origin. This represents 123,400 more students than in 2006, an increase of 4.6 per cent. The global number of mobile students has grown by 53 per cent since 1999; and the number of female mobile students has increased at an even faster rate.

China sends the greatest number of students abroad, amounting to almost 421,100. Other major countries of origin are: India (153,300), the Republic of Korea (105,300), Germany (77,500), Japan (54,500), France (54,000), the United States (50,300), Malaysia (46,500), Canada (43,900) and the Russian Federation (42,900). These ten countries account for 37.5 per cent of the world's mobile students, reported by 153 host countries with such data.

In contrast, the United States hosts the largest number and share of the world's mobile students at 595,900 and 21.3 per cent respectively. It is followed by the United Kingdom (351,500), France (246,600), Australia (211,500), Germany (206,900), Japan (125,900), Canada (68,500), South Africa (60,600), the Russian Federation (60,300) and Italy (57,300). These 11 countries host 71 per cent of the world's mobile students, with 62 per cent of them studying in the top six countries (UNESCO, *Global Education Digest*, 2009).

2 Funding crises, market forces and centralisation

All this significant increase in education – at primary, secondary and tertiary levels – has led to the need for more and more funding. So much so, it is reasonable to talk of a 'funding crisis' in education across the world. Just how is it all to be paid for?

The United States model suggests the importance of market structures, competition and profit. Unlike the UK and most of Europe, for instance, it has a clear two-tier university system – with the most prestigious colleges and universities (the Ivy League, etc.) being in the private sector, and the rest being run by the public sectors (such as the State of California). In the UK, the Blair–Brown government did not suggest the privatisation of universities but introduced a system of student loans, replacing the previous system of grants. The later coalition government is continuing this – and increasing the size of loans.

In the school system, the Education Act 1988 introduced the devolution of the financial management of schools from Local Education Authorities to boards of governors, and gave schools with over 300 students the right to 'opt out' of the LEA system. They would then become 'grant maintained' – in effect, a business funded from central government. In 1994, 592 of 3,773 secondary schools and 334 of 18,828 primary schools exercised this option.

The main thrust of the 1988 changes was to introduce market forces (supply, demand, competition and choice) into all levels of the education system. By more heavily assessing schools and publishing the results of assessments in 'league tables', the government of the time believed it would instil competition between schools and enable parents and students to make informed choices about where to study.

While the Labour government reversed some aspects of the 1988 policy in 1997, it largely continued the process of marketisation in higher education, introducing student loans and fees in the name of making students keener consumers (and saving public money), and also promoting the repackaging of knowledge into short, non-cumulative 'modules' – often with mass-marketed textbooks, such as this one.

Yet while there is a concern with free markets at one level, at another level there has been increasing central state intervention in matters linked to the syllabus and assessment. A 1992 Education (Schools) Act introduced new centralised arrangements for school inspection (the Office for Standards in Education, Ofsted). Textbooks geared to mass education and new standard curricula may mean much less flexibility.

3 'Excellence and quality': the culture of auditing

In many nations, concern has arisen about the standard of education. Some people in many industrialised

Ethics in educational fieldwork and life stories

Harry Wolcott researches in the field of education. In his book, *Sneaky Kid and Its Aftermath* (2002), he looks at the experience of educational failure, especially how there is so little support for those who are failed by our educational systems. He does this through the life story of Brad, a troubled 19-year-old. The life story is organised by themes, taking us through issues like 'I don't have to steal, but . . .', 'A new life', and 'Being sneaky'. Intriguingly, the book also presents a short dramatic version of the story (with a heavy rock score!) which has been performed in some universities. Ever since its publication, it has been controversial. What is not told in the original story are the background details of how Wolcott met Brad, how Brad lived on his property, and how Wolcott regularly had sex with him. All this happened before he got him to tell his life story. *Sneaky Kid* tells how Brad develops schizophrenia and returns to Wolcott's house and burns it down in an attempt to kill him. Brad is screaming, 'You fucker. I'm going to kill you. I'm going to kill you. I'm going to tie you up and leave you in the house and set the house on fire' (Wolcott, 2002: 74). Luckily, Harry escapes; unluckily, his house does not. It goes up entirely in flames, with all his and his partner's belongings. There is a serious court case, where despite Brad's guilt, Wolcott is himself scrutinised for his relationship with Brad. Brad's family is especially unhappy about the relationship with Wolcott, but so are many academics. Ultimately, Brad is institutionalised.

This life story raises a lot of issues. Most apparently, can there ever be a justification for having sex with a (vulnerable) research subject? It is true that the sex came before the research, but there will also be many who worry about the age difference. Wolcott himself takes a strident tone against his critics. Almost in anger against those who preach at him, he says: 'one can be ethical or one can conduct social research, but one cannot be both ethical and a researcher in such settings. I'll opt for the label of researcher. I'm prepared to take my bumps' (Wolcott, 2002: 145).

This certainly goes against the current tide of work on the need for more ethics in research, not less. All social life is ethical. There is no getting away from how people treat people, and often one makes a mess of it. What Wolcott seems to say is that the mess is one thing and the research is another. Yet, surely, the minute you start meddling around in other people's lives, you develop responsibilities. We have responsibilities as teachers, as friends, as sociologists. We cannot simply shunt them aside, as Wolcott seems to want to do.

In the final chapter of his book, Wolcott reviews ethics and ethics boards. Once again, he does not mince his words. He has no time for them. These Institutional Review Boards are another example of the bureaucratisation of research. Above a simple risk analysis done by the researcher, there is no need for them. As he says:

> Some awfully petty personnel find comfort in enforcing some awfully petty rules, which takes up the valuable time of others from completely closing down the discovery-oriented approach qualitative researchers follow.
>
> (Wolcott, 2002: 148)

In our view, there should be some checks on students. Research training should include ethical dimensions, but so should economics, business studies, social work and psychology. There is no need to separate out social research. We should all become ingrained to take seriously how we conduct our work. What do you think of this case and the issues it raises?

---

nations fear that schools have done an increasingly poor job of motivating and training students, allowing general intellectual and performance standards to slip. Others, however, argue that the increasing focus on market forces in some countries is itself undermining standards.

Likewise, UK politicians of many colours have expressed alarm that 40 per cent of 11-year-olds and 30 per cent of 14-year-olds were not meeting national numeracy and literacy standards – well below international averages. The Labour government which swept to power in the UK in 1997 claimed in its first White Paper, *Excellence in Schools*, that its main priorities were 'education, education and education'. Following on from the preceding government, Labour has striven to expand monitoring of schools, through an improved Office for Standards in Education (Ofsted). Ministers have proposed testing children from the moment they start school, requiring primary schools to provide an hour a day on literacy and numeracy; weeding out the ranks of so-called incompetent teachers; and setting performance targets for each school, with those that fail to meet targets facing closure.

Some critics of both the former Conservative and the Labour governments have suggested that the language of concern over decline has scapegoated teachers and LEAs for all the wider problems with education. Without a workforce able to feel confidence in itself, they claim, teachers can hardly encourage confidence among children. Some academics at the university level reject Labour's marketisation push as undermining the authority of 'pure knowledge' (Coffey, 2001).

The culture of auditing

In Chapter 6, we looked at the growth of a culture of auditing – and saw how it has been developed in the field of health, policing and education. In education, debates over standards have become part of a wider movement of auditing, accountability and measuring 'outcomes'. We see it in:

- The creation of targets and tiers: education now has set syllabi, 'key stages' and 'bench marking' for measuring successful outcomes. In universities, the creation of the Research Assessment exercise in 1985 more or less suggests that every tutor should produce at least four good publications in the assessed period, and these are then evaluated by peer review.
- The surveillance of schools and inspection of teachers, largely through Ofsted.
- The creation of published league tables for all stages of education – primary, secondary and tertiary.

All this not only has the outcome of identifying the 'best' schools; it also leads to the phenomenon of the 'failing school'. At their extremes, such schools can be closed down or taken out of the hands of the local authority, or new 'super heads' can be brought in. Such schools seem intensively to encourage a labelling process. As teachers become more and more demoralised, hurt and angry, so children start to find their own experiences invalidated even more. A blame culture weakens both pupils and staff, lowering self-respect and self-esteem, and destroying confidence. This usually means a complete disruption and

discontinuity of schooling, as old teachers leave and new ones are brought in. The schools, in practice, tend to be ones in inner-city areas or areas of significant deprivation.

4 Dangerous schools

In recent years, there has been growing concern about levels of violence and misconduct in schools. Thus, for instance, in a few notorious cases in the United States there have been prominent shootings at schools, which have necessitated high-security policing around school buildings. In the most infamous case, at Columbine High School, two boys killed a teacher, 12 students and themselves. Although such killings are very rare, they almost always achieve much publicity and fuel the idea of 'dangerous and violent schools' (*Newsweek*, 23 August 1999).

In April 2007, student Seung-Hui Cho killed 32 people, wounded many more and then killed himself in two separate attacks at Virginia Tech in the United States. It was the deadliest school shooting in US history.

Such shootings have been much less prominent in the UK, though it has been estimated that there are something like three cases of arson per week in UK schools (*Guardian Education*, 30 October 2001: 2). More and more teachers worry about their working conditions when some of their pupils are willing to abuse, fight or even stab them. This seems to be one of the major reasons cited by teachers for leaving the profession.

Linked to this, many children now find themselves outside the educational system, as schools say they cannot cope with 'problem children'. In 2001/2 some 10,000 children were permanently excluded from schools – 4 per cent higher than in the previous year, but lower than in 1996/7 (when 13,000 were excluded). Boys outnumbered girls by nearly five to one; and were highest among some ethnic groupings (Black Caribbean). The age group where exclusions were most common was those aged 13 and 14 (*Social Trends*, 2007: 29).

5 Parent power: parentocracy

Education in England and Wales (Scotland and Northern Ireland operate separate education systems) has gone through three phases: a concern for imparting basic information to the working classes, followed by a shift to a meritocratic ideology, followed by a new

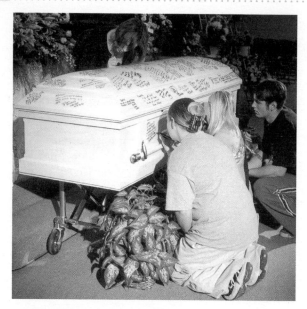

The massacre of 12 schoolchildren and one teacher at Columbine High School brought their friends together to consider their emotional and spiritual response to their deaths

Source: Rick Wilking/Reuters.

phase labelled **parentocracy**, *a system where a child's education is increasingly dependent upon the wealth and wishes of parents, rather than the ability and efforts of pupils* (P. Brown, 1990).

In part, the emphasis on parental choice in primary schools has fuelled this shift. One study of parents exercising choice over their children's schooling found that class plays a major influence. For working-class parents, school had to be fitted into the demands of work and other family matters, while middle-class parents tended to reorganise their household arrangements to accommodate school. With the ideology of parentocracy, schools may be seen once again to disadvantage the less flexible working classes.

Another aspect of parentocracy is the rise of 'parent power' in the running of schools. Parents are invited to make their voices heard at school governors' meetings and, in the UK, vote on such matters as whether schools should 'opt out' of the LEA system. One study found that 'middle-class white males still dominate the powerful positions in secondary schools governorship', although women have increasing influence at the primary school level (Deem et al., 1995; Deem, 1997: 28). Worryingly, though, the same study found that 'governors may turn out to have quite different characteristics from those of the pupils who attend the school they govern and to have much less interest in

social justice than might be thought appropriate for those overseeing a public education service' (Deem, 1997: 31).

6 Credentialism

Randall Collins (1979) coined the term *credential society* for societies where people view diplomas and degrees as evidence of ability to perform specialised occupational roles. As modern societies have become more technologically complex, culturally diverse and socially mobile, a CV or résumé often says more about 'who you are' than family background does.

Credentialism, then, is *evaluating a person on the basis of educational qualifications*. Functional analysis views credentialism as simply the way our modern society goes about ensuring that important jobs are filled by well-trained people. But Collins points out that credentials often bear little relation to the responsibilities of a specific job, and maintains that degrees serve as a shorthand way to sort out the people with the manners and attitudes sought by many employers. In short, credentialism operates much like family background as a gatekeeping strategy that restricts prestigious occupations to a small segment of the population. Finally, this emphasis on credentials can encourage *over-education*, by which many workers have more schooling than they need to perform their jobs. As a result, although we see more and more people with degrees, there are relatively fewer jobs calling for highly educated workers, while the proportion of low-skilled service jobs is expanding.

7 Education and the Information Revolution

One key trend now reshaping education involves technology. Just as the Industrial Revolution had a major impact on schooling in the nineteenth century, so computers and the Information Revolution are transforming formal education today. At the start of the twenty-first century, all educational institutions require computers and computing skills. It is a major change that has effectively taken one generation – about 20 to 25 years – to more or less complete. But we still cannot quite see where this is leading. The new high-tech world is a world of uncertainty.

The promise of new information technology goes beyond helping students learn basic skills to improving the overall quality of learning. Interacting with computers prompts students to be more active learners and has the added benefit of allowing them to progress at their own pace. For students with disabilities who cannot write with a pen or pencil, computers permit easier self-expression. The introduction of computers into schools at all levels of education appears significantly to increase learning speed and retention of information.

Looking ahead

This chapter has suggested just how important – and how full of problems – educational systems are across the world. Since the nineteenth century, most countries have seen the provision of education systems as central social institutions. Education can improve literacy, raise general standards of knowledge and awareness, and provide a better-trained workforce. But at the same time it may work to reproduce social divisions across class, gender and ethnicity.

In many low-income countries, children have few opportunities to pursue education beyond a basic level, while in richer countries students are often processed in school via a bureaucratic system, increasingly organised through credentialism, league tables and the 'audit culture'. In all countries there are major problems of funding.

SUMMARY

1　Education is the major social institution for transmitting knowledge and skills, as well as teaching cultural norms and values.

2　Three classic perspectives can be used to study education. Functional theories examine the functions of a school – such as intellectual, economic and social. Symbolic interactionists search for everyday meanings in schools and have observed classroom interactions often through ethnography. Conflict analysis points out how differences in class, race, gender and sexuality promote unequal opportunities for schooling. Formal education also serves as a means of generating conformity to produce compliant adult workers. When children get labelled as achievers or as failures at school, they learn to become the type of person which the label suggests they are.

3　Five factors serve to perpetuate social inequalities in schools: the home background, the local environment, the culture of the school, the marketplace of schools and the reproduction of class across generations. Streaming, in theory, groups students of similar needs to maximise the appropriateness of teaching materials and the pace of learning. Critics maintain that schools stream students according to their social background, thereby providing privileged youngsters with a richer and more challenging education.

4　Educational inequalities are found at all stages of the educational system right throughout the world. At higher levels it is even more marked. Nevertheless, the twenty-first century is witnessing more and more students across the world in higher education. There is also a significant growth in 'mobile students'.

5　The UK government has introduced market forces into the education system. Some believe that the market will improve services and choice, but others suggest that market forces are increasing inequalities and undermining the traditional principles of education.

6　Many education systems encourage people to get credentials which are not necessarily related to the available jobs.

7　Contemporary issues facing education include funding, auditing, parentocracy, credentialism and the Information Revolution.

CONNECT UP: Turn to Part 6 of this book for key resources and link up
with the book's website, which links to these resources
SEE: www.pearsoned.co.uk/plummer

MYTASKLIST

Ten suggestions for going further

1 Connect up with Part Six and the Sociology Web Resources

As you work through ideas and think about the issues raised in this chapter, look at the accompanying website and the resource centre at the end of this book which connects to it. There is a lot here to help you move on. To link up, see: www.pearson.co.uk/plummer.

2 Review the chapter

Briefly summarise (in a paragraph) just what this chapter has been about. Consider: (a) What have you learned? (b) What do you disagree with? Be critical. And (c) How would you develop all this? How could you get more detail on matters that interest you?

3 Pose questions

(a) Why did widespread schooling develop in Europe only after the Industrial Revolution?
(b) Referring to various countries, including the UK, describe ways in which schooling is shaped by economic, political or cultural factors.
(c) How valuable do you find classroom interaction studies? Do one of your own, looking around your campus and class. Do the themes outlined in the text still apply?
(d) Examine the controversy over why girls seem to be achieving more than boys in UK schools. Consider also how girls 'achieve' in low-income societies. Discuss how cultures may shape such achievement.

4 Explore key words

Many concepts have been introduced in this chapter. You can review them from the website or from the listing at the back of this book. You might like to give special attention to just five words and think them through – how would you define them, what are they dealing with, and do they help you see the social world more clearly or not?

5 Search the Web

Be critical when you look at websites – see the box on p. 940 in the Resources section. For this chapter look at the following:

World information

UNESCO
www.unesco.org
The UNESCO website is a useful starting point for world analyses of education.

UK information

Department for Education and Skills (UK)
www.dfes.gov.uk
For UK government policy and information on funding.

National Literacy Trust
www.literacytrust.org.uk
Covers all aspects of education.

6 Watch a DVD

- Laurent Cantent's *The Class* (2008). Teacher and novelist François Bégaudeau plays a version of himself as he negotiates a year with his racially mixed students from a tough Parisian neighbourhood.
- Alan Bennett's play *The History Boys* (2006) becomes a film about grammar school boys and their teacher(s).
- Ken Loach's *Kes* (1969): a classic film set in the 1960s, it is the standard bearer of all flims about education and the working class.
- Peter Weir's *Dead Poets' Society* (1989): Robin Williams in an elite US school challenging his students.

- Mike Newell's *Mona Lisa Smile* (2003): Julia Roberts does the same as the above for girls, but not as well.

7 Think and read

Sally Tomlinson, *Education in a Post-welfare Society* (2nd edn, 2007). This is an excellent and critical study of education in the UK over the past 60 years – and has a strong concern with current issues. Her more recent book, *Race and Education* (2008), is another excellent review of this field.

Amanda Coffey, *Education and Social Change* (2001). A lively discussion of the major issues facing education in the contemporary UK (and much of it is relevant to other Western cultures too).

A. H. Halsey, Hugh Lauder, Phillip Brown and Amy Stuart Wells, *Education: Culture, Economy and Society* (1997). A very valuable collection of up-to-date readings which mark out the field of the contemporary sociology of education.

Gender and schooling

Paul Willis, *Learning to Labour* (1977). The classic UK ethnography: a study of a small group of working-class boys moving from school to work. Its fame may, however, be curiously misplaced: it studies only 12 boys and overlays the observation with a rather dense theoretical Marxism.

Mairtin Mac an Ghaill, *The Making of Men: Masculinities, Sexualities and Schooling* (1994). A vivid study of gender, class and ethnicity in a secondary school.

Sue Sharpe, *Just Like a Girl: How Girls Learn to Become Women* (2nd edn, 1994). Updates her original 1976 study and finds that girls have changed.

 Think about what a university is for. To help you with this, two lively books are:

Mary Evans, *Killing: The Death of the Universities* (2004)

Frank Furedi, *Where Have All the Intellectuals Gone?* (2006)

8 Relax with a novel

The classic books on university life include David Lodge's *Small World* and Malcolm Bradbury's *The History Man*. Both are now quite old, but remain very telling about the follies of academic life. Lionel Shriver's *We Need to Talk about Kevin* is ostensibly about a pupil who kills at school, but it is about so much more.

9 Connect to other chapters

- To link labelling processes to labelling theory, see Chapters 14 and 17.
- To link education to social class, see Chapter 10.
- To link education to gender and ethnicity, see Chapters 11 and 12.

10 Engage in THE BIG DEBATE

Is education being dumbed down? The case of mass higher education

There has been a marked expansion in numbers going to universities and other institutions of higher education across the world, but especially in the industrialised world. In one sense, 'schooling' has now been extended for many young people to over 20 years of age. It has almost become compulsory for middle-class groups. Figure 20.4 shows figures for 18-year-olds in education for selected countries in 2004.

This change has meant a shift from an *elite system* of higher education (where a very select few went to university, who then automatically got the 'best jobs') to a *mass system* (where a much larger – if still selected – group go to university). Over the past century, the UK has seen a shift from something like 1 per cent to 30 per cent of young people attending university, and a government goal is that some 50 per cent should eventually attain this. In the United States, such a system has existed for a long time, and it is now starting to appear everywhere.

There are many strands of the modern university which we can see as being shaped by some of the themes already discussed in this book. Universities have become large bureaucracies. Standardisation has become the norm for courses and assessments. There has been a *McDonaldisation of the university* as mass textbooks and PowerPoint slides take over from library searching and creative lecturing. Universities have become part of the

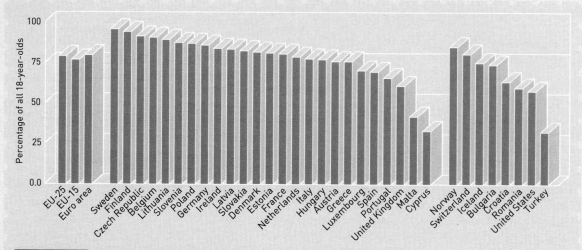

Figure 20.4	Percentage of 18-year-olds in education: selected countries, 2004
	Source: After Eurostat, *Europe in Figures – Eurostat Yearbook 2006–07*, p. 88.

market. They are now much more vocational and tied into market forces. Indeed, even within the universities the market dominates so that students now become 'customers'. There is an upside to this in so far as students may now have their immediate demands satisfied: 'We are paying after all!' they say. But there is also a downside: concern over long-term thinking and the values of university life may now have to recede as they are not part of market values. Academics too may come to have more concern with patenting and intellectual property rights than with the search for truth. Instead of the classics of a culture being studied, new courses such as cultural studies, tourism and even golf course studies have appeared in the new curriculum. And the universities have become more and more involved in commercial practices. Contemporary changes in higher education may be closely linked to changes in the work situation. Post-Fordism (discussed in Chapter 15) may now be found in universities. Just as the work system has to become more flexible and adaptable (and this brings growing uncertainty), so too modern university systems need to do this.

Some argue that we are entering the phase of the *postmodern university*. Frank Webster suggests that the idea of 'differences' is central to this. Universities may once have been elite institutions where a common background led to a common search for a common knowledge provided through tutors and libraries. All this has now gone. We have, as Webster says, differences in 'courses, students, purposes, academics and disciplines' (2000: 319). There seem to be very few common traits that now bind the universities together. Along with this, they have declined in general standing: getting a degree has now become a commonplace, and it no longer has a major role in gaining employment or status in society. Elite universities prided themselves on their autonomy and freedom, but mass universities have become much more restrained by business and governments: they have become much more accountable. At the same time, universities have moved from being closed to open – expert knowledge was limited and now there is much more openness.

Continue the debate

1   Just what is happening to universities today? How have they changed? What do you see as their major problems?

2   Has 'more' meant 'worse'?

Source: Evans (2004); Furedi (2006); Smith and Webster (1997); Webster (2000).

CHAPTER 21

HEALTH, MEDICINE AND WELL-BEING

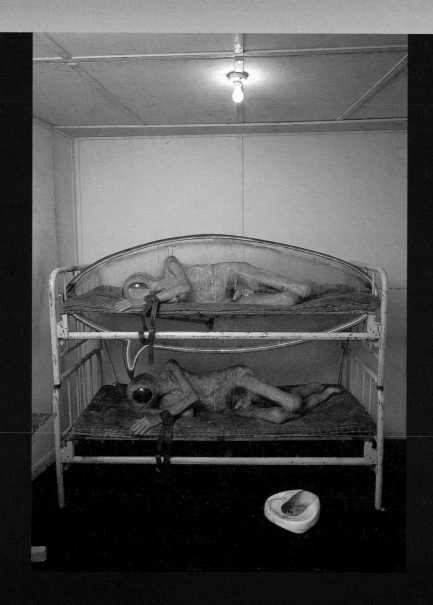

Defecation and urination are universal features of social life. Every day, every human emits an average of 100 grams of faeces and roughly one and a half litres of urine which contain billions of viruses, bacteria and parasites. Yet across the world of nearly 7 billion people, some 40 per cent of people have no access to sanitation. This does not simply mean that they do not have a toilet in their house, or that they have no access to an outside toilet. It does not even mean that they have no access to an outhouse that empties into a nearby drain. These are people who have no access at all to any latrine of any kind. They practice 'open defecation' – they go behind bushes, dump in streams, find distant spots.

This lack of hygienic facilities experienced by 2.6 billion people is a fundamental cause of disease which leads to 2 million deaths – mainly of children – each year. Every year, around 60 million children in the developing world are born into households without access to sanitation; and children living in such households are twice as likely to get diarrhoea as those with a toilet. *Diarrhoea kills more children every year than AIDS, malaria and measles combined*. At any one time, half of the hospital beds in developing countries are filled with people suffering from diarrhoea.

Yet when industrialisation arrived in the Western world, it also brought this same terrible problem. It led eventually to a public health revolution, which required large investments of public funds. Toilets, drainage, plumbing and water enabled a change in living arrangements which eventually brought down illness on a large scale. This is scarcely 150 years ago and now we take our toilets for granted; indeed, luxuriate in them. But in much of the world, good sanitation is rarely given a priority and it is one of the great unspoken indignities of the poor: to live with shit and to die from shit-linked illnesses. No one wants to mention the problem. It is disguised as the clean water problem – not the 'shit problem'.

Our health is intimately linked to our environment: as this chapter will explore.

tip If this major world problem interests you, read: Rose George, *The Big Necessity* (2008) and Maggie Black and Ben Fawcett, *The Last Taboo* (2008), and look at the website of WaterAid: www.wateraid.org/international/ what_we_do/statistics/default.asp

Men make use of their illnesses at least as much as they are made use of by them.

Aldous Huxley, *Collected Essays*

How well I should be if it were not for all those people shouting that I am ill!

André Gide, *Pretexts*

'*Sanitation is more important than independence*

Mahatma Gandhi

In this chapter, we ask:

- **What is health?**

- **What are key health differences and inequalities across the world?**

- **How is illness linked to social factors?**

- **What are the different kinds of health system?**

- **What are the main sociological approaches to the study of health?**

- **What sociological lessons can be learnt from three case studies: obesity, AIDS and death?**

(Left) Edward Kienholz, *The State Hospital* A chilling, invented view of patients in a mental hospital.

See: Robert L. Pincus (1994) *On a Scale that Competes with the World: The Art of Edward and Nancy Kienholz.*

Source: Moderna Museet, Stockholm.

Q Edward Kienholz (1927–94) was an American installation artist whose work was highly critical of aspects of modern life. What do you think he was trying to say here?

We tend to think of illness and disease as matters for doctors and biologists. But what this chapter will show is that disease is also very much a matter for sociologists. What happens to our bodies is a product of the kind of society we live in. How we and others treat our bodies are social acts through and through. Moreover, looking after our bodies has necessitated a major set of social institutions around medicine. In this chapter, we will start an exploration of all this.

What is health?

Billions of people around the planet face major health problems, and some are in a position to cope more successfully than others. The World Health Organization famously defined **health** in 1946 as *a state of complete physical, mental and social well-being* (1946: 3). This definition underscores the major theme of this chapter: *health is as much a social as a biological issue*. And it provides major clues as to how a society or nation works. Societies with a lot of sickness and early deaths are likely to be socially organised very differently from those where people live longer lives and experience less illness.

Health and society

The health of any population is shaped by traits of the surrounding society. Key aspects of health include the following:

1 *People judge their health relative to others*. Standards of health vary from society to society. In the earlier part of last century, the contagious skin disease, yaws, was so common in sub-Saharan Africa that people there considered it normal (Dubos, 1980; orig. 1965). Health is sometimes a matter of having the same diseases as one's neighbours.

2 *People often equate 'health' with morality*. In some cultures, for instance, the disabled may themselves be seen as in some way to blame – albinos, dwarfs and hydrocephalic children may be seen as supernatural (Barnes et al., 1999: 14); and those who contract a sexually linked disease may be looked upon as morally suspect. Indeed, some countries require potential immigrants to take HIV and syphilis tests before they are given visas. In short, ideas about good health constitute a type of social control that encourages conformity to cultural norms.

3 *Cultural standards of health change over time*. In the nineteenth century masturbation (or onanism) was denounced as a threat to health. Today, such notions are rejected (and some therapists view masturbation very positively). Conversely, few people 60 years ago spoke of the dangers of cigarette smoking, a practice that is now widely regarded as a threat to health.

4 *Health and living standards are interrelated*. Poor societies routinely contend with malnutrition and poor sanitation, which promote high levels of infectious disease. Industrial development, taking little account of people's health, likewise has often lowered living standards.

5 *Health relates to social inequality*. Every society distributes resources unequally. The physical, mental and social health of the wealthy is far better than that of poor people. This pattern starts at birth, with infant mortality highest among the poor. Affluent people enjoy a greater chance of recovering from major illnesses and accidents than poor people.

Health and the body

As we saw in Chapter 7, sociologists have taken an increasing interest in the ways in which our bodies are social. And the sociology of health and illness can be seen as looking at the way in which the body breaks down in society and needs to be socially repaired. Medical regimes are then required to organise all this work around birth, disease, decay and death. From the moment the foetus is identified to the final inability to repair the body, resulting in death, social organisation is needed to deal with these 'bodies'. And as we shall see later, the size of our bodies – from thin and anorexic to fat and obese – is linked to our wider health.

Health: a global survey

Because health is an important dimension of social life, we find pronounced change in human well-being over time. Historians of disease have identified three phases in human health. In a pre-agricultural phase, people lived short but healthy lives with few infectious diseases. The Agricultural Revolution improved food security, but the accompanying increases in social inequality allowed elites to enjoy better health, while peasants and slaves often laboured for long hours and lived in crowded, insanitary shelters. In the cities of medieval Europe, human waste and other refuse fuelled infectious diseases, including plagues that periodically wiped out entire towns (Mumford, 1961).

By the industrial era, people started to learn how to control many infectious diseases, but suffered from a range of diseases linked to environment, pollution and stress (such as cancers, strokes and heart disease). Contemporary ailments are more often helped by a change in lifestyle than by medication. Hence, as we shall see, medical work is increasingly preventive rather than curative (McKeown, 1976).

Health in low-income countries

The burden of disease is much greater in low-income societies than wealthy ones: it is literally a matter of life and death which part of the world you are born into. Thus the average global life expectancy is around 67 years: in Japan it is 82 whilst in Swaziland it is 31.8. In Afghanistan it is 44. Healthier countries have far lower levels of child mortality than poorer ones. In 2008, low-income countries had a level of *child mortality of 109 deaths per 1,000 live births, compared with 5 per 1,000 in high-income countries*, representing a more

The global patterns of disease

WORLD WATCH

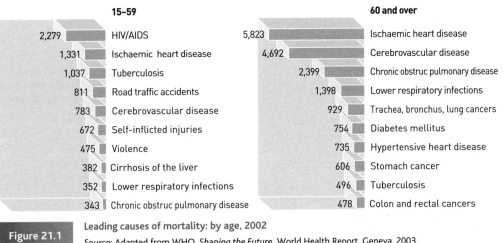

15–59	
2,279	HIV/AIDS
1,331	Ischaemic heart disease
1,037	Tuberculosis
811	Road traffic accidents
783	Cerebrovascular disease
672	Self-inflicted injuries
475	Violence
382	Cirrhosis of the liver
352	Lower respiratory infections
343	Chronic obstruc pulmonary disease

60 and over	
5,823	Ischaemic heart disease
4,692	Cerebrovascular disease
2,399	Chronic obstruc pulmonary disease
1,398	Lower respiratory infections
929	Trachea, bronchus, lung cancers
754	Diabetes mellitus
735	Hypertensive heart disease
606	Stomach cancer
496	Tuberculosis
478	Colon and rectal cancers

Figure 21.1   Leading causes of mortality: by age, 2002

Source: Adapted from WHO, *Shaping the Future*, World Health Report, Geneva, 2003.

Table 21.1   **Numbers of deaths by cause and region: estimates for 2002 (thousands)**

	Africa	Western Pacific	Europe	The Americas	Eastern Mediterranean	Southeast Asia	Total worldwide
Infectious and parasitic diseases	5,787	794	212	394	959	2,968	11,114
Cardiovascular diseases	1,136	3,817	4,857	1,927	1,080	3,911	16,728
Cancers	410	2,315	1,822	1,115	272	1,160	7,094
Respiratory infections	1,071	511	273	228	365	1,393	3,841
Perinatal and maternal causes	585	371	69	192	371	1,183	2,771
Injuries	747	1,231	803	540	391	1,267	4,979

Source: Adapted from WHO, *Shaping the Future*, Geneva, 2003, calculated from Annex Table 2.

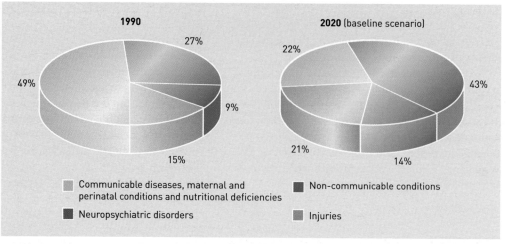

Figure 21.2	Anticipated shift in global burden of disease: by disease group in developing countries, 1990–2020

Source: After WHO, *Evidence, Information and Policy*, 2000.

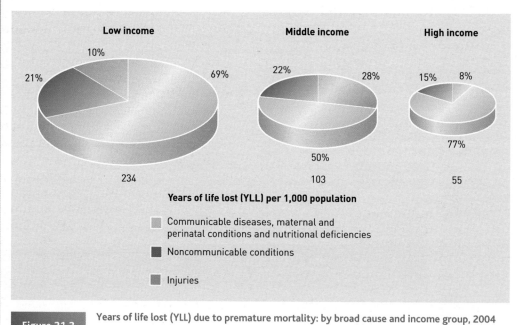

Figure 21.3	Years of life lost (YLL) due to premature mortality: by broad cause and income group, 2004

Note: Income categories are as defined by the World Bank's *World Development Report*, 2004.

Source: WHO, *World Health Statistics* (2010).

than 20-fold difference (*World Health Statistics*, 2010). Indeed, 10 per cent of the world's children die before the age of one. In most parts of the world, once you survive childhood, there is a good chance of living as long as most people do in the richer countries. (See Chapter 24 for more on population.)

Around *1 billion people around the world suffer from serious illness linked to poverty*. Poor sanitation and malnutrition kill people of all ages, especially children (Calvert and Calvert, 2001: 58). The diagrams and table in the box suggest some of the striking differences in health which distinguish societies of the world today.

Health is compromised not just by having too little to eat, but also by being restricted to consuming only one kind of food. In impoverished countries, sanitary drinking water may be as scarce as the chance of a balanced diet. Contaminated water breeds many of the infectious diseases that imperil both adults and children. The leading causes of death in Europe a century ago, including influenza, pneumonia and tuberculosis, remain widespread killers in poor societies. Thus largely preventable diseases are still common:

- *Diarrhoeal disease*: some 1.5 million children under five die from diarrhoea – in which a lack of good sanitation plays a major role.

- *Measles*: remains a leading cause of death among young children, despite the availability of a safe and effective vaccine for the past 40 years. An estimated 164,000 people, the majority of them children, died from measles in 2009.

- *Malaria*: in 2008, there were an estimated 243 cases, causing nearly 900,000 deaths – mainly infants, young children and pregnant women, and most of them in Africa. A child dies of malaria every 30 seconds.

- *Schistosomiasis (blood flukes)*: affects about 200 million people worldwide.

- *Tuberculosis*: someone in the world is newly infected with TB bacilli every second (140 per thousand population in 2008). Overall, one-third of the world's population is currently infected with the TB bacillus. It is estimated that 1.7 million deaths resulted from TB in 2009. Both the highest number of deaths and the highest mortality per capita are in Africa.

- *Yellow fever*: there are 200,000 estimated cases of yellow fever (with 30,000 deaths) per year. However, due to underreporting, only a small percentage of these cases are identified (WHO, 2007).

In addition, poor societies are further plagued by a shortage of doctors and other medical personnel, along with a lack of funding for medicines.

Illness and poverty form a vicious cycle in much of the world – poverty breeds disease, which, in turn, undermines people's ability to earn income. Moreover, when medical technology does curb infectious disease, the populations of poor nations soar. Without resources to ensure the well-being of the people they have now, poor societies can ill afford surging population growth. At present, the WHO reports that things are getting worse. Over 35 per cent of Africa's children are at higher risk of death than they were ten years ago. Every hour more than 500 African mothers lose a small child (WHO, 2003: 1). Thus, efforts to lower death rates in poor countries will ultimately succeed only if they simultaneously reduce birth rates as well. The damage this causes is vast: for example, there are some 11 million 'AIDS orphans' in sub-Saharan Africa – children whose parents have died from HIV/AIDS. Older brothers and sisters (and sometimes grandparents) are left to raise large families (UNICEF, 2004b).

Although 'death' is a clear and simple measure of a population's health, recently a new useful measurement of **disability-adjusted life years** (DALYs) has been introduced. This *measures the lost years of 'healthy' life.* DALYs combine years of life lost (YLLs) through premature death with years lived with disability (YLDs).

Health as a human right

The 'Global Strategy' of *Health for All* by 2000, adopted by the WHO in 1982, saw health as a basic human right. It argued that 'all the people in all the countries should have at least such a level of health that they are capable of working productively and participating actively in the social life of the

The Global Burden of Disease (GBD)

METHODS & RESEARCH

The Global Burden of Disease (GBD) analysis provides a comprehensive assessment of mortality and loss of health due to diseases, injuries and risk factors for all regions of the world – a measure that makes comparisons possible. The overall burden of disease is assessed using the disability-adjusted life year (DALY), a time-based measure that combines years of life lost due to premature mortality and years of life lost due to time lived in states of less than full health. The WHO GBD project draws on a wide range of data sources to quantify global and regional effects of diseases, injuries and risk factors on population health.

Perhaps surprisingly in the twenty-first century, there are still leper colonies. About 750 patients are living in Abu Zaabal, Egypt's biggest leper colony, 40km north of Cairo. Another 3,000–4,000 cured lepers are living in the adjoining Abdel Moneim Riad village. Abu Zaabal was built in 1933 encompassing a hospital and agricultural land in order to be self-sustainable. Warda, 80, lived more than 35 years at Abu Zaabal. Leprosy left her very disfigured, October 2008

See: http://claudiawiens.wordpress.com/2009/02/12/leprosy-colony-abu-zaabal-in-egypt/.

Source: © Claudia Wiens/Corbis.

community in which they live'. The WHO aimed at ensuring that all peoples have adequate access to safe water, sanitary facilities, immunisation against major infections and local healthcare. 2000 was set as the target year for 'health for all' but it soon became clear that this would not be achieved (WHO, 2000; World Bank, 2000).

In some low-income countries such as Sri Lanka, the People's Republic of China and Costa Rica, there have been successes: life expectancy is generally more than 65 years. Four factors have been suggested to assist this process: an ideological commitment to equity in social matters; equitable access to and distribution of public healthcare provision; equitable access to and distribution of public education; and adequate nutrition at all levels of society (Calvert and Calvert, 2001: 57). Where these factors are present, health becomes more available for all.

Health in high-income countries

Industrialisation dramatically changed patterns of human health in Europe, though at first not for the better. By 1800, as the Industrial Revolution was taking hold, factories were choking the cities with people drawn from the countryside in search of economic opportunity. Unprecedented population concentration spawned serious problems of sanitation and overcrowded housing. Moreover, factories continuously fouled the air with smoke, a health threat unrecognised until well into the twentieth century. Accidents in the workplace were also common.

But as the nineteenth century progressed, health in western Europe and North America improved. This change was mainly due to a rising standard of living

Some questions to ask about a nation's health

1 What is average life expectancy of a country?
In the UK in 1849 it was 38.5 years for a woman and 36.8 years for a man. In 2008 it was 82 years for a woman and 77.9 for a man.

2 How many people work in health professions?
In the UK in 2008, 1.7 million people worked in the National Health Service, which was the country's largest employer.

3 How many doctors are there per 100,000 people?
In Cuba there are 59, in the USA there are 26, and in the UK there are 23. In South Africa and Pakistan there are 8, in Zambia, Kenya, Indonesia and the Ivory Coast there is just 1 doctor per 100,000 people.

4 How much is spent per head on health?
The highest are the USA with $6,714 and Norway with $6,267 per head. Middling is much of Europe with France at $4,056, Germany $3,669 and the UK at $3,361; below $500 we find much of the Caribbean and South America, eastern Europe and Africa.

5 What are the most prevalent illnesses?
In 2008, three sets of disease were dominant in the UK:

- Circulatory diseases – heart attacks, diseases, brain haemorrhage, diseases of the arteries (168,328).
- Cancers and neoplasms (141,143).
- Respiratory diseases – pneumonia, lung disease, bronchitis, asthma (71,751).

 Answer these questions for your own country. Examine national statistics, such as UK *Social Trends* and quarterly health statistics, www.statistics.gov.uk/hsq/hsqissue; and global statistics such as the WHO's Annual World Health Statistics, www.who.int/whosis/whostat/2010.

that translated into better nutrition and safer housing for the majority of people. After 1850, medical advances had further promoted health, primarily by controlling infectious diseases. To illustrate, in 1854 John Snow noted the street addresses of London's cholera victims and traced the source of this disease to contaminated drinking water (Rockett, 1994). Soon after, scientists linked cholera to specific bacteria and developed a protective vaccine against the deadly disease. Armed with this knowledge, early environmentalists campaigned against age-old practices such as discharging raw sewage into rivers used for drinking water. As the twentieth century dawned, death rates from infectious diseases had fallen sharply.

With the decline of infectious diseases, chronic illnesses, including heart disease and cancer, are left to claim almost two-thirds of the population of Europe, generally in old age. In short, while nothing alters the reality of death, industrial societies manage to delay our demise for decades. Table 21.2 shows how we report on long-standing illness in the UK.

The rise of a medical model

Industrialisation facilitated a 'medical model' of health. The majority of the most significant changes in health in industrialised societies occurred as a consequence of changes in society (such as improved sanitation and cleanliness, education and better food). At the same time, the scientific method started to shape thinking about illness in Western societies through the gradual emergence of a medical model. In an ideal-type mode, this model claims:

1 Diseases arise from a biological breakdown within the individual.
2 Diseases have specific causes (like viruses) which can be located.
3 The focus of attention is, therefore, upon the body of the ill person, rather than on general well-being.
4 The correct response to illness, therefore, is treatment within a medical environment and/or through pharmaceuticals.
5 Treatment is 'scientifically neutral': that is, free of value judgements (Hart, 1985).

Table 21.2	Self-reported longstanding illness in the UK: by sex and age,[1,2] 2008							
	Rates per 1,000 population							
	Men				Women			
	16–44	45–64	65–74	75 and over	16–44	45–64	65–74	75 and over
Musculoskeletal								
Arthritis and rheumatism	11	64	114	118	15	97	193	236
Back problems	21	47	33	31	18	41	31	36
Other bone and joint problems	13	37	46	87	12	41	67	117
Heart and circulatory								
Heart attack	*	22	54	58	*	8	26	45
Stroke	1	6	24	33	*	6	16	27
Other heart complaints	4	50	110	117	5	23	59	111
Other blood vessel/embolic disorders	*	9	20	29	1	5	7	18
Respiratory								
Asthma	29	30	30	41	47	45	52	44
Bronchitis and emphysema	0	4	26	33	*	6	16	16
Hay fever	5	3	*	0	3	*	*	0
Other respiratory complaints	3	17	24	34	3	6	13	27

[1] Population aged 16 and over reporting a longstanding illness or disability that limited their activities.
[2] In 2008 the General Household Survey was renamed the General Lifestyle Survey.

Source: Social Trends, 40 (2010) Table 7.16, p. 102.

Such a model is widespread, yet each of the factors outlined above can be challenged. Critics reject the focus on biology, contending that biology plays only one part in the total 'health life' of an individual. Social factors, including stress, difficulty coping with a changing social environment or a personal tragedy, can also affect health. Addressing one aspect of the problem may not cure the whole person. Moreover, some would critique the medical establishment for distancing people from their own bodies. They argue that doctors should help people to understand how their bodies work, rather than using baffling jargon and handing down judgements that remove people's control of their own bodies.

Some social links to illness

Given these problems with the medical model, sociologists often highlight the many social factors that play a role in producing illness. A UK government report on inequalities and health, the Acheson Report (Acheson, 1998) (discussed below), suggests a full spectrum of factors that need to be identified in understanding the main determinants of health. They are depicted in Figure 21.4 and range through the following:

- The broadest features of the society: – we have already seen how low-income and high-income societies are likely to have different disease patterns.
- Specific living conditions such as work and housing: poor work conditions and housing can be highly correlated with poor health.
- Social and community networks of support: isolation and lack of support can trigger or exacerbate health problems.
- Individual lifestyle factors: for example, drinking alcohol heavily or smoking may be linked to health disruption.
- Age, sex and constitutional factors.

Social epidemiology and inequalities in health

Most people in Europe are healthy by world standards. Some categories of people, however, enjoy far better health and well-being than others. Here we will look at some of the social patterns of health in the UK – which is another way of saying that we will be looking at social inequalities. The patterns in the UK are fairly typical of those in many Western societies. Once again, as we have seen throughout this book, one of the major mechanisms of social organisation is inequality. And just as we have seen that inequalities shape disease and health in low-income societies, so too they shape them in high-income societies.

Social epidemiology is *the study of how health and disease are distributed throughout a society's population.* Just as early social epidemiologists examined the origin and spread of epidemic diseases, so researchers today find links between health and physical and social environments. Such analysis rests on comparing the health of different categories of people.

Social class

We have known for over a century a major fact: *that social class and illness are intimately connected.* In her classic study, Lesley Doyal has argued that: 'Class differences in morbidity and mortality . . . provide strong evidence to support the argument that social and economic factors remain extremely important in determining the ways in which people live and die' (Doyal, 1979: 65). In 2002, in England and Wales, the infant mortality among babies born inside marriage whose fathers were in semi-routine occupations was 7.5 per 1,000 live births, almost three times the rate of 2.7 per 1,000 live births of those whose fathers were in higher managerial occupations (*Social Trends*, 2004: 107). Note, though, that for all groups there have been significant long-term declines in infant mortality. Thus, in 1921, 84 children per 1,000 live births died before the age of one, yet by 2002, the rate had dropped to only 4.8. (But as we have seen, this is certainly not true in all parts of the world where, in many places, infant mortality has remained very high indeed.)

The Black Report

Perhaps the most important study to look at health inequalities in the UK came in the 1980s in the form of the Black Report (1980): *The Report of the Working Party on Inequalities in Health* (updated in 1992 as *The Health Divide*). In this, Townsend and Davidson (1982) argued that:

1 Inequalities in health are found at birth (as above), in childhood, in adolescence and throughout adult life.
2 Some of these inequalities are among the worst in Europe.
3 Inequalities have also been growing.

How to make sick societies healthier

Do wealthier societies become healthier? Richard Wilkinson is the author of a major research study, *The Impact of Inequality* (2005), which examines international health statistics, their patterns across different countries, and their links with social inequalities. We have met him before in Chapter 8 (see p. 261), where we looked more generally at inequalities. Looking at world statistics, he claims that the healthiest countries in the world are not necessarily the richest. Rather, the healthiest countries are those where income and wealth are more equally distributed.

Wilkinson's prime concerns are threefold:

1 He looks at the quality of our lives, primarily in terms of the ways in which we 'see ourselves in the eyes of others', and the importance of being valued in society.

2 His second concern is with health problems – this includes a range of issues, but mortality ranks high among his concerns.

3 Finally, he looks at the levels of inequality across societies (as measured by a tool known as the Gini coefficient).

Wilkinson finds that there are correlations between mortality rates and inequality as measured by income. Thus, countries like Japan and Sweden – which are seen to be among the most egalitarian in the world – are also ones that enjoy much better health and are generally seen to promote well-being. Life expectancy in rich nations correlates with levels of equality.

On this analysis, much of his data suggests how badly the USA performs. The USA is both the richest and yet the most unequal country in the world. Notably, it has the lowest life expectancy in the developed world. He shows, for instance, that the variation in life expectancy between rich areas and poor black areas in the USA was close to 16 years.

The higher people's status, the longer they live. In a sense this is not news: sociologists of medicine and epidemiologists have long known that social class correlates with disease. But Wilkinson is saying something more. He is concerned with the stresses that come from living at the bottom of the social order. Drawing from the famous study by Robert Putnam, *Bowling Alone*, (introduced in Chapter 6, p. 195), which measures levels of community involvement (and social capital), he suggests that the widening gap in income distribution can weaken social cohesion. Increased inequality leads to poorer relations.

The crucial dimension in health is not simple wealth or income, but a sense of low status, a lack of control over life and social injustice; of being at the bottom of the pecking order, on the lowest rung. It is this that leads to damaged lives without a sense of well-being. A sense of respect and self-esteem matter most. Inequality may be much worse for our health than smoking: it seems to lie at the heart of our illness.

As he says:

> The esteem in which we are held in other's eyes matters to us. We want to feel valued and appreciated rather than looked down on and ignored. Social exclusion or imputations of inferiority are painful. The impact of these experiences is neither fleeting nor a sign of undue sensitivity: it is formative.
>
> (Wilkinson, 2005: 290)

See: Richard G. Wilkinson, *The Impact of Inequality: How to Make Sick Societies Healthier* (2005) and his book with Kate Pickett, *The Spirit Level* (2009).

 See the website of the Equality Trust for more detail: www.equalitytrust.org.uk. Fernando de Maio discusses Wilkinson's work in *Health and Social Theory* (2010: Chapter 4).

One of its most famous findings was that the child of an unskilled manual worker will die around seven years earlier than a counterpart born to professional parents.

Linked closely to this is inequality in healthcare. Some research suggests that working-class patients are treated somewhat differently. They may, for example, be given less time and be less well known to their doctors. More than this, there may be an 'inverse care law' – those whose need is less may get more resources, while those in greatest need get less – and the poorest may not get such good treatment from within the NHS (Tudor-Hart, 1971; Hart, 1985).

All in all, the link between class and inequality seems evident. But the question that is then posed concerns why. The Black Report looked at four main arguments which might explain social class differences around health. The four arguments have framed much of the debate in recent years. The competing arguments are:

1 *Statistical artefacts*. This suggests that there are real problems of measurement and the statistics themselves may not be reliable indicators.

2 *Natural-health selection explanations*. This suggests that health status itself may influence positioning in the class structure. The healthy drift upwards, the sick drift downwards. (Note that this has a social Darwinism ring to it.)

3 *Materialist explanations*. This suggests that material deprivations – poverty, low incomes, bad housing conditions, pollution at work – shape the experiences of health.

4 *Cultural explanations*. This suggests that certain class ways of life – more smoking in working-class groups, poorer diets, less exercise – shape the health experiences.

PUBLIC SOCIOLOGY

The Acheson Report: social divisions and health in the UK

Death rates

Although death rates have fallen over the last 20 years, the difference in rates between those at the top and bottom of the social scale has widened. For example, in the early 1970s, the mortality rate among men of working age was almost twice as high for those in class V (unskilled) as for those in class I (professional). By the early 1990s, it was almost three times higher.

Average life expectancy at birth

For men in classes I and II combined, life expectancy increased by two years between the late 1970s and the late 1980s. For those in classes IV and V combined, the increase was smaller, 1.4 years. The difference between those at the top and bottom of the social class scale in the late 1980s was five years: 75 years compared with 70 years. For women, the differential was smaller, 80 years compared with 77 years.

Life expectancy at age 65

Again, in the late 1980s, this was considerably higher among those in higher social classes, and the differential increased

over the period from the late 1970s to the late 1980s, particularly for women.

Infant mortality rates

These were lower among babies born to those of higher social classes. In 1994–6, nearly five out of every 1,000 babies born to parents in class I and II died in their first year. For those babies born to families in classes IV and V, the infant mortality rate was over seven per 1,000 babies.

Obesity

Being overweight is a measure of possible ill health, with obesity a risk factor for many chronic diseases. There is a marked social class gradient in obesity which is greater among women than among men. In 1996, 25 per cent of women in class V were classified as obese compared to 14 per cent of women in class I. For men, there was no clear difference in the proportions reported as obese, except that men in class I had lower rates of obesity, 11 per cent, compared to about 18 per cent in other groups. Overall, rates of obesity are rising. For men, 13 per cent were classified as obese in 1993 compared to 16 per cent in 1996. For women, the rise was from 16 per cent to 18 per cent.

Raised blood pressure

There is a clear social class differential among women, with those in higher classes being less likely than those in the manual

classes to have hypertension. In 1996, 17 per cent of women in class I and 24 per cent in class V had hypertension. There was no such difference for men, where the comparable proportions were 20 per cent and 21 per cent respectively.

Major accidents

Among men, major accidents are more common in the manual classes for those aged under 55. Between 55 and 64, the non-manual classes have higher major accident rates. For women, there are no differences in accident rates until after the age of 75 when those women in the non-manual group have higher rates of major accidents.

Mental health

This also varies markedly by social class. In 1993–4, all neurotic disorders, such as anxiety, depression and phobias, were more common among women in classes IV and V than among those in classes I and II – 24 per cent and 15 per cent respectively. This difference was not seen among men. However, there were striking gradients for alcohol and drug dependence among men (but not women). For example, 10 per cent of men in classes IV and V were dependent on alcohol compared to 5 per cent in classes I and II.

Source: Acheson (1998).

 For an update of Acheson, see Hilary Graham's *Unequal lives*.

The Black Report concluded that the last two explanations were the most satisfactory.

The Acheson Report

More recently, the Acheson Report (1998) has drawn together a number of studies to provide a review of the state of health in the UK. It notes that:

> **Inequalities in health exist, whether measured in terms of mortality, life expectancy or health status; whether categorised by socioeconomic measures or by ethnic group or gender. Recent efforts to compare the level and nature of health inequalities in international terms indicate that Britain is generally around the middle of comparable western countries . . . Although in general disadvantage is associated with worse health, the patterns of inequalities vary by place, gender, age, year of birth and other factors, and differ according to which measure of health is used.**
>
> (Acheson, 1998)

The *Public sociology* box shows some of the major findings.

Ethnicity

Diseases can also affect ethnic groups significantly differently. In general, people in black (Caribbean, African and other) groups and Indians have higher rates of limiting long-standing illness than white people. Those of Pakistani or Bangladeshi origin have the highest rates. In contrast, the Chinese and 'other Asians' have rates lower than the white population. Large inequalities in infant mortality rates exist between white and ethnic minority groups in England and Wales. Caribbean and Pakistani babies are more than twice as likely to die before the age of one as White British or Bangladeshi babies, in part due to a higher prevalence of preterm birth and congenital anomalies, respectively, in these particular groups. There is considerable heterogeneity between different ethnic groups in both the causes and the risk factors for infant mortality.

There are also some diseases which disproportionately affect certain groups: sickle-cell anaemia affects mainly Afro-Caribbeans, while rickets affects mostly Asians. Admission rates for mental illness are also higher for Afro-Caribbeans (with a much greater likelihood of a schizophrenia diagnosis). And there is some evidence that there is a much higher risk of heart disease among Asians and a much higher risk of a stroke among Afro-Caribbeans (Skellington, 1996: 113–21).

Gender issues

Women generally fare better than men across the life course. At each age, the age-specific mortality rate for boys is higher than for girls, although recently death rates have decreased by 29 per cent for males and by 25 per cent for females, narrowing the differential in death rates slightly. Although the life expectancy gap between males and females is decreasing, this is not the case for healthy life expectancy. Healthy life expectancy of females is only two to three years more than that of males.

Despite women having a longer life expectancy (and this seems to be increasing across the world), they are more likely to be ill. They are more likely to visit doctors than men, and more likely to be admitted to hospitals. (Much of this seems connected to issues of reproduction.) All this is compounded by class. Women tend to be poorer, for example, and this creates a greater potential for ill health. Women are also supposed to put the needs of children (and others) first (Graham, 1993).

Smoking is higher among girls than boys, but in later life the proportions of men and women smoking even out (at 29 and 28 per cent, respectively). For both children and adults, males are more likely to drink alcohol heavily than females, but the rate among women is on the increase. Men are more likely to become more aggressive, resulting in higher rates of accidents, violence and suicide. In the European Union (as elsewhere), violent deaths (suicides and accidents) are the single most important cause of death among young men between ages 15 and 24 (Eurostat, 1995b: 228).

In general, perceptions of what it is to be a man (see Chapter 15) create pressures for adult men to be more competitive, to repress their emotions and to engage in hazardous behaviour such as smoking cigarettes and drinking alcohol to excess.

Age

In industrialised countries, death is now rare among young people, with two notable exceptions: a rise in mortality resulting from accidents and, more recently, from acquired immune deficiency syndrome (AIDS). (See Map 21.1 later in this chapter for a global perspective on HIV infection.)

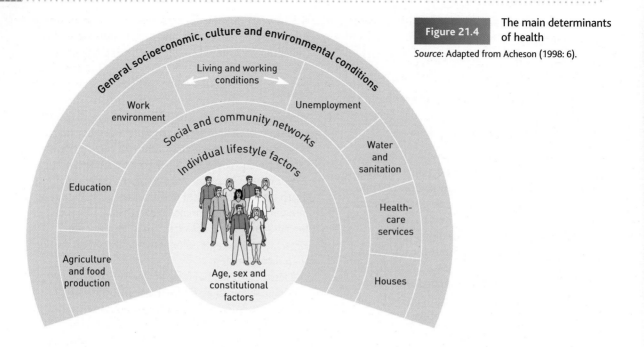

Figure 21.4   The main determinants of health

Source: Adapted from Acheson (1998: 6).

Healthcare provision and medicine

Medicine is *a social institution concerned with combating disease and improving health*. Medicine is a vital part of a broader concept of **healthcare**, which is *any activity intended to improve health*. Through most of human history, healthcare was the responsibility of individuals and their families. Medicine emerges only as societies become more productive, assigning their members formal, specialised roles. Such medical practitioners recognise the healing properties of certain plants and offer insights into the emotional and spiritual needs of the ill. From our point of view, traditional healers such as acupuncturists and herbalists may seem like unscientific 'witch doctors', but, in truth, they do much to improve human health throughout the world. As a society industrialises, healthcare becomes the responsibility of specially schooled and legally licensed healers, from anaesthetists to X-ray technicians.

Healthcare systems

According to a World Health Report (2000), a healthcare system includes '*all the activities whose primary purpose is to promote, restore or maintain health*' (2000: 5). Healthcare systems exist wherever societies create an attempt deliberately to protect and promote health alongside treating diseases. (In some societies, people may be fatalistic about their health; but in most they do something actively to promote it.)

Modern healthcare systems or networks as we know them today hardly existed a hundred years ago (and in much of the low-income/poor world they hardly exist even today). These systems or networks include myriad different forms. We could identify *hospitals, doctors, home care, community and nursing care, health education, environmental safety, media campaigns, pressure group activities and cyber-health*. In modern societies, they employ large numbers of people and cost huge sums of money. Often these health provisions cannot really be seen as a system, as they do not connect up very well or at all. Indeed, modern healthcare systems are often criticised for failing to integrate, for not knowing what each other is doing, and for not being 'joined up'. Sometimes services needlessly repeat each other; at other times they may leave gaps. Often this is due to the inefficiencies of bureaucracies, which we have met before (in Chapter 6). All of this can be very costly.

Comparative healthcare systems

The World Health Organisation suggests that, at a world level, 'three generations of health system reform' have happened during the twentieth century (WHO, 2000: 13). These are:

1   *Founding of national health systems* – nominally 'universal' (though often used more by privileged groups). It establishes the broad principle that governments should play a major role in the health of their people. The development of the National Health Service in the UK from 1948 is always cited as a major example. As we shall see, some countries have been better at this than others. There have been many problems, especially in poorer countries.

2   *Emphasis on 'primary care'* – a much contested term. It establishes a basic 'front line' approach to care. This is often low-cost work and very direct. In India, for example, community health workers were trained and placed in some 100,000 posts intended to serve nearly two-thirds of the population. Nevertheless, training was insufficient, funding was inadequate, referral systems were weak and the quality of care turned out to be pretty poor (2000: 14).

3   *A new universalism.* This requires a high-quality delivery of essential care for everyone, rather than all possible care for the whole population or only the simplest and most basic care for the poor. Originally, the modern health system was built around hospitals (largely in the nineteenth century) and the rising professions of medicine, especially doctors. But over time, the system has become more and more diversified, complex and fragmented. And the individual hospital's central role in healthcare is no longer so indisputable (Armstrong, 1998).

Most industrial societies have comprehensive public systems of healthcare, the major exception being the United States. However, they work in very different ways. Socialised (or nationalised) medical systems are collective, take inequalities seriously and aim to provide comprehensive coverage for all. They are funded centrally. By contrast, privatised systems tend to work by market forces and allow choices for many while creating a 'health underclass' for whom services are minimal. Below, we sketch a few different systems.

In societies with predominantly **socialist** economies, the government provides medical care directly to the people. It is an axiom of socialism that all citizens have the right to basic medical care. To translate this ideal of equity into reality, people do not rely on their private financial resources to pay doctors and hospitals; rather, the government funnels public funds to pay medical costs. The state owns and operates medical facilities and pays salaries to practitioners, who are government employees.

People's Republic of China

As we have seen (Chapter 4), this was a poor, agrarian society that is now moving rapidly to modernise. It also faces the daunting task of attending to the health of more than 1.3 billion people. Traditional healing arts, including acupuncture and the use of medicinal herbs, are still widely practised in China. In addition, a holistic concern for the interplay of mind and body marks the Chinese approach to health (Sidel and Sidel, 1982b). Over its history, medicine in China has been shaped by Confucian, Taoist, Buddhist and Marxist ideas. Modern

Healthcare in Europe

Taken as a whole, the health of Europe is among the best in the world (only Japan is better) with life expectancy high and increasing, and mortality rates low and declining. The southern European countries have seen the most substantial improvements. But stubborn differences linked to inequalities remain.

In general, there is a growing emphasis upon primary healthcare (provision focused upon whole communities and their general health status). Healthcare costs present problems for all countries and the newer technologies are prohibitively expensive. Some countries finance their health systems from collective taxation (the UK, Sweden), some by state-run health insurance funds (Germany, Norway, Denmark, Belgium), some have private schemes (Greece, Austria, the Netherlands) and others have a mixed system of private and state (Ireland, France, Switzerland).

In 1891 Sweden instituted a compulsory, comprehensive system of government medical care. Swedes pay for healthcare with their taxes, which are among the highest in the world. In most cases, doctors receive salaries from the government rather than fees from patients, and most hospitals are managed by government. Because this medical system resembles that of socialist societies, it is often described as **socialised medicine**, *a healthcare system in which the government owns and operates most medical facilities and employs most doctors.*

 For detailed information on all European health systems see: www.euro.who.inf/en/home/ projects/observatory.

systems are hence a mix of many ideas, but contemporary health care in China is now overwhelmingly publicly provided – even though such provision is still very uneven in such a large country. Communicable diseases and malnutrition have a major impact on health, especially in less developed and more isolated areas, and particularly among young children. The emergence of severe acute respiratory syndrome (SARS) in southern China in 2003 demonstrated the need to strengthen public health, including surveillance, hospital infection control and health information systems.

In 2009, major reforms were announced to improve the health care system. This included spending more than $120 billion to build hospitals and clinics as part of an effort to provide basic, universal health care. The government will also subsidise insurance to extend coverage to more of its citizens. Prevention programmes are also planned.

In recent years, there has been a reduction in traditional infectious diseases but an increase in chronic disease as lifestyle changes. An increasing emphasis is on prevention. For example, in China smoking is linked to the deaths of at least 1 million people each year. (China accounts for a third of all cigarettes smoked worldwide.) But in 2011, legislation banned smoking in public places. Public venues are now required to prominently display 'No Smoking' signs and employers are encouraged to ask their staffers not to smoke (c.f. Unschuld, 2010).

Healthcare in the United Kingdom

In the UK, as a result of the Beveridge recommendations, the National Health Service (NHS) was introduced in 1948 as a tripartite system of hospitals, local health authorities and an 'executive council sector' responsible for GPs, dentists and the like. Thus all UK citizens are entitled to medical care provided by the National Health Service, but those who can afford to may purchase more extensive care from doctors and hospitals that operate privately. Doyal has suggested that this system is more of a nationalised system than a socialised one because it remains full of inequalities: the upper class and wealthy choose the private system, leaving the middle and working classes to be the recipients of the National Health Service.

During the 1980s (the 'Thatcher years') basic changes to the NHS were introduced to make the system more efficient and cost-effective. These changes centred on the 'internal market', another version of Thatcher's emphasis on **marketisation** (*goods and services working on market principles of supply and demand*) and **privatisation** (*the transfer of state assets/property from public to private*

ownership). The private system of hospitals and insurance was encouraged. Between 1979 and 1989, private hospitals increased by 30 per cent and the number of private beds by 58 per cent. Private insurance grew from 5 per cent to 13 per cent (Gabe et al., 2004: 209). Hospitals could opt to become self-governing trusts; general practitioners (doctors) could opt to become 'fund-holders'; there was an emphasis on performance indicators; compulsory tendering for contracts was made mandatory; and 'consumer sovereignty' was embodied in a *patients' charter*, part of a consumer-led range of services. The new National Health Service, then, is much more market-driven than the old one, and it works with a much more interventionist style of management derived from the private sector and often linked to total quality control (TQC). Ranade (1994) suggests that it became post-Fordist (see Chapters 6 and 15). There was a shift from mass needs and mass delivery to welfare pluralism as NHS organisations became 'flexible firms'. With this NHS, there was the growth of information technology, fragmented and pluralistic management, polarisation, flexibility and 'value for money', along with a decline in the number of professionals and an increase in the number of ancillary workers.

All this is about to change again as a major change in health policy and direction for the NHS was being announced by the new UK government of 2010 as this book went to press. Hospitals were to be encouraged to move outside of the NHS and general practitioners were being asked to get together in groups to take on responsibility for spending much of the NHS budget. Ostensibly, this was to create more information and choice for patients. But a concern was being voiced that this flagged the dismantling of the National Health Service.

Healthcare in the United States

The United States stands alone among industrialised societies in having no government-sponsored medical system that provides care to every citizen. Called a **direct-fee system**, the US system is *a medical care system in which patients pay directly for the services of doctors and hospitals*. Thus while Europeans look to government to cover about 80 per cent of their medical costs (paid for through taxation), the US government pays less than half its country's medical bills (US Bureau of the Census, 1999).

The mostly private US medical care system allows affluent people to purchase their medical care, yet the poor fare worse than their counterparts in Europe. This disparity can be seen in the relatively high death rates among both infants and adults in the United States compared to many European countries.

There are nevertheless public insurance programmes. In 1965 Congress created Medicare and Medicaid. Medicare pays a portion of the medical costs of men and women over 65; in 2007 it covered 41 million women and men, about 14 per cent of the population. During the same year, Medicaid, a medical insurance programme for the poor, provided benefits to nearly 40 million people, or about 13 per cent of the population. In all, 36 per cent had some medical care benefits from the government, but most also participate in a private insurance programme.

In all, 85 per cent of the US population has some medical care coverage, either private or public. Yet most plans pay only part of the cost of treating a serious illness, threatening even middle-class people with financial ruin as medical costs escalate. And most programmes also exclude many medical services, such as dental care and treatment for mental health problems. Most seriously, 46 million people (about 15 per cent of the population) have no medical insurance at all. Many more people lose their medical coverage temporarily each year due to layoffs or job changes. While some of these people choose to forgo medical coverage (especially young people, who simply take their good health for granted), most work part time or full time for small businesses that provide no healthcare benefits. In general, then, the people caught in a medical care bind are those (most commonly women, minorities and their children) with limited incomes who can afford neither to get sick nor to purchase the medical care they need to stay healthy (Health Insurance Association of America, 1991; Hersch and White-Means, 1993; Smith, 1993). It would appear that healthcare in the United States is in a very sorry position: excellent for the rich, disastrous for the poor. There have been a number of attempts to change this system, but it is always politically very difficult. President Barack Obama has recently instigated a major health reform.

Recent developments in healthcare provision

1 Changing ideas on public health

In the nineteenth century, public health was concerned with the control of epidemics like cholera, measles and tuberculosis. Its central concerns highlighted the significance of improving housing and sanitation – two factors which had a major impact on the general level of health (McKeown, 1976). A century later, the WHO proposed a 'new public health' (NPH) to be focused upon 'lifestyles and living conditions' which influence health. It led to claims that more and more financial resources should be given to programmes or policies which 'create, maintain and protect' healthy lifestyles and 'supportive environments for health' (Nutbeam, 1998). In the UK, for instance, we have seen this in major campaigns around 'healthy living'. There have been 'healthy living centres', 'health demonstration centres' and 'food and health action' groups; major social policies have been developed around smoking, drinking, obesity, cancers and the like; and all this has been linked to advertising and education. 'Health promotion' is the key phrase. And this connects to the wider culture – for instance, in the concerns with food, television chef Jamie Oliver tried to convert the UK to healthier school food in 2004. The NPH is no longer a matter of health education: it works on social prevention and social justice to provide a much wider programme. Closely linked to environmental and ecological issues (see Chapter 25), the new public health has a lot to do with nutrition and combating problems generated by new eating habits (see Lang and Heasman, 2004; and Interlude 2).

2 Self-help activism and new social health movements

Much activity now aims to promote the health and well-being of members of society. As we have seen throughout this book, the new social movements are a feature of life in the twenty-first century (see especially Chapter 16). Such movements range from patient and patient support groups to radical action groups. These days they often have to be both media aware and 'web savvy' in order to bring their concerns to a wider public.

Some are geared towards research and education, some are fund raising, some are politically active (from lobbying governments to challenging general perceptions of the illness), some provide general mutual support for their members, some offer treatment: many offer all or most of these things. They can be looked at as social movements, pressure groups, resistance to professional power, charities, philanthropy and as models of new selves. In general, they divide between those that aim for assimilation (i.e. that want improvements and support within the terms of the existing society) and those that aim for radical change (i.e. that see the need for fundamental changes before the issues around the problem can be resolved).

These are often worldwide movements. Two examples are:

- *The women's movement*. During the 1970s, women made a major critique of the ways in which women's health needs were being treated. They created new accounts, books, health centres, critiques of reproduction, childbirth, contraception and a wide-ranging critique of what was seen as patriarchal knowledge and male professional dominance. They raised questions about women as passive and 'victims'. Many of their actions have brought about significant changes to the workings of contemporary health systems.

- *HIV/AIDS*. Right from the discovery of HIV in 1981, social movements started to appear which focus on healthcare delivery to gay men (and subsequently this spread out more widely). The Gay Men's Health Crisis was set up by 1982 in New York; others have followed throughout the world (in the UK the main body was the Terrence Higgins Trust and this is now fully established with government funding). These bodies provided a constant critique and campaigns against government policies – which were complacent, ineffective and often stigmatising of certain groups.

By the start of the twenty-first century, social movements and self-help groups had established themselves as an integral part of modern health systems and had provided a marked shift in the power base of these systems from 'experts' to 'patients'.

3 Cyber-medicine

Of increasing significance is the growth of modern information technologies in healthcare. The case of the UK is instructive. In 1998, the NHS introduced NHS Direct – a telephone helpline which provides access to health advice and information. In 2005/6, the service handled over 6.8 million calls. A year later they introduced NHS Direct Online, a website to provide health information. This has also grown rapidly and now has over a million visits a year. But it is much more pervasive than this. Most diseases now have their own websites where immediate information on help can be provided, along with intricate medical details and case studies. Self-help groups can provide additional support and plans for activism if needed. Cyber-medicine is expanding rapidly and is making 'patients' more active in pursuing their own health (*Social Trends*, 2007: 106). The issue is for the client/patient to be more informed, more knowledgeable and more active in their own health. And as this happens, so the character of the health system changes.

 See Andy Miah and Emma Rich, *The Medicalization of Cyberspace* (2008).

A sample of self-help groupings in the UK

Self help UK provides a guide to support and self-help in the UK. This organisation lists every major illness and then provides details of its self-help groupings – for research and for care. There are hundreds of such organisations in the UK alone; worldwide now there are probably millions. A listing for the UK can be found at www.selfhelp.org.uk.

Some examples include:

AIDS
- Terrence Higgins Trust: www.tht.org.uk
- National AIDS Trust www/nat.org.uk
- Positively Women www.positivelywomen.org/uk

Cancer
Given there are over 200 different cancers, and many have their own support groupings, it is not surprising to find that the list is long here. But see:

- Cancer Research UK http://info.cancerresearch.org
- Macmillian Cancer Support www.macmillan.org.uk/Home.aspx

Alzheimer's disease
- Alzheimer's Society www.alzheimers.org.uk/site/index.php

Diabetes
- Diabetes UK www.diabetes.org.uk

Bowels
- Irritable Bowel Syndrome The Gut Trust www.theguttrust.org

Chronic fatigue syndrome
- Action for ME www.afme.org.uk

Heart disease
- British Heart Foundation www.bhf.org.uk

4 Holistic, alternative or complementary medicine

The scientific model of medicine has recently been tempered by the more traditional notion of **holistic medicine**, an approach to healthcare that emphasises prevention of illness and takes account of a person's entire physical and social environment.

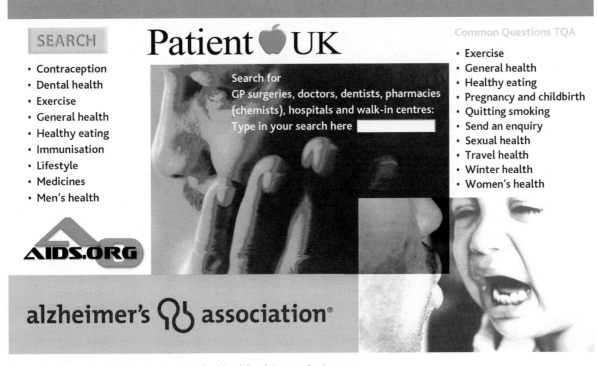

Cyber-health: you can find a vast network of health advice on the internet

Sources: With permission from AIDS.ORG, Alzheimer's Association and EMIS EKBS.

It covers a range of treatments, such as herbalism, homeopathy, acupuncture and osteopathy. Saks (1992) suggests that in the UK there are some 11,000 therapists working in alternative medicine and a further 17,000 non-registered practitioners. They are usually 'holistic': that is, covering the whole person rather than just a specific illness (Pietroni, 1991). In 1993, the British Medical Association (BMA) recognised both the need for and the value of these 'alternatives', while stressing also the need for 'good practice' within them, including sound training, ethical codes, a register of members and an organised structure (British Medical Association, 1993). They are becoming increasingly popular because biomedicine has been distancing itself from its patients and not matching its promise to treat many illnesses effectively. Patients have therefore been becoming more and more alienated from doctors.

The following are foundations of holistic healthcare (Duhl, 1980):

1 *Patients are people.* Holistic practitioners are concerned not only with symptoms but with how each person's environment and lifestyle affect health. For example, the likelihood of illness increases under stress caused by poverty or intense competition at work. Holistic practitioners extend the bounds of conventional medicine, taking an active role in combating environmental pollution and other dangers to public health.

2 *Responsibility, not dependency.* The complexity of contemporary medicine fosters patients' dependence on doctors. Holistic medicine tries to shift some responsibility for health from doctors to patients themselves by enhancing their abilities to engage in health-promoting behaviour. Holistic medicine favours a more *active* approach to health, rather than a *reactive* approach to illness.

3 *Personal treatment.* Conventional medicine locates medical care in impersonal surgeries and hospitals, which are disease-centred settings. Holistic practitioners favour, as much as possible, a personal and relaxed environment such as the home. Holistic medicine seeks to re-establish the personal social ties that united healers and patients before the era of specialists.

Clearly, holistic care does not oppose scientific medicine, but it shifts its emphasis away from narrowly treating disease towards the goal of achieving the highest possible level of well-being for everyone.

Table 21.3	The transformation of health and disease				
	I Traditional/ agrarian	II Industrialising	III Modernising	Moving into . . .	IV Postmodern
Illness	High rates of acute infectious diseases Regular epidemics 'Short lives'	Infections start to be contained (now mainly concentrated in urban poor) but chronic illness grows Ageing populations	Increasing life expectations	Lower rates of infectious disease Higher rates of chronic respiratory disease	The immortality movement
Management	Herbal Religious Local	Environmental and public health Growth of healthcare systems The hospital Professions of medicine	'Preventive care'	'Managed care' Law and bureaucracy High-tech medicine	Health education Self-help organising Cyber-medicine Big pharma and high-tech surveillance Remission society
Beliefs	Folk models	Rise of biomedical model Ideas of curing illness From 'disease'	The language of 'health'	Care back in the community From 'the patient' to 'the person' Medicalisation of everything Importance of prevention	The language of 'well-being'
Demography	High death rate High birth rate Low population	Falling death rate High birth rate Rapid population growth	Low death rate Low birth rate Slowing population growth		Contrasting rates across the world
Death	'Natural'	Home death	Hospital death	Assisted death	The immortality movement
Noted for	Epidemics	Gout Melancholy TB	Heart disease Cancer		Postmodern illnesses (AIDS, CFS, bipolar, anorexia, Alzheimer's)

Understanding health and medicine

We can, once again, return to each of the major theoretical paradigms in sociology introduced in Chapter 1 to find ways of understanding health and illness sociologically.

1 The functions of sick roles

The dominant functionalist theorist of the mid-twentieth century, Talcott Parsons (1902–79), viewed medicine as a social system's way of keeping its members healthy. From this point of view, illness is dysfunctional, undermining the performance of social roles and thus impeding the operation of society.

The sick role

The normative response to disease, according to Parsons, is for an individual to assume the **sick role**, *patterns of behaviour defined as appropriate for people who are ill.* As explained by Parsons, the sick role has four characteristics.

1 *Illness suspends routine responsibilities.* Serious illness relaxes or suspends normal social obligations, such as going to work or attending school. To prevent abuse of this licence, however, people do not simply declare themselves ill; they must enlist the support of others, especially a recognised medical expert, before assuming the sick role.

2 *A person's illness is not deliberate.* We assume that sick people are not responsible for their ailments; illness is something that happens to them. Therefore, the failure of ill people to fulfil routine responsibilities should carry no threat of punishment.

3 *A sick person must want to be well.* We also assume that no one wants to be sick. Thus, people suspected of feigning illness to escape responsibility or to receive special attention have no legitimate claim to the sick role.

4 *An ailing person must seek competent help.* People who are ill have an obligation to seek competent assistance and to cooperate with healthcare practitioners. By failing to accept medical help or to follow 'doctor's orders', a person gives up any claim on the sick role's exemption from routine responsibilities (Parsons, 1964; orig. 1951).

The doctor's role

The doctor's role centres on assessing claims of sickness and restoring sick people to normal routines. This responsibility, Parsons explained, rests on specialised knowledge. Doctors expect patients to follow 'doctor's orders', and to provide whatever personal information may reasonably assist their efforts.

Although it is inevitably hierarchical, the doctor–patient relationship varies from society to society. In Japan, for example, tradition provides doctors with great authority over patients. One manifestation of this elevated position is that Japanese doctors routinely withhold information about the seriousness of an illness on the grounds that such knowledge might undermine a patient's fighting spirit (Darnton and Hoshia, 1989). Even three decades ago, doctors in

Europe acted in much the same way. But the patients' rights movement embodies the public demand that doctors readily share more medical information and offer patients a choice of treatment options. A more egalitarian relationship between doctor and patient is also developing in European societies and, gradually, in Japan as well.

Critical comment

Parsons' notion of the sick role illuminates how society accommodates illness, as well as some non-illness situations, such as pregnancy. In this scheme, the doctor operates as the 'gatekeeper', regulating access to the sick role.

2 The social construction of health and illness

Both health and medical care can be seen as human constructions that indicate various meanings around illness. Research in the constructionist perspective looks at doctors' and other healthcare professionals' ideologies around different diseases. It examines the 'lay health beliefs' (people's commonsense views of illness), it delves into the construction of medical knowledge and its application, and it analyses the biographical construction of the illness career and the changing sense of self as a sick person. Constructionists investigate a wide range of matters, and we will look at a few of these below (Bury, 1986).

The social construction of illness

How we respond to illness is based on social definitions that may or may not square with medical knowledge. For instance, people with AIDS contend with fear and sometimes outright bigotry that have no basis in medical fact. Students have been known to ignore signs of illness on the eve of a vacation, yet dutifully march into the health centre before a difficult examination and claim their medical certificate. Health, in short, is not an objective fact but a negotiated outcome. Even the 'expert opinions' of medical professionals are influenced by non-medical factors.

Moreover, how people define a medical situation often affects how they actually feel. Medical experts have long marvelled at psychosomatic disorders (a fusion of Greek words meaning 'mind' and 'body'), in which state of mind guides physical sensations (Hamrick et al., 1986).

The social organisation of medical knowledge

Constructionists look at the ways in which medical knowledge is produced and organised: for example, how an illness such as schizophrenia is identified and used by psychiatrists, and the ways in which people come to be classified into routine, normal cases (Scheff, 1967). Social constructionists make problematic the very issues which might appear self-evident in health practice, such as the nature of medical knowledge and medical 'facts'. Far from being obvious, 'scientific' or given, they are found to be bound up with culture. They ask how diagnoses are made and where this knowledge comes from.

To take what may seem an unproblematic example: dentistry. Dentistry has not always been with us, and Sarah Nettleton has shown how 'the dental examination' emerged from nineteenth-century public health programmes and worked to establish the notion of the 'normal mouth', which could be used as the baseline for comparing all other mouths. Progressively, this led to the development of a new profession which claimed the field and built up its own specialist routines and ideas. Ideas in health do not just happen: they have to be socially (and historically) constructed, and interactionists ask how this happens (Nettleton, 1992, 1995).

The social construction of treatment

In Chapter 7, we used the dramaturgical approach of Erving Goffman to explain how doctors craft their physical surroundings ('the office') and present themselves to others to foster specific impressions of competence and power. Joan Emerson (1970) illustrates this process of reality construction by analysing a situation familiar to women, a gynaecological examination carried out by a male doctor. After observing 75 such examinations, she explains that this setting is especially precarious, because it is so vulnerable to misinterpretation. The man's touching of a woman's genitals – conventionally viewed as a sexual act and possibly even an assault – must, in this case, be defined as impersonal and professional.

To ensure that people construct reality in this way, doctors and nurses remove sexual connotations as completely as possible. They furnish the examination room with nothing but medical equipment; all personnel wear medical uniforms. Staff members act as if such examinations are simply routine, although, from the patient's point of view, they may be quite unusual. Further, rapport between doctor and patient is established before the examination begins. Once under way, the doctor's performance is strictly professional, suggesting to the patient that inspecting the genitals is no different from surveying any other part of the body. A female nurse is usually present during the examination, not only to assist the doctor but to dispel any impression that a man and woman are 'alone in a room'.

Emerson's analysis has practical implications. It suggests that understanding how reality is socially constructed in the examination room is just as crucial as mastering the medical skills required for effective treatment. Aware of this, some medical training now incorporates instructions which get medical students actually to climb on to an examination table and place their feet in the metal stirrups, with their legs spread apart, to gain an appreciation of the patient's point of view. It is claimed that 'The only way to understand a woman's feelings is to be there.'

The social organisation of illness

Constructionists also look at the ways in which people live their lives through illnesses, at their 'regimes' of health. They are concerned with how people give meaning to their illness, how they organise their days around medications, and how they develop various strategies for 'coping' with illness. They have been particularly keen to examine various chronic diseases, such as multiple sclerosis, Parkinson's disease and cancers, all of which have long-term effects. Bury distinguishes three concepts which help us to see the different ways in which people respond to their illnesses. *Coping* shows how people (passively) 'put up' with illness; *strategies* show what people do when faced with illness; and *style* refers to the ways in which people actively respond to and present their illnesses (Bury, 1991). Corbin and Strauss have made a linked set of distinctions. First, there is *illness work*: how people manage their symptoms, medications and illness crises. Secondly, there is *everyday life work*: how people keep their routine lives going – shopping, eating, cleaning, child-rearing. And thirdly, there is *biographical work*: how people provide narratives and stories of their lives to make sense of their illness and to account for their medical history (Corbin and Strauss, 1985; Kleinman, 1988).

Narratives of illness

Closely linked to this, then, are the stories and narratives that people produce of their illness. Arthur Kleinman's influential book, *The Illness Narratives* (1988), examines life narratives of distressing illnesses – chronic pain, AIDS, dying, colostomy. Distinguishing the bodily disease from the socially located illness, he suggests that doctors hitherto have given too much primacy to the former, neglecting the needs patients have for making sense of their lives and illness, learning from the social narratives of illness that others have provided. Pain on its own needs a sense-making frame, which patients should be encouraged to find. As he says: 'The illness narrative is a story the patient tells, and significant others retell, to give coherence to the distinctive events and long-term course of suffering' (Kleinman, 1988: 49). He provides an opening checklist of the kinds of question that could be asked by a patient:

> **What is the cause of the disorder? Why did it have its onset precisely when it did? What does the illness do to my body? What course is it following now, and what course can I expect it to follow in the future? What is the source of improvements, and exacerbations? How can I control the illness, its exacerbations and its consequences? What are the principal effects the illness has had on my (our) life? What do I most fear about this illness? What treatment do I wish to receive? What do I expect of the treatment? . . . Such questions are not asked simply to gain information. They are deeply felt. The facial expression, the tone of voice, posture, body movements, gait, and especially the eyes expose the emotional turmoil that is so much part of the long-term experience of chronic illness.**

(Kleinman, 1988: 43–4)

Awareness of illness

Constructionists look not just at the ill but also at all those who surround them. In a classic study, Glaser and Strauss looked at the ways in which friends and families deal with the person who is known to be dying of cancer. In particular, they researched the difficult issues of whether the patient knows – or does not know – they are dying, and how friends and families cope in different ways with this. In some instances, families may know the patient is dying while the patient may not; in other cases, it may be the other way around. All of this can lead to different forms of interactions around the death bed: not least to problems of deception and lying (Glaser and Strauss, 1967).

Medical settings

Interactionists also study medical settings – the dentist's surgery, the abortion clinic, the hospital – looking at daily routines and rituals. For instance, in a classic study, tellingly entitled *The Ceremonial Order of the Clinic* (1979), the late British sociologist Phil Strong looked at over 1,000 consultations between children, parents and doctors in outpatient clinics in Scotland. In all the situations, an enduring feature of the ritual was the doctor's ability to control what was happening. But within this control, four standard ritual patterns emerged. In the *bureaucratic ritual*, rules are followed, people are polite to each other and mothers are presumed to be 'technically incompetent'. In the *clinical ritual*, the mothers assume the doctor's 'authority'. In the private ritual, the doctor's competence is accepted because it is 'sold'. And in a fourth *charity pattern*, doctors reveal the mother's inadequacy (Strong, 1979). In such studies, interactionists point to a core feature of medical work: that it is ritualistic and stable.

The medicalisation process

Constructionists often talk about **medicalisation**, *the process by which events and experiences are given medical meaning and turned into medical problems.* They suggest that many behaviours seen as moral or personal concerns at one time have recently become part of the orbit of medical work. Birth is a good example. For centuries, women gave birth without medical help (and in most parts of the world they still do), but in modern industrial societies it is seen almost as a heresy to employ 'natural childbirth methods' away from a medical regime. Likewise, with many forms of so-called deviance: everything from eating problems ('anorexics', 'bulimics', 'obesity') and school truancy to alcohol use ('alcoholism') and excessive sex ('sex addiction') has been brought into the field of medicine and therapy (Conrad and Schneider, 1990). Here, moral issues become medical ones and medicine becomes a major institution of social control.

Critical comment

One strength of the symbolic-interaction paradigm lies in revealing the relativity of sickness and health. What people view as normal or deviant, healthful or harmful, depends on a host of factors, many of which are not, strictly speaking, medical. This approach also shows that all medical procedures involve a subtle process of reality construction between patient and doctors.

But the approach also raises the problem of objective standards of well-being. Certain physical conditions do indeed cause specific negative changes in human capacities, whether we think so or not. People who lack sufficient nutrition and safe water, for example, suffer from their unhealthy environment, however they define their surroundings. The constructionist position can be overstated to the point when all medical knowledge is seen as suspect. But a more balanced view can incorporate interactionist/constructionist insights into a wider approach.

3 Inequalities, conflict, and health and illness

Conflict analysis ties health to various dimensions of social inequality, some of which have been discussed above. To take gender as an example, a number of feminist sociologists have analysed the ways in which inequalities can seriously affect women (for example, in creating extra stress) and they have provided case studies of the ways in which medical power may well be exerted over women (for example, in dealing with reproduction). Further, doctors are most frequently men, while health carers are usually women: a hierarchy of inequality around health work is reproduced (Doyal, 1995).

Another example would highlight world inequalities. As we have seen in the earlier parts of this chapter, while the industrial world may be enjoying unprecedented 'good health', poorer countries are still experiencing high levels of disease and morbidity.

More broadly, researchers working in a conflict paradigm have focused on three main issues: *access to medical care*, the effects of *the profit motive* on treatment, and the *politics of medicine*.

The access issue

Personal health is the foundation of social life. Yet, from a Marxist-conflict perspective, capitalist societies make health a commodity, so that health follows wealth. This problem is probably more serious in the United States than in other industrialised societies because that country has no universal healthcare system. Capitalism may provide excellent healthcare for the rich; it simply does not provide it very well for the rest of the population.

Indeed, the concentration of wealth in capitalist societies makes the goal of equal medical care impossible to achieve. Only a wholesale redistribution of economic resources, say the Marxists, would allow medical care to be uniformly available (Navarro, 1977).

The profit motive

Beyond the access issue, radical critic John Ehrenreich (1978) argues, the profit motive turns doctors, hospitals and the pharmaceutical industry into multibillion-pound corporate conglomerates. The pharmaceutical industry is the most profitable of all industries. In 2002, their total drug sales reached $430 billion. The quest for ever-increasing profits encourages questionable medical practices, including ordering needless tests, performing unnecessary surgery and overly prescribing drugs (Blech, 2006). While a third of the world cannot afford essential drugs, the rich West proliferates 'blockbuster drugs', such as the wonder drug Viagra to enhance sexual potency, which can bring in billions of dollars. In the United States, more than 2 million women have undergone silicone breast implant surgery, under the assumption that the plastic packets of silicone were safe. Recently, however, it became clear that these implants are not safe enough – a fact apparently known to some manufacturers for decades.

The decision to perform surgery often reflects the financial interests of surgeons and hospitals more than the medical needs of patients. And, of course, any drugs or medical procedure prescribed for people subjects them to risks, which harm between 5 and 10 per cent of patients (Illich, 1976; Sidel and Sidel, 1982a).

Sometimes, too, doctors may have a direct financial interest in the tests and procedures they order for their patients (Pear and Eckholm, 1991). In short, conflict theorists conclude, healthcare should be motivated by a concern for people, not profits.

Medicine as politics

Although medicine declares itself to be politically neutral, scientific medicine frequently takes sides on significant social issues. The history of medicine, critics contend, is replete with racial and sexual discrimination, defended by 'scientific' facts (Leavitt, 1984). Consider the diagnosis of 'hysteria', a term which has its origins in the Greek word *hyster*, meaning 'uterus'. In coining this word, medical professionals apparently suggested that being a woman is synonymous with being sick or crazy.

Surveying the entire medical field, some critics see political mischief in today's scientific medicine.

TOP 10

Pharmaceutical companies, 2009: companies ranked by healthcare revenue

Rank	Company	Country	Rough guide to total revenue ($)
1	Johnson & Johnson	USA	64 billion
2	Pfizer	USA	48 billion
3	Glaxo Smith Kline	United Kingdom	45 billion
4	Roche	Switzerland	44 billion
5	Sanofi-Aventis	France	42 billion
6	Novartis	Switzerland	41 billion
7	AstraZeneca	UK	32 billion
8	Abbot Laboratories	USA	30 billion
9	Merck & Co.	USA	24 billion
10	Wyeth	USA	23 billion

Note: There are over 35 companies with revenues in excess of $3 billion. These companies are often called The Big Pharma.

Source: Based on information from 'Fortune Global 500 2009 Pharmaceutical Industry'. *Fortune,* 160(2) July (2009).

Scientists explain illness in terms of bacteria and viruses, ignoring the effects of social inequality on health. From the scientific perspective, in other words, poor people get sick because of a lack of sanitation and an unhealthy diet, even though poverty may be the underlying cause of these ills. In this way, critics charge, scientific medicine depoliticises health by reducing complex political issues to matters of simple biology.

Critical comment

Conflict analysis offers another approach to the relationships among health, medicine and our society. According to this view, social inequality is the reason why some people have far better health than others; moreover, conflict theorists denounce the profit motive as inconsistent with the interests of patients.

The most common objection to the conflict approach is that it minimises the overall improvement in health through the years and scientific medicine's contribution to the high standard of living in the West today. Even though they could certainly do better, health indicators rose steadily over the course of the twentieth century.

In sum, sociology's three major theoretical paradigms convincingly argue that health and medicine are social issues. Indeed, advancing technology is forcing us to confront the social foundations of this institution. The famous French scientist Louis Pasteur (1822–95) spent much of his life studying how bacteria cause disease. Before his death, he remarked that health depends much less on bacteria than on the social environment in which bacteria operate (Gordon, 1980: 7). Explaining Pasteur's insight is sociology's contribution to human health.

HIV/AIDS and sociology

HIV stands for human immunodeficiency virus – a virus which causes slow but constant damage to the immune system. AIDS stands for acquired immune deficiency syndrome and is the condition diagnosed when there are a group of related symptoms that are caused by advanced HIV infection, making the body vulnerable to life-threatening illnesses called opportunistic infections. Early symptoms of the disease include heavy night sweats, chronic diarrhoea, pneumonia, skin cancers and a general malfunctioning of the body as its immune system breaks down. AIDS is at present an incurable disease, but it can be forestalled by anti-retroviral therapy (ART). Most people who are taking HIV treatments in rich countries are taking two or more medications at the same time. This is called highly active anti-retroviral therapy (HAART). It may also be called combination therapy or 'the cocktail'. Combination therapy has been found most effective at combating HIV by attacking the virus in many different ways.

The recent historical patterns of disease suggested a marked shift from contagious diseases (still prominent in low-income countries) to degenerative diseases such as cancers and strokes (common in high-income societies). The arrival of AIDS seemed to change all this, for it had all the hallmarks of a major infectious epidemic not dissimilar to the 'plagues' of much of history. Indeed, for a while it was often dubbed 'the twentieth-century plague'. It continues to grow in the twenty-first century but its shape is constantly changing.

The United Nations estimated that by the end of 2009, some 60 million people had been infected and 25 million had died of HIV-related causes. By 2010, around 33.5 million people across the world were living with HIV/AIDS. There were 15.7 million women, 15. 3 million men and 2.4 million children. Perhaps most significant of all, in Africa there were 14 million AIDS orphans (*UNAIDS Update*, 2009; *Outlook Report*, 2010).

In the UK at the end of 2008, an estimated 83,000 people were living with HIV, of whom more than a quarter (27 per cent) were unaware of their infection. In 2008, there were 7,298 new diagnoses of HIV, contributing to a cumulative total of 105,625 cases reported by the end of June 2009. There have been 25,470 diagnoses of AIDS in the UK, and 18,787 people diagnosed with HIV have died (Avert: www.avert.org).

AIDS/HIV is now present in all countries throughout the world, but its 'shape' – its rates, how it is transmitted and whom it impacts – differ greatly. Map 21.1 shows the global estimates for different continents. The highest rates are to be found in sub-Saharan Africa (with 38 per cent of 15- to 49-year-olds in Swaziland and Botswana being infected). The most rapid expansion seems to be taking place in the People's Republic of China and eastern Europe. The smallest numbers are to be found in the West, where expensive medications (ART) have slowed the infection a little. Each area has its own pattern, but everywhere it is a major health concern (see Table 21.4).

The nature of HIV and AIDS

AIDS was first identified in 1981 among small clusters of gay men in North America and was for a short while called GRID (gay-related immune deficiency). Soon it was recognised to exist in many other groups, including haemophiliacs, heroin users, Haitians, prostitutes and, ultimately, heterosexuals. It was renamed AIDS in 1982.

Its prime cause was identified in the mid-1980s as a virus which breaks down the immune system (HIV – human immunodeficiency virus). The main risk of transmission happens through the exchange

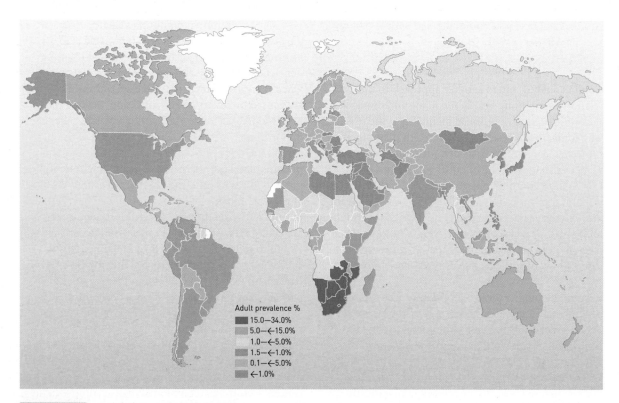

Adult prevalence %
- 15.0–34.0%
- 5.0–<15.0%
- 1.0–<5.0%
- 1.5–<1.0%
- 0.1–<5.0%
- <1.0%

Map 21.1   A global view of HIV infection

Source: http://data.unaids.org/pub/GlobalReport/2006. Reproduced by kind permission of UNAIDS.

Table 21.4	Regional HIV and AIDS statistics, 2001 and 2008			
	Adults and children living with HIV	Adults and children newly infected with HIV	Adult prevalence (%)	Adult and child deaths due to AIDS
Sub-Saharan Africa				
2008	22.4 million [20.8 million–24.1 million]	1.9 million [1.6 million–2.2 million]	5.2 [4.9–5.4]	1.4 million [1.1 million–1.7 million]
2001	19.7 million [18.3 million–21.2 million]	2.3 million [2.0 million–2.5 million]	5.8 [5.5–6.0]	1.4 million [1.2 million–1.7 million]
Middle East and north Africa				
2008	310,000 [250,000–380,000]	35,000 [24,000–46,000]	0.2 [<0.2–0.3]	20,000 [15,000–25,000]
2001	200,000 [150,000–250,000]	30,000 [23,000–40,000]	0.2 [0.1–0.2]	11,000 [7,800–14,000]
South and southeast Asia				
2008	3.8 million [3.4 million–4.3 million]	280,000 [240,000–320,000]	0.3 [0.2–0.3]	270,000 [220,000–310,000]
2001	4.0 million [3.5 million–4.5 million]	310,000 [270,000–350,000]	0.3 [<0.3–0.4]	260,000 [210,000–320,000]
East Asia				
2008	850,000 [700,000–1.0 million]	75,000 [58,000–88,000]	<0.1 [<0.1]	59,000 [46,000–71,000]
2001	560,000 [480,000–650,000]	99,000 [75,000–120,000]	<0.1 [<0.1]	22,000 [18,000–27,000]
Oceania				
2008	59,000 [51,000–68,000]	3,900 [2,900–5,100]	0.3 [<0.3–0.4]	2,000 [1,100–3,100]
2001	36,000 [29,000–45,000]	5,900 [4,800–7,300]	0.2 [<0.2–0.3]	<1,000 [<500–1,200]
Latin America				
2008	2.0 million [1.8 million–2.2 million]	170,000 [150,000–200,000]	0.6 [0.5–0.6]	77,000 [66,000–89,000]
2001	1.6 million [1.5 million–1.8 million]	150,000 [140,000–170,000]	0.5 [<0.5–0.6]	66,000 [56,000–77,000]
Caribbean				
2008	240,000 [220,000–260,000]	20,000 [16,000–24,000]	1.0 [0.9–1.1]	12,000 [9,300–14,000]
2001	220,000 [200,000–240,000]	21,000 [17,000–24,000]	1.1 [1.0–1.2]	20,000 [17,000–23,000]
Eastern Europe and central Asia				
2008	1.5 million [1.4 million–1.7 million]	110,000 [100,000–130,000]	0.7 [0.6–0.8]	87,000 [72,000–110,000]
2001	900,000 [800,000–1.1 million]	280,000 [240,000–320,000]	0.5 [0.4–0.5]	26,000 [22,000–30,000]
Western and central Europe				
2008	850,000 [710,000–970,000]	30,000 [23,000–35,000]	0.3 [0.2–0.3]	13,000 [10,000–15,000]
2001	660,000 [580,000–760,000]	40,000 [31,000–47,000]	0.2 [<0.2–0.3]	7,900 [6,500–9,700]
North America				
2008	1.4 million [1.2 million–1.6 million]	55,000 [36,000–61,000]	0.6 [0.5–0.7]	25,000 [20,000–31,000]
2001	1.2 million [1.1 million–1.4 million]	52,000 [42,000–60,000]	0.6 [0.5–0.7]	19,000 [16,000–23,000]
TOTAL				
2008	33.4 million [31.1 million–35.8 million]	2.7 million [2.4 million–3.0 million]	0.8 [<0.8–0.8]	2.0 million [1.7 million–2.4 million]
2001	29.0 million [27.0 million–31.0 million]	3.2 million [2.9 million–3.6 million]	0.8 [<0.8–0.8]	1.9 million [1.6 million–2.2 million]

Source: World Health Organization, *UNAIDS Update*, December 2009.

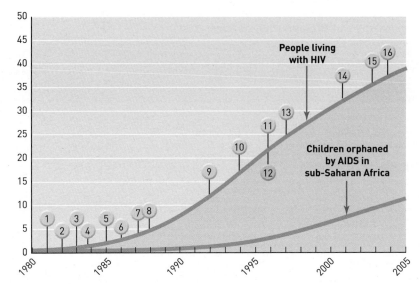

1 First cases of unusual immune deficiency are identified among gay man in USA, and a new deadly disease noticed
2 Acquired immune deficiency syndrome (AIDS) is defined for the first time
3 The human immune defiency virus (HIV) is identified as the cause of AIDS
4 In Africa, a heterosexual AIDS epidemic is revealed
5 The first HIV antibody test becomes available
6 Global Network of People living with HIV/AIDS (GNP+) (then International Steering Committee of People Living with HIV/AIDS)
   founded
7 The World Health Organization launches the Global Programme on AIDS
8 The first therapy for AIDS – zidovudine, or AZT – is approved for use in the USA
9 In 1991–3, HIV prevalence in young pregnant women in Uganda and in young men in Thailand begins to decrease, the first
   major downturns in the epidemic developing countries
10 Highly active anti-retroviral treatment launched
11 Scientists develop the first treatment regimen to reduce mother-to-child transmission of HIV
12 UNAIDS is created
13 Brazil becomes the first developing country to provide antiretroviral therapy through its public health system
14 The UN General Assembly Special Session on HIV/AIDS. Global Fund to fight AIDS, tuberculosis and malaria launched
15 WHO and UNAIDS launch the 3×5 initiative with the goal of reaching 3 million people in developing world with ART by 2005
16 Global Coalition on Women and AIDS launched

Figure 21.5   25 years of AIDS

Source: http://data.unaids.org/pub/GlobalReport/2006. Reproduced by kind permission of UNAIDS.

of bodily fluids – notably blood, semen and/or a mother's milk – in which the HIV virus can be found. Wherever the virus may be passed on to others, people are 'at risk'. As a result, some of the major roots of transmission include sexual activities, intravenous drug use and blood contamination (such as blood transfusion). Women with HIV can give it to babies during pregnancy. Once people are infected, they can pass it on to others.

The virus can be tested for through the presence of its antibodies. Although the search is on for some kind of preventive vaccine, the main medical advances to date have been through various drug treatments which slow down the progress of the disease. There are now a whole array of (usually very expensive) drugs, such as AZT, 3TC and Combivir, which can be taken. By the mid-1990s many people with AIDS in high-income

countries were living with little disruption and with little fear of imminent death. This was not true of people in lower-income countries, however, where AIDS had become a major killer and where the costs of such treatments were prohibitive.

 You can find a wealth of information country by country in the world on the United Nations website for AIDS. You may also like to ponder the enormous amount of work and planning needed to assemble such data across the world – and the problems that arise in making sense of such data.
See: www.unaids.org.
See also the AIDS timeline at:
www.avert.org/aids-timeline.htm.

Sociological implications of AIDS

The social implications of AIDS are so many that it becomes almost a test case for the relevance of sociology to health. Here are just a few.

AIDS raises issues about the social causes of illness and health and the patterns of social epidemiology. There are a number of distinctive social patterns of AIDS distribution. It is quite wrong (and dangerous), for example, to say (as it once was) that AIDS is a feature of younger gay men in the big cities, as this is only one of a range of patterns. In many cities, it may be linked to intraveneous drug use; sometimes it is linked to networks of prostitution; sometimes to casual sex patterns. In some parts of the world, it is overwhelmingly linked to heterosexual transmission and often to the refusal of men to wear condoms. In many parts of the world it is also linked to infected women passing it to their children. *Each 'local' epidemic has local features and is changing all the time.* There may be one epidemic among sexually active African men and women in eastern Africa, another kind of epidemic among drug injectors and their partners in Russia, and a third among men who have sex with men in Rio de Janeiro, and so on. *Sociologists need to study local contexts which shape disease.*

Second, HIV transmission is largely gendered. 'Worldwide, women may be more affected by the consequences of HIV/AIDS, but it is the sexual and drug taking behaviour of men which enables the virus to spread' (Foreman, 1999: vii). Men are at risk; women are vulnerable. Men's behaviour is often influenced by harmful views about 'what it is to be a man', and this in turn is often linked to being powerful in sexual relations. Some suggest that masculinity may well be the prime cause of the epidemic, so much so that in 2001 the theme of the World AIDS Conference was 'Men make a difference' (UNAIDS.org, 24 May 2001). Men refuse to stop passing it on; and women have little choice in getting it. It is bound up with the man's sense of masculinity and the need to establish this through having sex.

Third, it is linked to stigma and prejudice. Many groups have been blamed for the illness: gay men, Africans, drug users, sex workers. AIDS is the classic case of a disease being used for racism, sexism and a more general scapegoating.

Fourth, the illness has a major impact on children, especially in low-income countries. Many children contract HIV early in life – it is estimated at 20 per cent in a number of African countries. They die young. But many children also find that their parents

The NAMES project AIDS Memorial Quilt began in 1987 as a panel of quilts remembering those who had died of AIDS. It was displayed for the first time in Washington DC on 11 October 1987 when it had 1,920 panels and covered a space larger than a football field. It has continued to grow, and in 2010, it had over 46,000 blocks (over 91,000 people) and weighed an estimated 54 tons – making it now impossible to display in its entirety. Panels can, however be viewed. It is the largest community art project in the world. See www.aidsquilt.org

Source: The AIDS Memorial Quilt, © 2010 The NAMES Project Foundation.

have died of the disease and they become 'AIDS orphans'. In Zimbabwe, in 2007, there were over a million AIDS orphans (which counted as 77 per cent of all orphans).

Fifth, it also raises issues over how a disease or illness comes to be represented in various forms of media. AIDS is not only a disease but a discourse. It is represented in health documents, in media images and films, and in health campaigns, and it is represented not only in words but in images. The imagery around AIDS has changed from the cautious concerns of a popular film like *Philadelphia* (1993), which won Tom Hanks an Oscar. Now the focus is increasingly on AIDS globally.

Sixth, AIDS raises measurement problems. To identify people with HIV requires a medical test for antibodies. Figures from organisations such as the United Nations are usually based on this. But there are many ways in which these figures cannot be relied on. People are unwilling to take the test. People may not even begin to recognise that they have the early stages of the disease and hence have no reason to be tested. In many countries throughout the world, awareness may be so low, and the facilities for testing so thin on the ground, that estimates become impossible. For instance, in 2000, China had a very low recorded rate – about 20,000. But it is likely that the disease was severely underreported. With improved measuring and greater openness, 650,000 cases of HIV were recorded in 2006 (and 75,000 people with AIDS). Hence one needs to be aware, when reading any AIDS statistics, that they are often very unreliable and need to be approached critically.

Seventh, it raises issues of generation and change. HIV has been around for 30 years. A full generation has been brought up with the background awareness of this new disease. Some people have never lived in a world where it did not exist. At the same time, the enormous concern about AIDS which was prevalent in the 1980s (the UK government, for example, leafleted every household in the country about it) has now declined, and with this decline in awareness of AIDS, prevention has declined too. At the same time, the arrival of anti-retroviral drugs has placed a kind of cure within the reach of many. Thus, whereas during much of the 1980s and early 1990s there were clear signs that many gay men changed their sexual practices to 'safer sex', by the late 1990s and throughout the 'noughties' there is clear evidence that the sexual behaviour of young gay men had reverted to unsafe sexual practices. AIDS as a disease raises the continuing issue of social change.

Finally, AIDS raises major political and cross-cultural issues. AIDS is a pandemic: that is, it is found in virtually all countries across the world. But the focus until recently has been on Western countries, where the numbers, though large, are small by comparison with the poorer countries of the world. For much of its history, the epidemic outside the West has been less well noticed and much less well funded. While in North America and the UK medications have been found which can control and delay AIDS, so that many people with the disease can now function well for long periods, in Africa the medical services were initially far too expensive. They could not be afforded, and the big medical companies did not supply them. In 2001, the pharmaceutical industry spent roughly 80 per cent of its products on 20 per cent of the world's population (*Newsweek*, 19 March 2001), with GlaxoSmithKline (GSK) leading the way (through a merger between Glaxo Wellcome and SmithKline) and claiming that every minute 1,100 people receive a prescription for a GSK product.

In low-income countries, AIDS drugs had long been unaffordable, but in April 2001, after the threat of a South African lawsuit, the global drug companies came under attack and faced a major reputation scare: drugs executives became the 'new villains'. 'Big Pharma' found itself in the firing line. A United Nations initiative led to GSK agreeing to supply a combination drug for $2 a day to low-income countries. By 2010, for most Africans living with HIV, ARVs are still not available – in 2010, less than 4 in 10 of those in need of treatment were receiving it. But it has improved over the past decade: the number of people receiving ARVs in Africa doubled in 2005 alone. By the end of 2009, almost 4 million people in Africa were receiving antiretroviral treatment, or 37 per cent of those in need according to the WHO's latest treatment guidelines (Alert: www.avert.org/hiv-aids-africa.htm).

But even with such large reductions, poor countries may not be able to afford such drugs without assistance from high-income countries. Kenya, for example, has an annual health budget of around $9 billion; with 2.2 million AIDS patients, caring for them would cost around $12 billion a year, even with 85 per cent discounts (*Newsweek*, 19 March 2001: 23).

In 2006, in developing low-income societies, 7.1 million people were in immediate need of life-saving AIDS drugs; of these, only 2.015 million (28 per cent) were receiving them.

Transplant bodies

LIVING IN THE C21ST

Transplantation surgery started to appear in the 1950s and has now become a fairly routine (if difficult) form of surgery which affects thousands of people worldwide. Between April 2009 and March 2010, there were 3,709 transplants and 2,021 donors in the UK (but some 8,000 were actively on the list awaiting transplant surgery – there is always a shortage of organs). Across the world, in 2005, 66,000 kidney transplants were performed, 60 per cent of which were in industrialised countries;

75 per cent of the more than 21,000 liver transplants and 6,000 heart transplants were performed in industrialised and emerging economies (UK Transplant, 2010; Transplant Observatory, 2007). Transplantation can also be seen as quintessentially postmodern: it challenges traditional views of what the body is and the boundaries of life and death are; it raises cyborg issues – of the links between bodies/nature and the world of technology.

Transplant surgery involves the surgical removal of a donor's organ (most commonly a kidney, liver, lung/heart, cornea, pancreas, etc.) which can be transplanted into a living (but usually very ill) person.

It involves at least three interconnected social worlds:

- the social worlds of the donors
- the social world of surgery
- the social worlds of the transplant patients

In the first, issues are raised of obtaining and procuring (just how the organs are to be obtained, and the impact on the donor's nearest and dearest). In the second, issues can be raised about the organisation of social networks embedded in transplant surgery (coordinators, surgeons, doctors, nurses, counsellors, social workers, administrators, educators working in hospitals, intensive care units, surgical operating

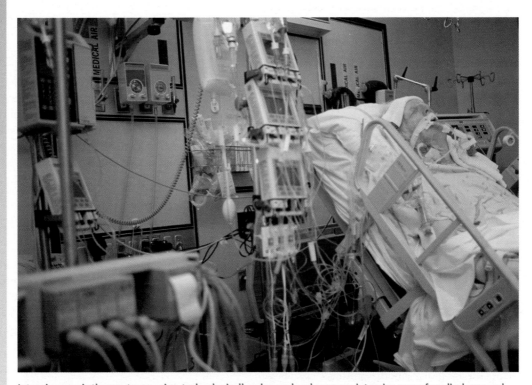

Intensive care is the most expensive, technologically advanced and resource-intensive area of medical care and suggests why health is now becoming so expensive in the twenty-first century. It can be traced back to the work of Florence Nightingale in the Crimean War in 1854 but the modern 'Urgency & Emergency' room started in the 1950s. Intensive care is an incredibly expensive healthcare service: in 2006, the average cost of funding an intensive care unit in the UK was £1,328 per bed per day for an Adult and £1,702 per bed per day for a child

Source: © Grafton Marshall Smith/Corbis.

LIVING IN THE C21ST

theatres and the like). And in the third, issues are raised about the 'careers' of patients – from being usually very ill people commonly confronting death to being almost 'rebirthed' through another's body part into a living person while living with 'death's shadow'.

Many sociological concerns are raised:

- The ways in which this 'body work' gets organised – through a gift relationship or a market relationship? Problems of scarcity and so on arise.
- The creation over the past 60 years or so of regimes of transplantation – just how did the routine works of transplantation come to be established in particular ways?
- The gathering of organs, along with some of the bad forms – from the Burke and Hare problem to modern trafficking of body parts

(Scheper-Hughes), from aggressive to domesticated.
- Social decision making: how to locate the moment of death (the brain dead, the cadavre, the social death, etc.).
- Cross-cultural variations.

See: Lesley A. Sharp, *Strange Harvest* (2006); Kieran Healy, *Last Best Gifts* (2006).

Observatory link: www.transplant-observatory.org. Global Knowledge Base link: www.who.int/transplantation/knowledgebase/en.

Death, dying and sociology

AIDS has brought the phenomenon of young people dying in the prime of their life to the fore. Throughout most of human history, confronting death has been commonplace. Until recently, no one assumed that a newborn child would live for long, and indeed this situation remains the case in most low-income societies of the world today. For those fortunate enough to survive infancy, illness prompted by poor nutrition, accidents and natural catastrophes such as drought or famine combine to make life uncertain, at best. Indeed, in times of great need, death was (and is) often deliberate, the result of a strategy to protect the majority by sacrificing a group's least productive members. *Infanticide* is the killing of newborn infants; *geronticide*, by contrast, is the killing of the elderly. If death was routine in the past, it was also readily accepted. Medieval Christianity assured Europeans, for example, that death fitted into the divine plan for human existence.

As some societies gradually gained control over many causes of death, death became less of an everyday occurrence. Fewer children died at birth, and accidents and disease took a smaller toll among adults. Except in times of war or catastrophe, people came to view dying as quite *extra*ordinary, except among the very old. In 1900, about one-third of all deaths in Europe occurred before the age of five, another third occurred before the age of 55, and the remaining one-third of men and women died in what was then defined as old age. By 1995, 85 per cent of our population died *after* the age of 55. Thus death and ageing have become fused in our culture: this has not always been so.

The modern separation of life and death

Sociologists have become increasingly interested in the sociology of death. If social conditions prepared our ancestors to accept their deaths, modern society, with its youth culture and aggressive medical technology, has fostered a desire for immortality, or eternal youth. In this sense, death has become separated from life.

Death is *physically* removed from everyday activities. The clearest evidence of this is that many of us have never seen a person die. While our ancestors typically died at home in the presence of family and friends, most deaths today occur in impersonal settings such as hospitals and nursing homes. Even hospitals commonly relegate dying patients to a special part of the building, and hospital morgues are located well out of sight of patients and visitors alike (Sudnow, 1967; Ariès, 1974).

Death and dying

Two of the first sociologists to study death were Barney Glaser and Anselm Strauss (1967). In the 1960s they conducted fieldwork in a hospital ward full of patients dying from cancer. Among their concerns were:

- *The learning of new roles and statuses as one moved towards death.* There was in fact a dying role with its own expectations.

- *The timing of death.* They examined the sequences around the death process and the stages through which the dying and their families and friends moved.

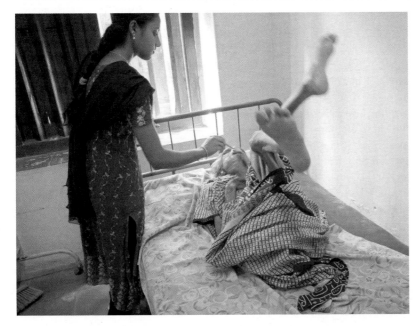

Aide feeding Madhavi at
Harmony House
Another one of Cathy Greenblat's
photos – see Chapter 3. Greenblat
uses Mother Theresa's observation
that 'we cannot do great things, only
little things with great love'.
Source: © Cathy Greenblat.

- *Awareness of dying*. They examined 'who knew what about the death' and this meant looking at a range of devices in which friends or families could sometimes be prevented from knowing about the possibility of death, and sometimes how even the patient could be misled.

- *Anguish*. The life history of one woman – Mrs Abel – dying of cancer.

The revival of death

Tony Walter (1994, 1998) has looked not just at death and dying, but also at the shifts in funeral patterns and bereavement. He asks some interesting questions. How, for example, does a country (say, the UK) each year care for half a million dying people, dispose of half a million corpses, manage more than half a million bereaved people and, depending on your point of view, help half a million souls on to the next life, not to mention represent all this in art, television and other media? Societies resolve these problems in very different ways and this is all part of the sociology of death and dying.

One of Walter's claims is that contemporary death is becoming more and more prominent. There was a period (for much of the twentieth century in the Western world) when death was hidden away from sight, but this is no more. He suggests that there are two strands to this process. One, which he calls a later modern strand, is driven by experts such as

Kübler-Ross (1969) and informs people how to cope with death. Thus Kübler-Ross famously takes us through five stages of dying. She claims that individuals initially react with *denial*, then swell with *anger*, try to *negotiate* a divine intervention, gradually fall into *resignation* and finally reach *acceptance*. Those who will grieve the loss of a significant person must also adjust to the approaching death.

According to some researchers, bereavement parallels the stages of dying described by Kübler-Ross. Those close to a dying person, for instance, may initially deny the reality of impending death, reaching the point of acceptance only in time. Many, however, question the validity of any linear 'stage theory', arguing that bereavement may not follow a rigid schedule. But all the experts agree that how family and friends view a death influences the attitudes of the person who is dying. Specifically, acceptance by others of the approaching death helps the dying person do the same. Denial of the impending death may isolate the dying person, who is then unable to share feelings and experiences with others.

One recent development intended to provide emotional and medical support to dying people is the *hospice*. Unlike hospitals, which are designed to cure disease, hospices help people have a 'good death'. These care centres work to minimise pain and suffering – either there or at home – and encourage family members to remain close by. Founded by Dame Cecily Saunders in 1967, there are now over 200 hospices in the UK (Lawton, 2000).

A postmodern strand of thinking about death has also developed. This suggests that dealing with death is increasingly driven by ordinary people, and allows for an enormous array of variety and difference in individual experiences of death. These days, for instance, people are much more likely to plan their own funerals, selecting music and sometimes pre-recording a speech, and people sometimes stipulate that mourners should follow their funerals with parties and even revelry. The traditions of the church funeral are also increasingly breaking down for some groups (Walter, 1994). Some of this started with the arrival of young men dying from AIDS-related illness throughout the 1980s. Here was the (tragic) sight of lots of young (generally gay) men dying. In their youthfulness, the old rituals and ceremonies just did not seem right.

Taking stock and looking ahead: health in the twenty-first century

To speak of illness at the end of the nineteenth century was to speak of deaths from infectious disease, which were widespread. Scientists had yet to develop basic antibiotics such as penicillin. Thus, even common infections represented a deadly threat to health. By the middle of the twentieth century it was a world dominated by doctors, hospitals, nurses and drugs. People started to take for granted that good health and long life were the rule – not the exception, as a century ago. Today, at the start of the twenty-first century, to talk of health conjures up a much wider range of images.

Another encouraging trend is public recognition that, to a significant extent, we can take responsibility for our own health (Caplow et al., 1991). Every one of us can live better and longer if we avoid tobacco, eat sensibly and in moderation, and exercise regularly.

The remission society

Part of the future will be the growing number of people who live in states which are neither wholly well nor wholly sick. These are the people living on medications, who function with transplants and prostheses of all kinds. We cannot see they are ill, and in some senses they are not, but they are dependent on technologies for their daily health. Arthur Frank (1995) calls this 'the remission society' and suggests that we are in need of new maps to shape our lives so that we can deal with this. He writes:

> These people are all around, though often invisible. A man standing behind me in the airport security check announces that he has a pacemaker; suddenly his invisible condition becomes an issue. Once past the metal detector, his 'remission' status disappears into the background.

(Frank, 1995: 8)

Continuing disease

Yet certain health problems will continue to plague society in the decades to come. Eating problems are fast coming to gain a significant focus. With no ultimate cure in sight, it seems likely that the AIDS epidemic will persist for some time. At this point, the only way to steer clear of contracting HIV is to make a personal decision to avoid any of the risky behaviours noted in this chapter.

The changing social profile of people with AIDS, which increasingly afflicts the poor in Africa and Asia, reminds us that health must be seen as a world issue. Even if Europe falls short in addressing the health of marginalised members of society, it also neglects the much wider devastations to be found in low-income societies. Problems of health are far greater in the poor societies of the world than they are in Europe. The good news is that life expectancy for the world as a whole has been rising – from 48 years in 1950 to 65 years today – and the biggest gains have been in poor countries (Mosley and Cowley, 1991). But in much of Latin America, Asia and especially in Africa, hundreds of millions of adults and children lack adequate food and safe water, and need medical attention. Improving health in the world's poorest societies remains a critical challenge in the twenty-first century.

SUMMARY

1 Health is a social as well as a biological issue, and well-being depends on the extent and distribution of a society's resources. Culture shapes both definitions of health and patterns of healthcare.

2 Through most of human history, health has been poor by today's standards. Health improved dramatically in western Europe and North America in the nineteenth century, first because industrialisation raised living standards and later as medical advances controlled infectious diseases.

3 Infectious diseases were the major killers at the beginning of the twentieth century. Today most people in Europe die in old age of heart disease, cancer or stroke.

4 Health in low-income countries is undermined by inadequate sanitation and hunger. Average life expectancy is about 20 years less than in Europe; in the poorest nations, half the children do not survive to adulthood.

5 In Europe, more than three-quarters of children born today can expect to live to at least age 65. Throughout the life course, however, people of high social position enjoy better health than the poor.

6 Cigarette smoking increased during the twentieth century to become the greatest preventable cause of death in Europe. Now that the health hazards of smoking are known, social tolerance for consumption of tobacco products is declining.

7 The incidence of sexually transmitted diseases has risen since 1960, an exception to the general decline in infectious disease.

8 Historically a family concern, healthcare is now the responsibility of trained specialists. The model of scientific medicine underlies the UK medical establishment.

9 Holistic healing encourages people to assume greater responsibility for their own health and well-being, and urges professional healers to gain personal knowledge of patients and their environment.

10 Socialist societies define medical care as a right that governments offer equally to everyone. Capitalist societies view medical care as a commodity to be purchased, although most capitalist governments support medical care through socialised medicine or national health insurance.

11 The United States, with a direct-fee system, is the only industrialised society that has no comprehensive medical care programme. Most people in the United States purchase private health insurance, government insurance or membership in a health maintenance organisation. One in six adults in the United States cannot afford to pay for medical care.

12 Functional analysis links health and medicine to other social structures. A concept central to functional analysis is the sick role, by which the ill person is excused from routine social responsibilities.

13 The symbolic-interaction paradigm investigates how health and medical treatments are largely matters of subjective perception and social definition. It researches medicine at work in everyday medical settings.

14 Conflict analysis focuses on the unequal distribution of health and medical care. It criticises the US medical establishment for relying too heavily on drugs and surgery, for giving free rein to the profit motive in medicine and for overemphasising the biological rather than the social causes of illness.

15 Two case studies of health issues and sociology are provided: AIDS and HIV, and death and dying.

CONNECT UP: Turn to Part 6 of this book for key resources and link up with the book's website, which links to these resources
SEE: www.pearsoned.co.uk/plummer

MYTASKLIST

Ten suggestions for going further

1 Connect up with Part Six and the Sociology Web Resources

As you work through ideas and think about the issues raised in this chapter, look at the accompanying website and the resource centre at the end of this book which connects to it. There is a lot here to help you move on. To link up, see: www.pearson.co.uk/plummer.

2 Review the chapter

Briefly summarise (in a paragraph) just what this chapter has been about. Consider: (a) What have you learned? (b) What do you disagree with? Be critical. And (c) How would you develop all this? How could you get more detail on matters that interest you?

3 Pose questions

(a) Compare the presentation of health and treatment in any two television programmes, such as *ER, House* and *Casualty*. What kind of sociological issues do they raise?

(b) In a global context, what are the 'diseases of poverty' that kill people in poor countries? What are the 'diseases of affluence', the leading killers in rich nations? Why are there such different patterns of disease?

(c) The United States health system is simultaneously seen as 'the best' and 'the worst' in the world. How can this be?

(d) Think of any health issue that interests you (cancer, multiple sclerosis, depression, disability, etc.) and consider how the issues raised in the chapter around AIDS and HIV could be applicable to these areas too. Discuss the ways in which matters such as gender, statistics, global politics, epidemiology and social movements may be key issues in the sociological study of health.

(e) Is the world of health and care undergoing radical transformations (which some might call the postmodernisation of health) in the twenty-first century?

4 Explore key words

Many concepts have been introduced in this chapter. You can review them from the website or from the listing at the back of this book. You might like to give special attention to just five words and think them through – how would you define them, what are they dealing with, and do they help you see the social world more clearly or not?

Good guides can be found in:

Jonathan Gabe, Mike Bury and Mary Ann Elston, *Key Concepts in Medical Sociology* (2004).

Kevin White, *The Sage Dictionary of Health and Society* (2005). This contains some 900 words commonly used in the health field, including global terms.

5 Search the Web

Be critical when you look at websites – see the box on p. 940 in the Resources section. For this chapter look at the following:

General

World Health Organization
www.who.int/home-page

UK Department of Health
www.dh.gov.uk/Home/fs/en

Euthanasia

International Task Force on Euthanasia and Assisted Suicide
www.internationaltaskforce.org/holland.htm

Materials and information on euthanasia in the Netherlands.

AIDS

UNAIDS
www.unaids.org

UNAIDS, the Joint United Nations Programme on HIV/AIDS, brings together the efforts and resources of ten UN system organisations for a global AIDS response.

On the pharmaceutical industry and AIDS, see: www.icaso.org
The website of the International Council of AIDS Service Organisations.

See also a series of activist reports from a leading New York AIDS campaigning organisation, ACT UP, available at: www.actupny.org/reports.

6 Watch a DVD

- Randa Haines' *The Doctor* (1991): a sick doctor changes his view on care.
- John McTiernan's *Medicine Man* (1992): ecology, medicine and romance in a South American rainforest.
- Fernando Mereilles's *The Constant Gardener* (2005): Nairobi conflict around pharmacy/corporate exploitation.
- Michael Moore's *Sicko* (2007): uses his usual style to attack the US health system.

Two very contrasting films on gay men and AIDS in the earlier years of the illness are:

- Gregg Araki's *The Living End* (1992): take a harrowing road trip with two dying HIV gay men.
- Norman Rene's *Longtime Companion* (1990): though it plays like a soap opera, this warm and compassionate film focuses on a group of friends on Fire Island and the emergence of AIDS in their community.

7 Think and read

Mildred Blaxter, *Health* (2004). A lively introduction to the whole field.

Sarah Nettleton, *The Sociology of Health and Illness* (2nd rev. edn, 2006) and Kevin White, *An Introduction to the Sociology of Health and Illness* (2nd edn, 2009) provide valuable textbook overviews.

Fernando de Maio, *Health and Social Theory* (2010). Delves into key health issues whilst integrating his research to key sociological theories.

Hilary Graham, *Unequal Lives: Health and Socioeconomic Inequalities* (2007). A must read on the inequalities of health.

The Alternative Health Report, Global Watch 2 (2008). A valuable critical analysis of global health issues.

Andy Miah and Emma Rich, *The Medicalization of Cyberspace* (2008). Provides a critical tour of the widespread move to 'cyberhealth'.

Although the above books have different emphases, they all provide excellent introductions to aspects of the sociology of medicine. On other topics, see:

Tony Barnett and Alan Whiteside, *AIDS in the Twenty-First Century: Disease and Globalization* (2nd edn, 2006).

Lesley Doyal, *What Makes Women Sick* (1995). The classic on women and health.

Susan Bordo, *Unbearable Weight: Feminism, Western Culture and the Body* (1993). A collection of papers around anorexia, eating disorders and the body, all written from a feminist perspective.

Glennys Howarth, *Death and Dying* (2007) and Clive Seale, *Constructing Death* (1998). Good introductions to the sociology of death, dying and bereavement.

8 Relax with a novel

To put some flesh on this chapter, it is useful to read some 'illness biographies'. These tell the non-medical stories of illness which are often so very different from the medical stories. There are many of these covering nearly all illnesses – see: Arthur Kleinmann, *The Illness Narratives: Suffering, Healing and the Human Condition* (1988).

Stories of being ill

Ann Oakley, *Fracture: Adventures of a Broken Body* (2007).

Audre Lorde, *The Cancer Journals* (1980).

Paul Monette, *Borrowed Times: An AIDS Memoir* (1988).

Jean-Dominique Bauby, *The Diving-Bell and the Butterfly* (2002/2008).

Arthur W. Frank, *The Renewal of Generosity: Illness, Medicine and How to Live* (2004).

Irving Zola, *Missing Pieces* (1982).

Arthur W. Frank, *At the Will of the Body: Reflections on Illness* (2002).

Virginia Woolf, *On Being Ill* (2002; orig. 1930).

9 Connect to other chapters

- Connect world health patterns to global inequalities (Chapter 9), urbanisation (Chapter 24) and environmental change (Chapter 25).
- Link health to social class (Chapter 10).
- Consider AIDS in relation to gender studies (Chapter 12) and low-income societies (Chapter 9).
- Connect health to the ageing process (Chapter 13).
- Link interactional health studies to classroom interactional studies (Chapter 19) and symbolic interactionism (Chapter 1).
- Link health with disability (Chapter 14).

10 Engage with THE BIG DEBATE

When is the right time to die? The 'right to die' debate

Because death struck at any time, often without warning, our ancestors would have found the question 'can people live too long?' to be absurd. But as increasing numbers of people live longer and longer, new questions arise about the best time and ways to die. One issue is the right of the elderly (and terminally ill) to die when they choose – the euthanasia debate. Another issue concerns the medical prolonging of life. While there is widespread support for using technology to prolong life, the high cost of nursing care for the elderly puts impossible burdens on the health service, prompting people to wonder how much old age we can now afford.

Recent decades, with a surge in the elderly population, have thus generated major new ethical debates. The question of how we die – by natural causes, self-inducement or physician-assisted death (PAD) – is on the worldwide agenda. And it is an issue that divides philosophers, doctors, ethicists, politicians and religious leaders around the world.

The Netherlands decision

In April 2001, the Netherlands became the first country in the world to legalise euthanasia, recognising a practice that had already been tolerated for over two decades. The Dutch (and some 90 per cent supported the law) believe legalising euthanasia will clear up a confused area of law which left doctors open to being prosecuted for murder. The US state of Oregon allows physician-assisted suicide, and Belgium passed euthanasia legislation in October 2001.

The new Dutch law insists that adult patients must have made a voluntary, well-considered and lasting request to die, that they must face a future of unbearable suffering and that there must be no reasonable alternative. A second doctor must be consulted and life must be ended in a medically appropriate way.

Euthanasia is possibly quite common – if covertly practised – in many other countries, and the Dutch argue that it is better to legislate than to leave it precariously practised 'underground'. There is now the worry, however, of 'death tourism' – people might travel to the Netherlands for help in finding euthanasia.

In some ways, the Dutch decision is a momentous one. While the new reproductive technologies give us a major control of birth, so now euthanasia has given us a major control over death.

In the same year in the UK, a 47-year-old woman with motor neurone disease received her doctor's assistance in easing her death, prompting a British Medical Association inquiry. Everywhere these issues are arriving on the agenda of public debate. And even though euthanasia is against the law in most countries, there are organisations developing which counsel the terminally ill into a 'peaceful and painless death'. The Swiss organisation Dignitas has seen some 146 people die since its inception in 1998, more than two-thirds of them foreigners.

The Hemlock Society

In the United States, Derek Humphrey is a founder and executive director of the Hemlock Society. Since 1980, this organisation has offered support and practical assistance to people who wish to die. Humphrey argues that the time has come for people to have straightforward information about how to end their own lives. Hence he published the book *Final Exit* in 1991 – a 'suicide, how to' manual that gives specific instructions for killing (swallowing sleeping pills, self-starvation, suffocation, etc.). It was an immediate and remarkably popular best-seller, especially among the elderly, suggesting that millions of people agree with him. Not surprisingly, when *Final Exit* was published, it sparked controversy. While supporters view the work as a humane effort to assist people who are painfully and terminally ill, critics claim that it encourages suicide by people who are experiencing only temporary depression. Yet the book has been translated into 12 languages, a second edition was released in 1997, and in 2000 a supplement was added to update some of the techniques!

The appearance of *Final Exit* also raises broader questions that are no less disturbing and controversial. Older people are, on the one hand, fearful of not being able to afford the medical care they may need and, on the other, alarmed at the prospect of losing control of their lives to a medical establishment that often seeks to prolong life at any cost. People of all ages worry whether the healthcare system can meet the escalating demands of seniors only by short-changing the young.

Against the spiralling costs of prolonging life, then, we may well have to ask if what is technically possible is necessarily socially desirable. In the new century, warns gerontologist Daniel Callahan (1987), a surging elderly population ready and eager to extend their lives will eventually force us either to 'pull the plug' on old age or to short-change everyone else. Raising this issue highlights the problem of priorities and selectivity in the health service. Callahan makes a bold case for limits. He reasons, first, that to spend more on behalf of the elderly we must spend less on others. With a serious problem of poverty among children, he asks, can we continue to direct more money towards the needs of the oldest members of our society at the expense of those just growing up?

Second, Callahan reminds us, a longer life does not necessarily make for a better life. Costs aside, does stressful heart surgery that may prolong the life of an 84-year-old person by a year or two truly improve their quality of life? Costs considered, would those resources yield more 'quality of life' if used, say, to transplant a kidney into a ten-year-old boy? Third, Callahan urges us to reconsider our notion of death. Today many people rage against death as an enemy to be conquered at all costs. Yet, he suggests, a sensible healthcare programme for an ageing society must acknowledge death as a natural end to the life course. If we cannot make peace with death for our own well-being, limited financial resources demand that we do so for the benefit of others (Callahan, 1987).

A compelling counterpoint, of course, is that those people who have worked all their lives to make our society what it is should, in their final years, enjoy society's generosity. Moreover, in light of our tradition of personal independence and responsibility, can we ethically deny an ageing individual medical care that this person is able and willing to pay for? What is clear from everyone's point of view is that, in the twenty-first century, we will face questions that few would have imagined even 50 years ago. Is optimum longevity good for everyone? Is it even possible for everyone?

Continue the debate

1 Should governments devise legislation to permit euthanasia? If yes, what safeguards need to be incorporated?

2 Evaluate the suggestion that doctors and hospitals should devise a double standard, offering more complete care to younger people but more limited care to society's oldest members.

3 Do you think we have a cultural avoidance of death that drives us to extend life at all costs?

4 Is the idea of rationing medical care really new? Hasn't our society historically done exactly this by allowing some people to amass more wealth than others?

CHAPTER 22

COMMUNICATION AND THE NEW MEDIA

SOCIOLOGIST KIRK JOHNSON spent some years in the small Indian village of Danawli, studying the impact of television. At the time of his research, some 25 of the 104 households in the village had TV sets. The elders of the village worried a great deal about the arrival of this new medium. One, for example, argued that *'TV is the devil . . . It has only caused us pain and is very bad for us.'* Another said: *'Television is ruining our culture . . . People no longer speak like they used to. They all, especially the young people, talk about the life in the cities or in England and America. They don't know anything about own history or traditions. I have heard some even talk about love marriage.'* Another said: *'Children used to come to hear the stories of olden days. Everyone used to listen to me. The young people today only want to watch television and movies and go to Panchgani until late at night'* (Johnson, 2000: 216 and 192).

But for many the television had broadened their horizons into the modern world. They saw a whole array of new experiences: different kinds of gender and class relations; different kinds of marriage and the 'desire for fewer children'; they saw the shift from success by heredity to achievement by merit and a change in the perception of caste relations. Television challenged the positions of traditional leaders. *'We have learned,'* says one man, *'that our leaders are corrupt, even the national leaders are corrupt. On TV they show us about how corrupt our parliament members are . . .'* (Johnson, 2000: 218).

Television promotes a greater receptiveness to new values and an openness to change. Many families may not have had TV in their home, but they would visit the homes of others to watch TV, and it had helped to bring some people together. New kinds of relationship are being formed, and this is particularly noticeable among the young and children.

Danawli reveals a transitional phase in the spread of television in rural India, and Kirk Johnson concludes that 'the one material commodity which has most dramatically influenced social change in rural India has been the television set' (Johnson, 2000: 15). Again, another older man speaks:

> There is no doubt about it. You can ask anyone. TV is the one thing that has most changed the way people live. You see how people watch TV. They are also so into TV that nothing else matters. The house could be burning down and no one would realise it. TV is very powerful. Our young people see things on the TV that we never saw, and this has changed the way they behave. They want everything they see. They are not satisfied any more with working the field and providing for the family.
>
> (Johnson, 2000: 213)

The Medium is the Message: it is the medium that shapes and controls the scale and form of human association and action.

Marshall McLuhan

In this chapter, we ask:

- **How has communication changed over time?**

- **How can we think about the way media work; what sorts of question can we ask?**

- **How has globalization changed the contemporary media?**

(Left) Max Ferguson, *News Vendor*, 1986
Max Ferguson's work paints a vanishing world, mainly in New York City. See his website at http://maxferguson.com.

See also: http://www.artnet.com/artist/155558/max-ferguson.html.

Source: News Vendor, 1986 (oil on panel), Ferguson, Max (Contemporary Artist)/Private Collection/The Bridgeman Art Library.

 Old media and new media? What does the image of the news vendor suggest?

The media age

This is the time of the media. Many of us live our lives increasingly in and through the media. We live what sociologists sometimes call mediated lives – lives immersed in the technologies of media communication. As we have seen (Chapter 1), it has been estimated that in 2010, young people in the USA spent at least seven hours a day hooked up to some kind of electronic communication (Pew Internet and American Life Project, 2010). Similarly, watching television is the most common home-based leisure activity for men and women in the UK. Virtually everyone watches it. Ninety-nine per cent of households in the UK own one television; 86 per cent have a video recorder, renting an average of ten films per year. But this is now almost an older technology: the arrival of digital communications – via websites, iPods, iPhones and iPads – has brought extensive and intensive changes to human social life. Between 1996/7 and 2005/6 the proportion of households owning a mobile

TV watching in outdoor public groups is very popular – as this group of Zambian Soccer fans shows
Source: © Gideon Mendel/Corbis.

phone shifted from 17 per cent to 79 per cent. DVD was launched in the UK in 1998 and has become the fastest-selling electronic format of all time – the numbers owning a DVD player grew from 31 per cent in 2002/03 to 79 per cent in 2005/6 – a growth of 48 per cent in three years. In 2010, 19.2 million households in the UK had internet access, or 73 per cent of households. This compares with 57 per cent in 2006, equivalent to 14.3 million households. Similar changes have been happening across the world. Note again, though, that the growth is unequal: in the UK, households in the highest 10 per cent income group were over three-and-a-half times as likely as those in the lowest 10 per cent to have an internet connection: 96 per cent of households compared with 26 per cent (*Social Trends*, 2010).

What is important about the new media technologies is the way in which they have come to play a prominent role in many aspects of our everyday lives. All the institutions discussed in this book have been changed by them. Political elections, for example, are geared up to television and the press; it is hard to imagine elections without the constant 'spin' and 'hype' in all the media. Likewise, religion has its 'televangelical' networks; and business and finance depend upon the new technologies for rapid information as well as a constant stream of advertising. And where would public events – sport or parliament or news – be if they were not relayed in our homes on television? Sports spectacles, from the Olympics and World Cups to golf and racing, depend on the television for their mass audiences.

Even the family has changed dramatically because of television. Until very recently, many homes had a TV centred in their living room, draped with family photos – symbolic of its importance. In the twentieth century, television gradually became a major part of everyday life, marking out family time and routines. It was the intimate machine, giving impressions of talking to you through chat programmes, advice programmes and close-up interviews with all kinds of people. The medium became friend and family. Indeed, much of what is shown on the screen actually depicts friends and families – the most popular programmes remain the 'soap operas', which are always about this (in the UK, *Coronation Street* has been running for over 50 years). But then we take to university or work all the details of the soap lives we have seen on TV and start to discuss them with friends. TV characters invade our lives as new friends. And the taste for 'reality television' over the past decade – from *Survivor* and *Big Brother* to *Strictly Come Dancing* and the *X Factor* – holds large

audiences for events that dissolve the boundaries between television and reality. This feature is brought home in films such as *The Truman Show*. Here a man is born on to a massive television set, becomes the focus of a major soap opera, and does not know it (till the end of the film, that is, when he breaks out of the programme to find his 'real' life). We are media saturated. Indeed, one commentator has tellingly remarked that:

> in one hour's television viewing, each one of us is likely to experience more images than a member of a non-industrial society would in a lifetime. The quantitative difference is so great as to become categorical; we do not just experience more images, but we live with a completely different relationship between the image and other orders of experience.

(Fiske, 1991: 58)

But now, of course, it has gone much further than just television. As we have seen throughout this book, the twenty-first century has now become the digital, networking and information age. Television is slowly receding into the corner for many, and the new digital technologies are taking over and reshaping life again. As we saw earlier, the Spanish sociologist, Manuel Castells, has argued that 'new information technologies are transforming the way we produce, consume, manage, live and die' (Castells, 1989: 15; see also Chapter 6, p. 200). In this chapter, we will look at some aspects of how our modern mass media system developed and examine some of the theories that have tried to explain how it works. We will show how media research needs to look at what media messages contain, how media messages are made and how they are understood by their audiences. Finally, we will glimpse their importance in the new century, as the media become increasingly globalised. (In the next chapter we will say more about the new digital media.)

Communications and social change

The history of societies can partially be written as the history of media communications. We have seen in Chapter 4 how social life changed between hunting and gathering societies and industrial society, and how technology is one guiding feature of social change. Technology can do nothing in itself: it takes people to act on the media to bring about change. But without the media themselves, no change would be possible. What we can see is direct one-to-one, face-to-face communication developing into the **mass media**, *any social or technological devices used for the selection, transmission or reception of information.*

One aspect of that technology is the means of communication. As the means of communication change, so do social lives. The major developments in human culture and consciousness are linked to changes in our modes of communication – the evolution from words and primitive speech through writing to typeface and now modern electronic worlds (Ong, 1982).

Our focus here is not upon the content of the media but on their form. In a famous phrase, US media guru Marshall McLuhan proclaimed that *The Medium is the Message* (McLuhan, 1964). What he meant by this is that independently of what is being said, it is the kind of 'medium which shapes and controls the scale of human association and action'. McLuhan sees the history of media as falling into three major periods. The first is an oral culture, where the ear is the important sense. Listening to the words is a harmonious, circular way of thought. The second is the writing and printing culture, where 'the ear' is exchanged for 'the eye'. It brings more linear thought. The third is the electronic culture. And here the media bring radical shifts again.

Consider Table 22.1, which outlines the evolution of the main forms of communication in society. We can return to our image of the world's history scaled to a 24-hour clock starting at midnight and continuing till the next midnight, introduced in Chapter 5. Here, speech is invented around 9.30 in the evening. Writing is not invented till about 8 minutes before midnight. Electronic devices appear some 11 seconds, and digital electronics 2 seconds, before the clock strikes midnight (Neuman, 1991: 7). The *Timeline* box gives some landmarks in media history.

Oral cultures

For most of our history, then, societies have been entirely dependent upon face-to-face grunts.

Table 22.1	Stages in the development of human communication	
1	The Age of Signs	No speech or writing, only sounds and bodily gestures. Maybe 70 million years ago?
2	The Age of Speech	Oral cultures, pre-literate, started to appear at most 100,000 years ago. Cro-Magnon and other prehistoric cultures. Linguists can identify around 50 prehistoric vocabularies.
3	The Age of Writing	Writing started to appear around 5,000 years ago. Sumerians, Egyptian civilisation, Turkey, Iraq, Iran. Initially pictographs, hieroglyphics, clay tablets. Later papyrus – a light and portable medium. Alphabets slowly replaced images and songs, and this promoted linear, rational and abstract thought. Problems of censorship started to appear. Chirography – or manuscripts – became the main form in the Middle Ages.
4	The Age of Print	First printing press in West c. 1445–56 (printing appeared in China nearly 800 years earlier). Gutenberg published Bible. Greatly amplified reach and impact of alphabet. Media censorship by church. Typography dominated. Printing speeded up with the Industrial Revolution.
5	The Age of Electronics	Electrical and electronic media, from late nineteenth century. Emergence of photography. Rise of recorded music. The Cinema Century.
6	The Information Age	Digital, high-tech, computing: games playing, mobile phones, iPods, iPhones and iPads.

Timeline Some modern landmarks in media history

1456	Gutenberg Press: printing of first book (The Bible) in Western world (but evidence of printing in China some 800 years earlier).
17th century	***Press started to develop***
1620–1	Corantos (news sheets) in Holland reporting (with King's authority) on wars.
1665	Oxford – court news (later *London Gazette*).
1690	First American newspaper reporting on colonies.
1785	*The Times* first published, followed by *The Observer* in 1791.
1838	*The Times* of India founded. Morse code invented.
1839	First photographs and sales of Daguerrotype camera.
19th century	Many of today's newspapers started in mid-19th century: *News of the World* in 1843, *The Daily Telegraph* in 1855 (when stamp duties were abolished). *The Daily Mail* was the first million-selling mass circulation newspaper.
1876	Alexander Graham Bell initiated the telephone.
1877	Edison patented the phonograph; first replayable recordings.
1891	Kinematography and 'peep scopes' arrived.
1896	First permanent cinema: 400-seater Vuitascope Hall, New Orleans.
20th century	In late 1890s and 1900s, short films like *How Bridget Served the Salad Undressed* and in 1903 *The Great Train Robbery*.
1910	Nickelodeon – some 10,000 family-orientated exhibition halls existed in the United States.
1915	*Birth of a Nation*: first 'major' film.
1921	First US radio station: KDKA Pittsburgh.
1922	Radio arrived in Britain with the British Broadcasting Company.
1926	50 million people per week went to the movies in the United States.
1936	Television arrived in Britain at Alexandra Palace, for a small audience; but with the onset of the Second World War was not fully developed until the 1950s. ITV came in 1955; BBC2 in 1962; Channel 4 in 1982; Channel 5 in 1997.
1950	UNIVAC (Universal Automatic Computer): first mass-produced computer.
1952	First video recorder demonstration in United States.
1960s	Emergence of internet through US Department of Defense; development of global satellite communications.
1967	First local BBC; first colour TV in UK.
1971	First successful video game reached United States arcades.
Early 1970s	Early development of optical fibre systems of communication.
1981	MTV first televised (started in United States on 1 August 1981). Developed like a radio station, always on the air, appealing to same market niche; VCR became widespread.
1985	First 'multiplex' cinema in the UK (The Point in Milton Keynes).
1992	Internet took off.
1995	'Privatised Cyberspace': internet became commercial when United States government pulled out; first commercial DVDs appeared.
1999	Rapid increase in usage of DVDs.
1990s	Rapid expansion of cell/mobile phones and their development as all-purpose means of communication.
21st century	The routinisation of hi-technologies globally. Mobile phones, digitalisation, laptops, MP3, iPods, iPads, etc. ubiquitous.

Language and speech only started to appear with more sophisticated societies, about 100,000 years ago. These were oral cultures, and culture here depended a great deal upon the ability to remember and to tell stories that were passed on from generation to generation. Without such stories, cultures and knowledge would have died out. Certainly, these were 'slow societies' where not a great deal could be retained. For continuity, memory must have been vital. And stories played a crucial role.

Writing cultures

Significant changes started to happen when the spoken word was written down. This depended upon first, a written language system – an alphabet or code of some kind – and second, a means for writing and an object to write upon. Oral cultures depend upon memory. Poetry and stories became very important in trying to pass on from generation to generation a sense of continuing culture. But writing makes it much easier to pass on this history.

And such a form will depend upon an alphabet or other system of writing. In China, some time around 3,000 years ago, a writing system developed with some 50,000 characters! And with this emerged an elite who could master it: the mandarins. Phonetic alphabets, based on sounds, are more recent and mark a major advance in ease of use.

In some ancient civilisations, writing was carved on stone, which was not at all easily transportable. Stone drawings are hard to change or revise – this medium therefore makes for relatively unchanging and stable societies. In Egypt, the dominance of stone as a medium gave a monopoly to those who owned it. But once papyrus was introduced, it played a major role in communication becoming more flexible.

The next major change came when the churches started to develop significant manuscript writings. The medieval church had a monopoly over religious and all other information, which was controlled in manuscripts by a special class of priests. Again, these were far from available to most people.

Print cultures

And so we reach a time, just a few hundred years ago, when the method of print was invented. This was truly a revolution. Now the control of the elite church's scribes could be bypassed, because for the first time in history there arose the possibility that large numbers of

people could become literate (able to read and write). This brought with it:

- an ability to store and transmit culture much more readily
- the potential to include those people previously excluded from knowledge
- a potentially different way of thinking in which the person 'engages' with a text rather than another person
- the potential for mass culture, mass society and mass education
- the development of new minds in which literate modes of thought become part of our everyday consciousness
- a new sense of 'authorship' and control over the text.

Despite the slow spreading of print, it was really only in the nineteenth century – with the birth of mass newspapers – that whole societies started to become literate (see Table 22.2). And at the same time, a mass education system was required to equip people for the new social order (see Chapter 20). Again, it was also a means of excluding people. There were constant fears of how this new literacy was 'dangerous'.

Electronic cultures

With the new electronic media, our experiences are no longer limited by where or who we are. Media, and especially television, weaken the strong sense we used to have of being in a place. Limited confines such as the family home, the office or the prison are now invaded by the television, which starts to shift the boundaries of how we experience the world.

In an important study, *No Sense of Place*, Joshua Meyrowitz (1986) looks at how the pattern of information flow changes with television. With television we 'eavesdrop' on a host of different worlds. We can gain access to worlds that in the past were not accessible. Thus, for example, children's worlds and adults' worlds, men's worlds and women's worlds could in the past be kept separate. There were things that adults could talk about when children had gone to bed; things that men could talk about when women were not there. But television cuts out these separate spaces. We now inhabit 'no sense of place'. Our sense of place has changed.

Television weakens the traditional distinction between physical place and social situations. Public spheres now enter the living room; public and private get blurred. Television has changed our way of

Table 22.2	Readership of national daily newspapers in Great Britain, 1971–2009 (%)[1]					
	1971	1978	1981	1991	2001	2009
Sun	17	29	26	22	20	16
Daily Mail	12	13	12	10	12	10
Daily Mirror	34	28	25	22	12	7
Daily Telegraph	9	8	8	6	5	4
The Times	3	2	2	2	3	4
Daily Express	24	16	14	8	4	3
Daily Star	.	.	9	6	3	3
Guardian	3	2	3	3	2	2
Independent	.	.	.	2	1	1
Financial Times	2	2	2	2	1	1
Any national daily newspaper[2]	.	72	72	62	53	42

[1] In the 12 months to June each year. Proportion of adults aged 15 and over who have read or looked at the individual newspaper for at least two minutes on the day before interview.
[2] Includes the above newspapers and *The Daily Record* in 1981, and *The Sporting Life* and the *Racing Post* in 2001 and 2009.

Source: *National Readership Survey* in *Social Trends*, 40 (2010), Table 13.6, p. 189.

Studying micro-media in the world of Goths

The methods of contemporary sociology are less and less dependent upon standard interviews and questionnaires. Access to new media forms has changed all that. Recent work on youth styles, for example, has looked at the significance of such new media in the creation of youth and club cultures. While there may be dominant media forms, club cultures and the like develop their own niche media – in the form of music and style magazines – and micro-media. Thornton defines the latter as: 'Flyers, fanzines, flyposters, listings, telephone information lines, pirate radio, e-mailing lists and internet archive sites . . . an array of media from the most rudimentary of print forms to the latest in digital interactive technologies are the low circulating narrowly targeted micro-media' (Thornton, 1995: 137).

In his research on Goths, Paul Hodkinson (2002) employs a

People often think that the sociological method is about interviewing. But there are many other tools of research – and many new ones in the making. Here are some 'fanzines' that were used in Paul Hodkinson's study of Goths. They tell a great deal about the lifestyles and cultures of Goths

Source: © S. L. Hodkinson.

range of research methods, from interviewing and observation to questionnaires and media analysis. He looks, for instance, at various Goth fanzines, analysing their content but also interviewing the producers and readers about them. Fanzines are local, they are not circulated widely, they have no mass distribution. Instead, they are picked up at concerts and have widely dispersed markets. What they do is help construct the values of the Goth scene, creating shared identities.

Fanzines can be very influential. As one interviewee puts it:

> J (female): It has a big role because it's a central point for all the reviews, gig dates, current interviews, where people discover who they like and who they don't. You have to be careful what you put in because to a certain extent you can influence the gothic community as a whole . . . You're in a position where you have a bit of power I guess.
>
> (Hodkinson, 2002: 168)

In addition, Paul Hodkinson looked at Goth websites. Here there were 'pages and pages of relevant sites' (2002: 176). Many Goths had their own home pages and most pages brought with them a cluster of further links. A key aspect of all this was the availability of Goth discussion groups. Groups such as the early *alt.gothic* and *uk.people.gothic* not only attracted local Goths but enhanced worldwide participation.

Consider the use of these new media in your own researches.

experiencing the world because it has changed what we know about everything. Television parades before us an array of differences: men can learn about women, children about adult worlds, heterosexuals about gays, whites about blacks, the poor about the rich, the mass about the elite (Meyrowitz, 1986). In earlier times, they could have been kept in separate spheres.

But electronic cultures are now extending way beyond this. Not only do we spend more and more time talking about and living around various media (television, video, DVD), we are shifting our ways of relating, making the PC, the laptop, the mobile phone, text messaging and the full range of new communications from twitter to YouTube more and more central to our lives. We have seen from Chapter 1 onwards (see the box on p. 24) and in almost every chapter of this book that new technologies are shifting the ways in which we live (for example, in Chapter 7, pp. 226–7; in Chapter 23, pp. 814–18). We now have mediated friends and mediated lives – coming to find our lives in and though the vast array of media communications available to us. We talk to friends and pick up new friends through the media. We watch the media and learn about celebrities. You may like to consider the role of new celebrities and what role they play in your life (see *Living in the twenty-first century*).

Living with a celebrity culture: from Princess Diana to Michael Jackson

The celebrity is a person who is well known for their well knowness.

(Daniel Boorstin, *The Image*, 1961: 58)

The deaths of Michael Jackson (in June 2009) and Princess Diana (31 August 1997) led to mass public displays of affection across the world. Over a million people lined the four-mile route from Kensington Palace to Westminster Abbey for Diana and there was global television coverage. But many seemingly less prominent celebrities also attract much attention. Until 150 years ago, it was unlikely that we could have many 'celebrities' or stars – if any. But now we live in celebrity times. This is the age of the superstar. We search out the X factor or the winner of *Big Brother*, award endless glittering 'prizes' – for music and sport, for books and philanthropy. Celebrities are found everywhere – in magazines, press, the news and current affairs, on television, in reality TV, and increasingly in the world of webcam culture (the first, long defunct, being the JenniCam (1996)). We can now become a celebrity overnight with the help of YouTube, Twitter or a blog. And often for the most banal reasons.

For some, this celebrity culture suggests the rise of extraordinary people with extraordinary talents whom we can admire: they excel in sport, have wonderful singing voices, write great novels, do great deeds. For others, it is mere sensationalism – another sign of a 'here today, gone tomorrow' society with a low attention span and a passion for simple momentary heroes.

And sociologists have started to research and ask questions about celebrities in contemporary cultures. They see celebrities as mass media constructs and ask how these come about and what effects they have. Celebrities are cultural forms which serve certain key functions. Sociologists examine how such celebrities are constructed; they develop typologies of celebrities; they ask about the functions they perform in a society. They examine fan cultures and the audiences they create. And they see new forms of 'mediated relationships' in which the media and their celebrities come to play significant roles in our personal lives.

One simple distinction to draw is between the celebrity who is *ascribed* their position (by blood: for example, royalty), one who *achieves* it (for example, in a sports competition) and one who derives it from certain attributes – for example, as a TV personality. For their fame to be developed, they will always need the work of a host of media workers – journalists, photographers, 'publicists'.

Celebrities perform a number of key functions in the modern world. They:

- provide role models and new identities (e.g. sports stars become someone to look up to)

- become scapegoats (someone to hate or blame)
- establish dialogues (the celebrity leads to public debate)
- create new emotional bondings and attachments through which we live our lives – they become our new 'intimate friends'
- facilitate 'parasocial interaction': a one-sided interaction where one person knows a lot about another, who knows nothing about them, which appeals to those who experience loneliness and shyness.

See: Graeme Turner, *Understanding Celebrity* (2004).

The twentieth century: harbinger of new media

In this section, we briefly trace some of the media developments over the past hundred years.

The century of film

The twentieth century has been called the century of film. Certainly it was born, grew rapidly across the world and became a dominant form of culture and entertainment during this time. Depositing millions of films of all genres in its wake, the twentieth century also produced a massive worldwide industry.

The film industry came into being through a complex interaction of inventions, and the first movie audience was created in 1895. Initially, the focus was on simple observations, but they soon blossomed into much more complex (but black and white and silent) films that attracted huge crowds (films like D. W. Griffiths' *Intolerance* and the Charlie Chaplin comedies). Sound was invented around 1927 (with Al Johnson in *The Singing Fool*). Colour followed, but did not become widespread until the 1950s. It was an international phenomenon – Germany, France, the UK, India, Russia and Latin America all became major film-makers. Nevertheless, from the 1920s onwards,

Hollywood became dominant. Today the dominant film-making countries are the USA, Japan, South Korea, Hong Kong and India.

In the 1970s, the 'blockbuster' appeared, a film which attracted huge crowds on its opening, achieved massive publicity, developed a merchandise empire around it and 'broke all box office records'. Stephen Spielberg's *Jaws* was probably the very first such blockbuster (in 1975), but it was soon followed by George Lucas's *Star Wars* (1977). Nowadays these 'blockbusters' are a major staple of the American film industry and they have a global impact. They also come in multiples: The *Harry Potter* series, the *Pirates of the Caribbean* series. They need to have a broad family appeal, and must especially appeal to children and teenagers – the largest cinema-going populations.

The top grossing films globally of all time (as of June 2010) are shown in the *Top 10* box. Note that not too much store should be put on these statistics. All amounts are in US dollars and only include theatrical box office receipts (movie ticket sales); they do not include video rentals, television rights and other revenues. Totals may include theatrical re-release receipts. Figures are not adjusted for inflation. The tendency is for this list to become simply a list of recent popular children's films, which tells little about the wider and more complex film industry. *Gone With the Wind*, which was the first major box office runaway success when it was shown in 1939, and which for three

TOP 10
All-time worldwide box office hits, 2010

		Receipts
1	*Avatar* (2009)	$2,734,434,950
2	*Titanic* (1997)	$1,835,300,000
3	*The Lord of the Rings: The Return of the King* (2003)	$1,129,219,252
4	*Pirates of the Caribbean: Dead Man's Chest* (2006)	$1,060,332,628
5	*Alice in Wonderland* (2010)	$1,019,689,394
6	*The Dark Knight* (2008)	$1,001,921,825
7	*Harry Potter and the Philosopher's Stone* (2001)	$968,657,891
8	*Pirates of the Caribbean: At World's End* (2007)	$958,404,152
9	*Harry Potter and the Order of the Phoenix* (2007)	$937,000,866
10	*Harry Potter and the Half-Blood Prince* (2009)	$933,956,98

Source: IMDb, the Internet Movie Database.

decades was seen as the top grossing film, now comes in at position 122 (with a gross income of $390,500,000. All these films are from the USA, even though this is a (non-US) world listing, which suggests something of the global power of the American hegemony.

Broadcasting and television

Broadcasting began life as a 'wireless' version of the telephone. In 1924, in the UK, the British Broadcasting Company (with Lord John Reith at its helm) was licensed by the Post Office to function as a monopoly. Reith saw that the BBC should have a role as 'a trustee of the national interest' and defender of middle-class Christian standards. The aims of the BBC were 'to educate, inform and entertain' (Reith, 1924). The historian Asa Briggs has summarised the BBC as displaying four key characteristics: its programming is for public good, not profit; it should provide a 'national' coverage for a community of the 'British';

Bollywood and the diaspora

The Indian film industry is the largest in the world and one of the oldest. In 2010, it was worth about US$1,256 million and nearly one thousand films are produced every year. India's film industry is the largest in the world, both in number of movies produced and in tickets sold. This Hindi film industry is based in Mumbai (Bombay). Much of the music industry is also based in Mumbai.

The film industry fragments into many different forms – from the highbrow and much esteemed films of the intelligentsia, such as the 1950s 'Apu Trilogy' of Satyajit Ray (1921–92), through to a very widespread, popular form which deals with key elements of romance, passion and music in lush settings – they are

(right) Posters for Bollywood films, Bombay, India

Source: Corbis © Catherine Karnow.

melodramatic and romantic musicals. This has come to be known as Bollywood (though the Indian film industry predates Hollywood and the first silent feature was made in 1913; maybe Hollywood should be renamed Mumbiwood?). They are available worldwide on DVDs, and they have spawned a large culture and spin-off industry: music albums, international film magazines, worldwide websites, Bollywood stars and celebrities. A 'Bollywood' stage musical *Bombay Dreams* (featuring the lives of Mumbai castrati) opened with moderate success in London in 2002, and in New York in 2004.

In their earliest manifestations, Bollywood films were simply romantic stories of traditional Indian life with music; they grew into lavish romantic musicals. In their more recent manifestations they have become influenced by Western images, music and dance. As Indians have migrated around the world, they have established the Indian film as a major worldwide genre with world appeal. The films are popular in Nigeria, Egypt and Zanzibar. Birmingham in England hosts the 'Bollywood Oscars'. It is estimated that at least 11 million Indian people have migrated around the world, and this diaspora has added to the global impact of these films.

Once the films were watched on large screens in open spaces in small villages (see the opening story to this chapter) and in tattered old cinemas. But as India becomes more and more economically successful, so the films are increasingly shown in Indian multiplexes.

The films have also generated their own UK spin-offs: films like *East is East* (1999) and *Bend it like Beckham* (2002) play jokes with some of the Bollywood forms; in their turn, Bollywood made *Bride and Prejudice*.

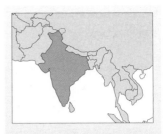

COUNTRY FACT FILE

INDIA

Population	1,156.9 million
Per capita GDP	$3100
Life expectancy	65.13 male
	67.13 female
Adult literacy	61%
Key languages	Hindi 41%,
	Bengali 8.1%
Key religions	Hindu 80.5%,
	Muslim 13.4%
Key city	New Delhi
Human development index	0.519 (119th, 2010)

In all of this we can see postmodern capitalist hybridic media worlds at work.

Source: Rajinder Kumar Dudrah, *Bollywood: Sociology goes to the Movies* (2006).

it should be a monopoly; and it should always provide high moral standards (Briggs, 1961). The BBC came to be seen as part of the 'establishment', embodying the values and power of the dominant class.

After the Second World War, new stations like the 'Third', the 'Light' and the 'Home Services' appeared under the aegis of the BBC, suggesting differences in audience and catering to different classes. The late 1950s and the 1960s brought 'pirate broadcasting' (Radio Luxembourg and offshore broadcasting, which challenged the dominance of the BBC) as well as a more critical and satirical approach to broadcasting that challenged the dominance of Reith's earlier goals. In 1967, it was reorganised (as Radios One, Two, Three and Four) and new commercial services were increasingly facilitated.

Early days of the media which now, a hundred years on, have come to pervade everyday life across the world

Sources: Pearson Education Ltd/Photodisc; Pearson Education Ltd/C Squared Studios/ Tony Gable; Pearson Eduction Ltd/ Photodisc/C Squared Studios.

Timeline Landmarks of British TV, 1990–2010

1990	Opening of British Satellite Broadcasting (BSB).
1990	Sky and BSB merged to form BSkyB.
1997	Start of Channel 5.
1998	Digital satellite service started.
1998	Digital terrestrial service started, including widescreen broadcasts.
2001	BBC's first digital interactive programme.
2002	Opening of Freeview digital terrestrial service.
2003	Regulation of commercial TV passes to Ofcom following merger of ITC with other regulatory bodies.
2004	BBC Chairman of Governors and Director General both resigned in wake of Hutton Report.
2004	Merger of Granada and Carlton completed. Merged company called ITV plc.
2006	Start of high definition service.
2007	First analogue switch-off: BBC2 signal at Whitehaven, Cumbria.

Source: Adapted from British TV History, Landmark Dates: http://www.tvhistory.btinternet.co.uk/html/landmark.html.

Television started in the UK in 1936 with the BBC in London but was relatively underdeveloped when the Second World War intervened. It was given a boost by the televising of the coronation of Queen Elizabeth in 1953. Independent television with advertising also arrived, with initially an eight-year franchise. In the USA cable started in 1950 (with 625 resolutions for screens) and colour began in 1953. In 1962, Telstar was launched as the first television satellite. Video appeared in 1965, and became popular in the late 1970s and early 1980s (by 2007, it had almost become obsolete). In 1976 the first flat-screen LCD television appeared. The *Timeline* box shows its more recent history.

Creating popular music recordings

Until the late nineteenth century, most music was live: it played out in small community events, 'bourgeois homes' and, by the eighteenth century, a growing number of theatres and concert halls. But as modern forms of communication started to appear during the nineteenth century, so mediated music became increasingly common. Music popular for its time became 'pop music', and became available first in sheet form and later in electrically recorded forms. The initial recordings appeared at the end of the nineteenth century, but only spread out into the wider Western culture through gramophones and 78 r.p.m. records in the 1920s and onwards. In the 1950s the records technology (their production and the means of playing them) shifted first into vinyl long-playing records (less easy to break and containing much more sound), and then into the relatively short-lived tape. The 1980s and 1990s saw new developments with compact discs (CDs), personal stereo systems and television channels such as MTV. A key time in the development of the music industry was in the post-Second World War period (the 1950s). The pop 'charts' were introduced in 1952, but they had more or less died by 2007 when record sales slumped, musical forms were recognised as very fragmented, and 'play lists' and the iPod had developed.

Musical forms can be traced through an array of genres: jazz, operetta, blues, film scores, song and dance routines, music hall, the dance bands era, crooning, cabaret and 'war songs'. Recently, they have proliferated further: to rock and roll, ballads, reggae, punk, heavy metal, rap, indie, house and 'boy bands'. As the world became more diversified, so too did its musical forms. Although certain stars and music forms dominate the contemporary market, it is now open to a wide range of niche markets – even the young of today can become fans of the Beatles or Elvis from 50 years ago, or the crooner Bing Crosby from nearly 80 years ago. It is the age of a paradoxical mass culture where everyone both listens to the same music and a highly differentiated niche market catering to smaller and smaller groupings. This shift in consumption has generally been called 'the long tail' (Anderson, 2007).

The growth of digital music

As widespread downloading of music from the internet and the growth of iPod/MP3 technology developed, major changes were needed in the music industry. Eight million people are said to have downloaded illegally in 2004, and annual global music sales started to fall. But the digital music business has continued to expand. In 2008 it had an estimated trade value of some US$3.7 billion – and growing. Recorded music is at the forefront of the online and mobile revolution, generating huge revenue through digital platforms (in percentage terms it is bigger than the newspaper, magazine and film industries combined). Music consumption is becoming far more ubiquitous as companies are expanding and diversifying.

tip To read about the latest issues on the music industry, download the Annual Report of IFPI (International Federation of the Phonographic Industry), which represents the recording industry worldwide with some 1,400 members in 66 countries and affiliated industry associations in 45 countries. See: www.ifpi.org.

New styles of communications in the twenty-first century

While cinema, television and radio were dominant forms of media in the twentieth century, there are distinct signs of major communication shifts taking place at the start of the twenty-first century that could have radical consequences for social life. As we have seen, mobile phones are now ubiquitous, and have made texting, emailing, photographing, games, audio listening, and film watching something which can now be small, portable and very personal – designer-matched for clothes and lifestyles. IPhones and iPads have become a central accessory for parts of the twenty-first-century world. We have also already seen in Chapter 7 some of the ways in which this is changing our relationships (see pp. 226–7). Table 22.3 suggests some of the key ways in which new and old media differ. We have also seen just how extensive is the penetration of the internet globally. By 2010, nearly 29 per cent of world population (2 billion people) were using the internet. Recent growth has been highest in Africa, the Middle East and Latin America; there are over a billion internet users in developing countries (one-third of these are in China).

Gaming cultures, YouTube and new entertainment

With the development of new media technologies, new forms of entertainment have also emerged. For example, YouTube, a video-sharing website on which users can upload, share and view videos was formed early in 2005 but by 2010 it claimed to have over 2 billion views a day.

Gaming is another part of the new entertainment world – but has a much longer history. The widespread growth of gaming and gaming cultures have become a key pastime in many countries round the world, initially amongst the young but now across a wider range of ages.

In the UK, 75 per cent of those aged 8 to 11 and 68 per cent of those aged 12 to 15 use the internet to play games (*Social Trends*, 2007: 173). In the 12 months to the end of September 2009, £1.73 billion was spent on video games, according to the data company GFK Chart-Track. The number of games consoles being used in Britain has shot up from 13.5 million in 2008 to well over 25 million in 2010, with enough consoles for nine out of every ten households in the country to have one. Globally, it is reckoned to be a $25 billion industry.

Gaming can be traced through several generations back to the 1940s and 1950s. Periods are often divided into the kinds of platform used: arcade, mainframe, console, personal computer and handheld game. By the 1970s, gaming was to be found in arcades and public places. Soon hand-held games and consoles started to take over; and more recently it has been developed through both the internet and easy downloading on to mobile phones and iPads. The first commercially viable video game was Computer Space in 1971, which laid the foundation for a new entertainment industry in the late 1970s. Arcade games, although still relatively popular in the early 1990s, begin a decline as home consoles became more common. PaRappa the Rapper popularised rhythm or music video games in Japan with its 1996 debut on the PlayStation. Subsequent music and dance games like beatmania and Dance Dance Revolution became ubiquitous attractions in Japanese arcades. Mortal Kombat, released on both SNES and Genesis consoles, was one of the most popular game franchises of its time. In 2009, *Call of*

Table 22.3	The movement from old media to new media
The old media technologies	**The new media technologies**
Analog	Digital
Corporation based	More and more 'networked'
Separate media (e.g. print, computing, photos)	All media converge (e.g. through the iPhone)
Separate professions	Increased DIY and blogging
Live and lived culture	'Virtual' culture

Source: Based on Flew (2007).

Duty: Modern Warfare 2, was considered the fastest-selling game in history (selling more than 1.2 million units in just 24 hours); it was attacked for encouraging violent behaviour. In 2010, the top console/hand-held games were Wii Play (Wii – 27.38 million), New Super Mario Bros (DS – 24.13 million), Mario Kart Wii (Wii – 24.01 million), Nintendogs (DS – 23.26 million) and Wii Fit (Wii – 22.61 million).

Gaming cultures are part of a new integrated world of entertainment where the differing media converge with each other – video links with YouTube, films with video, music with phones, network groups with photos, books with iPads and Kindles. It becomes difficult to maintain the borders of media that were possible in the twentieth century. Table 22.4 shows the top-selling media in 2009 (note how significant the games culture is).

Table 22.4	The Entertainment Chart 2009					
Overall position	Sector	Position in sector chart	Title	Artist	Company	2009 sales total
1	Game	1	Call of Duty: Modern Warfare 2		Activision Blizzard	2,926,637
2	Video	1	Harry Potter & The Half Blood Prince		Warner Home Video	2,193,700
3	Game	2	FIFA 10		Electronic Arts	2,155,697
4	Video	2	Quantum of Solace		20th Century Fox	2,040,229
5	Video	3	Twilight		E1 Entertainment	1,815,543
6	Album	1	I Dreamed a Dream	Susan Boyle	Sony Music	1,714,369
7	Game	3	Wii Sports Resort		Nintendo	1,488,797
8	Album	2	The Fame	Lady Gaga	Universal Music	1,458,289
9	Video	4	Slumdog Millionaire		20th Century Fox	1,383,838
10	Video	5	Transformers – Revenge of the Fallen		Paramount	1,362,020
11	Video	6	Micheal McIntyre – Hello Wembley		Universal Pictures	1,286,863
12	Album	3	Crazy Love	Michael Buble	Warner Music	1,257,292
13	Game	4	Wii Fit		Nintendo	1,246,461
14	Video	7	Madagascar – Escape 2 Africa		Paramount	1,223,805
15	Video	8	Angels & Demons		Sony Pictures	1,153,425
16	Album	4	The End	Black Eyed Peas	Universal Music	1,144,722
17	Album	5	Only By The Night	Kings of Leon	Sony Music	1,132,483
18	Video	9	High School Musical 3 – Senior Year		Walt Disney	1,084,911
19	Video	10	Ice Age 3 – Dawn of The Dinosaurs		20th Century Fox	1,074,651
20	Album	6	Now That's What I Call Music 74	Various Artists	EMI/Universal	1,053,574

Source: *Era Yearbook 2010* (and online at www.eraltd.org/-attachments/Resources/Yearbook.pdf).

Theories of the media

In this section we review a number of the key accounts that have been developed to understand media. We start with the classic hypodermic model, which is rarely taken seriously these days, and end with more recent global theories.

1 The classical 'hypodermic' model

The earliest theory of the mass media at the turn of the century – often called the magic bullet theory or the 'hypodermic' model of the media – is the simplest propaganda theory of the media. It assumes that people are passive and that the media message has a direct impact upon them. It suggests the following:

- Media messages are presented to members of a mass society, who receive them more or less uniformly.
- These messages are stimuli which influence the individual strongly.
- The stimuli lead individuals to respond in a similar, uniform fashion.
- The effects of mass communication *are powerful, uniform and direct* (our italics, adapted from Lowery and De Fleur, 1988: 23–4).

Although this theory is still popularly used in everyday discussions (especially among those who see the media as dangerous), such an account has long been discredited. Indeed, each point raised above can be taken as a critical issue of exactly what does not happen with the media! We will now look at some of the theories that have been developed to replace this 'hypodermic syringe' model.

2 Functionalist theories of the media

Functionalist theories of the media look at the ways in which the media serve to integrate society in different ways, and examine the role of media effects in doing this. As part of the social system, media can provide information, education, entertainment and diversion. Five functions have been particularly noted:

1 *The surveillance function.* The media provide a continuous flow of data about the world we live in. They can warn us of dangers (from hurricanes to wars to dangerous criminals) and be instrumental in providing information on traffic jams and the stock market, for example, as well as all kinds of information linked to personal welfare. (They can also be dysfunctional – stirring up undue anxiety, for example.)

2 *The status conferral function.* Here, the media give status to people, public issues, organisations and social movements. Enhanced status comes to all who feature in the media – they become more known about, for good or bad. Not only do major events such as political elections or famous criminal trials come to attention, but many minor issues can be accorded status. Thus, a child with a life-threatening illness, an old person on her 100th birthday or environmental activists protesting about a local pollution problem can all be accorded 'status'.

3 *The 'enforced application of social norms' function.* This highlights the public announcement of social norms, and publicity serves to close the gap between 'private attitudes and public morality'. The leading media analyst Dennis McQuail sees the media as fostering public communication values, which stress freedom, equality and order. The media can promote values by dramatising deviance of all kinds. By bringing to our attention 'youth crime', 'rape', 'child sex offenders', 'drugs' or 'serial killers', the community's awareness is heightened and moral boundaries are drawn (see Chapter 17). Later in this chapter we describe how this often works as a 'moral panic'.

4 *The transmission of culture function.* The media have become prime modern agents of socialisation (see Chapter 7). From young children's programmes such as *Teletubbies* to teenage chat shows, the media serve a key role in passing on elements of a society's culture and heritage.

5 *The narcotising function.* This is more of a dysfunction than a function and refers to the way in which a flood of information can lead to superficiality (Lazarsfeld and Merton, 1996: 16–18; see also Wright, 1967; McQuail, 1994).

Critical comment

Functionalist theories were popular during the mid-twentieth century but have been much in decline since. The above listing suggests why. In many ways, all functionalist theories do is provide a descriptive listing of how an institution works in the current society. The functions listed here may be important, but it is not always clear that they add much depth of understanding.

3 Symbolic interactionism

Herbert Blumer, the founder of symbolic-interactionist analysis, was one of the first sociologists to conduct audience research on cinema-going. As part of a widespread concern about the impact of films on young people, a series of investigations were set up in the late 1920s and early 1930s (popularly known as the Payne Studies, they were initiated by a pro-film censorship group, the Motion Picture Research Council). Blumer was involved with one of these that looked at young people. Straightforwardly, he asked some 1,500 young people to write 'motion-picture autobiographies', backed up with more selective interviews, group discussions and observations. He argued that to know what impact media had on young people's lives, it is best simply to ask them. Following on from this, much of his ensuing book *Movies and Conduct* is given over to young people's first-hand accounts of the films they have seen – how they provide the basis of imitation, play, daydreams, emotional development and 'schemes of life'. He let the people speak for themselves. One entry, dealing with stereotypes, reads:

> **Female, 19, white college senior: – One thing these pictures did was to establish a permanent fear of Chinamen in my mind. To this day I do not see a Chinese person but what I think of him as being mixed up in some evil affair. I always pass them as quickly as possible if I meet them in the street, and refuse to go into a Chinese restaurant or laundry.**
>
> (Blumer, 1933: 145)

Quite rightly, others have recently been more critical of his straightforward naiveté of approach. Denzin, for example, has recently been very critical of Blumer, suggesting that the study, while progressive in method, was shrouded with Blumer's assumptions ('pro-middle class and anti-film', Denzin, 1992: 107). It was also open to being used to crusade against film content and viewed texts unproblematically (Clough, 1992). True, Blumer's initial studies in the 1930s now look somewhat simple, but he was the first to take seriously audience responses.

Norman Denzin has focused on the importance of 'the movies' for understanding social life in the twentieth century. He considers the film and going to the cinema to have been the key mode of narrative in that century. Talking of the 'cinematic society', he suggests that watching films shifted much of that century's experience by encouraging a more visual, looking society – a society which he sees as increasingly voyeuristic. Denzin's method is to look at films, ranging from *Blue Velvet* to *Rear Window*, to see how they display the cultural logic of society (Denzin, 1992, 1995).

The theory of moral panics

Drawing heavily on the symbolic-interactionist tradition, Stanley Cohen investigated an emerging youth phenomenon in the UK in the 1960s: that of the Mods and Rockers (see Chapter 5). These young people appeared on the beaches and around the town centres of several south coast holiday resorts in England (including Clacton) over the Easter holiday of 1964. Although Cohen discovered that the amount of serious violence and vandalism was relatively little, he found that the media 'blew it up out of all proportions'. The media – and other 'moral crusaders' – saw the Mods and Rockers as terrorising the town and being 'hell bent on destruction'. Cohen saw this as a 'moral panic' and defined it in the following way:

> **Societies appear to be subject, every now and then, to periods of moral panic. A condition, episode, person or group of persons emerges to become defined as a threat to societal values and interests; its nature is presented in a stylised and stereotypical fashion by the mass media; the moral barricades are manned by editors, bishops, politicians and other right thinking people; socially accredited experts pronounce their diagnoses and solutions; ways of coping are evolved . . .**
>
> (Cohen, 2003: 28; orig. 1972)

Like Durkheim (in Chapter 4), Cohen argued that when societies entered times of anxiety and crisis, 'folk devils' were created through moral panics to reassert dominant values. For moral panics to exist, these responses have to be out of all proportion to the actual threat or danger. The media played a central role in stirring up concern, often amplifying the problem. From a small initial issue, major hysteria could be created which often served the interest of specific groups worried about specific social issues, such as teenage crime getting out of control.

Since Cohen's influential study, a great many 'folk devils and moral panics' have been identified. The media have mounted major concerns over drugs, mugging, baby battering, granny battering, child abuse of all forms, dole scroungers and welfare cheats, AIDS, video nasties, rapists and serial killers, paedophiles, Satanism and ritual abuse, religious cults, militant trade unionism, 'blacks' and pornography. In some cases the problems behind such issues have been found to be quite major, but in other cases the hysteria is out of all proportion to the actual problem. Phillip Jenkins has shown, for example, that although there is often massive concern over serial killers, they are in fact very rare indeed, and serial killings have remained at roughly the same low rate for the last 100 years (P. Jenkins, 1992).

To understand the workings of a moral panic, it is important to look at the way in which the media – newspapers and TV in particular – come to identify a 'problem' and present it in a particular way, and how this may 'fit' into a particular set of social anxieties or worries. Many moral panics, for example, depict dangerous threats to the traditional moral values of family life. When AIDS first appeared in the early 1980s, the media often handled it in a sensational way, depicting it as a dangerous threat to traditional sexuality (Cohen, 2003, orig. 1972; P. Jenkins, 1992).

4 Conflict theories of the media

Much European work on the mass media has adopted a conflict (and often Marxist) approach to the media. Within this paradigm, the media are seen to be owned by dominant classes who use them as a mechanism to serve their own interests. The media thus come to play a major role in the transmission of ideologies. Broadly, conflict theories highlight two important matters. The first concerns the economic base of the media, particularly the ways in which they follow a profit motive and the ways in which big business conglomerates come to shape them. The second concerns the ideological structuring of the media, particularly the ways in which certain conflicting interests – often of class, ethnicity and gender – are 'screened out' of the messages.

The political economy of the media

This stresses how the major means of communication in society come to be owned by private economic interests. Increasingly, it can be shown that these interests form giant interlocking directorates and are in the hands of powerful tycoons, such as Rupert Murdoch and Silvio Berlusconi. (Berlusconi – who owns Finevest, with a virtual monopoly of Italian commercial television – was elected twice as prime minister after much campaigning on his own television!) It has been true for some time that a country's media have been in the hands of a few powerful economic groups. Table 22.5 shows the approximate concentration of media ownership in the UK in the mid-1990s. But even in the early 1970s, the top five media firms in the UK accounted for 71 per cent of daily newspaper circulation, 78 per cent of admissions to cinemas, 76 per cent of record sales and 74 per cent of homes with commercial television. But what has been happening since that time has been an increasing concentration of ownership globally. Thus Murdoch's transnational company has holdings in the United States, Latin America, Europe (especially the UK and Germany), Australia and Asia. This is discussed further below. Table 22.6 shows circulation figures for the UK press in 2010.

These powerful economic interests work consistently to exclude 'those voices lacking economic power or resources'. All kinds of minority – from ethnic groups to disabled groups, from 'women' to 'gays' – may not be represented in media coverage. But more, much of the media will find that 'the voices which survive will largely belong to those least likely to criticise the prevailing distribution of power and wealth' (Murdock and Golding, 1977: 39).

Table 22.5	Ownership of press media in the UK	
	Approximate share of market	
News International	35%	*Sun, Times, Sunday Times, News of the World*
Mirror Group	23–27%	*Mirror, Sunday Mirror, People*
United Newspapers	14% (9% for Sundays)	*Daily Express, Daily Star, Sunday Express*
Associated Newspapers	15%	*Daily Mail, Mail on Sunday*
Hollinger	7%	*Daily Telegraph, Sunday Telegraph*

Note: These figures are approximate and meant only to indicate a broad level of concentration of the media in a few large firms.

Table 22.6	National daily newspaper circulation, July 2010						
	July 2010	July 2009	% change	June 2010	July 2010 (without bulks)	February– July 2010	% change on last year
Sun	3,042,406	3,121,407	−2.53	2,979,999	3,042,406	2,983,257	−1.41
Daily Mirror	1,242,446	1,340,028	−7.28	1,248,919	1,242,446	1,242,304	−6.69
Daily Star	843,229	887,106	−4.95	809,992	843,229	821,448	−2.14
Daily Record	324,229	343,165	−5.52	323,235	322,266	328,064	−6.42
Daily Mail	2,117,839	2,178,640	−2.79	2,092,643	2,004,131	2,097,778	−3.75
Daily Express	663,871	734,045	−9.56	664,293	663,871	666,469	−8.14
Daily Telegraph	678,391	818,937	−17.16	681,322	678,391	685,370	−14.23
The Times	502,588	580,483	−13.42	503,642	502,588	505,752	−14.75
Financial Times	378,497	397,600	−4.80	391,865	341,457	391,702	−5.60
Guardian	277,246	328,773	−15.67	286,220	277,246	286,496	−15.03
Independent	183,975	189,013	−2.67	187,135	121,542	186,760	−7.15

Source: ABCs: National daily newspaper circulation July 2010, Guardian.co.uk, 13 August 2010. Copyright Guardian News & Media Ltd 2010.

The big media corporations

Although they are constantly merging and buying each other up, the leading media firms in the world are usually said to include TimeWarner (with sales approaching £25.8 billion in 2009), Disney (with £36.1 billion) (see Figure 22.1), Bertelsmann (£19 billion in 2006; the only Europe-based firm), Viacom (£12 billion) and News Corporation (£30.4 billion). Typically, these firms have media holdings in a wide range of enterprises.

For example, News Corporation, owned by Rupert Murdoch, has holdings in Twentieth Century Fox (film, television and video and Fox News), 132 newspapers (in Australia, the UK and the USA), 25 magazines, book publishing, Asian Star Television and BSkyB satellite television. It also has large stakes in Germany's Vox channel, Sky Latin America, Japan Sky Broadcasting, Australian Foxtel Cable, Spanish El Canal Fox, India Sky Broadcasting, Channel V (an Asian music video channel) and Hong Kong Phoenix satellite. As of 30 June 2006, News Corporation owned a particularly large number of subsidiary enterprises in the USA, but equally had a strong presence in Europe, Latin America, Asia and Australia. In the UK, it owns newspapers such as *The Times*, the *Sun*, and the *News of the World*, and it has a large investment in British Sky Broadcasting. Well-known Hollywood film companies it owns include Twentieth Century Fox Film, Searchlight Pictures and numerous others.

Another example is TimeWarner. With an international labour force of around 340,000, it has holdings in 24 magazines (including *Time*), the second largest book publishing business in the world, Warner Bros films, Warner music group, cinemas, comics, Home Box Office (the largest cable channel in the world), Six Flags theme parks, Warner Bros retail stores, several global cable channels including CNN, TBS and TNY, Turner Classic movies, the Cartoon Network and CNN-SI all sports news channel, and on, and on (Herman and McChesney, 1997: Chapter 3). In January 2001, it merged with America Online (AOL), making it the world's biggest media company.

Bertelsmann is one of the largest European media corporations. In 2006, it reported revenues of more than €19 million. It currently owns publishing houses, such as Random House, the RTL television group and many other media companies in different sectors. It is also involved in Sony BMG Music Entertainment, in a joint operation with Sony, which controls well-known labels such as RCA Records and Columbia Records.

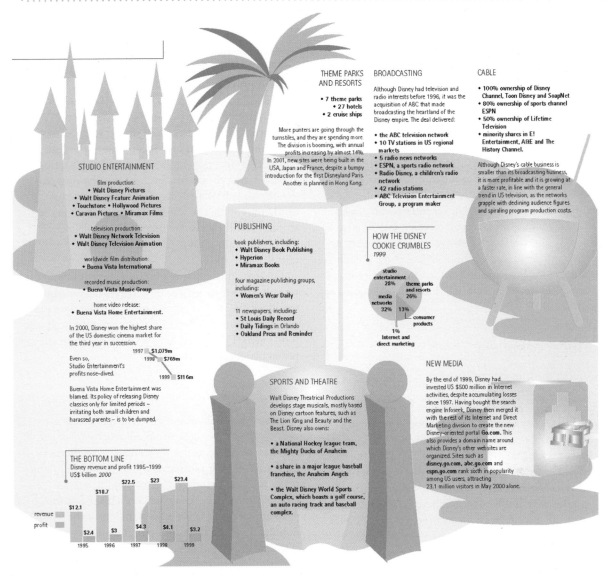

THEME PARKS AND RESORTS

• 7 theme parks
• 27 hotels
• 2 cruise ships

More punters are going through the turnstiles, and they are spending more. The division is booming, with annual profits increasing by almost 14%. In 2001, new sites were being built in the USA, Japan and France, despite a bumpy introduction for the first Disneyland Paris. Another is planned in Hong Kong.

BROADCASTING

Although Disney had television and radio interests before 1996, it was the acquisition of ABC that made broadcasting the heartland of the Disney empire. The deal delivered:

• the ABC television network
• 10 TV stations in US regional markets
• 5 radio news networks
• ESPN, a sports radio network
• Radio Disney, a children's radio network
• 42 radio stations
• ABC Television Entertainment Group, a program maker

CABLE

• 100% ownership of Disney Channel, Toon Disney and SoapNet
• 80% ownership of sports channel ESPN
• 50% ownership of Lifetime Television
• minority shares in E! Entertainment, A&E and The History Channel.

Although Disney's cable business is smaller than its broadcasting business, it is more profitable and it is growing at a faster rate, in line with the general trend in US television, as the networks grapple with declining audience figures and spiraling program production costs.

STUDIO ENTERTAINMENT

film production:
• Walt Disney Pictures
• Walt Disney Feature Animation
• Touchstone • Hollywood Pictures
• Caravan Pictures • Miramax Films

television production:
• Walt Disney Network Television
• Walt Disney Television Animation

worldwide film distribution:
• Buena Vista International

recorded music production:
• Buena Vista Music Group

home video release:
• Buena Vista Home Entertainment.

In 2000, Disney won the highest share of the US domestic cinema market for the third year in succession.

Even so, Studio Entertainment's profits nose-dived.

1997 $1,079m
1998 $769m
1999 $116m

Buena Vista Home Entertainment was blamed. Its policy of releasing Disney classics only for limited periods – irritating both small children and harassed parents – is to be dumped.

PUBLISHING

book publishers, including:
• Walt Disney Book Publishing
• Hyperion
• Miramax Books

four magazine publishing groups, including:
• Women's Wear Daily

11 newspapers, including:
• St Louis Daily Record
• Daily Tidings in Orlando
• Oakland Press and Reminder

HOW THE DISNEY COOKIE CRUMBLES
1999

studio entertainment 28%
theme parks and resorts 26%
media networks 32%
13%
consumer products
1% Internet and direct marketing

SPORTS AND THEATRE

Walt Disney Theatrical Productions develops stage musicals, mostly based on Disney cartoon features, such as The Lion King and Beauty and the Beast. Disney also owns:

• a National Hockey league team, the Mighty Ducks of Anaheim

• a share in a major league baseball franchise, the Anaheim Angels

• the Walt Disney World Sports Complex, which boasts a golf course, an auto racing track and baseball complex.

NEW MEDIA

By the end of 1999, Disney had invested US $500 million in Internet activities, despite accumulating losses since 1997. Having bought the search engine Infoseek, Disney then merged it with the rest of its Internet and Direct Marketing division to create the new Disney-oriented portal **Go.com**. This also provides a domain name around which Disney's other websites are organized. Sites such as **disney.go.com, abc.go.com** and **espn.go.com** rank sixth in popularity among US users, attracting 23.1 million visitors in May 2000 alone.

THE BOTTOM LINE
Disney revenue and profit 1995–1999
US$ billion 2000

revenue
profit

$12.1 $18.7 $22.5 $23 $23.4
$2.4 $3 $4.3 $4.1 $3.2
1995   1996   1997   1998   1999

Figure 22.1	The wonderful world of Disney's media empire

Source: Reproduced with permission from *The Global Media Atlas*, p. 64. Copyright © Myriad Editions, www.MyriadEditions.com.

The culture industry and ideology

German critical theorists Adorno and Horkheimer saw the development of a 'culture industry' which 'transfers the profit motive naked on to cultural forms'. The multibillion-dollar Hollywood empire sells its wares – from *Star Wars* to *Pirates of the Caribbean* – for huge profits. True 'culture' dissolves in the face of this commercial marketplace. And even 'great culture' will be dug up and recycled for new profits. For instance, the work of the eighteenth-century novelist Jane Austen has been repackaged into films, television mini-dramas and reworked books. Often this leads to her work becoming 'just like everything else': flattened for profit. Likewise, almost every novel by Charles Dickens has been turned into a musical (*Oliver!* being just the most famous). And every aspect of the media is saturated with this. There are extremes, as in the hype of 'world concerts' by leading rock stars such as Eminem and Madonna. Everywhere, media products 'are commodities through and through' and 'human beings are once more debased'. 'The colour film demolishes the genial old tavern to a greater extent than bombs ever could: the film exterminates its image.' It is 'mass deception', 'anti-enlightenment', and leads to subservience to blind authority (Adorno, 1991: 85–92).

Ideological state apparatuses

The French Marxist philosopher Louis Althusser (1918–90) saw a number of institutions (the media, but also education, religion, the family) as being independent of the state but functioning to reproduce the dominant ideologies through what he called the **ideological state apparatuses** (or ISAs, as some have called them more popularly). These are *social institutions which reproduce the dominant ideology, independent of the state*. (In contrast, repressive apparatuses such as police and army employ more direct power.) Ideologies construct imaginary relations for people to live in, which help obscure the actual things that are going on (Althusser, 1971).

Critical comment

Conflict theories are persuasive in alerting us to media capital and bias. There is a growing world concentration of the mass media in the hands of a few major corporations, and the research evidence suggests pervasive biases (especially over what is not allowed to be said in the media). But conflict theories may suffer from exaggeration. People are sometimes seen as being too much like passive victims and capital is seen as moving too coherently in favour of one outcome. In fact, media practices are complex and varied.

5 Postmodern media theory

Over the past decade, a group of newer social theorists have come to highlight the centrality of the media in our lives. In particular, they have suggested that we now live increasingly through the products of the mass media, which have come to have an autonomous existence of their own. We are media consumers. And the media messages, from Madonna's video to the soap opera *EastEnders*' murders, become a new form of reality. We are awhirl and awash in signs.

Baudrillard (1929–2007) sees modern societies as concerned with the consumption of signs. While in his earlier work he explored media 'codes', in his later work 'simulation' becomes the core of social life. Broadly, whatever is really happening in the world no longer matters because people are coming to live so much in a media-mediated world that reality is bypassed. All we are left with are exploding (imploding) signs and **simulacra**, *worlds of media-generated signs and images*. Just what these signs refer to in the world is no longer clearly distinguished.

One of Baudrillard's most famous (and disturbing) remarks concerned the Gulf War (16 January–28 February 1991). He argued that it was a hyper-real representation on our television screens: the real battlefields were now replaced by media saturation. We can watch the bombings, hear the planning, see the war and all its atrocities from the comfort of our living room. The war is a simulation: we are not there, nor will we ever be there. All we will know is the hyper-reality that media messages convey to us (Baudrillard, 1991).

Once the media tried to provide copies of reality, but now they are their own reality. This is the postmodern world we live in. The masses for Baudrillard are mass media consumers. Everything is now reproduced – be it on video, TV, CDs or film. It comes to us already as a pre-experienced hyper-reality.

Critical evaluation

This is a fashionable view that certainly places a great deal of importance on media images. But in that lies the critique. For Baudrillard is accused of excess. For him, it is often as if the Gulf War did not really happen, or indeed that any reality outside the media does not really happen. This is a serious problem, not least since large numbers of the world's population are not caught up in the media – millions still have no access to the media. And of those that do, many can clearly distinguish between signs and realities.

News is a central media product in modern societies. Not only was the news press the first major means of mass communication in the nineteenth century, but today most TV channels adopt specific mechanisms for the delivery of news. Many radio stations in the UK punctuate their programmes with hourly or half-hourly news bulletins. And since the 1980s there have been continuous 'wall-to-wall' news channels such as CNN, which circulate around the world. Functionalist analysis may suggest that news serves an important information function. Conflict theories, by contrast, see the media as ideological, mystifying what is really going on. Action theories focus on the ways in which people come to make sense of the media and the ways in which audiences read their messages.

Three key questions in media analysis

The pioneering media analyst Harold Laswell once said that the goal of media research is to answer the question: *who* says *what*, in *which channel*, to *whom* with *what effect* (Laswell, 1948)? Following this, and putting it simply, we can say that media analysis directs our attention to three broad areas: media texts, media construction and media consumption, which are locatable within codes, encoding and decoding (see Figure 22.2). **Codes** are *rule-governed systems of signs*, **encoding** involves *putting a message of any kind into a language*, and **decoding** is *the process by which we hear or read and understand a message*.

The first area thus highlights the codes in **media texts**: that is *all media products, such as television programmes, films, CDs, books, newspapers and website pages*. We look for the *logics and rules* that pattern

these messages, for they are not usually random. The focus here is on the contents of the media and what organises them. It involves looking at specific contents such as chat shows (on television and radio), film genres (for example, comedies or musicals) and 'stars' or 'celebrities' such as Madonna or Brad Pitt. Media texts are analysed for the messages they are trying to get across and their various biases.

A second area concerns the ways in which these media texts are produced. This involves looking at the technologies that emerge to present texts, along with the people who make programmes and their wider social locations. This involves a process of *encoding*, and it enables messages to be put into a language – be they spoken or written, verbal or pictorial. It involves looking at such matters as how journalists produce the news, how specific technologies such as the iPod are manufactured for music production, and the *organisation of finance and the ownership of media*.

A third question looks at how messages are received and consumed. This involves a process of *decoding* and the focus is on ***the audience***. This involves looking at such matters as how families watch television, studying soap opera fans, or looking at the way gender may shape how films are viewed.

All three of these act as a feedback loop.

1 Looking at media content

A number of theories have been developed to help us analyse and 'read' the texts and images of the media. We will look at just two: genre theory and semiology. (Others that could be looked at include narrative theory and code analysis.)

Genre theory

Genre theory (from Latin *genus*, meaning 'type') helps us make sense of the seemingly chaotic flux of media programmes by identifying recognisable categories (Table 22.7). Each may then have its own set of rules and codes through which it is turned into a recognisable form.

As an example, consider the soap opera – a very popular topic for media analysis. Whether one is a fan of *EastEnders*, *Neighbours*, *Emmerdale*, *Coronation Street* or countless others, certain broad features make them identifiable as a type of programme. (They all, by the way, have their own elaborate websites as well as fanzines and regular features in soap magazines.) Of course, the specific contents, characters and plots

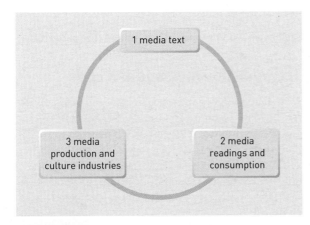

Figure 22.2 Questions a media analysis must address

1 What is the nature of the media text to be analysed – a film, a celebrity, a news item, a Facebook entry? How is it coded – what is its message?
2 How is this text consumed by its readers, its audiences, its fans?
3 How is this text produced – what are the organisations, people and corporations behind it? The process and flows of linkage become very important. Here we ask:
   (a) How does a media text come to be encoded – the link between 1 and 3?
   (b) How does a media text come to be decoded – the link between 1 and 2?
   (c) What is the full flow between text, reader and producer?

Table 22.7	Genres of television programmes viewed in England:[1] by sex, 2007/8 (%)		
	Men	Women	All aged 16 and over
News[2]	73	71	72
Films	68	64	66
Comedy	64	54	59
Live sport coverage	72	37	54
Wildlife	52	50	51
Soaps	29	58	44
History	44	34	39
Food and cookery	30	46	39
Contemporary or period drama	25	45	35
Quiz shows	31	37	35
Current affairs or politics	36	29	33
Other sport	46	17	31

[1] Respondents were asked 'Thinking about when you watch television, what type of programmes do you watch nowadays?'
[2] National or local news.

Source: *Taking Part: The National Survey of Culture, Leisure and Sport*, Department for Culture, Media and Sport, in *Social Trends*, 40 (2010), Table 13.3, p. 187.

will vary. But as a type, soap operas are all likely to have the following:

- *A never-ending story*. Storylines must always carry over to the next episode – there can be no closure, as in a one-hour drama.

- *Regular cliff-hangers*. Each episode must come to some sort of climax. Every hour or half-hour, the programme needs to have a crisis which will make the viewer wish to watch the next episode. The programme has to be a 'tease'.

- *Core characters*. The viewers become very familiar with the characters – they come to know a lot about them through watching many episodes. There are a lot of 'regulars' in soaps.

- *Interweaving storylines*. There are never just one or two plots, but a number. There are always several narrative strands proceeding at the same time.

- *The unfolding text*. Narrative progression has to be fairly slow. Often a storyline unfolds over weeks.

- *A woman's genre*. Women are more likely to feature in soaps, and women are more likely to watch them (see Geraghty, 1991; Allen, 1992, 1995).

 See BARB – British Audience Research Board figures for breakdowns of popular programmes: see www.barb.co.uk.

Semiology and the study of signs

As we have seen in Chapter 5, semiology is the study of signs. Semiology studies all signs: 'images, gestures, musical sounds, objects and the complex associations of all these, which form the content of ritual, convention or public entertainment' (Barthes, 1967: 9). Signs have no intrinsic or fixed meanings. Instead, their meaning is arbitrary and derived from the way they relate to other words and signs. Language has two components: *langue* (language) and *parole* (speech). The former is the rules and structures of language; the latter is its practice in actual speech and writing. Studying langue would enable the analyst to get at the underlying structures of language. Applied to the media, we become concerned with analysing the content of media as a system of signs, tracing out their relationships to each other – and possibly to an underlying pattern.

The television message as a code

All the programmes and images on TV can be examined for the kinds of values and messages they get across. Take the example of television news: many of us watch it every day. But 'textual sociologists' attempt to see it as a system of codes and values, and if the news does not fit these values, it will not work. Golding and Elliot, in a classic study, suggest that news values include:

- *Featuring of personalities*. Stories need a human angle – people and personalities who have a story to tell. Abstractions and theories are not favoured, but interesting personal stories are.

- *Elites and celebrities*. The featuring of big or well-known names is better than featuring 'nobodies'.

- *Narrative structures that contain key elements of human drama*. Joy, sorrow, shock, fear: these are the stuff of news.

- *Spectacle, good visuals and aesthetics*. Since television is a visual medium, news stories without good images become less newsworthy than those with good images. Sometimes news stories may be included simply because there are good images!

- *Entertainment value to attract large audiences.* News must provide materials which are captivating, humorous, titillating, amusing or generally diverting.

- *Importance.* The news item must have significance for large numbers of people in the audience.

- *Proximity.* News stories must be recent and relatively local. Foreign news must have local significance. The news in Norway cannot be the same as the news in Brazil.

- *Brevity.* Nothing can last too long and everything must be packed with information. News is part of what has been called the 'three-minute blip culture'.

- *Negativity.* Bad news is good news. It registers potential threats to social order.

- *Recency.* A premium is put on being first with the news. Once a competitor has the story, it becomes less significant (adapted from Golding and Elliott, 1979: 114–23).

Specific forms of news, such as crime news, may also bring other special values. Thus, for example, Pauline Jewkes (2004) suggests that crime newsworthiness increases when it features violence, sex, or threatened or dangerous children, as well as having a strong focus on particular individuals.

2 Constructing the message

A second concern of media analysis highlights the ways in which media messages actually get constructed. To take an example: just how is a television 'newscast' made? How is a 'news story' actually produced? Sociologists have done much work on this, and they have highlighted various layers of production.

A first layer looks at the actual *demands of the news programme itself*. Here there is an immediate daily time cycle, a planning structure which creates a routine agenda of predictable stories that provide the background of each day's production requirement (Schlesinger, 1978: 79). Far from being 'news', much of it is planned and routine. Slots need filling: an opening story, a limited number of stories required to fill a 15-minute space, good visuals, all following a regular schedule. Slots must be produced three times a day at the correct time (if there is no news, something has to be found; and if there is too much news, some of it has to be edited out).

A second layer looks at the *day-to-day practices of news journalists*. Here a specific culture of work helps journalists look out for certain kinds of news and not others. It is 'purposive behaviour' (Molotch and Lester, 1974).

A third layer sees the news as being structured by the *organisational demands of a bureaucracy*. We have seen in Chapter 6 how modern organisations tend to be highly rule-governed agencies: news is produced through such rules. Most noticeable are the rules of news production that are tightly linked to a 'stopwatch culture' (Schlesinger, 1978: 83).

Fourth, the news may be linked to wider concerns such as *community needs and dominant ideologies*. The Glasgow Media Group (1982) found that wider influences were at work, such that 'impartial news' often reflected a particular mindset of middle-class values.

Finally, news needs to be seen in the wider context of the *workings of the corporations*. Here such matters as financial structure become important. News that is too offensive or disturbing may lose advertising revenue. News, like all media outputs, becomes part of an industry and can be analysed this way. We looked briefly at the 'business of media' in a previous section (p. 778).

3 Looking at media audiences

A final major concern in contemporary approaches to the mass media is that of the audience and the impact of media upon them. Modern audiences differ from those of the past. Once – in theatres and stadia – audiences were linked to a specific public setting, planned, organised and collectively shared. These days, audiences have become much more fragmented and individualised. It is the difference between watching a film in a cinema and watching a video at home. One is public and shared; the other private and personalised.

The main concern of researchers has been to look at the ways in which media impact audiences. One classic study which looked at the impact of television on children's lives gives a typically cautious conclusion:

For some children under some conditions some television is harmful. For other children under the same conditions, or for the same children under other conditions, it may be beneficial. For most children under most conditions, most television is neither harmful nor potentially beneficial.

(Schramm, 1961)

Although there has been a long tradition of examining so-called media effects – what the media do to people – it is only fairly recently that researchers have switched the question from what the media do to people to what people do to the media. The classical 'effects literature' has tended to see audiences as fairly passive recipients of media messages. As we have seen above, the most extreme version of this is the hypodermic syringe model – where people are seen to be passively injected with media messages. While no media analyst holds such a view today, it remains popular among public and media moralists. For instance, in the aftermath of the murder of a young child, James Bulger, in the UK in 1993 by two young boys, the video of *Child's Play 3* (in which a similar kind of murder was to be seen) was evoked as a cause of the murder. While it is possible to say that the film may have played a part in the murder – along with many other factors – it cannot be said simply to have caused it.

More recent approaches to the media audience tend to conduct ethnographic research on specific audiences. Thus, the researcher may enter a 'fan group' and see how they watch their favourite star. Or the researcher may observe and interview women as to how they watch soap operas and, indeed, what they like about them. In one celebrated study, David Morley entered families and observed the ways in which they watched the media.

Looking at 18 south London working-class families, Morley observed how they used television. One of his key themes is the way such viewing is structured by gender. Among his findings, which have to be seen as very provisional because of the scale of his study, he suggests:

- Adult men have most control over the programme choice, and the video is more likely to be controlled by 'dad'.
- Women are usually engaged in other domestic activities, and watch television more sporadically (except in 'solo' watching by daytime). Husbands seem to watch more than wives.
- Men are more systematic and focused: they watch more attentively.
- Men prefer sport and news, while women prefer drama and fiction features.
- Women are more likely to express guilt over their viewing habits; they also use it as a conversation piece more (Morley, 1986: Chapter 3).

The fragmentation of the mass audience

Although many critics have argued that this is the age of 'mass society', others have argued that what we are seeing is a breakdown of the population into hundreds of very different audiences. To take an example: the world of music used to be divisible into a few broad groupings. There was 'classical music', 'popular music', maybe 'jazz' and a few others. Now, as any browser in a record 'megastore' will find, audiences for music have splintered in many directions: New Age, ethnic, rock, classic rock, show tunes, country and western, punk, reggae, folk. But these are broken down into further categories. Show tunes has its Sondheim aficionados who would not go near an Andrew Lloyd Webber score. And there are those who seek out the most obscure musicals that only run for one night. And so on. What has happened is the emergence of many media markets – niche markets. At the same time, some 90 per cent of all albums sold in Europe are for rock or light music, while 5–10 per cent are classical (Therborn, 1995: 224).

This may be depicted, as in Figure 22.3, as a move from media having elite audiences, through those having mass audiences to those having more specialised audiences. When a new medium appears it is usually adopted by an educational elite, before spreading out to a wider mass audience. After a while this splinters into a host of specialist groupings. What this means is that much media expansion takes place through increasingly specialised audiences (Figure 22.4).

Watching the news

The decoding issue turns to how actual audiences may interpret and watch the news. Here, the task is to get close to actual audiences to see the ways they make sense of the programmes they watch. Often this has a strongly gendered pattern; it may also be shaped by such things as class, age, ethnicity and sexuality. How we 'read' the media is known as *audience ethnography* (see below).

In one celebrated study, the UK media sociologist David Morley examined the audiences of *Nationwide* (a popular UK 1970s news programme). He worked from the premise that the programme can be 'read' or viewed in a number of different ways. The text is *polysemic, open to many interpretations*. He was interested

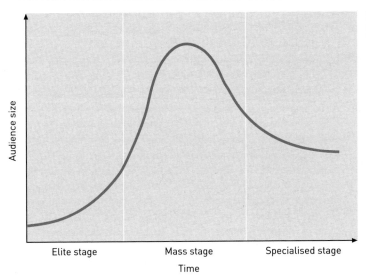

Figure 22.3 A model of media specialisation

Source: Adapted from Neuman (1991).

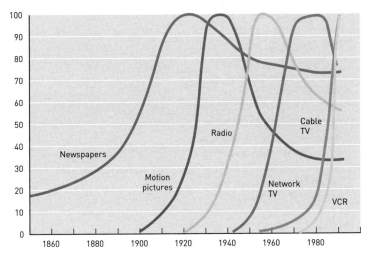

Figure 22.4 Size and fragmentation of audiences

Source: Adapted from Neuman (1991).

in showing the programme to a range of different groups (university arts students, trade unionists, apprentices, etc.) and getting their feedback. From this, Morley aimed to generate a typology of the 'decodings' made and to analyse their variety.

Broadly, what he found were three main positions in which the 'decoder' stood in relation to the text. For some, the meaning was taken fully within the framework which the message itself suggested (he calls this '*the dominant code*'). For others, the meaning was broadly encoded this way, but through relating it to some specific concrete context that reflected the reader's own position, the meaning was modified ('*the negotiated code*'). For still others, they recognised what was trying to be said, but rejected it and imposed a meaning that worked in an opposite way (an '*oppositional reading*') (Morley, 1992: 89).

What is important about this approach is the way in which it never sees viewers as passive dummies just soaking up the news. Instead, the news is approached actively and audiences have to work to give it meanings.

The Eurovision Song Contest: globalising music, queering worlds?

Popular music became 'European' somewhere in the mid-1950s, for that was when the European Song Contest came into being. Established in 1956 (at Lugano, Switzerland with 14 delegate countries participating), it was set up by the European Broadcasting Union (EBU) and aimed to be the 'Grand Prix of European Song'. Since then, it has been an annual television event celebrating its fiftieth anniversary in 2006 (with 25 countries in the final, and 38 countries in the semi-final). It has become 'bigger, better and more popular than ever' (O'Connor, 2007: 4). 'The Eurovision Song Contest' is a good example of globalised television. Several sociological issues can be raised.

First, just what does the contest say about musical forms and how a nation's identity presents itself through music? The song contest occupies a curious position with the world of pop music, since very few of its songs ever become 'hits', and usually look way outside the boundaries of what is seen as pop music in Europe. It is usually mocked, for example, by young people who are into other forms of more widespread music. Each country displays a music form which in some way is common to all of Europe while also being very distinctive about its own culture. It is hybridic and glocalised (see Chapter 2).

Secondly, it suggests the political coalitions of Europe. What has become clear over the years is the way in which voting patterns become predictable according to country alignments. Often country proximity shapes the voting: it is not the music that calls the tune, but the politics of each country.

But finally, the contest has generated a cult status among many different groups in each country. One of the most interesting is the way in which gay or 'queer groups' have appropriated much of the style and substance of the programme. The song contest has always been 'camp' – it displays exaggerated musical forms, especially of men and women, and outlandish dress, etc. Abba won in 1974 with 'Waterloo'; Bucks Fizz won in 1981 with a cutish number in which the pretty boys took the pretty girls' skirts off; in 1998 the transsexual Dana International won in Jerusalem (as controversy raged in Israel about her); and in 2007 an out lesbian singer took the stage to win. Queer parties and gay clubs celebrate each year with the Eurovision Song Contest.

Source: John Kennedy, O'Connor, *The Eurovision Song Contest: The Official History*, London: Carlton Books (2007).

The globalisation of the media

As media of various kinds proliferated throughout the world during the twentieth century, the claim was increasingly made that the mass media have become one of the central mechanisms through which globalisation is taking place. Indeed, the vast interconnections across cultures through internet, television satellites and cables have now become a key feature of twenty-first-century life.

We can see the potential of media globalisation across three major areas.

The globalisation of media content

As internet groups, games, films, music, news and the entertainment industry all come to 'travel' the world, so their languages and images become commonly available across cultures. The *content* of programmes has also become increasingly global. There are 'global totemic festivals' (Barker, 1997: 14) such as the royal marriage of Prince William and Catherine Middleton in April 2011, the World Cup, the Olympics, the funeral of Michael Jackson and earlier the funeral of Diana, Princess of Wales with an estimated 2.5 billion global audience, where it seems as if everyone in the world may be experiencing the same events. This is also true of much live global coverage of many news events:

world disasters like the Asian Tsunami of 2005 and acts of terrorism like the 9/11 suicide bombing of the New York Twin Towers, for example, are screened around the world instantly and simultaneously.

Some commentators have suggested that some genres of television are indeed being recycled everywhere in approximately the same forms throughout the world. Thus, news and soap operas seem to travel very well. There *are* differences across cultures: there are still some 150 cultures to which the Australian soap *Neighbours* has not been exported (Crofts, 1995: 102)! But overall, Barker suggests that a certain kind of international style may be developing. This includes: high production values (glossy and expensive); pleasing visual backgrounds (the landscapes of Australia, the beaches of California); more action than in traditional soaps; a Hollywood-style narrative mode; elements of melodrama over realism (Barker, 1997: 95). Likewise, Barker finds news narration similar. What is news is fairly consistent from country to country, although there are some variations.

The globalisation of media forms

The new technologies have become more and more pervasive and have started to hook up with each other. During the 1990s, there was a massive shift to 'digital transmission' of all kinds of data, and this, combined with satellite, meant the rapid expansion of the 'information superhighway', with three cores in North America, Europe and east Asia. Nowadays, there is a major convergence of electronic forms – for example, as hand-held mobile phones come to incorporate DVD, CD, news programmes, internet groupings, gaming cultures and other features.

The rise of super corporations

Traditionally in Europe, radio and television have received *public finance* (via licences and taxes) to provide a *universal service for citizens* by producing programmes which have some form of public *accountability*, some *regulation of content* and some *protection from competition*. The British Broadcasting Corporation (BBC) is one classic instance of this. It used to account for over half of the viewing time, but that proportion is now in serious decline as the new television channels stream online. The BBC World Service, with a long history, is being overtaken by groups such as CNN and MTV. And the story is the same throughout the world. What we are now

seeing is the rise of major mega corporations which dominate media life across the world (see above).

The myth of media globalisation

Although claims about the importance of the media shaping globalisation are widespread, critics claim that it is overstated. There is much evidence that most cultures have developed their own distinctive major media channels, and although they may 'borrow' from other cultures, they maintain an independence. Bollywood may borrow from Hollywood but it is *not* Hollywood. The China internet blocks the use of much Western material. Muslim television is not the same as Western television. And so on.

Kai Hafez (2007) has made a strong argument against the globalisation of the media. At the very least, he claims, there are three very different responses to cultural change, media and globalisation. These are:

- the adoption of the 'other' culture (this is the globalisation model and often presumes a 'Westernisation' of the media)
- the emergence of 'glocalised' hybrid cultures – in which local and global elements are mixed together
- the revitalisation and reassertion of traditional and other local cultures as a reaction to globalisation (see Hafez, 2007: 14).

The growth of Al-Jazeera

One interesting 'global' television service (recently much talked about) is that of Al-Jazeera (a term that in Arabic means 'The Peninsula'). Arab television developed from 1996 after the decline of the London-based BBC Arabic network. Based in Qatar (in the Gulf region), it is a state-sponsored Arabic news channel, having (in 2002) a regular audience of 35 million (and being available to some 310 million worldwide). It exists in a region stigmatised for decades and open to huge censorship. After 11 September 2001, this satellite television station became prominent in its coverage of the Afghanistan war, especially exclusive video tapes of Osama bin Laden.

Although the United States has tried setting up its own Arab language news channel in the Middle East, it has not proved popular. Al-Jazeera provides the 'other side of the story', giving global coverage to news that is usually dominated by the English-speaking Western world (especially the USA and the UK) (Miladi, 2003).

THINKERS & THEORY

Jürgen Habermas: the changing public sphere

The German sociologist Jürgen Habermas (1929–) is considered one of the world's foremost contemporary social theorists.

Habermas has been concerned with the 'life world' (the immediate environment of the 'social actor'), with knowledge and communication, and how it changes in the modern world. He is concerned with what he calls the changes in the public and private spheres of modern societies. The public sphere is 'a domain of our social life in which such a thing as public opinion can be formed . . . and is open in principle to all citizens' (Habermas, 1989; orig. 1962). The public sphere is an arena where public debate flourishes, and ideas and opinions can grow. Habermas traces its history, suggesting that it was in seventeenth- and eighteenth-century Europe that it developed a clear form. Between the realm of the state (see Chapter 16) and the private sphere of the family, there emerged a new public sphere which allowed people to exercise judgement and to engage critically in public debate. This may have been in the salons and coffee houses of the big European cities.

But nowadays, he worries, such debates have been narrowed by the collapse of this sphere into the mass media. It was originally the newspapers and the mass tabloids that first significantly brought about this change. They developed a much more commercial and consumer-based culture which was linked to the privatised worlds of money and commerce rather than a public forum of debate.

He worries about the future of democracy as the media expand and proposes a theory of communicative action. He sees three forms of knowledge at work in society. First is instrumental knowledge, which is technical and scientific. Much of this has worked against human

Jürgen Habermas
Source: © Rex Features/SIPA.

progress and has impoverished human lives. Second is hermeneutic knowledge, where the focus is on understanding. But Habermas looks for a third form of knowledge, which could be 'emancipatory'. Believing in progress and modernity, he argues that societies can move forward only if people can peel away all the irrationalities partially bestowed on them by media messages and arrive at a 'pure speech' situation in which they can understand clearly each other's ideas. At present this is made impossible because of technology.

Looking ahead: the future of the media

Sociology has come increasingly to recognise that throughout the twentieth century the mass media came to play a growing importance in the lives of societies. This is true not just of the industrial West, but of nearly all cultures. Global 'mediasation' has become a major process in the twenty-first century. The full implications of this have yet to be grasped, but we need to consider at least three questions.

First, it seems likely that more and more of our lives – and those of our children – will come to be lived away from the real world and inside a media-created one. Once the full implications of home multimedia start to be realised, will we spend less and less time in public space confronting real events and more and more time in a virtual space? Is the simulacrum arriving?

Secondly, the media world seems set to become an increasingly commercialised global one, dominated by huge transnational corporations. To the extent that this happens, will this mean not only an increasing homogenisation of different cultures, but also a real threat to democracy as more and more of what we see in the world is regulated by high finance?

But third, the top internet countries are overwhelmingly in the West: 90 per cent of users in 1995 were in North America and western Europe. At least 80 per cent of the world's countries still lack communications technologies. And overwhelmingly, the typical user of the Net is a North American male looking for entertainment. Although globalisation may be taking place, is this a process that will have serious consequences for the wider inequalities in society?

SUMMARY

1 We live our lives increasingly through the media. Patterns of communication have changed through five main kinds of culture: sign, oral, writing, print and most recently electronic cultures. We now live in a mediated or media-saturated world.

2 Initially, sociologists looked at the media through the hypodermic model: this suggests media messages are presented to members of a mass society, who receive them more or less uniformly and are strongly influenced by them. The stimuli lead individuals to respond in a similar, uniform fashion. The effects of mass communication are powerful, uniform and direct. This view has long been discredited and newer theories show that the reverse of these assumptions is more or less true.

3 There are many theories of the media. Hypodermic theories of simple media cause and effect are generally discredited. Functionalist theories focus on the ways in which media perform key functions. Marxist and conflict theory tends to look at the control function of the media and the concentration of media ownership. Interactionist theories focus on meanings and the interpretations of audiences. And postmodern theories tend to focus on the way media assumes a life of its own in the postmodern world, seeing social life as increasingly dominated by simulacra and signs.

4 There are three main areas for a media analysis: media messages, encoding and decoding. Codes are rule-governed systems of signs, encoding involves putting a message of any kind into a language, and decoding is the process by which we hear or read and understand a message.

5 Media texts are analysed through what the media says, how it is produced and how people (audiences) make sense of it.

6 Although there exist public forms of ownership of the media, such as the BBC in the UK, increasingly the media are concentrated in the ownership of a few major companies, such as TimeWarner, Bertelsmann and Viacom.

CONNECT UP: Turn to Part 6 of this book for key resources and link up with the book's website, which links to these resources
SEE: www.pearsoned.co.uk/plummer

MYTASKLIST

Ten suggestions for going further

1 Connect up with Part Six and the Sociology Web Resources

As you work through ideas and think about the issues raised in this chapter, look at the accompanying website and the resource centre at the end of this book which connects to it. There is a lot here to help you move on. To link up, see: www.pearson.co.uk/plummer.

2 Review the chapter

Briefly summarise (in a paragraph) just what this chapter has been about. Consider: (a) What have you learned? (b) What do you disagree with? Be critical. And (c) How would you develop all this? How could you get more detail on matters that interest you?

3 Pose questions

(a) For the next few days, keep a detailed record of 'you and your media'. Keep a detailed log of just when you engage with the mass media, what the kinds of media were, what messages were sent, and how they impinged on your life. Note all the media you use, from papers and magazines to television and film, and from CD and PC to mobile. It may surprise you just how much of your life is now 'mediated'.

(b) Outline the major 'areas of media' study. Select any one media item, such as a TV programme or a film, and examine the kinds of question you would ask about it.

(c) Who owns the media? Using a reference book such as *Who Owns Whom?* examine the ownership of the media and assess the concentration in a few powerful hands.

(d) How far do you think mass media have now become globalised? Discuss the implications of this.

4 Explore key words

Many concepts have been introduced in this chapter. You can review them from the website or from the listing at the back of this book. You might like to give special attention to just five words and think them through – how would you define them, what are they dealing with, and do they help you see the social world more clearly or not?

Helpful here are:

Nicholas Abercrombie and Brian Longhurst, *Penguin Dictionary of Media Studies* (2007).

Anne Hill and James Watson, *Dictionary of Media and Communication* (2006).

5 Search the Web

Be critical when you look at websites – see the box on p. 940 in the Resources section. For this chapter look at:

OECD and the information economy
www.oecd.org/topic

UNESCO
http://portal.unesco.org

The Blackwell listing for cultural studies
www.blackwellpublishing.com/subjects/SI

The Al-Jazeera television station and its website
http://english.aljazeera.net/HomePage

Al-Jazeera is a 24-hour news and current affairs channel, headquartered in Doha. It provides news in English and Arabic.
Freepress
Working for reform, it documents 'who owns the media'.
www.freepress.net/resources/ownership

6 Watch a DVD

- Orson Welles's *Citizen Kane* (1941): classic 'media mogul' story, based on the life of Randolph Hearst.
- Sydney Lumet's *Network* (1976): Peter Finch and Faye Dunaway in a major media battle – a powerful film.
- Peter Weir's *The Truman Show* (1998) and Gary Ross's *Pleasantville* (1998): two films where 'tele-reality' blurs with reality. Very provocative.

- Robert Redford's *Quiz Show* (1994): media corruption around a 1950s quiz show.

7 Think and read

Terry Flew, *Understanding Global Media* (2007), Kai Hafez, *The Myth of Media Globalization* (2007) and Tehri Rantanen, *The Media and Globalization* (2005). Good guides to the contemporary debates on the global media.

Kevin Williams, *Understanding Media Theory* (2003) and Denis McQuail, *McQuail's Mass Communication Theory* (5th edn, 2005). Two textbooks: the first is recent, the other classic.

Sue Thornham, Caroline Bassett and Paul Marris (eds), *Media Studies: A Reader* (3rd edn, 2009). A well-established reader which covers the field well (since it was first published, it has developed many rivals).

Joshua Meyrowitz, *No Sense of Place: The Impact of Electronic Media on Social Behavior* (1986). A major, and now classic, study which draws upon Goffman (1959) and McLuhan (1964) to show the way in which television is changing the way we experience the world.

8 Relax with a novel

Guy de Maupassant's *Bel-Ami* (1885) is a classic early study of journalism; Evelyn Waugh's *Scoop* (1938) is a classic satire of sensational journalism; and F. Scott Fitzgerald's *The Last Tycoon* is a classic tale of Hollywood.

9 Connect to other chapters

- For links to inequalities, see Chapters 8–13.
- For links to globalisation, see Chapter 2.
- For links to functionalist, conflict and interactionist theories, see Chapter 1.
- For links to theories of culture, see Chapter 5; and for links to societal development, see Chapter 4.
- For links to cyberspace media, see Chapters 6 and 23.

10 Engage with THE BIG DEBATE

Are the media destroying social life?

Ever since their inception, the mass media have always been attacked as dangerous. They have been at the centre of controversy. In the very earliest days, when books and novels started to be published, there were worries that these could be corrupting. As the earliest popular literature slowly became available to the 'masses', so it was denounced. In 1806, a Samuel P. Jarvis said that 'The evil consequences attendant upon novel reading are much greater than has generally been imagined' (Starker, 1989: 61). Much later, in the 1930s, radio programmes caused great alarm, and Lyman Bryson wrote:

> All great human inventions, even printing, even language itself, have proved to be two-edged swords. They can do as much evil as good. Radio is as great – and as dangerous – as any . . . and it can broadcast injury and discord and ugliness into the farthest reaches of inhabited space. To be lightminded about the radio is to jig along a precipice . . .
>
> Starker (1989: 115)

These days every new media form comes under attack. When Dungeons and Dragons (D&D) was first marketed in 1973 (with 8 million copies sold by 1985), it was accused of 'dabbling in the demonic' by *Christianity Today*. And attempts were made to link teenage suicides and murders to it. In 1992, the issue became 'rap and race' with the song 'Cop Killer' by Ice-T prompting a boycott of Warner Bros. records by parents anxious about the lyrics. (To see the lyrics, go to www.metrolyrics.com/cop-killer-lyrics-body-count.html.)

This may be extreme. But every form of media has had its critics: the early tabloids and newspapers, Hollywood movies from the start of the twentieth century till now, children's comics, the 'plug-in drug' of television, 'video nasties', pop music, reality TV, 'games', computers. Over and over again, the media have been posed as a threat and a danger.

Media critics have claimed that the media can have serious effects on their audience. Among the many dangers they pose are the following:

- The fostering of passivity: the 'couch potato' syndrome of inertly watching.
- The growth of crime, violence and moral decline: the media shape low values and provide bad role models.

- Trivialisation: we are, in the words of one critic, 'amusing ourselves to death'. Authentic sports, religion and politics get trivialised. Even education becomes 'infotainment'.
- The promotion of materialism and commercial values: most media come with advertising to the forefront and this leads to a 'promotional culture'. Even the weather or the news gets identified with sponsorship.
- Brainwashing, manipulation and mass conformity.
- The 'simulation' of the world, giving us pseudo-images and false realities: at its most extreme we come to inhabit an unreal media world, cut off from more authentic experiences.

In short, mass media lead to a degenerating mass culture. As Bernard Rosenberg says: 'At its worst, mass culture threatens not merely to cretinise our taste but to brutalise our sense, while paving the way to totalitarianism' (cited in Starker, 1989: 13).

In contrast, media defenders reject these criticisms and argue that the media can do the following.

- Increase participation and creativity: viewers can be active and critical and use the media – they respond by writing letters, engaging in debates and the like.
- Enhance the information a society has and help keep us aware of what is going on.
- Increase public debate.
- Extend access to all kinds of information and entertainment that previously were restricted to an elite class.
- Provide diversity.

- Reduce crime and enhance morality through making people more aware of issues.

In short, mass media can enhance a diverse, active and participatory culture.

Some modern media analysts such as Joli Jensen (1990) see the worry over the media as part of a continuing concern over modernity. The 'dangerous media', they suggest, are repeatedly compared with some mythical golden age in the past and taken to symbolise all the dangers of the modern world – rapid change, differences, a loss of clear authority, etc. They are constantly under attack because they are potent symbols of rapid change and a modern world hurtling into an unknown future. But media are in fact human made and here to stay, and we can shape them in the direction that we wish. They cannot in themselves be blamed for anything.

Continue the debate

1 Do you think that watching soap operas and reality television – the most popular forms of television – can play any useful social role?
2 Do you think 'sport' has been degraded through being turned into a mass media event?
3 Look around you and see what form the attack on the media is currently taking. Dissect this latest example.
4 Look back at earlier forms of media scare. Do the concerns of those times seem tame compared to those of today? Have the media got more outrageous and more threatening?
5 Weigh up the pros and cons of the new global communications systems.

CHAPTER 23

SCIENCE, CYBERSPACE AND THE RISK SOCIETY

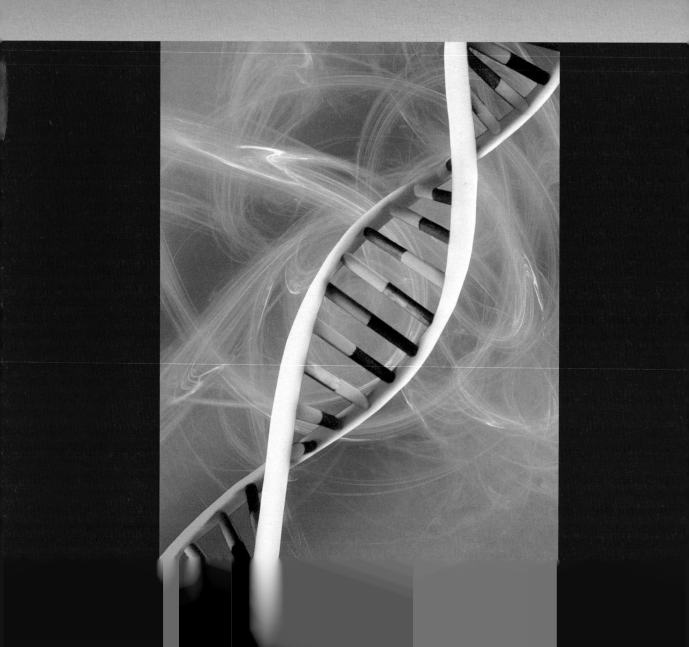

MICHIO KAKU IS A PHYSICS PROFESSOR and one of those scientists who have a mission to help people see just how much science will change the world. His website describes him as a 'famed futurist' and a 'best selling physicist', and you can find him on YouTube illustrating the marvels of modern science. For his best-selling book *Physics of the Future: How Science Will Shape Human Destiny and our Daily Lives by the year 2100* (2011), he interviewed over 300 scientists, asking them to predict some of the key changes that were imminent in the world. Some of them we are already very familiar with today: telephones, cameras, PCs, faxes, mobile phones, planes, videos, laptops, DVDs. Some we can already see in the making: people walking on the moon; computers that read our voices and talk back to us; children made in test tubes; babies cloned from other babies; smartcards for everything. Ideas that were not on the agenda even 100 years ago, which sounded like pure science fiction, have already happened – and are spreading widely. But he goes much further than this.

He suggests that over the coming decades, we will be developing 'smart homes' where our living spaces are fully wired to deal with our every need through hundreds of mini-computers. We will be solving major problems of health through the Human Genome Project's ability to identify major illness linked to genes. Longevity will be radically increased and the possibility of perpetual life will no longer be science fiction. We will be harnessing the energy from the universe to meet our daily needs. And we will create a 'planetary civilisation' capable of regular travel to, living on and communicating with other planets.

He goes even further and suggests that the Internet will be in your contact lenses and will recognise people's faces and display their biographies; that sensors will be in your clothes and appliances to scan for DNA and potential dangers; and that radical new spaceships may serve as elevators to propel you hundreds of miles into space!

Reading his book would have been reading science fiction even 50 years ago; but now more and more of it is becoming a reality. He claims that this is the scientific future. And if it is, what kind of new society will this bring? And what will sociologists make of it? In this chapter, we explore the sociology of science and its explorations around three key scientific revolutions: the quantum revolution, the biomolecular revolution and the computer revolution.

We should be on our guard not to overestimate science and scientific methods when it is a question of human problems; and we should not assume that experts are the only ones who have a right to express themselves on questions affecting the organization of society.

Albert Einstein, cited in Webster (1991: 126)

In this chapter, we ask:

- **What is the nature of scientific change in the modern world and how could a sociology of science help us understand how science is done?**

- **Can there be a sociology of the cosmos and what might it look like?**

- **What is the biotechnology revolution?**

- **What is the impact of cyberspace on social life?**

(Left) The Double Helix, taken from the DNA, is often taken to symbolise the late twentieth century. As the properties of the DNA were explored in the Human Genome Project (see the discussion at the end of this chapter), so this image became widespread.

Source: © Denis Scott/Corbis.

Q Discuss the idea that an image – a factory, a heart, a matrix, a hologram – can be used to raise ideas about the very nature of a society?

Dr Kaku's 'visions' are developed on his website at: www.mkaku.com.

As we saw in Chapter 1, sociology was born out of a concern with the changing character of this modern, industrial world, with where we have come from and where we are heading. Behind some of these changes was the rapid growth of science as a form of knowledge, and along with it the rise of many new technologies. This chapter looks at the role of knowledge and science in the modern world, and asks about some of the social issues that are raised around them.

Risk and the three scientific revolutions of the twentieth century

Michio Kaku talks of the 'three pillars of science', which he sees as matter, life and mind. Matter leads to the science of the universe, and the *quantum revolution*. Life leads to the science of biogenetics and leads to the *biomolecular revolution*. Mind leads to the science of information and the *computer revolution*. With these, science in the twentieth century brought three great 'discoveries': the atom, the gene and the computer. Indeed, there has been a move from 'an age of discovery' to 'an age of mastery' (Kaku, 1998: 5).

Science on its own can be 'purely academic'. It may be theoretical and abstract and of little consequence to the daily life of most of the world. Once it starts to be applied through technology, however, each one of its concerns comes to raise vast social and political implications.

Thus, for example, the quantum revolution may have discovered the atom, but it took technology to harness this enormous energy to put people on the moon *and* to create the atom bombs which were dropped on Hiroshima and Nagasaki, killing an estimated 75,000 people.

The biomolecular revolution may have discovered the gene, but it took people to turn it into a technology called the Human Genome Project, which aimed to map out the complete genetic structure of the human being *and* to raise the spectre of cloning, designer babies, racial eugenics and even immortality.

The Information (computer) Revolution may have discovered digitalisation, but it took people to turn it into modern information technology, which has generated unparalleled communication possibilities *and* unleashed a whole array of ethical and political

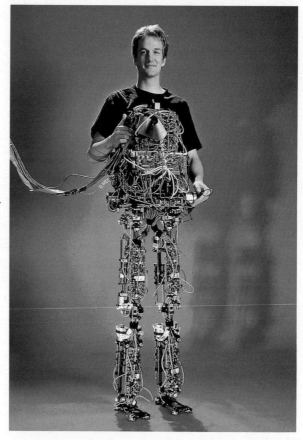

This walking robot is a composite image of the M2 robot with the torso of roboticist Dan Paluska. Designed to walk like a human, using fluid rather than stiff robotic movement, it follows rules from computer simulations, making changes in response to local conditions
Source: Peter Menzel/Science Photo Library.

issues, from the 'surveillance society' to the potential for cyborg machines (eventually) to take over from human life. At times, the genre of science-fiction writing seems to come close to reality! We will return to this later in the chapter.

Science, technology and the risk society

Recall how in Chapter 2 we introduced the ideas of Ulrich Beck on a *world risk society*. We will now start to see in this chapter how the new sciences are generating new technologies which 'manufacture' risks that are different from those found in more traditional societies. These new technologies are humanly produced yet often quite invisible: we just do not know where they may lead us and what dangers they may bring. Scientific 'experts' have the skills and knowledge of science, but the social, ethical and political implications of what they do are a matter not simply for them – 'the experts' – but for everyone in society. In this chapter we shall consider a number of areas, from genetic engineering to computers, which have consequences that we cannot easily predict. In Chapter 25 we shall take this further by considering changes in the environment. Right now, we start our discussion by considering just what science is.

Knowledge and science: traditions of study

Simply put, we know commonsensically what science is through its various manifestations. We do not just see it at work as we use our everyday objects (from mobiles to computers, from cars to planes), but we also grasp it as we look at the world: the infinity of space and its vastness; the random evolutionary mutations that may have brought us human beings about; the existence of DNA. The *Timeline* box suggests some of the major developments. Aspects of scientific thought have long existed across civilisations, often as 'natural philosophy', but they were heavily infused with metaphysical and religious assumptions. The so-called *Age of Science* arrives when the belief in our ability to transform the world through 'objective' knowledge becomes a major mode of thought. Human beings become capable of radically transforming, controlling and innovating their worlds. And this is surely one of the keys to industrialisation and social change – the world now looks radically different because of the uses of scientific knowledge.

Sociologists have long been interested not only in seeing whether the study of society could be scientific (see Chapters 2 and 3), but also in studying just what is meant by knowledge and science. Karl Mannheim (1893–1947) is generally seen as the founder of what has come to be known as the **sociology of knowledge**, *that branch of sociology which sees an association between forms of knowledge and society*. Born in Hungary, moving to Germany but leaving there in 1933 for the London School of Economics, he is a key figure in shaping this sociology. He agreed with Marx that

belonging to certain groups could shape the kind of beliefs we held. But unlike Marx, he did not always see those groups as class or economic groups. His basic insight was that all knowledge, ideas or 'science' depend upon social structures and situations to shape them.

In what follows, we will start to look at some of the issues that sociologists and others have raised in understanding 'science'.

Paradigms and the philosophy of science

Thomas S. Kuhn (1922–96) suggested that scientists are socialised into scientific communities. These have their own conventions of knowledge and ways of doing science. They generate their own 'puzzle solving' within an almost unquestioned set of beliefs. Thus, **paradigms** are born: *general ways of seeing the world which suggest what can be seen, done and theorised about in science*. Paradigms provide 'normal science'. Everyday scientists engage in puzzle solving. There is no objective truth, only a consensus about the truth. As work proceeds, anomalies start to pile up: things that do not fit, or make sense. This leads eventually to a 'paradigmatic crisis' from which a new paradigm may emerge. For Kuhn, there is strictly no clear logical reason why this shift happens: Aristotelian physics was not simply bad Newtonian physics, it was based on a different paradigm, a radically different way of seeing the world.

Many philosophers of science are critical of this view. Karl Popper (1902–94) was one such major critic and Kuhn's major opponent. For Popper, science can never prove the facts of the world: its task is to *falsify* and show what is not or cannot be. One negative case will tell you that a theory or hypothesis is not true. For Popper, scientists should start with a theory and then test it against the world of evidence. They establish very specific hypotheses from which predictions may be made. (For example, Newton's Law of Gravitation suggests specific hypotheses around the movement of bodies.) For Popper, then, 'objective knowledge' could be approached through falsification, not verification, and through deduction, not induction. These are the keys to science, and we discussed some of this in Chapter 3. The debates between Kuhn and Popper are largely philosophical ones, but they anticipated the arrival of a tradition of sociological enquiry into science.

Timeline Landmarks of science

Year*	Science	Technology	Society
1600	Kepler – planetary orbits Galileo – mechanics Descartes – mechanical philosophy, analytical geometry Harvey – circulation of blood Classification of plants	Problems of navigation Use of telescope Bacon's view of research	Early colonists in America Persecution of witches Thirty Years' War – religious discord in Europe Growth of early capitalism
1650	Rise of English science Boyle – gas law Alchemical experimentation Huygens – pendulum and wave theory of light Newton – calculus, gravitation, optics	Mercury barometer Improved microscopes Study of pumps and gases	English Civil War Growth of ideas of liberty, toleration and possessive individualism Founding of Royal Society and Académie des Sciences Constitutional monarchy in England Louis XIV in France
1700	Linnaean classification of living things Stagnation in English science	Savery's steam pump Newcomen's steam engine Growth of small-scale manufacture Improved iron and steel making	Establishment of public banks Classical architecture and art English mercantilist colonial policies
1750	Studies in electrostatics Early debates on origin of earth, fossils, flood, etc. Phlogiston theory in chemistry Scientific expeditions Science influenced by nature – philosophy Discovery of chlorine and oxygen Overthrow of phlogiston theory	Birth of scientific engineering Agrarian revolution Growth of ideas of technical progress Hot-air balloons Improved textile machinery Much-improved steam engines Vaccination	The Enlightenment The Age of Reason British conquest of India Science as liberatory force French *Encyclopédie* American independence Adam Smith's economics French Revolution: 'Liberty, Equality, Fraternity'
1800	Foundations of geology Foundations of electromagnetism Principle of conservation of energy Theory of thermodynamics Theory of biological cells Lead in science shifts from France to Germany	Rapid industrialisation of Britain – factories, machine tools, coal, textiles Growth of transport – canals, roads, railways, shipping Telegraph Growth of gas industry	The Romantic Movement Malthus on population Population increase and shift to cities German university system
1850	Advances in agricultural chemistry Theory of evolution Organic chemistry Periodic table of the elements Cell division, heredity Electromagnetic theory Physical chemistry X-rays, radioactivity, electrons	Industrialisation of the United States and Europe Internal combustion engine Antiseptic surgery, germ theory of disease, public health	Free trade – ethos of competition, survival of the fittest Writings of Marx American Civil War Franco-Prussian War Growth of trade unions Colonial imperialism Growth of monopolies

Year*	Science	Technology	Society
1900	Theory of relativity Development of biochemistry Quantum theory Lead in science shifts to the United States Genetics	Introduction of electronics and radio Aeroplanes Poison gas in warfare Car industry, oil US technological dominance	First World War Russian Revolution Depression of 1930s Rise of Fascism and Nazism Second World War
1950s on	Nuclear physics New tools, e.g. electron microscope, radio telescope, computers Science policy studies Molecular biology – genetic code High-energy physics Space explorations	Industrialisation of Japan Nuclear weapons, missiles Electronic communications Synthetics, plastics, nylon Artificial fertilisers TV and consumer goods Nuclear power Space technology and exploration High-technology medicine – new drugs, transplants, etc.	Dominance of the United States East–West Cold War Growth of mass entertainment Increased spending on science Growth of military–industrial complex Independence for colonies Widening gap between rich and poor countries Man on the moon
1980	Extensions in cosmology Microelectronics	Computers, information technology Environmental concern Increasing automation	Energy crisis
1990s	The Human Genome Project Digitalisation	New reproduction technologies Digitalisation Possibility of cloning Mobile phones New medicines for AIDS, Viagra, etc.	Postmodernism Globalisation Risk society Awareness of the environment
2000s	Publishing of Human Genome Project Continuing discovery of new star galaxies Stem cell research Man-made DNA – possibility of a synthetic life flow (artificial life)	High-speed broadband and Wi-Fi YouTube, Hydrogen fuel cell cars Multimedia mobiles iPod (2002) Partial face transplants (2005) iPhones, iPads (2010)	'Dolly Dies' (2003) Space travel for private citizens (2004) Partial face transplant (2005) Science and the environment issues Genetically engineered life and its ethical problems. Talk of the 'posthuman' Over 1.5 billion internet users, 100 million websites and I trillion URLs worldwide by 2008

* Nearest half-century (approx.).

Source: Developed from Boyle et al. (1984: 16, 18, 22).

For more: see Science Timeline at www.intute.ac.uk/sciences/timeline10.html.

The institutional sociology of science

Robert King Merton (1910–2003), a leading functionalist, originally presented his sociology of science in 1942. He saw that science – emerging in the seventeenth century – was analogous to the rise of the Protestant ethic (which is discussed in Chapter 4). Both were opposed to dogma and both fostered forms of hard work. In part, Merton's work was a critique of Soviet and Nazi claims that science was shaped by factors of class or race. He focused especially on the rise of the sciences in the seventeenth century, and suggested that science developed its own 'ethos' (or way of life) with its own distinctive community and culture. Four key norms organised scientific work. These were:

1 *Universalism*. Science should be guided by the search for wider, universal truths and should not be biased by more particular claims linked to, say, class or gender.

2 *Communalism*. Scientists should believe in the earlier findings of science as a common heritage.

3 *Disinterestedness*. Scientists should be impartial and should subject their work to rigorous examination by their scientific peers.

4 *Organised scepticism*. Scientists should suspend judgements till the facts are in. 'They should engage in the detached scrutiny of beliefs in terms of empirical and logical criteria' (Merton, 1996).

In some ways, Merton's work created a 'wish list' of what a scientific community should be like, and many subsequent examinations have not found a scientific community where these norms are put into practice. To the contrary, much scientific work proceeds on the basis of idiosyncratic, individualistic and independent beliefs. Much of Merton's work may in fact be prescriptive, as he tried to link 'science' to the bases of liberal democracy.

THINKERS & THEORY

Actor Network Theory (ANT)

Actor Network Theory, or ANT, studies human–non-human relationships – our relationship with 'things'. It connects up the full range of material objects, people and activities into relational networks, and asks how they all work together even as they keep changing and moving on. More formally, it studies the networks, institutions and practices of social worlds – with an emphasis on both human and non-human (actants). Actants take their role in social life because of the way they hold relationships together. As Bruno Latour, a key thinker in this tradition says: 'Society is not what holds us together, it is what is held together' (Latour, 1986: 276).

ANT is concerned with how relatively stable network nodes are stablished. Let's take a very simple example – and these theorists do not usually choose simple examples! We go for a drink in a bar. It cannot be explained simply as us – humans – being motivated by the desire of a drink. In a sense it is equally caused by the existence of the drink, the bar itself, the money we have in the pocket – and, of course, the bar persona and any friends we go with. Together they are an ensemble, a network that enables drinking to happen. If anything is on its own, the drink will not happen. Material worlds and human worlds collide.

There is neither a society out there, nor an individual in here. The focus in this approach is on the intermediary and the contingent. ANT examines the flows of actions and where they lead; and material 'things' take on active roles in social life. Things – materials, stuff – are agents in social life. The focus is on the ways in which these worlds composed of people, material objects, machines and technologies 'act' and relate – and how they keep on the move, changing and relating to each other. As a theory, it is most clearly identified with the science scholars Bruno Latour and Michel Callon, and the sociologist John Law, who originally developed empirical studies of science, organisations, technologies and markets (and ultimately 'space' and the 'natural world'). Its prime method is the detailed ethnographic case study. It studies the persistent relations around things: if the relationships cease to persist, so does the thing.

See: Bruno Latour, *Reassembling the Social* (2005).

A useful resource on this is *The Actor Network Resource*, although it has got a little out of date recently. See: www.lancs.ac.uk/fass/centres/css/ant/antres.htm.

Science as a social construction: the sociology of scientific knowledge

During the 1970s, a growing body of researchers did sociological fieldwork and ethnographies on scientific work as it was conducted in laboratories. They examined just how science was done, not only in regular science such as physics and chemistry, but also in irregular or 'deviant' science such as parapsychology, astrology and acupuncture. Their concern was to investigate the content (theories, methods and techniques) of actual scientific work. Scientists were studied like a foreign tribe. The research needed to identify the relevant groups and people, the actors who participate in networks (often global) who work to shape and define a field of enquiry.

These sociologists study what Bruno Latour (1947–) has called 'science in the making' through 'Laboratory Life' (see Latour and Woolgar, 1986). It is sometimes called ANT (Actor network theory: see the *Thinkers and theory* box). For example, Latour conducted fieldwork in the science laboratories at the Salk Institute in California, observing work on barium peptides. The study looks at how scientists talk about their work, the paperwork they generate, their publications. All these are examples of ways of constructing a scientific fact. Likewise, Harry Collins examined disputes within physics over 'gravitational waves' and showed how accusations mixed technical and non-technical claims. This position leads to what has been called **epistemic relativism**, the idea that *knowledge is rooted in a particular time and culture* (Webster, 1991: 15).

Overall, the sociology of science studies adopts one of two approaches. The *interests approach* suggests that science's claims to be true knowledge are actually shaped by certain interests. Sometimes these are

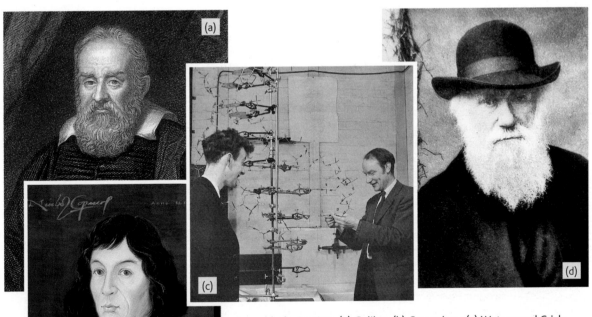

A world of scientists: (a) Galileo; (b) Copernicus; (c) Watson and Crick; (d) Darwin

Source: Science Photo Library (a) Sheila Terry/Science Photo Library; (b) Deltlev van Ravenswaay/Science Photo Library; (c) A. Barrington Brown/Science Photo Library; (d) Science Photo Library.

political: much research, for example, depends upon sponsorship, especially such things as medical sponsorship. On an even wider level, certain biases may go to the heart of science – it may have a class, race or gender bias. Thus, for example, some feminist scientists have argued that there have been major male biases in science because it is largely a male institution. This is to be found in the kinds of question that science sets itself, in its tools of work, and indeed in a certain kind of male 'clubbiness' among scientists (Fox Keller, 1985). Others have suggested that much science is also shaped by commercial interests, where funding is dependent upon major corporations.

Part of this commercial science may be seen as **Big Science**, which refers to *a particularly strong sense of expertise and its dominance*, one that is usually strongly backed by money (capital and industry), supported by governments and given a lot of symbolic prestige. During the mid-twentieth century this was largely associated with nuclear physics; indeed, it gave rise to both the space race and the nuclear bomb. Both the USSR (Russia) and the United States used these projects as major tools in

their symbolic Cold Wars with each other, while at the same time spending billions on these projects. In more recent times, the science of genetics has become almost as important with its major Human Genome Project (see the *Big debate* at the end of the chapter). Accidents are dismissed as part of the learning curve; critics are silenced as ignorant, uninformed, irrational; the strong march of science equals progress and cannot be halted (De Solla Price, 1963).

An alternative approach to this 'interest' model sees this as inadequate because even its own claims could be open to such arguments. The need, therefore, is for a much more refined *discourse analysis*. Science is now analysed like a text. How do the propositions, claims and ideas of scientists come to take on the status of 'facts'? This kind of study looks at the ways in which science presents itself as a solid and unquestionable body of evidence, whereas in fact the objectivity of science derives from its rhetorical power. Whatever science we are presented with, there is usually a large amount which we have to take on trust and which even the scientists take on trust.

PUBLIC SOCIOLOGY

The 'Science Wars'

The 'Science Wars' is the term given to a conflict fought between some 'scientists' and some critics of science, such as the sociologists of scientific knowledge described in the text. The former claim that their work must have the 'objective status of knowledge'. They suggest that the sociological critics, by focusing on the social situations that produce knowledge, minimise, even trivialise, the importance of science in the advance of humankind. Science puts people on the moon; invents computers that change the world; discovers causes and cures of major illnesses. This is serious work and serious science. By contrast, the sociologists who say otherwise are not to be taken seriously: they are often frauds,

intellectually pretentious and seriously misleading.

But the sociologists and cultural critics of science who do what is known as 'Science and Technology Studies' (STS) claim they are studying how science actually does get done in the laboratory. It is a legitimate social activity to study. They are, however, often very disillusioned with the way in which science – especially physics – has been used, and they become disaffected with it.

Indeed, it is not just sociologists who worry about this. Many distinguished scientists have also found objections to science, at least in so far as it is to be seen as the saviour of the world, the harbinger of modernity. The 'Scientific Revolution' was a problem. For as science became more and more prominent, it seemed to take on a life of its own – a bit like that mad Frankenstein and his machine.

It became divorced from society and politics. We have only to think of the use of the atom bomb.

Steve Fuller (1998) has suggested how the debate is in part based on a series of misunderstandings between the two groups. Table 23.1 suggests how.

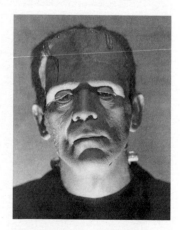

Close-up of Boris Karloff as the monster in a scene from the film *Frankenstein*

Source: © Bettmann/Corbis.

PUBLIC SOCIOLOGY

Table 23.1	A map of misreading: how scientists 'socially construct' science studies
Where science studies says . . .	**Scientists read this as meaning . . .**
Science is socially constructed.	Science is whatever enough people think it is.
The validity of scientific claims must be understood in relation to the claimant's perspective.	There is no distinction between reality and how people represent it.
Science studies has its own aims and methods.	Science studies willfully ignores the aims and methods of science.
Science is only one possible way of interpreting experience.	Science is merely an interpretation that distorts experience.
Gravity is a concept scientists use to explain why we fall down, not up. There are other explanations.	Gravity exists only in our minds and, if we wanted, we could fall up, not down.
Scientists' accounts of their activities are not necessarily the best explanation for those activities.	Scientists' accounts of their activities can be disregarded when explaining those activities.

Source: Based on Fuller (1998).

The idea of the *black box* (borrowed from cybernetics) is used here. This is a quick way of suggesting a very complex process that is going on inside (in the 'black box') which nobody need explain and others need not understand. Scientists might claim that it is simply beyond ordinary folk to understand this, yet what is happening may actually be incomprehensible to all, and very messy indeed. But science and scientists develop a rhetoric which justifies itself even when it cannot really explain what it is doing or what is going on. In this view, much science becomes both a rhetorical skill in persuasion as well as an act of faith.

Steve Epstein, for example, has studied the claims made around the causes of the disease HIV/AIDS. He suggests that the claim that HIV is the absolute causal agent in AIDS is the guiding assumption behind billions of dollars' worth of research progammes for HIV antibody testing, antiviral drug development and treatment, and vaccine research development around the world. It is the cornerstone of 'what science knows about AIDS' (Epstein, 1998: 26). And yet, he says, there are still controversies of different kinds over the causes and nature of HIV, but they are regarded as heresies and can hardly be heard. Science, then, is socially structured in this way to include core assumptions and exclude rival views. It is not quite as neutral and objective as it is often claimed.

The quantum revolution: human society and the cosmos

The 'science of the universe' is the first of our three major scientific revolutions to be considered. It raises a concern about the relationship of human beings both to the wider cosmos and to the existence of atomic energy (and its use in atomic bombs). Albert Einstein (1879–1955) is possibly the most famous scientist of the twentieth century. For him 'mass' and 'energy' were the same things and could be converted into each other. He claimed, among many other things, that 'nothing moves faster than the speed of light', that this speed is always constant, and that objects become heavier as they move faster. But he is most famed for his theory of relativity, and the equation that $E = mc^2$, where energy (E) was equal to mass (m) times the speed of light (c) squared. This is the basis of the atomic bomb. Nuclear physics also links us to 'the Big Bang theory of the universe', 'the theory of the expanding universe' and the growth of ways of measuring and defining space – the development, for example, of the Hubble space telescopes. All of these matters of science have major implications for society.

Sociology in outer space

Relatively few sociologists have taken any interest in the cosmos, outer space and interplanetary travel. But recent work suggests this is about to change (Dickens and Ormrod, 2007). Indeed, 'the cosmos' does raise many social issues. Five issues seem prominent. Four are discussed below, and another in the *Living in the twenty-first century* box.

1 Satellite surveillance

The first artificial (humanly made) satellite – Sputnik I – was launched by the Soviets (Russia) in October 1957 – although it had been dreamed of in science fiction a century earlier in the writings of Jules Verne and others. Currently there are around some 600 satellites orbiting the earth, and they have transformed much social life on earth. They range from satellites working on scientific fronts (such as space exploration) and military/intelligence (usually top secret), to satellites which provide our weather information, anti-satellite weapons designed to destroy enemy satellites, space observation satellites, navigational satellites (Satnav), earth satellites for environmental monitoring, and, of course, a whole range of communications satellites, which enable our networks of radios, television and mobile phones to function effectively. Cyberspace depends on it heavily. Indeed, much of social life on earth now seems to have become reliant on space satellites. At present, these satellites have been launched by only a handful of countries and one region, Europe – through the European Space Agency ESA (Wikipedia provides an interesting timeline on all of this).

2 Space research as a tool for understanding human life

The study of life in outer space speaks a lot about life on earth. To send people into space requires huge research efforts to understand just how human beings can react under these extreme conditions. Many issues are raised: weightlessness, sensory deprivation and long periods (several years) of travel, radiation, food management – generally the workings of everyday life in space craft and the management of the body in confined areas and body functions, as well as social isolation from the earth. In *Spacefaring: The Human Dimension*, Harrison focuses primarily on the people doing the travelling. On the technological side, he explores astronaut selection and training, medical and environmental hazards and issues of life support and habitation. He pays equal attention to 'soft' science aspects of human space travel, such as the stresses that arise from working and surviving in space, group dynamics among astronauts, and even off-duty time (and it is here that Harrison boldly goes where few space authors have gone before – into the realm of sex in space).

3 The militarisation of space: star wars

The 'space race' and 'star wars' have played an important political and symbolic role over the last half-century. Space wars signify the ownership and potential use of spacecraft, as well as the potential for nuclear war. Until the end of the Cold War (at the end of the 1980s) there were significant clashes between Russia and the USA. Control of space seems to signify control over life on earth, and the race to be a superpower is closely connected.

4 The role of space in the imaginary life

'Outer space' also plays a role in the imaginary life of society, and seems to have done for millennia. It signals the transcendent and what is beyond the everyday. In the modern world, films, television shows, magazines, games and theme parks have made a constant feature of such worlds. The literature of science fiction is the key, and it has a best-selling market. The world of outer space is everywhere. Indeed, in the United States, it has been suggested that space programmes tap into America's cultural dreams, where past history has provided a model of limitless frontiers, heroes, explorers and the progress of society through technology (McCurdy, 1999).

Dickens and Ormrod have investigated the role of space weapons, satellites and private space travel and examined plans to use space resources to colonise outer space. They suggest that these have been means through which outer space has been humanised and brought into everyday earth life. Large sections of our economy are now organised through it, and a new kind of imperialism may be taking over the near regions of outer space. Over time we can expect it to increasingly influence our daily lives – as indeed it has in the past 50 years or so. We are, in their words, entering a new kind of cosmic society (Dickens and Ormrod, 2007).

LIVING IN THE C21ST

The possibility of space travel

For some, space travel is now on the agenda. The space industry has been through a number of stages (see the *Timeline* box). But most recent is the goal of 'spaceports for rocket-bound tourists' – the imminent development of commercial space travel. Most will be planned by governments (around 35 spaceports have been suggested), but others are private. Space travel for a very limited few commercial travellers started in 2001, but it is very expensive and will usually involve quite short journeys. In 2010, Virgin Galactic was booking places for around $200,000 for a ticket. It is also very risky and dangerous – since 1957 only a scarce 500 people have ever made an out-of-earth journey. For the very rich, however, this may well become a new form of thrill-seeking and vacation time, and a way of celebrating their symbolic position in a stratified world!

There are many problems with space travel. First, the cost is huge. Second, human beings have short lives – and travelling in space involves huge periods of time. To get to Mars would take eight months (a round trip would take that much longer!). No human has so far stayed in space for anything like that period of time. Finally, humans are also very expensive in terms of life support – 'they eat masses of food, drink masses of water, breathe masses of air, and they need to sleep for several hours a day. Robots have none of these disadvantages' (Hart-Davis and Bader, 2007: 92). Although there will be a rise in space travel in the twenty-first century, it is most unlikely to become a possibility for most of earth's inhabitants.

Source: M. Hastings et al., 'The new space race', *Newsweek*, 7 August 2006: 46–7.

Timeline Space exploration

1957	USSR launched Sputnik.
1958	NASA was established to run the American space programmes.
1961	The USSR sent first man into space (Yuri Gagarin in Vosstok 1).
1969	The USA landed first men on the moon (Apollo 11).
1971	USSR launched first space station (Salyut I).
1981	Launch of the space shuttle Columbia, first reusable spacecraft.
1990	NASA and Europe launched the Hubble space telescope.
1998	International Space Station started (due to be completed in 2010).
2001	First Trip by a 'space tourist', Dennis Tito.
2003	The Columbia disaster (crew of 7 killed).
2004	SpaceShipOne was first privately run flight.
2009	Phoenix mission to Mars landed on the planet.
2010	Virgin Galactic plans space tourism flights at $200,000 per person.

Source: Modified from: Hart-Davis and Bader, *The Cosmos: A Beginner's Guide* (BBC Books, 2007: 61).

Nuclear proliferation

In August 1945, atom bombs were dropped over Japan. They established a worldwide desire never to use such bombs again. The *Enola Gay* dropped its deadly load on Hiroshima on 6 August, killing some 80,000–120,000; a second bomb was dropped on 9 August on Nagasaki. The war between the USA and Japan was brought to an end, but it is usually seen as the single most destructive event in the history of warfare. (The survivors – known as Hibakusha – have provided detailed accounts of living with this horror, and the whole experience is well documented on www.pcf.city.hiroshima.jp.)

In 1963, a Nuclear Test Ban Treaty was signed. As we have seen (Chapter 16, p. 562), currently there are nine states which have detonated nuclear weapons. Five are recognised by the Nuclear Non-Proliferation Treaty (NPT), which was signed in 1968: they are the United States, Russia, the United Kingdom, France and China. Although the aim of the NPT was elimination of nuclear weapons, little has happened in practice. Since then, other states have developed nuclear weapons, including India, Pakistan and North Korea. Israel is also widely believed to have an arsenal of nuclear weapons, and many other countries such as Iran and Libya regularly speak of developing their programmes. South Africa alone has dismantled its armoury.

In 2007, four senior US statesmen made appeals for abolition. In 2009, US President Barack Obama made a speech which indicated a desire for a 'nuclear-free world' and a year later Russia and the United States signed a new comprehensive nuclear arms reduction agreement. The long-term and growing fear of nuclear proliferation motivates some nuclear weapons states to contemplate 'going to zero' because they believe that otherwise it may prove impossible to prevent other countries developing nuclear weapons.

Since their invention and use, nuclear weapons have been the object of major worldwide protest movements such as the British Campaign for Nuclear Disarmament (CND). Nuclear weapons are often seen as symbolic of modern times – the 'Nuclear Age'. They symbolise both the scientific abilities of humans and their dreadful capacities for war, terror and annihilation (Lifton, 1996) (see Chapter 16).

The 'biotechnology revolution': social issues

The biotechnology revolution comes in many forms and in this section we will consider a few of the arguments. At their most general, these biological arguments are not just about science: they have become a mass way of thinking. 'The gene is an icon of our time' (Rothman, 1998: 14). They are seen as the prime movers of life and a cause for almost everything. Whatever the question is, genetics becomes the answer. From the problems of race and war, to rape and cancer, from sexuality to crime, from addictions to disease, almost every issue of our time has been placed within this biological frame. The explanation lies 'in the genes'. Nor is this a new way of thinking: ideas of 'instincts', 'bad seeds', 'good and bad blood', 'nature', etc. have been its precursor and around for a long time. Two core – but interconnected – themes are those which highlight the new disciplines of **sociobiology** (*a theoretical paradigm that explores ways in which our biology affects how humans create culture*) and evolutionary psychology; and those which highlight the importance of specific DNA codes and gene mapping. We will consider each in turn.

1 Science, biology and genetic politics

Major recent developments in the biological sciences have focused upon the gene, and these have often been linked theoretically to sociobiology and evolutionary psychology (EP). Edward O. Wilson (1975, 1978) is generally credited as the founder of this field, and optimistically claimed that sociobiology would reveal the biological roots of human culture. Both these theoretical paradigms explore ways in which our biology, and especially our genes, shape how humans become social and how cultures exist (see Chapters 5 and 7). In these arguments, the role of biology is given primacy as a science in explaining the social. Usually such approaches look for distant (distal) causes of our contemporary culture and behaviour thousands of generations ago in our evolutionary pasts. Nowhere is the power of gene analysis clearer than in the development of the Human Genome Project, which is the issue for discussion at the end of the chapter.

The logic of evolution

Both sociobiology and evolutionary psychology rest on the logic of evolution. In his book *On the Origin of Species*, Charles Darwin (1979; orig. 1859) claimed that living organisms change over long periods of time as a result of *natural selection*, a matter of four simple principles. First, all living things live to reproduce themselves. Secondly, the blueprint for reproduction lies in the genes, the basic units of life that carry traits of one generation into the next. Genes vary randomly in each species; in effect, this genetic variation allows a species to 'try out' new life patterns in a particular environment. Thirdly, due to genetic variation, some organisms are more likely than others to survive and to pass on their advantageous genes to their offspring. Fourthly, over thousands of generations, specific genetic patterns that promote reproduction survive and become dominant. In this way, as biologists say, a species *adapts* to its environment and dominant traits emerge as the 'nature' of the organism.

Many social traits have been linked back to evolution. Thus, the difference between the sexes, the development of different sexual orientations (for example, homosexuality), the persistence of crime and aggression, the links between race and IQ, the connections between language and the brain, and the universality of rape have all been connected to evolution.

The 'Darwin Wars'

It will not be surprising to learn that many social scientists hotly contest the views of these biologicial evolutionists. The conflict has been called the 'Darwin Wars', whereby new genetics theorists, such as Steven Pinker, Richard Dawkins, Daniel Dennett and Helena Cronin, find themselves disagreeing with both sociologists and some biologists, such as Richard Leowontin, Stephen Jay Gould, Noam Chomsky, and Steven and Hilary Rose, about the role of biology in understanding society.

Now it is not the case that critics are dismissive of Darwin or that they suggest there is no role for biology to play. Quite the contrary, the role of biology has to be taken very seriously and social scientists do misleadingly tend to minimise it. But they suggest that the claims that are made by evolutionary psychologists and sociobiologists often seem too overstated and wide ranging.

A controversial case: Thornhill and Palmer – the evolutionary role of rape

Take the example of a recent study of rape by US sociobiologists Randy Thornhill and Craig Palmer (2000). Drawing on the evolutionary theory of sex, they claim that rape is a necessary part of the evolutionary process. They see it as completely congruent and compatible with the development of sex differences.

Broadly, and in line with many evolutionary theorists, they suggest that for reproductive potentials to be fulfilled and humans to reproduce themselves satisfactorily, there is an evolutionary necessity for men to have sexual intercourse with as many women as they can. Meanwhile, for women the task is different: it is to find the best man and the best seed. The male is seen as more likely than the female to desire sex with a variety of partners.

All this rests on the argument that the biological significance of a single sperm and a single egg differ dramatically. For healthy men, sperm represents a 'renewable resource' produced by the testes throughout most of the life course. A man releases hundreds of millions of sperm in a single ejaculation – technically, enough to fertilise many millions of women (Barash, 1981: 47). A newborn female's ovaries, however, contain her entire lifetime allotment of follicles or immature eggs. A woman commonly releases a single mature egg cell from her ovaries each month. So, while a man is biologically capable of fathering thousands of offspring, a woman is able to bear only a relatively small number of children.

Given this biologically based difference, each sex is well served by a distinctive reproductive strategy. From a strictly biological perspective, a man reproduces his genes most efficiently by being promiscuous – that is, readily engaging in sex. This scheme, however, opposes the reproductive interests of a woman, whose relatively few pregnancies demand that she carry the child for nine months, give birth and care for the infant for some time afterwards. Thus, efficient reproduction on the part of the woman depends on carefully selecting a mate whose qualities (beginning with the likelihood that he will simply stay around) will contribute to her child's survival and successful reproduction (Remoff, 1984).

Evolutionary biology suggests that cultural patterns of reproduction, promiscuity, the double standard and indeed rape, like many others, have an underlying bio-logic. Simply put, they have developed around the world because women and men everywhere tend towards distinctive reproductive strategies. Men prefer a higher number of sex partners; women do not.

In this view, rape is seen as universal – across humans and animals. It also goes back a long way in time. Its distant roots in our make-up lie with men competing for women. Rape thus becomes a device in which men can gain reproductive benefits.

This account is well defended by its authors, who have little time for social science, which they see as ideological. But likewise, very few social scientists have taken their work at all seriously. This illustrates very clearly the way in which different scientific communities often speak across each other and do not listen to each other's arguments. What are some of the key issues in these debates?

Key issues

First, critics claim that gene theorists are often too reductionist. This is to say that they reduce the complexity of human life histories, imaginations, minds, bodies, knowledges and selves to a 'seed': to a moment when a sperm joins an egg. Ultimately, they claim, and despite the huge variations of cultures and histories, these seeds contain the potential for all human beings. It is important therefore to ask what is missing from these rather grand claims. Often there is little attempt to look for immediate causes in a culture or a life, but instead an attempt to look back to causes that may have appeared thousands of years ago. The tendency is to give priority to distant (or distal) causes rather than more immediate (or proximal) causes.

Critics claim that genetic theorists often ignore time. DNA is called a code, a blueprint, but life unfolds through time and space. Human evolution is a lifelong building project involving history and interactions with many others in the wider social environment. DNA will have its part to play in this lifelong project, of course, but it is surely facile to suggest that it all simply 'unfolds' from a genetic base.

And this leads to the claims that many of these accounts may be too deterministic. While Darwin's evolutionary theory certainly recognised the importance of chance, contingencies and more or less random moments with unpredictable outcomes, many of the newer theories are much more restrictive. The central feature of his theory was that of adaptations constantly taking place. So although there may be broad biological bases, contingency plays an important role too. We need to distinguish here between long-term trends and causes, and enabling adaptations that take place in contexts and local environments. We can speak of long-term evolved human capacities or capabilities without then saying what they cause.

But the key is culture. Even if it is true that men are evolutionary rapists or genetically aggressive, this would not really begin to explain the different levels of aggressiveness and rape across different cultures, ages, classes, ethnicities and times. For rape and violence are not static, fixed things. Likewise, even if some theorists suggest that rape is an evolutionary necessity, this does not begin to explain the variations in rape rates.

On top of all this, there are also ideological concerns. Some critics fear that sociobiology may revive biological arguments, common a century ago, touting the superiority of one race or sex. In general, though, defenders these days counter this by rejecting the past pseudo-science of racial superiority. On the contrary, they contend, new genetic theories may actually unite all of humanity by asserting that all people share a single evolutionary history. With regard to sex, sociobiology does rest on the assumption that men and women differ biologically in some ways that culture cannot overcome – if, in fact, any society sought to. But, far from asserting that males are somehow more important than females, sociobiology emphasises how both sexes are vital to human reproduction. They claim that science is on their side, and that objections made on moral or political grounds by feminists or anti-racists are just that, and cannot be taken as science.

But critics counterclaim that this raises the problem of the 'authority of the scientist'. Almost everything that these theories touch – from crime to medicine,

from gender to race – raises profound ethical and political issues which cannot be ignored. Yet very often the scientist steps over the line of science to become an 'expert' on ethics and morality. The field of bioethics can often become an apologia for the scientist.

Finally, although sociologists are often not in a position to evaluate this, we should note that there is actually a great deal of research from biologists themselves which suggests that many of the claims of the evolutionary psychologists do not match the findings of biological researchers and suffer from being seriously overstated. Thus, Anne Fausto-Sterling finds a much wider range of male and female behaviours than evolutionary psychologists would allow us to believe (Fausto-Sterling, 1992).

2 Issues of genetic modification

Many of the developments in genetic modification will be available mainly to the wealthy West. With our greater knowledge and mapping of genes, we can already see *gene mapping*, *profiling*, *therapy* and *modification* taking place in plants and animals, including human beings.

Thus, *genome profiling* will enable the decoding of the genetic basis of many illnesses, giving medicine more effective mechanisms for diagnosis and treatment. Increasingly, medical practitioners will be able to predict from particular genes the health of an individual. This will lead to more and more knowledge about the pre-born child, as well as a wider range of options for treating disease. But at the same time, this will bring untold risks. For instance, it may lead to higher insurance policies for giving birth to people with suspected 'sick genes'; it may lead to more abortions; it may lead to what Lee Silver suggests may be seen as two human species: a genetically enhanced superior species and a genetically deficient inferior one (Silver, 1998). 'Designer children' may be engineered.

The new genetic discoveries are also open to commercial exploitation. Already companies have claimed to patent certain genes. Commercial companies such as Celera Genomics (under the US scientist Craig Venter, in particular) have raised billions of dollars on the US stock market in an attempt to sell patented genes to industry. (However, international protests followed, and a joint declaration from US President Clinton and UK Prime Minister Blair argued that genetic data should be available to everyone and not commercially patented.) The point is that these new 'sciences' bring many unknown potentials that we may well have to live with in the future.

LIVING IN THE C21ST

The politics of life itself

In his book, *The Politics of Life Itself*, the sociologist Nikolas Rose concludes that 'new spaces are emerging for the politics of life in the twenty-first century' (2007: 8). He argues that somewhere in the twentieth century – as the new 'biotechnology revolution' was taking place – a new politics quietly entered our lives. It is one that is being shaped by biologists of all stripes. As he says: 'in all manner of small ways, most of which will soon be routinized and taken for granted, things will not be quite the same again'. What are these new politics?

Rose draws from the earlier work of Michel Foucault (see Chapter 17) who was interested in the new ways in which the body was surveyed and disciplined. We saw this in the case of the developing prison with its rules. Rose contends that the new biology has more recently taken over. He suggests that five emerging pathways are shaping our lives. These are:

1 The significance now given to the biological molecule as a bedrock of social life (e.g. in the Human Genome Project).

2 The hope and belief we now have that biology will help us get the best possible future we can.

3 The development of a new idea of what it means to be human – which puts our bodily existence at the centre of thinking. Here we start to find the significance of what might be called 'biological citizenship'.

4 The importance of a wide array of new experts on the body, ranging from stem cell researchers and genetic counsellors to the pharamaceutical industry and the arrival of 'bioethicists'.

5 The development of new markets that can cash in on all this: a new form of economy – the pharmaceutical industry, the market in body parts.

(Like many sociologists, Rose gives these processes a complex terminology. In his language, these developing social processes display molecularization, optimization, subjectification, somatic expertise and economies of vitality.)

We now live in the middle of the making of multiple new histories with no clear sense of where we might be heading. We have already witnessed it in the way many of us now take for granted the tools of EEGs, PET and CAT scans, and MRI exams in hospitals. But here now are major new worlds of genetic screening, genetic therapy, body part donation and transplantation, drug control and a massive pscyhopharmaceutical industry. All kinds of changes in the regulation of our bodies are taking place.

For Nikolas Rose, the future lies in grasping what he calls 'biocapital' and the new 'mutations in biopower', grasping the new emphasis on treating disease susceptibilities rather than disease. It will lead to a shift in our understanding of the patient and the emergence of new forms of medical activism. A new conception of 'biological citizenship' is taking shape that recodes the duties, rights and expectations of what it means to be a human being, and which is changing the ways in which human beings relate to each other and their bodies. Contemporary politics will increasingly call 'life itself' into question.

Genetically modified foods

Modifying the genetic composition of crops and animals through 'selective breeding' has been known as part of agriculture for centuries, but the newer techniques mean that artificial transfers between completely unrelated organisms become a reality. Genetic modification of foods is much more radical than cross-breeding: there is a manipulation of the genetic composition.

GM crops are currently being grown in around 13 countries and being tested in many more. They are being widely grown in China, and America has grown some 3.5 trillion genetically modified plants since 1994.

The most prevalent kinds of plant so far have been maize (20 per cent of the US maize crop in 1998) and soya (30 per cent, or 21 million tons). They can give more vitamins and make 'superfoods', such as 'super-rice'.

Since present farming techniques may not be able to deal with the world's starvation problems, developments in biotechnology are sometimes seen as the solution. But they have generated significant conflicts. The United Nations Development Programme, for instance, generally favours their development. It claims that GM crops may give greater yields for farmers and lift people out of poverty. Such crops could help farmers cultivate marginal land prone to drought or salt. They may enhance nutritional

THINKERS & THEORY

Donna Haraway: the cyborg society

Donna Haraway (1944–) has been a long-time professor at the University of California, Santa Cruz, in the History of Consciousness programme and Feminist Studies. She was trained as a biologist/natural scientist, and much of her work has focused on the natural body and its relation to the human sciences. In her writing and research (and life), she radically transgresses the conventionally assumed different borders of academic disciplines like biology, physics, literature and sociology. Like most of our contemporary social thinkers, her work can be hard to read because it is creating a new way of thinking.

Her most telling and provocative book – published in 1991 – is *Simians, Cyborgs and Women*. Here, Simians are the higher primates – the monkeys, apes and us – and cyborgs are 'hybrid creatures': mixes of our 'natural bodies', other organic creatures, and especially technology and machines. Her 'cyborg manifesto', published first in 1985, suggests the making of new bodies that will transgress the boundaries of nature and conventional bodies. 'Cyborg' is a term originally derived from the study of scientists working and living in outer space, where the conditions of human survival changed dramatically and required much technological aid for humans to survive. This image of the cyborg helps us rethink what it all means to be human, especially as we move into postmodern times. The idea was captured brilliantly in the *Terminator* films. Haraway is credited with suggesting the so-called 'cyborgification of society'.

Critical of seemingly natural science accounts for their presumed objectivity and 'disembodied gaze', Haraway's analysis of human bodies suggests how all our old categories around the body are really just locally produced conventions: they need not be that way. Science often reinforces these categories. In her view, science always needs to be located in specific times and places; and examined critically for its political and ethical engagement. Thus, for example, Haraway sees the divisions of sex/gender (see Chapter 12), nature/culture, body/mind as conventions that need to be transgressed. The history of science can be seen as a set of stories that construct matters such as gender, sex, sexuality and race. And these need challenging. Part of this argument has clearly been of great interest to feminists.

More recently, Haraway's fascination has increased with those interested in the links between humans and other animals. In some of her work she looks at the ways in which people have meaningful relations with their animals: a recent book considers the links between *Dogs, People and Significant Otherness* (2003).

See: Haraway (1991, 2003); and David Bell, *Cyberculture Theorists* (2007). There is also a useful website: www.thecore.nus.edu.

Donna Haraway (1944–)
Source: Permission from Donna Haraway.

qualities of foods, improve their appearance, and be more resistant to general herbicides and plant killers.

Yet, once released into the environment, their impact is hard to predict. There are all kinds of knock-on effect which can produce risks, and these may alter the food production chain. Poor farmers may become locked into technologies that they cannot afford to sustain. In any event, many poorer farmers actually live in countries with food surpluses – the problem is not production of food but its distribution. Direct action has led to many supermarkets banning such foods.

Assisted conception and the new reproductive politics

In 1978, in Britain, Louise Brown became the world's first 'test-tube' baby. Now, in the twenty-first century, such techniques have almost become commonplace worldwide. Technically speaking, test-tube babies are the product of *in vitro fertilisation* (IVF), a procedure whereby the male sperm and the female ovum are united 'in glass' rather than in a woman's body. In this complex medical procedure, doctors use drugs to stimulate the woman's ovaries to produce more than one egg during a reproductive cycle. Then they surgically harvest eggs from her ovaries and combine them with sperm in a laboratory dish. The successful fusion of eggs and sperm produces embryos, which surgeons then either implant in the womb of a woman who is to bear the child, or freeze for use at a later time.

The immediate benefit of *in vitro* fertilisation is to help couples who cannot conceive normally to have children. Infertile couples – and infertility is on the increase – can hence now have children. Looking further ahead, new birth technologies may eventually reduce the incidence of birth defects. By genetically screening sperm and eggs, medical specialists expect to increase the chances of a healthy baby (Thompson, 1994).

In 2004, in the UK alone there were:

- 3.5 million couples having difficulty conceiving (one in seven couples)
- 30,818 patients undergoing IVF (see below)
- 8,275 successful births via IVF, giving rise to 10,175 children
- 708 successful births due to donor insemination, and
- around 1 per cent of all births were the result of IVF and donor insemination.

At the same time, the success rate is not especially high. The average success rate is around 28 per cent for women using IVF who are under 35; for all older categories the success rate is much lower (HFEA, 2007: www.hfea.gov.uk/25.html).

Dolly's story

The story of a baby lamb known as Dolly was introduced to the UK public on 23 February 1997 (though she was actually born on 5 July 1996). Her claim to fame was that she was cloned from a single cell taken from the breast tissue of a single donor. Until this time, as far as we know, all new mammalian life had originated in an embryo through the merger of gametes from a male and female, a mother and a father.

Once the issue of animal cloning has been proved possible, it is but a few steps to the issue of human cloning. Although at present most governments oppose such developments, there have already been maverick scientists who claim to have cloned people. Once again this raises many moral and ethical issues to be considered in the future. Dolly died in 2003, but the issues she raised continue (Wilmut and Highfield, 2006; Rose, 2007).

Timeline The 'new reproduction': key events in the UK

1978	Birth of Louise Brown: the first test-tube baby.
1982	Warnock Committee – advised on ethical issues around new reproduction.
1985	Surrogacy Arrangements Act – banned commercial surrogacy in the UK.
1987	The Pope condemned the new technologies (in his Instruction and Respect for Human Life).
1990s	Growth of stem cell research, infertility research.
1990	Human Fertilisation and Embryology Act.
1991	Human Fertilisation and Embryology Authority established (HFEA).
1996–7	The Dolly story involving a 'cloned' sheep.
2000	President George W. Bush outlawed cloning.
2003	Death of Dolly.
2007	Debate on human–animal hybrids developed by HFEA.
2009	President Barack Obama reversed the Bush decision in his first 100 days: 'medical miracles do not happen simply by accident'.

Ethics and risk

The new reproductive politics brings a wide array of new ethical and political issues. Among the concerns are:

1 The rights and choice to reproduce (or not). Problems of infertility and childlessness no longer mean that you cannot have children by other means.

2 Ovary and egg donation, raising issues about who is donating and ultimately who the parents may be.

3 Egg and sperm banks, raising issues of sperm and eggs being frozen for later use; even the foetus can now be brought 'alive' at a later time.

4 Embryo research, where the use of frozen embryos for medical – and maybe other? – research starts to raise concerns about the moral status of the embryo as a research object.

5 Surrogacy, where the issue of someone else's body being used to carry your child is raised.

6   Commercial surrogacy, whereby the selling and buying of babies, embryos, eggs and sperms often by commercial agencies for 'needy' and infertile 'would-be parents' creates new international markets. In some parts of the world (including much of northern Europe), such markets are generally outlawed; in other countries (for example, the United States), they can be widespread.

7   Much more general issues around the rights to choose exactly the kind of child you want – from choosing the sex of a baby, to avoiding illness and disabilities, to 'age and generation hopping', to cloning for perfection, to gene therapy. In popular language these raise the ethics of 'designer babies', 'cloning' and 'perfect babies'.

All these conflicts raise questions over what it means to give birth and raise children – features that go to the heart of intimacy. But the outcomes of all such decisions have to be seen as unanticipated and risky: we are right on the edge of what Aldous Huxley described in his novel as a *Brave New World*. These new decisions may flow from scientific advances, but they bring in their wake not just a string of medical concerns, but also – once again – many unpredictable risks. Who, for instance, are the children being born this way? What will be their identities? Who are their 'real parents'? And what happens when some of these procedures go wrong?

As doctors, politicians and lawyers decide when to employ or withhold these *new reproductive technologies* (NRTs), they move into a new position to define what constitutes 'families'. In most cases, doctors and hospitals, for instance, have restricted *in vitro* fertilisation to women under 40 years of age who have male partners. Single women, older women and lesbian couples are only slowly gaining access to this technology. In 1991, for example, Arlette Schweitzer, a 42-year-old librarian living in Aberdeen, South Dakota, became the first woman on record to bear her own grandchildren. Because her daughter was unable to have a baby, Schweitzer agreed to have her daughter's fertilised embryos surgically implanted in her own womb. Nine months later, her efforts yielded healthy twins – a boy and girl (Kolata, 1991). Such a case strikingly illustrates how new reproductive technology has created new choices for families and sparked new controversies for society as a whole. The benefits of this rapidly developing technology are exciting, but its use raises daunting ethical questions about the creation and manipulation of life itself. All types of new reproductive

Nirmala Devi and her lawyer Navjit Brar leave Chandigarh court on 9 June 1997 after she sought permission from a judge to 'rent her womb'. Devi offered her womb to a childless couple for 50,000 rupees (£1,000) to bear a child, after conferring with her bedridden and paralysed husband. Police in the northern Indian city of Chandigarh were threatening to prosecute Devi under the Suppression of Immoral Traffic Act. Devi approached the court to declare her 'renting of womb' as legal and said she had no other source of income and cannot bear the medical expenses of 700 rupees (£15) each month for her ailing husband
Source: Rajesh Bhambi/Reuters.

technology – from laboratory fertilisation to surrogate motherhood, in which one woman bears a child for another – force us to confront the inadequacy of conventional kinship terms. Is Arlette Schweitzer the mother of the twins she bore? The grandmother? Or both?

Then, too, we need to consider that, when it comes to manipulating life, what is technically possible may not always be morally desirable. While many women and some feminists have welcomed these developments as a way for women to gain more control over their bodies, others are more sceptical. For Andrea Dworkin, this heralds the arrival of a 'farming model' towards women, and one which signals 'the coming *gynocide*'. The new reproductive technologies 'will give conception, gestation and birth over to men – eventually, the whole process of the creation of life will be in their hands' (Dworkin, 1983: 188). Likewise, Gena Corea writes that '[t]he new reproductive technologies represent an escalation of violence against women, a violence camouflaged behind medical terms' (Corea, 1988: 85). British sociologist Diane Richardson has summarised the key objections. She writes:

> the new reproductive technologies are being used to uphold traditional notions of motherhood and femininity, have serious eugenic implications, have a low success rate and are expensive, pose health risks to women and, most importantly, they can be seen as extending control over women's reproductive capacities.

(Richardson, 1994: 87)

Recognising some of these issues, in 1982 the Warnock Committee was set up by the UK government to consider the ethical implications of such new reproductive issues. In its final report, it advocated very close regulation of such activities through a new body, the Human Fertilisation and Embryology Authority (HFEA), with the power, for example, to license IVF clinics. Unlike the system in the United States, the Warnock Committee (1984) was firmly against the commercialisation of such practices – where wombs can be sold (or rented)!

The computer revolution and the information society

Throughout this book, we have noted how the information technology (IT) revolution has refashioned capitalism. 'Globalisation' (Chapter 2), 'postmodernity' and the 'post-industrial society' (Chapter 4), the 'network society' (Chapter 6), the 'information society' (Chapter 15) and the 'media society' (Chapter 22) are all terms that connect to these changes. The Information Revolution is really a shorthand name for all those high-tech machines (such as faxes, satellite dishes, the internet and mobile phones) which deal with information.

Cees Hamelink (2000) usefully distinguishes four major roles of these new technologies. These are:

1 *Capturing technologies*: those which gather data, such as scanners and remote satellites.
2 *Storing technologies*: those which make data retrievable, such as discs, CD-Roms, and smartcards.
3 *Processing technologies*: those which enable the manipulation of data, such as laptops and gameboys.
4 *Communication technologies*: those which disseminate data, such as broadcasting, mobile phones, faxes and email.

The spread of IT across the world has been an extraordinarily rapid development. In many Western countries it has become part of mainstream life in less than 20 years. Bearing in mind that the World Wide Web was not launched until 1991, already over 180 countries are connected and there are now over 100 million users in the United States alone. A new generation, the Net Generation, for whom the use of personal computers, information technology and the Net is taken for granted, is growing up. Brought up on Nintendo games and computers, they create a huge generation gap, often reversing adult–child roles as children come to know so much more about these things than either their teachers or their parents. Many 'users' are young, male and relatively wealthy: these are what Douglas Rushkoff (1999) calls the 'Digital Kids'. That said, more and more women are becoming involved; information technology is spreading through the classes and ethnicities; and it is moving through more groups across the world. The *Top 10* box shows the countries where it is most in use.

TOP 10
Computers per 100 people, 2008

1	Israel	122.1
2	Switzerland	96.2
3	Canada	94.2
4	Netherlands	91.2
5	Sweden	88.1
6	United States	80.6
7	United Kingdom	80.2
8	Australia	75.7
9	Singapore	74.3
10	Saudi Arabia	69.8

Source: Adapted from *Pocket World in Figures*, Profile Books (2011: 93).

The growth of computing

Briefly, we can see the rise of the new information technologies as passing through three phases:

1 *The mainframe phase.* A first phase was dominated by large, mainframe computers pioneered by IBM and others. In 1946 Philadelphia engineers switched on a machine the size of a large room (yet this 'mother of all computers' was no better (that is, could do no more) than today's four-pound, hand-held calculator). Computers were large and expensive, as well as hard to use and different from each other. There were few around and many people were required to operate each one.

2 *The PC phase.* A second phase started in the 1970s when the first PC (ALTO) was built (in 1972). Now the promise of cheaper, smaller and personal computers began. At roughly the same time, the first internet exchanges started to occur (in November 1969). The Net has its origins in the Pentagon's Advanced Research Projects Agency (ARPA) and gradually spread from the military to the universities. From 1990 private companies came to dominate the space. Between 1998 and 2000 usage in the UK jumped enormously: from 18 to 34 per cent, with some 45 per cent of adults aged 16 and over saying they had accessed the internet at some time (*Social Trends*, 2001: 233–4).

3 *Ubiquitous computing.* A third phase is known as 'ubiquitous computing'. Here computers are everywhere and blend into the background of social life. In this stage, most computers are connected to each other, most people have access to computers, and there are many computers per person. Computer usage becomes routinely linked to the internet. Although we may be in this era already, it may not be till 2020 that it will be in full flower. Computers today are cheap and convenient, most work in similar ways and they can be easily carried around – in laptops, in mobile phones, in watches, in pocket calculators and the like.

Key themes in the 'Digital Age'

Within this information society, some clear themes are emerging. Among the major changes that sociologists note are:

- *Digitalisation.* A common language is replacing earlier analogue systems everywhere. It has been called the 'bar coding' of the world – almost every item now comes 'machine readable' with its bar code. It is there at the supermarket checkout and on almost every 'commodity' being produced, and soon it may even be that our body parts become digitalised as, for example, our eyes instead of passports are scanned at airports.

- *Pervasiveness.* IT is to be found everywhere: in the home from kitchen to bathroom, in offices, on the streets, in finance, government, education, health, etc. We carry it with us in smartcards, smart mobiles, smart homes, smart offices, smart weapons. It is present too in the arrival of surveillance (see Chapter 17).

- *Convergence.* Increasingly, all systems start to adopt this new process, and systems start to look more and more alike.

- *Information and ideas.* There is less concern with things and more concern with ideas. It is no longer the factory assembly line but the computer screen which is the dominant image and metaphor of our time.

- *Shift in space and time.* This is a world less bound to physical reality and, as such, we find it shifts our understanding of many classic things that were bound into a material world. Our sense of space and time changes, as we may now move around the global world instantly. Even our sense of a bounded body may shift as we increasingly engage with ideas in space rather than with embodied people. Virtual realities come to exist.

- *A networking logic.* Finally, as we started to see in Chapter 6, the nature of social groups starts to change. Not only do primary and secondary groups become transformed, but more and more we relate to others through 'networks'.

The social impact of information technologies

The changes we have been discussing may well have an impact on almost every topic we have discussed in this book, from health and cities to education and politics. They touch lives in many ways. Indeed, once again we can see the new technologies as part of the risk society, for we cannot at this stage in our history begin really to see the consequences of the widespread development of cyberspace. There is more 'manufactured uncertainty'. In many countries throughout the world, the 'dangers' of the information society have indeed been recognised, and the state has placed restraints on its use. In what follows we will briefly look at some of the currently identifiable impacts and then consider some of the more negative possibilities.

In Chapter 2, we saw how globalisation itself means a shift in time and space, in part because IT has brought this about. The world has shrunk and become more immediate because of email, websites, mobile phones and the like.

Digital economies

A very central part of this must be the digitalisation of the economy, which has shaped everything from global finance markets and shopping on the Net to 'bar codes' and new forms of work. The global financial economy is absolutely dependent on IT. As Castells (1996: 93) comments:

> Capital is managed around the clock in globally integrated financial markets working in real time for the first time in history: billion dollars-worth of transactions take place in seconds in the electronic circuits throughout the globe.

The Information Revolution is also changing the character of the workplace and even of work itself. Even 30 years ago, Shoshana Zuboff (1982) pointed to four ways in which computers are altering the character of work. She suggested they are:

1 *Deskilling labour.* Just as industrial machinery 'deskilled' the master crafts workers of an earlier era, so computers now threaten to make the skills of managers obsolete. More and more business decisions are based not on executive decision-making but on computer modelling, in which a machine determines whether to buy or sell a product or to approve or reject a loan.

2 *Making work more abstract.* Industrial workers typically have a 'hands on' relationship with their product. Post-industrial workers manipulate words or other symbols in pursuit of more 'user-friendly' software or some other abstract definition of business success.

3 *Limiting workplace interaction.* The Information Revolution forces employees to perform most of their work at computer terminals. This system isolates workers from one another.

4 *Enhancing employers' control of workers.* Computers allow supervisors to monitor each worker's output precisely and continuously, whether employees are working at computer terminals or on an assembly line (see Rule and Brantley, 1992). Technology is not socially neutral; rather, it *shapes* the way we work and alters the balance of power between employers and employees.

Digital democracies

A new shape is also being suggested for politics. In Chapter 16, we suggested how new social movements were partly reshaping politics: such movements as we saw in Seattle, etc., are organised largely in and through networks. We could say that the Web is reshaping the public sphere (see the box featuring Jürgen Habermas on p. 788). More and more people can communicate online about matters that are of concern to them through newsgroups, chat rooms, web links, etc.

Digital relationships

As we saw in Chapter 6, new ways of relating start to appear with mobile phones, email and the internet. One aspect of this is the arrival of online dating. Not only are there highly specialised markets such as CatholicSingles.com and GoodGenes.com, but there are also very large generic sites such as Matchmaker.com, SocialNet.com, and Match.com and Altmatch.com (for gays and lesbians). In China, in 2001, one million (mainly young) people had signed up for Club Yuan, the dating section of the Chinese Sina.com, which is breaking down centuries-old traditions. 'When you talk to girls on the Internet, what you think and feel is more important than how much money you have, or other status symbols that carry so much weight in the outside world,' a Beijing university student who calls himself Supersheng is quoted as saying (*Newsweek*, 'Love Online', 12 March 2001: 46–9).

Creating new cultures and social worlds on the Web

One of the most striking implications for sociologists of the new chat lines, emails, websites and the like is the way in which they are fashioning networks of new cultures and communications. At the simplest level, a personal homepage becomes a new mode for the presentation of a self (see Chapter 7). People can select, embellish or even radically transform a publicly available sense of who they are through the design and content of their personal page.

Interest groups of all kinds can establish worldwide communications with the like-minded: hobbies, fanzines and all soap operas seem to have their sites (*Star Trek* is suggested to have some 1,200 websites alone: Pullen, 2000). Artists can make their work available on sites – not just their art images and their sales programmes, but also a space for discussion among artists. Vast new sexual communities appear online, creating sites for every imaginable sexual fetish and experience. Major world religions and the thousands of breakaway groups and 'new religious movements' all have their sites, and often they are extremely elaborate and detailed. Indigenous peoples, such as the Cherokee Indians, establish sites to 'strengthen tribal ties while asserting sovereign rights and fostering self determination' (Arnold and Plymire, 2000: 192). Diaspora groups such as Indians can create new digital diasporas that serve to fashion new communities. The women's movement can now stretch across the globe – even in poorer and low-income societies – to raise issues and information on the 'cyberfight to stop violence against women', or to discuss and update women's experience at the Beijing Conference on Women's Human Rights. New political organising becomes possible, such as that seen in Seattle or Genoa. It is hard for sociology to ignore the creation of all these new worlds in which self, politics, community are now so intertwined on a global scale (see Gauntlett, 2000, for an expansion of most of these examples and details of websites).

The 'risks' of cyberworlds

As with all technologies, we can ask about how such changes might have invited new social worlds of 'risk' upon us. These are not quite like the worlds of the past where risk may have been even more prominent through natural catastrophe, because these risks are largely unknown and uncertain. To put it simply, as the world of websites, emails and mobile phones has extended rapidly into our lives, what may be the hidden consequences of this quite profound change? More and more people are spending more and more time sitting at and communicating with machines. Might this change their posture, their writing skills, their sense of self, their communities, their communication abilities? We have suggested above that to some extent it already has. Below we consider just four of the more worrying aspects.

Cyberpower, cyberclasses and stratification

One scenario is to see a new world of stratification appearing which is based upon the 'information haves' and the 'information have nots'. This can already be seen in the Western world, where older people without computing skills increasingly find themselves cut off from a new generation that live their everyday lives through these new media and were brought up on 'Gameboys'. Although IT may well have touched most countries across the world, it still does not really touch directly most of the world's 6 billion population. There is a global digital divide. Thus, while some commentators believe that cyberspace will enhance democracy and create greater access to power for all (even suggesting that the new virtual hierarchies may well work to undermine offline 'official hierarchies'), critics suggest that cyberspace could generate a world of **cyberclasses**, *a stratification system based on the information 'haves' and 'have nots' linked to the rise in new information technologies.* Political theorist Zillah Eisenstein comments that:

> Cyberspace is accessible to only a small fraction of people outside the west. Eighty-four percent of computer users are found in north america and northern europe. Sixty-nine percent are male, average age thirty-three, with an average household income of $59,000. The top twenty internet-connected computer countries are significantly homogeneous. They are first world, except for singapore . . . Approximately 80 percent of the world's population still lacks basic telecommunications access. Asia has 1.5 million users, two-thirds of whom are in japan. There are more telephone lines in Manhattan than in all of sub-saharan africa. The united states has thirty-five computers per hundred people; japan has sixteen; taiwan has nine. Ghana, on the other hand, has one computer per thousand people.

(Eisenstein, 1998: 72–3)[1]

It is early days to be clear what the shape of cyberpower will be, but it is interesting to speculate how it may lead to new patterns of social stratification. We may be entering a world where only those with access to

---

[1] Cyberspace is growing so fast that these figures will be seriously out of date. They are only meant to be indicative of the issues that should be raised. Latest figures are available at www.c-i-a.com. Note too that the lack of capitals for countries is a feature of Eisenstein's writing and not a printing error!

information technology have a significant say (and when this is combined with the prospects of the new genetic classes described briefly above becoming a possible future risk, the issues start to multiply).

Information overload

Another scenario looks to the glut of information and how the new society is leading to information overload. We can already see that one consequence of the Web is not simply access to information, but access to too much information. A search may be conducted which tells you there are several million pages available for you to browse. A link may be taken which hurls you deeper and deeper into the trivia of the Net. New skills become necessary to manage, sort, handle and select the vast and growing array of data available. We need to be able to distinguish types of information, to be able to assess the validity of information, to be able to streamline, systematise and sort through masses of data to find key materials, otherwise we will be overloaded and incapacitated.

Cybercrimes

Another striking, though not surprising, feature of the new information technologies is the way in which they are generating new worlds of crime. There is already much concern over hacking (entering computer systems without the owner's permission), the unleashing of viruses that can instantly paralyse world communication systems, computer use for the distribution of illegal materials (from drugs and money-laundering to baby-selling and people-selling, and on to a massive world of erotica and pornography). New forms of 'trouble' are starting to appear – cyber-rape, cyber-harassment, cyber-stalking (see the images in films such as *War Games*, *The Net* and *Hackers*). Many of these crimes are 'virtual'

because they are much less obviously 'bodily' (they involve digital communications in space) and they seem much harder to control and monitor (Hackers. com is a major site full of hacking news and resources!)

The dysfunctionality of IT

Some of the changes that come with the new cyberworlds suggest possibilities of deep, social changes within the social organisation of human nature. Writers within this field of study now talk quite cheerily of an era when we become 'cyborgs' and when we enter the 'post-human society'. Human beings are moving beyond their humanness. We are creating new forms of life – finding new forms of time, breaking down classic life rhythms, reordering our sense of time and space, generating a new impersonality. On the internet, nobody knows you at all, nobody knows who you are, where you are, or even your age, race or gender. For some it is a way of hiding from others and 'real-time' life, a kind of escape and addiction into a new world.

Looking to the future: technology and the risk society

This chapter has looked briefly at three major revolutions taking place in science technology: the quantum revolution, the biomolecular revolution and the computer revolution. Each of these is bringing major changes to society and, indeed, to the very nature of human life at the start of the twenty-first century. From putting people into space to making babies in test tubes, human life is being reconstructed in novel ways.

Cybersexualities

Just as when photography and film were first introduced they generated the pornographic photograph and film, so as soon as the newer information technologies appeared, an erotic world of cybersex and intimacy appeared alongside and embedded within it. New information technologies are used in ways that can facilitate new patterns of sexuality and intimacy. And this is no small world. Surfing the internet gives access to a medium full of intimate words and images: from guidance pages on infertility (over a million sites on sperm banks) to sites engaged in bride-mail ordering; from images of the most 'extreme' sexual fetishes ('Extreme' is indeed the name given to one such site) to access to potentially endless partners on email. The sheer range, number and intense flow of unregulated intimacy and erotica of all kinds that becomes available at the press of a button could never have happened before in history.

These new technologies have generated multiple new forms of intimacy: sex messaging, sex chat rooms, sex news groups and bulletin boards, email discussion groups, camcorder sex, new forms of porn, access to relationships of all kinds, new social movement campaigns around sexuality, even so-called cyborg sex, teledildonics, virtual sex, and new approaches to the body and emergent 'techno-identities' and 'techno-cultures'. Along with this a new language has emerged that mirrors new forms of sexualities – *cyber-porn, cyber-queer, cyber-stalking, cyber-rape, cyber-victim, cybersex*. Although such new forms can result in people meeting in real space for 'real sex', there is also a great deal of masturbatory sex being generated through these media, as well as virtual sex taking place in these virtual spaces.

What this means is that in recent years many new sexual practices have unfolded along with an array of new issues. Sociologists are starting to study just what is going on. Dennis Waskul in *Self Games and Body*

Play: Personhood in Online Chat and Cybersex (2003) applies the theoretical work of Erving Goffman (see Chapter 7) on self-management and the presentation of self in sexual communications online, and Aaron Ben-Ze'ev has examined *Love Online* (2004), providing detailed accounts of how people meet online. Others have documented some of the pitfalls of cybersex – how it can generate infidelity, the growth and routinisation of pornography, the development of sexual harassment online and the growth of 'sexual addiction' on the internet (e.g. Maheu and Subotnik, *Infidelity on the Internet* and Patrick Carnes, *In the Shadow of the Net*, 2001).

On a wider level, sociologists have suggested the moral panics and hysteria gathering around such sexualities. Most prominently there has been the concern with paedophilia on the net, and the ways in which young people can be misled, 'groomed' and ultimately seduced and abused (see Philip Jenkins, *Beyond Tolerance: Child Porn Online*, 2001).

Cybsersexualities, then, are becoming an increasingly important means of sexual communication in the twenty-first century. And they have both positive and negative impacts. Cybersex is a new phenomenon raising many new questions. At the start of the twenty-first century,

there are signs that sociologists are taking significant interest in it.

The idea of 'risk society' starts to alert us to some of the unanticipated dangers that such changes may also bring. In this chapter we have only started to consider some of the issues that this raises.

SUMMARY

1 The 'three pillars of science' are matter, life and mind. Matter leads to the science of the universe and the *quantum revolution*. Life leads to the science of biogenetics and the *biomolecular revolution*. Mind leads to the science of information and the *computer revolution*. With these, science in the twentieth century brought three great 'discoveries': the atom, the gene and the computer. The chapter is roughly structured around these concerns.

2 New technologies bring new risks and are part of the risk society.

3 Sociologists study science in a number of ways. Thomas Kuhn introduced the idea of normal science and paradigms. Robert K. Merton saw science as an institution and outlined four key features of it: universalism, communalism, disinterestedness and organised scepticism. More recently, the sociologists of scientific knowledge have seen science as a social construction and examined how science is socially produced in the laboratory by conducting fieldwork studies.

4 The 'Science Wars' indicate the conflicts between those who see science as neutral objective knowledge and those who see it as socially organised and produced.

5 Advances in the new reproductive technologies, *in vitro* fertilisation, aim to help couples who cannot conceive normally to have children, but they raise many new issues of 'risk': the rights and choice to reproduce (or not); sperm and eggs being frozen for later use; embryo research; surrogacy and commercial surrogacy; cloning for perfection; and the ethics of 'designer babies'.

6 The Information Revolution has developed across the world over the past 20 years. Key themes include its pervasiveness, the importance of digitalisation, the shifts in time and space and the convergence of forms into common networks. It is shifting all aspects of social life and creating digital economies, digital democracies, digital relationships and new cyber-communities. At the same time it brings risks of cyberclasses, cybercrimes, information overload and dysfunctionality.

CONNECT UP: Turn to Part 6 of this book for key resources and link up with the book's website, which links to these resources
SEE: www.pearsoned.co.uk/plummer

MYTASKLIST

Ten suggestions for going further

1 Connect up with Part Six and the Sociology Web Resources

As you work through ideas and think about the issues raised in this chapter, look at the accompanying website and the resource centre at the end of this book which connects to it. There is a lot here to help you move on. To link up, see: www.pearson.co.uk/plummer.

2 Review the chapter

Briefly summarise (in a paragraph) just what this chapter has been about. Consider: (a) What have you learned? (b) What do you disagree with? Be critical. And (c) How would you develop all this? How could you get more detail on matters that interest you?

3 Pose questions

(a) What problems do you find with the idea that 'technology shapes social life'?
(b) Reconsider what you understand by Beck's notion of the 'risk society'. Provide illustrations from contemporary science and technology.
(c) Examine the Science Wars. How far do you think 'sociology of science studies' undermines scientific work?
(d) Examine the ethical issues developed from the Human Genome Project.

4 Explore key words

Many concepts have been introduced in this chapter. You can review them from the website or from the listing at the back of this book. You might like to give special attention to just five words and think them through – how would you define them, what are they dealing with, and do they help you see the social world more clearly or not?

5 Search the Web

Be critical when you look at websites – see the box on p. 940 in the Resources section. For this chapter look at the following:

Human Fertilisation and Embryology Authority
www.hfea.gov.uk
The Human Fertilisation and Embryology Authority is the UK's independent regulator, overseeing safe and appropriate practice in fertility treatment and embryo research.

Human Genome Project
www.genome.gov
The site of the US National Human Genome Research Institute.

Space exploration
http://www.solarviews.com/eng/history.htm
History of space exploration.

On science, more generally, see:

Earlier science
www.sullivan-county.com/id2/index.htm
Looks at the history of major Muslim/Islamic scientists who antedated the European Renaissance.
Also try: http://fugu.biology.qmul.ac.uk and www.geneservice.co.uk/home or more advanced resources on genetic research.

6 Watch a DVD

A chance for science fiction freaks to think about society through science fiction. Does science fiction anticipate social worlds to come? Take a look at:

- James Whale's *Frankenstein* (1931): mad scientist creates a living monster. Changed the original Mary Shelley

(1818) classic novel but now seen as a classic. There have been many spin-offs and remakes of all kinds (including *The Rocky Horror Show*).

- Fritz Lang's *Metropolis* (1926): futuristic tale full of striking images and disturbing politics.

On cyberspace, see:

- Brett Leonard's *The LawnMower Man* (1992): the classic for special effects of virtual reality. Had some claims to be a first in showing this, but a very minor film in fact.
- Andy Wachowki's *The Matrix* (triology): *The Matrix* (1999), *The Matrix Reloaded* (2003), *The Matrix Revolutions* (2003): many have suggested that these are the state-of-the-art 'science' fictions.

See also:

- Joseph Sargent's *The Forbin Project* (1969).
- John Carpenter's *Dark Star* (1974).
- Ridley Scott's *Blade Runner* (1982).
- Chris Columbus's *Bicentennial Man* (1999).
- James Cameron's *The Terminator* (1984) (and the subsequent *Terminator II* (1991) through *Teminator IV* (2008)).
- Jonathan Mostow's *Terminator III: Rise of the Machines* (2003).
- Andrei Tarkovsky's *Solaris* (1972).
- James Cameron's *Avatar* (2009) – the last in a long line of space tales.

7 Think and read

Nikolas Rose, *The Politics of Life Itself* (2007). A major book examining the new 'bio' developments around the body.

Peter Dickens and James Ormrod, *Cosmic Society: Towards A Sociology of the Universe* (2007). Provides a stimulating entrance to a critical sociological account of human beings in the universe.

Ulrich Beck, *Risk Society* (1992). This is the classic and key statement of the emergence of a risk society, though it is far from being an 'easy read'. He has developed his argument further in *World Risk Society* (1999), and it is evaluated from a number of perspectives in Barbara Adam, Ulrich Beck and Joost Van Loon (eds), *The Risk Society and Beyond* (2000).

Marcia C. Inhorn, *Local Babies, Global Science* (2003). One of a number of books studying IVF across the world – this one focuses upon the somewhat unlikely country of Egypt.

See also Faye Ginsburg and Rayna Rapp, *Conceiving the New Order* (1995) and Gay Becker, *The Elusive Embryo* (2000), a study of people who face the problems of infertility and the solutions to such concerns through the new reproductive technologies.

Hilary Rose and Steven Rose, *Alas Poor Darwin: Arguments against Evolutionary Psychology* (2001); Richard Lewontin, *It Ain't Necessarily So: The Dream of the Human Genome and Other Illusions* (2000); and Barbara Katz Rothman, *Genetic Maps and Human Imaginations: The Limits of Science in Understanding Who We Are* (1998) look at the controversies surrounding the 'biological debates'. Rothman's book is a beautifully written and passionate critique of the worst excesses of science. The balance needs to be redressed by looking at Richard Dawkins, *Unweaving the Rainbow: Science, Delusion and the Appetite for Wonder* (2006b).

Stephen Wilkinson, *Bodies for Sale* (2003). Provides a very helpful philosophical guide to the many issues surrounding medical ethics involved in the new 'human body trade'.

Ben Agger, *The Virtual Self: A Contemporary Sociology* (2004). Very readable account – an 'older' sociologist's excitement at virtual reality and society.

On science more generally, see:

David J. Hess, *Science Studies: An Advanced Introduction* (1997). Remains an excellent guide to the sociology of science.

8 Relax with a novel

The literature of science fiction is vast. See Jeff Prucher's *Brave New Words: The Oxford Dictionary of Science Fiction* (2007). Cyberspace can also be found in science fiction, in the work of writers such as William Gibson in his trilogy *Neuromancer* (1984), *Count Zero* (1986) and *Mona Lisa Overdrive* (1988).

9 Connect to other chapters

- Connect reproductive technology debates to Chapter 18 on families.
- Connect cyberworlds to interaction (Chapter 6), power (Chapter 16) and class (Chapters 8–10).
- Connect science to methods (Chapter 3).
- Connect to war in Chapter 16.
- Connect to media in Chapter 22.

10 Engage with
THE BIG DEBATE

The language of life: can the Human Genome Project solve our problems?

For 13 years, until 2003, teams in the UK, Europe and the United States worked hard to unpack the three-billion-letter DNA alphabet. For many, the Human Genome Project represents perhaps the greatest medical breakthrough of all time: the key to DNA. DNA is the spiralling molecule found in each cell of the human body, the molecule that contains the blueprints of our being and makes each one of us different from every other human. Bit by bit, human beings have been decoded.

And now you can read about it on the internet. If it were all to be typed single-spaced on A4 paper, the blueprint for a single human being would fill 750,000 pages! Great hopes are held for it in increasing food production, reducing pollution, combating disease and enhancing the quality of life. Look at www.genome.gov/Education.

In medical terms, the human body is composed of some 100 trillion cells, most of which contain a nucleus of 23 pairs of chromosomes (one of each pair comes from each parent). Each of these chromosomes is packed with DNA, segments of which are called genes. Genes guide the production of proteins, the building blocks of the human body.

If genetics sounds complex (and it is), the social implications of understanding genetics are no simpler. Scientists have known about DNA since 1952, and studied it since then. But now we have the map: our genetic landscape can be set out before our eyes. The ambitious goal of the Human Genome Project was nothing less than to understand the operation of each bit of DNA; in essence, the human genome is the collection of all human genes. Researchers argue that knowing them will help us read and understand the computer program that drives our existence. And therein lies the greatest question of all: do we really want to learn the secrets of life itself?

Many scientists offer strong support for the Human Genome Project. They envisage for the future a completely new approach to medicine: rather than treating symptoms, doctors would address the basic causes of illness. Research, they point out, has already identified the genetic abnormalities that cause some forms of cancer, sickle-cell anaemia, muscular dystrophy, Huntington's disease, cystic fibrosis and a host of other crippling and deadly afflictions. In this twenty-first century, with information from the genetic 'crystal ball', screening will allow us to identify people destined to develop serious illnesses, and doctors will be able to manipulate segments of DNA to prevent the onset of diseases before they start.

But many people, both within and outside the scientific community, urge caution in taking such research too far. The problem, they claim, is that no one is sure how genetic information should be used. At its worst, genetic mapping opens the door to Nazi-like efforts at breeding a super-race.

It seems inevitable that some parents will seek to use genetic testing to evaluate the future health (or even the eye and hair colour) of their unborn child. Should people be permitted to abort a foetus that fails to meet their expectations? Or, further down the road when genetic manipulations become possible, should parents be able to design their own children?

Then there is the issue of 'genetic privacy'. Should a prospective spouse be able to request a genetic evaluation of her fiancé before agreeing to marry? Should life or health insurance companies be allowed to demand genetic testing before writing policies? Should a corporation be permitted to evaluate job applicants in order to weed out those whose future illnesses might drain their healthcare funds? Clearly, what is scientifically possible is not always morally desirable. Our society is already grappling with questions and an important new field of bioethics has come about to consider how to use the ever-expanding knowledge about human genetics. These ethical dilemmas will only mount as genetic research pinpoints the roots of our make-up in the years to come.

Continue the debate

1 Discuss some of the ways in which understanding your genetic code might assist in big life questions like: who will have your baby? Some parents might want to genetically design their children. Would this lead to a class of 'superhumans'?

2 Consider what 'bioethics' is and the issues it raises, and debate some of the concerns that have been raised in this chapter.

3 Where do we turn to devise standards for the proper use of genetic information?

Source: www.genome.gov.

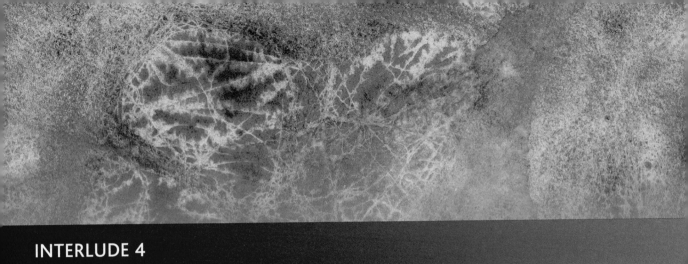

Researching our generational biographies

Simone de Beauvoir, the famous French feminist existentialist philosopher, once pondered in her biography, *All Said and Done* (1977):

> Every morning before I open my eyes, I know I am in my bedroom and my bed . . . I wake up with a childish feeling of astonishment – why am I myself? What astonishes me . . . is the fact of finding myself here, and at this moment, deep in this life and not in any other. What stroke of chance brought this about? . . . It seems to me that a thousand different futures might have stemmed from every single movement of my past; I might have fallen ill and broken off my studies; I might not have met Sartre [the philosopher]; anything at all might have happened. Tossed into the world, I have been subjected to its laws and contingencies, ruled by will other than by own, by circumstances and by history; it is therefore reasonable for me to suggest that I am myself contingent. What staggers me is at the same time I am not myself contingent.
>
> (p. 1)

Are you 'contingent'? What does contingent mean? Does it mean your life is ruled by chance factors? Lives are contingent. They are subject to seemingly chance events, to accidents. We cannot know where a life will lead us, and sometimes the most accidental happening takes us down a path and closes off others – a path we had not foretold in any way.

But if our lives were ruled entirely by chance, surely this would mean we could not predict anything. And one guideline of sociology is that our lives do indeed slip into routines: patterns, structures and institutions. We saw this debate in our second chapter – the action/structure debate (see p. 59) but we have encountered it throughout the book. All the statistics you have encountered suggest big trends in the social world: but no one unique individual has to fit into these trends. In this section of the book, we have outlined some of the major patterns, structures and practices that you were born into and which you confront – almost as the 'social facts' which Durkheim analysed: you cannot wish them away. You act within these institutions – sometimes they enable you to act, and sometimes they frustrate you and you resist them.

In this part of the book, then, we have been examining key historical social institutions and their practices. We have looked at families, economies, politics, religions, education, science, knowledge and means of communications as major institutions that organise societies. They are central to every sociologist's toolbox. But recall C. Wright Mills's famous observation which we introduced in Chapter 1. Here he encourages sociologists to go further – to connect the institutional to the biographical. As he says:

> The sociological imagination enables us to grasp history and biography and the relations between the two. That is its task and its promise.
>
> (Mills, 1967: 4; orig. 1957)

In this interlude, we give brief attention to the biographical elements of sociology and ask you to ponder a little how your own life is constrained or enabled by these institutions. Are your lives contingent upon social structures?

The biography in sociology

There is a small but significant tradition in sociology which uses biography as a research tool. It is seen as a major humanistic mode of understanding. Looking at lives and how they experience the world helps us to grasp the connections between our innermost feelings and the wider outer world of social change. It helps us put the uniqueness of a life with the more general features of a social world. It helps us connect the emotional and the rational, the scientific and the artistic, the objective and the subjective. It bridges what in Chapter 3 we called 'the bridgeable divide'

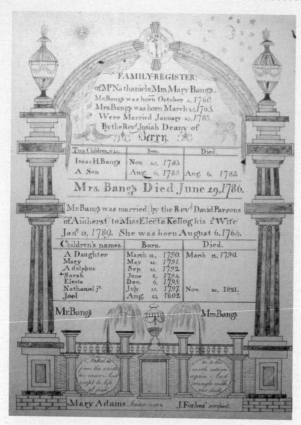

The life and times . . . Useful biographical information for sociological research

Source: Corbis/Catherine Karnow.

share a similar kind of fate: war babies, depression babies, boom babies. We talk about the 'hippy generation', Thatcher's children and the millennial generation. Douglas Coupland's novel *Generation X* (1996) tell the tales of 'twenty somethings' living through the 1980s, and his *Generation A* (2009) tells the tale of youth living at some time in the near future. What is your generation?

3 A biography deals with *phases and sequences* – it tells the story of a life as it moves from birth to death. There are phases and sequences; people move through lives and the world changes with this. So people face key turning points; they have epiphanies; they have major landing stages in their lives. When they look back they can often see stages and what sociologists call 'careers' and 'status passages'. Often a life can be marked out in key turning points (or epiphanies). What kinds of stages have you been through so far?

4 Finally, autobiographies are *stories* told of lives. They are not actually the life – indeed, we can never really grasp the life in all its glory and gory detail. They are instead narratives about ourselves – they tell the tale of what we think (or even want others to think). Think for a bit about the way our lives are story telling – we tell ourselves stories in order to live. What kinds of stories are you telling of your life and how do these stories come to play a role in your life?

Your life in sociology

The parts in this section deal with key concerns of all societies. But in some ways you can now take all these societal concerns and translate them into biographical concerns. All lives (as all societies) have to deal with issues or problems of economy, power, control, household, religion, education, health, communication and knowledge/science. These are features of all societies. They have to be dealt with. But they are also historically and culturally specific – different practices and institutions are developed at different times. And the life experience that goes along with them is hence very different. Your life is partially trapped in all this. Table 1 suggests the most basic way in which this works.

In this section, we can now get a bit more personal. Think about your own life (or that of a friend, family member, or anyone you know quite a lot about). Maybe look back at some of the discussions on biographies and auto/ethnographies raised earlier (in Chapters 3 and 13). And then try to locate your own life as it is touched by the institutions discussed in this part.

between humanistic and positivistic research (Table 3.1) and what in Chapter 1 we called the action and structure debate (see the *Big debate* at the end of that chapter).

There are several useful features about a biography worth noting before we make a few connections to the concerns of this part of the book. These are:

1 A biography exists in a *historical moment* – it tells the story of the moment, and not another moment, in history. Who knows where you will end up when you are born? People born at the start of the twentieth century could hardly have grasped the technologies that had arrived by its end; nor could they have foreseen the horrors of the Holocaust. Yet for many the history of their lives is the history of these changing institutions – technologies, wars, politics. So where do you situate yourself historically? What is your own historical moment?

2 A biography exists in a *generation* – a particular group of people who are born at a similar time often

METHODS & RESEARCH

Studying unfolding lives through longitudinal research

Most sociological research takes a snapshot of people at one particular moment in time. But we also need to grasp the ways in which lives develop over their own life stages within wider historical and social change. The world for a 50-year-old in 2011 is very different from the world they were born into in 1961; and it will be very different around their likely death 50 years on in 2061. Significant change – in life and society – is often overlooked in sociological research. The study of this change over time is called **longitudinal research**, which *provides information about what has happened to the research subjects over time*.

In popular culture, an example of this is the *Up* television series of documentaries produced by Michael Apted, which have followed 14 children since 1964 when they were 7 years old. They were chosen to represent different social classes and have been followed up every seven years (the next study is due in 2011 or 2012). Similar programmes have been made in Australia, Belgium, France, the Czech Republic, Denmark, Germany, Japan, the Netherlands, South Africa, Sweden, the USA and the USSR. In 2000, the BBC started *Child of our Time* to follow the lives of 25 children who were born around the turn of the millennium. (See the Wikipedia entry for a tour: there are DVDs available from the series.)

Sociological researchers have developed this much more. Some follow large numbers of people across the age cycle – these are often called *panel or cohort studies*. Others follow smaller numbers more intensively. The former are usually quantitative and statistical and are illustrated in the work of the British Household Panel in the UK (which can be found on the BHPS website at www.iser.essex.ac.uk/survey/bhps). It is household-based, interviewing every adult member of sampled households. The wave 1 panel consisted of some 5,500 households and 10,300 individuals drawn from 250 areas of Great Britain. The latter are qualitative, usually known as QLR (qualitative longitudinal research). An example of this is the Inventing Adulhoods Project between 1996 and 2006 which studied 100 young people over ten years from different parts of the country. It is now partially digitalised and can be accessed at the Inventing Adulthoods site (www1.lsbu.ac.uk/inventingadulthoods).

For a detailed introduction to these studies, see: Jane Elliott, *Using Narrative in Social Research* (2005: Chapter 4) and Julie McLeod and Rachel Thompson, *Researching Social Change* (2009: Chapter 4).

Table 1	Our problems in living and the habits we build around them
Core problems in social living which people face	**Ways societies handle this: structures, institutions, practices**
Getting basic resources – food, shelter	The economic (including work and consumption)
Getting organised – achieving goals	The polity
Keeping things orderly	The law – and socialisation
Reproducing the society	The family, kinship, intimacies
Fostering good relations	Civic life, citizenship, welfare
Developing communications	Language and media
Acquiring and developing knowledge	Science and education
Cultivating a spiritual side to life	Religion
Others	*Note: This is NOT meant as an exhaustive list.*

Generational biographies: going further

These short introductions to fields of study cannot go far. But consider that each institution discussed in this part of the book can be applied back to your own life. Then ask what it was like for your grandparents' generation. Finally, take a glimpse into an imagined future – just what might these institutions be like in your grandchildren's time, 50 years hence.

Ponder: how is your (any) life shaped by:

- *Economy*: What kind of economic system do you live in? What is your work, your income and wealth, your consumption? And what about that of your grandparents? Your grandchildren?

- *Political process*: Who has power? How much control do you have over your governments? And what about that of your grandparents? Your grandchildren?

- *Social control*: How does society deal with order and breakdown? How do you live with crimes? And what about your grandparents? Your grandchildren?

- *Family*: How do you find ways of living together? And what about your grandparents? Your grandchildren?

- *Religion*: How do you come to believe in your gods? And what about your grandparents? Your grandchildren?

- *Education*: How do you learn about a culture and the world? And what about your grandparents? Your grandchildren?

- *Health*: How do you deal with your body and its ailments? And what about your grandparents? Your grandchildren?

- *Communications*: How do you talk and interact with others and our machines? And what about your grandparents? Your grandchildren?

- *Knowledge and science*: How do you develop wider understandings of the world? And what about your grandparents? Your grandchildren?

Two quick examples. Those born between, say, 1990 and now have only ever known a world organised through television, computers and mobile phones, or, on a wider level, AIDS as a disease. When I was born, I knew of no such things. Indeed, I did not have a computer till 1984 – when I was moving towards being aged 40! So my initial experience of such commonplaces of the present day was a challenging one. I can recall when we wondered whether computers would catch on; when people said mobile phones were just a silly phase; when AIDS was called GRID and people were unsure what it was. There again, the generation before me would have found the worlds of television, automobiles and land phones to have been a novelty. More politically, they would have known the horrors of living through the Second World War – and indeed the depression that preceded it. I have moved through my life with direct contact with this. Language, dress, media, politics – everything keeps on changing across the generations and any understanding of the social requires a deep taking on board of these different generational meanings and standpoints.

Further reading

Terhi Rantanen, *The Media and Globalization* (2005). Uses the details from the lives of three families (from Finland, China and Latvia) across four generations (born roughly in 1900, 1925, 1950 and 1975). A key focus is on the ways in which the media have influenced their lives.

Ken Plummer, *Documents of Life – 2: An Invitation to a Critical Humanism* (2001a). Now an e book and is an introduction to this whole field. It has a chapter on doing life stories and narratives.

PART 5

SOCIAL CHANGE AND THE TWENTY-FIRST CENTURY

CHAPTER 24

POPULATIONS, CITIES AND THE SPACE OF THINGS TO COME

Winning eight Oscars in 2008, Danny Boyle's *Slumdog Millionaire* was the hit film of that year. A homage to Indian commercial cinema, it is based on an Indian novel *Q & A* by Vikas Swaru. It tells the story of Jamal Malik (Patel), an 18-year-old orphan from the dharavi slums of Mumbai, who is about to win 20 million rupees on India's *Who Wants To Be A Millionaire?* It is a rags to riches tale. As the whole country watches, he is arrested on suspicion of cheating and tortured by the police. How could a street kid know so much? To prove his innocence, he tells his story. There are some great musical numbers.

The film is set in the slums of Mumbai, one of the world's largest modern urban cities, and was criticised for being 'poverty porn' and exploitative. Colourful and romantic, it showed the 'West' a glimpse of the new poverty cities of the world. With a population between 14 and 19 million, Mumbai is one of the biggest cities in the world – one of a whole breed of new slum megacities in low-income societies. It sprawls; it smells; it is chaos. Most notedly it is two cities – a rich city with smart hotels, tourism and billionaires living extravagant lives; and a desperately poor one where millions struggle to survive every day with no sanitation, no work, no money, no electricity and very little in the way of housing. Here most Indians live in *chawls* – dilapidated all-purpose rooms cramming six people into 15 square metres with 10 to 20 tenements on four or five floors. The latrine is usually shared with many other families. These 'homes' are so small that most of the time is spent on the street away from them. Mike Davis, author of *City of Slums*, highlights the stark contrast: 'The rich have some 90 per cent of the land and live in comfort in open areas, the poor live crushed together on 10 per cent of the land' (Davis, 2006: 34, 96). Most urban dwellers in India live in slums with tin roofs, little sanitation and no electricity. Welcome to the slums of the modern world . . .

In the same year, the Man Booker prize for best fiction was awarded to Aravind Adiga's *The White Tiger*. This too is set in India and gives a portrait of the 'two Indias': 'the bleak, soul-destroying poverty of village life and the glittering prizes to be found in the big city'. Through the eyes of the protagonist, Balram Halwai, we see more of the dark side of modern India.

 tip Watch: Danny Boyle's *Slumdog Millionaire* (2008).
Read: Aravind Adiga's *White Tiger* (2008).
Study: Mike Davis's *City of Slums* (2006).

The city is a world of strangers

Lynn Lofland

In this chapter we ask:

- **What is demography and how are populations shaped?**

- **What are the key issues around the 'population explosion'?**

- **How have cities grown?**

- **What kinds of problem do the new cities raise?**

(Left) Aerial view of a market in St Paul, Reunion
The aerial photographs of Yann Arthus-Bertrand are stunning. Look at his work on YouTube, at www.yannarthusbertrand.org, or his book *The Earth From the Air* (2004).
Source: © Yann Arthus-Bertrand/Corbis.

 Consider how 'society' can be analysed from the air in striking ways.

This chapter examines both population growth and urbanisation – two powerful forces that have worked hand in hand to shape and reshape our planet for thousands of years. A steadily increasing population has been one of the most serious challenges facing the world, and this has been linked to the growth of urban regions of unprecedented size. Interest in these issues is linked to what is called 'the sociology of space', an area of sociology which looks at the changing ways in which we create and organise the spaces we live through (Hubbard et al., 2004).

The sociology of space

For sociologists, spaces are not simple givens or things we can take for granted. All space is socially organised and transformed: we build the places we live in and the spaces in which we move around. This is obvious when we look at maps: they seem to tell us where we stand in relation to things. It also seems obvious when we look at the buildings we inhabit: the houses, the offices, the factories, the shops, the museums. But in fact these are all things we have built – they are socially produced. For example, maps are not simply maps. Looking at history, and different cultures, it becomes clear that maps of the world take on very different shapes. Most of us are so used to the modern Western map of the world that it is hard to imagine any other. But many are possible and it is interesting to ponder just why we have the map we do.

This is also true of the way we make our own private, more personal spaces. We construct our own little worlds of space: the rooms of our own, the landscapes that pattern our neighbourhoods, the 'maps' of our lives.

Sociologists call all this 'the social construction of space' – the ways in which humans come to make, organise and transform the locations through which lives are then conducted. A simple way to grasp this is to consider what your 'spaces' would be like if you lived in a favela or shanty town in Rio, you hung around on street corners in downtown Los Angeles taking drugs, you worked in a smart office block in the City of London, or you slept all day in your own small bedroom. Or if you live in a gated community, go partying, or enjoy Disneyland. All societies are characterised by an enormous number of spaces and socially organised locations. These are all spaces we have invented, and sociology discusses how we make them, live in them, and transform them. We will focus

later in the chapter on the move to cities and the ways in which this process – urbanisation – has transformed lives.

Demography and population

From the point at which the human species emerged about 250,000 BCE until several centuries ago, the population of the entire earth was never more than 500 million – less than the number of Europeans today. Life for our ancestors was anything but certain; people were vulnerable to countless diseases, frequent injury and periodic natural disasters. Powerless in the face of such calamity, one might well be amazed that our species has managed to survive for hundreds of generations.

About 250 years ago, however, world population began to push upward and the population is now more than six times larger than it was in 1800. People spoke of the 'population time bomb', as fears were expressed about whether the globe could take such a steep and rapid expansion. The numbers rose to about 3 billion in 1960. Since then the population has grown by around a billion every 12 to 14 years. In 2011, it was roughly 7 billion. Overall, the world population is expected to increase by roughly 2.6 billion during the next 45 years, from 6.4 billion in 2004 to around 9 billion in 2050 (see Figure 24.1). The populations of higher-income regions of the world, however, are increasing at a very low rate (around 0.25 per cent) while those in lower-income societies are increasing nearly six times as fast (and a subset of these – 49 of the least developed societies – are growing at 2.4 per cent per year). By 2050, high-income societies will have populations in steep decline (and getting older and older – see Chapter 13), while low-income societies will still have populations growing at an annual rate of 1.2 per cent.

The causes and consequences of this human drama form the core of **demography**, *the study of human population*. Demography (from Greek, meaning 'description of people'), a close cousin of sociology, analyses the size and composition of a population as well as how people move from place to place. Although much demographic research is a numbers game, the discipline also poses crucial questions about the effects of population growth and its control. The following sections explain basic demographic concepts.

Table 24.1	Trends in global population: population of the world, major development groups and major areas, 1950, 1975, 2009 and 2050

Major area	Population (millions)			Population in 2050 (millions)			
	1950	1975	2009	Low	Medium	High	Constant
World	2,529	4,061	6,829	7,959	9,150	10,461	11,030
More developed regions	812	1,047	1,233	1,126	1,275	1,439	1,256
Less developed regions	1,717	3,014	5,596	6,833	7,875	9,022	9,774
Least developed countries	200	357	835	1,463	1,672	1,898	2,475
Other less developed countries	1,517	2,657	4,761	5,369	6,202	7,123	7,299
Africa	227	419	1,010	1,748	1,998	2,267	2,999
Asia	1,403	2,379	4,121	4,533	5,231	6,003	6,010
Europe	547	676	732	609	691	782	657
Latin America and the Caribbean	167	323	582	626	729	845	839
Northern America	172	242	348	397	448	505	468
Oceania	13	21	35	45	51	58	58

Source: Population Division of the Department of Economic and Social Affairs of the United Nations Secretariat (2009). *World Population Prospects: The 2008 Revision. Highlights.* New York: United Nations.

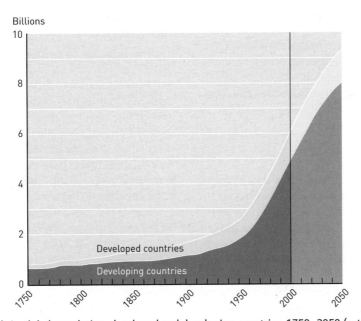

Figure 24.1	Trends in global population, developed and developing countries, 1750–2050 (estimates and projections)

Note: Each day 200,000 more people are added to world food demand. The world's human population has increased nearly fourfold in the last 100 years; it is projected to increase from 6.7 billion (2006) to 9.2 billion by 2050. It took only 12 years for the last billion to be added, a net increase of nearly 230,000 new people each day, who will need housing, food and other natural resources. The largest population increase is projected to occur in Asia, particularly in China, India and southeast Asia, accounting for about 60 per cent and more of the world's population by 2050. The rate of population growth, however, is still relatively high in Central America, and highest in central and part of western Africa. In relative numbers, Africa will experience the most rapid growth, over 70 per cent faster than in Asia (annual growth of 2.4 per cent versus 1.4 per cent in Asia, compared to the global average of 1.3 per cent and 0.3 per cent in many industrialised countries) (statistics from UN Population Division, 2007). In sub-Saharan Africa, the population is projected to increase from about 770 million to nearly 1.7 billion by 2050.

Source: Hugo Ahlenius, Nordpil; http://maps.grida.no/go/graphic/trends-in-population-developed-and-developing-countries-1750-2025-estimates-and-projections.

TOP 10

Largest world populations, September 2009 (to nearest million)

1	China	1,339
2	India	1,157
3	United States	307
4	Indonesia	240
5	Brazil	190
6	Pakistan	175
7	Bangladesh	156
8	Nigeria	149
9	Russia	140
10	Japan	127

Note: UK is 22nd with 62m, Australia is 51st with 22m, Hong Kong is 98th with 7m.

Source: Based on US Census Bureau data in www.internetworldstats.com/stats8.htm.

Key factors shaping the population

In any country, three factors play a crucial role in shaping its population. These are **fertility**, which shapes the numbers born; **mortality**, which shapes the numbers who die; and **migration**, which shows the patterns of people moving in and out of a country. Below we briefly consider each of these.

1 Fertility

The study of human population begins with how many people are born. **Fertility** is *the incidence of child-bearing in a country's population*. During their child-bearing years, from the onset of menstruation (typically in the early teens) to menopause (usually in the late forties), women are capable of bearing more than 20 children. But *fecundity*, or maximum possible child-bearing, is sharply reduced in practice by cultural norms, finances and personal choice.

Most simply, demographers use the measure of **crude birth rate** to describe *the number of live births in a given year for every thousand people in a population*. (In 2000, the birth rate for the world was 22, but because it conceals so much variation, this is a quite useless figure!) A more sophisticated measure is the **total period fertility rate** (TPFR), *the average number of children each woman would have in her lifetime if the average number of children born to all women of child-bearing age in any given year remained constant during that woman's child-bearing years*. This measure tells us the average number of children women have had in the past and allows us to project how many they may be likely to have in the future. In 1964, the TPFR for women in the UK was 2.95 children. By 2002, it had fallen to 1.6 (*Social Trends*, 2004).

This measure has gained favour among demographers because the calculation is not affected if the proportion of women in different age groups changes. This flexibility is important, as was noted in Chapter 13, because the proportion of elderly women (as well as men) is increasing in industrialised societies. As will be discussed later in this chapter, the proportion of young people is increasing in many less developed countries. The TPFR thus allows for valuable comparisons between countries in the modern world.

The accuracy of the projections can weaken, however, if women change the average age at which they start having children. In Europe, women are generally waiting longer to have their first baby. While many women became pregnant in their teens prior to the Second World War, the average age of first birth had risen to the late twenties in many European countries by the 1990s. In the new century, European women have more educational and career opportunities than they enjoyed in earlier decades, as well as having access to more reliable family planning methods. Many women are choosing to seize these opportunities before they start a family. Even so, some demographers predict that women who have children are, on average, unlikely to wait much longer than they are now to have their first baby, and TPFRs may increase very slightly in the coming years (*Social Trends*, 1997: 32).

2 Mortality

Population size is also affected by **mortality**, *the incidence of death in a country's population*. In addition to the TPFR, demographers use a **crude death rate**, *the number of deaths in a given year for every thousand people in a population*. In 1995 there were 642,000 deaths in the UK population of 58.6 million, yielding a crude death rate of 10.9. The crude death rate in industrialised countries has fallen sharply over the last century. In the UK in 1900, over 17 of every thousand people died each year (*Social Trends*, 1997: 33). Higher crude death rates are still common in non-industrialised countries today.

Table 24.2	World demographic indicators, 2005–2010[1]					
					Life expectancy at birth (years)	
	Population (millions)[2]	Population density (sq. km)[2]	Infant mortality rate[3]	Total fertility rate	Males	Females
Asia	4,167	131	41.5	2.35	67.1	70.8
Africa	1,033	34	82.6	4.61	52.9	55.3
Europe	732	32	7.2	1.50	71.1	79.1
Latin America and the Caribbean	587	29	21.8	2.26	70.2	76.7
North America	352	16	5.8	2.04	77.0	81.5
Oceania	36	4	22.8	2.44	74.1	78.9
World	6,909	51	47.3	2.56	65.4	69.8

[1] Data are estimates and projections for the period 2005–2010, revised in 2008.
[2] Data are projections for 2010.
[3] Per 1,000 live births.

Source: *Social Trends*, 40 (2010), Table 1.14, p. 10.

TOP 10
Highest infant mortality rates

1	Angola	180.21
2	Afghanistan	153.14
3	Liberia	138.24
4	Niger	116.66
5	Mali	115.86
6	Somalia	109.19
7	Mozambique	105.80
8	Zambia	101.20
9	Guinea-Bissau	99.82
10	Chad	98.69

Note: North Korea is ranked 49th with 51.34 and Cyprus at 154th with 9.7.

Figures give the number of deaths of infants under one year old in a given year per 1,000 live births in the same year. This rate is often used as an indicator of the level of health in a country.

Source: www.cia.gov/library/publications/the-world-factbook/ rankorder/2091rank.html.

TOP 10
Highest life expectancy

1	Macau	84.36
2	Andorra	82.51
3	Japan	82.12
4	Singapore	81.98
5	Hong Kong	81.86
6	Australia	81.63
7	Canada	81.23
8	France	80.98
9	Sweden	80.86
10	Switzerland	80.85

Note: The UK is ranked 36th with a life expectancy of 79.01 years, Lithuania is ranked 87th with a life expectancy of 74.90 and Angola is ranked 224th with a life expectancy of 38.20. Caution: these figures are based on 2009 estimates.

Source: www.cia.gov/library/publications/the-world-factbook/ docs/notesanddefs.html#E.

Table 24.3 Demographic indicators: selected EU countries[1]

	1970				Life expectancy at birth (years)		2005–2010[2]				Life expectancy at birth (years)[2]	
	Population (millions)	Population density (sq. km)	Total fertility rate	Infant mortality rate[3]	Males	Females	Population (millions)[4]	Population density (sq. km)[4]	Total fertility rate	Infant mortality rate[3]	Males	Females
Germany	78.17	219	1.64	21.1	67.9	73.8	82.06	230	1.32	4.1	77.1	82.4
France	50.77	92	2.31	16.3	68.6	76.2	62.64	114	1.89	3.9	77.6	84.7
United Kingdom	55.66	229	2.44	17.4	69.0	75.2	61.89	253	1.94	4.7	77.2	81.6
Italy	53.36	177	2.35	26.7	69.1	75.1	60.10	199	1.38	3.9	78.1	84.1
Netherlands	13.04	314	2.06	11.7	71.1	77.0	16.65	401	1.74	4.5	77.8	82.0
Belgium	9.63	316	2.02	17.2	68.4	74.9	10.67	350	1.77	4.1	76.7	82.6
Denmark	4.93	114	1.97	12.0	70.9	76.4	5.48	127	1.84	4.4	76.0	80.6
Ireland	2.95	42	3.82	18.1	68.9	73.8	4.59	65	1.96	4.5	77.5	82.3
Luxembourg	0.34	131	1.72	17.1	67.2	74.1	0.49	190	1.66	4.2	76.7	82.1

[1] The nine EU countries after the UK joined in 1973.
[2] Data are estimates and projections for the period 2005–2010, revised in 2008.
[3] Per 1,000 live births.
[4] Data are projections for 2010.

Source: Social Trends, 40 (2010), Table 1.16, p. 11.

Table 24.3 suggests how death rates and birth rates combine to show natural population change. Mortality data also permit the calculation of **life expectancy**, *the average age to which people in a given society are likely to live*. Males born in Britain in 2002 can expect to live 75.7 years, while females can look to over 80 years (*Social Trends*, 2004).

Another widely used demographic measure is the **infant mortality rate**, *the number of deaths among infants under one year of age for each thousand live births in a given year*. Again, even in Europe, with a generally low infant mortality rate, there are significant differences across countries. Thus, in eastern Europe the rates are actually quite high, but in the European Union they are among the lowest in the world.

In Europe, infant mortality has declined dramatically over the last 40 years. Baby girls have a slightly higher chance of survival than baby boys, though this gap is narrowing. Infant mortality can also vary between ethnic groups. In the United States, white and Asian babies are more likely to survive past infancy than African-American babies, for example.

3 Migration

Population size is also affected by **migration**, *the movement of people into and out of a particular territory*. As we have seen in Chapter 11, migration is sometimes involuntary, such as the forcible transportation of 10 million Africans to the Western Hemisphere as slaves (Sowell, 1981). Voluntary migration, however, is usually the result of complex 'push–pull' factors. Dissatisfaction with life in poor countries may 'push' people to move, just as the higher living standards of rich nations may exert a powerful 'pull'. Net migration to the UK increased to 198,000 in 2009 compared with 163,000 in the previous year. This was primarily as a result of decreased emigration. Some 1.25 million immigrants enter the United States each year.

People's movement into a territory, commonly termed *immigration*, is measured as an **in-migration rate**, calculated as *the number of people entering an area for every thousand people in the population*. Movement out of a territory, or *emigration*, is measured in terms of the **out-migration rate**, *the number leaving for every thousand people*. Both types of migration usually occur simultaneously; their difference is called the **net migration rate**. All nations also experience internal migration: that is, movement within their borders from one region to another.

Migration has become an issue of particular social concern in many parts of Europe. As was discussed in Chapter 11, some white Europeans fear the immigration of non-white peoples with different cultures and languages from other parts of the globe and, as a response, seek to restrict numbers of immigrants from outside Europe. Indeed, the rising number of racist attacks against immigrant communities in many European countries reflects the more extreme end of this spectrum. Many small rural communities also worry over the out-migration of young people and, in some cases, the in-migration of the elderly. Without new generations to carry on their traditions, some rural communities may disappear. Additionally, the member governments of the European Union periodically worry about so-called 'benefit tourists', people who move from one country offering less public support to the poor to another country with more generous benefits. For this reason, many politicians would like to standardise some benefits to spread the cost of supporting the less well-off more evenly.

Population growth

Fertility, mortality and migration all affect a society's population. The projected population growth of countries throughout the world, with the breakdown by region, is shown in Figure 24.2. In general, the earth's low-growth continents include Europe, North America and Oceania. Asia, with 1.7 per cent growth, stands near the global average, while Latin America (1.9 per cent growth) and Africa (2.8 per cent growth) comprise the high-growth regions of the world. *Natural increase* (more births than deaths) accounts for the majority of population expansion in the high-growth regions.

A handy rule of thumb is that dividing a society's population growth rate into the number 70 yields the *doubling time* in years. Thus, annual growth of 2.8 per cent means that the African population will double in 25 years. The population is growing most rapidly in countries with the fewest resources to cope with more people (Population Reference Bureau, 1995b).

Population composition

Demographers also study the composition of a society's population at a given point in time.

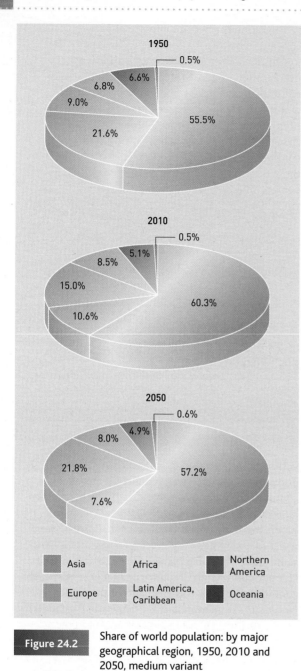

1950

0.5%
6.6%
6.8%
9.0%
21.6%
55.5%

2010

0.5%
5.1%
8.5%
15.0%
10.6%
60.3%

2050

0.6%
4.9%
8.0%
21.8%
7.6%
57.2%

- Asia
- Africa
- Northern America
- Europe
- Latin America, Caribbean
- Oceania

Figure 24.2 Share of world population: by major geographical region, 1950, 2010 and 2050, medium variant

Source: World Population Prospects, 2008 Revision.

One simple variable is the **sex ratio**, *the number of males for every hundred females in a given population.* Sex ratios are usually below 100 because women typically outlive men. In India, however, the sex ratio is 108. More males than females survive in India, as well as in parts of east Asia, much of the Middle East and north Africa, because parents value sons more than daughters. Thus parents are more likely to abort a female foetus or, after birth, to provide less care to females than to males.

A more complex measure is the **age–sex pyramid**, *a graphical representation of the age and sex of a population* (Figure 24.3). The rough pyramid shape of these figures results from higher mortality as people age. Looking at the high-income pyramid, the bulge corresponding to ages 20–49 reflects high birth rates from the mid-1940s to the late 1960s, resulting in the *baby boom*. The contraction just below this band represents the baby bust that followed as birth rates dipped.

Age–sex pyramids not only reflect a society's history, they foretell its future. The age–sex pyramid for lower-income nations is wide at the bottom (reflecting higher birth rates) and narrows quickly by what we would call middle age (due to higher mortality). They tend therefore to be much younger societies. But Figure 24.3 tells an interesting new story. By 2040 the pyramid shape common in the past now starts to widen again at the top. This starts to indicate a new age structure in which the old are living much longer.

History and theory of population growth

Throughout most of human history, societies favoured large families, since human labour was the key to productivity. Additionally, until the development of rubber condoms 150 years ago, controlling birth was uncertain at best. But if birth rates were high, so were death rates, as populations were periodically ravaged by infectious diseases. Thus world population at the dawn of civilisation, about 8000 BCE, hovered well below 100 million.

A demographic shift began in about 1800, as the earth's population reached the 1 billion mark. Humans reached the next billion by 1930, barely a century later! The global population reached 3 billion by 1962 – after just 32 years – and 4 billion by 1974, a scant 12 years later. The rate of world population increase has recently slowed, but in 2007, the world population was estimated at over 6.5 billion. In no previous century did the world's population even double. In the twentieth century, it increased *fourfold*.

Currently, global population is increasing by 90 million people each year, with more than 90 per cent of this growth in poor societies. At this rate, the earth's people will probably reach 8.3 billion by 2025 and pass 10 billion within a century from now.

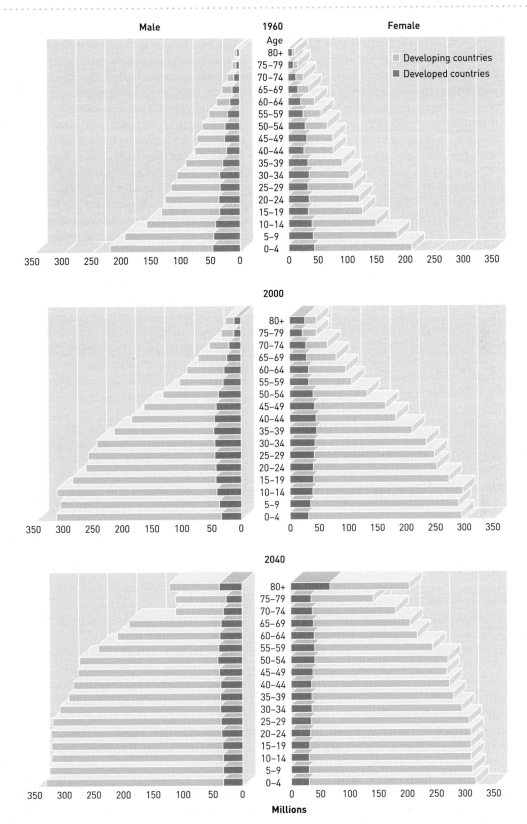

Male   **1960**   **Female**

Developing countries
Developed countries

2000

2040

Millions

Figure 24.3   Population in developed and developing countries: by age and sex, 1960, 2000 and 2040

Source: US Census Bureau, *An Aging World*, 2008.

Without a change in global consumption and living patterns, this increase will have dramatic social and environmental consequences. For this reason, a number of scholars have reflected on the potential impacts of population growth. This chapter now assesses some of the more influential perspectives.

Malthusian theory

The sudden population growth two centuries ago sparked the development of demography. Thomas Robert Malthus (1766–1834), an English clergyman and economist, noted that the number of people in the world had begun to increase geometrically (that is, doubling each time, 2, 4, 8, 16, 32, etc.). Even though people were improving farming technology and techniques, Malthus feared that the limited range of farmland could only sustain an *arithmetic increase* (as in the series 2, 3, 4, 5, 6) in the production of food (1926; orig. 1798). He concluded that the world might head towards a period of catastrophic starvation.

Malthus noted that people could slow the tide of population increase through *preventive checks*, such as family planning, sexual abstinence and delayed marriages; however, people objected to birth control on religious grounds, and his common sense told Malthus that people would not abstain from sex or marry very much later. He also predicted that such *positive checks* as famine, disease and war would slow – but not prevent – the progression towards the final catastrophe, a vision that earned him the nickname of 'the dismal parson'.

Critical evaluation

Fortunately for us, Malthus's predictions were flawed. By 1850, the birth rate in Europe began to drop, partly because children were becoming more of an economic liability than an asset and partly because people began to use condoms. Secondly, Malthus underestimated human ingenuity. Irrigation, fertilisers and pesticides have increased farm production far more than he imagined. Some critics also noted that poor regions suffer deaths from war and famine disproportionately and objected to viewing suffering as a 'law of nature' rather than the product of inequality.

Still, we should not entirely dismiss Malthus's distressing prediction. First, habitable land, clean water and fresh air are certainly finite. Greater industrial productivity has taken a toll on the natural environment. Additionally, as medical advances have lowered death rates, the world population has risen even faster. This planet cannot sustain an indefinite increase in its number of people.

Demographic transition theory

Malthus's rather crude analysis has been superseded by **demographic transition theory**, *a thesis linking population patterns to a society's level of technological development*. Why did world population soar after 1800? Why is population increase much higher in poor countries than in rich nations? Demographic transition theory answers these questions by analysing birth and death rates at four stages of a society's technological development. As shown in Figure 24.4, societies yet to industrialise, those at Stage 1, have high birth rates because of the economic value of children, the absence of effective family planning and the high risk that children will not survive to adulthood. Death rates, too, are high, due to periodic outbreaks of plague or other infectious disease, low living standards and a lack of medical technology. But deaths almost offset births, so population increase is modest.

Stage 2, the onset of industrialisation, brings a demographic transition as population surges upward. Technology expands food supplies and science combats disease. Death rates fall sharply but birth rates remain high, resulting in rapid population growth. It was in an era like this that Malthus formulated his ideas, and that goes a long way towards explaining his pessimism. Most of the world's least economically developed societies today are still in this high-growth stage.

In Stage 3, a mature industrial economy, birth rates drop, finally coming into line with death rates and, once again, curbing population growth. Fertility falls, because most children born do survive to adulthood, and rising living standards make raising children expensive. Affluence, in other words, transforms offspring from economic assets into economic liabilities. Smaller families, also favoured by women working outside the home, are made possible by the widespread availability of family planning. As birth rates follow death rates downward, population growth slows further.

The most recent stage corresponds to a post-industrial economy. The birth rate in such societies continues to fall, in part because dual-income couples gradually become the norm and partly because the costs of raising children continue to rise. This trend,

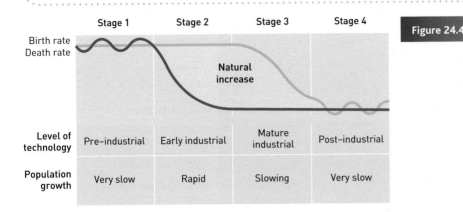

Figure 24.4 Demographic transition theory

coupled with steady death rates, means that, at best, population grows only very slowly. Recent years have witnessed a natural *decrease* in Europe's population.

Critical evaluation

Demographic transition theory suggests that technology holds the key to demographic shifts. Instead of the runaway population increase Malthus feared, this analysis foresees technology reining in population growth. Demographic transition theory dovetails with modernisation theory, one approach to global development examined in Chapter 9.

Modernisation theorists are optimistic that industrialisation will also solve the population problems that now are placing strains on poor countries. But critics, notably dependency theorists, counter that current economic arrangements only ensure continued poverty in much of the world. Unless there is a significant redistribution of global resources, they maintain, our planet will become increasingly divided into industrialised 'haves', enjoying low population growth, and non-industrialised 'have-nots', struggling in vain to feed soaring populations.

Global population today

A brief survey of population trends around the world today reveals a growing gap between events in richer and poorer nations. Understanding these trends is the first step to understanding the nature of the population problem.

The low-growth North

When the Industrial Revolution began, growth in western European and North American populations peaked at 3 per cent annually, doubling the population in little more than one generation. But since then, growth rates have eased downward throughout the Northern Hemisphere. The natural increase from births over deaths in Europe dropped from 7.7 per thousand in 1960 to 1.00 per thousand in 1990. As Europe entered Stage 4, the birth rate neared the replacement level of 2.1 children per woman, a point that demographers designate as **zero population growth**, *the level of reproduction, migration and death that maintains population at a steady state.* Demographers now predict a steep decline in populations of the developed world by 2050 – unless they are replaced by new migrants.

The high-growth South

Population growth is a serious and increasing problem in the poor societies of the Southern Hemisphere. Only a few nations lack industrial technology altogether, placing them at demographic transition theory's Stage 1. Most of Latin America, Africa and Asia has moved to Stage 2, still primarily agricultural but with some industry. In these nations, advanced medical technology (much supplied by rich societies) has sharply reduced death rates, but birth rates remain high. A look back at Figure 24.2 shows that poor societies now account for two-thirds of the earth's people, a proportion that continues to rise.

In poor countries, urban families average four to five children; in rural areas, the number is often six to eight (World Bank, 1991). No one doubts that world population simply cannot keep increasing at anything like its current rate. At a 1994 global population conference in Cairo, delegates from 180 nations not only agreed on the need for vigorous action to contain population growth, but also pointed

The busy streets in India's Uttar Pradesh are crammed with bicycle traffic. Uttar Pradesh is a state in the northern part of India, with a population of over 190 million people

Source: © Karen Kasmauski/Science Faction/Corbis.

WORLD WATCH

Empowering women: the key to controlling population growth

Sohad Ahmad lives in a village 50 miles south of Cairo, Egypt's capital city. Her husband is a farmer and her family is poor. At first glance, one might conclude that this woman's situation fits a stereotype all too typical in low-income countries: desperate poverty pushing families to have more and more children to work the fields and earn more income. But this is not the case.

Sohad Ahmad has had only two children, and she and her husband will have no more. Egypt's rising population has already created such a demand for land that her family could not afford more even if they could farm it. More importantly, Sohad Ahmad does not want her

life defined only by child-bearing. Thus she has made a personal decision to have no more children.

Women like Sohad Ahmad who are taking control of their fertility and seeking greater opportunities are more and more common across Egypt. Indeed, this country has made great progress in reducing its annual population growth from 3 per cent just 25 years ago to 2 per cent today – one of the lowest rates in the region. This is why the International Conference on Population and Development selected Cairo for its historic 1994 meeting.

The 1994 Cairo conference was not the first of its kind, but it stands out in several respects. First, it had an unprecedented base of participation, with representatives from 180 nations. Second, delegates from more than 1,200 non-governmental organisations also attended the meeting. Third, the Cairo conference reached virtual consensus on a new path towards effective control of

global population, elevating the standing of women.

In the past, population control programmes have been limited to making birth control technology available to women. This is a crucial objective, since only half the world's married women make use of effective birth control. But it has become clear that more than technology is needed to curb population increase. The larger picture shows that, even with available birth control, population continues to grow in societies that define women's primary responsibility as raising children.

Dr Nafis Sadik, an Egyptian woman who headed United Nations efforts at population control for some time, summed up the new approach to lowering birth rates: *give women more choices and they will have fewer children*. In other words, women with access to schooling and jobs, who can decide when and if they wish to marry and who bear children as a matter of choice, will limit their fertility.

The door to schooling must be open to older women too, Dr Sadik adds, since they often exercise great influence in local communities.

Evidence from countries around the world is that controlling population and raising the social standing of women are inseparable objectives.

Continue the debate

1 Discuss the ways in which a country can control the size of its population.

2 Do you agree that the key to population control is 'empowering women', or is this taking too much responsibility away from men?

3 Is population control really necessary in a world where some countries have such a low birth rate?

 tip Look back to the boxes on reproductive politics (p. 406) and birth control in low-income societies (p. 304).

out the crucial link between population control and the status of women. The *World watch* box offers a closer look.

In the last decade, the world has made significant progress in lowering fertility. At the same time, however, mortality rates are falling. Although few would oppose medical programmes that save lives, especially those of children, this trend exerts upward pressure on population. In fact, population growth in most low-income regions of the world is due *primarily* to declining death rates. After about 1920, when Europe and North America began to export advances in scientific medicine, nutrition and sanitation around the world, mortality tumbled. Since then, inoculations against infectious diseases and the use of antibiotics and insecticides have pushed down death rates with stunning effectiveness. For example, in Sri Lanka, malaria caused half of all deaths in the 1930s; a decade later, insecticides used to kill malaria-carrying mosquitoes cut the malaria death toll in half. Although we hail such an achievement, this technological advance sent Sri Lanka's population soaring. Similarly, India's infant mortality rate slid from 130 in 1975 to 74 in 1995, a decline that has helped boost that nation's population to 1,000 million.

Improvement in access to family planning in the developing world is clearly necessary, but how it should be introduced and who should direct the change in population is an open question. Many people in less developed countries view family planning initiatives coming from the West as racist, arguing that people in rich nations have little real regard for the welfare of the world's poor and instead only wish to curb the potential for immigration from the South to the North and the propensity for violence in overcrowded regions from which the North extracts natural resources. Policies of previous governments in India and China that have forced people to limit family size

have proved highly unpopular among many groups in each country. Some people in both richer and poorer countries suggest that the best way to control population growth is to distribute the world's resources and wealth more fairly between all countries, and to expand educational and career opportunities for women everywhere.

Urbanisation: space and the city

For most of human history, the sights and sounds of great cities such as Hong Kong, Rio de Janeiro, Paris or Los Angeles were completely unknown. The world's people lived in small, nomadic groups, moving as they depleted vegetation or searched for migratory game. Humans survived for tens of thousands of years without permanent settlements. Cities first emerged in the Middle East, then arose on all the continents, but held only a tiny fraction of the earth's people until very recently.

Today, the population of the world's five largest cities exceeds the total planetary population when cities first developed. By 1950, nearly 80 cities had populations in excess of 1 million; by 2000, that number exceeded 250. By 2010, half of the world's population lived in cities. These figures testify to the steady march of **urbanisation**, *the concentration of humanity into cities* (see Figure 24.5). Urbanisation both redistributes the population within a society and transforms many patterns of social life. We will trace these changes in terms of four differing patterns of urban life:

1 The evolution of early cities beginning 12,000 years ago.

2 The rise of industrial cities after 1750.

The malling of the world

Shopping or 'consumption', as we saw in Chapter 15, has now become one of the main social pastimes of many people in the twenty-first century and has come to organise large geographical landscapes. Of course, there have always been markets for the selling and buying of goods across many cultures and history – the agora of Athens and the oriental bazaar of Turkey or Persia (Iran), for example. But the modern expansion of shopping through 'arcades' really began in the nineteenth century. 'Department stores' like Bloomingdales appeared in the early twentieth century. And all of this indicated a reorganisation of 'space'. Today we live with huge shopping malls – a major feature of the landscapes of many countries. They are, as the sociologist George Ritzer (2004a) puts it, 'Cathedrals of Consumption'.

The first integrated shopping centre (of 28 stores) with parking accommodation seems to have been built in 1916 for the wealthy in the Chicago suburb of Lake Forest. Others continued to be built, but a landmark was reached in 1954 when the world's largest mall was built in Michigan – with 110 stores in a two-level complex (and a major department store within it). The first mall opened in the UK in 1957.

Since then malls have appeared all over the world: they have become a major feature of public spaces throughout the world. Malls were opened in Germany (1964), Brazil (1966), Japan (1968), Thailand (1981) and Argentina (1988). By 2003, there were some 53 in Hungary, 66 in Poland, 17 in Slovakia and another 17 in the Czech Republic (Blythman, 2005: 233). The Kingdom Centre – a three-storey glass and steel centre – appeared in Ryadh, Saudi Arabia. Smaller stores are right next to major ones, and hypermarkets stand on borders between town and country. China opened its first mall in 1990, and by the end of this decade, it will have opened at least seven of the world's ten largest malls. Currently, Asia is home to eight of the world's ten largest shopping malls, six of which have been built since 2004.

What is striking about many malls is the way they have become 'fantasy cities'. Our environments often become themed and 'spectacular' in their design. They proclaim their success and imbue the whole environment with a rich sense of well-being, and provide an escalating development of commodity fantasy themes.

Modern malls are strikingly illustrated at their most extreme in Las Vegas. Here 'Disneyland goes shopping'. A children's theme park becomes the model for adult shopping: a theme park with an amusement park, endless 'eateries', an ice skating rink, artificial lagoons and hotels. Local themes appear. In San Salvador, the Gallerias shopping arcade houses a Roman Catholic church that holds mass twice a day; there are also local banks, art galleries and government offices. This is a new (and maybe bizarre?) amalgamation of global social space, shopping and entertainment.

Source: *Forbes*, 9 January 2007; *Newsweek*, 5 December 2005; Ritzer (2004a).

---

3   The explosive growth of mega-cities in low-income countries in the late twentieth century.
4   The recent rise of global cities and the spread of vast urban regions and the 'endless city'.

1 The evolution of early cities

Cities are a relatively new development in human history. Only about 12,000 years ago did our ancestors found the earliest permanent settlements, setting the stage for the *first urban revolution*. As glaciers drew back at the end of the last ice age, people congregated in warm regions with fertile soil. At the same time, humans discovered how to domesticate animals and cultivate crops. Whereas hunting and gathering demanded continual movement, raising food could require people to remain in one place. Domesticating animals and plants also yielded a material surplus, which freed some people from concentrating on food production and allowed them to build shelters, make tools, weave clothing and take part in religious rituals. Thus the founding of cities, made possible by favourable ecology and changing technology, was truly revolutionary, enhancing productive specialisation and raising living standards as never before.

The first cities

Historians identify Jericho as one of the first cities. This settlement lies to the north of the Dead Sea in disputed

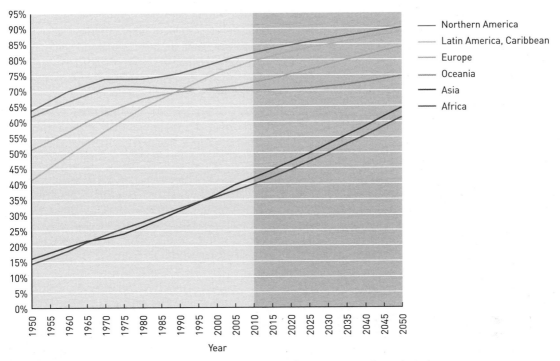

Figure 24.5 Urban population: by major geographical area (per cent of total population)
Source: World Urbanization Prospects, 2009 Revision.

land currently occupied by Israel. About 8000 BCE, Jericho contained about 600 people. By 4000 BCE, numerous cities were flourishing in the Fertile Crescent between the Tigris and Euphrates rivers in present-day Iraq, and urban settlement had begun along the River Nile in Egypt.

Some cities, with populations reaching 50,000, became centres of urban empires. Priest-kings wielded absolute power over lesser nobles, administrators, artisans, soldiers and farmers. Slaves, captured in frequent military campaigns, laboured to build monumental structures such as the pyramids of Egypt (Stavrianos, 1983; Nolan and Lenski, 2010).

In at least three other areas of the world, cities developed independently. Several large, complex settlements bordered the Indus river in present-day Pakistan, starting about 2500 BCE. Scholars date Chinese cities from 2000 BCE. And in Latin America, urban centres arose around 1500 BCE (Change, 1977).

Pre-industrial European cities

Urbanisation in Europe began about 1800 BCE on the Mediterranean island of Crete. Cities soon spread throughout Greece, resulting in more than 100 city-states, of which Athens is the most famous.

During its Golden Age, lasting barely a century after 500 BCE, Athenians made major contributions to the Western way of life in philosophy, the arts and politics. Yet Athenian society, numbering some 300,000, rested on the labour of slaves, who comprised a third of the population. Their democratic principles notwithstanding, Athenian men also denied the rights of citizenship to women and foreigners (Mumford, 1961; Stavrianos, 1983).

As Greek civilisation faded, the city of Rome grew to almost 1 million inhabitants and became the centre of a vast empire. By the first century CE, the militaristic Romans had subdued much of northern Africa, Europe and the Middle East. In the process, Rome spread its language, arts and technology. Four centuries later, the Roman Empire fell into disarray, a victim of its gargantuan size, internal corruption and militaristic appetite. Yet, between them, the Greeks and Romans founded cities across Europe from the Atlantic Ocean all the way to Asia, including Vienna, Paris, London and Constantinople.

The fall of the Roman Empire initiated an era of urban decline in Europe lasting 600 years. Cities became smaller as people drew back within defensive walls and competing warlords battled for territory. About the eleventh century, the 'Dark Ages' came to an end as a semblance of peace allowed trade to bring life to cities once again.

Expanding trade prompted medieval cities to tear down their walls. Amsterdam grew considerably from the fourteenth century, as it became more prominent in trade. Beneath towering cathedrals, the narrow and winding streets of London, Brussels and Florence soon teemed with merchants, artisans, priests, peddlers, nobles and servants. Typically, occupational groups such as bakers, key-makers and carpenters clustered together in distinct sections or 'quarters'. Ethnic groups also inhabited their own neighbourhoods, often because people kept them out of other districts. The term 'ghetto' (from the Italian word *borghetto*, meaning 'outside the city walls') first described the segregation of Jews in medieval Venice.

The growth of industrial European cities

Throughout the Middle Ages, steadily increasing commerce enriched a new urban middle class or *bourgeoisie* (from the French, meaning 'of the town'). By the fifteenth century, the power of the bourgeoisie rivalled that of the hereditary nobility. In the 1400s Paris became the largest European city with a population of over a quarter of a million people.

2 The rise of the modern industrial city

By 1750 industrialisation was well under way, triggering a *second urban revolution*, first in Europe and then in North America. Factories unleashed productive power as never before, causing cities to grow to unprecedented size. London, the largest European city in 1700, with 550,000 people, swelled to 6.5 million by 1900 (Weber, 1963; orig. 1899). Most of this increase was due to migration from rural areas by people seeking a better standard of living.

Cities not only grew but changed shape as well. The industrial-capitalist city replaced older irregular streets with broad, straight boulevards, which accommodated the increasing flow of commercial traffic. Steam and electric trams, too, crisis-crossed the expanding cities. Lewis Mumford (1961) adds that developers divided cities into regular-sized lots, making land a commodity to be bought and sold. Finally, the cathedrals that had guided the life of medieval cities were soon dwarfed by towering, brightly lit and frantic central business districts made up of banks, retail stores and office buildings. Built for business, cities became increasingly

crowded and impersonal. Crime rates rose. Especially at the outset, a small number of industrialists lived in grand style, while for most adults and children, factory work proved exhausting and provided bare subsistence.

In 1810, 20 per cent of the British population lived in cities and towns. By 1910 the figure was nearer 80 per cent (Kumar, 1978). Taking Europe as a whole, Therborn (1995: 184) notes that the proportion of European peoples living in cities escalated from a tenth in 1800, to a third by 1900, to two-thirds by 1989. Although European cities have often continued to grow significantly, they have usually had major geographical and political restrictions placed on their development. Consequently, European cities have not tended to reach the proportions of some cities in the newly industrialising world.

The great metropolis: 1860–1950

The twentieth century has seen living spaces changing in a number of directions, from the growth of central cities to expansion beyond suburbs. The pace of urban change has accelerated with time.

Following the First World War, waves of people deserted the countryside for cities in hopes of obtaining better jobs. This growth marked the era of the **metropolis** (from Greek words, meaning 'mother city'), *a large city that socially and economically dominates an urban area*. Metropolises soon became the manufacturing, commercial and residential centres. The concentration of industrial technology not only generated expansion of the population, but also changed the physical shape of cities. From the three- or four-storey towns in the United States in 1850, steel girders and mechanical lifts raised structures over ten storeys high in 1880. In 1930, New York's Empire State Building became an urban wonder, a true 'skyscraper' stretching 102 storeys into the clouds.

Decentralisation: commuter towns and the suburbs

The industrial metropolis reached its peak during reconstruction after the Second World War. Since then, something of a turnaround, termed 'urban decentralisation', has occurred as people have deserted the city centres. Many large cities stopped growing, and some lost considerable population, after 1950. During the 1970s, the populations of Paris and London dropped by around 20 per cent. Instead of clustering in densely packed central cities, urban populations expanded outwards.

Urbanism becomes a way of life

Commentators and theorists have increasingly realised that contemporary cities have given rise to distinctive social experience. The Parisian poet Charles Baudelaire (1821–67) described the **flâneur**, *a social type who wanders cities, enjoying the sights and the crowd.* Subsequently, a number of sociologists, Toennies, Durkheim, Simmel, Park and Wirth among them, started to analyse the city as a distinctly modern form which brought a pervasive newness, a concern with the transitory and obsessive individualism, along with a new excitement and sophistication.

We previously encountered the ideas of German sociologist Georg Simmel (1858–1918) when we looked at how size affects the social dynamics of small groups (Chapter 6). Simmel (1950; orig. 1905) also turned his characteristic micro-level focus to the city, probing how urban life shapes people's attitudes and behaviour. From the point of view of the individual, Simmel explained, the city is a crush of people, objects and events. Because the urbanite is easily overwhelmed with stimulation, he continued, a *blasé attitude* emerges as a coping strategy. That is, city people learn to respond selectively by tuning out much of what goes on around them. City dwellers are not without sensitivity and compassion for others, although they sometimes seem 'cold and heartless'. But urban detachment, as Simmel saw it, is better understood as a technique for social survival by which people stand aloof from most others so they can devote their time and energy to those who really matter.

Another key early thinker of the city was Louis Wirth (1897–1952),

one of the Chicago sociologists (see below). Wirth's best-known contribution is a brief essay in which he develops a comprehensive theory of urban life (Wirth, 1938). Wirth began by defining the city as a setting with a large, dense and diverse population. These traits, he argued, combine to form an impersonal, superficial and transitory way of life. Sharing the teeming streets, urbanites surely come into contact with many more people than rural residents do. But, if city people pay any mind to others, they usually know them only in terms of *what they do*: as bus driver, florist or shop assistant, for instance.

Decades of research have provided support for only some of his conclusions. Wirth correctly maintained that urban settings do sustain a weaker sense of community than do rural areas. But conflict is found in the countryside as well as the city. Furthermore, while urbanites treat many people impersonally, they typically welcome such privacy and, of course, they do maintain close personal relationships with many others. Where the analysis of Wirth and others falls short, too, is in painting urbanism in broad strokes that overlook the effects of class, race and gender. Herbert Gans (1968) suggested that there were many types of urbanite – rich and poor, Asian, black and white, women and men – all leading distinctive lives. In fact, cities often intensify these social differences. That is, we see the extent of social diversity most clearly in cities where different categories of people reside in the largest numbers (Spates and Macionis, 1987).

Modern societies have generally been ambivalent about urban life. As he assumed the US presidency in 1800, Thomas Jefferson repudiated the city as a 'pestilence to the morals, the health and the liberties of man' (quoted in Glaab, 1963: 52). Almost a century later,

English author and Nobel prize winner Rudyard Kipling echoed those sentiments after a visit to Chicago: 'Having seen it, I urgently desire never to see it again. It is inhabited by savages' (quoted in Rokove, 1975: 22). Others have disagreed, of course, siding with the ancient Greeks, who viewed the city as the only place where humanity can expect to find the 'good life'.

Cities then have long provoked spirited and divergent reactions. They have an ability to encapsulate and intensify human culture. Cities have been the setting for some of the greatest human virtues (from grand architecture to high-tech hospitals) as well as the greatest human failings (from ghettos of extreme poverty to concentrated pollution). Cities offer great economic opportunities, but also generate more extreme forms of social problems, from crime to racial tensions to social alienation. Indeed, a test of the balance between the promise and the failings of city life is emerging most intensely in newly expanding cities in the developing world.

Urban relationships are not only specialised and impersonal, Wirth explained, they are also founded on self-interest. For example, shoppers view grocers as the source of goods, while grocers see shoppers as a source of income. Urban people may pleasantly exchange greetings, but friendship is not the reason for their interaction. Finally, limited social involvement coupled with great social diversity also make city dwellers more tolerant than rural villagers. Rural communities often jealously enforce their narrow traditions, but the heterogeneous population of a city rarely shares any single code of moral conduct (Wilson, 1985, 1995).

As we shall see later in this chapter, many sociologists have found the city to be a place of great theoretical interest.

Just as central cities flourished a century ago, we have recently witnessed the expansion of both new towns and **suburbs**, *urban areas beyond the political boundaries of a city*. They began to grow late in the nineteenth century as railways and buses enabled people to work in city centres yet leave behind the centralised congestion when they went home to quieter dormitory communities. The suburban trend caught on more quickly in the United States than in Europe.

Cheaper cars and declining land prices, and the need to move from seriously overcrowded cities such as London, gradually also led to the development of planned new towns, such as Stevenage in Hertfordshire and Basildon in Essex. Here home ownership catered to more prosperous working-class people, and council housing estates catered for the less well-off.

Following the consumers, business, too, began moving to the new towns, and large, often impersonal, shopping centres started to replace the city centre stores of the metropolitan era. Manufacturing companies also decentralised into industrial parks far from the high property taxes, congested streets and the growing crime rates identified with inner cities. The development of the motorway system, with its ring roads encircling central cities, made moving out to the new towns or the suburbs almost irresistible for residents and business people alike.

Suburbanisation also came at the cost of conformity. In the United States, one of the most famous suburban sprawls was Levittown, the brainchild of the American developer Abraham Levitt. It was derided by critics as a field of look-alike boxes – a label which aptly suits many of the council estates in Britain as well. Additionally, as businesses have centralised into large chain stores, suburban shopping districts increasingly resemble each other. The main variation often is only the order in which the major department stores and so forth are arranged. But these suburbs also developed a more worrying form of conformity, as communities such as Levittown excluded black, Asian and Hispanic residents (Gans, 1982; orig. 1962). Indeed, racial prejudice against increasing numbers of immigrants and ethnic minorities fuelled the growth of suburbs, prompting many whites to flee to homogeneous, high-prestige enclaves.

Moreover, this rapid growth in suburbs and new towns soon threw older cities into financial problems. Population decline meant falling tax revenues. The overall result has often been inner-city decay. To many middle-class white people, the deteriorating inner cities became synonymous with slum housing, crime, drugs, unemployment, the poor and minorities.

This perception fuelled wave after wave of 'white flight' and urban decline. Suburbs may have their share of poor housing, congestion and crime, but they still appeal to many people because they remain largely white, unlike the inner cities whose populations encompass a greater share of ethnic minorities.

Gentrification

The location of ghettos and centres of urban prosperity, however, does change over time. This change largely results from the process of 'gentrification', whereby areas in decline are transformed into areas of prosperity. Businesses and politicians periodically cooperate, with businesses providing the money and labour to restore or rebuild facilities, and politicians providing tax and legal incentives to improve the profitability of these 'urban recycling' schemes. The London Docklands, eight and a half square miles of east London, has been transformed from run-down docks and poverty-stricken dwellings to a prosperous business community dotted with luxury flats and trendy boutiques. Gentrification is a process of moving wealth back into the metropolis, but this process carries a heavy price. Urban ghettos are the homes of many poor people, and cheap housing and low-wage jobs do not fit comfortably into high-profit renewal programmes. Often, the poor residents of gentrified areas get pushed aside and are left to relocate themselves in other poor and overcrowded areas. Like suburbanisation, gentrification in Europe and the United States is a process which has often worked to the benefit of white people at the expense of ethnic minorities.

3 Mega-cities and megalopolis: the rise of size

In 1950, only London (with 8 million residents) and New York (with 12.3 million residents) were **mega-cities**, defined as *a city with a population exceeding 8 million*. But by 2005, there were 20 mega-cities, with 16 in the developing world. Some such cities, like Shanghai and Seoul, are compact; others, like Bangkok and Manila, sprawl over a considerable area. The continuing decentralisation of cities has also produced vast urban areas that encompass numerous municipalities. In the early 1960s, the French geographer Jean Gottmann (1961) coined the term **megalopolis** to designate *a vast urban region containing a number of cities and their surrounding suburbs*.

Although a megalopolis is composed of hundreds of separate cities and suburbs, from an aeroplane at night one observes what appears to be a single continuous city. These are sometimes also called *agglomerations*, which link cities to suburbs to smaller cities. Among the major agglomerations are Tokyo, New York, Seoul, Mexico City, Mumbai (Bombay), São Paulo, Cairo, Manila, Shanghai and Lagos (www.citypopulation.de/World).

Table 24.4 includes a projection on the growth of such cities. It is clear that in the 1950s the 'big cities' tended to be both in the West and comparatively small when placed alongside the projections for 2025. Remember, these are only estimates: despite attempts to measure city sizes, it is exceedingly difficult.

Urban tensions

With so many processes involved in the rise of cities – from the expansion of work with very low wages, low job security and few benefits, to suburbanisation and gentrification – working against the poorest residents, it is small wonder that tensions between city elites and poor people result. Sometimes these tensions arise on a small scale, such as with acts of vandalism and petty crime. Occasionally, they erupt into riots. The UK has experienced a succession of such riots: in Bristol in 1980, in Brixton, Southall, Toxteth and Moss Side in 1981; again in Brixton and Toxteth, as well as in the Broadwater Farm estate (Tottenham) and Handsworth (Birmingham) in 1985; and in Bradford and Burnley in 2001. While these riots mainly reflected ethnic grievances, they provided a forum for youths and older poor people from many ethnic groups to vent their frustrations. Like the more internationally famous riots in Los Angeles following the acquittal of white police officers who had beaten the black motorist Rodney King unconscious, these riots generally broke out in response to an act of violence perpetrated against a poor person. Such riots may do little to solve the long-term problems of the poor and have often served to reinforce the stereotypes held by the residents of gentrified city areas and suburbs that the poor constitute a problem which has to be controlled.

Mega-cities in low-income societies

The world has experienced a revolutionary expansion of cities three times in human history. The first urban revolution began around 8000 BCE with the first urban settlements and continued as permanent settlements later appeared on different continents. The second urban revolution took hold about 1750 and lasted for two centuries as the Industrial Revolution touched off rapid growth of cities in Europe and North America. But a third urban revolution started around 1950. This time the change is taking place in the less developed nations.

In 1950, only a quarter of the people living in low-income countries inhabited cities; by 1995, the proportion had risen to 42 per cent. At the time of writing, it exceeds 50 per cent. Moreover, while only seven cities (two of which were in low-income countries) had populations over 5 million in 1950, by 2010 over 45 cities had passed this mark – a great many in poor nations. In 1950, eight of the top ten were in industrialised countries. By 2015, however, the majority will be in less economically developed countries.

Not only will these exploding urban areas be the world's largest, but also they will encompass unprecedented populations. Relatively rich countries such as Japan may have the resources to provide for cities with upwards of 30 million people, but for poor nations, such as Mexico and Brazil, such supercities will tax resources that are already severely strained. Shanty towns and *favelas* are homes for millions of the world's population.

To understand the third urban revolution, recall that many poor societies are now entering the high-growth stage of demographic transition. Falling death rates continue to fuel population growth in Latin America, Asia and, especially, Africa. For urban areas, the rate of population increase is twice as high because, in addition to natural increase, millions of migrants leave the countryside each year in search of jobs, healthcare, education and conveniences such as running water and electricity.

Cities often offer more opportunities than rural areas, but they provide no quick fix for the massive problems of escalating population and grinding poverty. In less developed societies, many burgeoning cities, including Mexico City described at the beginning of this chapter, are simply unable to meet the basic needs of much of their population. Thousands of rural people stream into Mexico City every day, even though more than 10 per cent of the *current* 25 million residents have no running water in their homes, 15 per cent lack sewerage facilities and the city can process only half the rubbish produced now. To make matters worse, exhaust from factories and cars chokes everyone, rich and poor alike.

Like other major cities throughout the developing world, Mexico City is surrounded by shanty towns,

Table 24.4   World cities, 1950–2025

1950			1975		
Rank	Urban agglomeration	Population	Rank	Urban agglomeration	Population
1	New York-Newark, USA	12.3	1	Tokyo, Japan	26.6
2	Tokyo, Japan	11.3	2	New York-Newark, USA	15.9
			3	Ciudad de México (Mexico City), Mexico	10.7

2009			2025		
Rank	Urban agglomeration	Population	Rank	Urban agglomeration	Population
1	Tokyo, Japan	36.5	1	Tokyo, Japan	37.1
2	Delhi, India	21.7	2	Delhi, India	28.6
3	São Paulo, Brazil	20.0	3	Mumbai (Bombay), India	25.8
4	Mumbai (Bombay), India	19.7	4	São Paulo, Brazil	21.7
5	Ciudad de México (Mexico City), Mexico	19.3	5	Dhaka, Bangladesh	20.9
6	New York-Newark, United States	19.3	6	Ciudad de México (Mexico City), Mexico	20.7
7	Shanghai, China	16.3	7	New York-Newark, United States	20.6
8	Kolkata (Calcutta), India	15.3	8	Kolkata (Calcutta), India	20.1
9	Dhaka, Bangladesh	14.3	9	Shanghai, China	20.0
10	Buenos Aires, Argentina	13.0	10	Karachi, Pakistan	18.7
11	Karachi, Pakistan	12.8	11	Lagos, Nigeria	15.8
12	Los Angeles-Long Beach-Santa Ana, United States	12.7	12	Kinshasa, Democratic Republic of the Congo	15.0
13	Beijing, China	12.2	13	Beijing, China	15.0
14	Rio de Janeiro, Brazil	11.8	14	Manila, Philippines	14.9
15	Manila, Philippines	11.4	15	Buenos Aires, Argentina	13.7
16	Osaka-Kobe, Japan	11.3	16	Los Angeles-Long Beach-Santa Ana, United States	13.7
17	Al-Qahirah (Cairo), Egypt	10.9	17	Al-Qahirah (Cairo), Egypt	13.5
18	Moskva (Moscow), Russian Federation	10.5	18	Rio de Janeiro, Brazil	12.7
19	Paris, France	10.4	19	Istanbul, Turkey	12.1
20	Istanbul, Turkey	10.4	20	Osaka-Kobe, Japan	11.4
21	Lagos, Nigeria	10.2	21	Shenzhen, China	11.1
			22	Chongqing, China	11.1
			23	Guangzhou, Guangdong, China	11.0
			24	Paris, France	10.9
			25	Jakarta, Indonesia	10.8
			26	Moskva (Moscow), Russian Federation	10.7
			27	Bogotá, Bolivia	10.5
			28	Lima, Peru	10.5
			29	Lahore, Pakistan	10.3

Source: United Nations Department of Economic and Social Affairs/Population Devision *World Urbanization Prospects: The 2009 Revision.*

settlements of makeshift homes built from discarded materials. As explained in Chapter 9 and as will be discussed further in Chapter 25, even city dumps are home to thousands of poor people, who pick through the waste hoping to find enough to ensure their survival for another day. In some cases, it can be hard to distinguish life on the congested streets from life in a dump. Paul Harrison, in a highly readable account of poverty in the city, described rush hour in Calcutta as:

> **the nearest human thing to an ant heap, a dense sea of people washing over roads hopelessly jammed as taxis swerve round hand-pulled rickshaws, buses run into handcarts, pony stagecoaches and private cars, and even flocks of goats fight it out for limited space.**

(1993: 165–6)

A few people have found riches in cities of the developing world. In some countries, such as Brazil, members of the urban poor are increasingly returning to the countryside and fighting with well-armed landowners for the right to farm to produce the food, shelter and textiles they need to survive.

Many of these cities can also be seen as 'postcolonial cities'. In them, the rich have lifestyles that are very similar to those of the wealthy in the West, while the urban poor face extremely limited services and incomes.

4 The endless cities: globalisation, global slums and the spread of mega-regions

In 1986, John Friedman developed the idea of world cities – large, urban regions, highly interconnected, through which finance, economic decision-making and international labour flow. The general idea of world cities is, of course, far from new: people have always travelled to and from major cities, which serve as huge magnets for cosmopolitanism. But from the latter part of the twentieth century onwards – and in large part linked to the growth of new informational networks and economies – cities started to transform themselves again.

Global cities are cities with considerable economic power, commanding global investments and the concentration and accumulation of capital. In Europe, only London and Paris can be seen as world cities, though other cities, including Frankfurt, Brussels, Amsterdam and Zürich, are also important. London,

Tokyo and New York emerged as three leading centres of world finance. While these cities are the homes of stateless corporations and international systems of finance, often housed in spectacular skyscraping buildings, they also have a growing number of poor people – often immigrants – who work for low wages.

For Saskia Sassen, global cities stand out as key command points in the organisation of the world economy, and are the key locations of the marketplaces for the leading industries (Sassen, 2000: 4). Hence, global cities are the prime location of major corporate headquarters of TNCs, international banks and an international division of labour, with privileged foreigners who 'jet set' around the world. They have to be major centres of communication, and a good air transport system is central. All global cities are connected by air to all other global cities.

These global cities have led to a large number of people now living not in one society but in several simultaneously. Although they are likely to have apartments in a number of cities across the world, their real home is probably the airport and the jet aircraft! These are what novelist Pico Iyer has called 'the global souls' (Iyer, 2000). See Figure 24.6, which illustrates the 'hierarchy of world cities'.

The twenty-first century: the urban millennium

In 2010, the United Nations organisation for human settlements, UN Habitat, published its biannual *State of World Cities* report which identifies the trends of developing mega-regions. While the world's urban population grew very rapidly (from 220 million to 2.8 billion), by 2009 over half of the world lived in cities. In the coming decades, UN Habitat claims we will see an unprecedented scale of urban growth in the developing world – especially in Africa and Asia, where the urban population is expected to double between 2000 and 2030. By 2050, over 70 per cent of the world will be urban dwellers (with only 14 per cent of people in rich countries living outside cities – and 33 per cent in poor countries). The towns and cities of the developing world will make up over 80 per cent of urban humanity. The projections are quite staggering. By 2025 there will be numerous conurbations that house some 25 million people (Shanghai, Jakarta, Dhaka, etc.); Mumbai could reach 33 million people (Davis, 2006).

The United Nations suggests that new 'mega-regions' are developing. These include:

Aerial view of Mexico City

Source: © Stephanie Maze/Corbis.

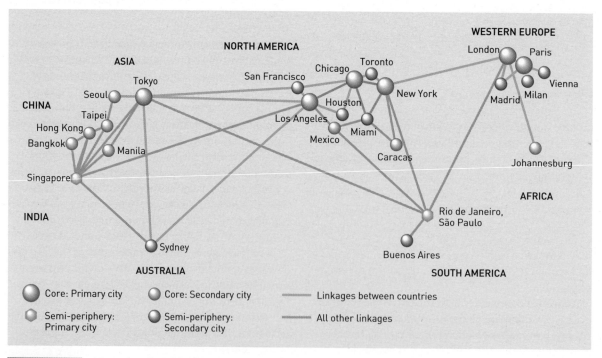

Figure 24.6   Hierarchy of world cities

Source: Adapted from *A Geography of the European Union* by Garrat Nagle and Kris Spencer (1996: 101), Oxford University Press.

- The Pearl river: Hong Kong–Shenzhen–Guangzhou, China – home to about 120 million people.

- Nagoya–Osaka–Kyoto–Kobe, Japan – home to around 60 million people.

- Rio de Janeiro and São Paulo with 43 million people.

- 'Urban corridors' which stretch in India from Mumbai to Delhi, and in West Africa along the Gulf of Guinea – with Lagos (23 million), Nigeria, Benin, Togo and Ghana.

Everywhere rural populations are in decline (see Figure 24.7). But the new cities are not taking on the

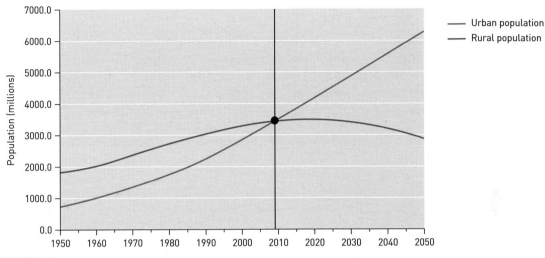

Figure 24.7   Growth of the urban population, 1950–2050
Source: World Urbanization Prospects, 2009 Revision.

Hong Kong
Source: Pearson Education Ltd/Corbis.

Table 24.5	Growth of urban population, 1950–2050								
	Percentage urban					Rate of urbanisation (percentage)			
Major area	1950	1975	2009	2025	2050	1950–1975	1975–2009	2009–2025	2025–2050
Africa	14.4	25.7	39.6	47.2	61.6	2.32	1.26	1.10	1.07
Asia	16.3	24.0	41.7	49.9	64.7	1.55	1.62	1.13	1.03
Europe	51.3	65.3	72.5	76.9	84.3	0.96	0.31	0.36	0.37
Latin America and the Caribbean	41.4	60.7	79.3	83.8	88.8	1.54	0.78	0.34	0.23
Northern America	63.9	73.8	81.9	85.7	90.1	0.58	0.30	0.28	0.20
Oceania	62.0	71.5	70.2	70.8	74.8	0.57	−0.05	0.05	0.22

Source: United Nations Department of Economic and Social Affairs/Population Division *World Urbanization Prospects: The 2009 Revision*.

same forms as the old industrialising cities. Rather, small villages become engulfed by urbanisation and lives are transformed. A central feature of this is the development of mega-slums.

The urban divide: planet of slums, wasted lives and inequalities

Life outside of the cities can entail extremes of poverty, and many people across the world flee from their desperately poor villages in search of a life in the city. But although cities do indeed produce wealth for many of their citizens (the five largest cities in India and China account for 50 per cent of those countries' wealth), they are also cradles of extreme inequality. Nestled right next to huge expensive shopping malls and wealthy business districts are slums of extreme poverty. Johannesburg is the least equal in the world; Latin America, Asian and African cities a little more equal – but they have high levels of slums and little sanitation. In the USA, some of the richest cities like New York and Washington are the most unequal, and foster major ghettoes – which lack access to good education, housing or political power (UN Habitat, 2010).

The most striking feature of the cities of the modern world is the scale of their slums. They are characterised by very poor housing, overcrowding, poor access to safe water and sanitation, and insecurity. In 2010, there were around 800 million people living in such slums. Table 24.6 gives the world slum population for 2010. The world slum population will probably grow by at

least six million each year, reaching an estimated 889 million by 2020.

The Challenge of Slums (UN Habitat, 2010) concludes that:

> Instead of being a focus for growth and prosperity, the cities have become a dumping ground for a surplus population working in unskilled, unprotected and low wage informal industries and trade.

(p. 32)

This is a kind of passive proletarianisation whereby traditional forms of work are dissolved and the great majority of people become part of a huge informal and unstructured labour market. Bauman's book talks of *Wasted Lives* (2004); Mike Davis (2006) of a 'surplus humanity'.

Contemporary slum cities have a different organisation when compared with older cities. In industrialising Britain, for example, the poor and the slums were mainly found right in the heart of the newly emerging cities. And indeed today there are still plenty of slums to be found in many inner cities, often where there are flop houses, government housing, tenements, squatters and street dwellers. But increasingly too they are to be found on the peripheries of the big new cities found in low-income societies. The slum and the shantytown now spread for miles at the outskirts of the city. Here are the huge rubbish tips that provide scavenging work; the refugee camps for the socially excluded; and miles and miles of 'make do' shelters. Table 24.7 suggests that many more poor now live on the outskirts than in the centre.

A crowded part of Kibera, one of Nairobi's slums. There are approximately 2.5 million slum dwellers in about 200 settlements in Nairobi, Kenya, representing 60 per cent of the Nairobi population. Kibera houses almost 1 million of these people. It is the biggest slum in Africa and one of the biggest in the world

Source: © Nigel Pavitt/JAI/Corbis.

Table 24.6	Slum living in the modern world	
Region/continent	**Numbers of people**	**Percentage of urban population (%)**
Sub-Saharan Africa	199.5 million	61.7
Southern Asia	190.7 million	35.0
Eastern Asia	189.6 million	28.2
Latin America and the Caribbean	110.7 million	23.5
Southeastern Asia	88.9 million	31.0
Western Asia	35.0 million	24.6
North Africa	11.8 million	13.3
Oceania	6.0 million	24.1

Source: UN Habitat (2010).

Anderson: Fieldwork and sociology

Elijah Anderson is one of North America's leading black sociologists and he has studied in intense detail the life of young black men in the inner city. His main style of research is fieldwork, or participant observation – he spends a lot of time just hanging around with black youth in the street as well as interviewing them and their relatives.

His most recent book, *Code of the Street* (1999), takes us to another world and grouping, one found in the midst of high-income societies. Many inner cities in North America are ostensibly ravaged by a pervasive violence: many young people come to live tormented lives in the midst of drugs, death and a decaying environment. It is a world also depicted in films such as John Singleton's film *Boyz n the Hood* (1991). Looking specifically at Germantown Avenue in Philadelphia, he

depicts an 8½-mile-long road running through the city from one end to the other, where the 'well-to-do, the middle classes, the working poor and the very poor' all live. It is a continuum of lifestyles with a 'code of civility' at one end and a 'street code' at the other. At one end lie the middle classes with busy, employed lives bustling with choices. Restaurants, farmers' markets and up-market stores thrive and there is little visible security. People get along and 'virtually every ethnic group is represented' (2000: 18). Although it is predominantly white, there is a flourishing sense of diversity.

At the opposite extreme the story is really not the same: exterior bars appear on rundown shops, discount stores appear, along with grafitti and very rundown buildings, many of which are no longer inhabited. It is here that groups of black youths start to appear, hanging around on street corners, outside stores, in the street and at major complexes (2000: 77). Both 'decent' and 'street' families can be found here (and overwhelmingly the former), but the air is thick with

danger and potential violence.[1] Street families seem to show a lack of consideration for others, but in effect they have their own 'street code'.

At the heart of the code, Anderson says, 'is the issue of respect – being treated "right". They need to be granted "props" (or proper due) or the deference one deserves.' In the street, this can become something which is 'ever more problematic and uncertain' (2000: 33). If you bother people, you will get disgraced and 'dissed' (disrespected). Often they involve minor issues of demeanour. It is hard to get away from it, even if you are a decent kid struggling to be good. As Anderson puts it:

> In impoverished inner-city black communities . . . particularly among young males and perhaps increasingly among females, such flight would be extremely difficult. To run away would likely leave one's self esteem in tatters, while inviting further disrespect.

(Anderson, 1999: 76)

Table 24.7	Where do the poor people live? (% of poor population)	
	Inner-city slums	Peripheral slums
Khartoum	17	83
Mexico City	27	73
Mumbai	20	80
Rio de Janeiro	23	77

Source: Adapted from Davis (2006: 31).

Understanding cities?

The Chicago School: Robert Park

The first major sociology programme in the United States took root a century ago at the University of Chicago. Chicago, then a new metropolis exploding with population and cultural diversity, became the research focus for generations of sociologists, and

[1] The terms 'decent families' and 'street families' are used by the residents themselves (Anderson, 1999: 35).

the work of these men and women yielded a rich understanding of many dimensions of urban life. Although inspired by European theorists such as Toennies, Durkheim and Simmel, their unique contribution to urban sociology was in making the city itself a laboratory for actual research.

Perhaps the greatest urban sociologist of all was Robert Ezra Park, who for decades provided the leadership that established sociology in the United States. Park is introduced in the *Thinkers and theory* box.

Urban ecology and the zonal theory of the city

Sociologists (especially members of the Chicago School) also developed **urban ecology**, *the study of the link between the physical and social dimensions of cities.* Chapter 25 spotlights cultural ecology, the study of how cultural patterns are related to the physical environment. Urban ecology is one application of this approach, revealing how the physical and social forms of cities influence one another. In cities there is a natural competition for space.

Consider, for example, why cities are located where they are. The first cities emerged in fertile regions where the environment favoured raising crops and, thus, settlement. Pre-industrial societies, concerned with defence, built their cities on mountains (Athens was situated on an outcropping of rock) or surrounded by water (Paris and Mexico City were founded on islands). After the Industrial Revolution, the unparalleled importance of economics led to the founding of cities near rivers and natural harbours that facilitated trade.

Urban ecologists also study the physical design of cities. In 1925 Ernest W. Burgess, a student and colleague of Robert Park, described land use in Chicago in terms of *concentric zones* that look rather like a bull's-eye (Park and Burgess, 1967; orig. 1925)

THINKERS & THEORY

Robert Ezra Park: walking the city streets

I suspect that I have actually covered more ground, tramping about in cities in different parts of the world, than any other living man.

(Park, 1950: viii)

Robert Ezra Park (1864–1944) was a man with a single consuming passion – the city. Walking the streets of the world's great cities, he delighted in observing the full range of human turbulence and triumph. Throughout his 30-year career at the University of Chicago, he led a group of dedicated sociologists in direct, systematic observation of urban life.

Park acknowledged his debt to European sociologists, including Ferdinand Toennies and Georg Simmel (with whom Park studied in Germany). But Park launched urban sociology in the United States by advocating the direct observation of the city rather than what amounted to 'armchair theorising' on the part of his European teachers. At Park's urging, generations of sociologists at the University of Chicago rummaged through practically every part of their city.

From this research, Park came to understand the city as a highly ordered mosaic of distinctive regions, including industrial districts, ethnic communities and vice areas. These so-called 'natural areas' all evolved in relation to one another, forming an urban ecology. To Park, the city operates like a living social organism, a true human kaleidoscope. Urban variety, Park maintained, is the key to the timeless attraction of people to cities:

The attraction of the metropolis is due in part to the fact that in the long run every individual finds somewhere among the varied manifestations of city life the sort of environment in which he expands and feels at ease; he finds, in short, the moral climate in which his particular nature obtains the stimulations that bring his innate dispositions to full and free expression. It is, I suspect, motives of this kind . . . which drove many, if not most, of the young men and young women from the security of their homes in the country into the big, booming confusion and excitement of city life.

(Park, 1967: 41; orig. 1925)

Park was well aware that many people saw the city as disorganised and even dangerous. Conceding an element of truth in these assertions, Park still found cities intoxicating. Walking the city streets, he became convinced that urban places offer a better way of life – the promise of greater human freedom and opportunity than we can find elsewhere.

Source: Based on Park (1950; 1967, orig. 1925).

(see Figure 24.8). City centres, Burgess observed, are business districts bordered by a ring of factories, followed by residential rings with housing that becomes more expensive the further it stands from the noise and pollution of the city's centre. Homer Hoyt (1939) refined Burgess's observations by noting that distinctive districts sometimes form *wedge-shaped sectors*. For example, one fashionable area may develop next to another, along a major road, or an industrial district may extend outwards from a city's centre along a railway line.

Chauncey Harris and Edward Ullman (1945) added yet another insight: as cities decentralise, they lose their single-centre form in favour of a *multi-centred model*. As cities grow, residential areas, industrial parks and shopping districts typically push away from one another. Few people wish to live close to industrial areas, for example, so the city becomes a mosaic of distinct districts.

Social area analysis adds another twist to urban ecology by investigating what people in specific residential areas have in common. Three factors seem to explain most of the variation: family patterns, social class and race/ethnicity (Johnston, 1976). Families with children gravitate to areas offering large flats or single family homes and good schools. The rich generally seek

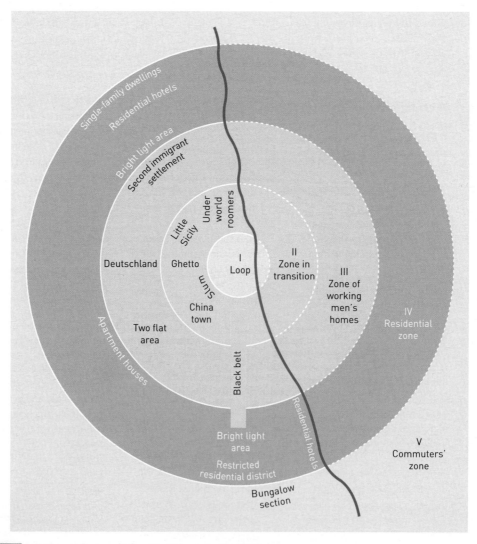

| Figure 24.8 | The zonal theory of the city: Chicago in the 1920s |

Source: Adapted from Park, R. E. and Burgess, E. W. 1967 (orig. 1925): *The City*, p. 55, University of Chicago Press.

high-prestige areas, often in the central city near many of the city's cultural attractions. People with a common social heritage tend to cluster together in distinctive communities.

Finally, Brian Berry and Philip Rees (1969) have managed to tie together many of these insights. They explain that distinct family types tend to settle in the concentric zones described by Ernest Burgess. Specifically, households with few children tend to cluster towards the city's centre, while those with more children live further away. Social class differences are primarily responsible for the sector-shaped districts described by Homer Hoyt as, for instance, the rich occupy one 'side of the tracks' and the poor the other. And racial and ethnic areas are found at various points throughout the city, consistent with Harris and Ullman's multi-centred model.

Critical evaluation

Chicago sociologists have been very influential but they have been found lacking. As the researchers themselves concede, their conclusions paint an over-simplified picture of urban life. Chicago urban ecologists have studied only US cities during a single historical period. Little of what we have learned about industrial cities applies to pre-industrial towns; similarly, even among industrial cities, socialist settlements differ from their capitalist counterparts. There is good reason to doubt that any single ecological model will account for the full range of urban diversity.

A major criticism started to develop in the 1970s. Critics claimed urban ecology errs to the extent that it implies that cities take shape simply from the choices that ordinary people make. Surely urban development responds more to powerful elites than to ordinary citizens (Molotch, 1976)? We look at these theories next.

The political economy of the city

More recent theories of the city have turned mainstream sociological opinion against the Human Ecology school. They argued that cities were not 'natural evolutions' but depended instead on the influence of institutions and political settings. The values of commercial property often come ahead of community values. Three highly influential studies – David Harvey, *Social Justice and the City* (1973); Manuel Castells, *The Urban Question* (1978) and John Logan and Harvey Molotch, *Urban Fortunes* (1988)

moved beyond the Chicago tradition of urban ecology to ask questions about the political economy of cities (using ideas they drew from Marx).

David Harvey examined the created environment developed by industrial capitalism. He argued that cities go wherever large firms choose to develop their factories, where investors place their money, and where property developers can make their money. City councils and managers play an increasing role in shaping the city with capital and their investments: overall his concern has been with the way space is produced under capitalism. What needs to be understood in the city are the workings of investments, markets and profits.

Manuel Castells saw the city as effectively a unit of labour power matched with consumption. More than anything, the modern city depended upon 'collective consumption', which was necessary to make its labour force happen. Alongside this the modern city's consumption and organisation depend more and more on the organisation of different social movements.

Harvey Molotch's work (1976) saw cities as 'growth machines', where growth and development/change become necessary for the well-being of city. This growth in turn depends upon real estate investors along with bankers, developers and corporate officials. Without these, the city cannot function. But more: it is this business and money making which shapes the city – cities are not simply places where people live, work and have social relationships. They are places to make money.

Doreen Massey (1984) sees the need to examine the 'relations of production' that shape space – not just the simple overt geographical mappings. Again, she sees the significance of 'layers of investment' and the need to study both single local regions and the ways in which they interconnect with other regions and often on mulilocational, multinational levels. The local is rarely just local: we need to develop 'a global sense of space'.

These theories of the city draw from Marx and rework the ideas of space. They argue that there is conflict between competing groups and that capitalism is the underlying force at work in modern urban–industrial communities. Increasingly, this has moved from local regulation to national and now global regulation – the modern city is shaped by the worldwide system of emerging global economy. Contemporary students of the city now have to look more and more at world cities and the relationships between the broad macro level of global economy and the more microsociological level of the local urban community or neighbourhood.

THINKERS & THEORY

Loïc Wacquant: urban outcasts and the rise of the hyperghetto

I don't have a job and I'll never have one. Nobody want to help us get out of this shit. If the government can spend so much money to build a nuclear submarine, why not for the inner cities? If fighting cops is the only way to get heard, then we'll fight them. **Teenage rioter from Bristol.**

(Wacquant, 2008: 31)

It is not just the slum cities of the South that suggest urban crisis: the big cities of the First World – London, Paris, Chicago – are also under stress, with huge divides between a wealthy and often super-rich visible surface, and a massive seething ghetto of underpriviliged, unequal and marginalised people. Loïc Wacquant's *Urban Outcasts* (2008) draws upon field, survey and historical data to examine the black ghetto of Chicago, the deindustrialising banlieue of Paris and the race conflicts in inner-city England. He stresses the unique character of each city, of course, but also suggests there are major forces in

common which are shaping their problems. The forces of neoliberal capitalism and the state play a critical role in shaping the life-chances of their residents. Critical here are the twin public policies of racial separation and urban abandonment. Wacquant does not, however, see this as the making of an underclass. Rather he highlights a number of factors which are generating a new logic within cities. These are:

- *Destruction of the old wage labour systems.* Everywhere and especially amongst the young, we find the growth of part-time, flexible work with short-term contracts, side by side with mass long-term unemployment. Youth unemployment has noticeably grown.
- *Decaying of local neigbourhoods.* Many areas in which people live have not just decayed physically; the areas people live in have become stigmatised and detached from the mainstream. These neighbourhoods start to 'taint' their people and create a massive sense of social indignity and demonisation.
- Systems of support and community from these

neighbourhoods start to weaken. The old bonds break, and the very spaces in which people live become alienating from within. The old class systems of support have been weakened.

Wacquant points to the growth of social inequality, the loss of a good wage system, the weakening of the welfare state, and the stigmatisation of whole city areas as key factors in this 'modernised misery' of First World cities.

Finally, Wacquant detects the rise of the 'penal state' and a 'punitive upsurge'. The poor are contained through criminalisation, with the prison becoming a major mechanism for their control. This also helps to make the social problems of the city less visible. He analyses the growth of prisons – and who gets to prison, suggesting they are overwhelmingly the cities' outcasts: 'unemployed youth left adrift, the beggars and the homeless, aimless nomads and dug addicts, post colonial immigrants without documents or support' (Wacquant, 2009: 4). The prison and the city live side by side.

See the research and theories of Loïc Wacquant: *Urban Outcasts* (2008) and *Punishing the Poor* (2009). He can also be easily found speaking on YouTube.

Looking ahead: population and urbanisation in the twenty-first century

The demographic analysis presented in this chapter points to some disturbing trends. We see, first of all, that the earth is gaining unprecedented population because of two parallel shifts: death rates are dropping even as birth rates remain high in much of the world. The numbers lead us to the sobering conclusion that controlling global population in the next century will be a monumental task.

Population growth is currently greatest in the least economically developed countries of the world: those that lack productive capacity to support their present populations, much less their future ones. Most of the privileged inhabitants of high-income nations are spared the trauma of poverty (but we do also see the rise of the urban superghetto). But supporting about 90 million additional people on our planet each year, 80 million of these added to poor societies, needs a global commitment to provide not only food but housing, schools and employment. The well-being of the entire world may ultimately depend on resolving many of the economic and social problems of poor, overpopulated countries and bridging the widening gulf between the 'have' and 'have-not' societies. We have seen this problem throughout the book.

Great concentrations of people have always had the power to intensify the triumphs and tragedies of human existence. Thus the world's demographic, environmental and social problems are most pronounced in cities, especially in poor nations. In Mexico City, São Paulo (Brazil), Kinshasa (Zaïre), Mumbai (India) and Manila (the Philippines), urban problems now seem to defy solution, and the end of remarkable urban growth in the world's low-income countries is nowhere in sight.

Earlier chapters point up many different answers to this problem. A classic view, linked with modernisation theory, holds that as poor societies industrialise (as western Europe and North America did a century ago), greater productivity will simultaneously raise living standards and this, in turn, will reduce population growth. A second view, associated with dependency theory, argued that such progress is unlikely as long as poor societies remain economically dependent on rich ones. More recent theories suggest that the roots of the problem are multiple and the problems need confronting from many different positions.

Throughout history, the city has improved people's living standards more than any other type of settlement. The question facing humanity now is whether cities in poor countries will be able to meet the needs of vastly larger populations in the coming century. The answer, which rests on a heady mix of sociological understanding, a grasping of international relations and global economic ties and, possibly above all, a concern for simple justice, will affect us all.

SUMMARY

1 Fertility and mortality, measured as total period fertility rates and crude death rates, are major components of population growth. The overall European population is shrinking slightly. Migration, the third component of population change, has altered the balance between urban and rural populations and has also become the focus of some social tension in the European Union.

2 Demographers use age–sex pyramids to represent the composition of a population graphically and to project population trends. The sex ratio refers to a society's balance of females and males.

3 Historically, world population grew slowly because high birth rates were largely offset by high death rates. About 1750, a demographic transition began as world population rose sharply, mostly due to falling death rates. Thomas Robert Malthus warned that population growth would outpace food production, resulting in social calamity. Demographic transition theorists argue that technological advances gradually prompt a drop in birth rates. Dependency theorists contend that the world's resources must be more evenly distributed to solve population problems equitably.

4 Research shows that lower birth rates and improved economic productivity in poor societies both result from improving the social position of women. World population is expected to reach 8 billion by 2025. Such an increase will probably overwhelm many poor societies, where most of the increase will take place.

5 Closely related to population growth is urbanisation. The first urban revolution began with the appearance of cities some 12,000 years ago. Urbanisation parallels a dramatic increase in the division of labour, as people assume a wide range of highly specialised, productive roles in society. Pre-industrial cities are characterised by low-rise buildings, narrow winding streets and personal social ties.

6 A second urban revolution began about 1750 as the Industrial Revolution propelled rapid urban growth in Europe. This brought about a change in the physical form of cities. Planners created wide, regular streets to facilitate trade. Their emphasis on commercial life and the increasing size of urban areas rendered city life more anonymous. Since the 1950s, European cities have decentralised. The growth of suburbs is one trait of the post-industrial society.

7 A third urban revolution is now occurring in poor societies of the world, where most of the world's largest cities will soon be found. In addition, we are seeing the development of global cities where large, urban regions become highly interconnected through finance, economic decision-making and international labour flows.

8 George Simmel, a European influence on the Chicago School, claimed that the over-stimulation of city life produced a blasé attitude in urbanites.

9 Urban ecology studies the interplay of social and physical dimensions of the city, and maps out the zonal theory of the city. Political economy approaches to the city focus upon the competiton of financiers.

MYTASKLIST

Ten suggestions for going further

1 Connect up with Part Six and the Sociology Web Resources

As you work through ideas and think about the issues raised in this chapter, look at the accompanying website and the resource centre at the end of this book which connects to it. There is a lot here to help you move on. To link up, see: www.pearson.co.uk/plummer.

2 Review the chapter

Briefly summarise (in a paragraph) just what this chapter has been about. Consider: (a) What have you learned? (b) What do you disagree with? Be critical. And (c) How would you develop all this? How could you get more detail on matters that interest you?

3 Pose questions

(a) Do governments have a right to regulate the number of children that people choose to have? Are there any moral dilemmas when people in rich countries strive to reduce fertility in poor countries?

(b) Over the course of history, how have economic and technological changes transformed the physical shape of cities?

(c) According to Ferdinand Toennies, Emile Durkheim, Georg Simmel and Louis Wirth, what characterises urbanism as a way of life? Note several differences in the ideas of these thinkers.

(d) Look at recent accounts of slum cities and global cities: what key social processes are at work here?

4 Explore key words

Many concepts have been introduced in this chapter. You can review them from the website or from the listing at the back of this book. You might like to give special attention to just five words and think them through – how would you define them, what are they dealing with, and do they help you see the social world more clearly or not?

5 Search the Web

Be critical when you look at websites – see the box on p. 940 in the Resources section. For this chapter look at:

United Nations population statistics
http://esa.un.org/unpd/wpp2008
www.un.org/popin/wdtrends
A wealth of tables, discussions and maps for every country in the world.

UN Habitat
www.unhabitat.org
The United Nations Human Settlements Programme, UN Habitat, is the United Nations agency for human settlements. It is mandated by the UN General Assembly to promote socially and environmentally sustainable towns and cities with the goal of providing adequate shelter for all.

Population Reference Bureau
www.prb.org
This website contains major files.

6 Watch a DVD

Many films of the *film noir* genre use the city as a backdrop and create major atmospherics around it.

- Yasujiro Ozu's *Tokyo Story* (1953): examines an elderly couple who move from a small town to their family in a big city, and details the contrasting ways of life. Considered a great and classic film.

- John Schlesinger's *Midnight Cowboy* (1969): the anomie and desperation of modern city life in the United States in the 1960s are well revealed in this classic with Dustin Hoffman and Jon Voight.
- Paul Schrader and Martin Scorsese's *Taxi Driver* (1976) and *Falling Down* (1992): the former sees Robert DeNiro in New York in the 1970s, the latter sees Michael Douglas in Los Angeles in the 1990s, but both films depict the sense of alienation and rage that may come from living in large urban environments.
- *Slumdog Millionaire* (2008) was an Oscar-winning story filmed in Mumbai with Mumbai actors. A bit of a Hollywood touch to world poverty.

7 Think and read

Massimo Livi-Bacci, *A Concise History of World Population* (rev. 4th edn, 2006) and John R. Weeks, *Population* (11th edn, 2011). General introductions to the whole field of demography.

Fred Pearce, *PeopleQuake* (2010). Provides a lively and readable tour of the 'population problems'.

Saskia Sassen, *Cities in a World Economy* (2006). An introduction to the ideas of a leading sociologist, but it is not always easy to read.

Mike Savage and Alan Warde, *Urban Sociology, Capitalism and Modernity* (2002). An earlier overview.

Doreen Massey, *World City* (2007). An important study from one of the world's leading thinkers about the city.

The work of Mike Davis on cities often proves controversial. But he is always a lively read and is packed with information and political concern. See his *City of Quartz* (1990) (on Los Angeles) and *Planet of Slums* (2006).

There are two readers which would prove excellent tour guides to this area of sociology. See:

The Urban Sociology Reader (2005) edited by Jan Lin and Christopher Mele.

The Global Cities Reader (2005) edited by Neil Brenner and Roger Keil.

Finally: UN Habitat, *State of the World's Cities 2010/11*. This is produced every two years and provides discussion and information on major world cities.

8 Relax with a novel

See Saul Bellow's *Herzog* (1964) (about Chicago), Edith Wharton's *The Age of Innocence* (1920) (early-twentieth-century New York), Tom Wolfe's *The Bonfire of the Vanities* (1988) (set in late-twentieth-century New York) and Colm Toibin's *The Story of the Night* (1997) (in Buenos Aires).

9 Connect to other chapters

- Connect demography to Chapter 25 on the environment.
- Link global cities to globalisation in Chapter 2.
- How does the city, and especially the zonal theory of cities, link to crime, as discussed in Chapter 17?

10 Engaged with THE BIG DEBATE

Apocalypse soon? Will people overwhelm the earth?

Are you worried about the world's increasing population? Think about this: by the time you finish reading this box, the number of people on the planet will have risen by more than a thousand. By this time tomorrow, 250,000 more will have been born. There are about six births for every death on the planet, so that the world's population is marching upwards by 80 million annually.

It is no wonder that many population analysts are deeply concerned about the future. The earth has an unprecedented population. In the 50 years from 1960 to 2010, the world population rose from 3 billion to 6.8 billion. Might Thomas Robert Malthus, who predicted that population would outstrip the earth's resources and plunge humanity into war and suffering, be right after all?

Lester Brown, a population and environmental activist, represents the neo-Malthusians who foresee a coming apocalypse if we do not change our ways. Brown concedes that Malthus failed to imagine how much technology (especially fertilisers and plant genetics) could boost the planet's agricultural output. But he maintains that the earth's burgeoning population is rapidly outstripping a host of finite resources. Families in many poor countries can find little firewood; members of rich societies are depleting oil reserves; everyone is draining our reserves of clean water (Brown et al., 2001).

Just as important, according to the neo-Malthusians, humanity is steadily poisoning the planet with waste. There is a limit to the earth's capacity to absorb pollution, they warn, and as the number of people continues to increase, our quality of life will inevitably decline.

But another camp of analysts sharply disagrees. Julian Simon (1981) points out that two centuries ago, Malthus predicted global catastrophe. Today, however, there are almost six times as many people on the earth and, on average, they live longer, healthier lives than ever before. As Simon sees it, the current state of the planet is cause for great celebration.

Simon argues that the neo-Malthusians err in assuming that the world has finite resources that are spread thinner and thinner as population increases. Rather, the anti-Malthusians counter, people have the capacity to improve their lives. We have yet to determine how many people the earth can support because humans are constantly rewriting the rules, in effect, by deploying new fertilisers, developing new high-yield crops and discovering new forms of energy. Simon points out that today's global economy makes available more resources and products than ever (including energy and a host of consumer goods), and at increasingly low prices. He looks optimistically towards the future, noting that technology, economic investment and, above all, human ingenuity have consistently proven the doomsayers wrong. And he is betting they will continue to do so.

Table 24.8	How the global population is increasing		
	Births	**Deaths**	**Net increase**
Year	141,000,000	51,000,000	90,000,000
Month	1,750,000	4,250,000	7,500,000
Day	391,000	141,000	250,000
Hour	16,300	5,875	10,425
Minute	270	98	172
Second	4.5	1.6	2.9

 Update your facts via world population clocks:
World Clock www.poodwaddle.com/clocks/worldclock
Worldometers www.worldometers.info/population

Continue the debate

1 Where do you place your bet? Do you think the earth can support 10 or 12 billion people? Why or why not?
2 What are some likely consequences of the fact that almost 90 per cent of current population growth is occurring in poor countries?
3 Does the world population problem only affect people in low-income countries? What must people in rich societies do to ensure our children's future?

CHAPTER 25

SOCIAL CHANGE AND THE ENVIRONMENT

SOME 800,000 RESIDENTS awoke coughing, vomiting, eyes burning when the Union Carbide pesticide chemical plant at Bhopal in India exploded around midnight on 3 December 1984. Trying to get away, those able to board a bicycle, moped, bullock cart or vehicle of any kind did. But for most of the poor, their feet were the only form of transportation available. Many dropped along the way, gasping for breath and choking on their own vomit. Families were separated; whole groups were wiped out at a time. Those strong enough to keep going ran 3, 6, up to 12 miles before they stopped. Most ran until they dropped. The explosion may well have killed from 3,000 to 6,000 people instantly. Whole families were wiped out. And a further 200,000 were maimed, brain damaged, deformed or killed by the 40 tonnes of lethal and noxious gases which were emitted into the atmosphere by the explosion, and which have taken their toll over many years.

Nearly 30 years on, at least 25,000 people exposed to the gas have died, and today in Bhopal tens of thousands more Indians suffer from regular water pollution and a variety of debilitating gas-related illnesses, such as respiratory and psychiatric problems, joint pains, menstrual irregularities, tuberculosis and cancers. The escalating number of birth defects in children include cleft palates, webbed feet and hands, twisted limbs, brain damage and heart problems. The Union Carbide disaster is commonly agreed to be one of the world's worst environmental accidents (although Chernobyl is a clear 'rival' for this claim).

Yet is it really fair to call all these deaths and continuing mutilations the outcome of 'an accident'? As has been clear for a long time, the 'accident' clearly resulted from corporate negligence and mismanagement. The plant used highly toxic chemicals in its production process, and when water somehow mixed with these, the resulting explosion was catastrophic. Of key importance here is the argument that far fewer people would have died or been injured if the plant had not been located so close to the shanty towns of the poor. The US owners of the company finally moved out in 1999, leaving behind a ruined site along with some 5,000 tonnes of waste, much of which had leaked into the soil. There had been little in the way of a serious clean-up operation and lives are still being ruined.

In 1989, Union Carbide agreed to pay the Indian government $470 million as compensation. This amounts to about $3,000 per family affected. The victims were prevented by law from suing Union Carbide in US courts. Still people go on dying and suffering.

 tip For details and images of the continuing damaged lives in Bhopal and corporate and government neglect, see: www.bhopal.org.

. . . the surface of the earth is truly a living organism. Without the countless and immensely varied forms of life that the earth harbours, our planet would be just another fragment of the universe with a surface as drab as that of the moon and an atmosphere inhospitable to man.

René Dubos (1970; orig. 1959)

. . . Some say the world will end in fire,
Some say in ice.

Robert Frost, 'Fire and Ice'

In this chapter, we ask:

- What is the relevance of sociology to the study of the environment?

- How is the problem of the 'environment' socially constructed?

- How do our human social activities change the state of the natural environment?

- What are the key social explanations of these environmental changes?

- How are social movements and other agencies responding to this?

(Left) Terrified children flee down Route 1 near Trang Ban, South Vietnam, in June 1972 after an accidental aerial napalm strike
Source: Nick UT/AP/PA Photos.

Q This is one of the most famous photographs of the twentieth century.
Consider what it says to you. What is it all about? Then look at the following websites:
http://tigger.uic.edu/~rjensen/vietnam.html
www.ibiblio.org/pub/academic/history/marshall/military/vietnam/short.history/chap_28.txt
www.mtholyoke.edu/acad/intrel/pentagon/pent1.html
www.pbs.org/battlefieldvietnam/history/index.html
www.lib.berkeley.edu/MRC/pacificaviet

There have been many disasters similar to Bhopal that have gained wider public attention: the slag heap slide at Aberfan in Wales, which buried a school in 1966; the spate of oil tanker groundings, which decimated sea life off the shores of Alaska, Britain and Ireland in the 1990s; the nuclear explosion at Chernobyl; the scare over 'mad cow disease' (BSE or bovine spongiform encephalopathy) and its links to CJD (Creuzfeldt–Jakob disease), and most recently the BP oil explosion in the Gulf of Mexico (2010), which spilled about 4.9 million barrels of oil, killing humans and wildlife, and wreaking havoc on the local environment. Such disasters cause enormous environmental damage: for instance, the *Torrey Canyon* oil slick deposited some 117,000 tons of oil in 1967 and killed between 40,000 and 100,000 birds. Humanity's remaking of the earth during the last two centuries may well exceed changes to our planet from all causes over the last billion years.

A high proportion of people in rich nations now enjoy a level of material comfort that our ancestors could scarcely have imagined. However, as those near to Bhopal learned, such achievements carry both costs and risks that endure over many decades. While many social changes have benefited some people, they have also had major environmental consequences, and disasters have become common. The way of life that has evolved in rich societies places such great strain on the earth's natural environment that it threatens the future of the entire planet. In this chapter we look at the sociology of these environmental issues and the problems – even crises – that we generate.

The global environment and its disasters

As Figure 25.1 clearly suggests, we are becoming more and more aware of the disasters in our midst. In the 1950s there were 20 great world catastrophes; in the 1970s there were 47; and by the 1990s there were 86 (Brown et al., 2001: 125). This may be due to increased media coverage and reporting, but the number of disasters seems to have escalated. In 1998–9 alone, over 120,000 people were killed in floods, earthquakes, fires and cyclones. In India, a cyclone in 1998 in Gujarat caused some 10,000 deaths.

There are no signs of this trend slowing in the twenty-first century. As we write in August 2010, in one week alone, some 150,000 people had died in monsoon floods in Pakistan and 4–5 million had had

their homes and lives destroyed. It is the worst flood ever recorded and will take decades to recover from. At the same time, more than 1,300 people are feared dead after flash floods and landslides struck northwest China. The disaster in Gansu province covered entire villages in water, mud and rocks. In Russia, a massive blast at the station in southern Siberia on 17 August 2010 blew out the plant's walls and caused the turbine room to flood. As of the morning of 20 August, 17 workers were confirmed dead and 58 were still missing. This kind of story is becoming a regular feature of global social life:

- Great Japan tsunami and earthquake (with a magnitude of 8.9) killed over 10,000 and left thousands missing in March 2011.
- Around 230,000 died after a 7.00 magnitude earthquake in Haiti in January 2010.
- 1,000 people were killed in Sumatra after a 7.6 magnitude earthquake in September 2009.
- An earthquake of 6.3 hit the Italian city of L'Acquila on 6 April 2009 with at least 300 dead.
- Some 87,000 people were killed in the Sichuan province of China, after an earthquake of 7.8 strikes the provincial town of Chengdu in May 2008.
- A double hurricane in the US Gulf of Mexico – Hurricane Katrina – brought heavy monsoon floods in July 2005. There was serious damage to the levees for which the government was very unprepared. Around 2,000 died, 1 million people became displaced, and 200,000 homes were destroyed.
- On 25 November 2005 the Kashmir earthquake killed 80,000 people, injured hundreds of thousands and made 3 million homeless.
- A tsunami on the south Asian coast on 26 December 2004 affected 11 countries, killing more than 225,000 people and displacing an estimated 1.2 million.

Throughout history such disasters have often happened, sometimes wiping out whole societies in one great flood. As these disasters seem to increase – and the reporting of them through global media becomes easier – there are major implications for societies, in costs to lives and social organisation. With these tsunamis, floods, hurricanes, earthquakes, fires, twisters, freezing and hot temperatures – so-called natural disasters – much government intervention is possible: building houses with earthquake-proof frames or fireproof roofs; stronger building structures; and not allowing building in places where 'disasters' can be predicted (e.g. coastlines beneath the sea level) would all help. Sociologists study the ways in which different

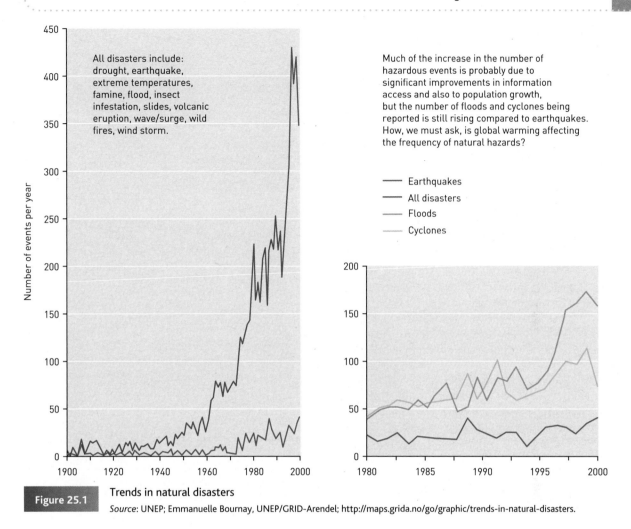

All disasters include: drought, earthquake, extreme temperatures, famine, flood, insect infestation, slides, volcanic eruption, wave/surge, wild fires, wind storm.

Much of the increase in the number of hazardous events is probably due to significant improvements in information access and also to population growth, but the number of floods and cyclones being reported is still rising compared to earthquakes. How, we must ask, is global warming affecting the frequency of natural hazards?

— Earthquakes
— All disasters
— Floods
— Cyclones

Figure 25.1   Trends in natural disasters

Source: UNEP; Emmanuelle Bournay, UNEP/GRID-Arendel; http://maps.grida.no/go/graphic/trends-in-natural-disasters.

kinds of infrastructure can facilitate or prevent natural disasters, as well as examining the social responses of people (from victims and their friends and families to help agencies such as the Red Cross). Very often inequalities of class and race permeate these disasters and the attempts to provide help. *Natural disasters can be lessened by social interventions.*

Sociologists have studied just what people do when natural disasters strike. How do they cope, and indeed how do governments cope? This 'sociology of natural disasters' looks at the shocks that people and communities experience when they are struck by a double hurricane – as with Katrina in New Orleans where the levee broke (see the film by Spike Lee, *When the Levees Broke: A Requiem in Four Acts* (2006)) or the responses of humanitarian agencies trying to help survivors of the Indian Ocean tsunami on 26 December 2004 (see the film by Abi Morgan

Tsunami: The Aftermath (2006), which shows the personal experience of the Boxing Day 2004 disaster in southeast Asia, the social inequalities and the corruption of governments). The *Research in action* box, below, shows one study that conducted such research.

War and the environment

Another area of growing concern about the environment lies in the spread of modern war. In the award-winning, classic but horrific opening picture to this chapter, we see children running for their lives from the terrible bombing destruction in the My Lai massacre in Vietnam. Throughout history, wars have been responsible for much devastation of the environment. Recently, we find them producing massive hazardous waste, pollution from all kinds

There were at least 220,000 deaths in the Haiti earthquake of 2010, out of a population of around just 9 million. The number of fatalities almost matched those experienced during the 2004 Indian Ocean Tsunami, which struck a far larger population

Sources: © NikoGuido/Corbis; © Kim Kyung-Hoon/Reuters/Corbis.

Heatwave: Disaster in Chicago

The Chicago School of Sociology used ethnographic fieldwork, in-depth interviewing, archival research, statistics and map-making to look at the structure of Chicago City in the 1920s and 1930s. A study by Eric Klinenberg uses similar methods to look at a 'natural disaster' which happened in Chicago in 1995. It is one of a series of studies that considers how society responds to natural crises – the sociology of disasters.

In this case, there was an exceptional climate – a 'heatwave': 521 people died because of heatstroke, dehydration, heat exhaustion and renal failure. This was an unusually high death toll for such an event. Many of the dead were stacked up in a mass grave in the mortuary 'old, alone and poor' (Klinenberg, 2003: 33). The heatwave had a particular impact on older women, who were already in poor health, on low income, and living in isolation and depression, and had few resources to survive the new weather conditions.

The heatwave was not just a natural event: it had many social consequences and was shaped by the ability of the Chicago city officials to cope with the elderly, who were deeply neglected. The study resulted in a book, which is full of interviews, records and observations; by looking at the areas with the highest death rates, it demonstrates that there was 'increasing spatial concentration and social separation of the affluent and the impoverished' (2003: 231).

Source: Eric Klinenberg, *Heat Wave: A Social Autopsy of Disaster in Chicago* (2003).

of gases, mass destruction of lands, and a littering of large areas with mines, waiting to be discovered by the unwary years later. The people of Fallujah in Iraq are suffering a huge increase in children born with severe deformities, the likely culprit being the weapons that US troops use. Childhood leukaemias have tripled in the Basra area since the conflict. The damage may have resulted from the Iran–Iraq conflict, but cases increased rapidly after the US and British involvement from 2003. In Afghanistan, too, bombing has reduced forests and generated cancers and psychological problems. Wars leave environments in devastation – often littered with bombs: none of this usually reaches the news headlines.

The environment, its degradations and its dangers, is the topic of this chapter. We start by looking at why sociologists take this topic seriously – it is, after all, a fairly new topic for them to study. We will then look at the ways in which the environment has been changing, in part through human actions and practices. Finally, we will look at the future and consider the different roles of social movements in changing what many see as the degradation of our planet.

Sociology and the natural environment

This chapter suggests links between sociology and **ecology**, *the study of the interaction of living organisms and the natural environment*. Researchers from many disciplines have contributed to this latter field, but this chapter will focus on those aspects of ecology that have a direct connection to human social interactions.

The concept of the **natural environment** refers to the *earth's surface and atmosphere, including all living organisms as well as the air, water, soil and other resources necessary to sustain life*. Like every other living species, humans are dependent on the natural environment for everything from basic food, clothing and shelter to the materials and advanced sources of energy needed to construct and operate our vehicles and all kinds of electronic devices. Yet humans stand apart from other species in our capacity for culture; we alone take deliberate action to remake the world according to our own interests and desires. Thus our species is unique in its capacity to transform the world, for better and worse.

The role of sociology

You may wonder what many of the topics found in this chapter – including solid waste, pollution, acid rain, global warming and loss of biodiversity – are doing in a sociology text. The answer is simple: all of these problems arise from human, social activities, not the 'natural world' operating on its own. Even in the case of natural disasters like tsunamis, we need to think about the human social response to them. Thus, all environmental issues are also issues for *social* understanding. Sociologists can bring at least four such understandings.

First, and perhaps most important, sociologists can demonstrate how human social patterns have caused mounting stress on the natural environment. That is, sociologists can spotlight how environmental problems are linked to particular global, historical and cultural changes. What we do in social life changes the environment. We discuss some of these below.

Secondly, sociologists can show how environmental damage is not equally distributed. For many reasons, poorer and disadvantaged communities are much more likely to experience the pains of environmental problems and have less resources to deal with them. Part Three of this book alerted us to many forms of social division, ranging from class and gender to ethnicity and culture; and the impact of environmental damage reinforces many of these divisions.

Thirdly, sociologists can conduct research on public opinion towards environmental issues, reporting people's thoughts and fears (whether grounded or not) about these controversies. Moreover, sociologists analyse why certain categories of people fall on one side or another of political debates over an environmental issue. Although environmental issues are often seen as key social problems in rich Western societies, poorer societies often have other priorities and do not place the environment as high in their lists of concerns.

Finally, sociologists can explore what 'the environment' and 'nature' mean to people of various cultures and social backgrounds. In many pre-industrial societies, and some contemporary cultures such as the Inuit today, nature demands respect and is seen to be alive and nurturing. It is often religious: gods and spirits inhabit the lakes and the skies. Animals may be eaten but they are also seen as part of the order of things. By contrast, modern industrial societies see 'nature' as something to be controlled, shaped, tamed. 'Nature' is something 'we' can regulate through 'science'.

The changing global environment

Environmental degradation is nothing new. But it was really only in the latter years of the twentieth century, as pollution accelerated, that global awareness of the problems grew. It is only in recent times that we have 'constructed' the environment as a social problem (see below).

It is now apparent that any understanding of the natural environment and its problems must also be global in scope. Regardless of humanity's political divisions into nation-states, the planet constitutes a single **ecosystem**, defined as *the system composed of the interaction of all living organisms and their natural environment*. The Greek meaning of *eco* is 'house', which reminds us of the simple fact that our planet is our home.

Even a brief look at the operation of the global ecosystem confirms that all living things and their natural environment are *interrelated*. Changes to any part of the natural environment ripple through the entire ecosystem, so that what happens in one part of the world inevitably has consequences in another. James Lovelock – a world-renowned scientist and maverick – claims that *planet earth itself should be seen*

PUBLIC SOCIOLOGY

The language and rhetoric of a social problem: a glossary of environmental terms

acid rain precipitation that is made acidic by air pollution so that it destroys plant and animal life

carbon footprint a personal measure of how much carbon dioxide you create and how much you contribute to climate change. It measures the effect of human activities on the climate in terms of the total of greenhouse gases: see the Guardian's *Quick Footprint Calculator* online

cultural ecology a theoretical paradigm that explores the relationship of human culture and the physical environment

ecological footprint human demand hectares per person. It looks at resources needed plus land on which to build and absorb CO_2 from burning fossil fuels. The USA measures 9.4, the world average is 2.23 and Africa is 1.1 (www.guardian.co.uk/conservation)

ecologically sustainable culture a way of life that meets the needs of the present generation without threatening the environmental legacy of future generations

ecology the study of the interaction of living organisms and the natural environment

ecosystem the system composed of the interaction of all living organisms and their natural environment

environmental deficit the situation in which our relationship to the environment, while yielding short-term benefits, will have profound, negative long-term consequences

environmental racism the pattern by which environmental hazards are greatest in proximity to poor people, especially minorities

global commons resources shared by all members of the international community, such as ocean beds and the atmosphere

greenhouse effect a rise in the earth's average temperature (global warming) due to increasing concentration of carbon dioxide in the atmosphere

Kyoto Protocol signed in Kyoto, Japan, in 1997 under a United Nations Framework, it aims to reduce greenhouse gas emissions (carbon dioxide, methane and four others) by 5.2 per cent of the 1990 level in each country. As of October 2010, a total of 191 countries had ratified the agreement

natural environment the earth's surface and atmosphere, including various living organisms as well as the air, water, soil and other resources necessary to sustain life

rain forests regions of dense forestation, most of which circle the globe close to the equator

risk society society in which risks are of a different magnitude because of technology and globalisation

sustainable development development that meets the needs of the present without compromising the ability of future generations to meet their own needs (Brundtland Commission) *as a living organism*, inside which humans and other species each have a vital part to play (see Lovelock, 1979). This is known as the **Gaia hypothesis**. Lovelock is now 90 (in 2010), and in his latest book, *The Vanishing Face of Gaia* (2009), he sees the world on an inevitable calamity course (and we had better enjoy it while we can!). A number of major claims have been made about why this 'calamity' is happening and we will be raising them through the chapter. An elaborate new language has come into being to explain this 'calamity'. Three major interlinked claims are outlined below (and see the box opposite for key terms).

1 Global warming

Climate change is now commonly regarded as fundamentally altering the planet. Average temperatures have climbed 1.4 °F (0.8 °C) around the world since 1880. With this, there has been a 30 per cent increase in carbon dioxide. In the twenty-first century, each year seems to bring new records in weather changes. Most scientists (but not all – see Lomborg (2001) – although even he has changed his mind!) agree that we must act soon to prevent further alterations, or we will see the end of humanity and the world as we know it.

Climate refers to long-term weather changes: heatwaves, ocean warming and sea level rising, glaciers melting and Arctic and Antarctic warming. They are not isolated weather events but long-term changes which foreshadow disease, population and animal changes along with flooding, storms, droughts and fires. They bring desertification and potential geopolitical instability.

 A useful summary of the UK weather over periods of time (climate) – and much more – can be found at the excellent website of the Met Office: www.metoffice.co.uk.

Natural scientists explain that rainforests play an important part in removing carbon dioxide (CO_2) from the earth's atmosphere. From the time of the Industrial Revolution, the amount of carbon dioxide that humanity has produced (most generated by factories and cars) has risen tenfold. Much of this CO_2 is absorbed by the oceans. But plants, which take in carbon dioxide and expel oxygen, also play a major part in maintaining the chemical balance of the atmosphere.

The problem, then, is that production of carbon dioxide is rising while the amount of plant life on earth is shrinking. To make matters worse, rainforests are being destroyed, mostly by burning, which releases even more carbon dioxide into the atmosphere. The atmospheric concentration of carbon dioxide behaves much like the glass roof of a greenhouse, letting heat from the sun pass through to the earth while preventing much of it from radiating back away from the planet. Thus ecologists talk about a **greenhouse effect** and a **carbon footprint** (see the *Public sociology* box).

Scientists note a small rise in global temperature (about 1 °C) over the twentieth century. Some go on to predict that the average temperature of our planet (about 15 °C in recent years) will rise by 5–10 °C during the twenty-first century. This warming trend would melt much of the polar ice caps, raise sea levels and push the oceans up over low-lying land around the world, flooding Bangladesh, for example, and much of coastal Europe.

Not all scientists share this vision of future global warming. Some point out that global temperature changes have been taking place throughout history, and rainforests have had little or nothing to do with those shifts. Moreover, higher concentrations of carbon dioxide in the atmosphere might actually accelerate plant growth (since plants thrive on this gas), which would serve to correct this imbalance and nudge the earth's temperature downward once again.

2 The 'hole' in the ozone layer

Consider the effects of our use of chlorofluorocarbons (CFCs) as a propellant in aerosol spray cans and as a gas in refrigerators, freezers and air conditioners. CFCs may have improved our lives in various ways, but as they were released into the atmosphere, they reacted with sunlight to form chlorine atoms, which, in turn, depleted ozone. The ozone layer in the atmosphere serves to limit the amount of harmful ultraviolet radiation reaching the earth from the sun. Thus, there is evidence of a 'hole' in the ozone layer (in the atmosphere over Antarctica) which may produce a rise in human skin cancers and countless other effects on plants and animals (Harrison and Pearce, 2000). While an international agreement has been reached to phase out the use of CFCs, many unscrupulous people continue to prefer to maximise their short-term convenience by continuing to use them. By 1997, the black market global trade in CFCs rivalled the trade in narcotics. Moreover, in spite of global efforts to cut other emissions, some soft drink companies are seeking to market a new self-cooling can, which will chill warm drinks in two minutes when opened – and release nearly as much pollution as the cars we drive today. Given the complexity of the global ecosystem, many threats to the environment go unrecognised. As the *World watch* box opposite explains, the popular, although seemingly innocent, act of eating fast food has significant environmental effects in other parts of the world.

3 Acid rain

The term refers to precipitation that is made acidic by air pollution so that it destroys plant and animal life. The complex reaction that generates acid rain (or snow) begins as power plants burning fossil fuels (oil and coal) to generate electricity release sulphur and nitrogen oxides into the air. Once the winds sweep these gases into the atmosphere, they react with the air to form sulphuric and nitric acids, which make atmospheric moisture acidic.

One type of pollution often causes another. In this case, air pollution (from chimneys) ends up contaminating water (in lakes and streams that collect acid rain). Notice, too, that acid rain is a global phenomenon because the regions that suffer the effects of acid rain may be thousands of miles from the site of the original pollution. Tall chimneys of British power plants have caused the acid rain that has devastated forests and fish in Norway and Sweden up to 1,000 miles to the northeast (Harrison and Pearce, 2000).

TOP 10
Consumers of energy

		Barrels of oil per day
1	USA	20,680,000
2	China	7,578,000
3	Japan	5,007,000
4	Russia	2,858,000
5	India	2,722,000
6	Germany	2,456,000
7	Brazil	2,372,000
8	Canada	2,371,000
9	Saudi Arabia	2,311,000
10	Korea South	2,214,000

Note: Chile is ranked 48th with a consumption of 253,000 barrels per day and Turkmenistan is ranked 69th with consumption of 156,000 barrels per day. The worst polluters are China, USA, Russia, India and Japan – in that order.

Source: www.nationmaster.com/red/graph/ene_oil_con-energy-oil-consumption&b_map=1#.

History, change and the environment

How did humanity gain the power to threaten the natural environment? We have already seen the role that population growth may play (see Chapter 24); here we will examine the role of culture and technology. As humans have devised new technologies, so we have gained the ability to make and remake the world as we choose. The *Timeline* suggests some of the historical issues.

Timeline A brief history of environment degradation

Pre-1500

Global extinctions of whole species – up to 90 per cent were lost at the end of the Permian and Cretaceous periods; many large mammals lost, some species through overhunting; microbe movements leading to epidemics; long-term natural climate changes

1500–1760

European ecological expansion and capitalist growth start to lead to rising resource shortages and land degradation; demographic movements and ecological transformation of the Americas

Modern: 1760–1945

Capitalist industrialisation, urbanisation, concentration, ecological expansion and colonialisation; local resource exhaustion, urban air, soil and water pollution, change in rural environments and forest loss; some global extinction of species and some contribution to global warming

Contemporary

Global warming, marine depletion, water in short supply, deforestation, desertification, soil exhaustion, overspills, hazardous waste, acid deposition, nuclear risks and decline of global ecosystem come with Western growth and consumption. Socialist industrialisation, industrialisation of the South, new risks from technology and warfare

Source: Adapted from Harrison and Pearce (2000), Held et al. (1999: 391).

Members of societies with simple technology are so directly dependent on nature that their lives are guided by the migration of birds and animals and the rhythm of the seasons. They remain especially vulnerable to natural events, such as fires, floods, droughts and storms. Nevertheless, horticulture (small-scale farming), pastoralism (the herding of animals) and even agriculture (the use of animal-drawn ploughs) started to radically alter the nature of our countrysides and landscapes.

It is, however, with the development of industrial technology that the most dramatic change in humans' relationship with the natural environment takes place. Industry replaces muscle power with combustion

---

WORLD WATCH

The global ecosystem: the environmental consequences of everyday choices

People living in high-income countries, such as most of those in Europe, have the greatest power to affect the earth's ecosystem for the simple reason that they consume so much of the planet's resources. Thus, small, everyday decisions about how to live can add up to large consequences for the planet as a whole.

Consider the commonplace practice of enjoying a burger. McDonald's and dozens of other fast-food chains serve billions of burgers each year to eager customers across the world. This appetite for beef creates a large market for cattle throughout the world. The UK briefly experimented with cheap feeding strategies to reduce the price of beef – only to gain problems with BSE, or 'mad cow disease', as a result. Yet even with the outbreak of the BSE scare in 1995, the European Community as a whole did not apply equally stringent regulations for the slaughter of cattle across member states until July 1997.

Other countries, particularly in Latin America, have responded

COUNTRY FACT FILE

BRAZIL

Population	198.7m
Per capita GDP	$9.567 (2007)
Life expectancy	68.7 male 76.0 female
Adult literacy	90% (2007)
Key languages	Portuguese
Key religions	Roman Catholic, Protestant
Key cities	Brasilia; São Paulo (17,833,757); Rio de Janeiro (5,850,544) (2000)
Human development index	0.699 (73rd, 2010)

to the demand for beef by expanding cattle ranching. As consumption of burgers has grown, ranchers in Brazil (the largest country in Latin America), Costa Rica and other countries are devoting more and more land to cattle grazing. Latin American cattle graze on grass. This diet produces the lean meat

demanded by the fast-food corporations, but it also requires that a great deal of land be dedicated to grazing.

Where is the land to come from? Ranchers in Latin America are solving their land problem by clearing forests at the rate of thousands of square miles each year. These tropical forests, as we shall explain presently, are vital to maintaining the earth's atmosphere. Therefore, forest destruction threatens the well-being of everyone – even the people back in Europe who enjoy burgers without giving a thought to the environment.

Enhancing global consciousness is thus a vital dimension of increasing environmental awareness. Ecologically speaking, our choices and actions ripple throughout the world, even though most of us never realise it. People in Europe are simply looking for a quick burger. Fast-food companies are making a profit by serving meals that people want. Ranchers are trying to earn a living by raising beef cattle. No one intends to harm the planet but, taken together, these actions can have serious consequences for everyone. All people on this planet inhabit a single ecosystem. In a world of countless environmental connections, we need to think critically about the effects of choices we make every day – like what's for lunch!

Source: Based on Myers (1984a).

engines that burn fossil fuels, including coal and oil. Such machinery affects the environment in two ways – by consuming natural resources and by releasing pollutants into the atmosphere. Humans armed with industrial technology become able to bend nature to their will far more than ever before, tunnelling through mountains, damming rivers, irrigating deserts and drilling for oil on the ocean floor.

The general pattern is clear. High-income, industrial societies place the greatest demands on the planet's ecosystem. While low-income societies use only 14 per cent of the total world energy, high-income societies use 57 per cent (World Bank, 1997: 93). The United States, home to 5 per cent of the world's population, consumes roughly one-third of the world's energy – more than any other country. The typical US adult consumes 100 times more energy annually than the average member of the world's poorest societies. Taking a broader perspective, *the members of all high-income societies represent 20 per cent of humanity, but utilise 80 per cent of all energy* (Connett, 1991).

But the environmental impact of industrial technology is not limited to energy consumption. Just as important, industrial societies produce 100 times more goods than agrarian societies do. While these products raise the material standard of living, they greatly escalate the problem of solid waste (because people ultimately throw away most of what they produce) and pollution (because industrial production generates smoke and other toxic substances).

People have been eager to acquire many of the material benefits of industrial technology, but a century after the dawn of industrial development, people began to gauge the long-term consequences of this new technology for the natural environment. Indeed, one defining trait of post-industrial societies is a growing concern for environmental quality. The 'environment' starts to be defined as a social problem by different groups.

From today's vantage point, we draw an ironic and sobering conclusion: as we have reached our greatest technological power, we have placed the natural environment – including ourselves and all other living things – at greatest risk (Voight, cited in Bormann and Kellert, 1991: ix–x). The evidence is mounting that, in our pursuit of material affluence, humanity is running up an **environmental deficit**, *a situation in which our relationship to the environment, while yielding short-term benefits, will have profound, negative long-term consequences* (Bormann, 1990).

The concept of environmental deficit implies three important ideas. First, it stresses that the state of the environment is a *social issue*, reflecting choices people make about how they live. Secondly, this concept suggests that environmental damage – to the air, land or water – is often *unintended*. By focusing on the short-term benefits of, say, cutting down forests or using easily disposable packaging, we fail to see (or choose to ignore) their long-term environmental effects. Thirdly, in some but not all respects, the environmental deficit is *reversible*. In as much as societies have created environmental problems, in other words, societies can undo most of them.

Growth and its limits

If the world as a whole were suddenly blessed with the material prosperity that people in much of the Western world take for granted, humanity would soon overwhelm the global environment. This conclusion suggests that our planet suffers not just from the problem of economic *under*development in some regions, but also from economic *over*development in others. For just how long can societies continue to grow in this way?

The logic of growth

One of the driving assumptions of modern Western societies is that of progress and material, economic advance. Moreover, we rely on *science*, looking to experts to apply technology to make our lives better. Taken together, such cultural values form the foundation for the *logic of growth*.

This logic of growth looks like an optimistic view of the world, suggesting, first, that people have improved their lives by devising more productive technology and, second, that we shall continue to do so into the future. The logic of growth thus amounts to the assertions that 'people are clever', 'having things is good (having more is better)', and 'life will improve'. A powerful force throughout the history of the Western, capitalist and industrial societies, the logic of growth has driven individuals to sail the seas, clear the land, build towns, railways and roads, and pursue material affluence.

But even optimistic people realise that 'progress' generates unanticipated problems, environmental and otherwise. The logic of growth responds by arguing that people (especially scientists and other technology experts) are inventive and will find a way out of any problems that growth places in our path. If, say, present resources should prove inadequate for our future needs, we will come up with new alternative resources that will do the job just as well.

To illustrate, most people in Europe would probably agree that cars have greatly improved our lives by providing us with a swift and comfortable means of travel. The counterargument, however, highlights some of the hazards that car culture raises. Cars have also made us dependent on petrol, and Europe has previously suffered when conflicts in the Middle East have slowed the sale of oil resources. Even if the logic of growth rightly suggests that scientists will develop cars needing an alternative fuel source by the time the planet's oil reserves run dry, today's millions of cars will make mountains of rubbish in the future.

This is one of many reasons why most environmental scientists criticise the logic of growth. Lester Milbrath (1989) argues that natural resources such as oil, clean air, fresh water and the earth's topsoil – all *finite* – simply cannot be replaced by technologically engineered alternatives. He warns that we can and will exhaust them if we continue to pursue growth at any cost.

And what of our faith in human ingenuity and especially the ability of science to resolve problems of scarcity? While conceding that humans are clever at solving problems, Milbrath adds that human resourcefulness, too, has its limits. Do we dare to assume that we will be able to solve every crisis that confronts us, especially those wreaking serious damage on the life-giving environment? Moreover, the more powerful and complex the technology (nuclear reactors, say, compared to petrol engines), the greater the dangers posed by miscalculation and the more significant the unintended consequences are likely to be. Thus, Milbrath concludes that as we call on the earth to support increasing numbers of people with finite resources, we will almost certainly cause serious injury to the environment and, ultimately, to ourselves.

The limits to growth

If we cannot 'invent' our way out of the problems created by the 'logic of growth', perhaps we have to come up with an alternative way of thinking about the world. Environmentalists, therefore, propose the counterargument that growth must have limits. The *limits to growth thesis*, stated simply, is that humanity must implement policies to control the growth of population, to cut back on production

and to use fewer resources in order to avoid environmental collapse.

The Limits to Growth, a controversial book published in 1972 that had a large hand in launching the environmental movement, uses a computer model to calculate the planet's available resources, rates of population growth, amount of land available for cultivation, levels of industrial and food production, and amount of pollutants released into the atmosphere (Meadows et al., 1972). The authors contend that the model reflects changes that have occurred since 1900, then projects forward to the end of the twenty-first century. Long-range predictions using such a complex model are always speculative and some critics think they are simply wrong (Simon, 1981). But many find the general conclusions of the study, shown in Figure 25.2, convincing.

Following the limits to growth logic, humanity is quickly consuming the earth's finite resources. Supplies of oil, natural gas and other sources of energy will fall sharply, a little faster or slower depending on policies in rich nations and the speed at which other nations industrialise. While food production per person should continue to rise through at least the early part of the twenty-first century, the authors calculate, millions will go hungry because existing food supplies are so unequally distributed throughout the world. By mid-century, the model predicts a hunger crisis serious enough that rising mortality

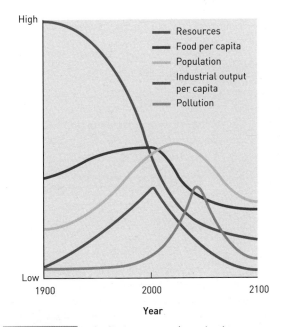

| Figure 25.2 | The limits to growth: projections |

Source: Based on Meadows et al. (1972).

rates will first stabilise population and then send it plunging downward. Depletion of resources will eventually cripple industrial output as well. Only then will pollution rates fall.

The lesson of this study is grim: current patterns of life are not sustainable for even another century. This leaves us with the fundamental choice of making deliberate changes in how we live or allowing calamity to force changes upon us.

How social actions degrade and damage our environment

We have reviewed some of the increasing demands on the natural environment. What, then, is the state of the natural environment today? The *World watch* box suggests an array of issues. Working from top to bottom, we see how all aspects of our environment – air, life, land, sea – are being degraded. Some of this we may see as an increase in *pollution* (for example, greenhouse gases in the air); others we may see as a *depletion of major resources* (for example, the loss of water, forests and animal species). In any event, social life is increasingly generating these problems and as such they become areas of major concern for sociologists in understanding the social mechanisms which generate environmental degradation. In what follows we look at some of the social practices employed by humans – the things we do in our daily lives – that degrade the environment.

1 Discarding waste in the 'disposable society'

As an interesting exercise, carry a rubbish bag over the course of a single day and collect all the materials you throw away. Most people would be surprised to find out how much waste they generate. Rubbish is a feature of all modern societies, but the most extreme case is the United States – the classic 'disposable society'. In the United States, an average person tosses out close to 5 pounds of paper, metal, plastic and other disposable materials daily (about 50 tons over a lifetime). For that country as a whole, this amounts to about 1 billion pounds of solid waste produced *each and every day*.

The United States is not the only culprit. In the European Union, legislation designed to facilitate the *safe* transport of goods around the common market and to protect consumer health has led to an escalating use of packaging. Everything (from baked goods to hammers to bicycle helmets) is increasingly sold with excessive packaging – a trend which many manufacturers and retailers have welcomed, as packaging can make a product more attractive to the customer (or harder to shoplift).

Consider, too, that manufacturers market soft drinks, beer and fruit juices in aluminium cans, glass jars or plastic containers, which not only consume

The world at risk: a dramatically changing environment

The air

The air: pollution

Depletion of the ozone level has now reached record levels. Fossil fuel burning releases about 6 billion tons of carbon into the air each year, adding about 3 billion tons annually to the 170 billion

tons that have settled since the Industrial Revolution. The rate of growth in carbon emissions is around 2 per cent per year. The good news is that there has been a 70 per cent reduction in ozone-producing substances since 1987, showing that change is possible with concerted action. Even so, according to NASA, the ozone hole in 2009 came to cover an area of 24 million square kilometres (down a

little from 26 million in 2004). (See: Ozone Hole Watch: http://ozonewatch.gsfc.nasa.gov.)

The weather: hotting up?

These are the hottest years for over a thousand years. The decade of 1998–2007 is the warmest on record, according to data sources obtained by the World Meteorological Organization (WMO). The global mean surface temperature for 2007 is currently estimated at 0.41 °C/0.74 °F above the 1961–90 annual average of 14.00 °C/57.20 °F. Within the next 40-year period, ocean temperatures could rise by 7 °C

WORLD WATCH

(enough to melt polar ice caps!) and there are risks of major 'climatic surprises' (see: World Metereological Office: www. wmo.int/pages/index_en.html).

The earth

Deforestation and urbanisation

Over the past half-century, the earth's vast forests of green have been reduced to tattered remnants. Some 3 billion hectares of the world's original forest cover – nearly half – has been lost. The world is losing 7 million hectares of fertile land a year due to soil degradation, and about 10 million hectares of forest land a year (about the size of South Korea). While there is less land, more food is needed. The world is becoming increasingly urbanised – 37 per cent in 1970, 60 per cent by 2030. Ten per cent of the world's trees face extinction.

Forests and biodiversity: species decline

'Life on earth is currently undergoing a sixth mass extinction event.' Rainforests once covered 14 per cent of earth's land surface; now they cover a mere 6 per cent. Around 150,000 square kilometres of tropical rainforest, equivalent to the size of England and Wales, is destroyed every year. Between 70 and 95 per cent of the earth's species live in the world's disappearing tropical forest. We are losing 50 species a day; 46 per cent of mammals and 11 per cent of birds are said to be at risk. By 2020, 10 million species are likely to become extinct. In 2003, scientists reported that industrial fishing had killed off 90 per cent of the world's biggest and economically

important fish species. 2010 was the UN International Year of Biodiversity – a year that celebrates the diversity of life on earth, including every plant, animal and micro-organism (see www.biodiversityislife.net).

People and population

World population has grown from 3 billion to nearly 7 billion in just 50 years. While the rate of growth is slowing, world population is still increasing by about 75 million people a year. It is fast becoming an ageing population (see Chapter 13). The current prediction is for a population of around 9 billion by the middle of the twenty-first century.

Transport

In 1997, according to the International Association of Motor Vehicle Manufacturers, more than 54 million cars were produced worldwide. By 2002, that number had risen to 58 million, and by 2008, it had reached 70.5 million. There has been some decline during the world recession. The key exception to this is China, now the largest automobile producer in the world, at nearly 14 million vehicles in 2009. Here, production increased by 48.3 per cent in comparison with the previous year. Kingsley Dennis and John Urry (2010) in their study of the global car industry have shown how much damage is done across the world by cars. Consider what they say:

> Worldwide, cars generate 1.2 million deaths and 20–50 million injuries a year ... the estimated global cost is $518 billion ... It is stimated that traffic injuries will become the third largest contributor to the global burden of ill health and physical impairment

by 2020 . . . The result is sheer carnage . . .

Indoor air pollution

In low-income societies, burning wood, animal dung and scraps inside can lead to deadly smoke in confined places. Indoor air pollution may kill between 3 and 4 million people a year.

The water

Water pollution

At present, more than a billion people are without access to clean water, and this may reach 2.5 billion by 2025; 2.5 billion lack sanitation services according to UNICEF. Freshwater ecosystems are in decline everywhere. Some 35 million people are dying from pollution through contaminated drinking water; deaths from waterborne illnesses are rapidly increasing and may have reached 120 million per year by 2020. Some 58 per cent of the world's reefs and 34 per cent of all fish may be at risk.

Data published by UNICEF, moreover, demonstrate highly unequal access to water and sanitation around the world. So, for instance, only 22 per cent of Ethiopians have access to fresh water, and only 6 per cent to sanitation facilities that meet international health standards. In Bolivia, 85 per cent of the population have access to fresh water coverage, and 45 per cent to salubrious sanitation facilities. In contrast, data collected by UNICEF and the World Health Organization show that access to improved water and sanitation facilities is practically universal in countries like the United Arab Emirates, Australia, Egypt, Lebanon and the United Kingdom.

Source: see sources quoted in the box and the list at the end of this chapter.

Turning the tide: a report from Egypt

Cairo, like many large cities, has become a mess of pollution. No sooner had we left the bus than smoke and stench, the likes of which we had never before encountered, swirled around us. Eyes squinting, handkerchiefs pressed against noses and mouths, we moved slowly uphill along a path ascending mountains of trash and garbage that extended for miles. We had reached the Cairo dump, where the refuse generated by 15 million people in one of the world's largest cities ends up. We walked hunched over and with great care, guided by only a scattering of light from small fires smouldering around us. Up ahead, through clouds of smoke, we saw blazing piles of trash encircled by people seeking warmth and enjoying companionship.

Human beings actually inhabit this inhuman place, creating a surreal scene, like the aftermath of the next global war. As we approached, the fires cast an eerie light on their faces. We stopped some distance from them, separated by a vast chasm of culture and circumstances. But smiles eased the tension and soon we were sharing the comfort of their fires. At that moment, the melodious call to prayer sounded across the city.

The people of the Cairo dump, called the Zebaleen, belong to a migrant religious minority – Coptic Christians – in a predominantly Muslim society. Barred by religious discrimination from many jobs,

the Zebaleen use donkey carts and small trucks to pick up the city's refuse and haul it here. For decades, the routine has reached a climax at dawn when hundreds of Zebaleen gather at the dump, swarming over the new piles in search of anything of value.

Upon our visit in 1988, we observed men, women and children picking through Cairo's refuse, filling baskets with anything of value: bits of metal, strips of ribbon, even scraps of discarded food. Every now and then, someone gleefully displayed a 'precious' find that would bring the equivalent of a few dollars in the city. Watching in silence, we became keenly aware of our sturdy shoes and warm clothing and self-conscious that our watches and cameras represented more money than most of the Zebaleen earn in a year.

Today, the Cairo Zebaleen still work the city's streets collecting trash. But much has changed, as they now represent one of the world's environmental success stories. The Zebaleen now have a legal contract to perform this work and, most important, they have established a large recycling centre near the dump. There, dozens of workers operate large machines that shred discarded cloth into stuffing to fill furniture, car seats and pillows. Others separate plastic and metal into large bins for cleaning and sale. In short, the Zebaleen are big business people. Using start-up loans from the World Bank, not only have the Zebaleen constructed an efficient recycling centre, they have also built for themselves a modern apartment complex, with electricity and running water.

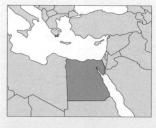

COUNTRY FACT FILE

EYGPT

Population	78,866.6 million
Per capita GDP	$6,000
Life expectancy	69.56 male 74.81 female
Adult literacy	66.4%
Key languages	Arabic (official)
Key religions	Muslim (mostly Sunni) 90%, Coptic 9%
Key city	Cairo
Human development index	0.620 (101st, 2010)

Source: Human Development Report (2009).

The Zebaleen are still poor by European standards. But they now own the land on which they live and work, and they are prospering. Certainly, they no longer inhabit the bottom rung of Egyptian society. And many international environmental organisations hope their example will inspire others elsewhere. When the 1992 environmental summit meeting convened in Rio de Janeiro, officials presented the Cairo Zebaleen with the United Nations award for environmental protection.

Source: Based on Macionis's visits to Egypt, 1988 and 1994. See also http://zabaleen.wordpress.com and www.facebook.com/thezabaleenproject.

WORLD WATCH

The Zebaleen people of Cairo have amazed the world with their determination and ingenuity, turning one of the planet's foulest dumps into an efficient recycling centre and providing new apartment units for themselves in the process

Source: © Barry Lewis/Alamy.

finite resources but also generate mountains of solid waste. Then there are countless items intentionally designed to be disposable. A walk through any local supermarket reveals shelves filled with pens, razors, flashlights, batteries and even cameras, intended to be used once and dropped in the nearest bin. Other products – from light bulbs to washing machines – are designed to have a limited useful life, and then become unwanted junk. As Paul H. Connett (1991) points out, even the words we use to describe what we throw away – *waste, litter, rubbish, refuse, garbage* – reveal how little we value what we cannot immediately use and how quickly we push it out of sight and out of mind.

Living in a 'disposable society', the average person in the United States consumes 50 times more steel, 170 times more newspaper, 250 times more petrol and 300 times more plastic each year than the typical individual in India (Miller, 1992). Comparable high levels of consumption in Europe mean that Western societies not only use a disproportionate share of the planet's natural resources, but also generate most of the world's refuse. Of the 435 million tonnes of waste disposed of each year in the UK, household dustbins account for only 6 per cent of the total; 36 per cent comes from commerce and industry. And half is produced by primary industries – mining, dredging, quarrying and farming (Lang and Heasman, 2004: 228).

Solid waste that is not burned or recycled never 'goes away'; rather, it ends up in landfills. The practice of using landfills, originally intended to improve sanitation, is now associated with several threats to the natural environment. First, the sheer volume of discarded material is literally filling up landfills. Especially in large cities such as London, there is

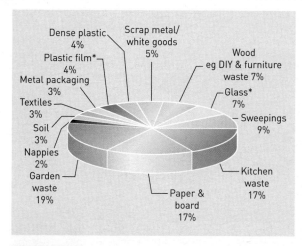

| Figure 25.3 | Waste in the UK: what we throw away |

Source: www.defra.gov.uk. Fortnightly rubbish collection leads to more recycling, says government, *The Guardian*, 26 April 2007. Copyright Guardian News & Media Ltd 2007.

simply little room left for disposing of rubbish. Second, material placed in landfills contributes to water pollution. Although laws now regulate what can be placed in a landfill, there are dump sites across Europe containing hazardous materials that are polluting water both above and below the ground. Third, what goes into landfills all too often stays there – sometimes for centuries. Tens of millions of tyres, nappies and other items that we bury in landfills each year do not readily decompose, leaving an unwelcome legacy for future generations. Figure 25.3 gives you some idea of what, when and how much we throw away in the UK.

2   Threatening the water supply

The oceans, lakes and streams supply the lifeblood of the global ecosystem. Throughout human history, people have relied on water for drinking, bathing, cooling, cooking, recreation and a host of other activities. Yet, the oceans have long served as a vast dumping ground for all kinds of waste, including nuclear submarines and human excrement. No one can calculate the precise amount of waste that has been poured into the world's oceans, but the total certainly exceeds millions of tons. The problems caused by disposing of solid waste in this way are crystal clear: polluted water kills fish or makes them dangerous to eat, and also spoils a source of great beauty and pleasure.

Through the process which scientists call the *hydrological cycle*, the earth naturally recycles water and

refreshes the land. The process begins as heat from the sun causes the earth's water, 97 per cent of which is in the oceans, to evaporate and form clouds. Next, water returns to earth as rain, which drains into streams and rivers and rushes towards the sea. The hydrological cycle not only renews the supply of water but cleans it as well. Because water evaporates at lower temperatures than most pollutants, the water vapour that rises from the seas is relatively pure and free of contaminants, which are left behind. Although the hydrological cycle generates clean water in the form of rain, it does not destroy pollutants that steadily build up in the oceans, and clean rain can collect pollutants in the air as it falls back to earth. Two key concerns, then, dominate discussions of water and the natural environment. The first is supply; the second is pollution.

Water supply

Talk about a 'drought', along with discussions of the amount of rainfall each month, has become a common concern in European societies, where the weather is relatively kind. But concern over an ample supply of water is hardly new. For thousands of years, since the time of the ancient civilisations of China, Egypt and Rome, water rights have figured prominently in codes of law. Throughout Europe, aqueducts of brick, built by the ancient Romans, stand as testimony to the historical importance of readily available water.

Today some regions of the world, especially the tropics, enjoy a plentiful supply of water, although most of the annual rainfall occurs over a relatively brief season. High demand for water, coupled with more modest reserves, makes water supply a matter of concern in much of Europe and North America as well as most of Asia. In these areas people look to rivers – rather than rainfall – for their water. Especially in the Middle East and parts of Africa, water supply has already reached a critical level. Egypt, for instance, is located in an arid region of the world, where people have long depended on the River Nile for most of their water. But, as the Egyptian population increases, shortages are becoming commonplace. Egyptians today must make do with a sixth as much water per person from the Nile as they did in 1900, and experts project that the supply will shrink by half again over the next 20 years (Myers, 1984c; Postel, 1993).

Within 30 years, according to current predictions, 1 billion people throughout the Middle East and parts of Africa will lack sufficient water. The world has recently witnessed the tragedy of hunger in the African nations of Ethiopia and Somalia. While we recognise the impact of food shortages there, an even more serious problem for these societies is the lack of adequate water for irrigation and drinking.

Surging population and complex technology – especially in manufacturing and power-generating facilities – have greatly increased our appetite for water. The global demand for water (estimated at about 5 billion cubic feet per year) has tripled since 1950 and is expanding faster than the world's population (Postel, 1993). As a result, even in areas that receive significant rainfall, people are using groundwater faster than it can be naturally replenished. Take the Tamil Nadu region of southern India, for example. There, the rapidly growing population is drawing so much groundwater that the local water table has fallen 100 feet over the last several decades.

In light of such developments, we must face the reality that water is a valuable, finite resource. Greater conservation of water by individuals (who consume, on average, 10 million gallons over a lifetime) is part of the answer. However, households around the world account for no more than 10 per cent of water use. We need to curb water consumption by industry, which currently uses 25 per cent of the global total.

Irrigation channels two-thirds of humanity's water use on to croplands. New irrigation technology may well reduce this demand in the future. But, here again, we see that population increase, as well as economic growth, is placing increasing strains on the ecosystem (Myers, 1984a; Goldfarb, 1991; Falkenmark and Widstrand, 1992; Postel, 1993).

Polluting water

In large cities – from Mexico City to Cairo to Shanghai – many people have little choice but to drink contaminated water. The poor people of the world suffer most as a result of unsafe water. As Chapter 21 noted, infectious diseases such as typhoid, cholera and dysentery, all caused by micro-organisms that contaminate water, run rampant in poor nations. Throughout the low-income regions of the world, then, the source of much illness and death can be traced to microbes thriving in polluted water (Falkenmark and Widstrand, 1992; Harrison and Pearce, 2000).

Thus, besides ensuring ample *supplies* of water, we must recognise that no society has done an exemplary job of protecting the *quality* of its water. In most areas of the world, tap water is not safe for drinking.

Most people living in Europe take for granted that tap water is free from harmful contaminants, and water quality in Europe is generally good by global standards. However, even here the problem of water pollution is growing steadily. The Rhine drainage basin (connecting the Netherlands, Germany, France and Switzerland) contains about 20 per cent of the EU's population, along with its industry. Large quantities of toxic waste – chemicals, heavy metals and sewage – have been found to be entering the river. Although actions have since been taken to reduce the quantities of waste, the possibility of contaminated water remains. Likewise, the pollution all round the Mediterranean is well known. And in the UK, pollution incidents in rivers have doubled in recent years (Pickering and Owen, 1994).

3 Polluting the air

Most people in Europe are more aware of air pollution than they are of contaminated water, in part because air serves as our constant and immediate environment. Then, too, many urbanites are familiar with the mix of smoke and fog (the origin of the word 'smog') that hangs over cities.

One of the unanticipated consequences of the development of industrial technology – especially the factory and the motor vehicle – has been a deterioration of air quality. The thick, black smoke belched from factory chimneys, often 24 hours a day, alarmed residents of early industrial cities a century ago. By the end of the Second World War, air pollution was commonplace in most industrial cities. In London, factory discharge, car emissions and smoke from coal fires used to heat households combined to create what was probably the worst urban air quality of the century. In the course of just five days in 1952, an especially thick haze – the infamous 'pea-souper' – that hung over London killed 4,000 people (Harrison and Pearce, 2000).

Recently, improvements have been made in combating air pollution brought on by industry. Laws now mandate the use of low-pollution heating fuels in most cities; the coal fires that choked London a half-century ago, for example, are now forbidden (the Clean Air Act of 1956 helped to end much of this pollution – though in December 1991, a severe smog did reappear). In addition, scientists have effectively devised new technologies to reduce the noxious output of factory chimneys and, even more important, to lessen the pollution caused by the growing number of cars and lorries. The switch to unleaded petrol, coupled with changes in engine design and exhaust systems, has reduced the car's detrimental environmental impact. Still, with cars accounting for around 80 per cent of all travel in Europe (and 96 per cent in the United States!), the challenge of cleaning the air remains daunting (*Social Trends*, 1997: 202). As the number of cars across the world increases (in 2002, around 41 million passenger vehicles were produced – five times as many as in 1950), so pollution grows. In 1961, the number of licensed vehicles in Great Britain was just under 9 million; in 1981, there were 19.3 million. By 2002, the figure was 30.6 million. Table 25.1 suggests the damage that the emissions from these cars can do (*World Watch*, 2004: *Social Trends*, 2004).

If the rich societies of the world can breathe a bit more easily than they once did, poor societies contend with an increasing problem of air pollution. For one thing, people in low-income countries still rely on wood, coal, peat or other 'dirty' fuels for cooking fires and to heat their homes. Moreover, many nations are so eager to encourage short-term industrial development that they pay little heed to the longer-term dangers of air pollution. As a result,

many cities in Latin America, eastern Europe and Asia are plagued by air pollution that rivals the toxic level found in London 50 years ago. All the major cities – from Bangkok to Mexico City – labour under intense city pollution that makes even breathing difficult!

4 Using transport systems that degrade the environment

Road transport dominates the transportation systems across the world, but air travel is the fastest growing; it has risen from 28 billion passenger kilometres in 1950 to 2.6 trillion passenger kilometres in 1998 (Sheehan, 2001: 106). All this has made rail – the great invention of the nineteenth century – less important. Cars and trucks have helped change the structures both of cities and of their surrounding landscapes. Increasingly, people use cars even for very short trips.

The high costs of modern car transportation include the following:

- Cars contribute to local and regional pollution, and in some parts of the world this pollution kills even more people than road accidents.
- Cars killed around 1.2 million people in 2004, according to a WHO World Report on Road Traffic in 2009.
- Cars damage ecosystems through the vast networks of roads created for their use.
- Cars make movement in cities difficult, hindering more efficient public transport and persuading those who can afford to fly to take more and more 'to the skies'.
- Cars perpetuate social inequalities: people in poorer countries cannot afford cars and spend a disproportionate amount of their time walking long distances for essential trips.

The United States Environmental Agency estimated that 60 per cent of all US carbon dioxide emissions come from motor vehicles. The USA has 30 per cent of the world's cars and produces some 45 per cent of the world's emissions (Dennis and Urry, 2010).

5 Destroying the land

Rainforests are *regions of dense forestation, most of which circle the globe close to the equator.* The largest tropical rainforests are in South America (notably Brazil), but west-central Africa and southeast Asia also have sizeable rainforests. In all, the world's

Table 25.1	The dangers of cars: what they release into the environment
Pollutant	**Hazard**
Carbon monoxide	Greenhouse gas – slows thought and reflexes
Ozone	Greenhouse gas – irritant on eyes, nose, lungs, etc.
	Damages trees – with acid rain
Nitrogen oxide	Greenhouse gas
	One-third of acidity of rainfall
Lead	Impairs mental development in children
Benzene	Cancer and impotence links
Hydrocarbons	Irritate lungs and are potentially cancerous
Carbon dioxide	Most significant greenhouse gas

rainforests cover an area of some 2 billion acres, which accounts for 7 per cent of the earth's total land surface.

Like the rest of the world's resources, the rainforests are falling victim to the needs and appetites of the surging human population. The demand for beef has sparked more cattle grazing in Latin America; ranchers typically burn forested areas to increase their supply of grazing land. Just as important is the lucrative hardwood trade. High prices are paid for mahogany and other woods by people in rich societies who have, as environmentalist Norman Myers (1984b: 88) puts it, 'a penchant for parquet floors, fine furniture, fancy panelling, weekend yachts, and high-grade coffins'. Under such pressure, the world's rainforests are now just half their original size, and they continue to shrink by about 1 per cent (65,000 square miles) annually. If this rate of destruction continues unchecked, these forests will vanish before the end of the twenty-first century and, with them, protection for the earth's climate and biodiversity.

6 Endangering the wildlife

Whatever the effects on this planet's climate, rainforest clearance has another undeniable impact. The disappearance of rainforests is a major factor eroding the earth's biodiversity, or, more simply, causing many thousands of species of plant and animal life to disappear for ever. While rainforests account for just 7 per cent of the earth's surface, they are home to almost half of the planet's living species. Estimates of the total number of species of animals and plants range from 1.5 million to as high as 30 million. Researchers, in fact, have identified more than 1,000 species of ant alone (Wilson, 1991).

Several dozen unique species of plants and animals cease to exist each day; but, given the vast number of living species on the earth, why should we be concerned with a loss of biodiversity? Environmentalists point to three reasons. First, our planet's biodiversity provides a vast and varied

The relations of human beings with other non-human animals is a key topic for sociologists. Unfortunately, destructive human activities have led to the current rate of species extinction, which is at least 100–1,000 times higher than the expected natural rate. For more information and details on the different endangered species, look at http://www.worldwildlife.org/species/

Source: PhotoDisc Volume 44; Photodisc Volume 6.

source of human food. Agricultural technology currently 'splices' familiar crops with more exotic plant life to yield crops that are more productive or resistant to insects and disease. In addition, geneticists, looking into the properties of unfamiliar plant and animal life, are working towards generating the quantity and quality of foods necessary to nourish our rapidly increasing population.

Secondly, the earth's biodiversity is a vital genetic resource. Medical and pharmaceutical industries depend on animal and plant biodiversity in their research to discover compounds that will cure disease and improve our lives. Children in Europe, for example, now have a good chance of surviving leukaemia, a disease that was almost a sure killer two generations ago, because of a compound derived from a pretty tropical flower called the rosy periwinkle. The oral birth control pill used by tens of millions of women is a product of the Mexican forest yam. Scientists have tested tens of thousands of plants for their medical properties, and they have developed hundreds of new medicines each year based on this research.

Thirdly, with the loss of any species of life – whether it is one variety of ant, the spotted owl, the magnificent Bengal tiger or the famed Chinese panda – the beauty and complexity of our natural environment is diminished. And there are clear warning signs. Three-quarters of the world's 9,000 species of birds are currently declining in number. Finally, keep in mind that, unlike pollution and other environmental problems, the extinction of species is irreversible and final. As a matter of ethics, then, should those who live today make decisions that will impoverish the world for those who live tomorrow (Myers, 1984b, 1991; Wilson, 1991; Brown et al., 2001)?

Constructing the social problem of the environment

Sociologists are often seen to be students of so-called 'social problems': the problems of 'drugs', 'crime' and 'poverty' are their concerns. Sociologists are often called upon to discuss sex, poverty and the like in the media and elsewhere. Looking at this book, you can probably see why they are seen this way.

But the issue goes much deeper than this. For sociologists are also interested in the ways social problems become constructed, organised and transformed. They are not just concerned with the problem as it seems to be; they also want to examine *the ways in which it has come to be seen as a problem*.

Thus, for example, throughout much of history, up until 50 years ago or so, people did not talk about the environment as a social problem. Nowadays, it is hard to read a newspaper or watch the news and not hear an item about some aspect of global warming, recycling or the environmental crisis. It is to be found everywhere: in the media, in films, in governmental reports, in social movements and in international congresses. Indeed, some would say the environment is the major problem facing the twenty-first century.

Social problems: objective conditions and constructed reactions

To look at this, sociologists provide two contrasting (and not necessarily antagonistic) ways of approaching social problems. One we can call the 'objective' approach and it is the approach we have adopted largely in this chapter. Objective here means 'real, tangible, and measurable'. We look at objective indicators, often measured by scientists – as we have here – to indicate the nature of the problem. And then we make

TOP 10	
Best environmental performance index, 2011	
1 Iceland	93.5
2 Switzerland	89.1
3 Costa Rica	86.4
4 Sweden	86.0
5 Norway	81.1
6 Mauritius	80.6
7 France	78.2
8 Austria	78.1
9 Cuba	78.1
10 Colombia	76.8

Note: The UK is ranked 14th with an index of 74.2 and Japan 20th with an index of 72.5. The index is based on a range of factors, including environmental health, biodiversity, air pollution, water use, agricultural methods and tackling climate change.

Source: Pocket World in Figures, Profile Books Ltd (2011).

suggestions – again as we hint at here – on ways that we can solve the problem.

Thus, we have shown the nature of environmental degradation created by human beings in their social life. They discard waste, threaten the water supply, pollute the air, destroy the land and endanger the wildlife. These things need to be modified or changed and we need action to do this. Hence we see social movements warning of the need for these changes, governments advocating policies of change and people all over the planet becoming more environmentally aware – charting their own carbon footprints and considering how their own actions can 'save the planet'.

But a second approach holds all this in abeyance and asks instead: *just how do human beings come to construct 'the environment' as a social problem?* This is the *claims-making approach* and it sees social problems as social constructions in which people make claims about what is and what is not a social problem. The emphasis now shifts to all the *responses to the environment* and their social causes, social patterns and social impact. Often sociologists have implied that many problems are invented when there are no problems, or they turn minor worries into major public concerns. Thus, we can trace the history of social problems – things like the problem of smoking, of alcohol, of child abuse, of poverty and so on.

These sociologists then look at the people who are involved in defining the problem, and the kinds of claim they make as to why it is a problem, and then they trace the evolution – or stages – of the problem defining. They trace the ways in which at one point in time nobody speaks of something as a problem (even though it may exist in our first sense above), and then at a later stage – maybe just a year or two hence – it comes to be seen as a major social problem. Just how did this happen? How did the 'problem of the environment' turn from being a non-problem to a major problem in a couple of decades?

The 'environmental social problem' is a very good example. There are large numbers of people who define it as a problem and make strong claims about it. And we can certainly trace key stages in its development (see the *Timeline* below). This is a very useful way for sociologists to look at these concerns: they do not just accept the nature of the problem as a given, but can show how society has worked at turning it into an identifiable problem, and they can show the exact procedures through which it has come into being (Loseke, 2003; Loseke and Best, 2003).

Timeline The environment: recent events

1962 **Silent Spring**
Marine biologist Rachel Carson published *Silent Spring*, calling attention to the threat of toxic chemicals to people and the environment.

1967 **Pollution disaster**
The *Torrey Canyon* oil tanker ran aground and spilt 117,000 tons of oil into the North Sea near Cornwall in the United Kingdom. The massive local pollution helped prompt legal changes to make ship owners liable for all spills.

1968 **The Population Bomb**
Paul Ehrlich published *The Population Bomb*, describing the ecological threats of a rapidly growing human population.

1971 **The Limits to Growth**
The Club of Rome, a group of economists, scientists and business leaders from 25 countries, published *The Limits to Growth*, which predicted that the earth's limits will be reached in 100 years at current rates of population growth, resource depletion and pollution generation.

1972 **United Nations Environment Programme**
Participants from 114 countries came to Stockholm, Sweden, for the UN Conference on the Human Environment. Only one was an environment minister, as most countries did not yet have environmental agencies. The delegates adopted 109 recommendations for government action and pushed for the creation of the UN Environment Programme.

1974 **Ozone layer**
Chemists Sherwood Rowland and Mario Molina published their landmark findings that chlorofluorocarbons (CFCs) can destroy ozone molecules and may threaten to erode the earth's protective ozone layer.

1982   **UN concern**

The UN Environment Programme organised the Stockholm +10 conference in Nairobi. The attendees agreed to a declaration expressing 'serious concern about the present state of the environment' and established an independent commission to craft a 'global agenda for change,' paving the way for the release of *Our Common Future* in 1987.

1983   **Climate**

The US Environmental Protection Agency and the US National Academy of Sciences released reports concluding that the build-up of carbon dioxide and other 'greenhouse gases' in the earth's atmosphere will probably lead to global warming.

1984   **Bhopal**

An estimated 10,000 people were killed and many more injured when Union Carbide's pesticide plant in Bhopal, India, leaked 40 tons of methyl isocyanate gas into the air and sent a cloud of poison into the surrounding city of 1 million people.

1985   **Ozone layers**

Scientists reported the discovery of a 'hole' in the earth's ozone layer, as data from a British Antarctic Survey showed that January ozone levels had dropped 10 per cent below those of the previous year.

1986   **Chernobyl**

One of the four reactors at the Soviet Union's Chernobyl nuclear power plant exploded and completely melted down. The explosion sent radioactive particles as far away as western Europe, exposing hundreds of thousands of people to high levels of radiation.

1989   **The Exxon Valdez**

The *Exxon Valdez* tanker ran on to a reef in Alaska's Prince William Sound, dumping 76,000 tons of crude oil – covering more than 5,100 kilometres of pristine coastline with oil and killing more than 250,000 birds.

1992   **Earth Summit at Rio**

Most countries and 117 heads of state participated in the groundbreaking UN Conference on Environment and Development (Earth Summit) in Rio de Janeiro, Brazil. It produced *Agenda 21*, a voluminous blueprint for sustainable development that called for improving the quality of life on earth.

Also: *The Convention on Climate Change* set non-binding carbon dioxide reduction goals for industrial countries (to 1990 levels by 2000).

World Scientists' Warning to Humanity stated that 'human beings and the natural world are on a collision course'.

1992   **Earth Summit at Rio**

Most countries and 117 heads of state participated in the groundbreaking UN Conference on Environment and Development (Earth Summit) in Rio de Janeiro, Brazil. It produced *Agenda 21*, a voluminous blueprint for sustainable development that called for improving the quality of life on earth.

Also: *The Convention on Climate Change* set non-binding carbon dioxide reduction goals for industrial countries (to 1990 levels by 2000).

World Scientists' Warning to Humanity stated that 'human beings and the natural world are on a collision course'.

1997   **Kyoto**

The Kyoto Protocol strengthened the 1992 Climate Change Convention by mandating that industrial countries cut their carbon dioxide emissions by 6 to 8 per cent from 1990 levels by 2008–12.

1998   **Ozone layer**

The ozone hole over Antarctica grew to 25 million square kilometers. (The previous record, set in 1993, was 3 million square kilometres.)

2001   **Bush and Kyoto**

Whilst the IPCC released a report citing 'new and stronger evidence that most of the observed warming of the last 50 years is attributable to human activities,' and stating temperatures will increase by 1.4 to 5.8 degrees Celsius by 2100, US President George W. Bush announced that the United States would not ratify the Kyoto Protocol, saying that the country could not afford to reduce carbon dioxide emissions.

2005   Kyoto finally came into force.

2006   *The Stern Report*: a 700-page UK report on the economics of climate change and warning of dangers.

2007   Ex-Vice President Al Gore won a Nobel Peace Prize (his film *An Inconvenient Truth* was a great success). He shared it with the IPCC for its fourth assessment of the environment.

2008 Election of Barack Obama as President in the USA signalled a more positive approach to the environment by the USA.

2009 Copenhagen Summit. 192 nations met in Denmark to move beyond Kyoto. The Copenhagen Accord was not legally enforceable and was regarded as a fiasco. Failure was blamed on both developing countries and developed countries.

The story continues ...

- UN reports that tropical countries lose more than 15 million hectares of forests a year to agriculture, logging and other threats.
- UN warns that the world's reservoirs are losing storage capacity as deforestation causes erosion and sedimentation behind dams.
- Some 3,250 square kilometres of Antarctica's Larsen B ice shelf collapse as regional temperatures warm.
- Survey finds that bleaching at Australia's Great Barrier Reef in 2002 may be the worst on record, affecting up to 60 per cent of reefs.
- 104 world leaders and thousands of delegates meeting at the World Summit on Sustainable Development in Johannesburg, South Africa, agree on a limited plan to reduce poverty and protect the environment.
- Amazon deforestation increases 40 per cent compared with 2001. Brazil registers second-highest figure in 15 years.
- Industrial fishing has killed off 90 per cent of the world's biggest and most economically important fish species.
- Study reports that within the past decade, war, hunting, mining, and other human pressures have wiped out 70 per cent of the global population of eastern lowland gorillas – leaving fewer than 5,000 worldwide.

Source: Adapted from www.worldwatch.org/taxonomy/term/59, where you can find a more elaborate version.

Environmental Milestones charts key events from the early 1960s to 2004.

Key shapers of 'the environmental problem'

The constructionist view of the environment asks how the following come to define the environment as a problem and what kinds of claim they make about the 'problem'. Key players include:

- *Scientists*: meteorologists, biologists, chemists, physicists, ecologists, etc.
- *Media*: press stories, films, documentaries, fund-raising concerts, etc.
- *Social movements*: Greenpeace, Friends of the Earth, World Wildlife Fund, etc.
- *'Research'*: Worldwatch Institute, Earthscan, People and Planet, etc.
- *Governments*: Green parties, policy units, budget advisers, officials, etc.
- *Global summits*: conferences, world reports.
- *Celebrities*: Al Gore, Bob Geldof, Bill Gates, Bono, Sting, etc.

Key claims on 'the environment problem'

While there are many arguments and positions taken on the environment, three major positions can be distinguished:

1 *The sceptics and critics.* These are largely politicians – but a few scientists are included – who argue that the changes in the environment have always been happening, that they are caused by 'natural events' outside of our control, and that they may even be being reduced by some human interventions. They often accuse 'environmentalists' of being 'doomsayers' and people who want to impede human progress (or human profit).

2 *The mainstream position* is a contrived consensus across governments which recognises the significance of climate change for the world, produces reports and organises conferences and summits on it. It is

spearheaded by the Intergovernmental Panel on Climate Change (IPCC) and regularly produces very large reports on the climate (The Fifth Assessment Report AR5 was under way in August 2010: see www.ipcc.ch. The need for environmental change is identified and programmes for change are planned.

3   *The radicals and critics.* These are largely those who work outside the mainstream frame and often in social movements. At the extreme, there are those who claim the disaster is already done and we can do little at this late stage to prevent a calamitous end. James Lovelock is an outspoken champion of this view (see above). Others see the source of the problem as capitalism and seek major changes in economic organisation and profit seeking in order to reduce the damage.

The environmental movement

The environmental movement is a major example of a contemporary social movement that aims to have a wide, global impact (see Chapter 16). Born of postmaterialist values, the movement itself has changed over time. It can be charted through a number of waves.

The 'first wave' of environmentalism was little more than a conservation movement that focused on protecting the natural environment. Its earliest manifestations may have appeared in Britain as long ago as the sixteenth century, with people's concerns for the changing countryside. The movement developed more focus in the nineteenth century through the emergence of groups such as the National Trust (1895) and the Royal Society for the Protection of Birds (created in 1889).

During the 1960s a 'second wave' of environmentalism took root in Europe and became decidedly more radical and critical. In 1962, in the United States, Rachel Carson's book *Silent Spring* explored the dangers of spreading pesticides across the land. Agricultural 'business as usual', Carson warned, was courting disaster. Before long, environmental concerns had become part of the activist culture that marked the decade with people chaining themselves to trees to halt logging and blocking ships armed with nuclear weapons.

By 1970, with the celebration of the first 'Earth Day', the environmental movement had come of age. Its adherents addressed a wide range of issues – including those covered in this chapter – and, increasingly, they directly challenged many of the practices and priorities that had long marked out the Western way of life.

By 1980, around 5 per cent of the population in the UK belonged to one of several thousand environmental groups. In 1989, a MORI poll revealed that 18 million people regarded themselves as environmentally conscious shoppers; and some 17–35 per cent of people rated the environment as the most important political issue (Garner, 1996: 62–3). At the forefront of these newer groups were *Friends of the Earth* and *Greenpeace*. Greenpeace emerged in the late 1960s and, by 1989,

Greenpeace is one of the world's leading social movements. Here we see a demonstration for a cleaner environment in Politeama Square, Palermo, Sicily. For more information, see: http://www.greenpeace.org/international/en/

Source: © Gianni Muratore/Alamy.

had attracted an estimated 3.5 million members. It has become a major NGO. Friends of the Earth was founded in 1969 in the United States, and by the early 1980s had branches in some 29 countries. Many feminist groups (*eco-feminists*) have also come to identify strongly with environmental change, especially those who argue that women are the sex who reproduce, nurture and care – more than men. As such, they have a major responsibility for reproduction and caring for their planet (Garner, 1996: 66).

At the same time, throughout all this, conservative administrations have often adopted a strong pro-business agenda and soon governments and the environmental movement were locking horns over population control, land development and other matters.

Today, the environmental movement is well established worldwide. It falls into three main groupings. One group comprises mainstream lobbyists, who usually work in NGOs such as Greenpeace and are often professional and well funded. A second group encompasses popular movements where people lobby for specific issues and work to change things in their own lives, such as picketing the transportation of livestock and concern over 'animal rights' in the UK, marching on railway carriages transporting nuclear waste in Germany, or landless peasants marching on Brasilia to address land rights issues. The third, more radical wing of environmentalism draws on Marxism and feminism and takes drastic action to instil a sense of urgency among governments.

Inequalities and the environment

Some sociologists argue that the background to all this is the global disparity of wealth and power. In the hierarchical organisation of societies, a small proportion of our population – what Chapter 16 called the 'power elite' – sets the national and global agenda by controlling the world's economy, law and view of the natural environment. Early capitalists shepherded Europe into the industrial age, hungrily tapping the earth's resources and frantically turning out manufactured goods in pursuit of profits. By and large, it was they who reaped the benefits of the new industrial wealth, while workers toiled in dangerous factories and lived in nearby localities blighted with smoke, racked with noise and shaken by the vibrations of the big machines.

As important: many societies have just ignored the most blatant instances of environmental destruction, even when elite perpetrators run foul of the law. Corporate pollution falls under the category of white-collar crime. Such offences typically escape prosecution. When action is taken, it is usually in the form of fines levied on a company rather than criminal penalties imposed on individuals. Thus, corporate executives who order the burning or burying of toxic waste have been subject to penalties no greater (and sometimes less) than ordinary citizens who throw rubbish from car windows.

Many critical thinkers argue that capitalism itself poses a threat to the environment. The logic of capitalism is the pursuit of profit, and that pursuit demands continuous economic growth. What is profitable to capitalists does not necessarily advance the public welfare and is not likely to be good for the natural environment. As noted earlier in this chapter, capitalist industries have long ensured ongoing profits by designing products to have a limited useful life (the concept of 'planned obsolescence'). Such policies may improve the 'bottom line' in the short term, but they raise the long-term risk of depleting natural resources as well as generating overwhelming amounts of solid waste.

A small share of the earth's population currently consumes most of its energy. Generally, members of rich societies use most of the earth's resources and, in the process, produce the most pollution. By exploiting both the earth and the poor of the less developed countries, these countries have poisoned the air and water in the process. From this point of view, rich nations are actually overdeveloped and consume too much. No one should expect that the majority of the earth's people, who live in poor societies, will be able to match the living standard in these countries; nor, given the current environmental crisis, would that be desirable. Instead, conflict theorists call for a more equitable distribution of resources among all people of the world, both as a matter of social justice and as a strategy to preserve the natural environment (Schnaiberg and Gould, 1994; Szasz, 1994).

Environmental racism

An important aspect of this inequality is the worrying growth of **environmental racism**, *the pattern by which environmental hazards are greatest in proximity to poor people, especially minorities.* For example, while many homes in rich countries can consume more than 2,000 litres of good-quality water every day, some 500 million people around the globe suffer from an almost total lack of drinking water! The World Health Organization suggests a basic requirement of 150 litres per day per household. This basic and quite low standard could well be achieved for the whole world if so much water was not squandered by the West (*New Internationalist*, 2001: 23).

Historically, factories that spew pollutants have been built in and near districts inhabited by the poor, who often work there. As a result of their low incomes, many could afford housing only in undesirable localities, sometimes in the very shadow of the plants and mills. Although workers in many manufacturing industries have organised in opposition to environmental hazards, they have done so with limited success, largely because the people facing the most serious environmental threats have the least social power to begin with.

Critical comment

This analysis raises important questions about who sets a society's agenda and who benefits (and suffers) most from decisions that affect us all. Environmental problems, from this point of view, are consequences of a global stratification (see Chapter 9). Yet, while it may be true that elites have always dominated industrial society, they have not been able to stem a steady tide towards legal protection of the natural environment. These protections, in turn, have yielded some significant improvements in our air and water quality. Arguably, however, much of this change has come about because of social movements directed towards environmental action.

So what of the charge that capitalism is particularly hostile to the natural world? There is little doubt that capitalism's logic of growth does indeed place stress on the environment. At the same time, however, capitalist societies have made some strides towards international agreements for environmental protection. And the environmental record of socialist societies is also very poor. For decades, industrialisation was pursued in neglect of environmental concerns, without challenge and with tragic consequences in terms of human health.

Finally, there is little doubt that high-income countries currently place huge demands on the natural environment. However, this pattern is already beginning to shift as global population swells in poor countries. And environmental problems are also likely to grow worse to the extent that poor societies develop economically, using more resources and producing more waste and pollutants in the process. In the long run, all nations of the world share a vital interest in protecting the natural environment. This concern leads us to the concept of a sustainable environment (see below).

Taking stock and looking ahead: for a sustainable world?

India's great leader Mahatma Gandhi once declared that societies must provide 'enough for people's needs, but not for their greed'. From an environmental point of view, this means that the earth will be able to sustain future generations only if humanity refrains from rapidly and thoughtlessly consuming finite resources such as oil, hardwoods and water. Nor can we persist in polluting the air, water and ground at anything like the current rates. The loss of global forests – through the felling of trees and the destructive effects of acid rain – threatens to undermine the global climate. And we risk the future of the planet by adding people to the world at the rate of 90 million each year.

Today, on every part of the earth inhabited by humanity, the environmental deficit is growing. In effect, our present way of life is borrowing against the well-being of future generations. As we have seen, members of rich societies, who currently consume so much of the earth's resources, are mortgaging the future security of the majority of people who live in the poor countries of the world.

In principle, we could solve the entire range of environmental problems described in this chapter by living in a more environmentally aware manner, one that makes environmental consequences central to our actions. This is the path to a culture that is sustainable, one that does not increase the environmental deficit. An **ecologically sustainable culture**, then, refers to *a way of life that meets the needs of the present generation without threatening the environmental legacy of future generations*. (The concept of 'sustainable development' was popularised through the 1987 UN Commission Report on the Environment – the Brundtland Commission.)

Sustainable living calls for three basic strategies. The first is the *conservation of finite resources*, balancing the desire to satisfy our present wants with the responsibility to preserve what will be needed by future generations. Conservation means using resources more efficiently, seeking alternative resources and learning to live with less. Technology is helping in providing some devices (from light bulbs to boilers) that are far more energy efficient than those available at present. Moreover, alternative energy sources need developing, including harnessing the power of the sun, wind and tides. While relying on help from new technology, a sustainable way of life will ultimately require a rethinking of the pro-consumption attitudes formed during decades of 'cheap electricity' and 'cheap petrol'. The consumer society discussed in Chapter 15 may have to be changed.

The second basic strategy is *reducing waste*. Whenever possible, simply using less is the most effective way to reduce waste. Governments will need to tighten regulations on pollution. They may need to foster this by shifting taxes on to environmental 'bads' such as carbon use or fuel emissions (e.g. fuel taxes). There will be a need to expand recycling programmes. Educational efforts need to enlist widespread support for these initiatives and for legislation requiring the recycling of certain materials.

The third key element in any plan for a sustainable ecosystem is *bringing world population growth under control*. As we showed in Chapter 24, the 2010 global population of 7 billion is straining the natural environment. Clearly, the higher world population climbs, the more difficult environmental problems will become. Global population is now increasing by about 1.5 per cent each year, a rate that will double the world's people in fewer than 50 years. Few analysts think that the earth can support a population of 10 billion or more. Controlling population growth will require urgent steps in poor regions of the world where growth rates are highest.

Technocentrism and ecocentrism

Although there is some common agreement about the need to *conserve resources, reduce waste and bring population under control*, there are many different positions on how to achieve this. As the *Big debate* at the end of the chapter discusses, some positions are radical and seek a fundamental change of the world; others believe the existing order just needs a little tinkering. Commonly, though, two positions have been identified: a technocentric one and an ecocentric one.

Those holding ecocentric positions (whom we might call Radical Greens) see economic growth as at odds with environmental objectives. There must be *limits to growth* (see above) as the valuing of growth in itself

will inevitably lead to more and more commodities, goods and waste. They are concerned that adopting technical and scientific solutions to the problems may just increase them: science has always had side-effects and these may well bring yet more damage (we have seen this both in Chapter 23 and in the idea of a risk society, discussed above). They suggest that major social and political changes become necessary for environmental change, and they argue that the planet is home not just for humans but for *all* living things. In contrast, technocentric positions put human beings and science at the centre of their arguments. They see the continued need for economic growth, but one in which technical solutions to problems of the environment may be found (see Table 25.2).

As with all such models, they set out polar positions which may help to clarify arguments but which in practice often need some compromise. Sweeping environmental strategies – put in place with the best intentions – will fail without some fundamental changes in the ways in which we come to think about the social and the natural world, and our place in them. By taking a view that sets up our own immediate interests as the standards for how to live, we have obscured several key connections.

First of all, we need to realise that, environmentally speaking, *the present is tied to the future*. Simply put, today's actions shape tomorrow's world. Thus, we must learn to evaluate our short-term choices in terms of their long-range consequences for the natural environment.

Secondly, rather than viewing humans as 'different' from or 'better' than other forms of life and assuming that we have the right to dominate the planet, we must acknowledge that *all forms of life are interdependent*.

Table 25.2	Models of technocentric and ecocentric solutions to environmental problems
Technocentric	**Ecocentric**
Modified sustainable economic growth	Growth seen as limited and undesirable
Technology can provide solutions	Distrust of science and technological fixes
Solutions within existing policy	Radical social and political change needed
Human-centred – human values	Nature-centred – wider values

Source: Based on Garner (1996: 30).

European environmental policy

Environmental issues are truly global. Many of the problems, like the releasing of CFCs into the atmosphere, have global effects and require global action. Some problems link to the exploitation of **global commons** – *the resources shared by the international community, such as ocean beds and the atmosphere.* Sometimes small local problems, such as poisonous gases leaking from landfills and water pollution, are multiplied so many times in many local contexts that they become major world hazards. The environment is a global concern requiring global policies.

The timeline below shows some major world issues in environmental change and world policies: 1972 saw a programme to manage the 'global commons', and established a UN Environment Programme. Subsequent world conferences include the Earth Summit held in Rio in 1992 and the Earth Summit 2 in New York in 1997.

Uniquely among international organisations, the European Union has 'the power to agree environmental policies binding on its members' (McCormick, 1991: 128). In 1997, the Worldwatch Institute remarked that: 'The European Union, consisting of some 15 countries and containing 360 million people, provides a model for the rest of the world of an environmentally sustainable food/population balance ... one seventh of humanity is already there' (Brown et al., 1997: 12–13). It has continued to do so since that time. Five periods of European policy can now be identified:

1957–72 The original Treaty of Rome did not raise environmental issues and there was minimal involvement.

1973–85 In the wake of the *Limits to Growth* report (see discussion in text), the First Environmental Action Programme gave the EU power to act whenever 'real effectiveness' on environmental issues seemed possible. Water quality, air quality and hazardous waste policies (120 directives, 27 decisions and 14 regulations) were implemented.

1986–92 A formal legal framework emerged.

1993–7 In the wake of Maastricht, integration curiously became weaker as the EU expanded to include new members and as members defended their national self-interest. Nonetheless, the EU continued to promote sustainable environmental policies through such measures as the regulation of fish stocks and the funding of sustainable development research.

2001 The Sixth Community Environmental Action Programme set out a plan for a wider programme of environmental action up to 2010.

2006 The Registration, Evaluation, Authorisation and Restriction of Chemicals (REACH) law of the European Union covered the production and use of chemical substances, and was one of the most complex European environmental initiatives.

2007 The European Union agreed to a policy obliging its member states to cut their carbon dioxide emissions by 20 per cent or more compared to the levels of 1990. On the basis of a possible international deal, emissions will be cut further in the future, and the use of renewable energy sources will also be increased to 20 per cent throughout the European Union.

Source: For updates, see the European Environmental Agency at www.eea.europa.eu.

Ignoring this truth not only harms other life forms, but will eventually undermine our own well-being. From the realisation that all life figures in the ecological balance must follow specific programmes that will protect the earth's biodiversity.

Third, and finally, achieving a sustainable ecosystem will require *global cooperation*. The planet's rich and poor nations are currently separated by a vast chasm of divergent interests, cultures and living standards. On the one hand, most countries in the northern half of the world are overdeveloped, using more resources than the earth can sustain over time. On the other hand, most nations in the southern half of the world are underdeveloped, unable to meet the basic needs of many of their people. A sustainable ecosystem depends on bold and unprecedented programmes of international cooperation. And, while the cost of change will certainly be high, it pales before the eventual cost of not responding to the growing environmental deficit.

Along with the transformations just noted, we will reach the goal of a sustainable society only by critically re-evaluating the logic of growth that has dominated our way of life for several centuries.

In closing, we might well consider that the great dinosaurs dominated this planet for some million years and then perished for ever. Humanity is far younger, having existed for a mere quarter of a million years. Compared to dinosaurs, our species seems to have the gift of intelligence. But how wisely will we use this ability? What are the chances that our species will continue to flourish on the earth a million years – or even a few hundred years – from now? It may be foolish to assume that our present civilisation is about to collapse, but it is certainly equally foolish to ignore the warning signs. One certainty is that the state of tomorrow's world will depend on choices we make today.

SUMMARY

1 Because the most important factor affecting the state of the natural environment is the way in which human beings organise social life, ecology – the study of how living organisms interact with their environment – is one important focus of sociology.

2 Societies increase the environmental deficit by focusing on short-term benefits and ignoring the long-term consequences brought on by their way of life.

3 Studying the natural environment demands a global perspective. All parts of the ecosystem, including the air, soil and water, are interconnected. Similarly, actions in one part of the globe have an impact on the natural environment elsewhere.

4 Social problems may be seen as objective conditions and constructed reactions. The social construction of social problems focuses upon claims making. It investigates the stages through which a problem moves, its key people and claims makers and the different kinds of arguments that can be made.

5 European and other Western countries have transformed into *disposable societies*, generating billions of pounds of solid waste each day. Even though *recycling* efforts have increased, the majority of waste continues to be dumped in landfills. Water consumption is rapidly increasing throughout the world. Much of the world – notably Africa and the Middle East – is currently approaching a *water-supply crisis*. The hydrological cycle purifies rainwater, but water pollution from dumping and chemical contamination still poses a serious threat to water quality in Europe. This problem is even more acute in the world's low-income countries. *Air quality* became steadily worse in Europe and North America after the Industrial Revolution. About 1950, however, a turnaround took place

and these societies have made significant progress in curbing air pollution. In low-income countries, particularly in cities, air quality remains at unhealthy levels due to burning of 'dirty' fuels and little regulation of pollution. *Acid rain*, the product of pollutants entering the atmosphere, often contaminates land and water thousands of miles away. *Rainforests* play a vital role in removing carbon dioxide from the atmosphere. Under pressure from commercial interests, the world's rainforests are now half their original size and are shrinking by about 1 per cent annually. *Global warming* refers to predictions that the average temperature of the earth will rise because of increasing levels of carbon dioxide in the atmosphere. Both carbon emissions from factories and cars and the shrinking rainforests, which consume carbon dioxide, aggravate this problem. The elimination of rainforests is also reducing the planet's *biodiversity*, since these tropical regions are home to about half of all living species. Biodiversity, a source of natural beauty, is also critical to agricultural and medical research.

6 A focus on capitalism highlights the importance of inequality in understanding environmental issues. This perspective blames environmental decay on the self-interest of elites, and notes the pattern of environmental racism whereby the poor, especially minorities, disproportionately suffer from proximity to environmental hazards. It also places responsibility for the declining state of the world's natural environment primarily on rich societies, which consume the most resources.

7 A sustainable environment is one that does not threaten the well-being of future generations. Achieving this goal will require conservation of finite resources, reducing waste and pollution, and controlling the size of the world's population.

CONNECT UP: Turn to Part 6 of this book for key resources and link up
with the book's website, which links to these resources
SEE: www.pearsoned.co.uk/plummer

MYTASKLIST

Ten suggestions for going further

1 Connect up with Part Six and the Sociology Web Resources

As you work through ideas and think about the issues raised in this chapter, look at the accompanying website and the resource centre at the end of this book which connects to it. There is a lot here to help you move on. To link up, see: www.pearson.co.uk/plummer.

2 Review the chapter

Briefly summarise (in a paragraph) just what this chapter has been about. Consider: (a) What have you learned? (b) What do you disagree with? Be critical. And (c) How would you develop all this? How could you get more detail on matters that interest you?

3 Pose questions

(a) What role can sociology play in understanding the natural environment? Can it also help in your own personal ways of dealing with the problems of environmental destruction?
(b) In what ways does environmental degradation link to patterns of social division and stratification?
(c) What is meant by 'sustainable development' and what evidence supports the contention that humanity is running up an 'environmental deficit'? Is there any evidence suggesting that some environmental problems are subsiding?
(d) Discuss the role of social movements in environmental change.
(e) Examine the idea of 'the risk society' and the problem of environmental degradation.

4 Explore key words

Many concepts have been introduced in this chapter. You can review them from the website or from the listing at the back of this book. You might like to give special attention to just five words and think them through – how would you define them, what are they dealing with, and do they help you see the social world more clearly or not?

See: Chris Park, *A Dictionary of Environment and Conservation* (2007).

There is a lot of basic information and key words on the environment in Robert Henson, *The Rough Guide to Climate Change* (2006).

Kristin Dow and Thomas Downing, *An Atlas of Climactic Change* (2006) looks at nature, causes and solutions to environmental issues through maps.

5 Search the Web

Be critical when you look at websites – see the box on p. 940 in the Resources section. For this chapter look at:

General

World environmental websites
www.webdirectory.com
A major listing of environmental websites.

United Nations Environment Programme (UNEP)
www.unep.org

Intergovernmental Panel on Climate Change (IPCC)
www.ipcc.ch

Worldwatch Institute
www.worldwatch.org
(also produces Vital Signs)

World Resources Institute
www.wri.org
This includes the very valuable resource:

Earth Trends
http://earthtrends.wri.org

Activist resources

These include the following groupings:

Friends of the Earth
www.foe.co.uk

Greenpeace
www.greenpeace.org.uk

People and Planet
www.peopleandplanet.net

UK government sites

www.defra.gov.uk
www.metoffice.gov.uk

6 Watch a DVD

- Steven Soderbergh's *Erin Brockovich* (2002): Julia Roberts plays a twice-divorced single mother who discovers a suspicious cover-up involving contaminated water in a local community causing devastating illness.
- Mike Nichols' *Silkwood* (1983): Meryl Streep is a whistleblower who speaks out about strange goings on at a factory plant.
- Spike Lee's *When the Levees Broke* (2006): well-known film producer makes a radical documentary about the racist response of US government to Hurricane Katrina.
- Al Gore's *An Inconvenient Truth* (2006): the former US Vice-President-turned environment campaigner. Award-winning documentary.
- Lucy Walker's *Waste Land* (2010): uplifting film about life on the landfills of Rio de Janeiro.

On a 'lighter' note, there is a long tradition of 'disaster movies' and you might like to watch a few to see what their key themes are. Wikipedia lists hundreds! Try: *The Towering Inferno* (1974), *Independence Day* (1996), *Volcano* (1997), *Armageddon* (1998), *The Day After Tomorrow* (2004), *Anna's Storm* (2007), *Cloverfield* (2008) and *The Road* (2009). See also: Stephen Keane, *Disaster Movies: The Cinema of Disaster* (2006).

7 Think and read

Phillip Sutton, *The Environment: A Sociological Introduction* (2007) and John Hannigan, *Environmental Sociology* (2006) are excellent introductions to the field.

Anthony Giddens, *The Politics of Climate Change* (2009). A world-leading sociologist guides you through the key issues and makes suggestions for a planned future to avoid the great catastrophe.

Donileen R. Loseke, *Thinking about Social Problems* (2003). The key introduction to the idea that social problems are socially constructed and organised.

Ulrich Beck, *Risk Society* (1992). The key statement on the emergence of a risk society, though it is far from being an 'easy read'. He has developed his argument further in *World Risk Society* (1999).

Classic writings on the environment

Rachel Carson, *Silent Spring* (1962). About the dangers of chemical pollution; helped launch the environmental movement in the United States and elsewhere.

Donella H. Meadows et al. (1972) *The Limits to Growth: A Report on the Club of Rome's Project on the Predicament of Mankind*. Predicts future ecological trends. Its conclusions support the 'limits to growth' thesis.

More information

An elegant visual account of the world's environment can be found in the work of the French photographer Yann Arthus-Bertrand. See his *Earth from the Air* project: book (2002) and website at www.earthfromtheair.com.

8 Relax with a novel

John Wyndham's *The Day of the Triffids* (1951): a powerful story about the sudden blinding of all human beings and the appearance of enormous, mobile predatory plants. A good novel, but Steve Sekely and Freddie Francis's film, *The Day of the Triffids* (1962) was a poorer version of the story.

9 Connect to other chapters

- Link to cities and demography as an issue in the environment in Chapter 24.
- Link to risk society and the environment in Chapter 23.
- Link to global inequalities in Chapter 9.
- Link to social movements in Chapter 16. The environmental movement is a major instance of a new social movement.

10 Engage with THE BIG DEBATE

Is an environmental catastrophe now inevitable? What is to be done? Armageddon and the environment

While many people believe that science and technology will improve their lives, environmentalists are not so sure. For them, the world is hurtling towards an ecological disaster. All the evidence described in this chapter must lead one to conclude that our environment is under severe risk, and planet earth could face its own destruction in the not too distant future.

Many environmentalists are saying that, in light of the risks we face, making basic changes is common sense. On the surface, at least, the public has come to accept environmentalism. And everywhere one looks, governments are acting to reduce the dangers, under the buzz phrase of 'sustainable development'.

But other environmentalists do not think the problem and solution are so simple. These 'ecological radicals' argue that basic changes are necessary in our way of life if we are to head off disaster down the road. In particular, they believe, we can no longer place economic growth at the heart of culture because this core value is causing an increasing environmental deficit. The materialist and consumerist vision of the good life can no longer be sustained because it leads to the degradation of the environment.

Going further, James Lovelock has been a long-time prophet of the environmental crisis. His latest best-selling book (2006, 2010) takes an even more pessimistic turn. In *The Revenge of Gaia*, Lovelock implies that it is now almost too late. The damage has been done. As he says:

> Like the Norns in Wagner's *Der Ring des Nibelungen*, we are at the end of our tether, and the rope, whose weave defines our fate, is about to break . . . humans, with breathtaking insolence have . . . thwarted Gaia's obligation to keep the planet fit for life; they thought only of their comfort and convenience.
>
> (Lovelock, 2006: 187)

Not all agree: Bjorn Lomborg's *The Skeptical Environmentalist* (2001) suggests that:

> the hole in the Ozone Layer is healing. The Amazon has shrunk by only 14 per cent since the arrival of Man. Only 0.7 per cent of species will be driven to extinction over the next 50 years. Even the poorest humans are getting richer by the year. Things are not good enough; but they are far, far better than we have been taught to believe.

He suggests that our sense of approaching human and environmental disaster is an artefact of the valid work of modern scientific, environmental and media institutions. Climate change is a long-term problem that cannot be fixed in a few years.

Perhaps society has come to accept the idea that environmentalism is good in principle, but it is far from clear that most people are willing to make the hard choices needed to achieve a sustainable way of life.

Continue the debate

1 Do you think limiting economic growth is necessary in order to secure our environmental future? Would you be willing to accept a lower standard of living to protect the natural environment?

2 What action have you ever taken (signing a petition, participating in a demonstration, modifying your consumption patterns) in support of the environment?

3 Does Kyoto matter? Where do you think the major European political parties stand on environmental issues?

4 Compare James Lovelock, *The Revenge of Gaia* (2006) and *The Vanishing Face of Gaia* (2007) with Bjorn Lomborg's *The Skeptical Environmentalist* (2001) and *Cool It: The Skeptical Environmentalist's Guide to Global Warming* (2007).

CHAPTER 26

LIVING IN THE TWENTY-FIRST CENTURY

HUMAN BEINGS ARE SOCIAL ANIMALS AND NEED SOCIETIES TO FUNCTION WELL. In this final chapter we will draw together strands about just how well the societies we live in today help us to function. Let's start with two extreme examples – from novels and film. One – *Into the Wild* (2007) – considers the idea that we might be better off to return to the wild, to go back to nature and leave modernity behind. Another – *The Road* (2010) – looks at a post-apocalyptic society, where most of society as we know it has been destroyed. Both create alternative worlds; both suggest that living without a society is not a good path to take.

Into the Wild is based on a true story. A successful student, Christopher McCandless, abandons all his possessions, gives his entire $24,000 savings account to charity and hitchhikes to Alaska where he tries to live alone in 'nature' in the wilderness. Ultimately he misses people, and dies from accidentally eating a poison berry and subsequent starvation. He survives a mere hundred days. A cheerful and likeable guy who is full of hope about getting back to nature and away from the horrors of the modern world, he dies alone. McCandless's story was reconstructed from his notes after his death: his tale joins a long line of those wanting to get back to nature. From Rousseau to Whitman, many writers have expressed the urge to 'return to nature'.

By contrast, *The Road* looks to the future. In this award-winning novel and film, we find a father and his young son taking a journey – we know not where – across a post-apocalyptic landscape caused by we know not

what. It is a tale of some time not so far in the future when civilisation has been wiped out and there is hardly any life left – people, animals and plants have died. The story is told in a cold, snowy, rainy, dark landscape where most of the few human survivors are marauding cannibals desperate for food, scavenging for human flesh. The father and son face one desperate situation after the other. There are roving bands of cannibals, new-born infants roasted and, most scary of all, living skeletal captives who have been harvested for food. Cormac McCarthy's novel joins a long line of post-apocalyptic stories that foretell the end of human society.

These are challenging stories. They make us think about the importance of society. And what kind of society? In this chapter, we draw together a number of strands about societies at the start of the twenty-first century.

tip Look at:
Into the Wild. Book by Jon Krakauer (1996) and film by Sean Penn (2007) with Emile Kirschner as McCandless.
The Road. Book by Cormac McCarthy (2006) and film directed by John Hillcoat (2009).

See also: William Golding's *Lord of the Flies* (1954) – twice made into a film; and P. D. James's *Children of Men* (1992), a film also in 2006.

Postmodernism is concerned with futures, not the future; there is never one future, but a plurality of diverse futures the move from modern

to postmodern is not a case of unilinear and universal change, nor a new grand narrative, but an eclectic mixing of old and new elements in a variety of distinct local and global forms. Postmodernity will not have a future but a variety of futures.

John Gibbins and Bo Reimer (1999: 140)

In this final chapter, we ask:

- **What are the major changes taking place in society?**

- **How can we examine social change?**

- **Can we draw up a balance sheet of 'progress' in the twenty-first century?**

- **Where might we be heading? Might science fiction help us?**

(left) R. B. Kitaj, *If Not, Not* (detail)

See: www.artcyclopedia.com/artists/kitaj_rb.html; www.ibiblio.org/wm/paint/auth/kitaj; http://wn.elib.com/Bio/Artists/Kitaj.html; www.glyphs.com/art/kitaj.

Source: © The Estate of R. B. Kitaj/Marlborough Fine Art/Scottish National Gallery of Modern Art.

Q This is one of Kitaj's strongest pictures and integrates modern catastrophes into a classical landscape, reminding us of Italian Renaissance paintings. He is known as a 'Pop Artist'. Is this postmodern? How and why?

Sociology tells one grand story, and a multitude of smaller ones

The Big Story – which runs throughout this book – is the story of the humanly created world we live in and its possible progress. Given the scale of human history (see Chapters 4 and 5), the past 300 years or so are a mere blip in time. But in this period, we have seen a continuous dramatic transformation of the social world, which sociologists might typically view as a shift from a *traditional* **society** through a *modern* one to something that is now in the making, which for convenience we could call a *high-tech, advanced capitalist postmodern* society (see Chapter 4, pp. 135–6). As we have seen (in Chapter 4 especially), there are many contrasting accounts of this change, and many ways to characterise it. Marx focused on conflict and the economic; Weber upon religion and rationality; Durkheim upon human bonding. And many others in their wake have also brought accounts to handle these changes. They are the big transformations and Table 26.1 attempts to bring a lot of these changes together. It is the big story of this book. (Hopefully, this table will also provide you with a useful framework to revise your understanding of the whole book – and of sociology.)

But there are also a multitude of much smaller stories. Indeed, sociology is probably at its very best when it studies a very specific group in the world to see what makes them work the way they do. Through this book we have had glimpses – only glimpses – of Japanese hip hop, delinquent gangs, people living with AIDS, gay partnerships, religious fundamentalisms, political institutions like the United Nations, people eating breakfasts, people wearing Muslim dress and so on. One task of sociology is to tell the myriad little stories of early-twenty-first century life, and hopefully this book has told you something of this. But of course, this is only an introduction – a little sample of what is to come if you decide to look more deeply into sociology.

In this final chapter, we take stock of this newly emerging world, its features and some of its problems.

Examining social change

In this chapter, we will review some of our key themes and hopefully suggest some tracks for the future.

We examine social change with both positive and negative consequences.

Almost every chapter of this book has been haunted by the idea of **social change**, *the transformation of culture and social institutions over time*. Recall how in Chapter 1 we argued that sociology was born of three revolutions: the Industrial Revolution, the political revolutions associated with democracy, and the urban revolution linked in part to the decline in community. But this broad process of social change is ubiquitous in society and has four key characteristics:

1 *Social change is ubiquitous and ceaseless*: it happens everywhere and we always live in its ever-flowing grandness. 'Nothing is constant except death and taxes', goes the old saying. Yet social patterns related to death have changed dramatically as life expectancy in the Western world has nearly doubled over the last two centuries. Taxes, meanwhile, unknown through most of human history, emerged only with complex social organisation several thousand years ago. In short, one is hard-pressed to identify anything that is not subject to the twists and turns of change.

Still, some societies change faster than others. As Chapter 4 explained, hunting and gathering societies tend to change quite slowly. Members of technologically complex societies, on the other hand, can sense significant change even within a single lifetime. Moreover, even in a given society, some cultural elements change more quickly than others. William Ogburn's (1964) theory of *cultural lag* (see Chapter 5) recognises that material culture (that is, things) usually changes faster than non-material culture (ideas and attitudes). For example, medical techniques that prolong life have developed more rapidly than have ethical standards for deciding when and how to use them. *One striking feature of the contemporary world is the speed of changes that take place.*

2 *Social change can be intentional but it is usually unplanned.* Industrial societies actively promote many kinds of change. For example, scientists seek more efficient forms of energy and advertisers try to convince consumers that life is incomplete without some new gadget. Yet even the experts rarely envisage all the consequences of the changes they promote. Thus, early car manufacturers certainly understood that cars would allow people to travel in a single day distances that had required weeks or months to traverse a century before. But no one foresaw how profoundly the mobility provided by cars would reshape European societies, scattering

Table 26.1	Traditional, modern and postmodern societies: a review chart

We all dwell simultaneously in traditional, modern and postmodern worlds – though to very different degrees.

Element of society	Traditional (agrarian)	Modernising (industrial capitalist)	Twenty-first century (global postmodern)	See Chapter
Economy and work	Agricultural, herding, fishing, maritime	Mercantile capitalism; factory	Global capitalism; IT and service	15
Technology	Human and animal energy	Industrial energy sources	Post-industrial, information, digital	15
Population	High birth and death: low population	Falling death and high birth: rapid growth	Low death and low birth: slowing population	24
Governance	Slavery, feudal, warlords, kings	Nation-states and new social movements (NSMs)	World organisations	16
Environment	'Natural disasters'		Eco catastrophe and environmental movements	25
Religions	Superstition, polytheism to monotheism	From monotheism to secularism	Fundamentalism, diversity, secularism	19
Communications	Signs, speech and early writing	Print to electronics	Mass media and digital culture	22
Community and networks	Tribal, village, face to face, local	Cities, associations, secondary	Networks, cyber-relations, global	6
Knowledge and ideas	Religion, folk, superstition	Rise of science	Relativism, reflexivity, relationalism	23
Control and law	Punitive, repressive, 'natural'	Increase of laws and formal institutions, restitutive	Massive legal system, heavily organised and financed	17
Disability and care				
Health	High death rate	Environmental health and 'sick model'	Managed care, high-tech medicine	21
Values	Traditional	'Make it new'	Postmodern pluralism	5
Groups	Primary	Secondary	Cyber-networked	6
Roles and self	Ascribed	Achieved	Open	7
Culture	Folk		Cosmopolitanism	5
Society	Simple	Industrial	Complex	4
Time and change	Very slow	Speeding up; invented traditions	Rapid – even within a generation	?
Military	Centrality of warfare but limited and focused	Massed national armies, all the people	'New wars'	16
		'Liberté, egalité, fraternité' and internal revolution		

Key processes of change include: industrialisation, rationalisation, capitalism, secularisation, medicalisation and globalisation.

Glossary: key words to consider here include: communities/associations, rural/urban, primary/secondary, monotheism/polytheism, local/global, individualism, nationalism.

Sociologists use versions of these ideas in many of their arguments, but there are many dangers of oversimplification and over-generalisation and they should never be seen as a simple evolutionary development. They are useful, though, as starting points for understanding deep contrasts and changes in society. Beware of the dangers of historicism – of seeing necessary, predictable change: societies develop contingently and unpredictably and are never homogeneous. These models are also derived largely from the standpoint of Western cultures and will not be so applicable elsewhere.

Further reading: books that discuss these kinds of change include: Gerhard Lenski and Patrick Nolan, *Human Societies* (11th edn, 2008).

Back to China: is China the country of the twenty-first century?

China became the world's second largest economy in 2010 (after the USA).

As we have seen in Chapter 4, China is a huge space with the largest population in the world and vast cultural and geographical differences. It is one of the world's nuclear powers and is the most pervasive language. It is both a very poor country and a potentially rich one. Literacy levels are high (about 90 per cent in 2001), and life expectancy (at 73 years in 2001) is good. It also has the highest rates of death penalty (see Chapter 17) and suicide (see Chapter 1) in the world.

Economically, it is a very divided country. In 2001, 16.6 per cent lived on less than $1 a day, and more than 700 million Chinese lived on less than $2 a day.

Millions of peasants flock from the country to take on work at very low wages – and this is a world of poor-quality products, exploited labour, corruption and human rights abuses. One report suggests that 'the gap between rich and poor is unprecedented, with the richest 20 per cent of the population accounting for 50 per cent of consumption, whilst the poorest 20 per cent struggle to consume just 5 per cent' (*Action Aid*, Spring 2005: 11).

More than anywhere else in the world, China today exemplifies the twentieth-century conflict between communism and capitalism. Officially it remains a communist society – and there are no democratic elections; in practice, a creeping programme of free market reforms have been introduced. In some parts of China there is abject poverty; in others, the world of consumerism and hypermarkets so common in the West are to be found. As we have seen earlier, Western-style shopping malls, discos and night scenes have become common in large cities. Many cities have seen the emergence of a consumer culture driven by the market, a culture which also intersects with the 'floating population' of vagrants, prostitutes and *liumang* (hooligans). And after the Maoist period, novel needs and experiences of private life came into being. There is a growing awareness of the body; the self can be indulged. Gay life is now flourishing in some of the bigger cities. At the same time, the Internet whilst widespread is very tightly regulated.

China hence looks two ways. One the one hand, it is a society of rapid economic development with increasing investment and growth alongside massive cultural change. But it is also an undemocratic society where most of its population still lives in dangerous rural poverty, and where for many – probably most – sanctions are extreme and life is hard. In areas like health, education and pensions, government planning is weak. If the twenty-first century is to belong to China, there are enormous tensions to overcome.

See: Will Hutton, *The Writing on the Wall: China and the West in the 21st Century* (2007).

TOP 10
Facts about China

	China	USA	Spain
Total population	1,336.3m	308.8m	44.6m
Urban population	42%	81%	77%
Life expectancy	73	78	80
GDP per capita	$13,270	$46,350	$35,220
Living under $1 a day	16.6%	*	*
Undernourished	11%	*	*
Adult literacy	93%	*	*
Telephones per hundred	25.5	49.6	45.4
Computers per hundred	5.7	80.6	39.3
Mobile phones per hundred	48.0	86.8	111.7

* These figures are not provided for 'First World' countries.

Source: Based on *World Guide* (2011).

family members, threatening the environment, and reshaping cities and suburbs. In addition, automotive pioneers could hardly have predicted the millions of deaths each year worldwide in car accidents. And as we saw in the previous chapter, the car has worked to degrade the environment in many ways. *These unplanned outcomes – often very dangerous and quite unpredictable – are what we have seen as the growth of the modern 'risk society'.*

3 *Social change often generates conflict, tension and controversy.* As the history of the car demonstrates, most social change yields both positive and negative consequences. Capitalists welcomed the Industrial Revolution because advancing technology increased productivity and swelled profits. Many workers, however, fearing that machines would make their skills obsolete, strongly resisted 'progress'. In the Western world, changing patterns of interaction between black people and white people, between women and men and between gays and heterosexuals give rise to misunderstandings, tensions and, sometimes, outright hostility. *Much change leads to generational tensions*: change means that each generation experiences the world in different ways. The world of computing and digitalisation which started to enter the mainstream world only in the 1980s has sharply divided generations, with younger digital generations only knowing this world, and older ones never being able to quite understand it in the same way.

4 *Some changes matter more than others.* Some social changes have only passing significance, whereas other transformations resonate for generations. At one extreme, clothing fads among the young burst on the scene and dissipate quickly. At the other, we are still adjusting to powerful technological advances such as television and computing half a century after their introduction. Some innovations, such as audio tapes and faxes, have had quite short lives; others, such as the car, are much less likely to 'die out' quickly. Looking ahead, who can predict with any certainty how computers will transform the entire world during the twenty-first century? The Information Revolution is turning out to be every bit as pivotal as the Industrial Revolution. As we have seen through this book, the high-tech digital world will have both beneficial and deleterious effects, providing new kinds of job while eliminating old ones, joining people together in ever-expanding electronic networks while threatening personal privacy.

Causes of social change

Throughout the book we have seen many different explanations of widespread social change. There is no reason to champion just one theory: it is much more likely that a number of factors come into play together. These include the following.

Economic change

Marx saw the tensions of capitalism as inevitably bringing change. Capitalism heralded class conflict as the engine that drives societies from one historical era to another. In industrial–capitalist societies the struggle between capitalists and workers propels society towards a different (socialist) kind of production. In the century since Marx's death, this model has been criticised. Yet, surely he correctly foresaw that the conflicts arising from inequality (now involving race, gender, disability, age and sexuality as well as social class) would force changes in every society, including our own. And many now argue that it is these tensions within capitalist economies that bring about major changes. As we see many inequalities still growing and not declining, who can say where the future will take us?

Cultural change

Culture is a dynamic system that continually gains new elements and loses others. Chapter 5 identified three important sources of cultural change. First, *invention* produces new objects, ideas and social patterns. Through rocket propulsion research, which began in the 1940s, we have engineered high-tech vehicles for space flight. Today we take such technology for granted; during the present century a significant number of people may well travel in space.

Secondly, *discovery* occurs when people first take note of certain elements of the world or learn to see them in a new way. Medical advances, for example, offer a growing understanding of the human body. Beyond the direct effects for human health, medical discoveries have also stretched life expectancy, setting in motion 'the greying of the Western world' (see Chapter 13).

Thirdly, *diffusion* creates change as trade, migration and mass communication spread cultural elements throughout the world. Ralph Linton (1937) recognised that many familiar elements of a culture have come to us from other lands. For example, cloth was developed in Asia while coins were devised in Turkey. Generally, material things diffuse more readily than non-material cultural traits.

Through much migration, the Western world has steadily changed in response to cultural diffusion. In recent decades, people from Africa, Asia and other parts of the world have been introducing new cultural patterns, clearly evident in the sights, smells and sounds of cities across European countries. From African music to Thai and Vietnamese food, non-Western cultures diffuse into the West. Conversely, the global power of the Western world ensures that much of Western culture – from the taste of beefburgers to the sounds of Pavarotti – is being diffused to other societies.

Ideas and change

Max Weber, too, contributed to our understanding of social change. While Weber acknowledged the importance of conflict based on material production, he traced the roots of social change to the world of ideas. He illustrated his argument by showing how people who display charisma can convey a message that sometimes changes the world.

Weber also highlighted the importance of ideas by revealing how the world-view of early Protestants prompted them to embrace industrial capitalism. By showing that industrial capitalism developed primarily in areas of western Europe where the Protestant work ethic was strong, Weber (1958; orig. 1905) concluded that the disciplined rationality of Calvinist Protestants was instrumental in this change.

Ideas also fuel social movements. Chapter 16 looked at social movements and showed how they may emerge from the determination to modify society in some manner (say, to clean up the environment) or from a sense that existing social arrangements are unjust. The international gay rights movement draws strength from the contention that lesbians and gay men should enjoy rights and opportunities equal to those of the heterosexual majority. Opposition to the gay rights movement, moreover, reveals the power of ideas to inhibit as well as to advance social change.

Ideas and conflict

One of the most striking developments since the mid-twentieth century has been the changing nature of war. Since the Second World War, with a few important exceptions, most wars have been waged within countries between rival ethnic groups – major conflicts have continued or resurfaced around ethnicity and religion. But as we saw in Chapter 16, these conflicts are also a major potential source of future world conflict – note the concern, for example, of Benjamin Barber (1995) over 'Jihad versus McWorld', or Samuel Huntington (1996) over the 'clash of civilisations'. When suicide bombers hijacked US passenger planes to crash into the twin towers of the World Trade Center and the Pentagon on 11 September 2001, killing about 6,000 people, the US government identified Islamic fundamentalists from the al Qaeda terrorist network as those responsible for the attacks and announced a long war to cleanse the world of such terrorism. This has led to the start of the twenty-first century becoming haunted by mass global conflict and old religious wars; ironically tensions which have dominated much of history are now back.

John Urry: mobilities and mobile lives

John Urry is the Director of the Centre for Mobilities Research at Lancaster University, where he has for a long time been a Professor of Sociology. His research has covered many fields from social movements to the changing nature of cities and capitalism. Most recently he has started to build a *Sociology beyond Societies* (2000) – one that focuses not upon societies but on the flows and movements of social processes. He locates them within modern science theories of complexities and argues for the analysis of *Global Complexity* (2003) through its key social flows.

His books lay out the ground for this new sociology and develop his ideas through major case studies. In *Mobilities* (2007), he looks at airports and flying, cars and roads, trains, pathways and wider forms of connecting through the flows of the media. He looks at how new technologies are leading to new *Mobile Lives* (with Anthony Elliott, 2010) – mobile relationships at a distance, and new patterns of 'mobile inequalities'. In *After the Car* (with Dennis Kingsley, 2010) he has looked at the rise of the car as a major (but environmentally and socially highly destructive) mode of travel which will have to change its character in the twenty-first century. He also suggests that a focus on mobilities will change every aspect of sociology – from its methods to its theories.

The world as it is now: the good news and the bad news

Here, and in Table 26.2, we briefly draw together some summary conclusions from various studies and reports which we have looked at during this book. You may like to consider them – along with the observations at the start of the chapter – as a way of making a progress report on the state of humankind at the start of the twenty-first century.

1   *Infant mortality* has fallen significantly throughout the world. In low-income societies there has been clear improvement: from 165 deaths per 1,000 live births in 1960 to about 56 in 2000. *Life expectancy* is up: again people in low-income countries lived for just about 41 years in 1960; they now live on average to 64 years. *But*: in much of sub-Saharan Africa, where AIDS is pronounced, there is still a 30-year lag from richer countries.

2   *Literacy* increased from around 16 per cent in 1960 to about 75 per cent in 2000 (and 82% by 2008). *But*: there are still around a billion people who are generally illiterate. And the new cyber-literacy may make this worse.

3   *Poverty* is generally down (but it is uneven). There has generally been more success in the war against poverty in the past 50 years than in the preceding 500 years. *But*: at least 1.2 billion people still live on less than $1 a day. Africa remains in a severe crisis, despite international aid.

4   *Hunger*. The number of starving and chronically undernourished in low-income societies declined from around 40 per cent in 1960 to less than 20 per cent in 2002. *But*: still over 800 million are chronically undernourished.

5   *Health*. There is more access to drinking water and reasonable sanitary conditions than ever before in the history of humankind. *But*: still 40% of the world has no sanitation, and AIDS has become the major killer disease of our time.

6   *Freedom and democracy*. Over the past 500 years, the struggle for and gaining of freedoms and justice for the ordinary person has been placed firmly on the agenda in ways it simply was not in the longer past. And more and more countries seem to be relatively more 'free' (maybe 46 per cent of the world). *But*: we have conflicts in Iraq, Palestine, Sri Lanka, Afghanistan, Uganda, Rwanda, Colombia, Sudan, Darfur and elsewhere. Thousands are being killed daily. Transnational organised crime flourishes – with a possible annual income of over $2 trillion. And there are more slaves in the world now than at the peak of traditional slavery.

7   *Technology*. Over a sixth of the world is now connected to the internet. *But*: whilst the 'digital divide' has been closing a little, it is still vast.

8   *Science and knowledge*. Looking at technical developments over the past century or so cannot fail to impress. It is probably fair to say that the last 200 years have brought more knowledge than all the previous centuries, and that the past 50 years have made it more accessible to more people than ever before in history. *But*: we go on being dehumanised by a lot of the technology – letting it use us rather than us using it.

9   *Art and culture*. The world history of art, culture, music, sport and human creativity is ceaseless and we can only stand in amazement at just what society managed to produce. *But*: we go on treating each other in the most degrading and appalling ways, with crime, corruption and damaged lives.

10 In 2006, the *rate of CO_2 emmisions* into the air was 2.6, some points down on previous years. *But*: this is just about the only good news we can hear on the environment!

If there were any conclusion to be drawn from this, it would probably have to be: doing OK, could do a lot better.

Table 26.2	The state of the future index
Where humanity is winning	**Where humanity is losing**
Life expectancy	CO_2 emissions
Infant mortality	Terrorism
Literacy	Corruption
GDP/per capita	Global warming
Internet users	Unemployment

Source: From *2007: The State of the Future* by J. C. Glenn and T. J. Gordon, copyright 2007 United Nations. Reprinted with the permission of the United Nations.

Sociology and some problems of the world

What kind of sense can be made of all these issues? Table 26.3 suggests some of the key concerns which have been identified by various 'publics' across the world as the 'most important problem facing the world today'. Poverty and the gap between rich and poor (inequalities) are identified everywhere as the major problem; others vary a little from country to country and region to region. 'Terrorism', for example, is much less identified as a problem in Africa, whereas HIV and AIDs are seen as more of a problem there than anywhere else in the world. The environment is seen as a problem is the Asia-Pacific region; less so in Latin America and Africa.

LIVING IN THE C21ST

The pursuit of happiness

In recent years, social scientists have been very busy examining what it means to be happy through empirical social research. A so-called happiness industry has developed with its own academic journal – the *Journal of Happiness Studies* – new research centres and a multitude of publications. In Britain, the key role has been played by Richard Layard, a professor at the London School of Economics, who also sits as a Labour member of the House of Lords. He is not a sociologist or a psychologist but an economist. His best-selling book is called *Happiness*. (He is also the author of a study called *The Depression Report: A New Deal for Depression and Anxiety Disorders*, which claims that one in six of us will be diagnosed as having depression or chronic anxiety disorder.) He has played a prominent role in shaping counselling and happiness services in the UK. He defines happiness subjectively:

> So what do I mean by happiness? By happiness I mean feeling good – enjoying life and feeling it is wonderful. And by unhappiness I mean feeling bad and wishing things were different. (cep.lse.ac.uk/ events/lectures/layard/ RL030303.pdf)

Other studies have taken a more sociological stance. Thus,

Robert E. Lane in *The Loss of Happiness in Market Economies* (2000) suggests that a key paradox of modern life is that, whilst most people seem to want more income, as societies become richer, they do not become happier. This is the conclusion of a growing amount of research from a number of countries which he reviews: the evidence suggests that people have grown no happier in the last 50 years, even as average incomes have more than doubled. The most apparent conclusion is that there is little evidence that money makes you happy or that capitalism and markets per se are good for you. In general, research suggests that, whilst people need to be above a certain level of poverty to be happy, income or wealth in itself does not make for happiness. Above a certain reasonable level, there is no evidence of increasing happiness.

A Happy Planet Index?

Just as economists have developed measurements around economic well-being, some social scientists are now focusing upon the less economic factors of 'subjective well-being'. They have developed an array of research tools to measure what happiness might be – for both individuals and whole societies. They have even come up with league tables of happy societies.

The Happy Planet Index (HPI) is a scale which combines environmental impact with well-being to measure the environmental efficiency with which people in each country live long and happy lives. The HPI is based on the key assumption that most people want to live long and fulfilling lives in a flourishing environment. Human well-being is operationalised as Happy Life Years. The scale examines three key factors:

1 Life expectancy
2 Human well-being
3 Damage via the Environmental Footprint.

In a way reminiscent of the Human Development Index (HDI) discussed in Chapter 9, each country's HPI value can be calculated as a function of its average subjective life satisfaction, life expectancy at birth, and ecological footprint per capita, which attempts to estimate the amount of natural resources required to sustain a given country's lifestyle. The HPI is *not* a measure of simply which are the happiest countries in the world. It links life satisfaction to environmental factors. The HPI is best conceived as a measure of the *environmental efficiency of supporting well-being* in a given country. Such efficiency could emerge in a country with a medium environmental impact (e.g. Costa Rica) and very high well-being (e.g. Panama), but it could also emerge in a country with only mediocre well-being, but very low environmental impact (e.g. Vietnam).

Table 26.3   Most important problems facing the world, by region

Q. What do you think is the most important problem facing the world today?	Total sample n = 53,749 (%)	Western Europe n = 3,573 (%)	Eastern and central Europe n = 11,476 (%)	Africa n = 7,746 (%)	North America n = 1,505 (%)	Latin America n = 3,718 (%)	Middle East n = 2,537 (%)	Asia-Pacific n = 11,151 (%)
Poverty: the gap between rich and poor	26	26	30	37	20	39	25	18
Terrorism	12	14	16	3	18	7	15	9
Unemployment	9	9	8	12	3	10	17	11
Wars and conflicts	8	9	8	4	9	5	10	10
Economic problems	7	5	6	9	6	8	7	11
Environmental issues	6	6	5	0	4	1	2	13
Drugs and drug abuse	5	5	5	1	8	5	3	4
Corruption	4	2	3	9	3	7	3	5
Crime	4	3	5	4	1	4	1	6
HIV/AIDS and other health issues	4	3	5	12	3	2	1	2
Globalisaton/fairer world trade	4	4	1	1	10	3	3	1
Human rights	2	3	4	2	3	1	2	1
Educational issues	2	2	1	1	3	2	4	2
Religious fundamentalism	2	4	1	1	2	1	1	1
Refugees, refugee and asylum problems	1	2	0	0	1	0	0	1
Other	1	2	1	1	2	1	1	1
Don't know/not applicable	2	2	1	3	2	1	4	4

Note: Statistically significant areas (that is, areas of particularly high concern – over 6%) are in bold.

Source: Gallup International Association, Voice of the People survey 2005.

Multiple modernities and their discontents

Throughout this book, we have used many terms that link to modern changes: capitalism, rationality and bureaucracies, nation-states, science and technology, to name a few (for more, see pp. 135–6). At the heart of this is a well-known sociological depiction of modernity. Simply put, this means:

1   *The decline of small, traditional communities.* Modernity involves 'the progressive weakening, if not destruction, of the concrete and relatively cohesive communities in which human beings have found solidarity and meaning throughout most of history' (Berger, 1977: 72). For thousands of years, in the camps of hunters and gatherers and in the rural villages of Europe, people lived in small-scale settlements with family and neighbours. Such traditional worlds, based on sentiments and beliefs passed from generation to generation, afford each person a well-defined place. These primary groups limit people's range of experience while conferring a strong sense of identity, belonging and purpose.

Small, isolated communities still exist in the Western world, of course, but they are now home to only a small percentage of people. Even for rural people, rapid transportation and efficient communication, including television, have brought individuals in touch with the pulse of the larger society and even the entire world.

2   *The expansion of personal choice.* To people in traditional, pre-industrial societies, life is shaped by forces beyond human control – gods, spirits or,

These images of the Twin Towers of the World Trade Center in New York – before and after the bombing on 11 September 2001 – may well have become the defining images of the early part of twenty-first-century life. Conflicts over modernity, ethnicity, religion and capitalism are now reflected on a global stage

Source: (a) Bruno Barbey/Magnum Photos; (b) Susan Meiselas/Magnum Photos.

simply, fate. Steeped in tradition, members of these societies grant one another a narrow range of personal choices. As the power of tradition erodes, however, people come to see their lives as an unending series of options, a process called individualisation. Many people respond to the alternatives in modern societies by changing their 'lifestyles' over time.

3 *Increasing diversity in beliefs*. In pre-industrial societies, strong family ties and powerful religious beliefs enforce conformity while discouraging diversity and change. Modernisation promotes a more rational, scientific world-view, in which tradition loses its force and morality becomes a matter of individual attitude. The growth of cities, the expansion of impersonal organisations and social interaction among people from various backgrounds combine to foster a diversity of beliefs and behaviour.

4 *Future orientation and growing awareness of time*. People in modern societies think more about the future, while pre-industrial people focus more on the past. Modern people are not only forward-looking but also optimistic that discoveries and new inventions will enhance their lives. In addition, modern people organise daily routines according to precise units of time. With the introduction of clocks in the late Middle Ages, sunlight and seasons faded in importance as measures of time's forward march, in favour of hours and minutes. Preoccupied with personal gain, modern people calculate time to the moment and generally believe that 'Time is money'.

This modern world touched off the development of sociology itself. As Chapter 1 explained, the discipline originated in the wake of the Industrial Revolution in western Europe, precisely where social change was proceeding most rapidly. Early sociologists tried to analyse and explain modernisation and its consequences – both good and bad – for human beings.

The rise of modernity is a complex process involving many dimensions of change, described in previous chapters and summarised in Table 25.1. These days the story of the past and the future may probably best be seen as one of multiple modernities. This was a phrase introduced by the sociologist S. N. Eisenstadt (2000) to capture the fact that there was and is no unified path of modernism – and certainly not a straightforward Western progress path. What we have found in this book are many different societies, each with its own

history, and plural pathways into a highly fragmented, multiple and ever-changing future. It is to this future that we now turn.

The future and change: new kinds of society in the making?

Recently, many sociologists have been conjecturing where future changes in society may take us. We have seen some of these conjectures throughout the book. To get a handle on the nature of the world's problems, for ten years between 1997 and 2007, the United Nations published a major report on *The State of the Future*, which distilled an enormous amount of information on the state of the world. In 2008, it was taken over by a non-profit organisation which continues its work. In regular debates and documentations, it suggests there are 15 significant global challenges confronting the world, as outlined in Figure 26.1. These are:

1 How can sustainable development be achieved for all while addressing global climate change?
2 How can everyone have sufficient clean water without conflict?
3 How can population growth and resources be brought into balance?
4 How can genuine democracy emerge from authoritarian regimes?
5 How can policy making be made more sensitive to global long-term perspectives?
6 How can the global convergence of information and communications technologies work for everyone?
7 How can ethical market economies be encouraged to help reduce the gap between rich and poor?
8 How can the threat of new and re-emerging diseases and immune micro-organisms be reduced?
9 How can the capacity to decide be improved as the nature of work and institutions change?
10 How can shared values and new security strategies reduce ethnic conflicts, terrorism and the use of weapons of mass destruction?
11 How can the changing status of women help improve the human condition?
12 How can transnational organised crime networks be stopped from becoming more powerful and sophisticated global enterprises?

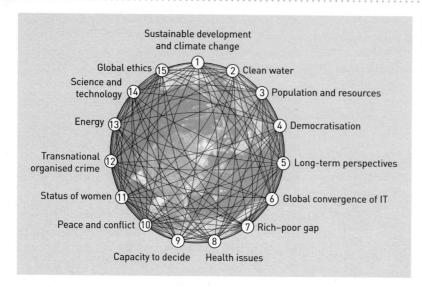

Figure 26.1 Fifteen global challenges facing humanity

Source: The Millennium Project, www.millennium-project.org/millennium/challenges.html.

13 How can growing energy demands be met safely and efficiently?

14 How can scientific and technological breakthroughs be accelerated to improve the human condition?

15 How can ethical considerations become more routinely incorporated into global decisions? (www.millennium-project.org/millennium/challeng.html)

Many of the chapters in this book have touched on such questions, but they have worked from a sociological approach where we sense the need to critically grasp the ways in which societies are working. We have seen possible pathways into the future, but they nearly always focus upon some ambivalent characteristics. This is to say, it is not clear where we are going, and there would seem to be inherent contradictions and tensions in future pathways. For instance, in Chapter 19 on religion we noted a trend (mainly in Europe) towards secularisation, while at the same time noting with Peter Berger that a much broader world-view would see a change towards desecularisation and the increasingly pervasive growth of new religious forms. Just when we thought religion was in decline, it bounced back with fury in the early twenty-first century. When we considered McDonaldisation, we saw a trend towards efficiency, predictability, calculability and control in many of our institutions; but as George Ritzer himself advocates, there are also signs that this pattern is being rejected by many (Ritzer, 2010). There is a resistance to McDonaldisation. And so we could continue. Many trends seem to bring their countertrend and no sociologist can really therefore predict where the future may lie.

Nevertheless, many sociologists at the start of the twenty-first century suggest that we are indeed moving into a different kind of social order. We saw some of these ideas in Chapter 4 (see the box on pp. 135–6). Ulrich Beck, for example, talks about the move from a 'first modernity' to a 'second modernity'. The former is what we have been calling modern society and its characteristics are now well known. In general, it involves a nation-state (and a welfare state), full employment, collective life and what he says is a 'heedless exploitation of nature'. But the 'second modernity' is different. He writes:

> The collective patterns of life, progress and controllability, full employment and exploitation of nature that were typical of first modernity have now been undermined by five interlinked processes: globalization, individualization, gender revolution, underemployment and global risks . . . The real theoretical and political challenge of the second modernity is the fact that society must respond to all these challenges simultaneously . . . There is a pluralization of modernity [which] opens up space for the conceptualization of divergent trajectories of modernity in different parts of the world.

(Beck, 1999: 2–3)

Beck is not alone in his vision. Among the many terms used for the emerging new kind of society we have been encountering in this book are:

- the unequal society
- the postmodern society
- the information society
- the network society

- the desecularised society
- the risk society
- the cyborg society
- the individualised society
- the human rights society
- the third way.

At work behind all these terms are a number of key processes which we have variously identified as 'globalisation', 'mediasation', 'digitalisation', 'disorganised capitalism', 'post-Fordism', 'McDonaldisation', 'desecularisation', 'democratisation' and a 'Third Way'. In part it is also *the world of the post*: post-feminism, post-history, post-identity, post-Marxism, postcolonialism and, of course, postmodernism.

But before we get carried away with all this talk of new things, it is important to recognise that in the new century, across the globe, *we all now live simultaneously in traditional, modern and postmodern worlds* (though at different paces and to differing degrees). Elderly folk and most of the 'developing/ majority/third-world/low-income' societies may still live overwhelmingly with tradition, whereas many younger folk and richer nations may find the postmodern to be more congenial to the organisation of their lives.

Thus, *traditional societies* are still to be found embedded in intense communities, surrounded by families, neighbours and strong bonding rituals embedded in strongly patriarchal and religious social orders. For most people in the world, traditional worlds remain their core: for many elderly in the West and probably many families outside the West, for example, the prevalence of new forms of society and intimacy is minimal.

Modern societies have emerged over the past 200 years or so and have become enmeshed in all the features of modernity discussed profusely by social scientists: urbanism, anomie, bureaucratisation, commodification, surveillance, individualisation. As societies become more and more 'modern', so all these features multiply rapidly. However, there is a downside and an upside to all this – a series of traps. On the one hand, our lives in modernity become engaged in a search for authenticity, meaning freedom: human relations become individualised in a world of choices. On the other hand, our lives become increasingly trapped within wider bureaucratising and commercialising forces: human relations can become McDonaldised, Disneyfied and subject to brutal exploitation. Lives can be located in contradictory tendencies.

Late-modern (or postmodern) societies incorporate the latter stages of the above with newer possibilities grafted on to the old in a high-tech and global world. We are just 'on the edge' of all this. Some people across the globe are not yet touched a great deal by it. But many are – and increasingly so.

THINKERS & THEORY

Jeffrey Alexander: the civil sphere and hope for the democratic life

Jeffrey Alexander is one of the world's leading contemporary sociologists. His most recent major work, *The Civil Sphere* (2006), provides a wide-ranging analysis of how contemporary societies do and should work. In it, he moves from a purely theoretical analysis to a *normative* one, i.e. one which is quite explicit about its values.

He claims the significance of the future of democratic societies and the maintenance of a 'civil sphere' where good social bonds, solidarity and community are maintained. Alexander charts different patterns of civil society and outlines key structures and process of the civil sphere which are fostered it in the twenty-first century: the new media, the law, democratic institutions like voting and parties, and the crucial role of social movements – especially around gender and race. He sees the civil society as a 'solidarity sphere in which a certain kind of universaling community comes to be culturally defined and to some degree institutionally

enforced'. It is socially organised and 'sustained by public opinion, deep cultural codes, distinctive organizations – legal, journalistic and associational – and such historically specific interactional practices as civility, criticism and mutual respect' (Alexander, 2006: 31).

Alexander is concerned throughout with the new ways in which solidarity and integration can be fostered in modern societies through a civil sphere, and can help to reduce conflict and tensions. For him: 'Civil society is a project. It inspires hope for a democratic life' (p. 553).

See: Jeffrey Alexander, *The Civil Sphere* (2006).

A note on knowledge and change

One further part of all this change has been shifts in the academy and in ways academics think, theorise and research. Moving under various (often contradictory and contested) guises over the past few decades, we have seen a paradigmatic shift, a continuous attack on and sustained critique of the orthodoxies of our time. Critical theory, feminism, multiculturalism, discourse theory, social constructionism, standpoint theory, queer theory, critical realism, postcolonialism and many others have all made their challenges.

At their hearts, they have made rendered 'knowledge' about social life much more problematic. Again, Beck and Beck-Gernsheim (2003) refers to 'zombie knowledge' from the past, a knowledge which simply has not taken on board the rapidly changing times in which we live. And he cites the importance of locating all our old 'knowledge' nowadays in a global frame – we always have to think beyond the local. Our social theorising is embedded in moral and political structures which need to be made much more explicit and part of our work. We become more and more reflective.

Four themes, introduced throughout this book, may help us to do this: globalisation, the cyber-information society, postmodernism and 'risk'.

Globalisation revisited

As we saw in Chapter 2 and subsequently throughout this book, the concept of globalisation has become an important one in contemporary sociology. We have seen it at work in almost every chapter.

Nowhere is the imagery of globalism more sharply drawn than in the prevalence of worldwide multicultural companies such as Coca-Cola, McDonald's, Nike and Disneyland. They capture the economic, social and cultural impact of this process and simultaneously symbolise what may be good and bad about it. They symbolise, for some, the good life; and yet for others, they are the butt of global social protest (Chapters 9, 15 and 16). Three critical features can be highlighted.

Glocalisation

The first is the relationship between the local and the global. Sociologist Roland Robertson (1992) has usefully coined the term 'glocalisation' as a way of matching the issues of globalisation to local contexts.

Glocalisation means that, while there are undeniable chains of economic and cultural change crossing the globe, each specific local context picks this up and moulds it uniquely: world processes are taken up through local communities and are transformed into something that clearly shows signs of a global culture while being modified into a unique form that connects to the local culture ('think globally, act locally'). **Glocalisation**, therefore, is the *process by which local communities respond differently to global changes*.

An instance of this is the way in which much food has become globalised: Thai cuisine moves all round the world, but in each local culture it gets modified. London's Thai cuisine is different from Californian Thai or New York Thai, and is clearly different from Bangkok Thai.

Hybridisation

A second and linked concern lies with the relationship between a trend towards homogeneity and a trend towards diversification. While a *McDonaldisation thesis* (see Chapter 6) suggests a certain global uniformity – predictability, calculability, efficiency, standardisation (which may be found not just in McDonald's but also in baby stores, package holidays, self-help books and even university textbooks!), a *hybridisation thesis* suggests a 'global mélange'. **Hybridisation** refers to *the ways in which forms of social life become diversified as they separate from old practices and recombine into new ones* (Pieterse, 1995: 47). The analogy starts with plants that become hybrids. Following Jan Nederveen Pieterse (1995: 45, 62), we can depict these trends as in Table 26.4.

Flows and 'scapes'

The anthropologist Arjun Appadurai (1996) has helpfully captured globalisation as a series of flows across the world. The world is moving and he sees it as a series of shifting 'landscapes' or horizons and perspectives. There are five major 'scapes' which he locates as:

- *finanscapes*, through which flows of money and capital cross the world

- *ethnoscapes*, where people constitute the shifting worlds we live in, such as tourists, immigrants, refugees, exiles, guest workers etc., who 'flow' across the globe

- *mediascapes*, where media messages, information, images, film, satellite communications and digital records flow through spaces across the world

Table 26.4	Globalisation as homogenisation or diversification?	
Globalisation as homogenisation	**Globalisation as diversification**	
Cultural imperialism	Cultural planetisation	
Cultural dependence	Cultural interdependence	
Cultural hegemony	Cultural interpenetration	
Autonomy	Synthesis, hybridisation	
Modernisation	Modernisations	
Westernisation	Global mélange	
Cultural synchronisation	Creolisation/crossover	
World civilisation	Global ecumene	

Source: Adapted from Pieterse (2004: 80).

- *technoscapes*, where technologies of all kinds – from atomic bombs and the Human Genome Project to discmen and computer games – glide through global spaces

- *ideoscapes*, where ideas, messages and ideologies move through different countries.

Critical comment

We have used the term 'globalisation' a great deal throughout this book, and the argument has been made that this is a major process at work in twenty-first-century societies. But we must stress too that such processes were well under way centuries ago; the world did not function as isolated countries for much of the second millennium, as the histories of wars, travel, exploration, trade and colonialism can attest.

But what we do see in the current era is a major speeding-up of this process (largely through the new technologies) and a greater involvement and awareness of it among more and more people. In this sense, it really does serve as a very important marker of a new world in the making (Giddens, 1999; Held et al., 1999).

The cyber-information society revisited

If modernity was the product of the Industrial Revolution, the emerging new era seems to be heavily influenced by the cyberspace, high-tech Information Revolution (which has also propelled us into the postmodern era). The past 50 years or so have seen a radical transformation in all aspects of social life as a consequence of these new technologies. Now at the start of the twenty-first century, they are firmly embedded and coming generations will just 'take them for granted'. At the same time, specialists in information technology predict that changes we shall see in the future are even greater than those we have seen in the past few decades. Life, then, is changing, and changing very rapidly, with the new technologies. You might like to review the book to see how often these issues have appeared. The box on p. 24 gives you a guide to this. You can see these issues appearing in every chapter of the book. You may like to return to the box in Chapter 4 (p. 116), which highlighted the many key changes we have discussed in in this book.

Postmodernism revisited

This is a term that a lot of sociologists reject. It is a term that has certainly been made to look ridiculous by those who focus upon its wilder excesses. But here we use it simply to flag all the big changes that are taking place right now in the world as it breaks from modern capitalism into some kind of new form (see Chapter 4, Table 4.1 to review this). Many of the old assumptions have to become weakened. The grand claims of the past are now seen to be oh-so overstated. And a certain modesty and scepticism is seen as a useful tool for careful thinking about society. In general, then, we use the term **postmodernity** to refer to *social patterns characteristic of newly emerging post-industrial societies*.

Looking more closely, however, we find disagreement about precisely what constitutes postmodernism. This term – long used in literary, philosophical and even architectural circles – has edged into sociology on a wave of social criticism that has been building since the surge of left-leaning politics in the 1960s and the confrontation with right wing neoliberal policies since the 1980s. Although there are many variants of postmodern thinking, all share the following five themes:

1 *In some important respects, modernity has failed.* The promise of modernity was multiple: of a life free from want, of a life over which one had more control, of the development of a rationality that would 'save us'. As many critics see it, however, the twentieth century was unsuccessful in eradicating

social problems such as poverty or even in ensuring health or literacy for many people. Indeed, it often fostered the most terrible authoritarian and genocidal systems.

2   *The bright light of 'progress' is fading.* Modern people typically look to the future, expecting that their lives will improve in significant ways. Today's citizens (even leaders), have much less confidence about what the future holds. Furthermore, the buoyant optimism that swept society into the modern era more than a century ago has given way to pessimism on the part of many adults that life is getting worse. A better balanced view of progress and utopia, regression and dystopia is needed.

3   *Science no longer holds all the answers.* The defining trait of the modern era was a scientific outlook and a confident belief that technology would make life better. But critics contend that science has created many problems. After all, it facilitated Hiroshima and the Holocaust. And it often seems to create more problems (such as degrading the environment) than it solves. Many postmodernist thinkers question the foundation of science – the assertion that objective reality and truth exists. Reality needs always to be seen as socially rather than simply naturally constructed, they claim; moreover, 'deconstructing' science shows that this system of ideas has often been widely used for political purposes, especially by powerful segments of society.

4   *Cultural debates are intensifying.* As we have already explained, modernity came wrapped in the bright promise of enhanced individuality and expanding tolerance. Critics claim, however, that the emerging postmodern society falls short of that promise. Queer theorists assert that heterosexism continues to shape society today. Multiculturalism seeks to empower minorities long pushed to the margins of social life and left to languish there. Religious interests are back on the agenda.

5   *Social institutions are changing.* Industrialisation brought sweeping transformation to social institutions; the rise of a post-industrial society is remaking society once again. We have seen this throughout the book. For example, just as the Industrial Revolution placed material *things* at the centre of productive life, now the Information Revolution has elevated the importance of *ideas*. Similarly, the postmodern family no longer conforms to any singular formula; on the contrary, individuals are devising new and varied ways of relating to one another.

Critical comment

Postmodern critics contend that the Western world has failed in important ways to meet human needs. Yet few would argue that modernity has failed completely; as we have seen, there have been marked increases in the length and quality of life over the course of the twentieth century for billions of people. Moreover, even if we were to accept postmodernist criticism that science and traditional notions about progress are bankrupt, what are the alternatives? Then, too, many voices offer strikingly different understandings of recent social trends.

The risk society revisited

As Chapters 23, 24 and 25 detailed, contemporary human societies are closely interconnected with science, population and the natural environment: change in one tends to produce change in the others.

Science, technology and change

Three new revolutions will haunt the twenty-first century: those of the atom, the gene and the computer. Each one (as we saw in Chapter 23) brings the potential for major social change. We live in a world where the unleashing of the atom may bring untold destruction in war and terrorism, where cyberworlds may well reshape just what it means to interact with other human beings, and where the new genetics will put within our reach the ability to clone and create designer babies. Notwithstanding any of this, we have already started to put people on the moon.

Such potential changes have also brought with them the need for consideration of ethical issues linked to science, and, as the twenty-first century proceeds, we shall probably witness more discussion not simply of science but also of the moral role of the scientist.

The natural environment and change

By and large, 'modern' culture has cast nature as a force to be tamed and reshaped to human purposes. From the onset of industrialisation and the rise of capitalism, people have systematically cut down forests to create fields for farming and to make materials for building; they have established towns and cities, extended roads in every direction and dammed rivers as a source of water and energy. Such human construction not only reflects a cultural determination to control the natural environment, it also points up the centrality of the idea of 'growth' in our way of life.

But the consequences of this thinking have placed increasing stress on the natural environment. Western societies confront problems from growing mountains of solid waste, as well as air and water pollution, all the while consuming the lion's share of global resources. A growing awareness that such patterns are not sustainable in the long term is forcing us to confront the need to change our way of life in some basic respects.

Demographic change

World population in 2010 was up to 7 billion from 6 billion in 2000. Ninety-five per cent of the increase was in developing countries, nearly all in rapidly expanding urban areas.

As Chapter 13 explained, many societies are growing older. Soon nearly one in five people in Western countries will be 65 or older. Medical research and healthcare services will come to focus more and more on people growing older. There will be increases in healthcare and pension costs. The relative size of the working population may fall and new opportunities for later life will have to be found. Common stereotypes about old people may well be undermined as more men and women enter this stage of life. Ways of life may change in countless additional directions as homes and household products are redesigned to meet the needs of growing ranks of older people.

Migration within and among societies is another demographic factor that promotes change. Between 1870 and 1930, millions of rural peoples in Western societies, along with millions of immigrants from poorer countries, swelled the industrial cities. As a result, farm communities declined, metropolises burgeoned and the Western world became for the first time a predominantly urban society. Similar changes are taking place today as people are moving across all the continents.

The shape of societies to come – a New World Order?

Social change is inherently complex, contradictory and controversial. Thus, in principle, almost everyone in our society supports the idea that individuals should have considerable autonomy in shaping their own lives. Many people will applaud the demise of tradition, viewing this trend as a sign of progress. Yet, as people exercise their freedom of choice, they inevitably challenge social patterns cherished by those who maintain a more traditional way of life. For example, people may choose to live with someone without marrying, or may feel more comfortable in an intimate same-sex partnership. To those who endorse individual choice, such changes symbolise progress; to those who value traditional family patterns, however, these developments signal societal decline.

New technology, too, sparks controversy. More rapid transportation and more efficient communication may improve our lives in some respects. However, complex technology has eroded traditional attachments to home towns and even to families. Industrial technology has also unleashed an unprecedented threat to the natural environment. In short, we know that change is accelerating over time, but views may differ sharply as to whether any particular change amounts to progress. Table 26.5 marks out some of the contradictory pushes and changes that the move towards a postmodern society brings.

John Gibbins and Bo Reimer, in their book *The Politics of Postmodernity* (1999), distinguished three types of vision of the future among social theorists. One group are the *pessimists*, who often see the world as moving towards some kind of final collapse. Another group are the *critics*, who see 'crisis' everywhere (often with little chance of real change). A third group are the *optimists* (1999: 142). Although optimists sense that many dangers are imminent (as we do in Table 26.5), they also believe that there are signs of a rise of 'more activist citizens dealing with more responsive political bodies in more areas of life and the globe' (1999: 145). They sense a new kind of politics in the making (which we described in Chapter 16), and a move towards what Giddens calls the democratisation of democracy (Giddens, 1999). So here, there is a positive and political look to the future, but one in which we are also aware of profound problems.

Towards 'the human rights society'

The twentieth century was not only the century of holocausts and wars, it was also the century when the idea of equality, human rights and the democratic state

Table 26.5	Some antagonisms of the New World Order	
The tragic 'dystopian' view	**The romantic 'utopian' view**
Widening inequalities, social divisions	Higher standards of living for large numbers of people
Fragmentation, post-Fordism, disorganisation, Balkanisation	The pluralisation ethos, differences recognised
Impersonality and loss of community	Participation and attachment in new 'social worlds'
Narcissism, egoism	'Individualism'
McDonaldisation, standardisation, dumbing down	'Choices', reflexivities
Moral decline and incivility	Citizenship, new ethics, moral effervescence
Entrenched hierarchies of exclusion	The democratisation of personhood and relationships
Uncertainty, chaos, a world out of control, risk	Chance for a New World Order, human rights

came into its own. In 1948, the Universal Declaration of Human Rights was adopted, acknowledging rights as a global concern. In its 30 articles, it stresses not only that people should not be held in servitude – 'slavery and the slave trade shall be prohibited in all their forms' – but also that many rights of equality should be upheld: the right to be equal before the law, the right to protection against discrimination, to education, to a standard of living adequate for the health and well-being of oneself and one's family, and the right to freedom of thought, conscience and religion.

Of course, such a document brings many problems. Some argue, for instance, that it is an imposition of Western views on the rest of the world, others argue that it is too idealistic to be fully implemented, and still others suggest that even in countries which have agreed to its principles, abuses of all kinds still occur. Despite this, the United Nations can claim that:

One of the 20th century's hallmark achievements was its progress in human rights. In 1900 more than half the world's people lived under colonial rule and no country gave all its citizens the right to vote. Today some three quarters of the world lives under democratic regimes. There has also been great progress in eliminating discrimination by race, religion and gender – and in advancing the right to schooling and basic health care.

(UNHDP, 2000: 1)

In conclusion

We can no longer isolate the study of the Western world from the rest of the world. At the beginning of the twentieth century, a majority of people in today's high-income countries lived in relatively small settlements with limited awareness of the larger world. Now, at the start of the twenty-first century, people everywhere participate in a far larger human drama. The world seems smaller and the lives of all people are increasingly linked. We now discuss the relationships among countries in the same way that people a century ago talked about the expanding ties among cities and towns.

The twentieth century witnessed unprecedented human achievement alongside unprecedented human tragedy. As this book has hopefully shown, while the everyday life of many has got better and better, for many more, solutions to some of the problems of human existence – inequalities, poverty, meaninglessness, disease, conflict, war, genocide – have eluded us. To this list of pressing matters new concerns have been added in recent years, such as controlling population growth and establishing a sustainable natural environment. Living in the twenty-first century, we must be prepared to tackle such problems with critical imagination, humanistic compassion and political will. The challenge is great, and sociology will be needed to keep critically alive our developing, wide-ranging understanding of human societies.

SUMMARY

1 Every society changes continuously, intentionally or not, and at varying speeds. Social change often generates controversy.

2 Social change results from invention, discovery and diffusion as well as social conflict.

3 Modernity refers to the social consequences of industrialisation, which include the erosion of traditional communities, expanding personal choice, increasingly diverse beliefs and a keen awareness of time, especially the future.

4 Social change is too complex and controversial simply to be equated with social progress.

5 In the twenty-first century, sociologists are discussing the current changes in society and many new kinds of society have been suggested. These include 'the postmodern society', 'the information society', 'the network society', 'the risk society', 'the cyborg society', 'the individualised society' and 'the human rights society'.

6 At work behind all these terms are a number of key processes which we have variously identified as 'globalisation', 'mediasation', 'digitalisation', 'disorganised capitalism', 'post-Fordism', 'McDonaldsisation', 'desecularisation', 'democratisation' and a 'Third Way'. All these ideas have been discussed earlier in this book.

7 Globalisation highlights the local and the global, hybridisation and 'scapes'.

8 Postmodernity refers to cultural traits of post-industrial societies. Postmodern criticism of society centres on the failure of modernity, and specifically science, to fulfil its promise of prosperity and well-being.

9 Human societies are closely interconnected to science, population and the natural environment: change in one tends to produce change in others. As changes in these areas become more unpredictable in outcomes, we increasingly face a 'risk society'.

10 Looking to the future, sociologists can see both utopian visions based upon human rights and democratisation, and dystopian visions based upon growing inequalities and sufferings.

11 The challenge of sociology is to keep alive a critical, wide-ranging understanding of human societies.

CONNECT UP: Turn to Part 6 of this book for key resources and link up
with the book's website, which links to these resources
SEE: www.pearsoned.co.uk/plummer

MYTASKLIST

Ten suggestions for going further

1 Connect up with Part Six and the Sociology Web Resources

As you work through ideas and think about the issues raised in this chapter, look at the accompanying website and the resource centre at the end of this book which connects to it. There is a lot here to help you move on. To link up, see: www.pearson.co.uk/plummer.

2 Review the chapter

Briefly summarise (in a paragraph) just what this chapter has been about. Consider: (a) What have you learned? (b) What do you disagree with? Be critical. And (c) How would you develop all this? How could you get more detail on matters that interest you?

3 Pose questions

(a) Look back over this text and consider whether Durkheim, Weber and Marx accurately predicted the character of the twenty-first-century world. How do their visions of society differ?
(b) Throughout this book we have used the term 'postmodern society'. What is a postmodern society? Are there any postmodern societies in the world today? What do they look like?
(c) Examine the tensions and contradictions in Table 26.5, and draw up both a utopia and a dystopia for the future based on some of these ideas.
(d) Look back over the book and review the main features of contemporary change suggested in each chapter.

4 Enhance key words

Many concepts have been introduced in this chapter. You can review them from the website or from the listing at the back of this book. You might like to give special attention to just five words and think them through – how would you define them, what are they dealing with, and do they help you see the social world more clearly or not?

5 Search the Web: make your own list of favourites

By now you should have developed a rather full source book of websites to draw upon. Review them with the help of the list of 100 best websites in the Resource List in Part Six (see pp. 937–47). Construct your own list of favourites.

6 Watch a DVD

During the course of this book, we have introduced a number of science fiction films. These included *Metropolis* (Chapter 1), *The Matrix* (Chapter 5), *The Stepford Wives* (Chapter 12), *Dr Strangelove* (Chapter 16), and in Chapter 23 *Frankenstein*, *Dark Star*, *Blade Runner* and the *Terminator* films. To these you could add:

- Robert Zemeckis's *Back to the Future Parts I–III* (1985–90): three films that raise the problem of time in different societies. Fairly lighthearted.
- Wim Wender's *Wings of Desire* (1987): slightly whimsical as angels visit Berlin. Some people connect it to Capra's *It's a Wonderful Life* (see Chapter 1).
- Stanley Kubrick's *2001: A Space Odyssey* (1968): the classic space film.
- Michael Anderson's *1984* (1956) and Michael Radford's *1984* (1984): two films of the classic Orwell novel. 1984 has now long passed, but some of the implications of these 'futuristic' scenarios are still open to analysis and discussion.

7 Think and read

- Göran Therborn, *The World: A Beginner's Guide* (2011): an invaluable guide to the sociology of the world and strongly recommended.

- *State of the World, 2011* (Worldwatch, 2011).
- Jeremy Rifkin, *The Empathetic Civilization: The Race to Global Consciousness in a World in Crisis* (2010).

8 Relax with a novel

In Part six of this book you will find a list of good novels and fiction that you could read to enhance your sociological imagination. But to close this section, you might like to consider the idea of utopia and a few novels that have been written about this. Utopia is an imagined ideal social world. Some of the earlier classics can be found in one volume edited by Susan Bruce in the Oxford World Classics Series: *Three Early Modern Utopias* (1999). It contains Thomas More's *Utopia*, Francis Bacon's *New Atlantis*, and Henry Neville's *The Isle of Pines*.

Twentieth-century classics would include H.G. Wells' *A Modern Utopia*. The idea of dystopia can be found in George Orwell's *1984* and Aldous Huxley's *Brave New World* (1932). A good general discussion on all this is Krishan Kumar's *Utopianism* (1991). A feminist account is Frances Bartkowski's *Feminist Utopias* (1989).

9 Connect to other chapters

It is time now to look over the whole book. But you might:

- Review Marx, Durkheim and Weber on modern societies in Chapter 4.
- Review shifts in identity in Chapter 7.
- Review theories of the global in Chapter 2 and elsewhere.
- Review postmodernity in Chapter 2 and elsewhere.

10 Engage with THE BIG DEBATE

Putting it all together: is the future postmodern?

Many sociologists have suggested that a rupture is happening within the modern world, and a new social order is starting to appear on a global scale. 'Postmodernism', 'late-modernism' and 'post-industrial' are all terms used to signify the emergence of this new social order. Jean-François Lyotard (1992: 80) has defined postmodernism as 'an incredulity towards metanarratives'. By this he means that we can no longer believe in one all-encompassing story or truth. We can now see there are many paths, routes, possibilities, truths. Indeed, for another leading French sociologist, Jean Baudrillard, the argument is that the postmodern is: 'the characteristic of a universe where there are no more definitions possible . . . It has all been done . . . So all that are left are pieces. All that remains to be done is play with the pieces – that is postmodern' (Baudrillard, 1991: 24).

These controversial theories and ideas have been used throughout this book, and it should be clear that not all sociologists agree with their use. Many reject the use of this term outright. In this chapter, we have brought together a number of significant changes that are happening in societies across the world. But is it wise to call these postmodern trends? If you look back to the box in Chapter 4 on different kinds of society

(see pp. 135–6), you will see sociologists have used many terms and ideas to characterise the world we are moving into. Look back on these and in the light of your searches, reading and thinking, consider which term might be best.

Almost every chapter in this book suggests that something is indeed happening at the start of the twenty-first century which must be seen as a significant change. Thus Chapter 2 ends by suggesting that new ways of approaching society through multiple voices are starting to happen: the old orthodoxies of functionalism, conflict and actions are being challenged. Chapter 3 suggests that new methods are in the making in sociological research. Chapter 4 captures the idea of a new kind of 'post-industrial' society in the making, and Chapter 5 highlights multiculturalism and postcolonialism. Then in Chapter 6, we see a new kind of postmodern organisation. In Chapter 15 we see a new kind of economy and pattern of work emerging that we call 'post-Fordist'. And so it goes on: new forms of 'postmodern family', new patterns of gender and sexual relations, new modes of consumption, new social movements, new forms of social control and even new religions. We have also seen debates around class which suggest that it may be becoming less important (Chapter 10), while ethnicity (Chapter 11), gender (Chapter 12) and age (Chapter 13) become more important. We have seen the rise of the new computer society – cybersociety – saturated with information and communication (Chapters 22 and 23), and the chapter on the environment (Chapter 25) hurtles us towards a new kind of 'risk society'. Even in this final chapter, we have highlighted how sociologists sense ever new forms of society emerging.

Along with all this has been another closely linked theme: globalisation. Here we start to see a major shift in the way the world exists in time and in space. The world becomes smaller and smaller as communications and finances flow around the globe. Hence we start to see global power structures appearing alongside global media, global cities and global inequalities. We are moving out of the era of the old nation-state and into a new period where countries are profoundly interconnected through global flows.

Continue the debate

1 Get clear what are the big social changes that this book has suggested are taking place.
2 Do you think that societies are really changing as dramatically as this book has been suggesting?
3 If yes, what is making these changes happen?
4 Discuss whether sociology has helped you understand them. What is the future role of sociology?
5 Do we need sociology to help in all this?
6 Drawing from trends you can detect in the social world now, invent a portrait of the future for your grandchildren. Will it be nearer utopia or dystopia?

The appeal of utopianism arises, I believe, from the failure to realise that we cannot make heaven on earth. What we can do instead is, I believe, to make life a little less terrible and a little less unjust in every generation. A good deal can be achieved in this way.

Karl Popper, 'Utopia and Violence', *Hibbert Journal*, 1948

Sociology, as we hope you have seen throughout this book, aims to be the systematic study of human society, where systematic means attending to the living (and lived) empirical world through (a) various means of 'data' collection and analysis, and (b) various theoretical stances that need evaluating. It aims at one level to be as neutral and objective as it can be in doing this task: to present 'facts', arguments, analyses and conclusions. In practice, though, as any reader will have noticed, value judgements creep in everywhere. Controversial issues are raised which cannot be resolved 'neutrally'. In the final analysis, values gently seep into what we assume about the social world, into where we come from and, perhaps most significantly, where we want to go.

Every chapter of the book has suggested to you social change (and as we saw in Chapters 1 and 2, sociology was born of these changes). If the book has one long story to tell, it is the story of the ways in which societies have changed from the past and will go on changing into the future. A vast web of ideas has been developed from data to capture this. Consider some of them: industrialisation, capitalism, *Gesellschaft*, urbanisation, rationalisation, mediasation, individualisation, democratisation, secularisation, population growth and so on (see Table 26.1 for a review). But the question is, where do values creep back in to all of this? They are never far away from our three old 'foundational' sociologists Marx, Durkheim and Weber. Marx, as is well known, was personally outraged at the exploitation and damaged lives he saw created by capitalistic industrialisation. He wanted a revolution for equality. Weber's work reeks of a kind of despair. However 'value free' he wanted to be, you sense his disenchantment with the world: indeed, he writes about it. Durkheim – trying to keep his study to 'social facts' – nevertheless hints at a future world where differences and diversities will be better organised. And when it comes to more recent sociologies, their values are proclaimed loud and clear. Feminist sociology declares the need to remove women's inequalities. Anti-racism sociology declares the need to critique signs of racism. Queer sociology actively seeks to break down stable categories of gender and sexuality which impede human possibilites. Postcolonial sociology sees the subordinations of groups all round the world, and challenges the supremacy of the European/American model that dominates thinking.

The importance of values in a value-free discipline

Values are actually so apparent in sociology that the student may well ask why sociology claims to be value free. The answer is straightforward: it will strive to do its best to be as objective and dispassionate as it can be within value judgements that it must also make itself aware of. So at the end of this book, it may be time for you to consider just why you want to study sociology and what your values might be. The box suggests some key values for you to think about, study and maybe bring to your life.

For us, the prime value of sociology might be seen as the progressive reduction of social suffering and the enhancement of 'good enough lives'. We study sociology in order ultimately to make this world a better place to live in – both in our own times and indeed for future generations. By implication, its tacit goal is to help remove the enormous amount of suffering this world creates and to celebrate the everyday experiences of humans creating their own liveable social worlds. It is a world they did not make, but a world that can be changed.

If we consider the sufferings we have encountered in this book, sociology could be a dismal science and a counsel of despair. We have not just encountered, but started to describe and explain, the widespread existence of poverty, wars, genocides, despotic rules, terrorism, ill health, shame . . . And we have shown some of the systems that seem to generate this: slavery, racism, poverty, stigma, sexism . . . But we have also shown that people fight back: there are myriad ways in which social actions create the worlds we live in, and either collectively or individually, we do indeed

LIVING IN THE C21ST

The need for a sociology of values

Meaning and values lie at the heart of human societies and sociology. We can find values in sociology in the baseline assumptions of our research, as guidelines in the practices of doing sociological theory and research (the research ethics we saw in Chapter 3), but also as topics to be studied and investigated in their own right (the sociology of values, ethics, morality). There are many values that interest sociology, but here are some prominent ones worth exploring.

- *Care and love*. Sociologists know that a recurring key feature of social life is the ways in which people look after each other in families, friendships and communities. There is even the kindness of strangers. Here sociologists can investigate caring relations, and they can also make sure their research relationships are grounded in care for the other.

- *Freedom and equality*. Sociologists know that these are often seen as in competition with each other in the modern world, but that they need not be. They also know that total freedom or total equality are both total nonsense: the social always constrains the free, and limits equalities. But there are many whose lives are damaged by lack of freedom and huge inequality, and much sociological work is hence concerned with enhancing freedom and opportunities of equality. In this sense, much sociology is emancipatory.

- *Human capabilities and human rights*. Sociologists are concerned with what it means to function well in a society – and hence draw up conceptions of human needs and their potentials, thwarting and flourishing (see Chapter 4 and the work of Sen and Nussbaum: p. 471). Meeting human needs and developing human capabilities often connect to the development of human rights. In research, sociologists think about the rights of their human subjects; more widely, there is a well-developed sociology of human rights.

- *Tolerance and cosmopolitanism*. Built into the heart of sociology is an awareness of the multiplicities of ways in which human social lives are different – across people, groups, cultures and nations. Ethnocentrism is a cardinal sin for sociologists and a wide-awake openness to the values of others is central. There is also a growing sociology of cosmopolitanism which looks at the justling contrasts of people who are very different being able to live together (see Bob Fine's *Cosmopolitanism* (2007) as an example).

- *Harm reduction*. Sociologists are interested in researching the ways in which human social enterprise often damages other people. Just as their interest in care suggests ways in which people look after each after, so their interest in human damage asks questions about the ways in which people may be damaged by certain social actions. At the simplest level, the human cost of war, the failure of massive imprisonment whilst crime still rages, and the failure of states to protect their peoples from environmental damage are all grounds of concern.

Source: Adapted from Plummer (2010: Chapter 8).

try to make this world a better place, at least for ourselves but often for others too.

Let us suggest, then, that a better definition of sociology than the one we started out with may be that it is *the critical, humanistic and systematic analysis of human society*. Critical because, as we saw in Chapter 1, the first rule of sociology is that *things are not what they seem*. Humanistic because this is a core value of sociology – to believe in *the value of the worthwhileness of all human beings and their social actions in all their richness and complexities*. And systematic because this is not simple journalism, but a quite profound journey to organise, observe and think ideas around human societies.

Put crudely, we are looking for a future world where respect is accorded to all human beings, where inequalities, violence and authoritarianism decrease, and where differences and variety are celebrated – not excluded. We do not want to see damaged lives or wasted lives. Sociology can help us become critical citizens in this long task.

At the end of one of the world's greatest novels, George Elliot's *Middlemarch*, she writes of the 'heroine':

> But the effect of her being on those around her was incalculably diffusive: for the growing good of the world is partly dependent on unhistoric acts; and that things are not so ill with you and me as they might have been, is half owing to the number who lived faithfully a hidden life, and rest in unvisited tombs.
>
> (1871; 1999: 758)

This is the everyday stuff of everyday life that makes up everyday societies. Sociology is at its best when it looks at the ceaseless human associations that people create; charts the divisions, inequalities and sufferings they generate; and provides a sense of the future, of 'better worlds'.

See: Iain Wilkinson, *Suffering: A Sociological Introduction* (2005).

PART 6

WEB RESOURCES FOR CRITICAL THINKING

CREATING SOCIOLOGICAL IMAGINATIONS

TWELVE PATHWAYS INTO CRITICAL SOCIOLOGICAL THINKING

This section is aimed to help you go way beyond the limits of a textbook. The book's website directly connects to this and makes it possible to link up with most of the items listed here. Look at: www.pearsoned.co.uk/ globalsociology

See this as an aid in your quest for understanding sociology and developing critical thinking. Suggestions have already been provided at the end of each chapter of this book. This final section provides a wide-ranging overall resource, listing many key websites in alphabetical order. Likewise, we suggest some key words for searching YouTube. Spend some time building up your own preference lists.

There is no shortage of data about society. The twenty-first century is a world cluttered with information, and sociologists can now plunder data on the World Wide Web. Looking at Wikipedia, doing a Google search or using YouTube can also bring undoubted speed in the search for information. Research that used to take days or weeks can now be done in hours or even minutes. But, as we have insisted throughout, there is always the need to adopt a critical and careful approach to the use of this material (see the *Big debate* in Chapter 1 on Wikipedia, and the tools for a critical cyber attitude on p. 939).

But this may also be the time to pause, think and consider some of the more classic ways of understanding the social world. So, in this part we also suggest that you can look at great works of art as a way of seeing society. Likewise, great novels always provide insights to humanity, human relations and social worlds. So in this resource section, we are not limiting our themes to those found on the Web. Older sources of stimulation can be found here too.

Here we suggest 12 key pathways for broadening and deepening your critical thinking about society. These are:

Be a good craftsman. Avoid any rigid set of procedures. Above all, seek to develop and to use the sociological imagination. Avoid the fetishism of method and technique. Urge the rehabilitation of the unpretentious intellectual craftsman, and try to become such a craftsman yourself. Let every person be their own methodologist; let every person be their own theorist; let theory and method again become the practice of a craft.

C. Wright Mills, *The Sociological Imagination* (1959: 224)

(Left) *Where do we come from? What are we? Where are we going?* Paul Gauguin (1897)
Eugène Henri Paul Gauguin (1848–1903) was a trailblazing French post-impressionist artist. In 1891, he left Paris for Tahiti where he found a more perfect world. *Where Do We Come From? What Are We? Where Are We Going?* was painted there in 1897 and has become one of his most famous paintings. Here Gauguin meditates on what we are and what we become. The title is scribbled in French in the upper left corner. It is all set in a paradise of tropical beauty.
Source: Photograph © 2011 Museum of Fine Arts, Boston.

See: Paul Gaugin: The Complete Works Web Site http://www.paul-gauguin.net/.

 How might art and sociology help us think about better worlds and lives?

THE SOCIOLOGY FILES
www.pearsoned.co.uk/plummer

Select from the links in the drop-down menu to access the student study materials.

1. **Internet sociologist** – improve your internet research skills using this tutorial.

2. **Web resources for critical thinking** – links to Part Six of the book. A range of materials that link to films, art and novels of sociological interest. It also includes links to the websites.

3. **Website links** – a major listing of websites of interest to sociologists.

4. **Chapter resources** – a collection of resources including PowerPoint slides for use in classes, interactive questions, an online glossary and revision flashcards.

5. **Reading supplements** – a selection of short pieces to read which will add to each chapter.

6. **Tutor's section** – some comments chapter by chapter which may be of particular interest to tutors.

7. **Podcasts** – introducing each part of the textbook and global voices on sociology.

8. **The Big Vote** – allowing you to give your view on key debates and see what other students think.

9. **The Sociology Blog** – check this regularly for current and 'hot' topics to update your knowledge.

10. **Pearson** – learn more about the textbook, including how to order this title or obtain an inspection copy.

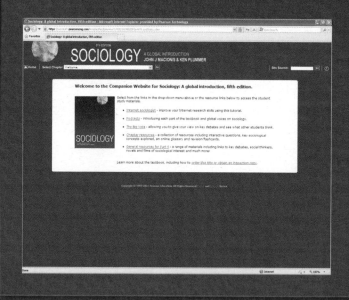

1 FILMS

www.pearsoned.co.uk/plummer/film

100 or so key films of sociological interest

The twentieth century was the century of film, and most films suggest ideas about the society we live in as well as providing resources for shaping the world we live in. This is a very short list of popular films of sociological interest – there are thousands more! You can probe more on the Internet Movie Database: www.imdb.com.

A very valuable book to help you make sense of film is: James Monaco, *How to Read a Film* (4th edition, 2008). See also Jean-Anne Sutherland & Kathryn Feltey *Cinematic Sociology: Social Life in Film* (2009) which shows how to use contemporary films to develop the sociological imagination.

Bodies and cyborgs

1   *The Fly*, David Cronenberg (1986)
2   *Frankenstein*, James Whale (1931)
3   *Terminator*, James Cameron (1984)

Crime and violence

4   *M*, Fritz Lang (1931)
5   *Twelve Angry Men*, Sydney Lumet (1957)
6   *Reservoir Dogs*, Quentin Tarantino (1992)
7   *The Godfather*, Francis Ford Coppola (1972)
8   *Goodfellas*, Martin Scorsese (1990)

Class

9   *Harlan County USA*, Barbara Kopple (1976)
10 *Blue Collar*, Paul Schrader (1978)
11 *Titanic*, James Cameron (1997)
12 *Gosford Park*, Robert Altman (2001)
13 *This is England*, Shane Meadows (2002)

Disability

14 *The Elephant Man*, David Lynch (1980)
15 *Sick: The Life and Death of Bob Flanegan Supermasochist*, Kirby Dick (1997)
16 *Inside I'm Dancing*, Damien O'Donnell (2004)
17 *Murderball Henry*, Alex Rubin (2005)
18 *The Diving Bell and the Butterfly*, Julian Schnabel (2007)

Documentary

19 *Nanook of the North*, Robert J. Flaherty (1922)
20 *Bowling for Columbine*, Michael Moore (2002)
21 *Freaks*, Tod Browning (1932)

Drug use

22 *Reefer Madness*, Louis J. Gasnier (1936)
23 *Trainspotting*, Danny Boyle (1996)
24 *Traffic*, Steven Soderbergh (2000)

Dying and Bereavement

25 *Shadowlands*, Richard Attenborough (1993)
26 *Away from Her*, Sarah Polley (2007)
27 *A Single Man*, Tom Ford (2009)

Education

28 *Kes*, Ken Loach (1969)
29 *If . . .* Lindsay Anderson (1968)
30 *Dead Poets' Society*, Peter Weir (1989)
31 *The History Boys*, Nicholas Hytner (2006)
32 *The Class*, Laurent Cantent (2008)

Environment

33 *Erin Brockovitch*, Steven Soderbergh (2000)

Everyday interaction

34 *Being There*, Hal Ashby (1979)
35 *Zelig*, Woody Allen (1983)
36 *Groundhog Day*, Harold Ramis (1993)
37 *Stranger than Fiction*, Marc Foster (2006)

Marlene Dietrich (1901–1992)
Marlene Dietrich was a major celebrity of the mid twentieth century. Today we have many new celebrities every year – who come and go. In Chapter 22 we ask just how important celebrities have become in the twenty-first century.

Family life

38   *Life is Sweet*, Mike Leigh (1990)
39   *In the Bedroom*, Todd Field (2001)
40   *American Beauty*, Sam Mendes (1999)
41   *Little Miss Sunshine*, Valerie Faris (2006)
42   *The Kids are Alright*, Lisa Cholodenko (2010)

Gay and lesbian

43   *The Celluloid Closet*, Rob Epstein and Jeffrey Friedman (1995)
44   *Fabulous! The Story of Queer Cinema*, Lisa Ades (2006)

Gender

45   *Stand by Me*, Rob Reiner (1986)
46   *Thelma and Louise*, Ridley Scott (1991)
47   *Boys Don't Cry*, Kimberley Pierce (1999)
48   *Brokeback Mountain*, Ang Lee (2005)

Holocaust

49   *The Pianist*, Roman Polanski (2002)
50   *Schindler's List*, Steven Spielberg (1993)

Music: a musical view of society

51   *The Wizard of Oz*, Victor Fleming (1939)
52   *West Side Story*, Jerome Robbins and Robert Wise (1961)
53   *Cabaret*, Bob Fosse (1972)
54   *Chicago*, Rob Marshall (2002)
55   *Sweeney Todd*, Tim Burton (2007)

Relationships

56   *Brief Encounter*, David Lean (1945)
57   *A Streetcar Named Desire*, Elia Kazan (1951)
58   *Fear Eats the Soul*, Rainer Wernder Fassbinder (1974)
59   *Annie Hall*, Woody Allen (1977)
60   *When Harry met Sally*, Rob Reiner (1989)
61   *The Human Stain*, Robert Benton (2003)

Poverty

62   *The Grapes of Wrath*, John Ford (1940)
63   *The Tree of Wooden Clogs*, Ermanno Olmi (1978)
64   *Angela's Ashes*, Alan Parker (1999)

Race and racism

65   *To Kill a Mockingbird*, Robert Mulligan (1962)
66   *The Long Walk Home*, Richard Pearce (1990)
67   *Malcolm X*, Spike Lee (1992)
68   *Do the Right Thing*, Spike Lee (1989)
69   *Mississippi Burning*, Alan Parker (1988)
70   *Crash*, Paul Haggis (2004)

Religion

71   *Inherit the Wind*, Stanley Kramer (1960)
72   *Of Gods and Men*, Xavier Beauvois (2010)

Science fiction

73   *Metropolis*, Fritz Lang (1927)
74   *2001: A Space Odyssey*, Stanley Kubrick (1968)
75   *Blade Runner*, Ridley Scott (1982)
76   *Back to the Future*, Robert Zemeckis (1985)
77   *The Matrix*, Andy and Larry Wachowski (1999)

Slavery and total institutions

78   *One Flew Over the Cuckoo's Nest*, Milos Forman (1975)
79   *Das Boot*, Wolfgang Petersen (1981)
80   *The Shawshank Redemption*, Frank Darabont (1994)
81   *Amistad*, Stephen Spielberg (1997)

Sports

82   *Hoop Dreams*, Steve James (1994)
83   *Remember the Titans*, Boaz Yakin (2000)
84   *Bend It Like Beckham*, Gurinder Chadha (2002)
85   *The Fan*, Tony Scott (1996)

Urban life and community

86   *Sunset Boulevard*, Billy Wilder (1950)
87   *On the Waterfront*, Elia Kazan (1954)
88   *Taxi Driver*, Martin Scorcese (1976)
89   *Manhattan*, Woody Allen (1979)
90   *Paris, Texas*, Wim Wenders (1984)
91   *Blue Velvet*, David Lynch (1986)
92   *Tokyo Story*, Yasujiro Ozu (1953)

Youth crime and delinquency

93   *Les Quatre Cent Coups*, François Truffaut (1959)
94   *A Clockwork Orange*, Stanley Kubrick (1971)
95   *American History X*, Tony Kaye (1998)

Youth cultures

96   *Rebel without a cause*, Nicholas Ray (1955)
97   *Les Quatre Cent Coups*, François Truffaut (1959)
98   *A Clockwork Orange*, Stanley Kubrick (1971)
99   *Saturday Night Fever*, John Badham (1977)
100   *Gregory's Girl*, Bill Forsyth (1981)
101   *Samson and Delilah*, Warwick Thorton (2010)

War

102   *The Deer Hunter*, Michael Cimino (1978)
103   *Saving Private Ryan*, Stephen Spielberg (1998)

See also:

104   *Chinatown*, Roman Polanski (1974)
105   *The Devils*, Ken Russell (1971)

Many of the above resources now have 'clickable' links from this book's website. Please visit www.pearsoned.co.uk/plummer/film to access them.

The Kite Runner
Study a novel and film together

Khaled Hosseini's *The Kite Runner* tells the story of an illiterate Afghan boy. Published in 2003, it is the tale of a boyhood friendship and growing up in the city of Kabul in the early 1970s. Running parallel with this is the story of modern Afghanistan. The kite is the book's central image. Banned in Afghanistan by the country's religious rulers, the novel became a best seller, not least because it was the first Afghan novel to be written in English. In 2007, it was turned into a film and nominated for an Oscar. Reading the book and then watching the film will give you a lot to think about concerning the changes taking place in Afghanistan.

2 NOVELS

www.pearsoned.co.uk/plummer/novels

101 or so novels of sociological interest

Alienation

Childhood and old age

Contingency in life

Crime

Cultures

Death and dying

Sociology as an Art Form

In his classic study, *Sociology as an Art Form* (1976), Robert Nisbet reflected:

> How different things would be . . . if the social sciences at the time of their systematic formation in the nineteenth century had taken the arts in the same degree they took the physical science as models.
>
> (1976: 16)

There is much that the humanities have to offer to the social sciences, and reading some great novels is as good a start as you can have. All good fiction stimulates the imagination about the kinds of society we live in. Here is a short list of classics by sociological theme. Although criticised by some for its seeming lack of multicultural awareness, the volume by Harold Bloom called *The Western Canon* (1994) is in fact a valuable distillation of the 'Western' classics. More details of many of the books can be found on The Literature Network at www.online-literature.com. Often the complete text is also available.

35   C. S. Lewis, *A Grief Observed* (1961)
36   Annie Proulx, *The Shipping News* (1993)

Diaries

37   Anne Frank, *The Diary of Anne Frank* (1947)
38   Samuel Pepys, *Diary* (1825)
39   James Boswell, *London Journal* (1763)
40   Doris Lessing, *The Golden Notebook* (1962)

Education

41   Alison Lurie, *Imaginary Friends* (1967)
42   Tom Wolfe, *I Am Charlotte Simmons* (2004)
43   James Hynes, *The Lecturer's Tale* (2001)
44   Norman N. Holland, *Death in a Delphi Seminar: A Postmodern Mystery* (1995)
45   Bernard Malamud, *A New Life* (1961)
46   David Lodge, *Small World* (1984)
47   Malcolm Bradbury, *The History Man* (1975)

Enlightenment

48   Voltaire, *Candide* (1759)
49   Jonathan Swift, *Gulliver's Travels* (1726)
50   Mary Shelley, *Frankenstein* (1818)

Gay and lesbian

51   Alan Hollinghurst, *The Swimming Pool Library* (1990)
52   Edmund White, *A Boy's Own Story* (1982)
53   Jeanette Winterson, *Oranges Are Not the Only Fruit* (1985)
54   Radclyffe Hall, *The Well of Loneliness* (1928)

Generations

55   Charles Dickens, *David Copperfield* (1850)
56   Edith Wharton, *The Age of Innocence* (1920)
57   Anthony Powell, *A Dance to the Music of Time* (1951–75)
58   Scott Fitzgerald, *The Great Gatsby* (1925)
59   Christopher Isherwood, *Goodbye to Berlin* (1939)
60   Jack Kerouac, *On the Road* (1957)
61   Colin MacInnes, *Absolute Beginners* (1959)
62   Douglas Copland, *Generation X* (1991)
63   Bret Easton Ellis, *American Psycho* (1991)
64   Saki, *When William Came* (1913)
65   Theodor Fontane, *Delusions, Confusions* (1888)
66   Tom Wolfe, *The Bonfire of the Vanities* (1987)
67   Thomas Mann, *Buddenbrooks: The Decline of a Family* (1901)
68   Gabriel García Márquez, *One Hundred Years of Solitude* (1967)
69   Ambrose Bierce, *Chickamauga* (1891)

Illness and mental illness

70   Charlotte Perkins Gillman, *The Yellow Wallpaper* (1892)
71   Thomas Mann, *The Magic Mountain* (1924)
72   Sylvia Plath, *The Bell Jar* (1963)
73   Maya Angelou, *I Know Why the Caged Bird Sings* (1969)

Marriage, personal life and community

74   Leo Tolstoy, *Anna Karenina* (1877)
75   Vladimir Nabokov, *Lolita* (1955)
76   Jane Austen, *Pride and Prejudice* (1813)
77   Virginia Woolf, *To the Lighthouse* (1927)
78   Alan Bennett, *Talking Heads* (1987)
79   Laurie Lee, *Cider with Rosie* (1959)
80   Lionel Shriver, *We Need to Talk about Kevin* (2003)
81   Zoe Heller, *Notes on a Scandal* (2003)
82   Tennessee Williams, *Collected Stories* (1928–81)
83   D. H. Lawrence, *Women in Love* (1920)
84   Daphne du Maurier, *Rebecca* (1938)
85   Hanif Kureshi, *Intimacy* (1998)

Narrative complexity in writing (see below: postmodern)

86   Marcel Proust, *Remembrance of Things Past* (1913–27)
87   Laurence Sterne, *The Life and Opinions of Tristam Shandy, Gentleman* (1760)
88   James Joyce, *Ulysses* (1920/22)
89   Mario Vargas Llosa, *Aunt Julia and the Scriptwriter* (1977)

Postmodern (see above)

90 Umberto Eco, *The Name of the Rose* (1980)
91 John Fowle, *The French Lieutenant's Woman* (1969)
92 Don DeLillo, *White Noise* (1985)
93 Cormac McCarthy, *The Road* (2006)
94 Italo Calvino, *If on a Winter's Night a Traveller* (1979)
95 Julio Cortázar, *Hopscotch* (1963)

Power

96 George Orwell, *Animal Farm* (1945)
97 Edmund Wilson, *To the Finland Station* (1940)
98 Gunter Grass, *The Tin Drum* (1959)
99 Isabel Allende, *Of Love and Shadows* (1987)
100 J. Coetzee, *Waiting for the Barbarians* (1980)
101 Heinrich Mann, *The Loyal Subject* (1919)

Racism

102 Harper Lee, *To Kill a Mockingbird* (1960)
103 Douglas Frederick, *Narrative of the Life of an American Slave* (1845)
104 Ralph Ellison, *Invisible Man* (1999)
105 James Baldwin, *Giovanni's Room* (1956)
106 Alice Walker, *The Color Purple* (1982)
107 Ernest J. Gaines, *The Autobiography of Miss Jane Pittman* (1971)

Social divisions

108 Elizabeth Gaskell, *North and South* (1855)
109 Robert Tressel, *The Ragged Trousered Philanthropists* (1914)
110 John Steinbeck, *The Grapes of Wrath* (1938)
111 George Orwell, *Down and Out in Paris and London* (1993)

Total institution experiences

112 Alexander Solzhenitsyn, *One Day in the Life of Ivan Denisovich* (1962)
113 Ken Kesey, *One Flew Over the Cuckoo's Nest* (1962)
114 Primo Levi, *If This is a Man* (1987)

Utopia/Dystopia

115 Aldous Huxley, *Brave New World* (1932)
116 George Orwell, *1984* (1949)
117 Anthony Burgess, *A Clockwork Orange* (1962)
118 Margaret Attwood, *The Handmaid's Tale* (1985)
119 Isaac Asimov, *Foundation Series* (1951–93)
120 Philip K. Dick, *The Man in the High Castle* (1962)
121 William Gibson, *Neuromancer* (1984)
122 Robert Silverberg, *Downward to the Earth* (1970)
123 Albert Camus, *The Fall* (1956)
124 Albert Camus, *The Stranger* (1941)

War

125 Robert Graves, *Good-bye to All That* (1929)
126 Pat Barker, *Regeneration* (1991)
127 Kurt Vonnegut, *Slaughterhouse-Five or, The Children's Crusade: A Duty-Dance With Death* (1969)

And a few more . . .

128 Benjamin Disraeli, *Sybil* (1845)
129 John Steinbeck, *Of Mice and Men* (1937)
130 Samuel Beckett, *Malone Dies* (1951)
131 Luigi Piranedello, *Six Characters in Search of an Author* (1925)
132 Salman Rushdie, *The Satanic Verses* (1988)
133 Toni Morrison, *Beloved* (1987)
134 Ian McEwan, *The Comfort of Strangers* (1981)
135 Albert Camus, *The Plague* (1947)
136 Lawrence Durrell, *The Alexandria Quartet* (1968)
137 Joseph Conrad, *Heart of Darkness* (1902)
138 W. Somerset Maugham, *Of Human Bondage* (1915)

Many of the above resources now have 'clickable' links from this book's website. Please visit www.pearsoned.co.uk/plummer/novels to access them.

3 ART AND SOCIOLOGY

www.pearsoned.co.uk/plummer/art

25 works or so of sociological interest

One picture is worth more than a thousand words
Ancient Chinese proverb

Below are listed the most prominent 'art works' in the book for you to consider.

- Pieter Brueghel the Younger, *The Battle between Carnival and Lent*, 1559, p. 2
- Michael Simpson, *World in Sky*, p. 32
- Leonardo da Vinci, *Vitruvian Man*, c. 1492, p. 60
- Chinese School, *Happy Together as One* (1963), p. 104
- Diego Rivera, *The Tribunal of the Inquisition*, p. 142
- Evelyn Williams, *Face to Face*, 1994, p. 174
- Lincoln Seligman, *Masked Ball*, p. 206
- Luigi Nono, *Abandoned*, p. 250
- Gerard Sekoto, *Yellow houses: a street in Sophiatown, South Africa*, 1940, p. 280
- William Hogarth's engraving *Gin Lane*, p. 316
- Ron Waddams, *We the Peoples . . .*, 1984, p. 346
- Lynn Randolph, *Cyborg*, 1989, p. 388
- Cathy Greenblat, *Felicitas, 99 years 364 days old, and Maria*, 2001, p. 426

Only connect

Studying society is greatly helped by the study of the great artists and contemporary ones.

Sociology is a social science, but it also has a very long and close relationship with the creative humanities – which include novels, drama, music, films and art. In this part of the book, we provide some resources for you to think even more widely about society. The ultimate task of the sociologist is to understand the ways in which a society works, and any means of doing this is helpful.

The book contains many images, some of which have been designated as great art and others of which are more like the photos you can take yourself. An interesting exercise now would be to read this book visually. Look back at each chapter, ignore the text, and just consider what the images tell you. Reading the visual – as well as the written – is very important. To help you in this task you could look at:

John Berger, *Ways of Seeing* (1972)
Howard S. Becker, *Telling about Sociology* (2007)
Austin Harrington, *Art and Social Theory* (2004)

- Pieter Breughel the Elder, *The Cripples*, p. 460
- Ford Madox Brown, *Work*, p. 494
- Soviet Art, Lenin addresses the workers to encourage them to support him, p. 536
- Prison artist, *Life in prison*, p. 580
- Carl Larsson, *My Loved Ones*, p. 622
- Aqa Mirak, *The Ascent of the Prophet Mohammed to Heaven*, sixteenth-century Persian manuscript, p. 658
- *Peter Wagner, Thomas 'Tim' Dyson, George Salmon, Jack Catlin and George Young, outside Lord's (1937)*, p. 690
- Edward Kienholz, *The State Hospital*, p. 722
- Max Ferguson, *News Vendor*, 1986, p. 760
- The double delix, p. 794
- Yann Arthus-Bertrand, *Aerial View of a Market in St Paul, Reunion*, p. 828
- *Terrified children flee down Route 1 near Trang Ban, South Vietnam, in June 1972*, p. 864
- R. B. Kitaj, *If Not, Not* (detail), p. 898
- Paul Gauguin, *Where do we come from? What are we? Where are we going?* (1897), p. 924

Questions and links for images in the book

Chapter 1

Q: Brueghel's painting is a world classic. Examine it closely. What issues of social life does it depict? Could you imagine what a contemporary version of this would look like?

See: www.artcyclopedia.com/artists/bruegel_the_younger_pieter.html

See also: http://wwar.com/masters/b/brueghel-pieter.html

Chapter 2

Q: Where are you in this image? What does the image say about you and your position in the world? What does it say about the billions of planet earth's population?

Chapter 3

Q: Leonardo Da Vinci (1452–1519) was one of the leading figures in Renaissance art. Why is this particular drawing so significant? Consider how you have seen it represented over and over again in the modern world. What does this suggest to you about studying social life?

See: www.artcyclopedia.com/artists/leonardo_da_vinci.html
www.willamette.edu/cla/exsci/info/history/vitruvian.htm
http://leonardodavinci.stanford.edu/submissions/clabaugh/history/leonardo.html

Chapter 4

Q: Look at this painting. What does it suggest to you about the nature of art under Chinese communist rule?

See: Chinese Art Portal: http://www.artzinechina.com/display.php?a=746
Chiu, M *Art and China's Revolution* 2008 Princeton University Press.

Chapter 5

Q: Rivera can be seen as a Marxist artist. Think how artists try to capture a sense of their own societies, often vast civilizations? Can you find parallels to Rivera's depiction of Mexico in the artists of other cultures around the world?

Look at: The Diego Rivera Virtual Web Museum: http://www.diegorivera.com/
See: Luis-Martin Lozano and Juan Coronel Rivera *Diego Rivera: The Complete Murals* (2008).

No amount of skillful invention can replace the essential element of imagination. If I could say it in words there would be no reason to paint.

Edward Hopper

Chapter 6

Q: Is this conformity or individuality?

See: www.evelynwilliams.com

Chapter 7

Q: What does the nature of the masked ball suggest about social life?

On Lincoln Seligman's work, see: www.lincolnseligman.co.uk.

Chapter 8

Q: How do we relate to images of the distant sufferer – here 'the abandoned'? How might art cultivate a disposition of care for and engagement with the sufferings of others?

See: Lilie Chouliaraki *The Specatorship of Suffering*. London: Sage, 2006.

Chapter 9

Q: Sekoto was a prominent artist in South Africa. Look at the websites and then consider how his art must have been shaped by his social situation. Do you think it is generally true that art is shaped by social situations? (And if so, might this also be true of sociology?)

http://wwar.com/masters/s/sekoto-gerard.html
www.art.co.za/gerardsekoto/default.htm
http://the-artists.org/artist/Gerard_Sekoto.html

Chapter 10

Q: William Hogarth's engravings are major social comments on life in eighteenth-century England, and his work is worth a study of its own for sociology. Examine this image carefully and look up a wide range of his work at:

http://exhibits.library.northwestern.edu/spec/hogarth/index.html and www.artchive.com/artchive/H/hogarth.html. The entry in Wikipedia is also helpful and locates this image.

Chapter 11

Q: What do you see here? The artist uses elements from the near and distant past to create a contemporary expression of spiritual and humanitarian concerns. Many of the works are reflections on living without conflict, and refer to the aims of the United Nations charter.

See his work online at: www.larrenart.org.uk.

Chapter 12

Q: This image is quite prominent in the world of cyber-art. What does it suggest to you about the human body and its transformation? What is the human being?

Lynn Randolph's work has been discussed by Donna Haraway, and debates and ideas on it can be found at her excellent site at: www.lynnrandolph.com.

Chapter 13

Q: What do you see as the advantages – and disadvantages – of using photography in sociology?

See: Alive with Alzheimer's (2002)
http://www.cathygreenblat.com/

Discussing photographs

Migrant Mother

This is an iconic image which comes from the Great Depression of the 1930s and was taken by Dorothea Lange (1895–1965). Sponsored by the Farm Security Administration, her photos are now universally known and much written about. Look at this photo and ask questions about it. There are a number of versions of it – it has been 'edited' or 'cropped' in different ways (sometimes with one child, sometimes with several). Much has been written about this photo, including comments from the Migrant Mother herself. For many years, her identity remained anonymous while the photo went on to become a symbol of the Great Depression. But in the late 1970s, Florence Owens Thompson wrote a letter to her local paper saying that she was the woman and she didn't like the image. Thompson stated:

> *I wish she hadn't taken my picture. I can't get a penny out of it. [Lange] didn't ask my name. She said she wouldn't sell the pictures. She said she'd send me a copy. She never did.*

Photography in social science raises many issues – and a lot of them are ethical and political.

See: Robert Hariman and John Louis Lucaites: *No Caption Needed: Iconic Photographs, Public Culture, and Liberal Democracy.* (University of Chicago, 2007) extracted on http://www.press.uchicago.edu/misc/chicago/316062.html

Linda Gordon: *Dorothea Lange: A life beyond limits illustrated.* W. W. Norton & Company (2009).

Source: Library of Congress, Prints & Photographs Division, FSA/OWI Collection, LC-USF34-9093C.

Chapter 14

Q: What does Breughel's *The Cripples* say to you? Little is known of the artist's politics or religion, so the exact nature of the moral is open to interpretation.

See Web Gallery of Art at: www.wga.hu/frames-e.html?/bio/b/breughel/pieter_e/index.html.

Chapter 15

Q: This painting shows a whole range of people from various social strata going about their daily tasks. How many kinds of work can you see in this painting, how are they organised, and does the painting have much to say about social class?

There is a lot about his life and art on the website: See www.european-artgallery.com/artist_page.cfm?painter=105 and www.manchestergalleries.org/the-collections/search-the-collection

Reading the visual: starting points

We need also to look at images by asking how they work in society – how to read the social image. Get into a questioning mode and pose some questions:

1 *Pragmatic and practical opening.* Look at the content and subject matter of the image – begin at the beginning and simply say what it is about. Pay no attention to fussy theories of hidden meanings and symbols – save those for later: start with the direct messages you get from it – what is the content of this picture? Describe what you see. Do not read about it – try to know nothing about it at all (which is often very hard) and approach it as simply, directly and raw as you can. Of course, this will immediately raise broader issues because it will become apparent that what you see and how you describe it will always involve some perception, selection and interpretaion.

2 *Locate it thematically – as a genre.* No image stands on its own. Usually all images can be connected in various ways to others. Thus images can typically be classified into such themes as portraits, still life, landscapes, historical, abstract, realist, humorous. They can also be classified by their themes – work, families, gender, war, class. Here sociological themes may become relevant. It may also be classified by history – when was this image produced and what point in history does it aim to represent? Think about how the image connects to others and ask questions that locate it within various traditions. It may be that later you will wish to think or read

around these themes – looking, for example, at the elderly in art (see Pat Thane's *The Long History of Old Age*) or suffering and pain in art (see Susan Sontag's *Regarding the Pain of Others*).

3 *Locate it formally.* We now move from what the picture is saying and become more interested in the ways – the manner – in which it is depicting something. The image is not real – it is an imaginative representation of something, and we need to ask why they present it this way and not some other way. Artists, for example, choose different ways to present their images – a Pollock is not a Rothko is not a Bacon. Look at the images in the book and you will soon see that they make their statements in different kinds of ways – they are different in their forms.

4 *Locate it semiotically.* See the image as system of signs, of signifers and signifieds. Here we ask questions less about content, or form, or genre – but about the communication of the meanings of the image. The meanings are not often obvious but hidden; and nor are they agreed upon by readers – they are usually ambiguous and open to argument. They are lodged in systems of communication and signs through which the meanings can be unravelled.

5 *Locate it culturally.* Think about the time and place in which the image was produced. How might images change with time and space – and how does this image reflect a time and space? Does it perform a political role? How might it have been interperted differently in the time it was made?

So:

- Describe the subject matter carefully.
- Locate it as a genre.
- Locate it formally and think about its formal properties.
- Look at it as a communications sign system? What is its meaning?
- Locate it culturally – what roles does it play in the wider society?

Chapter 16

Q: Soviet art rejected the trends of twentieth century art in much of the Western world. What might this image tell you about Soviet power?

See: www.marxists.org/archive/lenin/index.htm
www.aha.ru/~mausoleu/
www.stel.ru/museum/
http://azer.com/aiweb/categories/magazine/ai142_folder/142_articles/142_lenin_art.html

Chapter 17

Q: In summer 2007, the Institute of Contemporary Arts (ICA) in London organised a show of art by prisoners and others in confinement in Britain, including inmates at young offender institutions, high-security psychiatric hospitals, secure units and immigration removal centres, as well as people supervised by probation and youth offending teams. It included painting, sculpture, drawing, ceramics, textiles and other media. This chapter opens with an image from prisoner art (though not from this exhibition). Discuss the nature and role of prison art.

See: www.lsa.umich.edu/english/pcap and www.ica.org.uk/Insider%20Art+14012.twl

Chapter 18

Q: Carl Larsson is one of Sweden's most famous painters. Here the image of family life perhaps anticipates the homely style indicated these days in the furnishings of IKEA. What do you think? What is his image of family life about? How might it fit with the Diana Gittins' quote?

See his websites at: www.clg.se/ and www.carllarsson.se/

Chapter 19

Aqa Mirak was a sixteen-century Persian painter. Think how religious art is shaped by both history and culture.

For more on Islamic visual culture see www.islamic-art.org and www.metmuseum.org/toah/splash.htm

Chapter 20

Q: 'The camera never lies'. Trace the social history of this photo and show how the camera often lies.

Look online at the account of this photo: *see* Ian Jack: Five Boys: The Story of a Picture. *Intelligent Life. Spring 2010.* Downloadable at: http://moreintelligentlife.com/content/ian-jack/5-boys

Chapter 21

Q: Edward Kienholz (1927–94) was an American installation artist whose work was highly critical of aspects of modern life. What do you think he was trying to say here?

See: Robert L. Pincus, 'On a scale that competes with the world: The art of Edward and Nancy Kienholz' (1994).

Chapter 22

Q: Old media and new media? What does this image suggest?

Max Ferguson's work paints a vanishing world, mainly in New York City. See his website at http://maxferguson.com and also www.artnet.com/artist/155558/max-ferguson.html.

Chapter 23

Q: Discuss the idea that an image – a factory, a heart, a matrix, a hologram – can be used to raise ideas about the very nature of a society?

See: www.mkaku.com

Chapter 24

Q: Consider how 'society' can be analysed from the air in striking ways.

The aerial photographs of Yann Arthus-Bertrand are stunning. Look at his work on YouTube at: www.yannarthusbertrand.org, or his book *The Earth from the Air* (2004).

Chapter 25

Q: This is one of the most famous photographs of the twentieth century. Consider what it says to you? What is it all about? This photo won Nick Ut the Pulitzer Prize in 1972. Then look at the following websites:

www.famouspictures.org/mag/index.php?title=Vietnam_Napalm_Girl
http://tigger.uic.edu/~rjensen/vietnam.html
www.ibiblio.org/pub/academic/history/marshall/military/vietnam/short.history/chap_28.txt
www.mtholyoke.edu/acad/intrel/pentagon/pent1.html
www.pbs.org/battlefieldvietnam/history/index.html
www.lib.berkeley.edu/MRC/pacificaviet

Tate Modern

The Tate Modern on the South Bank Embankment, London is one of the world's leading art galleries. It helps for sociologists to regularly visit art galleries and sense the shifts in culture. *See*: http://www.tate.org.uk/modern/

Source: Pearson Education Ltd/Michael Duerinckx/Imagestate

Chapter 26

Q: This is one of Kitaj's strongest pictures and integrates modern catastrophes into a classical landscape, reminding us of Italian Renaissance paintings. He is known as a 'Pop Artist'. Is this postmodern? How and why?

See: www.artcyclopedia.com/artists/kitaj_rb.html
www.ibiblio.org/wm/paint/auth/kitaj
http://wn.elib.com/Bio/Artists/Kitaj.html
www.glyphs.com/art/kitaj

Twelve pathways into critical sociological thinking

Q: How might art and sociology help us think about better worlds and lives?

See: Paul Gaugin: The Complete Works Web Site
http://www.paul-gauguin.net/

Many of the above resources now have 'clickable' links from this book's website. Please visit www.pearsoned.co.uk/plummer/art to access them.

4 TIME AND SPACE

www.pearsoned.co.uk/plummer/time

Part of the argument of sociology is that all social understanding is bound up with particular times and places – it is shaped by history and geography. Sociology always asks you, then, to consider the social origins of social things – to ask just how anything has developed. How did the media develop? How have wars developed? How has love making changed across different times and places? And it also asks you to be specific about which place you are talking about – the world is a big place. So keeping in mind the importance of time and space, the book has constantly located its arguments in history and different world cultures. Keep asking: which society, when?

On the World Wide Web, see
Space: Google Maps at http://maps.google.co.uk
Time: Google Timelines at http://timelines.ws

Timelines

Look at:

Mao Tse Tung (1893–1976)

From Confucianism to Communism to Capitalism.

In January 2011, the population of China was estimated at 1,337,798,957 – the world's largest country. For much of its history it was influenced by Confucianism, but in the twentieth century it became a major communist society. Mao Tse Tung was the leading communist revolutionary of this time. He was the architect of the People's Republic of China from its establishment in 1949, and held control over the nation until his death in 1976. He claimed he was a theoretical Marxist–Leninist, and his own position is known as Maoism. Since his death there has been a slow drift towards capitalism. By the end of the twenty-first century, many think China will be the world's leading economy: at present it is the second major one (See Chapters 4 and 26).

Gustav Mahler (1860–1911)

Mahler was a leading Austrian composer who bridged tradition and modernism in his music. He became one of the most frequently performed and recorded of all composers. The links between music and society are explored a little in the Interlude of Part Two.

Queen Victoria (1819–1901)

Queen Victoria was the monarch of the U.K. from 1837 until her death in 1901. Sociology was born and shaped in this Victorian England.

On reading maps

Maps of:

Many of the above resources now have 'clickable' links from this book's website. Please visit www.pearsoned.co.uk/plummer/time to access them.

How to lie with maps

A good map tells a multitude of little white lies

(Monmonier, 1996: p. 25)

Throughout this book you will encounter many maps. But just like statistics, they never tell obvious and simple truths and need to be critically scrutinised. All maps distort reality. A complex changing three dimensional world is simplified for a particular purpose. The same phenomena can always – and often is – mapped differently. Always consider:

1   Maps are systems of signs – they reduce complex realities into a code. What are the features of this code? Its symbols and their meanings?
2   Maps are representations – ways of projecting reality. How do they relate to scale? What's being exaggerated? What's being suppressed?
3   What's been omitted? Every map is a small selection of what could be told – so what's missing?
4   What interests might it serve? Maps are made to look like they are 'natural' and the author of the map disappears. But maps are made by people with purposes in mind and usually are shaped by certain interests, world views and assumptions. Maps are made for purposes. So ponder why they were made and what interests work at work.

Increasingly, online maps are interactive. You can watch the process of making maps – and indeed assemble them yourselves.

See:

Mark Monmonier *How to Lie with Maps* (1996 2nd ed)
Dennis Wood *The Power of Maps* (1992)

5 WEBSITE LINKS

www.pearsoned.co.uk/plummer/websites

Look back to Chapter 1, the *Big debate* and the websites at the chapter end. Here you will find a discussion of how to use websites critically, and also a listing of a number of key websites. At the end of each chapter, you will find more suggested websites for each topic in the book. You will also find websites sprinkled around in each chapter.

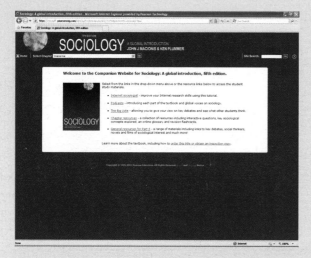

tip If you have not yet come to terms with surfing and evaluating items on the internet, a good introduction for sociological thinking is the online tutorial (which will take about half an hour). See: **the Internet Sociologist at: http://www.vts.intute.ac.uk/he/tutorial/sociologist**

Basic Sociology Websites include:
Sociolog http://www.sociolog.com/
Sociosite http://www.sociosite.net/index.php
Socioweb http://www.socioweb.com/

Below is a listing of selective sites organised by key theme. They have been selected because they appear to be a reliable and established resource, but they are only starting points for your researches.

AIDS
UNAIDS
http://unaids.org

AVERT
www.avert.org

Attitudes and values
Global Voice of the People
www.voice-of-the-people.net

World Values Survey
www.worldvaluessurvey.org

British Social Attitudes
www.britsocat.com/Body.aspx?control=HomePage

European Social Survey
www.europeansocialsurvey.org
http://ec.europa.eu/public_opinion/standard_en.htm

Bourdieu
HyperBourdieu© WorldCatalogue
http://hyperbourdieu.jku.at

An online bibliography of comments and elaborations of Bourdieu's work
http://web.archive.org/web/20080302205941/
http://www.massey.ac.nz/~nzsrda/bourdieu/byauthgr.htm

Capitalism
A short history of capitalism and its origins in European Enlightenment
www.wsu.edu/~dee/GLOSSARY/CAPITAL.HTM

What is Capitalism? at World Socialist Movement
www.worldsocialism.org/articles/what_is_capitalism.php

Children
UNICEF – The State of the World's Children
www.unicef.org/publications/index.html

Human Rights Watch: Children's Rights
www.hrw.org/campaigns/crp/index.htm

Cities
The State of the World's Cities
http://ww2.unhabitat.org/istanbul+5/statereport.htm

Citizenship
Citizenship Foundation
www.citizenshipfoundation.org.uk

Class
Working Class Movement Library
www.wcml.org.uk

History of the World's Working Class (The)
www.hartford-hwp.com/archives/26/index.html

Climate change (see also Environment)
DEFRA
www.defra.gov.uk/environment/

UN Climate Change website
www.un.org/climatechange
http://unfccc.int/essential_background/feeling_the_heat/items/2907.php
www.unep.org/themes/climatechange

Colonialism
Political Discourse: Theories of Colonialism and Postcolonialism
www.postcolonialweb.org/poldiscourse/discourseov.html

Crime and criminology
(see the webliography in Carrabine et al. 2009)
UK Criminal Statistics
www.homeoffice.gov.uk/rds/crime

United Nations Office of Drugs and Crime (UNODC)
www.unodc.org

Crime Theory
www.crimetheory.com

Paul's Crime Page: Reiman's *The Poor Get Prison*
http://www.paulsjusticepage.com/RichGetRicher/
summary2.htm

The World Factbook of Criminal Justice Systems
http://bjs.ojp.usdoj.gov/content/pub/html/wfcj.cfm
provides narrative descriptions of the criminal justice
systems of 45 countries around the world.

European Justice Forum
http://europeanjusticeforum.org

UN Centre for International Crime Prevention (CICP)
http://www.uncjin.org/CICP/cicp.html

Critical theory
Illuminations: the critical theory website
www.gseis.ucla.edu/faculty/kellner/Illumina%20Folder

Introductory Guide to Critical Theory
www.cla.purdue.edu/academic/engl/theory/index.html

Critical Theory Collective
www.critical-theory-collective.org

Critical thinking
Center for Critical Thinking
www.criticalthinking.org

UK A-Level Critical Thinking
www.criticalthinking.org.uk

Culture
Cultural studies and critical theory on EServer.org
http://theory.eserver.org

Cultural Studies Central
www.culturalstudies.net

Cyberspace
Resource Center for Cyberculture Studies
http://rccs.usfca.edu

A sociological tour through cyberspace, at Trinity University
www.trinity.edu/~mkearl

Death and dying
Archives of death-soccon@jiscmail.ac.uk
www.jiscmail.ac.uk/lists/death-soccon.html

Death studies
www.tandf.co.uk/journals/titles/07481187.asp

Sociology of death and dying
www.trinity.edu/MKEARL/death.html

Disability
Disability Alliance
www.disabilityalliance.org

Disability World
www.disabilityworld.org/links/International_Organizations

Drugs
United Nations Office of Drugs and Crime
www.unodc.org

Drug Alliance
www.drugpolicy.org/global

Drugs information at the UK Home Office
www.homeoffice.gov.uk/drugs

Release
www.release.org.uk

Drugscope
www.drugscope.org.uk

Durkheim
Durkheim
www.emile-durkheim.com

Emile Durkheim's sociology
www.faculty.rsu.edu/~felwell/Theorists/Durkheim/index.htm

Emile Durkheim Archive, The
http://durkheim.itgo.com

Economy
Statistics on work patterns, unemployment, consumption
and the economy generally can be found in sources already
mentioned: search under
Social Trends (UK)
Eurostats (Europe)
World Bank Fact Book (World)

United Nations Conference on Trade and Development
(UNCTAD)
www.unctad.org

International Labor Organization
www.ilo.org

New Economic Foundation (NEF)
www.neweconomics.org

OECD and the Information Economy
www.oecd.org/topic/0,2686,en_2649_
37413_1_1_1_1_37413,00.html

International Monetary Fund
www.imf.org

The New Economics Foundation (NEF)
www.neweconomics.org/about

Institute for Economic Affairs
www.iea.org.uk

The Work Foundation
theworkfoundation.com

Trades Union Congress
www.tuc.org
Information on unions in the UK.

Fortune Magazine
www.fortune.com

Cultivating a critical cyber attitude

As sociologists come to use websites more and more for their basic materials, they can come up with a huge amount of 'dross': websites, youtubes and twitters that are unreliable and even useless for the purposes of accurate information and ideas. Anybody can make a website after all, and what is to stop people putting large amounts of mis/disinformation on the site – either deliberately or out of ignorance? The sociologist has to routinely be able to assess the accuracy of different websites. It is part of their mundane work. They need a critical cyber-attitude. Here are the five C's to remember: credibility, comparison, contexts, changes and critique. Look at your web data in the light of these five criteria.

1 **Credibility**: look at the credentials of the site – consider who has written it and why? What is their agenda? Does the site give information about the author of the page and can you trust them? The most reliable sites are probably those of high-profile organisations, such as the United Nations or Amnesty International, or those of organisations such as universities. But even so, these will always have agendas. The least reliable are likely to be those of individuals, although there are plenty of dedicated individuals out there who simply want to bring all the work of Marx or Mead into a public forum. Think of the agenda behind the site.

2 **Comparison**: look at a range of websites in the area that interests you, not just one, and so get a feel for the different qualities, the common links and the central themes which appear across them. Compare and contrast: this will help you develop an independent and critical way of thinking, and help you check the sources of arguments or claims.

3 **Contexts**: put your cyberdata into broader perspective so that you can make sense of it. For example, think about its historical situation (where does this data sit on a timeline?), geography (which country is this from?), theory (how does it link to the theories you are studying?) and method (what is the validity, reliability and representativeness of this data?)

4 **Changes**: look at when the site was established and when it was last changed. Websites do indeed go out of date very quickly. Consider when the web page was assembled, and especially the page you are using. Good websites will show a date, and are kept up to date. If you have a very old date, it may be worth searching further to find a more recent update of the site. Check the refresh button.

5 **Critique**: always relate your cyberdata to wider frameworks for understanding. Never take anything as obvious evidence or truth simply because you find it in cyberspace. Beware and be critical!

The Economist
www.economist.com/index.html

Interbrand
www.interbrand.com/books_papers.asp

Naomi Klein
www.naomiklein.org/main

Paul Krugman
http://krugman.blogs.nytimes.com

World Bank
www.worldbank.org

Education
Education at the OECD
www.oecd.org/topic/0,3373,en_2649_
37455_1_1_1_1_37455,00.html

UNESCO IBE Database: information on almost every education system in the world
http://nt5.scbbs.com/cgi-bin/om_isapi.dll?clientID =
139318720&infobase=iwde.nfo&softpage=PL_frame
http://stats.uis.unesco.org/unesco/ReportFolders/
ReportFolders.aspx?CS_referer=&CS_ChosenLang=en

World education
www.worlded.org

Elderly
British Society of Gerontology
www.britishgerontology.org

UN Programme on Ageing: Towards a Society for All Ages
www.un.org/esa/socdev/ageing

The National Council on Ageing
www.ace.org.uk

The Centre for Policy on Ageing
www.cpa.org.uk

Emotion
Centre for Research into Emotion Work (CREW)
www.brunel.ac.uk/about/acad/bbs/research/centres/crew

Emotion at the Stanford Encyclopedia of Philosophy
http://plato.stanford.edu/entries/emotion

Enlightenment
British Enlightenment Research Network
www.utas.edu.au/history_classics/bern

A comprehensive history sourcebook for the Enlightenment
at Fordham University
www.fordham.edu/halsall/mod/modsbook10.html

A detailed website on the history of the European
Enlightenment, at Washington State University
www.wsu.edu/~dee/ENLIGHT/ENLIGHT.HTM

Environment
United Nations Environment Project
www.unep.org

Intergovernmental Panel on Climate Change
www.ipcc.ch

Worldwatch
www.worldwatch.org

Earth Trends
http://earthtrends.wri.org

Greenpeace
www.greenpeace.org/international

World Environmental websites
www.apec-vc.or.jp
www.worldwatch.org

People and Planet
www.peopleandplanet.net

Encyclopedia of Earth
www.eoearth.org

Environmental Knowledge and Change:
Maps and Graphics Library
http://maps.grida.no

Ethnicity
Race and Ethnicity Online
www.apsanet.org/~rep

Poverty and ethnicity in the UK
www.jrf.org.uk/knowledge/findings/socialpolicy/2059.asp

Focus on Ethnicity and Identity
www.statistics.gov.uk/focuson/ethnicity

Ethnography
ethnography.com
www.ethnography.com

An introduction to visual ethnography
www.youtube.com/watch?v=gD-Pjzz7LfU

Digital ethnography at Kansas State University
http://mediatedcultures.net/ksudigg

American ethnography
www.americanethnography.com

Ethnomethodology
International Institute for Ethnomethodology and
Conversation Analysis
www.iiemca.org

Ethnomethodology and Conversation Analysis
www.paultenhave.nl/EMCA.htm

Europe
EUROPA – Gateway to the European Union
http://europa.eu/index_en.htm

EUROSTAT
http://epp.eurostat.ec.europa.eu/portal/page?_pageid=
1090,30070682,1090_33076576&_dad=portal&_
schema=PORTAL

The annual yearbook of European Statistics can be accessed at:
http://epp.eurostat.ec.europa.eu/portal/page/portal/
publications/eurostat_yearbook

Family
United Nations Family Development
www.un.org/esa/socdev/family

Single parents
http://singleparents.about.com

Gay and lesbian couples
http://buddybuddy.com/partners.html

Morgan Centre for the study of relationships and personal
life (Manchester)
www.socialsciences.manchester.ac.uk/morgancentre

Families and Social Capital (Southbank)
http://www1.lsbu.ac.uk/families

Centre for Family Research (Cambridge)
www.ppsis.cam.ac.uk/CFR

Families, Life Course and Generations (FLaG) Research
Centre (Leeds)
www.sociology.leeds.ac.uk/flag/about

Feminism
Feminist Majority Foundation Online
www.feminist.org

Institute for Global Communication
www.igc.org/index.html

Feminism and Women's Studies
http://feminism.eserver.org/index.html

Feminism news archive at The Guardian
www.guardian.co.uk/world/feminism

Feminism at the Stanford Encyclopedia of Philosophy
http://plato.stanford.edu/entries/feminism-topics

Feminist theory
CultureCat
http://culturecat.net

Feminism and Women's Studies
http://feminism.eserver.org/index.html

Feminist Theory website
www.cddc.vt.edu/feminism

Food
Association for the Study of Food and Society (ASFS)
http://food-culture.org

International Commission on the Anthropology of Food (ICAF)
http://erl.orn.mpg.de/~icaf

Foucault
The world of Michel Foucault
www.csun.edu/~hfspc002/foucault.home.html

michel-foucault.com
www.michel-foucault.com

foucault.info
http://foucault.info

Freud
Sigmund Freud – life and work
www.freudfile.org

Sigmund Freud
http://users.rcn.com/brill/freudarc.html

Geertz
Video interview with Clifford Geertz
www.alanmacfarlane.com/ancestors/geertz.htm

Big Ideas: Clifford Geertz
www.thirteen.org/bigideas/geertz.html

HyperGeertz
www.iwp.uni-linz.ac.at/lxe/sektktf/GG/geertzstart.html

Gender
WomenWatch
www.un.org/womenwatch

GenderStats: database of gender statistics
http://devdata.worldbank.org/genderstats/home.asp

Gender Institute at the London School of Economics and Political Science
www.lse.ac.uk/collections/genderInstitute

International Gender Studies Centre at the University of Oxford
http://users.ox.ac.uk/~cccrw

Giddens
www.theory.org.uk/giddens.htm
www.faculty.rsu.edu/~felwell/Theorists/Giddens/index.htm

Globalisation
Forces of globalisation
www.humanities.uci.edu/critical/Projects.html#forces/Events/Forces.html

International Forum on Globalization (IFG)
www.ifg.org

World Bank: Globalization
www.worldbank.org/globalization

World Commission on the Social Dimensions of Globalization
www.ilo.org/public/english/wcsdg

The Globalization website
www.sociology.emory.edu/globalization

Globalization 101.org: a student's guide to globalization
www.globalization101.org

Health
World Health Organization
www.who.int/en

US National Center for Health Statistics
www.cdc.gov/nchs

UNECE Health Statistics (Europe)
www.unece.org/stats/links.htm

WHO European Observatory on Health Systems and Policies
www.euro.who.int/en/home/projects/observatory

UK Department of Health
www.dh.gov.uk/Home/fs/en

History
Royal Historical Society
www.rhs.ac.uk

Holocaust
Yad Vashem
www.yadvashem.org

Human development and capabilities
Human Development Report (and Index)
http://hdr.undp.org/hdr2007/statistics

Human Development and Capability Association
www.capabilityapproach.com/index.php

See also: *Journal of Human Development and Capabilities: A Multi-Disciplinary Journal for People-Centered Development*

Human reproduction
International Planned Parenthood Federation
www.ippf.org/en

Human Fertilisation and Embryology Authority
www.hfea.gov.uk

World Health Organization
www.who.int/reproductivehealth/en

Human rights
Human Rights Watch
www.hrw.org

Amnesty International
www.amnesty.org

Liberty
www.liberty-human-rights.org.uk

Women's human rights
www.hrw.org/women

International Gay and Lesbian Human Rights Commission
www.iglhrc.org/site/iglhrc

Hunger
World Food Programme
www.wfp.org

Identity
www.theory.org.uk

Indigenous peoples
Native Web
www.nativeweb.com/resources

Indigenous People: Issues and resources
http://indigenouspeoplesissues.com

Indigenous People: Literature
www.indigenouspeople.net/sidemenu.html

Survival International
www.survivalinternational.org

UN Permanent Forum on Indigenous Issues
www.un.org/esa/socdev/unpfii

Inequality
Global Policy Forum on Inequality
www.globalpolicy.org/social-and-economic-policy/
global-injustice-and-inequality.html

The Equality Trust (mainly UK)
www.equalitytrust.org.uk/about

Working group on extreme inequality (mainly US)
http://extremeinequality.org

Focus on the Global South
www.focusweb.org

Life Chances and Social Mobility: An Overview of the
Evidence
www.jrf.org/publications/migration-and-social-mobility-life-
chances-britain%E2%80%99s-minority-ethnic-communities

Online Atlas of the Millennium Development Goals
http://devdata.worldbank.org/atlas-mdg

Islam/Muslims
Muslim Association of Britain
www.mabonline.net

Middle East Policy Council
www.mepc.org/main/main.asp

Tabsir: insight on Islam and the Middle East
www.tabsir.net

Languages
UNESCO: Atlas of the World's Languages in Danger
www.unesco.org/culture/languages-atlas

Ethnologue: languages of the world
www.ethnologue.com

Liberties
Freedom House
www.freedomhouse.org/template.cfm?page=1

Statewatch
www.statewatch.org

Liberty
www.liberty-human-rights.org.uk

Libraries
British Library
www.bl.uk/index.shtml

Library of Congress
www.loc.gov/index.html

Maps
Environmental Knowledge and Change: Maps and
Graphics Library
http://maps.grida.no

Marx
www.marxists.org
www.spartacus.schoolnet.co.uk/TUmarx.htm
http://plato.stanford.edu/entries/marx

George Herbert Mead
The Mead Project
www.brocku.ca/MeadProject

The Internet Encyclopedia of Philosophy
www.iep.utm.edu/m/mead.htm

Media
British TV history
www.tvhistory.btinternet.co.uk

British Audience Research Board
www.barb.co.uk

Internet resources on media studies
http://bubl.ac.uk/link/m/mediastudies.htm
www.spartacus.schoolnet.co.uk/REVmedia.htm

Freepress
www.freepress.net

Methodology
European Association of Methodology
www.eam-online.org

SocioSite: Research Methodology and Statistics
www.sociosite.net/topics/research.php#STAT

Migration
United Nations High Commissioner for Refugees
www.unhcr.ch

Global Commission for International Migration
www.gcim.org

Age-of-migration website for book by Castles and Miller
www.age-of-migration.com/uk/resources/weblinks.html

European Migration Center
www.emz-berlin.de/start/animation.htm

Links on issues of migration and refugees
www.forcedmigration.org

Modernity
Modernist cultures
www.js-modcult.bham.ac.uk

Cultural Logic: An Electronic Journal of Marxist Theory and Practice
http://clogic.eserver.org

Vienna café: the Viennese café and fin-de-siècle culture
www.rca.ac.uk/viennacafe

Music
International Federation of the Phonographic Industry
www.ifpi.org

MTV
www.mtv.com

Royal Philharmonic Orchestra
www.rpo.co.uk

BBC Music
www.bbc.co.uk/music

Neoliberalism
What is Neoliberalism? by Dag Einar Thorsen and Amund Lie of the University of Oslo
http://folk.uio.no/daget/What%20is%20Neo-Liberalism%20FINAL.pdf

On Neoliberalism: An Interview with David Harvey
http://mrzine.monthlyreview.org/2006/lilley190606.html

Oral history
Oral History Society
www.ohs.org.uk

Oral history at the BBC
www.bbc.co.uk/history/trail/htd_history/oral/recording_oral_hist_01.shtml

Oral history recordings at the British Library (recordings on a very wide variety of issues, such as the Holocaust, the history of jazz in Britain, and the common cold)
http://sounds.bl.uk/BrowseCategory.aspx?category=Oral-history

Politics
Political sources on the net
www.politicalresources.net

Freedom House
www.freedomhouse.org

Transparency International
www.transparency.org

Parties and Elections
www.parties-and-elections.de

UK Government and its cabinet
www.cabinetoffice.gov.uk

Open Democraccy
www.opendemocracy.net/about

Populations
United Nations Populations Statistics
http://esa.un.org/unpd/wpp2008/index.htm
www.un.org/popin/wdtrends

Population Reference Bureau
www.prb.org

UNFPA
www.unfpa.org

Positivism
Auguste Comte and Positivism
http://membres.lycos.fr/clotilde

Postmodern theory
Contemporary Philosophy, Critical Theory and Postmodern Thought
http://carbon.ucdenver.edu/~mryder/itc/postmodern.html

Everything Postmodern: a postmodern webguide since 1995
www.ebbflux.com/postmodern

Baudrillard on the Web
http://intermargins.net/intermargins/TCulturalWorkshop/academia/scholar%20and%20specialist/Baudrillard/Baudrillard%20on%20the%20Web.htm

Postmodern Culture
www.iath.virginia.edu/pmc

Kritikos: Journal of Postmodern Cultural Sound, Text and Image
http://intertheory.org/kritikos

Poverty
developmentdata.org
www.developmentdata.org

World Bank
www.worldbank.org

United Nations
www.undp.org/poverty

Global monitoring report
www.un.org/milleniumgoals

Oxfam
www.oxfam.org.uk

The Conference on Poverty
www.poverty.org

The Poverty Site
www.poverty.org.uk

Child Poverty Action Group
www.cpag.org.uk

Low Pay Commission
www.lowpay.gov.uk

Policylibrary.com
www.policylibrary.com

Charles Booth Online Archive
http://booth.lse.ac.uk

Power
Power Elite: excerpts from the book
www.thirdworldtraveler.com/Book_Excerpts/PowerElite.html

Global Power Barometer
http://blog.washingtonpost.com/postglobal/drg/index.html

Prisons
International Centre for Prison Studies
www.prisonstudies.org

Prison Reform Trust
www.prisonreformtrust.org.uk

Her Majesty's Prison Service
www.hmprisonservice.gov.uk

A Victorian Prison at the National Archives
www.nationalarchives.gov.uk/education/lesson24.htm

Queer studies
Queer Resources Directory
www.qrd.org

One national gay and lesbian archive
www.onearchives.org

International Gay and Lesbian Association
www.ilga.org/countries
www.queertheory.com
www.queersymposium.org

Racism
European Network Against Racism
www.enar-eu.org

European Union Agency for Fundamental Rights
http://fra.europa.eu/fraWebsite/home/home_en.htm

European Commission against Racism and Intolerance
www.coe.int/t/dghl/monitoring/ecri/default_en.asp

Institute of Race Relations
www.irr.org.uk

The Runnymede Trust
www.runnymedetrust.org

Refugees
Refugee Council
www.refugeecouncil.org.uk

Refugee Action
www.refugee-action.org.uk

UNHCR – the UN Refugee Agency
www.unhcr.org/cgi-bin/texis/vtx/home

Religions
Adherents.com
www.adherents.com

Centres for the Study of Religion
www.princeton.edu/~csrelig
http://berkleycenter.georgetown.edu

World Council of Churches
www.oikoumene.org

Islam at a glance
www.islam-guide.com

Jewish culture and history
www.igc.apc.org/ddickerson/judaica.html

Hinduism Today
http://www.himalayanacademy.com

Zen Buddhism
www.dharmanet.org

Humanism
www.iheu.org

Sociosite
www.sociosite.net/topics/religion.php

Research methods
Social Research Update
http://sru.soc.surrey.ac.uk

Computer-assisted qualitative data analysis
www.surrey.ac.uk/sociology/research/researchcentres/caqdas

Qualitative Page
www.qualitativeresearch.uga.edu/QualPage

Risk society
Risk at the Royal Statistical Society
http://membership.rss.org.uk/main.asp?page=0

Risk and Society Study Group at the British
Sociological Association
www.britsoc.co.uk/specialisms/RiskandSociety.htm

Science
Centre for the Study of Knowledge Expertise Science (KES)
www.cardiff.ac.uk/socsi/research/researchcentres/kes

British Society for the History of Science
www.bshs.org.uk

Sexuality
Program in Human Sexuality Studies, San Francisco
State University
http://hmsx.sfsu.edu/About%20Us/Mission.htm

Simmel
Detailed overview, extracts and essays on Simmel at
University of Chicago
http://ssr1.uchicago.edu/PRELIMS/Theory/simmel.html

A detailed biography and appreciation of Simmel
http://socio.ch/sim/bio.htm

Slavery
Anti-Slavery International
www.anti-slavery.org

Contemporary slavery links
www.brandeis.edu/projects/fse/Pages/
linkscontemporaryslavery.html

Social movements
List of social movements
http://en.wikipedia.org/wiki/List_of_social_movements

Living the Legacy: The Women's Rights Movement 1848–1998
www.legacy98.org/index.html

América Latina en Movimiento
www.alainet.org

Postcolonial and Postimperial Literature in English
www.postcolonialweb.org

International Women's Tribune Centre
www.iwtc.org/index2.html

Social policy
www.historyandpolicy.org

Sociology (general introductions)
Sociolog
www.sociolog.com

Sociosite
www.sociosite.net/index.php

Socioweb
www.socioweb.com

The Internet Sociologist
www.vts.intute.ac.uk/he/tutorial/sociologist

A sociological tour through cyberspace
www.trinity.edu/~mkearl

Sociology Professor
www.sociologyprofessor.com

Statistics and databases
Data on the Net
http://3stages.org/idata

Sociology (organisations)
American Sociological Association
www.asanet.org

British Sociological Association (BSA)
www.britsoc.co.uk

European Sociological Association
www.europeansociology.org

International Sociological Association
www.isa-sociology.org

Sociology theorists
Sociology Professor
www.sociologyprofessor.com

Sport
Official website of the Olympic Movement
www.olympic.org

British Association of Sport and Exercise Sciences
www.bases.org.uk

Statisticians (general)
Royal Statistical Society
www.rss.org.uk

Statistics (sources)
United Nations (World)
http://unstats.un.org/unsd/pubs/gesgrid.
asp?mysearch=pocketbook

CIA World Factbook
www.cia.gov/library/publications/the-world-factbook

Eurostat (Europe)
http://epp.eurostat.ec.europa.eu/

UK national statistics
www.statistics.gov.uk

New Internationalist World Guide
www.newint.org/themes/map/world-map.htm

Infoplease
www.infoplease.com/ipa/A0004372.html

Data on the Net
http://3stages.org/idata

Suicide
Centre for Suicide Research, Oxford
http://cebmh.warne.ox.ac.uk/csr/statistics.html

Samaritans
www.samaritans.org

Befrienders
www.befrienders.org

Symbolic interactionism
Society for the Study of Symbolic Interaction
www.espach.salford.ac.uk/sssi/index.php

Celebrating Erving Goffman
www.jstor.org/stable/2067438

Anselm Strauss
http://sbs.ucsf.edu/medsoc/anselmstrauss/index.html

Transgender
Transgenderzone
www.transgenderzone.com

Trans-health
http://trans-health.com

Values
World Values Survey
www.worldvaluessurvey.org

Eurobarometer
www.social-science-gesis.de/en/data_service/
eurobarometer/ceeb
http://ec.europa.eu/public_opinion/index_en.htm

British Social Attitudes
www.natcen.ac.uk

War
Stockholm International Peace Research Institute
www.sipri.org

Global war on terrorism: Strategic Studies Institute
publications
www.strategicstudiesinstitute.army.mil/global-war-on-terrorism

Department for War Studies, Kings College
www.kcl.ac.uk/schools/sspp/ws

Weber
Verstehen: Max Weber's Home Page
www.faculty.rsu.edu/~felwell/Theorists/Weber/Whome.htm

Weberian sociology of religion
www.ne.jp/asahi/moriyuki/abukuma

Welfare
E-library for Global Welfare
www.globalwelfarelibrary.org

Welfare Reform and Management of Societal Change
www.kent.ac.uk/wramsoc

Women
(see also Feminism, Gender)

Women and politics
www.ipu.org/wmn-e/web.htm

WomenWatch
www.un.org/womenwatch

Work
International Labour Organization
www.ilo.org

The Work Foundation
http://theworkfoundation.com

Trades Union Congress
www.tuc.org

World
CIA World Factbook
www.cia.gov/library/publications/the-world-factbook/
index.html

United Nations Development Programme
www.undp.org

New Internationalist
www.newint.org

Youth
Youth at the United Nations
www.un.org/esa/socdev/unyin/index.html

National Youth Agency
www.nya.org.uk

Many of the above resources now have 'clickable'
links from this book's website. Please visit
www.pearsoned.co.uk/plummer/websites
to access them.

6 YOUTUBE

In recent years, YouTube has transformed our visual worlds. Now, at one click, we can be transported into a ceaseless stream of images. The implications of this for sociological analysis have not yet been fully worked out, but that should not – will not – stop you using it for your research and presentations. So here is an opening list of suggestions you might like to search. They are linked to each chapter.

Two important matters to note

1   As with all website links, there is a large amount of dross and drivel and material of dubious quality on YouTube. Take care in what you use – see the discussion of how to do this in Chapter 1.

2   Unlike website URLs, YouTube addresses are currently far too unreliable for us to list them. Instead, what we provide are just a few key words for you to surf with. We know there is good stuff there, as we have checked. But you will have to decide what is good stuff and what is not. For example, if you search for *Marx* you will soon find a lot on Richard Marx, a popular singer of the 1980s; and Groucho Marx, a comic of the 1930s. But you will find much less on Karl Marx – who is of more relevance to sociology! Type in *Karl Marx*, and the search will be much more successful. Likewise, there are a growing number of 'student presentations' on the net: they can be very good (but they can also be dreadful). It is of interest to see what others are up to, but never leave your critical judgement behind.

Chapter 1

- Karl Marx
- Suicide
- Durkheim
- Enlightenment history
- Comte

Chapter 2

- Japan Global Hip Hop
- Postmodernism
- Herbert Spencer
- Max Weber
- Globalisation

Chapter 3

- Yanomami
- Balinese cockfighting
- Margaret Mead
- Social constructionism
- Positivism

Chapter 4

- Margaret Thatcher
- Aboriginals or hunter tribes or agricultural societies
- Fritz Lang or Metropolis
- World cities
- Global development

Chapter 5

- Cultural studies
- Youth culture
- Civilisation
- Muslim cultures
- World languages

Chapter 6

- Bureaucracy
- Milgram experiments
- McDonaldisation
- Network society
- Managerialism

Chapter 7

- Socialisation
- Behaviourism/behaviorism
- Feral children (Kaspar Hauser)
- Identity sociology
- Body sociology

Chapter 8

- Social exclusion
- (modern) Slavery
- Social class
- Ideology
- Race, class, gender

Chapter 9

- (global) Poverty
- World Bank
- Modernisation
- Dependency theory
- Women poverty

Chapter 10

- Gender, class
- Class Britain (or UK)
- Working classes
- Engels working class
- Social stratification

Chapter 11

- Racism (Britain)
- Migration/migrants (Britain)
- Diaspora communities

- Ethnic segregation
- Ethnicity gender

Chapter 12

- Gender New Guinea (one link, but very good)
- Transsexual
- Patriarchy
- Sex trafficking/tourism
- Feminism (suffragettes)

Chapter 13

- Child marriage
- Child soldiers
- Global ageing
- Alzheimer's
- Ageism

Chapter 14

- Stephen Hawking
- Disabilities UK
- Elephant man
- Global disabilities
- Disability movements

Chapter 15

- Industrial Revolution
- Information Revolution
- Global capitalism
- Global sweatshops
- Consumer society
- Unemployment

Chapter 16

- Governance
- World Trade Organization
- World Social Forum (As related to introductory example; not mentioned in chapter)
- Globalisation politics
- Social movements

Chapter 17

- Deviance
- Crime UK
- Globalisation crime
- Foucault
- Surveillance (society)

Chapter 18

- Kinship anthropology/sociology
- Families anthropology/sociology
- Single-parent families
- Gay lesbian families
- Families Mexico

Chapter 19

- Salman Rushdie
- Religion sociology/anthropology
- World religions
- Religion UK
- God delusion/atheism

Chapter 20

- Global education
- Global literacy
- Education gender
- Education ethnicity
- Bourdieu

A YouTube selection

Here are some YouTube clips worth looking at:
A dark if amusing starting point might be the song by Tom Lehrer:
Search: Tom Lehrer on Sociology
But then, maybe listen to a lecture by a contemporary exponent:

Anthony Giddens
There are a great many full length lectures of Anthony Giddens on YouTube who is featured in Chapter 16. He is a brilliant spontaneous lecturer who speaks usually without jargon and you can almost choose which topic you want to hear him speak on. Just search with Anthony Giddens as key term.

The Conversations with History at the Institute for International Studies
A series of hour long interviews with key figures in social thinking which includes:
Manuel Castells
Michael Mann
Jurgen Habermas
Martha Nussbaum
David Harvey
Naom Chomsky

Pierre Bourdieu
Sociology is a Martial Art – Pierre Bourdieu

Zygmunt Bauman
How to survive death

Look also at clips and trailers from films mentioned in the book. For example:
Modern Times – trailer
Rashamon – trailer
Metropolis – Restoration trailer (2010)
It's a Wonderful Life – Tribute (2008)
Groundhog Day – Trailer
The Tree of Wooden Clogs – Trailer

Chapter 21

- Female circumcision
- Global health
- Health poverty
- Health UK
- HIV/AIDS

Chapter 22

- Global media
- Print culture
- Cyberculture
- Semiology
- Media theory

Chapter 23

- Risk society
- Space travel
- Charles Darwin
- Genetically modified foods
- Cybercrime

Chapter 24

- Demography
- World population (growth)
- Modern city
- Mega-cities
- Urbanism

Chapter 25

- Global environment
- Environmental sociology
- Ozone layer
- Global warming
- Global water supply

Chapter 26

- Manuel Castells
- Ulrich Beck
- Martha Nussbaum
- Anthony Giddens
- Donna Haraway

Oscar Wilde (1854–1900)

Wilde was certainly not a sociologist. But the insights of many creative thinkers and artists need to be taken seriously in sociology. They help us imagine better worlds and lives. As Wilde said famously: '*A map of the world that does not include Utopia is not worth even glancing at, for it leaves out the one country at which Humanity is always landing*'. (From his *The Soul of Man Under Socialism*)

Mohandas Karamchand Gandhi (1869–1948)

India is the world's second most populous country – with nearly a sixth of the world's population (1.18 billion estimated in 2010). Ghandi was the formative leader in India's transition to the modern world. His defining philosophy was based on resistance to tyranny through non violence. This idea helped India gain independence and inspired movements for civil rights and freedom across the world. For Ghandi:

'*Poverty is the worst form of violence*'.

Richard Attenborough's *Gandhi* is an award winning 1982 biographical film.

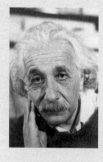

Albert Einstein (1879–1955)

'*Imagination is more important than knowledge*'.

Einstein was a major theoretical physicist who discovered the laws of relativity. But he was also a gifted and enthusiastic musician who once said that: 'Life without playing music is inconceivable for me . . . I live my daydreams in music. I see my life in terms of music . . . I get most joy in life out of music.' Most scientific thinking bridges the arts and the sciences. See Chapter 3.

7 THINKERS AND THEORY

www.pearsoned.co.uk/plummer/thinkers

One way of approaching sociology is via key social thinkers, and you have been introduced to a selection of these in this book. The table on p. 37 provides an opening set of images. If you would like to take this further, see:

Rob Stones, *Key Sociological Thinkers* (2nd edn, 2007)
John Scott, *Fifty Key Sociologists* (2006)

Here is a checklist of 36 thinkers for you to follow up on the web:

1 The Enlightenment and the Age of Reason, p. 14
2 Auguste Comte: The French Revolution and positivism, p. 16
3 C. Wright Mills: The sociological imagination, p. 21

Many of the above resources now have 'clickable' links from this book's website. Please visit www.pearsoned.co.uk/plummer/thinkers to access them.

8 WORLD STATISTICS

You can find a useful list of statistical sources in Chapter 9, p. 283. Here is a list of some key 'Top 10' boxes and other useful tables that you will find in the book; sources differ and are named with the list.

Countries, Country Fact Files and regions under examination
Note: all Country Fact Files are derived from: (a) United Nations Development Project: *Human Development Report 2010*; (b) *The Economist Pocket World in Figures*, 2011 Edition; (c) The World Bank; *The World Bank Data Bank of Development Indicators*, 2011 – see: http://data.worldbank.org/. Use the most recent versions of these for updates and also for examining other countries not considered in the text.

9 BIG DEBATES OF OUR TIME

www.pearsoned.co.uk/plummer/bigvote

See discussion materials in the end-of-chapter
Big debates

1 Debate Wikipedia and other digital tools for a digital generation, p. 29
2 The sociological puzzle: do we make social life or does social life make us? p. 59
3 Damned lies and statistics: so do statistics tell us the truth? p. 94
4 Progress: is society getting better or worse? p. 140
5 Whose culture is this? The problem of Eurocentrism, multiculturalism and postcolonialism in sociology, p. 172
6 Mobile phones and Facebook: what are they doing to our personal life? p. 205
7 Who am I?: Identity crisis in our time p. 239
8 Are the rich worth what they earn? p. 277
9 Will the world starve? p. 313
10 Why does poverty still exist in high income countries? p. 344
11 Dangerous extremists: Islamic fundamentalists or Islamophobes? p. 386
12 Does 'porn' degrade women? Gender, sexuality and the politics of pornography, p. 424
13 A sad or happy old age? What are the social implications of living longer? p. 458
14 Do the disabled have the right to a flourishing life? Bioethics and disability rights, p. 488
15 The crisis and the crash: will capitalism survive? p. 533
16 Are we moving beyond left and right? The politics of difference, p. 577
17 Is crime really decreasing – or increasing? p. 621
18 What is the future of the family? The family values debate, p. 656
19 Is religion in decline? The death of God or the triumph of religion? p. 689
20 Is education being dumbed down? The case of mass higher education, p. 719
21 When is the right time to die? The 'right to die' debate, p. 758
22 Are the media destroying social life? p. 791
23 The language of life: can the Human Genome Project solve our problems? p. 822
24 Apocalypse soon: Will people overwhelm the earth? p. 863
25 Is an environmental catastrophe now inevitable? What is to be done? Armageddon and the environment, p. 896
26 Putting it all together: is the future postmodern? p. 919

Many of the above resources now have 'clickable' links from this book's website. Please visit www.pearsoned.co.uk/plummer/bigvote to access them.

Now see the big vote

www.pearsoned.co.uk/plummer/bigvote

10 ABBREVIATIONS AND ACRONYMS

This is a list of abbreviations and acronyms, most of which are mentioned in this book. It is worth knowing as many of them as possible, as they inform you about what is going on in the world – once terms are abbreviated, the abbreviations often enter common use.

9/11	11 September 2001 terrorist attack on twin towers in New York
7/7	7 July 2005 London bombing
AIDS	acquired immune deficiency syndrome
ANC	African National Congress
ANT	Actor Network Theory
ART	anti-retroviral therapy
AOL	America Online
AS	assisted conception
ASBO	anti-social behaviour order (now defunct)
ASEAN	Association of South East Asian Nations
ASI	anti-slavery movement
BCS	*British Crime Survey*
BHPS	British Household Panel Study
BSE	bovine spongiform encephalopathy
CBS	Columbia Broadcasting System
CCTV	closed-circuit television
CEE	central-eastern European
CFC	chlorofluorocarbon

CIS	Commonwealth of Independent States	IVF	*in vitro* fertilisation
CJD	Creutzfeldt–Jakob disease	LGBTQ	Lesbian, gay, bisexual, transgender, queer
CND	Campaign for Nuclear Disarmament	MDG	Millennium Development Goal
CNN	Cable News Network	MTV	Music Television
CO_2	carbon dioxide	NAFTA	North American Free Trade Agreement
DALY	disability-adjusted life year	NATO	North Atlantic Treaty Organization
DIY	do-it-yourself	NBC	National Broadcasting Company
DNA	deoxyribonucleic acid	NGO	non-governmental organisation
DVD	digital video disc	NIC	newly industrialised country
DWP	Department of Work and Pension (UK)	NRM	new religious movement
ECHR	European Court of Human Rights	NRT	new reproductive technologies
EU	European Union	NSM	new social movement
FAO	Food and Agricultural Organization	OECD	Organization for Economic Cooperation and Development
G8	(formerly G7) The 'Group of Eight' advanced industrialised nations: Canada France, Germany, Italy, Japan, Russia, the UK and the USA	OPCS	Office of Population Census Survey
		OPEC	Organization of Petroleum-Exporting Countries
GATT	General Agreement on Tariffs and Trade	PIN	personal identification number
GBD	global burden of disease	PPC	purchasing power parity
GDI	Gender-related Development Index (a UN measurement)	QUANGO	Quasi-autonomous non-governmental organisation
GDP	gross domestic product	R&D	research and development
GLF	Gay Liberation Front	SARS	severe acute respiratory syndrome
GM	genetically modified	SD	sustainable development
GNP	gross national product	SEN	special educational needs
GSM	global social movement	SNG	Social network group
HBAI	households below average income	SNS	social network site
HDI	Human Development Index (a UN measurement)	SSA	sub-Saharan Africa
HFEA	Human Fertilisation and Embryology Authority	SSSI	Society for the Study of Symbolic Interaction
HIV	human immunodeficiency virus	TB	tuberculosis
HPI	Human Poverty Index	TNC	transnational corporation
ICT	information and communication technology	UN	United Nations
ICT4D	Information and Communication Technologies for Development	UNCED	United Nations Conference on Environment and Development
IDP	internally displaced person	UNCHR	United Nations Centre for Human Rights
IFPI	International Federation of the Phonographic Industry	UNDP	United Development Programme
		UNEP	United Nations Environment Programme
IGO	international governmental organisation	UNESCO	United Nations Educational, Scientific and Cultural Organization
ILO	International Labour Organization		
IMF	International Monetary Fund	UNHCR	United Nations High Commissioner for Refugees
IMR	infant mortality rate	UNICEF	United Nations International Children's Emergency Fund
INGO	international non-governmental organisation		
IOC	International Olympic Organization	UNPFA	United Nations Fund for Population Activities
IPCC	Intergovernmental Panel on Climate Change	URL	universal resource locator
IPEC	International Programme for the Elimination of Child Labour	USSR	Union of Soviet Socialist Republics
		VCR	video cassette recorder
IQ	intelligence quotient	WB	World Bank
ISCED	International Standard Classification of Education	WCED	World Commission on Environment and Development
ISDN	integrated services digital network	WFP	World Food Programme
IT	information technology	WHO	World Health Organization
ITU	international telecommunication union	WTO	World Trade Organization

GLOSSARY

These definitions aim at being succinct. For a further development of ideas, see also dictionaries and encyclopedias listed on p. 27.

A

absolute poverty a lack of resources that is life threatening (often measured as a per capita income equivalent to less than one/one and a half international dollars a day)

achieved status a social position that someone assumes voluntarily and that reflects personal ability and effort

acid rain precipitation that is made acidic by air pollution and destroys plant and animal life

action perspective a micro-theory that focuses on how actors assemble social meanings

activity theory a high level of activity enhances personal satisfaction in old age

actors people who construct social meanings

Afrocentrism the dominance of African cultural patterns

ageism prejudice and discrimination against the elderly

age–sex pyramid a graphical representation of the age and sex of a population

age stratification the unequal distribution of wealth, power and privileges among people at different stages in the life course

agriculture the technology of large-scale farming using, initially, ploughs harnessed to animals and later, more powerful sources of energy

alienation the experience of isolation resulting from powerlessness

animism the belief that elements of the natural world are conscious life forms that affect humanity

anomie lack of norms

anticipatory socialisation social learning directed towards gaining a desired position

anti-racism institutions, practices and theories which work to reduce the levels of racism in a society

ascribed status a social position that someone receives at birth or assumes involuntarily later in life

assimilation the process by which minorities gradually adopt patterns of the dominant culture

authoritarianism a political system that denies popular participation in government

authority power that people perceive as legitimate rather than coercive

B

behaviourism specific behaviour patterns are not instinctive but learned

beliefs specific statements that people hold to be true

Big Science a particularly strong sense of expertise and its dominance, one that is usually strongly backed by money, supported by governments and given a lot of symbolic prestige

bilateral descent a system tracing kinship through both men and women

biography a person's unique history of thinking, feeling and acting

blue-collar (or manual) occupations lower-prestige work involving mostly manual labour

body projects the process of becoming and transforming a biological entity through social action

bureaucracy an organisational model rationally designed to perform complex tasks efficiently

bureaucratic inertia the tendency of bureaucratic organisations to perpetuate themselves

bureaucratic ritualism a preoccupation with rules and regulations to the point of thwarting an organisation's goals

C

capabilities opportunities for human functioning

capitalism diverse economic systems which stress private ownership, profit, free markets and competition

caste system a system of social stratification based on inherited status or ascription

cause and effect a relationship in which change in one variable (the independent variable) causes change in another (the dependent variable)

census a count of everyone who lives in the country

charisma extraordinary personal qualities that can turn an audience into followers

charismatic authority power legitimised through extraordinary personal abilities that inspire devotion and obedience

church a type of religious organisation well integrated into the larger society

civilisations broadest, most comprehensive cultural entities

civil religion a quasi-religious loyalty binding individuals in a basically secular civil society

class conflict antagonism between entire classes over the distribution of wealth and power in society

class consciousness Marx's term for the recognition by workers of their unity as a social class in opposition to capitalists and to capitalism itself

class society a hierarchical, usually capitalist, society with pronounced social stratification and inequalities based on economic exploitation

class system a system of social stratification based on individual achievement

code rule – governed system of signs

cohabitation the sharing of a household by an unmarried couple

cohort a category of people with a common characteristic, usually their age

collective behaviour activity involving a large number of people, often spontaneous, and typically in violation of established norms

collectivity a large number of people whose minimal interaction occurs in the absence of well-defined and conventional norms

colonialism the process by which some nations enrich themselves through political and economic control of other countries

commodification aspects of life are turned into things – commodities for sale

communism an economic and political system in which all members of a society are socially equal

concept a mental construct that represents some part of the world, inevitably in a simplified form

conflict perspective a framework for building theory that envisages society as an arena of inequality that generates conflict and change

conglomerates giant corporations composed of many smaller corporations

control holding constant all relevant variables except one in order to observe its effect

conversational analysis a rigorous set of techniques to technically record and then analyse what happens in everyday speech

conversion a personal transformation or religious rebirth

corporation an organisation with a legal existence, including rights and liabilities, apart from those of its members

correlation a relationship by which two (or more) variables change together

cosmogony a tale about how the world/universe was created; a theodicy, a tale about how evil and suffering is to be found in the world

cosmopolitanism view that all people, despite their great differences, can share a common humanity

counterculture cultural patterns that strongly oppose those widely accepted within a society

credentialism evaluating a person on the basis of educational qualifications

crime the violation of norms that a society formally enacts into criminal law

crimes against property (property crimes) crimes that involve theft of property belonging to others

crimes against the person (violent crimes) crimes that direct violence or the threat of violence against others

criminal justice system institutional responses to alleged violations of the law (usually utilising police, courts and prison officials in bureaucratic processes)

criminal recidivism subsequent offences committed by people previously convicted of crimes

critical sociology all knowledge harbours political interests and the task of sociology is to critically unmask what is actually going on

crowd a temporary gathering of people who share a common focus of attention and whose members influence one another

crude birth rate the number of live births in a given year for every thousand people in a population

crude death rate the number of deaths in a given year for every thousand people in a population

cult a religious organisation that is substantially outside a society's cultural traditions

cultural capital a term often used to designate the practices where people can wield power and status because of their educational credentials, general cultural awareness and aesthetic preferences

cultural conflict political opposition, often accompanied by social hostility, rooted in different cultural values

cultural ecology a theoretical paradigm that explores the relationship of human culture and the physical environment

cultural hybridisation refers to the ways in which parts of one culture (language, practices, symbols) get recombined with the cultures of another

cultural integration the close relationship among various elements of a cultural system

cultural lag the fact that cultural elements change at different rates, which may disrupt a cultural system

cultural relativism the practice of judging a culture by its own standards

cultural reproduction the process by which a society transmits dominant knowledge from one generation to another

cultural transmission the process by which one generation passes culture to the next

cultural universals traits that are part of every known culture

culture the beliefs, values, behaviour and material objects that constitute a people's way of life

culture shock personal disorientation that comes from encountering an unfamiliar way of life

cyberclasses a stratification system based on the information 'haves' and 'have nots' linked to the rise in new information technologies

cybersociety society where information technologies become paramount

D

Davis–Moore thesis the assertion that social stratification is a universal pattern because it has beneficial consequences for the operation of a society

decentred a process by which a centre, core or essence is destabilised and weakened

decoding the process by which we hear or read and understand a message

decommodification the degree to which welfare services are free from the market

deductive logical thought reasoning that transforms general ideas into specific hypotheses suitable for scientific testing

degenerate war a deliberate and systematic extension of war against an organised armed enemy to a war against a largely unarmed civilian population

democide mass murders by governments

democracy a political system in which power is exercised by the people as a whole

democratic socialism an economic and political system that combines significant government control of the economy with free elections

demographic transition theory a thesis linking population patterns to a society's level of technological development

demography the study of human population

denomination a church, independent of the state, that accepts religious pluralism

dependency ratio the numbers of dependent children and retired persons relative to productive age groups

dependency theory a model of economic and social development that explains global inequality in terms of the historical exploitation of poor societies by rich ones

dependent variable a variable that is changed by another (independent) variable

descent the system by which members of a society trace kinship over generations

deterrence the attempt to discourage criminality through punishment

deviance the recognised violation of cultural norms

dialogic multiple voices in conversation, not a single voice or monologue

diaspora refers to the dispersal of a population from its 'homeland' into other areas

digitalisation social life becomes organised through new media technologies

direct-fee system a medical care system in which patients pay directly for the services of doctors and hospitals

disabilities the social side of impairments, usually involving discrimination of various kinds

disability-adjusted life years (DALY) measures the lost years of 'healthy' life by combining years of life lost through premature death with years lived with disability

discourses bodies of ideas and language often backed up by institutions

discrimination any action that involves treating various categories of people unequally

disengagement theory the proposition that society enhances its orderly operation by disengaging people from positions of responsibility as they reach old age

Disneyisation the process by which the principle of the Disney theme parks is coming to dominate more and more sectors of American society as well as the rest of the world

displaced peoples those who often find themselves homeless in their own land

division of labour specialised economic activity

documents of life research documents produced in the natural world by the subjects themselves, such as letters and diaries

dramaturgical analysis Erving Goffman's term for the investigation of social interaction in terms borrowed from theatrical performance

dyad a social group with two members

dysfunction *See* social dysfunction

E

ecclesia a church that is formally allied with the state

ecologically sustainable culture a way of life that meets the needs of the present generation without threatening the environmental legacy of future generations

ecology the study of the interaction of living organisms and the natural environment

economy the social institution that organises the production, distribution and consumption of goods and services

ecosystem the system composed of the interaction of all living organisms and their natural environment

education the social institution guiding the critical learning of knowledge, job skills, cultural norms and values

ego Freud's designation of a person's conscious efforts to balance innate, pleasure-seeking drives and the demands of society

electronic tagging a system of home confinement aimed at monitoring, controlling and modifying the behaviour of defendants or offenders

eliminationism *see* genocide

emotional labour the management of feeling to create a publicly observable facial and bodily display

empirical evidence information we can verify with our senses

encoding putting a message of any kind into a language

endogamy marriage between people of the same social category

environmental deficit the situation in which our relationship to the environment, while yielding short-term benefits, will have profound, long-term consequences

environmental racism the pattern by which environmental hazards are greatest in proximity to poor people, especially minorities

epistemic relativism knowledge is rooted in a particular time and culture

epistemology branch of philosophy that investigates the nature of knowledge and truth

essentialism the belief that qualities are inherent in (essential to) specific objects

estate a system based on a rigidly interlocking hierarchy of rights and obligations

ethical life, the how people should behave

ethnic antagonism hostilities between different ethnic groups

ethnic cleansing *See* genocide

ethnicity a shared historical and cultural heritage

ethnocentrism the practice of judging another culture by the standards of one's own culture

ethnography the description of ways of life – developed into a method for the social sciences as the tools of fieldwork to make sense of everyday life

ethnomethodology Harold Garfinkel's term for the study of the way people make sense of their everyday lives

Eurocentrism a view of the world which places Europe at the centre of its thinking

euthanasia (mercy killing) assisting in the death of a person suffering from an incurable disease

exogamy marriage between people of different social categories

experiment a research method for investigating cause and effect under highly controlled conditions

expressive leadership group leadership that emphasises collective well-being

extended family (consanguine family) a family unit including parents and children, but also other kin

F

fad an unconventional social pattern that people embrace briefly but enthusiastically

faith belief anchored in conviction rather than scientific evidence

false consciousness Marx's term for explanations of social problems grounded in the shortcomings of individuals rather than the flaws of society

family a social institution, found in all societies, that unites individuals into cooperative groups that oversee the bearing and raising of children

family of choice people with or without legal or blood ties who feel they belong together and wish to define themselves as a family

family unit a social group of two or more people, related by blood, marriage or adoption, who usually live together

family violence emotional, physical or sexual abuse of one family member by another

fashion a social pattern favoured for a time by a large number of people

feminisation of poverty the trend by which women represent an increasing proportion of the poor

feminism the advocacy of social equality for the sexes, in opposition to patriarchy and sexism

fertility the incidence of child-bearing in a country's population

flâneur a social type who wanders cities, enjoying the sights and the crowd

folkways a society's customs for routine, casual interaction

Fordism an economic system based on mass assembly-line production, mass consumption and standardised commodities

formal organisation a large, secondary group that is organised to achieve its goals efficiently

formal sociology studies social forms and developed in work of Simmel

fourth age an age of eventual dependence

functional illiteracy reading and writing skills insufficient for everyday living

functional paradigm a framework for building theory that envisages society as a complex system whose parts work together to promote solidarity and stability

fundamentalism a conservative religious doctrine that opposes intellectualism and worldly accommodation in favour of restoring a traditional, otherworldly and absolutist spirituality

G

Gaia hypothesis planet earth itself should be seen as a living organism

Gemeinschaft Toennies' term for a type of social organisation by which people have strong social ties and weak self-interest

gender the social aspects of differences and hierarchies between female and male

gender gap measure of level of inequality between men and women

gender gap index (GGI) a measure of the levels of inequality between men and women in access to resources

gender identity the subjective state in which someone comes to say 'I am a man' or 'I am a woman'

gender order the ways in which societies shape notions of masculinities and femininities through power relations

gender performance refers to ways of 'doing gender', the ways in which masculinities and femininities are acted out

gender regime the gender order as it works through in smaller settings

gender role refers to learning and performing the socially accepted characteristics for a given sex

gender stratification a society's unequal distribution of wealth, power and privilege between the two sexes

gender violence all those practices of domestic and sexual violence directed at maintaining gender hierarchies and punishing femininities

generalised other George Herbert Mead's label for widespread cultural norms and values that we use as references in evaluating ourselves

genocide the systematic annihilation of one category of people by another

genre a species or type of media programme

gerontocracy a form of social organisation in which the elderly have the most wealth, power and prestige

gerontology the study of ageing and the elderly

Gesellschaft Toennies' term for a type of social organisation by which people have weak social ties and considerable self-interest

Gini coefficient widely used and major statistical measure to compare and analyse social inequalities

global burden of disease a comprehensive measure of mortality and loss of health due to diseases for all regions of the world

global commons resources shared by all members of the international community, such as ocean beds and the atmosphere

global economy economic activity spanning many nations of the world with little regard for national borders

globalisation the increasing interconnectedness of societies

global perspective the study of the larger world and our society's place in it

glocalisation process by which local communities respond differently to global changes

governance the exercise of political, economic and administrative authority in the management of a country's affairs at all levels

government formal organisations that direct the political life of a society

greenhouse effect a rise in the earth's average temperature (global warming) due to increasing concentration of carbon dioxide in the atmosphere

gross domestic product (GDP) all the goods and services on record as produced by a country's economy in a given year

gross national product (GNP) all a country's goods and services, as for GDP, with the addition of foreign earnings

groupthink the tendency of group members to conform by adopting a narrow view of some issue

H

habitus the habits that we acquire in social life and carry around with us – they are 'durable dispositions through which people live in the world'; an idea developed by Bourdieu

hate crime a criminal act against a person or a person's property by an offender motivated by racial or other bias

Hawthorne effect a change in a subject's behaviour caused simply by the awareness of being studied

health a state of complete physical, mental and social well-being

healthcare any activity intended to improve health

health maintenance organisation (HMO) an organisation that provides comprehensive medical care to subscribers for a fixed fee

hegemonic masculinity the dominant or main ways of being a man in a society

hegemony the means by which a ruling/dominant group wins over a subordinate group through ideas

hermaphrodite a human being with some combination of female and male internal and external genitalia

hermeneutics studies which focus on the processes through which the world is interpreted and understood

heteronormative privileging heterosexual relations

heterosexism ideas organised around sexism and heterosexuality as dominant forms of sexual relations

hidden curriculum subtle presentations of political or cultural ideas in the classroom

high culture cultural patterns that distinguish a society's elite

high-income countries the nations with highest overall standard of living

holistic medicine an approach to healthcare that emphasises prevention of illness and takes account of a person's entire physical and social environment

homogamy marriage between people with the same social characteristics

homophobia the dread of being in close quarters with homosexuals

horticulture technology based on using hand tools to cultivate plants

humanising bureaucracy fostering a more democratic organisational atmosphere that recognises and encourages the contributions of everyone

humanism stance that takes the human subjects seriously and is concerned with their meanings

hunting and gathering simple technology for hunting animals and gathering vegetation

hybridisation ways in which forms of social life become diversified as they separate from old practices and recombine into new ones: a 'global mélange'

hypothesis an unverified statement of a relationship between variables

I

id Freud's designation of the human being's basic drives

ideal culture (as opposed to real culture) social patterns mandated by cultural values and norms

ideal type Weber's term for an abstract statement of the essential characteristics of any social phenomenon

ideal types an abstract statement of the essential, though often exaggerated, characteristics of any social phenomenon

identity *See* social identity

ideological state apparatuses social institutions that reproduce the dominant ideology, independent of the state

ideology cultural beliefs that serve to legitimate key interests and hence justify social stratification

imagined community mental images that suggest an affinity between people

impairment lives becoming biologically incapacitated

incest taboo a cultural norm forbidding sexual relations or marriage between certain kin

income occupational wages or salaries and earnings from investments

independent variable a variable that causes change in another (dependent) variable

indigenous peoples peoples with ties to the land, water and wildlife of their ancestral domain

individualisation process that gives more importance to the choices we can make about the personal life we wish to have

inductive logical thought reasoning that transforms specific observations into general theory

industrialism technology that powers sophisticated machinery with advanced sources of energy

industrial reserve army a disadvantaged section of labour that can be supplied cheaply when there is a sudden extra demand

infant mortality rate the number of deaths among infants under one year of age for each thousand live births in a given year

information society a society based on new information technologies

ingroup a social group commanding a member's esteem and loyalty

in-migration rate, calculated as the number of people entering an area for every thousand people in the population

institutional prejudice or discrimination bias in attitudes or action inherent in the operation of society's institutions

institutions established social routines and habits

instrumental leadership group leadership that emphasises the completion of tasks

interaction order what we do in the immediate presence of others

intergenerational social mobility upward or downward social mobility of children in relation to their parents

interpretive sociology focuses on meanings, understandings and subjectivities

intersectionality ways in which different forms of inequality and division interact with each other

interview a series of questions that a researcher administers personally to respondents

intragenerational social mobility a change in social position occurring during a person's lifetime

'Islamophobia' a hatred of all things Muslim

J

juvenile delinquency the violation of legal standards by the young

K

kinship a social bond, based on blood, marriage or adoption, that joins individuals into families

L

labelling theory examines nature, causes and impacts of deviant labels. Deviance and conformity result not so much from what people do as from how others respond to those actions; it highlights social responses to crime and deviance

language a system of symbols that allows members of a society to communicate with one another

latent functions consequences of any social pattern that are unrecognised and unintended

liberation theology a fusion of Christian principles with political activism, often Marxist in character

libertarianism takes individual freedom as the prime value

life expectancy the average age to which people in a given society are likely to live

linguistic determinism language shapes the way we think

linguistic relativism distinctions found in one language are not found in another

looking-glass self Cooley's term for the image people have of themselves based on how they believe others perceive them

low-income countries nations with little industrialisation in which severe poverty is the rule

M

macro-level orientation a focus on broad social structures that characterise society as a whole

macro-sociology the study of large-scale society

mainstreaming integrating special students into the overall educational programme

manifest functions the recognised and intended consequences of any social pattern

marginalisation people live on the edge of society and outside the mainstream with little stake in society overall

marketisation an economic system based on the principles of the market, including supply, demand, choice and competition

marriage a legally sanctioned relationship, involving economic cooperation as well as normative sexual activity and child-bearing, that people expect to be enduring

mass media any social or technological devices used for the selection, transmission or reception of information

mass society a society in which industry and expanding bureaucracy have eroded traditional social ties

master status a status that has exceptional importance for social identity, often shaping a person's entire life

material culture the tangible things created by members of a society

matriarchy a form of social organisation in which females dominate males

matrilineal descent a system tracing kinship through women

matrilocality a residential pattern in which a married couple lives with or near the wife's family

McDonaldisation of society a process by which the principles of the fast-food industry come to be applied to more and more features of social life

mean the arithmetic average of a series of numbers

measurement the process of determining the value of a variable in a specific case

mechanical solidarity Durkheim's designation of social bonds, based on shared morality, that unite members of pre-industrial societies

median the value that occurs midway in a series of numbers arranged in order of magnitude or, simply, the middle case

media texts all media products, such as television programmes, films, CDs, books, newspapers and website pages

mediasation the process by which the mass media enter and shape everyday experience

medicalisation the process by which events and experiences are given medical meaning and turned into medical problems

medicalisation of deviance the transformation of moral and legal issues into medical matters

medicine a social institution concerned with combating disease and improving health

mega-city a city with a population exceeding 8 million

megalopolis a vast urban region containing a number of cities and their surrounding suburbs

meritocracy a system of social stratification based on personal merit

methodology the study of different logics, epistemology and research tools

metropolis a large city that socially and economically dominates an urban area

micro-sociology the study of everyday life in social interactions

middle-class slide a trend towards declining living standards and economic security at the centre of industrial societies

middle-income countries nations characterised by limited industrialisation and moderate personal income

migration the movement of people into and out of a particular territory

military–industrial complex the close association among the national government, the military and defence industries

minority a category of people, distinguished by physical or cultural traits, who are socially disadvantaged

miscegenation biological reproduction by partners of different racial categories

mob a highly emotional crowd that pursues some violent or destructive goal

mode the value that occurs most often in a series of numbers

mode of production the way a society is organised to produce goods and services

modernisation the process of social change initiated by industrialisation

modernisation theory a model of economic and social development that explains global inequality in terms of differing levels of technological development among societies

modernity social patterns linked to industrialisation

monarchy a political system in which a single family rules from generation to generation

monogamy a form of marriage joining two partners

monopoly domination of a market by a single producer

monotheism belief in a single divine power

moral panic a condition, episode, person or group defined as a threat to social values which is presented in a stylised and stereotypical fashion by the mass media

mores a society's standards of proper moral conduct

mortality the incidence of death in a country's population

multiculturalism an educational programme recognising past and present cultural diversity in society and promoting the equality of all cultural traditions

multinational corporation a large corporation that operates in many different countries

multi-paradigms combination of different philosophies, epistemologies, theories and methods

multiple modernities different histories of societies lead through different routes to different forms of modernity

multiple perspectives takes on many perspectives for looking at social life rather than just one

N

narco state areas of governance that have been taken over and are controlled and corrupted by drug cartels and where law enforcement is weak or effectively non-existent

nation-state a political apparatus over a specific territory with its own citizens backed up by military force and a nationalistic, sovereign creed

natural environment the earth's surface and atmosphere, including all living organisms as well as the air, water, soil and other resources necessary to sustain life

neocolonialism a new form of global power relationship that involves not direct political control but economic exploitation by multinational corporations

neoliberalism economic theories based on the free market and individualism, derived from the work of Hayek and others

neolocality a residential pattern in which a married couple lives apart from the parents of both spouses

net migration rate the number of people who enter a territory (in-migration) minus the number of people who leave (out-migration) in a given year

network a web of social ties that links people who identify and interact little with one another

newly industrialising countries (NICs) lower-income countries that are fast becoming higher-income countries

new racism racism based upon cultural, rather than biological, values

new social movements (NSMs) transform identities and society in the post-industrial world

non-material culture the intangible world of ideas created by members of a society

non-verbal communication communication using body movements, gestures and facial expressions rather than speech

norms rules and expectations by which a society guides the behaviour of its members

nuclear family (conjugal family) a family unit composed of one or two parents and their children

nuclear proliferation the acquisition of nuclear weapons technology by more and more nations

O

objectivity a state of personal neutrality in conducting research

occupational gender segregation works to concentrate men and women in different types of job

occupational prestige the value that people in a society associate with various occupations

oligarchy the rule of the many by the few

oligopoly domination of a market by a few producers

ontology philosophical branch which studies the nature of being and existence

operationalising a variable specifying exactly what one intends to measure in assigning a value to a variable

oral culture tradition transmission of culture through speech

organic solidarity Durkheim's designation of social bonds, based on specialisation, that unite members of industrial societies

organisational environment a range of factors external to an organisation that affect its operation

orientalism a process by which the 'West' creates a stereotype of the 'East'

other-directedness a receptiveness to the latest trends and fashions, often expressed in the practice of imitating others

outgroup a social group towards which one feels competition or opposition

out-migration rate the number leaving for every thousand people

P

paradigm general ways of seeing the world which suggest what can be seen, done and theorised about in science

parentocracy a system where a child's education is increasingly dependent upon the wealth and wishes of parents, rather than the ability and efforts of pupils

participant observation a research method in which researchers systematically observe people while joining in their routine activities

pastoralism technology based on the domestication of animals

patriarchy a form of social organisation in which men dominate, oppress and exploit women

patrilineal descent a system tracing kinship through men

patrilocality a residential pattern in which a married couple lives with or near the husband's family

peace a state of international relations devoid of violence

peer group a social group whose members have interests, social position and age in common

penality the institutions and agencies that compare a penal system, including the economic, political, intellectual and cultural conditions

penal populism the idea that the public has a generally punitive stance towards crime and that politicians can benefit from exploiting this belief

personality a person's fairly consistent patterns of thinking, feeling and acting

personal space the surrounding area to which an individual makes some claim to privacy

plea bargaining a legal negotiation in which the state reduces the charge against a defendant in exchange for a guilty plea

pluralism a state in which racial and ethnic minorities are distinct but have social parity

pluralist model an analysis of politics that views power as dispersed among many competing interest groups

political action committee (PAC) an organisation formed by a special-interest group, independent of political parties, to pursue political aims by raising and spending money

political revolution the overthrow of one political system in order to establish another

politics the social institution that distributes power, sets a society's agenda and makes decisions

polyandry a form of marriage joining one female with two or more males

polygamy a form of marriage uniting three or more people

polygyny a form of marriage joining one male with two or more females

polysemic open to many interpretations

polytheism belief in many gods

popular culture cultural patterns that are widespread among a society's population

population the people who are the focus of research

positivism a means to understand the world based on science

postcolonialism recognises how many cultures have been made through oppressor–subject relationships and seeks to unpack these, showing how cultures are made

postcolonial theory refers to the wide critiques of (usually 'white') Western cultures that are made from people who have been colonised in the past

post-feminism ideas developed after second wave feminism, and linked to postmodernism

post-Fordism an economic system emerging mainly since the 1970s and based on flexibility (rather than standardisation), specialisation and tailor-made goods

post-industrial economy a productive system based on service work and high technology

post-industrialism computer-linked technology that supports an information-based economy

postmodernism ways of thinking which stress a plurality of perspectives as opposed to a unified, single core

postmodernity social patterns characteristic of post-industrial societies

poststructuralism postmodern theory which is critical of humanism, structures and simple divides in favour of theories that stress non-core or essential ideas of multiplicities and differences

poverty line threshold for measuring poverty, below which people are deemed poor (in the UK, often defined as 60 per cent of the median household income)

power the ability to achieve desired ends despite resistance from others

power elite model an analysis of politics that views power as concentrated among the rich

practices the practical logics by which we both act and think in a myriad of little encounters of daily life

prediction researchers using what they do know to predict what they don't know

prejudice a rigid and irrational generalisation about an entire category of people

pre-operational stage Piaget's term for the level of human development at which individuals first use language and other symbols

presentation of self an individual's effort to create specific impressions in the minds of others

prestige the value that people in a society associate with various occupations

primary group a small social group whose members share personal and enduring relationships

primary labour market occupations that provide extensive benefits to workers

primary sector the part of the economy that generates raw materials directly from the natural environment

primary sex characteristics the genitals, used to reproduce the human species

privatisation the transfer of state assets/property from public to private ownership

profane that which is an ordinary element of everyday life

profession a prestigious, white-collar occupation that requires extensive formal education

programmes films, CDs, books, newspapers, website pages, etc.

proletariat people who provide labour necessary to operate factories and other productive enterprises

propaganda information presented with the intention of shaping public opinion

public sociology aims to make sociological ideas more accessible, even popular, with wider audiences

Q

qualitative research investigation by which a researcher gathers humanistic, non-numerical, data

quantitative research investigation by which a researcher collects numerical data

queer once a negative word to denigrate homosexuals; now a positive term to capture a wide variety of sexualities and gender experiences that transgress or do not conform to established norms

queer theory the view that most sociological theory has a bias towards 'heterosexuality' and that non-heterosexual voices need to be heard

questionnaire a series of written questions that a researcher supplies to subjects, requesting their responses

R

race a category composed of people who share biologically transmitted traits that members of a society deem socially significant

racial formation links between structures and cultures where racial relations are organised

racialisation process of ranking people on the basis of their presumed race

racism the belief that one racial category is innately superior or inferior to another

rainforests regions of dense forestation, most of which circle the globe close to the equator

rationalisation of society Weber's term for the historical change from tradition to rationality as the dominant mode of human thought

rationality deliberate, matter-of-fact calculation of the most efficient means to accomplish a particular goal

rational–legal authority (bureaucratic authority) power legitimised by legally enacted rules and regulations

real culture (as opposed to ideal culture) actual social patterns that only approximate cultural expectations

realism scientific method that theorises a 'problematic' in order to see what is really going on

reference group a social group that serves as a point of reference in making evaluations or decisions

reflexivity reflecting on own actions and knowledge

refugees people who flee their own country for political or economic reasons, or to avoid war and oppression

rehabilitation a programme for reforming an offender to preclude subsequent offences

relative deprivation a perceived disadvantage arising from a specific comparison

relative poverty the deprivation of some people in relation to those who have more

reliability the quality of consistent measurement

religion a social institution involving beliefs and practices based upon a conception of the sacred

religiosity the importance of religion in a person's life

replication repetition of research by others

research method a systematic plan for conducting research

research tool a systematic technique for conducting research

resocialisation radically altering an inmate's personality through deliberate manipulation of the environment

retribution moral vengeance by which society inflicts suffering on an offender comparable to that caused by the offence

retrospective labelling the interpretation of someone's past consistent with present deviance

risk society society where risks are of a different magnitude because of technology and globalisation

ritual formal, ceremonial behaviour

role behaviour expected of someone who holds a particular status

role conflict incompatibility among the roles corresponding to two or more statuses

role set a number of roles attached to a single status

role strain incompatibility among roles corresponding to a single status

routinisation of charisma the transformation of charismatic authority into some combination of traditional and bureaucratic authority

S

sacred that which is extraordinary, inspiring a sense of awe, reverence and even fear

sample a part of a population that researchers select to represent the whole

Sapir–Whorf hypothesis the hypothesis that people perceive the world through the cultural lens of language

scapegoat a person or category of people, typically with little power, whom people unfairly blame for their own troubles

schooling formal instruction under the direction of specially trained teachers

science a logical system that bases knowledge on direct, systematic observation

secondary analysis a research method in which a researcher utilises data collected by others

secondary group a large and impersonal social group whose members pursue a specific interest or activity

secondary labour market jobs that provide minimal benefits to workers

secondary sector the part of the economy that transforms raw materials into manufactured goods

secondary sex characteristics bodily development, apart from the genitals, that distinguishes biologically mature females and males

sect a type of religious organisation that stands apart from the larger society

secularisation the historical decline in the importance of the supernatural and the sacred

segregation the physical and social separation of categories of people

self George Herbert Mead's term for the human capacity to be reflexive and take the role of others

self-employment earning a living without working for a large organisation

self-fulfilling prophecy a prediction that causes itself to become true

semiotics study of symbols and signs

sensorimotor stage Piaget's designation for the level of human development at which individuals experience the world only through sensory contact

sex the biological distinction between females and males

sexism the belief that one sex is innately superior to the other

sex ratio the number of males for every hundred females in a given population

sexual harassment comments, gestures or physical contact of a sexual nature that are deliberate, repeated and unwelcome

sexuality aspects of the body and desire that are linked to the erotic

sexual orientation an individual's preference in terms of sexual partners: same sex, other sex, either sex, neither sex

sexual scripts help define the who, what, where, when and even why we have sex

sick role patterns of behaviour defined as appropriate for people who are ill

simulacrum a world of media-generated signs and images

slavery a form of stratification in which people are owned by others as property

social capital friendships, networks and connections over time which create links and bonds and often shape the quality of a life; see Bourdieu

social change the transformation of culture and social institutions over time

social character personality patterns common to members of a particular society

social class social stratification resulting from the unequal distribution of wealth, power and prestige

social conflict struggle between segments of society over valued resources

social-conflict paradigm a framework for building theory that envisages society as an arena of inequality that generates conflict and change

social construction of reality the process by which people creatively shape reality through social interaction: linked to social constructionism

social control system planned and programmed responses to expected deviance

social democratic a mix of capitalist and socialist/welfare economies and politics

social divisions differences that are rendered socially significant (e.g. class, gender, ethnicity)

social dysfunction the undesirable consequences of any social pattern for the operation of society

social epidemiology the study of how health and disease are distributed throughout a society's population

social facts Durkheim's term for ways of depicting phenomena external to an individual and which constrain and coerce

social function the consequences of any social pattern for the operation of society

social group two or more people who identify and interact with one another

social identity our understanding of who we are and who other people are, and, reciprocally, other people's understanding of themselves and others

social institution a major sphere of social life, or societal subsystem, organised to meet a basic human need

social interaction the process by which people act and react in relation to others

socialisation a lifelong process by which individuals construct their personal biography

socialised medicine a healthcare system in which the government owns and operates most medical facilities and employs most doctors

socialism an economic system in which natural resources and the means of producing goods and services are collectively owned

social mobility change in people's position in a social hierarchy

social movement organised activity that encourages or discourages social change

social network a web of social ties that links people who identify with one another

social practices *See* practices

social protection (1) a means by which society renders an offender incapable of further offences temporarily through incarceration or permanently by execution

social protection (2) a set of benefits available (or not available) to the individual or household to reduce multidimensional poverty and deprivation

social reproduction the maintenance of power and privilege between social classes from one generation to the next

social stratification a system by which society ranks categories of people in a hierarchy

social structure recurrent and relatively stable patterns of social behaviour

society people who interact in a defined territory and share culture

sociobiology a theoretical paradigm that explores ways in which our biology affects how humans create culture

sociocultural evolution the Lenskis' term for the process of change that results from a society's gaining new information, particularly technology

socioeconomic status (SES) a composite ranking based on various dimensions of social inequality

sociology the systematic study of human society

sociology of knowledge that branch of sociology which sees an association between forms of knowledge and society

special-interest group a political alliance of people interested in some economic or social issue

spurious correlation an apparent, although false, relationship between two (or more) variables caused by some other variable

standpoint epistemologies all knowledge is grounded in standpoints and standpoint theory enables groups to analyse their situation (problems and oppressions) from within the context of their own experiences

state *See* nation-state

state capitalism an economic and political system in which companies are privately owned but cooperate closely with the government

state terrorism the use of violence, generally without the support of law, against individuals or groups by a government or its agents

status a recognised social position that an individual occupies

status frustration the process by which people feel thwarted when they aspire to a certain status

status set all the statuses a person holds at a given time

stereotype a prejudicial, exaggerated description applied to every person in a category of people

stigma a powerfully negative social label that radically changes a person's self-concept and social identity

streaming the assignment of students to different types of educational programme

structural–functional paradigm a framework for building theory that envisages society as a complex system whose parts work together to promote solidarity and stability

structural social mobility a shift in the social position of large numbers of people due more to changes in society itself than to individual efforts

structuration focuses on both action and structure simultaneously; a process whereby action and structure are always two sides of the same coin

structured dependency the process by which some people in society receive an unequal share in the results of social production

subaltern subordinate and outside power structure (often linked to **postcolonialism**)

subculture cultural patterns that set apart some segment of a society's population

suburbs urban areas beyond the political boundaries of a city

superego Freud's designation of the operation of culture within the individual in the form of internalised values and norms

surveillance society society dependent on communication and information technologies for administrative and control processes, resulting in the close monitoring of everyday life

survey a research method in which subjects respond to a series of items in a questionnaire or an interview

sustainable development development that meets the needs of the present without compromising the ability of future generations to meet their own needs

symbol anything that carries a particular meaning recognised by people who share culture

symbolic interaction a theoretical framework that envisages society as the product of the everyday interactions of people doing things together, linked to Mead and Blumer

T

technology knowledge that a society applies to the task of living in a physical environment

terrorism violence or the threat of violence employed by an individual or group as a political strategy

tertiary sector the part of the economy that generates services rather than goods

Thatcherism a system of political beliefs based on free markets and minimum state intervention

theocracy a form of government where a god or religion is recognised as the supreme ruler

theoretical paradigm a basic image of society that guides sociological thinking and research

theoretical perspective can be seen as a basic image that guides thinking and research

theory a statement of how and why specific facts are related

third age a period of life, often free from parenting and paid work, when a more active, independent life is achieved

Third Way a framework that adapts politics to a changed world, transcending old-style democracy and neoliberalism

Thomas theorem W. I. Thomas's assertion that situations we define as real become real in their consequences

total institution a setting in which people are isolated from the rest of society and manipulated by an administrative staff

totalitarianism a political system that extensively regulates people's lives

total period fertility rate the average number of children each woman would have in her lifetime if the average number of children born to all women of child-bearing age in any given year remained constant during that woman's child-bearing years

totem an object in the natural world collectively defined as sacred

tracking the assignment of students to different types of educational programme

trade unions organisations of workers collectively seeking to improve wages and working conditions through various strategies, including negotiations and strikes

tradition sentiments and beliefs passed from generation to generation

traditional authority power legitimised through respect for long-established cultural patterns

tradition-directedness rigid conformity to time-honoured ways of living

transnational corporation a firm that has the power to coordinate and control operations in more than one country, even if it does not own them

transsexuals people who feel they are one sex though biologically they are the other

triad a social group with three members

triangulation using many different research tools to understand a problem

tribalism the condition of living as a separate group or tribe

U

unconscious experiences which become too difficult to confront and so become hidden from the surface workings of life

underclass a group 'under the class structure' which is economically, politically and socially marginalised and excluded

underground economy economic activity generating income that is unreported to the government as required by law

urban ecology the study of the link between the physical and social dimensions of cities

urbanisation the concentration of humanity into cities

V

validity the quality of measuring precisely what one intends to measure

values culturally defined standards by which people assess desirability, goodness and beauty, and which serve as broad guidelines for social living

variable a concept whose value changes from case to case

verstehen German for 'understanding', linked to work of Max Weber

victimless crimes violations of law in which there are no readily apparent victims

W

war armed conflict among the people of various societies, directed by their governments

wealth the total value of money and other assets, minus outstanding debts

white-collar crime crimes committed by persons of high social position in the course of their occupations

white-collar occupations higher-prestige work involving mostly mental activity

world systems theory Marxist theory about the interdependence and exploitation of global economies

Z

zero population growth the level of reproduction, migration and death that maintains population at a steady state

Please visit www.pearsoned.co.uk/plummer/glossaryquiz to access the Glossary quiz.

REFERENCES

A

Aas, Katja Franko. *Globalization and Crime*. London: Sage, 2007.

Abbott, Pamela and Claire Wallace. *The Family and the New Right*. London: Pluto, 1992.

Abbott, Pamela, Claire Wallace and Melissa Tyler. *Introduction to Sociology: Feminist Perspectives*. Abingdon: Routledge, 2005.

Abercrombie, Nicholas. *Television and Society*. Cambridge: Polity, 1996.

———. *Sociology*. Cambridge: Polity, 2004.

Abercrombie, Nicholas and Brian Longhurst. *The Penguin Dictionary of Media Studies*. London: Penguin, 2007.

Abercrombie, Nicholas, Stephen Hill and Bryan Turner. *Penguin Dictionary of Sociology*. London: Penguin, 2006.

Acheson, D. *Independent Inquiry into Inequalities in Health Report*. London: HMSO, 1998.

Adorno, Theodore. *The Culture Industry*. London: Routledge, 1991.

Adorno, Theodore and Max Horkheimer. *Dialectic of Enlightment*. New York: Seabury, 1972.

Adorno, Theodore, et al. *The Authoritarian Personality*. New York: Harper & Brothers, 1950.

Agger, B. *The Virtual Self: A Contemporary Sociology*. Oxford: Blackwell, 2004.

Agustín, Laura Maria. *Sex at the Margins*. London: Zed Books, 2007.

Ahmed, Akbar S. *Discovering Islam: Making Sense of Muslim History and Society*. London: Routledge, 1988.

———. *Islam Under Siege: Living Dangerously in a Post-honor World*. Cambridge: Polity, 2003.

———. *Journey Into Islam: The Crisis of Globalization*. Washington, DC: The Brookings Institution, 2007.

Akeret, R. V. *Photoanalysis*. New York: Wyden, 1973.

Alam, Sultana. 'Women and poverty in Bangladesh'. *Women's Studies International Forum*, Vol. 8, No. 4 (1985): 361–71.

Alavi, Masrin. *We are Iran*. London: Portobello, 2006.

Albrow, Martin. *The Global Age*. Cambridge: Polity, 1996.

Alcock, P. *Understanding Poverty*, 2nd edn. Basingstoke: Macmillan, 1997.

Alexander, Cynthia and Leslie Pal. *Digital Democracy*. Oxford: Oxford University Press, 1998.

Alexander, Jeffrey. *The Civil Sphere*. Oxford: Oxford University Press, 2006.

Allan, Graham (ed.). *The Sociology of the Family: A Reader*. Oxford: Blackwell, 1999.

Allan, Graham and Graham Crow. *Families, Households and Society*. London: Palgrave, 2001.

Allen, Beverley. *Rape Warfare: The Hidden Genocide in Bosnia-Herzegovina and Croatia*. Minneapolis, MN: University of Minnesota Press, 1996.

Allen, R. *Channels of Discourse Reassembled*, 2nd edn. London: Routledge, 1992.

———. *Soap Operas around the World*. London: Routledge, 1995.

Allen, Sheila and Carol Walkowitz. *Homeworking: Myths and Realities*. London: Macmillan, 1987.

Allport, Gordon. *The Use of Personal Documents in Psychological Science*. New York: Social Science Research Council, 1942.

Allsop, Kenneth. *The Bootleggers*. London: Hutchinson, 1961.

Althusser, Louis. *Lenin and Philosophy and Other Essays*. London: New Left Books, 1971.

Altman, Dennis. *Global Sex*. Chicago: University of Chicago Press, 2000.

Amnesty International. *Crimes of Hate, Conspiracy of Silence*. London: Amnesty International, 2001.

Anderson, Benedict. *Imagined Communities*. London: Verso, 1989.

Anderson, Bridget. *Doing the Dirty Work: The Global Politics of Domestic Labour*. London: Zed, 2000.

Anderson, Chris. *The Long Tail: How Endless Choice Is Creating Unlimited Demand*. London: Random House, 2007.

Anderson, Elijah. *Code of the Street*. New York: W. Norton, 1999.

Andretta, Massimiliano and Donatella della Porta (eds). *The Global Justice Movement*. Boulder, CO: Paradigm, 2007.

Ang, Ian. *Watching Dallas: Soap Opera and the Melodramatic Imagination*. London: Methuen, 1985.

Anthias, Floya and Nira Yuval Davis. *Racialised Boundaries*. London: Routledge, 1993.

Appadurai, Arjun. *Modernity at Large: Cultural Dimensions of Globalization*. London and Minneapolis, MN: University of Minnesota Press, 1996.

Appiah, Kwame Anthony. *Cosmopolitanism: Ethics in a World of Strangers*. London: Allen Lane, 2006.

Appignanesi, L. and S. Maitland. *The Rushdie File*. London: Fourth Estate, 1989.

Appignanesi, Richard and Chris Garratt. *Postmodernism for Beginners*. Cambridge: Icon, 1995.

Arber, Sara and Jay Ginn (eds). *Connecting Gender and Ageing: A Sociological Approach*. Buckingham: Open University Press, 1995.

Archer, Louise. *Race, Masculinity and Schooling: Muslim Boys and Education*. Maidenhead: Open University Press, 2007.

Arendt, Hannah. *The Origins of Totalitarianism*. Cleveland, OH: Meridian, 1958.

Ariès, Philippe. *Centuries of Childhood: A Social History of Family Life*. New York: Vintage, 1965.

———. *Western Attitudes toward Death: From the Middle Ages to the Present*. Patricia M. Ranum, trans. Baltimore, MD: Johns Hopkins University Press, 1974.

Armstrong, David. 'Decline of the hospital'. *Sociology of Health and Illness*, Vol. 20, No. 4 (1998): 445–57.

Arnold, Ellen C. and Darcy C. Plymire. 'The Cherokee Indians and the internet', in David Gauntlett (ed.), *web.studies*. London: Arnold, 2000: 186–93.

Arthus-Bertrand, Yann. *The Earth from the Air*, revised edn. London: Thames & Hudson, 2002; orig. 1999.

Asante, Molefi Kete. *The Afrocentric Idea*. Philadelphia, PA: Temple University Press, 1987.

Asch, Solomon. *Social Psychology*. Englewood Cliffs, NJ: Prentice-Hall, 1952.

Ashford, Lori S. 'New perspectives on population: lessons from Cairo'. *Population Bulletin*, Vol. 50, No. 1 (March 1995): 1–44.

Atchley, Robert C. *Aging: Continuity and Change*. Belmont, CA: Wadsworth, 1983; 2nd edn, 1987.

Atkinson, Paul. *Everyday Arias: An Operatic Ethnography*. New York: Altamira, 2006.

Attwood, Feona (ed.). *Mainstreaming Sex: The Sexualization of Western Culture*. London: I. B. Tauris, 2009.

Aubert, Laurent. *The Music of the Other*. Farnham, Survey: Ashgate, 2007.

Auden, W. H. *Collected Poems*. London: Faber and Faber, 1976.

B

Baars, Jan, Dale Dannefer, Chris Phillipson and Alan Walker. *Aging, Globalization and Inequality: The New Critical Gerontology*. Amityville: Baywood, 2006.

Bachrach, Peter and Morton S. Baratz. *Power and Poverty*. New York: Oxford University Press, 1970.

Back, Les. *New Ethnicities and Urban Culture: Racism and Multiculturalism in Young Lives*. London: UCL Press, 1996.

Back, Les. *The Art of Listening*. London: Berg, 2007.

Back, Les and John Solomos (eds). *Theories of Race and Racism: A Reader*, 2nd edn. London: Routledge, 2009.

Bakardjieva, Maria. *Internet Society: The Internet in Everyday Life*. London: Sage, 2005.

Bales, Kevin. *Disposable People: New Slavery in the Global Economy*. Berkeley, CA: University of California Press, 2000.

——. *Understanding Global Slavery: A Reader*. Berkeley: University of California Press, 2005.

——. (opening essay) *Documenting Disposable People: Contemporary Global Slavery*. London: Hayward, 2008.

Bales, Kevin et al. *Modern Slavery: The Secret World of 27 Million People*. London: Oneworld Publications, 2009.

Bales, Robert F. 'The equilibrium problem in small groups', in Talcott Parsons et al. (eds), *Working Papers in the Theory of Action*. New York: Free Press, 1953: 111–15.

Ball, Stephen. *Beachside*. London: Routledge, 1981.

——. *Education Policy and Social Class*. London. Routledge, 2006.

Balnaves, Mark, James Donald and Stephanie Hemelryk. *The Global Media Atlas*. Brighton: British Film Institute and Myriad, 2001.

Baltzell, E. Digby. 'Introduction to the 1967 edition', in W. E. B. Du Bois, *The Philadelphia Negro: A Social Study*. New York: Schocken, 1967; orig. 1899.

Banks, Olive. *Faces of Feminism*. Oxford: Martin Robertson, 1981.

Bannock, Graham, R. E. Baxter and Evan Davis. *The Penguin Dictionary of Economics*. Harmondsworth: Penguin, 2004.

Banyard, Kat. *The Equality Illusion: The Truth about Women and Men Today*. London: Faber and Faber.

Barash, David. *The Whispering Within*. New York: Penguin, 1981.

Barber, Benjamin. *Jihad vs McWorld*. New York: Ballantine, 1995.

——. *Consumed: How Markets Corrupt*. New York: W. W. Norton, 2008.

Barker, Chris. *Global Television: An Introduction*. Oxford: Blackwell, 1997.

——. *The SAGE Dictionary of Cultural Studies*. London: Sage, 2004.

Barker, Eileen. 'Who'd be a Moonie? A comparative study of those who join the Unification Church in Britain', in Bryan Wilson (ed.), *The Social Impact of New Religious Movements*. New York: Rose of Sharon Press, 1981: 59–96.

——. *The Making of a Moonie*. Oxford: Blackwell, 1984.

——. *New Religious Movements: A Practical Introduction*, 4th edn. London: HMSO, 1995.

Barnaby, Frank. *The Future of Terror: A 21st Century Handbook*. London: Granta, 2007.

Barnes, Colin and Geoff Mercer (with Tom Shakespeare). *Exploring Disability: A Sociological Introduction*, 2nd edn. Cambridge: Polity, 2010; orig. 1999.

Barnett, Tony and Alan Whiteside. *AIDS in the Twenty-First Century: Disease and Globalization*, 2nd edn. New York: Palgrave Macmillan, 2006.

Barrett, Michele. *Women's Oppression Today*. London: Verso, 1980.

Barrow, J. 'West Indian families', in R. Rapoport et al. (eds). *Families in Britain*. London: Routledge, 1982.

Barry, Kathleen. *Female Sexual Slavery*. New York: New York University Press, 2003.

Barthes, Roland. *Elements of Semiology*. Annette Lavers and Colin Smith, trans. London: Cape, 1967.

Basmenji, Kaveh. *Tehran Blues: Youth Culture in Iran*. London: SAQI, 2005.

Bateson, Gregory and Margaret Mead. *Balinese Character*. New York: New York Academy of Science, 1942.

Baudrillard, Jean. 'Interview: game with vestiges'. *On the Beach*, Vol. 5, Winter (1984): 19–25.

——. *Jean Baudrillard Selected Writings*. Cambridge: Polity, 1988.

——. 'The reality gulf'. *Guardian* (11 January 1991): 25.

Bauman, Zygmunt. *Modernity and the Holocaust*. Cambridge: Polity, 1989.

——. *Modernity and Ambivalence*. Cambridge: Polity, 1991.

——. 'From pilgrim to tourist – or a short history of identity', in Stuart Hall and Paul Gu Gay (eds), *Question of Cultural Identity*. London: Sage, 1996.

——. *Globalization: The Human Consequences*. Cambridge: Polity, 1998.

——. *Wasted Lives: Modernity and Its Outcasts*. Cambridge: Polity, 2004.

Bauman, Zygmunt and Tim May. *Thinking Sociologically*, rev. edn. Oxford: Blackwell, 2001; orig. 1990.

Baumeister, Roy. *Identity: Cultural Change and the Struggle for Self*. Oxford: Oxford University Press, 1986.

——. *Evil: Inside Human Violence and Cruelty*. New York: Barnes and Noble, 2001.

Baudelot, Christian and Establet, Roger. *Suicide: The Hidden Side of Modernity*. Cambridge: Polity, 2008.

Baylis, John and Steve Smith (eds). *The Globalization of World Politics*, 5th edn. Oxford: Oxford University Press, 2010; 4th edn, 2008.

Baym, Nancy K. *Personal Connections in the Digital Age*. Cambridge: Polity, 2010.

Beahm, George. *Muggles and Magic: An Unofficial Guide to J. K. Rowling and the Harry Potter Phenomenon*. Charlottesville: Hampton Roads, 2007.

——. *Bedazzled: Stephanie Meyers and the Twilight Phenomenon*. London: J. R. Books, 2009.

Beasley, Chris. *What is Feminism?* London: Sage, 1999.

Beauvoir, Simone de. *The Second Sex*. London: Virago, 1997 (orig. 1949 in French; first English edn, 1953).

Beccaria, Cesare. *Essay on Crimes and Punishments*. Indianapolis, IN: Bobbs-Merrill Educational, 1963; orig. 1764.

Beck, Ulrich. *Risk Society*. London: Sage, 1992.

——. *The Reinvention of Politics*. Cambridge: Polity, 1997.

——. *World Risk Society*. Cambridge: Polity, 1999.

——. *The Brave New World of Work*. Cambridge: Polity, 2000a.

——. *What is Globalization?* Cambridge: Polity, 2000b.

Beck, Ulrich and Elisabeth Beck-Gernsheim. *The Normal Chaos of Love*. Cambridge: Polity, 1995.

——. *Individualization*. London: Sage, 2003.

Beck-Gernsheim, Elisabeth. *The Social Implications of Bioengineering*. Atlantic Highlands, NJ: Humanities Press, 1991.

——. *Reinventing the Family: In Search of New Lifestyles*. Cambridge: Polity, 2002.

Becker, Gay. *The Elusive Embryo*. Berkeley, CA: University of California Press, 2000.

Becker, Howard S. *Outside: Studies in the Sociology of Deviance*. New York: Free Press, 1963; 2nd edn, 1966.

——. *Doing Things Together*. Chicago: Aldine, 1986.

——. *Tricks of the Trade*. Chicago: University of Chicago Press, 1998.

——. *Telling about Society*, Chicago: University of Chicago Press, 2007.

Beeghley, Leonard. *The Structure of Social Stratification in the United States*. Needham Heights, MA: Allyn & Bacon, 1989.

Bell, Daniel. *The Coming of Post-industrial Society: A Venture in Social Forecasting*. New York: Harper Colophon, 1976.

Bell, David. *Cyberculture Theorists: Manuel Castells and Donna Haraway*. London: Routledge, 2007.

Bell, Judith. *Doing Your Research Project: A Guide for First-Time Researchers in Education and Social Science*, 5th edn. Buckingham: Open University Press, 2010.

Bellah, Robert N. *The Broken Covenant*. New York: Seabury Press, 1975.

Bellah, Robert N., Richard Madsen, William M. Sullivan, Ann Swidler and Steven M. Tipton. *Habits of the Heart: Individualism and Commitment in American Life*. New York: Harper & Row, 1985.

Benedict, Ruth. 'Continuities and discontinuities in cultural conditioning'. *Psychiatry*, Vol. 1 (May 1938): 161–7.

Benhabib, Seyla. *The Claims of Culture*. Princeton, NJ: Princeton University Press, 2002.

Benjamin, Walter. *The Work of Art in the Age of Mechanical Reproduction*. London: Cape, 1970.

Bennett, James. *Oral History and Delinquency*. Chicago: University of Chicago Press, 1981.

Bennett, Tony, Mike Savage, Elizabeth Silva, Alan Warde, Modesto Cayo-Cal, David Wright. *Culture, Class, Distinction*. London: Sage, 2009.

Benton, Ted (ed.), *The Greening of Marxism*. New York: Guilford Press, 1996.

Ben-Ze'ev, Aaron. *Love Online: Emotions on the Internet*. Cambridge: Cambridge University Press, 2004.

Berger, Alan L. *Children of Job: American Second-Generation Witnesses to the Holocaust*. New York: State University of New York Press, 1997.

Berger, Peter L. *Invitation to Sociology*. New York: Anchor, 1963.

——. *The Sacred Canopy: Elements of a Sociological Theory of Religion*. Garden City, NY: Doubleday, 1967; 2nd edn, 1997.

——. *Facing Up to Modernity: Excursions in Society, Politics and Religion*. New York: Basic Books, 1977.

——. *The Capitalist Revolution: Fifty Propositions about Prosperity, Equality and Liberty*. New York: Basic Books, 1986.

——. (ed.). *The Desecularization of the World*. Washington, DC: Ethics and Public Policy, 1999.

Berger, Peter, Brigitte Berger and Hansfried Kellner. *The Homeless Mind: Modernization and Consciousness*. New York: Vintage, 1974.

Berger, Peter and Hansfried Kellner. *Sociology Reinterpreted: An Essay on Method and Vocation*. Garden City, NY: Anchor, 1981.

Berger, Peter and Thomas Luckmann. *The Social Construction of Reality: A Treatise in the Sociology of Knowledge*. Garden City, NY: Anchor, 1967.

Bernard, Jessie. *The Female World*. New York: Free Press, 1981.

——. *The Future of Marriage*. New Haven, CT: Yale University Press, 1982; orig. 1973.

Bernstein, Basil. *Class, Codes and Control* (3 vols). London: Routledge, 1977.

Berry, Brian L. and Philip H. Rees. 'The factorial ecology of Calcutta'. *American Journal of Sociology*, Vol. 74, No. 5 (March 1969): 445–91.

Best, Joel. *Damned Lies and Statistics*. Berkeley, CA: University of California Press, 2001.

Best, Shaun. *A Beginner's Guide to Social Theory*. London: Sage, 2002.

——. *Understanding Social Divisions*. London: Sage, 2005.

Beveridge, William. *Social Insurance and Allied Services* (The Beveridge Report), Cmd 6404. London: HMSO.

Beynon, Huw. *Working for Ford*. London: Allen Lane, and Harmondsworth: Penguin, 1973.

Beynon, Huw, Ray Hudson and David Sadler. *A Tale of Two Industries: The Contraction of Coal and Steel in the North East of England*. Buckingham: Open University Press, 1991.

Bhadra, Bipul Kumar. *Sociology of C. Wright Mills*. Calcutta, India: Minerva Associates, 1998.

Bhavnani, Kum-Kum. 'Talking racism and the reality of women's studies', in D. Richardson and V. Robinson (eds), *Introducing Women's Studies*. London: Macmillan, 1993.

Biagioli, Mario (ed.). *The Science Studies Reader*. London: Routledge, 1999.

Birren, James et al. *Aging and Biography*. New York: Springer.

Black, Sir Douglas et al. *The Black Report*. London: HMSO, 1980.

Black, John. *A Dictionary of Economics*. Oxford: Oxford University Press, 2003.

Black, Maggie and Ben Fawcett. *The Last Taboo: Opening the Door on the Sanitation Crisis*. London: Earthscan, 2008.

Blackburn, Robin. *Banking on Death*. London: Verso, 2003.

——. *Age Shock: How Finance is Failing Us*. London: Verso, 2007.

Blaikie, Andrew. *Ageing and Popular Culture*. Cambridge: Cambridge University Press, 1999.

Blau, Peter M. *Exchange and Power in Social Life*. New York: Wiley, 1964.

Blau, Peter M. and Otis Dudley Duncan. *The American Occupational Structure*. New York: Wiley, 1967.

Blaxter, Mildred. *Health*. Cambridge: Polity, 2004.

Blech, Jorg. *Inventing Disease and Pushing Pills: Pharmaceutical Companies and the Medicalisation of Normal Life*. London: Routledge, 2006.

Blum, Edward J. *W.E.B. Du Bois, American Prophet*. Philadelphia, University of Pennsylvania Press, 2007.

Blumer, Herbert. *Movies and Conduct*. New York: Macmillan, 1933.

——. 'Collective behavior', in Alfred McClung Lee (ed.), *Principles of Sociology*, 3rd edn. New York: Barnes & Noble, 1969a: 65–121.

——. *Symbolic Interactionism*. Englewood-Cliffs. Prentice-Hall, 1969b.

Blumstein, Alfred and Joel Wallman (eds). *The Crime Drop in America*. Cambridge: Cambridge University Press, 2000.

Blythman, Joanna. *Shopped: The Shocking Power of British Supermarkets*. London: Fourth Estate, 2005.

Bogardus, Emory S. 'Comparing racial distance in Ethopia, South Africa, and the United States'. *Sociology and Social Research*, Vol. 52, No. 2 (January 1968): 149–56.

Bok, Lee. *Chav Guide to Life*. London: Crombie Jardine, 2006.

Booth, Charles. *Life and Labour in London*. London: Macmillan, 17 vols, 1901–2.

Bordo, Susan. *Unbearable Weight: Feminism, Western Culture and the Body*. Berkeley: University of California Press, 1993.

Boorstin, Daniel. *The Image: A Gude to Pseudo-events in America*. New York: Harper and Row, 1961.

Bormann, F. Herbert. 'The global environmental deficit'. *BioScience*, Vol. 40 (1990): 74.

Bormann, F. Herbert and Stephen R. Kellert. 'The global environmental deficit', in F. Herbert Bormann and Stephen R. Kellert (eds), *Ecology, Economics and Ethics: The Broken Circle*. New Haven, CT: Yale University Press, 1991: ix–xviii.

Bornat, Joanna (ed.). *Reminiscence Reviewed*. Buckingham: Open University Press, 1994.

Bornstein, Kate. *My Gender Workbook*. London: Routledge, 1998.

Boston Women's Health Book Collective. *Our Bodies, Ourselves*. Angela Phillips and Jill Rakusen eds. British edn. Harmondsworth: Penguin, 1978; orig. 1971.

Bott, Elizabeth. *Family and Social Network*. New York: Free Press, 1971; orig. 1957.

Bottero, Wendy. *Stratification: Social Division and Inequality*. London: Routledge, 2005.

Bottoms, Anthony F. 'Some neglected features of modern penal systems', in D. Garland and P. Young (eds), *The Power to Punish*. London: Heinemann, 1988.

Bourdieu, Pierre. *Distinction*. London: Routledge, 1984.

——. *The Logic of Practice*. Stanford, CA: Stanford University Press, 1990.

Bourdieu, Pierre et al. *The Weight of the World: Social Suffering in Contemporary Society*. Cambridge: Polity, 1999.

Bowker, John (ed.). *Concise Oxford Dictionary of World Religions*. Oxford: Oxford University Press, 2005.

——. *World Religions: The Great Faiths Explored and Explained*. London: Dorling Kindersley, 2006.

Bowles, Samuel and Herbert Gintis. *Schooling in Capitalist America: Educational Reform and the Contradictions of Economic Life*. New York: Basic Books, 1976.

Bowling, Ben and Coretta Phillips. *Racism, Crime and Justice*. Harlow: Longman, 2002.

Boyle, Charles, Peter Wheale and Brian Sturgess. *People, Science and Technology*. Brighton: Wheatsheaf, 1984.

Brabazon, Tara. *From Revolution to Revelation: Generation X, Popular Memory and Cultural Studies*. Aldershot: Ashgate, 2005.

Bradley, Harriet. *Fractured Identities: Changing Patterns of Inequality*. Cambridge: Polity, 1996.

Bradshaw, York W. and Michael Wallace. *Global Inequalities*. London: Pine Forge, 1996.

Brah, A. and Minhas, R. (1988) 'Structural racism or cultural difference: schooling for Asian girls,' in M. Woodhead and A. McGrath (eds), *Family, School and Society: A Reader*, London: Hodder and Stoughton.

Braham, Peter and Linda Janes (eds). *Social Differences and Divisions*. Oxford: Blackwell/Open University Press, 2002.

Branegan, Jay. 'Is Singapore a model for the West?', *Time*, Vol. 141, No. 3 (18 January 1993): 36–7.

Branston, Gill and Roy Stafford. *The Media Student's Book*. London: Routledge, 2006.

Bratlinger, Patrick. *Crusoe's Footprints: Cultural Studies in Britain and America*. New York: Routledge, 1990.

Braudel, Fernand. *A History of Civilization*. Harmondsworth: Penguin, 1995.

Brecher, Jeremy, Tim Costello and Brendan Smith. *Globalization from Below*. Cambridge, MA: South End Press, 2000.

Brenner, Neil and Roger Keil. *The Global Cities Reader*. London: Routledge, 2005.

Brierley, Peter. 'Religion', in A. H. Halsey with Josephine Webb (eds), *Twentieth Century British Social Trends*. London: Macmillan, 2000.

Briggs, Asa. *The Birth of Broadcasting*. London: Oxford University Press, 1961.

Brinton, Crane. *The Anatomy of Revolution*. New York: Vintage, 1965.

British Crime Survey. Published since 1984 and yearly since 2001. London: HMSO.

British Social Attitudes. Published annually; various publishers.

Brody, Hugh. *The Other Side of Eden: Hunters, Farmers and the Shaping of the Modern World*. London: Farrar, Straus and Giroux, 2000.

Brown, Andrew. *The Darwin Wars: The Scientific Battle for the Soul of Man*. London: Simon & Schuster, 1999.

Brown, Lester R. et al. (eds). *State of the World 1997*. London: Earthscan, 1997.

——. *State of the World 2001: A Worldwatch Institute Report on Progress toward a Sustainable Society*. London: Earthscan, 2001.

——. *State of the World 2004: The Consumer Society*. London: Earthscan, 2004.

Brown, P. ' "The Third Wave": education and the ideology of "parentocracy" '. *British Journal of Sociology of Education*, Vol. 11 (1990): 65–85.

Browning, Gary, Abigail Halci and Frank Webster (eds). *Understanding Contemporary Society: Theories of the Present*. London: Sage, 2000.

Bruce, Steven. 'The twilight of the gods'. *Sociology Review* (November 1992).

——. *Sociology of Religion*. Oxford: Oxford University Press, 1995.

——. *Religion in the Modern World: From Cathedrals to Cults*. Oxford: Oxford University Press, 1996.

——. *Sociology: A Very Short Introduction*. Oxford: Oxford University Press, 1999.

——. *Fundamentalism*. Oxford: Polity, 2000.

——. *Politics and Religion*. Oxford: Polity, 2003.

Brundtland, G. (ed.). *Our Common Future*. Oxford: Oxford University Press, 1987.

Bryman, Alan. *Disney and His Worlds*. London: Routledge, 1995.

——. *Social Research Methods*, 3rd edn. Oxford: Oxford University Press, 2008.

——. *The Disneyization of Society*, London: Sage, 2004.

Bryson, Bill. 'Of mice and millions'. *Observer Magazine* (28 March 1993): 16–23.

Bryson, Valerie. *Feminist Debates*. London: Macmillan, 1999.

Bulmer, Martin and Anthony M. Rees (eds). *Citizenship Today: The Contemporary Relevance of T. H. Marshall*. London: UCL Press, 1996.

Burawoy, Michael. 'The Soviet descent into capitalism'. *American Journal of Sociology*, Vol. 102, No. 5 (March 1997): 1420–44.

Burbidge, Mikey and J. Walters (eds). *Breaking the Silence: Gay Teenagers Speak for Themselves*. London: Joint Council of Gay Teenagers, 1981.

Burchard, Tania. 'Social exclusion: concepts and evidence', in David Gordon and Peter Townsend (eds), *Breadline Europe: The Measurement of Poverty*. Bristol: Policy Press, 2000.

Burke, Roger Hopkins. *An Introduction to Criminological Theory*, 3rd edn. Cullompton, Devon: Willan, 2009.

Bury, M. R. 'Social constructionism and the development of medical sociology'. *Sociology of Health and Illness*, Vol. 8 (1986): 137–68.

——. 'The sociology of chronic illness'. *Sociology of Health and Illness*, Vol. 13, No. 4 (1991): 451–68.

——. *The Sociology of Health and Illness: A Reader*. London: Routledge, 2003.

Busfield, Joan. *Women, Men and Madness*. London: Macmillan, 1997.

——. *Health and Health Care in Modern Britain*. Oxford: Oxford University Press, 2000.

Butler, Judith. *Gender Trouble*. London: Routledge, 1990.

Butler, Robert N. 'The life review'. *Psychiatry*, Vol. 26 (1963): 63–76.

Butler, Robert N. *Why Survive? Being Old in America*. New York: Harper & Row, 1975.

Butler, Tim and Paul Watt. *Understanding Social Inequality*. London: Sage, 2007.

Buxton, Julia. *The Political Economy of Narcotics: Production, Consumption and Global Markets*. London: Zed, 2006.

Byrne, Darren J. O. *Human Rights: An Introduction*. London: Pearson, 2003.

Bytheway, Bill. *Ageism*. Buckingham: Open University Press, 1995.

C

Calder, Martin (ed.). *Child Sexual Abuse and the Internet: Tackling the New Frontier*. Lyme Regis: Russell House, 2004.

Calvert, Peter and Susan Calvert. *Politics and Society in the Third World*, 2nd edn. London: Longman, 2001; 3rd edn, 2007.

Cancian, Francesca M. *Love in America: Gender and Self-Development*. Cambridge: Cambridge University Press, 1987.

Caplow, Theodore, Howard M. Bahr, John Modell and Bruce A. Chadwick. *Recent Social Trends in the United States, 1960–1990*. Montreal: McGill-Queen's University Press, 1991.

Carmichael, Stokely and Charles V. Hamilton. *Black Power: The Politics of Liberation in America*. New York: Vintage, 1967.

Carnes, Patrick, David Delmonico and Elizabeth Griffin. *In the Shadows of the Net: Breaking Free of Compulsive Online Sexual Behaviour*. Center City: Hazelden Information & Educational Services, 2001.

Carrabine, Eamonn. *Crime, Culture and the Media*. Cambridge: Polity, 2008.

Carrabine, Eamonn, Paul Iganski, Maggy Lee, Ken Plummer and Nigel South. *Criminology: A Sociological Introduction*, 2nd edn. London: Routledge, 2008.

Carrington, Christopher. *No Place Like Home: Relationships and Family Life among Lesbians and Gay Men*. Chicago: University of Chicago Press, 1999.

Carson, Rachel. *Silent Spring*. Boston, MA: Houghton-Mifflin, 1962.

Carter, Neil. *The Politics of the Environment*. Cambridge: Cambridge University Press, 2007.

Cashmore, Ellis. *Beckham*. Cambridge: Polity, 2004.

Cashmore, Ellis and Chris Rojek. *Dictionary of Cultural Theorists*. London: Arnold, 1999.

Castells, Manuel. *The Urban Question*, 1978.

——. *The Informational City*. Oxford: Blackwell, 1989.

——. *The Information Age* (3 vols). Oxford: Blackwell. Vol. 1, 1996; Vol. 2, 1997; Vol. 3, 1998.

Castles, Stephen and Mark J. Miller. *The Age of Migration: International Population Movements in the Modern World*, 4th edn.

London: Palgrave Macmillan, 2009; orig. 1993.

Castree, Noel, Neil Mccoe, Kevin Ward and Mike Samers. *Spaces of Work: Global Capitalism and the Geographies of Labour*. London: Sage, 2004.

Cavadine, Mick and James Dignan. *Penal Systems: A Comparative Approach*, 4th edn. London: Sage, 2005.

Central Intelligence Agency. *The World Factbook, 2000*. Washington DC: CIA, 2000 (www.cia/gov/publications/factbook).

Chang, Ha-Joon. *23 Things They Don't Tell You about Capitalism*. London: Allen Lane.

Change, Kwang-Chih. *The Archaeology of Ancient China*. New Haven, CT: Yale University Press, 1977.

Chatterton, Paul and Robert Hollands. *Urban Nightscapes: Youth Cultures, Pleasure Spaces and Corporate Power*. London: Routledge, 2003.

Cheal, David. *Families in Today's World: A Comparative Approach*. London: Routledge, 2008.

Chodorow, Nancy. *The Reproduction of Mothering*. Berkeley, CA: University of California Press, 1978.

Christie, Kenneth. *The South African Truth Commission*. London: Palgrave, 2000.

Christie, Nils. *Crime Control as Industry: Towards Gulags, Western Style*, 3rd edn. London: Routledge, 2000.

Clarke, Adele. 'Modernity, post modernism and human reproductive processes,' in Chris Hable Gray (eds), *The Cyborg Handbook*. New York: Routledge, 1995: 139–55.

Clarke, Candace. *Misery and Company: Sympathy in Everyday Life*. Chicago, IL: University of Chicago, 1998.

Clawson, Dan, Robert Zussman, Joya Misra, Naomi Gerstel, Randall Strokes, Douglas L. Anderton and Michael Burawoy. *Public Sociology: Fifteen Eminent Sociologists Debate Politics and the Profession in the Twenty-First Century*. Berkeley: University of California Press, 2007.

Clegg, Stuart R. *Modern Organisations: Organisation Studies in the Postmodern World*. London: Sage, 1990.

Clinard, Marshall and Daniel Abbott. *Crime in Developing Countries*. New York: Wiley, 1973.

Clough, Patricia Ticineto. *The Ends of Ethnography: From Realism to Social Criticism*. Newbury Park, CA: Sage, 1992.

Cloward, Richard A. and Lloyd E. Ohlin. *Delinquency and Opportunity: A Theory of Delinquent Gangs*. New York: Free Press, 1966.

Coakley, Jay and Eric Dunning (eds) *Handbook of Sports Studies*. London: Sage, 2000–2.

Cochrane, Alan and John Clarke. *Comparing Welfare States: Britain in International Context*. London: Sage, 1993.

Coffey, Amanda. *Education and Social Change*. Buckingham: Open University Press, 2001.

Cohen, Albert K. *Delinquent Boys: The Culture of the Gang*. New York: Free Press, 1971; orig. 1955.

Cohen, Phil. 'Subculture conflict and working class community', in S. Hall et al. (eds), *Culture, Media, Logica*. London: Hutchinson, 1980; orig. 1972.

Cohen, Robin. *Frontiers of Identity: The British and the Others*. Harlow: Longman, 1994.

Cohen, Robin. *Global Diasporas: An Introduction*. London: Routledge, 2008.

Cohen, Robin and Paul Kennedy. *Global Sociology*, 2nd edn. Basingstoke: Macmillan, 2007.

Cohen, Stanley. *Visions of Social Control*. Cambridge: Polity, 1985.

——. *Folk Devils and Moral Panics: The Creation of the Mods and Rockers*, 3rd edn. London: Routledge, 2003; orig. 1972.

Cohen, Stanley and Laurie Taylor. *Escape Attempts: The Theory and Practice of Resistance to Everyday Life*, 2nd edn. London: Routledge, 1995.

Cohen, Stanley and Jock Young (eds). *The Manufacture of News*, 2nd edn. London: Constable, 1981.

Coleman, Clive and Jenny Moynihan. *Understanding Crime Data*. Buckingham: Open University Press, 1996.

Coleman, David and John Salt. *The British Population: Patterns, Trends and Processes*. Oxford: Oxford University Press, 1992.

Coleman, P. *Aging and Reminiscence Processes*. New York: John Wiley, 1986.

Coleman, Richard P. and Lee Rainwater. *Social Standing in America*. New York: Basic Books, 1978.

Collier, Paul. *The Bottom Billion: Why the Poorest Countries are Failing and What Can be Done About It*. New York: Oxford University Press, 2007.

Collier, Richard. *Masculinities, Crime and Criminology*. London: Sage, 1998.

Collins, Patricia Hill. *Black Feminist Thought*. London: Routledge, 1990.

Collins, Randall. 'A conflict theory of sexual stratification'. *Social Problems*, Vol. 19, No. 1 (Summer 1971): 3–21.

——. *The Credential Society: An Historical Sociology of Education and Stratification*. New York: Academic Press, 1979.

Comte, Auguste. *Auguste Comte and Positivism: The Essential Writings*. Gertrud Lenzer ed. New York: Harper Torchbooks, 1975; orig. 1851–4.

Concise Oxford Dictionary of Sociology, The. 3rd edn. John Scott ed. Oxford: Oxford University Press, 2005.

Condry, Ian. *Hip Hop Japan: Rap and the Paths of Cultural Globalization*. Chapel Hill, NC: Duke University Press, 2006.

Connell, R. W. *Masculinities*. Cambridge: Polity, 1995.

——. *Gender*. Cambridge: Polity, 2002 (2nd edn, 2009).

Connell, R. W. *Southern Theory*. Cambridge: Polity, 2007.

Connett, Paul H. 'The disposable society', in F. Herbert Bormann and Stephen R. Kellert (eds), *Ecology, Economics and Ethics: The Broken Circle*. New Haven, CT: Yale University Press, 1991: 99–122.

Connor, Steven. *Postmodern Culture: An Introduction to Theories of the Contemporary*, 2nd edn. Oxford: Blackwell, 1997.

Conrad, Peter and Joseph Schneider. *Deviance and Medicalization: From Badness to Sickness*, 2nd edn. London: Routledge, 1990 (1st edn, Free Association Press, 1980).

Cooley, Charles Horton. *Human Nature and the Social Order*. New York: Schocken, 1964; orig. 1902.

Coombe, Vivienne and Alan Little. *Race and Social Work*. London: Routledge, 1986 (2nd edn, 1992).

Corbin, J. and Anselm Strauss. 'Managing chronic illness at home'. *Qualitative Sociology*, Vol. 8, No. 3 (1985): 224–47.

Corea, Gena. 'The new reproductive technologies', in Dorchen Leidholdt and Janice C. Raymond (eds), *The Sexual Liberals and the Attack on Feminism*. New York: Pergamon, 1988.

Coser, Lewis A. *Masters of Sociological Thought: Ideas in Historical and Social Context*, 2nd edn. New York: Harcourt Brace Jovanovich, 1977.

Council on Families in America. *Marriage in America: A Report to the Nation*. New York: Institute for American Values, 1995.

Coveney, Lal et al. *The Sexuality Papers*. London: Hutchinson, 1984.

Cox, Harvey. *The Secular City*, rev. edn. New York: Macmillan, 1971; orig. 1965.

Coxon, Anthony P. M. *Between the Sheets: The Sexual Diaries of Gay Men*. London: Cassell, 1997.

Craib, Ian. *Modern Social Theory*, 2nd edn. Hemel Hempstead: Harvester Wheatsheaf, 1992.

Cramer, Duncan and Dennis Laurence Howitt. *The SAGE Dictionary of Statistics: A Practical Resource for Students in the Social Sciences*. London: Sage, 2004.

Crewe, Ivor. 'Changing votes and changing voters'. *Electoral Studies* (December 1992).

Crofts, S. 'Global neighbours', in R. Allen (ed.), *Soap Operas around the World*. London: Routledge, 1995.

Crompton, Rosemary. *Class and Stratification*. Cambridge: Polity, 1993.

——. *Women and Work in Modern Britain*. Oxford: Oxford University Press, 1997.

Crouch, Colin. *Social Change in Western Europe*. Oxford: Oxford University Press, 1999.

Crystal, David. *English as a Global Language*. Cambridge: Cambridge University Press, 1997.

——. *The Cambridge Encyclopedia of Language*, 3rd edn. Cambridge: University of Cambridge Press, 2010.

——. *Txtng: The Gr8Db8*. Oxford: Oxford University Press, 2009.

Cuff, E. C. and G. C. F. Payne (eds). *Perspectives in Sociology*, 4th edn. London: Allen and Unwin, 1997; orig., 1979.

Cumming, Elaine and William E. Henry. *Growing Old: The Process of Disengagement*. New York: Basic Books, 1961.

Curtiss, Susan. *Genie: A Psycholinguistic Study of a Modern-Day 'Wild Child'*. New York: Academic Press, 1977.

D

Dahl, Robert A. *Who Governs?* New Haven, CT: Yale University Press, 1961.

——. *Dilemmas of Pluralist Democracy: Autonomy vs. Control*. New Haven, CT: Yale University Press, 1982.

Dahrendorf, Ralf. *Class and Class Conflict in Industrial Society*. Stanford, CA: Stanford University Press, 1959.

Daly, Martin and Margo Wilson. *Homicide*. New York: Aldine, 1988.

Daly, Mary. *Beyond God the Father*. Boston, MA: Beacon, 1973.

——. *Gyn Ecology: The Metaethics of Radical Feminism*. Boston, MA: Beacon, 1978.

Danaher, Geoff, Tony Schirato and Jen Webb. *Understanding Foucault*. Sage, 2002.

Dandaneau, Steven P. *Taking It Big: Developing Sociological Consciousness in Postmodern Times*. London: Pine Forge, 2001.

Daniel, W. W. *Racial Discrimination in England* (based on the PEP Report). Harmondsworth: Penguin, 1968.

Darnton, Nina and Yuriko Hoshia. 'Whose life is it, anyway?' *Newsweek*, Vol. 113, No. 4 (13 January 1989): 61.

Darwin, Charles. *The Illustrated Origin of the Species*, abridged by Richard Leakey. London: Faber and Faber, 1979; orig. 1859.

Da Silva, Filipe Carreira. *G. H. Mead: A Critical Introduction*. Cambridge: Polity, 2007.

Davidson, Julia O'Connell. *Prostitution, Power and Freedom*. Cambridge: Polity, 1998.

Davie, Grace. *Religion in Britain since 1945: Believing without Belonging*. Oxford: Blackwell, 1994.

——. 'God and Caesar: religion in a rapidly changing Europe', in J. Bailey (ed.), *Social Europe*, 2nd edn. London: Longman, 1998: 231–54.

——. *Religion in Modern Europe: A Memory Mutates*. Oxford: Oxford University Press, 2000.

Davies, Malcolm, Hazel Croall and Jane Tyrer. *Criminal Justice: An Introduction to the Criminal Justice System in England and Wales*, 4th edn. London: Pearson/Longman, 2009; orig. 1995.

Davis, Kingsley. 'Extreme social isolation of a child'. *American Journal of Sociology*, Vol. 45, No. 4 (January 1940): 554–65.

——. 'Final note on a case of extreme isolation'. *American Journal of Sociology*, Vol. 52, No. 5 (March 1947): 432–7.

Davis, Kingsley and Wilbert Moore. 'Some principles of stratification'. *American Sociological Review*, Vol. 10, No. 2 (April 1945): 242–9.

Davis, Lennard J. ed. *The Disability Studies Reader*, 3rd edn. London: Routledge, 2010.

Davis, Mila. *City of Quarts*. London: Verso, 1990.

——. *Planet of Slums*. London: Verso, 2006.

Davis, Murray. *Smut*. Chicago: University of Chicago Press, 1983.

Dawkins, Richards. *The God Delusion*. London: Black Swan, 2006a.

——. *Unweaving the Rainbow: Science, Delusion and the Appetite for Wonder*. London: Allen Lane, 2006b.

Dean, Malcolm. *Growing Older in the Twenty-First Century*. European Social Research Council, 2004. Also accessed at: www.shef.ac.uk/uni/projects/gap/Publications.htm.

De Beauvoir, Simone. *All Said and Done*. Harmondsworth: Penguin, 1977.

Deem, Rosemary (ed.). *Schooling for Women's Work*. London: Routledge and Kegan Paul, 1980.

——. 'Governing schools in the 1990s'. *Sociology Review*, Vol. 6, No. 3 (1997): 28–31.

Deem, Rosemary, K. J. Brehony and S. Heath. *Active Citizenship and the Governing of Schools*. Buckingham: Open University Press, 1995.

de Hennezel, Marie. *The Warmth of the Heart Prevents Your Body from Rusting: Ageing without growing old*. London: Macmillan, 2011.

Delaney, Tim and Tim Madigan. *The Sociology of Sports: An Introduction*. London: McFarland & Co, 2009.

Delanty, Gerard. *Social Science: Philosophical and Methodological Foundations*. Milton Keynes: Open University Press, 2005.

——. *Community*. London: Routledge, 2003.

——. *The Cosmopolitan Imagination: The Renewal of Social Theory*. Cambridge: Cambridge University Press, 2009.

Delanty, Gerard and Chris Rumford. *Rethinking Europe: Social Theory and the Implications of Europeanization*. London: Routledge, 2005.

DeNora, Tia. *Music in Everyday Life*. Cambridge: Cambridge University Press, 2000.

Delphy, Christine and Diana Leonard. *Familiar Exploitation: A New Analysis of Marriage in Contemporary Western Societies*. Cambridge: Polity, 1992.

De Maio, Fernando. *Health and Social Theory*. Basingstoke: Palgrave, 2010.

Dennis, Kingsley and John Urry. *After the Car*. Cambridge: Polity, 2010.

Dennis, Norman and George Erdos. *Families without Fatherhood*. London: IEA Health and Welfare Unit, 1993.

Dennis, Norman, Fernando Henriques and Clifford Slaughter. *Coal is Our Life: An Analysis of a Yorkshire Mining Community*. London: Eyre & Spottiswoode, 1956.

Denzin, Norman K. *The Research Act*. New Brunswick, NJ, 1970; 1999.

——. *Images of Postmodern Society: Social Theory and Contemporary Cinema*. London: Sage, 1991.

——. *Symbolic Interactionism and Cultural Studies: The Politics of Interpretation*. Oxford: Blackwell, 1992.

——. *The Cinematic Society*. London: Sage, 1995.

——. *Performance Ethnography: Critical Pedagogy and the Politics of Culture*. London: Sage, 2003.

——. *The Qualitative Manifesto: A Call To Arms*. Walnut Creek, CA: Left Coast Press, 2010.

Denzin, Norman K. and Yvonna S. Lincoln (eds). *Handbook of Qualitative Research*, 3rd edn. London: Sage, 2004.

Department of Education and Employment. *Excellence in Schools*. CM 3681. London: HMSO, July 1997.

Desai, Vandana and Robert B. Potter (eds), *The Companion to Development Studies*, 2nd edn. London: Hodder, 2008.

De Solla Price, D. *Little Science, Big Science*. New York: Columbia University Press, 1963.

Devine, Fiona. *Affluent Workers Revisited*. Edinburgh: Edinburgh University Press, 1992.

Devine, Fiona and Sue Heath. *Sociological Research Methods in Context*. London: Macmillan, 1999.

Devine, Fiona and Mary C. Waters. *Social Inequalities in Comparative Perspective*. Oxford: Blackwell, 2004.

Diamond, Jared. *Guns, Germs and Steel: The Fate of Human Societies*. New York: W. W. Norton, 1997.

——. *Collapse: How Societies Choose to Fail or Succeed*. New York: Penguin, 2005.

——. *The Third Chimpanzee: The Evolution and Future of the Human Animal*. London: Harper Perennial, 2006.

Dicken, Peter. *Global Shift: Mapping the Changing Contours of the World Economy*, 6th edn. London: Sage, 2010.

Dickens, Charles. *Oliver Twist*. 1886: 36; orig. 1837–9.

Dickens, Charles. *Bleak House*. London: Penguin, 2003.

Dickens, Peter and James Ormrod. *The Cosmic Society*. London: Routledge, 2007.

Dillon, Michelle. *Introduction to Sociological Theory*. Oxford: Wiley-Blackwell, 2009.

Dines, Gail. *Pornland: How Porn Has Hijacked our Sexuality*. Boston: Beacon, 2010.

Dobash, R. Emerson and Russell Dobash, 'Violence against women', in Laura O'Toole and Jessica Schiffman (eds), *Gender violence*. New York: New York Press, 1997.

Dollard, John. *Caste and Class in a Southern Town*. New Haven, CT: Yale University Press, 1937 (reprinted in the Sociology of Class series, New York: Routledge, 1998).

Dollard, John, L. Doob, N. Miller, O. Mowrer and R. Sears. *Frustration and Aggression*. New Haven, CT: Yale University Press, 1939.

Domhoff, G. William. *Who Rules America Now? A View of the '80s*. Englewood Cliffs, NJ: Prentice-Hall, 1983.

Dorling, Daniel. *Injustice: Why Social Inequality Persists*. Bristol: Policy Press, 2010.

Douglas, J. W. B. *The Home and the School*. London: MacGibbon and Kee, 1964.

Douglas, Mary. *Purity and Danger*. Harmondsworth: Penguin, 1966.

——. *Natural Symbols*. Harmondsworth: Penguin, 1970.

Dowd, Nancy E. *In Defense of Single-Parent Families*. New York: New York University Press, 1997.

Downes, David and Paul Rock. *Understanding Deviance*, 2nd edn. Oxford: Clarendon Press, 1988.

Downing, Lisa. *The Cambridge Introduction to Foucault*. Cambridge: Cambridge University Press, 2008.

Doyal, Lesley. *The Political Economy of Health*. London: Pluto, 1979.

——. *What Makes Women Sick*. London: Macmillan, 1995.

Du Bois, W. E. B. *Dusk of Dawn*. New York: Harcourt, Brace & World, 1940.

——. *The Philadelphia Negro: A Social Study*. New York: Schocken, 1967; orig. 1899.

——. *The Souls of Black Folk*. New York: Penguin, 1982; orig. 1903.

Dubos, René. *Mirage of Health: Utopias, Progress and Biological Change*. New York: Harper & Row, 1980; orig. 1959.

Dudrah, Rajinder Kumar. *Bollywood: Sociology Goes to the Movies*. London: Sage, 2006.

Du Gay, Paul. *In Praise of Bureaucracy: Weber, Organization, Ethics*. London: Sage, 2000.

——. *The Values of Bureaucracy*. Oxford: Oxford University Press, 2005.

Du Gay, Paul, Stuart Hall, L. Janes, H. MacKay and K. Negus (eds). *Doing Cultural Studies: The Story of the Sony Walkman*. Buckingham: Open University Press, 1996.

Duhl, Leonard J. 'The social context of health', in Arthur C. Hastings et al. (eds), *Health for the Whole Person: The Complete Guide to Holistic Medicine*. Boulder, CO: Westview, 1980: 39–48.

Duhring, Simon (ed.). *The Cultural Studies Reader*, 2nd edn. London: Routledge, 2006.

Duncombe, Jean and Dennis Marsden. 'Love and intimacy: the gender division of emotion and "emotion work"'. *Sociology*, Vol. 27, No. 2 (1993): 221–41.

Duneier, Mitchell. *Slim's Table*. Chicago: University of Chicago, 1994.

——. *Sidewalk*. New York: Farrar, Strauss and Giroux, 2000.

Durkheim, Emile. *The Division of Labor in Society*. New York: Free Press, 1964a; orig. 1895.

——. *The Rules of Sociological Method*. New York: Free Press, 1964b; orig. 1893.

——. *The Elementary Forms of Religious Life*. New York: Free Press, 1965; orig. 1915.

——. *Suicide*. New York: Free Press, 1966; orig. 1897.

——. *Selected Writings*. Anthony Giddens ed. Cambridge: Cambridge University Press, 1972; orig. 1918.

——. *Sociology and Philosophy*. New York: Free Press, 1974; orig. 1924.

Dworkin, Andrea. *Pornography: Men Possessing Women*. New York: Pedigree, 1981.

——. *Right Wing Women*, London: Women's Press, 1983.

——. *Intercourse*. New York: Free Press, 1987.

E

Eadie, Jo (ed.). *Sexuality: The Essential Glossary*. London: Arnold, 2004.

Ebaugh, Helen Rose Fuchs. *Becoming an EX: The Process of Role Exit*. Chicago: University of Chicago Press, 1988.

Economist. *Pocket Europe in Figures*. London: Economist Books, 2000.

Eder, Klaus. *The New Politics of Class*. London: Sage, 1993.

Edgell, Steven. *Class*. London: Routledge, 1993.

Edmunds, J. and B. Turner. *Generations, Culture and Society*. Buckingham: Open University Press, 2002.

Edwards, Jeanette, et al. *Technologies of Procreation*, 2nd edn. London: Routledge, 1999.

Ehrenreich, Barbara. *Nickel and Dimed: On (Not) Getting by in America*. New York: Henry Holt, 2001.

Ehrenreich, John. 'Introduction', in John Ehrenreich (ed.), *The Cultural Crisis of Modern Medicine*. New York: Monthly Review Press, 1978: 1–35.

Ehrlich, Paul R. *The Population Bomb*. New York: Ballantine, 1968.

Eichler, Margrit. *Nonsexist Research Methods: A Practical Guide*. Winchester, MA: Unwin Hyman, 1988.

Eisendstadt, S. N. 'Multiple modernities'. *Daedalus*, Winter 2000, 129: 1.

Eisenstein, Zillah R. (ed.). *Capitalist Patriarchy and the Case for Socialist Feminism*. New York: Monthly Review Press, 1979.

——. *Global Obscenities: Patriarchy, Capitalism and the Lure of Cyberfantasy*. New York: New York University Press, 1998.

Ekman, Paul. 'Biological and cultural contributions to body and facial movements in the expression of emotions', in A. Rorty (ed.), *Explaining Emotions*. Berkeley, CA: University of California Press, 1980: 73–101.

Ekman, Paul, Wallace V. Friesen and John Bear. 'The international language of gestures'. *Psychology Today* (May 1984): 64–9.

Elder, Glenn. *Children of the Great Depression*. Chicago: University of Chicago Press, 1974.

——. 'Perspectives on the life course', in Glenn Elder, *Life Course Dynamics*. Ithaca, NY: Cornell University Press, 1985.

Eldridge, John. *C. Wright Mills*. London: Tavistock/Routledge, 1983.

Elias, Norbert. *The Civilizing Process*. Edmund Jephcott, trans. Oxford: Blackwell, 1978a; orig. 1939.

——. *What is Sociology?* Stephen Mennell and Grace Morrissey trans. London: Hutchinson, 1978b; orig. 1970.

——. *Mozart: The Sociology of a Genius*. Cambridge: Polity, 1994.

Elliot, Faith Robertson. *Gender, Family and Society*. London: Macmillan, 1996.

Elliott, Anthony and Charles Lemert. *The New Individualism: The Emotional Costs of Globalization*, revised edn. London: Routledge, 2009.

Elliott, Antony and John Urry. *Mobile Lives*. London: Routledge 2010.

Elliott, Jane. *Using Narrative in Social Research*. London: Sage, 2005.

Emerson, Joan P. 'Behavior in private places: sustaining definitions of reality in gynecological examinations', in H. P. Dreitzel (ed.), *Recent Sociology*, Vol. 2. New York: Collier, 1970: 74–97.

Engels, Friedrich. *The Origin of the Family*. Chicago: Charles H. Kerr & Company, 1902; orig. 1884.

Enloe, Cynthia. *Bananas, Beaches, and Bases: Making Feminist Sense of International Politics*. Berkeley, CA: University of California Press, 1990.

Epstein, Steven. *Impure Science: AIDS, Activism and the Politics of Knowledge*. Berkeley, CA: University of California Press, 1998.

Erikson, Erik H. *Childhood and Society*. New York: W. W. Norton, 1963; orig. 1950.

——. *Identity and the Life Cycle*. New York: W. W. Norton, 1980.

Erikson, Kai T. *Wayward Puritans: A Study in the Sociology of Deviance*. New York: Wiley, 1966.

Erikson, Robert and John H. Goldthorpe. *The Constant Flux: A Study of Class Mobility in Industrial Societies*. Oxford: Clarendon Press, 1992.

ESPAD (1999) *European School Survey Project on Alcohol and Other Drugs: Report*. Stockholm.

Esping-Andersen, C. *The Three Worlds of Welfare Capitalism*. Cambridge: Polity, 1990.

Esposito, John L. *The Islamic Threat: Myth or Reality*. New York: Oxford University Press, 1992.

Etzioni, Amitai. *A Comparative Analysis of Complex Organization: On Power, Involvement and Their Correlates*, rev. and enlarged edn. New York: Free Press, 1975.

——. *The Spirit of Community: Rights, Responsibilities, and the Communitarian Agenda*. New York: Crown Publishers, 1993.

European Roma Rights Center. 'Time of the Skinheads: denial and exclusion of Roma in Slovakia'. Country Report Series, No. 3 (January 1997).

Eurostat. *Europe in Figures*, 4th edn. Luxembourg: Office for Official Publications of the European Communities, 1995a.

——. *Women and Men in Europe: A Statistical Portrait*. Luxembourg: Office for Official Publications of the European Communities, 1995b.

——. *Europe in Figures*. Luxembourg: Office for Official Publications of the European Communities, 2006.

Evans, Karen and Janet Jamieson (eds). *Gender and Crime: A Reader*. Maidenhead: Open University Press, 2008.

Evans, Mary. *Killing Thinking: The Death of the Universities*. London: Continuum, 2004.

——. *A Short History of Society*. Maidenhead: Open University Press, 2006.

Evans-Pritchard, E. E. *Kinship and Marriage amongst the Nuer*. Oxford: Clarendon Press, 1951; reprinted 1969.

F

Falkenmark, Malin and Carl Widstrand. 'Population and water resources: a delicate balance'. *Population Bulletin*, Vol. 47, No. 3 (November 1992). Washington, DC: Population Reference Bureau.

Farrer, James. *Opening Up: Youth, sex culture and market reform in Shanghai*. Chicago: University of Chicago Press, 2002.

Faulkner, Robert R. and Howard S. Becker. *Do You Know . . . ? The Jazz Repertoire in Action*. Chicago: University of Chicago Press.

Fausto-Sterling, Anne. *Myths of Gender: Biological Theories about Women and Men*. New York: Basic Books, 1992.

Featherstone, Mike (ed.). *Global Culture: Nationalism, Globalization and Modernity*. London: Sage, 1990.

——. *Consumer Culture and Postmodernism*. London: Sage, 1991.

Fennell, Graham, Chris Phillipson and Helen Evers. *The Sociology of Old Age*. Buckingham: Open University Press, 1988.

Ferrell, Jeff, Keith Hayward and Jock Young. *Cultural Criminology*. London: Sage, 2008.

Finch, Janet. *Family Obligations and Social Change*. Cambridge: Polity, 1989.

Finch, Janet and Dulcie Groves (eds). *A Labour of Love*. London: Routledge, 1983.

Finch, Janet and Jennifer Mason. *Negotiating Family Responsibilities*. London: Routledge, 1993.

Fine, Gary Alan. *Kitchens*. Chicago, IL: University of Chicago Press, 1995.

Fine, Robert. *Cosmopolitan*. London: Routledge, 2007.

Finnegan, Ruth. *The Hidden Musicians: Music Making in an English Town*, 2nd edn. Connecticut: Wesleyan University Press, 2007.

Fiske, John. 'Postmodernism and culture', in James Curran and Michael Gurevitch (eds), *Mass Media and Society*. London: Methuen, 1991.

Fitzpatrick, Mary Anne. *Between Husbands and Wives: Communication in Marriage*. Newbury Park, CA: Sage, 1988.

Flaherty, Jan, John Veit-Wilson and Paul Dornan. *Poverty: The Facts*. London: Child Poverty Action Group, 2004.

Flandrin, Jean-Louis. *Families in Former Times: Kinship, Household and Sexuality*. Richard Southern trans. Cambridge: Cambridge University Press, 1979.

Flew, Terry. *Understanding Global Media*. Basingstoke: Palgrave, 2007.

Foer, Franklin. 'Soccer vs. McWorld'. *Foreign Policy* (January/February 2004): 32.

Foreman, Martin (ed.). *Aids and Men: Taking Risks or Responsibility?* London: Zed, 1999.

Foster, Robert J. *Coca-Globalization*. Basingstoke: Palgrave, 2008.

Foucault, Michel. *Discipline and Punish: The Birth of the Prison*, Alan Sheridan trans. London: Allen Lane, 1977; orig. Paris: Editions Galliand, 1975.

——. *The History of Sexuality*, Vol. 1. London: Allen Lane, 1979 (orig. Paris: Editions Galliand, 1976).

Fowler, Brenda. *Iceman: Uncovering the Life and Times of a Prehistoric Man Found in an Alpine Glacier*. London: Pan, 2002.

Fox, Kate. *Watching the English: The Hidden Rules of English Behaviour*. London: Hodder & Stoughton, 2005.

Fox Keller, Evelyn. *Reflections on Gender and Science*. New Haven, CT: Yale University Press, 1985.

Francis, Mark. *Herbert Spencer and the Invention of Modern Life*. Stocksfield: Acumen, 2007.

Frank, André Gunder. *On Capitalist Underdevelopment*. Bombay: Oxford University Press, 1975.

Frank, Arthur. *The Wounded Storyteller: Body Illness and Ethics*. Chicago: University of Chicago Press, 1995.

Franklin, Sarah. *Embodied Progress*. London: Routledge, 1997.

Frayman, Harold. *Breadline Britain 1990s: The Findings of the Television Series*. London: London Weekend Television, 1991.

Frazier, E. Franklin. *Black Bourgeoisie: The Rise of a New Middle Class*. New York: Free Press, 1965.

——. *The Negro Church in America*. New York: Schocken, 1963.

Freedom House. *Freedom in the World*. New York: Freedom House, 2000.

Freire, Paulo. *Pedagogy of the Oppressed*. London: Sheed and Ward, 1972.

French, Marilyn. *Beyond Power: On Women, Men, and Morals*. New York: Summit Books, 1985.

Freud, Sigmund. *Civilisation and Its Discontents*. Harmondsworth: Penguin, 2004; orig. 1930.

Friedan, Betty. *The Feminine Mystique*. Harmondsworth: Penguin, 1963.

——. *The Fountain of Age*. New York: Simon & Schuster, 1993.

Friedman, John. 'The world city hypothesis'. *Development and Change*, Vol. 17: 69–83.

Friedman, Milton and Rose Friedman. *Free to Choose: A Personal Statement*. London: Secker and Warburg, 1980.

Friedman, Thomas L. *The World is Flat: Globalization in the Twenty-First Century*. Harmondsworth: Penguin, 2006.

Frisby, David. *Georg Simmel*, 2nd edn. London: Tavistock, 2002.

Frisby, David and Derek Sayer. *Society*. London: Routledge, 1986.

Fukuyama, Francis. *The End of History*. Washington, DC: Irving Kristol, 1989 (offprint from *The National Interest*, summer 1989 issue).

——. *Trust: The Social Virtues and the Creation of Prosperity*. London: Hamish Hamilton, 1995.

Fuller, Steve. *Science*. Minneapolis, MN: University of Minnesota Press, 1997.

——. 'Who's afraid of science studies?'. *Independent on Sunday* (28 June 1998).

Furedi, Frank. *Where Have All the Intellectuals Gone?*, 2nd edn. London: Continuum, 2006.

Furlong, Andy and Fred Cartmeal. *Young People and Social Change: Individualism and Risk in the Age of High Modernity*. Buckingham: Open University Press, 1997.

Furstenberg, Frank F., Jr. 'The new extended family: the experience of parents and children after remarriage'. Paper presented to the Changing Family Conference XIII: The Blended Family. University of Iowa, 1984.

G

Gagnon, J. and W. Simon. *Sexual Conduct*. Chicago: Aldine, 1973.

Gallup International, *Voice of the People 2006: What the World Thinks of Today's Global Issues*. Gallup International, 2006.

Gamble, Andrew. *The Spectre at the Feast: Capitalist Crisis and the Politics of Recession*. Basingstoke: Palgrave, 2009.

Gamer, Robert F. *Understanding Contemporary China*, 3rd edn. Boulder: Rienner, 2008.

Gane, Mike. *Auguste Comte*. London: Routledge, 2006.

Gannon, Martin J. *Understanding Global Cultures: Metaphysical Journeys through 23 Nations*, 4th edn. London: Sage, 2009.

Gans, Herbert J. *People and Plans: Essays on Urban Problems and Solutions*. New York: Basic Books, 1968.

——. *The Urban Villagers: Group and Class in the Life of Italian-Americans*. New York: Free Press, 1982.

Garca-Moreno et al. *WHO Multi-country Study on Women's Health and Domestic Violence against Women: Initial Results on Prevalence, Health Outcomes and Women's Responses*. Geneva: WHO, 2005.

Garfinkel, Harold. 'Conditions of successful degradation ceremonies'. *American Journal of Sociology*, Vol. 61, No. 2 (March 1956): 420–4.

——. *Studies in Ethnomethodology*. Cambridge: Polity, 1967.

Garland, David. *Punishment and Modern Society*. Oxford: Clarendon, 1990.

——. *The Culture of Control*. Oxford: Oxford University Press, 2002.

Garner, Robert. *Environmental Politics*. London: Prentice Hall, 1996; 2nd edn, 2001.

Gauntlett, David (ed.). *web.studies*. London: Arnold, 2000.

Gay, Peter. *The Enlightment: An Interpretation*. London: Weidenfeld and Nicolson, 1970.

Geertz, Clifford. *The Interpretation of Cultures*. New York: Basic Books, 1973; London: Hutchinson, 1995.

Geertz, Hildred and Clifford Geertz. *Kinship in Bali*. Chicago: University of Chicago Press, 1975.

Gelder, Ken and Sarah Thornton (eds). *The Subcultures Reader*, 2nd edn. London: Routledge, 2005; orig. 1997.

Gelder, Ken. *Subcultures: Cultural Histories and Social Practice*. London: Routledge, 2008.

George, Rose. *The Big Necessity: Adventures in the World of Human Waste*. London: Portobello Books, 2008.

George, Susan. *How the Other Half Dies: The Real Reasons for World Hunger*. Totowa, NJ: Rowman & Allanheld, 1977.

Geraghty, Christine. *Women and Soap Operas*. Cambridge: Polity, 1991.

Gergen, Kenneth J. *The Saturated Self: Dilemmas of Identity in Contemporary Life*. New York: Basic Books, 1991.

Gerth, H. H. and C. Wright Mills (eds). *From Max Weber: Essays in Sociology*. New York: Oxford University Press, 1946; London: Routledge and Kegan Paul, 1948.

Geschwender, James A. *Racial Stratification in America*. Dubuque, IA: Wm C. Brown, 1978.

Gibbins, John and Bo Reimer. *The Politics of Postmodernity*. London: Sage, 1999.

Giddens, Anthony. *The Constitution of Society*. Cambridge: Polity, 1984.

——. *Sociology: A Brief but Critical Introduction*. New York: Harcourt Brace Jovanovich, 1982; 2nd edn, London: Macmillan, 1986.

——. *The Consequences of Modernity*. Oxford: Polity, 1990.

——. *Self Identity and Late Modernity*. Cambridge: Polity, 1991.

——. *The Transformation of Intimacy*. Cambridge: Polity, 1992.

——. *Beyond Left and Right: The Future of Radical Politics*. Cambridge: Polity, 1994.

——. *The Third Way: The Renewal of Social Democracy*. Cambridge: Polity, 1998.

——. *Runaway World: How Globalization is Reshaping Our Lives*. London: Profile, 1999.

—— (ed.). *The Global Third Way Debate*. Cambridge: Polity, 2001.

—— (ed.). *The Progressive Manifesto: New Ideas from the Centre-Left*. Cambridge: Polity, 2004.

——. *The Politics of Climate Change*. Cambridge: Polity, 2009.

Giddens, Anthony and Jonathan Turner (eds). *Social Theory Today*. Cambridge: Polity, 1987.

Giele, Janet Z. 'Gender and sex roles', in Neil J. Smelser (ed.), *Handbook of Sociology*. Newbury Park, CA: Sage, 1988: 291–323.

Gilborn, David. *Racism and Anti-Racism in Real Schools*. Buckingham: Open University Press, 1995.

Gilleard, Chris and Paul Higgs. *Cultures of Ageing: Self, Citizen and Body*. London: Pearson, 2000.

——. *Contexts of Ageing*. Cambridge: Polity, 2005.

Gilligan, Carol. *In a Different Voice: Psychological Theory and Women's Development*. Cambridge, MA: Harvard University Press, 1982.

Gilroy, Paul. *There Ain't No Black in the Union Jack*. London: Hutchinson, 1987.

——. *The Black Atlantic: Modernity and Double Consciousness*. London: Verso, 1993.

——. *After Empire: Multiculture or Postcolonial Melancholia*. London: Routledge, 2004.

Ginsburg, Faye and Rayna Rapp. *Conceiving the New World Order*. Berkeley, CA: University of California Press, 1995.

Ginsburg Faye, Lila Abu-Lughood and Brian Larkin (eds). *Media Worlds: Anthropology on New Terrain*. Berkeley, CA: University of California, 2002.

Giroux, Henry. *Border Crossings: Cultural Workers and the Politics of Education*. London: Routledge, 1992.

Gittins, Diana. *The Family in Question: Changing Households and Familiar Ideologies*. Basingstoke: Macmillan, 1985; 2nd edn, 1993.

Giulianotti, Richard and Roland Robertson. *Globalization and Football*. Newbury Park, CA: Sage, 2009.

Glaab, Charles N. *The American City: A Documentary History*. Homewood, IL: Dorsey, 1963.

Glaser, Barney and Anselm Strauss. *Awareness of Dying*. London: Weidenfeld and Nicolson, 1967.

Glasgow Media Group. *Really Bad News*. London: Writers and Readers, 1982.

Glasner, Angela. 'Gender and Europe: cultural and structural impediments to change', in Joe Banks (ed.), *Social Europe*. London: Longman, 1992.

Glazer, Nathan and Daniel P. Moynihan. *Beyond the Melting Pot*, 2nd edn. Cambridge, MA: MIT Press, 1970.

Glendenning, F. 'What is elder abuse and neglect?', in P. Decalmer and F. Glendenning (eds), *The Mistreatment of Elderly People*. London: Sage, 1993.

Glock, Charles Y. 'The religious revival in America', in Jane Zahn (ed.), *Religion and the Face of America*. Berkeley, CA: University of California Press, 1959: 25–42.

——. 'On the study of religious commitment'. *Religious Education*, Vol. 62, No. 4 (1962): 98–110.

Glueck, Sheldon and Eleanor Glueck. *Unraveling Juvenile Delinquency*. New York: Commonwealth Fund, 1950.

Gobineau, J. A. Comte de. *Essay on the Inequality of the Human Races*. New York: Putnam, 1915; orig. 1853.

Goffman, Erving. *The Presentation of Self in Everyday Life*. Garden City, NY: Anchor, 1959.

——. *Asylums: Essays on the Social Situation of Mental Patients and Other Inmates*. Garden City, NY: Anchor, 1961.

——. *Stigma: Notes on the Management of Spoiled Identity*. Englewood Cliffs, NJ: Prentice-Hall, 1962.

——. *Interactional Ritual: Essays on Face-to-Face Behavior*. Garden City, NY: Anchor, 1967.

——. 'The Interaction Order'. *American Sociological Review*, Vol. 48 (1982): 1–17.

Goldberg, Steven. *The Inevitability of Patriarchy*. New York: William Morrow, 1974.

——. *Why Men Rule: A Theory of Male Dominance*. Chicago: Open Court, 1993.

Goldhagen, Daniel Jonah. *Worse than War: Genocide, Eliminationism and the Ongoing Assault on Humanity*. New York: Public Affairs, 2009.

Golding, Peter and Philip Elliott. *Making the News*. London: Longman, 1979.

Goldman, Robert and Stephen Papson. *Nike Culture*. London: Sage, 1998.

Goldsby, Richard A. *Race and Races*, 2nd edn. New York: Macmillan, 1977.

Goldthorpe, John H. (in collaboration with Catriona Llewellyn and Clive Payne). *Social Mobility and Class Structure in Modern Britain*. Oxford: Clarendon Press, 1980.

——. 'On the service class, its formation and future', in A. Giddens and G. Mackenzie (eds), *Social Class and the Division of Labour*. Cambridge: Cambridge University Press, 1982.

Goldthorpe, John H., David Lockwood, Frank Bechhofer and Jennifer Platt. *The Affluent Worker*. Cambridge: Cambridge University Press, 1968.

González-López, Gloria. *Erotic Journeys: Mexican Immigrants and Their Sex Lives*. Berkeley, CA: University of California Press, 2005.

Goode, William J. *World Changes in Divorce Patterns*. New Haven, CT: Yale University Press, 1993.

Gordon, David and Peter Townsend (eds). *Breadline Europe: The Measurement of Poverty*. Bristol: Policy Press, 2000.

Gordon, James S. 'The paradigm of holistic medicine', in Arthur C. Hastings et al. (eds), *Health for the Whole Person: The Complete Guide to Holistic Medicine*. Boulder, CO: Westview, 1980: 3–27.

Gordon, Raymond G. Jr (ed.). *Ethnologue: Languages of the World*. Dallas: SIL International, 2005.

Goring, Charles Buckman. *The English Convict: A Statistical Study*. Montclair, NJ: Patterson Smith, 1972; orig. 1913.

Gorringe, Hugo. *Untouchable Citizens: Dalit Movements and Democratisation in Tamil Nadu*. New Delhi: Sage, 2006.

Gorssberg, Lawrence, Cary Nelson and Paula Treichler. *Cultural Studies*. London: Routledge, 1992.

Gortz, André. *Farewell to the Working Class: An Essay on Post-industrial Socialism*. London: Pluto, 1982; orig. French edition, 1980.

Gottmann, Jean. *Megalopolis*. New York: Twentieth Century Fund, 1961.

Gould, Stephen. J. *Life's Grandeur*, London: Cape, 1996.

Gouldner, Alvin. 'The sociologist as partisan: sociology and the welfare state', in Larry T. Reynolds and Janice M. Reynolds (eds), *The Sociology of Sociology*. New York: Avon Books, 1970a: 218–55.

——. *The Coming Crisis of Western Sociology*. New York: Avon Books, 1970b.

Graham, Hilary. *Unequal Lives: Health and Socioeconomic Inequalities*. Maidenhead: Open University Press, 2007.

Gramsci, A. *Selections from the Prison Notebooks*. London: New Left Books, 1971.

Granovetter, Mark. 'The strength of weak ties'. *American Journal of Sociology*, Vol. 78, No. 6 (May 1973): 1360–80.

Gray, Ann. *Research Practice for Cultural Studies*. London: Sage, 2003.

Gray, Chris Hables (ed.). *The Cyborg Handbook*. London: Routledge, 1995.

Gray, John. *False Dawn: The Delusions of Global Capitalism*. London: Granta, 2002.

——. *Heresies: Against Progress and Other Illusions*. London: Granta, 2004.

——. *Black Mass: Apocalyptic Religion and the Death of Utopia*. London: Allen Lane, 2007.

Grayling, A. C. *Against All Odds*. London: Oberon, 2007.

Grayling, A. C. *The Good Book: A Secular Bible*. London: Bloomsbury, 2011.

Green, Gill. *The End of Stigma?* London: Routledge, 2009.

Green, Penny and Tony Ward. *State Crime: Governments, Violence and Corruption*. Pluto, 2004.

Greenblat, Cathy. *Alive with Alzheimer's*. Chicago: University of Chicago Press, 2004.

Greenhalgh, Susan. *Just One Child: Science and Policy in Deng's China*. Berkeley CA: University of California Press, 2008.

Grint, Keith. *The Sociology of Work: An Introduction*. Cambridge: Polity, 1991; 2nd edn, 1998.

Gubbay, Jon, Chris Middleton and Chet Ballard. *The Student's Companion to Sociology*. Oxford: Blackwell, 1997.

Gubrium, Jaber F. *Speaking of Life: Horizons of Meaning for Nursing Home Residents*. Hawthorne, NY: Aldine de Gruyter, 1993.

Gutmann, Matthew (1996). *The Meanings of Macho: Being a Man in Mexico City*. Berkeley, CA: University of California Press, 1996 (2nd edn, 2006).

H

Habermas, Jürgen. *Towards a Rational Society: Student Protest, Science, and Politics*. Jeremy J. Shapiro trans. Boston, MA: Beacon, 1970; latest edns 1989, paperback 1992; orig. 1962.

Hacker, Helen Mayer. 'Women as a minority group'. *Social Forces*, Vol. 30 (October 1951): 60–9.

Hafez, Kai. *The Myth of Media Globalization*. Cambridge: Polity, 2007.

Hall, David. *Cybercrime: The Transformation of Crime in the Information Age*. Cambridge: Polity, 2007.

Hall, Stuart. *Policing the Crisis*. London: Macmillan, 1978.

——. 'Encoding and decoding', in Stuart Hall et al. (eds), *Culture, Media, Language*. London: Hutchinson, 1980.

——. 'Our mongrel selves'. *New Statesman and Society* (19 June 1992a).

——. 'The question of cultural identity', in Stuart Hall, David Held and Tony McGrew (eds), *Modernity and Its Futures*. Cambridge: Polity Press in association with the Open University, 1992b.

Hall, Stuart and Martin Jacques. *New Times*. London: Lawrence and Wishart, 1989.

Hall, Stuart, David Held and Tony McGrew (eds). *Modernity and Its Futures*. Cambridge: Polity Press in association with the Open University, 1992.

Halliday, Fred. *The World at 2000*. London: Palgrave, 2001.

Halsey, A. H. *Change in British Society*. Oxford: Oxford University Press, 1986.

Halsey, A. H. with Josephine Webb (eds). *Twentieth-Century British Social Trends*. London: Macmillan, 2000.

Halsey, A. H., Jean Floud and C. Arnold Anderson (eds). *Education, Economy, and Society: A Reader in the Sociology of Education*. New York: Free Press; London: Collier-Macmillan, 1961.

Halsey, A. H., Hugh Lauder, Phillip Brown and Amy Stuart Wells. *Education: Culture, Economy and Society*. Oxford: Oxford University Press, 1997.

Hamelink, Cees. *The Ethics of Cyberspace*. London: Sage, 2000.

Hamilton, George. *Religion in the Medieval West*. London: Edward Arnold, 1996.

Hammond, Philip. *The Sacred in a Secular Age*. Berkeley, CA: University of California Press, 1985.

Hamrick, Michael H., David J. Anspaugh and Gene Ezell. *Health*. Columbus, OH: Merrill, 1986.

Hannerz, Ulf. 'Cosmopolitans and locals in world culture', in Mike Featherstone (ed.), *Global Culture: Nationalism, Globalisation, and Modernity*. London: Sage, 1990.

Hannigan, John. *Environmental Sociology*, 2nd edn. London: Routledge, 2006.

Haraway, Donna. *Simians, Cyborgs and Women: The Reinvention of Nature*. London: Free Association, 1991.

——. '"Cyborgs and Symbiants": living together in the New World Order', in C. G. Hay (ed.), *The Cyborg Handbook*. London: Routledge, 1995: xi–1.

——. *The Companion Species Manifesto: Dogs, People, and Significant Otherness*. Chicago: Prickly Paradigm, 2003.

Harding, Sandra. *Whose Science? Whose Knowledge? Thinking from Women's Lives*. Milton Keynes: Open University Press, 1991; 2nd edn, 1999.

Hare, Paul A., Edgar F. Borgatta and Robert F. Bales. *Small Groups: Studies in Social Interaction*, rev. edn. New York: Alfred A. Knopf, 1965.

Hargreaves, David. *Social Relations in a Secondary School*. London: Routledge, 1967.

Hargreaves, David H. *Interpersonal Relations and Education*. London and Boston, MA: Routledge and Kegan Paul, 1975.

Harne, Lynne and Jill Radford. *Tackling Domestic Violence*. Maidenhead: Open University Press, 2008.

Harper, Sarah. *Ageing Societies*. London: Hodder Arnold, 2006.

Harris, Chauncey D. and Edward L. Ullman. 'The nature of cities'. *The Annals*, Vol. 242 (November 1945): 7–17.

Harris, Colette. *Muslim Youth: Tensions and Transitions in Tajikistan*. Oxford: Westview, 2006.

Harris, Marvin. *Cultural Anthropology*, 2nd edn. New York: Harper & Row, 1987.

Harris, Sam. *The End of Faith*. New York: Free Press, 2006.

Harrison, K. David. *When Language Dies*. Oxford: Oxford University Press, 2007.

Harrison, Lawrence. 'Promoting cultural change', in L. E. Harrison and S. P. Huntingdon (eds), *Culture Matters*. New York: Basic Books, 2000a: 296–308.

Harrison, Lawrence E. and Samuel P. Huntington. *Culture Matters: How Values Shape Human Progress*. New York: Basic Books, 2000b.

Harrison, Paul. *Inside the Third World: The Anatomy of Poverty*, 2nd edn. New York: Penguin, 1984; 3rd edn, 1993.

Harrison, Paul and Fred Pearce. *AAAS Atlas of Population and Environment*. Berkeley, CA: University of California Press, for the American Association for the Advancement of Science, 2000.

Hart, Nicky. *The Sociology of Health and Medicine*. Ormskirk, Lancashire: Causeway, 1985.

Hartmut, Rosa and William Scheuerman, *High Speed Society*. Pennsylvania: University of Pennsylvania Press.

Harvey, David. *Social Justice and the City*. London: Edward Arnold, 1973.

——. *The Condition of Postmodernity*. Oxford: Blackwell, 1989.

——. *A Brief History of Neoliberalism*. Oxford: Oxford University Press, 2005.

——. *The Enigma of Capital and the Crises of Capitalism*. London: Profile, 2010.

Harvey, Mark et al. *Exploring the Tomato*. Cheltenham: Edward Elgar, 2002.

Haskey, J. 'Estimated numbers of one-parent families and their prevalence in Great Britain in 1991'. HMSO, 1992.

Havighurst, Robert J., Bernice L. Neugarten and Sheldon S. Tobin. 'Disengagement and patterns of aging', in Bernice L. Neugarten (ed.), *Middle Age and Aging: A Reader in Social Psychology*. Chicago: University of Chicago Press, 1968: 161–72.

Hay, Chris Gable (ed.). *The Cyborg Handbook*. London: Routledge, 1995.

Hay, D. *Europe: The Emergence of an Idea*, 2nd edn. Edinburgh: Edinburgh University Press, 1968.

Hayles, N. Katherine. 'The life cycle of cyborgs', in C. G. Hay (ed.), *The Cyborg Handbook*. London: Routledge, 1995: 321–38.

——. *How We Became Posthuman*. Chicago: University of Chicago Press, 1999.

Health Insurance Association of America. *Source Book of Health Insurance Data*. Washington, DC: The Association, 1991.

Healy, Kieran. *Last Best Gifts: Altruism and the Market for Human Blood and Organs*. Chicago: University of Chicago Press, 2006.

Hebdidge, Dick. *Subcultures: The Meaning of Style*. London: Routledge, 2007.

Heelas, Paul. *The New Age Movement*. Oxford: Blackwell, 1996.

Heider, K. G. *Ethnographic Film*. Austin, TX: University of Texas Press, 1976.

Held, David. *Global Transformations*, 2nd edn. Cambridge: Polity, 2007; orig. 1999.

Held, David and Anthony G. McGrew. *The Global Transformations Reader: An Introduction to the Globalization Debate*. Cambridge: Polity, 2003.

——. *Globalization/Anti-globalization: Beyond the Great Divide Polity Press*. Cambridge: Polity, 2007.

Henry, William A., III. *Guardians of the Flutes: Idioms of Masculinity*. London: McGraw-Hill, 1981.

Herdt, Gilbert. *Guardians of the Flutes: Idioms of Masculinity*. London: McGraw-Hill, 1981.

—— (ed.). *Gay and Lesbian Youth*. London: Haworth, 1989.

Herek, Gregory M. and Kevin T. Berrill. *Hate Crimes: Confronting Violence against Lesbians and Gay Men*. Newbury Park, CA: Sage, 1992.

Heritage, John. 'Ethnomethodology', in Anthony Giddens and Jonathan Turner (eds), *Social Theory Today*. Oxford: Polity, 1987: 224–72.

Herman, Edward S. and Robert W. McChesney. *The Global Media*. London: Continuum, 1997.

Herrnstein, Richard J. *IQ and the Meritocracy*. Boston: Little, Brown & Co., 1973.

Herrnstein, Richard J. and Charles Murray. *The Bell Curve: Intelligence and Class Structure in American Life*. New York: Free Press, 1994.

Hersch, Joni and Shelly White-Means. 'Employer-sponsored health and pension benefits and the gender/race wage gap'. *Social Science Quarterly*, Vol. 74, No. 4 (December 1993): 850–66.

Hervieu-Leger, Danièle. *Religion as a Chain of Memory*. Oxford: Polity, 2000.

Hesmondhalgh, David. *The Cultural Industries*, 2nd edn. London: Sage, 2007.

Hess, David J. *Science Studies: An Advanced Introduction*. London: New York University Press, 1997.

Hewitt, John P. *Self and Society*, 8th edn. London: Allyn and Bacon, 1999.

Hewitt, John P. and David Shulman. *Self and Society*, 10th edn. London: Allyn and Bacon, 2010.

Hewson, Claire, Peter Yule, Dianna Laujrent and Carl Vogel. *Internet Research Methods*. London: Sage, 2003.

Heywood, Andrew. *Global Politics*. London: Palgrave, 2011.

Hill, Anne and James Watson. *Dictionary of Media and Communication*. London: Hodder Arnold, 2006.

Hill, Michael. *Understanding Social Policy*, 5th edn. Oxford: Blackwell, 1997.

Hirsch, Jennifer. *A Courtship after Marriage: Sexuality and Love in Mexican Transnational Families*. Berkeley, CA: University of California Press 2003.

Hirsch, J. and Wardlow, H. (eds) *Modern Loves: The Anthropology of Romantic Courtship and Companionate Marriage*. Ann Arbor, MI: University of Michigan Press, 2006.

Hirst, Paul and G. Thompson. *Globalization in Question: The International Economy and the Possibilities of Governance*. Cambridge: Polity, 1996 (3rd edn, 2009).

Hitchens, Christopher. *God is not Great*. London: Atlantic Books, 2007.

Hobsbawm, Eric. *The Age of Revolution*. London: Weidenfeld and Nicolson, 1962.

——. *The Age of Capital*. London: Weidenfeld and Nicolson, 1975.

——. *The Age of Empire*. London: Weidenfeld and Nicolson, 1987.

——. *Age of Extremes: The Short Twentieth Century, 1914–1991*. London: Michael Joseph, 1994.

Hochschild, Arlie. *The Managed Heart*. Berkeley, CA: University of California Press, 1983.

——. *The Second Shift: Working Parents and the Revolution at Home*. London: Judy Piatkus, 1989.

Hodkinson, Paul. *Goth: Identity, Style and Subculture*. Oxford: Berg, 2002.

Hoffman, John and Paul Graham. *Introduction to Political Theory*, 2nd edn. Harlow: Pearson Longman, 2009.

Hoggart, R. *The Uses of Literacy*. Harmondsworth: Penguin, 1957.

Holland, Janet, Caroline Ramazanoglu, Sue Sharpe and Rachel Thomson. *The Male in the Head: Young People, Heterosexuality and Power*. London: Tufnell, 1998.

Holton, Robert J. *Cosmopolitans: New Thinking and New Directions*. Basingstoke: Palgrave, 2009.

Homans, George C. *The Human Group*. New Brunswick, NJ: Transaction, 1992; orig. 1950.

Hostetler, John A. *Amish Society*, 3rd edn. Baltimore, MD: Johns Hopkins University Press, 1980.

Howarth, David and Aleta J. Norval (eds). *South Africa in Transition*. London: Palgrave, 1998.

Howarth, Glennys. *Death and Dying: A Sociological Introduction*. Cambridge: Polity, 2007.

Hoyt, Homer. *The Structure and Growth of Residential Neighborhoods in American Cities*. Washington, DC: Federal Housing Administration, 1939.

Hubbard, Phil, Rob Kitchin and Gill Valentine. *Key Thinkers on Space and Place*. London: Sage, 2004.

Hughes, John, Wes Sharrock and Peter J. Martin. *Understanding Classical Sociology: Marx, Weber, Durkheim*. London: Sage, 2003.

Humphrey, Derek. *Final Exit: The Practicalities of Self-deliverance and Assisted Suicide for the Dying*. Eugene, OR: The Hemlock Society, 1991.

Hunt, R. and J. Jensen. *The School Report: The Experiences of Young Gay People in Britain's Schools*. Available at: www.stonewall.org.uk/documents/school_report.pdf.

Hunter, Floyd. *Community Power Structure*. Garden City, NY: Doubleday, 1963; orig. 1953.

Hunter, Susan. *Who Cares? Aids in Africa*. Basingstoke: Palgrave Macmillan, 2003.

Huntington, Samuel P. *The Clash of Civilizations: Remaking the World Order*. New York: Touchstone, 1996.

Hutton, Will and Anthony Giddens (eds). *On the Edge: Living with Global Capitalism*. London: Cape, 2000.

Huq, Rupa. *Beyond Subculture: Pop, Youth and Identity in a Postcolonial world*. London: Routledge, 2006.

Hyde, Mark. 'Disability', in Geoff Payne (ed.), *Social Divisions*. Basingstoke: Macmillan, 2006.

Hyland, Paul with Olga Gomez and Francesca Greensides. *The Enlightenment: A Sourcebook and Reader*. London: Routledge, 2003.

Hyman, Richard. *Strikes*. Basingstoke: Macmillan, 1989a.

——. *The Political Economy of Industrial Relations: Theory and Practice in a Cold Climate*. Basingstoke: Macmillan, 1989b.

I

Iannaccone, Laurence R. 'Why strict churches are strong'. *American Journal of Sociology*, Vol. 99, No. 5 (March 1994): 1180–1211.

Ignatieff, Michael. *A Just Measure of Pain: The Penitentiary in the Industrial Revolution, 1750–1850*. London: Macmillan, 1978.

Illich, Ivan. *De-schooling Society*. Harmondsworth: Penguin, 1973.

——. *Medical Nemesis: The Expropriation of Health*. New York: Pantheon, 1976.

Innes, Anthea. *Dementia Studies*. London: Sage, 2009.

Ingham, Geoffrey. *Capitalism*. Cambridge: Polity, 2008.

Inglehart, Ronald. 'Globalization and postmodern values'. *Washington Quarterly*, Vol. 23, No. 1 (Winter 2000): 215–28.

Inglis, Fred. *Media Theory: An Introduction*. Oxford: Blackwell, 1990.

Inhorn, Marcia C. *Local Babies, Global Science: Gender, Religion, and In Vitro Fertilization in Egypt*. New York: Routledge, 2003.

Irvin, George. *Super Rich: The Rise of Inequality in Britain and the United States*. Cambridge: Polity, 2008.

Ishay, Micheline (ed.). *The Human Rights Reader: Major Political Writings, Essays, Speeches, and Documents from the Bible to the Present*. New York: Routledge, 1997.

Iyer, Pico. *The Global Soul: Jet Lag, Shopping Malls, and the Search for Home*. London: Bloomsbury, 2000.

J

Jackson, Brian and Dennis Marsden. *Education and the Working Class*. London: Routledge, 1963.

Jackson, Stevi. *Heterosexuality in Question*. London: Sage, 1999.

Jackson, Tim. *Prosperity without Growth*. London: Earthscan, 2009.

Jacobs, Jane. *The Economy of Cities*. New York: Vintage, 1970.

Jacobson, Jodi L. 'Closing the gender gap in development', in Lester R. Brown et al. (eds), *State of the World 1993: A Worldwatch Institute Report on Progress Toward a Sustainable Society*. New York: W. W. Norton, 1993: 61–79.

Jacoby, Russell and Naomi Glauberman (eds). *The Bell Curve Debate*. New York: Random House, 1995.

Jagarowsky, Paul A. and Mary Jo Bane. *Neighborhood Poverty: Basic Questions*. Discussion paper series H-90-3. John F. Kennedy School of Government. Cambridge, MA: Harvard University Press, 1990.

Jahoda, M., P. Lazersfeld and H. Zeizel. *Marienthal: Sociology of an Unemployed Community*, 2nd edn. London: Tavistock, 1972; orig. 1933.

James, Adrian L., Keith Bottomley, Alison Liebling and Emma Clare. *Privatising Prisons: Rhetoric and Reality*. London: Sage, 1997.

James, Allison, Chris Jenks and Alan Prout. *Theorizing Childhood*. New York: Teachers' College Press, 1998.

James, Allison and Adrian James. *Key Concepts in Childhood Studies*. London: Sage, 2008.

Jameson, Frederick. *Postmodernism or the Logic of Late Capitalism*. London: Verso, 1992.

Jamieson, Anne, Sarah Harper and Christian Victor (eds). *Critical Approaches to Ageing and Later Life*. Buckingham: Open University Press, 1995.

Jamieson, Lynn. *Intimacy: Personal Relationships in Modern Societies*. Oxford: Polity, 1998.

Jefferson, Tony. 'Masculinities and crime', in Mike Maguire, Rod Morgan and Rob Reiner (eds), *The Oxford Handbook of Criminology*, 2nd edn. Oxford: Clarendon Press, 1997; 3rd edn, 2003.

——. 'Masculinities and crime', in Mike Maguire, Rod Morgan, Rob Reiner et al. (eds), *The Oxford Handbook of Criminology*. Oxford: Clarendon Press, 1997; 3rd edn, 2003.

Jeffreys, Sheila. *The Sexuality Debates*. New York and London: Routledge & Kegan Paul, 1987.

Jencks, Christopher. 'Genes and crime', *The New York Review* (12 February 1987): 33–41.

Jencks, Christopher, et al. *Inequality: A Reassessment of the Effect of Family and Schooling in America*. New York: Basic Books, 1972.

Jenkins, Philip. *The Next Christendom: The Coming of Global Christianity*. Oxford: Oxford University Press, 2007.

Jenkins, Phillip. *Intimate Enemies: Moral Panics in Contemporary Great Britain*. New York: Aldine de Gruyte, 1992.

——. *Beyond Tolerance: Child Pornography on the Internet*. New York: New York University Press, 2001.

Jenkins, Richard. *Pierre Bourdieu*. London: Routledge, 1992.

——. *Social Identity*. London: Routledge, 1996.

——. *Rethinking Ethnicity*. London: Sage, 1997.

Jenkins, Richard. *Sociology*. London: Palgrave, 2002.

Jenks, Christopher. *Childhood*. London: Routledge, 1996.

Jensen, Joli. *Redeeming Modernity: Contradictions in Media Criticism*. Newbury Park, CA, and London: Sage, 1990.

Jewkes, Pauline. *Media and Crime*. London: Sage, 2004 (2nd edn, 2010).

Jewkes, Yvonne (ed.). *Crime Online*. Cullompton: Willan, 2007.

Johnson, Kirk. *Television and Social Change in Rural India*. London: Sage, 2000.

Johnson, Malcolm. *The Cambridge Handbook of Age and Aging*. Cambridge: Cambridge University Press, 2005.

Johnson, Paul. 'The seven deadly sins of terrorism', in Benjamin Netanyahu (ed.), *International Terrorism*. New Brunswick, NJ: Transaction, 1981: 12–22.

Johnston, R. J. 'Residential area characteristics', in D. T. Herbert and R. J. Johnston (eds), *Social Areas in Cities. Vol. 1: Spatial Processes and Form*. New York: Wiley, 1976: 193–235.

Jones, Andrew. *Dictionary of Globalization*. Cambridge: Polity, 2006.

Jones, Martin. *Feast: Why Humans Share Food*. Oxford: Oxford University Press, 2007.

Jordan, David C. *Drug Politics: Dirty Money and Democracies*. Norman, OK: University of Oklahoma Press, 1999.

Jordan, Tim. *Cyberpower: The Culture and Politics of Cyberspace and the Internet*. London: Sage, 1999.

Joseph Rowntree Foundation (Income and Wealth Inquiry Group). *Inquiry into Income and Wealth*. York: Joseph Rowntree Foundation, 1995.

Joseph Rowntree Foundation. *Progress on Poverty 1997–2003/4: Findings*. York: Joseph Rowntree Foundation, October 2003.

Juergensmeyer, Mark. *Global Rebellion: Religious Challenges to the Secular State*. Berkeley, CA: University of California Press, 2008.

Jung Chang. *Wild Swans: Three Daughters of China*. London: Flamingo, 1993.

Jung Chang and Jon Holliday. *Mao: The Unknown Story*. London: Jonathan Cape, 2006.

Jupp, Victor. *The SAGE Dictionary of Social Research Methods*. London: Sage, 2006.

K

Kadushin, Charles. 'Friendship among the French financial elite'. *American Sociological Review*, Vol. 60, No. 2 (April 1995): 202–21.

——. 'A short introduction to social networks'. Working paper for the CERPE Workshop, City University of New York, 21 May 2000.

Kaku, Michio. *Visions: How Science will Revolutionize the 21st Century and Beyond*. Oxford: Oxford University Press, 1998.

Kaku, Michio. *Physics of the Future: How Science will Shape Human Destiny and our Daily Lives by the Year 2100*. London: Allen Lane, 2011.

Kaldor, Mary. *New and Old Wars: Organized Violence in a Global Era*. Cambridge: Polity, 1999; 2nd edn, 2006.

Kallen, Evelyn. *Social Inequality and Social Injustice: A Human Rights Perspective*. London: Palgrave, 2004.

Kanagy, Conrad L. and Donald B. Kraybille. *The Riddles of Human Society*. London: Pine Forge, 1999.

Kanter, Rosabeth Moss. *Men and Women of the Corporation*. New York: Basic Books, 1977.

——. *When Giants Learn to Dance: Mastering the Challenges of Strategy, Management and Careers in the 1990s*. New York: Simon & Schuster, 1989.

Kaplan, E. Ann. *Rocking around the Clock: Music, Television, Postmodernism and Consumer Culture*. London: Routledge, 1987.

Karner, Christian. *Ethnicity and Everyday Life*. London: Routledge, 2007.

Katz, Jack. *Seductions of Crime: Moral and Sensual Attractions in Doing Evil*. New York: Basic Books, 1990.

Katz, James E. and Mark Aakhus (eds). *Perpetual Contact: Mobile Communication, Private Talk, Public Performance*. Cambridge: Cambridge University Press, 2002.

Katz, Jonathan. *Gay American History*. New York: Thomas and Cromwell, 1976.

Kaufman, Walter. *Religions in Four Dimensions: Existential, Aesthetic, Historical and Comparative*. New York: Reader's Digest Press, 1976.

Keller, Helen. *The Story of My Life*. New York: Doubleday, 1903.

Kelly, Liz. *Surviving Sexual Violence*. Cambridge: Polity, 1988.

Kempadoo, Kamal and Jo Doezema. *Global Sex Workers*. London: Routledge, 1998.

Kenyon, G. M. *Restorying Our Lives: Personal Growth through Autobiographical Reflection*. London: Praeger, 1977.

Khazanov, A. M. *Nomads and the Outside World*. Oxford: Oxford University Press, 1984.

Kidron, Michael and Ronald Segal. *The New State of the World Atlas*. New York: Simon & Schuster, 1991.

Kimmel, Michael S. *The Gendered Society*. London: Oxford University Press, 2000; 2nd edn, 2004.

King, Martin Luther, Jr. 'The Montgomery bus boycott', in Walt Anderson (ed.), *The Age of Protest*. Pacific Palisades, CA: Goodyear, 1969: 81–91.

Kinkead, Gwen. *Chinatown: A Portrait of a Closed Society*. New York: HarperCollins, 1992.

Kinsey, Alfred. *The Sexual Behaviour of the Human Male*. Philadelphia, PA: Saunders, 1948.

——. *The Sexual Behaviour of the Human Female*. Philadelphia, PA: Saunders, 1953.

Kishor, Sunita. '"May God give sons to all": gender and child mortality in India'. *American Sociological Review*, Vol. 58, No. 2 (April 1993): 247–65.

Kittrie, Nicholas N. *The Right To Be Different: Deviance and Enforced Therapy*. Baltimore, MD: Johns Hopkins University Press, 1971.

Kitzinger, Celia. *Feminism and Conversational Analysis*. London: Sage, 2003.

Klein, Naomi. *No Logo*. London: Flamingo, 2000.

——. *Shock Doctrine: The Rise of Disaster Capitalism*. London: Allen Lane, 2007.

Kleinman, Arthur. *The Illness Narratives*. New York: Basic Books, 1988.

Klineberg, Eric. *Heat Wave: A Social Autopsy of Disaster in Chicago*. Chicago: University of Chicago Press, 2003.

Klug, Francesca. *Values for a Godless Age*. Harmondsworth: Penguin, 2000.

Kocsis, Karoly. 'Ethnicity', in David Turnock (ed.), *East Central Europe and the Former Soviet Union*. London: Arnold, 2001: 88–103.

Kohlberg, Lawrence. *The Psychology of Moral Development: The Nature and Validity of Moral Stages*. New York: Harper & Row, 1981.

Kolata, Gina. 'When Grandmother is the mother, until birth'. *New York Times* (5 August 1991): 1, 11.

Komarovsky, Mirra. *Blue Collar Marriage*. New York: Vintage, 1967.

Kortre, J. N. and E. Hall. *Seasons of Life: The Dramatic Journey from Birth to Death*. Ann Arbor, MI: Ann Arbor Paperback, 1999.

Kotlikoff, Laurence J. and Scott Burns. *The Coming Generational Storm*. London and Cambridge, MA: MIT Press, 2004.

Kozinets, Robert V. *Netnography: Doing Ethnographic Research Online*. London: Sage, 2010.

Kozol, Jonathan. *Prisoners of Silence: Breaking the Bonds of Adult Illiteracy in the United States*. New York: Continuum, 1980.

——. 'A nation's wealth'. *Publisher's Weekly* (24 May 1985a): 28–30.

——. *Illiterate America*. Garden City, NY: Doubleday, 1985b.

——. *Savage Inequalities: Children in America's Schools*. New York: Harper Perennial, 1992.

Krasno, Jean (ed.). *The United Nations: Confronting the Challenge of a Global Society*. Boulder: Lynne Rienner, 2004.

Kraybill, Donald B. *The Riddle of Amish Culture*. Baltimore, MD: Johns Hopkins University Press, 1989.

Kraybill, Donald B. and Marc A. Olshan (eds). *The Amish Struggle with Modernity*. Hanover, NH: University Press of New England, 1994.

Kriesi, Hanspeter, Ruud Koopmans, Jan Willem Dyvendak and Marco G. Giuni. *New Social Movements in Western Europe*. London: UCL Press, 1995.

Kübler-Ross, Elisabeth. *On Death and Dying*. New York: Macmillan, 1969.

Kuhn, Manford and T. S. McPartland. 'An empirical investigation of self attitudes'. *American Sociological Review*, Vol. 19, No. 4 (1954): 68–76.

Kuhn, Thomas. *The Structure of Scientific Revolutions*, 2nd edn. Chicago: University of Chicago Press, 1970.

Kumar, Krishan. *Prophecy and Progress: The Sociology of Industrial and Post-Industrial Society*. Harmondsworth: Penguin, 1978.

——. *From Post-industrial to Post-modern Society: New Theories of the Contemporary World*. Oxford: Blackwell, 1995.

Kurtz, Lester. *Gods in the Global Village: The World's Religions in Sociological Perspective*, 2nd edn. London: Pine Forge, 2006.

Kushner, Tony and Katherine Knox. *Refugees in an Age of Genocide*. London: Taylor and Francis, 1999.

Kuznets, Simon. *Modern Economic Growth: Rate, Structure and Spread*. New Haven, CT: Yale University Press, 1966.

Kvale, Steiner. *Interviews: An Introduction to Qualitative Research Interviewing*. London: Sage, 1996.

L

Lacey, Colin. *Hightown Grammar*. London: Routledge, 1970.

Lambevski, Sasho A. 'Suck my nation: masculinity, ethnicity and the politics of (homo)sex'. *Sexualities*, Vol. 2, No. 4 (November 1999): 397–420.

Lane, Robert E. *The Loss of Happiness in Market Democracies*. New Haven and London: Yale University Press, 2000.

Lang, Tim and Michael Heasman. *Food Wars: Public Health and the Battle for Mouths, Minds and Markets*. London: Earthscan, 2004.

Layard, Richard. *Happiness: Lessons from a New Science*. London: Allen Lane, 2005.

Lappé, Frances Moore and Joseph Collins. *World Hunger: Twelve Myths*. New York: Grove/Food First, 1998.

Lash, Scott and John Urry. *The End of Organized Capitalism*. Cambridge: Polity, 1987.

Lash, Scott and Celia Lury. *Global Culture Industry: The Mediation of Things*. Cambridge: Polity, 2007.

Laslett, Peter (ed.). *Household and Family in Past Time: Comparative Studies in the Size and Structure of the Domestic Group over the Last Three Centuries in England, France, Serbia, Japan and Colonial North America, with Further Materials from Western Europe*. Cambridge: Cambridge University Press, 1972.

——. *The World We Have Lost: England before the Industrial Age*, 3rd edn. New York: Charles Scribner's Sons, 1984.

——. *A Fresh Map of Life: The Emergence of the Third Age*. Basingstoke: Macmillan, 1989; 2nd rev. edn, 1996.

Laswell, Harold. 'The structure and function of communication in society', in Lymon Bryson (ed.), *The Communication of Ideas*. New York: Harper & Row, 1948.

Latour, Bruno. *Reassembling the Social*. Oxford: Oxford University Press, 2005.

Latour, Bruno and Steve Woolgar. *Laboratory Life: The Construction of Scientific Facts*. Princeton, NJ: Princeton University Press, 1986.

Laumann, Edward O., John H. Gagnon, Robert T. Michael and Stuart Michaels. *The Social Organization of Sexuality: Sexual Practices in the United States*. Chicago: University of Chicago Press, 1994.

Lawson, Tony and Joan Garrod. *The Complete A–Z Sociology Handbook*, 4th edn. London: Hodder & Stoughton, 2009.

Lawton, J. *The Dying Process*. London: Routledge, 2000.

Layard, Richard. *Happiness: Lessons from a New Science*. London: Allen Lane, 2005.

Lazarsfeld, Paul F. and Robert K. Merton. 'Mass communication, popular taste and organized social action', in Paul Marris and Sue Thornham (eds), *Media Studies*. Edinburgh: Edinburgh University Press, 1996.

Leacock, Eleanor. 'Women's status in egalitarian societies: implications for social evolution'. *Current Anthropology*, Vol. 19, No. 2 (June 1978): 247–75.

Leavitt, Judith Walzer. 'Women and health in America: an overview', in Judith Walzer Leavitt (ed.), *Women and Health in America*. Madison, WI: University of Wisconsin Press, 1984: 3–7.

Lee, David and H. Newby. *The Problem of Sociology*. London: Hutchinson, 1983.

Lee, David and Bryan Turner (eds). *Conflict about Class: Debating Inequality in Late Industrialism*. London: Longman, 1996.

Lee, Nick. *Childhood and Society*. Maidenhead: Open University Press, 2001.

Lees, Sue. *Sugar and Spice: Sexuality and Adolescent Girls*. Harmondsworth: Penguin, 1993.

Le Grand, Julien. *The Strategy of Equality*. London: Allen & Unwin, 1982.

Lehne, Gregory. 'Homophobia among men', in D. David and R. Brannon (eds), *The Forty-Nine Per Cent Majority: The Male Sex Role*. London: Addison Wesley, 1976.

Leibfried, Stephan (ed.). *Welfare State Futures*. Cambridge: Cambridge University Press, 2001.

Leila. *Married by Force*. London: Portrait, 2007.

Lemert, Charles. *Social Theory: The Multicultural and Classic Readings*. Boulder, CO: Westview, 2004.

——. *Social Things: An Introduction to the Sociological Life*, 4th edn. Lanham: Rowman & Littlefield, 2008.

Lemert, Edwin M. *Social Pathology*. New York: McGraw-Hill, 1951.

——. *Human Deviance, Social Problems and Social Control*, 2nd edn. Englewood Cliffs, NJ: Prentice-Hall, 1972.

——. *The Trouble with Evil: Social Control at the Edge of Morality*. Albany: State University of New York Press, 1997.

Lengermann, Patricia Madoo and Ruth A. Wallace. *Gender in America: Social Control and Social Change*. Englewood Cliffs, NJ: Prentice-Hall, 1985.

Lenski, Gerhard. *Power and Privilege: A Theory of Social Stratification*. New York: McGraw-Hill, 1966.

Lenski, Gerhard, Patrick Nolan and Jean Lenski. *Human Societies: An Introduction to Macrosociology*, 11th edn. New York: McGraw-Hill, 2010.

Leonard, Eileen B. *Women, Crime and Society: A Critique of Theoretical Criminology*. New York: Longman, 1982.

Levinson, Daniel J., with Charlotte N. Darrow, Edward B. Klein, Maria H. Levinson and Braxton McKee. *The Seasons of a Man's Life*. New York: Alfred A. Knopf, 1978.

Levinson, Daniel, J., with Charlotte N. Darrow, Edward B. Klein, Maria H. Levinson and Braxton McKee. *The Seasons of a Woman's Life*. New York: Knopf, 1996.

Levi-Strauss, *The Raw and the Cooked*. Chicago: University of Chicago Press, 1983; orig. 1969.

Levitas, Ruth. *The Inclusive Society? Social Exclusion and New Labour*. London: Macmillan, 1998.

Levitas, Ruth and Will Guy (eds). *Interpreting Official Statistics*. London: Routledge, 1996.

Lewis, Gail, Sharon Gewirtz and John Clarke. *Rethinking Social Policy*. London: Sage/Open University Press, 2000.

Lewis, Jane. 'Gender and the development of welfare regimes'. *European Journal of Social Policy*, Vol. 2, No. 2 (1992): 159–74.

Lewis, Jeff, *Cultural Studies: The Basics*, 2nd edn. London: Sage, 2008.

Lewis, Oscar. *Five Families*. New York: Basic Books, 1959.

——. *The Children of Sanchez*. New York: Random House, 1961.

Lewontin, Richard. *It Ain't Necessarily So: The Dream of the Human Genome and Other Illusions*. London: Granta, 2000.

Lichtenstein, Nelson. *Wal-Mart: The Face of Twenty-First Century Capitalism*. New York: The New Press, 2006.

Lievrouw, Leah A. and Sonia Livingstone. *Handbook of New Media*. London: Sage, 2001.

Lifton, Robert Jay. *The Broken Connection*. New York: American Psychology Association, 2006.

Lin, Jan and Chistopher Mele. *The Urban Sociology Reader*. London: Routledge, 2005.

Linden, Eugene. 'Can animals think?' *Time*, Vol. 141, No. 12 (22 March 1993): 54–61.

Lindesmith, Alfred R., Anselm L. Strauss and Norman K. Denzin. *Social Psychology*. London: Sage, 8th edn, 1999; orig. 1949.

Ling, Rich. *New Tech, New Ties: How Mobile Communication is Reshaping Social Cohesion*. Cambridge, MA: MIT Press, 2008.

Linton, Ralph. *The Study of Man*. New York: D. Appleton-Century, 1937.

Lipset, Seymour Martin and Reinhard Bendix. *Social Mobility in Industrial Society*. Berkeley, CA: University of California Press, 1967.

Lister, Ruth. *Poverty*. Cambridge: Policy, 2004.

Livi-Bacci, Massimo. *A Concise History of World Population*, revised 4th edn. Oxford: Wiley-Blackwell.

Lloyd, Moya. *Judith Butler*. Cambridge: Polity, 2007.

Lockwood, David. *Solidarity and Schism: The Problem of Disorder in Durkheimian and Marxist Sociology*. Oxford: Clarendon Press, 1992.

Lockwood, David, John Goldthorpe, Frank Beckhoffer and Jennifer Platt. *The Affluent Worker*. Cambridge: Cambridge University Press, 1967.

Lockwood, Matthew. *The State They're In: An Agenda for International Action on Poverty in Africa*. London: ITDG, 2005.

Lodge, David. *The Modes of Modern Writing*. London: Arnold, 1977.

Lofland, J. *Doomsday Cult*, 2nd edn. New York: Irvington, 1996.

Logan, John and Harvey Molotch. *Urban Fortunes*. Berkeley, CA: University of California Press, 1988.

Lomberg, Bjorn. *The Skeptical Environmentalist*. Cambridge: Cambridge University Press, 2001.

Lomberg, Bjorn. *Cool It! The Skeptical Enviromentalist's Guide to Global Warming*. London: Cyan and Marshall Cavendish, 2007.

Lombroso, Cesare. *Crime: Its Causes and Remedies*. Montclair, NJ: Patterson Smith, 1911.

——. *L'Uomo Delinquents*. Turin: Fratelli, 1970.

Longino, Charles F., Jr. 'Myths of an aging America'. *American Demographics*, Vol. 16, No. 8 (August 1994): 36–42.

Lopez, Barry. *Arctic Dreams: Imagination and Desire in a Northern Landscape*. London: Picador, 1986.

Lorber, Judith. *Paradoxes of Gender*. New Haven, CT: Yale University Press, 1994.

Lord, Walter. *A Night to Remember*, rev. edn. New York: Holt, Rinehart & Winston, 1976.

Lorenz, Konrad. *On Aggression*. New York: Harcourt, Brace & World, 1966.

Loseke, Donileen R. *Thinking about Social Problems: A Constructionist Perspective*, 2nd edn. Chicago: Aldine, 2003.

Loseke, Donileen and Joel Best (eds). *Social Problems: Constructionist Readings*. Piscataway: Aldine Transaction, 2003.

Louie, Miriam Ching Yoon. *Sweatshop Warriors*. Cambridge, MA: South End Press, 2001.

Lovelock, James. *Gaia: A New Look at Life on Earth*. Oxford: Oxford University Press, 1979.

Loverlock, James. *The Revenge of Gaia*. Harmondsworth: Penguin, 2007.

Loverlock, James. *The Vanishing Face of Gaia*. Harmondsworth: Penguin, 2010.

Lowery, A. and Melvin L. De Fleur (eds). *Milestones in Mass Communication Research*. London: Longman, 1984; 2nd edn, 1988.

Lozano, Luis-Martin and Rivera, Juan Coronel. *Diego Rivera: The Complete Murals*. London: Taschen Books, 2008.

Lupton, Deborah. *Food, the Body and the Self*. London: Sage, 1996.

——. *The Emotional Self*. London: Sage, 1998.

Lutra, Mohan. *Britain's Black Population*. London: Arena, 1997.

Lutz, Catherine A. and Geoffrey M. White. 'The anthropology of emotions', in Bernard J. Siegel, Alan R. Beals and Stephen A. Tyler (eds), *Annual Review of Anthropology*, Vol. 15. Palo Alto, CA: Annual Reviews, 1986: 405–36.

Lynd, Robert S. *Knowledge for What? The Place of Social Science in American Culture*. Princeton, NJ: Princeton University Press, 1967.

Lynd, Robert S. and Helen Merrell Lynd. *Middletown in Transition*. New York: Harcourt, Brace & World, 1937.

Lyng, Stephen. *Edgework*. London: Routledge, 2004.

Lyon, David. *Surveillance Society: Monitoring Everyday Life*. Buckingham: Open University Press, 2001.

Lyotard, J. F. *The Postmodern Condition*. Manchester: Manchester University Press, 1992.

M

McAdam, Doug, John D. McCarthy and Mayer N. Zald. 'Social movements', in Neil J. Smelser (ed.), *Handbook of Sociology*. Newbury Park, CA: Sage, 1988: 695–737.

Mac an Ghail, Máirtín. *Making of Men: Masculinities, Sexualities and Schooling*. Buckingham: Open University Press, 1994.

McCallister, J. F. O. 'The British Disease'. *Time*, Vol. 19, December 2005, No. 23–7.

McCarthy, Jane Ribbens, Rosalind Edwards and Val Gillies. *Parenting and Step-Parenting*. Oxford: Centre for Family and Household Research, Oxford Brookes University, 2000.

McCarthy, John D. and Mayer N. Zald. 'Resource mobilization and social movements: a partial theory'. *American Journal of Sociology*, Vol. 82, No. 6 (May 1977): 1212–41.

McCormick, John. *British Politics and the Environment*. London: Earthscan, 1991.

McCurdy, Howard E. *Space and the American Imagination*. Washington, DC: Smithsonian Institution Press, 1999.

MacDonald, Robert. *Youth, the Underclass and Social Exclusion*. London: Routledge, 1997.

MacDonald, Robert and Jane Marsh, *Disconnected Youth: Growing Up in Britain's Poor Neighbourhoods*. London: Palgrave, 2005.

McGrath, Alister. *The Twilight of Atheism: The Rise and Fall of Disbelief in the Modern World*. London: Rider & Co., 2004.

McIlroy, John. *Trade Unions in Britain Today*, 2nd edn. Manchester: Manchester University Press, 1995.

Macionis, John J. 'Intimacy: structure and process in interpersonal relationships'. *Alternative Lifestyles*, Vol. 1, No. 1 (February 1978a): 113–30.

Mack, Joanna and Stewart Lansley. *Poor Britain*. London: Allen & Unwin, 1985; 2nd edn, London: Routledge, 1993.

McKeown, T. *The Role of Medicine: Dream, Mirage and Nemesis*. London: Nuffield Provincial Hospital Trust, 1976.

MacKinnon, Catharine A. *Feminism Unmodified: Discourses on Life and Law*. Cambridge, MA: Harvard University Press, 1987.

Mackinnon, Donald, June Statham and Margaret Hales. *Education in the UK: Facts and Figures*. Buckingham: Open University Press, 1996; 3rd edn, 1999.

McLaughlin, Eugene and John Muncie (eds). *Sage Dictionary of Criminology*. London: Sage, 2001.

McLean, Gill L. *Facing Death: Conversations with Cancer Patients*. Edinburgh: Churchill Livingstone, 1993.

McLean, Martin. 'The politics of curriculum in European perspective'. *Educational Review*, Vol. 45, No. 2 (1993): 125–35.

McLellan, David. *Karl Marx: Selected Writings 2000*, 2nd edn. Oxford: Oxford University Press, 2000.

McLeod, Julie and Rachel Thompson. *Researching Social Change*. London: Sage, 2009.

McLuhan, Marshall. *The Medium is the Message*. London: Routledge, 1964.

McMichael, A. J. *Planetary Overload: Global Environment Change and the Health of the Human Species*. Cambridge: Cambridge University Press, 1993.

Macpherson, Sir W. *The Stephen Lawrence Inquiry*. Cm 4262. London: HMSO, 1999.

McNair, Brian. *Striptease Culture: Sex, Media and the Democratisation of Sex*. London: Routledge, 2002.

McQuail, Denis. *Mass Communication Theory*, 3rd edn. London: Sage, 1994; *Mass Communication Theory: An Introduction*, 5th edn, 2005; orig. 1978.

McRae, Susan. *Cross-Class Families: A Study of Wives' Occupational Superiority*. New York: Oxford University Press, 1986.

McRobbie, Angela. *Feminism and Youth Culture*. London: Macmillan, 1991.

Maguire, Mike, Rod Morgan, Rob Reiner et al. (eds). *The Oxford Handbook of Criminology*. Oxford: Clarendon Press, 1997; 4th edn. 2008.

Mahbubani, Kishore. *Can Asians Think? Understanding the Divide Between East and West*. South Royalton: Steerforth, 2004.

Mai, Mukhtar. *In the Name of Honour*. London: Virago, 2007.

Majka, Linda C. 'Sexual harassment in the Church'. *Society*, Vol. 28, No. 4 (May–June 1991): 14–21.

Malcolm, Noel. *Bosnia: A Short History*, rev. edn. London: Macmillan, 1996.

Malcolm X (with Alex Haley). *The Autobiography of Malcolm X*. Harmondsworth: Penguin, 1966.

Malthus, Thomas Robert. *First Essay on Population*. London: Macmillan, 1926; orig. 1798.

Mann, Michael. *Encyclopedia of Sociology*. London: Macmillan, 1983.

Mann, Michael. *The Dark Side of Democracy: Explaining Ethnic Cleansing*. Cambridge: Cambridge University Press, 2005.

Manning, Philip. *Erving Goffman and Modern Sociology*. Cambridge: Polity, 1992.

Marchbank, Jennifer and Gayle Letherby. *Introduction to Gender: Social Science Perspectives*. London: Longman, 2008.

Marcuse, Herbert. *One-Dimensional Man*. Boston, MA: Beacon, 1964.

Marfleet, Paul. *Refugees in a Global Era*. Basingstoke: Palgrave Macmillan, 2006.

Markham, A. N. *Life Online: Researching Real Experiences in Virtual Space*. London: AltaMira, 1998.

Marris, Paul and Sue Thornham (eds). *Media Studies: A Reader*. Edinburgh: Edinburgh University Press, 1996.

Marshall, Gordon, David Rose, Howard Newby and Carolyn Vogler. *Social Class in Modern Britain*. London: Hutchinson, 1988.

Martell, Luke. *Ecology and Society: An Introduction*. Cambridge: Polity, 1994.

——. *The Sociology of Globalization*. Cambridge: Polity, 2010.

Martin, Gus. *Understanding Terrorism*. London: Sage, 2004; 3rd edn, 2010.

Martin, John M. and Anne T. Romano. *Multinational Crime: Terrorism, Espionage, Drug and Arms Trafficking*. Newbury Park, CA: Sage, 1992.

Martin, S. I. *Britain's Slave Trade*. London: Channel 4 Books, 1999.

Marty, Martin E. and R. Scott Appleby (eds). *Fundamentalisms Comprehended*. Chicago: University of Chicago Press, 1995.

Marullo, Sam. 'The functions and dysfunctions of preparations for fighting nuclear war'. *Sociological Focus*, Vol. 20, No. 2 (April 1987): 135–53.

Marx, Karl. 'Excerpt from "A Contribution to the Critique of Political Economy"', in Karl Marx and Friedrich Engels, *Marx and Engels: Basic Writings on Politics and Philosophy*. Lewis S. Feurer ed. Garden City, NY: Anchor, 1959: 42–6; 2nd edn, 1977; orig. 1859.

——. *Early Writings*. Tom Bottomore ed. New York: McGraw-Hill, 1964a.

——. *Karl Marx: Selected Writings in Sociology and Social Philosophy*. T. B. Bottomore trans. New York: McGraw-Hill, 1964b.

——. *Capital*. Friedrich Engels ed. New York: International Publishers, 1967; orig. 1867.

——. 'Theses on Feuer', in Robert C. Tucker (ed.), *The Marx–Engels Reader*. New York: W. W. Norton, 1972: 107–9; orig. 1845.

Marx, Karl and Friedrich Engels. 'Manifesto of the Communist Party', in Robert C. Tucker (ed.), *The Marx–Engels Reader*. New York: W. W. Norton, 1972: 331–62; orig. 1848.

——. *The Marx–Engels Reader*. Robert C. Tucker ed. 2nd edn. New York: W. W. Norton, 1978.

Mason, David. *Race and Ethnicity in Modern Britain*, 2nd edn. Oxford: Oxford University Press, 2000a.

Massey, Doreen. *Spatial Divisions of Labour*. London: Macmillan, 1984.

——. *World City*. Cambridge: Polity, 2007.

Massey, Douglas S. and Nancy A. Denton. 'Hypersegregation in US metropolitan areas: black and Hispanic segregation along five dimensions'. *Demography*, Vol. 26, No. 3 (August 1989): 373–91.

Matthiessen, Peter. *Indian Country*. New York: Viking, 1984.

Matza, David. *Delinquency and Drift*. New York: Wiley, 1964.

Mauss, Armand L. *Social Problems of Social Movements*. Philadelphia, PA: Lippincott, 1975.

Mayhew, Henry. *London's Underworld*. P. Quennel ed. London: Spring Books, 1861.

Mead, George Herbert. *Mind, Self and Society from the Standpoint of a Social Behaviourist*. Charles W. Morris ed. Chicago: University of Chicago Press, 1962; orig. 1934.

Mead, Margaret. *Coming of Age in Samoa*. New York: Dell, 1961; orig. 1928.

——. *Sex and Temperament in Three Primitive Societies*. New York: William Morrow, 1963; orig. 1935.

Meadows, Donella H., Dennis L. Meadows, Jorgan Randers and William W. Behrens, III. *The Limits to Growth: A Report on the Club of Rome's Project on the Predicament of Mankind*. New York: Universe, 1972.

Meltzer, Bernard N. 'Mead's social psychology', in Jerome G. Manis and Bernard N. Meltzer (eds), *Symbolic Interaction: A Reader in Social Psychology*, 3rd edn. Needham Heights, MA: Allyn & Bacon, 1978.

Melucci, Alberto. 'The new social movements: a theoretical approach'. *Social Science Information*, Vol. 19, No. 2 (May 1980): 199–226.

Menchú, Rigoberta. *I, Rigoberta Menchú: An Indian Woman in Guatemala*. London: Verso, 1984.

——. *Crossing Borders*. London: Verso, 1998.

Mennell, Stephen. *All Manners of Food: Eating and Taste in England and France from the Middle Ages to the Present*. Oxford: Blackwell, 1985.

Merton, Robert K. 'Social structure and anomie'. *American Sociological Review*, Vol. 3, No. 6 (October 1938): 672–82.

——. *Social Theory and Social Structure*. New York: Free Press, 1968.

——. 'Discrimination and the American creed', in *Sociological Ambivalence and Other Essays*. New York: Free Press, 1976: 189–216.

Messerschmidt, James. *Masculinity and Crime*. Lanham, MD: Rowman and Littlefield, 1993.

——. *Nine Lives: Adolescent Masculinities, the Body and Violence*. London: Sage, 2000.

Meston, Cindy M. and David M. Buss. 'Why humans have sex'. *Archives of Sexual Behavior*, Vol. 36 (2007): 477–507.

Meyerhoff, Barbara. *Remembered Lives: The Work of Ritual, Storytelling and Growing Older*. Athens, GA: University of Georgia Press, 1992.

Meyrowitz, Joshua. *No Sense of Place: The Impact of Electronic Media on Social Behavior*. New York and Oxford: Oxford University Press, 1986.

Miah, Andy and Emma Rich, *The Medicalization of Cyberspace*. London: Routledge, 2008.

Michels, Robert. *Political Parties*. Glencoe, IL: Free Press, 1949; orig. 1911.

Miladi, Noureddine. 'Mapping the *Al-Jazeera* phenomenon', in D. K. Thussu and D. Freedman (eds), *War and the Media*. London: Sage, 2003: 149–60.

Milbrath, Lester W. *Envisioning a Sustainable Society: Learning Our Way Out*. Albany, NY: State University of New York Press, 1989.

Milburn, Alan. *Unleashing Aspiration: The Final Report of the Panel on Fair Access to the Professions*. London: Cabinet Office, 2009.

Milgram, Stanley. 'Behavioral study of obedience'. *Journal of Abnormal and Social Psychology*, Vol. 67, No. 4 (1963): 371–8.

——. 'Group pressure and action against a person'. *Journal of Abnormal and Social Psychology*, Vol. 69, No. 2 (August 1964): 137–43.

——. 'Some conditions of obedience and disobedience to authority'. *Human Relations*, Vol. 18 (February 1965): 57–76.

Miliband, Ralph. *The State in Capitalist Society*. London: Weidenfeld and Nicolson, 1969.

Miliband, Ralph and Leo Panitch. *Socialist Register, 1993: Real Problems, False Solutions*. London: Merlin Press, 1993.

Mill, John Stuart and Harriet Taylor Mill. *The Subjection of Women*. London: Dover, 1997; London: Virago, 1983; orig. 1869.

Miller, Arthur G. *The Obedience Experiments: A Case of Controversy in Social Science*. New York: Praeger, 1986.

Miller, Daniel (ed.). *Acknowledging Consumption*. London: Routledge, 1995.

Miller, G. Tyler, Jr. *Living in the Environment: An Introduction to Environmental Science*. Belmont, CA: Wadsworth, 1992.

Miller, Walter B. 'Lower class culture as a generating milieu of gang delinquency', in Marvin E. Wolfgang, Leonard Savitz and Norman Johnston (eds), *The Sociology of Crime and Delinquency*, 2nd edn. New York: Wiley, 1970: 351–63; orig. 1958.

Millet, Kate. *Sexual Politics*. Garden City, NY: Doubleday, 1970.

Mills, C. Wright. *The Power Elite*. New York: Oxford University Press, 1956.

——. *The Sociological Imagination*. New York: Oxford University Press, 1959; 2nd edn, 1967; 3rd edn, 1970.

——. *Power, Politics, and People: The Collected Essays of C. Wright Mills*. London and New York: Oxford University Press, 1967; orig. 1957.

Millstone, Eric and Tim Lang. *The Atlas of Food: Who Eats, What, Where, When, Why*. Brighton: Earthscan, 2002.

Mirza, Heidi. *Young, Female and Black*. London: Routledge, 1992.

Mirza, Heidi Safia (ed.). *British Black Feminism*. London: Routledge, 1997.

Modood, Tariq. 'Political blackness and British Asians'. *Sociology*, Vol. 28, No. 4 (1994): 859–76.

——. *Multicultural Politics: Racism, Ethnicity and Muslims in Britain*. Edinburgh: Edinburgh University Press, 2005.

Modood, Tariq, R. Berthoud, J. Lakey, J. Nazroo, P. Smith, S. Virdee and S. Beishaon. *Ethnic Minorities in Britain*, 4th edn. London: Policy Studies Institute, 1997.

Molotch, Harvey. 'The city as a growth machine'. *American Journal of Sociology*, Vol. 82, No. 2 (September 1976): 309–33.

Molotch, Harvey and Marilyn Lester. 'News as purposive behaviour'. *American Sociological Review*, Vol. 39 (1974): 101–12.

Monahan, Torin (ed.). *Surveillance and Society*. London: Routledge, 2006.

Mooney, Jayne. *Gender, Violence and the Social Order*. Basingstoke: Macmillan, 2000.

Moores, Shaun. *Interpreting Audiences: The Ethnography of Media Consumption*. London: Sage, 1993.

Morgan, David. *Farewell to the Family*. London: Institute of Economic Affairs, 1995.

——. *Family Connections: An Introduction to Family Studies*. Cambridge: Polity, 1996.

——. 'Risk and family practices', in Elizabeth B. Silva and Carol Smart (eds), *The New Family?* London: Sage, 1999.

Morgan, Patricia. *Delinquent Fantasies*. London: Temple Smith, 1978.

Morgan, Rod and Tim Newburn. *The Future of Policing*. Oxford: Clarendon Press, 1997.

Morin, S. and E. Garfinkle. 'Male homophobia'. *Journal of Social Issues*, Vol. 34, No. 1 (1978): 29–47.

Morley, David. *Family Television: Cultural Power and Domestic Leisure*. London: Comedia, 1986.

——. *Television: Audiences and Cultural Studies*. London: Routledge, 1992.

Morley, David and K.-H. Chen (eds). *Stuart Hall: Critical Dialogues in Cultural Studies*. London: Routledge, 1996.

Morris, Lydia. *Dangerous Classes: The Underclass and Social Citizenship*. London: Routledge, 1994.

Morrison, Kenneth. *Marx, Durkheim, Weber: Formations of Modern Social Thought*, 2nd edn. London: Sage, 2006.

Mosley, W. Henry and Peter Cowley. 'The challenge of world health'. *Population Bulletin*, Vol. 46, No. 4 (December 1991). Washington, DC: Population Reference Bureau.

Muggleton, David and Rupert Weinzierl (eds). *The Post-Subcultures Reader*. Oxford: Berg, 2003.

Mullan, Phil. *The Imaginary Time Bomb: Why an Ageing Population is not a Social Problem*. London: I. B. Tauris, 2002.

Mullins, Christopher. *Holding your Square: Masculinities, Street Life and Violence*. Willan, 2006.

Mumford, Lewis. *The City in History: Its Origins, Its Transformations and Its Prospects*. New York: Harcourt, Brace & World, 1961.

Murdock, George Peter. 'The common denominator of cultures', in Ralph Linton (ed.), *The Science of Man in World Crisis*. New York: Columbia University Press, 1945: 123–42.

——. *Social Structure*. New York: Free Press, 1965; orig. 1949.

Murdock, Graham and P. Golding. 'Capitalism, communication and class relations', in James Curran et al., *Mass Communication and Society*. London: Edward Arnold, 1977.

Murray, Charles. *Losing Ground: American Social Policy 1950–1980*. New York: Basic Books, 1984.

Musello, C. 'Family photography', in J. Wagner (ed.), *Images of Information Still Photography in the Social Sciences*. Beverley Hills, CA: Sage, 1979.

Musgrove, Frank. *Youth and the Social Order*. London: Routledge, 1968.

Myers, Norman. 'Humanity's growth', in Sir Edmund Hillary (ed.), *Ecology 2000: The Changing Face of the Earth*. New York: Beaufort, 1984a: 16–35.

——. 'The mega-extinction of animals and plants', in Sir Edmund Hillary (ed.), *Ecology 2000: The Changing Face of the Earth*. New York: Beaufort, 1984b: 82–107.

——. 'Disappearing cultures', in Sir Edmund Hillary (ed.), *Ecology 2000: The Changing Face of the Earth*. New York: Beaufort, 1984c: 162–9.

——. 'Biological diversity and global security', in F. Herbert Bormann and Stephen R. Kellert (eds), *Ecology, Economics and Ethics: The Broken Circle*. New Haven, CT: Yale University Press, 1991: 11–25.

N

Nakx, K. 'The "eclipse" of folk medicine in Western society'. *Sociology of Health and Illness*, Vol. 13, No. 1 (1991): 203.

Narayan, Deepa. *Voices of the Poor: Can Anyone Hear Us?* Oxford: Oxford University Press for the World Bank, 2000.

National Intelligence Council. *Global Trends 2015*. Washington, DC: US Government Printing Office, 2000.

Navarro, Vicente. 'The industrialization of fetishism or the fetishism of industrialization: a critique of Ivan Illich', in Vicente Navarro (ed.), *Health and Medical Care in the US: A Critical Analysis*. Farmingdale, NY: Baywood, 1977: 38–58.

——. *Crisis, Health and Medicine*. London: Tavistock Institute, 1986.

Nayak, Anoop. *Race, Place and Globalization: Youth Cultures in a Changing World*. Oxford: Berg, 2003.

Nelan, Bruce W. 'Crimes without punishment'. *Time*, Vol. 141, No. 2 (11 January 1993): 21.

Nettle, Daniel and Suzanne Romaine. *Vanishing Voices: The Extinction of the World's Languages*. Oxford: Oxford University Press, 2000.

Nettleton, Sarah. *Power, Pain and Dentistry*. Buckingham: Open University Press, 1992.

——. *The Sociology of Health and Illness*. Cambridge: Polity, 1995.

Neugarten, Bernice L. and Dail A. Neugarten. *The Meanings of Age: Selected Papers of Bernice L. Neugarten*. Chicago: University of Chicago Press, 1996.

Neuman, W. Russell. *The Future of the Mass Audience*. Cambridge: Cambridge University Press, 1991.

Newburn, Tim (ed.). *Key Readings in Criminology*. Cullompton, Devon: Willan, 2009.

New Internationalist (compiled by Andy Crump and edited by Wayne Ellwood). *The A to Z of World Development*. Oxford: New Internationalist Publications, 1998.

Newman, Katherine S. *Declining Fortunes: The Withering of the American Dream*. New York: Basic Books, 1993.

Nielsen, Joyce McCarl (ed.). *Feminist Research Methods: Exemplary Readings in the Social Sciences*. Boulder, CO: Westview, 1990.

Nisbet, Robert A. *The Sociological Tradition*. New York: Basic Books, 1966.

——. *The Quest for Community*. New York: Oxford University Press, 1969.

——. 'Sociology as an art form', in *Tradition and Revolt: Historical and Sociological Essays*. New York: Vintage, 1970. (Published as *Sociology as an Art Form*. London: Heinemann, 1976.)

——. *A History of the Idea of Progress*. New York: Basic Books, 1989.

Nolan, Patrick and Gerhard Lenski. *Human Societies: An Introduction to Macrosociology*, 11th edn. New York: McGraw-Hill, 2010.

NORC (National Opinion Research Center). *General Social Surveys, 1972–1994: Cumulative Codebook*. University of Chicago: National Opinion Research Center, 1994.

Norden, Martin F. *The Cinema of Isolation: A History of Physical Disability in the Movies*. New Brunswick, NJ: Rutgers University Press, 1994.

Norris, C. and G. Armstrong. *The Maximum Surveillance Society: The Rise of CCTV*. Oxford: Berg, 1999.

Norris, Pippa (ed.). *Critical Citizens*. Oxford: Oxford University Press, 1999.

Nussbaum, Martha. *Sex and Social Justice*. Oxford: Oxford University Press, 2000.

——. *Frontiers of Justice: Disability, Nationality and Species Membership*. Cambridge, MA: Harvard University Press, 2006.

Nussbaum, Martha. *Creating Capabilities: The Human Development Approach*. Cambridge, MA: Harvard University Press, 2011.

Nussbaum, Martha C. and Amartya Sen. *The Quality of Life*. Oxford: Clarendon, 1993.

Nutbeam, D. *Health Promotion Glossary*. Geneva: World Health Organization, 1998.

O

Oakes, Jeannie. 'Classroom social relationships: exploring the Bowles and Gintis hypothesis'. *Sociology of Education*, Vol. 55, No. 4 (October 1982): 197–212.

——. *Keeping Track: How High Schools Structure Inequality*. New Haven, CT: Yale University Press, 1985.

O'Brien, Joanne and Martin Palmer. *The Atlas of Religion*. Brighton: Earthscan, 2007.

O'Brien, Jodi and Judith Howard. *Everyday Inequalities: Critical Inquiries*. Oxford: Blackwell, 1998.

O'Byrne, Darren J. *Human Rights: An Introduction*. New York: Longman, 2001.

O'Connor. John Kennedy. *The Eurovision Song Contest: The Official History*. London: Carlton, 2007.

O'Donnell, Mike. *Classical and Contemporary Sociology: Theories and Issues*. London: Hodder and Stoughton, 2001.

O'Donnell, Mike and Sue Sharpe. *Uncertain Masculinities: Youth, Ethnicity and Class in Contemporary Britain*. London: Routledge, 2000.

Offe, Claus. 'New social movements: challenging the boundaries of institutional politics'. *Social Research*, Vol. 52 (1985): 817–68.

Ogburn, William F. *On Culture and Social Change*. Chicago: University of Chicago Press, 1964.

Okin, Susan Moller. *Justice, Gender and the Family*. New York: Basic Books, 1989.

Oliver, Mike. *Understanding Disability: From Theory to Practice*, 2nd edn. Basingstoke: Palgrave, 2010; orig. 1996.

Omi, Michael and Howard Winant. *Racial Formation in the United States: From the 1960s to 1990s*. London: Routledge, 1995.

Ong, A. *Orality and Literacy*. London: Sage, 1982.

Oeppen, Ceri and Angela Schlenkhoff (eds). *Beyond the 'Wild Tribes': Understanding Modern Afghanistan and Its Diaspora*, 2010.

Oppenheim, C. *Poverty: The Facts*, 2nd edn. London: Child Poverty Action Group, 1993.

O'Reilly, Karen. *The British on the Costa del Sol*. London: Routledge, 2000.

——. *Ethnographic Methods*, 2nd edn. London: Routledge, 2011; orig. 2004.

Osborne, Richard and Borin Van Loon. *Sociology for Beginners*. Cambridge: Icon, 1996.

P

Pahl, Jan. *Money and Marriage*. Basingstoke: Macmillan Education, 1989.

Pahl, Ray. *Divisions of Labour*. Oxford: Blackwell, 1984.

Parekh, Bhikhu. 'The Rushdie affair and the British press'. *Social Studies Review* (November 1989): 44.

Park, Robert E. *Race and Culture*. Glencoe, IL: Free Press, 1950.

——. 'The city: suggestions for the investigation of human behavior in the human environment', in Robert E. Park and Ernest W. Burgess, *The City*. Chicago: University of Chicago Press, 1967; orig. 1925: 1–46.

Park, Robert E. and Ernest W. Burgess. *The City*. Chicago: University of Chicago Press, 1967; orig. 1925.

Parker, Richard and Herbert Daniel. *Sexuality, Politics and AIDS in Brazil: In Another World?* Bristol, PA: Taylor & Francis, 1993.

Parkin, Frank. *Class Inequality and Political Order: Social Stratification in Capitalist and Communist Societies*. London: MacGibbon & Kee, 1971.

Parkinson, C. Northcote. *Parkinson's Law and Other Studies in Administration*. New York: Ballantine Books, 1957.

Parsons, Talcott. 'Age and sex in the social structure of the United States'. *American Sociological Review*, Vol. 7, No. 4 (August 1942): 604–16.

——. *The Social System*. New York: Free Press, 1964a; orig. 1951.

——. *Essays in Sociological Theory*. New York: Free Press, 1964b; orig. 1954.

Parsons, Talcott and Robert F. Bales (eds). *Family, Socialization and Interaction Process*. New York: Free Press, 1955.

Pascoe, C. J. *Hey, Dude, You're a Fag: Masculinity and Sexuality in High School*. Berkeley: University of California, 2007.

Patten, Marguerite. *A Century of British Cooking*. London: Grub Street, 2001.

Payne, Brian. *Crime and Elder Abuse*. Springfield, IL: Charles C. Thomas, 2005.

Payne, Geoff (ed.). *Social Divisions*. London: Macmillan, 2000; 2nd edn, 2005.

Pear, Robert with Erik Eckholm. 'When healers are entrepreneurs: a debate over costs and ethics'. *New York Times* (2 June 1991): 1, 17.

Pearce, Fred, *PeopleQuake*. London: Eden Project, 2010.

Pearson, Geoffrey. *Hooligan: A History of Respectable Fears*. London: Palgrave Macmillan, 1983.

Penguin Dictionary of Sociology, The, 4th edn. Nick Abercrombie, Stephen Hill and Bryan Turner eds. Harmondsworth: Penguin, 2000.

Peter, Laurence J. and Raymond Hull. *The Peter Principle: Why Things Always Go Wrong*. New York: William Morrow, 1969.

Pew Internet and American Life Project. *Social Media and Mobile Internet Use Among Teens and Young Adults*. Washington: Pew Research Center, 2010.

Phillipson, Chris. *Capitalism and the Construction of Old Age*. London: Macmillan, 1982.

Phillipson, Chris. *Reconstructing Old Age: New Agendas in Social Theory and Practice*. London: Sage, 1998.

Phizacklea, Annie. *One Way Ticket: Migration and Female Labour*. London: Edward Arnold, 1993.

——. *Unpacking the Fashion Industry: Gender, Racism and Class in Production*. London: Routledge, 1995.

Pickering, K. T. and Lewis A. Owen. *An Introduction to Global Environmental Issues*. London: Routledge, 1994.

Pieterse, Jan Nederveen. 'Globalization as hybridization', in Mike Featherstone et al. (eds), *Global Modernities*. London: Sage, 1995.

——. *Globalization and Culture: Global Melange*, 2nd edn. Lanham, MD: Rowman and Littlefield, 2009a; orig. 2004.

——. *Development Theory*. London: Sage, 2009b.

Pietroni, P. *Reader's Digest Guide to Alternative Medicine*. London: Reader's Digest Association, 1991.

Pilcher, Jane and Imelda Whelehan. *Fifty Key Concepts in Gender Studies*. London: Sage, 2004.

Pillemer, Karl. 'Maltreatment of the elderly at home and in institutions: extent, risk factors, and policy recommendations', in US Congress, House, Select Committee on Aging, and Senate, Special Committee on Aging, *Legislative Agenda for an Aging Society: 1988 and Beyond*. Washington, DC: US Government Printing Office, 1988.

Pines, Maya. 'The civilization of Genie'. *Psychology Today*, Vol. 15 (September 1981): 28–34.

Pink, Sarah. *Doing Sensory Ethnography*. London: Sage, 2009.

Pirandello, Luigi. *The Pleasure of Honesty*. Harmondsworth: Penguin, 1962.

Pitt, Malcolm. *Introducing Hinduism*. New York: Friendship Press, 1955.

Piven, Frances Fox and Richard A. Cloward. *Regulating the Poor: The Functions of Public Welfare*. London: Tavistock, 1972.

Pizzey, Erin. *Scream Quietly or the Neighbours Will Hear*. Harmondsworth: Penguin, 1974.

Plant, Martin. *Binge Britain: Alcohol and the National Response*. Oxford: Oxford University Press, 2006.

Plant, Martin and Moira Plant. *Binge Britain*. Oxford: Oxford University Press, 2006.

Platt, L. *Parallel Lives? Poverty among Ethnic Minority Groups in Britain*. London: Child Poverty Action Group, 2002.

——. 'Poverty', in Geoff Payne (ed.), *Social Divisions*. London: Macmillan, 2001; 3rd edn, 2006.

——. *Poverty and Ethnicity in the UK*. Bristol: Polity Press, 2007.

Platt, L. *Understanding Inequalities*. Cambridge: Polity, 2011.

Plomin, Robert and Terryl T. Foch. 'A twin study of objectively assessed personality in childhood'. *Journal of Personality and Social Psychology*, Vol. 39, No. 4 (October 1980): 680–8.

Plummer, Ken. *Documents of Life: An Introduction to the Problems and Literature of a Humanistic Method*. London: Allen & Unwin, 1983.

——. 'Organising AIDS', in Peter Aggleton and Hilary Homans (eds), *Social Aspects of AIDS*. London: Falmer, 1988.

——. 'Speaking its name: inventing gay and lesbian studies', in Ken Plummer (ed.), *Modern Homosexualities*. London: Routledge, 1992.

Plummer, Ken. *Documents of Life 2: An Invitation to a Critical Humanism*. London: Sage 2001a; orig. 1983.

——. 'The square of intimate citizenship'. *Citizenship Studies*, Vol. 5, No. 3 (November 2001b): 237–53.

——. *Intimate Citizenship*. Seattle: University of Washington Press, 2003.

——. *Sociology: The Basics*. London: Routledge, 2010.

Pogge, Thomas. *World Poverty and Human Rights*. Cambridge: Polity, 2002.

Pogge, Thomas. *Politics as Usual: What Lies behind the Pro-poor Rhetoric*. Cambridge: Polity, 2010.

Pollak, Otto. *The Criminality of Women*. New York: Basic, 1950; 2nd edn, 1961.

Polsby, Nelson W. 'Three problems in the analysis of community power'. *American Sociological Review*, Vol. 24, No. 6 (December 1959): 796–803.

Popenoe, David. 'Family decline in the Swedish welfare state'. *The Public Interest*, No. 102 (Winter 1991): 65–77.

——. 'The controversial truth: two-parent families are better'. *New York Times* (26 December 1992): 21.

——. 'American family decline, 1960–1990: a review and appraisal'. *Journal of Marriage and the Family*, Vol. 55, No. 3 (August 1993): 527–55.

——. 'Scandinavian welfare'. *Society*, Vol. 31, No. 6 (September–October, 1994): 78–81.

Population Reference Bureau. 'Past and future population doubling times, selected countries'. *Population Today*, Vol. 23, No. 2 (February 1995): 6.

Postel, Sandra. 'Facing water scarcity', in Lester R. Brown et al. (eds), *State of the World 1993: A Worldwatch Institute Report on Progress Toward a Sustainable Society*. New York: W. W. Norton, 1993: 22–41.

Postman, Neil. *Amusing Ourselves to Death*. London: Methuen, 1986.

Poulantzas, Nicos. 'The problem of the capitalist state'. *New Left Review*, 1969.

Power, Michael. *The Audit Society: Rituals of Verification*. Oxford: Oxford University Press, 1997.

Pratt, John. *Penal Populism*. London: Routledge.

Procter, James. *Stuart Hall*. London: Routledge, 2004.

Pryce, Ken. *Endless Pressure*, 2nd edn. Harmondsworth: Penguin, 1986; orig. 1979.

Pullen, Kirsten. 'I-love-Xena.com', in David Gauntlett (ed.), *web.studies*. London: Arnold, 2000: 52–61.

Putnam, Robert. *Bowling Alone: The Collapse and Revival of American Community*. New York: Simon and Schuster, 2001.

Q

Quinney, Richard. *Class, State and Crime: On the Theory and Practice of Criminal Justice*. New York: David McKay, 1977.

R

Rademaekers, William and Rhea Schoenthal. 'Iceman'. *Time*, Vol. 140, No. 17 (26 October 1992): 62–6.

Rahman, Momin and Stevi Jackson. *Sexuality and Gender*. Cambridge: Polity, 2010.

Ranade, Wendy. *A Future for the NHS? Health Care in the 1990s*, 2nd edn. London: Longman, 1994.

Rantanen, Terhi. *The Media and Globalization*. London: Sage, 2005.

Rathje, William and Cullan Murphy. *Rubbish: The Archeology of Garbage*. New York: HarperCollins, 1991.

Rebick, Marcus. *The Changing Japanese Family*. London: Routledge, 2009.

Redfern, Catherine and Kristin Aune. *Reclaiming the F Word: The New Feminist Movement*. London: Zed, 2010.

Reid, Ivan. *Social Class Differences in Britain*, 3rd edn. London: Fontana, 1989.

——. *Social Class in Britain*. Cambridge: Polity, 1998.

Reiman, Jeffrey and Paul Leighton. *The Rich Get Richer and Poor Get Prison*. London: Pearson, 2009.

Reinharz, Shulamit. *Feminist Methods in Social Research*. New York: Oxford University Press, 1992.

Reith, John. *Broadcasting Over Britain*. London: Hodder and Stoughton, 1924.

Remoff, Heather Trexler. *Sexual Choice: A Woman's Decision*. New York: Dutton/Lewis, 1984.

Rex, John and Robert Moore. *Race, Community and Conflict*. London: Oxford University Press, 1967.

Richards, Janet. *The Sceptical Feminist: A Philosophical Enquiry*. Harmondsworth: Penguin, 1982.

Richardson, Diane. *Women, Motherhood and Children*. London: Macmillan, 1993.

——. *Women, Motherhood and Childrearing*. London: Macmillan, 1994.

Ridge, Tess and Sharon Wright (eds) *Understanding Inequalities, Poverty and Wealth: Policy and Prospects*. Bristol: Policy Press, 2008.

Rieff, Philip. 'Introduction', in Charles Horton Cooley, *Social Organization*. New York: Schocken, 1962.

Riesman, David. *The Lonely Crowd: A Study of the Changing American Character*. New Haven, CT: Yale University Press, 1970; orig. 1950.

Rifkin, Jeremy. *The Empathetic Civilization*. Cambridge: Polity, 2010.

Riley, Matilda White, Anne Foner and Joan Waring. 'Sociology of age', in Neil J. Smelser (ed.), *Handbook of Sociology*. Newbury Park, CA: Sage, 1988: 243–90.

Ritzer, George. *Sociological Theory*. New York: Alfred A. Knopf, 1983: 63–6; 3rd edn, New York: McGraw-Hill, 1992.

——. *The McDonaldization of Society: An Investigation into the Changing Character of Contemporary Social Life*. Thousand Oaks, CA: Pine Forge, 1993; 6th edn, 2010.

——. *Expressing America*. London: Sage, 1995.

——. *Enchanting a Disenchanted World*. Thousand Oaks, CA: Pine Forge, 1999.

—— (ed.). *The McDonaldization Reader*. Thousand Oaks, CA: Pine Forge; London: Sage, 2002.

——. *Cathedrals of Consumption*. Thousand Oaks, CA: Pine Forge, 2004a.

——. *Handbook of Social Problems*, Thousand Oaks, CA: Sage, 2004b.

Ritzer, George. *Globalization: A Basic Text*. Oxford: Wiley-Blackwell, 2010.

Rivolim Pietra. *The Travels of a T-Shirt in the Global Economy*, 2nd edn. New York: Wiley, 2009.

Roald, Anne Sofie. *Women in Islam: The Western Experience*. London: Routledge, 2001.

Roberts, Brian. *Biographical Research*. Buckingham: Open University Press, 2002.

Roberts, Ken. *Class in Modern Britain*. London: Palgrave, 2001.

——. *Youth in Transition: Eastern Europe and the West*, Basingstoke: Palgrave, 2009.

Robertson, Roland. *Globalization: Social Theory and Global Culture*. London: Sage, 1992.

Rockett, Ian R. H. 'Population and health: an introduction to epidemiology'. *Population Bulletin*, Vol. 49, No. 3 (November 1994). Washington, DC: Population Reference Bureau.

Roethlisberger, F. J. and William J. Dickson. *Management and the Worker*. Cambridge, MA: Harvard University Press, 1939.

Rogers, Anne and David Pilgrim. *A Sociology of Health and Illness*, 4th edn. Maidenhead: Open University Press, 2010.

Rojek, Chris. *Stuart Hall*. Cambridge: Polity, 2002.

——. *Cultural Studies*. Cambridge: Polity, 2007.

Rokove, Milton L. *Don't Make No Waves, Don't Back No Losers*. Bloomington, IN: Indiana University Press, 1975.

Roopnarine, Jaipaul and Uwe Gielen (eds). *Families in Global Perspective*. London: Pearson, 2005.

Roper, Lyndal. *Oedipus and the Devil: Witchcraft, Sexuality and Religion in Early Modern Europe*. London: Routledge, 1994.

Rose, Gillian. *Visual Methodologies: An Introduction to the Interpretation of Visual Methodologies*, 2nd edn. London: Sage, 2007.

Rose, Hilary and Steven Rose. *Alas, Poor Darwin: Arguments against Evolutionary Psychology*. London: Cape, 2001.

Rose, Nikola. *The Politics of Life Itself: Biomedicine, Power and Subjectivity in the Twenty-First Century*. Princeton: Princeton University Press, 2007.

Rose, T. *Black Noise*. Hanover: Wesleyan University Press, 1994.

Rosen, Lawrence. *The Culture of Islam: Changing Aspects of Contemporary Muslim Life*. Chicago: University of Chicago Press, 2004.

Rosenbaum, Alan S. (ed.). *The Philosophy of Human Rights: International Perspectives*. London: Aldwych Press, 1980.

Rosenhan, D. L. 'On being sane in insane places'. *Science*, Vol. 179, No. 70 (1973): 250–8.

Rosenthal, A. *The New Documentary in Action*. Berkeley, CA: University of California Press, 1971.

Rossi, Alice S. 'Gender and parenthood', in Alice S. Rossi (ed.), *Gender and the Life Course*. New York: Aldine, 1985: 161–91.

Rostow, Walt W. *The Stages of Economic Growth: A Non-Communist Manifesto*. Cambridge: Cambridge University Press, 1960.

——. *The World Economy: History and Prospect*. Austin, TX: University of Texas Press, 1978.

Rothman, Barbara Katz. *Genetic Maps and Human Imaginations: The Limits of Science in Understanding Who We Are*. New York: W. W. Norton, 1998.

Rothman, M., P. Entzel and B. Dunlop (eds). *Elders, Crime and the Criminal Justice System*. New York: Springer-Verlag, 2000.

Rowbottom, Sheila. *A Century of Women: The History of Women in Britain and the United States*. London: Viking, 1997.

Rowe, David C. and D. Wayne Osgood. 'Heredity and sociological theories of delinquency: a reconsideration'. *American Sociological Review*, Vol. 49. No. 4 (August 1984): 526–40.

Rowntree, Seebohm. *Poverty: A Study of Town Life*. London: Macmillan, 1902.

Roxborough, Ian. 'War, militarism and national security', in George Ritzer (ed.), *Handbook of Social Problems*. Thousand Oaks, CA: Sage, 2004: 335–54.

Rubin, Gayle. 'Thinking sex', in Carole S. Vance, *Pleasure and Danger*. London: Routledge, 1984.

Rubin, Lillian Breslow. *Worlds of Pain: Life in the Working-Class Family*. New York: Basic Books, 1976.

Rule, James and Peter Brantley. 'Computerized surveillance in the workplace'. *Sociological Forum*, Vol. 7, No. 3 (September 1992): 405–23.

Rummel, R. J. *Death by Government*. New Brunswick, NJ: Transaction, 1996.

——. *China's Bloody Century: Genocide and Mass Murder since 1900*. New Brunswick, NJ: Transaction, 2007.

Runciman, W. G. 'How many classes are there in society?'. *Sociology*, Vol. 24 (1990): 377–96.

Runnymede Trust. *Multi-ethnic Britain – Facts and Trends*. London: Runnymede Trust, 1994.

——. *Islamophobia: A Challenge for Us All*. London: Runnymede Trust, 1997.

Rushdie, Salman. *Midnight's Children*. London: Picador, 1982.

Rushkoff, Douglas. *Playing the Future: What We Can Learn from Digital Kids*. New York: Riverhead, 1999.

Russell, Diana E. H. *Rape in Marriage*. New York: Macmillan, 1982.

Russell, James. *Double Standards: Social Policy in Europe and the United States*, 2nd edn. Lanham, MD: Rowman and Littlefield, 2010.

Ryan, William. *Blaming the Victim*, rev. edn. New York: Vintage, 1976.

Rymer, Russ. *Genie*. New York: HarperPerennial, 1994.

S

Sachs, Jeffrey. *The End of Poverty: How We Can Make It Happen in Our Lifetime*. London: Penguin, 2005.

Sagan, Carl. *Cosmos*. New York: Random House, 1980.

Said, Edward. *Culture and Imperialism*. London: Chatto, 1993.

——. *Orientalism*. London: Penguin, 2003; orig. 1978.

Saks, M. *Alternative Medicine*. Oxford: Clarendon Press, 1992.

Salmon, G. *E-moderating: The Key to Teaching and Learning Online*. London: Taylor & Francis, 2004.

Samson, Colin. *A Way of Life That Does Not Exist: Canada and the Extinguishment of the Innu*. London: Verso, 2003.

Sanders, Teela, Maggie O'Neill and Jane Pitcher. *Prostitution: Sex Work, Policy and Politics*. London: Sage, 2009.

Sanghera, Jasvinder. *Shame*. London: Hodder & Stoughton, 2007.

Sapir, Edward. 'The status of linguistics as a science'. *Language*, Vol. 5 (1929): 207–14.

——. *Selected Writings of Edward Sapir in Language, Culture and Personality*. David G. Mandelbaum ed. Berkeley, CA: University of California Press, 1949.

Sassen, Saskia. *The Global City: New York, London, Tokyo*. Princeton, NJ: Princeton University Press, 1991.

——. *Cities in a World Economy*, 2nd edn. London: Sage, 2000.

——. *Cities in a World Economy*. Newbury Park, CA: Pine Forge Press, 2006.

Sato, Ikuyo. *Kamikaze Biker: Parody and Anomie in Affluent Japan*. Chicago: University of Chicago Press, 1991.

Savage, Jon. *Teenage: The Creation of Youth 1875–1945*. London: Chatto and Windus, 2007.

Savage, Mike. *Walter Benjamin and Urban Meaning*. Keele: University of Keele Press, 1993.

Savage, Mike and Alan Warde. *Urban Sociology, Capitalism and Modernity*. London: Macmillan, 1993.

Savage, Mike, J. Burlow, P. Dickens and T. Fielding. *Property, Bureaucracy and Culture: Middle-Class Formation in Contemporary Britain*. London: Routledge, 1992.

Sayers, Janet. *Biological Politics*. London: Tavistock, 1982.

Scaff, Lawrence A. 'Max Weber and Robert Michels'. *American Journal of Sociology*, Vol. 86, No. 6 (May 1981): 1269–86.

Scarce, Rik. *Eco-warriors: Understanding the Radical Environmental Movement*. Walnut Creek, CA: Left Coast Press, 2006.

Scarman, Leslie George. *The Brixton Disorders, 10–12 April 1981: Report of an Inquiry: Presented to Parliament by the Secretary of State for the Home Department, November 1981*. London: HMSO, 1981.

Scharf, T., C. Phillipson, P. Kingston and A. E. Smith. 'Social exclusion and older people: exploring the connections', *Education and Ageing*, Vol. 16, No. 3 (2001): 303–20.

Scharping, Thomas. *Birth Control in China 1978–1994*. New York: Curzon, 2000.

Scheff, Thomas J. *Mental Illness and Social Processes*. New York: Harper & Row, 1967.

——. *Being Mentally Ill: A Sociological Theory*, 2nd edn. New York: Aldine, 1984; orig. 1966.

Schellenberg, James A. *Masters of Social Psychology*. New York: Oxford University Press, 1978: 38–62.

Scheper-Hughes, Nancy. *Death Without Weeping: The Violence of Everyday Life in Brazil*. Berkeley, CA: University of California Press, 1992.

——. 'The global traffic in organs'. *Current Anthropology*, Vol. 41, No. 2 (2000): 191–224.

Scheper-Hughes, Nancy and Loic Wacquant (eds). *Commodifying Bodies*. London: Sage, 2002.

Schlesinger, Philip. *Putting 'Reality' Together: BBC News*. London: Constable, 1978.

Schlosser, Eric. *Fast Food Nation*. Harmondsworth: Penguin, 2002.

Schmidt, Roger. *Exploring Religion*. Belmont, CA: Wadsworth, 1980.

Schnaiberg, Allan and Kenneth Alan Gould. *Environment and Society: The Enduring Conflict*. New York: St Martin's Press, 1994.

Schramm, Wilbur. *TV in the Lives of our Children*. Stanford, CA: Stanford University Press, 1961.

Schumann, Hans Wolfgang. *Buddhism: An Outline of Its Teachings and Schools*. Wheaton, IL: The Theosophical Publishing House/Quest Books, 1974.

Scott, John. *Who Rules Britain?* Cambridge: Polity, 1991.

——. *Poverty and Wealth*. London: Longman, 1994.

——. *Corporate Business and Capitalist Classes*. Oxford: Oxford University Press, 1997.

——. *Social Network Analysis: A Handbook*, 2nd edn. London: Sage, 2000.

——. *Fifty Key Sociologists: The Contemporary Theorists*. London: Routledge, 2006a.

——. *Fifty Key Sociologists: The Formative Theorists*. London: Routledge, 2006b.

——. *Sociology: The Key Concepts*. London: Routledge, 2006c.

Scott, Peter. *The Meanings of Mass Higher Education*. Buckingham: Open University Press, 1995.

Scott, Susie. *Making Sense of Everyday Life*. Cambridge: Polity, 2009.

Scott, W. Richard. *Organizations: Rational, Natural and Open Systems*. Englewood Cliffs, NJ: Prentice-Hall, 1981.

Scott, Joan Wallach. *The Politics of the Veil*. Princeton, NJ: Princeton University Press, 2007.

Scrambler, Graham. *Health and Social Change: A Critical Theory*. Oxford: Oxford University Press, 2002.

Seabrook, Jeremy. *In the Cities of the South*. London: Verso, 1996; 2nd edn, 2001.

Seager, Joni. *The Atlas of Women in the World*, 4th edn. New York: Penguin, 2009; orig. 1997.

Seale, Clive. *Constructing Death: The sociology of dying and bereavement*. Cambridge: Cambridge University Press, 1998.

Sedgwick, Eve Kasofsky. *The Epistemology of the Closet*. Berkeley, CA: University of California Press, 1990.

Seekings, Jeremy and Nicoli Nattrass. *Class, Race, and Inequality in South Africa*. New Haven: Yale University Press, 2006.

Segal, Lynne. *Is the Future Female? Troubled Thoughts on Contemporary Feminism*. London: Virago, 1994.

——. *Straight Sex: The Politics of Pleasure*. London: Virago, 1994; 2nd edn, 1997.

——. *Why Feminism*. Cambridge: Polity, 1999.

Seidman, Steven (ed.). *Queer Theory/Sociology*. Oxford: Blackwell, 1996.

Sekulic, Dusko, Garth Massey and Randy Hodson. 'Who were the Yugoslavs? Failed sources of common identity in the former Yugoslavia'. *American Sociological Review*, Vol. 59, No. 1 (February 1994): 83–97.

Sen, Amartya. *Development as Freedom*. New York: Alfred A. Knopf, 1999.

Sen, K. M. *Hinduism*. Baltimore, MD: Penguin, 1961.

Sennett, Richard and Jonathan Cobb. *The Hidden Injuries of Class*. New York: Vintage, 1973.

Sewell, Tony. *Black Masculinities and Schooling*. London: Trentham, 1996.

Sharma, Ursula. *Caste*. Buckingham: Open University Press, 1999.

Shakespeare, Tom. *Disability Rights and Wrongs*. London: Routledge, 2006.

Sharp, Lesley A. *Strange Harvest: Organ Transplants, Denatured Bodies, and the Transformed Self*. London: University of California Press, 2006.

Sharpe, Sue. *Just Like a Girl: How Girls Learn to Become Women*, 2nd edn. Harmondsworth: Penguin, 1994.

Sharrock, W. W., D. W. Francis and E. C. Cuff. *Perspectives in Sociology*. London: Routledge, 2005.

Shaw, Clifford S. *The Jack Roller*. Chicago: University of Chicago Press, 1966; orig. 1930.

Shaw, Martin. *War and Genocide: Organized Killing in Modern Society*. Cambridge: Polity, 2003.

——. *What is Genocide? A New Social Theory*. Cambridge: Polity, 2007.

Sheehan, Molly O'Meara. 'Making better transportation choices', in Lester R. Brown et al. (eds), *State of the World 2001*. London: Earthscan, 2001: 103–22.

Sheehy, Gail. *Passages: Predictable Crises of Adult Life*. New York: Dutton, 1976.

Sheldon, William H., Emil M. Hartl and Eugene McDermott. *Varieties of Delinquent Youth*. New York: Harper, 1949.

Sherman, Sharon R. *Documenting Ourselves: Film, Video, Culture*. Lexington, KY: University of Kentucky Press, 1998.

——. *The Body and Social Theory*, 2nd edn. London: Sage, 2003.

Shilling, Chris. *The Body and Society*. London: 1993.

Short, Philip. *Mao: A Life*. London: Hodder & Stoughton, 1999.

Shweder, R. A. *Welcome to Middle Age (and Other Cultural Fictions)*. Chicago: University of Chicago Press, 1998.

Sidel, Ruth and Victor W. Sidel. *A Healthy State: An International Perspective on the Crisis in United States Medical Care*, rev. edn. New York: Pantheon, 1982a.

——. *The Health Care of China*. Boston, MA: Beacon, 1982b.

Sills, David L. 'The succession of goals', in Amitai Etzioni (ed.), *A Sociological Reader on Complex Organizations*, 2nd edn. New York: Holt, Rinehart & Winston, 1969: 175–87.

Silva, Elizabeth B. and Carol Smart. *The New Family?* London: Sage, 1999.

Silver, Lee. *Remaking Eden*. London: Phoenix Giant, 1998.

Simmel, Georg. *The Sociology of Georg Simmel*. Kurt Wolff ed. New York: Free Press, 1950: 118–69; orig. 1902.

——. 'The metropolis and mental life', in Georg Simmel, *The Sociology of Georg Simmel*. Kurt Wolff ed. New York: Free Press, 1950: 409–24; orig. 1905.

Simon, Jeff. *Cultural Studies: The Basics*. London: Sage, 2002.

Simon, Julian. *The Ultimate Resource*. Princeton, NJ: Princeton University Press, 1981.

Simpson, George Eaton and J. Milton Yinger. *Racial and Cultural Minorities: An Analysis of Prejudice and Discrimination*, 4th edn. New York: Harper & Row, 1972.

Sinfield, Adrian. *What Unemployment Means*. Oxford: Martin Robertson, 1981.

Skeggs, Beverley. *Formations of Class and Gender: Becoming Respectable*. London: Sage, 1997.

Skellington, R. *'Race' in Britain Today*, 2nd edn. London: Sage, 1996.

Skelton, T. and Gill Valentine (eds). *Cool Places: Geographies of Youth Cultures*. London: Routledge, 1998.

Skocpol, Theda. *States and Social Revolutions: A Comparative Analysis of France, Russia and China*. Cambridge: Cambridge University Press, 1979.

Slater, Nigel. *Toast: The Story of a Boy's Hunger*. London: Fourth Estate, 2003.

Slater, Philip E. 'Contrasting correlates of group size'. *Sociometry*, Vol. 21, No. 2 (June 1958): 129–39.

Smart, Barry. *Michel Foucault*. London: Routledge, 1985.

——. (ed.). *Resisting McDonaldization*. London: Sage, 1999.

Smart, Carol. *Women, Crime and Criminology: A Feminist Critique*. London: Routledge and Kegan Paul, 1977.

——. *The Ties that Bind*. London: Routledge, 1984.

——. *Personal Life, Relationships and Families: New Directions in Sociological Thinking*. Cambridge: Polity, 2007.

Smart, Carol and Bren Neal. *Family Fragments?* Cambridge: Polity, 1999.

Smart, Ninian. *Atlas of World Religions*. Oxford: Oxford University Press, 1999.

Smith, Adam. *An Enquiry into the Nature and Causes of the Wealth of Nations*. New York: The Modern Library, 1937; orig. 1776.

Smith, Anthony D. *Nationalism: Theory, Ideology, History*. Cambridge: Polity, 2001.

——. *The Cultural Foundations of Nations: Hiererachy, Covenant and Republic*. Oxford: Blackwell. 2008.

Smith, Anthony and Frank Webster (eds). *The Postmodern University? Contested Voices of Higher Education in Society*. Buckingham: Open University Press, 1997.

Smith, Dan (ed.). *The State of the World Atlas*. Harmondsworth: Penguin, 2008; orig. 1999.

Smith, David. *Third World Cities*, 2nd edn. London: Routledge, 2002.

Smith, David and Shelagh Armstrong. *If the World were a Village*. London: A&C Black, 2003.

Smith, David J. 'Ethnic origins, crime and criminal justice', in M. Maguire, R. Morgan and R. Reiner (eds), *Oxford Handbook of Criminology*. Oxford: Oxford University Press, 2010.

Smith, David J. and Sally Tomlinson. *The School Effect: A Study of Multi-racial Comprehensives*. London: Policy Studies Institute, 1989.

Smith, Greg. *Erving Goffman*. London: Routledge, 2006.

Smith, Philip (ed.). *The New American Cultural Sociology*. Cambridge: Cambridge University Press, 1998.

Smith, Robert B. 'Health care reform now'. *Society*, Vol. 30, No. 3 (March–April 1993): 56–65.

Smith, Stephen. *Ending Global Poverty: A Guide to What Works*. New York: Palgrave Macmillan, 2005.

Smith-Lovin, Lynn and Charles Brody. 'Interruptions in group discussions: the effects of gender and group composition'. *American Journal of Sociology*, Vol. 54, No. 3 (June 1989): 424–35.

Snell, Marilyn Berlin. 'The purge of nurture'. *New Perspectives Quarterly*, Vol. 7, No. 1 (Winter 1990): 1–2.

Snodgrass, Jon. *The Jack-Roller at Seventy*. Lexington, MA: DC Heath/Lexington Books, 1982.

Snyder, Sharon L. and David T. Mitchell. *Cultural Locations of Disability*. Chicago: University of Chicago Press, 2006.

Social Trends, 2010. London: HMSO, 2010.

Sorokin, Pitrim and C. Berger. *Time Budgets of Human Behaviour*. Cambridge, MA: Harvard University Press, 1938.

Sowell, Thomas. *Ethnic America*. New York: Basic Books, 1981.

——. *Migrations and Cultures: A World View*. New York: Basic Books, 1996.

Soysal, Yasemin. *Limits of Citizenship: Migrants and Postnational Membership in Europe*. Chicago: University of Chicago Press, 1994.

Speer, James A. 'The new Christian Right and its parent company: a study in political contrasts', in David G. Bromley and Anson Shupe (eds), *New Christian Politics*. Macon, GA: Mercer University Press, 1984: 19–40.

Spencer, Liz and Ray Pahl. *Rethinking Friendship: Hidden Solidarities Today*. Princeton, NJ: Princeton University Press, 2006.

Spender, Dale. *Man Made Language*. London: Routledge and Kegan Paul, 1980.

——. *Women of Ideas and What Men Have Done to Them: From Aphra Behn to Adrienne Rich*. London: Routledge and Kegan Paul, 1982.

Spike Peterson, V. and Anne Sisson Runyan, *Global Gender Issues in the New Millennium*, 3rd edn. Boulder, CO: Westview, 2010.

Spindler, Konrad. *The Man in the Ice*. London: Phoenix, 2001.

Spitzer, Steven. 'Toward a Marxian theory of deviance', in Delos H. Kelly (ed.), *Criminal Behavior: Readings in Criminology*. New York: St Martin's Press, 1980: 175–91.

Stacey, Judith. *Patriarchy and Socialist Revolution in China*. Berkeley, CA: University of California Press, 1983.

——. *Brave New Families: Stories of Domestic Upheaval in Late Twentieth-Century America*. New York: Basic Books, 1990.

——. 'Good riddance to "the family": a response to David Popenoe'. *Journal of Marriage and the Family*, Vol. 55, No. 3 (August 1993): 545–7.

——. *In the Name of the Family: Rethinking Family Values in the Postmodern Age*. Boston, MA: Beacon, 1996: 8.

——. *Unhitched: Love, Marriage and Family Values from West Hollywood to Western China*. New York: New York University Press, 2011.

Stanley, Liz (ed.). *Feminist Praxis: Research, Theory and Epistemology in Feminist Sociology*. London: Routledge and Kegan Paul, 1990.

Stanley, Liz and Sue Wise. *Breaking Out: Feminist Consciousness and Feminist Research*. London: Routledge and Kegan Paul, 1983.

Stanworth, M. D. *Gender and Schooling: A Study of Sexual Divisions in the Classroom*. London: Hutchinson in association with the Explorations in Feminism Collective, 1983.

Stark, Rodney and William Sims Bainbridge. 'Of churches, sects and cults: preliminary concepts for a theory of religious movements'. *Journal for the Scientific Study of Religion*, Vol. 18, No. 2 (June 1979): 117–31.

——. 'Secularization and cult formation in the jazz age'. *Journal for the Scientific Study of Religion*, Vol. 20, No. 4 (December 1981): 360–73.

Starker, Steven. *Evil Influences: Crusades against the Mass Media*. New Brunswick, NJ: Transaction, 1989.

Stavrianos, L. S. *A Global History: The Human Heritage*, 3rd edn. Englewood Cliffs, NJ: Prentice Hall, 1983.

Stein, Dorothy. *People Who Count: Population and Politics, Women and Children*. London: Earthscan, 1995.

Stein, Stuart. *Sociology on the Web: A Student Guide*. Harlow: Pearson, 2003.

Stephens, John D. *The Transition from Capitalism to Socialism*. Urbana, IL: University of Illinois Press, 1986.

Stern, Steve J. *The Secret History of Gender: Women, Men, and Power in Late Colonial Mexico*. Chapel Hill, NC: University of North Carolina Press, 1997.

Stinchcombe, Arthur L. 'Some empirical consequences of the Davis–Moore theory of stratification', *American Sociological Review*, Vol. 28, No. 5 (October 1963).

Stockman, Norman. *Understanding Chinese Society*. Cambridge: Polity, 2000.

Stone, Lawrence. *The Family, Sex and Marriage in England 1500–1800*. New York: Harper & Row, 1977.

Stones, Rob. *Sociological Reasoning: Toward a Past-Modern Society*. London: Macmillan, 1996.

——. *Key Sociological Thinkers*. Basingstoke: Palgrave, 2008; orig. 1998.

Storey, John. *Cultural Studies and the Study of Popular Culture*. Edinburgh: Edinburgh University Press, 1996.

Storr, Merl. *Latex and Lingerie: Shopping for Pleasure at Ann Summers Parties*. Oxford: Berg, 2004.

Storry, Mike and Peter Childs (eds). *British Cultural Identities*. London: Routledge, 1997.

Stouffer, Samuel A. et al. *The American Soldier: Adjustment during Army Life*. Princeton, NJ: Princeton University Press, 1949.

Strathern, Marilyn. *Audit Cultures: Anthropological Studies in Accountability, Ethics and the Academy*. London: Routledge, 2000.

Straus, Murray A. and Richard J. Gelles. 'Societal change and change in family violence from 1975 to 1985 as revealed by two national surveys'. *Journal of Marriage and the Family*, Vol. 48, No. 4 (August 1986): 465–79.

Streib, Gordon F. 'Are the aged a minority group?', in Bernice L. Neugarten (ed.), *Middle Age and Aging: A Reader in Social Psychology*. Chicago: University of Chicago Press, 1968: 35–46.

Strong, Philip. *The Ceremonial Order of the Clinic*. London: Routledge, 1979.

Stryker, Susan and Stephen Whittleeds. *The Transgdender Studies Reader*, London: Routledge, 2006.

Sudnow, David N. *Passing On: The Social Organization of Dying*. Englewood Cliffs, NJ: Prentice-Hall, 1967.

Sumner, William Graham. *Folkways*. New York: Dover, 1959; orig. 1906.

Suoranta, Juha and Tere Vaden. *Wikiworld*. London: Pluto, 2010.

Sutherland, Edwin H. 'White collar criminality'. *American Sociological Review*, Vol. 5, No. 1 (February 1940): 1–12.

Sutherland, Holly, T. Sefton and D. Pichaud. *Poverty in Britain: The Impact of Government Policy since 1997*. York: Joseph Rowntree Foundation, 2003.

Sutherland, Jean-Anne and Feltey, Kathryn. *Cinematic Sociology: Social Life in Film*. Newbury Park, CA: Pine Forge Press, 2009.

Sutton, Philip W. *The Environment: A Sociological Introduction*. Cambridge: Polity, 2007.

Swain, J., S. French, C. Barnes and C. Thomas (ed.). *Disabling Barriers, Enabling Environments*. London: Sage, 2004.

Swann, Lord. *Education for All*. Cmmd 9453. London: HMSO, 1985.

Swartz, David. *Culture and Power: The Work of Pierre Bourdieu*. Chicago: University of Chicago Press, 1997.

Szasz, Thomas S. *The Manufacturer of Madness: A Comparative Study of the Inquisition and the Mental Health Movement*. New York: Dell, 1961.

——. *The Myth of Mental Illness: Foundations of a Theory of Personal Conduct*. New York: Harper & Row, 1970; orig. 1961.

——. 'Mental illness is still a myth'. *Society*, Vol. 31, No. 4 (May–June 1994): 34–9.

Sznaider, Natan. *The Compassionate Temperament: Care and Cruelty in Modern Society*. Lanham, MD: Rowman and Littlefield, 2000.

T

Taeuber, Karl and Alma Taeuber. *Negroes in Cities*. Chicago: Aldine, 1965.

Tannen, Deborah. *You Just Don't Understand Me: Women and Men in Conversation*. New York: Wm Morrow, 1990.

Tannenbaum, Frank. *Crime and the Community*. Boston, MA: Ginn & Co., 1938.

Tapscott, Don and Anthony Williams. *Wikinomics: How Mass Collaboration Changes Everything*. London: Atlantic Books, 2007.

Taylor, Ian. *Crime in Context*. Cambridge: Polity Press, 1999.

Taylor, Ian, Paul Walton and Jock Young. *The New Criminology*. London: Routledge, 1973.

Terkel, Studs. *Working*. New York: Pantheon Books, 1974 (UK edn, London: Peregrine, 1977).

Thane, Pat. *The Long History of Old Age*. London: Thames and Hudson, 2006.

—— (ed.). *Unequal Britain: Equalities in Britain since 1945*. London: Continuum, 2010.

Theen, Rolf H. W. 'Party and bureaucracy', in Erik P. Hoffmann and Robbin F. Laird (eds), *The Soviet Polity in the Modern Era*. New York: Aldine, 1984: 131–65.

Therborn, Göran. *European Modernity and Beyond: The Trajectory of European Societies 1945–2000*. London: Sage, 1995.

—— (ed.). *Between Sex and Power: Families in the World 1900–2000*. London: Routledge, 2004.

——. *Inequalities of the World*. London: Verso, 2006.

——. *The World: A Beginner's Guide*. Cambridge: Polity, 2011.

Thomas, Janet. *The Battle in Seattle*. Colorado: Fulcrum, 2000.

Thomas, T. *Sex Crime: Sex Offending and Society*. Cullompton, Devon: Willian, 2000.

Thomas, W. I. *W. I. Thomas on Social Organization and Social Personality*. Morris Janowitz ed. Chicago: University of Chicago Press, 1966; orig. 1931.

Thomas W. I. and D. S. Thomas. *The Child in America*. New York: Knopf, 1928.

Thomas, W. I. and Florian Znaniecki. *The Polish Peasant in Europe and America*. New York: Dover, 1958; orig. 1918.

Thompson, E. P. *The Making of the English Working Class*. Harmondsworth: Penguin, 1963.

Thompson, John. *The Media and Modernity: A Social Theory of Media*. Cambridge: Polity, 1995.

Thompson, Kenneth (ed.). *Readings from Emile Durkheim*. London: Routledge, 1985.

Thompson, Paul. *Voices of the Past: Oral History*. Oxford: Oxford University Press, 1974; 3rd edn, 2000.

Thompson, Paul, Catherine Ibsen and Michele Auerldstern. *I Don't Feel Old: The Experience of Later Life*. Oxford: Oxford University Press, 1990.

Thorne, Burrie and Z. Luria. 'Sexuality and gender in children's daily worlds'. *Social Problems*, Vol. 33, No. 3 (1985): 176–90.

Thornham, Sue, Caroline Bassett and Paul Marris (eds). *Media Studies: A Reader*, 3rd edn. Edinburgh: Edinburgh University Press, 2009.

Thornhill, R. and C. Palmer. *A Natural History of Rape: Biological Bases of Sexual Coercion*. Cambridge, MA: MIT Press, 2000.

Thornton, Sarah, *Club Cultures*. Cambridge: Polity, 1995.

Thornton, Sarah. *Club Cultures: Music, Media and Subcultural Capital*. London: Routledge, 2005.

Tilly, Charles. *Social Movements 1768–2004*. London: Paradigm, 2004.

Timonen, Virpi. *Ageing Societies: A Comparative Introduction*. Maidenhead: Open University Press, 2008.

Tocqueville, Alexis de. *The Old Regime and the French Revolution*. Stuart Gilbert trans. Garden City, NY: Anchor/Doubleday, 1955; orig. 1856.

Toennies, Ferdinand. *Community and Society* (*Gemeinschaft und Gesellschaft*). New York: Harper & Row, 1963; orig. 1887.

Tolson, A. *The Limits of Masculinity*. London: Tavistock, 1977.

Tolson, Jay. 'The trouble with elites'. *The Wilson Quarterly*, Vol. 19, No. 1 (Winter 1995): 6–8.

Tomlinson, Sally. *A Sociology of Special Education*. London: Routledge, 1982.

——. *Education in a Post-Welfare Society*. Buckingham: Open University Press, 2007.

——. *Race and Education: Policy and Politics in Britain*. Maidenhead: Open University Press, 2008.

Tong, Rosemarie. *Feminist Thought: A More Comprehensive Introduction*, 3rd edn. Boulder, CO: Westview, 2008.

Totten, Samuel et al. *Century of Genocide*. New York: Garland, 1997.

Townsend, Peter. *The Family Life of Old People*. Harmondsworth: Penguin, 1957.

——. *Poverty in the UK*. Harmondsworth: Penguin, 1979.

——. *Poverty and Labour in London: Interim Report of a Centenary Survey*. London: Low Pay Unit, in conjunction with the Poverty Research (London) Trust, 1987.

Townsend, Peter and Nick Davidson (eds). *Inequalities in Health: The Black Report*. Harmondsworth: Penguin, 1982.

Toynbee, Polly. *Hard Work: Life in Low-Pay Britain*. London: Bloomsbury, 2003.

Travers, Max. *The New Bureaucracy: Quality Assurance and Its Critics*. Bristol: Policy Press, 2007.

Trebilcot, Joyce (ed.). *Mothering: Essays in Feminist Theory*. Totowa, NJ: Rowman & Allanheld, 1984.

Trenchard, I. and H. Warren. *Something to Tell You: The Experiences and Needs of Young Lesbians and Gay Men in London*. London: Gay Teenage Group, 1984.

Troeltsch, Ernst. *The Social Teaching of the Christian Churches*. New York: Macmillan, 1931.

Truth and Reconciliation Commission of South Africa, *Report* (5 vols) and CD-Rom. London: Palgrave, 2000.

Tudge, Colin. *The Day Before Yesterday: Five Million Years of Human History*. London: Cape, 1995.

Tudor-Hart, J. 'The inverse care law'. *The Lancet* (27 February 1971): 405–12.

Tumin, Melvin M. 'Some principles of stratification: a critical analysis'. *American Sociological Review*, Vol. 18, No. 4 (August 1953): 387–94.

——. *Social Stratification: The Forms and Functions of Inequality*, 2nd edn. Englewood Cliffs, NJ: Prentice-Hall, 1985.

Tunstall, Jeremy. *Old and Alone: A Sociological Study of Old People*. London: Routledge and Kegan Paul, 1966.

Turino, Thomas. *Music as Social Life*. Chicago: University of Chicago Press, 2008.

Turkle, Sherry. *Life on the Screen: Identity in the Age of the Internet*. London: Weidenfeld and Nicolson, 1996.

Turner, Brian. *The Body and Society*. Oxford: Blackwell, 1984.

——. *Medical Power and Social Knowledge*. London: Routledge, 1987; 2nd edn, 1996.

Turner, Bryan F. 'Outline of a theory of citizenship'. *Sociology*, Vol. 24, No. 2 (1990): 189–217.

Turner, Charles Hampden and Fons Trompenaars. *The Seven Cultures of Capitalism*. London: Piatkus, 1993.

Turner, Graeme. *Understanding Celebrity*. London: Sage, 2004.

Turner, Ian, Paul Walker and Jack Young. *The New Criminology*. London: Routledge, 1977.

Turner, Jonathan. *Herbert Spencer*. London: Sage, 1985.

U

UNAIDS. *The Impact of AIDS on People and Societies*. New York: UN Publications, 2004.

UNDP (United Nations Development Programme). *Overcoming Barriers: Human Mobility and Development*. London and New York: Palgrave Macmillan, 2009.

——. *Human Development Report 20th Anniversary Edition. The Real Wealth of Nations: Pathways to Human Development*. London and New York: Palgrave Macmillan, 2010.

UNESCO Institute for Statistics. *Global Education Digest 2009*. Montreal: UNESCO, 2009 (and on UNESCO Statistics website: www.unesco.org).

UNFPA (United Nations Population Fund). *Lives Together, Worlds Apart: Men and Women in a Time of Change. The State of the World Population*. New York: UNFPA, 2000 (and on UNFPA website: www.unfpa.org).

Ungerson, Clare. *Policy is Personal: Sex, Gender and Informal Care*. London: Tavistock, 1987.

UN Habitat. *State of the World's Cities: Bridging the Urban Divide 2010/2011*. London: Earthscan, 2010.

UNHCR (United Nations High Commission for Refugees). *The State of the World's Refugees: Fifty Years of Humanitarian Action*. Oxford: Oxford University Press, 2000.

UNHDP (United Nations Human Development Programme). *Human Development Report*. New York: Oxford University Press, 2010 (and annual reports since 1990).

UN House of Representatives. *Street Children: A Global Disgrace*. Washington, DC: US Goverment Printing Office, 1992.

UNICEF. *The Progress of Nations*. New York: UNICEF, 1996.

——. *Early Marriages, Child Spouses*. New York: UNICEF, March 2001.

United Nations. *World Urbanizing Prospects: The 1999 Revision*. New York: United Nations, 1999.

——. *World Population Prospects: The 2002 Revision*. New York: United Nations, 2002.

——. *Urban Agglomerations*. New York: United Nations, 2003a.

——. *World Urbanizing Prospects: The 2003 Revision*. New York: United Nations, 2003b.

——. *Africa's Orphaned Generation*. New York: UNICEF, 2004a.

——. *The Official Summary of the State of the World's Children*. New York: UNICEF, 2004b.

UNODC. *Global Report on Drugs*. New York: United Nations, 2010.

Unschuld, Paul. *Medicine in China*. Berkeley: University of California Press, 2010.

Urry, John. *Sociology Beyond Societies*. London: Routledge, 2000.

——. *Global Complexity*. Cambridge: Polity, 2003.

——. *Mobilities*. Cambridge: Polity, 2007.

——. *Mobile Lives*

US Bureau of Justice. *Sourcebook of Criminal Justice Statistics 1990*. Timothy J. Flanagan and Kathleen Maguire eds. Washington, DC: US Government Printing Office, 1991.

——. *Criminal Victimization*. Washington, DC: Bureau of Justice, 1998.

US Bureau of the Census. Prepublication data on income and wealth provided by the Census Bureau. Washington, DC: Government Publications, 1999, 2001, 2002, 2003.

US Bureau of the Census. *Report on Marriage and Divorce*. Washington, DC: US Government Printing Office, 2002.

US Immigration and Naturalization Service. *Legal Immigration, Fiscal Year 2000*. Washington DC: US Immigration and Naturalization Service.

V

Van Biema, David. 'Parents who kill'. *Time*, Vol. 144, No. 20 (14 November 1994): 50–1.

Vance, Carole S. (ed.). *Pleasure and Danger*. London: Routledge, 1984.

Vattimo, Gianni. *The Transparent Society*. Cambridge: Polity, 1992.

Veblen, Thorstein. *The Theory of the Leisure Class*. New York: The New American Library, 1953; orig. 1899.

Venkatesh, Sudhir. *Gang Leader for a Day*. London: Allen Lane, 2008.

Vincent, John A. *Inequality and Old Age*. London: UCL Press, 1996.

Vincent, John, Chris Phillipson and Murna Downs (eds). *The Futures of Old Age*. London: Sage, 2005.

Vogel, Ezra F. *The Four Little Dragons: The Spread of Industrialization in East Asia*. Cambridge, MA: Harvard University Press, 1991.

Vogel, Lise. *Marxism and the Oppression of Women: Toward a Unitary Theory*. New Brunswick, NJ: Rutgers University Press, 1983.

Vold, George B. and Thomas J. Bernard. *Theoretical Criminology*, 3rd edn. New York: Oxford University Press, 1986.

Volti, Ruth. *An Introduction to the Sociology of Work and Occupations: Globalization and Technological Change into the Twenty-First Century*. Newbury Park, CA: Pine Forge Press, 2008.

von Hirsch, Andrew. *Past or Future Crimes: Deservedness and Dangerousness in the Sentencing of Criminals*. New Brunswick, NJ: Rutgers University Press, 1976.

Vonnegut, Kurt, Jr. 'Harrison Bergeron', in *Welcome to the Monkey House*. New York: Delacorte Press/Seymour Lawrence, 1968: 7–13; orig. 1961.

Vuillamy, Ed. *Amexica: War along the Borderline*. London: Random, 2010.

W

Wacquant, Loic. *Urban Outcasts: A Compararive Sociology of Advanced Marginality*. Cambridge: Polity, 2008.

——. *Punishing the Poor: The Neoliberal Government of Social Insecurity*. Durham, NC: Duke University Press, 2009; orig. 2004.

Walby, Sylvia. *Theorizing Patriarchy*. Cambridge: Polity, 1990.

——. *Globalization and Inequalities*. London: Sage, 2009.

Walker, Alan and Tony Maltby. *Ageing Europe*. Buckingham: Open University Press, 1997.

Walkerdine, Valerie, H. Lucey and J. Melody. *Growing Up Girl: Psychosocial Explorations of Gender and Class*. Basingstoke: Palgrave, 2001.

Walkgate, Sandra. *Gender and Crime: An Introduction*. Cullompton, Devon, Willian.

Wallace, Mia and Klint Spanner, *How to Get an ASBO*. London: Virgin.

Wallerstein, Immanuel. *The Modern World-System: Capitalist Agriculture and the Origins of the European World-Economy in the Sixteenth Century*. New York: Academic Press, 1974.

——. *The Capitalist World-Economy*. New York: Cambridge University Press, 1979.

——. *The End of the World as We Know It: Social Science for the Twenty-First Century*. Minneapolis: University of Minnesota Press, 1999.

Wallis, Roy. *The Road to Total Freedom: A Sociological Analysis of Scientology*. London: Heinemann, 1976.

Walmsley, Roy. *World Prison Population List: Findings*, No. 188. London: Home Office, 2003.

——. *World Prison Population List*. London: International Centre for Prison Studies, King's College, 2007.

Walter, Natasha. *Living Dolls: The Return of Sexism*. London: Virago, 2010.

Walter, Tony. *The Revival of Death*. London and New York: Routledge, 1994.

——. *On Bereavement: The Culture of Grief*. Buckingham and Philadelphia, PA: Open University Press, 1998.

Warleigh, Alex. *European Union: The Basics*. London: Routledge, 2008.

Warner, W. Lloyd and J. O. Low. *The Social System of the Modern Factory*. Yankee City Series, Vol. 4. New Haven, CT: Yale University Press, 1947.

Warner, W. Lloyd and Paul S. Lunt. *The Social Life of a Modern Community*. New Haven, CT: Yale University Press, 1941.

Warnock Committee. *Report of the Committee of Inquiry into Human Fertilisation and Embryology*. CM9314. London: HMSO, 1984.

Waskful, Dennis D. *Self-games and Body-play: Personhood in Online Chat and Cybersex*. New York: Peter Lang, 2003.

——. (ed.). *Net.SeXXX: Readings on Sex, Pornography and the Internet*. New York: Peter Lang, 2004.

Waters, Malcolm. 'Inequality after class', in David Owen (ed.), *Sociology after Postmodernism*. London: Sage, 1997.

Waters, Malcolm. *Globalization*. London: Routledge, 2000.

Watson, James and Mellisa Caldwell. *The Cultural Politics of Food and Eating*. Oxford: Blackwell, 2004.

Watson, James and Anne Hill. *Dictionary of Media and Communication Studies*, 5th edn. London: Arnold, 2000.

Watson, John B. *Behaviorism*, rev. edn. New York: W. W. Norton, 1930.

Weber, Adna Ferrin. *The Growth of Cities*. New York: Columbia University Press, 1963; orig. 1899.

Weber, Max. *Max Weber on the Methodology of the Social Sciences*. E. A. Shils and H. A. Finch trans. and eds. Glencoe, IL: Free Press, 1949.

——. *Rational and Social Foundations of Music*. Carbondale, IL: Southern Illinois University Press, 1958.

——. *The Protestant Ethic and the Spirit of Capitalism*. New York: Charles Scribner's Sons, 1958; orig. 1905.

——. *Economy and Society*. G. Roth and C. Wittich eds. Berkeley, CA: University of California Press, 1978; orig. 1921.

Webster, Andrew. *Science, Technology and Society*. Basingstoke: Macmillan, 1991.

Webster, Colin. *Understanding Race and Crime*. Maidenhead: Open University, 2007.

Webster, Frank. 'Higher education', in Gary Browning, Abigail Halci and Frank Webster (eds), *Understanding Contemporary Society: Theories of the Present*. London: Sage, 2000: Chapter 22.

——. *Theories of the Information Society*, 3rd edn. London: Routledge, 2006.

Weeks, J. *Coming Out: Homosexual Politics in Britain from the Nineteenth Century to the Present*. London: Quartet, 1977.

——. *Sexuality*, 3rd edn. London: Routledge, 2009; orig. 1986.

Weeks, J., Brian Heaphy and Catherine Donovan. *Same Sex Intimacies: Families of Choice and Other Life Experiments*. London: Routledge, 2001.

Weeks, Jeffrey. *Against Nature: Essays on History, Sexuality and Identity*. London: Rivers Oram, 1991.

——. *The World We Have Won*. London: Routledge, 2007.

——. *The Language of Sex*. London: Routledge.

Weeks, John R. *Population*, 11th edn. Florence, KY: Wadsworth.

Weidenbaum, Murray. 'The evolving corporate board'. *Society*, Vol. 32, No. 3 (March–April 1995): 9–20.

Weinberg, George. *Society and the Healthy Homosexual*. New York: Doubleday, 1973.

Weine, Stevan M. *When History is a Nightmare: Lives and Memories of Ethnic Cleansing in Bosnia-Herzegovina*. New Brunswick, NJ: Rutgers University Press, 1999.

Wells, Karen. *Childhood in a Global Perspective*. Cambridge: Polity, 2009.

Weller, Paul. *Religions in the UK: Directory 2001–03*, 3rd edn. Derby: University of Derby, 2003.

Wellings, Kaye et al. *Sexual Behaviour in Britain: The National Survey of Sexual Attitudes and Lifestyles*. Harmondsworth: Penguin, 1994.

Wellman, Barry. *Networks in the Global Village*. Boulder, CO: Westview, 1999.

Wellman, Barry et al. 'Networks as personal communities', in B. Wellman and S. D. Berkowitz (eds), *Social Structures: A Network Approach*. Cambridge: Cambridge University Press, 1988: 130–84.

Wells, Liz (ed.). *Photography: A Critical Introduction*, 2nd edn. London: Routledge, 2003.

Wesolowski, Wlodzimierz. 'Transition from authoritarianism to democracy'. *Social Research*, Vol. 57, No. 2 (Summer 1990): 435–61.

West, Candace and Don Zimmerman. 'Doing gender'. *Gender and Society*, Vol. 1, No. 1 (1987): 125–51.

Weston, Kath. *Families We Choose: Lesbians, Gays, Kinship*. New York: Columbia University Press, 1991.

Westwood, Sallie and Parminder Bhachu (eds). *Enterprising Women: Ethnicity, Economy, and Gender Relations*. London: Routledge, 1988.

White, Kevin. *An Introduction to the Sociology of Health and Illness*, 2nd edn. London: Sage, 2009.

Whitely, Sheila. *Women and Popular Music: Sexuality, Identity and Subjectivity*. London: Routledge, 2000.

Whorf, Benjamin Lee. *Language, Thought and Reality*. Cambridge, MA: MIT Press, 1956; orig. 1941.

Whyte, William H., Jr. *The Organization Man*. Garden City, NY: Anchor, 1957.

Wichterich, Christa. *The Globalized Woman*. London: Zed, 2000.

Wilkinson, Iain. *Suffering: A Sociological Introduction*. Cambridge: Polity, 2004.

Wilkinson, Richard. *The Impact of Inequality: How to Make Sick Societies Healthier*. London: Routledge, 2005.

Wilkinson, Richard and Kate Pickett. *The Spirit Level: Why More Equal Societies Almost Always Do Better*. London: Allen Lane, 2009.

Wilkinson, Stephen. *Bodies for Sale*. London: Routledge, 2003.

Williams, Kevin. *Understanding Media Theory*. London: Hodder Arnold, 2003.

Williams, Raymond. *Keywords*. London: Fontana, 1975; reissued 2010.

Williams, Raymond. *Culture and Society: Coleridge to Orwell*. London: Hogarth, 1987; orig. 1958.

Williams, Robin M., Jr. *American Society: A Sociological Interpretation*, 3rd edn. New York: Alfred A. Knopf, 1970.

Williams, Simon. *Emotion and Social Theory*. London: Sage, 2001.

Williamson, Jeffrey G. and Peter H. Lindert. *American Inequality: A Macroeconomic History*. New York: Academic Press, 1980.

Willis, Paul. *Learning to Labour*. London: Ashgate, 1978.

Wilmut, Ian and Roger Highfield. *After Dolly: The Uses and Misuses of Human Cloning*. London: Little, Brown, 2006.

Wilson, Bryan. *Religion in Sociological Perspective*. New York: Oxford University Press, 1982.

Wilson, D. R. and D. L. Carlson. *Researching Sociology on the Internet*. Florence: Wadsworth, 2004.

Wilson, Edward O. *Sociobiology: The New Synthesis*. Cambridge, MA: Belknap Press of the Harvard University Press, 1975.

——. *On Human Nature*. New York: Bantam, 1978.

Wilson, James Q. *Bureaucracy: What Government Agencies Do and Why They Do It*. New York: Basic Books, 1991.

Wilson, James Q. and Richard J. Herrnstein. *Crime and Human Nature*. New York: Simon & Schuster, 1985.

Wilson, Thomas C. 'Urbanism and tolerance: a test of some hypotheses drawn from Wirth and Stouffer'. *American Sociological Review*, Vol. 50, No. 1 (February 1985): 117–23.

——. 'Urbanism and unconventionality: the case of sexual behavior'. *Social Science Quarterly*, Vol. 76, No. 2 (June 1995): 346–63.

Winlow, Simon and Steve Hall. *Violent Night: Urban Leisure and Contemporary Culture*. Oxford: Berg, 2006.

Wintle, Michael (ed.). *Culture and Identity in Europe*. London: Avebury, 1996.

Wirth, Louis. 'Urbanism as a way of life'. *American Journal of Sociology*, Vol. 44, No. 1 (July 1938): 1–24.

Witte, Rob. *Racist Violence and the State: A Comparative Analysis of Britain, France and the Netherlands*. Harlow: Longman, 1996.

Wolcott, Harry F. *Sneaky Kid and Its Aftermath: Ethics and Intimacy in Fieldwork*. London: Alta Vira, 2002.

Wollstonecraft, Mary. *A Vindication of the Rights of Woman*. London: Everyman's Library, 1992; orig. 1792.

Wood, Julian. 'Groping towards sexism: boys' sex talk', in A. McRobbie and M. Nava (eds), *Gender and Generation*. London: Macmillan, 1984.

Woods, Peter. *The Divided School*. London: Routledge, 1979.

Woofitt, Robin and Ian Hutchby. *Conversational Analysis: Principles, Practices and Applications*. Cambridge: Polity, 1998.

World Bank. *World Tables 1991*. Baltimore, MD: Johns Hopkins University Press, 1991.

——. *World Development Report 1993*. New York: Oxford University Press, 1993.

——. *World Development Report 1995: Workers in an Integrating World*. New York: Oxford University Press, 1995.

——. *World Development Report 1997: Workers in an Integrating World*. New York: Oxford University Press, 1997.

——. *World Development Report 2000: Entering the Twenty-First Century*. New York: Oxford University Press, 2000.

——. *World Development Report 2000/1: Attacking Poverty*. Washington, DC: World Bank, 2001.

——. *World Development Indicators 2003*. Washington, DC: World Bank, 2003a.

——. *World Development Report 2003*. Washington DC: World Bank, 2003b.

——. *World Development Report 2004*. Washington DC: World Bank, 2004.

World Health Organisation (WHO). *Constitution of the World Health Organisation*. New York: WHO Interim Commission, 1946.

——. *World Health Report 2000. Health Systems: Improving Performance*. New York: WHO, 2000.

——. *Reducing Risks – Promoting Healthy Life*. New York: WHO, 2002.

——. *Shaping the Future*. New York: WHO, 2003.

——. *Controlling the Global Obesity Epidemic*. Nutrition reports. www.who/int/not/obs.htm, 2004.

Wright, Charles R. *Mass Communications*. New York: Random House, 1967.

Wright, Erik Olin. *Classes*. London: Verso, 1985.

Wright, Erik Olin and Bill Martin. 'The transformation of the American class structure, 1960–1980'. *American Journal of Sociology*, Vol. 93, No. 1 (July 1987): 1–29.

Wright, Erik Olin, Andrew Levine and Elliott Sober. *Reconstructing Marxism: Essays on Explanation and the Theory of History*. London: Verso, 1992.

Y

Young, Iris Marion. *Justice and the Politics of Difference*. Princeton, NJ: Princeton University Press, 1990.

Young, Jock. *The Exclusive Society*. London: Sage, 2000.

——. *The Vertigo of Late Modernity*. London: Sage, 2007.

Young, Jock and John Lea. *What Is to be Done about Law and Order?* Harmondsworth: Penguin, 1984.

Young, Michael and Peter Willmott. *Family and Kinship in East London*. Basingstoke: Penguin, 1957.

——. *The Symmetrical Family*. London: Routledge and Kegan Paul, 1973.

Z

Zangwill, Israel. *The Melting Pot*. New York: Macmillan, 1921; orig. 1909 (also London: William Heinemann, 1919 and Ayer Company Publishers (USA), 1994).

Zeitlin, Irving M. *The Social Condition of Humanity*. New York: Oxford University Press, 1981.

Zimbardo, Philip. *The Lucifer Effect: Understanding How Good People Turn Evil*. New York: Random House, 2007.

Zubaida, Sami. *Islam, The People and The State*, rev. edn. London: I. B. Tauris, 2009.

Zuboff, Shoshana. 'New worlds of computer-mediated work'. *Harvard Business Review*, Vol. 60, No. 5 (September–October 1982): 142–52.

Zuckerman, Phil. 'Atheism', in M. Martin, *The Cambridge Companion to Atheism*. Cambridge: Cambridge University Press, 2006.

——. *Invitation to the Sociology of Religion*. London: Routledge, 2003.

——. *Society without God: What the Least Religious Nations Can Tell Us about Contentment*. New York: New York University Press, 2008.

NAMES INDEX

SUBJECT INDEX

ABOUT THE AUTHORS

Ken Plummer

is Emeritus Professor of Sociology at the University of Essex, and has been actively involved in teaching introductory sociology for the past thirty years. He has been a Senior Lecturer at Middlesex University, and a visiting Professor at the University of California (Santa Barbara) and the University of New York (Stony Brook), as well as giving lectures in many countries around the world.

Apart from a passion for introductory teaching, his major research interests lie in the fields of sexuality, stigma, humanism, story telling, methodology and symbolic interactionist theory. He is the author of *Sexual Stigma* (1975), *Telling Sexual Stories* (1995), *Documents of Life-2* (2001) and *Intimate Citizenship* (2003) as well as the editor of *The Making of the Modern Homosexual* (1981), *Symbolic Interactionism* (1991, 2 vols), *Modern Homosexualities* (1992), *The Chicago School* (1997, 4 vols) and *Sexualities: Critical Assessments* (2001, 4 vols). His most recent book is *Sociology: The Basics* (2010). He is also the founder (and continuing) editor of the journal *Sexualities*.

After the third edition of *Sociology: A global introduction* (2005) Ken became seriously ill and underwent life-saving transplant surgery. He was and is truly grateful to all those involved in saving his life, and was delighted to make the new revisions for this text, his first major task after recovery! He is still in very good health for this fifth edition. And still crazy after all these years, he believes that sociology at its best has a lot to contribute to the modern world, but that it needs to become more accessible and less pretentious and pompous. He hopes this textbook will help towards this.

John J. Macionis

is Professor of Sociology at Kenyon College in Gambier, Ohio, having graduated from Cornell University and the University of Pennsylvania. At Kenyon, he has chaired the Anthropology–Sociology Department, directed the multidisciplinary programme in Humane Studies and presided over the College's Faculty. He has also been active in academic programmes in many other countries.

His publications are wide-ranging, focusing on community life in the US, interpersonal intimacy in families, effective teaching, humour and the importance of global education. He is co-editor of *Seeing Ourselves: Classic, Contemporary and Cross-Cultural Readings in Sociology*, co-author of *Cities and Urban Life* and author of the concise introductory text, *Society: The Basics*.

Professor Macionis considers himself 'first and foremost . . . a teacher' who wishes to share his expertise and experience with students both in person and through his textbooks.

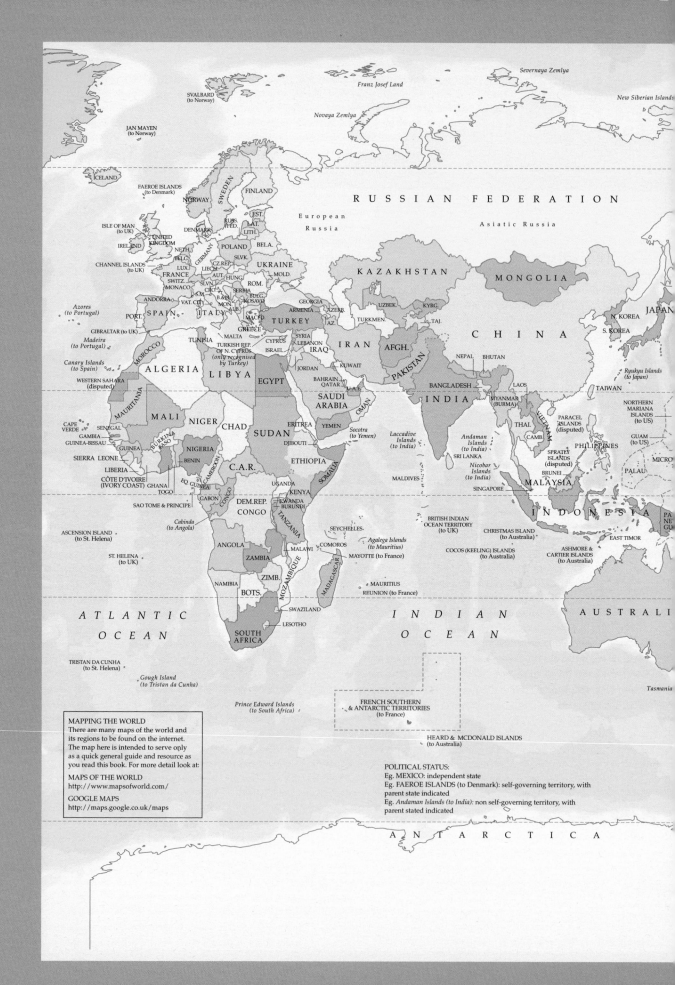

Severnaya Zemlya

Franz Josef Land

New Siberian Islands

SVALBARD
(to Norway)

Novaya Zemlya

JAN MAYEN
(to Norway)

ICELAND

FAEROE ISLANDS
(to Denmark)

NORWAY

SWEDEN

FINLAND

RUSSIAN FEDERATION

European
Russia

Asiatic Russia

ISLE OF MAN
(to UK)

UNITED
KINGDOM

IRELAND

DENMARK

RUSS.
FED.

EST.
LAT.
LITH.

POLAND

BELA.

CHANNEL ISLANDS
(to UK)

NETH.
BELG.
LUX.
FRANCE
SWITZ.
MONACO

GERMANY
LIECH
AUT.
SLVN.
S.M.
VAT. CITY

CZ.REP.
SLVK.
HUNG.
CRO.
B.&H.
MON.
ALB.

UKRAINE

MOLD.

ROM.

SERBIA
BULG.
KOSOVO
MACED.

KAZAKHSTAN

MONGOLIA

N. KOREA

JAPAN

Azores
(to Portugal)

ANDORRA

PORT.

SPAIN

ITALY

GREECE

GEORGIA

ARMENIA

AZERB.

AZ.

UZBEK.

KYRG.

TURKMEN.

TAJ.

CHINA

S. KOREA

GIBRALTAR (to UK)

Madeira
(to Portugal)

Canary Islands
(to Spain)

MOROCCO

TUNISIA

MALTA

TURKISH REP.
OF N. CYPRUS
(only recognised
by Turkey)

CYPRUS
LEBANON
ISRAEL

TURKEY

SYRIA

IRAQ

IRAN

AFGH.

NEPAL

BHUTAN

Ryukyu Islands
(to Japan)

TAIWAN

WESTERN SAHARA
(disputed)

ALGERIA

LIBYA

EGYPT

JORDAN

KUWAIT

PAKISTAN

BANGLADESH

INDIA

MYANMAR
(BURMA)

LAOS

NORTHERN
MARIANA
ISLANDS
(to US)

MAURITANIA

MALI

NIGER

CHAD

SUDAN

ERITREA

YEMEN

BAHRAIN
QATAR

SAUDI
ARABIA

U.A.E.

OMAN

Socotra
(to Yemen)

Laccadive
Islands
(to India)

Andaman
Islands
(to India)

SRI LANKA

THAI.

CAMB.

PARACEL
ISLANDS
(disputed)

PHILIPPINES

GUAM
(to US)

MICRO

CAPE
VERDE

SENEGAL

GAMBIA

GUINEA-BISSAU

GUINEA

SIERRA LEONE

LIBERIA

CÔTE D'IVOIRE
(IVORY COAST)

BURKINA
FASO

NIGERIA

BENIN

GHANA

TOGO

C.A.R.

ETHIOPIA

DJIBOUTI

SOMALIA

Nicobar
Islands
(to India)

MALDIVES

SINGAPORE

SPRATLY
ISLANDS
(disputed)

BRUNEI

MALAYSIA

PALAU

INDONESIA

PA
NE
GU

CAMEROON

EQ. GUINEA

SAO TOME & PRINCIPE

GABON

CONGO

DEM.REP.
CONGO

Cabinda
(to Angola)

UGANDA

RWANDA
BURUNDI

KENYA

TANZANIA

BRITISH INDIAN
OCEAN TERRITORY
(to UK)

CHRISTMAS ISLAND
(to Australia)

EAST TIMOR

ASCENSION ISLAND
(to St. Helena)

ANGOLA

ZAMBIA

ZIMB.

MALAWI

MOZAMBIQUE

COMOROS

MADAGASCAR

SEYCHELLES

Agalega Islands
(to Mauritius)

MAYOTTE (to France)

COCOS (KEELING) ISLANDS
(to Australia)

ASHMORE &
CARTIER ISLANDS
(to Australia)

ST. HELENA
(to UK)

NAMIBIA

BOTS.

SWAZILAND

LESOTHO

MAURITIUS

REUNION (to France)

AUSTRALI

ATLANTIC

OCEAN

SOUTH
AFRICA

INDIAN

OCEAN

TRISTAN DA CUNHA
(to St. Helena)

Gough Island
(to Tristan da Cunha)

Tasmania

Prince Edward Islands
(to South Africa)

FRENCH SOUTHERN
& ANTARCTIC TERRITORIES
(to France)

HEARD & MCDONALD ISLANDS
(to Australia)

MAPPING THE WORLD
There are many maps of the world and
its regions to be found on the internet.
The map here is intended to serve only
as a quick general guide and resource as
you read this book. For more detail look at:

MAPS OF THE WORLD
http://www.mapsofworld.com/

GOOGLE MAPS
http://maps.google.co.uk/maps

POLITICAL STATUS:
Eg. MEXICO: independent state
Eg. FAEROE ISLANDS (to Denmark): self-governing territory, with
parent state indicated
Eg. Andaman Islands (to India): non self-governing territory, with
parent stated indicated

ANTARCTICA

SOCIETY IN HISTORY: TIME LINES

A time line is a visual device that helps us understand historical change. The upper time line represents 5 billion years of the history of the planet Earth. This time line is divided into three sections, each of which is drawn to a different scale of time. The first section, **The Earth's Origins**, begins with the planet's origins 5 billion years before the present (B.P.) and indicates that another full billion years passed before the earliest forms of life appeared. The second section, **Our Human Origins**, shows that plants and animals continued to evolve for billions more years until, approximately 12 million years ago, our earliest human ancestors came onto the scene. In the third section of this time line, **Earliest Civilisation**, we see that what we term civilisation is relatively recent, indeed, with the first permanent settlements occurring in the Middle East a scant 12,000 years ago. But the written record of our species' existence extends back only half this long, to the time humans invented writing and first farmed with animal-driven ploughs some 5,000 years B.P.

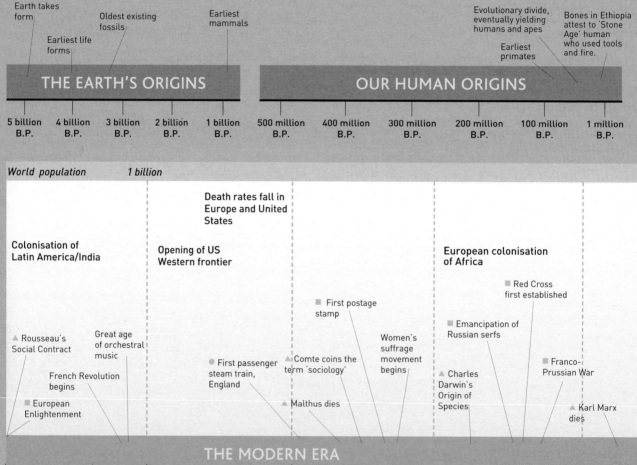

Age of dinosaurs   All humans are hunters and gatherers

Earth takes form

Oldest existing fossils

Earliest mammals

Earliest life forms

Evolutionary divide, eventually yielding humans and apes

Bones in Ethiopia attest to 'Stone Age' human who used tools and fire.

Earliest primates

THE EARTH'S ORIGINS

OUR HUMAN ORIGINS

| 5 billion B.P. | 4 billion B.P. | 3 billion B.P. | 2 billion B.P. | 1 billion B.P. | 500 million B.P. | 400 million B.P. | 300 million B.P. | 200 million B.P. | 100 million B.P. | 1 million B.P. |

World population   1 billion

Death rates fall in Europe and United States

Colonisation of Latin America/India

Opening of US Western frontier

European colonisation of Africa

■ Red Cross first established

First postage stamp

■ Emancipation of Russian serfs

▲ Rousseau's Social Contract

Great age of orchestral music

Women's suffrage movement begins

● First passenger steam train, England

▲ Comte coins the term 'sociology'

■ Franco-Prussian War

French Revolution begins

▲ Charles Darwin's Origin of Species

■ European Enlightenment

■ Malthus dies

▲ Karl Marx dies

THE MODERN ERA

| 1775 | 1800 | 1825 | 1850 | 1875 |

▲ Adam Smith dies

● Steam locomotive invented

● Photography invented

● Telegraph invented

● Telephone invented

● Light bulb invented

● Rubber condoms invented

● Pasteur evolves germ theory of disease

● Coca Cola invented

Industrial Revolution transforms Europe

Industrialisation underway

Adam Smith applauds capitalism

Comte coins term 'sociology'

Marx challenges capitalist class conflict

Comte

Malthus warns of perilous population increase

Spencer

Darwin's 'Origin of the Species' published (1859)

Sociology came into being in the wake of the many changes to society wrought by the Industrial Revolution over the last few centuries – just the blink of an eye in evolutionary perspective. The lower time line provides a close-up look at the events and trends that have defined **The Modern Era**, most of which are discussed in this text.

Innovations in technology are charted in the panel below the line and provide a useful backdrop for viewing the milestones of social progress highlighted in the panel above the line. Major contributions to the development of sociological thought are traced along the very bottom of this time line.

Events are coded according to the broad themes as follows:

- Technology
- National/global events and trends
- Sociology as a discipline

For Time Lines on the world wide web, see www.

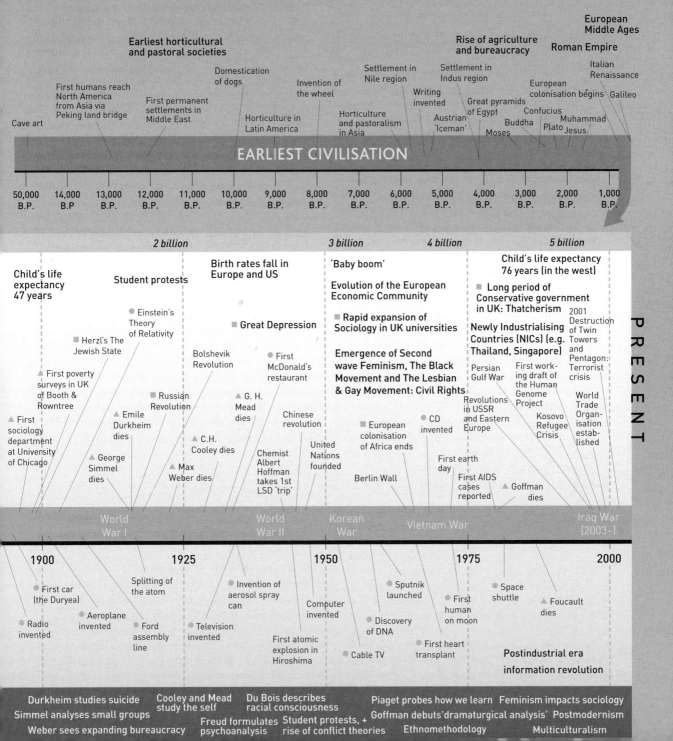

Durkheim studies suicide   Cooley and Mead study the self   Du Bois describes racial consciousness   Piaget probes how we learn   Feminism impacts sociology

Simmel analyses small groups   Freud formulates psychoanalysis   Student protests, + rise of conflict theories   Goffman debuts 'dramaturgical analysis'   Postmodernism

Weber sees expanding bureaucracy   Ethnomethodology   Multiculturalism

ACKNOWLEDGEMENTS

Ken Plummer wishes to thank Daniel Nehring in helping with this edition, and especially for his work on the website and the resources. Carlos Gigoux also provided much valuable help with the website. He has been a marvellous support. Assistance with earlier editions came from Kimberley Fisher, Travis Kong, John Stevens, Annemarie Naylor, Agnes Skamballis and Beverley Chaplin. It is still appreciated and remembered. Former colleagues and students at Essex have always been stimulating and enjoyable to be with; and I thank especially Rob Stones, Colin Samson, Eamonn Carrabine, Pam Cox, Cathy Greenblat, Ewa Marokowska, Roísín Ryan-Flood, Paul Thompson, Nigel South, Leonore Davidoff, and Hiroko Tanaka for their continuing support and friendship. Steve Smith and Travis Kong helped me to think about China.

At Pearson Education, I have always had a legion of colleagues who have provided me with massive support. This is the fourth edition of the book on which I have worked with Andrew Taylor and he has always been the greatest of pleasures to work with – and a wonderful editor: I thank him here too for his kindness to me during my illness and his tolerance of my quirky ways. I am also very grateful to my ever-accommodating desk editor, Mary Lince, to Maggie Wells for her work on the book's design and to Jodie Mardell-Lines for her work on the book's website.

Finally, as always, my dear partner, Everard Longland, read the entire proofs and commented with interest. So having just nursed me through major illness for three years, he cheerfully and calmly continues to support me in my work. I am indeed a very fortunate person.

Ken Plummer
Wivenhoe, March 2008

Publisher's acknowledgements

We would like to thank the anonymous panel of reviewers for their valuable comments on the book.

The publishers would like to record a huge debt of gratitude to Ken Plummer for his continued dedication, good humour and generosity with his expertise during the production of this 5th edition. This new edition continues to display all his joie de vivre and desire to innovate, as well as his great passion for his subject and the rich diversity of the world.

The publishers gratefully thank Everard Longland for use of his artwork in sections of the book and on the cover.

We are grateful to the following for permission to reproduce copyright material:

Figures

Figure 1.1 from *Sociology: The Basics*, Routledge (Plummer, K. 2010) p. 192; Figure 1.2 from Internet World Stats, http://www.internetworldstats.com/stats.htm, Copyright © 2010, Miniwatts Marketing Group; Figure 4.1 adapted from *Human Societies: An Introduction to Macrosociology*, 10th ed., Paradigm Publishers (Lenski, G., Nolan, P. and Lenski, J. 2006) p. 52, Fig. 3.1; Figure 6.3 from Spencer, Liz; *Rethinking Friendship: Hidden solidarities today.* © 2006 by Princeton University Press. Reprinted by permission of Princeton University Press; Figure 7.2 adapted from *The Seasons of a Man's Life*, Alfred A. Knopf (Levinson, D. et al. 1978) p. 57, copyright © 1978 by Daniel J. Levinson, reprinted by permission of SLL/Sterling Lord Literistic, Inc. Copyright by Daniel Levinson; Figure 7.3 adapted from *Documents of Life 2: An Invitation to a Critical Humanism*, Sage Publications Ltd. (Plummer, K. 2001) pp. 126–127; Figure on page 242 from More than 1.02 billion hungry people, http://www.fao.org/hunger, Food and Agriculture Organization of the United Nations; Figures 9.1, 9.2, 15.1 from Macionis, John J., *Sociology, 13th*, © 2010. Printed and Electronically reproduced by permission of Pearson Education, Inc., Upper Saddle River, New Jersey; Figure 9.3 from http://www.avert.org/worlstatinfo.htm, data from UNAIDS (2010) UNAIDS Report on the Global AIDS Epidemic, with permission from AVERT, www.avert.org and

UNAIDS/ONUSIDA 2010; Figure 10.1 from Factfile UK: Wealth and Poverty – How much we earn . . . and what we're worth, *The Guardian*, 20 November 2010, Copyright Guardian News & Media Ltd 2010; Figure 10.2 from EU Survey of Income and Living Standards, Eurostat, in, *Social Trends*, 40, Fig. 5.15, p. 69 (2010), Crown Copyright material is reproduced with permission under the terms of the Click-Use Licence; Figure on page 325 from *Optimise the value of your customers and locations, now and in the future – Mosaic UK – the consumer classification of the United Kingdom* (http://www.experian.co.uk/assets/business-strategies/brochures/mosaic-uk-2009-brochure-jun10.pdf) p. 6, © 2010 Experian Ltd. All rights reserved; Figure 11.2 from Long-Term International Migration (LTIM), International Passenger Survey (IPS), ONS, http://www.statistics.gov.uk/cci/nugget.asp?id=260, Crown Copyright material is reproduced with permission under the terms of the Click-Use License; Figure 12.1 adapted from Thinking Sex, *Pleasure and Danger: Exploring Female Sexuality*, edited by Carol S. Vance, Pandora Press, 1989, Fig. 2, p. 282 (Rubin, C. 1989); Figure 13.3, Figure 13.4 from *United Nations Programme on Ageing, 2007*, © United Nations, 2007. Reproduced with permission. The United Nations is the author of the original material; Figure 13.5 from The old-age security motive for fertility, *Population and Development Review*, 11, no.1, pp. 75–97 (Nugent, J. B. 2006), Copyright © 2006 The Population Council, Inc. Reproduced with permission of Blackwell Publishing Ltd; Figure 13.6 adapted from data from Office for National Statistics and General Register Office for Scotland. Crown Copyright material is reproduced with permission under the terms of the Click-Use License; Figure 14.1 from *Social Trends*, 40, 2010, p. 31, Fig. 3.5, Department for Children, Families and Schools, Crown Copyright material is reproduced with permission under the terms of the Click-Use License; Figure 14.2 adapted from *Adult psychiatric morbidity in England, 2007 Results of a household survey* (McManus, S., Meltzer, H., Brugha, T., Bebbington, P. and Jenkins, R. (eds) 2011) A survey carried out for The NHS Information Centre for health and social care by the National Centre for Social Research and the Department of Health Sciences, University of Leicester, Copyright © 2011, Re-used with the permission of The Health and Social Care Information Centre. All rights reserved, in *Social Trends*, 40, 2010, Fig. 7.19, p. 104; Figure 14.4 from *Social Trends*, 40, 2010, p. 197, Figure 13.18 Charities Aid Foundation; National Council for Voluntary Organisations, Crown Copyright material is reproduced with permission under the

terms of the Click-Use License; Figure 15.2 from *Social Trends*, 40, 2010, p. 45, Figure 4.2, Labour Force Survey, Office for National Statistics, Crown Copyright material is reproduced with permission under the terms of the Click-Use License; Figure 15.3 from *Trade Union Membership 2009*, Department for Business, Innovation and Skills (Archur, J. 2010) Chart 1.1, p. 3, http://stats.bis.gov.uk/UKSA/tu/TUM2009.pdf, Crown Copyright material is reproduced with permission under the terms of the Click-Use License; Figures 15.4, 15.5 from *Eurostat, Europe in Figures: Eurostat Yearbook 2009* (Eurostat 2009), © European Union, 2009; Figure 16.1 adapted from *European Parliament Elections 2009, Research Paper 09/53*, 17 June 2009 p. 25, Parliamentary material is reproduced with the permission of the Controller of HMSO on behalf of Parliament; Figure on page 557 from *SIPRI Yearbook 2010: Armaments, Disarmament and International Security*, Oxford University Press: Oxford (Stockholm International Peace Research Institute 2010) Fig. 2A.1; Figure on page 571 from *The United Nations System, Principal Organs, United Nations Department of Public Information 06-39572 – August 2006 – 10,000 – DPI/2431* United Nations (United Nations Department of Public Information) © United Nations, 2006. Reproduced with permission. The United Nations is the author of the original material; Figure 17.1 from *Social Trends*, 40, 2010, Figure 9.12, p. 133, Office for Criminal Justice Reform, Ministry of Justice, Crown Copyright material is reproduced with permission under the terms of the Click-Use License; Figures 17.2, 17.3 from *Criminal Statistics: England and Wales 2008* (Ministry of Justice 2010), http://www.justice.gov.uk/publications/docs/criminal-stats-2008.pdf, Crown Copyright material is reproduced with permission under the terms of the Click-Use License; Figure on page 613 from *The Jack-Roller: A Delinquent Boy's Own Story*, University of Chicago Press (Shaw, C. R. 1966) Cover design by James Bradford Johnson, photographer: Clifford R. Shaw; Figure 18.1 from *Social Trends*, 40, 2010, Figure 2.9, p. 19, Office for National Statistics, Crown Copyright material is reproduced with permission under the terms of the Click-Use License; Figure 18.2 from *Social Trends*, 40, 2010, Figure 2.19, p. 24, Office for National Statistics; Eurostat, Crown Copyright material is reproduced with permission under the terms of the Click-Use License; Figure 18.3 adapted from *Social Trends*, 2002, p. 32, Office for National Statistics; Eurostat, Crown Copyright material is reproduced with permission under the terms of the Click-Use License; Figure 18.4 from *Social Trends*,

2007, Fig. 2.9, Office for National Statistics; General Register Office for Scotland; Northern Ireland Statistics and Research Agency, Crown Copyright material is reproduced with permission under the terms of the Click-Use License; Figure 18.5 adapted from http://www.statistics.gov.uk, Office for National Statistics, Crown Copyright material is reproduced with permission under the terms of the Click-Use License; Figure 18.6 adapted from *Social Trends*, 37, 2007, Crown Copyright material is reproduced with permission under the terms of the Click-Use License; Figure 18.7 adapted from *Social Trends*, 2007, p. 16, Fig. 2.6, Census 2001, Office for National Statistics; Census 2001, General Register Office for Scotland, Crown Copyright material is reproduced with permission under the terms of the Click-Use License; Figure 19.1 after http://www.adherents.com/Religions_By_Adherents.html. © 2005 www.adherents.com; Figure 19.2 from World Religions joke from greetings card. Original design by Barbara Shoolery © Game Plan Design. Published as greeting card by Recycled Paper Greetings, Inc. All rights reserved; Figure 19.3 from *Social Trends*, 40, 2010, Figure 13.20, p. 198, YouGov, Crown Copyright material is reproduced with permission under the terms of the Click-Use License; Figure 20.1 from *Unleashing Aspiration: The Final Report of the Panel on Fair Access to the Professions*, Cabinet Office (The Panel on Fair Access to the Professions 2009) Figure 1f, p. 18, Crown Copyright material is reproduced with permission under the terms of the Click-Use License; Figures 20.2, 20.3 from *Global Education Digest 2009: Comparing Education Statistics Around the World*, UNESCO (UNESCO Institute for Statistics 2009) © UNESCO-UIS 2009; Figure 20.4 after *Europe in Figures – Eurostat Yearbook 2006–07* (Eurostat 2007) Figure 2.3, p. 88, reprinted by permission of the European Communities; Figure 21.1 adapted from *Shaping the Future* (WHO 2003) World Health Report, Geneva, World Health Organization; Figure 21.2 after *Evidence, Information and Policy* (WHO 2000), World Health Organization; Figure 21.3 from *World Health Statistics 2010* (WHO 2010) p. 60, with permission from World Health Organization; Figure 21.4 from *Independent Inquiry into Inequalities in Health Report*, HMSO (Acheson, D. 1998) p. 6, Crown Copyright material is reproduced with permission under the terms of the Click-Use License; Figure 21.5 from http://data.unaids.org/pub/GlobalReport/2006, Reproduced by kind permission of UNAIDS, www.unaids.org; Figure 22.1 from *The Global Media Atlas*, British Film Institute and Myriad Editions (Balnaves, M. et al. 2001) p. 64, Copyright © Myriad Editions, www.MyriadEditions.com; Figures 22.3, 22.4 from *The Future of the Mass Audience*, Cambridge University Press (Neuman, W. R. 1991), © Cambridge University Press 1991, reproduced with permission; Figure 24.1 from Trends in population, developed and developing countries, 1750–2050 (estimates and projections) by Hugo Ahlenius, Nordpil, http://maps.grida.no/go/graphic/trends-in-population-developed-and-developing-countries-1750-2050-estimates-and-projections, UNEP/GRID-Arendal/data sources: Goldewijk, Kees Klein. 2008. HYDE 3.0 population estimates 'RE: Population data'. November 17, 2008 personal email (November 17, 2008), UNEP/GRID-Arendal; Figure 24.2 from *World Population Prospects: The 2008 Revision*, United Nations (Population Division of the Department of Economic and Social Affairs of the United Nations Secretariat 2009) Figure 5, © United Nations, 2009. Reproduced with permission. The United Nations is the author of the original material; Figure 24.5 from *World Population Prospects: The 2009 Revision*, United Nations (Population Division of the Department of Economic and Social Affairs of the United Nations Secretariat 2010) Fig. 1, http://esa.un.org/unpd/wup/Fig_1.htm, © United Nations, 2010. Reproduced with permission. The United Nations is the author of the original material; Figure 24.6 adapted from *A Geography of the European Union*, Oxford University Press (Nagel, G. and Spencer, K. 1996) p. 101; Figure 24.7 from *World Population Prospects: The 2009 Revision, Highlights*, United Nations (Population Division of the Department of Economic and Social Affairs of the United Nations Secretariat 2010) Fig. I, p. 2, http://esa.un.org/unpd/wup/Documents/WUP2009_Highlights_Final.pdf, © United Nations, 2010. Reproduced with permission. The United Nations is the author of the original material; Figure 24.8 adapted from *The City* (Park, R. E. and Burgess, E. W. 1967) p. 55, originally published 1925, published and reprinted by permission of The University of Chicago Press; Figure 25.1 from Trends in natural disasters, http://maps.grida.no/go/graphic/trends-in-natural-disasters by Emmanuelle Bournay, UNEP/GRID-Arendal/data sources: Center for Research on the Epidemiology of Disasters (CRED), UNEP/GRID-Arendal; Figure 25.4 from www.defra.gov.uk. Graph from 'Fortnightly rubbish collection leads to more recycling, says government', *The Guardian*, 26/04/2007, Copyright Guardian News & Media Ltd. 2007; Figure 26.1 from The Millennium Project, Global Futures Studies and Research, Global Challenges for Humanity, http://www.millennium-project.org/millennium/challenges.html, The Millennium Project, global futures research think tank.

Logos

Logo on page 739 from Patient UK logo, with permission from EMIS EKBS; Logo on page 739 from Aids.org; Logo on page 739 from Alzheimer's Association

Maps

Map 4.1 adapted from *Nomads and the Outside World*, Cambridge University Press (Khazanov, A. M. 1984) p. 185, with permission from the author; Map 4.4 from *The World Guide*, 11th ed., Oxford: New Internationalist Publications (Brazier, C. and Hamed, A. (eds) 2007) p. 60, Reprinted by kind permission of the New Internationalist. Copyright New Internationalist. www.newint.org; Maps 5.1, page 936 from 'Inglehart-Welzel Cultural Map of the World' by Ronald Inglehart http://www.worldvaluessurvey.org/statistics/some_findings.html; Map 5.2 from *Discovering Islam: Making Sense of Muslim History and Society*, Ahmed, A. S., pp. 146–7, Copyright © 1988 Routledge. Reproduced by permission of Taylor & Francis Books UK; Map on page 242 from 2009 Hunger Map, http://documents.wfp.org/stellent/groups/public/documents/liason_offices/wfp185786.jpg, World Food Programme; Map 16.3 adapted from Life after Communism: The facts, *New Internationalist*, 366, April 2004, Reprinted by kind permission of New Internationalist. Copyright New Internationalist. www.newint.org; Map 17.1 adapted from *Amnesty magazine*, Issue 117, Jan./Feb. 2003, http://www.amnesty.org; Map 21.1 from http://data.unaids.org/pub/GlobalReport/2006, Reproduced by kind permission of UNAIDS, www.unaids.org.

Tables

Table 1.2 adapted from Suicide rates per 100,000 by country, year and sex (Table), Most recent year available; as of 2009 http://www.who.int/mental_health/prevention/suicide_rates/en/index.html, with permission from World Health Organization; Table 1.3 from *Sociology: The Basics*, Routledge (Plummer, K. 2010) p. 77; Table 1.4 from Internet World Stats, http://www.internetworldstats.com/stats.htm,

Copyright © 2000–2010, Miniwatts Marketing Group. All rights reserved worldwide; Table on page 96 from *Social Trends*, 40, 2010, Table 13.12, p. 193, from Taking Part: The National Survey of Culture, Leisure and Sport, Department for Culture, Media and Sport, Crown Copyright material is reproduced with permission under the terms of the Click-Use License; Table 5.1 from *National Geographic Visual History of the World* National Geographic (2005); Table 5.2 adapted from Summary by language size, http://www.ethnologue.com/ethno_docs/distribution.asp?by=size, Table 3: Languages with at least 3 million first-language speakers, used by permission, © SIL, *Ethnologue, 16th Edition*, M. Paul Lewis, ed., 2009; Table 5.3 adapted from Summary by area, http://www.ethnologue.com/ethno_docs/distribution.asp?by=area, Table 1: Distribution of languages by area of origin, used by permission, © SIL, *Ethnologue, 16th Edition*, M. Paul Lewis, ed., 2009; Table 8.1 adapted from *Sociology: The Basics*, Routledge (Plummer, K. 2010) Table 7.3; Table 9.1 adapted from United Nations Development Programme, *Human Development Report 2010*, published 2010, Palgrave Macmillan, reproduced with permission of Palgrave Macmillan; Table 9.2 from Special Report: The World's Billionaires http://www.forbes.com/lists/2010/10/billionaires-2010_The-Worlds-Billionaires_Rank.html, Reprinted by Permission of Forbes Media LLC © 2011; Table 9.3 from AIDS Orphans, http://www.avert.org/aids-orphans.htm, data from UNICEF/UNAIDS (2010) Children and AIDS: Fifth Stocktaking Report, with permission from AVERT, www.avert.org and UNAIDS/ONUSIDA 2010; Table 9.5 from The State of the Worlds Toilets, http://www.wateraid.org.uk, with permission from WaterAid; Table 10.1 from *Statistical Bulletin: 2009 Annual Survey of Hours and Earnings*, Office for National Statistics (2009) p. 10, Median gross weekly earnings by occupation, Crown Copyright material is reproduced with permission under the terms of the Click-Use License; Table 11.4 from *Social Trends*, 40, 2010, Table 1.4, p. 4, Annual Population Survey, Office for National Statistics, Crown Copyright material is reproduced with permission under the terms of the Click-Use License; Table 13.1 from *Accelerating Action Against Child Labour*, ILO (2009) Table 1.4, p. 10, http://www.ilo.org/wcmsp5/groups/public/---dgreports/---dcomm/documents/publication/wcms_126752.pdf, Copyright © International Labour Organization 2009; Table 13.4 adapted from General Household Survey (Longitudinal), Office for National Statistics, *Social Trends*, 37, 2007, p. 89, Table 7.3, Crown Copyright material is reproduced with permission under the terms of the Click-Use License; Table 14.1 from *Understanding Disability: From theory to practice*, Macmillan (Oliver, M. 1996) p. 34, reproduced with permission of Palgrave Macmillan; Table 14.3 from *A Caring Society? Care and dilemmas of human service in the 21st century*, Palgrave (Fine, M. D. 2007) p. 200, reproduced with permission of Palgrave Macmillan; Table 14.5 from *Social Trends*, 40, 2010, p. 196, Table 13.16, Taking Part: The National Survey of Culture, Leisure and Sport, Department for Culture, Media and Sport, Crown Copyright material is reproduced with permission under the terms of the Click-Use License; Table 15.2 from *Social Trends*, 40, 2010, p. 49, Short-Term Employment Surveys, Office for National Statistics, Crown Copyright material is reproduced with permission under the terms of the Click-Use License; Table 15.4 from *Labour Force Survey*, Eurostat (2008), © European Union, 2008; Table 15.5 adapted from Annual Survey of Hours and Earnings 2009, Table 2.6a, www.statistics.gov.uk/downloads/theme_labour/ASHE-2009/tab2_6a.xls, access date September 4 2010, Crown Copyright material is reproduced with permission under the terms of the Click-Use License; Table 15.6 from Unemployment rates, http://epp.eurostat.ec.europa.eu/statistics_explained/index.php?title=File:Table_unemployment_rates.PNG&filetimestamp=20110401095503, © European Union, 2010; Tables 16.3, 16.4 from http://www.elections2009-results.eu/en/turnout_en.html, Source: TNS opinion in cooperation with the European Parliament; Tables on page 557, page 558 adapted from *SIPRI Yearbook 2010: Armaments, Disarmament and International Security*, Oxford University Press: Oxford (Stockholm International Peace Research Institute 2010); Table 17.1 from *Social Trends*, 40, 2010, Table 9.3, p. 128, British Crime Survey, Home Survey, Crown Copyright material is reproduced with permission under the terms of the Click-Use License; Table 17.2 from *World Drug Report 2008*, United Nations (UNODC 2009), © United Nations, 2009. Reproduced with permission. The United Nations is the author of the original material; Table 17.3 from *Sociology: The Basics*, Routledge (Plummer, K. 2010); Table 18.1 from *Engendered housework: A cross-european analysis*, IRISS Working Paper 2007-07, CEPS/INSTEAD, Differdange, Luxembourg (Voicu, B., Voicu, M., Strapkova, K. 2007) Table 1, with permission from Malina Voicu; Table 18.2 from *Social Trends*, 40, 2010, Table 2.2, p. 15, Census, Labour Force Survey, Office for National Statistics, Crown Copyright material is reproduced with permission under the terms of the

Click-Use License; Table 18.3 from *Eurostat, Europe in Figures: Eurostat Yearbook 2009* (Eurostat 2009) Table 3.14, p. 157, © European Union, 2009; Table 19.1 from *Social Trends*, 2004, Crown Copyright material is reproduced with permission under the terms of the Click-Use License; Table 20.1 adapted from *The State of the World's Children*, Special Edition (UNICEF 2009) Tables 1 and 5, with permission from UNICEF; Table 20.2 from *The Official Summary of the State of the World's Children*, UNICEF (UNICEF 2004) p. 121; Table 20.3 from *A View Inside Primary Schools* (UNESCO Institute for Statistics 2008), with permission from UNESCO Institute for Statistics; Table 20.4 adapted from *Social Trends*, 40, 2010, Table 3.3, p. 29, Department for Children, Schools and Families; Welsh Assembly Government; Scottish Government; Northern Ireland Department of Education, Crown Copyright material is reproduced with permission under the terms of the Click-Use License; Table 20.5 from *Social Trends*, 40, 2010, Table 3.16, p. 38, Longtitudinal Study of Young People in England, and Youth Cohort Study, from the Department for Children, Schools and Families, Crown Copyright material is reproduced with permission under the terms of the Click-Use License; Table 20.6 from *Social Trends*, 40, 2010, Table 3.14, p. 37, Department for Children, Schools and Families, Crown Copyright material is reproduced with permission under the terms of the Click-Use License; Table 21.1 adapted from *Shaping the Future* (WHO 2003) World Health Report, Geneva, 2003, calculated from Annex Table 2, World Health Organization; Table 21.2 from *Social Trends*, 40, 2010, Table 7.16, p. 102, General Lifestyle Survey 2008 (Longtitudinal), Office for National Statistics, Crown Copyright material is reproduced with permission under the terms of the Click-Use License; Table 21.4 from *2009 AIDS Epidemic Update* (UNAIDS 2009) p. 11, UNAIDS/ONUSIDA 2009; Table 22.2 from *Social Trends*, 40, 2010, Table 13.6, p. 189, National Readership Survey, Crown Copyright material is reproduced with permission under the terms of the Click-Use License; Table 22.6 from ABCs: National daily newspaper circulation July 2010, guardian.co.uk, Friday 13 August 2010, Copyright Guardian News & Media Ltd. 2010; Table 22.7 from *Social Trends*, 40, 2010, Table 13.3, p. 187, Taking Part: The National Survey of Culture, Leisure and Sport, Department for Culture, Media and Sport, Crown Copyright material is reproduced with permission under the terms of the Click-Use License; Table 24.1 from *World Population Prospects: The 2008 Revision. Highlights*, United Nations

(Population Division of the Department of Economic and Social Affairs of the United Nations Secretariat 2009) Table I.1, p. 1, © United Nations, 2009. Reproduced with permission. The United Nations is the author of the original material; Table 24.2 from *Social Trends*, 40, 2010, Table 1.14, p. 10, United Nations, Crown Copyright material is reproduced with permission under the terms of the Click-Use License; Table 24.3 from *Social Trends*, 40, 2010, Table 1.16, p. 11, Office for National Statistics; United Nations, Crown Copyright material is reproduced with permission under the terms of the Click-Use License; Table 24.4, Table 24.5 from *World Urbanization Prospects: The 2009 Revision*, United Nations (United Nations Department of Economic and Social Affairs, Population Division 2009), © United Nations, 2010. Reproduced with permission. The United Nations is the author of the original material; Table 24.6 from *World Slum Population Explosion*, United Nations (UN-HABITAT 2010), © United Nations, 2010. Reproduced with permission. The United Nations is the author of the original material; Table 24.7 adapted from *Planet of Slums*, Verso (Davis, M. 2006) p. 31; Table 26.2 from *2007: State of the Future*, United Nations (Glenn, J. C. and Gordon, T. J. 2007) p. 6, © United Nations, 2007. Reproduced with permission. The United Nations is the author of the original material; Table 26.3 from *Voice of the People Survey 2005* (Gallup International Association 2005), with permission from WIN-Gallup International (www.gallup-international.com); Table 26.4 adapted from Globalization as hybridization, *Global Modernities*, edited by Featherstone, M. et al., Sage Publications Ltd., p. 80 (Pieterse, J. N. 1995).

Text

Box on page 100 from 50 Highest Paid Footballers in the World: Be Prepared to be Slightly Surprised by Mark Apostolou, http://www.caughtoffside.com/2010/02/17/50-highest-paid-footballers-in-the-world-be-prepared-to-be-slightly-surprised/, with permission from the author; Box on page 155 adapted from *Sociology: The Basics*, Routledge (Plummer, K. 2010) p. 108; Boxes on page 292, page 597, page 813 adapted from *Pocket World in Figures*, Profile Books (The Economist 2007); Extract on pages 368–369 from Weine, Stevan M., *When History is a Nightmare: Lives and Memories of Ethnic Cleansing in Bosnia-Herzegovina*. Copyright © 1999 by Stevan M. Weine. Reprinted by permission of Rutgers University Press; Extract on page 409 from *Pornography: Men Possessing Women*, Pedigree: New York (Dworkin, A. 1981) p. 1, Copyright © 1979, 1980, 1981 by Andrea Dworkin, with permission from Elaine Markson Literary Agency; Box on page 416 from *The World We Have Won*, Routledge (Weeks, J. 2007), with permission from Taylor & Francis Books UK; Box on page 441 from *Pocket World in Figures*, Profile Books (The Economist 2010); Poetry on page 450 by Dylan Thomas, from *The Poems of Dylan Thomas*, copyright © 1952 by Dylan Thomas. Reprinted by permission of New Directions Publishing Corp. and pub. Orion, with permission from David Higham Associates Ltd; Poetry on page 450 from 'Do Not Go Gentle into that Good Night' by Dylan Thomas from *The Poems*, pub. Orion (Thomas, D. 1939), with permission from David Higham Associates Ltd; Extract on page 510 from *I, Rigoberta Menchu: An Indian Woman in Guatemala*, edited and introduced by Elizabeth Burgos-Debray, translated by Ann Wright, pub. Verso (imprint of New Left Books) (Menchú, R. 1984), Verso/New Left Books Ltd; Boxes on page 556, page 557 adapted from Corruption Perceptions Index 2010, http://www.transparency.org/policy_research/surveys_indices/cpi/2010, Copyright 2010 Transparency International: the global coalition against corruption. Used with permission. For more information, visit http://transparency.org; Box on page 587 from *Crime in England and Wales, 2008–9* (Home Office 2009) Home Office Statistical Bulletin, Crown Copyright material is reproduced with permission under the terms of the Click-Use License; Box on page 596 adapted from *World Population List*, 8th ed., ICPS (Walmsley, R. 2009), with permission from International Centre for Prison Studies (ICPS); Box on pages 598–599 from *The Maximum Surveillance Society: The Rise of CCTV*, Oxford: Berg (Norris, C. and Armstrong, G. 1999) pp. 40–42, © C. Norris and G. Armstrong, *The Maximum Surveillance Society*, Berg Publishers, an imprint of Bloomsbury Publishing Plc; Boxes on page 694, page 884 from *Pocket World in Figures*, Profile Books Ltd. (The Economist 2011); Extract on page 701 adapted from *The Autobiography of Malcolm X*, by Malcolm X, published by Hutchinson, published by Hutchinson. Reprinted by permission of The Random House Group Ltd; Box on page 713 from Times Higher Education World University Rankings, http://www.timeshighereducation.co.uk/world-university-rankings/, with permission from Times Higher Education; Box on page 772 adapted from British TV History, Landmark Dates, http://www.tvhistory.btinternet.co.uk/html/landmark.html,

P. T. Mathias; Box on page 805 adapted from *The Cosmos: A Beginner's Guide by Adam Hart-Davis and Paul Bader*, published by BBC Books. Reprinted by permission of The Random House Group Ltd and Watson, Little Ltd; Poetry on page 865 excerpt from 'Fire and Ice', from the book, *The Poetry of Robert Frost* edited by Edward Connery Lathem, Copyright 1923, 1969 by Henry Holt and Company, copyright 1951 by Robert Frost. Reprinted by permission of Henry Holt and Company, LLC. Published by Jonathan Cape. Reprinted by permission of The Random House Group Ltd; Box on page 872 from http://www.nationmaster.com/red/graph/ene_oil_con-energy-oil-consumption&b_map=1#, with permission from Nationmaster.com; Extract on pages 909–910 from The Millennium Project, Global Futures Studies and Research, Global Challenges for Humanity, http://www.millennium-project.org/millennium/challenges.html, The Millennium Project, global futures research think tank.

In some instances we have been unable to trace the owners of copyright material, and we would appreciate any information that would enable us to do so.

The publisher would like to thank the following for their kind permission to reproduce their photographs:

(Key: b-bottom; c-centre; l-left; r-right; t-top)

2 Bridgeman Art Library Ltd: The Battle between Carnival and Lent (oil on canvas). Brueghel, Pieter the Younger, (c. 1564–1638) / Private Collection, Johnny Van Haeften Ltd., London / The Bridgeman Art Library. **6 Stock Illustration Source:** Paul Schulenburg / Stock Illustration Source. **7 Getty Images:** Getty Photodisk (tl, tr, bl, br). **Pearson Education Ltd:** BananaStock (c). **16 akg-images Ltd:** akg-images. **21 Getty Images:** Archive Photos / Stringer. **32 Getty Images:** Taxi / Michael Simpson. **40 Corbis:** © Hulton-Deutsch Collection / Corbis (bl); © Bettmann / Corbis (tr). **www.granger.com:** The Granger Collection, New York (c). **Pearson Education Ltd:** The Illustrated London News Picture Library / Ingram Publishing / Alamy (tl). **46 Alamy Images:** © Mike Goldwater / Alamy (tl); © Homer Sykes Archive / Alamy (bl). **Magnum Photos Ltd:** © Eve Arnold (r). **47 Corbis:** © Bettmann / Corbis. **49 Corel. 50 Alamy Images:** © Jenny Matthews / Alamy. **54 Alamy Images:** © PYMCA / Alamy. **60 Bridgeman Art Library Ltd:** Galleria dell'Academia, Venice, Italy /

BAL. **66 Alamy Images:** © Jenny Matthews / Alamy. **72 Corbis:** © Reuters / Corbis. **75 Nick Broomfield:** from the film Ghosts. **80 Cathy Greenblat. 81 Reprinted with permission of the New York Academy of Sciences, www.nyas.org. 97 Alamy Images:** © Aflo Foto Agency / Alamy. **104 Bridgeman Art Library Ltd:** Happy Together As One, August 1963 (colour litho) by Chinese School, (20th century) Private Collection / © The Chambers Gallery, London / The Bridgeman Art Library. **106 Reuters:** Reuters / Funai-Frente de Proteção Etno-Ambiental Envira / Handout (Brazil). **113 Getty Images:** Getty Photodisk. **121 Katz Pictures Ltd:** Frank Spooner / Gamma. **136 Corbis:** © Robert Essel NYC / Corbis. **142 Bridgeman Art Library Ltd:** The Tribunal of the Inquisition, detail from mural cycle (mural) by Rivera, Diego (1886–1957) Palacio Nacional, Mexico City, Mexico / Index / The Bridgeman Art Library / © DACS, © 2011 Banco de Mexico Diego Rivera Frida Kahlo Museums Trust, Mexico, D.F./DACS. **146 Ingram Publishing:** The Creative Symbol Collection. **160 Corbis:** © Wael Hamzeh / Corbis (br); © Antonio Dasiparu / Epa / Corbis (t). **162 Corbis:** © Peter Turnley / Corbis. **164 Eamonn McCabe. 172 Corel. 174 Bridgeman Art Library Ltd:** Face to Face, 1994 (oil on canvas) (pair of 173317), Williams, Evelyn (Contemporary Artist) / Private Collection / The Bridgeman Art Library. **179 Yale University Library / Manuscripts and Archives:** Stanley Milgram Papers (MS 1406). Manuscripts and Archives, Yale University Press / Courtesy of Alexandra Milgram, From the film Obedience copyright © 1968 by Stanley Milgram; copyright renewed 1993 by Alexandra Milgram, and distributed by Penn State Media Sales. **182 Everard Longland. 186 Alamy Images:** © World History Archive / Alamy. **189 Corbis:** © Bernard Bisson / Sygma / Corbis. **190 Corbis:** © Oleg Popov / Reuters / Corbis. **191 Alamy Images:** © Iain Masterton / Alamy. **199 Corbis:** © Al Rod / Corbis. **200 Manuel Castells. 206 Bridgeman Art Library Ltd:** Berkley Hotel Mural – 1, Seligman, Lincoln (Contemporary Artist) / Private Collection / The Bridgeman Art Library. **211 Science Photo Library Ltd:** CCI Archives. **212 Pearson Education Ltd:** The Illustrated London News Picture Library / Ingram Publishing / Alamy. **214 www.granger.com:** The Granger Collection, New York. **216 Corbis:** © Louie Psihoyos / Corbis. **222 American Sociological Association:** www.asanet.org. **234 Pearson Education Ltd:** Photodisc / Jack Hollingsworth. **245 Corbis:** © Peter Dench / Corbis SRC. **250 Bridgeman Art Library Ltd:** Abandoned, 1903 by Nono, Luigi (1850–1918) Museo d'Arte Moderna di Ca' Pesaro,

Venice, Italy / The Bridgeman Art Library. **256 Corbis:** © David Orr / Sygma / Corbis (bl). **Getty Images:** Popperfoto / Getty Images (t); AFP / Getty Images (br). **259 Getty Images:** Walter Dhladhla / AFP. **263 Corbis:** © Nogues Alain / Corbis Sygma. **272 Corbis:** © Strauss / Curtis / Corbis (b); © David Turnley / Corbis (t). **280 Bridgeman Art Library Ltd:** Yellow Houses: a street in Sophiatown, c.1940 (board), Sekoto, Gerald (1913–93) / © Johannesburg Art Gallery, South Africa / The Bridgeman Art Library / Courtesy of The Gerard Sekoto Foundation. **287 Magnum Photos Ltd:** © Chris Steele-Perkins. **291 Alamy Images:** © Picture Contact BV / Alamy. **297 Alamy Images:** © HJB / Alamy. **299 Pearson Education Ltd:** Digital Vision. **300 Pearson Education Ltd:** Digital Vision. **303 Pearson Education Ltd:** Digital Vision. **307 Corbis:** © Reuters / Corbis. **316 The Art Archive. 318 Corbis:** © Richard Baker / In Pictures / Corbis. **329 Ronald Grant Archive:** Courtesy Dirty Hands Prods / RGA. **332 Corbis:** © Bettmann / Corbis (l). **346 Bridgeman Art Library Ltd:** We the Peoples . . . 1984 (acrylic on board), Wadams, Ron (Contemporary Artist) / Private Collection / The Bridgeman Art Library. **348 Corbis:** © Radu Sigheti / Reuters / Corbis. **355 akg-images Ltd:** africanpictures / akg-images. **361 Corbis:** © Bettmann / Corbis (b). © **Equality and Human Rights Commission:** (t). **362 Corbis:** © Peter Turnley / Corbis. **364 Getty Images:** AFP / Staff. **367 Corbis:** © Peter Turnley / Corbis (br); © Patrick Robert / Corbis (bl); © Faisal Mahmood / Reuters / Corbis (tl); © Ed Kashi / Corbis (tr). **381 Press Association:** AP / Press Association Images. **388 Lynn Randolph. 390 University of Chicago Press. 391 Getty Images:** Michael Steele / Staff. **392 TopFoto:** © ullsteinbild / TopFoto TopFoto.co.uk. **393 Corbis:** © Bettmann / Corbis. **395 courtesy Sylvia Walby. 397 Corbis:** © Jeffrey L. Rotman / Corbis. **408 Getty Images:** Popperfoto (r); Hulton Archive (l). **419 Press Association:** Gail Burton / AP / APA Photos. **426 Cathy Greenblat. 430 Corbis:** © Robert van der Hilst / Corbis. **431 Alamy Images:** © John Warburton-Lee Photography / Alamy. **435 Alamy Images:** © Roger Cracknell 01 / classic / Alamy (tl); © Howard Barlow / Alamy (tr). **Magnum Photos Ltd:** © Chris Steele-Perkins (br). **Press Association:** PA Photos (bl). **437 Kobal Collection Ltd:** Globo Films. **445 Cathy Greenblat. 460 Bridgeman Art Library Ltd:** Bridgeman Art Library Ltd / Louvre, Paris / France / BAL. **461 Corbis:** © Prashant Nadkar / Reuters / Corbis. **464 Getty Images:** AFP. **467 Kobal Collection Ltd:** MGM. **468 Press Association:** PA Photos. **471 Martha Nussbaum. 472 Press Association:** PA Photos. **481 Corbis:** © Howard Davies / Corbis (t).

Getty Images: News (b). **494 Bridgeman Art Library Ltd:** Preliminary study for 'Work', 1863, 1852–65 (oil on canvas) (see also 62924 & 100701), Brown, Ford Maddox (1821–93) / © Manchester Art Gallery, UK / The Bridgeman Art Library. **498 Corbis:** © Jason Lee / Reuters / Corbis. **510 Sophie Herxheimer. 513 Press Association:** Richard Vogel / AP / PA Photos. **514 Pearson Education Ltd:** Eyewire. **518 Ulrich Beck. 528 Corbis:** © Viviane Moos / Corbis. **536 Bridgeman Art Library Ltd:** Vladimir Ilyich Lenin (1870–1924) Addressing the Red Army of Workers on 5th May 1920, 1933 (oil on canvas), Brodsky, Isaak Israilevich (1883–1939) / Private Collection, RIA Novosti / The Bridgeman Art Library. **537 Corbis:** © Christopher J. Morris / Corbis. **539 Corbis:** © Ahmad Halabisaz / Xinhua Press / Corbis. **546 Corbis:** © Olivier Hoslet / epa / Corbis. **554 Corbis:** © Reuters / Corbis. **555 Corbis:** © David Turnley / Corbis. **559 Press Association:** David Guttenfelder / AP / Press Association. **565 Alamy Images:** © Janine Wiedel Photolibrary / Alamy. **570 Corbis:** © Brooks Kraft / Corbis. **578 Getty Images:** Tom Stoddart / Hulton Archive. **580 Stock Illustration Source:** Alan E. Cober / Stock Illustration Source. **593 Getty Images:** AFP. **595 Reuters. 598 Corbis:** © George Steinmetz / Corbis. **601 Stanley Cohen. 604 Mary Evans Picture Library. 608 Corbis:** © Jérome Sessini / Corbis. **609 Agentur Bilderberg GmbH:** © Michael Ende / Agentur Bilderberg GmbH. **622 © the Nationalmuseum, Stockholm:** Carl Larsson, My Loved Ones. **631 Corbis:** © Wong Adam / Redlink / Corbis. **645 Corbis:** © David Turnley / Corbis. **649 Corbis:** © Mario Guzman / epa / Corbis. **650 Alamy Images:** © Barry Lewis / Alamy. **652 Corbis:** © DaZo Vintage Stock Photos / Images.com / Corbis. **658 Bridgeman Art Library Ltd:** OR2265 Ascent of the Prophet Mohammed to Heaven, Mirak, Aqa (FL.c.1520–76) British Library, London, UK, © British Library Board. All Rights Reserved / The Bridgeman Art Library. **660 Magnum Photos Ltd:** Raghu Rai. **670 Reuters:** Gleb Garanich / Reuters. **672 Alamy Images:** © David Pearson / Alamy (br). **Reuters:** Reuters / Str Old (t, bl). **673 Alamy Images:** © Victor Paul Borg / Alamy. **679 Getty Images:** Paul Popper Popperfoto. **682 Reuters:** Reuters / Alexei Dityakin. **685 Corbis:** © Enny Huraheni / Reuters / Corbis. **690 Getty Images:** Jimmy Sime / Stringer / Hulton Archive. **692 Corbis:** © Atlantide Phototravel / Corbis. **701 Corbis:** © Bettmann / Corbis. **709 Corbis:** © Thorne Anderson / Corbis (l); © Alain Nogues / Corbis Sygma (r). **711 Corbis:** © Corbis. **716 Reuters:** Rick Wilking / Reuters. **722 Moderna Museet, Stockholm. 728 Corbis:** © Claudia Wiens / Corbis.

749 The NAMES Project Foundation: © 2010 The NAMES Project Foundation. **751 Corbis:** © Grafton Marshall Smith / Corbis. **753 Cathy Greenblat. 760 Bridgeman Art Library Ltd:** News Vendor, 1986 (oil on panel), Ferguson, Max (Contemporary Artist) / Private Collection / The Bridgeman Art Library. **762 Corbis:** © Gideon Mendel / Corbis. **767** © **S. L. Hodkinson. 770 Corbis:** © Catherine Karnow / Corbis. **771 Pearson Education Ltd:** Photodisc. C Squared Studios (r); Photodisc / C Squared Studios / Tony Gable (c); Photodisc (l). **788 Rex Features:** SIPA. **794 Corbis:** © Denis Scott / Corbis. **796 Science Photo Library Ltd:** Peter Menzel. **801 Science Photo Library Ltd:** (tr); Sheila Terry (tl); Detlev vab Ravenswaay / Science Photo Library (bl); A. Barrington Brown / Science Photo Library (c). **802 Corbis:** © Bettmann / Corbis. **810 Donna Haraway. 812 Reuters:** Rajesh Bhambi / Reuters. **824 Corbis:** © Catherine Karnow / Corbis. **828 Corbis:** © Yann Arthus-Bertrand / Corbis. **840 Corbis:** © Karen Kasmauski / Science Faction / Corbis. **850 Corbis:** © Stephanie Maze / Corbis. **851 Pearson Education Ltd:** Corbis. **853 Corbis:** © Nigel Pavitt / JAI / Corbis. **864 Press Association:** Nick Ut / AP / PA Photos. **868 Corbis:** © Niko Guido / Corbis (l); © Kim Kyung-Hoon / Reuters / Corbis (r). **877 Alamy Images:** © Barry Lewis / Alamy. **884 PhotoDisc:** PhotoDisc Volume 6 (bl); PhotoDisc Volume 44 (tl, tr, br). **888 Alamy Images:** © Gianni Muratore / Alamy. **898 Scottish National Gallery of Modern Art:** © The Estate of R. B. Kitaj/Marlborough Fine Art. **908 Magnum Photos Ltd:** Susan Meiselas (r); Bruno Barbey (l). **924 Museum of Fine Arts, Boston:** Paul Gauguin, French, 1848–1903, Where Do We Come From? What Are We? Where Are We Going?, 1897–98, Oil on canvas, 139.1 x 374.6cm (54 3 / 4 x 147 1 / 2in.) Museum of Fine Arts, Boston, Tompkins Collection – Arthur Gordon Tompkins Fund, 36.270. Photograph © 2011 Museum of Fine Arts, Boston. **932 Library of Congress:** Library of Congress, Prints & Photographs Division, FSA / OWI Collection, LC-USF34-9093-C. **934 Pearson Education Ltd:** Michael Duerinckx. Imagestate.

In some instances we have been unable to trace the owners of copyright material, and we would appreciate any information that would enable us to do so.